A STUDENTS MANUAL
OF
THE HISTORY OF INDIA
FROM THE EARLIEST PERIOD TO THE PRESENT

A STUDENTS MANUAL
OF
THE HISTORY OF INDIA
FROM THE EARLIEST PERIOD TO THE PRESENT

BY

MEADOWS TAYLOR,

C.S.I., M.B.A.S, M.R.I.A., &C.

AUTHOR OF 'CONFESSIONS OF A THUG' 'TARA' ETC. ETC.

GYAN

Published by

Gyan Publishing House
5, Ansari Road
Daryaganj, New Delhi-110002
Phone: 011-47034999, 9811692060
E-mail: books@gyanbooks.com

Distribution Network
gyanbooks.com
India, USA, Canada, UK, Australia, France

ISBN : 978-81-212-2210-5 (HB)
First Published, 1870

2nd Impression 2021

Printed at: Gyan Press, Delhi.

A Students Manual of The History of India
Author: Meadows Taylor

A STUDENT'S MANUAL

OF

THE HISTORY OF INDIA

FROM THE EARLIEST PERIOD TO THE PRESENT.

BY

MEADOWS TAYLOR,

C.S.I., M.R.A.S., M.R.I.A., &c.

AUTHOR OF 'CONFESSIONS OF A THUG' 'TARA' ETC. ETC.

LONDON:

LONGMANS, GREEN, AND CO.

1870.

TO MY COUSIN

HENRY REEVE, D.C.L.

MEMBER OF THE INSTITUTE OF FRANCE

&c. &c.

MY FAITHFUL FRIEND OF MANY YEARS

I Dedicate this Volume.

INTRODUCTION.

To my Readers.—I have been induced to write this Manual of the History of India to supply a want which I have observed to exist among all classes of English people. Most of my young friends tell me 'they are never taught anything about India;' and while I deplore this, I also see that many persons of mature age are deterred by their length, and other causes, from attempting the perusal of the larger Indian histories. It occurred to me, therefore, that a complete, but easy history, might be acceptable and useful to all; and I was the more led to this consideration from my own experience; for I do not know of any work from which enough can be learned without difficulty—either to satisfy present requirements, or to induce a more general study. The large Histories of India, besides being voluminous, are costly; most of them are out of print, and thus beyond the reach of ordinary students. Many of them are only fragments—histories of peculiar periods or peoples; and thus reference is required to many works by the student who desires to follow the complete history of India in all its branches.

The historical events of the ancient classic nations of Greece and Rome still possess a charm which time has not diminished; but the condition of their people has become altogether changed. It is not so, however, with India; and it is strange to us now to see Hindoos, who hold the same Pagan faith and follow the same customs as their forefathers who fought with Alexander the Great on the banks of the Indus, submitting themselves to a Christian nation so far distant from them as ours, and vying with ourselves in loyalty to our gracious Queen.

Surely, then, it is worth knowing how this came about!—this strange romance, of which in the whole world's history there has been no parallel; and it is this that I purpose to relate as briefly, as simply, and yet as completely as I can.

Many people tell me that they are deterred from reading any work on India by the difficulty of the proper names. This, however, is more imaginary than real, for in point of fact they are very easy; and I offer the following short rules for the pronunciation of Indian words as I have written them. I have not adopted the most modern system of orthography—as yet undecided—first, because I do not altogether understand it; and, secondly, because, with an intimate knowledge of Indian languages and orthography, I am unable to reconcile that system with the original. In this view I may be considered presumptuous, but I cannot help it. I have, in fact, adhered, in most respects, to the orthography of Thomson's 'Oordoo Dictionary,' which is printed in the English characters. I have written for English people, finding in English letters every equivalent for Indian pronunciation without the many diacritical marks which the other systems have required, or the adoption of foreign vowels which are not understood by all; and I am well assured that the native words of this work will be as well understood in India as in England.

VOWELS.

A. When a is accented as á, it is broad, as in far, large, fall, &c. *Examples*, Patán, Shitáb Rái, Nawáb.

When a is not accented, it is short, as in rat, can, &c. *Examples*, Patna, Madras, Hattras, &c.

E. When e is accented as é, it is broad, as in there, where, &c. *Examples*, Shére Khan, Péshwah, Bégum.

When e is not accented, it is short, as in yet, set, get, &c. *Examples*, Mecca, Vellore.

EE. Double e is long, as in feet, steel, &c. *Examples*,

Runjeet, Kurreem, which are less liable to error than Ranjit, Karim.

I is never accented, so as to represent ee; it is invariably short, as in fit, sit. *Examples*, Sindia, Krishna, Tippoo.

O. When o is not accented, it is short, as in got, lot. *Examples*, Arcot, Balloba.

When accented, ó is long, as in shore, more. *Examples*, Bhóslay, Mórád. O, unaccented, has also a medium sound according to situation, as Holkar, Gwalior, &c.

OO is always long, as in poor, moor. *Examples*, Rámpoor, Poorun, Poona, Oordoo, Mahdoo, Hindoo. Double o has been adopted in preference to the accented ú, not only because it is a nearer equivalent to the Indian character, but because the pronunciation cannot be mistaken.

OU, when used, has the sound of ow, as in loud, proud. Thus Oudh is not Oodh, as too frequently pronounced, but Owdh, Joudhpoor, &c.

U is always short, as in run, but, &c. *Examples*, Meerut, Pátun, Guntoor, Gunput, &c.

Y, as a termination, is always short, as, in English, very, boundary, anxiety. *Examples*, Cauvery, Ally, Godavery, Dehly. When y is not a terminal letter, it is long, as in Hyder.

In consonants no directions are needful, as they are perfectly intelligible.

KH, it may however be mentioned, is hard, as in the Scottish loch. *Example*, Khan.

GH has also a guttural sound, as Afghan, Ghatgay, but has no equivalent in English.

Whenever h, as an aspirate, occurs with any consonant, it is a simple and divided aspirate, as in Bithoor, Dabha, Thug, &c. The sound of th, as in thing, length, &c., is unknown.

Lastly, I pray my readers not to allow any difference of belief, or race or colour, to prejudice them; and to believe, as this history will, I trust, prove to them, that India has produced men as great and memorable in many respects as those of Western nations. When Europe, now so highly civilised, was wrapt in the darkest gloom of barbarism and ignorance, and its people were painted savages, India was the seat of the highest intellectual sciences. Its philosophers ranked with those of Greece; its people produced the most beautiful and delicate manufactures; and the records of their social polity exhibit the existence of elaborate codes of law and diplomacy, with provisions for mutual security and protection of property, to which the nations of the West were long strangers. If, under the direction of Divine Providence, we English have outstripped the bounds of early Indian progress, its people are not the less entitled to our admiration and sympathy for what they have preserved.

Up to the close of the eighteenth century I have added chronological dates regarding memorable events, which may serve to assist the student's memory.

MEADOWS TAYLOR.

OLD COURT, HAROLD'S CROSS, NEAR DUBLIN:
1870.

LIST OF WORKS CONSULTED.

1. Prinsep's Indian Antiquities.
2. Fergusson's Indian Chronology—Journal of Royal Asiatic Society, March 1869.
3. Voyages of M. Cæsar Fredericke—Asiatic Miscellany.
4. India in the 15th Century—Hakluyt Society.
5. Catalogue of Mackenzie's Collection of Inscriptions, by H. H. Wilson.
6. Walter Elliot's Canarese Inscriptions, part i. vol. xx.—Asiatic Researches.
7. Briggs's Translation of Ferishta's History.
8. Scott's Deccan.
9. Dow's History of Hindostan.
10. Syr-ool Muta Khereen.
11. Elphinstone's History of India.
12. Mill's History of India, with Wilson's Continuation.
13. Thornton's History of India.
14. Marshman's History of India.
15. Montgomery Martin's History of India.
16. Beveridge's Comprehensive History of India.
17. Trotter's History of India.
18. Grant Duff's History of the Mahrattas.
19. Wilks's History of Mysore.
20. Tod's Rajasthan.
21. Williams's History of Guzerat.
22. Malcolm's Central India.
23. Malcolm's Life of Clive.
24. Orme's History.
25. Cambridge's War in Coromandel.
26. Buchanan's Report on Mysore.
27. Cunningham's History of the Sikhs.
28. Prinsep's Narrative.
29. Lake's Sieges and Operations.

30. Dixon's Mairwarra.
31. Faria De Souza's History of the Portuguese in India.
32. Campbell's Personal Narrative.
33. Kaye's Afghan War.
34. Kaye's Sepoy War, vol. i.
35. Havelock's Narrative (Afghan War).
36. Eyre's Narrative of Military Operations (Afghanistan).
37. Napier's Conquest of Sinde.
38. Napier's Administration of Sinde.
39. Outram's Commentary (Sinde).
40. The Nizam, by H. G. Briggs.
41. Our Ally the Nizam, by Major Hastings Fraser.
42. Chesney's Polity.
43. Prichard's Administration of India.
44. Raikes's Revolt in North-West Provinces.
45. Trevelyan's Cawnpoor.
46. Edwards's Reminiscences.
47. Malleson's History of the French in India.
48. Parliamentary Returns and Blue Books.
49. Asiatic Register.
50. The Homeward Mail, &c., &c., &c.

To each and all of these works, I beg to record my sincere obligations.

M. T.

CONTENTS.

BOOK I.

BOOK II.

BOOK III.

BOOK IV.

BOOK V.

BOOK VI.

BOOK VII.

BOOK VIII.

BOOK IX.

TO THE READER.

In the first Book of this Manual, the orthography of proper names has been retained, for the most part, as found in the sources from whence the narrative was derived:—Menu for Menoo, Siva for Seeva, Sûdra for Soodra, &c. Reference to the subjoined list will enable the student to judge in what respect they differ from the system elsewhere followed.

It was also deemed advisable not to alter the orthography, conventionally established, of such words as Deccan (Dekhun), Carnatic (Karnatik), Concan (Kónkan), &c.

Page	3,	*for*	Aravulli	*read*	Aravully.
„	„	„	Injadri	„	Injádry.
„	4,	„	Deccan	„	Dekhun.
„	5,	„	Concan	„	Kónkan.
„	21 and elsewhere,	*for*	Menu	*read*	Menoo.
„	22,	*for*	Sûdra	*read*	Soodra.
„	31,	„	Bhagwat Gita	„	Bhugwut Geeta.
„	„	„	Visheshika	„	Vishéshika.
„	32,	„	Sivite	„	Seevite.
„	39,	„	Yuga	„	Yooga.
„	41,	„	Delhi	„	Dehly.
„	„	„	Saruswati	„	Suruswuty.
„	42 and elsewhere,	*for*	Oude	*read*	Oudh.
„	44,	*for*	Muni	*read*	Munee.
„	46,	„	Panjab	„	Punjáb.
„	54,	„	Sanchi	„	Sanchy.
„	59,	„	Keneri	„	Kenery.
„	60,	„	Vishnu	„	Vishnoo.
„	62,	„	Vullabhi	„	Vullabhee.
„	65,	„	Tulu	„	Tooloo.
„	66,	„	Kanchi	„	Kunchy.
„	67,	„	Kurki	„	Kurky.
„	68,	„	Chalûkya	„	Chalookya.
„	69,	„	Bhûrya	„	Bhoorya.
„	73,	„	Narupati	„	Narooputee.
„	76,	„	Dahu	„	Dahoo.

&c. &c. &c.

LIST OF ILLUSTRATIONS.

MAPS.

PLANS.

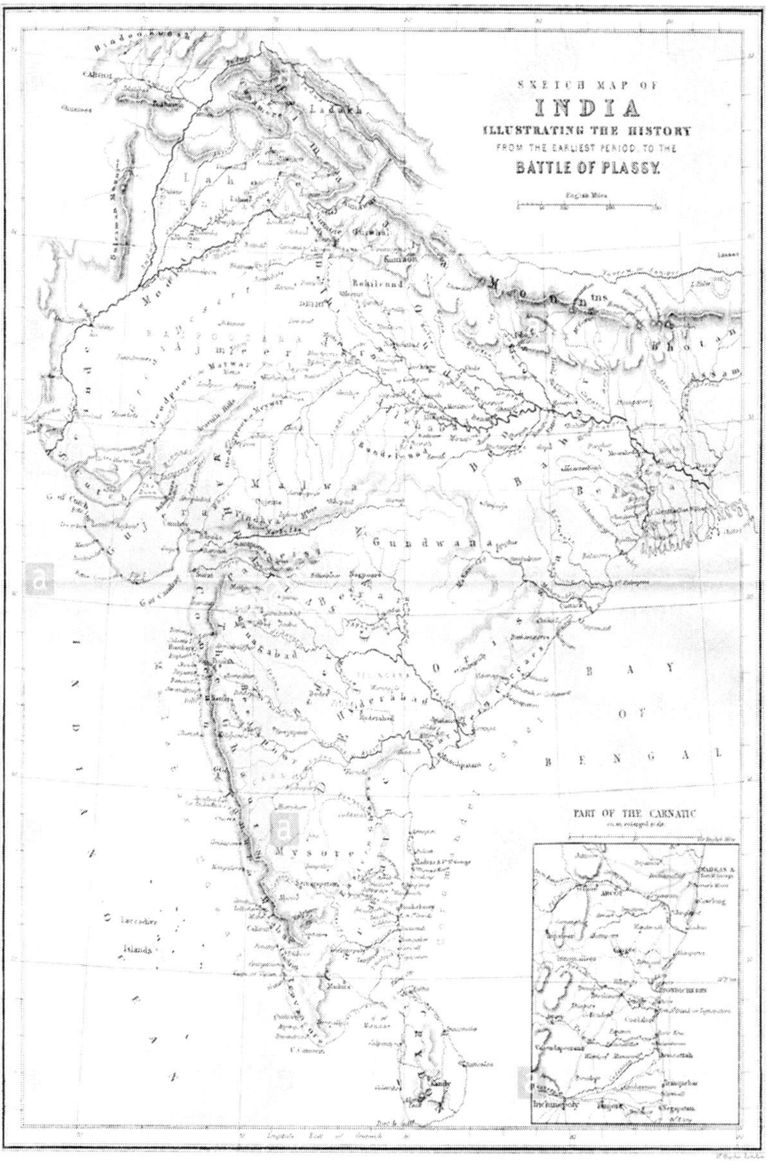

SKETCH MAP OF
INDIA
ILLUSTRATING THE HISTORY
FROM THE EARLIEST PERIOD, TO THE
BATTLE OF PLASSY.
English Miles
BAY OF BENGAL
PART OF THE CARNATIC
Mysore
Gundwana
Malwa
Ladakh
Rohilcund
Bhotan
Assam
Laccadive Islands
Arcot
Trichinopoly
Kandy

MANUAL

OF

INDIAN HISTORY.

BOOK I.

CHAPTER I.

A BRIEF DESCRIPTION OF INDIA.

Before entering upon its history, it may be interesting for the student to know a little of the character and features of the great continent of India; and it is the more necessary that something should be known of them, in order that the histories of its various peoples may be followed with the greater precision. In their general geographical definitions, the present maps leave nothing to be desired, and they are accessible to all. To the north, the great chain of the Himalaya mountains separates India from Tartary, extending eastward to the frontiers of China, and to the west and north-west into Central Asia, whence, by a succession of smaller ranges, elevated plateaux, and tablelands, they descend into the sea eastwards of the Indus. Into the great continent of India the descent from them is broken and precipitous. Deep rugged ravines and beds of rivers separate one chain of mountains from another, leaving in a few instances stupendous natural passes, which have served as a means of communication between India and the countries lying beyond it, on the east, north, and west.

To the north and east, such means of access to India are comparatively few. The footpaths which exist, lead over mountain-ridges covered with perpetual snow, and rise to an immense height, some of them being from 15,000 to 20,000 feet above the sea. It is only in the summer season, therefore, and for a brief period, that they are practicable even for sheep or goats which carry small loads, or for the yâks or mountain oxen of Tibet, that are used as beasts of burden. These mountains, rude and inaccessible as they appear, are inhabited by various races and tribes; some Tibetian, others mixed or purely Indian. The rigour of the climate does not affect them; and they are, for the most part, a robust, peaceful, and industrious people, subsisting by agriculture. To the west and north-west, however, the character of the inhabitants changes. They are found to be fierce and warlike, a distinction they have maintained from the earliest ages. The passes which lead into India from Central Asia, through Afghanistan, are practicable for horses and camels, and in some instances for wheeled vehicles; and it is through these passes, and by this warlike population, that the greatest invasions of India have taken place, and the greatest trade with Central Asia is now carried on.

Thus, it will be observed, that the northern frontier of India is protected by an almost impassable barrier on three sides. The whole of this tract possesses the most magnificent scenery in the world; its mountains are the highest, and its rivers—the Ganges, the Indus, and the Berhampooter[1]—among the longest and most famous. Most of the mountains, up to heights which define the growth of trees, are richly clothed with forests; and above these tower the magnificent snow-clad peaks and glacier hollows of the upper ranges, which far exceed in sublimity the most stupendous of the Alpine chains of Switzerland. In some places, indeed, one Mont Blanc piled upon another would not equal the height which the Himalayan peaks attain, and the elevations of some of the loftiest of them have not yet been accurately determined. Along the southern bases of most part of these mountains lie forest tracts, which are filled with deadly malaria, and are unfit for the residence of human beings; but as the lower heights are reached, a purer climate, not unlike that of Southern Europe, is found to exist, healthy and bracing, and in which the inhabitants are robust and vigorous. Many of these lower slopes of the Himalayas have proved well adapted for the culture of tea, several sanitary stations for Europeans have been established, and the whole region produces grain and fruit in abundance.

If the map be examined, it will be seen that the northern drainage of these stupendous mountains forms the supply of two noble rivers. From a point near the centre, the Berhampooter flows eastward, piercing the range at a point on the north-east of Bengal, whence it flows to the sea parallel with the Ganges. Nearly from the same central point the Indus takes its rise, and like the Berhampooter finds a passage through the mountains into the

[1] Properly Brumha-Pootr, son of Brumha.

north-west portion of India, which is called the Punjâb, and thence, joined by other great tributaries which have their rise from the southern faces of the Himalayas, and flowing through Sinde, falls into the sea on the opposite side of India to the Berhampooter. To the north of the valleys of these two great rivers lie the bleak, arid, elevated plains and steppes of Tartary, separated from India by almost impenetrable mountain defiles and passes covered with eternal snow. To the south the Ganges and Jumna rivers carry the mountain drainage through their broad valleys, opening out into hot, glowing, fertile India, stretching forth in all her luxuriant beauty to the Southern Ocean.

The great plains of the Ganges and Jumna are bounded to the south by a range of mountains of much less height than the Himalayas, for they rarely attain an elevation of even 4,000 feet above the sea. They form the buttresses, as it were, of the elevated tableland of Central India, which declines on all sides to lower elevations. To the west, bordering the valley of the Indus, these mountains are called Aravulli; to the east and south, Vindhya, whence they pass into two other ranges, called Sátpoora and Injadri, and from them into the plains of the Deccan and Southern India.

Along the west of the continent stretch mighty mountain buttresses, which are named the Ghauts in general terms, but have many local designations. They begin south of the valley of the rivers Nerbudda and Tapty, which run westward into the ocean, separating them from the Aravulli range; and stretching along the western coast, almost without a break, rise generally to about 4,000 feet. In two localities however the Neilgherries and Mahabuleshwur form tablelands of from 6,000 to 8,000 feet above the sea, which possess delightful and salubrious climates with very lovely scenery, and as sanataria have become the resort of invalids from many parts of India.

After rising from the sea into the range of Ghauts, the rest of India slopes gradually towards the eastern coast of Coromandel. Of this tract, the river Godavery, with the Krishna and Bheema, which unite and afterwards bear the former name, receive the general drainage, and fall into the Bay of Bengal; while further to the south the Pennaar, the Palar, and the Cauvery or Coleroon, follow in succession; and, rising in the elevated western districts, carry their waters to the sea at various points on the coast of Coromandel.

It is obvious, therefore, that after passing the broad valley of the Ganges and Jumna, the central portion of India becomes an exceedingly diversified tract, crossed by several ranges of mountains and hills of moderate heights, among which there are many broad plateaux of tableland; and that these fall away into Bengal on the east, the Deccan on the west, and the lower part of India on the south. Bengal is comparatively flat, but the Deccan is undulating and varied in character; sometimes opening into wide downs and rolling plains, in other places broken by ravines and low ranges of hills. To the south-west of the Deccan the large tableland of Mysore joins the main range of Ghauts, and breaks into the lower southern districts by deep ravines and mountain-spurs, some of them attaining a very considerable elevation; while offsets from the western mountains stretch, in some places, nearly across the southern portion of the peninsula, breaking the monotonous character of its plains, and affording a great diversity of scenery and of climate.

Hindoo geographers have divided India into portions which are still recognised. The valley of the Ganges and all Central India nearly as far as the line of the Nerbudda river, is called Hindostan;[1] adjoining it, to the south and east, lie Bundelkhund and Orissa, and further east, the great provinces of Bahar and Bengal; while to the west and south are Rajpootana, or the country of the Rajpoots, and Malwah, with the provinces of Guzerat and Kutch. All these are bounded to the south by the broad valley of the Nerbudda and Tapty rivers, south of which rises the great tableland of the Deccan, which stretches nearly across the continent; bounded upon the west by the Ghauts, and on the east by Berar and Orissa, with part of Telingana, and to the south by the rivers Tumboodra and Krishna.

Here the designation of the country as far as the southern boundary of Mysore, again changes to that of Carnatic, passing into what is termed 'Drawed,' which includes all the southern portion of the continent. Between the range of Ghauts and the sea lies a long strip of territory, the northern half of which is called Concan, and the southern Malabar. It is a tract of great natural beauty, bordering the sea, and broken by numberless spurs from the Ghaut mountains, abounding with more diversified scenery than any other portion of India, except the Himalayas.

The climate.

A very general impression among those who have no experience of India is, that the climate is uniformly hot; but this is by no means the case. In the northern portions the winter months are frequently very cold: and as far south as the Deccan, though frosts seldom occur south of the Nerbudda, yet cold is decidedly felt, which decreases gradually to the south. As the cold weather in England gives place to a warmer temperature in spring, so in India the heat increases from the month of March

[1] From Hindoo and Sthan—settled habitation.

to June with great intensity. Hot, scorching winds blow day and night; the earth is parched, vegetation withers up, and many trees shed their leaves. The heat is most especially felt in broad low valleys like Hindostan Proper and Bengal, and in the wide plains of Drawed; but in the central tablelands and in the Deccan, it exists in a less degree, and the nights are for the most part cool and pleasant. This heat season, so peculiar to India, is followed by one equally remarkable and interesting as a natural phenomenon. When the heat is at its greatest, in June, the sky becomes overcast with clouds, great piles of which rise up every day, and generally disperse at night; and with little warning the south-west monsoon, as it is called, bursts upon the land in all its grandeur. The thunder and lightning are for a time almost beyond conception, and are accompanied by furious storms of wind and heavy torrents of rain; but this war of the elements does not last long: gloomy skies give place to light clouds and cheerful sunshine, and the whole land bursts into the vivid green of new vegetation, with a rapidity and beauty which can hardly be conceived. Then, until September, pleasant showery weather continues, which resembles that of an English summer; and on the highlands of Central India and the Deccan this is perhaps the pleasantest season of the year. The south-west monsoon does not, however, reach the Coromandel coast. There, in the month of November, another monsoon comes across the Bay of Bengal from the north-east, and is similar in character to that of the south-west. It is a curious provision of nature, resulting from ascertained causes—in the prevalence of certain wind currents, and the existence of two great oceans which bound the shores of India—that these periodical seasons of rain should occur. At other times rain seldom falls, and indeed is hardly needed. For months together the skies are almost without a cloud; but the heavy dews of the cold season descend plentifully, and maintain the vegetation which the monsoon created. As the monsoons close the air becomes colder, and the so-called winter begins.

Productions.

In a country so diversified by nature and possessing such differences of climate and soil, the productions necessarily vary with situation. In Bengal, in much of the southern part of the peninsula (Drawed), in the Concan and Malabar, rice is the principal food of the people. Rice cannot be grown without water, as the plants require to live in water until the seed or grain begins to ripen; and it is only therefore where water is readily procurable and can be applied to the soil, that rice can be grown. In Bengal, from the great rivers which run through it, water is abundant. In Drawed and the Concan, artificial irrigation is almost universal; and the mountain streams, and even the large rivers, as the Krishna, Palar, Pennaar, Coleroon, and Cauvery, are skilfully dammed up, and their waters turned upon the land as far as they can be used. But rice is not the only product which needs a regular supply of water. Sugar-cane, indigo, mulberry-trees for silk, ginger and turmeric, orchards and gardens with their numberless provisions for the luxuries and necessities of man, all require it; and where means of irrigation from rivers and artificial reservoirs are wanting, wells are used and the water is raised by cattle. Such irrigation, however, is very limited in extent in comparison with the others. In the south of India, where much of the soil is naturally dry, sandy, or gravelly, the necessity of storing up water was known to the people even before the Christian era. Dams of stonework were built across considerable rivers and streams; and by earthern embankments, faced with stone, thrown across valleys, large lakes were formed, some many miles in circumference, with an infinite number of small ones; from all of which the water is drawn off by sluices, and applied to the land. The periodical rains fill these reservoirs, and water is stored up, which enables cultivation to be carried on through the seasons of drought, until the next monsoon commences.

This method of storing up water is, however, by no means universal in India. From a line above the northern boundary of the Carnatic, except in a few localities, it is hardly practised at all. The people of the central and northern provinces of India do not use rice except as a luxury. They feed upon wheat, barley, and many kinds of millet and pulse. They are a hardier people, and require more substantial food than those who eat rice. Some of these cereals grow in the rainy season, and ripen at its close. Others, wheat and barley, as also cotton and oil seeds, are sown in the deep black soil of these regions at the close of the monsoon; and though there is no rain, the moisture retained by the soil, and the heavy dews, are sufficient for their growth until they ripen. In these tracts wells are used for what partial irrigation is required, or the small brooks are turned to use, as far as they provide means; but recently the government of India has constructed canals from the Ganges, the Jumna and the rivers of the Punjâb, for the purposes of irrigation: and there can be little doubt that the application of water to the land, in seasons when none falls from the skies, will become very extensive and productive.

It is a subject of general belief that India is a land of palm-trees, of luxurious vegetation, of deep cool groves, and umbrageous forests, of many rivers and streams, of gorgeous flowers and luscious fruits—in fact, a kind of warm, sensuous paradise. But though poets may write of these, and painters depict scenes like those in which fancy has revelled, it is not reality. Here and there, the beauty of India is truly all that can be imagined, and even more; but such localities are rare. In the Himalayas, as previously stated, the scenery is the most sublime in the world. Stupendous mountain peaks, rising from eternal snow, are fringed by the luxuriant vegetation of Indian forests and valleys. In Bengal, owing to the redundant fertility of a prolific soil, watered by great rivers, adorned with noble trees and groves, and inhabited by a teeming population, which tills every available spot, the scenery is soft, and of a dreamy sensuous character. In the Concan and Malabar there is a combination of grandeur and beauty hardly to be described; but the rest of India is of a very homely character, if not indeed frequently very dreary in aspect. In the wide plains and downs of the central provinces and the Deccan, the traveller may pass for miles without seeing a tree to break the monotony of the scene, or afford him shelter. They are covered, it is true, with waving crops of grain and cotton, and admirably tilled, but they possess no charm for the eye, and are wearisome in their almost unchanging character; while in the wooded portions of the central mountain ranges, the absence of population, the sameness of outline, and the want of water, are no less repulsive. Through such scenes, great rivers run in deep channels; flooded to their brim in the monsoon, they dwindle to threads of water in the streams and to deep pools in the dry season—never beautiful, conveying no fertility to the countries through which their courses run, and impossible of navigation. Towns and villages occur every few miles, separated from each other only by the extent of their township lands; but no neat farmhouses are dotted over the country as in England, for the population, as it has ever done, still lives in communities for mutual security and protection, and will not separate.

And yet, with all its defects, India is a noble, gorgeous land, teeming with natural wealth, and possessing an orderly, industrious population of varied races and character; of which, and their history, it is purposed, in succeeding chapters, to give some account.

CHAPTER II.

OF THE PEOPLE—HINDOOS AND MAHOMEDANS.

IN the preceding chapter, a very brief and general sketch of the character of the country and some of its natural features has been given, with the object, not only of making the aspect of the great continent of India somewhat better understood than it generally is, but because there is a strong desire in the mind of every intelligent person to follow by description what is detailed in a map, to realise the differences of situation and scenery—in short, to get a footing, as it were, in a strange land, among a strange people. It is also equally interesting to know by what classes of people it is inhabited; how they live, how they are fed, what clothes they wear, and what is their general character. And in regard to all these, and many other simple details, so much misapprehension exists, that a few pages seem necessary for their explanation. A book, and a very large and interesting one it would be, might be written on these subjects; for the differences in religion and caste among Hindoos, which separate whole classes of the people from each other as decidedly as if they were different nations—the distinctions which arise from situation, local customs, usages and languages, as well between classes of Hindoos as of Mahomedans, would all furnish matter for description and illustration. All Europe is Christian; but Russians could not be described as Spaniards, or Italians, or Greeks, as English, French, or Germans; yet the continent of India contains many more separate peoples than Europe, and many more languages, which have no connection one with another; and though all have become blended together, under the influence of two great religions, Hindooism and Mahomedanism, they still preserve the marks of original nationalities. In our own country an Englishman is known from an Irishman or a Scotchman; there is a common language for all, yet they vary in character, and still preserve distinctive national customs. But apply this to India, and the difference is still greater and more marked. The language of the Hindoos of Northern India is as utterly incomprehensible by the Hindoos of the south, as that of a Spaniard would be to a Russian, or a native Greek to an Englishman. Thus a common religion, in the case of the Hindoos as with Christians, unites them in some degree, though in a very limited one; and as regards social customs or sympathy one with another, there is little or no unity. While, therefore, it is impossible to follow every variation of local character and custom, a general idea may yet be given of characteristics which belong to the people at large.

Divisions of the population of India.

The population of India is divided in a general sense into two great portions, Hindoos and Mahomedans. There are besides the aboriginal races who are not Hindoos, Boodhists, Christians and other sects, as will be hereafter detailed. Of all, the Hindoos are by far the most numerous, and in proportion to the Mahomedan, are about five to one—that is, the Hindoos would represent 150,000,000, and the Mahomedans about 30,000,000 of the whole. Of the entire population, about 151,500,000, are British subjects; and their subdivisions are shown by the following table, which has recently been compiled in India. The rest belong to the independent native States, of which there are 153 great and small, whose population is computed to amount to about 50,000,000. The whole therefore, in round numbers, may be estimated with safety at 200,000,000.

The population of the British provinces exclusively, is thus classified:—

Asiatic Christians	1,100,000
Booddhists	8,000,000
Aboriginal races	12,000,000
Mahomedans	25,000,000
Hindoos	110,000,000
Parsees	180,000
East Indians	91,000
Europeans (including troops)	156,000
Jews	10,000
Armenians	5,000
Total	151,542,000

Hindoos are those who follow the Brahminical faith. They are pagans, and for the greater part worshippers of idols; and they are divided not only into many religious sects, but into castes which do not eat or intermarry with each other, though they belong to the same social communities, and live together harmoniously.

Hindoos.

Mahomedans are believers in Mahomed, and are as much separated from Hindoos as Christians are; but from their numbers and long existence in the country, and in many cases descent from Hindoos who were converted to Mahomedanism in early times, they have become assimilated with them in more respects than is possible for Christians to be. Though they are opposed to Hindoos in religion as much as Christians are, and cannot eat with or intermarry with them, yet they share together labour of all kinds, trades and professions, military service, landed property, and distinctions of local rank. It will be obvious, therefore, that these two great classes are entirely different, and have little real sympathy one with another; and it will be shown hereafter, that the Hindoos were the original possessors of India till they were conquered by the Mahomedans, who held sway over them for many centuries, and indeed till the English conquered both.

Mahomedans.

It may be doubted whether, in all essential respects, there is a more courteous and intelligent population in the world than that of India at large, whether Hindoo or Mahomedan, though they naturally differ in many respects. The Hindoo is cheerful, pliant, social, and for the most part amiable. The Mahomedan is graver, more formal, more proud

Character and manners.

and reserved, yet courtly and polite. Many of the highest virtues of humanity may be claimed for both, while they exhibit many of the vices common to all people. Hindoos, among themselves, are kind to their children, perhaps over-indulgent; they honour their parents and elders; are extremely charitable, for it is part of their religion to be so; honest in their transactions one with another, industrious, and in religious matters tolerant, unless specially excited. As soldiers, brave and patient; as merchants and traders, enterprising and persevering. Their vices need not be particularised, and it is enough to say, perhaps, that they are those common to human nature everywhere in which civilised elements exist.

Hindoo characteristics.

Hindoos are accused by many writers of being habitually untruthful. This, however, may be denied in many respects, and doubted in others, for the examples before those writers were chiefly taken from the lower classes, and from legal experiences in which their worst qualities were developed. If their own standard of truth is not so high as we profess ours to be, it may be ascribed to the teaching of their religion, under which it is only wonderful that they are what they are. In this respect also there is a great difference between precept and practice; and while Hindoos profess to believe in the immoralities and crimes of the gods and demigods whom they worship, it would be impossible for them to put these in practice without incurring the penalties and censure, not to say the reprobation, of their castes, and of the communities in which they live. Thus when vicious, the vices of Hindoos are less obtrusive than our own; nor is undisguised depravity anywhere offensively apparent. The restraints of caste are repressing and injurious in many respects, but there is no question that the means possessed by caste divisions, of enforcing the at least outwardly moral conduct of their members, preserve Hindoo society in a great degree from any flagrant and habitual indulgence in vicious practices. In a general aspect, then, the Hindoos present an orderly, intelligent and amiable character, and the deeper the knowledge attained of Hindoo society may be, the stronger those qualities will be found to prevail.

Mahomedan characteristics.

The more the Mahomedan character approaches to the Hindoo, the softer it becomes. Many Mahomedans, as has been previously stated, are descended from Hindoo converts, and in agricultural districts there is only the difference of faith between the people; but the Mahomedans descended from the original warlike stock of invaders and conquerors are very different. Here is met the rigid formality and deep fanaticism of the race and faith: hating Hindoos because they are idolators and pagans; hating Christians even with a more bitter hatred everywhere, but in India more especially as their conquerors. Bigoted, narrow-minded, and too often stained with vice more deeply either than the Hindoos or ourselves, they remain what their faith has made them. On the other hand. courteous, brave, faithful, more truthful habitually than the Hindoos, and more self-reliant and independent in bearing and conduct. As subjects, however, of a great empire, by no means so useful. Too proud to work, they are bad farmers, and except in a few instances, as weavers, &c., unskilful artisans. Wanting in the bright, facile, intellectual qualities of mind which mark Hindoos, they refuse, for the most part, modern means of education; and either rest in profound and sullen ignorance, or do not advance beyond the bounds, even in the best instances, of their ancient limits of knowledge. Thus, in lagging behind, they find those employments fall away from them which, in the times of their emperors, were the hereditary and prescriptive rights of their class, and are in consequence moody and discontented. And yet, examples could be given of Mahomedans in trying positions, in which, for vigour and integrity, and for honourable and decisive conduct and action, they have exceeded the Hindoo, and approached, if they did not rival, the European.

Food of the people—Hindoos.

The Brahmins form the highest and most exclusive classes of Hindoos, and affect the greatest purity in their diet. All animal food is prohibited to them, as well as carrots, onions, turnips, and some other vegetables, and only a few of the lower grades, in peculiar localities, eat fish. In the northern and central parts of India, Brahmins eat unleavened bread; in Bengal, the south of India, rice—and these are accompanied by savoury dishes of vegetables and pulse, with ghee or boiled butter, which is esteemed very nourishing. They also use milk and curds in large quantities, vermicelli and sweetmeats of many kinds. This diet is also adopted by all the highest castes, who affect equal purity with the Brahmins, and they abstain entirely from the use of fermented or spirituous liquors, drinking nothing but milk and pure water. The lower classes of Hindoos, and some of the higher, as the Rajpoots, eat animal food, except beef: but sparingly, and not as an article of common diet. In other respects, and for the most part, they feed like the upper classes, and a vow or resolution not to eat meat is considered meritorious. In regard to spirits and opium, however, there is no restriction, and in some localities these are used to a great extent without reproach.

At their meals, Hindoos appear to Europeans, and indeed in comparison with most other nations, singularly unsociable. Women are never allowed to eat with men, not even a wife with her husband. Meals are always served in the kitchen, a portion of which is set apart for an eating-place, and the food is supplied from the fireplace as required. In great festivals at temples, or entertainments in private houses, open courtyards, and not unfrequently open streets, are swept and watered; long lines of platters made of leaves sewn together are placed on the ground, and when the guests are seated, attendants bearing huge copper vessels and trays of cooked bread or rice serve a portion to each, accompanied by the various savoury or sweet dishes which have been provided. Women do not mix with men on these or any other festive proceeding; they take their meals apart, and when the men have finished eating.

Mahomedans.

Mahomedans are not restricted in animal food, except in regard to hog's-flesh, which to them, as to the Jews, is an abomination. They are much better cooks than Hindoos, and their system of cookery amounts to a science. They dress meat in various savoury dishes—pilaus, curries, ragouts and the like—but never eat it plain roasted or boiled. Vegetables are dressed with meat or separately, and with all they eat rice, or leavened or unleavened bread. Spirits, wine, or other distilled or fermented liquors, are forbidden by their religion; but many, nevertheless, indulge in them to a great extent, especially in Southern India. As with Hindoos, women do not eat with men, but there is no particular place in the house set apart for eating. Some of the upper classes of Mahomedans now eat their meals at table, using knives and forks, with the usual table services; but these are very rare, and for the most part Mahomedans, as is the case with all classes of Hindoos, take their food with their fingers. While, however, Mahomedans do not object to earthenware and china plates and dishes, with Hindoos they are esteemed unclean, and they use silver or brass plates, or plantain or other fresh leaves, which, when procurable, are always preferred.

CHAPTER III.

OF THE PEOPLE—*continued.*

Hindoo costume—men.

The costume of the male Hindoos, as depicted in ancient sculptures, is still used. It consists of two pieces of broad cotton cloth, one of which is folded round the waist, reaching to the calf of the leg, the other cast gracefully over the shoulders. These cloths are generally ornamented by coloured borders of silk or cotton, and with a turban, shawl, or handkerchief, tied round the head, completes the costume. For the women, a single piece of broader silk or cotton cloth, plain or coloured, and from ten to twelve yards long, is first partly tied round the waist, forming a petticoat which touches the feet, and the rest being passed round the body and over the head, falls to the right side and down the back. A tight boddice is worn underneath, except by some classes in Southern India. This costume is very graceful and simple, completely covering the body; and the figures of women and girls, as they carry their water-vessels from village wells or river-banks, are very picturesque and beautiful.

Women.

Until after the Mahomedan conquest, no clothes, cut out and sewn together, appear to have been worn by Hindoos; and by many such are still esteemed unlawful. But for the most part male Hindoos now wear tunics as upper garments, with the dhoty or waist-cloth beneath. Others have even adopted the Mahomedan fashion of loose and tight drawers and trousers, and can only be distinguished from them by the fastenings of the tunic or vest being on the right side, while those of Mahomedans are on the left. The materials used for made-up clothes are generally plain English or native calico or muslin; but the wealthier classes, both male and female, particularly on occasions of general or household festivals, use the rich fabrics of their own country; brocades of gold and silver, gorgeous silks and satins, and the finest muslins, which no other country can produce.

made garments.

For the most part there is little difference between the present Hindoo and Mahomedan costume as regards made-up clothing; but Mahomedans do not generally use the single waist-cloths which distinguish Hindoos. They wear instead drawers, or trousers, tight and loose; and a tunic, long or short, with a turban and waist-scarf. Although, like the Hindoos, they indulge in the richest garments they can afford for festivals, yet ordinarily they affect great plainness of dress. Mahomedan women usually wear a full petticoat, a boddice and a scarf, which, fastened at the waist, is passed once round the body and over the head. The scarf is also used in conjunction with drawers, tight and loose. If the male Mahomedans use a plainer style of dress than Hindoos, the same cannot be said of their women, who, according to their means, wear the richest brocades and finest muslins, trimming their dresses with gold and silver lace and tissue. Hindoos and Mahomedans wear shoes or sandals when they walk abroad. In the south of India, sandals are perhaps more common than shoes, or slippers; but Hindoo women wear only sandals. Whatever the covering of the feet may be, it is never worn in the house—that

Mahomedan costume—males.

Females.

would be considered unclean; as also, the entering of another person's house with shoes or sandals would be discourteous. Shoes and sandals, therefore, are left at the door, and the feet of men and women are naked.

Ornaments and jewels.

Both Hindoos and Mahomedans are inordinately fond of jewels and ornaments of gold and silver; and even the very lowest classes contrive to invest some of their earnings in them. At festivals, Hindoo men wear necklaces, earrings and bracelets; but this costume is not followed by male Mahomedans. By women, however, both Hindoo and Mahomedan, there is no limit within their means to decoration of themselves and their children. Diamonds, rubies, and emeralds, all uncut, are set in every conceivable form; and massive necklaces, rings, bracelets, armlets, and anklets, with toe-rings of solid gold or silver, and pearls, are worn habitually. Natives of India reject all false jewellery, and even the lower classes of precious stones, such as amethyst, topaz and the like. Adornments, however humble in character or value, must be real of their kind; and thus possessing intrinsic value, form part of the actual wealth of the family, and pass from generation to generation as hereditary family property.

Amusements.

Among Hindoo children there is much more freedom and diversity of amusement than among Mahomedans. It may be said, indeed, that the latter are brought up as men and women before their time, and are much more secluded than Hindoos, particularly among the higher ranks. Except the very lowest classes, they are seldom seen at play; and they have no free outdoor games like the Hindoos, except what are shared with them. But among Hindoos, boys have marbles, prettily made of strong sealing-wax, and games for them not unlike our own: the marble is shot by being placed against the tip of the left forefinger, which is drawn back and let go suddenly, and not with the right forefinger and thumb. There are also peg-tops, hop-scotch, and a kind of trap, played with a bat, and a short stick set in a hole in the ground, instead of a ball, the rules of which are precisely like our own. Each of these games, and many others, has its appropriate season as with ourselves.

Kites.

Kite-flying is common both to Hindoos and Mahomedans, and is much more amusing and ingenious than ours. Kites are generally oval in shape, made of the lightest material; they require no tails, and carry, according to size, a great deal of string. When boys or men fly kites against each other, the object is to cut away or break their adversary's kite; and for this purpose a certain length of the string, nearest the kite, is armed with a paste in which fine pounded glass is mixed, and which, when dry, makes the string extremely sharp. When two kites are flying, the object is to get most to the windward side, and higher than the adversary; having attained this, the kite, by a turn of the wrist, is made to descend head-foremost very rapidly, and if the direction and distance be true, the string of the other kite is cut, or the kite itself is broken. If, however, the aim is missed, the adversary has the advantage, and does not fail to use it. Thus, in the hands of skilful players, kites are seen to ascend and descend, to attack and avoid each other; now to swoop head-foremost nearly to the earth, and then as rapidly to rise till one is cut away. While the season for kite-flying lasts, numbers may be seen in the afternoons over every town and city, nay over every village, the players being absorbed in their game, and frequently betting heavily upon it.

Athletic exercises.

For outside and more active amusements, there are gymnasia in almost every town and village, and they are used chiefly by Hindoos, who are fonder of athletic exercises than Mahomedans. In them, wrestling, leaping, the use of the sword and spear, the wielding of heavy clubs, throwing weights, exercises on the cross-bars and poles, are taught, and many of our present gymnastic feats have an Indian origin. Once a year all the frequenters of the gymnasium assemble, crown their instructor with wreaths of flowers, and, attended by music, march in procession round the town or village, to a place set apart for the purpose, when trials of skill are made before the assembled people, and rewards and prizes given. Several hardy outside games like prison-bars are played by young men and boys, especially in bright moonlight nights when the air is cool; and the tendency to active spirited games and amusements among the people is far more prevalent throughout the country in every part, than is generally supposed.

Toys.

Toys and playthings for young children are common in all parts of India; they are made both of wood and earthenware, and being mentioned in the earliest dramas and poems, appear to have existed from very remote times. If they are not so perfect and ingenious as those used by European children, they appear to answer all the purposes for which they are intended.

Dolls.

What the girls of India, whether Hindoo or Mahomedan, would do without dolls, it is hard to say, and they are at least as numerous as they are among English or French children. Not, however, certainly so beautiful, nor have they blue eyes, flaxen hair and waxy skins; they are of wood, painted, and are frequently frightful enough; but O the benign mystery of dolls, which inspire such universal love and care as is bestowed upon them everywhere! In India the Hindoo or Mahomedan girl of good family and ample means has her doll's-room specially set apart; she may have many, perhaps, and each in turn requires something to be done for it. One may be ill, and the doctor is sent for, who prescribes sugar and water with a grave face, and leaves the patient to be nursed. If all are well, they have to be amused by songs and house games. They are put to bed and taken up again, bathed, dressed and undressed. Sometimes one has to be married, and an elaborate marriage festival is performed, which lasts several days, and to which all friends, young and old, are invited. Sometimes one dies, and there is mourning. Dolls' ornaments and clothes are frequently very expensive, and I have known instances, in a princely family, of a doll's trousseau and jewels costing some thousands of rupees. Dolls sometimes need change of air, and there is a children's party at a garden-house, or in the fields under trees, and a feast, with a happy gathering of young people and a merry return home by moonlight. Were it not for dolls, therefore, Hindoo and Mahomedan girls might have a dull time; but whether from the young princess, with her dolls clothed in brocade and fine muslin and her splendid feasts, to the poor labourer's child who makes a dirt house in the village street, set round with gaily-coloured pebbles from the brook, and seats her rag doll thereon, sharing, for her festival, a pennyworth of coarse sugar with her playmates—the interest and affection is the same, and may not have varied for thousands of years.

Household employment.

Needlework, as understood among ourselves, is almost unknown among Hindoo girls, and in a limited degree among Mahomedans. The former do not need to sew their clothes. As they grow up they may help their mothers to make patchwork quilts or sew up boddices, but that is all. Mahomedan girls, however, frequently sew very neatly, and are able to cut out and make up clothes that are required in the house. They also embroider in silk and gold-thread very beautifully, and some make a livelihood by their work. There is one thing, however, which all learn at a comparatively very early age, and that is the useful accomplishment of being good housewives; looking after the servants where any are kept, learning how to cook, and in poor families, cooking themselves, or assisting their mothers to do so; helping to wash clothes and to sweep out the house, and when all work is done, spinning thread for the weaver. Except those of very rich people, female children in India can never be idle; there is always something to do, and it is very pleasant to see them do it; for few girls learn to read or write except in the higher classes, and they are thus thrown upon household employment to pass their time; and to take a pride in their household management, which, as they marry, is counted their husbands' honour as well as their own, is their chief desire. It may be hoped, nevertheless, that the means of female education which have been so happily commenced in India may progress rapidly.

The amusements of women are fewer than those of their children perhaps, and of no great variety. A few play chess, or a kind of draughts, or cards, or spin. They pay and receive visits; but above all they have their continuous household duties to perform, and the care of their children. They cannot walk abroad if they be Mahomedans, unless they conceal their persons. If the ancient descriptions of Hindoo society are true, women then, of all ranks, moved everywhere freely; but most of the upper classes of Hindoos, except the Brahmins, have followed the Mahomedan custom of seclusion, and their women would consider themselves dishonoured by exposure abroad. Among most of the middle classes of Hindoos, however, especially in Central and Southern India, no restriction of women is practised, and they go everywhere unveiled.

Amusements of women.

The foregoing amounts to a very sorry enumeration of women's amusements; but where husbands are themselves ignorant, they look for no accomplishments in their wives, and are content; and until the education of men in India has attained a higher general standard than it possesses at present, female education, did it even exist, would hardly perhaps be appreciated. The men are not, however, the less tender and affectionate to their wives; and the wife, as the head of the house, whether Hindoo or Mahomedan, is held in honour by every good husband, and exerts her legitimate authority as her best occupation. It will not be denied that there are bad husbands, as there are bad wives; but, on the whole, native married life appears to carry with it a fair average, at least, of domestic comfort and happiness. In ancient times, Hindoo women seem to have been far better educated than at present, and to have taken a more decided part in the ordinary public transactions of their stations. They appear also to have been instructed in accomplishments, and to have held a higher position in social life than they do now. At a very early period in Hindoo history, they and their property were protected by special laws, which are still observed, and the utmost respect to them in all classes of life was enjoined. In regard to the position of widows, in some portions of India, and peculiarly in Bengal, much reform is needed; for, in becoming widows, they suffer degradation which is unmerited, sad, and miserable. In other localities, however, this is not the case, and they are treated with the honoured respect which is due to them.

With Hindoos, as with Mahomedans, amusements are much of the same character. A few of both are sportsmen, in all grades of society; and large and small game is pursued with perseverance and success. Comparatively few are fishermen.

Amusements of men.

Hawking still survives as a field sport, and is followed alike by the noble with his train of attendants and hawk-bearers, as by the peasant with a sparrow-hawk or falcon on his wrist. Leopards are trained to run down deer; hounds are kept to bring wild boars to bay; and, in short, sporting holds its full place among men's amusements. Among Hindoos, however, it is only the martial classes who are attached to field sports; to priests, merchants, and traders, they are unknown. Both Hindoos and Mahomedans who can afford to keep them are fond of horses, and are for the most part good riders, and partial to horse exercise. Foot exercise, as an amusement, is unknown in any class, and the common expression 'to take a walk' would be incomprehensible. Indoor amusements are chess, draughts, and cards, with, sparingly, reading or study of any kind. Men who have little to do, and who are not occupied by trades or professions, pay visits at each other's houses; and small evening parties are common—for conversation, or at times music, professional singers and players being engaged. Among Hindoos, readings and recitations of ancient Sanscrit literature, especially portions of the Ramáyan and Máhábhárut, with dramas and poems, form a continual source of amusement both to males and females. Public festivals are nearly always of a religious character, and belong to both classes; and their celebration is never omitted; while a great number of household observances, such as anniversaries of births, commemoration of deaths, performances of vows, and ceremonies of purification, betrothals, marriages, naming of children, and the like, are frequent in most families, and draw together relatives and friends, so far as the observance of caste restrictions will allow. Hospitality is universal, and freely rendered; and its companion, charity, is denied by none, and is frequently almost too profuse.

Public amusements, in the European sense, hardly exist at all.

Public amusements.

There are no public shows, theatres, races, picture-galleries, or concerts. In some parts of India, individuals of the poorer classes, weavers and other artisans, learn portions of Sanscrit and vernacular plays and farces, and act them after a rude fashion; and there are also professional reciters of epic and other poetry, who are, for the most part, Brahmins. Strolling players, who manage marionnettes very cleverly, singers both male and female, all exist, and are hired by families at domestic festivals, or by village communities, and paid by subscription. Such performances take place in the open air, generally at night, in a garden, a courtyard, or the village square or street, and are heartily enjoyed by the people. Again, there are jugglers, acrobats, snake-charmers, monkey and bear leaders, and other vagrant performers of like character, who wander over every part of India, and contribute, after their humble fashion, to public amusement.

Some of the pleasantest public sights in India are the fairs and great markets, held periodically in stated places. For these the people put on their gayest apparel, and enjoy themselves very heartily. There are swings and merry-go-rounds, jugglers, acrobats, and marionnette players; stalls of children's toys, of sweetmeats, of gay cloths, and brass and copper vessels which sparkle in the sun. The people are cheerful, sober, and orderly; and for the time seem to throw aside the reserve they usually exhibit. At most of these fairs a large amount of business in horses, sheep, cattle, local produce, and merchandise is transacted, and engagements entered into for further dealings.

Habitations.

Throughout India the people, for the most part, are well and comfortably housed, though their habitations are not like those of Europe. In Bengal they are made of reeds and bamboos thatched for the lower classes, and for the higher, of brick, frequently of two stories. In Upper India, the houses of the lower and middle classes have walls built of clay, with tiled roofs; and the same in the south. In the Deccan and Central India, houses are built of clay, or rough stone and clay with flat-terraced roofs, covered with clay beaten down. The plan of a house does not vary much anywhere, and consists of a court with rooms round it, some walled in, others open, which can be closed by curtains. The houses of rich people are built on the same principle, and many of them are fine palaces, beautifully finished in cut stone, ornamented brickwork, or stucco; but the rooms are generally too small for comfort.

Furniture.

Many natives of rank, both Hindoo and Mahomedan, have now furnished their houses in the European style; but they have crowded into them chandeliers, sofas, tables, and chairs, without taste or discrimination. Such apartments are, however, never used by the family; and whether rich or poor, Hindoo or Mahomedan, the ordinary furniture is of the simplest character: a carpet or cotton mattress covered with a white cloth, a large pillow or pillows, form the only sofa, for the family sit on the ground. In poor families, a mat takes the place of a carpet. Accommodation for sleeping is equally primitive. If the family do not sleep on the floor, or bare ground, on mats or carpets, bedsteads are used with stout legs on which a carpet or mattress is placed with pillows and sheets. All these are removed in the daytime, the bedding is rolled up and put away, and the bedstead placed upright against the wall.

It may not be necessary to pursue these illustrations of the habits of the people further, and enough has perhaps been stated in these brief and general sketches, to introduce them generally to the reader.

CHAPTER IV.

OF THE OCCUPATIONS OF THE PEOPLE.

I WISH it to be understood by this chapter, that the people of India are not, as many may have thought, rude or uncivilised. Communities like theirs require a great many different professions and trades to manage the ordinary affairs of their lives; and it has always been esteemed one of the highest proofs of civilisation when a people is divided into classes which minister to each other's wants, and share each other's burdens. Men in a state of nature, as savages, have no such wants or distinctions.

Among the most ancient of Hindoo books there is a very curious one, the Institutes of Menu, which was translated into English from the Sanscrit by Sir William Jones, an eminent Indian judge, many years ago, and it is one which students of Indian history will do well to read. It treats, in the fullest manner, of the religious and social polity of the Hindoos, as they existed 1,300 years before our Lord appeared on earth—that is, more than 3,000 years ago—and to a great extent still continue. From that book alone can a true perception of the foundation of the Hindoo system be gained. In it are laws for diplomacy; for princes and their people; for priests and soldiers; for professional persons, tradesmen, and artisans, even to the lowest degree. It has been said of these Institutes, that they are too theoretical ever to have been practised; but though there is undoubted foundation for this opinion, there is at least no question that they present a picture of the Hindoos as they were when this compilation took place, which is alike graphic and truthful. The classes described, for the regulation of which the laws are made, must all have existed; and thence the conclusion is irresistible, that the Hindoo people formed civilised communities which time, and progress elsewhere, have very little altered. When it is considered what Europe was 3,000 years ago, and how few populations there were then on the earth who were civilised in any material degree, it is impossible to repress a feeling of respect for those who, at that remote period, maintained so high a standard, and transmitted it to their posterity.

Now, therefore, as then, setting apart princes, there are in India classes of priesthood of many kinds, some hereditary, some assumed, who expound sacred books, recite rituals, and direct ceremonies for the people; that is, name them, marry them, direct their funeral rites, and perform for them acts of sacrifice and oblation, and other offices of their religion, including spiritual direction and instruction through life, for them and their families. The highest classes of hereditary priesthood are called Brahmins, and by the code of Menu they form the first of the four degrees in caste. There are, however, other priests, hereditary and otherwise, who belong to Hindoo sects, and are not Brahmins; or, having been born Brahmins, have abandoned their peculiar distinction. Of all, however, the Brahmins are the chief, and are perfectly exclusive. No Brahmin can marry into another sect, and no one can become a Brahmin; he must be born in the order. In some Hindoo sects, persons withdrawing themselves from worldly employments may educate themselves as priests, but they can never attain the exclusive rank or sanctity of Brahmins.

The Brahmins.

Soldiers in very ancient times belonged to the order called Kshéttrya, which was as exclusive as that of the Brahmins, and only second to it in the social scale; but they are now much divided, and the profession has ceased to be exclusive. The present Rajpoots of India hold themselves to represent the ancient Kshéttryas; but this is denied by many, and it is questionable whether any of the pure original race have married. Any one so disposed can now become a soldier; and in the British army, as also in the forces of native princes, there are men of all sects and classes, even Brahmins, who have adopted military service as a means of livelihood.

Kshéttryas.

Next in order, according to Menu, come the Váishya, or professions; and, by the ancient rules, these also are exclusive and hereditary, and to some extent still remain so—physicians, lawyers, bankers, and the higher degrees of merchants and traders, of scribes, clerks, agents, factors, and the like, belonged to the order in the days of Menu, and still belong to it; but time has wrought a great change here, as with the military, and to all classes, professions are now open.

Váishyas.

The laws of Menu disclose how thoroughly the science of trading was known 3,000 years ago. Then, bankers understood and followed the fluctuations of money value; they kept account-books, day-books, and ledgers by single and double entry. They charged interest, simple and compound; they made insurances by sea and by land; they granted bills of exchange, and provided for protests; in short, they followed the practices of modern times, which are little changed from the ancient rules. Now, everywhere in India, are bankers who rival

Trading.

our own in the value and regularity of their transactions. They employ distant agencies, they make advances, and they lend money on every kind of security. Their books are kept with the same correctness and fidelity as those of English merchants; and it is rare to hear of failures among them, for they are farsighted and prudent in their dealings. Many of them are very wealthy, and the whole of the money-trade of India may be said to be in their hands.

While the higher grades of merchants have these establishments in large cities, those of humbler classes are to be found in every village of India; advancing money to farmers upon their crops, purchasing local produce, and dispatching it to large markets on their own account, or acting as agents for the merchants of towns and cities. Indian merchants in great cities, as Calcutta or Bombay, now send produce to England, France, or America; and import in return the products of those and other countries to supply the wants of their own. So also, it appears by Menu, that 3,000 years ago ships from India sailed to other parts, laden with Indian produce, and returned with what was required; and independent of the trade by sea, that by land, with western nations, was perhaps even greater.

The classes of shopkeepers in India, which are esteemed of lower grade than bankers and merchants, are as numerous as with ourselves. There are drapers, grocers, sellers of provisions of all kinds, druggists, dealers in hardware, in carpets, and in jewels and ornaments; in short, in every conceivable article of demand or consumption. There are not the magnificent shops which adorn European cities; but the vendors have the means of storing up all that their customers require. An Indian bazaar has not even the picturesque attractions of those of Cairo or Constantinople, yet it contains goods in as great profusion and of as great a value.

Súdrás.

The fourth division of Menu was called 'Súdrá,' and embraced many of the lower classes of traders just enumerated; and with them agricultural classes and citizens. These classes are very much diversified, and are the most numerous in India, which is essentially an agricultural country. In some localities the tillage of the soil is indifferent; but such instances are rare, and for the most part the cultivators of India are sound practical farmers, who fully understand the proper changes and rotations of crops, the use of manures, the difference between crops which grow from the rain which falls, and those which need to have water applied to them. They produce cotton, sugar-cane, ginger, turmeric, pepper, and vegetables; wheat, rice, millet, pulse of many kinds, with other cereals. They rear cattle and horses, and everywhere are peaceful, industrious, and persevering. It has been often represented in England, by interested parties, how the poor Indian ryot, or farmer, barely contrived to scratch up his land and throw the seed upon it, without care or thought as to how it might grow or ripen. This, however, is very untrue. Land in India requires to be ploughed very deeply at times, cleared from weeds, and in some cases richly manured; nor is there any part of the country in which there would be a chance for the farmer from any negligent or haphazard proceedings. The Indian farmer was using a drill plough to sow his land, centuries and centuries before that very instrument was introduced into England; and the farming implements, though rough and rude in appearance, are more efficacious there than our own.

Lastly, in the Súdrá or lowest class come artisans and labourers. In regard to the former, the trade of the father descends to the son almost without exception; and as trades have, for the most part, become castes, there is little change, and perhaps no advance in skill, in many of them. Yet there is all that the people need, and some of the principal may be enumerated. Goldsmiths, blacksmiths, and carpenters are the highest in social rank and importance. After them come weavers of many kinds, from the producer of the coarsest cotton cloths to those exquisite filmy muslins, brocades, and cloth of gold and silver which excite wonder and admiration, and are, as yet, unapproached by the most skilful European workmen. Some classes of weavers are Mahomedan; but the three first-named artisans are rarely of that religion. Tailors, potters, painters, masons, stonecutters, boatmen, fishermen, carpet-makers, mat and basket-weavers, saddle and harness-makers, dyers, brass and coppersmiths, barbers, cutlers, armourers, paper-makers, inlayers, marble and ivory-workers, embroiderers, lime-burners, brick-makers, rope-makers, silk-winders, cotton-cleaners, spirit-sellers, distillers, confectioners, cooks, butchers, dairymen—the list need not be prolonged, for it will be understood from those enumerated that they could only be supported by a people who need the artificial wants of civilised life to be supplied. Some of these and other trades are exclusively Hindoo, some as exclusively Mahomedan, and some mixed; but by far the most numerous are the Hindoos of the Súdrá division. Some common European trades are wanting in India—a miller's, for instance; for there are no wind or water mills in India Proper. All flour is ground in the hand-mill or quern, either by the women of every household, or by those who support themselves by grinding. Bakers too are very rare, for, except in large Mahomedan cities, and in stations of English troops, no one eats leavened bread; and there are no public ovens. Tanners, leather-dressers, and shoemakers there are in abundance, but they belong to the very lowest class, and are esteemed outcasts.

Last of all, there are labourers of all kinds—agricultural, helpers in trades and in warehouses, porters, and constructors of those mighty railway works which are now being led through the length and breadth of the country. And when are added to these employed persons, as clerks, accountants, assistants, attendants, servants, messengers, and the like, it will be evident that, in the great land of India, its teeming population has found enough to do, and that few are idle.

CHAPTER V.

OF CASTE AND ITS EFFECTS.

Separation of classes—Brahmins.

In the preceding chapter, the division of the Hindoo people into four classes, at a very early period, as provided by the Institutes of Menu, has been briefly explained. This was the foundation of their present separation into castes, which have still further divided the original four classes, and rendered their recognition in many respects extremely difficult. Caste, as originally devised, was not supposed to extend to Brahmins, who, as the head of the four orders, are sacred, and professedly beyond its influence; but, in point of fact, it does exist among them, and appears under many forms. First, in the sections into which the Brahmins have become subdivided, which differ in an extraordinary degree, in every part of India. For these minute subdivisions it is nearly impossible to account. They have proceeded from families and members of families who, having emigrated from one part of India to another, have retained peculiar customs and traditions; or, from pride of race, or other causes, have become exclusive. Or they have arisen from the adoption of peculiar doctrines, or customs of spiritual teachers, or from the exclusive worship of certain divinities—Vishnu, or Seeva, or Krishna, an incarnation of Vishnu; or from adherence to the ancient Monotheistic tenets of the Védas, and rejection of idolatry. Secondly, from impurity of descent, or having mixed with aboriginal or secondary classes. These separations have virtually produced caste, which affects social relations. Many of the present subdivisions of Brahmins will not eat with or intermarry with others; and any transgression of sectarian rules would involve a suspension or denial of caste privileges. Some classes will eat with each other, but will not intermarry. Brahmins who follow the profession of the priesthood only, frequently hold themselves superior to, and distinct from, others who are soldiers or merchants, or who have betaken themselves to any secular callings for a livelihood. Hence an immense variety of Brahminical castes have been created, which, though in general terms they have not affected the peculiar sanctity and exclusiveness of their original foundation, have yet broken the unity of their order, and reduced its power.

Regulation of castes.

The rules of caste among Brahmins are enforced by Swamees or spiritual princes or popes, and by Gooroos or religious instructors, who hold spiritual dominion over divisions of the country, and the peculiar sects of which they are the chiefs. These high authorities make tours among their people, holding confirmations, and performing other solemn rites. Persons who are charged with irregular conduct of any kind offensive to the rules of their order, are cited before their tribunals, and, on conviction, are suspended from caste privileges, fined, or ordered penance and pilgrimage in expiation of their faults or crimes. Agents or delegates from these spiritual authorities are constantly moving among the people, receiving information of transgressions, examining candidates for confirmation (moodra), and presenting them to the Swamee or Gooroo on his arrival at stated places; and by these means a strict moral surveillance and discipline is maintained.

Further development of caste.

Among the second, third, and fourth orders of class division, the disruption is even more complete. Professions and trades have become hereditary, as was recommended by Menu, and out of them castes have been formed. By inferior alliances, illegitimacy, and other causes, additional separation to a very wide extent has occurred; and the same effects descend to the lowest classes, and even to labourers. Each caste must observe its own rules and distinctions, which, for the most part, depend upon oral tradition. None can intermarry or eat with another. As a familiar example of such impassable boundaries, it may be stated that a banker or merchant of high degree could not marry with a rich tradesman's daughter of lower caste, without forfeiture of caste privilege; or, in regard to the children of such a union, if made, escape the necessity of establishing them as a new caste, which must seek similarly situated individuals for settlement in life. An infinite number of castes have sprung up, and are being created by such *mésalliances*. On the other hand, no reproach whatever would follow such a person's marriage with a poor man's daughter of his own caste, let their social station in the scale of wealth or position be never so far separate. Again, it would be as impossible for a blacksmith to marry a weaver's daughter, or to give his daughter to a potter, as it would be for a grocer to marry his daughter to a carpenter or a goldsmith.

Government of lower castes.

The government of each of the lower grades of caste is conducted by its own elders, in conjunction with their peculiar priests, who are not, as a rule, Brahmins, though Brahmins officiate on solemn occasions for all; and to its influence the protection of the morality of Hindoo society is mainly attributable. Immoral conduct, openly and defiantly persisted in, irregular connections with women, flagrant dishonesty, neglect or breach of caste rules in regard to marriages, to provision for children, maintenance of widows and other helpless family connections; neglect of religious ceremonials, eating or drinking with disqualified persons; habitual intoxication, slander, and the like—are punishable by fine and penance, imposed upon the offender by caste decisions; and although the English laws of India afford protection from any oppression or unjust awards of caste tribunals, such decrees are very rarely appealed against, and are for the most part efficacious. For the suspension of caste privileges is too serious to be overlooked, or, except in rare cases, even questioned. While it exists, the convicted person is, so to speak, socially dead. He cannot receive even water from his own family. He cannot contract marriage himself or be a party to the settlement of his children. The loss or suspension of caste follows him into every transaction of life, and would not be expiated even by death, since no religious ceremony could be performed for him. The preservation of his caste is, therefore, the untiring effort of every good Hindoo, and for its redemption, if he have erred, the utmost sacrifice is made. Religious morality, or a moral life which is the effect of religious principle, becomes of secondary rank in the social scale. Neglect of, or offence to, religion, unless it involves a breach of caste rules, bears with it only a distant contingency of punishment after death, and may be disregarded; but an offence against caste is punished promptly and severely, and cannot be evaded. It is a result ever present and threatening, which even a meritorious profession of religion does not avert. There may be, and doubtless are, persons who defy caste rules, and die impenitent and alone; but they are comparatively very few indeed.

It is not either as though a person of a higher grade, under the ban of caste, can betake himself for refuge or sympathy to a lower. No lower caste could or would receive him. To give aid to one so situated would involve a breach of the rules of the inferior caste, and would be punishable on the same grounds as those of the higher. No rejected or convicted person, for instance, could marry a daughter to a man of lower caste; the alliance would be scornfully rejected even by the most inferior grades. Every Hindoo has therefore his own peculiar caste alone to look to for the exercise and maintenance of social privileges; he has nothing above it, or below it; thus the preservation of this condition of his life is the leading principle of every Hindoo's mind, and the dread of damaging or losing it is hardly to be appreciated by any who are ignorant of all that it involves.

Caste in other Hindoo sects, not Brahminical.

The above remarks do not apply solely to the classes who are under the general or distinctive religious supervision of Brahmins, and accept the Hindoo faith as it is expounded by them, or by caste priests of lower degree who are subordinate to them. There are many other sects in India which have separated from orthodox Hindooism, which deny the authority and sacred character of Brahmins, and, in their peculiar religious profession, are entirely independent. Such are the Jains and Lingâyets, both very numerous, and others in various parts of India. None of these, however, permit breaches of caste rules to pass unpunished; indeed, in many respects, there appears to be greater stringency and severity of caste discipline among them than among the others.

Caste among Mahomedans.

The Hindoo system of caste control has extended, either by example, or of necessity in default of other means, for the enforcement of morality, in some degree to the Mahomedans. It is by no means uncommon for an incorrigible offender to be excluded from social privileges for offences against propriety, and to be subjected to punishment by fine, or otherwise, under a decree by his elders. Such proceedings are proved to be very valuable in regard to a class of people which might, and often do, become extremely dissolute; nevertheless, it cannot be said that Mahomedans have the same respect for, or dread of, caste rules as Hindoos. Among native Christians also, who exist in great numbers in Southern India, caste restrictions, very much like those of Hindoos, are still known to prevail, and with good effect.

Thus caste, it will be seen, has not an exclusively religious basis; nor is it, on the other hand, exclusively social in its aspect. It is a combination of both, serving to maintain the professed religious faith, and apart from that faith, to uphold the decent moralities of social life. As the religious belief of the Hindoos exists at present, were all caste restrictions suddenly withdrawn, they would give place to the wildest and most uncontrollable license, which, by their religion only, would be wholly unchecked. Caste discipline, therefore, is an aid to preservation of the outwardly decent morality of the people, and the observance of laws, which no profound jurist would desire to see abolished, until, by a purer faith, its aims, as well as its practical effects, could be accomplished.

CHAPTER VI.

OF THE RELIGION OF THE HINDOOS.

Where religious observances form a great part of the ordinary daily life of all Hindoos, it seems necessary to explain the motive, and as far as possible the tenets or principles upon which they depend; and, indeed, without this key, as it were, to the feelings of the people, many important points in their character could not be understood; nor, in a religious sense, the difference between mere superstition and a deep reverence for sacred things. Perhaps because Hindoos are pagans and idolators, it has been, and still is, the practice of writers to contrast their religion with the Christian faith; and, trying it by that standard only, to reject it as abominable. In this chapter it is proposed to review modern Hindoo religion as it is, leaving any comparison out of sight altogether, or to be supplied by the student; as a religion professed by 150,000,000 of souls, with a place of its own in the world's history apart from any other, and from its great antiquity, and preservation during centuries of change and revolution, being entitled to consideration.

Daily ordinary ceremonials.

To every European resident in India it will be evident that Hindoos perform a number of daily religious ceremonies. If he study the customs of the people, he will come to understand their purport; otherwise they will be necessarily unintelligible. A few of these may be briefly detailed. If a Brahmin, the Hindoo, as he wakes from sleep, repeats a sacred text, to guide him during the day. Many of these texts, chosen from the Védas, are of a highly devotional and supplicatory character. He then bathes, either in his house or by preference at a well, or in a stream, when he repeats the liturgy of the ceremony with invocations to the elements; and he pours libations to the manes of his progenitors. He then puts on clean garments which have been freshly washed, and returns home, where, in the room or closet in which, in every family, the household gods are kept apart, he reads a portion of the scripture, or repeats hymns and texts, in company with the women of his household and his children, who have also bathed. He then marks his forehead with the sacred emblem of his caste, and afterwards those of his wife and children. In some families, rich enough to maintain one, these ceremonies are performed by the family priest; and, after their conclusion, the morning meal is eaten, and the worldly business or calling can be pursued. It is the custom among many Hindoo families to worship daily at the public temple of their tutelary divinity, and present flowers or other offerings as part of their morning service; this follows the bathing, which is indispensable. In a necessarily brief sketch, the minute details of Brahminical worship cannot be followed; and what has already been stated may serve rather to represent the ordinary observances of those middle classes of Hindoos who have been educated sufficiently to read the liturgies, or to repeat them by rote. With the lower orders of Hindoo artisans and labourers, the details differ only as being less complete, in consequence of less instruction, or less capability of observance; but there is not a Hindoo farmer, artisan, or even common labourer, who does not possess household gods, who does not worship them in his house, and thus purify himself before he, or his family, can eat, or he goes to his daily labour, whatever it may be. During the day, a devout Hindoo will repeat the name of his tutelary divinity upon his rosary; no one gets up, sits down, enters or leaves a room, yawns, sneezes or coughs, without invoking his protection. No Brahmin opens his book for study, no merchant or trader his day-book or ledger, no blacksmith, carpenter, weaver or other artisan or labourer uses his tools, without the same form. But it is by no means necessary to follow the Hindoo through every act of his daily existence, which, from morning till night, is a continual series of religious observances; it is only intended to show that a system of religion pervades every Hindoo's life in its most ordinary and matter-of-fact relations, and, however humble or unpretentious that life may be, cannot be separated from it.

This, however, becomes largely magnified when more particular ceremonials are considered, which form epochs in the Hindoo's life; nor is there a single domestic occurrence which has not one appropriated to it from birth until death. Betrothals, marriages, birth of children, purification after childbirth, birthdays, performance of vows made on any special occasion, sacrifices, oblations, penances, pilgrimages, cremations, or burials and rites for the repose of the souls of relations—all, and many more events of life which it is needless to detail, involve the performance of religious ceremonies. Added to these, are the high festivals of the gods, visitation of particular temples and shrines, the worship and entertainment of Brahmins by Brahmins themselves and inferior castes; and there are many others, which have their place in turn, while of all, comparatively few are neglected or evaded.

Effects of ceremonial observance—Faith.

It would be out of place to discuss the influence which the outward observances of Hindooism have upon the people. The great processions, the often gorgeous and imposing temple ceremonies, no doubt excite them to enthusiasm, if not to fanaticism; but the religious lives and impressions of Hindoos rest upon a deeper and more enduring foundation than this. They are based upon faith, which, as the main doctrine of their religion, is the motive from which their practical religion springs. It does not concern them that the lives of the gods they believe in, as represented in the Puranas and other popular scriptures, are cruel, capricious, immoral, or on the other hand benevolent; or that the legends regarding them are filled with events which are utterly incredible or absurd. It is enough that the gods are believed to be as they are represented; that their actions cannot be tried by human standards, and that they have the power and the will to grant what is besought of them. Absolute, unconditional faith in them rises superior to all objections or impossibilities; reverence, even amounting to childish credulity, holds the believer in thrall; and a practical devotion follows, which is the habitual condition of mind in which the devout Hindoo desires to live. In the new system of doctrine promulgated by the Brahmins, on the resuscitation of Hindooism and the decline of Boodhism, the quickening influence of faith was undoubtedly the most important. The new doctrines are founded on the tenets of the Védas, but are simplified and purged from metaphysical subtleties, which had become, under these great amplifications, incomprehensible by the ordinary masses of the people, and the discussions on which are confined to the Brahmins themselves. Faith in the mercy and power of God, or of any divinity, male or female, as part of the divine principle or essence, efficacious to hear and grant prayer; the assurance that prayer addressed would be heard by one who had sympathies with human life and its needs, was a doctrine which accorded with the cravings of human souls, entered into their daily lives, and became part of their being. No matter who, of the whole Pantheon might be adopted as the tutelary divinity of a man and of his family, to that being they gave unreserved faith, and through all vicissitudes, he, or she, as it might be, became the object of adoration and of confidence.

Secondary influence of instruction.

Knowledge of sacred works, of the Védas, the Shastras, and Puranas may belong almost exclusively to the Brahmins, and out of them the people are instructed in the popular legends of the gods, and fragments of philosophy and moral principles; but the influence these exercise upon Hindoo life is of a secondary character to the faith or belief which has just been noticed. Tenets and texts, in the form of precepts, may be learned by rote, and the repetition of them be esteemed highly meritorious; but comparatively few, except Brahmins, understand them—ignorance prevents their application to the necessities of life, and thus they become of little or no avail in the guidance of everyday observance of religion. But if Vishnu, or Seeva, or any other god, or demi-god, be the tutelary deity of a house, a father or mother will pray to him for the life of a child, for offspring, or in any sore need. They will make pilgrimages to distant shrines, attended with inconceivable bodily pain or privation; they will swing by hooks, measure their lengths on the ground in journeys of hundreds of miles, burn themselves with fire, and give all they possess, as propitiatory acts for the aid they implore, or for the pardon of sin they have committed. Such acts are the voluntary emanations of the faith professed, which not even failure in the object will lessen.

Faith, degenerated into credulity, becomes at last superstition; and it will be admitted that Hindoos in general, not excepting Brahmins, are deeply superstitious. Among Hindoos the grossest superstitions are as notorious as they are lamentable; but for the most part they have no concern with the professed religion. They are terrors of evil demons, of serpents, of deities and spirits, who have no place in orthodox Hindoo mythology—sprites who can vex and afflict by disease or misfortune. There is no faith in these imaginary beings; they are never prayed to for aid; but terror of their malign influence is universal, and they may be deprecated by sacrifice and appeased. Such superstitions are the remains of the ancient aboriginal faith of India, everywhere observable as underlying Hindooism, and still existent, in its original condition, among the wild tribes of India who are not Hindoos.[1] This most ancient belief is as much the basis of the countless superstitions of Hindoos, as faith is of their religious principle; and is for the present uneradicable. Hindooism may even be replaced by Mahomedanism or Christianity, as has indeed occurred in some localities, but it is very questionable whether either has dispelled, or in any way affected, the Shakti superstitions.

To enter into a detail of the Pantheon or mythology, or other particulars of Hindoo belief, would far exceed the scope and intention of this chapter, which concerns the popular religion only. Students, curious to follow out the subject, may consult many of the original Hindoo works of which translations have been made. Of these, Schlegel's Latin version of the 'Bhugwat Geeta,' the most popular exposition of faith; Essays by Sir W. Jones, Colebrooke, Elphinstone, Mill, Ward, Professor Wilson, and many others; in particular, an admirable recent Commentary by Mrs. Manning will be found replete with information and instruction. The metaphysical systems of Patánjula, of Goutama, of the Sankya Sára, the Nyáya, and Vishéshika, which are still professed by sections of Brahmins,

[1] Hunter's 'Rural Bengal.'

may be examined; but these abstruse works, now hardly understood by their professors, form no part of the popular religion of India; they are the principles of schools of philosophy which, like those of the Greeks, were confined to the philosophers themselves and their immediate disciples. Among them will be found as sublime thoughts and aspirations as can be expressed by language, but disfigured by puerilities which are hardly conceivable.

Good works.

Next to faith, good works have a large part in the everyday religion of Hindoo life. To be kind to relatives and dependants; to be charitable to the full extent of means, and to be hospitable, are duties enjoined by every sacred and moral treatise, constantly preached or expounded, and cheerfully obeyed. To perform ceremonials, to make sacrifices and oblations, to present gifts to Brahmins and religious devotees, in the name of a tutelary divinity; to build temples or tanks, plant groves, construct bathing-places on sacred rivers, or dig wells, are works acceptable to divinity, and to be performed therefore as frequently as possible. The merits of such good works are preached by all classes of priests to all classes of people; and they are taught in schools with the more ordinary moral precepts of honesty, sobriety, truth, reverence for elders, justice, and the like, all of which, as antagonistic to sin, are counted as good works, and are believed to be highly acceptable to God. Nor are the consequences of sin—that is, not only positive commission of evil, but neglect of good works—omitted. Here, however, the religion of the people falls into caste discipline, which is a more direct and efficient means of preserving general Hindoo morality than is religion in the abstract, as indeed has been previously explained. Without the restrictions of caste, it will be admitted that the religion of faith alone, earnest and vivid as it may be, would prove a weak defence against immorality of all kinds; and it is under the joint action of the two, strengthening and supporting each other, that the Hindoos have not only preserved both, but that there is a vitality in them at present which at no period of Hindoo history would seem to have been exceeded.

Connection between caste discipline and religion.

Sects of Hindoos.

Among Hindoos, sects have sprung up from time to time, which have been secessions from exclusive Brahminical direction and superiority. Of these the Jains, as the successors of the Booddhists, is perhaps the oldest, and in it many of the Booddhist tenets are incorporated. The Lingáyets, who arose in the Deccan, in the eleventh century A.D., are extremely numerous in Southern India. They are a pure Seevite sect, worshipping no idols but the Phallic emblem and the bull, and rejecting the ministration of Brahmins for that of priests of their own. The

Sikhs also, who date from the seventeenth century, reject idolatry and refuse the doctrines and domination of Brahmins. Recently also there has sprung up in Calcutta a sect styled Brahmo Somaj, which aspires to the re-institution of the most ancient and most pure Monotheism, rejecting Christianity equally with idolatry and caste. Its intentions are benevolent, and it has met with some success, as its disciples amount to several thousands; but whether the movement has any vitality remains to be proved. There are many Brahmins also, in all parts of India, belonging to all sects and divisions of that order, who style themselves 'Vedanta,' who follow the tenets of the Védas, reject idolatry for the most part, and aspire to a pure Theism; but they have few followers. These various sects may, collectively, number among them several millions of souls; but they have no perceptive effect upon the mass of popular Hindoo belief, which, whether in its professed worship of idols, or otherwise, remains undisturbed.

In the popular religion, there is no doubt that idol-worship is considered not only necessary, but efficacious. Some classes of Brahmin and other scholars allege that the idol is but the inanimate object, which serves to fix the mind of the worshipper upon the being worshipped, and that in any other sense it is mere wood or stone; but this is not the popular belief at all. Images are held to be possessed by the spirit of the god represented. He is believed to be present at the time of sacrifice; he eats, he sleeps, he is bathed and clothed. The worshipper believes in a real spiritual presence, as an act of faith which it would be shocking heresy to deny. In some favoured places, where miracles are still claimed, there are more popular images than in others, because the god prefers to dwell in them more than elsewhere, and it is to these places that great pilgrimages are made from all parts of India, attended with an amount of faith and devotion that is difficult to define or express: and there is not a hamlet, much less a village, throughout India which has not one or more temples, possibly of a very humble character in many cases; but still each enshrining an image, of popular gods or demi-gods, for general worship. There are besides these the Grám Déotás, or village tutelary gods, which have no place in established mythology. They are benevolent spirits, who are believed to watch over village and other communities, protect their boundaries and crops, and avert famine and pestilence. They are worshipped and propitiated by a general annual sacrifice, at which all members of the community assist, generally before or after harvest; and offerings made to them are delivered to priests, who are rarely Brahmins.

It may seem strange and wonderful to the reader, that the

paganism which has been briefly sketched, should exist among an intelligent and intellectual people like the Hindoos, face to face with the enlightenment and civilisation of the nineteenth century; and that a religion which arose before the birth of Abraham, should have survived with, comparatively speaking, so little change. Such, however, is a fact which cannot be ignored in any history of the Hindoo people: and whether, by the present existing influences in India, it may be changed or modified, is a problem which, for the present, defies speculation.

CHAPTER VII.

OF INDIA BEFORE THE ARYANS.

Ancient inhabitants.

FROM the very earliest ages, and long before the Aryans, who will be described in the next chapter, invaded India, its inhabitants were wild and savage tribes, widely dispersed over the country; but all, in a greater or less degree, resembling each other in features and habits, and speaking rude languages, which are connected one with another in certain points. These tribes are now generally classed as Turanian, and belong to a very large section of one of the most ancient people on the earth, who inhabited India, the Eastern and part of the Pacific Islands, and Australia. They have been also termed Negritós, because of certain points of similarity with the negroes of Africa, though in other and very material respects the two races differ altogether. The present Negritós are, for the most part, very dark in colour, some of them being almost black. They have coarse and occasionally woolly hair, thick lips, and short broad noses. They are seldom tall, and never corpulent; but they are strong and active, and are able to live in deep forests and other unhealthy places without suffering. They subsist by the chase, and on fruits, herbs, and roots known to them, and they wear little or no clothing. Their weapons—bows and arrows, spears and javelins, and in some places that curious invention the boomerang—have a common resemblance to each other, which is at once curious and interesting. Modern researches have done much to bring together these strange points of agreement: and in museums, where they are all classified, it is impossible to withstand the conviction, that however widely separated by position, the Turanian Negritós now, as in the most remote prehistoric times, have the same instincts as to food and the means

Their habits and weapons.

of obtaining it, and the same habits of life; and that their weapons not only agree in form and method of use, but can hardly be distinguished one from another. A striking instance of this agreement is afforded in the boomerang, which was first met with in Australasia, and was supposed to be peculiar to its inhabitants; but the wild tribes of Southern India possess exactly the same weapon, and use it in the same manner. So also the science of language, when applied to all the tongues of this widely-spread people, finds agreement in construction, in roots of words, in idioms and phrases, and often in the very words themselves. These languages and dialects form a distinct group of their own, having no connection with other equally distinct groups of languages, which are traceable to remote times.

Languages.

It will naturally be asked how this is known, and whether any of these prehistoric tribes, as they may be called, still exist in India. Certainly they do exist, and in some localities in great numbers. The aggregate of the whole is computed at 12,000,000. Some of them still retain their original condition of savagery, being naked, or almost naked; inhabiting dense unhealthy forests and jungles, where no other human beings could live; shunning civilised men, and living in the rudest huts. These are among the lowest types of human beings known upon the earth. Others, probably from contact and connection with Aryans and other western invaders of India, are more advanced in manners and customs. They cultivate the soil, though rudely; they wear clothes to some extent, and are collected into communities and villages. They hold intercourse with civilised people, and trade with them, interchanging the products of their hills and forests for cloths, brass vessels, and such other articles as they cannot themselves produce; but, for all this, completely different in habits, in religious belief (if what they profess can be called religion), and in language. It is quite possible that all the aboriginal tribes of India were once in the same low scale of existence which is to be seen in the very lowest of them at present; and that those among them who have partly emerged from this condition, have done so under the example or influence of the Hindoos. But, notwithstanding their approaches, in some degree, to civilised life, these tribes retain their ancient peculiarities in manners, customs, rites and superstitions so strongly, that they cannot be classed with Hindoos, and indeed remain for the most part as distinctly separated from them in all respects as if Hindoos had never existed.

Present representatives.

Differences between present aboriginal tribes and Hindoos.

It may be taken for granted, therefore, that these wild, and at best semi-savage tribes, formed the aboriginal population of India, and were dispersed all over the country. India, in remote ages, may have been for the most part covered by forests, chequered here and there by tracts of open grassy downs and undulating plains, like those of the Deccan, Mysore, and the central provinces. Hardy, active tribes, which preferred an open country, abounding in deer, antelopes, wild hog, and feathered game, would most likely live on these wide plains and downs. Those, on the other hand, more timid perhaps, to whom the shelter and seclusion of forests, and the fruits, vegetables, and roots they afforded, were most suitable, remained in them; and thus the representatives of both are to be seen existing to the present day.

Along the bases of the Himalaya mountains, from the Punjâb to Eastern Bengal, lie dense unhealthy forests, of which some classes of aboriginal tribes form the only population. The climate, indeed, is so deadly, that, beyond a few months in each year, no other persons can live in it. Some of these tribes have become intermixed with Mongolians; but by far the greater number are Turanians or Negritós, and they extend till they meet with the Shans, Karens, and Burmese, to the east and south-east, and the Chinese to the east and north. None of them are, however, found among the mountains on the west and north-west boundaries of India—that is, west of the river Indus. A few of the most numerous of the sub-Himalayan tribes, classed as aboriginal, may be here enumerated; these are, Garrows, Tharoos, Boksas, Kacháries, Nagas, Kookies, Lepchas, and Loshais, with other wholly distinct, or of mixed origin between Indian and Tibetian, Chinese or Burmese races.

Sub-Himalayan aborigines.

Now, it will be remembered that, in the first chapter, the broad valley of the Ganges and Jumna rivers, and the hilly waving tracts of Central India, which rise out of it on the southern side, were described. No pure aboriginal classes are now to be found in the valley itself; but there are many different tribes all preserving the same general family likeness, though living entirely apart from each other, and speaking different languages and dialects, inhabiting the most hilly and hitherto inaccessible parts of these central tracts. Those nearest to the Ganges are the Santáls, a very numerous and powerful tribe. To the south and east, bordering upon Western Bengal and Kuttack, are the Kórewahs, the Lurka Koles, Ooraons, and Hós. South-west of these, in the mountains which divide Orissa from the open Deccan, are the Khônds, who were altogether unknown until of late years, when their horrible rites of human sacrifice, and practice of kidnapping children from the British provinces, attracted the notice of Government, and led

Aboriginal tribes of Central and Western India.

to measures for their suppression. All these aboriginal tribes are very numerous and warlike. All, in turn, have engaged in wars with ourselves; have been defeated, and brought under subjection and control. They are not entirely savage, but they retain their ancient rites and customs, and are pure in descent, without intermixture with Hindoos. Among some of these tribes, as the Koles and Ooraons, missionaries of the Christian faith have made remarkable progress, and it does not seem improbable that the whole may not gradually embrace Christianity.

Again, in Central India, among the mountain ranges of the Vindhyá, Sátpoora and Aravulli chains, are found Góands, Bheels, and Kólees. Further to the west Meenas, Mhairs, Waghurs, and others, all separate from each other and more or less imbued with Hindooism; yet still preserving their aboriginal distinctive customs and language. Of these, some are warlike and robber tribes, as the Bheels, Meenas, Waghurs, &c.; others, as the Góands, are peaceful and industrious.

Tribes in the Deccan and Southern India.

In the Deccan proper and Mysore, as also in the South of India, the Máhars, Mangs, Beydurs, and Chamárs, with Wuddurs, Whalleás, Puriars, and others, are the present representatives of aboriginal races; and have never perfectly united with Hindooism. They are superior in features and intelligence to the forest tribes; and, since their original subjection, have intermingled with Hindoo communities, and become, in point of fact, part of them; but traces of their ancient languages are still retained in their dialects, and underlying their profession of the Hindoo religion, are the aboriginal superstitions and worship of demons and spirits, as also of natural objects, which have never been forsaken. South-west of Mysore, among the Neilgherry and other mountain ranges of the southern end of the peninsula, Caramburs, Paliars, Irulars, and other strictly forest tribes are found inhabiting the wildest portions of the dense forests, most of whom are of the lowest type of humanity, corresponding with their sub-Himalayan representatives. These savages are at present as irreclaimable as the cannibals of the Andaman Islands or the Bushmen of Australia.

From the foregoing details, it will be evident that throughout India many of the forest and wild tracts are still inhabited by the descendants of the earliest races of its population, among whom their original languages and superstitions have been preserved. None of them have written languages, and few preserve even traditions of the past; yet it can hardly be doubted that all belonged to one great family, which inhabited India. Though Hindooism has existed in great power for more than three thousand years, and its civilisation extended to all accessible parts of the country, it is evident that little, if any, impression was ever made by it upon these portions of the aboriginal inhabitants.

Causes for present location by aboriginal tribes.

It is no less evident, that as the great Aryan race progressed in its conquest and possession of India, all tribes which remained unsubdued were driven to the hills, forests, or other fastnesses which they now inhabit; while others, uniting with the Aryans, formed the mixed races now represented by the cultivators, the artisans, and, for the most part, the civilised middle classes of the country. For those portions of the aboriginal tribes which did not join with them, the Aryan Hindoos appear to have had no concern. If they ever made raids upon the settled districts, they were driven back, and possibly invaded in turn; but there is no appearance of possession having been taken of their places of retreat, and there are no records of their having been ever brought within the pale of the Hindoo belief, or social system of polity or caste. In an equal degree, strange to say, they were neglected, or overlooked by the Mahomedans, who planted no missions or colonies among them, or strove to convert them either by force or by missionary priests; and to this day the aboriginal tribes are more familiar with Hindoos than with their conquerors, the Mahomedans.

What has been stated in this chapter is but a very brief sketch of a wide and very interesting subject for study, on which a good deal of light has already been thrown, while deeper investigations are in progress; but the readers of this work could hardly understand what was meant by the aboriginal tribes of India, unless some explanation of what they have been, and continue to be, were afforded.

CHAPTER VIII.

OF THE ARYAN CONQUEST OF INDIA.

Period of the Aryan invasion and conquest undefinable.

The most industrious compilers of Indian history have in vain attempted any definition of the period at which the Aryan race, or races, first penetrated to India, and established themselves there. They were a people, it is believed, from Central Asia, who brought with them the arts and polity of a civilised nation, and a language, the Sanscrit, which is one of the most expressive and perfect in the world. Their emigrations were not confined to India. At some very remote period, equally undefinable as that of their invasion of India, tribes, speaking the same language, had turned westwards, penetrated to Europe, and established themselves in Greece, and in different parts of Scandinavia, Germany, and perhaps Italy; and from the Teutons, as one of their divisions, we English are in a great measure descended. We, therefore, can claim a common ancestry with the Hindoos; but it was to them and to the Greeks that mental progress was first vouchsafed, while we, and the Teutons, long remained in a condition of comparative barbarism and ignorance.

The early portions of Hindoo chronology are undefinable. In the last degree uncertain and fabulous, there is no one point in them on which historic reliance can be placed. Efforts have been made to reduce their immense assumptions of time to correspond with other chronologies, but with little practical result. What are given as three of the successive ages of the world, amount to several millions of years; and while one king is said to have reigned 1,728,000 years, and another 10,000, it would serve no practical purpose if details were given here of what is so entirely incomprehensible. But there is a fourth era of their world's history, now fixed at 3,001 years before our Lord's advent, which does not partake of the same extravagance or inprobability. It is termed by the Hindoos the Kálé Yoog, and serves to express a date or epoch at which the Aryan Hindoos attained power; or it may possibly be that of their first invasion of, or settlement in, India: and is at least a starting-point from which other epochs may be reckoned. The Aryan was not, however, the only remote foreign invasion. Branches of a Turanian people from Central Asia, and of the Cushites from Arabia, have penetrated to India during successive Aryan invasions; but these portions of the ancient history of the world are too dim to be defined, and the chronology of the period before and after the establishment of the Assyrian and Egyptian kingdoms, is too uncertain to be quoted in reference to the Aryans of India.

Ancient Hindoo chronology.

The fourth era.

Other pre-historic invasions of India.

It is certain, however, that remains exist in India which are not Aryan, and may be Cushite, Turanian or Scythian. These are cairns, dolmen, and cromlechs; huge rocks which have been placed in certain forms as temples; barrows and tumuli. All these, and the contents of the cairns and barrows, iron arms, spears and arrow-heads, with rude pottery, and urns in which the ashes of the dead have been buried, agree almost exactly with similar remains in England and in Europe generally, which have been termed Celtic, and, both in Europe and in India, are, to all appearance, the work of the same people. Again, as in Europe, flint knives, celts, and other tools and weapons made of stone, have been found in various localities of India in great numbers; which, neither in workmanship nor intention, can be distinguished

Prehistoric monuments and remains.

from each other. It is a remarkable fact also, that these prehistoric remains in India are for the most part found south of a line which may be represented on the map between Goa on the western coast, Jubbulpore in Central India, and Orissa: and are further marked as lying within the boundaries of the southern groups of Indian languages, which are termed Dravidian, to distinguish them from the northern, which are Aryan. These Dravidian languages are found by philologists to be akin to the Turanian or Scythian of remote times. They are highly cultivated, and co-existent with, or possibly, as some consider, anterior to, the Aryan Sanscrit; and it may be assumed therefrom that a Turanian or Scythian race became settled in the southern portions of India, after an invasion, or invasions, by a more southern route than the Aryans, and that the prehistoric monuments may have been constructed by them, and are memorials of their progress. Certain it is, that in the purely Aryan and northern provinces of India no such structures have been found. These prehistoric remains in India have been only of comparatively recent discovery, and serve to prove how widely traces of occupation by kindred races have been diffused over the world in those remote periods of time to which there is no clue of historic record; nor is it by any means improbable that many successive waves of invasion may have swept over India, in whole or in part, all traces of which, except the imperishable monuments of Southern India, have passed away. Whatever they may have been, any opinion in regard to them must for the present be purely speculative, and therefore out of place in this work; and the course of the Aryans must be followed, who, as the most powerful and civilised of early foreign conquerors, left memorials of their own peculiar character which have endured to the present time.

Boundary of discovery of prehistoric remains.

Connection between Dravidian and Scythian languages.

The first authentic record of the Aryans which is at present in existence in its original purity, is a religious work called the Védas. It consists of four books, written in the Sanscrit language, and is esteemed the most sacred, as it is the most ancient, of the Hindoo scriptures. From these four books it can be understood that the Aryan Hindoos were a simple pastoral people, of nomadic habits; that they worshipped one God, with adoration also of the elements and attendant spirits. Some portions of the Védas are written in a language so rugged and unpolished, that they are presumed to belong to the very earliest periods of Aryan existence; others are fluent, poetical, and graceful, showing the progress that had been made towards civilisation. All the four books consist of hymns, liturgies and rituals; no historical facts can be gathered from them, and they are evidently a compilation

Religious works of the Aryans.

of sacred legends and ritualistic observances, previously perhaps traditional. The date of this compilation[1] has been variously computed. The Hindoos claim for it the epoch 3001 B.C., before noticed; Sir William Jones attributed it to 1580 B.C.; but Mr. Colebrooke,[2] by an ingenious series of calculations on astronomical data, fixes it in the fourteenth century B.C., or about the era of the writing of the Pentateuch. The compiler was a Brahmin, named Vyása. There is little doubt that before this period the Aryans had become united under royal dynasties. After the Greeks had invaded India, a philosopher named Megasthenes, who was an ambassador at one of the Aryan courts, obtained from the Brahmins a list of kings, which are quoted by Arrian and Pliny, 184 in number; which, allowing an average of eighteen years to each reign, leads back to the era 3001 B.C. previously mentioned. There is no historic record beyond this, and recent investigations[3] agree with those made by the Greek philosopher 2,000 years ago, almost exactly.

Pentateuch, 1452 B.C.

The next Aryan date which can be fixed with approximate correctness is that of the writing or compilation of the Institutes of Menu. They contain no historical facts, or genealogies of kings; but they are very valuable as affording a complete exposition of Aryan society and the peculiar divisions into which it had been separated. In comparison with what can be gathered from the Védas, it is evident that great progress in essential civilisation and settlement had been made in the period that had elapsed between their compilation and that of the Institutes, which, according to the best authorities, may be assumed as 600 years, or in the ninth century B.C. The Institutes contain the laws for a complete State, and its social polity, of which a king is the head. Portions of them may be theoretical, as regards the higher obligations between men and classes of men; but the details bear with them the impress of careful truth, and are evidently derived from the classes of the Aryans, and those with whom they had become intermixed.

Code of Menu.

Ahab king of Israel, 923 B.C.

The first settlement of the Aryans in India seems to have been made between the site of the modern Delhy and the Punjâb, which, as also Kashmere, there can be little doubt they had already overrun. This territory was called Brahma-Vérta, and lay between the Saraswáti and Kaggar rivers; its capital was Hastinapoor, and the whole tract is still considered sacred ground. From it, the Aryans gradually spread to the eastward and southward; but less to the latter than the

Locality of the first Aryan settlement.

[1] Elphinstone, App. I.

[2] 'Asiatic Researches,' vol. viii.

[3] Fergusson's 'Indian Chronology.'

former, as they followed the courses of the Ganges and the Jumna through a country of great fertility and beauty, in preference to attempting the invasion of the Aravulli hills, then no doubt inhabited, as now, by tribes of warlike aborigines. As they went forward, the wild aboriginal races retreated into the mountains north and south; though there were also many who became united with the Aryans, and formed the mixed races which exist at present.

This progress may have continued for a thousand years or more. During that period the Aryans had divided into two great sections, the solar race and the lunar, and each formed separate monarchies in Oude, in Maghada of Bengal, and other localities; but there are no strictly historical facts which can be discovered to establish particular events, and a mere list of names of kings is given in some of the later sacred writings of the Hindoos, without value or interest.

The Máhá-bhárut.

Where no historical events were regularly chronicled, and there were no edifices on which dates or dynasties were inscribed, two great epic poems, the subjects of which are drawn from early Aryan history, have survived the past, and afford illustration of two remarkable events—the great war between the solar and lunar races, the subject of the Máhábhárut, and the war of Ráma with Ceylon, which is that of the Ramáyan. The latter event is perhaps the earliest in history, but to the former is generally assigned the first place, in record of the great battle fought on the plains near Delhy, which resulted in the victory of the solar race, then represented by Yudistheer, its king, over the lunar. The solar race are termed Pandoos, from the king Yudistheer's four brothers, who are the real heroes of the war; the lunar, Kooroos. These distinctions seem afterwards to have ceased, and the two to have become blended together. Some of the Rajpoot clans, however, to the present day claim descent from one or other of the great divisions of warriors. The war is believed to have occurred about 1300 B.C.; it was therefore nearly contemporary with the alleged compilation of the Védas; but the poem was not written until long afterwards by Vyása, who, in the second century before Christ, collected the events described from existing traditions. The poem, however, bears the mark of much Brahminical interpolation and addition; and it is not improbable that much of it may have been written, as far as the events of the contest are concerned, at a much earlier period than Vyása's part in it, and the Brahminical and metaphysical episodes which have been supplied. However this may be, its details give a vivid picture of the social condition of the early Aryan period, of their mili-

Belus reigned in Babylon, B.C. 1322.

tary and political power, of their religious ceremonies, feasts, and entertainments, and even of their domestic life and clothing; and in these respects it is confirmatory of the general tenor of the Institutes of Menu. Many tributary and allied princes and people are mentioned as belonging to both sides in the contest; and it can thence be assumed that the whole of Hindostan Proper, from the bases of the Himalayas on the north, to the line of the Nerbudda river on the south, Guzerat on the west, and Bengal and Bahar on the east, was under the dominion of monarchs of pure Aryan descent, and that the Hindoo religion of the Védas, the social system of caste, and the laws of Menu, prevailed among their people. Many portions and episodes of the Máhábhárut are of great poetic beauty, and at the period of its compilation the Sanscrit language had perhaps attained the highest perfection. If possible, the Máhábhárut is more popular among the people than the Ramáyan, and the recitation of it, and its beautiful episodes, form a never-failing gratification to countless numbers of listeners.

The event which is the subject of the second great epic is the invasion of Ceylon by Ráma, a king of Oude. He was married to Seeta, the daughter of the king of Mithila; and during one of their excursions in the southern forests, she was surprised and carried off by Rawun, king of Ceylon. Ráma assembled a powerful army for her recovery, and for the first time the Aryan warriors marched southward. Among the forests and mountains of Central India they found wild aboriginal races in considerable force, who are described as savages, apes, and demons; but as the Aryans approached the south, they encountered people in a state of civilisation equal, if not indeed superior, to their own. With the invasion of Ceylon and rescue of Seeta the contest ends. The work is still in existence, and, like the Máhábhárut, forms the subject of popular recitation all over India. The existence of King Ráma has been questioned by many; but his name appears as a king of Oude in the most authentic of Hindoo genealogies, and his place in them gives him a date of about 2000 B.C. Possibly the civilised people found by the Aryans in Southern India and Ceylon may have been the descendants of Turanian or Cushite invaders, before alluded to, who had settled there; but in regard to them, even the Ramáyan, diffuse in other respects, is entirely silent. It is possible also that Aryan colonies may have been founded in the south by Ráma, which led to a gradual amalgamation of the northern and southern races.

The Ramáyan.

Semiramis, 2075. Abraham, 1996.

The student is directed to Volumes I. and II. of the 'History of India,' by Mr. J. Talboys Wheeler, which give not only copious translations of the two great epic poems, but much valuable comment and illustration of the Vedic and early Brahmanic periods of Aryan history.

CHAPTER IX.

OF THE BOODDHISTS, 598 TO 543 B.C.

The establishment of the doctrine of Booddhism in India embraces a period of great historic interest, and is perhaps the first event which can be fixed with precise accuracy. At the period when the great reformer Sakya Muni, or Gautama, as he is variously designated, preached his new doctrines, the original purity of the Hindoo religion and its simplicity had become debased; and the spiritual domination of the Brahmins, rigidly enforced as it was under the terrible provisions of the code of Menu, was oppressive and intolerable. Idolatry had commenced, and the worship of one God had been extended to Seeva and Vishnu, who had many votaries. A licentious and lascivious spirit had been introduced by the Brahmins, or was the result of lax moral discipline: and from these causes, the success of a new and purer faith of less exclusive character became not only possible, but probable. Sakya Muni was born in the year 598 B.C. He was descended from a princely Aryan family, who ruled over part of modern Oude, and was of the Kshéttrya, or warrior caste. He was well educated, and until his twenty-eighth year lived at his father's court. Becoming, however, disgusted with the licentiousness and frivolity which prevailed, unable to obtain religious consolation from the ceremonials or preaching of the Brahmins, and deeply affected by the sin and sorrow which existed in the world, he suddenly quitted his family, and betook himself to the abode of certain holy Brahmins, celebrated for their learning and the austere rigour of their lives, in order to discover the true way to salvation. They did not, however, satisfy him; and he left them for entire seclusion, from which he did not emerge until he had arranged and perfected the principles of his new doctrine. After that, Booddh, or the Enlightened, as Sakya Muni now styled himself, wandered from place to place, preaching his own tenets, defying the Brahmins, vanquishing them in arguments, and obtaining a great number of disciples; and it certainly affords a high testimony to the tolerant spirit of that age, and proves the comparatively small

Birth of Sakya Muni.

Cyrus born, 599 B.C.

Prophet Jeremiah, 600 B.C.

Sakya Muni's retirement from his father's court.

His entire seclusion and subsequent mission.

esteem in which Brahminism was held, that this vigorous preacher of a new and entirely antagonistic doctrine should have been afforded such free scope for his purpose. Before his death, which occurred in 543 B.C., Sakya Muni had connected his own family with many other royal and noble persons, and the Booddhist faith had been extended to the central portions of Hindostan and Bengal.

His death, 543 B.C.

The 60th Olympiad, B.C. 540.

The first Booddhists were therefore Aryans; and, despite of the Brahmins, and their hereditary and exclusive priesthood, the new creed was rapidly diffused, by means of missionaries, to all parts of India. It did not openly declare itself until the reign of Asóka, two hundred years afterwards; but the progress made meanwhile, must have been very extensive and sure to have admitted of the subsequent triumphant result. The main features of the creed were the subduing evil desire by contemplation, the practice of benevolence and charity, as means of overcoming earthly sin and sorrow, and obtaining a final reward by rest and absorption into the divine essence after death. The doctrines of Booddhism are extremely subtle, metaphysical, and difficult of comprehension; and any discussion of them would be out of place here. They professed, however, a purer and simpler faith than that held by the Brahmins, and seem to have satisfied the religious desires of thoughtful men. Idolatry was not permitted, and while the fanciful legends, and the licentious legends and proceedings of Hindoo gods were rejected, Booddhism retained the metaphysical philosophy of the Hindoo sages. It did not alter the social or political character of the Aryans, nor does it appear to have affected distinctions of caste: but while it was paramount in India, the people became freer and less exclusive, and their rulers more practically awakened to the duties and responsibilities of their position. The progress of Booddhism in India, its decline, and final extinction, will be detailed hereafter.

Diffusion of Booddhist tenets.

CHAPTER X.

OF THE INVASIONS OF INDIA BY DARIUS AND ALEXANDER THE GREAT, 518 TO 327 B.C.

In the year 518-521 B.C. the first invasion of India from the west, of which there is any authentic record, was made by Darius, then king of Persia. His army advanced to the Indus, where a fleet of boats was built by a Greek

Jews begin to build the second Temple, 530 B.C.

navigator, named Scylax, who sailed down the river to the sea. Scylax then followed the coast westwards; but it seems doubtful whether he returned by the Persian Gulf, which is most probable, or whether he coasted round Arabia, and reached the head of the Red Sea Owing to his report of the fertility of the countries traversed, Darius conquered them, and they were for some time tributary to Persia; but it is by no means certain that these conquests extended beyond the banks of the river Indus.

First invasion of India by Darius, king of Persia.

There is little doubt that the success of the first Persian invasion of India became afterwards known in Greece, and stimulated the desire of the Greeks to advance eastwards, through Persia, their hereditary enemy, to the rich country beyond. In the year 334 B.C. Alexander the Great invaded Persia, and won the victory of the Granicus; a success which, in 331, was crowned by the battle of Arbela, giving him possession of the whole of the country. In the year 327 B.C., excited by the accounts he received of the splendour and wealth of India, Alexander again advanced eastwards, and traversing the rugged mountains of the Hindoo Koosh and the wild passes of Afghanistan—sometimes having to fight his way, and sometimes received with honour by local rulers and their people—his host of 120,000 men debouched from Afghanistan, probably by the route of the Khyber, and crossed the Indus at Attock. Between the Indus and the Hydaspes or Jhelum, Alexander was royally entertained by Taxiles, the ruler of the country; but, beyond that river, he was met by Pórus, who held sway as far as Delhy, at the head of the Aryan chivalry. In the battle which ensued Alexander was victorious, and Pórus having submitted, was honourably treated, and his dominions restored to him. Alexander now crossed the two remaining rivers of the Punjâb, the Chenab and the Ravee, and arrived at the right bank of the Beyas, or Hydraotes.

The Grecian progress eastwards.

Alexander reaches the Punjâb.

Having already penetrated so far, and with his mind filled with accounts of the splendour and extent of the Eastern Aryan kingdoms, Alexander would have marched onwards, regardless of risk, and most probably would have carried all before him; but his Greeks would move no further, and he was obliged, for the present at least, to give up his project of subduing India. His Greek sailors prepared a fleet of boats on the Hydaspes, or Jhelum, and at the confluence of that river with the Ascesines, or Chenab, Alexander embarked with all his European forces and a few chosen allies, and sailed down the Indus to the sea.

He sails down the Indus to the sea.

It is not necessary here to repeat the details of the voyage, nor the dangers he encountered from local tribes who opposed him, and whom he conquered; neither is it necessary to follow him in his celebrated march back into Persia, nor the course of his admiral, Nearchus, who adopted the route of Scylax, by sea. All this is told at length, in other works which are familiar to every student of history: it is only needful to note the state of India at that period, and the effect of the Grecian invasion.

The period lay nearly midway between the establishment of Booddhism and the Christian era; and the Greeks have transmitted an account, in many respects very amply and faithfully drawn up, of the condition in which they found the Indian people. There is no mention of public edifices, for as yet architecture was unknown; or of magnificent cities, for the best habitations were as yet probably of wood or of clay; but of the population the details are very interesting. The system of caste prevailed, and trades and professions had become separate castes, the members of which did not intermarry or eat with each other. The country was thickly peopled and well cultivated, and each village formed a municipal community, which was governed by means of its elders and village officers, who were hereditary. There were manufactures of cotton and silk, of great beauty and costliness, and gold and silver ornaments were worn by men and women. The Indian warriors were not only well armed, and used elephants as well as cavalry and infantry in battle, but appear to have understood the art of war better even than the Persians; and their valour was very great. In other countries the discipline of the Greeks had enabled them to win great victories with very trifling losses; but in their Indian battles they lost many more in proportion, and the gallant resistance made by the Malli and other tribes of the Indus, surprised even Alexander himself, who was severely wounded on one occasion. The religion of the people was idolatrous, and it is evident had become greatly debased from the comparatively pure and simple faith of the Védas. Widows occasionally burned themselves on the funeral pyres of their husbands; but women in general held an honourable place, and do not appear to have been secluded. There were religious devotees and their monasteries, and other classes of mendicants, who, in pursuance of vows, underwent the most frightful penances. The power of the Brahmin priesthood in all spiritual matters was very great, and they were esteemed holy: as yet they had not adopted secular employments, and lived apart as professors of religion. There is no mention of the Booddhist schism, which appears to have been unknown to the Greeks at that period. Several great kingdoms existed in India, and many smaller principalities and States, most or all of which

Condition of the people.

were in feudal dependence upon the larger ones. It must be borne in mind, however, that the Greeks knew only of the kingdoms of Northern India; all to the south of the boundary of Hindostan Proper was as yet very dark. There is no evidence of the prevalence of any shocking barbarity or savagery; on the contrary, the manners and polite demeanour of the people are highly praised. The Hindoos were decently, not to say often richly, clothed; they were courteous and intelligent; they observed their laws, and indeed appear, in all essential respects, to have possessed the elements of civilised life in as great a degree as the Greeks themselves. In sciences, the Hindoos had progressed beyond the Greeks; they were better astronomers and mathematicians; and in metaphysics they had displayed as profound thoughts. They had cultivated their language, Sanscrit, to the utmost perfection, and had rules for prosody, for poetry, and prose composition. In discussing the most abstract problems of philosophy and logic, they at least equalled many of the most eminent of the Greeks. Learning, however, was still confined almost exclusively to the Brahmins, and by any other classes could only be procured at great risk, and under the frightful penalties of the laws of Menu. In all respects, therefore, the testimony of the Greeks to the existing condition of Hindoo society is most valuable, not only in relation to its peculiar period, but as exhibiting how little, comparatively speaking, that society has since changed.

Effects of the Greek expedition.

The expedition of Alexander, and the intercourse so long maintained afterwards with India by the Greeks, opened out, as it were, not only eastern stores of knowledge, but of traffic to western nations. It was claimed by a Greek philosopher, Diodorus Siculus, for Alexander, that the real foundation for his eastern expedition was the philanthropic hope of uniting all the peoples of the countries he should pass through with his own, and the collection of all the products of the eastern world at his great emporium Alexandria; and had he survived to undertake another, there is little doubt the result would have been much more complete and effective. It is certain, however, that a great increase of traffic followed the close of the Indian expedition; and as products could not be bought or sold without local agents, it resulted that Greek, Persian, Syrian, Babylonian, and perhaps Egyptian merchants visited, and even resided in, different parts of India. Intercourse, therefore, between the east and west became more frequent and more materially and practically useful. It broke down the exclusiveness which, owing to their situation, the Hindoos had as yet maintained; and though it was not immediately realised in the complete manner which the great Greek monarch had hoped for, yet was never afterwards interrupted, and never ceased to increase.

CHAPTER XI.

FROM THE INVASION OF ALEXANDER TO THE END OF THE MAURYAN DYNASTY, B.C. 327 TO 195.

ABOUT two years after his return from India, and before another expedition could be arranged, or any of his magnificent plans carried out, Alexander the Great died, in 324 B.C.; he had reached only his thirty-second year. After his death, Seleuchus, one of his most able commanders, became possessed of the province of Babylon, with those portions of the Indian conquests that had been maintained, including Bactria, which, as contiguous to North-Western India, produced very considerable intercourse between the Greeks and the Hindoo kings. It was mentioned in the last chapter, that when Alexander reached the Hydraotes, his desire was to march onwards into India, and subdue the Prasii, or Eastern kingdoms, which were represented to him as far more extensive and magnificent than that of Pórus. One of these kingdoms was Maghada, the capital of which was Palibóthra, a city on the Ganges, the exact site of which has never been ascertained. The monarch who ruled over it was Nandá, of the Nága, or serpent-worshipping dynasty, which commenced in the year 691 B.C. These Takshuk, or, as they are termed in India, Nága[1] kings, were descended from a powerful Tartar race, who, as Nága princes mentioned in the Máhábhárut, are supposed to have invaded India at a remote period, first possessing themselves of Kashmere, and afterwards, extending their conquests, became possessed of the Maghada kingdom, which had been in existence from the period of the Máhábhárut.

Death of Alexander the Great.

The Maghada kingdom.

Of Maghada, several kings in succession bore the name of Nandá; hence they are sometimes mentioned as the Nandá dynasty. The last Nandá was put to death by his chief minister; and a person named Chandra Goopta—called Sandracottus by the Greeks—a man of low extraction, but of great ability, became king, and founded what was styled the Mauryan dynasty. Chandra Goopta had served in the army of Pórus, on the invasion of Alexander, and after his departure headed an insurrection by which the Greek posts were

Establishment of the Mauryan dynasty.

[1] From Nág, a serpent (Cobra di Capella).

driven out of the Punjâb. At this time also, according t Justin,[1] he possessed himself of the kingdoms of Pórus and of Taxiles, and was therefore independent at the time of his election to the throne of Maghada: or he may have been powerful enough to seize the throne after the murder of the king.

The revolution in Maghada happened in 325 B.C., only two years after Alexander's invasion of India, and one year before his death, which, as already mentioned, occurred at Babylon, in 324. During the early portion of Chandra Goopta's reign, India was invaded by Seleuchus, who was opposed by him; but peace having ensued, Seleuchus sent Megasthenes, an eminent Greek philosopher, as his representative to the Maghada court, and he resided at Palibóthra for many years. He was a man with shrewd, intelligent powers of observation; and it is from the portions of his writings which have survived, that the accounts of the Hindoo people of that period are derived. Chandra Goopta consolidated the whole of the northern, and much of the eastern, portion of India into one monarchy; and during his reign great progress was made in traffic, not only with western nations by land, but by sea with those of the east. Hindoos founded colonies in Java and Siam, and introduced their religion into those countries. In India, roads were marked out for travellers, resting-places or inns were established, and the police is mentioned by Megasthenes in high terms of praise. As yet the national religion of Northern India was not altered, for Chandra Goopta was a Hindoo, and followed the established Brahminical tenets.

Reign of Chandra Goopta.

Sakya Muni, or Booddh, as has been explained in Chapter IX., died in 543 B.C., so that the doctrines he preached had been prevalent for upwards of 200 years. Although they had made very extensive progress, they had by no means, as yet, greatly affected Hindooism, though they may have checked its idolatry, and restrained the power and broken the exclusive character of the Brahmins. Hitherto, learning had been confined to them, and to the Sanscrit language as its medium; but Chandra Goopta began to cultivate the spoken language Páli, a dialect of Sanscrit, and thus threw open the acquisition of knowledge to his people. This, and many other popular and benevolent measures, were carried out in Chandra Goopta's reign, which continued for twenty-five years. He died in 300 or 301 B.C., and was succeeded by his son, Mitra Goopta, or Bimbisórá, as he is variously styled. He also was a Hindoo; but the Booddhists were tolerated, if not actually pro-

Progress of Booddhism.

Death of Chandra Goopta. Mitra Goopta succeeds.

Seleuchus founds An-

[1] Lib. xv. p. 4.

tected, by him. He renewed the treaties with Seleuchus, and maintained the honour and glory of his kingdom, till his death, 275-6 B.C., after a reign of twenty-five years, and was succeeded by Asóka, who, during the reign of his grandfather, Chandra Goopta, had given promise of great ability.

tioch, &c., B.C. 300.

Death of Mitra Goopta.

Asóka, his son, succeeds.

When Asóka ascended the throne of Maghada, the kingdom extended from the mouths of the Ganges on the east to those of the Indus on the west, thus embracing not only all the northern provinces of India as far as Bactria, but portions of the Deccan. The limits of this widely-spread dominion are marked by stone pillars with inscriptions recorded upon them, in the Páli language, many of which still remain. They are traced from Orissa, on the west of Bengal Proper, to beyond Kabool, in Afghanistan. At Girnar, in Kutch, Asóka's edicts were carved upon granite rocks, and are still perfectly legible; and their collection and translation by Mr. James Prinsep, who first discovered a key to the character used by Asóka, and other eminent Oriental scholars, has thrown a flood of light upon the transactions of this remote period. They prove Asóka to have been a singularly wise and benevolent monarch, ardent in the advancement of civilisation, and earnest in the protection of his subjects. By him, the first popular courts of justice known in India were established; they were of several degrees, civil and criminal, suitable to the wants of the people, and by them capital punishment was abolished. Means of traffic and communication by roads were also extended. At an early period after his accession to the throne, Asóka renounced the Hindoo faith, and joined the Boodhist, which became that of the nation at large. After a great synod, held in 286 B.C., religious and political missions were dispatched to neighbouring and distant countries, and Tibet, China, Burmah, Cambodia, Siam, Java, and Ceylon received the Boodhist missionaries with a strange and fervent ardour, so that millions of converts were made; nor is it improbable that Boodhism may have been preached in Britain, as it was in Greece.

His dominions.

Asóka's character and acts.

His adoption of the Boodhist faith.

Boodhist missions.

Asóka maintained friendly intercourse with Grecian and Syrian monarchs, and with Egypt, and brought many of the useful arts and sciences of those countries into his own. To him can be traced the commencement of architecture and sculpture in India, as applied to religious and other public edifices, which may have been introduced from Bactria, or possibly from Greece itself. It has been ascertained beyond a doubt, that before his reign architecture was not applied to public buildings, as temples and the like; in fact, that none existed: and

Commencement of architecture.

it may be assumed that even up to Asóka's period, the most populous cities consisted of little better than clay or wooden dwellings. This too may account for the disappearance—as in the cases of Palibóthra, Paithána, and other cities known to the Greeks—of all traces of them at the present time. It may be concluded, therefore, from the perfectly authentic details of Asóka's reign, that the Aryan population was not only materially advanced in civilisation and political power, but became less exclusive in character and religious belief. While he lived, Booddhism attained, perhaps, its greatest extent and authority in India. Hindooism was not, however, entirely suppressed, and the Brahmins, while they were no longer recognised as the dominant heads of religious society, were yet respected as learned men, and were not interfered with so long as they did not come into collision with the progress of the new religion.

Victory of the Romans over the Gauls, 225 B.C.

Asóka dies. Division of his empire follows.

Extinction of the Mauryan dynasty.

Battle of Lama, and end of Second Punic War, 196 B.C.

Asóka died in the year 226 B.C., having reigned thirty-seven years, in great usefulness and splendour. After that event his noble empire declined. His three sons divided it between them; and, with their descendants, the great Mauryan dynasty, established by Chandra Goopta, ceased to exist about 195 B.C., having lasted about 139 years. It was the first which came into intimate and prolonged connection with the Greeks, and from this cause, and the inscriptions and edicts recorded by Asóka and others, becomes actually historical, without the mist of mere tradition and allegory which accompanies all its predecessors. One of the earliest specimens of architecture perhaps in India is the Booddhist stupa, or shrine, at Sanchi, in Central India, which was commenced in 255 B.C., the celebrated seventeenth year of Asóka's reign. It is a noble and curious work, which, with a similar but later erection at Amravati, on the Krishna river, have lately been brought to public notice.[1] Several of the cave temples and Viharas, or monasteries, excavated from the solid rock in various localities, belong to this dynasty, which, till its close, appears to have consistently professed the Booddhist faith.

[1] They form the subject of a noble volume illustrative of Tree and Serpent Worship in connection with Booddhism, written by J. Fergusson, Esq., F.R.S., and published under the authority of the Secretary of State for India, 1868.

CHAPTER XII.

FROM THE END OF THE MAURYAN DYNASTY TO THE CHRISTIAN ERA, 195 B.C. TO A.D. 1.

FOR this unsatisfactory period in Indian history several reasons may be assigned. The Greek connection with the great Maghada dynasty had ceased, and the historian can no longer draw from Grecian sources what the local records do not supply. Nor were passing events, as in the case of Asóka's reign, commemorated by inscriptions so full and so authentic; but from genealogical lists in the Hindoo Puranas, or later sacred scriptures, and from occasional inscriptions upon cave temples and monasteries, something has been done to redeem the otherwise hopeless uncertainty which had previously existed.

After the death of Asóka, in 226 B.C., seven princes successively occupied the throne of Maghada, till 195 B.C., a period of only thirty-one years, giving an average of a little more than four years to each. This is distinctive of many revolutions and possible contentions; for when the kingdom had been once divided, it was impossible, according to the usual course of Eastern political events, that continued disputes and efforts to obtain the mastery should not have occurred. Out of the Mauryan, therefore, other royal, but much smaller, dynasties may have proceeded, of which no account, or even tradition, has been preserved. There are, however, several dynasties co-existent with the Mauryan, which may be mentioned.

Successors of Asóka.

Second Punic War ends, 196 B.C.

The kingdom of Mithila, now represented by Benares, had survived from the period of the Ramáyan, 1400 B.C.; for King Ráma's wife, Seeta, the innocent cause of the war with Ceylon, was a daughter of the 'king of Mithila.' Although unquestionably one of the most ancient of the Aryan States, it does not appear at any time to have possessed extensive territories or power; and in the period under notice was most probably subject to Maghada. In like manner, Gour, in Bengal, a city of even greater antiquity than Mithila, was the capital of a local kingdom; both serving to prove the progress and settlement of the Aryans eastward, and their establishment of monarchies.

Kingdom of Mithila.

Kingdom of Gour.

Among these varied dynasties may be mentioned that of the Sangás, which, following the Mauryan, commenced B.C. 188, and, in a succession of ten princes, continued for 112 years; that is, to B.C. 86. They were Booddhists, and were famous for their religious zeal in the construction of religious edifices, and excavation of cave temples. To them the Booddhist caves in Kuttack may be attributed. The second great 'tope' at Sanchi was the work of Pushpamitra, the first of the dynasty, in B.C. 188. The cave temples at Bája are attributed to King Pulindáka, B.C. 127; and the best known, and in most respects most beautiful and still perfect of these excavated temples, the great cave at Karlee, between Bombay and Poona, to King Dévabhuti, in B.C. 86.[1] The inscriptions on these great works have preserved the names of the kings of this dynasty, which appears to have ceased with Dévabhuti, and the localities of the memorials themselves may indicate the extent of their jurisdiction.

Sangā dynasty.

Romans enter Asia, B.C. 190.

Mithridates defeated by Scylla, B.C. 86.

At Kanouj, in Oude, under the hills of Nipal, another great Hindoo dynasty sprang up, or at least materially increased in power during the period under notice. Their princes did not join the Booddhist movement; they were exclusively Hindoos, and perhaps Brahmins. It is at least certain, that they protected vast numbers of Brahmins during their persecution by the Booddhists; for one of the most numerous of the northern Brahminical sects is termed Kanoujya. Grants of land were made to them, and they became farmers, as many continue to be. The Kanoujya Brahmins are not esteemed as of the purest rank by others; they seldom hold priestly offices, and many of them enter the military service. They are, perhaps, the finest physical race in India, and of the true Aryan type.

Kanouj.

The greatest Indian monarch of the first century before Christ was Vikram-Aditya, a prince of the Andhra dynasty, which, both at Maghada, to which it succeeded, and at Warungul, south of the Godavery river, which it founded, rose to great power, and ruled over Malwah and Central India, as well as Maghada, for several centuries. The commencement of the reign of Vikram-Aditya, B.C. 56, was established as a Hindoo era, and is still continued. He was a very popular and enlightened ruler, and at his court literature was highly patronised, many of the best Hindoo plays, poems, and philosophical works having been there composed. An authentic event, connected with Vikram-Aditya's reign, was an invasion of Western India by the Tue-Che, or Huns, about 26 B.C. They were defeated in a great battle by King Vikram, but do not appear to have left the country, as they

Andhra dynasty and Vikram-Aditya.

Nero emperor of Rome, B.C. 54.

Octavius emperor.

[1] Fergusson's 'Chronological Table.'

are traceable, as holding Western India for 248 years afterwards.[1] These Huns were Scythians; and either to them, or to prior invasions by the same people, the prehistoric remains mentioned in Chapter VIII. probably belong.

Sáh dynasty.

Cæsar in Gaul.

Contemporary with the rise of the Andhra dynasty may be mentioned the Sáh, founded by Náhápána in 57 B.C., which was destined to become very powerful.

Kanwa dynasty.

The Kanwas, who commenced to reign in 76 B.C., and in a succession of four princes, were extinct in B.C. 31. These and other smaller States appear by inscriptions of their own, or are included in those of others; but the extent of their dominions, their capital cities, and, with few exceptions, the events of their reigns, are unintelligible.

Battle of Actium.

To add to the confusion of northern dynastic history belonging to the two centuries before Christ, it is believed that there were several invasions of Northern India by the Greek Bactrians, under Demetrius and Menander, and by 'Yavanas' from Kashmere. 'In the reign of Bhoja,' writes Mr. Stirling, in 'Asiatic Researches,' vol. xv., 'the "Yavanas," from Sindha (Sinde) Dés, invade the country in great force, but are driven back. Then follows Vikram-Aditya. If, therefore, the dates are to be depended on, these invasions took place before the Christian era. Other Yavana invasions occur in the next four reigns; but the most important of all occurred in the reign of Subhan Deo, who ascended the throne in the year 318, the year of the Bullabhi era. In the ninth year of his reign a Yavana, Rakta Bahu, invades the country (Orissa) by sea, and conquers it. . . . . His son succeeds, but is murdered by the invaders. A Yavana dynasty then ruled over Orissa for a space of 146 years, or down to A.D. 473.'

Invasions by Yavanas by land and sea.

By these admixtures of foreign races, the original Aryan stock no doubt became greatly modified. This also was a period of much religious excitement and disturbance; for, after the existence of Booddhism as a national religion, so long as there were dynasties of princes to maintain it, Hindooism, never eradicated, sprang suddenly into renewed strength, and a deadly persecution of the Booddhists ensued, which in time spread all over India, and ceased only with their expulsion. It was not only that the Brahminical faith had never been extinguished, but that the Booddhist creed did not, after experience, sit easily upon the Indian people. In essentials it was too cold, too abstract, and too self-mortifying, to attract many real worshippers; and, by the common population, it is questionable

Revival of Brahminism and persecution of Booddhists.

[1] 'Bhan Dajee,' quoted by Fergusson.

whether its ultra-metaphysical doctrines could even be understood at all, while its rigid penances, fasts, vigils, and contemplations, could not be undertaken. Booddhism had moreover split up into a number of sects, and it seemed never decided whether it was not in effect a covert atheism, without any distinct indications of a future state, except the annihilation of the Nirvana, or absorption into the Divine Being. This did not suit a lively and imaginative people like the Aryan Hindoos; and the Brahmins, men of powerful intellect, and great experience of human nature and of the people, employed themselves, during the predominance of Booddhism, in drawing up that new system of Hindoo belief and practice which still exists in India.

The new Hindoo faith.

To the old simple faith of the Védas they added an immense Pantheon like that of the Greeks, only infinitely more fanciful and grotesque; and it is quite possible, that they may have moulded their Pantheon on the model of that of the Greeks, with which they had become acquainted during the period which followed the invasion of Alexander. To this was added the doctrine of faith, and other philosophic tenets that belonged especially to early Hindooism. Such was the new creed which the Booddhist formalists had to encounter. As the Booddhist dynasties—the Mauryans, Sangás, Kanwas—became weaker, they were replaced by vigorous Hindoo kingdoms, like the Andhras, under Vikram-Aditya, and others, who became the prominent supporters and propagators of the new Hindoo faith.

The beginning of the movement is ascribed to the miraculous appearance of four brothers, styled Agni-Kool, or sons of fire, who, according to the legend, were produced out of the fire-fountain of sacrifice on Mount Aboo, in Guzerat, under the powerful incantations of a Brahmin, named Vashishta. They are supposed to have been Rajpoot princes, and descent from them is still claimed by Rajpoot clans.[1] It is certain that the warlike classes of India, who probably never embraced Booddhism, were early enlisted on the side of persecution, and assisted their priesthood; and that the Booddhists were driven from their monasteries, which were destroyed, or having been purified, were converted into Hindoo temples. Brahmins preached the renewed Hindooism boldly through India, and the people heard with wondering ears of the existence of gods and goddesses, under the new revelation of the sacred Puranas; of their loves and contests, and passions akin to humanity; of new and different heavens and hells; of miracles of the gods, and of deified heroes, and their interest in the affairs of men. There were too many elements of popular faith mingled

[1] Tod's 'Rajasthan,' &c.

with these strange legends to escape the belief of the Hindoo people. The whole of the new scheme of religion was accepted with an avidity of which the persecution of the Booddhists was an earnest proof; and the Brahmins, as the receivers of a fresh and divine revelation, became more powerful than ever. Then idol-worship recommenced. The images of gods and demi-gods were created after a rude fashion which has never altered, and set up in religious edifices, which had never before existed; and these were mingled with the pre-existent Seevite adoration of the Pillar and the Calf followed by the Israelites, and of trees and serpents, until the present elements of Hindoo faith were completed, and no matter how old, or how incongruous, were believed. Splendid festivals, liturgies, and ceremonial observances were combined with a licentious faith and practice, and proved irresistible to the Hindoo people of all ranks; and it is consistent with their character that Booddhism declined. It was not, however, altogether extinguished; there were still princes and their people powerful enough to preserve it for the present, and indeed for four centuries afterwards.

In other respects, up to the Christian era, India does not seem to have much changed. The system of the divisions of the people by Menu still prevailed. Literature and the science of astronomy, mathematics and logic, as well as religious and metaphysical philosophy, had attained their greatest height; and though as yet no union of India under one particular dynasty or empire is apparent, yet individual kingdoms were locally powerful, the people were civilised, and, as far as can be ascertained, content and prosperous.

During this period also, the progress of the Aryans towards the south of India was an active one. There are no records, it is true, of that progress, nor of the faith which may have been professed before Hindooism; but that powerful States arose which were Hindoo, there can be no question, nor any that Booddhism was established in some localities; but, on the whole, there is great historic darkness in regard to the condition of the south until the era of Ptolemy, A.D. 140. It is, however, extremely 160th
probable that Egyptian and Greek, and possibly also Olympiad.
Roman, merchants visited the southern portions of India before, as they undoubtedly did after, the Christian era; and that, in the period now under consideration, there was comparatively little difference between the population of the north of India and of the south.

CHAPTER XIII.

OF THE NORTHERN MEDIÆVAL DYNASTIES, A.D. 100 TO 700.

At the period of the Christian era, the northern portion of India was ruled over by several powerful dynasties, of which a brief summary is necessary.

Andhras. I. The Andhras held part of North-Eastern India, which included Maghada, as their northern capital, and of Telingána, the tract which intervenes between the Deccan and the sea. Another capital for the southern provinces was founded at Wurungul. In a series of twenty-nine princes, Vandals in Africa. whose names and dates of succession have been ascertained, the Andhras are traceable as far as 436 A.D., and will appear again, in however a reduced condition, in contact with the Mahomedans.

Pálás. Pálá dynasty. II. Eastward from the Andhras lay the great kingdom of Bengal, ruled by a dynasty known under the designation of Pálá, which, according to inscriptions of various periods, claims to have ruled over all India and Ceylon at one period, and to have included even Tibet in its dominions.[1] It has always, however, been found difficult to decide, in relation to the text of early Indian inscriptions, whether to admit the facts they profess to record, or, on the other hand, to attribute them to the ingenuity of the scribes who, in order to magnify the records of their patrons, mingled together the most incongruous materials and traditions of conquest and dominion. There is no doubt, Séna dynasty. however, that the Pálá dynasty, and its successor the Séna, reigned in Bengal up to the Mahomedan conquest of that province; and as communication by sea was easy and frequent with Ceylon, they may have shared with others the occasional sovereignty of that island.

III. Shortly before the Christian era, a Tartar race established Tartar dynasties of Kashmere. themselves in Kashmere, and became Booddhists. In the year 21 A.D., the reigning king, Abhimánya, erected 200th Olympiad. the gateways of the celebrated tope or shrine at Sanchi,[2] in Central India, as one of the established memorials of the dynasty, which appears to have ceased with him, and was Gonardhás: I. succeeded by the Gonardhás, who added snake-worship to their Booddhism, though it is very probable that this peculiar faith was that of the original Tartar invaders.

[1] Elphinstone's 'History,' vol. i.; Colebrooke, &c.
[2] Fergusson's 'Chronology.'

The Gonardhás were large contributors to the Booddhist monuments and remains of India. The third of their line, Ravánâ, constructed some of the early cave temples at Ajunta, in the Deccan, about the close of the first century A.D. The eleventh prince, Mihirakála, about the second century A.D., raised the central building of the Booddhist shrine of Amravati,[1] on the Krishna river. The seventeenth in succession built the Booddhist tope called Tukht-i-Soliman, in the Punjâb; and to his successor Gokárna, the Booddhist excavations near Nassúk are attributed; as also to the last but one of the dynasty, Narendráditya, the beautiful outer rail of the Temple of Amravati.[1] With the next prince, Yudishthéra, the Gonardhá dynasty ceased for an interval of six 'Aditya' kings, who also appear to have been great constructors and excavators. By Tunjisia, in the close of the third century A.D., the inner rail of the Amravati tope was added;[2] and by Jayendra, the fifth Aditya, the great Booddhist caves and monasteries at Keneri, near Bombay, were excavated. About A.D. 450, the Gonardhá dynasty was again raised to power by Méghaváhána; and the beautiful zodiac cave temple at Ajunta, 530 A.D., the temple of Martund, in Kashmere, and that of Bhuvanéshwar, in Orissa, 622 A.D.,[3] still remain as memorials of this dynasty.

Construction of cave temples.

Adityas.

Gonardhás: II. restored.

Marcian emperor of the East.

Pope Boniface II.

Hejira of Mahomed.

Although its works, in temples, &c., lie as far south as Amravati, on the banks of the Krishna, they can hardly be accepted as proofs of the actual dominion of these Kashmere dynasties so far to the southward in the early period of their existence. The Booddhists, priests and monks, had fixed upon wild lonely spots as localities for their worship; and of this peculiar taste, or perhaps necessity, there is no more striking example than the secluded ravine of Ajunta. In such places, works of excavation or construction were permitted to distant parties, most probably under the countenance or assistance of local rulers. At a later period, however, the power of the Kashmere dynasty seems to have increased very materially, and the 'Raja Turangiri,' or history of Kashmere, supplies many facts in the mediæval age of India which are worthy of credit. The period of this history extends from Kanishka, the third prince of the original Tartar dynasty, who is placed at 17 to 24 A.D.,[4] to 40 A.D.,[5] down to 622 A.D., or about six centuries.[6]

Dynasty of Kashmere.

Tiberius emperor of Rome.

[1] Fergusson's 'Tree and Serpent Worship.'

[2] Ibid.

[3] Ibid.

[4] General Cunningham's 'Numismatic Chronicle.'

[5] Lassen, 'Ind. Alterthumskirche.'

[6] 'Abstract of Raja Turangiri,' by Professor Wilson.

Marcian emperor. Attila invades Germany.

In or about 450 A.D. Méghaváhána, the first prince of the restored Gonardhá line, is recorded to have invaded Ceylon, and usurped that kingdom; an event which is in some measure confirmed by Ceylon annals. In A.D. 525 Matrigoopta, the fifth king, abdicated, and the throne was then taken possession of by Vikram-Aditya the Great, King of Malwa, at that time lord paramount of India. On his death, however, Pravaraséna re-occupied the throne: invaded the territories of Siladitya, the successor of Vikram; defeated him, and took him prisoner, but subsequently restored the kingdom to him. These events, and the many celebrated and still existing memorials of the Kashmere dynasty, entitle it to a high place in the records of the first five centuries of the Christian era in India.

Sáh dynasty of Sauráshtra.

IV. Although hitherto the peninsula of Kattiawar has not been alluded to in particular terms, yet under its Hindoo or Sanscrit appellation of Saurâshtra, it became the seat of Aryan colonies at a very early period of their invasion, and from its natural fertility, as well as its commanding maritime position, rose into a powerful kingdom. At the time of the Máhábhárut, Saurâshtra was possessed by Krishna, who took an active part in the great war; and, as an incarnation of Vishnoo, is still worshipped by perhaps the majority of the Hindoos, while his temple of Dwarka, as well as that of Somnâth, continue to be very holy places of pilgrimage. From the death of Krishna, however, up to the period under notice, no historical facts have come to light: and the traditions of the Yadoo race, to which Krishna belonged, supply no materials on which dependence can be placed. In Kattiawar, the Sáh dynasty was founded in the first century B.C., by Náhápána, and subsequently attained great power. The dynasty displaced was probably Mauryan, which, under King Asóka, undoubtedly possessed Saurâshtra and the adjacent countries. The most important of Asóka's edicts, previously mentioned in Chapter XI., were engraved upon the rocks of the hill forts of Girnar and Joonargurh, in this province; and it will be remembered that after his death, his empire, which had extended east to west from sea to sea, became dismembered and broken up into separate States and dynasties, of which no authentic record has survived. The establishment of the Sáh dynasty is, however, more perfectly authenticated than any contemporary event; and it is by their coins, a nearly complete series of which has been collected, that the dates of successive princes have been defined in a great measure, though not as yet to a complete extent.

The Sáhs are believed to have been a Parthian race, one of the numerous bands of Central Asian warrior invaders who, from time to time, poured by hordes into India, and settled there; their descendants still exist in Kattiawar, and preserve the fair complexion of their race separate from other inhabitants of the province, and their peculiarly fine breed of horses possesses a lineage as old as their own. During the period of the Mauryan dynasty, and indeed long before it, Sauráshtra became highly civilised, and an active trade was carried on with Egypt by sea, as well as with Persia by land. The Sáhs would seem, therefore, to have followed the track of commerce, and invaded Sauráshtra by the western passes and Sinde. In a series of twenty-seven successions, they reigned in Sauráshtra until A.D. 235, or in all 313 years;[1] or, by another calculation, 376 years. Sehore was their capital, and their dominions extended as far as Sattara and Kolapore, in the Deccan. In the first instance they appear to have adopted the Booddhist faith; and the excavation and construction of the wonderful cave temple at Karlee, between Bombay and Poona, was the work of Náhápána, the founder of the dynasty, in conjunction with King Dévabhuti, of the Sangá dynasty, B.C. 86, whose works then were probably completed. One inscription of the Sáhs, that on the bridge of King Rudra Damán, is of the year 15 A.D. It commemorates the conquest of the Deccan from Satakarni I. of the Andhra dynasty, who reigned from A.D. 10, and by this the authenticity of both monarchs is determined. Mr. Fergusson is of opinion[2] that these Sáhs were Tue-Che, mentioned in the last chapter as having conquered Western India, B.C. 26; and the dates given agree on various grounds so nearly, that there can be little question on the subject. Whether, however, the Sáhs were Parthians, according to Colonel Tod, or Indo-Bactrians; or, as Mr. Elphinstone prefers to consider, Persians of the Sassanian race, is undecided, and signifies, perhaps, very little; they were at least foreigners, and as the sun appears on their coins as the distinctive emblem of their dynasty, it favours the presumption that they were Sassanian Persians, fire and sun worshippers, who adopted Booddhism as the then existent faith of their new country.

Maximinius emperor.

Tiberius emperor.

V. The dynasty of the Gooptas, better known, perhaps, under their local appellation of Bullabhi or Vullabhi, who conquered Sauráshtra from the Sáhs, and established themselves at Vullabhi in Kattiawar, in or about the year 318 A.D., was apparently of northern origin, but their chronology is confused, and has been perplexing to antiquarians in a great degree; nor can it be said to be yet entirely cleared up. That they were a powerful race of mediæval kings,

The Gooptas, Bullabhis or Vullabhis of Sauráshtra.

Constantine emperor.

[1] Fergusson's 'Chronology.'

[2] 'Indian Chronology,' p. 51.

is evident from the Vishnoo Purana, in which a list of them is given. This list includes the names of six monarchs who held the proud title of 'Maharaja Adiraj,' or Emperor of India; and from inscriptions at Allahabad, on the Ganges, and elsewhere, it may be inferred that their actual dominion extended over the whole of Hindostan Proper, including possibly several minor States, as well as over India in general. In the Allahabad inscription, translated by Mr. Prinsep, Samoodrá Goopta, the second monarch in the series, claims sovereignty over Sinhála, or Ceylon, as having been conquered by him; and affords additional confirmation of that island having been, for a considerable period in the fourth and fifth centuries after Christ, if not indeed earlier, a dependency of the Indian monarchs.

The Goopta dynasty professed the Hindoo faith, and the ruins of their western capital, Vullabhi, attest its former extent; but as most of their coins belong to what is called the Kanoujya series, it may be assumed that that ancient city was their northern capital, and, in conjunction with their inscriptions, show that their real seat of power was in Northern India, from whence their conquests extended to Vullabhi in the west, and eventually reached Ceylon in the course of 150 years. Toramána, the last king of the dynasty, bears the date of A.D. 498, which agrees with that of Toramána, the fourth in succession of the kings of Kashmere. It is possible, therefore, as there are no traces of the Gooptas after 498 A.D., that the two dynasties had become united in the person of Toramána, and this view of the subject is adopted from the tenor of inscriptions at Gwalior and Eran, and other data, by several authorities.[1] In his annals of the Rajpoots, Colonel Tod traces the Bullabhis, or what remained of them after the subversion of their dynasty, to Mewar, where they founded a new principality, which still exists. They had been driven out of Kattiawar by a fresh invasion from the westward, and as their latest dates upon copper-plate grants is 525 A.D., their removal to Mewar may have occurred at, or soon after, that period.[2]

Franks converted to Christianity.

All through the mediæval period, however, much confusion exists, on account of names of kings of different dynasties being identical with each other; and great ingenuity and perseverance have been exercised by those who have had, so to speak, to grope their way through these dark ages, to distinguish one from another. The fact that these northern dynasties had coins, has been of great importance and assistance, not only in arranging

[1] Fergusson's 'Bhan Dajee Rajenshahal.'

[2] Elphinstone, 'History,' vol. i. p. 407.

lists, and dates of succession, but of proving a common foreign origin of the royal race from Sassanian or Persian invaders, in contra-distinction to the more ancient Aryan dynasties which had no coinages. These Indo-Sassanian kings, as the Gooptas, form a separate group of themselves in the mediæval period of India, and the ancient Aryan dynasties appear to have been absorbed by them, except that of the Pálás of Bengal, and to some extent the Andhras.

In the foregoing summary of the northern dynasties of India, only those have been mentioned of which authentic details exist, gathered from inscriptions and coins. These details are being followed up by discoveries from newly-translated inscriptions and from coins, so that the subject is, as yet, not by any means as complete as it may hereafter become. Besides those already enumerated, there were others in northern India at the period under review, a valuable table of which is given by Mr. Elphinstone,[1] which contains the following names:—Maghada (Andhra), Gour, Malwah, Guzerat (Sáh and Goopta), Kanoujo (Goopta), Mithili, Benares Dehly, Ajmere, Mewar (Bullabhi), Jesselmere, Jeipoor—the last three still existing—Sinde and Cashmere. These probably comprised the whole of the major States of Northern India, and existed from periods extending, in the cases of Maghada, Gour, Malwah, Mithili, Dehly, Kashmere, and Sinde, far beyond the Christian era, down to the tenth, twelfth and thirteenth centuries A.D., that is, until subverted by the Mahomedans. Over these States, at various periods, and by monarchs of different dynasties who were powerful enough to assume and maintain it in turn, the authority of Maharaja Adhiraj, or emperor, was exercised. There never appears to have been any confederation of States with an emperor at its head, nor did the authority of emperor belong to any line or dynasty by hereditary right; but the power exercised may be assumed to represent that of the strongest for the time being. The following detail, quoted from Mr. Fergusson's 'Chronology of the Mediæval Period,' shows not only the persons, but the States, which exercised the privilege of emperorship at various periods, and the comparatively short intervals between some, may serve to show the rapid fluctuations of power, and the perpetual contentions of the kings of India with each other.

Hindoo Emperors of India.

[1] 'History,' vol. i. p. 412.

Maharaja Adhiraj, or Emperors of India.

		A.D.
1.	Vikram-Aditya, of Malwah	490
2.	Siladitya, of Malwah	530
3.	Prabhárakára, of Kanouj	580
4.	Raja Varadhána	605 ?
5.	Pula Kesi II., of Kulyan	609
6.	Sri Dharaséna III., of Bakabhi	650 ?
7.	Vikram-Aditya, of Kulyan	660
8.	Vinayaditya, of Kulyan	680
9.	Vijayaditya, of Kulyan	695
10.	Vikram-Aditya II.	733

This list contains four names of kings of Kulyan, a State which has not as yet been alluded to, as it belonged to the southern group of Indian kingdoms, and its history will be explained hereafter.

CHAPTER XIV.

OF THE SOUTHERN MEDIÆVAL DYNASTIES: HINDOO—B.C. 900 TO A.D. 800.

Obscurity of Southern Indian history.

THE progress of the Aryan Hindoos southwards is involved in the last degree of obscurity. In regard to the northern Aryans, there are at least some historic points upon which, as will have been understood, no doubt can be cast. Others, uncertain in many respects, perhaps, but still seeming to illustrate each event, may be accepted in general terms until the advent of the Greeks; and the progressive communications with them, for several centuries, furnish historical particulars and dates, which tally with those of foreign sources, and cannot be refuted. For the south, however, there are no such data. The conquest of Ceylon by Ráma, King of Oude, though admitted as a remote historical fact, may nevertheless be open to as much doubt as the siege of Troy. There are, however, many portions of the Ramáyana which, putting aside more modern Brahminical interpolations, bear a strong impress of truth. It is not to be gathered from the Ramáyana that the northern Aryans had any previous knowledge of the people of the south. Their progress southwards had been stopped apparently by the central forests and jungles; and, in like manner, the southern people seem only to have reached the southern boundaries of those tracts. Ráma, however, is recorded to have established kingdoms at Kishkinda, a small district near Beejanugger, on the Tumboodra river, still held sacred by Hindoos, and also in Lunka or Ceylon; and after the Ceylon war, intercourse between the north and south no doubt increased, and may have been maintained for many centuries before the Christian era; but there is no record of any kind on which historic dates or facts can be based, and the whole has to rest, necessarily, upon conjecture or inference. All the royal races of the south evidently trace their origin to persons of northern origin. The Seevaic faith and worship had extended to the south at a very early age, and though Brahmins are not mentioned till a later period, the people appear to have been divided into castes.

In Chapter VIII. a speculation was hazarded as to the original invaders of the south being Turanian or Scythian, as well because of analogies in languages, as on account of existing prehistoric remains. The original language, whatever it may have been, became converted into Tamul as the head, Teloogoo, Canarese, Malialum, Tulu, and some other minor dialects. Each of those named possessed, and still possesses, a geographical limit of its own, which has probably never varied; and though all differ in many respects, yet their family likeness to each other, as a distinct group, has never been questioned. Mr. Elphinstone, 'History,' vol. i. ch. ii. book iv., adopts the opinion of Mr. Ellis in regard to the great antiquity and perfection of the Tamul language before the Aryan Sanscrit; and if this hypothesis be tenable, it opens out a length of period which defies speculation. The original literature of this language has a character which is not Aryan, and it was only affected by Sanscrit at a later period, when that language was introduced by Brahmin missionaries. The ancient Tamul literature possesses no tradition of its antiquity; but, on the fact of its existence, and the concurrent testimony of the Ramáyana, it may be accepted that the earliest settlers in Southern India were at least as civilised as those of the north.

Languages of the south.

Three separate conquests of Ceylon, subsequent to that of Ráma, were noticed in the last chapter as claimed by Hindoo monarchs of India. The first by Chandra Goopta, about A.D. 400 to 401; the second by Mégháváhaná, of the Gonardya dynasty of Kashmere, A.D. 430; and the third at a probably much later period, by Devá Pal Déb, king of Bengal. These circumstances are mentioned to prove that intercourse was maintained between the north and south at these, as at earlier, periods. The Chinese Booddhist traveller Fah-Hian sailed in a 'great merchant vessel' from the mouth of the Ganges to Ceylon about A.D. 400. The Booddhist relics had been transferred there at an earlier period; and probably about A.D. 600, the island, according to Booddhist chronology, was

Successive conquests of Ceylon.

Pope Innocent.

invaded and taken possession of by 'Vijáyo,' who crossed from the southern portion of India. But there are earlier records of the existence of southern monarchies than these. Mr. Elphinstone quotes Strabo as authority for an embassy from 'King Pandion' to Augustus, shortly before the Christian era, perhaps about 20 B.C., when Pórus, a northern king, sent a similar mission—or the two may be identical; and also that the Pandyan dynasty is mentioned in the 'Periplus,' which has many details of provinces and cities still distinctly traceable by name. It is evident, therefore, that two powerful kingdoms had been established in the south—one the Pandyan, which had its permanent capital at Madura; the other Chôla, the first capital of which was Kanchy, or Conjeveram, on the Cauvery, the second, Tanjore.

Early connection with Greece.

There can be little doubt, also, that at the period of the Christian era, intercourse by sea from the western coast of India was maintained with Egypt, and perhaps with Arabia; and though absolute corroboration is wanting, the visit of the Apostle Thomas to Southern India, his conversion of large numbers of the inhabitants to Christianity, and his martyrdom at Malliapoor, near Madras, are supported as well by local tradition and the observance of the anniversary of his death, as by the fact that the Christian Churches founded by him continued to exist until, about the fifth century, they placed themselves under the spiritual authority of the Bishop or Patriarch of Mosul, in Armenia, and still remain subject to his jurisdiction. In these early ages, the Indian Christians do not seem to have suffered persecution by the Hindoos. Cooroorangon Perumal, probably a king of Madura or of Chéra, in the sixth century, is recorded to have afforded protection to the Christians, whose merchants were rich, and traded with Egypt and Persia.

Mission and death of the Apostle Thomas.

Of the southern kingdoms, the Chôla was undoubtedly the largest, though not perhaps the most ancient. Its alleged founder was Tayaman Nálé, who came from the north of India, and appears to have gained possession of the country near the modern Arcot. Kanchy, or Conjeveram, which afterwards became the capital, was founded by Adánda. About 350 B.C. the Chôla dynasty merged into the Pandya by marriage, and so continued for 570 years; but in 214 A.D. the States became separated again, and the Chôlas removed their capital to Tanjore, which was founded in that year by Kullotunga, the head of a new dynasty which flourished there till A.D. 886. Grants and endowments by separate Chôla princes can be traced down to the fourteenth century; but the

Chôla dynasty.

Darius Ochus subdues Egypt.

Leo emperor of the East.

historical facts are rare and obscure. There is no question, however, that the Chôla dominions were very extensive; they met those of the Andhras on the north, the Pandyas and Chéras on the south and west, and on the east they were bounded by the sea. To this dynasty countless temples and other works may be traced by their inscriptions, and the peculiar style of architecture — Dravidian, which was founded in the south, is recognised by Mr. Fergusson as one of the distinct orders of India. It is possible, also, that some of the excavated temples of Ellora, especially that of Kylas, the most modern and most magnificent, may, from its style, have been the work of the Chôlas.

Their dominions.

The founder of the Pandyan dynasty is named Pandya, a person of the agricultural class, who came from Ayodya, or Oude. From him, seventy-four successions are reckoned up to Kuna, or Guna, in the third century A.D., which, on the generally assumed average of sixteen years to each, would place the establishment of the Pandyan dynasty about the ninth century B.C. Their first capital was Kurky, which is mentioned in the 'Periplus,' the second Kalyanpoor, and the third Madura, founded by Kulasikhárá. In the third century A.D. the kingdom was ruled by a princess, who was conquered by an incarnation of Seeva, whom she married; and this event probably records the introduction of the Seevaic faith, which, both in the Pandyan and Chôla kingdoms, appears to have been the established religion. Both these dynasties, however, lapsed into Jainism at various periods, and a conversion of the Pandyan king Kuna, in A.D. 1028, forms the subject of a special inscription. The Pandyas reigned over the whole of the extreme southern portion of India, and the dynasty was prolonged until its final extinction by the Mahomedans.

Pandya dynasty.

The Chéra dominions embraced the western districts of Mysore with Malabar, and may have been separated from the Chôlas about A.D. 500. Little, however, is known of the dynasty.

Chéra dynasty.

In these southern Turanian kingdoms, the science of architecture was developed at an early period, possibly before, but certainly soon after, the Christian era; and more progress was made in it, by the execution of temples and other great public monuments, than in the north. Not only were their dimensions larger, but their style was more confirmed, and their ornamentation richer, and of a more distinct character. But as an almost higher proof of their civilisation, it may be adduced that artificial irrigation of the soil had been commenced upon a scale of extended usefulness, which existed probably in no other country except Babylon. The exact period at which the system was commenced is not known; but existing inscriptions relate to periods shortly after the Christian era, and it is not improbable that it had then been long in operation. In this particular, the southern people of India left the northern far behind.

Not only were stone dams, or weirs, thrown across large rivers, and their streams directed over the lands on their banks, but reservoirs of all sizes, from the humblest village tank to those noble lakes still in existence, which are from one to ten square miles and upwards in area, were distributed over every part of the country, furnishing then, as now, means of irrigation to thousands of acres of land, which would otherwise be sterile. These reservoirs were formed by dams thrown across the courses of brooks and streams of all sizes, at some point where the comparative flatness of the river valley above, and projections of high land on each bank towards the stream, afforded at once the site of a basin and its dam; and thus the water of the stream, when flooded by the periodical rains, was stored up until it was needed for the dry seasons. The dams of these reservoirs were of earth faced with large blocks of rough stone set without mortar; nor can the most scientific processes of the present day improve either the principles of construction of such dams, or the simple but efficacious sluices with which they were fitted for the regulated discharge of water. Of such useful works, upwards of fifty thousand are still in working order in the Madras Presidency, and the total number of these enduring monuments of past ages must be immense.

CHAPTER XV.

OF THE SOUTHERN MEDIÆVAL DYNASTIES: HINDOO (*continued*), A.D. 250 TO 1200.

Chalúkya dynasty of Kulyan.

CONTEMPORARY with the Chólas and Pandyas of the extreme south, a dynasty named Chalúkya had arisen at an early period, and in the middle of the fourth century A.D. had attained great power in the Carnatic. The first authentic date of this family, obtained from a fine and still perfect inscription, is 489 A.D., by Púlakési, the son of Jaya Sinha. The genealogy of the family extends to fifty-nine princes, or, on an average of sixteen years to each, a period of 944 years. Of these, forty-three princes reigned in Ayodya, or Oude, and the remaining sixteen in the Carnatic, which would fix the rise of the southern Chalúkya family about A.D. 250. The founder of the Carnatic dynasty was a prince named Héma Syn, who had wandered to the

Theodoric king of Italy.

Decius emperor of Rome

Deccan and Carnatic, and, marrying a princess of the latter country, settled there. Their first capital was Nagávy, near the Bheema river, and thence, as their power increased, they moved to Kulyan, the present Kalliany of the Nizam's dominions, which became a famous city. In their inscription at Yeeoor, the Chalúkyas claim authority over the Chólas and Pandyas of the south, and also over the Andhras, on the eastern side of the peninsula; and for a time the Chalúkya princes, as indeed is proved from other sources, were lords paramount in India. The Chalúkyas were magnificent temple-builders, and some of the most beautiful edifices in Western India bear their dynastic emblem, the boar. It is doubtful how much of the Ellora excavations belong to them, but they are assumed to have taken a large part in them; and at the village of Khurósa, not far from Kalliany, there is a fine series of cave temples, containing emblems of Seeva, executed by them. The fourth and fifth centuries A.D. are the periods of the greatest power of this dynasty, and victories over the Chôlas, and even the burning of their capital, Kanchy, are recorded, as well as military operations which extended into Malwah. After the fifth century the dynasty declined, though very gradually, under attacks by the Chólas from the south, the Yádávás from the north, and probably the Andhras from the east; but in the year 733 A.D. a king named Teila is recorded as having reinstated the power of the kingdom, and his grandson, Dása Várána, to have overcome the Chôlas, driving them southwards, and again burning their capital. The Chalúkya dynasty lasted till the year 1182 A.D., when the throne was usurped by one of the feudal nobles, from which it may be inferred that the kingdom had fallen into a distracted condition.

Cave temples excavated.

Dynasty declines, but is restored.

Andronicus emperor of the East.

The Kala Bhúryas, who subverted the great Chalúkya dynasty in the year 1182, were originally feudal chiefs of the Chalúkyas, and ruled over a small territory to the west of Kalliany. They also appear to have had an Aryan origin, as the founder of the family had emigrated from Kalinga, in Northern India, to the Deccan at a very early period, and attached himself to the Chalúkya family, as is recorded in their inscriptions. Towards the close of the Chalúkyan power, serious contentions arose between them and their powerful vassal, and sometimes one party, and again the other, are recorded to have been dominant, until the final disappearance of the Chalúkyas. Nor were the Kala Bhúryas long destined to survive them.

Kala Bhúrya dynasty of Kulyan.

At that period a new sect was springing up in the Carnatic, which, alike hostile to the Jain as it was to the Brahminical faith, became the means of accomplishing a great dynastic and religious revolution. A Brahmin named Bussappa, of obscure birth, began the new movement, preaching a pure Theism, the abolition of idolatry, and the adoration only of the Phallic emblems of Seeva. The new faith, under the appellation of Lingáyet, soon attracted notice, and on account of the divine revelations claimed by him, Bussappa was invited to Kulyan, then in possession of the King Vijala Kalabhúrya, who had usurped the throne. Bussappa was taken into favour by the Minister of the State, and having married his daughter, resided at Court. At this period the King became enamoured of Bussappa's beautiful sister Pudma, married her, and raised her brother to the rank of minister and head of the army. Bussappa then conceived the project of establishing his new tenets by force, the first step to which would be to usurp the throne. He boldly proclaimed that he was an incarnation of Seeva, and was followed by an immense number of his disciples. The King took the field against him, and in a battle which ensued was defeated with great loss. Satisfied with his success, however, Bussappa, who might then have usurped the throne, besought pardon, and was reinstated in office. His real object was to obtain the throne for his sister's child, and to become regent of the kingdom; and by some means the King was induced to abdicate and become an ascetic; but, as he disappeared, it is more than probable he was put to death in A.D. 1166, nine years after his usurpation of the kingdom. Bussappa could not however maintain his position, or his authority over his nephew, and being obliged to fly from Kulyan, was pursued and put to death; but the tenets he had promulgated had been accepted by multitudes of the people, who now venerated him as a martyr; they were preached after his death with great effect by another nephew, Chun-Bussappa, and remain to the present time, professed by perhaps the majority of the middle classes in Southern and South-Western India.

Rise of the Lingáyet sect.

Bussappa's proceedings.

William king of Scotland.

Vijála Kalabhúrya's death terminated the Chalúkya dominion, and the kingdom was immediately afterwards invaded, and annexed by the Yádávás or Jadows of Déoghur, the modern Dowlatabad. The Chalúkyas appear in the first instance to have been Hindoos professing the Seevaic faith, but they afterwards became Jains, a religion which had been introduced from Kattiawar and Guzerat, and so continued till the Lingáyet revolution, under Bussappa. Most of the splendid temples erected by the Chalúkya and by a minor dynasty, the Rattás, absorbed by them, were dedicated to the Jain faith: with many Viharas or colleges and monasteries, all of which suffered

The Yádávás conquer Kulyan.

severely, as well by the irruptions of the Brahminical Chólas in the fierce period of religious contention between the Lingáyets and the Jains, which followed the death of Bussappa. The architecture of the Chalúkya period is peculiar, but extremely elegant, having a character of ornamentation of its own, which is not without suspicion of Greek assistance.

The Bellály were the successors of the Chéra dynasty in Western Mysore and Malabar; they occupied a place, as it were, between the Chalúkyas and the Chólas, and by their inscriptions appear to have maintained constant warfare with both. By an inscription of A.D. 1235, seventeen successions are enumerated up to the founder of the family, which, according to the usual average computations, would place his date in A.D. 980, or thereabouts; and an inscription in the Mackenzie collection makes it A.D. 984. One of the Chalúkyan records commemorates a great victory over the Belláls near Moodgul, when the Belláls had invaded the kingdom; but temples erected by both dynasties, bearing their distinctive emblems, the boar of the Chalúkyas, and the tiger or *shardúla* of the Belláls, are found in the same localities, denoting their alternate possession of the country. For some time the town of Lukhoondy, in Dharwar, was the capital of the Belláls, whence they retired southwards to Dwára Samoodra, in North Mysore. They were Jains in the first instance; but in 1133, Vishnoo Verddhána, the king, was converted to Brahminism by the great Brahmin missionary Ramanuja, to commemorate which event, the splendid temple at Belloor was dedicated to Vishnoo. The dynasty continued till A.D. 1268, as will be hereafter mentioned.

Hól Sálá, or Bellál dynasty.

Henry I. king of Scotland.

The Silhárás were local princes, tributary to the Chalúkyas. Their territories lay around Kolapoor, which was then their capital, and their inscriptions upon temples, and copper tablet grants, prove them to have held extensive, though not perhaps independent, sway over a large portion of what is now styled the Southern Mahratta country. An inscription of A.D. 1135 enumerates eight successions up to the founder of the family, which would place their origin about 907 A.D.

Silhárás.

Stephen king England.

A legend concerning the Kadámba family, which is certainly one of the most ancient of the southern dynasties, records that the founder was the offspring of Seeva, born under a Kadámba tree, and hence the family appellation. They were sovereigns of Banawassy, which is a district mentioned in Ptolemy, as also the name of its prince, Trinetra Kadámba, in A.D. 168. A memorial inscription of the family recounts successions up to

Kadámbas.

A.D. 578, or contemporary with the Chalúkyas; but claims to have been independent at the period of the establishment of the Chalúkyas. To the founder of the family, Mayura Varma, is attributed the introduction of Brahmins and the Brahmin faith. Banawassy, and a portion of the Dharwar collectorate, was the seat of the family; but their possessions extended to the sea-coast, north and south, for a considerable distance, their inscriptions being traceable in temples and other buildings; and it was no doubt owing to their maritime position that they became known to the early Greek navigators.

Tiberius emperor.

Mention of the Rattá dynasty occurs in inscriptions incidentally with the Chalúkyas, who subverted them; they were Jains, and lords of Samdati, in Dharwar; they are traceable by these inscriptions up to A.D. 1097; and, though in a reduced condition, the family was in existence up to the Mahomedan conquest.

Rattá.

The era of Shaliváháná, A.D. 77, is still maintained among the Hindoos of the Deccan, over which country, and perhaps part of Malwah, he reigned at that period; but comparatively little is known of him, except his era, on which historical dependence can be placed. He was a Hindoo, and took an active part in the persecution of the Booddhists, by the assistance of the Agni Kool warriors of Rajpootana. By tradition, Shaliváháná was the son of a potter, born in a miraculous manner of a virgin to be the saviour and protector of the then persecuted Brahmins, and a regenerator of the Hindoo faith; but to what dynasty he belonged, or whether he was the founder of one, there is no record. The capital of Shaliváháná is believed to have been Paitan, on the Godavery, which still remains. In the 'Periplus,' two great cities in the Deccan are mentioned as marts of trade, one of which is Plithana; and Mr. Elphinstone conjectures that the Greek ΠΛΙΘΑΝΑ may be a clerical error for ΠΑΙΘΑΝΑ or Paitan. The other city is Tagára, in regard to which no definite conclusion has been arrived at. It seems, however, far from improbable, that the ruins of a once extensive city on the tableland between the fort of Déogurh, or Dowlatabad, and the caves of Ellora may be the place. This ruined city was not apparently known to Mr. Elphinstone, and the Greeks may, in this instance also, have committed a clerical error, by writing ταγάρα for the Hindee ναγάρα, 'the city.' The local power of Shaliváháná, and his zeal for the Hindoo faith, renders it possible that he followed the Booddhists in the excavations at Ellora; and it would be by no means inconsistent with probability that the Tagára or Nagara of the Greek merchants, near Déogurh, was one at least of his capitals. One of the appellations of the Silhárá family was Tagára-poor;

Shaliváháná.

and Mr. Elphinstone ('History,' ch. ii. book iv. p. 431) states that the Rajpoot family of Silhar possessed Tagára as its capital in the eleventh century. The city itself, however, has never been discovered under its recorded name.

The Yádává dynasty had probably existed for a considerable period before it rose to its zenith of power. Its foundation is attributed to Ramjee, a shepherd, five centuries B.C.; but there is no distinct record of its genealogies, though it claimed, like many others, a descent from one of the Pandoos of the Máhábhárut. Whether it was the successor to Shalivâháná, or not, has never been traced. In 1190 A.D. one of its inscriptions records conquests of the western provinces of the Chalúkya kingdom; and while by it the kingdom of the Chalúkyas, on the fall of the Kalabhúryas, was annexed, victories are also recorded over the Bellâls of Dwára Sumoodra. The capital of the Yádávás was Déogurh, and their history, as connected with the Mahomedan invasion, will be related hereafter.

Yádává dynasty of Déogurh.

Henry VI. emperor of Germany.

The ancient and powerful dynasty of the Andhras seems to have split into four portions after the Christian era. The original stock still held Maghada, in Bahar, and in A.D. 53 the Ganapati branch settled south of the Godavery, under Kákateya; another branch, the Narupati, became masters of Telingána, of which the capital was Wurungul; and a third, the Gajupati, ruled over Kuttack. Nothing of accurate historic record is known of these dynasties, till the Mahomedans found the Narupati Andhras at Wurungul, and this event in their history will be recorded in its proper place.

Andhras.

Nero emperor.

From Déogurh and Malwah the Hindoo kingdoms and dynasties pass into those of the north. What have been reviewed in the present chapter contain those only of the south so far as inscriptions or other memorials have served to perpetuate them for more than a thousand years, and those of the Chalúkyan group are curiously exact and complete. It may be gathered from the recorded history of their contentions, that not only did no confederation of States exist, but that there was no sympathy or bond of union between any of them. On the contrary, indeed, a perpetual strife for superiority was maintained, which resulted in the domination, now of one, now of another, as had been the case in Northern India up to the period of the Mahomedan invasion of the south. From the fifth century the history of the Carnatic is, of all, the clearest portion, and is well illustrated by the inscriptions of the ruling families, the absence of which, in other localities, is so much to be regretted. The country appears to have been well peopled and well cultivated; and the sea-coast afforded means of communication by sea with Egypt and Arabia. In most respects little change can be traced, and the names of towns and villages mentioned in inscriptions and now existing have not been altered. From the Christian era up to the seventh century the Jain faith was the prevailing religion; and, as in Guzerat and other localities where it existed, its richly decorated temples remain as proofs, not only of the highest architectural skill of the period, but of a refinement in taste which is perhaps traceable to Greek influence. On the mission of Shunkur Achárya, in the eighth century, most of the people forsook the Jain faith, and returned to the Brahminical tenets preached by him, which enjoined the worship of Seeva. The village communities were governed on the same principles as at present, by their hereditary officers. Colleges and schools had been established for education, and endowed by their founders; hereditary district officers, deans of guild, and other functionaries presided over the administration of the laws and the collections of revenue; agriculture was well protected, and flourished; and so far as the inscriptions[1] afford particulars, there seems to be no reason to doubt the existence of a high and then progressive civilisation, equal in all respects to that of Northern India.

[1] Sir Walter Elliot's collection.

BOOK II.

CHAPTER I.

OF THE EARLY MAHOMEDAN INVASIONS OF INDIA, A.D. 664 TO 997.

IN the year 622 A.D. Mahomed fled from Mecca to Medina, and the date was accepted as the commencement of the Mahomedan era, under the title of the Hegira. Before a hundred years had expired, Egypt, Syria, Northern Africa, and part of Spain had been subdued by the Arabs, and the religious belief of Mahomed was diffused as widely as the conquests of his votaries had extended. While Mahomedanism spread thus rapidly to the west, it progressed even in a more permanent degree through Arabia and Persia into Central Asia. Westwards, the new faith had been checked by Christianity; eastwards there was nothing to oppose its progress but an effete fire-worship in Persia, and beyond that, a semi-savage Paganism, of which no distinct traces are obtainable, but which may have been allied to the observances of the ancient Scythians. The warriors of Islam, urged on by fanatical zeal on the one hand, and love of plunder and dominion on the other, quickly overran Central Asia, and as early as 664 A.D., forty-four years after the Hegira, had penetrated to Kabool, while the intervening tracts of Persia had been already brought within the pale of Mahomedanism and its governments, and were subject to the Arab caliphs established in them.

Mahomedan progress.

This history has no concern with the fluctuations of power which followed the first Arab settlements in Afghanistan; but, of them, the results were the acceptation of the Mahomedan faith, and a nominal, if not in some instances actual, submission to the central Mahomedan government. On the south side of Persia the Mahomedan progress was no less rapid than on the north-east. Bussora was founded by the Caliph Omar, and from thence expeditions against Sinde and Beloochistan were undertaken, but with only partial success. In the year 711 A.D.,

Expedition from Bussora to Sinde.

however, an Arab vessel was detained at the mouth of the Indus; and the prince of the country, Rajah Dáhu, was called upon for its restitution. It was in vain he urged that the locality was not in his territory; the Mahomedans would hear of no excuse, and sent a small detachment of troops to enforce the demand, which was overwhelmed. The governor of Bussora, Hejáz, now dispatched a larger force, of 6,000 men, under his nephew Kassim, who, having succeeded in taking by storm a celebrated temple, in which he obtained a large booty—probably Dwarka—followed its defenders along the Indus, defeated a numerous army assembled by the Rajah, who perished in the battle, and finally reached his capital, Brahminabad, which was defended by his widow. Kassim, though well provided with catapults and other engines of war, made little impression on the place; but a scarcity of provision rendered the defenders desperate, and in a hopeless sally against the Mahomedans, the Hindoo queen and body-guard of Rajpoots perished. Kassim then advanced to Mooltan, which was weakly defended, and the capture of a few less important cities completed the conquest of Sinde.

Phillipinus Bardanes emperor of the East.

First conquest of Sinde.

It is alleged by some writers, that the youthful conqueror, having re-equipped his army, and received reinforcements, marched across India to the Ganges. This, however, does not rest upon authority sufficient to establish it as an historical fact; and the forces at his disposal, which never exceeded 8,000 men, render it improbable that he should have even attempted such an expedition. On the contrary, he seems to have been satisfied with his conquest, and set himself diligently to conciliate the people, and confirm them in their rights of property; but his miserable end prevented the accomplishment of his plans. Two beautiful daughters of the Rajah Dáhu had been despatched by Kassim to the Caliph's harem. On their arrival at Damascus, one of them denounced Kassim as having dishonoured her, and a mandate was sent to Sinde for him to be sewn up in a raw hide, and sent to the Caliph. When the body arrived at Damascus, the princess declared her falsehood, but triumphed in having thus avenged her father's death. Whether this legend be strictly true, is perhaps questionable, though related by various Mahomedan historians; it is however certain, that by Kassim's death, or recal from Sinde, the Mahomedan power then was much weakened, and after an occupation by his successors of about forty years, they were expelled by the Rajpoot tribe of Suméra, who took possession of the province: nor were any further attempts to regain a footing in India made by the Arab caliphs. The Mahomedan faith, lacking the military

Death of Kassim.

The Mahomedans expelled from India.

support which had accompanied it elsewhere, did not progress in Sinde; and after a time the Arab invasion had become little more than tradition. According to Rajpoot authority, however, it is related, that in the reign of Khomán, Rajah of Chittore, an invasion of Mahomedans took place between A.D. 812 and 836, under Mahmood, son, or other relative, of the Caliph Haroun-al-Rasheed, and then governor of Khorassán, and that the Mahomedans were defeated and expelled from India; but this alleged event is not confirmed by Mahomedan historians, and may be doubtful, or perhaps the mere repression of a predatory raid. If it really happened, it forms additional proof that early Mahomedan enterprises against the Hindoos, with the exception of that of Kassim, were unsuccessful, and that they were found more united, and more powerful and warlike, than the people of the west, over whom the Mahomedans had triumphed.

Egbert Saxon king.

After the death of the Caliph Haroun-al-Rasheed in A.D. 806, the empire of the Arab Caliphate did not preserve its integrity. The great provinces of Khorassán and Trans-Oxania had rebelled, and in the course of sixty years had become independent under the Tahirites, or successors of Tahir, who had begun the movement. They were succeeded by the Sofarides, in A.D. 872, the founder of which short-lived dynasty was Yakoob, a brazier of Seistan, who became a military adventurer of much celebrity: and these were subverted in turn by the Samánis, in 903 A.D., a dynasty which continued to exist in Central Asia for 120 years. The fifth prince, Abdúl Melek, possessed a Toorky slave, named Alptugeen, who held the high office of governor of Khorassán. On the death of his patron, in A.D. 961, he fell under the suspicion of the successor to the throne, and having escaped with a few followers, betook himself to Ghuzny, an outlying province to the south-eastward, among the Soliman mountains, where, aided by the rude Afghan population of the tract, he became independent. In or about A.D. 976 Alptugeen died, and was succeeded by Subooktugeen, also a slave, who had married his daughter. Ferishta states that Alptugeen had a son named Isákh, who succeeded his father, and died in less than two years, without issue, and that on his death Subooktugeen was elected king, and married as already stated.

Disruption of the Caliphate.

Alfred king of England.

Edward king of England.

Edgar reigns.

Monarchy of Ghuzny established.

Edward II. king of England.

Although a slave, having been purchased by a merchant in Toorkistan when a boy, Subooktugeen yet claimed illustrious descent from Yezdijerd, the last of the Persian kings. He displayed great talent at an early age, and was entrusted by Alptugeen with military expeditions,

Subooktugeen's expeditions into India.

some of which were directed against the Indian tribes on the Indus, from whom the mountain ranges of Afghanistan separated the Mahomedans, and thus he seems to have become acquainted with India, and desirous of penetrating into it. Having therefore subdued and annexed Kandahar, he determined to invade the territories of Jeypal, then prince of the Punjâb, including Kashmere and Mooltan, and having marched eastwards, in A.D. 977, taken certain forts, built mosques, and obtained a large booty, he returned to Ghuzny. Jeypal was by no means willing to rest under this act of aggression. He assembled a large army, and crossing the Indus, advanced to Lumghan, where he was met by Subooktugeen; but before the armies engaged, a furious storm occurred at night, which so disheartened and dispersed the superstitious Hindoos, that Jeypal sued for terms, and agreed to give up fifty elephants, and pay a large sum of money, to receive which he requested ambassadors might be sent with him to Lahore. Safely protected in his own capital however, the Hindoo king repudiated the promises he had made: and instigated by his Brahmin counsellors, imprisoned the Mahomedan envoys. Subooktugeen was little disposed to brook the insult, and had already gained experience of the weakness of the Hindoo troops before his mountain warriors. He had returned to Ghuzny, but on receiving news of the Hindoo advance, retraced his steps to Lumghan, where the vast Hindoo forces were arrayed to meet him. Jeypal had enlisted the kings of Dehly, Ajmere, Kalinga, and Kanouj in the national cause, and his army is represented to have amounted to 100,000 horse and an immense body of infantry. As in the case of Alexander's invasion, the best of the Aryan chivalry had assembled to hurl back the Mahomedans. This was not, however, fated to happen. Subooktugeen, an experienced general, directed successive attacks of 500 fresh cavalry at a time against a weak point of the Hindoo position; their line was broken, and a general advance of the Mahomedans completed their victory. Subooktugeen did not follow up his success; he was content with levying heavy contributions on the country west of the Indus, and took possession of Peshawur and Lumghan, making that town his boundary.

Thus was the first permanent occupation of Indian territory by Mahomedans accomplished, which was soon afterwards relinquished. Subooktugeen did not renew his attacks upon India, and for the rest of his life appears to have been engaged in military operations to the north-westward, residing chiefly at Balkh; but falling ill there, he commenced a journey to Ghuzny for change of air, and died by the way, at Tormooz, in the month of August, 997 A.D., in the fifty-sixth year of his age and twentieth of his reign, his remains being carried to

Death of Subooktugeen.

Ghuzny. In his last moments he had nominated as his successor his second son Ismail, who was crowned at Balkh, and is esteemed to have been legitimate, whereas Mahmood, the eldest son, was otherwise; Mahmood, however, was determined to assert his right to the throne. He first wrote to his brother, offering him Balkh and Khorassán as an independent kingdom, if he would resign his pretensions to the rest; and this having been refused, both parties prepared for an issue in war. They met near Ghuzny, when Ismail was defeated, and without further resistance the whole kingdom was taken possession of by Mahmood, who kept his brother under an honourable restraint during his life.

His son Mahmood succeeds him.

CHAPTER II.

OF THE INVASION OF INDIA BY SOOLTAN MAHMOOD OF GHUZNY, SURNAMED 'BOOT-SHIKUN,' OR IDOL-BREAKER, A.D. 997 TO 1030.

MAHMOOD was now thirty years old, having been born on December 15, A.D. 967. He was in the prime of life, and having been his father's constant companion in war, and entrusted with many independent operations, had gained a large experience. His first act was to profess allegiance to the royal house of Samány; but this having been rejected, and a new governor of Khorassán appointed, Mahmood not only maintained his position, but on the occasion of a revolution, in which the Samány sooltan, Mansoor II., was dethroned and blinded, declared his independence. This event took place in the year 999 A.D., soon after which he received a robe of honour from the Caliph, and assumed the title of sooltan. Since his accession Mahmood had employed himself in the settlement of the civil affairs of his kingdom; and to obviate any chances of disturbances to the westward, he entered into alliance with Elik Khan, the usurper of the Samány dynasty, and received his daughter in marriage. Elik Khan, therefore, became the undisputed master of Trans-Oxania, and Mahmood was left at liberty to pursue his great plans in regard to India, which he had most at heart. He had become highly popular with the people and with his army; and his zeal for the propagation of Islamism, as well as the consciousness of power arising from the security of his position, impelled him to undertake operations against the Hindoo Pagans and idolators on his eastern frontier, as well for their conversion to his country's

Mahmood declares independence, A.D. 999.

Sylvester pope.

Mahmood assumes the title of sooltan.

faith, as affording him a new field of operations, infinitely more inviting than the poor and distracted regions of the west.

Afghanistan was naturally a poor country, thinly inhabited. India was rich in general wealth, in the possession of countless Hindoo shrines and temples, overflowing with gold and precious stones, and possessing a teeming population, from which an abundance of slaves could be carried away to be added to the sparse people of his own country. With part of India, on the shores of the Indus, Mahmood was already familiar; and the accounts borne to him by traders, and general report of the splendour of the countries beyond, was too tempting a prospect to be neglected. But it was not till the year 1001 A.D. that he made any movement eastward.

Henry II. emperor of Germany.

In the month of August in that year he set out from Ghuzny with ten thousand chosen horsemen,

First invasion by Mahmood, A.D. 1001.

and on November 27 met Jeypal, the Rajah of Lahore, at Peshawur, at the head of 12,000 horse and 30,000 foot. The battle which ensued was obstinately contested by the Hindoos, but they were utterly defeated, five thousand of their troops were slain, and Jeypal himself, with many of his

Rajah Jeypal defeated.

relations and chiefs, were taken prisoners. Mahmood, however, released Jeypal, on promise of his paying an annual tribute; but the aged king, deeming himself unfit to reign longer, abdicated in favour of his son Anundpál, and perished by fire on a funeral pile—a death to which he had devoted himself.

In the year A.D. 1004 Mahmood having returned from a mili-

Second invasion, A.D. 1004.

tary expedition into Seistan, found that the Indian tribute had not been fully paid. Anundpál had contributed his quota; but the Rajah of Bhateea, Beejy Rái, a Rajpoot prince, had refused his share, and could not be compelled to furnish it. Mahmood, therefore, advanced upon Mooltan, and thence into the Rajah's territories; but was opposed with such desperation by the Rajpoots, that he was repulsed in several attacks. On the evening of the battle, Mahmood prostrated himself towards Mecca in sight of his troops, and rising, with a shout 'that the prophet had given him the victory,' again led on his men, and drove the enemy into their fort, which he invested. As the siege was closely pressed, Beejy Rái abandoned the place, and took refuge in a wood, where he was attacked by Mahmood, and after an obstinate defence put an end to his own existence. A great booty was obtained in the city, which, with Beejy Rái's territories, was annexed to Mahmood's dominions.

It is not clear from the Mahomedan history how Mooltan had

Third invasion, A.D. 1005.

by this time become a Mahomedan province. Shekh Hameed Lody, the first Mahomedan ruler, had paid tribute to Subooktugeen, and by his name must have been an Afghan. In A.D. 1005, however, his grandson, Abool Futteh Dáwood, revolted, and being in alliance with Anundpál of Lahore, that prince detached a part of his army to oppose Mahmood, who was advancing on Mooltan by way of Peshawur. Again the Hindoos were defeated. Anundpál fled to Kashmere, and Mooltan having been invested by Mahmood, its rulers submitted on the promise of paying a heavy annual tribute. The sooltan would probably have continued his march into India, but was obliged to return immediately to Ghuzny, his western territories having been invaded by his father-in-law, Elik Khan, king of Kashgar. In a series of rapid marches Mahmood traversed Khorassán, and met his enemies (for a confederation against him had been formed) within a short distance of Balkh, and the armies drew up for battle. The engagement was a bloody one, and sharply contested; but Mahmood had brought with him 500 elephants, which he posted at intervals in his line, and which seem to have mainly contributed to the victory he obtained. Elik Khan was forced to retreat, and thenceforward molested his son-in-law no more; but, it being winter, Mahmood's army suffered severely by the snow on their return.

Mahmood defeats Elik Khan, king of Kashgar.

Meanwhile, however, events had occurred in India which obliged the sooltan to return thither, and it is impossible not to admire his energy on this occasion. Sewukpál, a renegade Hindoo rajah, had been entrusted with the charge of Sooltan Mahmood's conquests, and had rebelled. Without staying at Ghuzny, Mahmood followed up the offender, defeated and took him prisoner; a heavy fine was exacted, and Sewukpál imprisoned for life. Anundpál, however, had not been punished for his treacherous support of the Mooltan rebel; and in the year 1008, Sooltan Mahmood, early in the spring, set out from Ghuzny to attack him. His intentions were perfectly well known, and Anundpál appealed to the Hindoo princes of India to second him in his efforts for the expulsion of the Mahomedans from their sacred soil. His appeal was speedily, if not heartily, responded to, and an immense army assembled at Peshawur. Money from all quarters was supplied for the war, and Hindoo women even melted their ornaments, and offered the gold and silver to aid the national cause. The Gukkurs, a powerful hill tribe in the north-west of the Punjáb, were induced to join the confederation, with 30,000 men, and Sooltan Mahmood, on debouching from the passes, was forced to entrench his camp.

Fourth invasion, A.D. 1005-6.

Fifth invasion, A.D. 1008.

In this position he remained inactive for forty days, doubtful whether he could advance, but unwilling to retire. The mutual inactivity was broken by the Hindoos, who attacked the Mahomedan intrenchments, headed by the wild Gukkurs, who, for a time, were successful; but the elephant on which the Hindoo general rode, frightened by naphtha balls and flights of arrows, fled. A panic ensued, and the Arabian and Afghan horse, about 16,000 in number, issuing from the intrenchments, pursued the Hindoos with vast slaughter. The Hindoo confederates were not pursued by the sooltan. He attacked the sacred town of Nagrakote, and for the first time began the destruction of idols and their temples. The fort of 'Bheem,' one of the holy shrines of the Punjâb, where fire issued from the rock, was taken by storm, and an immense booty in solid gold and silver ingots, plate, and precious stones obtained, with which Mahmood returned to Ghuzny, and displayed to his wondering subjects at a great festival, as well as a proof of his victories, as to stimulate their desire for further conquests; and in the year 1011 he again set out with the intention of taking Thanésur, near Dehly, which was represented to be the holiest place in India.

Plunders Hindoo temples.

It may be gathered from the sequel, that Mahmood, having defeated the Hindoos at Peshawur in 1009, again admitted Anundpál to terms; for by treaty Mahmood was now entitled to pass through the domains of that prince with his army. Anundpál, however, wrote to the sooltan, that while he should be welcomed with fitting hospitality, he trusted that Thanésur might be spared, and that he would ensure its revenues being paid regularly. But Mahmood spurned the offer, and declared that, with the assistance of God, he would root out idol worship from all India. Anundpál vainly endeavoured to rouse again the national spirit of the Hindoo princes for the defence of Thanésur; and Mahmood, by rapid marches, having reached the place, plundered it, broke down temples and idols, the chief of which, Jugsôma, was sent to Ghuzny to be trampled upon in the streets. Mahmood desired to press on to Dehly, but Anundpál, who lay in his rear, was not to be depended upon, though, on the sooltan's return, his hospitality was profuse; Mooltan was doubtful, and, under the circumstances, a return to Ghuzny was deemed the safest policy. 200,000 captives were taken to that city and dispersed over the country, and the general booty was again enormous.

Sixth invasion, A.D. 1010.

Temple of Thanésur plundered.

The years 1012 to 1017 A.D. passed without any further invasion of India; but in the latter year Sooltan Mahmood, with an army of 100,000 horse and 20,000 foot, set out with the determination of reaching Kanouj, one of the most ancient and most wealthy of Indian cities, known to Persian tradition as having been invaded by King Gooshtasp. The Mahomedan host paused nowhere, and

Edward II. and Canute kings of England.

Seventh invasion, A.D. 1017.

encountered no opposition of any moment. The rajah, Koowur Rái, was unprepared for defence, and made the best terms he could, in unconditional submission. Mahmood then passed on to Meerut, which also submitted: and thence to Muttra and the sacred shrines of Krishna, which were found so splendid as to excite even the sooltan's admiration. All the gold and silver idols were melted down, and many of the temples destroyed; but some were spared on account of their beauty. From Muttra the sooltan appears to have turned homewards, attacking and subduing all petty princes who fell in his way. These were Rajpoots, and the same miserable results were observable everywhere, in the destruction of their women by the men, followed by a frantic attack upon the Mahomedans, in which they perished. On his return to his capital, Mahmood, emulating the beautiful architecture he had seen in India, erected a splendid mosque, which was called 'the Celestial Bride,' and this example was followed by the nobility of his court, who vied with each other in adorning the capital.

Kanouj attacked.

The year 1021 was remarkable for a confederation of the Hindoo sovereigns against the Rajah of Kanouj, who had maintained friendly relations with the sooltan; and to assist him, Mahmood again advanced into India, but was too late to save Kanouj, which had been taken by the Rajah of Kalinga, in Bundelkund, and its sovereign put to death. To avenge this act, Sooltan Mahmood proceeded to Kalinga, but the rajah fled before the Mahomedan army, and after devastating the country, the sooltan proceeded homewards. Anundpál, the rajah of Lahore, had probably joined the Hindoo confederation against Kanouj; for, on this occasion, Mahmood returned from Kashmere, whither he had proceeded, and took and sacked Lahore, while Anundpál fled to Ajmere.

Eighth invasion, A.D. 1021.

Kanouj attacked by the Rajah of Kalinga.

Mahmood attacks Kalinga.

Although foiled in his purpose of reducing Nandá Rái of Kalinga, in 1021, Sooltan Mahmood did not forego it; and in A.D. 1023 marched against him by way of Lahore. Passing by Gwalior, he laid siege to the fort, but its rajah submitted, and was not interfered with; Nandá Rái also made no resistance, and having presented some valuable gifts, was confirmed in his possessions.

Ninth invasion, A.D. 1023.

Sooltan Mahmood had long heard of the sanctity and wealth of the temple of Somnâth, situated on the sea-coast, in the province of Kattiawar, and as it was a place of pilgrimage for Hindoos from all parts of India, burned to destroy so notorious an example of idolatry. In September 1024 A.D., therefore, he marched from Ghuzny with

Tenth expedition, A.D. 1024.

Pope John XIX.

his army, accompanied by 30,000 volunteers who served without pay, for the express purpose of destroying Somnâth. Having reached Mooltan, Mahmood struck across the desert to Ajmere, which had been evacuated by its rajah, and thence reached Anhulwara, the capital of Guzerat, now ruled over by a prince of the Solunkee or Chalúkya dynasty, which had succeeded the Chowras in A.D. 942. The rajah, however, had retired into the mountains, and the Mohamedans pushed on to Somnâth. The temple fortress was bravely defended by the Rajpoots, and the assaults were continued for three days, but without effect; while a diversion against the besiegers was made in their rear by Bheem Déo, the rajah of Guzerat, which had well-nigh proved successful. Mahmood, however, as on a former occasion, prostrated himself in prayer before his troops, and remounting his horse, cheered them on to victory. 5,000 of the garrison were slain, and the remainder escaped by boats, pursued however by the Mahomedans, who slew many more of them. Although Mahmood had seen many noble Hindoo temples, he was not prepared for the magnificence of Somnâth. Entering the great hall, the idol, nine feet in height above the ground, was before him, and with a blow of his mace he struck off its nose. The Brahmins offered an immense sum if he would spare it, but the sooltan replied that he desired to be known to posterity as 'Mahmood the idol-breaker, not as the idol-seller,' and the image was broken to pieces. In its inside were found precious stones and pearls, of a value far exceeding what had been offered, and the wealth of the temple was immense.

Mahmood invades Guzerat.

Temple of Somnâth captured.

Vast booty obtained.

After a short stay at Somnâth, the sooltan followed Rajah Bheem Déo, who had retired to the fort of Gundaba, probably Gundava, in Kutch, which was stormed and taken, but the rajah escaped. Believing the place to be impregnable, the rajah had lodged all his valuables there, which fell into the sooltan's hands. Mahmood then proceeded to Anhulwara, which was a magnificent capital, and contemplated making it his permanent abode; but being dissuaded from such a step, and having conferred the throne of Guzerat upon a prince of the country, he marched for Ghuzny by way of Sinde, avoiding Rajah Bheem Déo, who had occupied the ordinary route; but the army narrowly escaped destruction by heat and thirst in the desert. This expedition, and the campaign and residence in Guzerat, had occupied two years and a half; and though in the year 1027 the sooltan undertook a campaign against the Juts, or Jâts, a tribe on the river Indus, who had molested his army on its return from Somnâth, and reduced

Gundaba taken.

Anhulwara occupied.

them to obedience, yet no further invasion of India on a large scale was attempted. He became seriously afflicted with the stone, and died on April 29, 1030, in the sixty-third year of his age, having reigned thirty-three years.

Hugh Capet reigns in France.

Sooltan Mahmood's character is a favourite one with all Mahomedan historians, and doubtless possessed many elements of greatness and of generosity, though of a variable character. While he could be liberal to profusion to some, he was niggard to others; and the famous satire of the poet Ferdousi, whom he had invited to his court, and treated inhospitably, is a bitter memorial against him, redeemed too late by his generosity to the poet's daughter. Mahmood was, nevertheless, a sincere patron of learning and of literature. He established colleges and schools at Ghuzny, and endowed them richly; and he beautified the city by many noble buildings. His justice was inflexible, and by his natural strength of character and personal bravery, he possessed himself, in an eminent degree, of the affections of his people. It will have been seen by the detail of his invasions, that he had no desire to make any permanent settlement in India, and took no part in its politics. The fierce iconoclasm of his nature, and lust of booty, were the foundations of all his Indian campaigns, and after he had plundered and devastated any Indian territory, and carried off thousands of its people to become slaves, he left it to its ancient rulers, to recover gradually from the desolation he had caused. It is probable that thousands of forcible conversions were made as a principle of faith; but Islamism took no root in India, and the destruction and plunder of their temples, and the slaughter of their priests and bravest warriors, established in the hearts of the Hindoo people a terror and hatred of the Mahomedans which was never afterwards redeemed. No instances, it may be said to his credit, are recorded of wanton or revengeful massacre or executions; and in his dealings with Hindoo princes he was in all cases merciful, even though they had proved unfaithful to their promises. Tried by the standard of his times, therefore, Mahmood must be considered on the whole humane, and his unquenchable thirst for gain by plunder is the worst feature in his character. In regard to the Hindoo princes, it is evident that their efforts to resist the invaders were comparatively feeble. Their greatest coalition, in A.D. 1006, did not amount to a representation of the warlike power of India, and was so quickly overthrown, that it scarcely deserves the name of resistance; while Anundpál of Lahore, the head of the Rajpoot dynasty of the Chôhans, was the only prince who appears to have had the national honour really at heart. At his death,

Character of Sooltan Mahmood.

the dominions of Mahmood extended as far as Isfahan westward, and their extent, already great, only perhaps prevented a permanent occupation of the greater part of India. Thirteen invasions of India are claimed for him; but ten only, as detailed, are of consequence.

CHAPTER III.

FROM THE DEATH OF SOOLTAN MAHMOOD TO THE END OF THE GHUZNEVY DYNASTY, A.D. 1030–1186.

Mahomed succeeds Sooltan Mahmood.

MAHMOOD left twin sons, Mahomed and Musaood: and by his will, created Mahomed his successor. The brothers had never been on good terms, and while their father kept Mahomed near him, on account of his docile and tractable disposition, he conferred on Musaood the government of Isfahan, in order that his turbulent nature might find employment in the subjugation of the warlike tribes around him. On his father's death, Musaood wrote to his brother relinquishing his claim to succession, provided the Persian provinces were assigned to him, and his name were read first in the public prayers; this, however, was refused by Mahomed, who, contrary to the advice of the officers of state, marched with an army to meet his brother. By the way, Mahomed halted for the forty days' fast of the Rumzán, during which time a conspiracy was formed against him in camp by his uncle and two other chief officers, and he was seized and imprisoned. The confederates then marched to Herat with the army, and joining Musaood, swore allegiance to him. Musaood, however, though he did not release his brother, hanged one and beheaded the other of the two treacherous officers, and imprisoned his uncle for life. According to the cruel custom of the time, Mahomed was blinded and deposed, after a reign of five months, and Musaood became sooltan of the whole Ghuznevy dominions.

Mahomed, blinded and deposed, succeeded by his brother Musaood, 1031.

From the period of his accession, in 1031 A.D., till 1033, Musaood was engaged in warfare with the Seljuk Tartars; but peace being concluded with them, he turned his attention to the affairs of India, whither he proceeded; captured the fort of Sursooty, in the Kashmere hills; and while he was engaged in this campaign, heard of the defeat of his general by the Seljuks, and was obliged to proceed to that part of his dominions to restore order. In the year 1036, having returned to India, Musaood reduced the fort of Hansy, before deemed impregnable, established

Musaood's invasion of India.

Renews the expedition.

Harold Harefoot king of England.

a garrison in it, and also in Sonput, near Dehly; and returning to Lahore, left his son Mâdood in possession, and proceeded to Ghuzny. Here he found the kingdom in confusion from repeated attacks by the Seljuks, and in May 1040 himself received a sore defeat by them, by which he was so disheartened, that he determined to reside for the future in India. As he proceeded to Lahore in 1042, his army mutinied, deposed him, and put him to death, raising to the throne his blind brother Mahomed, whom he had brought with him. Musaood had reigned nine years. Though of a warlike temperament, he was fond of the society of learned men; he built and endowed schools and colleges, and for a period was very popular; but he lacked the energy of his father, and perhaps the Ghuznevy dominions, already spread over an immense tract of country, were become too large to be governed efficiently. Shortly after his deposition, Musaood was put to death by his cousin Soliman, in the fort of Kurry, where he had been confined. During his reign he had appointed his son Módood governor of Balkh; who, on hearing of his father's murder, repaired to Ghuzny, where he was received with enthusiasm, assumed the crown, and immediately marched upon Lahore to avenge his father's death. The blind king Mahomed opposed him at Duntoor, was defeated, and taken prisoner, and, with several officers who had taken part in the deposition of King Musaood, put to death. Finding his brother Mâdood, who had continued in charge of Lahore, was not disposed to accord his allegiance, Módood marched against him; but, before any engagement occurred, Mâdood was found dead in his bed, and all opposition ceased. Meanwhile the Seljuks had recommenced hostilities, and the king left India to oppose them. During his absence, the Hindoo princes of Northern India, taking advantage of the difficulties of the new king, organized an insurrection against the Mahomedans, which for a time threatened serious consequences. The Rajah of Dehly, in conjunction with other confederates, retook Hansy and Thanésur, with their dependencies. The fort of Nagrakote capitulated, and an idol was replaced there with great pomp. This success encouraged other rajahs of the Punjâb; who, having coalesced, invested Lahore; but it was desperately defended by its Mahomedan garrison, street by street: and when, in despair of receiving aid, and in sore strait from famine, the garrison sallied forth, the Hindoos fled, and the siege ceased. This event seems to have broken up the Hindoo confederation;

Musaood defeated by the Seljuks.

And is deposed by the army.

Mahomed succeeds him.

Módood, son of Musaood, assumes the crown, and proceeds to India.

He returns to oppose the Seljuks.

Hindoo insurrection, A.D. 1043.

Turks conquer Persia.

The Hindoos besiege Lahore, but are defeated.

for though the troubles on the western frontier of the kingdom never ceased, its Indian possessions remained at peace till the king's death, which occurred December 24, A.D. 1049. His son Musaood, a child of four years old, was proclaimed king, but almost immediately deposed by his uncle Abool Hassan, who became king, and at once recovered the Punjâb, Sinde, and other Indian territory from a rebel officer who had coalesced with the inhabitants. Abool Hassan was, however, deposed in 1051 by Abdool Rusheed, a son of the Sooltan Mahmood; who, after a reign of a year, was in time deposed by Farókhzád, son of King Musaood, who reigned six years, and died in A.D. 1058; but no event of Indian interest is recorded of this period. He was succeeded by his brother Ibrahim without opposition, who reigned in peace till his death, in A.D. 1098, with the exception of one Indian campaign in A.D. 1079, which was confined to a portion of the Punjâb. Ibrahim was a religious devotee, and employed himself in translating the Korán and other religious works. His son Musaood III., who succeeded him, was of a bolder and more martial character, and his love of justice was distinguished by the compilation of all existing laws of the kingdom into one code. Although he does not appear to have entered upon any Indian campaign in person, yet his generals carried the Mahomedan arms beyond the Ganges, and returned with much spoil of temples and cities. During the reign of Musaood III. Lahore became the real capital of the Ghuznevy dynasty, and their possessions in India had become consolidated.

King Módood's death, A.D. 1049.

Pope Leo IX.

Abool Hassan deposed A.D. 1051 by Abdool Rusheed. Farókhzád deposes him 1052, and reigns till A.D. 1058.

Ibrahim succeeds, and reigns till A.D. 1098.

Edgar king of Scotland.

Musaood III. succeeds, and reigns till A.D. 1118.

Makes Lahore his capital.

Arslan, a son of the late king, now imprisoned his brothers, and was crowned; but the princes who had been put aside appealed through their mother, who was sister of Sanjur, sooltan of the Seljuks, to him for aid, which was promptly rendered, and Arslan defeated in a bloody battle by the sooltan in person. Arslan fled to India, and collecting all the troops there, attempted to recover Ghuzny, but was again defeated, and put to death in the twenty-seventh year of his age and third of his reign.

Arslan usurps the throne, 1118.

Put to death, 1121.

When the Seljuk sooltan interfered, in 1118 A.D., on behalf of his nephews, and defeated Arslan, he placed another nephew, Béhrám, brother of Arslan, upon the throne, and the date of his reign is reckoned from that period—there being then in fact two kings of the same kingdom. After quelling a rebellion in India, Béhrám reigned in peace for some time, but having executed one of the Ghoory family, his son-in-law, the

Béhrám sooltan, 1118.

Prince of Ghoor, Seif-ood-deen Soor, in order to avenge his brother's death, invaded Ghuzny, when Béhrám was forced to fly, and Seif-ood-deen took possession of the city. Béhrám, however, recovered it during the winter, and took Seif-ood-deen prisoner, whom he executed in a barbarous manner. Alla-ood-deen, brother of Seif-ood-deen, now sooltan of Ghoor, marched at once to avenge the act, defeated Béhrám, and having taken possession of Ghuzny, gave it up to indiscriminate pillage and slaughter for seven days. Most of the noble edifices raised by the Ghuznevy kings were destroyed, and even learned and inoffensive men of high station were put to death in cold blood. The city never afterwards recovered from this spoliation, and Alla-ood-deen obtained the appellation of 'Jehan-soz,' or 'burner of the world,' by which, and for his infamous cruelties, he was afterwards distinguished. These events have perhaps no direct concern with Indian history, but it is necessary to relate them in regard to the family of Ghoor, which succeeded the Ghuznevies in India.

Ghuzny plundered by Alla-ood-deen Seljuk.

After the engagement with Alla-ood-deen, Sooltan Béhrám fled towards India, but died by the way of a broken heart, in the year 1152, having reigned 35 years.

Frederick I., Barbarossa, emperor of Germany.

Béhrám died, A.D. 1152.

Khoosroo, his son, succeeds.

Dies at Lahore, A.D. 1160.

The Ghoory family conquer Ghuzny.

Philip Augustus king of France

His son Khoosroo, who reached Lahore safely, was received with joy, and became king. He would have made an effort to regain Ghuzny, but owing to the defeat of the Seljuk sooltan by the Toorkomans, this became impossible, and he remained content with his Indian possessions, over which he ruled for seven years without troubles. He died at Lahore, in the year 1160, leaving his dominions to his son, Khoosroo Mullik, who was destined to be the last of the dynasty. After a protracted struggle, the whole kingdom of Ghuzny had fallen into the possession of the Ghoory family, and in the year 1180, Shahab-ood-deen Mahomed Ghoory, brother of Gheias-ood-deen, sooltan of Ghoor, who had succeeded his uncle Alla-ood-deen, overran the Indian possessions of Sooltan Khoosroo, and invested Lahore, which he was unable to take, and peace was concluded between them, Sooltan Khoosroo giving up his son Khoosroo Mullik as a hostage. Four years afterwards Mahomed Ghoory invaded the Punjâb again, and established some garrisons in the province, which Sooltan Khoosroo was unable to expel: and being desirous of getting the sooltan into his power, wrote to him that he had despatched his son with overtures of peace. The message was not open to suspicion, and the sooltan, very desirous of meeting the son from whom he had been so long separated, went to meet him, attended only by a small escort. Mahomed Ghoory's plan had so far succeeded: and by a rapid march, at the head of 20,000 cavalry, he threw himself between the sooltan and Lahore, and while part of the force surrounded the unfortunate sooltan's camp and made him prisoner, the rest, headed by Mahomed Ghoory, passed on to Lahore, of which he took possession without opposition, in the name of his brother, the Sooltan of Ghoor. Thus the house of Ghuzny ceased to reign; Sooltan Khoosroo had reigned twenty-eight years, and was the last of the race of Subooktugeen who held royal power. He and his family were sent to Ghoor and confined there, and their ultimate fate is not known. The great Ghuznevy dynasty had lasted from A.D. 962 to 1186, or 224 years.

Mahomed Ghoory deposes Sooltan Khoosroo, and establishes the dynasty of Ghoor.

CHAPTER IV.

OF THE CONQUESTS OF SOOLTAN SHAHAB-OOD-DEEN, MAHMOOD GHOORY, COMMONLY CALLED MAHOMED GHOORY, A.D. 1156–1205.

ALLA-OOD-DEEN, sooltan of Ghoor, who had taken possession of Ghuzny, died in 1156 A.D., after a reign of four years. He had confined his nephews Gheias-ood-deen and Shahab-ood-deen, and his son Seif-ood-deen became sooltan. His first act was to release his cousins, and restore them to the government they had previously held; and having reigned barely a year, he was assassinated by a person whose brother he had put to death. To him Gheias-ood-deen succeeded; and it is a strange feature of those times, when the first act of every succeeding monarch seems to have been to slay, blind, or confine every possible pretender to the throne, that he should have trusted his brother Mahomed with powers virtually as extensive as his own; a trust which was fulfilled to the day of his death by Mahomed Ghoory with the most scrupulous and devoted faith.

Sooltan Alla-ood-deen Ghoor dies, A.D. 1156.

Seif-ood-deen, his son, succeeds, and reigns only a year.

Sooltan Gheias-ood-deen succeeds.

Mahomed Ghoory, after Ghuzny had been taken possession of by his brother, Sooltan Gheias-ood-deen, and the officers of the Ghuznevy kings displaced, was despatched to India, to annex the provinces which belonged to the subverted dynasty. Mooltan was taken, and the fort of Oocha, the scene of Alexander's memorable attack and severe wound, was invested. The gates were opened by the raja's widow, who desired to marry her daughter to the Mahomedan general, and

First Indian campaign of Mahomed Ghoory.

had put her husband to death; and he returned with his Hindoo bride to Ghuzny. In A.D. 1179–80 he invaded Sooltan Khoosroo Mullik's territory of Peshawur; and, as has been already related in the last chapter, gained possession of Lahore, and sent the royal captives to his brother Gheias-ood-deen, by whom they were confined.

Second campaign, A.D. 1179–80.

Philip Augustus King of France.

In 1191 Mahomed Ghoory again advanced into India, and retook the fort of Bitunda from the Hindoos. Here he learned that the Rajah of Ajmere, Prithy Rái, with the Rajah of Dehly, Chawund Rái, were advancing to meet him with 200,000 horse and 3,000 elephants; and the adverse forces met near the village of Narrain, on the banks of the Soorsutty or Saraswaty river, which, to the Hindoos, was the holy ground of the Máhábhárut. In this engagement, Mahomed Ghoory was defeated with great loss; himself severely wounded, and his army pursued for forty miles. But the Hindoos did not follow up their advantage: Bitunda was besieged for a time, but abandoned; and, as had been the case before, the Hindoo princes relapsed into inactivity.

Third campaign, A.D. 1191–92.

Richard I. in Palestine.

Battle of Narrain, and defeat of the Mahomedans.

For a time Mahomed rested with his brother Sooltan Gheias-ood-deen at Ghoor; but the shame of the defeat he had sustained rankled at his heart, and proceeding to his government of Ghuzny, he organised an army of 120,000 picked horsemen, with which he marched suddenly into India by the route of Peshawur. Having reached Lahore, he dispatched an ambassador to the Rajah of Ajmere, offering him friendship should he embrace Islamism, otherwise the issue of war; a fair challenge perhaps, according to the customs of the times, but one which, he must have known, would be refused. It was impossible, indeed, to have offered to the head of the Chôhan Rajpoots, the descendant of one of the princes of the fire-fountain of Mount Aboo, a greater insult. At this period the ruling families of the Hindoos of Northern India were all Rajpoots. Prithy Rái, rajah of Ajmere, was the head of the Chóhan tribe; and, subordinate to him were the Hárás, under Hamira and others. The Aditya dynasty of Mewar was ruled over by Ragakuna. The Tomáras were rajahs of Dehly, the Rahtores of Kanouj, and the Baghilas, who had succeeded the Chalúkyas, of Guzerat. To all these, the chosen champions of the Hindoo faith, and representatives of the Aryan chivalry, Prithy Rái made a powerful appeal, which was heartily responded to. Their splendid victory over Mahomed Ghoory was not more than two years old, and nothing had occurred to damp the ardour it had reawakened; nor at any period in its history were the

Fourth campaign, A.D. 1193.

Rajpoots of India better united, or more fitted to encounter a national enemy than on the present occasion.

Second great battle of Narrain or Tirouri.

The Hindoos took up their position on their old ground at Tirouri or Narrain, on the Soorsutty river, and awaited the arrival of the Mahomedans, with the river bed, for it contained little water, between them. Ferishta quotes the letters which passed between the commanders; that of the Hindoos is arrogant and vaunting, but offering not to molest the Mahomedans if they retired. Mahomed's reply is that of a simple soldier, whose sense of duty forbids him to retreat. The Hindoos spent the night in thoughtless revelry, the Mahomedans in preparation, and before dawn Mahomed had advanced to the hostile camp. He directed attacks to be made by fresh bodies of horse on the Hindoo centre as rapidly as possible, retreating at the same time, till watching his opportunity, he charged at the head of 12,000chosen mail-clad warriors, and rode through the Hindoo host, scattering it on all sides. 'Like a great building,' writes Ferishta, 'it tottered to its fall, and was lost in its own ruins.' Chawund Rái, rajah of Dehly, Hamira Hárá, and many noted leaders fell on the field. Prithy Rái was taken and put to death, and the whole of the *matériel* and private property of the Hindoo army fell into the conqueror's hands. This great battle virtually decided the fate of India, nor was any coalition of similar magnitude attempted, or indeed was it possible, in after years.

Victory of the Mahomedans.

Decides the fate of India.

The glory of the victory was stained by the massacre of unresisting Hindoos at Ajmere, which was plundered; and having made over the country to an illegitimate son of Prithy Rái, Mahomed proceeded northwards, and returned to Ghuzny, leaving as his deputy Kootub-ood-deen Eibuk, who took Dehly with its dependencies from the rajah, and in 1193 A.D. established it as the seat of Mahomedan government.

Kootub-ood-deen Eibuk captures Dehly.

Fifth campaign, A.D. 1194.

Kanouj and Benares taken.

In the succeeding year, Mahomed Ghoory returned to India, and marching eastwards, Jeychund Rái, rajah of Kanouj, was defeated by the vanguard of the army under Kootub-ood-deen Eibuk, and a fort, in which the rajahs of Kanouj kept their treasures, fell before the Mahomedans, who passed onwards to Benares, where Mahomed Ghoory broke the idols in all the temples, and consecrated the buildings to Islamism. He then proceeded to return to Ghuzny, having created Kootub-ood-deen viceroy. In 1194 A.D. Kootub-ood-deen was summoned to the aid of the prince who had been nominated to Ajmere and had been expelled. Hemraj, who had created the revolution, was, however, defeated and slain in battle, and a Mahomedan governor was appointed to protect and control the rajah—a course which has often since been followed by ourselves under similar circumstances. Having settled Ajmere, Kootub-ood-deen proceeded to Anhulwara, in Guzerat, where he defeated Bheem Déo, the rajah, and would probably have annexed the kingdom, but was recalled to Dehly, by orders from Ghuzny.

Kootub-ood-deen Eibuk defeats the Rajah of Guzerat.

The sixth campaign was of short duration, for Mahomed Ghoory, after taking Byana, in Rajpootana, left the field operations to be concluded by Kootub-ood-deen, when Gwalior fell after a long siege; and marching into Guzerat, he took Anhulwara and all its dependencies. In this year, while engaged in affairs on the western frontier, Mahomed Ghoory heard of the death of his brother, Gheias-ood-deen, and was crowned sooltan without opposition. He now recommenced his western campaign against the King of Kharizm, but was defeated in a severe battle, and narrowly escaped with his life, being obliged to pay a heavy ransom.

Sixth campaign, 1195.

Anhulwara in Guzerat taken by Kootub-ood-deen.

Sooltan Gheias-ood-deen dies.

Is succeeded by Mahomed Ghoory, 1195.

Meanwhile the Gukkurs, mention of whom has been made on previous occasions, revolted, and committed dreadful atrocities in the Punjâb, which they overran, and even captured Lahore. The sooltan, therefore, marched from Ghuzny to Mooltan, which had also rebelled, defeated the rebel Zeeruk, who had been in charge of the province, and then attacked the Punjâb in conjunction with Kootub-ood-deen, who had been summoned from Dehly. The Gukkurs were quickly reduced, and for the most part became Mahomedans: and the sooltan was on his return to Ghuzny, when, being encamped near the town of Rohtuk, on the Indus, and his tents opened at nights to admit fresh air from the river, a body of Gukkurs swam the stream, cut down the sentinel in the sooltan's tent, and before the guards could assemb e, had succeeded in forcing an entrance and in murdering him; he was found to have received no less than twenty-two wounds. This event happened on March 14, A.D. 1205. His remains were carried to Ghuzny, and interred there. Mahomed Ghoory left no male issue. He had accumulated an immense amount of treasure, the results of his Indian campaigns, the possession of which, with the succession to the kingdom, was disputed for a time; but eventually his nephew, Mahmood, son of the late king, Gheias-ood-deen, was crowned as sooltan.

Rebellion of the Gukkurs.

Sooltan Mahomed Ghoory murdered at Rohtuk, 1205.

The character of Mahomed Ghoory is hardly, perhaps, appreciated by the Mahomedan historians. He was faithful to his brother, just and liberal; and his military exploits equalled, if they did not in some respects exceed, those of his great ancestor, Sooltan Mahmood I. He overcame greater combinations by the Hindoo princes than it had ever fallen to the lot of Sooltan Mahmood to encounter, and his generalship and calm courage in the great battle which virtually decided the fate of India were of the highest character. Sooltan Mahmood's exploits were against a people who had not, within the memory of man, scarcely indeed of tradition, encountered a foreign invasion; they were taken unawares, and for the most part made a comparatively trifling defence. Mahomed Ghoory, on the contrary, had to contend with the combined military forces of Northern India, now thoroughly aroused to a sense of common danger, actuated by national honour for the defence of their country, and inspirited by their previous victory. The results of his Indian campaigns were not merely plunder. As Mahomed Ghoory advanced he annexed the districts he occupied, and provided means for their administration, and they laid the real foundation of the subsequent Mahomedan empire of India, of which his comparatively early death prevented the probable realisation in his own person.

Character of Sooltan Mahomed Ghoory.

CHAPTER V.

OF THE SLAVE KINGS OF DEHLY IN SUCCESSION, A.D. 1205 TO 1239.

At the period of Sooltan Mahomed Ghoory's death, three Turkish slaves, who had been brought up by him, held viceregal appointments. Kootub-ood-deen Eibuk was viceroy in Northern India, Nasir-ood-deen Kubáchá in Mooltan and Sinde, and Eldooz in Ghuzny. Mahomed Ghoory's successor, his nephew Mahmood, immediately after his accession, sent a warrant of investiture as king, with all the insignia of royalty, to Kootub-ood-deen, and he was crowned, as first Mahomedan king, at Lahore on July 24, 1206. The king had already served in India for twenty years, and had exercised viceregal power for the whole of that period. He was not therefore new to the situation. Born of obscure parents, he had become the slave of a Kázi or law-officer in Toorkistan, who had him educated. On this person's death the boy was sold by his executors, and presented by the purchaser to Mahomed Ghoory, then engaged in one of his western campaigns. Thenceforward the fortunes of Kootub-ood-deen experienced no check; his natural

Kootub-ood-deen Eibuk created king of India, A.D. 1205.

Henry emperor of Constantinople.

Origin of Kootub-ood-deen.

talents had free scope for action, and whether as a soldier, a general, or a political administrator, he gained equal distinction.

To him, indeed, the details of the conquests in India are due. In 1192 A.D., after Mahomed Ghoory had returned to Ghuzny, Kootub-ood-deen took Dehly, after a fierce conflict, and established the seat of Mahomedan government there. In the succeeding year he drove back the Guzerat forces, and in 1194 accompanied the sooltan in his campaign towards Benares. His establishment of a Mahomedan administration in Ajmere has been already noticed, as also the campaign which ensued in Guzerat; and in the same year Kootub-ood-deen was invited to Ghuzny, where he was received with all the honour and respect due to his position. He had scarcely returned to Dehly when the Mairs of Rajpootana rebelled. Kootub-ood-deen proceeded to attack them, but was worsted in a skirmish, in which he received six or seven wounds, and had a narrow escape from death. In the year 1202 he captured the strong fort of Kalinga, in Bundelkund, obtaining an immense booty, and completed the subjugation of the provinces lying between that place and Dehly. In the year 1205, as has been related, he became king of India, and a quarrel having arisen between him and Eldooz, governor of Ghuzny, he marched thither and was crowned there; but, unable to hold the city, he returned almost immediately to India. Here, until his death, which occurred by a fall from his horse in the year 1210, Kootub-ood-deen occupied himself in the regulation of his dominions, and attempted no further conquests. There can be no question of the ability by which he had raised himself from the condition of a slave to that of a king, and Mahomedan historians attest not only his vigour, but his social virtues, and his profound, generous liberality. To commemorate the conquest of Dehly the celebrated minaret, called the Kootub Minar, still perfect, with a splendid mosque, were commenced by Kootub-ood-deen, and completed by his successor, Shumsh-ood-deen Altmish.

Indian campaigns of Kootub-ood-deen Eibuk.

Takes Ghuzny and is crowned, but returns to India, where he dies, 1210.

Crusade against the Albigenses.

Kootub-ood-deen left one son, Arám, who at once ascended to the throne, but appears to have been deficient in vigour and resolution. Nasir-ood-deen Kubáchá became independent in Sinde, and Mahmood Bukhtyar Khiljy, another of Sooltan Mahomed Ghoory's slaves, possessed himself of Bengal, while other chiefs, imitating their example, became independent. A deputation of the nobles of the State, therefore, waited upon Shumsh-ood-deen Altmish, the son-in-law and adopted son of the late king, and besought him to save the kingdom by accepting the throne. He complied with their request,

Arám, his son, succeeds, 1210.

Shumsh-ood-deen Altmish

defeated Arám in an engagement near Dehly, and was crowned king. All these events happened in the same year, 1210, and before he had well established his authority the Toorky cavalry in his service rebelled and advanced upon Dehly, but were defeated by the king, who had now no one to oppose him. In the year 1215, Táj-ood-deen Eldooz, king of Ghuzny, made an effort to recover the Indian dominions, and advanced upon Dehly with a large army, but was defeated by Altmish on the plain already memorable from former battles, and taken prisoner.

Defeats Arám, and becomes king, 1210.

Shumsh-ood-deen Altmish called to the throne, 1210.

Magna Charta signed by King John.

Táj-ood deen Eldooz attacks Altmish, but is defeated.

In 1217 Altmish next endeavoured to reduce Nasir-ood-deen Kubáchá, who was independent in Sinde, but failed in his purpose after a severe struggle. Meanwhile the dominions of the Sooltan of Kharizm had been invaded by the Moghuls under Chengiz or Jengiz Khan, who overran the country, and penetrated as far as Ghuzny. Jelal-ood-deen, the son of the Sooltan of Kharizm, vainly endeavoured to save the eastern portion of his dominions, but was pursued to the Indus, and narrowly escaped with his life. He repaired to Altmish, and endeavoured to induce him to act against the Moghuls, but in the face of their overwhelming numbers and power he declined the expedition. Jelal-ood-deen, however, subsequently recovered part of the Ghuzny dominions in Persia.

Henry III. king of England.

Invasion of Ghuzny by Moghuls under Jengiz Khan.

In 1217 Shumsh-ood-deen Altmish again invaded Sinde, and having defeated his brother-in-law, who was afterwards drowned in the Indus, annexed the province to his dominions. It must be understood, however, that this conquest relates to Northern Sinde and Mooltan only. Southern Sinde was still in possession of the Suméra Rajpoots, and there is no record of any attempt to subdue them having been made by the Mahomedans up to this period. In A.D. 1226 Malwah, including the celebrated fort of Mandoo, was conquered, which was followed in 1231 by the recapture of Gwalior, which had again fallen into the hands of the Hindoos; and in this campaign Oojeyn, the former capital of Rajah Vikram-Aditya the Great, and one of the oldest and most famous Hindoo cities of India, fell into the king's hands, when all the idols of the celebrated temples there were destroyed. Altmish also re-established his authority over the provinces of Bengal, which had been interrupted by the rebellion of its governor. Thus before his death, which occurred on April 30, 1235, Shumsh-ood-deen Altmish had established the Mahomedan sovereignty over the whole of Northern India, from the Indus to the Ganges, and in

Altmish invades Northern Sinde and annexes it.

Malwah conquered.

Gwalior recaptured.

Oojeyn taken.

Shumsh-ood-deen Altmish dies, 1235.

this large tract, the power of the Hindoos was completely broken. Such of the native chiefs as were permitted to govern their hereditary dominions paid tribute; but the largest portion of the country appears to have been under a direct Mahomedan administration. Shumsh-ood-deen Altmish had reigned twenty-six years with honour, and forms another instance of self-elevation by his talent, from his originally low condition.

Rookn-ood-deen, the eldest son of the late king, was governor of Budaoon, and was at Dehly on his father's death. He was crowned without opposition on May 1, 1235, but at once abandoned himself to every species of licentiousness, of which the consequences were immediately apparent in several serious rebellions. His mother, a cruel woman, virtually conducted the administration; but the nobles of the kingdom were so disgusted with the conduct both of the mother and son, that they put forward Ruzeea Sooltana, his eldest sister, to supersede him; and the princess, having put herself at the head of an army and marched against him, he was delivered up to her, and placed in confinement. Ruzeea Sooltana was no ordinary woman. It is rare among the families of Eastern princes to find any example of vigour or heroism in the female members; but Ruzeea possessed both in an eminent degree. Ferishta writes of her, comparing her with the late king's sons:—'She had a man's head and heart, and was better than twenty such sons;' she had no fault, 'but that she was a woman.' She was well educated, and had been her father's constant companion; and while engaged in his Gwalior campaign, he had appointed her his regent at the capital. She was well acquainted not only with the routine of ordinary current affairs, but with the political transactions of the State. After her assumption of the royal authority she gave public audiences, sat in the royal seat, and transacted all business in public. Such a person must needs have had, and perhaps made, many enemies, and there were many intrigues against her; but for a time she succeeded in breaking them up, and in establishing full order in the State and its most distant dependencies. The princess was unmarried, and the favour with which she regarded her master of the horse, who was permitted to lift her on her horse when she rode out, gave offence to many.

Rookn-ood-deen Feroze, his son, succeeds.

Deposed and succeeded by Ruzeea Sooltana.

Her character.

In the year 1239, the popular feeling was expressed in the rebellion of the Viceroy of Lahore; but the queen marched promptly against him, and reduced him to obedience. A second revolt was that of Mullik Altoonia Toork, governor of Bitunda. In proceeding thither from Lahore, the Toorky chiefs of the army mutinied, and carried the queen to Altoonia, by whom she was detained, and to whom she was shortly after married. Meanwhile the Prince Beiram, her brother, had been elected king, and when the queen marched from Bitunda, to re-establish her authority, at the head of an army which she and her husband had collected, they were met by the forces of Beiram, and after a severe action the queen was defeated. She rallied her army, however, but was defeated finally on August 24, 1239. In her flight from the fatal field of Keithul, the unfortunate lady and her husband were taken prisoners, and put to death, on November 14 of the same year. Ruzeea Begum Sooltana had reigned three and a half years.

The queen marries Altoonia and is deposed by her brother.

She attempts to regain power, but is defeated twice.

Put to death, 1239.

CHAPTER VI.

THE SLAVE KINGS OF DEHLY (*continued*), A.D. 1239 TO 1288.

MOIZ-OOD-DEEN BEIRAM ascended the throne on April 21, 1239–40, but in an unquiet reign of two years displayed no ability. On November 22, 1241, the Moghuls, advancing from Ghuzny, had seized Lahore; the viceroy had fled, and the vizier, Yekhtyar-ood-deen, was dispatched from Dehly to oppose them at the head of such troops as could be collected. When the danger was past, as the Moghuls did not remain, the vizier formed a plot to depose the king: and on his return to Dehly besieged the capital, which, after a long siege, was taken on May 10, 1241, and the king imprisoned and afterwards put to death. He had reigned little more two years. He was succeeded by Alla-ood-deen Musaood, son of Rookn-ood-deen, whose reign of four years is remarkable only for two partial invasions by the Moghuls—one of Bengal by way of Tibet, the other of a part of the Punjâb—both of which were repelled by the local authorities. Musaood entered upon a career of detestable profligacy and cruelty, and the nobles at court, wearied of his vices, requested his uncle Nasir-ood-deen to come to the capital. On his arrival, on June 10, 1246, he found the king already deposed, and in confinement, where he remained till his death.

Beiram, brother of Ruzeea Sooltana, succeeds, 1239–40.

Imprisoned and put to death.

Alla-ood-deen Musaood succeeds.

Beiram deposed, 1246.

Nasir-ood-deen Mahmood, in many respects, was a remarkable character. He was the son of Shumsh-ood-deen Altmish, and had been nominated by his father to the government of Bengal, but was too young to undertake

Nasir-ood-deen Mahmood succeeds, 1246.

the charge. The widow of his father, who was not his mother, had confined him; but he was released by King Musaood, and appointed to the government of Byraich, which he conducted in an able manner. His personal habits were very simple; and during his imprisonment he had supported himself by making copies of the Korán, an occupation which he never abandoned. Ferishta writes of him, that he had but one wife, whom he obliged to do all homely offices, refusing even the assistance of a servant; and when she complained one day of having burnt her fingers in baking bread, he exhorted her to persevere and God would reward her; as for himself, he was only a trustee of the State funds, and would allow of no extra expenses. If the king had been earlier employed in large public affairs, as his father intended, it is probable he would have made a better ruler, and trusted less to others; nevertheless, his reign brought no disaster on the State, and his virtuous private character was an admirable contrast to the profligate princes who had preceded him.

His habits and character.

Having removed some of the oldest and most disaffected officers from frontier posts, he replaced them by others, and thus established powerful and harmonious garrisons on the west, whence Moghul invasions might be apprehended. He then reduced many of the petty Hindoo princes of the Dooáb, or tract between the Ganges and Jumna, to obedience; and, between 1247 and 1250, the territory between Malwah and the Jumna, with the greater part of Rajpootana, was thoroughly subjected. In the principality of Nurwur, in Bundelkund, he was opposed by the rajah, according to Ferishta, at the head of 5,000 horse and 200,000 foot; and though the numbers may be exaggerated, they go far to establish the extent of the opposition which the king had to encounter in the subjugation of a partially conquered and martial people. It was an interesting circumstance of the year 1250, that Sheer Khan, the viceroy in charge of the western frontier, availed himself of an opportunity of driving the Moghuls out of Ghuzny, and taking possession of it in the name of the king. Another incursion by them into the Punjâb was also repelled. In spite of some domestic intrigues and minor campaigns, the king seems to have enjoyed peace till 1258, when the Mewatees and other Rajpoot tribes broke into rebellion, and were only subjected after a great loss of life on both sides; and in the same year, an envoy from the prince of the Moghuls arrived and was entertained with great honour and splendour. On February 18, 1265-6, the king, who had been long suffering from disease, died.

The acts of his government.

Rebellion of the Mewatees

Nasir-ood-deen dies, 1266.

It is doubtful whether he left any children, for none are mentioned by the Mahomedan historian; and Gheias-ood-

Gheias-ood-deen Bulbun

deen Bulbun, who had been vizier during the twenty years of the late king's reign, ascended the throne without opposition.

succeeds him.

Gheias-ood-deen had, like other great men of the time, been originally a Toorky slave. In his youth he had belonged to Altmish I., and had raised himself to the highest ranks in the State. His court, after his accession, was esteemed the most dignified and learned in Asia; and he gave refuge to no less than fifteen princes of Central Asia, who had been dispossessed of their dominions by the Moghuls, and allotted to each a sumptuous establishment at Dehly. The etiquette of his court was very strict, and his public ceremonies and processions the most magnificent that had ever been seen in India. In his early youth he had been addicted to wine: but after his accession to the throne, he not only gave up the use of it, but prohibited its sale or manufacture in his dominions, while he repressed all public immorality with the utmost strictness, and not unfrequently with cruelty. In 1266, the year of his accession, the Mewatees again rebelled, but were hunted down, and put to death indiscriminately, while the greater part of their country was cleared of forest, and cultivated. Several other rebellions were suppressed with equal severity and effect. It will be remembered that Sheer Khan, an officer of great bravery and merit, had been placed in charge of the western frontier by the late king. In 1267 he died, and the king appointed his eldest son and heir, the Prince Mahomed, as Sheer Khan's successor. His fate will be related hereafter. The greatest rebellion during the king's reign was that in 1279, of Toghral Khan, viceroy of Bengal, who had assumed the title of king. Two successive expeditions sent against him had failed; at last the king, notwithstanding his advanced age, proceeded in person to Bengal; and Mullik Mokunder, one of his officers, having discovered the rebel camp, charged into it at the head of only forty men, and in his own tent of audience cut down the rebel's adherents, but Toghral himself escaped. This strange and desperate exploit so terrified the rebels, who considered the king's army was upon them, that they fled. Toghral, however, was pursued and killed. When the king arrived next day, he reproved Mullik Mokunder for his rashness, but afterwards rewarded him. On all concerned in this rebellion, however, he poured out his utmost vengeance. Nor were even women and children spared; and after his return to Dehly, executions of the most cruel character were inflicted upon those

Origin of Gheias-ood-deen.

The magnificence of his court, and maintenance of public morality.

Renewed rebellion of the Mewatees and others subdued.

Insurrection in Bengal quelled.

Exploit of Mullik Mokunder.

Cruel executions in Bengal.

who had been taken prisoners, or who were sent from Bengal. In the end, however, on a remonstrance being made by the law officers and religious men of the court, the king desisted from his barbarous conduct.

Some time after this event, the Prince Mahomed arrived from Lahore on a visit to his father, but had not been with him three months when news reached him of a serious incursion of the Moghuls. The prince departed to his post, engaged the Moghuls, and defeated them: but in a chance medley at the close of the action was killed. The death of his beloved son had the effect of completely prostrating the king, now upwards of eighty years of age, and he sank gradually. Believing himself on his death-bed, he sent for his second son Kurra Khan, then governor of Bengal, in order to nominate him as his successor; but finding his father better than he expected, Kurra Khan returned to Bengal without taking leave of him, which so incensed the old king, that he invited his grandson, Kei-khoosroo, from Mooltan, and made a will in his favour. A few days afterwards, being upwards of eighty years of age, the king expired, having reigned in great splendour and glory for twenty-one years.

Death of Prince Mahomed.

Gheias-ood-deen Bulbun dies, 1286.

Margaret queen of Scotland.

His disposition of the kingdom was not however carried out. The nobles were apprehensive that Kurra Khan would dispute it and thus raise a civil war, and Kei-kobád, his son, then in Dehly, was selected and crowned, Kei-khoosroo retiring to his government of Mooltan. Kei-kobád was a handsome and engaging youth, who had been brought up with great strictness by his father, and expectations were formed from his previous character that he would prove a good king. These, however, were sorely disappointed, for he gave himself up to a course of riotous debauchery, which was encouraged by the vizier, Nizam-ood-deen, who retained the executive power in his hands. The principal events of the short reign of Kei-kobád were an invasion by the Moghuls, which was repelled, and followed by the execution of all the Moghul officers in the royal service, on pretence of their complicity with their countrymen; and the visit of the king's father, Kurra Khan, to Dehly, which, though it caused apprehensions of a war between them at first, ended amicably and even affectionately, Kurra Khan warning his son as he departed homewards against the designs of his vizier. For a time the advice of his father was observed by Kei-kobád, but he was again thrown into the vortex of pleasure by the minister, and failing to check his power, effected his death by poison through parties who were inimical to him.

Kei-kobád crowned.

The Moghul officers put to death.

The vizier poisoned.

The king attacked by paralysis.

His excesses had, however, so entirely ruined the constitution of the young king, that he became paralytic, and the executive power of the kingdom fell into the hands of three nobles, of whom Mullik Julal-ood-deen Feroze, of the Khiljy tribe, was the chief. After a brief struggle between the rivals for superiority, Julal-ood-deen prevailed: and at his instigation, the king, who was lying helpless in his country palace, was soon afterwards murdered by a Tartar, whose father had been unjustly executed. This event happened in the year 1288, and with it the dynasties of the slave kings ceased to exist. Julal-ood-deen Khiljy was proclaimed king, and to ensure his position, caused the infant son of Kei-kobád, who was in his power, to be put to death. From A.D. 1205 to 1288, a period of eighty-three years, ten kings, originally slaves, and their descendants, had reigned over India.

Kei kobád murdered, 1288.

Pope Nicholas I.

Pope Nicholas IV.

Julal-ood-deen Khiljy becomes king

CHAPTER VII.

OF THE KHILJY OR GHILZYE DYNASTY OF DEHLY, A.D. 1288 TO 1304.

The Khiljies were a tribe who, according to Ferishta, had been driven from Toorkistan and had settled in the mountains west of the Punjâb, where they still remain. Being a warlike race, many of them entered the service of the kings of Ghuzny and of India, and among them some rose to high offices. Julal-ood-deen was the son of the governor of Samárá, and had risen into favour with the late king, by whom he was promoted; but he was already advanced in age, being seventy years old when he became king; and he seems to have undertaken the office, for it was to him little more, with much distrust of his own powers. He professed great humility, he would not ascend the throne, or ride into the court of the palace; and his elevation produced no change in relation to his intimate associates, whom he entertained without pomp or ceremony as he had been used to do. Dehly became a point of attraction for all the learned men of Asia; and poets, musicians, and singers were liberally patronised and rewarded. Ameer Khoosroo, one of the sweetest of Persian poets, was ennobled and made librarian to the king. In the suppression of the first rebellion against him, Julal-ood-deen displayed such entire absence of revengeful feeling, that his courtiers, only used to the wholesale executions of former

Origin of Julal-ood-deen Khiljy.

His court and habits.

reigns, remonstrated with him. 'My friends,' he replied, quietly, 'I am now old, and I wish to go down to the grave without shedding more blood.' His courtiers, however, were partly in the right. The people were unused to such clemency, and sadly took advantage of it: crime of all descriptions increased; many of the governors of provinces were rebellious; and a conspiracy was set on foot to dethrone him. At a meeting of its members, one of them retired secretly and gave information to the king, who sent a party of his guards, and the conspirators were brought into the royal presence. They expected no less than death; but the king, drawing his sword, flung it before them, and challenged the boldest to use it against him. One of them replied, that the king should not care for words spoken under the influence of wine, and all prostrated themselves before the monarch, who forgave them.

Anecdote of his clemency.

His treatment of conspirators.

Nevertheless, it could not be concealed that the king's great lenity was causing much mischief as well as disquiet in the provinces. Sidy Mowla, a celebrated Dervish, was executed for a plot against the king's life; and his curse as he died, against him and his posterity, seems to have affected the king very deeply. The year 1291 was one of severe famine, in which thousands perished, and the king's eldest son, Khan Khanan, fell a victim to an existing epidemic, both of which events were attributed by the superstitious to the execution of the holy Dervish. The king, however, seems to have at last roused himself to a sense of duty, and marched against the rebels in Malwah; but the campaign was inconclusive, owing to his aversion to bloodshed.

Sidy Mowla, a Dervish, executed.

In the following year, 1292, however, he repelled, with much vigour, an invasion of the Moghuls, and one of their chiefs joined the king with 3,000 of his followers, and received his daughter in marriage. Ferishta mentions incidentally, that these Moghuls became Mahomedans, which proves that that faith had not as yet been received in some of the distant provinces of Northern Asia.

In 1293, the king marched into Malwah, which was reduced to obedience, and his nephew, Alla-ood-deen, now rising into notice, reduced the Hindoos of Bhilsa and other districts in Central India, for which he was rewarded with the government of Oude, in addition to that of his own province. Encouraged by his success, Alla-ood-deen now requested permission to make an expedition southwards, into countries as yet unpenetrated by the Mahomedans; and with 8,000 horse set out, in the year 1294, for the Deccan. Alla-ood-deen evidently marched by the line of Saugor and Jubbulpoor, for he debouched from the tableland of Central India

Rebellion in Malwah reduced.

Expedition by Alla-ood-deen to the Deccan, 1294.

Pope Boniface VIII.

by the passes into Berar, upon its capital, Ellichpoor, then held, according to tradition, by the Hindoo, or Jain rajah, Eel, who was a feudatory of the rajahs of Déogurh. A severe engagement took place on the plain between Ellichpoor and the hills, and the memory of the field of combat is still preserved by the mounds of the Mahomedan soldiers killed in the action, which are called 'Gunj Shaheed,' or the heaps of the martyrs. From Ellichpoor, the young leader pushed on rapidly to Déogurh, the impregnable stronghold of the Jadow or Yádává rajahs, who then held sway over the country of Máhárashtra. This place had originally been a conical hill, rising out of the plain, and separated rather more than a mile from the tableland to the north. Its sides all round had been scarped perpendicularly for 130 feet, probably at the period of the excavation of the cave temples of Ellora; a broad ditch had been excavated round the hill, and there was no passage to its summit but through a tunnel which, commencing in the ditch, had been led through the interior of the hill itself, which was composed of solid trap-rock. Such a work was unique in India then, as it is at present; it was utterly inaccessible, and in itself impregnable; but the city at its foot, where the rajah dwelt, was an open one.

Meets the Hindoos near Ellichpoor and defeats them.

Description of Déogurh.

Alla-ood-deen could make no impression on the fort; but he beleagured the city, and though it was stoutly defended by Ram Déo, the rajah, as long as provisions lasted, yet he was ultimately obliged to capitulate. The rajah, after informing Alla-ood-deen that he had been taken unawares, offered 1,500 pounds weight of gold as a ransom for the place, with a quantity of precious stones; and the Mahomedans consented to withdraw. At this juncture, the rajah's son, Shunkul Déo, arrived with the main army, and repudiated his father's negotiations. An action therefore ensued, in which the Mahomedans would have been defeated but for the officer left at Déogurh, who, with a thousand horse, retrieved the day; the Mahomedans rallying, drove the Hindoos from the field with heavy loss, and the siege was resumed. It was in vain that the rajah protested he had had no hand in his son's conduct. Alla-ood-deen was inexorable as to further payment for ransom; and in the end consented to receive pearls, diamonds, precious stones, silver, and pieces of silk of a value which seems almost incredible, but without question must have been very great; Ellichpoor and its dependencies were also ceded.

The rajah accepts terms, which are broken by his son;

who is defeated.

Final ransom.

Ellichpoor ceded.

Meanwhile, no news had been received of Alla-ood-deen's progress, and the king, becoming anxious, marched to Gwalior, where flying reports reached him of the success of the expedition. It was then debated whether Alla-ood-deen should be intercepted, and obliged to give up his plunder, or permitted to return to Kurra; but the king, with his accustomed unsuspiciousness, protested against the former, and in due time Alla-ood-deen reached Kurra safely. Almas Bey, the brother of Alla-ood-deen, an officer in the king's confidence, had, however, conspired against his sovereign in his brother's interest, and represented to Alla-ood-deen that the king really desired his death.

Alla-ood-deen returns to Kurra.

This seems to have suggested the infamous course which Alla-ood-deen pursued. The aged king was invited to Kurra, and having no suspicion, and being anxious to meet his nephew after his perilous expedition, went slightly attended, in a barge, by the Ganges. As he disembarked from his vessel, Alla-ood-deen met him with a show of the greatest affection; but while the king was caressing him and leading him back to the barge, two of Alla-ood-deen's guards, at a signal from him, fell upon the old man and murdered him. This event happened on July 19, 1295. There were many who now remembered the curse of the Dervish, and believed it fully fulfilled, not only as regarded the actual murderer, but afterwards in the person of Alla-ood-deen himself, who, though at first fortunate, and even glorious, ended his days in misery.

Julal-ood-deen murdered, 1295.

Michael Andronicus emperor of the East.

Alla-ood-deen did not at once become king. The Queen-Dowager, on receiving news of the murder, placed the crown on the head of her youngest son, and seated him on the throne. The real heir, however, was his elder brother, Arkully Khan, then in his government at Mooltan, but he declined to come to the capital. Alla-ood-deen, whose project had been to establish an independent kingdom in Oude, now aspired to the throne itself, and marched upon Dehly, where the young king at first opposed him; but seeing resistance would be futile, left the city with his mother and the royal treasures, and proceeded rapidly in the direction of Mooltan. Alla-ood-deen did not follow him, but entering Dehly with great pomp, was crowned king about the end of 1296. His great object at first seems to have been to obliterate the memory of his treachery to his uncle by unlimited largesse to the mob of Dehly, and as Ferishta writes, 'He who ought to have been received with detestation, became the object of admiration to those who could not see the blackness of his deeds through the splendour of his munificence.' He next despatched a force to Mooltan, under his brother Aluf Khan, who

The Queen-Dowager causes her youngest son to be crowned.

Alla-ood-deen marches on Dehly.

The young king marches towards Mooltan.

Alla-ood-deen crowned, 1296.

Sir William Wallace defeats the English at Stirling.

laid siege to the place for two months, when it was given up by the troops, who made over to him Arkully Khan and Kudr Khan, the late king's sons, on condition that their lives should be spared, and with these captives he set out for Dehly. By the way he received his brother's orders to blind the two princes; and after this barbarous act, they were confined in the fort of Hansy, and soon afterwards put to death.

Two of the late king's sons taken at Mooltan.

Blinded and put to death.

Alla-ood-deen's position was now secure, and he commenced an earnest, and in many respects at first, a beneficial, government; and from the varied and romantic events of the period, the several expeditions into Southern India, as yet unknown to the Mahomedans, and the strange character of the king himself, the reign of Alla-ood-deen is one of the most interesting of the early Mahomedan sovereigns of India. All the weakness and irresolution of the previous reign was quickly redeemed. A force was sent to Guzerat under Aluf Khan, in 1297, and Anhulwara was again taken. The rajah, Rái Kurrun, fled: but his beautiful wife, Kowla Dévy, and all his family and treasure, fell into the hands of the Mahomedans. The rich city of Cambay was held to ransom, and a vast sum obtained; and Aluf Khan obtained a slave named Kafoor from a merchant there, who afterwards became famous. On the return of the expedition to Dehly, Alla-ood-deen became enamoured of the Rajpoot queen, and married her.

Alla-ood-deen's government.

Anhulwara, in Guzerat, taken.

Marries the Hindoo queen of Guzerat.

The Guzerat campaign was no sooner ended, than the king had to encounter a very dangerous invasion of the Moghuls, with 200,000 horse, under Kootloogh Khan. They drove the inhabitants of the country before them, who crowded into Dehly, and the peril of absolute famine was added to that by the enemy. His counsellers would have had the king retreat; but he had received reinforcements, and at the head, as Ferishta writes, of 300,000 horse and 2,700 elephants, marched out of the city. The action which ensued was bravely fought on both sides; but the Moghuls were forced to retreat, and evacuated India, with the same expedition they had entered it. Elated with his prosperity, Alla-ood-deen now entertained the idea of propagating a new faith of his own, and of conquering the world like Alexander; but these wild projects were after awhile abandoned, and in 1299 he undertook a campaign against Runtunbhore, in which he was severely wounded and left for dead by his uncle, Rookn Khan, who, reporting the king's death in camp, ascended the throne. Meanwhile, Alla-ood-deen had recovered, and though barely able to sit his horse, repaired to camp, where he was re-

The Moghuls invade India. 1298.

The first Turkish empire.

ceived with enthusiasm by the soldiery, and Rookn Khan, who had fled, was taken and beheaded. In the sequel the fort of Runtunbhore was carried by storm; but the king's cruel nature was only satisfied by the execution of those who had so bravely defended it.

Runtunbhore taken, and its defenders put to death.

His dominions being at peace, Alla-ood-deen turned his attention to civil affairs. He had been reproached with an undue use of wine, and he not only destroyed all he possessed, but actually prohibited its use throughout his dominions. The roads were rendered secure, and highway robberies ceased. He introduced changes in the collection of revenue, by enhancing the demand to half the value of the produce, which created much distress; but under the bigoted application of the tenets of the Korán, there was little mercy then shown to Hindoos. The rich, however. of both denominations, were called upon to give up their wealth, and the king's extortions created immense dissatisfaction and unpopularity; nor was there a department of the State, or of trade and commerce, or condition of social existence, which the king's curious edicts, some salutary and others mischievous, did not affect. His character in this, and in many other respects, strongly resembles that of Tippoo Sooltan, and much of his capricious and ill-regulated policy proceeded, if not from insanity, at least from his want of education. In the course of the year 1303 he dispatched an army, by way of Bengal, to Wurungul, the capital of Telingána, and then ruled over by the Naraputty branch of the Andhra dynasty; for his own expedition to Déogurh had, in fact, opened the way to the Mahomedan conquest of the South of India. With other troops at his disposal, he undertook a campaign against Chittore, in Rajpootana, which was reduced, and thence he would have proceeded into the Deccan; but receiving intelligence of an invasion by 20,000 Moghul horse, he returned to Dehly. Here for a time he was in a sore strait, for half his army was gone to the South of India, and the Moghuls plundered unchecked up to the very gates of the capital. At length a sudden panic seemed to possess them, for all at once they retreated precipitately to their own country. It is most probable, perhaps, that they were sated with plunder; but in 1304, Ali Beg Moghul, with 40,000 horse, penetrated as far as Amroha, in Rajpootana; but was defeated with heavy loss by Toghluk Khan, governor of the Punjâb, and these two leaders, who, with 9,000 soldiers, were taken prisoners, were all, as Ferishta states, put to death. One of the most romantic incidents of this reign was the escape of the Rajah of Chittore from confinement in Dehly. He had

The civil administration.

Expedition to Wurungul, 1303.

A renewed Moghul invasion.

Their unexpected retreat.

Moghuls defeated in Rajpootana.

Noble conduct of a

a beautiful daughter, whom the king demanded as the price of his release. The rajah feigned consent, and on the terms being communicated to the princess, she determined on making them the means of her father's release. She therefore proceeded towards Dehly, being furnished with the king's pass to visit her father, and when near the city, filled litters with some devoted adherents as if they had been her female attendants. All were admitted unsuspiciously to the place where her father resided, when the guards were overpowered, and horses having been previously prepared, the father and daughter rode through the city and escaped. The rajah recovered Chittore, which he afterwards retained, becoming tributary to the king, and furnishing a contingent of 5,000 horse and 10,000 foot to the royal army.

Princess of Chittore.

CHAPTER VIII.

THE KHILJY DYNASTY OF DEHLY (*concluded*), A.D. 1305 TO 1321.

1305 A.D. Another Moghul invasion defeated.

In the year 1305 A.D. a fresh invasion of Moghuls occurred; but they were intercepted by Ghazy Beg Toghluk, on the banks of the Indus, and sorely defeated, while most of the survivors perished in the deserts of Central Asia on their return. The captives sent to Dehly were, as before, put to death by the king, and a pillar built of their skulls; but even these severe losses did not deter them, and once again in the same year the Moghuls appeared, only to be defeated by Toghluk, who, on this occasion, pursued them into Kabool and Ghuzny, and every year afterwards levied heavy contributions from those cities, which restrained Moghul incursions for many years afterwards.

They renew the attack, and are pursued to Kabool and Ghuzny.

Expedition of Mullik Kafoor to the Deccan, 1306.

In the year 1306 A.D., as Ram Déo, the rajah of Déogurh, had neglected to send his tribute for three years, an expedition against him was determined on; and Mullik Kafoor, the eunuch slave who had been purchased at Cambay, and who had by this time risen to high rank and favour, was selected to command it. Nor did he disappoint the expectations the king had formed of him. 100,000 horse marched from Dehly under his command, and their numbers were increased by quotas from several provinces on the route. Kowla Dévy, the king's wife, urged that her favourite daughter, Déwul Dévy, whom she had left with her husband, should, if possible, be returned to her; and this formed the object of a special

Robert Bruce king of Scotland.

attack upon Kurrun Rái, rajah of Guzerat, who had refused to give her up. Aluf Khan, who had defeated the rajah in several skirmishes, now found that he had escaped him and gone to Déogurh, taking his daughter with him, whom he had promised in marriage to Shunkul Déo, the son of the rajah. This event gave Aluf Khan great concern, as he could find no track of the fugitive. He nevertheless proceeded in the direction of Déogurh, and while halting for two days in the vicinity of the caves of Ellora, which are about eight miles from the fort, a party of 300 of his men, who had gone to see the caves, came suddenly on a body of Hindoo horse, which proved to be the escort of Déwul Dévy herself; and in the skirmish which ensued, she was captured and taken to Aluf Khan's camp, who, well knowing the importance of his prize, returned to Dehly, where the princess was restored to her mother. Soon after her arrival, the king's son, Khizr Khan, fell in love with her, and the parties were married with great pomp. This event formed the subject of a beautiful poem by Ameer Khoosroo, the poet-laureate at the Dehly court, which still survives.

Déwul Dévy, the daughter of Kowal Dévy, captured near Ellora.

She is taken to Dehly, and marries Khizr Khan, the king's son.

Meanwhile Mullik Kafoor had proceeded to Déogurh, where the rajah, being in no condition to oppose him, welcomed him hospitably, and returned to Dehly with him, where he was received with all honour, and had titles with an estate conferred upon him, his expenses on return being also paid. This honourable treatment completely ensured the fidelity of the Rajah of Déogurh during his life.

Mullik Kafoor at Déogurh.

It will be remembered that the king had despatched in the year 1303 an expedition against the Hindoo kingdom of Wurungul by way of Bengal. This, however, failed, and the army was obliged to retreat after severe sufferings. In 1309, therefore, another expedition was placed under command of Mullik Kafoor, to invade Wurungul by the route of Déogurh, which succeeded, though not without a brave resistance, from Luddur Déo, its rajah. After a long siege, the fort of Wurungul was captured; and the rajah made terms by the payment of a heavy sum of money, besides consenting to pay tribute annually. On his return to Dehly, Mullik Kafoor was received with great rejoicings, and in the year following he again proceeded southwards, to reduce the Hindoo State of Dwára Sumoodra, in the Carnatic, of the power and wealth of which he had received information in the Deccan. Dwára Sumoodra was the capital of the Hôi Salá or Bellál kingdom, which has been brought to notice in

Expedition of Mullik Kafoor to Wurungul, 1309.

Edward II. king of England.

His success.

Expedition to Dwára Sumoodra, 1310.

Rhodes taken by the Knights of St. John.

Chapter XIV. Bk. I. It had survived the destruction of the Chalúkyas of Kulyan, by the Yádávás of Déogurh, and was in the highest state of prosperity. On his arrival at Déogurh, Mullik Kafoor found that the old rajah, Ram Déo, was dead, and had been succeeded by his son Shunkul Déo, who was not as well affected to the Mahomedans as his father had been; but Mullik Kafoor pressed on, and finally reached the sea-coast of Malabar, where he built a mosque to commemorate the event. The Bellál kingdom was easily overpowered; Dwára Sumoodra, its capital, was sacked, and the magnificent temple of Seeva there, though uncompleted, severely injured. The temple still exists in much of its original beauty and perfection, one of the most admirable specimens of florid Hindoo architecture in India. The booty obtained by Mullik Kafoor was immense; 312 elephants, 20,000 horses, and 96,000 maunds of gold are stated by Ferishta; an amount which appears incredible: but it is a curious circumstance that no silver was found; the idols, ornaments public and private, and plate, being all of beaten gold.

Immense booty obtained.

It will be remembered that many of the Moghuls who had been captured became converts to Mahomedanism, and the king had taken them into his service. For some unaccountable reason, however, he conceived an aversion to them, and discharged them. In their distress, some of the most desperate conspired against him, which, becoming known, the whole were put to death, to the number of 15,000, in a single day, no one daring to remonstrate with the king against such barbarity. The spoils of the south, with the punctual collection of the increased revenue, had filled Dehly with wealth; and the number of public buildings, mosques, mausoleums, and colleges which were built, exceeded those of any previous period. The magnificence of the king's dominions was now at its zenith, and with it, the king's temper, always eccentric, began to alter. Instead of directing public affairs himself, he gave them over to Mullik Kafoor: and he appointed his own sons, still mere children, to offices of the highest trust, which had to be managed by corrupt deputies.

All Moghuls in the royal service put to death.

Increase of wealth in Dehly.

Mullik Kafoor seems, however, to have been by no means easy in his elevated position, and in 1312 proposed that he should be sent again to the Deccan to receive the royal tribute. On his arrival at Déogurh, he found Shunkul Déo in rebellion; but he was quickly reduced, and put to death, and having again overrun the Carnatic, and received the tribute from Wurungul, dispatched the treasure to Dehly, remaining himself at Déogurh. The king's infirmities were now fast gaining upon him, and he could not live without his favourite. Mullik

Third expedition of Mullik Kafoor, 1312.

Kafoor was therefore recalled; and seeing the king's condition, conceived the project of succeeding him. To this end it was necessary to alienate his affections from his sons, of whom he was very fond. Khizr Khan, the eldest, though in some respects a wild and thoughtless youth, was yet much attached to his father, and when he heard of his illness, vowed to walk from his seat of government to the capital as a penance, a feat he actually accomplished. But Mullik Kafoor's plans against him were too deeply laid; and the prince, with his younger brother and their mother, were confined. To add to the king's vexations, Guzerat broke into rebellion, and the troops sent there were defeated. The Rajpoots of Chittore expelled the Mahomedans, and Hurpal Déo, the son-in-law of Ram Déo, of Déogurh, revolted and defeated many of the Mahomedan garrisons in his territories. On receiving these accounts, writes Ferishta, the king 'bit his own flesh with fury;' but he had been stricken with mortal illness, and died on December 19, A.D. 1316.

The king recalls Mullik Kafoor, who conspires against him.

The king's sons confined and various insurrections break out.

Philip V. king of France

Alla-ood-deen Khiljy dies, 1316.

After the king's death Mullik Kafoor produced a deed, said to have been executed by the king, in which Oomur, his fourth son, was nominated successor, under the regency of Mullik Kafoor; and the boy was placed on the throne. The two eldest princes, then imprisoned, were blinded; and the king's third son, Moobaruk, would have been murdered but for his presence of mind in distributing his jewels to the men sent for the purpose. These ruffians having quarrelled over their booty, the affair became known to the officer who commanded the royal guards, who attacked Mullik Kafoor in his own apartments, and put him to death. The Prince Moobaruk was then proclaimed king, but was not crowned till March 22, 1317. Meanwhile he had caused his brother Oomur to be blinded and confined. His first measures were beneficial and just. Many captives were released, and all restrictions upon trade and agriculture removed; but he gave himself up to licentiousness, and the natural cruelty of his nature was hardly concealed. In 1318 he marched to Déogurh, with the purpose of chastising the rebel Hurpal Déo, who was defeated, taken prisoner, and most inhumanly flayed alive. On his return to the capital the king's excesses increased; he was rarely sober, and perpetrated the most frightful cruelties. To such a length did his disgraceful conduct proceed, that, as Ferishta states of him, he used to dress himself constantly as a common actress, and go, with public women, to dance at the houses of the nobility.

His son Oomur succeeds.

The princes are blinded.

Mullik Kafoor put to death.

Oomur deposed by Moobaruk, who blinds him.

Mullik Khoosroo, originally a Hindoo slave, who had risen to the king's favour, had been sent from Déogurh with an army into the Carnatic, and the spoil he obtained was so great that he conceived the project of declaring independence in the Deccan. Though this became impossible, it did not prevent his conspiring against the king's life, on his return to Dehly; and the plot became so notorious, that the king was warned of it: but in vain; and on the night of March 9, 1321, he was murdered by the conspirators, Mullik Khoosroo assisting in the act. Nor were the conspirators content with the king's death. The royal princes, and the younger children of Alla-ood-deen, perished in the massacre. Thus was the murder of Gheias-ood-deen avenged according to the curse and prophecy. The last days of Alla-ood-deen were terrible to all around him, and the conduct of his son Moobaruk, according to Ferishta, was too shockingly indecent and profligate to be recorded. Next day Mullik Khoosroo ascended the throne, under the title of Nasir-ood-deen, and took Déwul Dévy, the widow of Khizr Khan, to himself; while every one who had a pretension of relationship to the late king was put to death. News of this horrible revolution quickly spread through the provinces, and Ghazy Beg Toghluk, the brave viceroy of Lahore, and other chiefs, marched upon the capital. Mullik Khoosroo was not without courage and led the royal guards and such troops as he could collect to oppose them; but before the hardy veterans of the frontier marches these effeminate soldiers had no chance. Mullik Khoosroo was defeated on the field of the Soorsutty, and fled; but on August 22, 1321, was captured in a tomb, where he had concealed himself, and forthwith executed for his crimes. Ghazy Beg Toghluk received next day the congratulations of the nobles of the city, who presented him with the keys, and he accompanied them thither. On arriving at the Palace of the Thousand Minarets, he, as Ferishta writes, 'wept bitterly,' declared that he had been induced to draw his sword only to rid the world of a monster, and if none of the royal race survived, he would serve whoever among the nobility might be chosen king. The multitude, with a shout, cried that he only was fit to reign; that he who had often delivered them from the Moghuls, had now freed them from a horrible tyranny; and thereupon, taking him up, they carried him into the great hall of audience, and seating him on the throne, hailed him as 'Shah Jehan,' king of the world. It is difficult to imagine any scene of history more impressive and exciting than this. The dynasty of the Khiljies had

Moobaruk Khiljy murdered, 1321.

Charles IV. king of France.

Mullik Khoosroo usurps the throne, and all the late king's family are destroyed.

The chiefs rebel against him and march on Dehly.

The king is defeated.

Mullik Khoosroo put to death, 1321.

Ghazy Beg Toghluk elected king.

passed away in a storm of revolution and murder, attended with horrible excesses, and that of Toghluk took its place, amidst the enthusiastic acclamations of a people who, as will have been observed, had suffered so deeply and so long. The Khiljy dynasty had continued from A.D. 1288 to 1321, or for thirty-three years.

CHAPTER IX.

OF THE DYNASTY OF TOGHLUK, A.D. 1321 TO 1351.

Previous career of Toghluk.

GHAZY BEG TOGHLUK, on ascending the throne, did not adopt the proud title with which he had been hailed by the populace of Dehly, but chose the more unassuming one of Gheias-ood-deen. He was a man of mature age and great experience, as well as personal courage. For many years he had acted as viceroy of Lahore, and had charge of that important frontier from the Himalayas to the borders of Sinde; and his able services in repelling the frequent incursions of the Moghuls have been already noticed. His first measures at once restored confidence, and regularity in the public administration of affairs was established. Codes of law were compiled and put in practice in the civil and criminal courts; and under his care even the city itself, under all the repairs made by him, wore a new aspect. The western frontier was strengthened by forts and garrisons, and the incursions of the Moghuls for the present effectually prevented. Déogurh and Wurungul had, however, revolted: and the king dispatched his eldest son, the Prince Aluf Khan, to the Deccan with a large army to restore order. Déogurh submitted; but Luddur Déo, rajah of Wurungul, made a stout resistance in the field, and when obliged to retire into Wurungul, defended it desperately. During the siege, a malignant epidemic—probably cholera—swept off hundreds of the troops every day, which not only terrified the rest, but prevented the siege operations; and a fresh panic was caused by reports from Dehly that there had been a revolution, and the king was dead. Several of the officers actually fled with their troops, and the prince was left in a sore strait. He retired from Wurungul, and of the whole army only about 3,000 reached Dehly. In two months, however, he had organised a new force, and with it proceeded against Wurungul to redeem his honour, and with more care and circumspection than on the first occasion. Beeder, afterwards to be the seat of a great

His active and beneficent measures.

Operations against Déogurh and Wurungul.

Mortality during the siege of Wurungul, which is abandoned.

Operations against the Deccan renewed.

monarchy, with Kowlas, and other strong places, were taken and garrisoned as the main army advanced; and Wurungul finally fell in the siege which ensued. Luddur Déo and his family were sent to Dehly, and Mahomedan officers were appointed to govern the country. The complete success which had attended this expedition was the subject of great public rejoicing in Dehly, where, on his return, the Prince Aluf Khan was welcomed with enthusiasm.

Wurungul taken by Prince Aluf Khan.

In 1325 the king visited his eastern frontier, and met there Kurra Khan, son of Gheias-ood-deen Bulbun, who had retained his position as virtual king through all the revolutions. He was now confirmed in his government, and allowed to assume the ensigns of royalty. The king returned to Dehly in the month of February, where his son had prepared a pavilion for his reception, on the plain beyond the city. On the conclusion of the entertainments, the prince and the nobles, preceding the king, had just left the building, when the roof fell in and the king and some of his attendants were killed. It is quite possible that the occurrence was purely accidental; but there were many suspicions at the time that it was not so. Ferishta, however, after a careful review of the historians of the period, acquits the prince of design in the catastrophe. Gheias-ood-deen Toghluk had reigned four years and some months.

Gheias-ood-deen Toghluk accidentally killed, 1325.

Edward II. king of England.

The new king was one of the most accomplished men of his age. He was eloquent in speech, and his writings, especially his letters, were models of style and composition. His memory was very retentive, and he had studied all the sciences of the period, especially mathematics and medicine, with much exactness; and in remarkable cases had used to attend patients himself, and note down the progress of their complaints. He had studied also the philosophy of the Greeks, and was fond of metaphysical discussions with learned men. His own religious conduct was very strict; he omitted no prayers or ceremonials, and did not tolerate their omission by others. But, as Ferishta observes, 'with all these admirable qualities, he was totally devoid of mercy, or of consideration for his people;' and Mr. Elphinstone speculates as to whether his nature had not a strong tincture of insanity. On his accession, when he assumed the designation of Mahomed Toghluk, the king distributed immense largesses to his nobles and courtiers, and on one day expended more than 500,000*l.* sterling.

Aluf Khan, or Mahomed Toghluk, succeeds him.

His character.

Almost the first great event of his reign was a vast irruption of Moghuls, who could not be repressed, and who overran the country up to Dehly without a check. In this instance the king displayed an unaccountable and mischievous

Irruption of the Moghuls.

weakness, foreign to his character, in ransoming his dominions by the payment of a vast sum of money, which, as was proved in the sequel, only stimulated the Moghuls to renewed invasions. This danger overcome, however, the king marched to the Deccan, of which he was very fond, and not only completely subjugated it, but returning, annexed Lukhnow and Chittagong. These successes were, however, more nominal than real; for the internal administration of affairs was deeply neglected; the currency had become so debased, that copper, instead of silver, became the circulating medium, and the king endeavoured to introduce a paper currency, which added to the confusion. Agriculture was impossible under the exactions imposed on the land and its produce, and whole tracts began to be deserted, the people becoming plunderers, and devastating the country. The king further impoverished his resources by raising 370,000 horse for the conquest of Persia; but the pay of the troops fell into arrears, they dispersed, and pillaged the districts they passed through on return to their homes.

They retire on payment of ransom.

General neglect and its effects.

Affairs continued in this unsettled state till 1337, when the king dispatched 100,000 horse under Khoosroo Mullik, his sister's son, to invade China by the Himalaya passes. The expedition reached the Chinese frontier, after incredible toil in the mountains, only to meet a Chinese force which forbade further progress; and in the retreat to India nearly the whole perished miserably, the few survivors being put to death by the king on their arrival at Dehly. Meanwhile the viceroy of the Deccan, Baha-ood-deen, the king's nephew, had rebelled. Khwaja Jehan, the governor of Guzerat, was ordered against him, and a battle was fought near Déogurh, in which the rebel was defeated, and fled to Kumpila, in the Carnatic, near which the Hindoo monarchy of Beejanugger was founded about this time. The rebels' position was so formidable, that the king himself returned to the Deccan; and after several contests, Baha-ood-deen, who had taken refuge with the Bellál rajah—who had removed his capital from Dwára Sumoodra to Tonoor, in Mysore—was given up to the king, and inhumanly flayed alive.

Expedition to China, 1337.

Edward III. king of England.

Its failure and destruction.

The king now determined on making Déogurh his capital. He changed its name from Déogurh to Dowlatabad, which it has since retained, and fortified the city with three lines of walls and ditches, erecting also mosques and palaces. The people of Dehly were now ordered to evacuate that city, and proceed to the Deccan by a road lined with full-grown trees, transplanted for the purpose; but thousands of

The king changes the capital from Dehly to Déogurh, or Dowlatabad.

helpless creatures—women, children, and aged persons—perished by the way. Dehly was, however, for a time almost deserted. In 1340 news arrived of the rebellion of the viceroy of Mooltan; and the king proceeded in person to subdue it, which he effected, and executed the viceroy, who had been taken in his flight. Instead, however, of returning to Dowlatabad, the king proceeded to Dehly, where he remained two years; but again abandoning that city, he repaired in 1340 to Dowlatabad, with his family, carrying with him a multitude of the people. It is revolting to follow the career of this capricious and inhuman monster; but it is worthy of record that, incensed with the people of the Dooáb, or tract between the Ganges and Jumna, for abandoning cultivation, he drove them out of the woods in which they had taken refuge, massacred them without mercy, and thousands of their heads were hung over the city walls of Dehly. As he proceeded to Dowlatabad, the king heard of a successful rebellion in Bengal, which he was unable to repress. Malabar also had risen, and the king proceeded thither, by way of Wurungul. On this journey he fell ill, and his life was despaired of; but having recovered, he returned by way of Bheer, where a tooth he had lost was interred with great ceremony in a fine stone mausoleum, still existing. He now revisited Dehly, permitting those of the inhabitants of Dowlatabad who chose to do so, to return; but a terrible famine prevailed in Northern India, and most of those who set out perished in it.

Many persons perish by the way.

Gunpowder invented in Europe.

Massacre of the inhabitants of the Dooáb.

Rebellion in Bengal.

Burial of one of the king's teeth at Bheer.

A whimsical idea now possessed the king, that his misfortunes were caused by not having been confirmed as king by the caliph; and he sent an embassy for that purpose to Arabia, which returned in 1344 with an envoy from the caliph, who was sumptuously entertained, and the caliph's name struck on all the coinage. In the same year, Krishn Nâik, son of the Rajah Luddur Déo of Wurungul, removed to the city of Beejanugger, which had been previously founded; and in concert with Bellál Déo of Dwára Sumoodra, aided by all the martial Hindoos of their dominions, drove the Mahomedan garrison from Wurungul to Dowlatabad, and cleared the country of all their posts. It may be easily believed how greatly the king was exasperated by this news; and his cruelties, if it were possible, increased.

Success of the Hindoos against the Mahomedans.

From 1344 to 1347, the record of the king's reign is little more than a series of rebellions and insurrections in the distant provinces. In the latter year he proceeded to Guzerat, and while employed there against a local insurrection,

Battle of Crécy, 1346.

heard that most of his troops in the Deccan Proper had mutinied and set up a new king. The Ameer Judeeda, who had been viceroy, was at the head of this movement, and a severe battle was fought between him and the king in person, without any decided result. Dowlatabad was in possession of the rebels, and the king besieged it. While thus employed, a fresh rebellion broke out in Guzerat; the governor had been put to death, and the capital had been taken by Mozuffer Khan, the Naib, or deputy-governor. The king, therefore, left the siege of Dowlatabad to be carried on by Ismail-ool-Moolk, viceroy of Berar, and returned to Guzerat, where, for a time, the disaffection was checked; but meanwhile his general at Dowlatabad had been defeated by an officer named Hussun Gungoo, and all the royal troops expelled by him. The new king, Ismail, had given up his position, which had been taken by Hussun Gungoo, who had become king, under the title of Alla-ood-deen Hussun Gungoo Bahmuny, and who was destined to become the founder of a noble and long-enduring dynasty in the Deccan. Before commencing the reduction of the great Deccan rebellion, however, the king determined to place the affairs of Guzerat on a sound footing. A friend, Zea-ood-deen Burny, the historian, at this juncture even advised him to abdicate, but the king replied, he had no one whom he could trust, and, whatever happened, was determined to punish rebellion. While in Guzerat, the king projected an invasion of the Lower Sinde territory, where the Sooméra Rajpoots had given refuge to some insurgents, and on his way thither, having reached the Indus, he eat fish to excess, which brought on fever, of which he died on March 20, 1351. He had reigned twenty-seven years, in an almost uninterrupted succession of rebellions and bloody reprisals, executions, and massacres, which are unparalleled, even in the history of Dehly.

Various rebellions and insurrections.

Alla-ood-deen Hussun founds a kingdom in the Deccan, 1347.

Mahomed Toghluk dies 1351.

John II. king of France.

CHAPTER X.

THE DYNASTY OF TOGHLUK (*continued*), A.D. 1351 TO 1398.

At the death of Mahomed Toghluk, the dominions of the Mahomedan empire in India Proper had reached the utmost limit they attained, until, in after times, the Emperor Aurungzebe united the whole of the continent under one government. To the north, the provinces of the Punjâb, Dehly and its dependencies, with Oude

Extent of Mahomedan dominion in India, and general political condition of the country, 1350-51.

and Bengal, formed an unbroken line of possessions, from which all former Hindoo kingdoms and principalities had disappeared. In Central India, Malwah and Bahar were conquered and annexed; but in Rajpootana, the principalities of the Rajpoot princes were still held by them, on payment of tribute. In the west, Guzerat was a royal province, as was Mooltan; but Lower Sinde as yet remained under the Sooméra Rajpoots, of the Jám dynasty, who had not been interfered with. The dominions of the Yádávás of Déoghur had been incorporated in the empire, and their dynasty was extinct; but some members of the family had escaped to their estates near the Western Ghauts, where they were not molested. Wurungul had fallen, and the eastern territory of the Andhras had been annexed; but a branch of the family had removed to Beejanugger, on the Tumboodra, and founded a kingdom there, which, as will be seen in the sequel, long resisted the Mahomedans of the Deccan, and rose to great power and eminence. In the Deccan Proper, the dominions of the late Yádává kingdom bounded the conquests of the Toghluks. They included Berar to the north, Déogurh and its dependencies, and extended west to the Malabar coast, and part of the Northern Koncan, including Raichore, Moodgul, Goolburgah, Beeder, Beejapoor, and Gunjooty; but the Mahomedan possession of the western part of the Deccan, that is of the present Sattara, Kolapoor and Poona, is doubtful, and was still under the sway of the native Mahratta princes.

Edward III. king of England. Order of the Garter instituted.

The line of boundary to the south and south-west may be represented by the Tumboodra and Krishna rivers. Beyond this, southwards, the Bellál dynasty ruled over Mysore, its capital being Tonoor—to be absorbed afterwards by the princes of Beejanugger. The Chôla dynasty, still powerful and independent, reigned at Tanjore, and the Pandávas at Madura. It seems very doubtful whether any of the Mahomedan incursions had reached these States; and though Mullik Kafoor is supposed, by some authorities, to have penetrated as far as Ramisseram, on the coast opposite to Ceylon, and built a mosque there in commemoration of the event, the fact is not supported by the Mahomedan historians of the time. This vast empire was, however, already beginning to break up. Before Mahomed Toghluk's death, the royal troops in the Deccan had revolted successfully, and Hussun Gungoo Bahmuny had been crowned king; nor was any attempt to subdue him made afterwards. Wurungul had also revolted, and expelled the Mahomedan garrisons. Guzerat was the scene of constantly recurring insurrections. Bengal was virtually independent, and the provinces immediately surrounding Dehly were wasted and impoverished under the late king's exactions and monstrous cruelties.

It is not certain whether Mahomed Toghluk left any male offspring; but as soon as his death was known at Dehly, Khwaja Jehan, a relative, placed a boy of six years old on the throne, and he was locally acknowledged as king. But Mahomed Toghluk on his death-bed had declared the Prince Feroze, his cousin, then with the army, to be his successor, and he was proclaimed accordingly. The army was in the utmost disorder, and some of the Moghul officers mutinied, plundered the treasury, and decamped with their spoils. They were, however, pursued and defeated; and Feroze resumed his progress to Dehly. On his arrival there, the pretensions of the boy who had been set up were withdrawn; and on September 14, 1351, Feroze was crowned, under the title of Feroze Toghluk. In 1353 the king made an attempt to regain the royal authority over Bengal, but was obliged by heavy rains to withdraw from the field. On the succession of a new king of Bengal the effort was renewed; but, by a treaty made with him, the independence of that province was recognised, and though there, as well as in the Deccan, the royal supremacy was acknowledged, and tribute remitted, their kings remained independent.

Mahomed Toghluk succeeded by Prince Feroze Toghluk.

Feroze Toghluk crowned, 1351.

The year 1354 was rendered memorable by the founding of a new city adjoining Dehly, which was named Ferozabad, and on July 12 the king opened the great canal he had constructed for purposes of irrigation from the Sutlej to the Kugger rivers. In 1356 another canal was constructed from the Jumna, by which water for irrigation of a peculiarly arid tract was carried as far as Hansy. A third canal connected with the Sutlej was also the work of Feroze Toghluk. All these great undertakings, admirable for their period, have been enlarged and restored by the British Government, after the neglect of centuries. The reign of the King Feroze was otherwise rendered memorable by his public works; and Ferishta, quoting the local Mahomedan historian Zea-ood-deen Burny, enumerates 50 dams across rivers to promote irrigation, 40 mosques, 30 colleges with mosques attached, 20 palaces, 100 caravanserais, 200 towns, 30 reservoirs or lakes for irrigation, 100 hospitals, 5 mausoleums, 100 public baths, 10 monumental pillars, 10 public wells, and 150 bridges; all of which were endowed with lands for their future maintenance. No works for irrigation had been constructed in Upper India before the era of Feroze Toghluk, even by

Ferozabad founded.

Sutlej canal opened.

Jumna canal opened, 1356.

The third canal.

Works of irrigation.

the Hindoos; and it is most probable that, having seen the irrigation system of Telingána in active operation, and understood the immense benefits which resulted from it, he was induced to commence it in the arid districts around his capital. The king did not always reside at Dehly; on the contrary, he made frequent tours in his dominions, which were much more efficiently and peacefully governed than during the reign of his uncle; and up to the year 1385 no very remarkable event occurred. The king had now reached his eighty-seventh year, his powers were fast declining, and his vizier, in order to remove an obstacle to his own schemes, secretly accused the king's son, Prince Mahomed Khan, of a design against his father's life; but the prince, unable to endure the calumny, went secretly to his father, declared his innocence, and having unmasked the vizier's plots, he fled precipitately from the capital.

Feroze Toghluk abdicates, 1387.

Nasir-ood-deen Toghluk crowned, 1387.

Eventually, in August 1387, Feroze Toghluk abdicated in favour of his son, who ascended the throne under the title of Nasir-ood-deen Mahomed. This prince, however, sadly belied the expectations of his father. He was dissolute and idle; and a plot was formed against him by his cousins, who raised a large army, and the parties fought in the streets of Dehly for three days, deluging the capital with blood; when the people, weary of the strife, brought the old king out of his palace, and set his palankeen down in the streets between the combatants. On this, the troops rallied round their old master, and the new king was obliged to fly. For a short time Feroze Toghluk continued to exercise authority; but finally breaking down, he nominated his grandson, Gheias-ood-deen, to succeed him, and died on October 23, 1388, in the ninetieth year of his age. The memory of this benevolent monarch remained dear to the people. He had abolished the practice of mutilation for crimes, which had long existed, and had been carried to a fearful extent. In the edict he issued, which is engraved upon the mosque of Ferozabad, are enumerated—cutting off hands and feet, noses and ears; putting out eyes, pulverizing the bones of living criminals with mallets, burning the body with fire, crucifixion, nailing down hands and feet, ham-stringing and cutting to pieces: which exemplify the cruel rigour of the early Mahomedan rule. All the former vexatious imposts on trade and upon cultivation were withdrawn, and the increase in tillage and in revenue was most remarkable. The king records also, that he had discovered, as far as possible, the heirs of such persons as had suffered from his uncle's cruelties, and pensioned or otherwise provided for them; but the reader is referred to the edict

Battle of Otterburn.

Feroze Toghluk dies, 1388. His benevolent reforms and acts.

itself, which is given in the Appendix, as a remarkable illustration of the period.

Gheias-ood-deen proved a very unworthy successor of so good a monarch as his grandfather, and after a brief reign of five months in continued debauchery, was put to death on February 18, 1389, in a revolt by his own brother and cousins. Aboo Bukr, another grandson of the late king, succeeded him; but, after reigning till November 27 of the same year, was deposed by Mahomed, who had fled from Dehly after his father's abdication, and who was now recalled to the capital by the united desire of all parties, and ascended the throne under the appellation of Nasir-ood-deen Mahomed Toghluk, on February 21, 1390. His rival, Aboo Bukr, had however many partisans, and resided in the city; and on April 18, being reinforced by Bahadur Nahir of Meerut, probably a converted Hindoo chieftain, he attacked Nasir-ood-deen, and drove him out of Dehly. But throughout this year the contention for the capital continued, and it was sometimes in the hands of one and sometimes of the other of the rivals: at length Aboo Bukr fled to Meerut, and Nasir-ood-deen was again seated on the throne. Until his death the kingdom seems to have been at peace, except from a few unimportant insurrections by the turbulent Rajpoots, and an attempt by the Mewatees under Bahadur Nahir to plunder Dehly, which was defeated by the king in person; and his exertions on this occasion brought on a severe fever, of which he died on February 19, 1394. His son Hoomayoon succeeded him; but also died suddenly, after a reign of forty-five days. Much confusion ensued on the unexpected death of the last king, and the choice of a successor was difficult. However, Mahmood, son of the late King Nasir-ood-deen Mahomed, was at length chosen; but the kingdom was already distracted by factions, and serious disorders began to arise. The vizier assumed the title of Mullik-oos-Shurk, and was the first to declare independence, at Joonpoor, in Bengal; the Gukkurs had risen in rebellion; Guzerat revolted, and became an independent kingdom; and Malwah and Khandésh followed the same example. Meanwhile factious disputes among the nobles ran high at Dehly. Some remained with the king, others espoused the cause of Noosrut Khan, the grandson of the late Feroze Toghluk. One party possessed Old Dehly, and the other Ferozabad; and the civil war between them, in which the provinces took no part, continued at the capital for three years, or until 1396, during which period constant bloodshed prevailed. In that year King Mahmood fell

Gheias-ood-deen Toghluk succeeds, 1388.

Put to death, 1389.

Aboo Bukr succeeds, 1389.

Deposed in the same year.

Nasir-ood-deen Mahomed Toghluk succeeds, 1390.

Robert III. king of Scotland.

Nasir-ood-deen Toghluk dies, 1394.

Hoomayoon succeeds and dies.

Mahmood succeeds.

into the power of Ekbál Khan, and became a mere cipher in his hands; but Ekbál Khan had succeeded in expelling Noosrut Khan and his partisans from the city, and might have succeeded in restoring order to the government, when Teimoor, or Tamerlane, whose advanced army under his son was already engaged in the western provinces, crossed the Indus on September 12, 1398, and marched rapidly upon Dehly.

Teimoor crosses the Indus, 1398.

CHAPTER XI.

OF THE INVASION OF TEIMOOR, AND CONCLUSION OF THE TOGHLUK DYNASTY; AND ESTABLISHMENT AND TERMINATION OF THE SYED DYNASTY, A.D. 1398 TO 1478.

INTELLIGENCE of the disorders at Dehly, and the general distraction of the empire, appears to have reached Teimoor at Sarmacand in 1396. Previous to this, his grandson, Peer Mahomed, had overrun the countries west of the Indus, and now advanced into India. Instead, however, of marching at once upon Dehly, he turned southwards, and attacked Mooltan, of which, after a siege of six months, he obtained possession; but here most of his horses died, and he was unable to undertake further operations. Teimoor himself, as has been already stated, crossed the Indus on September 12, 1398. The governor of the Punjâb, Moobaruk Khan, made an ineffectual attempt to oppose the advanced guard of the Moghuls, and after a short resistance in an intrenched camp, left his force, sailed down the Chenab, and escaped; and Teimoor's army encountered no further resistance in that province. Without waiting to besiege Toolumba, he sent 30,000 horse to reinforce his grandson, and following them in person, was met by the prince on the road. Bhutnáir, the rajah of which had acted against the prince during his investment of Mooltan, was taken by assault, and the defenders and inhabitants of the city massacred without distinction. Teimoor had appointed Kelthul as the place of general rendezvous for the army, which, during his absence from it, had meanwhile pillaged the Punjâb and Mooltan and now advanced upon Dehly by the route of Paniput.

Prince Peer Mahomed captures Mooltan.

Teimoor occupies the Punjâb, and rejoins his grandson.

As Teimoor was reconnoitring, the king and his vizier sallied out of the city at the head of 5,000 horse; but in the skirmish that ensued were driven back, and the next day Teimoor took up a new and more commanding position. When he had been attacked by the king, the captives

The army marches on Dehly, which Teimoor invests.

in his camp, Hindoos and Mahomedans, brought on by the army, expressed their joy at the hope of speedy deliverance; whereupon Teimoor, considering that so large a number might endanger his position, directed them all, above the age of fifteen years, to be put to death in cold blood. Ferishta states they were 100,000 of all classes, which may be an exaggeration; but this does not diminish the atrocity of the deed. On January 13, 1399, Teimoor encamped on the plain of Ferozabad, and on the 15th formed his line of battle. The King Mahmood and his vizier, with all the available troops and 120 elephants, marched out of Dehly to encounter him, but were defeated, and fled back to the city, from which the king and his vizier escaped during the night, the king in the direction of Guzerat. Teimoor did not, however, enter the city; but on the next Friday, being the Mahomedan sabbath, he caused himself to be proclaimed emperor of India, and the public prayers to be read in his name. His next step was to impose a contribution upon the inhabitants; and the refusal of many of them to pay brought on a collision with the Moghul troops, which, after continuing for several days, ended in a general and indiscriminate massacre of the people, and the city was given up to pillage, during which Teimoor was employed in giving a great entertainment to his officers, and does not seem to have taken any steps to check the proceedings of his brutal soldiery. He remained at Dehly only fifteen days, and then set out on his return homewards. Meerut was taken, and the garrison put to the sword; Lahore fell to a detachment, and whoever opposed his progress was in turn defeated or destroyed. Teimoor left no garrisons in India; but he appointed Syed Khizr Khan, the viceroy of Lahore, as his deputy.[1]

He puts all his prisoners to death.

Battle of January 15, 1399.

King Mahmood Toghluk is defeated.

He escapes towards Guzerat.

Teimoor is proclaimed emperor of India.

His exactions and massacre of the people.

Teimoor returns to his country.

Henry IV. king of England.

After an attempt to retain the capital, made by Noosrut Khan, who was expelled by the Vizier Ekbál Khan, some order was restored by the latter; but his authority extended only to a few districts outside the city. All the other provinces of the empire were held by the several viceroys as independent kingdoms. They are thus enumerated by the Mahomedan historian:—'Guzerat, by Mozuffer Khan; Kanouj, Oude, Kuna, and Joonpoor, by Khwaja Jehan, commonly called Shah Shurk; Lahore, Depalpoor, and Mooltan, by Khizr Khan; Sámáná, by Ghalib Khan; Byana, by Shumsh Khan Abdy;

Independent provinces.

[1] The student is recommended to read the 'Mulfuzát-Timuri,' or Autobiography of Teimoor, translated by Major Stewart.

Kalpy and Mahoba, by Mahomed Khan; all of whom styled themselves kings.' In the year 1401, King Mahmood, who had been the guest of Mozuffer Shah of Guzerat, left his court and returned to Dehly, still held in his name by the vizier Ekbál Khan; but he took no part in public affairs, receiving a pension which was allotted to him. Soon afterwards, on the death of the King of Joonpoor, an attempt was made by the vizier to recover that territory, which ended in failure: and the king, instead of occupying Dehly, went to reside at Kanouj. The vizier now employed the forces under his command against several of the revolted chiefs, with various success, between 1402 and 1405; and on November 14 of that year was slain in a battle between the troops of the Punjâb and his own. The king now visited Dehly, on the invitation of Doulut Khan Lody; but returned to Kanouj, from which place, however, he was expelled; and again reached the capital, where he resided till his death, from fever, in February 1412, after an inglorious and unfortunate reign of twenty years. With him closed the Toghluk dynasty, as it is not mentioned that he left any heirs. He was succeeded, according to an election by the nobles, by Doulut Khan Lody Afghan, who, after the death of Ekbál Khan, had acted as vizier and commander of the army, and had done his utmost to restore order. He ascended the throne in April 1412; but was obliged to defend himself against Khizr Khan, viceroy of Lahore, who, in the interests of Teimoor, attacked Dehly, and forced the king to surrender. He was thereupon imprisoned, and died on June 4, 1416.

King Mahmood Toghluk returns to Dehly.

Attempts made by the vizier to recover revolted provinces, in one of which he is slain, 1405.

Mahmood Toghluk dies, 1412, and his dynasty ceases.

Doulut Khan Lody succeeds, 1412.

Battle of Agincourt, 1415.

And dies in prison, 1416.

There now ceased to be any king of Dehly. Khizr Khan held his authority on behalf of the Emperor Teimoor, and supported his position by aid of the Punjâb and Mooltan forces, which had been under his orders. Khizr Khan was an active and successful general, and recovered many of the outlying provinces. He was engaged in constant operations in the field from 1416 to 1421, when he died at Dehly on May 20, to the great grief of the people, who had become deeply attached to him on account of the justice and moderation of his character. He was succeeded in his authority by his son Moobaruk, who lived till January 28, 1435, when he was murdered by some Hindoos in the pay of parties to whom he had given offence. It does not seem necessary to follow the particular events of the successions of the Syeds, as the condition of Dehly did not change. No impression was made upon the new kingdoms which had been

Syed Khizr Khan conducts the government.

Dies, 1421.

Syed Moobaruk succeeds.

Murdered, 1435.

established, and the records of the local historians only furnish details of minor campaigns against subordinates who revolted from time to time. The successions of the Syeds after Moobaruk are as follows:—Syed Mahomed, 1435 to 1445, when he died; Syed Alla-ood-deen, his son, from 1445 to 1478, of which period he reigned seven years, and having nominally abdicated in favour of his brother, resided for the rest of the time at Budaoon. He had adopted Bheilole Lody as his successor, who, in fact, had conducted the affairs of state since Alla-ood-deen's retirement. The administration of the four Syeds in succession had lasted from 1416 to 1478, or 62 years.

Syed Mahomed succeeds, and dies, 1445.

Alla-ood-deen succeeds.

Abdicates, 1452, and dies, 1478.

Constantine Palæologus emperor.

CHAPTER XII.

OF THE AFGHAN DYNASTY OF LODY, A.D. 1478 TO 1526.

Origin of Bheilole Lody.

BHEILOLE LODY was descended from a rich family of Afghan merchants, who traded between Kabool and India; some of whom, as was common at the period, entered the service of the sovereign of India from time to time. The uncle of Bheilole, in the action between Khizr Khan, the viceroy of Lahore, and the vizier Ekbál Khan, had slain the latter in single combat, and was rewarded by the governorship of Sirhind. It is related by Ferishta, that the wife of this person's brother, when pregnant, was killed by the fall of her house; but the child being still alive, was taken from her body, and under the name of Bheilole grew up to be a favourite with his uncle, received his daughter in marriage, and on his death, succeeded to his command. In course of time, the Afghan party at Sirhind became too powerful to escape notice, especially when they began to take the adjoining districts into their possession; and they were attacked and driven into the mountains, where many perished; but Bheilole, to whom a superstitious influence was attached, on account of his birth, escaped. After some vicissitudes, he recovered Sirhind; and when he found himself strong enough, marched upon the capital, to which he laid siege; but this expedition was not successful. During the reign or administration of Syed Alla-ood-deen, however, he was invited to Dehly by the vizier, whom he ultimately supplanted and deprived of power, and remained there after the abdication or retirement of Alla-ood-deen until his death, as has been recorded in the last chapter.

His birth and career.

The Mahomedan historians reckon Bheilole's accession to the throne from the abdication of the king, in A.D. 1450. The principal event of Bheilole Lody's reign was the recovery of the kingdom of Joonpoor from the Shurky dynasty, which disappeared in the contention, and its re-incorporation with the dominions of Dehly; an event which, after many years of struggle on both sides, occurred in A.D. 1478.

The kingdom of Joonpoor recovered.

Bheilole Lody reigned till 1488, when he died of a disease from which he had long suffered. By will, he had divided his dominions between his five sons; but the nobles of the State, foreseeing in this arrangement serious elements of strife, besought him to alter it and to nominate his grandson to succeed him. The queen was anxious to secure the throne for her son, Nizam Khan, and in the midst of these intrigues the king died. Bheilole Lody had governed his people wisely and well. He had repressed disorder, and at his death the dominions of the State extended from the Punjâb to the eastern frontier of Bengal in an unbroken line.

Bheilole Lody dies, 1488.

James IV. king of Scotland.

Intrigues for the succession.

On the king's death, setting aside the grandson who had been nominated by him, and Burbik Khan, the eldest son, the nobles of the State elected the prince Nizam Khan to be king, who accordingly ascended the throne under the title of Sikunder Lody. Burbik Khan was at this time governor of Joonpoor, and refusing to acknowledge his brother's election to the throne, took up arms to assert his own right. He was however defeated, and afterwards pardoned; but his bad government of the province caused his removal from office. Subsequently the king, at various periods of his reign, employed his army in reducing the Hindoo rajahs and chieftains who occupied Bundelkund and Northern Malwah; and in 1517 he was making preparations to reduce Gwalior, when he was attacked by a quinsy, and died on December 14 of that year, having reigned nearly twenty-nine years in much prosperity. Although the king undertook many minor campaigns, and for the most part conducted them in person, yet he enjoyed long intervals of peace, when he employed his great talents and learning in amending the civil administration of his dominions. He was humane and charitable; his police, and the horse posts and other public communications of his dominions, were excellent; and his great legal acquirements, and patient dispensation of justice, acted as salutary checks upon all laxity or oppression. The king was also a poet, and his literary accomplishments were considerable. With all his generosity and liberality to his Mahomedan subjects, how-

Prince Nizam Khan elected king, who takes the name of Sikunder Lody.

Sikunder Lody dies, 1517.

Luther's reformation begins.

His character and measures.

ever, he had no tolerance for Hindoos; and whenever it was possible, he destroyed their temples and idols, prohibited their religious ceremonies, and built mosques in their sacred places. In this respect, and in zeal for his religion, Sikunder Lody is esteemed by Mahomedan historians as one of the champions of the faith of Islam.

His intolerance of Hindoos.

In this case there was no dispute for the succession, and Ibrahim, the late king's eldest son, ascended the throne without opposition; but was very soon afterwards called upon to suppress a serious rebellion by his younger brother Julal Khan, then governor of Kalpy, who, at the head of a party of discontented Afghan chiefs and their adherents, proceeded to Joonpoor, captured it, and declared himself king. This event aroused the suspicion of all his other brothers, whom King Ibrahim now confined in the fort of Hansy. He then followed his brother Julal Khan, who by this time had obtained some successes; but the rebel was defeated and obliged to fly to Gwalior, and thence to the court of Sooltan Mahmood Khiljy of Malwah; but being ill received there, was travelling to another place of refuge, when he was pursued and taken prisoner by the Gônds of the hills, and sent to the king's camp. He was there sentenced to imprisonment in Hansy with his brothers, but on his way thither was put to death by the king's order. This act, and other cruelties and severities, produced further rebellions, and much general dissatisfaction among the nobility. No one felt sure that he might not at any time be denounced as a traitor by a secret enemy, and be imprisoned or put to death. Bahadur Khan Lohany, governor of Behar, declared his independence, and defeated the Dehly troops on several occasions. Doulut Khan Lody, viceroy of the Punjâb, also revolted, but instead of proclaiming his independence, went to Kabool, and besought Babur, a descendant of the Emperor Teimoor, then ruler of Kabool, to accompany him to India, as well to assert his right to the throne in virtue of his ancestor's conquests, as to put an end to the cruelties of Ibrahim Lody and the general distraction of the kingdom. In the year 1526, therefore, Babur invaded India and advanced upon Dehly, where, in a bloody battle fought on April 21, 1526, on the plain of Paniput, where the fate of India had already been so often decided, Ibrahim Lody was slain, and a new dynasty under the Moghuls commenced. The dynasty of Lody, in three successions, had virtually lasted from A.D. 1450 to 1526, or seventy-six years.

Ibrahim, his son, succeeds, 1517.

Rebellion of his brother Julal Khan.

Who is defeated.

Captured and put to death.

Further rebellions ensue from the king's cruelties.

Doulut Khan Lody invites Babur to India.

Babur invades India.

Treaty of Madrid.

Battle at Paniput, when Ibrahim Lody is slain.

Before proceeding further with the history of the monarchy of Dehly and the Moghul dynasty, it is necessary to revert for a while to those independent Mahomedan kingdoms which, from the death of Mahomed Toghluk in A.D. 1351, had arisen in various localities in India, and which, as well for their power and magnitude as for their effects upon India at large, cannot be overlooked. By a review of them, the chronological events of India will be connected and maintained up to the establishment of the Moghul dynasty.

BOOK III.

CHAPTER I.

OF THE MAHOMEDAN KINGS OF KASHMERE.

Historical records of Kashmere recapitulated.

There is no portion of India perhaps of which the genealogical records are so complete and indisputable as those of Kashmere, which, from the very earliest ages until its annexation to the Moghul empire, had held independent existence. The 'Raja Turangiri,' a genealogical record of the province, the authority of which is not questioned by any of the most eminent Indian chronologists, begins with the Kauráva dynasty, in 3714 B.C., which continued till B.C. 2448, when the first Gonardya dynasty commenced, and continued till 1217 B.C. After an interval not accounted for, the second Gonardya line began, which lasted 1013 years, and ended in 216 B.C., and was followed by the Aditya, for 192 years—168 B.C. to 23 A.D. —when the Gonardya being restored, ruled for 433 years, or till A.D. 579, and was succeeded by the Nágas or Karkotás, in A.D. 615, who continued for 260 years, or till A.D. 873. The Utpála dynasty in succession lasted 84 years, or from A.D. 875 to 959; and the last Hindoo or mixed dynasty, from 960 A.D. to 1275 A.D., or more properly to 1294, if a single reign of a Bhóta king and his wife be reckoned. The whole of the foregoing dynasties were Hindoos, Booddhists, and snake and fire worshippers, which, with adoration of the sun, seem to have been the pervading faiths in Kashmere from B.C. 3714 down to A.D. 1294, or 5008 years.

Shah Meer becomes minister.

The Mahomedan chronicle does not begin till 1315 A.D., when a Hindoo rajah, named Séna Déo, reigned in Kashmere, and a Mahomedan, one Shah Meer, was admitted into his service, who rose gradually to the office of prime minister, under Séna Déo's son, Rajah Runjorn. On the latter's death, the throne was claimed and occupied by Rajah Anund Déo of Kashgar, by whom, however, the Mahomedans were expelled from court. A revolt was the consequence, the vexation attendant on which caused the rajah's death in 1326. His wife, Kowla Dévy, for a short time endeavoured to maintain her late husband's authority, but, being defeated by Shah Meer, ultimately married him, when Shah Meer declared himself king, under the title of Shumsh-ood-deen. The king became famous in Kashmere for his reduction of vexatious imposts, light taxation, and the vigour with which he repelled Tartar invasions; but, having attained a great age, he abdicated the throne in A.D. 1349, and died in the same year.

Who, under the title of Shumsh-ood-deen, becomes king, 1326.

Edward III. king of England.

Shah Meer abdicates and dies, A.D. 1349.

The late king had left his dominions divided between his two sons, Jumsheed and Ally Sheer, and the latter immediately claimed part of the government. This brought on a civil war, in which Jumsheed was defeated; when he seems to have withdrawn his pretensions altogether, and, after a troubled reign of fourteen months, retired from the contest; and was succeeded by Ally Sheer, under the title of Alla-ood-deen, who reigned till A.D. 1363, when he died. The prince Siah Mookh, or 'black face,' succeeded his brother under the designation of Shahab-ood-deen. He was an enterprising and warlike monarch, who, passing the natural mountain boundary of the province, carried his arms southward, till he encountered the Jám of Sinde, on the Indus, who was sorely defeated by him. On his return, the Rajah of Nagrakote tendered his submission, and became a dependant of Kashmere.

Jumsheed, 1349.

Retires, 1351.

Alla-ood-deen, 1351.

Dies, 1363.

Shahab-ood-deen, 1363.

Shahab-ood-deen died in 1386, having nominated his brother Hindál as his successor, who ascended the throne under the title of Kootub-ood-deen, and died A.D. 1396. He had left a son, by name Sugga, who took the title of Sikunder, to which afterwards he added 'Boot-Shikun,' or Iconoclast, from the number of idols and temples which he destroyed in Kashmere. At the instance of his minister, a converted Brahmin, he broke up all the idols of gold and silver, and destroyed, as far as it was possible to do, the Cyclopean temples of the ancient faith in Kashmere. In other respects Sikunder would appear to have been a temperate and virtuous monarch. He died in 1416, leaving three sons, and he declared that the eldest, Ameer Khan, should succeed him.

Dies, 1386.

Tamerlane conquers Georgia.

Kootub-ood-deen, 1386.

Dies, 1396.

Sikunder, 1396.

Dies, 1416.

Ally Shah, 1416.

Ameer Khan was a minor; but, out of respect for his father, he was placed on the throne as Ally Shah, and continued to reign for some time, when he formed a desire to travel into India, and left the government under charge of his younger brothers Shady

Khan and Mahomed Khan. The consequences, as may be supposed, were revolt. Ally endeavoured to regain his kingdom, but failed; and Shady Khan was crowned in his stead in 1422, under the designation of Zein-ool-abid-deen. His first acts were to withdraw the edicts against Hindoos. Brahmins were permitted to return to the country, and worship after their old manner; temples were rebuilt, and the profession of all religions tolerated. He constructed canals and reservoirs, and his general administration was wise, just, and effective. He was a great patron of literature and of the arts and music; the science of the latter being improved by treatises written on the subject. In his personal habits he was temperate and virtuous, having only one wife, to whom he was strictly faithful. These qualities did not, however, secure him against the jealous disputes of his sons, which, though quelled as they broke out, continued in a greater or less degree to embitter his life, till his death in 1472, at the age of 69. On his father's death, Hajy Khan was crowned, under the appellation of Heidur. His conduct belied the expectations that had been formed of him; and, after a vicious and profligate career of fourteen months, he was accidentally killed. His son Hassan succeeded him, who, after a reign troubled by domestic feuds and intrigues, died in 1486. The eldest son of the late king, the Prince Mahomed, was a minor, aged seven years; he was, however, placed on the throne, the prime minister, Syed Hassan, acting as regent. The very strict seclusion in which the young prince was kept by the Syed party excited great public suspicion and discontent, and became the source of a war at the capital between the people and the Syeds, who defended themselves desperately; but the city of Serinugger, in which they resided, was at length stormed by the populace, who rescued their young king, and he was formally crowned. The discordance of the early part of his reign continued till its close. Futteh Khan, the grandson of King Zein-ool-abid-deen, opposed him, and civil war ensued; but Mahomed was finally deserted by his adherents, and fell into the hands of Futteh Khan in 1496, by whom he was confined.

Deposed.
Zein-ool-abid-deen, 1422.
Dies, 1472.
Heidur, 1472.
Killed, 1473.
Hassan, 1473.
Dies, 1486.
Mahomed, 1486.
America discovered, 1495.
Mahomed deposed, 1496.

Futteh Khan now ascended the throne, and continued to reign till 1505, when a party was formed in favour of King Mahomed. Futteh Khan was defeated, and deposed; but having assembled an army, again deposed Mahomed, who had reigned about ten months. Mahomed now sought refuge at the court of Sikunder Lody of Dehly,

FuttehKhan, 1496.
Deposed, 1505.
Mahomed succeeds.

who sent an army with him for the recovery of his kingdom. The Kashmere forces were defeated, and while Mahomed for the third time recovered his kingdom, Futteh Khan fled into India, where he died in 1507. From this period till 1524 no event of particular interest appears to have occurred: but in that year, Mullik Atchy, a former minister, rebelled, defeated the king, and placed him in confinement, raising to the throne the Prince Ibrahim. These constant revolutions brought upon Kashmere the interference of the Emperor Babur, who sent an army into the province to restore order. Ibrahim was deposed, and Nazook, grandson of Mahomed, placed on the throne by the imperial general; but as soon as the force had retired, Abdool Makry, the former prime minister, who was again in authority, sent for the old King Mahomed, who was in confinement at Lohkote, and replaced him on the throne, and he reigned till 1532, when he declared his grandson, Nazook, to be his successor. In the same year the Tartars of Tibet invaded Kashmere, and were repulsed, but not without having caused much damage and loss. King Mahomed reigned till the year 1535, when he died of fever, after a troubled and chequered career of nearly fifty years. This brings the history of the kings of Kashmere up to the accession of the Moghul emperors, and what remains of it belongs to that period, and will be detailed in its proper place.

Is again deposed by Futteh Khan; but recovers his kingdom.

Futteh Khan dies, 1507.

Mahomed deposed, 1525.

Ibrahim succeeds, 1525, and is deposed.

Nazook, 1525.

Deposed, 1525.

CHAPTER II.

OF THE MAHOMEDAN KINGS OF GUZERAT, A.D. 1305 TO 1443.

The remote Hindoo dynasties of Sauráshtra, or Guzerat, have been already traced in Chapter XIII. Bk. I. down to the Vullabhis or Bullabhis, A.D. 525. After that period, the local dynasties, if there were any who aspired to rule the whole of the country, became very obscure; and it is most probable that individual chiefs retained their territories, and ruled them, without any attempt at confederation, for more than a hundred years after the Bullabhis. From A.D. 696, however, a restoration of the Balhára line was made at the capital, Anhulwara, which continued till A.D. 935. And in A.D. 746 the Chowra clan rose to power at Anhilpoor, and continued till A.D. 942, in seven successions. Sawunt Singh was the reigning prince in A.D. 935, and bestowed his eldest sister in marriage upon Mool Raj,

Early Hindoo dynasties up to the Mahomedan conquest.

one of three brothers of the Salunki or Chalúkya tribe of the dynasty of Kulyan in the Deccan, who had emigrated into Guzerat in the troubled period which preceded the dissolution of their own dynasty. By Mool Raj the throne of Guzerat was usurped in A.D. 942, and the Salunki dynasty continued till A.D. 1210. The Salunkis were great patrons of architecture; and many of their splendid memorials still exist; in particular, Mool Raj's temple of Budra Mala, on the banks of the Suruswutty. Mool Raj greatly extended the Hindoo kingdom of Guzerat, carried his arms into the Deccan, and for a while united Kulyan with Anhulwara and Guzerat, but he closed his career as an ascetic. He was succeeded by his son Chamund Rái, in A.D. 1025, when Guzerat was invaded by Sooltan Mahmood of Ghuzny; and from that period forward, Guzerat had to sustain its share of Mahomedan invasions. They were, however, less frequent than those directed against the northern Hindoo dynasties; for Guzerat, except by sea, was very inaccessible from the west. Bheem Déo, who reigned in 1032, was remarkable for the noble Jain temples of Aboo; and Somnâth was rebuilt by him. The reign of his successor, Kurun, was made equally memorable by temples at Girnar and Modheyra, and by the construction of the Kurun Ságor, or sea of Kurun, a fine reservoir for the purposes of irrigation—and the first on historical record—which was several miles in circumference. The embankment of this fine work was destroyed by a flood as late as 1814. Bheem Déo, the last of the Salunkis—a dynasty to which Guzerat owed all its splendour and good government—reigned in A.D. 1209, and died in 1215, when the throne was occupied by a chief of the Waghila or Baghila tribe, who retained it for a hundred years, until Guzerat was occupied by the Mahomedans, and annexed to the empire by Alla-ood-deen Khiljy. Before that time, the vigour of an united kingdom had been frittered away into small principalities; yet the prolonged resistance of independent chiefs of the country forms a remarkable feature in the history of Guzerat; and though their inroads in the province were frequent, the Mahomedans, until a comparatively late period, possessed, in reality, none of the country.

Mool Raj attains great power.

His splendid temples.

Unites Kulyan with Guzerat.

Is succeeded by his son.

Temples of Rajah Bheem Déo,

and works of irrigation.

Eventual conquest by the Mahomedans, 1305.

It is a strange circumstance to find recorded in a Mahomedan history of a period of high religious fanaticism in India, that the viceroy of one of the most important of the imperial provinces should have sympathised with Hindoos to such an extent, as Ferishta writes, 'that he promoted, rather than suppressed, the worship of idols.' This was, however,

Tolerance of the Mahomedan viceroy.

the case in the person of Furhut-ool-Moolk, imperial viceroy of Guzerat in the year 1391, when the Emperor Mahomed Toghluk II. was reigning at Dehly. It is very possible that Furhut-ool-Moolk designed to effect his independence, and, as a preliminary measure, made friends of the Rajpoots, who were still a very powerful and strictly military class, by allowing them free exercise of their faith. His conduct, however, excited the alarm of the learned and religious professors in the province, and they despatched petitions to the emperor for his removal. These were submitted to a council of holy persons at Dehly, the result of

Furhut-ool-Moolk, viceroy, recalled, 1391.

Mozuffer Khan appointed viceroy, 1391.

Manuel II. emperor of the East.

which was the recall of Furhut-ool-Moolk, and the appointment, on March 6, 1391, of Zuffur, a nobleman of the court, to the office of viceroy, under the title of Mozuffer Khan. It is recorded, also, that he was presented with a white canopy, or perhaps umbrella, and scarlet pavilion, such as were used by kings only; and it may be presumed that the emperor was prepared to acknowledge him as a tributary king, provided he could establish his position. Mozuffer Khan was a man of no ancient family; he was descended from a Rajpoot; his immediate progenitors had been menial servants, and one historian of the period mentions that Zuffur Khan had been wine-distiller to the court. Be this as it may, Mozuffer Khan proceeded to Guzerat, and was opposed by Furhut-ool-Moolk with an army of Hindoos. These,

Furhut-ool-Moolk slain.

however, were defeated in an action at Sidpoor or Chitpoor, in which Furhut-ool-Moolk was slain, and Mozuffer Khan took quiet possession of the capital, Anhulwara, and its dependencies. His first acts appear to have been a display of furious religious zeal against the Hindoo chiefs, several of whom he reduced between 1393 and 1395, and for the second

Temple of Somnâth destroyed.

Mozuffer Khan proclaimed king, A.D. 1396.

time, the temples at Somnâth, found standing, which had been erected in 1032 by Bheem Déo, with all their idols, were broken down, and mosques built in their stead. In the year 1396 Mozuffer Khan caused himself to be proclaimed king, and coins were struck in his name. He had left his son, Tartar Khan, at Dehly, who espoused the cause of Noosrut, the rival king, with Mahmood Toghluk. Their contention for superiority has been already alluded to in Chapter X., Book II., and Tartar Khan fled to his father, as Teimoor invaded India in A.D. 1398. Mahmood Toghluk followed him, but Mozuffer Khan declined to receive him, and it was thus evident that the invasion of the Moghuls had only seated the King of Guzerat more firmly in his dominions. The life of any king of India at that period could hardly pass without war: but till his death, on July 27, 1411, Mozuffer Shah appears to have enjoyed a tranquil and prosperous reign. He was succeeded, though not without some opposition, by his grandson Ahmed, son of Tartar Khan, who had died intermediately. Feroze Khan, by some accounts the son, by others the nephew, of the late king, gained a party in his favour, was proclaimed king, and resisted Ahmed, but having submitted, was restored to favour. As soon as peace was secured, the king set about building a new city, which was named Ahmedabad, and is still the capital of Guzerat, while its present interesting remains attest the extent and grandeur of its original condition. The buildings which survive, many of them in a complete state of preservation, show the transition from Hindoo or Jain architecture to Mahomedan, and it is evident from them that the Mahomedans, in Guzerat at least, had no architects of their own. Arches were not used till a later period, and while the carved oriels, perforated windows, with the ornamental courses of carved stone masonry, are essentially Hindoo, the style is adapted to Mahomedan requirements. The architecture of Ahmedabad has been recently illustrated by a beautiful work published by the Antiquarian Society of Western India,[1] and the city, as recorded by the Mahomedan historian, was, at its period, considered the handsomest in India. The dominions of Guzerat at this time consisted of Guzerat and Kattiawar; but the latter was more nominal than real, as the Rajpoot chiefs had not been subdued. In 1413, however, the king made the flight of two rebellious officers into Kattiawar a pretext for the invasion of that province, when he reduced the important fortress of Girnar, or Joonagurh, which, up to that time, had remained in the hands of the Hindoos. Ahmed Shah seems to have been thoroughly imbued with the fanatical hatred of Hindoos by which his grandfather obtained his position; for, in 1414, an officer, Táj-ool-Moolk, was deputed to destroy all idolatrous temples in Guzerat; and in 1416 the king himself marched against Nagore, where he did the same.

Mozuffer Shah dies, 1411.

Sigismund emperor of Germany.

Feroze Khan proclaimed king.

Ahmedabad founded.

Peculiar style of architecture.

Kattiawar reduced.

Hindoo temples destroyed.

On his eastern frontiers were the dominions of the king, or, as he styled himself, the Sooltan of Malwah, who had become independent, as well as the King of Khandésh; and frequent raids on the Guzerat territory were made by them conjointly, or independently. In 1419 the king marched against Sooltan Hooshung of Malwah, defeated him in a great battle at the village of Kulliada, and pursued him to Mandoo, his capital; but the rainy season having set in, he was

Wars with the Kings of Malwah and Khandésh.

Battle of Kulliada.

[1] 'Architecture of Ahmedabad,' Hope and Fergusson. (Murray, 1866.)

unable to invest the place, and peace was concluded in 1420. This, however, did not continue, being broken by the Sooltan of Malwah, who obtained some decided advantages and took possession of several of the Guzerat districts. In the sequel, however, Ahmed Shah retrieved his losses, and defeated the sooltan, who escaped with much difficulty. In 1428, the king was drawn into a war with Ahmed Shah Bahmuny of the Deccan, who, at the instance of his son-in-law, the King of Khandésh, espoused the cause of a fugitive rajah of the Guzerat dominions. The Deccan monarch had taken possession of the island of Tanna, near Bombay, which became the scene of a fierce and long-contested struggle between the rival parties; but the troops of Ahmed Shah, commanded by his son Zuffur Khan, were in the end victorious, and the Deccanies retreated with great loss. The contest was, however, renewed in Khandésh in 1431, when the Deccan king made a great effort to retrieve his honour; but was again defeated. The last military enterprise of the king was an attempt to restore the grandson of the Sooltan of Malwah to the throne, from which he had been expelled by a rebellious officer who had usurped the government. In this, however, the king was unsuccessful. He was unable to take Mandoo, and the plague breaking out suddenly in his army, he was forced to retire to his capital, where he died, July 4, 1443, after a reign of nearly thirty years.

Madeira discovered.

Joan of Arc.

Ahmed Shah dies, 1443.

Henry VI. king of England.

CHAPTER III.

OF THE MAHOMEDAN KINGS OF GUZERAT (*continued*), A.D. 1443 TO 1526.

It is a remarkable circumstance that the first act of the new king was to marry the daughter of the Rajah of Edur,[1] a Rajpoot, whose flight to Khandésh had been the cause of the war with the Kings of the Deccan and Khandésh; and to restore to him all his dominions. King Mahomed does not seem to have possessed the martial character of his father; the only military operation he undertook being in 1490, when he invaded the dominions of the Rajah of

Mahomed Shah succeeds, 1443.

Marries the daughter of the Rajah of Edur.

[1] The principality of Edur still exists, having descended to its possessors from a period long anterior to the Mahomedan invasion, and survived all the revolutions of the last four hundred years. It is an interesting fact that the last prince, H. H. Maharajah Sri Jowan Singjee, K.C.S.I., who died in 1869, was a member of the Legislative Council of Bombay up to the period of his decease.

Champanair, but was obliged to retreat and destroy his baggage. In 1451 the Sooltan of Malwah, encouraged by the king's timidity, advanced into Guzerat at the head of 100,000 men; and the king, unable or unwilling to oppose him, took refuge in the Island of Diu, where, at the instigation of the officers of the State, poison was administered to him on February 12, by his wife. He had reigned nearly nine years, and, from his inoffensive disposition, had obtained the appellation of 'Kurreem,' or the Merciful. He was succeeded by his eldest son Kootub Khan, who ascended the throne under the title of Kootub Shah. He reigned nearly eight years, and is remarkable only for his cruel, vindictive character, and disgraceful profligacy and debauchery. He died May 25, 1459. His uncle Dáwood succeeded him, but was immediately afterwards deposed in favour of his nephew Mahmood, who was entitled Bégurra.

Mahomed Shah poisoned, 1451.

Kootub Shah succeeds, 1451; and dies, 1459.

Mahmood I. Bégurra succeeds, 1459.

Mahmood was a brave and warlike king, and displayed considerable talent in civil government, redeeming the neglect and profligacy of his predecessor Kootub Shah; and though he was only fourteen years of age at the period of his accession, the prompt suppression by himself of a revolt by the nobles of the State gave evidence of unusual energy, and he soon grew to be respected by his people. Up to 1462 the king seems to have had a peaceful reign. In that year his aid was besought by Ahmed Nizam Shah, king of Ahmednugger in the Deccan, who had been reduced to extremity by the Sooltan of Malwah; and he took command of the army in person, relieved his ally, and prevented any further combination against him.

Edward king of England.

In 1469 the strong and hitherto impregnable fort of Girnar was finally reduced, the rajah tendering his submission rather than abiding the issue of a siege. Many Hindoo temples, it is recorded, were destroyed on this occasion. In the ensuing year, however, the rajah again resisted, and, being unable to oppose the king, consented to become a Mahomedan, and received the title of Khan Jehan. This led to the founding of a city near Girnar, which was named Moostufabod, and which was the favourite residence of the king for many years. Passing over campaigns in Kutch and the borders of Sinde, the reduction of the fort of Champanair, and the capture of its Chowhan Rajpoot rajah, Bénee Rái, is recorded in 1483. The Rajpoots had bravely defended the place, and when further resistance became hopeless, they put their women to death, set fire to the palaces, and, as the smoke ascended, sallied out to meet their

Girnar again rebels, and is reduced.

The rajah becomes a Mahomedan.

Charles VIII. king of France.

death; but the victory was sorely tarnished by the execution of the brave Rajpoot, on his refusal to become a Mahomedan.

Madagascar discovered by the Portuguese.

Naval action with the Portuguese.

In 1507 King Mahmood, in command of his own fleet, acted in concert with a Turkish fleet, sent from the Red Sea by the Sooltan of Constantinople, against the Portuguese, who are, for the first time, mentioned in an action with Guzerat history. The Mahomedan historian claims the victory, but though one of the Portuguese ships was blown up, the Mahomedans were defeated by Almeida. The action had, nevertheless, the effect of restraining the Portuguese for some time from further attacks upon the coast towns. In 1509 the king had the satisfaction of receiving an embassy from Dehly, by which the independence of Guzerat was acknowledged. He was, if possible, much more powerful in reality than Sikunder Lody, who sent it; but the supremacy of Dehly was always acknowledged by all the independent Mahomedan kings, and their official recognition by the emperor was an honour highly prized. On November 23, 1511, King Mahmood I. died, in his seventieth year. He had reigned fifty-five years in great prosperity and honour. He had not only extended his dominions to the Indus and the desert, but had consolidated them by an efficient civil administration; and his power, and martial character, restrained all attempts to molest him by the neighbouring Kings of Malwah and the Deccan. He was the greatest, both in power and character, of all the Mahomedan kings of Guzerat, and traditions of his familiar life and exploits are still recited in the country, mingled, however, with laments for the subjugation of the ancient and more romantic Hindoo dynasties of that remote antiquity which is still dear to the people. During the last hundred years, architecture had made great progress, and the king was its liberal patron, as well at the new cities he had founded, as at Ahmedabad; and reference to the work mentioned at p. 135 will prove the exquisite taste and skill by which it was distinguished.

Henry VIII. king of England.

Mahmood I. dies, 1511.

His character and acts.

Mozuffer Shah II. succeeds, 1511.

Cuba conquered by the Spaniards.

The king marches to Malwah.

The eldest son of the late king, Mozuffer, ascended the throne on his father's death without opposition, under the title of Mozuffer Shah II. He was born on April 10, 1470, and was in his forty-first year when he began his reign. In 1517 the reigning Sooltan of Malwah had been expelled from his capital by the Rajpoots, and the king marched thither in person to succour his ally. Since the early contention between Malwah and Guzerat for superiority, which ended in the triumph of the latter, the kings of Malwah had ceased from aggression, and there are no records of disputes on either side. Mozuffer Shah took the strong fort and capital of Mandoo by assault, and the garrison—19,000 Rajpoots, according to Ferishta—were slain. On taking possession of the place, Mozuffer Shah restored Sooltan Mahmood Khiljy to his throne, without stipulation of any kind—a circumstance which, for the times, redounds much to his honour. The Ráná Sanka, chief of Chittore, had been the aggressor against Malwah; and Mozuffer Shah undertook a campaign against him in 1519 and 1520, but little impression seems to have been made upon the rajah, who, though he made a nominal submission to the Guzerat king, continued to retain his independence. On February 17, 1526, the king, who had long been afflicted with a painful disorder, died, having nominated the Prince Sikunder as his successor. At the period of his death, the king was fifty-six years old and had reigned fifteen years. He had come to the throne at mature age, and was a man of simple habits and even disposition, though he was warlike and enterprising; he was well educated and accomplished, and made several copies of the Korán during his life; and his liberality to learned men caused many, from distant countries, to settle in Guzerat.

Inconclusive campaign against Chittore.

Mozuffer Shah dies, 1526.

His son Sikunder succeeds.

In the year 1526, the Moghuls under Babur invaded Hindostan, and the reign of Mozuffer Shah II. completes the history of Guzerat up to that period.

CHAPTER IV.

OF THE MAHOMEDAN KINGS OF MALWAH, A.D. 1387 TO 1482.

FERISHTA gives the following definition of the boundaries of Malwah, which is substantially correct:—'It is bounded on the south by the river Nerbudda; to the north it has the Chumbul; to the west is Guzerat, and on the east are the districts of Bundelkund and Gurra Mundalah.' The whole comprises some of the most beautiful and fertile provinces of Central India, and being for the most part a high tableland, enjoys a cool and salubrious climate. One of the most ancient and illustrious Hindoo dynasties of India had ruled over Malwah from the year 840 B.C., in a succession of fifty-six monarchs, to A.D. 1192, the most celebrated of them being Vikram-Aditya, in the year 56 B.C., and Rajah Bhôj, A.D. 483; both, probably, having been Maha-Rajah Adhiraj, or emperors of all India. Oojeyn was the Hindoo capital; and as early as the

Boundaries of Malwah.

Ancient Hindoo dynasties.

reign of Vikram-Aditya was the seat of learning and science of the best days of Hindoo literature. It was under him also that the great effort for the renewal of the Brahminical faith and the extirpation of Boodhism was made; and it is probable that the Puranas, and other sacred works now followed, were composed or compiled by the Brahmins, who were supported by him and his immediate predecessors. There was no tract of India, except Rajpootana, which more patriotically resisted the Mahomedans than Malwah; and the histories of the early kings and emperors of Dehly are full of accounts of campaigns in this province, waged with varying fortune till, in 1310, during the reign of Gheias-ood-deen Bulbun, king of Dehly, the province was annexed to the Mahomedan dominions, and the old Hindoo line disappeared, after an almost perpetual contest of 300 years.

Resistance to Mahomedan progress.

In the year 1387 Dilawur Khan Ghoory, a nobleman of the court of Dehly in the reign of Feroze Toghluk, who claimed descent from the Ghoory sooltans of Damascus, was appointed governor; and, during the unsettled period which ensued, threw off his allegiance to Dehly, and became independent. Instead of occupying the ancient Hindoo capital, Oojeyn, he resided chiefly at Dhar and Mandoo; and the latter place became, ultimately, the capital of the Malwah dominions, and one of the strongest, as it is still one of the most picturesque, mountain fortresses in India. In 1398 Mahmood Toghluk, king of Dehly, who had fled before the invasion of Teimoor, and had been denied refuge in Guzerat, received a hospitable welcome from Dilawur Khan Ghoory, and resided with him at Dhar for three years; at the expiration of which period he returned to Dehly, and Dilawur Khan, at the instance of his son, Alp Khan, who, during the king's residence at Dhar, had been fortifying Mandoo, declared himself king in 1401, assumed the ensigns of royalty, and had coins struck in his name. He only survived this event four years, and died in A.D. 1405.

Dilawur Ghoory becomes independent.

Dilawur Khan Ghoory becomes king, 1401; and dies, 1405.

Death of Tamerlane.

He was succeeded by his son Alp Khan, who ascended the throne under the title of Sooltan Hooshung Ghoory, without immediate opposition; but a strong belief prevailed that he had poisoned his father; and Mozuffer Shah of Guzerat, who had been an intimate friend of the deceased monarch, invaded Malwah to avenge his death, or probably by covert invitation from the disaffected nobility. The issue has been already stated in the detail of the events of Mozuffer Shah's reign, in the preceding chapter. Sooltan Hooshung was beleaguered in Dhar and forced to surrender,

Sooltan Hooshung Ghoory succeeds.

Sooltan Hooshung deprived of his authority.

and the kingdom was placed under charge of Noosrut Khan, the brother of Mozuffer Shah. Very shortly afterwards, Noosrut Khan, in a panic, abandoned his government, and the Malwah court placed Moosy Khan, a nephew of the late king, upon the throne. Sooltan Hooshung now besought the King of Guzerat to allow him to regain his kingdom, and declared his innocence of all the allegations made against him; when the king, releasing him from his confinement, sent with him a force under the Prince Ahmed, his own grandson. Hooshung was not immediately successful; but some of the principal officers of State having joined him, Moosy Khan abandoned his pretensions, and gave up the fortress of Mandoo, where Sooltan Hooshung now established himself in security. In 1410 Mozuffer Shah died, and the Prince Ahmed succeeded him. He was opposed by his uncles, who sought aid from Sooltan Hooshung. It might be supposed that the sooltan, who owed his throne to the exertions made on his behalf by the Guzerat king, would have refused connection with the movement; but the first invasion of Malwah was still rankling in his heart, and he had determined to avenge it. His present intentions were frustrated by the submission of the insurgents in Guzerat, but in 1418 he attacked the Guzerat dominions in person, and sustained the defeat at Kulliada which has been already mentioned in the preceding chapter. Nor was this his last attempt upon Guzerat. In 1422 and 1423 Sooltan Hooshung again made war against it: but, after some successes, was in the end obliged to fly to Mandoo. It was said of the sooltan that victory never smiled on him; and in 1428 he was defeated by Ahmed Shah Bahmuny of the Deccan, when the ladies of his family were taken prisoners, but restored to him with all honour. The restless career of the sooltan came to an end on September 7, 1432, when he died, after a reign of thirty years. In the intervals of his wars, Sooltan Hooshung had devoted himself to the completion and adornment of his capital Mandoo, which remains, though deserted and ruined, a noble memorial of him. The Hindoos had occupied the position before the Mahomedans came to Malwah; but not as a city. It is a large table mountain, which forms a bold promontory as it were, projecting from the Vindhyá range into the valley of the Nerbudda, but is almost isolated from the tableland by a deep ravine. On all sides but one, the mountain is steep; and its rugged sides are almost inaccessible. The circumference of the summit, which is nearly level, is estimated at twenty-eight miles. While the King of Dehly had been the guest of his father at Dhar, the sooltan, then the Prince Alp

The King of Guzerat assists him;

and he recovers Mandoo.

The sooltan attacks Guzerat, but is defeated.

Amurath besieges Constantinople.

Defeated Ahmed Shah.

Sooltan Hooshung Ghoory dies, 1432.

His capital Mandoo described.

Khan, had fortified this natural stronghold till it became impregnable against all military operations of the period. Natural scarps of the summit rock were made more perfect, and walls and towers built along the dizzy steeps of all the faces. During his lifetime, and when Mandoo was thickly inhabited as a city, Sooltan Hooshung built the noble Jumma mosque, one of the finest specimens of Mahomedan architecture in India: the beautiful water palace, situated between two lake reservoirs; with many other public edifices which still remain to attest the magnificence of the period; and, unfortunate in many respects as he was, wilful, headstrong, and ungrateful, he was yet popular with his people. He did not molest his Hindoo subjects, nor break down their temples; and even at the distance of nearly five hundred years, his warlike achievements and romantic adventures and amours, are still the subjects of popular tales and ballads of the country. In this respect, indeed, Sooltan Hooshung, and the brave but unfortunate Báz Bahadur, the last of the royal races of Malwah, have, as Mahomedans, few rivals in romantic interest.

CHAPTER V.

OF THE MAHOMEDAN KINGS OF MALWAH (*concluded*), A.D. 1482 TO 1526.

Ghizny Khan succeeds as Sooltan Mahomed Ghoory, 1432.

Is poisoned in the same year by the vizier, who usurps the throne.

Sooltan Mahmood Khiljy succeeds, 1435.

THE king left two sons, Ghizny and Othman, and some demonstrations ensued in favour of the latter. Ghizny Khan, however, succeeded to the throne under the title of Sooltan Mahomed Ghoory. He proved weak and dissolute, and was poisoned, at the instigation, as was alleged, of his vizier, Mahmood Khan, who, setting aside the son of the deceased king, and all the claimants to the throne, himself became sooltan, and was crowned under the title of Sooltan Mahmood Khiljy in 1435. The Ghoory dynasty of Malwah was not, however, extinct. The cause of Prince Ahmed, son of the late king, was warmly espoused by the King of Guzerat, Ahmed Shah; but on the death of that prince, and the settlement of other members of the late royal family on estates judiciously allotted to them, all opposition to the new dynasty ceased. Sooltan Mahmood Khiljy proved to be a brave general and soldier, and an equally good administrator of the civil details of his government. During the reign of Syed Mahomed, king of Dehly, he received an invitation from a party at the capital to become emperor; and he marched thither in 1440, but finding himself opposed, gave up the project. His unsuccessful expedition to Guzerat in 1451 has been already noticed in connection with King Kootub Shah, by whom he was defeated; and after this event he refrained from further molestation of the Guzerat dominions.

With the Hindoo chiefs around him, however, he was at constant variance from one cause or other. The Rajpoots had, in fact, grown to be very powerful; and the king appears to have had no resource, in order to check their marauding propensities, but to follow them to their strongholds. In 1455 he took Kerowly, Ajmere, and Runtunbhore, and compelled their rajahs to pay tribute. The Rajah of Kéhrla, on the southern frontier, proved more difficult of subjection; and his cause having been espoused by the Bahmuny king of the Deccan, Sooltan Mahmood was drawn into a war with that power, which he prosecuted vigorously, and defeated the Deccanies under the walls of their capital, Beeder; but on his return to Guzerat, his army suffered heavily, and the retreat became little better than a flight. In 1467, however, after some severe fighting on both sides, Ellichpoor, in Berar, was taken by the sooltan's general, Mukbool Khan, and having been ceded to Malwah, peace ensued. Two years afterwards the sooltan died in his camp, while engaged in a campaign against the Rajpoots of Keechwara, on May 27, 1469, at the age of sixty-eight. He was thirty-four years old when he ascended the throne, and reigned as nearly as possible the same period. During his reign, many noble buildings were erected in Mandoo, and its fortifications much improved. The great mosque began by Sooltan Hooshung was entirely completed in 1439 as one of the first acts of his reign; it had 360 arches and 200 minarets. To his Hindoo subjects he was kind and just, and it was only when he passed his own frontier that he occasionally destroyed the temples in the territories of the Rajpoot chiefs. In his own dominions the profession of the Hindoo faith seems to have been perfectly tolerated.

Operations against the Rajpoots.

Kerowly, Ajmere, and Runtunbhore taken.

The Deccan invaded.

West Berar annexed to Malwah.

Sooltan Mahmood Khilji dies, 1469.

His public buildings and improvements.

His toleration of the Hindoos.

Sooltan Mahmood was succeeded without opposition by his eldest son, Gheias-ood-deen, a man of mature age, who, during the greater part of his father's reign, had been his constant companion, and had led the troops of the State in many a hard-fought field, with distinguished gallantry. He had, however, determined upon a peaceful reign, and for a period of thirty-three years seems neither to have molested any one nor been himself molested. He maintained 15,000 women in his seraglio, of all professions and trades, and possessed of all possible accomplishments;

Sooltan Gheias-ood-deen succeeds, 1469.

His peaceful reign and habits.

and among them were a body-guard of 500 Abyssinians, armed with firearms, and dressed in uniform. He was much attached to his feathered favourites—pigeons, parrots, mynas, and other birds—and yet with all this appearance of sensual indolence, the sooltan was not in reality neglectful of his public affairs. Malwah was never more prosperous, nor its people better governed, than under this strange king. In the latter end of his life his intellect became clouded, and a contest began among his sons for the succession in 1497, which ended on October 22, 1500, when Nasir-ood-deen, his eldest son, who had been obliged to fly from Mandoo, regained his place, imprisoned his younger brother, Alla-ood-deen, who had opposed him, and ascended the throne. A few days afterwards the old sooltan died. Ferishta acquits Nasir-ood-deen of having poisoned his father, as alleged by some. He had already been crowned with the sooltan's consent, and was, with his sanction, conducting the government when his younger brother conspired against him. The aged sooltan was imbecile, and his death or life made little difference in Nasir-ood-deen's position; but Alla-ood-deen had won over one of his father's mistresses to aid his designs, and had thus gained an advantage, which, as has been related, was the cause of his imprisonment. With the exception of an expedition to Chittore, where the rajah did not resist, but paid tribute, and the king married one of the princesses of the country—there is no remarkable event connected with this reign. The sooltan's eldest son, Shahab-ood-deen, had revolted and fled to Dehly, from whence he refused to return, and the sooltan, being taken ill, nominated his third son, Mahmood, as his successor, and died in 1512, having reigned a little more than eleven years.

The king's mind fails, and disputes ensue for the succession.

Sooltan Gheias-ood-deen dies, A.D. 1500.

Nasir-ood-deen, his eldest son, succeeds.

His peaceful reign.

Sooltan Nasir-ood-deen dies, 1512.

Gaston de Foix.

The sooltan's death was no sooner known in the country than his son returned from Dehly to Mandoo, and a struggle between the brothers ensued, in which Sooltan Mahmood was victorious, and his brother was obliged to fly; but his success—mainly attributable to the exertions of Medny Rái, a Rajpoot chieftain, who supported him when the Mahomedan officers held aloof—was dearly bought in the favour extended to that person, who introduced his own tribe and other Hindoos into the executive government, to the exclusion of the old Mahomedan officers. Some allowance must be made for the prejudices of the Mahomedan historians of the period, and Medny Rái's conduct may be exaggerated by them; but there can be little doubt that he overstepped the

Sooltan Mahmood Khiljy succeeds.

Medny Rái exerts objectionable influence.

proper bounds of his position, and that the king's suspicions were ultimately confirmed. He attempted to discharge the whole of the Rajpoots, but was foiled, and reduced to such extremity that he fled from Mandoo, leaving it in possession of Medny Rái, and took refuge in the Guzerat territory. Mozuffer Shah, as has already been related, warmly espoused his cause, and marched with a large army to Mandoo, which was taken by escalade; when the Rajpoots, who were unable to escape from the fortress, and had already put their women and children to death, were slain, to the number of 19,000 men. Medny Rái had, however, escaped, and taken refuge with Ráná Sanka of Chittore; and it was an interesting and romantic incident of the war which followed, that when the sooltan had been badly wounded in a charge against the Ráná's army, and lay on the field unable to move, he was taken to the Ráná's tent, where his wounds were dressed, and, as soon as he had recovered, was forwarded honourably to his own dominions. Had the situations been reversed, the Hindoo chief would either have been put to death on the field, or held to ransom by the sacrifice of his treasures or dominions. In the year 1525 Mozuffer Shah of Guzerat died, and his son Bahadur Shah succeeded, but was opposed by his brothers. Bahadur Shah was too powerful to be dethroned by them; but the princes intrigued against him at Dehly, and one of their agents was very cordially received at Mandoo. Bahadur Shah, therefore, remonstrated with Sooltan Mahmood, who, by his conduct, seems to have been really implicated in the plot against him, and refused to confer with him in person. This conduct so incensed Bahadur Shah, that he marched at once upon Mandoo, and captured it by escalade, in the night of May 20, 1526. Sooltan Mahmood was taken prisoner, and was ordered into confinement at Champanair. On the way thither, the camp of his escort was attacked by some marauders, when, in an attempt to escape, the sooltan was killed by the guards who had charge of him. This event happened on May 25, 1526, and Malwah thenceforward ceased to exist as a separate kingdom. It was annexed to Guzerat, and continued as a dependency of that kingdom till its final annexation to the great Moghul empire. The two dynasties of Malwah, Ghoory and Khiljy, had lasted 139 years.

King escapes from Mandoo.

The city is retaken and the Rajpoot garrison slain.

Humane treatment of the king by Ráná Sanka.

The King of Malwah supports a conspiracy against the King of Guzerat.

Mandoo is besieged and taken, and the king made prisoner.

Sooltan Mahmood II. killed, 1526.

Malwah is annexed by Guzerat.

CHAPTER VI.

OF THE MAHOMEDAN KINGS OF KHANDÉSH, A.D. 1370 TO 1520.

Situation and boundaries of Khandésh.

KHANDÉSH is a province which intervenes between the table-land of Malwah on the north and that of the Deccan on the south. To the north it is bounded by the Sátpoora and the Vindhyá range of mountains; to the south by the plateau of the Deccan, which breaks into it by deep rugged ravines, clothed with forests; to the east is Berar, and to the west the southern portion of Guzerat. It is for the most part a broad, low-lying valley, with the river Tapty running through it from east to west, and receiving the drainage of the mountains north and south, by innumerable small rivers and brooks. The soil everywhere is extremely fertile, and during the Mahomedan occupation of the province was cultivated like a garden, the streams supplying means of irrigation, which was largely used. In after years, when it was perpetually harried by the Mahrattas, Khandésh became nearly desolate. Many of its most fertile tracts had become unhealthy jungles, and were without inhabitants; but its reclamation commenced from the period of its possession by the British after the Mahratta war, and it has again attained a high degree of prosperity, being, with Berar and Guzerat, celebrated for its production of cotton.

Its great fertility.

Mullik Rajah Farooky, its first Mahomedan governor.

To this province Mullik Rajah Farooky was appointed as governor by Feroze Toghluk, king of Dehly, in the year 1370; and a romantic incident is related of his rise under the patronage of that king. Mullik Rajah was descended from a noble but reduced family, which traced its pedigree to the Caliph Farook, and held himself aloof from the court, but belonged to the body-guard of King Feroze. He was a great sportsman, and having once met the king, who had separated many miles distance from his attendants, and was alone, he dressed a rough repast of game for him, and was invited to court, where he was promoted to the command of 2,000 horse, and nominated to the government of Khandésh, the capital of which was then Talnair, on the Tapty river. Such frontier commands, with freedom for exertion, were acceptable posts for the adventurous spirits of the time; and having taken possession of his province, Mullik Rajah speedily reduced some of the Hindoo chiefs about him, and caused himself to be feared as well as respected. On the death of his patron King Feroze, and when

His origin.

Dilawur Ghoory, governor of Malwah, and Mozuffer Shah of Guzerat, had declared their independence of Dehly, their example was followed by Mullik Rajah, who, to strengthen his political connection, married the daughter of Sooltan Dilawur Ghoory. For a time he entered into the schemes of his father-in-law for the subjugation of Guzerat; but having been sharply defeated on one occasion by Mozuffer Shah, and followed to his capital, peace ensued, which was never afterwards broken by the parties. Nor was Mullik Rajah Farooky of a restless and intolerant spirit, like his great neighbours. He applied himself sedulously to the extension of agriculture and cotton manufactures, he protected his Hindoo subjects, and at his death, on April 28, 1399, after a reign of twenty-nine years, he left a compact and prosperous kingdom to his successor, Mullik Nusseer, his eldest son.

Assumes independence.

Mullik Rajah Farooky dies, 1399.

Henry IV. king of England.

One of the first acts of Mullik Nusseer's reign was his seizure of the celebrated fortress of Aseergurh, which had been so called after Asa Aheer, a descendant of one of the ancient Aheer, or cowherd kings, who, being Hindoos, had ruled over the wild tracts of Góndwáná, and parts of Khandésh and Berar, long antecedent to the Mahomedan invasion, and had possession of fastnesses like Aseergurh, Gawilgurh, Narnalla, and other mountain positions, where they had remained secure and independent; tributary, however, to the Yádávás of Déogurh, or to the Hindoo dynasties of Malwah, as long as they existed, and afterwards acting independently, until their final extinction by the Mahomedans.

Mullik Nusseer succeeds, 1399.

The ancient Hindoo shepherd kings.

Aseergurh was situated in the north-eastern portion of Khandésh, and commanded the upper or eastern division of the valley of the Tapty, which is chiefly used as grazing land, even to the present day. It was a huge mass of basalt, rising seven hundred feet above the plain, with perfectly precipitous sides, except at one corner, where a steep pathway led to the summit. It contained water in abundance, and, rising as it did out of a nearly level country on all sides, was, for the period, quite impregnable. With Mullik Rajah the Hindoo prince Asa had been on excellent terms, and he had no suspicion of his son. When, therefore, Mullik Nusseer wrote to him, begging shelter for his family, pending other arrangements, his request was at once acceded to, and the first procession of palanquins which arrived was welcomed with honour, and the ladies it contained hospitably received. The next day 200 other litters arrived, and the unsuspicious Hindoo, accompanied by his family, went to meet them; but they found, too late, that these litters were filled with armed men, who,

Description of Aseergurh.

King Mullik Nusseer's treachery to Asa.

having surprised the garrison, put the unfortunate Asa and the whole of his family to death; and Mullik Nusseer, arriving shortly afterwards, took possession of the fort and of the wealth of the Hindoo prince, which was very great. This exploit was considered so important, that Zein-ood-deen, a celebrated Mahomedan saint, came expressly from Dowlatabad to tender his congratulations upon the 'victory over the infidels,' and the town of Zeinabad, on the left bank of the Tapty, was founded in his honour; and Boorhanpoor on the right bank, opposite to Zeinabad, being also founded at the same time, was named after the equally celebrated saint, Boorhan-ood-deen, and became the capital of the province. In 1417 a dispute having arisen between Mullik Nusseer and his brother, Mullik Ifty Khan, to whom Talnair had been left by his father, the king besieged and took Talnair, confining his brother in the fort of Aseergurh. Khandésh was thus once more united under one power. The king's wars with the Bahmuny kings of the Deccan, which arose out of the marriage of his daughter to the Bahmuny king, Alla-ood-deen, are of little interest; and he fared so badly in them that, after a severe defeat, he died of vexation, on September 10, 1437, after a reign of forty years.

Asa and his family are put to death.

The towns of Zeinabad and Boorhanpoor founded in honour of the event.

Mullik Nusseer dies.

James II. king of Scotland.

He was succeeded by his son, Meerun Adil Khan Farooky, who reigned a little more than three years, and was assassinated in the city of Boorhanpoor, on April 28, 1441, and was in turn succeeded by his son Meerun Moobaruk Khan Farooky, who enjoyed a perfectly peaceful reign of seventeen years, which he devoted to the improvement of his dominions, keeping himself aloof alike from the political transactions and the military expeditions of Guzerat, Malwah, and the Deccan. He died on May 17, 1457. His eldest son, Adil Khan Farooky, followed in succession; and for a time endeavoured to free himself from the supremacy of Guzerat. In this, however, he failed; and for the rest of his long and prosperous reign of forty-six years enjoyed entire peace. He died on April 8, 1503, deeply regretted by his people. He had resided almost continuously at Boorhanpoor; and though that city had been greatly increased by his predecessors, and adorned by many fine buildings, yet it was under his own hand that it grew to be one of the most beautiful in India. By Adil Khan Farooky, the noble palace citadel which was named the Ark, and commands the only ford leading to the city, was entirely constructed, and of which the splendid and massive ruins still

Meerun Adil Khan Farooky succeeds, 1437.

Printing invented, 1440.

Meerun Adil Khan assassinated, 1441.

Meerun Moobaruk Khan Farooky succeeds, 1441.

Dies, 1457.

Adil Khan Farooky succeeds, 1457.

Dies, 1503.

Pope Pius III.

Description of Adil Khan's works in Boorhanpoor.

Fortified palaces.

exist. Rising almost from the river-bed to the summit of the lofty northern bank of the Tapty, in tiers of fine arches, and terraces which were once gardens, the level portion of the summit, connected with the town, was filled with sumptuous buildings in a fine style of architecture. The interiors of some of the apartments, which have vaulted roofs, are fitted with fountains, and marble slopes honeycombed, over which, in the hot weather, pure water flowed with a rippling murmur; while the spacious halls and private rooms, with their open arches, and oriel windows once fitted with screens of carved woodwork, show an appreciation of comfort in fresh air and ventilation foreign to the habits of the present people of India. The elegant Jumma mosque, in the market-place, the fortifications, garden-houses and hunting-pavilions in many parts of the picturesque environs of the city; the deer park; and, above all, the noble and never-failing supply of water, brought to the city by pipes from the neighbouring hills, prove Adil Khan Farooky to have been a person of no ordinary public spirit, benevolence, and taste. The city, even in its present reduced condition, shows evidences of its former wealth in the carved woodwork of balconies, verandahs, and architraves of doors and windows, and in the style and size of many of the dwelling-houses. The king completed the fortifications of Aseergurh, and the paved road up to the summit; and the remains of pavilions and gardens, and the mosques and mausoleums, which appear on every side of Boorhanpoor, testify to the wealth and good taste of the period. Boorhanpoor and Aseergurh, situated twelve miles north of the city, and now a military station of the Bombay army, are to the present day most interesting to the traveller, and well worthy of a visit. The branches of manufacture introduced or perfected in the time of the Farooky kings, of gold and silver thread, tissues, ribbons, cloth of gold and silver, and brocaded silks and muslins, still survive, and are the main support of the population; and the processes of manufacture of these valuable and elegant fabrics are at once curious and ingenious.

Water supply.

Manufactures.

Adil Khan Farooky left no male issue, and his younger brother, Dáwood, succeeded him. With the exception of a short war with the Ahmednugger State, nothing remarkable is recorded of his reign, and he died on August 6, 1510, having reigned nearly eight years. At his death, his son, Ghizny Khan, a minor, was placed on the throne by the chief minister; but almost immediately afterwards poisoned, and the direct line of the house of Farooky ceased to exist. There were, however, several collateral relatives who laid claim to the throne; and,

Dáwood Khan Farooky succeeds, 1503.

Dies, 1510.

Henry VIII. king of England.

Dáwood Khan's son, Ghizny Khan, succeeds, and is poisoned.

Disputed succession.

as was inevitable, intrigues arose among them; but Mahmood Shah Bégurra of Guzerat summarily put an end to these factions by marching into Khandéeh, and placing Adil, the son of Hussun, and grandson of Nusseer Khan by the daughter of Mahmood Shah of Guzerat, upon the throne, under the title of Adil Khan Farooky II. The first act of Adil Khan was the recovery of Talnair and its dependencies, which had been alienated and usurped by the vizier of the late king; and having married a daughter of King Mozuffer Shah of Guzerat, and assisted him in his campaigns in Malwah, the king lived in peace till his death in 1520, after a reign of nine years. His son Meerun Mahomed succeeded him, whose fortunes will be hereafter noticed.

Adil Khan Farooky succeeds, 1511.

Dies, 1520.

Meerun Mahomed succeeds, 1520.

CHAPTER VII.

OF THE MAHOMEDAN KINGS OF BENGAL AND BAHAR, A.D. 1341 TO 1523.

In the reign of Mahomed Toghluk, king of Dehly, Mullik Fukhr-ood-deen revolted, and having slain Kuddur Khan, the viceroy of the eastern provinces of Bengal, proclaimed himself king over Lukhnow, Soonargaum and Chittagong. This event happened in the year 1341. He was, however, opposed by Mullik Aly Moobaruk, by whom he was defeated and put to death, after a short reign of two and a half years. Mullik Aly, who had assumed the title of Alla-ood-deen, now became king, but was put to death in less than two years afterwards. Ferishta's records of this monarch are very meagre, and it is probable that Bengal had no good court historian. Hajy Elias, who succeeded Alla-ood-deen, under the title of Shumsh-ood-deen Poorby, is not accounted for as a relative or otherwise; but he was a wise and benevolent prince, and so active in defence of his dominions, that the forces of Dehly could make no impression upon him. In 1353 he was obliged to take refuge in the fort of Yekdalla, which was besieged by Feroze Toghluk without effect; and in 1354 and 1357 he sent embassies to Dehly, when his independence appears to have been recognised as a tributary. He died in the latter year, 1357, and was succeeeded by his eldest son, Sikunder Poorby, who, being again attacked by Feroze Toghluk, consented to pay tribute, which was most

Mullik Fukhr-ood-deen becomes king, 1341.

Executed, 1344.

Alla-ood-deen succeeds, 1344.

And is assassinated.

Shumsh-ood-deen Poorby succeeds, 1344.

Dies, 1357.

Sikunder Poorby succeeds, 1358.

Dies, 1367.

likely the cause of the war. He afterwards reigned in peace until 1367, when he died.

Little more than the date of accession and deaths of the succeeding sovereigns of this dynasty are to be found in the Mahomedan chronicle, and those recorded are as follows:—Gheias-ood-deen Poorby succeeded his father Sikunder in 1367, and died in 1374; he was followed in the same year by Sooltan Oos-Sulateen Poorby, his son, who is described as brave, benevolent, and merciful. He reigned nearly ten years, and died in 1383. His son, Shumsh-ood-deen Poorby II., succeeded him. He was a weak prince, and after an inglorious reign of three years died. During the reign of the last king, the Poorby authority seems to have been greatly weakened; for Rajah Kans, a Hindoo zemindar, seized the throne after the king's death, and reigned until 1392, when he died. He was succeeded by his son Jeetmul, who, strange to say, being a Rajpoot, professed a desire to become a Mahomedan, and was admitted to that faith with great pomp, under the title of Julal-ood-deen.

Gheias-ood-deen succeeded, 1367.
Died, 1374.
Sooltan Oos-Sulateen succeeds, 1374.
Dies, 1383.
Shumsh-ood-deen succeeds, 1383.
Dies, 1386.
Rajah Kans usurps the throne, 1386.
Dies, 1392.
Jeetmul, afterwards Julal-ood-deen, succeeds, 1392.

Julal-ood-deen proved to be a wise and benevolent monarch, and reigned for seventeen years, or till the end of 1409, in great prosperity. His son, the Prince Ahmed, succeeded him, and reigned nearly eighteen years; and after his death, the throne was usurped by a slave, named Nasir-ood-deen Gholam, who was shortly after deposed. As Ahmed had left no male heirs, Nasir Shah, a lineal descendant from Shumsh-ood-deen, was placed on the throne, but died after a brief reign of two years, and was succeeded by Burbik, who reigned peaceably for seventeen years, and died in 1445. Yoosuf followed him, who died in 1457, when Sikunder was placed on the throne; but immediately deposed, and Futteh elected, who, though distinguished for liberality and justice, was murdered by one of his eunuchs, in 1461. This person seized the throne: but was deposed by Mullik Andeel, an Abyssinian chief, who became king under the title of Feroze Poorby, and died in the year 1493, after a long and prosperous reign, at his famous capital of Gour. His son Mahmood succeeded him, but was put to death by an Abyssinian slave, named Sidy Budr, who adopted the title of Mozuffer and ascended the throne. In the year 1496 he was besieged in his capital, Gour, by the nobles who had revolted, and in a sally made by the garrison under his command,

Dies, 1409.
Ahmed, 1409.
Dies, 1426.
Nasir Shah succeeds, 1426.
Dies, 1428.
Burbik succeeds, 1428.
Dies, 1445.
Yoosuf succeeds, 1445.
Dies, 1457.
Murdered, 1461.
Feroze Poorby succeeds, 1461.
Dies, 1493.
Mahmood succeeds, and is murdered, 1493.
Mozuffer succeeds, 1493.

which brought on a bloody general action, he was slain; though by another account he was put to death by the captain of his body-guard. He was succeeded by his vizier, Syed Shureef, who had been at the head of the revolt, and who ascended the throne under the title of Alla-ood-deen Poorby. He dismissed the Abyssinian and the Bengal levies, probably Rajpoots, who had proved rebellious and fickle, and reigned in quiet prosperity and great splendour till 1523, when he died, and was succeeded by his eldest son Nuseeb, whose history will be followed hereafter. During this period of broken successions, however, Bengal rose to great wealth and prosperity, and its capital, Gour, was one of the finest and most populous cities of India. It is now completely in ruins, and for the most part overgrown with jungle, and uninhabited.

Is killed, 1496. Alla-ood-deen succeeds. Died, 1523.

CHAPTER VIII.

OF THE MAHOMEDAN KINGS OF JOONPOOR, THE SHURKY DYNASTY, A.D. 1394 TO 1476.

On the accession of Mahmood Toghluk to the throne of Dehly he raised his minister, Kwajah Jehan, who was a eunuch, to the title of Mullik-oos-Shurk, and conferred upon him the government of the eastern provinces, of which Joonpoor became the capital. The confusion which attended King Mahmood's reign enabled the viceroy to declare his independence; and he assumed the title of Sooltan Oos-Shurk, or king of the East, and the dynasty was continued under the appellation Shurky till its close. The viceroy had declared his independence in 1394, and died in 1399. He left an adopted son, Mullik Kurrunful, who ascended the throne under the title of Moobaruk Shah Shurky. On hearing of this event, Mulloo Yekbál Khan, the vizier of Mahmood Toghluk, who had usurped the throne of Dehly, marched against Moobaruk Shah; but was unable to enforce the royal authority, and obliged to return to the capital, where Mahmood Toghluk had resumed the government. Shortly afterwards Moobaruk Shah died, in 1401, and was succeeded by his son Ibrahim, under the title of Ibrahim Shah Shurky. Mulloo Yekbál Khan and Mahmood Toghluk now again conjointly invaded the Joonpoor territory; but Mahmood Toghluk separated from his minister, and betook himself to the city of Kanouj, where he was suffered to remain

Mullik-oos-Shurk declares independence, 1394. Dies, 1399. Moobaruk Shah Shurky succeeds, 1399. Dies, 1401. Ibrahim Shah succeeds, 1401.

unmolested by both parties. On the death of Mulloo Yekbál Khan, in 1405, Mahmood Toghluk removed to Dehly, and Kanouj was taken by Ibrahim Shah, after a short siege. With this consolidation of his dominions the king appeared to have been content, and applied himself with much success to the improvement of the agriculture and civil government of his territory. In 1427 he was engaged in a short but indecisive campaign with Syed Moobaruk, king of Dehly, and in 1435 endeavoured, without effect, to prevent Kalpy falling into the hands of Sooltan Hooshung, of Malwah. These seem to have been the only military events of his reign, which lasted, for the most part in profound peace and prosperity, for forty years. He died at an advanced age, in 1440.

Kanouj taken.

Ibrahim dies, 1440.

Ibrahim was succeeded by his eldest son, Mahmood, who captured Kalpy in 1444, but restored it, at the instance of the Sooltan of Malwah, to its original possessor. In 1452 the king endeavoured to possess himself of Dehly, which he besieged; but was obliged to abandon his project on the approach of the Emperor Bheilole Lody, who pursued him and captured much of his baggage. Reprisals followed on both sides; and up to the period of the king's death, in 1457, peace had not been concluded between them. Mahmood Shah was succeeded by his eldest son Bheekun, who ascended the throne under the title of Mahomed Shah Shurky, and a hollow peace with Dehly was concluded; but Kootub Khan, the cousin of the King of Dehly, was not released, which furnished pretexts for a fresh war with Joonpoor. Mahomed was a warlike king, and a man of great personal bravery; but his cruelties at Joonpoor had alienated many persons from him, and his having caused his younger brother Kootub to be put to death, had inspired almost universal detestation of him. His army fell away from him and joined his surviving brothers, Hoosein Khan and Julal Khan; upon which Mahomed Shah fled, but was overtaken and killed. The Mahomedan historian relates that the queen-mother, eager to revenge the murder of Kootub Khan, her favourite son, persuaded the armour-bearer of her son Mahomed Shah to remove the points of all the arrows in his quiver; and in this defenceless condition he was put to death.

Mahmood Shah succeeds, 1440.

Frederick III. emperor of Germany.

Dies, 1457.

Mahomed Shah Shurky succeeds, 1457.

His cruelties.

Defeated by his brothers.

And killed.

Killed, 1457.

Mahomed Shah's reign, though full of tragic incidents, had only lasted five months. He was succeeded by his brother Hoosein, under the title of Hoosein Shah Shurky. The province of Orissa, then governed by a descendant of the ancient local Hindoo dynasty, had been invaded by his father,

Hoosein Shah Shurky succeeds, 1457.

but without effect; and the king now again attempted its subjection. He invaded the province at the head of an army of 30,000 horse and 100,000 foot, and the rajah, being unable to resist so vast a force, submitted at once; but the occupation of the province was not attempted, and the king returned, satisfied with the booty he had obtained. In 1465 Gwalior was attacked, and its rajah forced to pay tribute; and in 1473, the king, incited thereto by his wife, Mullika Jehan, a princess of Dehly, aspired to become emperor, and marched against Bheilole Lody, who, at first, endeavoured to make terms with the Shurky king; but his offers being refused in arrogant terms, the emperor marched out of Dehly at the head of such troops as he could hastily assemble, defeated the Shurky army in three successive actions, and pursued it to Joonpoor, of which, and its dependencies, he took possession. The kingdom was not, however, finally subdued till the reign of Sikunder Lody, son of Bheilole, who annexed it to Dehly in 1476. Hoosein Shah Shurky found refuge with Alla-ood-deen Poorby of Bengal, with whom, till his death, he continued to reside, and the dynasty of the Shurky kings ceased with him.

Invasion of Orissa. Gwalior attacked. Hoosein Shah attempts to take Dehly. Is defeated, and loses his kingdom. Which is incorporated with Dehly. Edward IV. in France. Hoosein Shah loses his kingdom, and dies in Bengal.

CHAPTER IX.

OF THE MAHOMEDAN KINGS OF MOOLTAN, THE LUNGA (AFGHAN) DYNASTY, A.D. 1443 TO 1524.

THE accounts of the rulers of the province of Mooltan, from the period of its annexation by the Mahomedans up to the year 1443, are extremely obscure. It appears at one time to have been held as a province of Ghuzny, at others by viceroys from Dehly, and again to have reverted to the Hindoos. In 1443, however, during the troubled reign of Syed Mahomed, king of Dehly, the people of Mooltan, having no viceroy or governor, and suffering under attacks of marauders on all sides, elected Sheikh Yoosuf, a person of good family and high character, to be ruler over them. Among others who tendered their submission was Rái Sehra, an Afghan chief of the Lunga tribe, who offered his daughter in marriage to Sheikh Yoosuf, and the ceremony was performed with great pomp. Rái Sehra had, however, conceived the design of securing Mooltan for himself; and during a visit to his son-in-law, contrived to throw him off his guard and to seize his person. He then caused him-

Sheikh Yoosuf becomes ruler.

self to be proclaimed king, under the title of Kootub-ood-deen Lunga. This event happened in the year 1445. Sheikh Yoosuf was allowed to proceed to Dehly, where he became the proud guest of the Emperor Bheilole Lody, but made no attempt to recover his position at Mooltan, and Kootub-ood-deen Lunga reigned in peace, till his death in 1469.

Kootub-ood-deen Lunga king, 1445.

Dies, 1469.

His son Hoosein succeeded to the throne, and an attempt was made by the Emperor Bheilole Lody to recover Mooltan for Sheikh Yoosuf, by despatching an army under the Prince Burbik and Tartar Khan; but the invasion was bravely repulsed by the Mooltan king; he received no further molestation from the emperor, and after Bheilole's death, King Hoosein sent ambassadors to his son Sikunder Lody, who were honourably received. Towards the close of his reign, the king abdicated in favour of his son Feroze, but this prince having been soon afterwards assassinated, Hoosein resumed his authority, until August 29, 1502, when he died at an advanced age, having reigned nearly thirty-four years. He was celebrated for his literary attainments, and founded many colleges and schools during his lifetime. On the king's death the heir-apparent, Prince Mahmood, was placed on the throne by the minister, Jám Bayezeed; but proving licentious and dissolute, the minister revolted and endeavoured to possess himself of a large portion of the kingdom. In this he eventually succeeded; the river Ravee (Hydraotes), being decided by Doulut Khan Lody, the governor of the Punjâb, on the part of the Emperor of Dehly, as the boundary between them. In the year 1524 the Emperor Babur directed the viceroy of the Punjâb to assume the management of Mooltan affairs, which had become greatly disordered; but before these instructions could be fully carried into effect, King Mahmood Lunga died, in 1524. His son, Hoosein Lunga II. was a minor, but he was placed on the throne by the nobles of the State. Mooltan was now invested by Shah Hoosein Arghoon, viceroy of the Punjâb, on behalf of the Emperor of Dehly. The garrison made a brave resistance, and though in sore distress for provisions, being reduced, according to the letter of a person present in Mooltan, to the historian Ferishta, to eating 'the dogs and cats of the place,' they refused to surrender the fortress, which was finally taken by escalade, with great slaughter of the people. The young king was confined as a State prisoner, and the Lunga dynasty ceased to exist, the province being annexed to the dominions of the empire of Dehly.

Hoosein Lunga succeeds, 1469.

Abdicates.

But resumes authority, and dies, 1502.

Mahmood Lunga succeeds, 1502.

Revolt of his minister, who divides the kingdom.

Dies, 1524, and is the last of his dynasty.

Mooltan besieged and captured, and the province annexed to Dehly.

CHAPTER X.

OF THE MAHOMEDAN KINGS OF SINDE AND TATTA, A.D. 1214 TO 1523.

THE earliest Mahomedan invasion of Sinde, by Mahomed Kassim, in A.D. 711, and its result, has been already related in Chap. I. Bk. II., and the history of the province is resumed from that period. After the death of Kassim, the conquests he had made were not maintained by the Arabs, and a Rajpoot tribe, the Sooméras, established themselves in Sinde, and maintained independence during the progress of the conquest of Mooltan and Guzerat by the Mahomedans, or for about five hundred years; but no genealogical detail of them has been discovered; and except a partial invasion of their territory by the Emperor Mahomed Toghluk, in 1351, the prosecution of which was prevented by his death, the Hindoo princes of Sinde remained unmolested by the Mahomedans of India.

The Sooméra Rajpoots.

At various periods, however, in the thirteenth century, Sinde and Mooltan were invaded by Mahomedan leaders from the west, one of whom, Nasir-ood-deen Kubáchá—a Toorky slave of Mahomed Ghoory, king of Ghuzny, and who had married a daughter of King Kootub-ood-deen Eibuk, the successor of Mahomed Ghoory in India—subdued the Sooméras, and declared himself King of Sinde. The date of his assumption of royal dignity does not appear in the Mahomedan history; but, in A.D. 1214, he repelled an attack on his Sinde territories, made from the west, by the forces of the King of Kharizm. In 1217 Nasir-ood-deen had conquered Sirhind, and endeavoured to possess himself of Lahore, but was defeated by King Shumsh-ood-deen Altmish, of Dehly. His territories, with the whole of the western frontier of India, would probably have fallen before Jelál-ood-deen, the gallant son of the King of Kharizm, who, for awhile, appeared desirous of establishing his independence in India. He had gained most of the Punjâb, defeated Nasir-ood-deen in several engagements, and even penetrated as far south as Tatta, on the Indus; but in 1222 he returned to his brother, the King of Irak, and did not renew his connection with India. In 1224–5 Shumsh-ood-deen Altmish, king of Dehly, dispatched an army for tha conquest of Sinde, and Nasir-ood-deen became so straitened in consequence, that he was forced to abandon Mooltan and Upper Sinde, and in an attempt to reach the

Alexander II. king of Scotland.

Nasir-ood-deen Kubáchá

lower country from the fort of Bukkur, by water, he and his family perished in a storm. Nasir-ood-deen Kubáchá had reigned twenty-two years, and left no successor.

drowned, 1224-5.

His dynasty becomes extinct.

The next dynasty which arose in Sinde was at first Hindoo, of the Soomána tribe of Rajpoots, entitled Jám, which had risen to power after the decline of the Sooméras, and the intermediate reign of Nasir-ood-deen Kubáchá. After that king's death, in 1224-5, Sinde continued subject to the kings of Dehly until A.D. 1336, when Jám Afra declared his independence, but died in 1339. Jám Chobán succeeded him, and it was probably to attack this prince that Mahomed Toghluk made his expedition from Guzerat into Sinde. Jám Chobán died in 1353, and was followed by Jám Bany. Up to this period, the Sinde State appears to have paid tribute to Dehly; but in 1360, on the refusal of Jám Bany to remit it, and his declaration of entire independence, King Feroze Toghluk invaded Sinde from Guzerat. The Jám was at first successful, inasmuch as the royal army was obliged to retreat for want of forage; but the campaign being renewed by the king in person, Jám Bany was obliged to submit, and was taken by Feroze Toghluk, honourably, to Dehly, where he was received into favour, restored to his possessions, and reigned till 1367. His brother, Jám Timmajee, succeeded him, and reigned till 1380. At the ensuing succession, the Jám family, hitherto Hindoos, embraced the Mahomedan faith, though for what reason, or under what circumstances, is not mentioned. Their history, indeed, is a mere list of successions, as follows.

JÁM DYNASTY.

Jám Afra, 1336.

Dies, 1339.

Jám Chobán succeeds, 1339.

Dies, 1353.

Jám Bany, 1353.

King Feroze Toghluk of Dehly invades Sinde.

Dies, 1367.

Jám Timmajee, 1367.

Dies, 1380.

Jám Sulah-ood-deen, who succeeded Timmajee, died in 1391; Jám Nizam-ood-deen in 1393. Jám Ali Sheer, a benevolent monarch, died, deeply lamented by his people, in 1409. Jám Girán succeeded, but died on the second day after his accession; and Jám Futteh Khan, a collateral relation, was elected king, and died in 1423. His younger brother, Jám Toghluk, succeeded him, and died in 1450. During his reign the Viceroy of Guzerat declared independence; and there being no actual imperial government in existence at Dehly, Jám Toghluk entered into relations with Guzerat, and probably paid tribute. On his death, his kinsman, Jám Moobaruk, was placed upon the throne, but almost immediately deposed, and Jám Sikunder succeeded, who died in 1452. He also seems to have left no male

Sulah-ood-deen, 1380.

Died, 1391.

Jám Nizam-ood-deen, 1391.

Died, 1393.

Jám Ali Sheer, 1393.

Died, 1409.

Jám Futteh Khan, 1409.

Died, 1423.

Jám Toghluk, 1423.

Died, 1450. — Jám Moobaruk, 1450, deposed. — Jám Sikunder, 1450. — Died, 1453. — Jám Sunjur, 1453. — Died, 1460. — Jám Nizam-ood-deen Nunda, 1460. — Died, 1492. — Jám Feroze, 1492. — Deprived of his dominions, 1519. — Charles V. emperor of Germany.

issue, for Sunjur, a descendant of a former royal race, was elected to fill the throne, on account of his high personal character, and died in 1460. Jám Nizam-ood-deen Nunda, who followed, was subjected, in the latter part of his reign, to various invasions by the Toorkomans of Kandahar, by which he lost the northern portion of his dominions, with the fort of Bukkur, and he died of a broken heart, in 1492. His son, Jám Feroze, succeeded him, but was opposed by Jám Sulah-ood-deen. He was related by marriage to Mozuffer Shah of Guzerat, who espoused his cause. Sulah-ood-deen was not at first successful; but Mozuffer Shah having undertaken a campaign against Sinde, in 1519, drove out Jám Feroze, and occupied the country himself. In turn Feroze besought aid of Shah Beg Arghoon, now independent at Mooltan; and in an engagement which followed, Sulah-ood-deen was slain. Feroze would now have recovered his throne; but after a very brief interval, Shah Beg Arghoon advanced with a large army into Sinde, and in 1520 annexed the province to his own dominions. Jám Feroze attempted to collect an army for the recovery of his position; but, failing in this, entered the service of King Bahadur Shah of Guzerat, and the Jám dynasty ceased with him.

ARGHOON DYNASTY. — Shah Beg Arghoon king, 1520. — Solyman, the Magnificent, emperor of the Turks. — He died, 1523. — Is succeeded by Shah Hoosein Arghoon, 1523.

Shah Beg Arghoon was descended from an illustrious family of Khorassán, and became governor of the province of Kandahar, whence, taking advance of the civil war between Jám Feroze and Jám Sulah-ood-deen, he invaded Sinde in 1520–21, and ultimately became possessed of it. He survived the event, however, only two years, and died in 1523. He was succeeded by his son, Shah Hoosein Arghoon, who rebuilt the fort of Bukkur, and reduced the whole of Sinde to obedience. In 1524 the Emperor Babur, before his invasion of India, directed operations to be commenced against Mooltan and Sinde; and whether on his own account, or on that of the emperor, appears uncertain, but Shah Hoosein Arghoon besieged and captured Mooltan, extinguishing the Lunga dynasty, and for the present reigned over both Sinde and Mooltan. His future fortunes and those of the Sinde kingdom will be related in connection with the histories of the Moghul emperors of Dehly.

CHAPTER XI.

OF THE BAHMUNY MAHOMEDAN DYNASTY OF THE DECCAN, A.D. 1351 TO 1378.

THE commencement of the rebellion in the Deccan has been already noticed, in Chap. X. Bk. II., and on the death of the Emperor Mahomed Toghluk, in 1351, it had been virtually accomplished by Zuffur Khan, one of the most remarkable men of his time. According to the account by the Mahomedan historian, he was originally a menial servant in the employ of a Brahmin of Dehly, named Gungoo, and when ploughing one of his master's fields, chanced to turn up a pot filled with gold coins. These he took to the Brahmin, who, appreciating his honesty, constructed his horoscope, which disclosed that he should attain royal honours; and the Brahmin requested that should this prove true, his own name might be associated with that of the dynasty. It is perhaps the best confirmation of this story, that at a period in which a fierce fanaticism and hatred of Hindoo idolators was a proud distinction coveted by most Mahomedans of high rank, Zuffur Khan, when he became a king, should have assumed 'Gungoo Bahmuny,' as the distinguishing title of his dynasty, in preference to any Mahomedan appellation; a title which it continued to possess till its extinction. Zuffur Khan was recommended to the service of the King of Dehly, and rose in it till he attained a high military command in the Deccan.

John II. king of France.

Rebellion of Zuffur Khan.

His origin.

Curious prediction regarding him.

His career.

Although the emperor was absent in Guzerat, the struggle for superiority was for some time carried on by the viceroy, Imád-ool-Moolk; but the royal troops were, in the sequel, completely defeated in a general action near the town of Beeder, on which occasion Imád-ool-Moolkh was killed; and no further attempts for the recovery of its power being made by the kingdom of Dehly, the whole of its possessions in the Deccan fell to Zuffur Khan, who, on August 12, 1347, was crowned king under the title of Alla-ood-deen Hussun 'Gungoo Bahmuny.' He selected the city of Goolburgah as his capital, on account of its central position, and applied himself with great vigour and ability to the consolidation of the dominions he had obtained. It is recorded of him also, that he took into his service his old master Gun-

Alla-ood-deen Hussun Gungoo Bahmuny crowned, 1347.

Charles IV. emperor of Germany.

goo, the Brahmin, and made him his 'chief treasurer,' being the first record of any office hitherto having been bestowed upon a Hindoo by a Mahomedan monarch. In 1357 the king was invited by an ancient prince of Guzerat to occupy that province, and advanced towards it with a large army; but falling ill, the expedition was abandoned, and he returned to Goolburgah. The kingdom was now divided into provinces, and from the details it may be gathered that the northern frontier was Berar; the eastern extended from Berar, Mahore and Ramgeer, to Indoor and Kowlas; on the south was the line of the Krishna and Tumboodra rivers, and on the west the sea, with the ports of Dabul and Choule. This did not, however, include Dharwar, which belonged to the Hindoo kingdom of Beejanugger. Over the area included in these general boundaries, the Mahomedan government had been gradually established in the previous fifty-three years of invasion and partial control. The king did not recover from the illness he contracted on his Guzerat expedition, and died at Goolburgah on February 10, 1358, in the sixty-seventh year of his age and twelfth of his reign, and was succeeded by his son Mahomed.

Extent of the Bahmuny dominions.

Alla-ood-deen Hussun dies, 1358.

Mahomed Shah succeeds, 1358.

Hindoo kingdoms.

Although the Mahomedan power was now very considerable in the Deccan, it was nevertheless menaced by two great Hindoo kingdoms, that of Wurungul, now repossessed by its original dynasty, on the east and south-east, and Beejanugger, a more modern State, but more powerful than Wurungul, on the south and south-west. Any display of weakness or irresolution on the part of the Mahomedan king would have produced very dangerous consequences; but Mahomed Shah, unlike his father, whose calm valour and political dignity had won him the kingdom, was a fierce and daring character, burning with fiery zeal, and intolerant of all Hindoos; and it was with the utmost impatience that he received the demands now made, that he should restore portions of the dominions of both States which his father had conquered. Mahomed was not, however, able at once to enter upon a campaign with either or both Hindoo States, and while he kept their ambassadors at his court, watched his opportunity for action. Nor was it long denied him. On his brother's return from Mecca, his demands on the Rajah of Wurungul induced that prince to send his son Vináik Déo to recover Kowlas; but he was defeated, and the Mahomedans plundered the country up to Wurungul, receiving the expenses of the war.

Demands made by the Hindoos for restoration of conquests.

War with Wurungul.

Peace then continued for some time, when a party of horse

merchants having complained of the exactions by Vináik Déo, Mahomed Shah invaded the Wurungul kingdom, captured the fort of Velumputtun, when Vináik Déo was taken prisoner, and put to death in a cruel manner. On his return, however, the king's force was roughly handled by the Hindoos, and he only escaped by the sacrifice of his baggage. But in the contest with Wurungul he was ultimately successful, and obtained cession of the fort of Golcondah, with its dependencies, together with jewels of great value, and elephants; when a peace was concluded, which lasted many years. His ultimate success.

On the king's return to Goolburgah, a great festival was held in celebration of his success; and a band of minstrels having given him peculiar pleasure by their performance, he directed an order for their payment to be written on the treasury of the Hindoo King of Beejanugger. His minister did not immediately despatch the order; but when Mahomed Shah inquired next day in regard to it, and found it had been detained, he is said to have exclaimed:—'Think you a word without meaning ever escapes my lips? the order I gave you arose, not from intoxication, but from serious design.' It was therefore forwarded, and, as was evidently expected, was treated with contumely by the Hindoo rajah. The royal messenger was placed on an ass, and with his face blackened was led about the streets of the Hindoo capital. The rajah took the initiative in the war which ensued; and though it was the rainy season, attacked and took the fort of Moodgul, in the Raichore Dooáb, then in possession of Mahomed Shah, and put the garrison to the sword. These events, and in particular the slaughter at Moodgul, roused the fanatical spirit of the king and of his people to the utmost. A crusade was preached in the great mosque of the capital; and the king swore an oath on the Korán before the assembly, that 'he would not sheath the sword till he had put to death a hundred thousand infidels,' in revenge for the death of the martyrs of Moodgul. Insult to Beejanugger. The king's messenger disgraced. War with Beejanugger. King Mahomed's oath.

In the month of January, 1365, therefore, he crossed the Krishna river with 9,000 chosen horse, and fell upon the Beejanugger army near Raichore, amidst a storm of rain, and when its elephants were powerless in the muddy soil. The Hindoo host was routed with the loss of 70,000 men, and the boast of the Hindoo general, Bhój-Mul, that he would return with the head of the Mahomedan king upon a spear, was changed to lamentation. The Hindoos lost all their camp equipage; and it is especially recorded that on this occasion 300 gun-carriages were among the spoils. This led to the immediate forma- Artillery first mentioned.

tion of a field artillery, which, manned by 'Turks' and 'Europeans,' did excellent service. Artillery had been used at the battle of Créçy, in 1346: and it seems by no means improbable that European or Turkish adventurers who traded with Beejanugger, by Choule, Calicut, Goa, and other ports on the western coast, should have introduced cannon there, when they were as yet unknown to the Mahomedans of Goolburgah and Northern India. The campaign now continued, and in one action, fought on August 22, 1366, Mahomed Shah having been meanwhile employed in a fruitless investment of the fort of Adony, he was nearly defeated; but eventually gained a great victory, in which the Hindoo general, Bhôj-Mul, was killed.

Mahomed Shah now followed up his success; and the Hindoo king, unable to oppose him in the field, retreated to the jungles and forests south of the capital, and finally into the capital itself.

Massacre of the people.

During this time, Mahomed Shah, who had followed him from place to place, massacred the miserable inhabitants of the country without distinction; and finally invested

Beejanugger invested.

the capital, after surprising the rajah's camp at night, which had been pitched outside the fortifications. The massacre of Hindoos still continuing, the population of Beejanugger rose against their rajah, who now offered terms of peace.

The Mahomedan officers remonstrate against the massacre.

This proposal seems to have been seconded by the officers of King Mahomed's army, who reminded him that his vow of slaying only 100,000 infidels had been largely exceeded; but the king, while he admitted the fact, would be content with nothing less than the payment of his order to the minstrels, and the amount was finally disbursed to them from

The king's order is paid.

the rajah's treasury. 'Praise be to God,' exclaimed the king, when he heard of it, 'that what I ordered has been performed; I would not let a light word be recorded of me in the page of history.'

Peace ensues.

Peace then ensued, which was honourably observed by Mahomed Shah during his life; and as one of the conditions, the practice of putting prisoners to death was to be mutually discontinued. The desolation caused by the Mahomedans in this campaign had been terrible; and their historian records, with ill-concealed exultation, that from first to last 500,000 'infidels' had fallen before the swords of the true believers, 'and that the Carnatic did not recover this depopulation for ages.'

King Mahomed's civil government.

The war with Beejanugger was the most prominent event of King Mahomed's life and reign; and after quelling a rebellion at Dowlatabad, which had originated in false news of his death, he applied his great natural abilities to the government of his dominions in all departments. His measures were eminently successful; all marauders were exterminated, and cultivation was materially increased. He made yearly tours through his dominions, receiving petitions, and providing for the security of his people. He entered into no further wars, and at his death, which occurred on March 21, 1375, he left a compact and flourishing country, a full treasury, and an immense property, in jewels and elephants, with a well-appointed army, to his son, Mujahid Shah, who succeeded him.

Mahomed Shah dies, 1375.

Richard II. king of England.

On his accession to the throne, Mujahid Shah was nineteen years of age; tall and majestic in person, and possessed of great bodily strength. He did not long preserve the peace with Beejanugger, which his father had so well observed; and his first act was to send an imperious message to Krishn Rái, the reigning rajah, to give up the territory west of the Tumboodra, as also the district between the Tumboodra and the Krishna rivers. The former had constituted part of the ancient Chalúkya dominions, and had never hitherto been claimed by the Mahomedans. In reply, the rajah not only refused the demand, but haughtily claimed that the elephants taken by the late King Mahomed should be returned. War therefore ensued; Mujahid Shah invaded the Hindoo kingdom, and with a portion of his army invested Adony, proceeding with the remainder to attack Krishn Rái. The rajah, however, declined an engagement, and retreated into the woods and forests south and west of his capital, pursued by Mujahid Shah, who followed the track of Mullik Kafoor in 1310, to the sea. Krishn Rái now returned to Beejanugger, and the king, suddenly retracing his steps, invested the city. He could, however, make no impression on the works, and in one of the skirmishes outside the walls nearly lost his life. In another, he penetrated into the second line of works, where there was a celebrated image of the monkey god Hunoomán, which the Brahmins tried to save. They were, however, attacked and dispersed, and the king, dismounting, struck the image in the face, mutilating its features. A dying Brahmin, lying at the foot of the image, cursed the king. 'For this act,' he said, 'thou wilt die ere thou reachest thy kingdom.' A prophecy which was literally fulfilled. The image, hewn out of a large boulder of granite, still remains, and shows the marks of the king's mutilation.

Mujahid Shah succeeds, 1375.

He demands cession of territory from Beejanugger.

War ensues.

The king's death prophesied.

The last effort of the rajah to dislodge Mujahid Shah from his position proved successful; for, after a severe engagement, he retired with very heavy loss in officers and men, accompanied by from 60,000 to 70,000 captives, chiefly

King Mujahid retires from Beejanugger

women. But Mujahid Shah had observed his father's guarantee not to put to death any of the inoffensive inhabitants. Adony had not fallen; and peace was now concluded between the kingdoms. Dáwood Khan, the king's uncle, had command of a division of the army in the last battle before Beejanugger, and had been severely reprimanded by the king for withdrawing from the place in which he had been posted and joining in the engagement. Smarting under the affront, he now conspired against his nephew, and assassinated him with his own hand, when asleep in his tent, April 14, 1378. Mujahid Shah had reigned scarcely three years, and, having no children, Dáwood Khan, being heir presumptive, claimed the succession, and was acknowledged by the army.

Peace ensues.

Mujahid Shah assassinated by his uncle.

Dáwood Shah succeeds, 1378.

Dáwood Shah's succession was disputed by many, and by none more than Roohpurwur Agha, the sister of the late king, who instigated one of her late brother's most attached attendants to revenge his master's death; and as the king was kneeling in prayer in the mosque at Goolburgah he was cut down by the assassin and died on the spot. This event happened May 19, 1378. Dáwood Shah had reigned only a month and five days. An attempt was made by some of his adherents to place his son Mahomed, a boy of nine years old, on the throne, but this was resisted by the princess Roohpurwur Agha, and Mahmood, the youngest son of the first king, Alla-ood-deen Hussun, was crowned with the consent of all parties.

Pope Urban VI.

Dáwood Shah assassinated, 1378.

Mahmood Shah succeeds, 1378.

CHAPTER XII.

OF THE BAHMUNY MAHOMEDAN DYNASTY OF THE DECCAN (*continued*), A.D. 1378 TO 1435.

Mahmood Shah was fortunate in inducing his maternal grandfather, Seif-ood-deen Ghoory, his father's chosen companion and counsellor—whose wisdom had mainly contributed to the well-government of the kingdom since its foundation—to become his minister. Mahmood himself was of a peaceable and virtuous disposition, and during his reign both foreign wars and domestic insurrections were unknown. It is remarkable, for the time, that the king had but one wife, to whom he was constant; and in his literary tastes, and the daily affairs of his kingdom, he found ample and congenial occupation. It is recorded of him, that on

Seif-ood-deen Ghoory minister.

King Mahmood's amiable character.

an occasion of scarcity he employed 10,000 bullocks to bring grain from Malwah and Guzerat, which was distributed to the people at a cheap rate, and that he established orphan schools at Goolburgah, Beeder, and many other towns and cities, with ample endowments for their support; while his other charities, especially to the blind, were large and universal throughout his dominions. On April 20, 1397, Mahmood Shah Bahmuny I. died of fever, to the great grief of his subjects, and on the day following the venerable Seif-ood-deen Ghoory died also, at the extraordinary age of 107 years.

Mahmood Shah I. dies, 1397.

Mahmood Shah I. was succeeded by his son, Gheias-ood-deen, without opposition. The king was seventeen years old, and there appeared nothing likely to prevent a long and prosperous reign; but having given offence to Lallcheen, a Turkish slave who aspired to the office of minister, he was invited to a banquet on June 9, 1397, and there blinded and imprisoned. He had reigned little more than a month. Lallcheen, now supreme in the State, placed Shumsh-ood-deen, brother of Mahmood Shah I., upon the throne, and constituted himself prime minister. Matters did not long continue in this condition. Feroze Khan and Ahmed Khan, the sons of Dáwood Shah (who had been protected and educated by the late King Mahmood), were considered dangerous by Lallcheen, and he was on the point of seizing them, when they escaped to the fort of Sugger, the commandant of which was in their interest; whence, with the troops under his command, the brothers marched upon Goolburgah. As they halted at the ford on the Bheema, and were sitting on a terrace overlooking the river, a mad fakeer came up to the Prince Feroze, and cried out, 'I am come to conduct thee to Goolburgah and to make thee king.' The act was accepted as a good omen, and the brothers set out. The personal daring of Feroze Khan secured the revolution, and the king and Lallcheen were confined. Gheias-ood-deen, the previously deposed and blinded king, was sent for, and Lallcheen being placed before him, was killed by him with a single blow of his sword. Gheias-ood-deen then proceeded to Mecca, where he died at an advanced age. The deposition of Shumsh-ood-deen was effected upon November 15, 1397; and girding himself with the famous sword of Alla-ood-deen Hussun, the Prince Feroze ascended the throne on the same day, under the title of Feroze Shah, Róz Afzoon, Gungoo Bahmuny. Feroze Shah may be entitled to the epithet of the 'merry monarch' of the Deccan; and of all the kings of the great Bahmuny dynasty he is almost the only one who survives in local tradition and song,

Gheias-ood-deen Shah succeeds, 1397.

Blinded and deposed, 1397.

Shumsh-ood-deen succeeds, 1397.

Shumsh-ood-deen deposed, 1397.

Feroze Shah succeeds, 1397.

His character and habits.

after the lapse of nearly 500 years. He was passionately fond of music, and drank hard; but, as he said, never to affect his reason, and he hoped, if these were sins, he should be pardoned for them. He had an immense harem, and boasted that it contained a representative of every nation on earth, including Europeans, and that he could speak to each lady in her own tongue. He founded a town which was called Ferozabad, on the Bheema, where the mad fakeer had called him to be king, and built a fort-pálace there, which still exists, overlooking a large pool of the river, on which boats conveying musicians and fireworks floated for the amusement of his seraglio. Though he worked continuously at state affairs during the day, he devoted the evening to pleasure; and his assemblies were open to all his friends, who called for what they pleased. Every year his ships sailed from Goa and Choule to Arabia and Egypt, and brought back the choicest productions of Europe: and among all his extensive reading, there was none he more particularly enjoyed than the Old and New Testaments, for in religion he was perfectly tolerant of all sects and creeds. Few monuments of his reign survive him, except the half-finished mosque in the fort of Goolburgah, said to be a copy of the great mosque of Cordoba in Spain, and the palace-fort of Ferozabad. All else of the splendid palaces of Goolburgah, which overlooked the artificial lake constructed by him, are now mere masses of ruin.

Events of his reign.

Tamerlane invades Northern India.

The events of his reign were very varied. In 1398, as it began, Déo Rái, rajah of Beejanugger, encouraged by the news of constant revolutions at Goolburgah, invaded the Raichore Doóáb. Feroze Shah moved to meet him, but was obliged to detach part of his army to check an incursion of the Rajah of Kéhrla into Berar. With the remainder, however, he advanced to the Krishna, where an individual having volunteered to slay the Hindoo rajah or his son, received permission to make the attempt. Disguising himself as a minstrel, the man, with several companions, attended a performance before the rajah's son; and themselves being called upon, danced according to the custom of the country with naked weapons. Watching their opportunity, they assassinated the young prince and escaped. Before dawn the king had crossed the river, and Déo Rái having fled in the panic caused by his son's murder, his camp was taken possession of with booty to an immense amount. The Hindoos were pursued to Beejanugger, and the large sum of 440,000*l.* was paid to the king as arrear of tribute and ransom for Brahmin prisoners.

The son of the Rajah of Beejanugger assassinated.

Victory of King Feroze.

In 1399 the king in person conducted a campaign against Rajah Nursing Rái of Kéhrla, with great success; receiving a daughter of the rajah's into his seraglio, with money and elephants. In 1401, an embassy sent to Teimoor aroused the suspicions of the Kings of Malwah and Guzerat, who opened negotiations with the Rajah of Beejanugger for a defensive alliance, which might have brought about another war; but it occurred from another and remarkable cause.

A goldsmith of the town of Moodgul had a very beautiful daughter: and inflamed by the accounts of her, and the refusal of her parents to give her up, the Rajah of Beejanugger sent a body of horse to carry her off. The girl, however, escaped; and for revenge, the cavalry plundered the districts. Foláđ Khan, the governor of the Dooáb, chased them out of it across the Tumboodra with heavy loss; but King Feroze was by no means inclined to put up with this unprovoked insult; and, assembling his army at Ferozabad, marched across the Dooáb and invested Beejanugger, whence he despatched detachments westward and southward to overrun the country. That sent to the west succeeded in taking the fort of Bunkapoor with its dependencies; the other returned with a rich booty in captives and gold. Déo Rái had relied upon assistance from Malwah and Guzerat: but none having come, he was now in sore straits, for Feroze Shah not only demanded his daughter in marriage, but Bunkapoor and the western districts as her dowry. The proposal of the Mahomedan king was humiliating to the utmost degree, but it could not be evaded, and Feroze Shah was married to the Beejanugger princess, with the utmost pomp and ceremony on both sides. The Hindoo prince, however, failed in a point of etiquette on the departure of Feroze Shah, and the king declared he would one day avenge it, and so returned to his capital, where he married the goldsmith's beautiful daughter to his son Hussun Khan.

Remarkable war with Beejanugger.

Feroze Shah marries a princess of Beejanugger.

Nothing further of moment occurred till the year 1417, when the king endeavoured to possess himself of the fort of Paungul, which belonged to Beejanugger. Déo Rái took the field against his son-in-law, whom he completely defeated: and, as the Mahomedans had done on former occasions, laid waste the dominions of Feroze Shah with fire and sword. These disasters were redeemed by Khan Khanan, the king's brother; but Feroze Shah's health and intellects were both giving way: and after some years of troubled character he fell dangerously ill, and having sent for his brother, resigned the crown to him on September 15, 1422, dying himself on the 25th of the same month. He had reigned upwards of twenty-five years, for the most part in great prosperity and glory.

War with Beejanugger renewed.

Pope Martin V.

Feroze Shah dies, 1422.

Siege of Constantinople by Amurath.

On ascending the throne, Khan Khanan assumed the title of Ahmed Shah, to which was added 'Wully,'

Ahmed Shah Wully succeeds, 1422.

or saint; and as the King Feroze on his death-bed had not recognised his son Husaun, he was put aside and provided for liberally. The accession of Ahmed Shah was, therefore, unopposed. After providing for the safety of his northern frontier, Ahmed Shah declared war against Beejanugger, and as no reason is given by the historian, it can only be attributed to the king's fanatical character, in the desire for the extermination of 'infidels.' Although the agreement not to slaughter inoffensive persons had been observed since the days of Mahmood I., yet, probably to avenge the invasion of Déo Rái, the king now broke down Hindoo temples and colleges, desecrated sacred places, and 'whenever the slain amounted to twenty thousand, he halted three days and made a festival, in celebration of the bloody event.' Such at least is the statement of the Mahomedan historian, and it was most likely from such fanatical deeds that the king obtained his much-prized appellation of 'Wully.' In the sequel, the Rajah of Beejanugger paid up the arrear of tribute, and the parties separated with acts of mutual courtesy. In 1421, a war with Wurungul followed, in which its rajah was slain; and for several years afterwards the king appears to have been travelling through his dominions, for in 1425 he completed the fortifications of Gawilgurh in Berar, and in 1426 engaged in hostilities with Sooltan Hooshung of Malwah, who had invaded the Deccan kingdom, and defeated him. On his return, Ahmed Shah founded the city of Beeder, on the site of an ancient Hindoo capital of the country, which afterwards became the capital of the Bahmuny dynasty, and will be described hereafter. The fort was finished in 1432, and it apparently became a favourite resort of the king's until his death, which occurred there on February 19, 1432. He had reigned twelve years, and was buried where he died, at Beeder.

War with Beejanugger.

Massacre of Hindoos.

War with Wurungul.

The city of Beeder founded.

Ahmed Shah Wully dies, 1435.

CHAPTER XIII.

OF THE BAHMUNY MAHOMEDAN DYNASTY OF THE DECCAN (*continued*), A.D. 1435 to 1461.

AHMED SHAH WULLY BAHMUNY was succeeded by his son Alla-ood-deen Shah II.; and as the court was then at Beeder, he was crowned at that city. Contrary to the usage of Mahomedan monarchs, he was much attached to his brother the Prince Mahomed Khan, and provided liberally for him nstead of blinding or confining him.

Alla-ood-deen II. succeeds, 1435.

Paris retaken from the English, 1436.

This conduct, however, was not reciprocated; for when the Prince Mahomed was despatched, soon after his brother's accession, with an army to demand arrears of tribute from Beejanugger, he was induced by some discontented officers to conspire with the rajah to effect a revolution in his own favour; and with a force supplied by the rajah, he seized upon and occupied the Dooáb of Raichore, Beejapoor, and other provinces. So formidable a conspiracy and rebellion could only be subdued by force; and the armies of the brothers met in the field, the king proving victor in a hard-fought battle. The insurgent troops and their officers fled and dispersed, and the king induced his brother to surrender on promises of protection. It is pleasing to record that the king fulfilled all his engagements: not only pardoning his brother, but conferring on him the estate of Raichore and its dependencies, where Prince Mahomed lived undisturbed till his death.

Conspiracy of Prince Mahomed.

Prince Mahomed is defeated and surrenders.

In 1436 an army was sent to subdue the Konkan, the tract lying between the Ghâts and the sea, which was successful; the Rajahs of Ráiree and Lonekhair not only paying tribute, but the latter cementing the alliance by the gift of his daughter, a lady of great beauty, talents, and accomplishments, to the king, and she became his especial favourite, under the title of Perichehra or Fairy-face. This, however, brought about quarrels with his queen, the daughter of Nusseer Khan, king of Khandésh, and she appealed to her father for justice. Nusseer Khan, being too weak to enter into a war by himself, applied for aid to Ahmed Shah, king of Guzerat, who assisted him with troops, and the province of berar was invaded. To oppose this inroad, King Alla-ood-deen sent Mullik-oot-Toojár, one of his chief commanders, with a body of select troops, who defeated Nusseer Khan and pursued him to Boorhanpoor, which city was plundered and partially destroyed. Nusseer Khan had previously fled to Lulling, before which place another action was fought, which resulted in Nusseer Khan's complete overthrow, and Mullik-oot-Toojár returned in great triumph to Beeder, now established as the capital of the Bahmuny kingdom.

Invasion and reduction of the Konkan.

War with Khandésh and Guzerat.

The King of Khandésh finally defeated.

There is no more healthy or beautiful site for a city in the Deccan than Beeder. The fort had been already erected on the north-east angle of a tableland composed of laterite, at a point where the elevation, which is considerable, or about 2,500 feet above the level of the sea, trends southward and westward, and declines abruptly about 500 feet to the wide plain of the valley of the Manjera, which it overlooks. The fortifications, still perfect, are truly noble; built of blocks

Description of Beeder.

of laterite dug out of the ditch, which is very broad and has a peculiar mode of defence met with nowhere else, two walls of laterite, the height of the depth of the ditch, having been left at equal distances between the *fausse-braye* and the counterscarp all round the western and southern faces of the fort. There were large bastions at frequent intervals in the rampart, and the curtains are strong and lofty. Inside the fort, the royal palaces overlooked the walls; and their present ruins attest their great extent and former magnificence. To the west extended a level plain covered with groves of mango and tamarind trees, out of which rise the noble mausoleums of the later Beereed dynasty, and the ruins of garden-houses, mosques, and tombs in great profusion. The city adjoined the fort, space being left for an esplanade, and stretched southwards along the crest of the eminence, being regularly laid out with broad streets. There was a plentiful supply of beautiful water, though the wells are deep; and in every respect, whether as regards climate, which is much cooler and healthier than that of Goolburgah, or situation, the new capital was far preferable to the old one. At the present time, though the city has diminished to a provincial town, and the noble monuments of the Bahmuny kings are decayed, there is no city of the Deccan which better repays a visit from the traveller than Beeder.

War with Beejanugger.

In 1443 Déo Rái, rajah of Beejanugger, having largely augmented his army and taken a corps of Mahomedans into his service, became impatient of continual payment of tribute, and once more determined upon trying the issue of war. He therefore invaded the Raichore Dooáb, the old battlefield, and took up a position on the right bank of the Krishna river. Alla-ood-deen Shah, having assembled his troops at Beeder, found himself at the head of 50,000 horse, 60,000 foot, and a considerable train of artillery; and with as little delay as practicable, he marched to the scene of action. In two months three severe actions were fought on the wide plains of the Dooáb, in the first of which the Hindoos had the advantage, in the second the Mahomedans, and the third seems to have been doubtful; but two Mahomedan officers of distinction having been taken prisoners, the king sent word to Déo Rái that 'he valued the lives of each at 200,000 common men,' and swore, should Déo Rái put them to death, that he would revenge each by the slaughter of 100,000 Hindoos. Such grim threats on the part of the Bahmuny kings had not proved vain on former occasions, and there was little occasion to doubt them on the present.

Peace ensues.

Their effect was a proposal on the part of Déo Rái to make peace, which was duly concluded; the parties contracting to respect each other's dominions, and Déo Rái agreeing to pay tribute as before. The terms of this treaty were strictly observed on both sides to the close of the king's reign.

It is pleasing to read records of the king's benevolence in erecting and endowing hospitals, and of his vigorous prosecution of idle vagabonds and robbers, who were sentenced to hard labour in chains. Edicts also were issued against the use of fermented liquors; but it does not appear that the king himself set a good example to his subjects. He not only indulged largely in wine, but now gave himself up to a sensual life, neglecting the affairs of state, and seldom appearing in public. A considerable force, however, was despatched under Mullik-oot-Toojár to reduce the rebellious and hitherto independent rajahs of the Konkan; but in 1453, after some successes, Mullik-oot-Toojár with his army was treacherously entrapped in a frightful ambuscade, when the whole of the force, and its gallant commander, perished miserably.

The king's government beneficial.

Mullik-oot-Toojár with his army perish in an ambuscade.

The jealousies and rivalries between the foreign troops and the Deccanies had been gradually augmented during this reign; and a great number of the former were massacred in cold blood by the latter at the fort of Chakun, an event which laid the foundation of those commotions which eventually caused the decay of the dynasty. The king suppressed them for the time, and with much of his former vigour, notwithstanding the painful disorder in one of his feet, led his army in 1455 to oppose the King of Guzerat, who, however, retreated. On his return to Beeder in 1457, the king's disorder increased; and he soon afterwards died of mortification of the affected part, after a reign of nearly twenty-four years, appointing his son Hoomayoon as his successor.

Contention between foreign and native troops.

Alla-ood-deen II. dies, 1457.

A feeble attempt to raise the king's youngest son Hussun to the throne was frustrated by the Prince Hoomayoon himself, who, having blinded and imprisoned his brother, took possession of it without opposition, and appointed Khwajah Mahmood Gáwan, who had been steadily rising in public esteem, to the office of chief minister. Before his accession to the throne, the cruel and vindictive temper of Hoomayoon had shown itself on so many occasions that he was feared by all classes; and it was not long before it broke out in acts of the most hideous cruelty. During the king's absence on a campaign in Telingána in 1459, a few desperate individuals, in the interest of one of the state prisoners, succeeded in setting him at liberty, and with him the king's brothers, the Princes Hussun and Yeháyá, who, with some 7,000

Hoomayoon Shah succeeds, 1457.

Khwajah Mahmood Gáwan, minister.

The king's cruelties.

persons were confined on various counts. The rage of the king when he heard of this event was beyond bounds. 2,000 of the city guards were put to death, and 8,000 cavalry despatched after the fugitives, who were finally entrapped at Beejapoor, and sent to the capital. The king now glutted himself with revenge. Seating himself in a balcony, over the gate of the fort, still perfect, he ordered his brother to be cast before a ferocious tiger, which killed him instantly and partially devoured him; and all who had even the most distant connection with the affair of his release, even menial servants, were impaled upon stakes, hewn to pieces, or cast alive into caldrons of boiling oil. After this, Hoomayoon threw off all restraint; and his horrible cruelties continued to his death on September 3, 1461, by some accounts from fever, and by others, probably more accurately, from the hands of his servants, who, in one of his fits of intoxication, put him to death. By his will, drawn up during his illness, he appointed the queen-mother and Khwajah Mahmood Gáwan, with Khwajah Jehan Toork, to be a council of regency on behalf of his son Nizam Shah, then eight years of age. Hoomayoon Shah had reigned three years and a half, the last two of which were passed in the revolting and inhuman cruelties which have been related, and in the most terrible debaucheries, too indecent to be recorded.

Hoomayoon Shah dies, 1461.

Edward king of England.

Nizam Shah succeeds, 1461.

CHAPTER XIV.

OF THE BAHMUNY MAHOMEDAN DYNASTY OF THE DECCAN (*continued*), A.D. 1461 TO 1482.

Nizam Shah, king.

The queen-dowager's character.

Nizam Shah, the young king, was a boy of great promise, spirited, and yet amenable in all respects to his mother and her counsellors. The queen herself was one of the few remarkable women that have appeared among female Indian sovereigns. She did not sit in public; but she daily received all reports of the kingdom tendered to her by the members of the regency, and gave her opinion and orders upon them. She brought her son forward in public, and directed that he should sit every day in the hall of audience while the business of the State was being transacted, in order that he should gain a full knowledge of current affairs. Under this attention to general affairs of State, the neglect and cruelty of Hoomayoon were speedily redeemed; but the dominion of a woman and a child could not be believed powerful by the neighbouring princes, and the Hindoos of Orissa and Telingána were the first to take the field, and advanced with a great army upon the capital. The queen, in nowise dismayed, put herself at the head of 40,000 troops: and when the Hindoos had advanced to within ten miles of Beeder, an unaccountable panic seized them, and they began to retreat. They were closely pursued by the royal army, until the Rajah of Orissa was obliged to take refuge in a fort, from which he was not allowed to depart without paying the expenses of the war. During these operations, the young king was daily in the field with Mahmood Gáwan, and was thus early initiated into the details of war. Hardly had the Hindoos retired, than Sooltan Mahmood Khiljy of Malwah invaded the Bahmuny kingdom, in the hope of annexing it to his own; and advanced, unchecked, to within a short distance of Beeder. The young king again appeared at the head of his army, and was present in a severe general action fought near Beeder, during which, for a time, the Bahmuny army was successful; but, at a critical point in the action, the Sooltan of Malwah charged the Bahmuny centre with his chosen horse and won the battle. The Sooltan of Malwah now invested Beeder; and the queen, under the advice of her counsellors, betook herself to Ferozabad on the Bheema, carrying the king with her. Ambassadors had also been despatched to the King of Guzerat, Mahmood Shah, who, unwilling to see the balance of power destroyed, marched at once with 80,000 horse into the Deccan, being met by Mahmood Gáwan, who had kept the field, and was cutting off the Sooltan of Malwah's supplies. Beeder had been invested by the sooltan, but the fort proved impregnable; and now threatened on his flank by the combined forces of Guzerat and the Deccan, he abandoned the siege of Beeder, and commenced his retreat to his own dominions. While Mahmood Gáwan directed 10,000 cavalry to harass the sooltan's retreat, he operated himself on the left flank of the enemy, declining a general action, until the Malwah army was reduced to sore straits for food. The sooltan burnt his baggage, and was pursued to the frontier of the Gónd districts, whence, through the desolate forest tracts which compose them, he retreated into Malwah, losing the greater part of his army by heat, starvation, and thirst. In the following year, 1462, the invasion was renewed by way of Dowlatabad; but the King of Guzerat again interfered in force, and the Sooltan of Malwah was obliged to retreat.

The kingdom invaded by the Hindoos of Wurungul.

They retreat.

Invasion by the Sooltan of Malwah.

The Bahmuny forces are defeated.

Beeder invested.

Relief from Guzerat.

The Sooltan of Malwah retires.

His privations and losses.

The Bahmuny dominions being now at peace, the queen-mother returned to Beeder with her son; and preparations for his marriage were in progress, when, to the great grief of all, he died suddenly on July 29, 1463, having reigned only two years.

Nizam Shah dies, 1463.

King Hoomayoon had left three sons, Nizam, Mahomed, and Ahmed; and the Prince Mahomed, now in his ninth year, was placed on the throne; the regency of the queen-mother, with her two counsellors, continuing as before. Of the latter, Khwajah Jehan Toork, who represented the Deccany party, was the executive minister at Beeder; and having contrived to keep Mahmood Gáwan employed at a distance, usurped the queen's authority, and so greatly misused it in peculations from the treasury, and other corrupt practices, that the queen determined to rid herself of him. She accordingly instructed her son the king, who sat daily in public, to denounce the minister; and as the boy one day took his seat, he cried to Nizam-ool-Moolk, one of the chief nobles, as he pointed to the minister, 'That wretch is a traitor, put him to death,' an order instantly obeyed. Mahmood Gáwan was now sent for, and to him the queen committed the executive details of the government. When the king had reached his fourteenth year he was married, and the queen, recognising his majority, retired from the regency; but her son continued to consult her on all important affairs of State for many years afterwards, indeed to the close of her life.

Mahomed Shah II. succeeds, 1463.

Misconduct of the minister,

who is executed.

The queen-dowager retires from office.

The first act of the king was to despatch an army to reduce Kéhrla, the rajah of which, in connection with Malwah, kept up much irritation on the northern frontier. This expedition was successful; but the brave Nizam-ool-Moolk, who commanded it, was treacherously killed by two of the enemy, after the place was taken, a loss deeply felt by the young king. The Sooltan of Malwah was not likely to submit tamely to the capture of Kéhrla, and remonstrated; and after a series of negotiations, which are very graphically detailed by Ferishta, a treaty resulted, by which Kéhrla was given up, and Malwah resigned all claim upon Berar or any part of the Bahmuny dominions, terms which were faithfully observed on both sides. In 1469, the kingdom being otherwise at peace, Mahmood Gáwan marched into the Konkan, where it will be remembered Mullik-oot-Toojár had perished with his army during the reign of Alla-ood-deen Shah Bahmuny II. The expedition was particularly directed against the Rajah of Kéhrla, who maintained a piratical fleet and intercepted the trade of the Mahomedans. These operations were perfectly successful. The whole of the Konkan, hitherto considered irreclaimable, was reduced to obedience in three years, and was taken with its

Kéhrla attacked and taken.

The Konkan reduced and annexed.

dependencies from the Rajah of Beejanugger; and Mahmood Gáwan was received on his return to Beeder with public honours.

Campaign in Telingána.

Battle of Barnet. Edward IV. restored.

The king himself undertook his first campaign in 1471, when he marched into Telingána, at the instance of Ambur Rái, a relative of the Rajah of Orissa, who promised to become tributary should he be restored to his rights. The king on this occasion took Condapilly and Rajahmundry, and brought the campaign to a successful conclusion. Yoosuf Adil Khan, governor of Dowlatabad, was also successful at the period in a campaign against the independent chieftains of the mountains bordering on Khandésh, and was rising steadily into notice and favour.

The king's second campaign.

Use of artillery.

In 1472 the king conducted his second field campaign, against Birkána Rái, rajah of Belgaum, then, as now, a strong fort with a wet ditch. The fort was regularly besieged, and artillery employed to breach the walls, as well as mines to blow in the counterscarp of the ditch. When the breach was reputed practicable, it was assaulted, and on the failure of the first attack the king himself led another, which was entirely successful. The queen-mother had accompanied her son on this campaign, and to his great grief died on the journey homewards, in camp near Beejapoor. Her remains were buried at Beeder. After about five years of peace another expedition into Orissa occurred in 1477; but it is doubtful whether the king, though he levied tribute from the rajah, ever completely possessed the country. He reduced, however, the Rajah Nursinga, whose dominions lay on the coast, near Masulipatam, and extended probably to those of the Beejanugger kingdom: and while engaged in these operations, he marched with a light force upon Conjeveram, and despoiled the great temples there of an immense amount of jewels and gold. It was the first occasion on which the Mahomedan arms had penetrated so far to the south of India, which, as yet, belonged exclusively to the Hindoos; and the event was considered so remarkable, that to commemorate it, the king assumed the title of Gházy, or holy warrior. On this occasion, however, the king had slain a Brahmin with his own hand, and as Brahmins had been hitherto spared out of consideration for Gungoo of Dehly, the circumstance was considered by the people a dire omen for the dynasty.

Death of the queen-dowager.

Second expedition against Orissa.

Conjeveram plundered, 1477.

By the recent conquests of the king and his generals, the Bahmuny territories had become considerably extended. They now stretched from sea to sea, and had attained their greatest limits, and a new division of them took place. Many other reforms were carried out under the suggestions of Mahmood

Gáwan, who, in the capacity of chief minister, had behaved with unexampled fidelity and ability. His reforms not only extended to every department of the State, to finance, to justice, to the army, and to public education, but embraced a new assessment and, in many instances, survey of the village lands, traces of which still remain in the country. By a note drawn up by the accomplished translator of Ferishta's history, it is evident that the Bahmuny army was better paid in 1470, when the value of money was greatly higher, than the English native army in 1830, the rates of which, since then, have been considerably reduced. The cost of a regiment of cavalry of 500 men, on the Bahmuny rates of 1470, was 31,500*l.* per year, that of an English native regiment of the same description in 1830, 21,900*l.* A private soldier, furnishing his own horse and arms, then received forty rupees per month; the allowance is now only twenty. It may be inferred, therefore, from this example, that the whole of the State establishments were in a highly creditable and practical working condition; and so efficient were the checks imposed by one part of the administration upon the other, that peculation was impossible.

Policy and acts of Mahmood Gáwan, the minister of State.

It has been previously recorded, that there were two great military parties in the State—the foreigners and the Deccanies. The foreigners were Moghuls, Persians, Turks, Arabians, and the like; and these, as well from natural sympathy as from their opposition to the Deccanies, held together. The Decannies and Abyssinians were the descendants of foreigners in perhaps many degrees, mixed up with converted Hindoos. They were equally numerous with the foreigners, indeed perhaps exceeded them; but they were seldom able or trustworthy as State servants in civil affairs, though brave in battle. At the period of Mahmood Gáwan's reforms, he, Yoosuf Adil Khan, a Turk by birth, and some others, were the chiefs of the foreign party; Nizam-ool-Moolk Bheiry and others, the leaders of the Deccanies and Abyssinians. Since the period of the execution of Khwajah Jehan, who had belonged to the Deccany party, the foreigners were in the ascendant; and the admirable conduct of Mahmood Gáwan left no room for cavil or complaint. He was in the almost exclusive confidence of the king, who had repeatedly conferred the highest honours on him that could be afforded to a subject, and these, instead of engendering arrogance, had only produced in the great minister additional exertions to make himself worthy of them. The Deccany party were, however, by no means idle; and their representative, Nizam-ool-Moolk Bheiry, and his creatures, began their execrable plot against the minister by

Military parties and factions.

Conspiracy against Mahmood Gáwan.

poisoning the king's mind with covert insinuations of the minister's faithlessness in public matters, of his peculations under cloak of reform, and of his mischievous interference with ancient vested rights and privileges of the nobility and the people. As these gradually had their effect, the conspirators determined upon a bolder and final effort. Yoosuf Adil Khan, the minister's adopted son, was absent, and the minister in sole attendance on the king in camp: accordingly a letter was drawn up, purporting to be from the minister to the Rajah of Orissa, representing the general discontent against the king, and the defenceless state of the eastern frontier; and urging him to march on Beeder, where he himself would join him, depose the king, and divide the kingdom between them. The minister's seal was obtained by drugging the slave who had charge of it, and an impression attached to the blank paper on which the forged letter was written. The letter itself was declared to have been taken from a messenger who had escaped. Such was the hellish plot.

Nizam-ool-Moolk was present when the letter was delivered to the king, and pretended that it was no more than he had long expected, and given warning of. Mahmood Gáwan was then sent for. He was apprised of his danger, and many of his adherents pressed him to escape, under their escort, to Yoosuf Adil Khan; but he refused. 'Such conduct,' he said, 'would be open rebellion;' and resolute in his own innocence of any crime, he went bravely to meet the accusation. The king was already intoxicated, and on the minister's entrance into the tent, sternly demanded what should be the punishment of a disloyal person? 'Let the abandoned wretch,' said the minister, 'who practises treason against his lord meet with no mercy.' The king then produced the letter, and while the minister was denouncing it as a forgery, the king rose from his seat, and ordered his Abyssinian slave Jowhur to put the minister to death on the spot. 'The death of an old man,' said Mahmood Gáwan to the king as he passed into the harem, 'is indeed of little moment; but to your Majesty it will be the loss of your character, and the ruin of an empire.' Kneeling down, Mahmood Gáwan repeated the creed of his faith, and at one stroke his head was severed from his body. This lamentable event occurred on April 5, 1481, in the seventy-eighth year of his age: and with him departed all the cohesion and the power of the great Bahmuny kingdom. Two Persian verses curiously mark the date by computation of letters, and express the cause of his death. One, which is carved on the architrave of his tomb at Beeder, is:—'Kutl-i-na huq—the unjust execution;' the other, 'Bé goonah, Mahmood Gáwan,

Bajazet II. emperor of the Turks.

Mahmood Gáwan executed, 1481.

shood shaheed—without fault, Mahmood Gáwan became a martyr.'

Character of Mahmood Gáwan.

The character of Mahmood Gáwan stands out broadly and grandly, not only among all his contemporaries, but among all the ancient Mahomedans of India, as one unapproachably perfect and consistent. The utter absence of selfishness or of self-aggrandisement in his public conduct and policy, his perfect and unaffected devotion to his sovereign the queen, through two trying and helpless minorities, when he might, as others had done at Dehly, and as his colleagues did after him at Beeder, have created an independent kingdom for himself; his noble and judicious reforms, his skill and bravery in war, his justice and public and private benevolence, have, in the aggregate, no equals in the Mahomedan history of India. Mahmood Gáwan was descended from an ancient family in Persia, which had filled the office of vizier to the princes of Geelan. He was of royal descent, and, apprehensive of the jealousy of Shah Tahmasp, declined office, and in his forty-third year set out to travel as a merchant. In this capacity he came to Beeder, by way of Dabul, during the reign of Alla-ood-deen Bahmuny II., who persuaded him to join his service, and thenceforward he rose steadily, by the sheer force of his great abilities, to the post he occupied at his death. His personal habits, though he kept up public state as befitted him, were curiously simple. At his death his treasurer rendered to the king an account of all the minister had possessed, which consisted of the capital he had brought from Persia—about 4,000*l.*—out of the profits of which he paid his private expenses for food and clothing, which were two larees, or four shillings a day; the rest being remitted to poor relations in Persia, and to humble friends, and the remainder disbursed to the poor. Out of the public revenues of his ample estates, while he paid the public establishments attached to him, he built and endowed the magnificent college at Beeder, which was partially destroyed by an explosion of gunpowder, in the reign of Aurungzebe, and which, while he lived at the capital, was his daily resort; and the grand fortresses of Owsah, Puraindah, Sholapoor, Dharoor, and many others, attest alike his military skill and science. He slept upon a mat, and none but earthern vessels were employed for cooking his simple meals. He had collected a library of 3,000 volumes, but they belonged to the college he had founded, and those works he wished to read were borrowed as he required them. Many affecting anecdotes of him are told by the local historians, but none more characteristic of the man than the following. When he returned from his great campaign in the

His origin.

His personal habits and benevolence.

Konkan, and honours and gifts were showered upon him; and when the king paid him a memorable visit, and put his own robes upon his minister, Mahmood, when the king had left him, went to his chamber, and casting himself on the ground, wept bitterly; after which, he sent for the holy men of Beeder, and distributed what he possessed among them. When asked why he had done this, he said gravely, 'When the king honoured me with a visit, and the queen-mother called me brother, my evil passions began to prevail against my reason, and the struggle between vice and virtue was so great in my mind, that I became distressed even in the presence of his majesty. I have, therefore, parted with my wealth, the temptation to evil.' Every Friday night he went disguised through the different wards of the city distributing alms to the poor, saying, as he gave them, 'This is sent by the king;' and his private charities from his estates, and from personal savings, reached poor and distressed persons in far distant cities of Mahomedan kingdoms.

Such was the practically benevolent and simple, but noble, character of the man so basely destroyed. 'O king,' said the fearless treasurer of the minister, when rendering an account of the funds in his charge, 'may many thousands such as Mahmood Gáwan be sacrificed for thy safety; but why didst thou not regard the claims of that minister, and ascertain who was the bearer of the letter to the Rái of Orissa, that his treason might be made manifest to us and to all mankind?' Too late the king discovered the horrible deceit which had been practised on him. Two of his principal officers at once separated themselves from him, and would not return till the arrival of Yoosuf Adil Khan, who was hastily summoned to camp. A fresh distribution of estates was ordered; but on their arrival at Beeder, the recipients of these honours would not enter the city, and sullenly withdrew to their possessions. It was the beginning of the end. When the king, restless at Beeder, soon afterwards marched to Belgaum, he dispatched Yoosuf Adil Khan to defend Goa, of which the Rajah of Beejanugger strove to repossess himself; and returned to Ferozabad. But Imád-ool-Moolk and Khodawund Khan, governors of Berar, with the whole of the Berar divisions of the army, refused to accompany him, and marched to their respective capitals. Mahomed Shah remained for three months at Ferozabad, afflicted with illness, and scared by the reproaches of his own conscience, vainly endeavouring to dispel care by sensual pleasures. When he arrived at Beeder, he had somewhat recovered from his fever, when excessive drinking brought on a relapse, from which he was partially relieved by his physicians; but in their temporary absence, he drank again, and fell into convulsions, from which he could not be relieved, and died on March 24, 1482, exclaiming constantly to the last, that Mahmood Gáwan was tearing him to pieces. Mahomed Shah had reigned twenty years, and was succeeded by his son Mahmood, then twelve years of age.

Mahomed Shah dies, 1482.

Mahmood Shah II. succeeds, 1482.

CHAPTER XV.

OF THE BAHMUNY MAHOMEDAN DYNASTY OF THE DECCAN (*concluded*), A.D. 1482 TO 1526.

Nizam-ool-Moolk Bheiry, the author of the detestable plot against the late minister, was too strong to be interfered with. He was the head of the Deccany party in the State, and now became executive minister and regent at Beeder. The young king was crowned with much pomp and ceremony, but all the chief foreign officers were absent, which gave rise to many rumours, and to not a little apprehension as to their ultimate designs. Shortly afterwards, Yoosuf Adil Khan arrived at the capital with his forces, and his entry into the city at the head of a thousand foreign cavalry, in glittering armour, as described by the local historian, must have been a grand sight, and reminds the reader of the Moorish chivalry of Spain. The minister and Yoosuf Adil Khan met in an apparently friendly manner, but they were each attended by some hundreds of their chosen personal guards, and their sentiments in regard to each other were well known: nevertheless, the offices of State were distributed afresh, and with a really fair consideration for the claims of both parties. Yoosuf Adil Khan, however, would accept no office, except his military command, and remained on his guard at the capital; but so long as he lived, Nizam-ool-Moolk was never certain that the late minister's death might not be suddenly avenged, and a plot was arranged to attack the foreign troops, and put Yoosuf Adil Khan to death. It was clumsily executed. The foreigners were attacked in the city unawares, and many of them killed; but they soon rallied, and in their turn did much execution. Eventually the holy men of Beeder mediated between the parties, and Yoosuf Adil Khan retired to his estate of Beejapoor, leaving the field to his rival. He never afterwards returned to Beeder, and declared his independence at Beejapoor in 1489, as will be related hereafter.

Mahmood II. crowned, 1482.

The rival ministers.

Plot against the foreign troops.

Nizam-ool-Moolk Bheiry was himself a native of the Deccan,

the son of the Brahmin 'Putwary,' or hereditary accountant of the town of Putree; or, by other accounts, the son of a Brahmin of Beejanugger, named Timapa. He had been taken prisoner when young, and, as was the usual custom, circumcised and educated as a Mahomedan. His abilities had raised him to the post he had gained before the death of Mahmood Gáwan, and his power and native origin secured to him the leadership of the Deccany party in the State. His disposition was, however, crafty and unfaithful. The queen-dowager soon suspected him, and endeavoured to rid herself of him; but this was not effected, and for a time the minister became stronger than ever, until the king entered upon the conduct of public affairs. From that time, the minister's influence began to decline, and he seems to have contemplated the establishment of an independent kingdom, like Yoosuf Adil Khan. Leaving the king's camp, then in Telingána, Nizam-ool-Moolk returned to the capital, and sending for his son, Mullik Ahmed, distributed to him much of the royal treasures, and dispatched him to Joonair, his seat of government, intending to follow with more; but Pusund Khan, governor of Beeder, delayed his departure, on various pretences, writing the particulars of his conduct to the king. Mahmood Shah replied, 'that if he were sincere he would send the traitor's head without delay,' and set out for Beeder; but Pusund Khan was faithful; he entered the minister's palace, strangled him, and sent his head to the king. Thus was the death of the great minister Mahmood Gáwan avenged, but too late to save the kingdom. Nizam-ool-Moolk's son, Mullik Ahmed, declared his independence on receipt of the news of his father's execution, and maintained it, as will be hereafter shown.

Origin and rise of Nizam-ool-Moolk Bheiry.

He meditates independence.

Is put to death.

His son declares his independence.

The king's own conduct was little suited to the emergency of the situation. Instead of proceeding in person against his rebellious officers, or checking the dissensions of his foreign and Deccany troops—on one occasion of which he narrowly escaped with his life—he gave himself up to pleasure. 'He totally neglected,' quaintly writes the historian, 'the affairs of his government, leaving them entirely to the direction of his favourites. Musicians and dancers flocked to his court from Lahore, Dehly, Persia, and Khorassán, as also story-tellers, reciters of the Shahnama, and other agents of pleasure. The people, following the example of their king, attended to nothing but dissipation: reverend sages pawned their very garments at the wine-cellars, and holy teachers, quitting their colleges, retired to taverns, and presided over the wine-flask.' Imád-ool-Moolk, the governor of Berar, who had been virtually

The king's imbecile conduct.

independent since he withdrew from Mahomed Shah at Ferozabad, as related in the preceding chapter, had already become king. The Bahmuny dominions had now lost their finest and most valuable provinces on the north, west, and south-west: and the districts round the capital, with Telingána, and the northern Circars, then under the government of Kootub-ool-Moolk, were all that remained. At the capital, Kassim Bereed, a Turk of great ability and craft, was minister, and the king became little more than a cipher in his hands. In the year 1493, however, on the complaint of the King of Guzerat, he entered on a campaign against Bahadur Khan Geelany, who was partially independent, at Goa, and in the sequel Bahadur Khan was killed in action. During this spirited campaign, the king displayed more energy than he had been believed capable of; but it did not last, and after betrothing his son to the daughter of Yoosuf Adil Shah, at Goolburgah, in 1497, he returned to Beeder. Here, in 1504, died Kassim Bereed, the minister, who was succeeded by his son Ameer, and henceforward the king's life was passed in entire dependence. Kootub-ool-Moolk, governor of Telingána, declared his independence in 1512, and all that remained to Beeder were the provinces immediately adjoining the capital. With the royal treasures, however, Ameer Bereed raised troops and endeavoured to win back portions of the old dominions, and in 1514 had invaded Beejapoor, taking the king with him, who was made prisoner in a general action near that city, when Ameer Bereed was defeated by Ismail Adil Shah, the successor of Yoosuf. The Beejapore king sent Mahmood Shah back to Beeder, under an honorary escort of his own cavalry, and for a time the king enjoyed comparative liberty; but shortly afterwards the Beejapoor troops withdrew, and the minister returning, resumed his power. Weary of this humiliation, the king, in 1514, escaped to Imád Shah, king of Berar, who sent an army with him to reinstate him at Beeder; but the treatment he received from Imád Shah appears to have been worse than that of Ameer Bereed, and as the hostile forces approached each other, in a general action, the king, leaving the army of Imád Shah, galloped across the field to Ameer Bereed, and was never afterwards allowed to escape. He was used as a pageant king for some years afterwards, whenever Ameer Bereed took the field; but had no power whatever, and died on October 21, 1518, after a reign of thirty-seven years, passed in constant vicissitudes. With him the dynasty of the Bahmuny kings

Imád-ool-Moolk becomes king of Berar.

Kassim Bereed minister.

Campaign against Goa.

Kassim Bereed dies.

Philip I. king of Spain.

Kootub-ool-Moolk becomes king of Golcondah.

The king's humiliation and subjection.

Mahmood Shah dies, 1518.

may be said to have virtually closed: but Ameer Bereed found a king necessary to his political existence. The Bahmuny family were still respected in their fall by their former vassals, and could not be interfered with, whereas had the minister declared independence, he could not have maintained it. The Prince Ahmed, eldest son of the deceased king, was therefore placed on the throne, as Ahmed Shah Bahmuny II., and died in 1520. He was replaced by Alla-ood-deen Shah Bahmuny II., the second son of Mahmood Shah, in the same year, who was a person of steady character and some determination, and formed a plan for arresting Ameer Bereed, and ridding himself of him. This plot was, however, accidentally discovered, and the king deposed, after a nominal reign of two years, and shortly afterwards put to death. He was succeeded by Wully Oolla, the third son of King Mahmood, who, like his brother Alla-ood-deen, tried to liberate himself, and was poisoned in order to make way for the marriage of Ameer Bereed to his queen, of whom the minister had become enamoured, in the year 1524. He was again succeeded by Kulleem Oolla, the son of Ahmed Shah, by the daughter of Yoosuf Adil Shah of Beejapoor. The king was, however, kept in close confinement; but in 1526 he contrived to send one of his companions with a petition to the Emperor Babur, who, however, was in no condition to interfere, and he afterwards escaped to his uncle, Ismail Adil Shah, and resided for a time at Beejapoor. Nothing, however, being done on his behalf, he proceeded to the court of Ahmednugger, where he resided till his death, and the Bahmuny dynasty ended with him: it had reigned, for the most part, in great glory and power, from 1347 to 1526, or 179 years. From it had sprung five separate independent kingdoms: Imád Shahy, or kings of Berar; Nizam Shahy, or kings of Ahmednugger; Adil Shahy, or kings of Beejapoor; Kootub Shahy, or kings of Golcondah, and Bereed Shahy; for Ameer Bereed assumed the style and title of king after the departure of Kulleem Oolla Shah Bahmuny. The histories of these States must be sketched separately, until they are connected with the period already referred to, namely, 1526.

Leo X. pope.

Ahmed Shah II. succeeds, 1518.

Dies, 1520.

Alla-ood-deen Shah II. succeeds, 1520.

Deposed, 1522: and put to death.

Wully Oolla Shah succeeds, 1522.

Poisoned, 1524.

Kulleem Oolla Shah succeeds, 1524.

Sweden and Denmark became Protestant.

On reviewing the events of the dynasty of the Bahmuny kings of the Deccan, and notwithstanding the early cruelties to the Hindoo inhabitants of Beejanugger, in the reign of Mahomed Shah I., it is evident that they were, on the whole, considerate to their Hindoo subjects, and governed them with moderation. The reign of Mahmood Shah I. was one of entire peace, and evidently one of much progress and improve-

Review of the character of the Bahmuny dynasty.

ment in civil administration; while, throughout the whole period of 179 years, foreign and domestic trade had flourished. The aim of the Mahomedan historians of the Deccan was more directed to the record of war, and of political events and intrigues, than of the transactions of peaceful years; but, notwithstanding this, there are occasional pleasant glimpses of quiet times, and their beneficial effects, which are not to be found in the records of Dehly. Of the details of the government of the country little is apparent. It does not appear that the Hindoos were employed in public affairs; but it is evident that their ancient system of corporate village government and district administration was not interfered with, and became strengthened by use. Up to the regency of Mahmood Gáwan, the revenue had been probably raised in kind, on a proportion of the crops; but his system evolved a commutation for money payment upon the value of the land, much on the principle of that afterwards perfected by the Emperor Akbar, and the great Ahmednugger minister, Mullik Umber. The country was probably as well cultivated and populated as it is at present,

Description of the Deccan by Athanasius Nitikin, 1470.

and Athanasius Nitikin, a Russian Armenian, who, in 1470, visited Beeder as a merchant, gives in his diary an interesting description of the country and its capital. There were villages at every cóss, or two miles, about the present complement; the land was laid out in fields, and the ground well tilled; the roads were well guarded, and travelling secure. Beeder is described as a noble city, with great salubrity of climate, and the King Mahmood Shah II. as a little man, twenty years old, with an army of 300,000 men, well equipped. Artillery is not mentioned; but there were many elephants, to the trunks of which scythes were attached in action, and they were clad in bright steel armour.

Architecture of the period.

The architecture of the Bahmuny dynasty is not remarkable. The royal mausoleums at Goolburgah are heavy gloomy buildings, with domes, roughly built and finished; but some of the stone terraces around them show specimens of good arabesque carving. The material, basaltic trap, did not, perhaps, invite more finished works. If, however, the mosque in the interior of the fort at Goolburgah, begun by Feroze Shah, had ever been completed, it would have been one of the grandest buildings in India. The city of Goolburgah is still a con-

City of Goolburgah.

siderable town, and the head of a province of H.H. the Nizam's dominions, carrying on a large trade in cotton and oilseeds with Sholapoor and Bombay. The fort is still perfect, but the rich palaces of Feroze Shah are masses of undistinguishable ruins. Without, the tombs of the early Bahmuny kings form noble groups of buildings; and deserted mosques and tombs of all descriptions, with ruins of pavilions and garden-houses, mark the once great extent of the royal city. Goolburgah is situated upon the railway from Sholapoor to Raichore, and is one of the principal stations on the line; and a line in extension will shortly connect it with Hyderabad. Could a greater contrast between India in the 15th and 19th centuries be imagined? When the court removed to Beeder it is evident that the style of architecture was much improved. The royal palaces were noble and spacious buildings, containing lofty halls and apartments, and the large oriel windows and arches, then filled up by carved woodwork, admitted air and light freely. The noble college of Mahmood Gáwan, in the city of Beeder, was perhaps the grandest completed work of the period. It consisted of a spacious square, with arches all round it, of two storeys, divided into convenient rooms. The minarets at each corner of the front were upwards of a hundred feet high, and, as also the front itself, covered with enamel tiles, on which were flowers on blue, yellow, and red grounds; and sentences of the Korán in large Kufic letters; the effect of which was at once chaste and superb. The fortresses built by the Bahmuny kings are, however, perhaps their greatest and most indestructible monuments, and far exceed any of the same period in Europe. They are of all kinds, both on the plains and on the crests of mountains, from baronial castles to forts of the grandest dimensions. Gawilgurh and Narnalla in Berar, especially the latter, are choice specimens of grandeur of design of mountain fortresses, and tasteful and munificent execution. At Narnalla, the first gateway near the crest of the mountain is covered with stone carving, in the most elegant designs, as perfect now as, when it was built, 450 years ago. In the plains, Puraindah, Kulliany, Sholapoor, Owsah, Nuldroog, Dharoor, Mahore, Kandhar, Yatgeer, Shahpoor, Oodgeer, and many others, are equally remarkable and beautiful; and of all, Puraindah and Owsah are the most perfect, according to military science. They consist of a wide deep ditch, and counterscarp with a covered way, and glacis rising to the height of the *faussebraye*. The gates were defended by traverses and redoubts; and the rampart and *faussebraye* are of cut stone, with round bastions fitted for the heavy guns of the period; which, many of them of immense size, and used for throwing stone shot, were composed of bars of iron welded together.

College at Beeder.

The Bahmuny fortresses.

To this dynasty, the origin of the present Mahomedan population of the Deccan in the rural districts is still traceable. The foreign troops, that is the Persians, Tartars, Moghuls, and Arabs, intermarried with the women of the country, or took them, forcibly at first, as slaves and concubines, and

Warlike classes and their descendants.

from them descended the Deccanies or mixed breeds, also soldiers, but counted of lower estimation, who have gradually merged into the present agricultural classes, and in some places still preserve their ancient haughty distinction of Alla-ood-Moolks, Bhylemees, Kálachuttrees, and other designations derived from their original leaders. Their warlike spirit, however, has not remained, and in this respect they are perhaps inferior to their fellow-farmers and labourers, the Mahrattas. In respect to education, the Bahmuny kings were liberal for their time. Mosques, often perhaps small and rude, were built in all the principal villages and market-towns, and well endowed as part of the existing village system. To each a moolla was appointed, who acted as schoolmaster and priest, while kazies and higher officers of civil law superintended the whole; colleges existed at the chief cities, all richly endowed. Thus means of education were free to all who chose to learn Persian or Arabic; and in most of the Deccan villages the endowments still exist. The Hindoos, it may be presumed, were neither assisted nor interfered with, and their literature was confined to the Sanskrit language, and to its professors the Brahmins. In the Telingá country, the example of the ancient Hindoo rulers in regard to irrigation works was followed in a liberal and spirited manner by the Mahomedans, and many of the noblest lake reservoirs now existing were built by them. On all these points, and in a general amelioration of manners, there is no question that the Mahomedan occupation of the Deccan during the existence of the great Bahmuny dynasty had not been barren of good effects.

Education.

Works of irrigation.

CHAPTER XVI.

OF THE SOUTHERN HINDOO STATES, SUBSEQUENT TO THE FIRST MAHOMEDAN INVASION—THE DYNASTY OF VIJYANUGGER OR BEEJANUGGER, A.D. 1119 TO 1524.

In Chapters XIV. and XV., Book I., the histories of several of the southern mediæval Hindoo dynasties have been sketched; but in them, that of Beejanugger could have no place, for it was not in existence at the period of the dissolution of the Chalúkya dynasty of Kulyan, and the extension of their dominions by the Yádávás of Déogurh. The family of Beejanugger claimed a very ancient origin, and a detail obtained by Mr. Edward Ravenshaw, of the Bengal Civil Service, from the Rajah of Anagoondy, its lineal descendant and present

Great antiquity of the Beejanugger family.

representative, and published in the 'Asiatic Researches,' vol. xx., gives a list of eighty-five princes from Pandoo, the original founder, to Yésha Nandi, whose fourteen sons divided his dominions, and being conquered by another power, Nandá Maharaja, one of them, fled to Wurungul, in Telingána, and established a dynasty there. It would appear, therefore, that he belonged to the Andhra race. Nandá died in A.D. 1076; and the succession proceeds to Vijála Raya, of Kulyan, in A.D. 1119, who, it will be remembered, had usurped the throne; but his brother Vijya Raya established himself about the same period at Vijyanugger, which he named after himself, and became the founder of a new dynasty.

Era of Nandá.

Henry IV. emperor, deposed.

Now, comparing the foregoing with the history of Kulyan, as shown by its inscriptions (vide Chapter XV., Book I.), some confusion is apparent. Vijála, who occupied the throne of Kulyan in 1162 A.D., was a Kála Bhúrya, and a feudal noble of the Kulyan kingdom; and it is quite possible that his brother or descendant Vijya, in the troublous times which succeeded the deposition of the Chalúkyas, may have established a new dynasty at Beejanugger, and incorporated with it the former Kála Bhúrya possessions, which lay directly west of that city. Vijya's line, however, of five successions, ended with Bhoop Raya, who having no male issue, adopted Bukka Rajah, son of the Rajah of Kumpila, or Kumply, near Vijyanugger, from whence an unbroken line descended.

By another account, however, Bukka and Hárihárá alone are stated to be the founders of the Beejanugger dynasty, and to have been fugitives from Wurungul, after its first conquest by the Mahomedans in 1322. The probability of the first account is questionable, from the fact that Beejanugger lay in the route of Mullik Kafoor, when he traversed the country from Déogurh or Dowlatabad to the sea, and when Dwára Sumoodra fell, would not have been overlooked; but, on the other hand, the sudden growth of the dynasty, if only established in 1322, to a power which could dispute the empire of the south of India with the Mahomedans after the death of Mahomed Toghluk, is hardly conceivable. A third hypothesis is founded upon the record of the great Brahmin missionary, Máhádéva Achárya, who states that he was the minister for a time of Sangama, a prince whose dominions extended to the southern, western, and eastern seas—that is, embraced the whole of the southern peninsula—and that Bukka and Hárihárá were his sons, and the inscriptions of these princes, given in Vol. IX of the 'Asiatic Researches,' confirm this account.

Bukka and Harihará.

The historian Ferishta, too, seems to have been at much pains to make out the origin of the remarkable family of Beejanugger. His statement is, that in 1344 Krishna Náik, son of the Rajah of Wurungul, had fled to Bellál Déo, rajah of the Carnatic, and that they entered into a contract to oppose the Mahomedans. To this end, a stronghold was established on the frontier, and given to his son Beeja, or Vijya, after whom it was named Beejanugger or Vijyanugger, and the Mahomedan posts, after the death of Mahomed Toghluk, were expelled from their country.

Ferishta's accounts of the family.

Whatever, therefore, be their exact origin, whether as an independent family, an offshoot from the Kála Bhúryas, from Wurungul, or from the Bellál dynasty of Dwára Sumoodra, there is no question that the kingdom of Beejanugger had risen to a high condition of power and prosperity at the period of the declaration of independence by Zuffur Khan in 1347. Assuming the line of the Tumboodra river to its junction with the Krishna, and afterwards the Krishna to the sea, as its northern boundary, it possessed the whole of the present Southern Mahratta country; and Mysore, as far as the boundary of the Chôla dominions. It had extinguished, or at least subdued, the Bellál dynasty of Dwára Sumoodra and Tonoor, and held possession of the sea-coast from Goa to Calicut. The extent and consolidation of this dominion may favour the hypothesis that the Beejanugger State could not have attained its dimensions in the short period between 1294 and 1347, and that it must have grown out of the ruins of former dynasties. At the same time it must be considered that, under the rapid effects of Indian revolutions, much might have been accomplished by active and spirited princes in fifty, or even in twenty-five years, in the national consolidation of the Hindoo power of the south, which had become so seriously threatened. Of the founders of the dynasty, Bukka reigned from A.D. 1334 to 1367; Hárihárá from 1367 to 1391. The city which had been founded was, as to situation, one of the most remarkable in India. An irregular plain on the right bank of the Tumboodra, near the sacred ground of Kishkinda, celebrated in the Ramáyana, was sufficient, but no more, for its enceinte. On the east and west it was bounded by rocky granite hills, through which were a few rugged passes. On the south the spurs of the lofty range of Ramanmullay, descended into it; on the north, the river Tumboodra, in a line of extremely deep pools and violent rapids, formed an almost impassable boundary; and immediately beyond, and rising out of its bed, a range of still more rugged and impassable granite hills, which has only one outlet, constituted an outer line of

Probable boundaries of the kingdom, in 1347.

Bukka reigned, 1334-67.

Hárihára, 1367-91.

Manuel emperor of the East.

Description of Beejanugger.

fortification, as it were, of great strength; and when the passes and hills had been fortified by bastions and curtains, the whole was rendered almost impregnable. The enceinte of the city comprised about ten square miles, and the ruins which everywhere fill it now, attest the great amount of its population, while the temples, monasteries, and receiving-houses for pilgrims to Kishkinda, are some of the finest in Southern India, many of them still in perfect preservation. Whether, therefore, from the sequestered situation of the city, the wild strange beauty of the river scenery, the temples and ruins of palaces, or its historical interest, there are few places in India more worthy of the attention of the traveller than Beejanugger.

It is not easy to determine what prince reigned in Beejanugger at the period of the accession of Mahomed Shah to the throne of Goolburgah, as none of the genealogical lists agree one with one another. The most probable is Déva or Déo Rái, who is termed Krishn Rái by Ferishta. It would be superfluous here to recapitulate the events of the war which ensued upon the wanton insult of Mahomed Shah Bahmuny, king of Goolburgah, or those of the war with Mahomed's successor, Mujahid Shah, which have been adverted to in Chapter XI. of this book. Unfortunately Beejanugger had no Hindoo historian, and had it not been for the Mahomedan records, this great Hindoo dynasty, like others, would have left no memorials except inscriptions. It is therefore impossible to follow the detail of its internal condition or successive conquests during the periods in which it was not engaged with the Mahomedans; but there is no question that the extent of its dominions, as also its wealth, far exceeded those of the Mahomedans, who, as Ferishta observes, only maintained their superiority by their valour.

Whether the third war with the Mahomedans occurred from the act of the same Déo Rái already mentioned or another, it is very difficult to determine; but the Déo Rái who reigned from 1391 to 1414, according to Mr. Ravenshaw's list, was on this occasion the aggressor, and invaded the Raichore Dooáb with 30,000 horse and a vast number of foot. Feroze Shah Bahmuny was now king of Goolburgah, who met the Hindoos on the bank of the Krishna river, and procured the assassination of the rajah's son by a fanatic, who disguised himself as a player, and performed in the rajah's presence. This tragical event dismayed Déo Rái, and he fled to his capital followed by Feroze Shah, who laid waste the country south-west of Beejanugger, occupied it in force, and was only stayed from further proceedings by the payment of eleven lacs of hoons—about half a million sterling. It might be supposed that so severe a lesson would have restrained the Hindoo prince from further aggressions, but this was not the case. In 1406 he heard of a very beautiful girl, the daughter of a goldsmith of Moodgul, then held by the Mahomedans, and sent a large body of cavalry to carry her off. She had, however, escaped, and the Beejanugger horse, in revenge, ravaged the country. Feroze Shah Bahmuny immediately resented the insult, and as has been related in the account of his reign, Chapter XII., Book III., obliged the rajah, not only to give him his daughter in marriage, but to cede Bunkapoor and other districts to the west as her dowry, and to give also ten lacs of hoons, 450,000*l.*, five *muns* (120lbs. weight) of pearls, 50 elephants, and 2,000 slaves, and thus a third peace was concluded.

Vijya Rái, 1414.

Council of Constance.

After the accession of Ahmed Shah Wully Bahmuny I., war again broke out between Goolburgah and Beejapoor. Déo Rái, according to Mr. Ravenshaw's list, had been succeeded by Vijya Rái, in 1414, who was besieged in his capital, but finding resistance fruitless, paid the arrear of tribute, and sent his son to escort the Mahomedan king to the frontier. In 1435, however, a fresh arrear of five years' tribute had occurred, and Mahomed Khan, the brother of Alla-ood-deen Bahmuny II., was sent to enforce payment. Vijya Rái had reigned till 1424, and Pandára Déo Rái had succeeded him. The campaign had a strange termination in the rebellion of the Prince Mahomed Khan, already related in Chapter XII., Book III., but the event had excited in the mind of Pandára Déo Rái a desire to conquer the whole of the Bahmuny kingdom. He admitted Mahomedans into his army, allotted to them a quarter of the city, and even built a mosque for their use, allowing them free practice for the rites of their religion. These haughty Moslem warriors would not salute an infidel prince, even on his throne, and made their salutations to a copy of the Korán placed before him, and it is very doubtful whether they were ever perfectly faithful. Having made his preparations, the Hindoo prince, in 1443, crossed the Tumboodra, and overran the country as far as Sugger and Beejapoor.

Vijya Rái dies, 1424.

Pandára Déo Rái succeeds, 1424.

It is an interesting fact that this war, and the events that followed it, are confirmed by the journal of Abd-el-Ruzzak, an ambassador to India from the King of Khorassán in 1442–3, which has been translated for the Hakluyt Society by Mr. W. Major, and published under the title of 'India in the Fifteenth Century.' It is an extremely interesting record of events at Beejanugger, and full of quaint descriptions of the city, and of the ceremonies performed at the great Hindoo festivals. Three great battles were fought on the plain between Moodgul and the Tumboodra, in the course of this war, with no decisive result; but two of the Mahomedan officers having been taken prisoners, the king wrote to the rajah that he valued their lives at 100,000 Hindoos each—a grim but significant threat which brought him to terms. The arrears of tribute were paid, and peace ensued, which from 1442-3 up to 1489, a period of forty-six years, was not disturbed on either side. There are, however, no records of the local events of the Beejanugger kingdom during this long period, except that of its various successors. Pandára Déo Rái died in 1450, and was succeeded by Ramchunder Rái, who died in 1473, and was succeeded by Narsinha Rajah, who died in 1490. The last prince is authenticated by his inscriptions, and left three sons, Achootya, Suda Seeva, and Trimala. The Bahmuny Mahomedan monarchy had now broken up, and the State of Beejapoor was declared independent by Yoosuf Adil Shah in 1489. Immediately after that event, Kassim Bereed, minister of Mahmood Shah Bahmuny, incited the Rajah of Beejanugger to attack Yoosuf Adil Shah, promising him Beejapoor if he could take it. The danger to Yoosuf Adil Shah was imminent: but local quarrels between the rajah and his minister delayed the projects for some time, and when the Beejanugger army advanced in 1493, it was defeated with immense slaughter by the Beejapoor monarch, and the rajah died of wounds received in the action. Between 1493 and 1524 some confusion exists as to the successions, and by Ferishta's account, it would appear that there had been several local revolutions in this period. In 1524, however, Krishn Rái Maharaya was the reigning sovereign, and it is for many reasons doubtful whether he belonged to the original Beejanugger family, or was the illegitimate son of Rajah Narsinha of Telingána, who had usurped the throne. In either case, he proved to be a man of vigour and ability. He was the only ruler of Beejanugger who ever competed evenly with the Mahomedans in the field; he carried his arms into Orissa, and married the daughter of its Hindoo king; and it was under him that the kingdom attained its greatest eminence and extent. During the long peace with the Mahomedans, its conquests had progressed; and at the period under notice, A.D. 1524, the localities recorded in inscriptions as being subject to the kingdom are as follows: Kanchy and Chôldesh, the country of the Chôlas; Pandoodesh or Madura, the original dynasties of both kingdoms having long since entirely disappeared; the whole of Mysore and the country eastwards to the sea; the midland dominions of the ancient State of Chéra, which had been conquered by the Belláls, and the Raichore Dooáb, and other

Pandára Déo Rái dies, 1450.

Ramchunder Rái, 1450.

Dies, 1473.

Narsinha succeeds, 1473.

Dies, 1490.

Krishn Rái, 1524.

western provinces. At this stage of its history, and when, in its modern condition, it had existed from 1322 to 1524, or 202 years the record of Beejapoor is, for the present, discontinued, and will be resumed and concluded in connection with the details of the Adil Shahy dynasty of Beejapoor.

CHAPTER XVII.

OF THE IMÁD SHAHY DYNASTY OF BERAR, A.D. 1484 TO 1527.

FUTTEH OOLLA IMÁD SHAH was the first of the great military commanders of the Bahmuny kings to declare his independence. He was a native of the Carnatic, was originally a Hindoo, and having been taken prisoner in one of the wars with Beejanugger, was brought up as a Mahomedan by Khan Jehán, governor and viceroy of Berar, in whose service, and afterwards in that of Mahmood Shah of Beeder, he much distinguished himself. At the recommendation of Mahmood Gáwan, he received the title of Imád-ool-Moolk, and succeeded his patron as viceroy of Berar. In 1482 he was summoned with his forces to join King Mahmood in his campaign against Bahadur Khan Geelany; but he obeyed sullenly, and at the close of the field service, when the king remained at Ferozabad, proceeded direct to Berar, and declared his independence. This event occurred in 1484, and he soon after died, and was succeeded by his eldest son, Alla-ood-deen.

Pope Innocent VIII., 1484.

Origin of Futteh Oolla Imád Shah.

Futteh Oolla Imád Shah becomes king, 1484.

Dies, 1484.

Alla-ood-deen continued the dynastic title of Imád chosen by his father, and was crowned king at Gawilgurh, then the capital of Berar, where he continued to reside. Gawilgurh is a noble mountain, rising 2,400 feet above the valley of Berar; and projecting from the Sátpoora range, to which it is joined by a narrow neck, or isthmus, and from its rugged and precipitous sides a natural stronghold almost impregnable. The summit was an extensive undulating area, then closely covered with dwellings, which extended to another elevation to the north, communicating with the level tableland of the range. Gawil was a grand and most picturesque position; and was fortified with great care by a wall and bastions all round the crest of the exterior precipice. A mosque, and part of the king's palace, are all that remain of the fort buildings; and the dynasty was probably never rich enough

Alla-ood-deen Imád Shah succeeds, 1484.

Description of Gawilgurh.

to indulge in architectural works of any magnitude. The most perfect of them is a pavilion in a small artificial lake, near Ellichpoor, called the Houz Kutora, which is a perfect specimen of the florid Saracenic style.

No attempts had been made by the Bahmuny king or his ministers to reclaim Berar, and Alla-ood-deen Shah reigned in peace. In 1514 Mahmood Shah Bahmuny escaped from Beeder, and threw himself on his protection; and he marched from Berar with a large army to reinstate him. Mahmood Shah, however, had not relished the treatment he had met with; and, on the field of battle, left the Berar king and rejoined his minister, Ameer Bereed. When his father, Futteh Oolla, separated himself from King Mahmood Bahmuny, Khodawund Khan, governor of Mahore and Ramgeer, had followed his example, and become independent. In 1516 Ameer Bereed marched against Mahore, and took it by storm, when Khodawund Khan was killed. This act was resented by Alla-ood-deen Shah, who marched to the relief of Mahore; and fearing the result of a war, Ameer Bereed retreated, leaving the sons of Khodawund Khan in possession. Alla-ood-deen, however, displaced them, and retained the forts himself, in virtue of the general treaty of partition entered into with Ameer Bereed. The young men took refuge with the King of Ahmednugger, and a war ensued, which continued for some time; but in the end, the King of Ahmednugger captured and retained both Mahore and Ramgeer. The ill-will between the States continuing, Alla-ood-deen, and his ally the King of Khandésh, attacked the King of Ahmednugger in 1527; but they fared worse than on the former occasion, losing much of their dominions. In his extremity, Alla-ood-deen applied for help to the King of Guzerat, who, with a view of taking advantage of these quarrels, marched into the Deccan, and soon displayed his real intentions; and as the only means of preserving what remained of his dominions, Alla-ood-deen did homage to the Guzerat king, and held Berar nominally in his name. Soon after this, though the date is not recorded by the Mahomedan historian, Alla-ood-deen Imád Shah died, and was succeeded by his eldest son, Duria Imád Shah, who enjoyed an entirely peaceful reign; but its duration is not recorded. He was succeeded by his son, Boorhan Imád Shah, an infant: and during the period of regency, Berar was annexed by the King of Ahmednugger to his dominions, as will appear in the history of that State.

Effort to replace Mahmood Shah at Beeder.

Ameer Bereed takes Mahore.

Its recapture by King Alla-ood-deen.

War with Ahmednugger.

Interference of the King of Guzerat.

Alla-ood-deen Imád Shah dies.

Duria Imád Shah succeeds.

CHAPTER XVIII.

OF THE ADIL SHAHY DYNASTY OF BEEJAPOOR, A.D. 1489 TO 1510.

Origin of Yoosuf Adil Shah.

YOOSUF ADIL KHAN, the founder of this noble dynasty, was the son, as generally believed, of Agha Moorád, or Amurath, sooltan of the Turks, who died in 1451. On the accession of his eldest son, Mahomed, an order was issued for all other male children of the late sooltan to be destroyed; but his mother, with extraordinary presence of mind, saved her son Yoosuf, and made him over to the charge of Khwajah Imád-ood-deen, a merchant of Sava, in Persia, with whom she was acquainted. To represent her son, the queen substituted a Circassian slave, who was strangled, and the real Yoosuf conveyed safely to Persia, where he was brought up. The sooltana subsequently maintained communications with her son; and sent to him his nurse, with her son Ghuzunfer Beg, and her daughter Dilshád Agha, who accompanied Yoosuf Adil Khan to India. The reason of his selecting India is attributed to a dream, in which it was revealed to him that he should attain royalty; but it is equally possible that Persia was insecure, and India a more noble field for exertion. Yoosuf, therefore, embarked at Shiraz, and reached Dabul, in the Konkan, in 1459. He was then seventeen years old, and of a handsome and engaging presence; and becoming acquainted with a Georgian merchant, was taken by him to Beeder, and sold as a Georgian slave to Khwajah Mahmood Gáwan, the minister, for the royal body-guard. He did not divulge his real rank, and probably permitted his own sale, both as a means of introduction to court, and as the best means of cutting off all trace of his position. From the rank of a private soldier, Yoosuf gradually rose to the command of the body-guard, and to be master of the horse; but becoming attached to Nizam-ool-Moolk Toork, who procured for him the title of Adil Khan, he accompanied that nobleman to Berar, on the campaign against Kéhrla, and behaved with much distinguished bravery in the storm of the fort. His friend, Nizam-ool-Moolk, having been killed on that occasion, Yoosuf Adil Khan succeeded to the command of his forces, with which he returned to Beeder. By his ability in civil government, and bravery in the field, Yoosuf Adil Khan rose gradually to the highest grades of rank and

He proceeds to India.

and is sold to Mahmood Gáwan, minister of Beeder.

His rise in the royal army.

employment. Mahmood Gáwan loved him, and adopted him as a son; and at his death, Yoosuf Adil Khan was looked up to as the leader of the foreign party in the State. The commands and estates of the late minister were bestowed upon him, and it has been already detailed in Chapter XIV. of this Book, how he withdrew from Beeder to Beejapoor, and did not return to the capital. In 1489 he declared his independence, and was crowned at Beejapoor, the capital of his dynasty—destined to become one of the largest and most magnificent cities of India, or indeed of Asia—under the title of Abool Mozuffer, Yoosuf Adil Shah.

Withdraws from Beeder.

Declares independence.

Beejapoor was an ancient Hindoo city: and a Hindoo building in the fort bears an inscription of the Chalúkya dynasty, as a college, with a large endowment. It was probably a considerable provincial town on the accession of the Bahmuny king, Alla-ood-deen Hussun; for it became the the seat of the provincial government of the western provinces of the Bahmuny dominions. Beejapoor stands nearly on the crest of one of the great trap waves of the Deccan, the watershed of the Deccan and Carnatic, at a considerable elevation, perhaps 2,000 feet, above the sea; but there is nothing picturesque in its situation for around it are undulating downs, and the country for the most part, though fertile, is stony and uninviting. To the east, however, where the trap formation breaks into the granitic plains of the Carnatic, lies the broad valley of the Dône river, a region of unsurpassed productiveness of grain. 'If the crop on Dône ripens, who can eat it? if it fail, who can eat?' is an old Mahratta proverb, expressive of its value. From this tract, and the wide range of Shorapoor, the Raichore Doоáb and Dharwar, supplies of grain for a large city or army were unfailing; and in these respects, and its healthy climate, the situation of Beejapoor was excellent; but the dominions of Yoosuf Adil Shah were by no means extensive, the maintenance of a large army as yet was impossible, and his enemy, Kassim Bereed, was not idle in stirring up intrigues against him. Kassim Bereed's plan was a subtle one. He incited Timraj, the regent of Beejanugger, by a promise of the Raichore Dooáb, to attack Beejapoor on the south-west; he made profuse promises to Mullik Bheiry, king of Ahmednugger, for co-operation on the north; he requested Bahadur Geelany to act on the west; while he himself, with the whole of the Beeder army, should join from the east. To oppose this immense combination against him, Yoosuf Adil Shah had only 8,000 cavalry and 200 elephants. He could not pretend to oppose Timraj, and made peace with him. He then fell upon Bahadur Geelany, and defeated him, forcing him back

Description of Beejapoor.

Intrigues of Kassim Bereed.

into his own territory with heavy loss. He then turned northward, met the combined armies of Beeder and Ahmednugger near Nuldroog, and in the partial action which ensued, Kassim Bereed fled to Beeder, leaving his ally to extricate himself as best he could; when the King of Ahmednugger, having no desire for a war on his own account, made peace and departed homewards. The confederacy was thus broken up; but the Beejanugger regent, Timraj, had been excited by the promise of the Raichore Dooáb, and determining to wrest it from Yoosuf Adil Shah, advanced with a large army for the purpose. The king proceeded to meet him; but in the first partial encounter, his troops were broken; then, hearing that the Hindoos had dispersed to plunder, he fell upon them with his reserve, with such fury, that the whole Hindoo army broke and fled to Beejanugger, leaving their camp to be plundered leisurely by the Mahomedans. The booty obtained was enormous. Sixty lacs of gold hoons were found in the treasury—about 2,500,000*l.* sterling—with many valuable jewels; and 200 elephants were captured. This remarkable action was fought in April 1493. The consequences of it were serious to the Beejanugger State, for its young rajah died of wounds received in the action, and the long peace which had subsisted between the Hindoos and Mahomedans, since the treaty of Ahmed Shah Wully Bahmuny, in 1425, or for nearly seventy years, was now broken.

The king defeats the confederates.

War with Beejanugger.

The Hindoos are defeated.

Maximilian I. emperor of Germany.

In 1495 Dustoor Deenar, an Abyssinian eunuch who held the government of Goolburgah, under Beeder, determined to declare his independence, and would have succeeded, but for the assistance given to King Mahmood by Yoosuf Adil Shah. In the previous year he had co-operated in the reduction of Bahadur Geelany, and he now rendered an equally efficient service to his former sovereign. It seems almost unaccountable how, in the course of a short period, the authorities of the Deccan could, as it were, suddenly change sides, and forget, even for a time, mutual rivalries and animosities. On this occasion, Dustoor Deenar's pretensions were supported by the King of Ahmednugger; and Kassim Bereed, in his emergency, sought the aid of Yoosuf Adil Shah, the man whom he had so recently endeavoured to destroy. It was given cheerfully, though not perhaps without a political purpose; the eunuch was defeated and humbled, but restored to his office; and Goolburgah was fixed upon as the place to celebrate the marriage of the Beejapoor princess to Ahmed Shah, son of Mahmood Shah, in fulfilment of their former betrothal. On this occasion, Yoosuf Adil Shah proposed to the king the dismissal

The king assists Beeder against Dustoor Deenar.

of Kassim Bereed from office, on condition that he himself should receive the districts held by Dustoor Deenar; and the king consenting, the orders were made out. Kassim Bereed resisted, as might have been—probably was—expected; and was defeated near Allund. There were other parties, however, who were dissatisfied by the arrangement. The Kings of Ahmednugger and Berar put in claims for other portions of territory, in order to create a balance of power; and after a long series of negotiations, a division was made, with which all appeared satisfied for the present, except Dustoor Deenar, who had been altogether thrown out. He had amassed much treasure, and was the leader of the Abyssinians, who supported him; and with them, and other troops, he took the field. Yoosuf Adil Shah offered honourable terms to him, and these being rejected, the parties met, and a severe general action was fought with great bravery on both sides. Dustoor Deenar was slain in the battle, and the King of Beejapoor suffered a severe loss in the death of his foster-brother, Ghuzunfer Beg, from the effects of wounds received in the last desperate charge which had decided the action.

Kassim Bereed defeated.

Dustoor Deenar slain in battle.

In 1502 Yoosuf Adil Shah, in pursuance of a vow, and with the concurrence of his principal officers and advisers, changed the State profession of faith from the Soony, or orthodox, to the Sheea, or heretical, in which he had been brought up in Persia. He experienced some opposition in this as yet unprecedented public declaration of that faith in India; but, as he allowed every one to follow his own judgment, he was not opposed in his own dominions; in regard to others, however, he was not so successful. A great league was made against him, in the name of a holy crusade, by the Kings of Ahmednugger, Golcondah, and Berar, with Ameer Bereed, who had succeeded his father at Beeder, and possessed, if possible, a more intriguing and restless spirit. Mahmood Shah was made the nominal leader of the league, and the Beejapoor territories were invaded. Yoosuf Adil Shah, finding himself too weak to encounter the united armies of the confederacy, took with him 6,000 horse, marched northwards to Dowlatabad and Berar, plundering the country, and made his way to Imád Shah of Berar, his son-in-law, who had not as yet moved. Imád Shah would not, however, openly espouse his cause; he advised him for the present to restore the Soony faith at Beejapoor, and to retire into Khandésh till the storm was past; advice which Yoosuf Adil Shah at once followed. Imád Shah was an experienced politician, and of great age and wisdom. He wrote

The State creed changed from Soony to Sheea.

A league against him ensues.

Beejapoor invaded.

The king proceeds to Berar.

to the leaders of the confederacy, to put them on their guard against Ameer Bereed, who, it was evident, had contrived the movement in order that he should be put in possession of Beejapoor; and should this occur, that he would then turn his forces against each of his allies in succession. This warning had the desired effect. The Kings of Ahmednugger and Golcondah saw, at once, that Ameer Bereed had made tools of them, and both suddenly left his camp with their forces. Yoosuf Adil Shah now returned to Gawil, and after routing the army of Ameer Bereed, who had fled to Beeder with the king, and plundering its camp, returned triumphant to Beejapoor, where, until 1510, he reigned without further molestation. In that year, the Portuguese, as yet little known, took Goa; but the king immediately proceeding thither, retook it, and expelled them. It was his last effort. He had had a tendency to dropsy for some time, which was aggravated by his exertions, and he died soon afterwards, in the seventy-fifth year of his age and twentieth of his reign. He was not buried at Beejapoor, but at the town of Gógy, in the district of Shorapoor, about sixty miles to the eastward, near the grave of a local saint, Peer Chunda Hooseinee, whom he had venerated. No mausoleum was built over him; and in the precincts of the holy burying-ground his open tomb is as simple as many others, and an endowment, which has been preserved, still provides a covering of cotton chintz for it, renewed from year to year. Thus, as the people of Gógy assert, with an honourable pride, there are not, as yet, faithful servants wanting to the noble king, to light a lamp at night at his grave, and to say *fatehas* for his soul's peace; while the tombs of the great Bahmuny kings, and of all his enemies in life, are desecrated. Soon after his first appointment to Beejapoor, Yoosuf Adil Khan had reduced a Mahratta chieftain, Mookund Ráo, to submission; and he married his sister, to whom he gave the Mahomedan title of Booboojee Khanum. By this lady he had three daughters and one son, Ismail, who, as a minor, succeeded to the throne. Of his daughters, Muryam or Mary, the eldest, married Boorhan Nizam Shah Bheiry, of Ahmednugger; Khoodeija, Alla-ood-deen Imád Shah, of Berar; and Beeby Musseety, the youngest, Ahmed Shah Bahmuny of Beeder.

The confederacy breaks up.

Ameer Bereed defeated.

The king returns to Beejapoor.

Portuguese take Goa, and it is retaken by the king.

Yoosuf Adil Shah dies, 1510.

Henry VIII. king of England.

Yoosuf Adil Shah is buried at Gógy.

Reverence still paid to his memory.

Marriage with a Mahratta lady.

Their children.

Among the sovereigns of the Deccan, there is no one of his period who can be compared with Yoosuf Adil Shah. In political ability, in learned accomplishments, and

Character of Yoosuf Adil Shah.

skill and personal bravery in the field, he had no equal, and was only perhaps inferior to his great patron, Mahmood Gáwan. He was perfectly tolerant of all religions, and his consideration for his Hindoo subjects may have proceeded in some degree from the influence of his wife, whom he loved with a rare affection, and to whom he was entirely faithful. Under him Hindoos were freely admitted to offices of trust, and Mahratta became the ordinary language of accounts and local business. From the means afforded by the booty of the Beejanugger army, the king built the fort and citadel of Beejapoor of stone—enormous and magnificent works of their class. The fort walls surrounded the town, as it was then, of Beejapoor, and consisted of a deep ditch and wall crowned with handsome machicolated battlements, with fine round and octagon bastions at intervals, fitted for artillery. Here and there, on weaker points, there is a *faussebraye*. In the citadel were the royal palaces and public offices, and its defences were similar to the outer walls, except that its ramparts were loftier, its bastions larger, and its ditch, partially filled with water, wider and deeper; and in addition to the ramparts there is a *faussebraye* all round. These works are, for the most part, still perfect. But in the time of Yoosuf Adil Shah, the splendour of Beejapoor was only in its infancy.

CHAPTER XIX.

OF THE ADIL SHAHY DYNASTY OF BEEJAPOOR (*continued*), A.D. 1510 TO 1534.

WHEN Ismail Adil Shah succeeded his father, he was about nine years old; and the late king, on his death-bed, had appointed Kumál Khan, who had followed him from Beeder, and proved faithful on many trying occasions, to be regent, in conjunction with the queen-mother. Kumál Khan at once restored the public profession of the Soony faith. The Portuguese had retaken Goa, and he made peace with them, on condition that they should not extend their possessions. It was soon observable, however, that the regent was strengthening his own party; and, as Ferishta observes, the Deccan then supplied examples, in Ameer Bereed of Beeder, and Timraj of Beejanugger, of the success of ministers and regents against their lawful princes. In the crafty and unscrupulous Ameer Bereed, Kumál Khan found an ally ready to further any desperate intrigue. He proposed that he should assist Ameer Bereed to conquer Ahmed-

Ismail Adil Shah succeeds, 1510.

Kumál Khan regent.

Portugese retake Goa.

Intrigues of the regent with Ameer Bereed.

nugger, if he would further his own projects for usurping the crown of Beejapoor; and these nefarious terms were ratified by a secret treaty, which provided that Kumál Khan was at liberty to imprison Ismail Adil Shah, or put him to death, as might be most expedient. The first act of the confederates was to besiege the fort of Sholapoor. Ameer Bereed had moved to Goolburgah and invested it; and Kumál Khan, confining the queen-dowager and her son to the citadel of Beejapoor, proceeded to Sholapoor, the possessor of which, Zein Khan, surrendered the fort to him. He then returned to Beejapoor, and to secure his own position, dismissed the foreign guards, who were to a man faithful to the king, while he took into his service a body of Mahratta horse, by which his own adherents were raised to the large number of 20,000 men.

Kumál Khan purposes to usurp the throne.

The queen, who possessed information of these proceedings, and of the fact that Kumál Khan had actually fixed, by his astrologers, a date for ascending the throne, now determined upon his destruction, if possible, as the only available means for escape; and she urged Yoosuf Toork, the foster-father of her son, of whose devotion to the family she had no doubt, to effect it—a commission he readily accepted. Kumál Khan had feigned to be ill, and had shut himself up for some days, as the astrologers had predicted certain malign influences against him. The queen, pretending to be solicitous as to his health, sent an old female attendant, whom she knew was acting as Kumál Khan's spy, to him with a complimentary message and wave offering, and requested her to take with her Yoosuf Toork, who desired an audience for leave to depart on a pilgrimage to Mecca. There was nothing in the message or in the individual to excite suspicion, and after its delivery, Yoosuf Toork was summoned to receive an honorary dismissal. On such an occasion it is customary for the superior to give some leaves of pân, rolled up with betel-nut, to the petitioner: as Yoosuf Toork advanced to receive the pân on his extended scarf, the naked hands being considered a disrespectful breach of etiquette, he concealed a naked dagger beneath it, and as the regent stretched out his hand, Yoosuf Toork suddenly plunged the dagger into his breast, and he died instantly, with a loud groan; while the attendants, hearing the noise, rushed in, and dispatched the assassin and the woman ere they could leave the apartment. Kumál Khan's body was then dressed and placed in the balcony by his mother, as though he were alive; and a message sent to the troops to hasten to salute him as king, and seize Ismail Adil Shah and his mother. Sufdur Khan, the minister's son, considering he had troops enough for this purpose, shut the gates

The queen's counter plot.

Kumál Khan assassinated.

of the fort, and proceeded in person against the queen's palace, which was separate from the rest, with a body of 5,000 men.

The queen did not as yet know of the fate of her messenger, and supposing he had been killed, and that Kumál Khan still lived, proposed to make the best terms she could; but Dilshad Agha, the foster-sister of her husband, at once saw the danger of such a step, and determined to resist. The palace gates were shut, and a faithful eunuch dispatched to the few foreign soldiers in the fort, to warn them of the king's situation. On their arrival, they undauntedly withstood the storm of shot and arrows poured against them, Dilshád Agha and the queen, clad in armour, encouraging them in person; but when cannon were brought up against the palace, its brave defenders began to despair, and some fled. Dilshád Agha's message to the few foreigners still in the city had, however, reached them: and they gained admittance to the palace from the fort ditch, by ropes thrown over the wall. This reinforcement augmented the defenders to nearly two hundred men, and with these, Booboojee Khanum and Dilshád Agha continued to fight gallantly. As Sufdur Khan broke open the gateway of the palace, he was received with a sharp volley of arrows and shot, totally unexpected; and being himself wounded in the eye, retired, and was leaning against the palace wall, when the young king, recognising him, pushed over a heavy stone from the terrace roof above, which killed him on the spot. His followers fled, and in a short time all the loyal population had rallied round their monarch. The body of Yoosuf Toork was buried with honour, and a mausoleum raised over it; nor did the king, when at the capital, fail to visit the place once in every month, and join in the ceremonies for the repose of the soul of the faithful servant to whose devotion he owed his life. As may be conceived, so romantic an event took a strong hold of the imagination of the people, and the facts are still recited by the minstrels of the country, with unfailing interest; while the traveller, if he knows the history, will be shown the scene of the tragedy and its consequences. The account of Ferishta is amply confirmed by the local narratives.

Heroic conduct of the queen-dowager.

Although still a mere boy in years, the events of the time, and his natural high spirit, imparted a decision to Ismail Adil Shah's mind which never left him. He at once assumed the direction of his own government. He dismissed the faithless Deccanies and Abyssinians, and re-enlisted the Toorks and Moghuls who had been discharged; and these, with his father's gallant veterans, who flocked to him from all quarters, soon composed a sufficient army. Ameer Bereed, on hearing of the death of Kumál Khan, had raised the siege of Goolburgah,

The king assumes the government.

and retired to Beeder; but he was not the less active in his designs against the young king, and eventually succeeded in inducing the Kings of Golcondah, Berar, and Ahmednugger to join him, on the part of Mahmood Shah Bahmuny, in an effort to uproot the Adil Shahy dynasty. These sovereigns sent quotas of troops; and, in 1514, Ameer Bereed and King Mahmood Shah Bahmuny advanced on Beejapoor at the head of 25,000 horse. Ismail Adil Shah was in nowise dismayed. He allowed the Beeder army to advance to Allapoor, within a mile and a half of the eastern gate of his capital; and as it debouched upon the great plain before the city, he fell upon it with 12,000 foreign cavalry, and leading the principal division himself, won a complete victory. Mahmood Shah and his son Ahmed had both been unhorsed in the action, and were captured; but were received as honoured guests by the young king, himself only fourteen years old, and treated with respect and dignity. The sequel to this invasion, was the proposal of Mahmood Shah to solemnise the marriage of his son to Beeby Musseety, the king's sister; and the two monarchs proceeded together to Goolburgah, where the marriage was concluded, amidst great rejoicings. Mahmood Shah and his son, with his bride, were then forwarded to Beeder, with an escort of 5,000 select cavalry, and for a time Ameer Bereed did not appear.

League against Beejapoor.

The king defeats the confederates.

From 1514 to 1519 peace prevailed; but the Rajah of Beejanugger had succeeded in getting possession of the Raichore Dooáb; and this being an original portion of the Beejapoor State, Ismail Adil Shah determined to regain it. Timraj, the regent of Beejanugger, had poisoned his ward, and now exercised regal power; and he was by no means disposed to admit Ismail Adil Shah's demands. He took up a position on the right bank of the river Krishna; and in an attempt to cross the river while excited by wine, Ismail nearly lost his life, and sacrificed many of his best troops. He was obliged to retreat; but the event had the good effect of inducing him to abandon the use of wine, to which it had been feared he was becoming addicted. All further attempt upon the Raichore Dooáb was for the present abandoned. Soon afterwards Boorhan Nizam Shah, king of Ahmednugger, proposed to marry the king's sister Muryam, and the ceremony was performed at Sholapoor, in May 1524, which fort, with its dependencies, was fixed as her dowry. The cession was not, however, immediately made; and Boorhan Shah, taking offence, invaded the Beejapoor dominions in 1535, assisted, as usual, by Ameer Bereed. The issue of this campaign was favourable to Ismail Adil Shah, who defeated his brother-in-law in a general action, with great

War with Beejanugger.

War with Ahmednugger.

Battle of Pavia.

loss of men and matériel of war, both being present in the field and leading their respective armies. In 1528, however, Boorhan Shah and Ameer Bereed renewed the contest, and were allowed to advance to within forty miles of Beejapoor, where they were attacked by Assud Khan, the Beejapoor general, and utterly routed, with the loss of their guns and elephants.

The King of Ahmednugger defeated.

These, as it were, family quarrels, did not, however, prevent the parties from assisting each other on emergent occasions; for in the same year, 1528-9, when the King of Ahmednugger was attacked by the King of Guzerat, Ismail Adil Shah sent him 6,000 horse and a sum of money equal to half a million sterling, to enable him to refit his army. It transpired, however, that while employed in this service, Ameer Bereed had tampered with the Beejapoor troops, and had promised their commander an independent estate if he would desert and join in an attack upon Beejapoor. This provoked Ismail Adil Shah beyond endurance; and he proposed to his brother-in-law that they should join to punish the man who contrived, by his malicious and unceasing intrigues, to keep the Deccan in perpetual turmoil; or, if he pleased, he might remain neutral, which would answer the same purpose. Boorhan Shah preferred the latter alternative; and in 1529 the Beejapoor king invaded the territory of Beeder with 10,000 of his best cavalry. In all his campaigns, the king seems to have trusted to archery as his chief weapon in war, and it was the national arm of the Persians, Tartars, Moghuls, and Turks, who composed his best troops; but at Beeder he had to encounter artillery and musketry, and a hard-fought action outside the walls of the city tested the bravery of his troops to the utmost. The king displayed great personal valour in this battle, killing in single combat two of the sons of Ameer Bereed, who had attacked him successively. At the close of the action, a large body of fresh cavalry was seen approaching from the right, which proved to be a contingent of 4,000 Golcondah horsemen sent to the assistance of Ameer Bereed. The king would have attacked these at once with his own division, and was with great difficulty persuaded to witness the final charge instead of taking a part in it. He therefore handed his own bloody sword to Syed Hoosein, his Arab general, and seated himself on a mound overlooking the field of battle, by which the place is still to be recognised. Syed Hoosein, and Assud Khan were completely successful, and on their return the king presented his own horse to Syed Hoosein.

Renewed intrigues of Ameer Bereed.

Ismail Adil Shah invades Beeder.

Peace of Cambray.

General action at Beeder.

The king's victory.

The fort of Beeder was now closely invested, Ameer Bereed

retired to Oodgheer, leaving the defence to his sons, and wrote to the King of Berar to come to Beeder as a mediator. When Imád Shah arrived, he found that Ismail Adil Shah would be content with nothing less than Ameer Bereed's unconditional submission; but the fort was impregnable, and Ameer Bereed would not come to terms. Hearing that his camp was pitched near that of the King of Berar, and that he was neglectful of it, Assud Khan was sent with 2,000 horse to make a night attack upon it, when the scouts sent on, returned, and declared they had reached the royal tent without a challenge. Assud Khan, conducted by these men, took twenty-five horse and a few foot with him, and found Ameer Bereed drunk, lying on his bed, and surrounded by guards, musicians, singers and dancers, all intoxicated and asleep. The bed of Ameer Bereed was now gently lifted as he lay on it and carried off, and it was only when he found himself at a considerable distance from his camp, travelling as it were through the air, that he awoke, crying out that he was in the power of evil spirits, and praying God to forgive him. Assud Khan now rode up to him, and told him what had happened; but promised his good offices with the king. Ismail Adil Shah was overjoyed with the result of the night expedition, which indeed was more like romance than reality; and at first seemed disposed to put the aged Ameer Bereed to death, for he was led out bareheaded in the hot sun for execution. Then he humbly begged his life, and promised to give up the fort and the Bahmuny treasures if it were spared; but his son, who held the fort, replied to his father's message to surrender, that he would not, and that his father's life, at his age, was not worth such a ransom. This was, however, only a feint to get better terms, for even in this extremity the merciful and chivalrous disposition of the King of Beejapoor was relied on. Ameer Bereed now begged to be taken before one of the towers of the fort where his sons were, accompanied by the elephant which the king declared should trample him to death; when at last, believing him to be in real danger, the sons offered to give up the fort if they were allowed to depart with their families to Oodgheer; and it was afterwards discovered that they had loaded themselves with the most valuable of the crown jewels before they departed. The kings now entered the city and fort in state, and seated themselves together on the throne. All the money in the treasury, about half a million sterling, the jewels, clothes, china, and other valuables, were distributed to the armies, or in charity, and King Ismail refused to take a single article for himself; he had not made war, he said, for booty, but for his honour, which

Ameer Bereed captured.

The fort of Beeder given up.

The king distributes the treasures of Beeder to his army.

was satisfied. The disposal of Ameer Bereed alone remained, and at the intercession of the King of Berar, an estate was conferred upon him, and he was allowed the command of 3,000 horse in the Beejapoor army.

Campaign in the Raichore Dooab.

The king now proceeded into the Raichore Dooáb, which, with the forts of Raichore and Moodgul, he recovered. Ameer Bereed, having rendered important service, was forgiven, and assured that his government of Beeder would be restored to him; and he was soon afterwards allowed to proceed to Beeder, on condition of surrendering two forts and their dependencies. But he was no sooner free than he recommenced his old practices, and renewed his intrigues with Boorhan Shah of Ahmednugger, who was sore at having had no part in his brother-in-law's last successful expeditions. Ismail Adil Shah had given notice to his brother-in-law that he was about to make a tour of his dominions, and that the officers on the frontier should not be alarmed; to which the King of Ahmednugger replied contemptuously, 'that it would be better if he stayed at home and minded his own business.' Ismail Adil Shah received this uncourteous message at Bahmunhully, when at evening prayer, and was so incensed, that he marched at once with a slight escort, and did not draw rein till he arrived next evening at Nuldroog. Here he dismissed the Ahmednugger ambassadors, and awaited the advance of their troops. Boorhan Nizam Shah had equipped a fine army, and his train of artillery was unusually large. He brought 25,000 horse into the field on this occasion; but they were chiefly Mahrattas and Deccanies, and had no chance against the veteran foreigners of Beejapoor. Boorhan Nizam Shah was defeated with the loss of all his guns and camp equipage, and fled to his capital; but the brothers-in-law met afterwards on the frontier, and agreed mutually that Ahmednugger should annex Berar to its dominions, leaving Beejapoor at liberty to proceed against Golcondah. In 1533, therefore, King Ismail opened a campaign against Golcondah—which State he averred had attacked him treacherously, and without cause, in the affair at Beeder—by the siege of Kowilkonda. Here the king fell ill of a violent fever, and died on September 6, 1534, after a glorious and successful reign of twenty-five years. In all his military enterprises the king had suffered only one reverse, that at the Krishna river, by the Beejanugger army, which was only attributable to his own rashness: and in the subsequent campaign, he not only retrieved that disaster, but recaptured the Raichore Dooáb, which had been in possession of the Hindoos for nearly twenty years. The king's body was carried from Kowil-

War with Ahmednugger.

Boorhan Nizam Shah defeated.

Ismail Adil Shah dies, 1534.

Reformation in England.

konda to Gôgy, and interred beside his father, a simple tombstone alone marking the spot. Ismail's character. The character of this king is well given in the words of a local historian, quoted by Ferishta. 'He was just, patient, and liberal; extremely generous, frequently pardoning State criminals, and averse to listening to slander. He never used passionate language, and possessed great wit, to which he added a sound and accurate judgment. He was an adept in the arts of painting, varnishing, making arrows, and embroidering saddlecloths; and in music and poetry excelled most of his age. He supported literary men and scholars munificently at his court; and had a great fund of humour, which he displayed at his private parties and in familiar intercourse with his courtiers.' His personal bravery was beyond question, as was proved by his acts of valour in all his wars, and he shared the fatigues and privations of his soldiers, who loved him deeply, and deplored his loss. No record of his civil administration has been preserved; but, it may be inferred from his general abilities and kind disposition, that it had flourished abundantly. On his death-bed he appointed his friend Assud Khan to be protector of the kingdom; and though he had no confidence in his eldest son Mulloo, he declared him his successor. Mulloo Adil Shah succeeds, 1534. This prince was therefore raised to the throne at Goolburgah, but his father's opinion was confirmed by his conduct, which so disgusted Assud Khan, that he retired to his estate of Belgaum, leaving the regency to the old queen-dowager, Booboojee Khanum, and Ismail Khan Deccany. He is dethroned, 1534. After enduring Mulloo Adil Shah's vices for six months, the queen-dowager determined to depose him; Ibrahim Adil Shah I. succeeds, 1534. and with the full approbation of Assud Khan, Mulloo Adil Shah was dethroned and blinded, and his brother Ibrahim crowned king, to the satisfaction of all parties in the State.

These transactions have brought the history of the Adil Shahy dynasty somewhat beyond the date previously mentioned, namely, 1526; but the details of the reign of Ismail Adil Shah could not be interrupted; and those of his successor, Ibrahim Adil Shah I., will be resumed hereafter.

CHAPTER XX.

OF THE NIZAM SHAHY DYNASTY OF AHMEDNUGGER, A.D. 1489 TO 1532.

THE death of Nizam-ool-Moolk Bheiry, who succeeded Mahmood Gáwan as minister of the Bahmuny State, after his execution, has been before related in Chapter XV. of this Book, as also the declaration of independence by his son Mullik Ahmed, which immediately followed that event. He had been previously employed in the royal service, both by Mahmood Gáwan and his own father; and, at the period under notice, was engaged in reducing the Northern Konkan, which formed part of his father's public estate, to obedience. In these operations he had been singularly successful; and had captured all the Mahratta strongholds, which, up to this period, had defied the Mahomedan arms. Ferishta states, that though he assumed independence, he was not crowned, nor did he style himself shah or king, until a later period. An attempt was made by the Bahmuny State, soon after his declaration of independence, to recover Mullik Ahmed's possessions; but the generals dispatched for the purpose were successively defeated; on the last occasion with the loss of all their baggage. A third attempt by Azmut-ool-Moolk, with 18,000 men, on the part of Mahmood Shah Báhmuny, was equally unsuccessful. Mullik Ahmed evaded them, marched suddenly upon Beeder, a distance of nearly 300 miles, surprised the city guards, and carried off the females of his family without loss; an exploit which considerably added to his fame. He then rejoined his forces, and after some manœuvres by both parties, a general action ensued, on May 28, 1490, in which the Bahmuny troops suffered a severe defeat on the plain near the town of Bingar, which was commemorated by the erection of a palace, surrounded by a garden and park, which still remain. The occurrences of the reign of Ahmed Nizam Shah were so much mixed up with those of Mahmood Shah Bahmuny, and his contemporaries, that they need not all be reviewed. Joonair as yet had been the capital of the new kingdom; but it was inconvenient in many respects, and was not sufficiently central. Mullik Ahmed Shah had determined to gain possession of Dowlatabad and its dependencies, which included the broad and fertile valley of the upper Godavery, and eventually to extend his power into Berar; and he fixed upon a spot near

Ahmed Nizam Shah assumes independence, 1489.

The Bahmuny generals defeated.

Bingar, where he had already erected a palace for the new capital, which was named Ahmednugger, the fort of Ahmed. The position, in every point of view, was an excellent one. It commanded all the passes into Khandésh and Dowlatabad, and its elevation, near the crest of one of the principal Deccan ranges of hills, secured a cool and salubrious climate. The city soon sprang up, and with the noble fort palaces of the Nizam Shahy dynasty, forms one of the most valuable military stations of the British army in the Deccan.

Ahmednugger founded, 1494.

America discovered by Columbus.

The Bahmuny officer, Mullik Wujoo, in charge of the province of Dowlatabad, had, like others, declared his independence; and there had since occurred a domestic revolution, in which his younger brother, Mullik Ashruf, had obtained the power. Ahmed Nizam Shah had not as yet been able to make any impression on Dowlatabad; but he devastated its districts in every season of harvest, and determined on continuing this policy till it should be given up. In 1499 he was engaged in besieging the fort, when Mahmood Shah of Guzerat moved southwards with the purpose of reducing Khandésh and relieving Dowlatabad. This had the effect of obliging Ahmed Nizam Shah to raise the siege; and a subsequent night attack upon the Guzerat army near Sooltanpoor, in Khandésh, caused its king to retreat. Ahmed Nizam Shah now advanced once more towards Dowlatabad, the garrison of which sent him word that their master had engaged to acknowledge the King of Guzerat as his sovereign, and as they could not submit to this, they would admit him if he would come. So favourable an offer could not be neglected, and the king marched with 3,000 horse, and encamped without the walls. Mullik Ashruf was then ill, and died in a few days; and the keys of the fort were delivered up to Ahmed Nizam Shah, who, rejoiced at his good fortune, directed the whole of the works to be repaired, and placed in them a trusty garrison of his own troops. The possession of Dowlatabad, with its large dependencies, very much increased the king's power; and though frequently threatened by Guzerat, no war actually took place. Ahmed Nizam Shah Bheiry fell ill in 1508, and died in the course of the year. He was buried at Rózah, near Dowlatabad, a place to which, as well for the mausoleums and colleges of holy Mahomedan saints established there, as from its beautiful situation and delightful climate, he had become deeply attached.

Dowlatabad besieged.

Brazil discovered.

The fort is given up to him.

Ahmed Shah Bheiry dies, 1508.

League of Cambray.

The king was succeeded by his son Boorhan Nizam Shah, then a boy of seven years old. The public affairs were in the hands of experienced officers, and the young king's

Boorhan Nizam Shah, his son, succeeds, 1508.

education was carefully conducted by them. Ferishta states, that he saw in the royal library at Ahmednugger, a treatise on the duties of kings, neatly copied by him when he was ten years old. In 1510 the kingdom was placed in some danger by the desertion of 8,000 cavalry to Alla-ood-deen Imád Shah of Berar, who, assisted by them, invaded the Ahmednugger dominions, being led to believe they would fall an easy prey; but he was resolutely opposed by Khwajah Jehán of Paraindah—who, partially independent, was yet tributary to Ahmednugger—and the young king himself: and was defeated with great loss, flying from the field of battle at Ranoory to Ellichpoor. The young king in this battle rode before Ajdur Khan, his tutor, on the same saddle, in the thickest of the fight. It was after this war that the Brahmin relations of the king claimed their hereditary rights as 'Putwaries,' or accountants of Putry. The regent, Mokumil Khan, proposed an exchange of territory for Putry, which belonged to Berar, and this being refused, he took forcible possession of the town, and it was afterwards retained as a family point of honour.

An invasion by troops from Berar defeated.

In 1523 the king was married at Sholapoor to Muryam, the sister of Ismail Adil Shah of Beejapoor: and their subsequent quarrel in regard to that fort, and the defeat of the King of Ahmednugger, when he was carried off the field fainting from the weight of his armour, have been already mentioned. Ferishta adds of this battle, 'it was so bloody a one, that nature revolts at the remembrance.' In 1527 Putry became the subject of a war. Alla-ood-deen Imád Shah of Berar retook and fortified it, when Boorhan Nizam Shah in person drove out the Berar garrison, razed the fortifications of the place, and bestowed it as 'a charitable gift' on his Brahmin relations, by whom it was held successively till the reign of the Emperor Akbur, and whose descendants still represent the family.

The king marries a princess of Beejapoor.

Solyman takes Belgrade.

Rome taken by Charles V.

In 1529 Boorhan Nizam Shah was severely pressed by the junction of Guzerat to the confederation of the Kings of Khandésh and Berar against him. The two latter he had defeated: but the accession of Guzerat to their league was very formidable. The timely assistance rendered by his brother-in-law, the King of Beejapoor, on this occasion, to Boorhan Nizam Shah, will be remembered; but the final success may be attributed to the judicious conduct of Kawur Sein, a Brahmin, who became Péshwa, or prime minister, being the first instance as yet recorded of any Hindoo being raised to an office of the highest rank. The Brahmin seems to have been as brave a soldier as he was a skilful administrator, but

League against the king.

The king defeated.

Boorhan Nizam Shah was nevertheless defeated, and obliged to sue for peace, and acknowledge the supremacy of the Guzerat king, which was considered a sufficient humiliation. In 1530 the king sent an embassy to the monarch of Guzerat, to congratulate him on his conquest of Malwah, but he was informed that he must do homage in person—a further humiliation, at which the king's pride revolted. 'Should he who had won his independence from the great house of Bahmuny stoop to that of Guzerat?' Shah Tahir, the holy saint who had been his ambassador, now dexterously delivered him from the dilemma. At the interview between the kings, he carried on his head a Korán, written by Ally; and the Guzerat king, descending from his throne to pay it reverence, saluted Boorhan Nizam Shah, who was following his ambassador. The two kings then entered into conversation, and became good friends; Bahadur Shah, before he returned to Guzerat, formally resigning all his assumed honorary pretensions as king of the Deccan. His Brahmin minister now rendered more excellent service to Boorhan Shah, in reducing the Mahratta chiefs of the mountain tracts who had as yet not submitted, and all these princes were very judiciously confirmed in their estates.

Mahratta chiefs reduced to obedience.

The last quarrel between Boorhan Nizam Shah and Ismail Adil Shah, in 1531, resulted, as has been recorded, in the former's utter defeat; but the letter written by Ismail on receipt of the rude message 'to stay at home and mind his own business,' has been preserved in Ferishta's history, and is too characteristic of the period to be omitted. 'Have you so soon,' writes the Beejapoor king, 'forgotten your late condition at Ahmednugger? If you pride yourself on the tattered rags of the King of Malwah, the boast is ridiculous. Nor need you be too vain of the title of shah, conferred on you by the King of Guzerat, since I derive my royal lineage from a race of sovereigns, and am so styled by the kings of Persia, descendants of the Prophet. I advise you to repent of your folly and arrogance, or I shall compel you to quit the enjoyments of your Bagh-i-Nizam, and try how you like the clashing of steel in the field of battle.' No doubt much of the royal correspondence between the brothers-in-law and their neighbour was in the same strain; and could Ferishta have introduced more specimens of the familiar and political letters and transactions of his period into his history, its interest and importance, great as both are, would have been highly enhanced. The King of Ahmednugger did not, it may be presumed, like the clashing of steel in battle, to which his gallant brother-in-law invited him, though he did not evade it: and the

Remarkable letter from Ismail Adil Shah.

defeat which followed was one of the worst he had experienced. In 1532 Ismail Adil Shah died, while Boorhan Nizam Shah lived for twenty years longer. The review of the latter part of his reign is therefore postponed.

Treaty of Nuremburg.

CHAPTER XXI.

OF THE KOOTUB SHAHY DYNASTY OF GOLCONDAH, A.D. 1512 TO 1550.

THE conquests of the Bahmuny dynasty had gradually progressed eastward after the establishment of the kingdom of Goolburgah; and the Hindoo principality of Wurungul, which made a gallant resistance, was finally reduced in A.D. 1421 by King Ahmed Shah Wully Bahmuny. Beyond this, to the east, were the provinces of the Ráis or Rajahs of Orissa, as yet very imperfectly known to the Mahomedans at that period, and consisting of some very fertile and productive possessions bordering on the sea, divided from the Deccan and western Telingána by a range of mountains, covered with thick and almost impenetrable forests, and inhabited by aboriginal races, unknown in any degree to the Mahomedans, and perhaps in a very limited one to the Hindoos. The last Bahmuny campaign, in 1477, had established garrisons as far north on the sea-coast as Rajmundry; and southwards, as far as the Krishna river, the country had been conquered from Nursingah, or Nursing Rái, a powerful prince who held an independent kingdom or principality, bordering upon the Hindoo kingdoms of Beejanugger, and probably the Chôlas of Kanchy, or their successors of Tanjore. It is equally probable, however, that the tract from the Krishna south to Madras, and west to the mountains which border Mysore, was in the possession of Palligars, or small independent princes who ruled over semi-civilised aboriginal tribes, which had not escaped the influence of Hindooism, and probably professed a nominal allegiance, either to Beejanugger or one of the southern Hindoo kingdoms. The Mahomedan possessions, however, lay north of the Krishna only; for King Mahmood Shah Bahmuny's rapid march on Conjeveram, in 1479, had been productive of no accession of territory. To the west, the Krishna and Tumboodra continued the boundary, and while Beejapoor possessed the Raichore Dooáb, Golcondah followed the left bank of the river up to its confluence with the Bheema, and then stretched in an irregular line to the hills south-

John VI. emperor of the East.

Southern Mahomedan conquests.

Boundaries.

west of Golcondah, which form the frontiers of the province of Beeder.

This area was therefore very considerable, and the country was highly productive. At a very early age—probably about the Christian era, or perhaps anterior to it—the Hindoos had commenced the works of irrigation on which the rice crops of the province depended: and up to the conquest of the Mahomedans, these useful works had been continued by the later Andhra dynasty of Wurungul, and the smaller native dynasties which were subject to it. Over this valuable tract, Koolly Kootub-ool-Moolk, a nobleman of the Bahmuny dynasty, was appointed governor by Mahmood Gáwan, the regent and minister; and was in attendance on the king in the camp at Peerkónda when he was executed. Kootub-ool-Moolk accompanied the king to Beeder after that event; but withdrew, like other great nobles, from court, to Golcondah, which had become the capital of the viceroyalty.

Hindoo works of irrigation.

Origin of Kootub-ool-Moolk.

Kootub-ool-Moolk was descended from the Baharloo tribe of Toorks or Turanians, and arrived in the Deccan with a body of his countrymen, who were taken into the royal service in the reign of Mahmood Shah Bahmuny. He had been well educated, and was employed as a secretary in one of the public departments for some years. In this capacity he volunteered on one occasion to go into Telingána, to adjust disputes with the Hindoo landholders; and having succeeded by peaceable negotiation in this duty, was ennobled, and became viceroy and governor of the province. He did not immediately follow the example of Yoosuf Adil Khan and Mullik Ahmed Bheiry, in declaring his independence in 1489: but remained loyal to Mahmood Shah, until the ascendency of Kassim Bereed became unendurable, and in 1512 was crowned as sooltan, under the title of Sooltan Koolly Kootub Shah, which was continued as the designation of his dynasty.

His services.

Koolly Kootub Shah declares independence, 1512.

Battle of Ravenna.

Ferishta's history of his reign is meagre; but his translator, Colonel Briggs, discovered and appended a history of the several reigns of the Golcondah kings, written by a local author, which is full of interesting details, and of particulars of the various conquests and annexations of Hindoo territory made by Sooltan Koolly during his long reign. Golcondah, previously an insignificant village, lying under a small hill-fort, was selected as the capital, on account of its central situation, and became a strongly fortified city. The king gradually extended his power over the whole of eastern Telingána to the sea. He captured Dewarcónda and other forts from the Rajah of Beejanugger, and established the river Krishna as his southern boundary; and the last account of the famous fort of Wurungul, appears in its capture by the sooltan. Koolly Kootub Shah did not enter into the quarrels which were maintained among the other kings of the Deccan. The only act of interference that can be traced to him is the dispatch of a contingent force to assist Ameer Bereed, in 1532–33, an act which drew upon him the retaliation of the King of Beejapoor in the siege of Kovilcóndah, in 1534; in the campaign connected with which, he received a wound in the face, which terribly disfigured him for the rest of his life. Towards the close of his reign, the king, content with the dominions he had gained, applied himself earnestly to the regulations of their civil government. He had attained the great age of nearly ninety years; and retained perfect enjoyment of his faculties, though he was infirm. Some years before, he had imprisoned his son Jumsheed for conspiracy—an act which the young man never forgave; and as the king was kneeling down to prayer in the mosque of the fort, on September 4, 1543, he was killed by the commandant, at the instigation of the prince, who, as had been previously arranged among the conspirators, succeeded him.

Sooltan Koolly Kootub Shah assassinated, 1543.

Sooltan Koolly Kootub Shah was in his ninetieth year, and had reigned as king forty-four years. Very little detail is given of the events of the reign of Jumsheed. He assisted Boorhan Nizam Shah in a war against Beejapoor, when he invested the fort of Etgeer, or Yatgeer, near the Bheema; but being obliged by Assud Khan, the Beejapoor general, to raise the siege, was pursued by him to his capital with great loss in men and camp-equipage. After this event, he withdrew himself from Deccan politics, and entered into minor wars with Hindoo chiefs, many of whom he reduced. Latterly, however, he fell ill, and became cruel and morose, and died in 1550, after a reign of nearly seven years, being succeeded by his son Soobhan, a boy of seven years; when the celebrated general Seif Khan, who was in exile at Ahmednugger, was recalled as regent. This arrangement was not, however, popular, and the nobles at court offered the crown to the late king's brother, Ibrahim, who had been residing at Beejanugger under the protection of Ramraj. In pursuance of this invitation, Ibrahim arrived at the capital, which he entered in state, and was crowned on July 27, 1550.

Jumsheed Kootub Shah succeeds, 1543.

Mary queen of Scotland.

Jumsheed Kootub Shah dies, 1550.

Is succeeded by his son Soobhan, who is deposed.

Ibrahim Kootub Shah crowned, 1550.

Pope Julius III.

CHAPTER XXII.

OF THE PORTUGUESE IN INDIA, A.D. 1415 TO 1501.

It is impossible to estimate the antiquity of the trade between India and Europe. From the dim ages of the Assyrian and Egyptian monarchies it had continued to the Grecian, and Alexander's invasion gave it an enormous impetus. Through the Romans, and by the Emperor Justinian, who, in A.D. 531, introduced the culture of silk into Italy, down to the Venetians and the Genoese, the trade descended with unflagging increase and prosperity. The spices, the manufactures, the sugar, the silk, and the pearls and precious stones of India, were welcome and indispensable commodities in all European markets; and the manner of the quickest and safest route of transport became a question of the highest national importance. The channels of trade were many. Through Afghanistan and Central Asia, merchandise from Northern India went first to Kabool or Kandahar, and thence, by Balkh, Sarmacand, Astrakhan, and the Caspian, reached the Black Sea. A more southern line was through Persia to Damascus, or Alexandria; and, in a greater or less degree, the whole of the coast of Asia Minor and Syria served as an *entrepôt* for the Indo-European trade. From Central and Southern India, as well as from its eastern portion, the sea was the only means of communication, and was largely used; and long before the Christian era, the Hindoo (Aryan) ships of Bengal took its productions to Ceylon, and at the proper season stretched across to Africa and Egypt. The western coast of India, from north to south, seems, from the earliest times, to have been a busy scene of export in the north-east monsoon, and of import in the south-west. The Indian vessels leaving Cochin, Calicut, Goa, Dabul, Choule, or Guzerat, from November to January or February, with a fair wind, made safe and rapid voyages to the Persian Gulf, or to Aden, perhaps also to the coasts of Egypt; and discharging their cargoes at Berenice, Cossien, Mocha, or Jeddo, in the Red Sea, Busheir or Bassora, in the Persian Gulf, returned with equal certainty on the change of wind to the south-west. The emporiums for the southern trade were Alexandria, Smyrna, and other ports in the Mediterranean; and from these the Venetians first, and afterwards the Genoese, had almost a monopoly of the carrying trade to Europe. When Constantinople

Early trade with India by Egypt.

Trade by land through Asia.

Trade by sea from the western coast.

was taken by the Turks, in 1453, the special protection the Genoese had received from the Greek emperors ceased, and the Venetians enjoyed a renewal of their prosperity for a considerable period.

But other means of communication with India were, after many attempts, considered practicable. Prince Henry of Portugal, in 1415, before the birth of Columbus, had explored much of the west coast of Africa, and had indicated a route by which its southern point might be passed; and it was well argued, that once Africa could be crossed, there was nothing to prevent access to India. Subsequently Columbus discovered America, but not, as he had hoped, a passage westwards to India; and it was Alonzo V., and after him King John II., who followed up the course of previous West African exploration. Portugal was poor, and the expense of fitting out expeditions very considerable. King John, therefore, offered shares in the discoveries that might be made to several European courts, on the condition that they should assist him, or otherwise allow him the full benefit of his national exertions. None, however, felt sufficient confidence in King John's theories to venture ships and men in their elucidation, and he determined to pursue them himself. He obtained the sanction of the Pope to his proceedings: and sent an expedition, under Diego Cam, who explored the coast of Africa to latitude 22° south, whence he dispatched messengers to find out where the Venetians obtained their drugs and spices. One of them, Pedro de Covillam, succeeded in reaching India, but before his discoveries were known in Portugal, Bartholomew Diaz, who had followed Diego's track in 1486, found he had rounded the Cape while driven out to sea in a storm; for when he again made land, he found it trended north-east, lying on his left hand, while to the east all was open ocean. His crew now mutinied, and, to his infinite mortification, refused to enter upon the unknown sea. On his way homeward by the coast, he discovered the southern Cape of Africa, which he called the Cape of Storms, but which was afterwards named the Cape of Good Hope.

Portuguese enterprises.

Battle of Agincourt.

Efforts of King John II.

Portuguese expedition under Diego Cam.

Second attempt by Bartholomew Diaz.

No immediate result followed this remarkable voyage. The attention of the European world had been temporarily dazzled by the discovery by Columbus of the American continent, and it was not till after King's John's death that his successor Emmanuel determined to continue the discoveries of Diaz. An expedition of three small vessels, carrying 100 men, was fitted out under Vasco de Gama, already favourably known by his qualities as a seaman, and Diaz ac-

King Emmanuel sends an expedition under Vasco de Gama.

companied him in a subordinate capacity. The ships sailed from the Tagus on May 8, 1497. Diaz quitted the expedition at Santa Maria: and Vasco de Gama, pursuing his voyage, rounded the Cape of Good Hope on November 20 of the same year. By Christmas he had discovered that part of the south-east coast which he named Tierra de Natál, and having stretched out to sea to avoid dangerous currents, he missed Sofala, then an emporium of trade with India, but reached Mozambique, a Mahomedan city, and then Melinda, a larger city than any hitherto met with. Ships from India were lying in the harbour, and there was every evidence of large trade in the Indian manufactures and commodities with which they were laden. Here he obtained the services of a Guzerat pilot, Mélémo Kana, as he is styled—most probably Maalim Khan—and sailed for India on April 22, 1498.

Vasco de Gama sails, 1497.

He reaches Melinda.

and thence sails for India.

The pilot proved an excellent navigator, and was familiar with the use of the Portuguese quadrant, and other nautical instruments; and on Friday, May 17, the high land of India was sighted, and on the 20th they cast anchor near the beautiful city of Calicut. Here De Gama sent ashore one of the criminals whom he had brought with him to be employed on desperate services, who, not being able to make himself understood, was taken by the people to the house of a Moor of Tunis, who spoke both Portuguese and Spanish. This man went off to De Gama's ship, and on approaching it cried out from his boat, 'Good luck, good luck! many rubies, many emeralds! Thou art bound to thank God for having brought thee where there are spices, and precious stones, and all the riches of the world.' This fortunate meeting with one who could speak their language filled the Portuguese with joy: and De Gama lost no time in reporting his arrival to the Zamorin, or sovereign of the country, who, being absent at a little distance, sent him a courteous invitation and welcome, and had his ships conveyed to a safe anchorage. On May 28 De Gama set out with twelve men to pay his respects to the prince, but not without many misgivings on the part of his crew. He was, however, honourably placed in a palankeen, and, attended by an immense concourse of people, finally reached the Zamorin's palace, at Poniany. The magnificence by which the Zamorin was surrounded, seems to have struck De Gama and his companions with amazement: and the public reception having been concluded, they were taken into a private apartment, where they detailed the object of their mission, which was favourably listened to. Next day the Portuguese presents were to be delivered, and were

Vasco de Gama reaches Calicut.

They meet with an interpreter.

The Zamorin welcomes the Portuguese.

The Portuguese presents.

certainly in nowise calculated to impress the Zamorin with the importance or wealth of the European strangers. Four pieces of scarlet cloth, six hats, four branches of coral, six almasars, a parcel of brass, a box of sugar, two barrels of oil and one of honey, were selected from the stock; and, as may be supposed, these homely articles were laughed at, while the Moors, jealous of any interference with their trade and privileges, commenced an intrigue in the palace, in which they represented De Gama to be a pirate. The letters sent by the King of Portugal, one of which was fortunately written in Arabic, were, however, honourably received by the Zamorin, who gave permission to De Gama to open trade.

The Moors intrigue against the Portuguese.

The Portuguese narrative of subsequent proceedings is very interesting, as well exhibiting the meanness and intrigue of a small Hindoo court; and De Gama was delayed on one pretence or other till August 10. His two officers, Diego Diaz and Braga, had been detained by the Zamorin; but on their release, there was no further pretext for remaining, and he weighed anchor, followed by a fleet of forty ships, which had been assembled to capture him, taking with him four natives. The Portuguese guns kept the enemy's fleet at a distance, till a breeze springing up, De Gama escaped in safety, and in September 1499 reached home.

Vasco de Gama quits Calicut.

A new expedition was now organised, under Pedro Alvarez Cabral, consisting of 13 vessels and 1,200 men, which sailed on March 9, 1500. De Gama had for the present retired; but Bartholomew Diaz and his brother Diego accompanied Cabral. On the voyage out, Brazil was discovered; and between that country and the Cape, a violent storm overtook the fleet, in which Bartholomew Diaz's ship foundered with all on board. The remainder, on the recurrence of fine weather, had, it was found, doubled the Cape of Good Hope without knowing it; and the fleet soon afterwards anchored at Melinda, where, as before, Guzerat pilots were obtained, and under their guidance the Portuguese arrived at Calicut on September 13. Cabral was received with the same imposing ceremonies as his predecessor; but the Mahomedans of Calicut were, if possible, more hostile and intriguing. Nevertheless permission was given to establish a factory, whereupon disagreements increased, till the Mahomedans one day stormed the factory unawares, and killed Ayres Correa, the officer in charge of it. Cabral's retaliation was severe. He took ten large vessels belong to the Mahomedans, and after transferring their cargoes to his own ships, set them on

The expedition under Cabral.

Diaz drowned at sea.

The expedition reaches Calicut,

and is well received.

Hostility of the Mahomedans.

Cabral retaliates.

fire. He then cannonaded the city, with destructive effect, and sailed to Cochin. Here the Portuguese were received with kindness, and underwent no difficulties in respect to loading their ships or trading with the people; and they received messengers from Cannanore and Quilon, belonging to the Hindoo kingdom of Travancore, offering them protection and trade on favourable terms. The Zamorin of Calicut, however, dispatched a fleet of twenty-five large and many smaller vessels, containing 15,000 men, to intercept Cabral, who, however, not remaining to return the hostages on board his vessels, set sail from Cochin, and got away from the enemy, to Cannanore, where, completing his cargoes, he sailed for Europe, and arrived on July 31, 1501.

And proceeds to Cochin.

His kind reception there, and trade.

Cabral returns to Portugal.

Before his arrival, three ships and a caravel had sailed under Juan de Nueva, who first touched at Anchidéva, an island near Goa, and thence proceeded to Cochin, where he found the rajah had behaved in a friendly manner to the Portuguese left in the factory. The Rajah of Cannanore also gave him pepper and other goods on credit; but the Zamorin of Calicut was still revengeful, and dispatched a large fleet against De Nueva. The Rajah of Cochin advised him to intrench himself on shore; but Juan de Nueva was a brave sailor, and as a hundred of the enemy's vessels came within shot, he handled them so severely, that they hung out a flag of truce, and presently departed. Had Cabral, with a much larger force, behaved in an equally spirited manner, the Zamorin's fleet might have been captured. De Nueva's conduct had, however, inspired respect, and he received an invitation from the Zamorin to visit Calicut, and enter upon negotiations. This he declined to do, fearing treachery; and having completed the cargoes of his ships, sailed for Europe.

Juan de Nueva's expedition.

Naval action with the Zamorin's fleet, which is defeated.

His return to Europe.

CHAPTER XXIII.

OF THE PORTUGUESE IN INDIA (*continued*), A.D. 1501 TO 1527.

De Nueva's voyage home was prosperous; and the accounts given by him of the power of the native princes of India and the population of the country, convinced the king that if the enterprises to India were to be continued at all, they must be of a more formidable character. Small vessels, carrying limited crews, for mere trading, were a mark

The Portuguese determine to send larger expeditions to India.

for the cupidity of small sovereigns like the Zamorin of Calicut, and were only tolerated by less powerful States and rulers such as Cochin and Cannanore. Of the greater powers in India, the Portuguese as yet appear to have gained no information; yet from the visits of European merchants to Beejanugger and Beeder, which seem to have been of ordinary occurrence, as 'Nazarenes' resided at Beeder, and traded as merchants in the reigns of the Bahmuny kings, the existence of some of the powerful monarchies must have been as well known to the Venetians and to the Genoese as they were to the Turks. The Christian merchants to India had apparently come, in Mahomedan or Hindoo vessels, to ports to the north of Calicut; but there is no record of any Christian settlement for trade, and it appears strange that the Nestorian Christians of Travancore and the south of India generally, should have remained undiscovered by the Portuguese till a much later period. The whole of the western trade of India, there is no doubt, had at this time fallen into the hands of Mahomedan merchants from Arabia and Southern Persia; and it is by no means impossible that they had extinguished the trade carried on by Christians and Hindoos, which had existed before the rise of Mahomedanism. It was now the great hope of the Portuguese to extinguish the Mahomedan trade in turn altogether, and to direct it into their own channel. The expedition of 1502, therefore, was composed of twenty ships, manned with a large proportion of soldiers. Cabral declined the command, and it was given to Vasço de Gama, who, with his brother Stephen, and Vincento Sodré, were to suppress the Mahomedan trade at all hazards. While Vasco de Gama himself should drive them from the coast of India, the two other captains should cruise through the Indian Ocean, and at the mouth of the Red Sea, cutting off all Moorish ships that appeared.

Early Christian merchants in the Deccan.

Mahomedan trade.

Expedition of 1502, under Vasco de Gama.

Its projects.

The fleet had assembled at Melinda, after establishing factories on the African coast, and now sailed across to the west coast of India. When near Cannanore, a large ship carrying pilgrims to Mecca, and the property of the Sooltan of Egypt, was captured, after a spirited resistance; and a scene of cruel massacre and piracy ensued, which would be hardly credible, but that it is related with every impress of truth and most minute detail by the Portuguese historian, Faria y Souza, whose account cannot be discredited. When the children of the captives were removed to the Portuguese vessels as slaves or converts, the crews of the captured vessels, with the passengers, were confined to the hold and the ship set on fire. The first attempt was not successful; but at the second, the whole, about

Wanton destruction of a Mahomedan pilgrim ship.

300 persons, perished in the flames. Vasco de Gama then proceeded to Cannanore, where he was sumptuously received, and thence sailed to Calicut, to revenge himself upon the Zamorin.

The Portuguese are well received at Cannanore.

The Zamorin's conduct, as incited by his Mahomedan subjects, had been faithless and hostile, but not barbarously cruel. As De Gama sailed into the bay, he captured the crews of fishing craft and other small vessels, and then sent his demands to the Zamorin, declaring that if they were not settled instantly, he should execute all the natives he had taken. And he literally fulfilled his threat, hanging the prisoners at the yard-arm of his ships; and cutting off their hands and feet, sent them ashore, without further negotiation. He then cannonaded the town, destroying much of it, and set sail for Cochin. The Zamorin sent a message thither, imploring De Gama to come to him, when all would be settled, and De Gama went, taking only his own ship; but he had a narrow escape from a light fleet, by which he was intercepted, and nearly captured, and matters between the Portuguese and the Zamorin became worse than ever. De Gama did not, however, remain long in India, and sailed for Portugal on December 20, 1503; but, before that period, he had formed an alliance with the Rajahs of Cochin and Cannanore; and he left his deputy, Vincento Sodré, to protect Portuguese interests at both places.

Cruelty of Vasco de Gama.

The Zamorin's treachery.

De Gama returns to Portugal.

On De Gama's departure, the Zamorin took up arms against his subject, the Rajah of Cochin, and demanded the surrender of the Portuguese. The rajah, however, resisted gallantly, and defeated the force sent against him. Sodré was unwilling or unable to risk anything in the contest, and remained at sea with his squadron. Meanwhile, assistance was at hand from Portugal, for nine ships had sailed from Lisbon, in three divisions, under the command of Alonzo Albuquerque, his brother Francisco, and Antonia Saldanha. On their arrival, the Zamorin's combination was rendered impossible, and he was defeated and obliged to sue for peace; and Triumpára, the rajah of Cochin, being satisfied of the power and, to him, good faith of the Portuguese, gave them permission to build a fort, while a factory was established at Quilon. At this juncture, the brothers Albuquerque sailed for Europe, leaving Duarte Pachéco with a small force to defend Cochin: and the Zamorin conceived he had now the Portuguese in his power. It is probable that he obtained aid from the Rajah of Beejanugger, whose vassal he was; for he now advanced upon Cochin, with a fleet carrying 400 pieces of ordnance, and by land

Albuquerque arrives with reinforcements.

The Zamorin defeated.

Portuguese fort built at Quilon.

The Zamorin attacks Cochin.

with an army of 50,000 men. Triumpára believed such a force to be invincible; but the gallant Pachéco bade him fear nothing, and with his handful of men and the rajah's troops, not only defeated the Zamorin in several bloody fights, but forced him eventually to retire with the loss of 18,000 men. These gallant operations were barely concluded, when Lopé Soarez arrived with a fleet of thirteen ships, the largest that had as yet been built in Portugal; and with them he sailed to Calicut, where the Zamorin agreed to all his demands, except the surrender of a Milanese, who was employed as an engineer in his service. Soarez resented this creditable refusal by again bombarding Calicut, and destroying much of the city; and on his passage from Cannanore, which had shared the same fate, he fell in with the Zamorin's fleet, and seventeen large Moorish vessels, all of which, after a smart action, he captured. These proceedings had afforded him a vast booty, and he sailed home, arriving on July 22, 1506, and leaving four ships to protect Cochin.

He is defeated by Pacheco.

Lopé Soarez arrives with thirteen ships.

Calicut is attacked.

The Zamorin's fleet captured.

In 1507 Don Francis Almeida, with the rank of Viceroy of India, arrived in command of a magnificent fleet of twenty-two ships and 1,500 trained soldiers. After building a fort at Anchidéva, near Goa, he sailed to Cochin, bearing a crown of gold and jewels which had been specially manufactured for Triumpára; but the old rajah had retired from the cares of government, and his nephew, the reigning prince, was invested with it in his stead. Almeida now gained intelligence of a formidable combination of native powers against the Portuguese. The Zamorin had not only drawn the court of Beejanugger, or Beejapoor—it is not very clear which—but the King of Guzerat, into an offensive and defensive alliance. The Mahomedans, who had so long enjoyed an exclusive western trade, found it to be very seriously interfered with, if not entirely intercepted; for the Portuguese squadrons cruised in the Indian Ocean, up to the mouth of the Red Sea, and intercepted most of the Moorish vessels. Through Mahmood Shah I., then king of Guzerat, the assistance of the Mameluke Sooltan of Egypt was invoked; and the Venetians, who took up the subject with ardour, furnished him with timber and artificers. By these means, in 1507, a fleet of twelve ships, under Ameer Hoosein, was sent to Guzerat from Suez in the Red Sea, and united with the fleet of Mahmood Shah, under his admiral, Mullik Eyáz. The combined fleets sailed southwards; and the Egyptian fleet being in advance, found the Portuguese

Madagascar discovered.

Don Francis Almeida first viceroy.

Combination of native powers against the Portuguese.

A Mahomedan fleet arrives from the Red Sea.

Naval engagement near Choule.

at Choule, and immediately engaged it with an ardour and skill as yet unknown to the Portuguese. The Guzerat fleet followed, and the close of the action found the Portuguese so disabled, that they were obliged to retreat, losing their flag-ship, which carried Lorenzo Almeida and a crew of 100 men, of whom only nineteen escaped.

The Portuguese severely defeated.

The accounts given by Faria y Souza, and the Mahomedan historian, differ widely as to the loss in men; but they agree as to the flag-ship and the death of Lorenzo, and there is no doubt that the Portuguese on this occasion experienced a severe check.

Arrival of Portuguese reinforcements under D'Acunha and Albuquerque.

It might have been difficult indeed for them to hold the sea, but for the opportune arrival, in 1508, of thirteen ships and 1,300 soldiers, under Tristan d'Acunha, and another fleet of twelve ships, under Alfonso Albuquerque.

Mahomedan positions captured.

These combined armaments attacked the Mahomedan positions in the Persian Gulf and Red Sea; and Muscat and Ormuz, the most important of all, fell in succession. Ormuz could not, however, be retained with the force at the admiral's disposal; and having received news of his appointment as viceroy, he crossed to the Indian coast. Almeida, however, who was bent on taking revenge for his defeat at Choule, would not resign his office; and proceeded in search of the combined Mahomedan fleets. They had sailed northwards, and being presently out of reach, Almeida attacked the fort of Dabul, then the property of the King of Ahmednugger, on the plea that it belonged to one who had joined the Zamorin's confederacy.

Almeida destroys Dabul.

This was not probable, perhaps; but it may be easily supposed that the admiral knew little of the divisions of Deccan kingdoms.

Naval engagement at Diu, and victory of the Portuguese.

After destroying Dabul by a cannonade, Almeida did not land his troops—he sailed northwards, and found the Mahomedan fleets at Diu. He at once attacked them, and the Egyptian admiral, in a chivalrous spirit, weighed anchor and engaged him. The result was a splendid victory to the Portuguese, and a complete satisfaction for the defeat of Choule; but it was stained by a savage act of Almeida, who put his prisoners to death.

Almeida's cruelty.

Of this engagement there is no trace in the history of Guzerat; but Faria y Souza's account of it is too circumstantial to be doubted.

Arrival of a fleet under Coutinho.

Almeida still refused to give up his authority, and actually imprisoned Albuquerque; but the arrival of a new fleet under Dom Fernando Coutinho, in 1510, obliged him to resign.

Fate of Almeida.

Almeida perished in a quarrel with some Kaffirs on the African coast; and he had been told.

it is related, by an Indian astrologer, that he should not reach Portugal.

Albuquerque's first act was to attack Calicut. Coutinho led the assault; but, drawn on too far by his ardour, was killed, and Albuquerque himself severely wounded. For the present, therefore, the viceroy withdrew from Calicut, and proceeded towards Ormuz; but by the way turned against Goa, then in possession of Ibrahim Adil Shah, king of Beejapoor, which fell, almost without resistance. In 1511 Goa was retaken by Ismail Adil Shah's general, Kumál Khan; but Albuquerque had seen the beauty and value of its position, and determined to regain it, and soon afterwards, suddenly appearing before the city, carried it by assault. The Beejapoor troops defended the place bravely; but they could not withstand the ardour of the Europeans, who inflicted a loss upon them of 6,000 men. No attempt was made by the King of Beejapoor to retrieve his loss, and the Portuguese were allowed to retain this most valuable possession under a covenant not to increase their territories. Albuquerque now declared Goa to be the capital of the Portuguese dominions in India —a distinction it still preserves. From the capture of Goa till his death in 1573, the viceroy was actively employed against Malacca, Pegu, Aden, Ormuz, and Diu. Ormuz was attacked in 1514, and a fort built there, and the Portuguese power was fully recognised by the King of Persia.

Calicut attacked.

Goa captured.

Cuba conquered by the Spaniards.

Goa retaken by Ismail Adil Shah.

Goa recaptured by Albuquerque.

Goa becomes the Portuguese capital.

These glories did not, however, protect the viceroy from the intrigues of his enemies at court; and, instead of receiving the title of Duke of Goa, as he had hoped, he was superseded by his avowed enemy Soarez. He was ill when he received the news, and it hastened his death. On December 16, 1515, the great viceroy died, commending his son and a small property to his sovereign. 'In regard to the affairs of India,' he said with his last breath, 'they will speak for him and for me.' Albuquerque had literally fulfilled the object of his mission; he had made his nation master of the Indian seas, and he had carried its arms victoriously into the Eastern Archipelago, from whence, to Aden and Ormuz, there was none to dispute them. As nearly as possible all the Mahomedan trade with Western India had now been intercepted: and the European traders, instead of Genoa and Venice, now sought Indian drugs and manufactures at Lisbon. He had committed his sovereign to no territorial acquisition which would have cramped his proceedings: and when he took Goa, he restricted

Albuquerque superseded and dies of grief.

Francis I. king of France.

Effects of Albuquerque's proceedings.

Policy and character of the viceroy.

himself to the city and fort, giving its dependencies to his native ally, Timoja, who governed them for him. Albuquerque was a brave and honourable gentleman; his acts have no stain of cruelty or deceit upon them, and he was respected, as much as feared, by his enemies.

His successors were men of a different stamp: less soldiers than merchants. Lopé Soarez made an unsuccessful attempt to take Aden; and Malacca was threatened, only to be saved by the spirit of its garrison. In 1517, however, Fernando Perez de Andrada reached Canton, and established the first European trading relations with the Chinese. Diego Lopez de Siquéra was a viceroy of much the same character as Soarez. He had a fleet of forty ships and 3,000 men. With these, in 1521, he sailed to Diu, and made the old demand in regard to a site for a fort; but meeting with a stern refusal from the old Guzerat admiral, abandoned the enterprise, and retired, but not unmolested, for Mullik Eyáz harassed his rear, took one of his vessels, and followed him to Choule, where he was again shamefully defeated. That the Portuguese were cowardly, began to be believed by the Kings of Guzerat and the Deccan; and in 1522, the King of Beejapoor attacked Goa, which he was however unable to take; but the Portuguese could not defend the territory of their native ally, Timoja, which was annexed to the Beejapoor dominions. It is true that this pusillanimity was redeemed by Hector di Silviera, in 1527; but a review of his proceedings will be better deferred to the history of Bahadur Shah, king of Guzerat, over whom a great victory was obtained.

His successors.

First intercourse with Chinese.

Diego Lopez defeated by the Mahomedan admiral.

Rhodes taken by the Turks.

BOOK IV.

CHAPTER I.

OF THE INVASION AND REIGN OF BABUR—INTRODUCTORY.

BEFORE entering on the details of the last Moghul invasion and its consequences, and the establishment of an imperial dynasty, in many respects differing very materially from its predecessors—a dynasty which, after attaining the utmost degree of splendour and power, was finally extinguished in misery and shame within the last few years—it seems an appropriate stage in this history to review, very briefly, the effects of the early Mahomedan rule upon India, and upon its people, up to the period referred to.

If this period be reckoned from the first invasion of Mahmood Shah of Ghuzny, in A.D. 1001, to the establishment of the Emperor Babur at Dehly, in 1526, it amounts to 525 years; but as the Mahomedan expeditions to India, up to the reign of Mahomed Ghoory—nearly 200 years later—may be considered more as military and predatory operations than affecting the government of the country, then only partially occupied by military posts, it becomes necessary to date the establishment of Mahomedan government from the reign of Kootub-ood-deen Eibuk, whose administration may be said to have commenced immediately after the battle of Narrain, in 1193; for, after that period, the various dynasties of the Mahomedan kings succeeded each other, as has been exhibited in detail, without interruption, down to the extinction of that of Lody, by Babur, in A.D. 1526. The period of actual administration, therefore, becomes reduced to 333 years. It was at first necessarily partial and circumscribed; but was gradually extended over the whole of India to the north, and as far as the Krishna river to the south, which as yet defined the extent of the Mahomedan possessions. South of the Krishna, as late as 1526, the country, up to this period, was exclusively Hindoo.

It is always difficult to realise the progress of time by mere numbers. If reduced to practical application, the figures 333 may serve to represent the period between the reigns of Henry VIII. and King John of England; or, as a later standard, between Henry VIII. and the present year, 1870, in the reign of Queen Victoria. The events of the intervening periods may be followed mentally, and the progress made estimated; and hence a deduction follows in regard to the time which has been needed to produce the changes that are evident. It is by no means so easy, however, to deal with the variations of a distant period, in a country entirely differing, in all respects, from any European standard; and while there is nothing on record among Hindoos, it is from the histories of the Mahomedans alone that the deficiency can be supplied; and from the details of their progress up to 1526, the conclusions to be arrived at are eminently unfavourable. This period has been shown to have been one continuous struggle for dominion, and, for the most part, for the suppression of Hindooism; and though the former had succeeded, the latter had made no progress whatever. It was in vain that millions, perhaps, of the Hindoos had been sacrificed under the fanatic zeal of an intolerant faith; equally vain that their temples had been destroyed, the idols they contained broken to pieces, and their holiest shrines desecrated. Hindooism yet remained, in every part of India, dear to the people, and its rites were practised in defiance of edicts, and of Mahomedan terrorism. There is hardly a reign of the early Mahomedan kings, in which expeditions for the express purpose of the extermination of idolatry and infidels are not chronicled with undisguised exultation by the Mahomedan historians; and the details of wholesale brutal massacres, or making slaves of tens of thousands of captives at a time, up to the period under notice are at once savage and repulsive. If here and there they are varied by the comparatively benevolent toleration of one monarch, he is almost invariably succeeded by another of the hereditary stamp.

Up to the period of 1526 there is no appearance of the Hindoos having enjoyed the continuance of their own peculiar laws; and indeed, under the tenets of the Mahomedan faith, and its practice, it would have been impossible for Mahomedan law officers to have administered, or even recognised them. It can only be assumed, therefore, that they were continued in secret, and were applied to questions of inheritance after a manner which avoided, or did not provoke, interference; and that their social ranks of caste protected them from disabilities which would otherwise have ensued. The Emperor Babur mentions in his Memoirs, that when he arrived in India, the officers of revenue, merchants, and workpeople were all Hindoos. In regard to the two last, the statement is no doubt literally correct. Mahomedan merchants, or dealers in money, were very rare, and with few exceptions Mahomedan artisans equally so; but his statement as regards the first classes must be received with reservation: and it is most probable that the employment of Hindoos extended only to the lower order of collectors of revenue, scribes and clerks—offices for which Mahomedans had neither qualifications nor tastes. In their dealings with the people, who spoke only vernacular languages, Hindoos were indeed indispensable, as interpreters and local managers; but, with very few exceptions, there is no trace of them having been admitted to public offices, or to any share in the government of their own people. Nor was it until after-times that their abilities were put to use, and they were allowed to rise in the imperial service to the rank to which they were entitled.

There was not only no progress in Hindoo literature or science, which before the Mahomedan invasion had attained great perfection, but what they possessed had grown obsolete from actual desuetude. Their trade had become impoverished, and that with foreign countries, except on the western coast, appears to have ceased altogether. Every Hindoo State, except a few of the Rajpoots in Rajpootana, had disappeared from the records of history; and while those that remained had as yet held their position only by their indomitable valour, they were tributary to the paramount power. In the whole of India there remained but one unconquered and independent, which was the kingdom of Beejanugger, and that was soon to follow the fate of the rest.

Had, however, these great national revolutions been attended with any corresponding benefit to the people? Had the Mahomedan Government introduced any civilizing influence of its own in furtherance of what had existed before? It is difficult to discover any whatever; nay, it is evident that in the destruction of the Hindoo nationality, the Mahomedans had supplied none of their own spirit or energy. They had not sought to raise the Hindoos to their own level, but to depress them as much as it was possible to effect; and they lay, as it were, at the feet of their conquerors, humbled and helpless, the sport of every succeeding tyrant, or breathing awhile in peace under the rule of a monarch comparatively merciful and considerate. In one point, however, the Mahomedans could make no impression upon the ancient Hindoo system, which would in any degree tend to their own benefit, and for the most part it underwent no interference. This was the independent government of villages by their local and hereditary corporations; and it was this system which secured to the Hindoo people, and perpetuated, the only freedom they retained.

The antiquity of village administration cannot be estimated;

but that it descended from the Aryan period can hardly be doubted. As lands were occupied by communities, which supported themselves by agriculture, members of trades and handicrafts were necessary to the general wants, and to retain their services, became hereditary officers. The carpenter, the blacksmith, the goldsmith, the potter, and others, were servants of the village, and were paid by dues levied on the produce at harvest. Over these was placed a chief authority or magistrate, and an accountant and registrar, whose offices also became hereditary. The head men, with the artificers and some others, formed the village council, which managed all local affairs, regulated the distribution of lands, settled local disputes, agreed with the officers of State for the revenues to be paid, collected them and transmitted them. Revolutions in general governments, of kingdoms or provinces, did not affect the constitution of these village republics: they were independent in the management of their own affairs; sometimes paying more, sometimes paying less, according to the rigour or mercy of the demand, but still preserving independence as far as social government was concerned. Nor did it much signify whether their government were Hindoo or Mahomedan. Over these communities the storms of dynastic revolution passed without effect; and as they were in 1526, so for the most part they remain, still practically free. The Mahomedans made no change in them; they must have seen that they could substitute nothing more simple or more efficient. A brutal monarch like Mahomed Toghluk might, for a time, impose cesses or taxes which rendered cultivation impossible, and when the villagers fled, might hunt them down like wild beasts; but even such misery had only a temporary result. When the storm passed over, the people resumed their old habits, and their old system, which, throughout India, might be modified by local existing circumstances, but was never wholly changed or eradicated. It was the only condition of freedom which remained to the Hindoos, and it was maintained. The Hindoo system had involved payment in kind—a fifth generally of the produce. This was changed by the Mahomedans into a commuted payment in coin, when coin became plentiful, and was probably of mutual advantage to both parties. It may also be stated, to the credit of the Mahomedan Governments, that their demands and assessments were seldom excessive or tyrannical, except when a poll-tax was imposed in addition to the demand upon the cultivation; and when this took place, it was attributable to the fanatic zeal which sought to abolish general idolatry by taxation of individuals.

It has been often said in praise of the Mahomedan period, that its monuments are unsurpassable in grandeur; and this is true to a certain extent, though that grandeur belongs to the period to come, rather than that which has been described. Up to 1526, architecture had made comparatively little progress, and their magnificent fortresses were only perfected after the introduction of artillery. Feroze Toghluk had constructed canals, and introduced from the south of India the system of irrigation; but his is a solitary instance of this public benevolence, and personally, in all respects, he was one of the most considerate of the early emperors of Dehly. Of the rest there are but few remains of any beauty or grandeur; even their mausoleums and palaces are insignificant in comparison with those which followed at Agra and Dehly, and in the Deccan; and it was in Guzerat and Malwah only, where the local monarchs applied the principle of Jain architecture to their public edifices, that up to this period, 1526, any remarkable buildings had been constructed.

In regard to education, the Mahomedans founded many colleges and schools at their capitals, and in some instances extended their school system into villages in connection with the endowments of mosques; but the languages taught in them, Persian and Arabic, were foreign to the people, and even to Mahomedans who became gradually part of the general population, and spoke vernacular languages. The range of acquirement was confined to religious works and a few elementary sciences, inferior to those of the Hindoos, and were unattainable by the people at large. It may be presumed that ordinary Hindoo village-schools were not interfered with, but they formed no part of the State system. It is recorded of many of the kings, that they patronised literature; that they themselves were authors and poets; but the learned men who assembled at their courts were not Indian; they came from Syria, Arabia, Persia, and even Spain; that is, from those countries to which the best era of Mahomedan literature belongs. Some local historians made records of their times; but the best of them, Ferishta, was a Persian, and belonged to a later period. Any progress in science which distinguished other Mahomedan countries did not appear in India. In poetry, and in novels and tales, there is an equal blank as regards native Mahomedans; for Ameer Khoosroo, and other Dehly authors, were foreigners. It has been already stated, that Hindoo literature was dead.

In the general improvement of the country no progress appears. Main tracks between the capital and the chief towns of provinces might be cleared of impediments and jungles; but it has not been discovered that any permanent road or causeway was ever attempted or executed. There were horse-posts, and post-houses in some instances; but these were for the use of Government servants and messengers, not for the people at large. In other respects, the communications through the country, whether by wheeled carriages or bullocks, remained as they were before the advent of the Mahomedans.

It will be admitted, perhaps, that such a system of government was capable of no enlightened progress, and was not fitted for initiating any. It had never attempted any centralizing influences of amelioration, and was one of brute force and conquest only, without other aim or consequence. In its turn, and without any principle of co-adhesion, it had fallen to pieces, as was its inevitable destiny; and it may be believed that in 1526, the inhabitants of Northern India regarded their deliverance from their gloomy and dissolute Afghan tyrants with a grim satisfaction, though they might not have much hope from their Moghul successors.

CHAPTER II.

OF THE MOGHUL DYNASTY—THE REIGN OF BABUR, A.D. 1526 TO 1530.

BABUR was a lineal descendant of Teimoor, or Tamerlane, and the sixth in descent from him. His father, Oomur Sheikh Mirza, had first been placed in charge of Kabool, by his father, Abu Said; but he was removed to Ferghana, on the Juxartes, where Babur was born. His mother was a Moghul of the race of Ghengis Khan; but Babur had no liking for the tribe, and indeed has recorded that he detested them. It is strange, therefore, that the dynasty he founded in India should ever have been termed Moghul; it was essentially Tartar; but the most recent invasions from the west having been by Moghuls, all Mahomedans had become known under that appellation, and the emperors themselves never seem to have desired to alter what was assigned to them by the people. It would be foreign to the scope of this work to follow the early fortunes of Babur. They are full of romance, and the student will find in the Autobiography of this prince, translated by Mr. Erskine, not only a fund of information in regard to transactions in Central Asia in the beginning of the sixteenth century, but a delightful record of his own tastes, feelings, and adventures, written with truth, and under a high sense of enjoyment of the beauties and pleasures of nature and of life, which is very charming. When he was only twelve years old, he lost his father, and became king of the family dominions; and at the age of fifteen, he had conquered for himself his ancestors' capital of Sarmacand. This he was too weak to retain—his conquest, and even his own dominions, alike passed away from him, and he was reduced to such straits of poverty, that his servants even abandoned him. When in his twenty-third year, Babur was driven out of Trans-Oxania, and this seems to have been the turning-point in his fortune; for in 1504, abandoning Central Asia, he had possessed himself of the kingdom of Kabool, where he reigned, in a constant state of chronic warfare with his neighbours, and of watchfulness to preserve his own possessions. In 1511 he had again taken Sarmacand; but, as before, could not retain it; and by a combination of Persians and Uzbeks, in 1514, he was deprived of all his dominions except Bactria. It was now that he turned his attention to India. The news of the distractions and repeated revolutions at Dehly reached him through Doulut Khan Lody, viceroy of the Punjâb, from time to time; and he conceived it a favourable opportunity for establishing the empire, to which, by his ancestor Teimoor's conquest, he had at least a better claim than any of the adventurers who had successively filled the throne. His first advance into India took place in 1519; but he had only reached Peshawur, when an invasion of Budukshân by the King of Kashgar obliged him to return. He had been unable to establish communication with Doulut Khan Lody; but he had written to the Emperor Ibrahim Lody, that the Punjâb should of right belong to him, and he requested its cession. In 1520 he again marched into India, but was obliged to return as suddenly as before, to repel an invasion from Kandahar. In 1524 Doulut Khan renewed his invitations, and Babur advanced as far as Lahore; but Doulut Khan had now turned against him, and in the uncertainty of his position, Babur returned to Kabool, having left governors in the districts he had occupied. Meanwhile the Prince Alla-ood-deen Lody, uncle to the King of Dehly, who had been residing at Kabool, made an attempt, under the assistance of Doulut Khan, to gain the throne of Dehly; but was defeated, and returned to his place of refuge. This seems to have encouraged Babur to make a final attempt. He crossed the Indus on December 15, 1525, at the head of only 10,000 chosen horse, and was met by Doulut Khan Lody and his son Ghazy Khan, at the head of 40,000 Dehly cavalry; but they declined an action, and reconciliation between Babur and Doulut Khan ensued soon afterwards. Invitations from many parties disaffected to the emperor now came in rapidly, and the sequel has already been related in Chapter XII., Book II.; the battle at Paniput, and the death of Ibrahim Lody in the action. Sending on his eldest son Hoomayoon to occupy Agra, Babur entered Dehly on May 10, 1526, and was proclaimed Emperor of India.

Babur had probably been misinformed as to the true condition of the monarchy of Dehly; he may have considered that it extended over all India, whereas he found it to be confined to a narrow tract, north-west of Dehly, communicating with the Punjâb. All else, to the south and east, was in the possession of revolted chieftains, and must be reconquered. His army too was probably affected by this discovery, as much as by the heat of the weather: for it became discontented, and even among the nobles and courtiers of Dehly an expectation appears to have arisen that Babur, like his ancestor Teimoor, would be content with a ransom, and leave them to their usual intrigues and revolutions. Babur, however, was equal to the emergency. He had come to conquer India, and would do so. His appeal to his own army was successful; under his resolute demeanour, many who had revolted made submission, and in four months his son Hoomayoon had recovered Joonpoor, and with it much of Bengal and Behar.

While the power of the Dehly kings was on the decline, that of the Hindoos in Rajpootana was on the increase, and had become in a great measure consolidated under Sunga, rajah of Chittore. In 1519 he had defeated and taken prisoner Mahmood Khiljy, king of Malwah, and since then had very materially increased in power. So long as Babur was merely opposed to a King of Dehly, anything that would tend to weaken that monarchy was welcome to the Hindoo prince, and he had sent Babur friendly communications; but when he became emperor, the situation was changed. Rajah Sunga summoned to his aid all the choicest warriors of the Rajpoot tribes: and exciting them by an appeal to their former chivalrous deeds in defence of Hindooism and their country, received an enthusiastic response. Once overthrown, the Mahomedans could not again rise, and the national faith would be restored. War was now declared, Mahomedan outposts were driven into the fort of Byana, and the Hindoo army advanced towards Dehly, and was met by Babur near Sikry. His Memoirs afford ample evidence of the anxiety he suffered on this occasion. An astrologer from Kabool had foretold the defeat of his army; his best veteran troops were dismayed; his Indian horse either deserted to the enemy or left his camp. He became penitent before God, he says: forswore drinking, gave away his gold and silver cups, and vowed to let his beard grow; but he did more than this—he assembled his best officers, and appealed to their honour, and the glory they had already achieved in many a fight. Were men of Islam to quail before the infidels? The reply was a fervent shout of devotion. As he drew up his army before the action, he rode down the lines cheering the men, and giving his instructions, and saw with joy that their old spirit had not departed. The Rajpoots fought with a valour and desperation that astonished even Babur himself; but they sustained a bloody defeat, and fled. In the sequel, Rajpootana was reduced to order, and Mahomedan garrisons placed in strong positions; and this having been accomplished, Babur turned his arms towards Mahmood Lody, who, having assumed the title of sooltan, had declared independence, and advanced to Benares with 100,000 men. This great but incongruous levy was also defeated, and afterwards dispersed, Mahmood himself retiring beyond the Soane river. Babur was now in possession of the Dehly territory south of the Ganges. North Behar was still held by the King of Bengal; but he made little resistance, and was admitted to terms. Soon afterwards a body of Afghans, who had separated from the Bengal army, rallied under Bayezeed Khan, and had taken Lukhnow; but these also were pursued and dispersed, and at the conclusion of this glorious and memorable campaign, Babur returned to Agra. It had been his last effort.

At Agra Babur was joined by his son Hoomayoon, who had left his government of Badukshan without leave, but was nevertheless affectionately welcomed. It is very possible that he had received intimation of his father's indifferent state of health, and wished to be near him. He himself, however, fell ill, and so dangerously, that his life was despaired of. When Hoomayoon had been altogether given up by the physicians, his father, in accordance with a strange superstition of his country, and despite the entreaties of his courtiers, determined to give his own life for his son's, and take his son's illness on himself; he accordingly walked thrice round his bed praying. In a short time afterwards he was heard to exclaim, 'I have borne it away, I have borne it away!' and began to decline. But, as has been stated, his health had already been affected by the climate of India, and the immense personal exertions made in the last campaign: and an illness began, before which he gradually sank, and expired at Agra, on December 26, 1530, in the fiftieth year of his age, and the thirty-eighth of his reign.

Of all the varied acts of his romantic life, there was none which, for daring valour, resolution, and consummate ability, could compare with Babur's short but brilliant Indian career. In less than four years, he had not only founded the dynasty of a great empire, but had recovered most of the ancient possessions of Dehly. He had himself selected a place for his grave, by a sparkling stream, near Kabool, and he was buried there; while to this day the garden around his tomb is a favourite holiday resort of the people of that city. Mr. Elphinstone has recorded an eloquent tribute to the memory of this great man ('History,' Book VII.), and quoted from his Memoirs many curious and interesting passages; but the Memoirs themselves are hardly to be estimated from extracts, and should be read in their entirety, as the only means of understanding the great but simple wisdom, habitual generosity, and light-hearted cheerfulness, indomitable bravery and perseverance, wit, humour, and refreshing boon-companionship, of this most natural and extraordinary monarch.

CHAPTER III.

THE MOGHUL DYNASTY (*continued*)—THE FIRST REIGN OF HOOMAYOON, 1538 TO 1540.

On Hoomayoon's accession to the throne of Dehly, he had to make provision, agreeably with his father's dying request, for his own three brothers: Kamrán, Hindál, and Mirza Askari. Of these, Kamrán was employed as governor of Kabool and Kandahar; the others had as yet received no offices. Hoomayoon would have preferred retaining Kabool and Kandahar as an appanage to his Indian dominions; nay, very possibly, might have preferred them to India itself; but he had little choice in the matter. Kamrán was by no means disposed to give up the territory over which he ruled, and Hoomayoon had no means of compelling him to do so. He, therefore, made over Afghanistan to his brother, and with it, the whole of the Punjâb. In following this course, however, he very materially weakened his own position; four years had not sufficed for consolidating the power of the new Indian dynasty, and Hoomayoon was by no means possessed of the talent or of the prestige of his father. He depended entirely upon his army, which was in fine condition; but he had alienated from himself the provinces from which fresh supplies of men could be drawn, the Indian soldiery had already the reputation of being mercenary and unfaithful, and he had no trust in them. To his brother Hindál he allotted the government of Sumbhul, and to Mirza Askari that of Mewat in Northern Rajpootana.

The emperor's first campaign was directed against the Hindoos of Bundelkund, always turbulent and disaffected. Kalinjer, so many times the subject of contention, was again being besieged, when the Afghan chieftains of Bengal, Bayezeed and Bábun, again rebelled. This insurrection was speedily repressed, and the emperor proceeded to attack Chunar, then held by Shére Khan, another powerful Afghan feudatory. He however submitted, on condition of retaining his fort; and the emperor, in 1532, returned to Agra. At this period, the kingdom of Guzerat, as will be elsewhere related, had attained its greatest eminence. Bahadur Shah was its king, who, as related in Ch. III., Book III., had succeeded Mozuffer Shah in 1526. He had annexed Malwah and some Hindoo States to his dominions; and as far south as Ahmednugger the kings of the Deccan acknowledged him as a paramount power. Bahadur Shah was by no means disposed to acknowledge the new dynasty of Dehly. If he owed allegiance at all, it was to the house of Lody, which had afforded him honourable protection in his absence from Guzerat; none certainly to the house of Teimoor. Nevertheless Bahadur Shah might have been as little noticed by Hoomayoon as he had been by Babur, had he chosen to keep neutral; but he did not remain so. His first offence was the protection of Hoomayoon's brother-in-law, who, under an accusation of treason, had fled from Dehly; and while negotiations regarding him were in progress, Alla-ood-deen Lody, the uncle of the late Ibrahim Lody, whose unsuccessful attempt to possess himself of Dehly has been related in the last chapter, suddenly left Afghanistan, and claimed his assistance. Bahadur Shah dare not, perhaps, openly espouse his cause; but he gave him money, by which Alla-ood-deen was enabled to equip a considerable force, and dispatch it against Dehly, under the command of his son Tartar Khan. It was, however, defeated by the emperor in a general action fought near Byana, in which Tartar Khan was slain. Hoomayoon was not now to be restrained from following up his victory over the malcontents in an advance into Guzerat; and this was delayed on a serious point of honour peculiar to the times. Bahadur Shah was engaged in war with the Rajah of Chittore, and had invested that fort. Were he to be attacked in that position, it would not only be at a disadvantage, but as a corresponding relief to 'the Infidels.' Hoomayoon waited therefore for the fall of Chittore; and in November 1534 advanced upon Bahadur Shah's camp, which was entrenched at Mundesoor. He had placed great confidence in his guns, which were served by the Portuguese, who had enabled him to prevail at Chittore; but they were of no avail: Hoomayoon cut off the supplies, and on his final attack in March 1535, Bahadur fled precipitately to Mandoo, and thence, finding himself pursued by the emperor in person, to Cambay, and eventually to the Island of Diu. Bahadur did not attempt to defend his territories, of which the emperor took possession; but the fort of Champanair long held out, and was only taken by escalade, the emperor himself being one of the three hundred men who gained entrance by climbing its almost perpendicular side, by means of steel spikes driven into crevices in the rock, while the attention of the garrison was drawn off by a feint against the gate. Believing his occupation of Guzerat to have been secure, Hoomayoon left the province under charge of his brother

Mirza Askari, the history of whose brief administration will be given in connection with the reign of Bahadur Shah, and marched for Bengal, about 1537, according to Mr. Elphinstone's computation of time, against Shére Khan, who had again rebelled, and on this occasion in a most formidable manner. The details of Shére Khan's progress will be more fitly given in the history of his career and reign than in this place. Hoomayoon, as he advanced eastwards, found Shére Khan was engaged in subduing Bengal: and he therefore laid siege to Chunar, which lay in the direct line of his advance, and of his communications. Chunar was taken—the pass of Chikragully, on the bank of the Ganges, was found unoccupied, and Hoomayoon's army debouched without opposition into the plains of Bengal. Gour was taken possession of almost without resistance, but still Shére Khan was at a distance. He had, however, followed a wise course. He had allowed the emperor to advance, as it were, into a decoy. The Ganges began to inundate the country, and the rains rendered it impassable. The emperor held his ground near Gour during the monsoon, but when the dry season enabled him to advance, he found that Shére Khan had thrown himself between Gour and the upper provinces, and was intercepting his communications. The advanced force of his army, on its return towards the upper provinces, was defeated near Mongyr, and before he could form any plans of his own, Shére Khan with his whole army had taken up a position across his very path. This campaign is one of the few of Indian occurrence in which military manœuvres were resorted to which can be followed with accuracy; and Shére Khan is entitled to high credit as a general, for the disposition and management of his forces. The emperor did not attack him at once, as he might have done with advantage, but allowed him, during a delay of nearly two months, to entrench his camp; out of which he sallied on the night of June 15, 1539, leaving enough force to mask his movements, and at daybreak the following morning assaulted the emperor in three divisions. The emperor's bridge of boats had not been finished, and escape was next to impossible—Shére Khan's attack was irresistible. Hoomayoon, as a last resource, plunged on horseback into the river, and would have been drowned with his horse, had not a water-carrier, floating on an inflated water-bag, rescued him. His army, including the best portion of his father's veterans, perished for the most part by the sword and in the inundations. The empress, who had been taken prisoner, was afterwards sent by Shére Khan to Agra, with every mark of respect.

Hoomayoon reached Agra safely, and found public affairs in great confusion. His defeat, and the loss of his army, had reduced his prestige. His brother Hindál had conspired against him, and

Kamrán, who had arrived from Kabool, was hardly to be trusted. Eventually, however, they were all reconciled. They expected that Shére Khan would follow up his successes, and were prepared to meet him; but instead of doing so, he remained in Bengal, reducing the whole to order, and establishing his own government. Growing weary of delay, and seeing how greatly Shére Khan was improving his position, the emperor moved against him in April 1540; and near Kanouj, met Shére Khan, who had advanced to encounter him. Hoomayoon had constructed a bridge of boats across the Ganges, over which he was allowed to pass his army without molestation. No sooner had he done so, however, than he was attacked by Shére Khan on May 16, and sustained an irreparable defeat. His army was driven back upon the bridge and into the river, where it perished for the most part; and Hoomayoon, whose horse was wounded, would have perished also, but for a eunuch, who guided an elephant on which the emperor had mounted, into the river and swam it across. Here, too, escape would have been impossible, for the elephant could not mount the steep bank on the other side; but two soldiers, who saw what had happened, tied their turbans together, threw them to the emperor, and so drew him to the shore. He was now joined by his brothers Hindál and Askari, and rallying a few troops, they made the best of their way back to Agra, whence, collecting such treasures and valuables as they could, the brothers pursued their route to Lahore, expecting that Kamrán, who was there, would enable them to hold their ground. In this, however, the emperor was mistaken; for Kamrán made peace with Shére Khan, by the cession of the Punjâb, and retired to Kabool.

Hoomayoon now proceeded to Sinde, then in possession of Hoosein Arghoon; and endeavoured to excite him to action in his behalf. But he was coldly received, and in the end opposed by this prince, who forced him to leave Sinde; and in his extremity, the emperor determined to cross the desert, and threw himself upon the protection of Mal Déo, rajah of Joudpoor. The march was one of misery and privation, many of his followers perished from thirst; and when the unfortunate monarch reached Joudpoor, he found the rajah hostile to him, and was obliged once more to resume his wanderings in the desert between that city and the Indus. It was a tract of burning sand, with hardly a break, unrelieved by the shade of a single tree, and almost destitute of water. Wherever there was any in the deep wells, a few houses had been built, generally fortified, and defended by a bold race of hereditary robbers and marauders. These people guarded their water with the utmost jealousy, resisted the attempts of the emperor's escort to obtain it, and after sharp skirmishes in many places, the unhappy fugitives were frequently driven off, and, already exhausted, had to struggle, as best they could, to another halting-place further on. In addition to the men, the horses, and a few camels, there was a crowd of helpless women, including the empress, then far advanced in pregnancy, and her attendants. After many weary marches, attended with the loss of numbers of their company by exhaustion, thirst, and fighting, they found themselves pursued by a body of the Joudpoor cavalry, from whom escape was impossible; but they were not attacked, and it seemed the intention of their pursuers that they should perish in the waste; for parties of horse preceded them, cutting off all access to water and provisions. Yet the emperor and his devoted followers struggled on, until, in final despair, they prepared themselves for death. At this juncture, their pursuers appear to have been actuated by pity for their sufferings; for the son of the rajah advanced with a flag of truce, and after upbraiding the emperor for a wanton invasion, as it was considered, of the country, and the slaughter of cattle, provided him with water and a few coarse provisions, and suffered him to depart. Amerkote, upon which place his final hope of deliverance rested, was, however, still far distant, and the horrors of the preceding part of this sad march were almost exceeded before it was concluded; but finally the emperor, with but seven followers, arrived at the fortress, and obtained from its rajah, Ráná Persád, the hospitality and rest he so deeply needed. Here too was born, on October 14, 1542, the Prince Akbur, destined to become one of the most glorious monarchs that India ever possessed.

From Amerkote, with the assistance of its rajah, Hoomayoon made a fresh attempt to obtain a footing in Sinde. He was joined by other Hindoo princes, and found himself at the head of 15,000 horse; but he made no progress against Hoosein Arghoon; and Ráná Persád, affronted by the conduct of some Moghuls, suddenly left Hoomayoon's camp, his example being followed by most of the others. The contest with Hoosein Arghoon did not last long after this. Glad to be rid of the emperor on any terms, he assisted him to proceed to Kandahar, and on July 9, 1543, Hoomayoon proceeded thither, all hope of re-establishing himself in India being for the present abandoned.

CHAPTER IV.

OF THE AFGHAN DYNASTY OF SOOR, 1540 TO 1545.

AFTER the flight of the Emperor Hoomayoon from India, his successful rival, Shére Shah Soor, succeeded him; and established the seventh Afghan dynasty. Shére Shah was descended from a family of purely military adventurers. His grandfather, Ibrahim Khan Soor, a member of the Afghan tribe of that name, belonged to the town of Róh, in the province of Peshawur; and on the accession of King Bheilole Lody, came to Dehly in search of employment. The Soor family claimed descent from the princes of Ghoor, one of whom, Mahomed Soor, settled among the Afghans of Róh, married the daughter of a chieftain, and transmitted his name to his posterity. The Soor tribe were thus distinguished as illustrious from the other Afghans of the country. Ibrahim Soor did not enter the royal service of Dehly; he was employed by Jumál Khan, a nobleman of distinction, who, being afterwards appointed governor of Joonpoor, in Bengal, took Hussun, the son of Ibrahim Soor, with him, conferred upon him the command of 500 horse, and granted estates for their maintenance. This person had eight sons, the two elder of whom, Fureed and Nizam, were legitimate; but they seem to have been neglected and ill-treated, and Fureed left his father, and entered the service of Jumál Khan, as a private soldier. His father wrote for him to be sent back 'for his education;' but the young man could not be persuaded to return home, and applied himself diligently to study.

After the lapse of several years, Hussun Soor visited Jumál Khan at Joonpoor, and being reconciled to his son Fureed, now made over to him the management of the family estate, which he conducted with great success: but he was eventually displaced by his father, at the instance of a favourite concubine, in favour of one of her sons, Sooliman. Fureed then left Bengal, and proceeded to Agra, where he took service with Doulut Khan Lody, a relative of the king, Ibrahim Lody, who endeavoured to interest the king in favour of his *protégé*; but failing in this, Fureed made no other effort to disturb his father's arrangements, and on his death was recognised as his heir, and received the royal confirmation of the family estates. He was not opposed by Sooliman, who retired to the court of Mahomed Khan Soor, a distant relative, now governor of Joonpoor, who seems to have endeavoured to make an arrangement between the brothers, and was preparing to enforce his award, when Ibrahim Lody, the king, fell in battle, and was succeeded by the Emperor Babur.

Fureed Soor would have been unable to resist the combination against him, but for the protection of Mahomed Shah Lohany, who had assumed independence in Behar. On one occasion, during a hunting party, Fureed slew a tiger with a single blow of his sabre, and received on the spot the title of Shére Khan, by which he was ever afterwards distinguished, and was also appointed tutor to the king's son. This did not, however, preserve him from the efforts of the family combination against him; and eventually Mahomed Khan Soor, taking advantage of his temporary absence, sent a force into the district, and placed Sooliman and his brother Ahmed in possession of the family estate. Shére Khan took refuge with the governor of Kuna, and obtained from him a body of troops to recover his territories, in the name of the new Emperor Babur. In this he was perfectly successful; and he recovered also other districts in the emperor's name, besides his own, obliging Mahomed Khan Soor to fly. Shére Khan thus became locally very powerful; but he recalled Mahomed Khan Soor, and generously put him in re-possession of his estate, thus converting his greatest foe into his warmest friend. Shére Khan had doubtless thus early perceived the necessity of strengthening the Afghan party in Bengal to the utmost of his power. Having thus settled his Bengal affairs, Shére Khan returned to Kuna, and accompanied his friend the governor on a visit to the Emperor Babur's camp.

Here he seems to have first conceived the possibility of recovering the throne of Dehly for the Afghan race. He said to a friend one day, 'that he thought it would be no difficult matter to drive those foreigners, the Moghuls, out of the country. If the Afghans, who were now at enmity among themselves, could be brought to unite, the work might be effected; and should fortune ever favour him, he imagined himself equal to the task.' Ferishta gives also a characteristic anecdote of Shére Khan. He was seated one day at dinner in the emperor's tent, when solid dishes of meat were before him, and he had only a spoon. His call for a knife was not attended to, and drawing his dagger, he cut up what he needed, and made a hearty meal. The emperor, who had been watching his guest, turned to the steward of the household and said, 'This Afghan is not to be disconcerted with trifles, he may come to be a great man yet.' Shére Khan was perhaps sensible of the imprudence of his conduct, for he left the emperor's camp suddenly, on pretence that his estate had been attacked, and proceeded to King Mahomed Khan Lobany, with whom he became an especial favourite; and it is evident that the manner and society of his own countrymen, the Afghans, were more acceptable to him than those of the court of the Moghul emperor.

Not long afterwards, King Mahomed Shah Lohany died, leaving a son—a minor; and his wife, the Sooltana Ladoo, as regent. Shére Khan acted as her minister; and, on the lady's death, succeeded to the chief power in the State, which was increased by a decisive victory obtained over the forces of the King of Bengal. It would appear as though it were impossible for any Afghan to endure the success or prosperity of another, and this national failing had proved the ruin of their several royal dynasties. Although Shére Khan's government of the Joonpoor State had been singularly beneficial and successful, his countrymen urged the young king, Julal Khan, to fly to the King of Bengal, already smarting under Shére Khan's defeat, and secure his aid in driving the minister from his position. Shére Khan could only protest his fidelity; but this had no effect, for the young king threw himself upon the protection of Mahmood Shah Poorby of Bengal, who, believing his statements, dispatched a large army against Shére Khan. This, however, like the former, was utterly routed, with the loss of its guns and elephants, by Shére Khan in person; and the young king, who had been present with it, again fled to Bengal, and made no further attempt to recover his kingdom.

This event materially increased Shére Khan's reputation, and also his actual power. He had now no rival in Behar, and by his marriage with Ladoo Mullika, the beautiful widow of Taj Khan, late governor of the fort of Chunar, secured that strong fort and its dependencies; while, about the same time, the successes of Mahomed Shah Lody against the Moghuls had secured Joonpoor and its dependencies, as far as Manukpoor, to the Afghans. This powerful Afghan confederacy did not, as has been already related in the life of the Emperor Hoomayoon, escape notice; and Hoomayoon marched against them from Kalinjer, which he was besieging. Whether from pique against Mahomed Shah Lody, or from a conviction that the proper time had not yet arrived, Shére Khan withdrew his forces from his ally, and an easy victory over him was obtained by the Moghuls. The Emperor Hoomayoon, who had supposed Shére Khan to be in his interest, now sent an officer—Hindoo Beg—to request the surrender of Chunar. This, however, being refused, the emperor proceeded in person to attack it, when Shére Khan protested his loyalty, and offered to send his son with 500 horse to serve in the royal army. These terms were accepted; Chunar was secured by a royal grant, and while the emperor was employed against Guzerat, Shére Khan, joined by his son from the emperor's camp, reduced the whole of Behar, and afterwards Bengal. Shére Khan had now completely thrown off the mask; and on the emperor's return from Guzerat, he besieged Chunar, which was taken, after a defence of six months, forced the pass of Gurhy, and entered Bengal. Shére Khan was, however, in nowise dismayed. As Chunar had been captured, what he most needed was a safe place for his family, and where his treasure could be protected; and he proposed to Hurree Krishn, a Hindoo chief who held possession of the impregnable fort of Rhotas, to admit him. The Hindoo, trusting to possess himself of Shére Khan's valuables, gave a ready assent. But Shére Khan had determined upon ejecting the Hindoo, and establishing a garrison of his own in the place. This was accomplished by sending a number of armed men in covered litters into the fort, as had been done in the case of the capture of Aseergurh by the King of Khandésh; and, after a short struggle, Hurree Krishn fled. Shére Khan, who was not far off, now took possession of Rhotas, established a strong garrison in it, and was free to prosecute the campaign against the emperor, now engaged at Gour, in Bengal. He, therefore, took up a position which he knew the royal army must pass on its way back to Agra, where the rebellion of Hindâl Mirza had rendered the emperor's presence indispensable; and the emperor's entire defeat has been already recorded. Shére Khan might have pursued the emperor with success, but 5,000 Moghul horse had been left in Gour, and this force was attacked without delay, and eventually routed, with the loss of its general.

Shére Khan Soor, king of Bengal, 1540.

Shére Khan now considered it a fitting period to assume the title of king, and he was crowned in 1539; and in the next year, marched to meet the Emperor Hoomayoon, who was advancing from Agra at the head of 100,000 men. The engagement which ensued, and which decided the fate of the empire of India for the time, has been already related in the first reign of Hoomayoon. The emperor was pursued to Agra, and through the Punjâb, by Shére Khan; who, having laid the foundations of a new Rhotas, and appointed his faithful and able general, Khowas Khan, as viceroy of the province, returned to Agra. Here he heard of a new attempt to create a kingdom in Bengal by Khizr Khan, whom he had left as viceroy, and he proceeded thither, suppressed the rebellion, and divided the territory into provinces. In 1542 the emperor, as he was now styled, took the field on a campaign against the always rebellious Hindoo States of Central India. Gwalior was taken, as also Runtunbhore; and on his return to Agra, Shére Khan applied himself diligently to the civil administration of the kingdom. In 1543 he again took up arms against the Hindoos. Raiseen was invested, and after a gallant defence, the garrison surrendered on condition of retaining their arms and property. One of the holy men attached to the emperor, however, decided that no faith could be kept with infidels, and Shére Khan directed the Hindoos to be attacked. None escaped this massacre, which appears to have been revolting even to the Mahomedans employed in it, and whose loss was very severe. After a brief rest, Marwar was invaded from Agra: and the emperor, finding how resolutely he was opposed by the Rajpoots, contrived, by means of a forged letter, to excite dissension and mutual suspicion among them. But while Mal Déo, prince of the country, retreated, Koonbha, one of his chieftains, discovered the deception; and being unable to 'convince Mal Déo of his error,' determined to subdue Shére Shah with his own tribe, or in any case to remove the stain upon their reputation. Shére Shah had 80,000 men in the field, Koonbha only 12,000; yet such was the fury of the Rajpoots' attack, that the emperor would have been defeated, but for the opportune arrival of a reinforcement, at the head of which he charged the Rajpoots, broke them, and slew the greater part of them. In allusion to the poverty of the country, and the bravery of its people, 'he had nearly,' he said, 'lost the empire of India for a handful of millet.' Chittore surrendered, and the emperer advanced to Runtunbhore, where he established his son Adil Khan. The Rajah of Kalinjer was next summoned, but he had heard of the emperor's treachery to the garrison of Raiseen, and refused to surrender. His fort, too, was one of the very strongest in India. The emperor invested it, and the siege had made much progress, when a shell burst in the battery, where the emperor was standing, blew up the magazine, and with it himself and many of his officers. He survived, however, till the evening, though in great agony; and when he heard that the fort had been taken by assault, he cried out, 'Thanks be to Almighty God!' and expired. This event occurred on May 22, 1545.

Shére Shah dies, 1545.

The emperor had reigned about five years, and had, notwithstanding his wars, done more for his country than most of his predecessors. He had built caravanserais, and dug wells—one at every two miles—from Soonargaum, in Bengal, to the Indus. He had erected mosques on the highways, and travellers were entertained at every stage at the public expense. Fruit-trees were planted along the lines of road, and horse-posts established for the public convenience. It is impossible to say what reforms might not have followed in the general administration, but for the emperor's death, in, as it may be said, the prime of his life. He had thoroughly effected what he had believed and declared to be possible—the expulsion of the Moghuls—and he had no rival in Northern India.

In comparison with most of the Afghan monarchs of India, the character of Shére Shah takes a high rank; nor is there any stain of the national cruelty attached to it, except in the instance of the massacre of the brave garrison of Raiseen. Shére Shah's subjects in Bengal were for by far the most part Hindoos. Yet he had governed them without any display of bigotry, which renders the event at Raiseen the more inexplicable. Stratagem, however, was a national characteristic, and was exhibited in a remarkable manner in the capture of the stronghold of Rhotas. As a general, Shére Khan takes a very high rank among Indian commanders. His military operations against the Emperor Hoomayoon, on both occasions of invasion of Bengal, were directed by great skill in strategy; and the combination of his comparatively weak forces against the flower of the Moghul army, hitherto unchecked, and the personal bravery by which they were directed, met with deserved success. There is no instance in the attainment of empire by military adventurers in India, which can be compared with that of Shére Shah Soor. From a private soldier, he had raised himself, in comparatively few years, to the rank in which he died, and that too without any of those crimes of murder or assassination which were the characteristics of his predecessors; and from his antecedents, had his life been spared, there is every reason to think that India might have enjoyed the effects of a firm and beneficent reign. Shére Shah's remains were carried to Sasseram, his family estate in Behar, and interred in the noble mausoleum there, which is still perfect. Surrounded by a reservoir of water, a mile in circumference, it is one of the noblest specimens of Afghan architecture in Bengal.

CHAPTER V.

OF THE DYNASTY OF SOOR (*concluded*), 1545 TO 1555.

SHÉRE SHAH SOOR left two sons—Adil Khan and Julal Khan—and had appointed the elder to be his successor; but the officers of the army, with whom Julal Khan was most popular, elected him to be emperor, and he was crowned in the fortress of Kalinjer, on May 25, 1545, three days after his father's death, under the title of Islam Shah, or more familiarly, Sulim Shah, by which he is best known. He wrote, however, to his brother, Adil Khan, then at Runtunbhore, to meet him at Agra, declaring that he had only taken up the authority as emperor till he should arrive; but near Agra he was met by Khowas Khan, the commander of all the forces, who had hastened from the Punjâb

Sulim Shah Soor emperor 1545.

on receiving news of Shére Shah's death, and who again caused him to be solemnly crowned, amidst the rejoicings of the army and the people. Sulim then renewed his invitation to his brother, and at his request deputed four officers whom he had named to escort him. The brothers met in a hunting-party near Futtehpoor Sikry, with much apparently real affection, and returned together to Agra, where Sulim attempted to seat his brother on the throne: but Adil Khan, by nature timid and indolent, well knowing also how little he had to expect from the nobles of the court, declined the honour, and leading forward Sulim Shah, placed him on the royal seat and saluted him, at the same time publicly disclaiming his birthright. He only stipulated for an estate; and being offered his choice, selected Byana, in Rajpootana. It would seem that the emperor would, on that occasion, have seized and imprisoned his brother, but for Adil Khan's conduct; but his suspicions remained, and two months afterwards he despatched a eunuch, with a pair of golden fetters, to bring Adil Khan to Agra. Of this intention Adil Khan had received intelligence, and he fled to Khowas Khan, in whom, as his father's most trusted friend, and a party to the settlement made at Agra, he had most reliance. Khowas Khan, shocked by Sulim Shah's perfidy, at once rebelled; and, aided by a number of the officers of the army, marched upon Agra. Sulim Shah was by no means prepared for such vigorous proceedings, and would have fled to Chunar; but being encouraged to try the event of a battle, marched out his troops, and attacked Khowas Khan, who was defeated. The Prince Adil Khan now fled to Patna; but disappeared soon afterwards, and was never traced. The insurgent chiefs protracted their rebellion, and retired to the Punjâb, where they were finally easily defeated at Umballa. Khowas Khan had, however, withdrawn from them on the eve of the action; and had he thrown himself on the emperor's mercy, would in all probability have been pardoned: instead of which, he wandered from place to place, till, in the year 1550, he was put to death by Taj Khan, the governor of Sumbhul, with whom he was residing. His remains were taken to Dehly and interred there, and such was the veneration in which his character had been held, that Ferishta informs us his tomb was considered sacred, and prayers were offered there, as to a saint, by all classes of suppliants.

Sulim Shah Soor died, 1553.

Sulim Shah Soor lived till 1553, when he died of a painful disorder which had long afflicted him. He had reigned about nine years. Like his father, in whose campaigns he had always taken an active part, he was a brave soldier, and in other respects followed his example in time of peace. He built intermediate post-houses between those of his father, on the road from Bengal to the Indus, and maintained an excellent police. In his general conduct he was spirited and energetic; and it is related of him, that when having leeches applied to him, he received news that the King of Kabool had crossed the Indus; he immediately started from his bed, ordered out his army, and had marched six miles before evening. As the gun-bullocks were at a distance grazing, he caused the field-artillery to be dragged by men as far as Lahore. This alarm, however, proved to be unfounded, and the emperor retired to Gwalior, where he died. It is remarkable that Mahmood Shah, king of Guzerat, and Boorhan Nizam Shah, of Ahmednugger, died in the same year.

Sulim Shah Soor had married his cousin Beebee Bye, the daughter of Nizam Khan Soor, and had by her one son, the Prince Feroze, who, at his father's death, was twelve years old. Ferishta relates that the emperor had frequently warned his wife of her brother, Mobariz Khan; and asked her, if she wished to preserve her child, to consent to his execution, 'for she might rely upon his putting his nephew to death.' Beebee Bye, would not, however, consent. The event proved that the emperor's suspicion was not without foundation; for, on the third day after his death, Mobariz Khan entered the females' apartments, and tearing the young prince from the arms of his mother, slew him with his own hand. He then caused himself to be crowned under the title of Mahomed Shah Soor, to which the appellation of Adily was added commonly, and by which he is distinguished.

Mahomed Shah Soor Adily succeeds, 1553.

Mahomed Shah was a profligate libertine, addicted to the lowest company. He could neither read nor write, and he began to confer the highest dignities of the State upon his low-born companions. He selected Hémoo, originally a Hindoo shopkeeper, and a man of much spirit and cleverness, who had been made superintendent of the markets by the late emperor, to be his minister, which gave dire offence to the proud Afghans of the court. Hémoo, however, did good service to his master, and was faithful to him to the last. It is impossible to conceive a court more profligate or disgraceful than that of Mahomed Shah Soor, who flung away his treasures, even in the streets, shooting golden arrows among the populace for his amusement. Brawls among the rough Afghan chiefs, even in the royal presence, were common; and one of them resulted in a rebellion which obliged the emperor to take the field for its suppression. Ibrahim Khan Soor, his brother-in-law, was also a cause of anxiety. An attempt to seize him drove that person into rebellion, in which he was very successful. He seized Dehly, and declared himself king, and proceeding to Agra, reduced the country about that city to some distance. During these proceedings, Mahomed Shah Adily was at Chunar, and from thence made a feeble attempt to suppress the usurpation. He found, however, that Ibrahim Khan was too strongly supported: and returning to Chunar, contented himself with the sovereignty of the eastern provinces. The empire was thus, for the present, divided into two portions. Meanwhile another strange revolution was in progress. Ahmed Khan, another nephew of the late Shére Shah, and brother-in-law of Mahomed Shah Adily, was in the Punjâb; and with the aid of some chiefs and nobles there, assumed the title of Sikunder Shah Soor, with royal state, and marched upon Agra at the head of 12,000 cavalry. Ibrahim Khan opposed him with a magnificent army of 70,000 cavalry, splendidly equipped: 200 of its officers possessed tents lined with velvet, and the gorgeous tent-equipage of the king himself had never been equalled. Before this imposing host Sikunder Shah's resolution failed for a time, and he made overtures for peace; but these were rejected, and he was attacked with impetuosity by Ibrahim's whole army. Part of his own was at once broken, but with a reserve he charged his adversary at a judicious moment, and completely defeated him. Ibrahim Khan fled, and the conqueror took possession of the capital; but he was not long able to enjoy his good fortune; the Emperor Hoomayoon was returning to India, and was to be opposed at all hazards.

Having been defeated by Sikunder, Ibrahim Khan fled to Kalpy. Here he was met by Hémoo, on the part of Mahomed Shah Adily, with a fine army, which had been collected at Chunar, to reconquer the western provinces. With this, Hémoo defeated Ibrahim Khan, and pursued him to Byana, which he besieged. But Mahomed Shah Soor of Bengal now appeared in the field against Mahomed Shah Adily, and Hémoo was recalled; when Ibrahim Khan fell upon his rear during the march, and was badly defeated. Ibrahim afterwards became chief of the Afghans of Meeana; but he continued restless till the end of his life, and was executed at Orissa, by one of the Emperor Akbur's generals, in 1567. After his recal from Byana, Hémoo followed Mahomed Shah Soor into Bundelkund: and, in an action which ensued at the village of Chuppurgutta, the Bengal king was defeated and slain. Hémoo was dispatched to Agra to oppose the Emperor Hoomayoon, and recovered both Agra and Dehly from the Moghuls; but he was finally defeated by Beiram Khan, the general of the Emperor Akbur, and executed, as will be hereafter related. He had been the main stay of Mahomed Shah Adily: and after his death the fortunes of that king declined, and he was eventually killed in a battle with the son of Mahomed Shah Poorby, of Bengal.

The reign of Sikunder Shah proved to be a very brief one.

He had been promised support by the Afghan chiefs; but no sooner had they placed him on the throne of Dehly (1554), than they fell to quarrelling among themselves for honours and estates; and, as Ferishta writes, 'the flames of discord were rekindled, and blazed fiercer than ever.' No one, in fact, seems to have been able to control these fiery and unstable Afghan chiefs but a man like Shére Shah Soor, with an indomitable will and iron hand; and Sikunder Shah, though a brave soldier, had neither. The army he sent to oppose Hoomayoon was defeated; and leading a second himself, he was beaten near Sirhind by Beiram Khan and the young Prince Akbur. Sikunder fled into the mountains, and continued a desultory contest against the Moghuls, which will be noticed in its proper place, until he was suffered to return to Bengal, where he reigned for some years; but the date of his death is not mentioned. With him the troubled reigns of the Soor dynasty ceased, and the family itself most probably became extinct, as it never afterwards rose to notice. The Emperor Hoomayoon had entered India in triumph: and it may well be supposed that the people, again weary of the rude and faithless Patáns, so long alike untrue to them and to each other, were content to expect better times from a new foreign dynasty, or to witness, with apathy, a fresh contest for superiority.

CHAPTER VI.

THE SECOND REIGN OF HOOMAYOON, AND RE-ESTABLISHMENT OF THE MOGHUL DYNASTY, 1555 TO 1556.

The circumstances connected with the Emperor Hoomayoon's expulsion from India have been already narrated in Chap. III. of this Book, and it is unnecessary to make further reference to them. He proceeded from Sinde to the Persian court of King Thamasp, and was hospitably received; but was perhaps at one time in some danger, owing to a desire on the part of King Thamasp to induce or compel his guest to adopt the Sheea doctrines, which he himself professed, and to introduce them into India, should he become repossessed of his authority there. In spite, however, of some eccentricity on the part of the Persian king, he eventually rendered Hoomayoon material assistance in furnishing 14,000 horse, under the command of his son, to aid the emperor's designs; while, on the other hand, the equivalent given was the cession of the province of Kandahar, if it could be recovered from the Prince Kamrán, who now reigned at Kabool. With his Persian allies, Hoomayoon appeared before Kandahar, in March 1545. The place was held by Mirza Askary, on the part of Kamrán, and made a brave resistance for six months: when, from want of provisions, it was surrendered, and the Persian prince put in possession of it. So far Hoomayoon had performed his promises; but there seemed little hope of further co-operation on the part of his allies, and Hoomayoon marched towards Kabool, intending to treat with his brother Kamrán. By the way, however, news of the death of the Persian prince reached him, and he returned to Kandahar, gained possession of the fort by a stratagem, and expelled the Persian garrison, which retreated into Persia. Having thus secured a strong footing in the country, Hoomayoon, encouraged by the accounts he heard of his brother Kamrán's unpopularity, marched upon Kabool, and on the road was joined by his brother Hindál, and great numbers of disaffected persons of rank; and the invasion was so formidable, that Kamrán, unable to attempt resistance, fled towards Sinde, pursued by Hindál, while Hoomayoon, on October 2, 1545, entered the city in triumph. Here he had the happiness of being reunited to his beautiful wife and his son Akbur, now four years old; and as he took up the boy in his arms, writes Ferishta, he cried, 'Joseph by his envious brethren was cast into a well, but he was eventually exalted by Providence, as thou shalt be, to the summit of glory!'

It might be supposed that Hoomayoon would now have turned his arms against India; but news of the death of Shére Khan Soor did not reach him till some time afterwards. His successor, Sulim Shah Soor, was strong and popular; and Hoomayoon, therefore, proceeded against Budukshán, the affairs of which had fallen into much disorder. During his absence, Kamrán, who had been ill received in Sinde, and was wandering about Afghanistan, contrived to surprise Kabool; but he was unable to retain it. Hoomayoon hurried back from Budukshán, defeated several detached parties of Kamrán's troops, and finally invested the city; which, after committing many cruel acts, Kamrán evacuated, and fled to the hills, and eventually to Balkh, where he received assistance by which he was enabled to repossess himself of Budukshán. The contest between the brothers now continued. Hoomayoon's attempt to expel Kamrán from Budukshán in 1550 was not successful; on the contrary, he had a narrow escape of his life, and was obliged to fly, only eleven attendants remaining with him; but, in the succeeding year, he recovered the power he had lost, and Kamrán became a fugitive among the wild Afghan tribes which inhabited the mountains between Kabool and the Punjâb. Here also he was pursued by Hoomayoon, and in a night attack upon his camp, November 19, 1551, the Prince

Hindál was killed. Hoomayoon had latterly loved his brother, who, by his good faith and bravery in the field, had redeemed his former errors, and was much afflicted at his loss; he now married Ruzeea Sooltana, Hindál's only child, to his son Akbur, and settled upon them the wealth Hindál had accumulated. Kamrán received no encouragement from Sulim Shah Soor to come to his court, and led a wild life among the Gukkurs and other hill-tribes of the Punjâb borders. At length, in 1552, he was seized and made over to Hoomayoon by the chief of the Gukkurs. It was the opinion of the Moghul officers of State, that Kamrán should be at once executed for his crimes; but this sentence was commuted by Hoomayoon into loss of sight, which was carried out. Some days afterwards, Hoomayoon went to see him, and Kamrán rising, advanced a few steps and said, 'The glory of the king will not be diminished by visiting the unfortunate;' and Ferishta adds, that Hoomayoon burst into tears, and wept bitterly. Mr. Elphinstone, Book vii. p. 173, vol. vi., gives a detailed account of the whole event from Hoomayoon's biographer; from which, as well as from Ferishta, it may be inferred that the emperor, while he had saved his brother's life, could not defend him from the only other alternative of State punishment.

Kamrán dies, 1556.

Kamrán asked to be allowed to proceed to Mecca, which was granted; but he got no further than Sinde, where he died in 1556.

Hoomayoon was now the undisputed ruler of all the Moghul territory in Afghanistan, and was free to commence his operations against India. The time was singularly propitious: a civil war was raging in India between the several representatives of the family of Soor, and the people were weary of the race. Hoomayoon's friends at Agra and Dehly wrote beseeching him to come to them; but he hesitated, as indeed was natural, considering the immense hazard of the stake. On the one hand, India might not receive him, and a common danger might unite the whole of the Soor family and Patáns against him; on the other, his ever restless Afghan subjects might break into rebellion. In his perplexity, a courtier suggested an old method of divination: which was, to send three messengers in different directions, to return with the names of the first person they met; and this was put to the test. The first who returned had met a man named 'Doulut,' or empire; the second one named 'Moorád,' or good fortune; the third, a villager named 'Saadut,' or the object of desire. Thus, according to the native historian—and his anecdote bears the impress of truth—the omens were declared propitious: and no delay was made. Hoomayoon could only assemble 15,000 horse, but they were veteran troops, and with them he marched from Kabool, in December 1554. At

Peshawur he was joined by his son Akbur, and his friend and general, Beiram Khan, with a select body of veterans from Ghuzny and Kandahar. It is worthy of remark, that the emperor, in the previous war, had despatched his son Akbur to his government of Ghuzny; and it was doubtless in this early training in public business, that his strength of character was developed. No opposition to the Moghuls was made by the Patán viceroy of the Punjâb, Tartar Khan. The fort of Rhotas was abandoned, and Hoomayoon entered Lahore without opposition. Here he halted to make some necessary arrangements in the country, sending on Beiram Khan in advance, with the Prince Akbur to check Sikunder Shah's army, which was advancing under Tartar Khan. Beiram Khan however did not hesitate to engage it, and defeated it at Machywara, near Sirhind, with the loss of elephants and baggage; while he sent out detachments which occupied the country nearly as far as Dehly. The resources of Sikunder Shah Soor were not, however, exhausted. On the defeat of Tartar Khan, he advanced in turn at the head of 80,000 men and a large train of artillery. Beiram Khan was too weak to oppose this host, but he wrote urgently to Hoomayoon to join him, and the emperor did not delay. On the morning of June 18, 1555, a memorable date in India, as well as in Europe in after years, as the young prince Akbur was inspecting the outposts, the Afghans under Sikunder Shah drew up and offered battle, and it was not declined. The contest raged for some time very hotly, the emperor, his noble son Akbur, and Beiram Khan being in the thickest of the fight; but the Moghuls, led by their young prince, were irresistible; the Patán army was defeated with immense slaughter, and Sikunder Shah fled to the hills. This victory once more decided the fate of the empire of India, and established a dynasty, which of all those heretofore existent, was to prove the most glorious and enduring. Dehly and Agra were successively taken possession of by an advanced force, and in the month of July the Emperor Hoomayoon re-entered Dehly after an absence of fifteen years of much vicissitude of fortune. Some revolts of minor character were summarily repressed, and the emperor was engaged in the general pacification of the country, when he met his death by a strange and untimely accident. On the evening of January 21, 1556, he was walking on the terrace of the library at Dehly, when, in the act of descending the steps to go to the evening prayer, the muezzin of the mosque announced the hour in the usual manner. Pausing to repeat the creed, the emperor sat down till the invocation to prayer was finished, and to assist himself to rise, made use of a pointed staff he usually carried. This slipped on the marble pavement, and he fell over the parapet into the

Hoomayoon re-enters Dehly, July 1555.

court below. He was taken up, and put to bed; but the injuries he had received were mortal, and he expired after some days of suffering on January 25, 1556. He was fifty-one years of age, and had reigned in India and Kabool for twenty-five years. Hoomayoon dies, 1556.

With many weaknesses, the character of Hoomayoon was yet noble and interesting. With greater firmness he might have preserved his empire against Shére Shah Soor; but in his youth, though personally very brave, he was a bad general, and his adversary was one of the best India had yet produced. It must be remembered also, that the Moghuls were as yet foreigners in India, and were far from popular. To the Hindoos indeed it might have mattered little whether Moghul or Patán was in the ascendant; but the native Mahomedans were of the latter party, and had attained under it power and wealth; the Moghuls were hereditary enemies of long standing, and it was only a natural consequence that when the first flush of Babur's conquest was past, the local Mahomedan party should have rallied under a vigorous leader, and thus they may have obtained the sympathy and assistance of the Hindoos. If the first reign of Hoomayoon had been one of rest and peace, it is probable India would have prospered greatly under his mild and tolerant government. As it was, the reigns of Shére Shah and Sulim Shah Soor were exceptions to the Patán or Afghan rule, and left little to be desired as to the well-being of the people; but in Mahomed Shah Soor Adily, the worst features of the Patán domination were resumed, civil war among the members of the family was desolating the country, and the well-timed advance of Hoomayoon was productive of general relief and peace. It is impossible not to sympathise with Hoomayoon in his early misfortunes, in his miserable wanderings in the desert, his struggles in Sinde, and his personal sufferings: nor to follow his variations of fortune at Kabool without interest; and the truthful memoirs of his servant Jouhur, exhibit him in all the conditions of his life as a simple, genial, good-humoured man, inferior in capacity to his great father Babur, but with a deep, fond love for his wife and child, so rare among eastern princes. Charitable and munificent, kind and courteous to all around him, and a pleasant companion, Hoomayoon's character is not tainted by crime; and the sorest test he was ever put to, was the blinding of his brother Kamrán, to save him from death. Passionately fond, as he was, of his boy Akbur, yet when he was only ten years old his father at once pushed him into public life at Ghuzny; and before he was twelve, he was fighting with his father and his gallant tutor and general, Beiram Khan, in the fierce battles with the Patáns of Sikunder Shah, which were to decide his future glorious empire of India. To the memory of his father, so deeply venerated, Akbur afterwards raised a splendid mausoleum of marble, which is still perfect; and it was from this building that the last royal representative of the family was led prisoner after the capture of Dehly, in 1857, and where his two sons were shot in its precincts.

CHAPTER VII.

OF THE REIGN OF THE EMPEROR AKBUR, 1556 TO 1558.

THE Emperor Akbur was not at Dehly at the period of his father's death. He was employed with his tutor, Beiram Khan, in the Punjâb; and when the news reached him at Kullanoor, he was at once raised to the throne, on February 15, 1556. Born on October 14, 1542, Akbur was thirteen years and three months old, or, according to Mahomedan reckoning, thirteen years and nine months, when he began his glorious and eventful reign; and in regard to his tender years and early strength of character, has only one competitor in Indian history, Ismail Adil Shah of Beejapoor, who, in his more limited sphere, was equally distinguished. The life and character of Akbur are so remarkable, and his reign so illustrious, that he became the subject of complete biographies and histories, by native authors of high reputation; while the records of the English Embassies, and the residence at Agra of Europeans of different nations, in considerable numbers, give undoubted confirmation on many points, which were entirely wanting in regard to many former monarchs of India.

It will have been seen by the previous narrative, that, as yet, public affairs in Northern and Eastern India were by no means settled. Sikunder Shah Soor, though defeated, was still in the field, at the head of some of the best of the old Patán chivalry. In the eastern provinces, the Patáns still held royal power; and Mahomed Soor Adily, with his followers and clansmen, was a formidable antagonist. The Rajpoots and Hindoos of Central India had as yet made no declaration, either of adherence to the old Mahomedan party, or the recognition of the new; and while many new estates and dignities had been granted by Hoomayoon to those who had served him best, the estates and allowances of the nobles and officers of the Patán court were as yet unconfirmed. It is almost impossible to conceive the existence of elements more profoundly disturbing or difficult to deal with; and to increase the embarrassment, the Moghul force in the country was singularly small, and may not at this period, even with reinforcements from

Afghanistan, have exceeded 30,000 cavalry; whereas, on the other hand, the united Patán clans could bring 100,000 into the field with ease; and Kabool and Kandahar, with Budukshán, ever restless and mutinous, were also to be controlled. Over this seething and unstable mass, a boy barely fourteen years of age, and his counsellors, inexperienced in Indian affairs, were to preside, and out of it to create one of the greatest empires of the world.

Akbur immediately appointed his tutor and general, Beiram Khan Toorkoman, now raised to the dignity of Khan Khanán, or lord of lords, as his prime minister: and committed to him the general regulation of civil and military affairs in detail: but, young as he was, and indeed from the very first, he never seems to have evaded the responsibility or the toil of the authority in chief, to have been drawn out of it into the pleasures of youth, or ever to have lost confidence in himself. He might have estimated, by the letters of congratulation which reached him on his accession, how slight was his hold on the country. They were those of his own officers only; all else held aloof, apparently watching the issue of events; and so long as Sikunder Shah Soor and Mahomed Shah Soor Adily were in the field, it is easily to be understood why they did so. Akbur's first act was to pursue Sikunder Shah, who had collected an army in the northern hills, and presented a formidable appearance; but he was totally routed in a general action near Umballa, and again fled into the mountains. Meanwhile Soliman Mirza, who had been placed in Budukshán as its governor, by Hoomayoon, rebelled, and marched against Kabool, which had so small a garrison, that Akbur was obliged to dispatch some of his own much-needed forces to the assistance of the governor; but they proved insufficient for the purpose. Suffering from want of provisions, the garrison at length capitulated, and Soliman Mirza was declared king, but returned to Budukshán. Akbur meanwhile had subdued the mountain tribes of the Punjâb about Nagrakote, and had received Dhuam Chund, their prince, into favour. Hitherto, therefore, he had made no attempt either to march eastwards to Dehly and Agra, or to strengthen them by reinforcements; and Hémoo, the active Hindoo minister of Mahomed Soor Adily, who had been watching his opportunity, now marched against them with a powerful army of 30,000 men and 2,000 elephants. The officer in charge of Agra had no means of opposing this invasion, and fell back upon Dehly; and an attempt was made by Khan Zemán, another Moghul commander, with 3,000 horse, to oppose the advance of Shady Khan, one of Hémoo's generals; but he was defeated, with the loss of nearly the whole of his force. Agra was taken, after a short siege, by Hémoo, who now advanced upon Dehly with the whole of his combined forces, and defeated Tardy Beg Khan, its governor, in a general action near Meerut. Dehly now surrendered, and the country was left open. During these events, Akbur was at Jullunder, in the Punjâb, where he was joined by Khan Zemán, and other officers, with the wreck of the Dehly and Agra forces: but he could see no way of retrieving the misfortunes, and in his extremity he submitted the whole question to the decision of Beiram Khan, in whose wisdom and foresight he reposed the utmost confidence. At a council of war, the officers of the army declared that with 20,000 men, which was all that could now be assembled, it would be madness to oppose the Patáns, who had 100,000 at least under Hémoo; and that the most advisable course was to retreat to Kabool. This course, however, was opposed by Beiram Khan, who, almost unsupported, was of opinion that the emperor ought to advance at once to give battle; and Akbur coinciding with his general, the movement was determined upon. It is evident from the sequel, that discipline among the Moghul commanders had been of a very loose description. For the most part semi-independent chieftains themselves, at the head of their clans, they had been used to act very much as they pleased; and though, when assembled together, they fought bravely and faithfully, yet they were not to be relied upon when separated. Beiram Khan, therefore, resolved upon making one serious example; and on the occasion of the emperor's temporary absence from camp, caused Tardy Khan Beg to be beheaded, on the ground of his having abandoned his post at Dehly. On his return, Beiram Khan informed Akbur what he had done, and of his grounds for so severe a measure, which involved the discipline of the army, and the safety of all. Akbur gave a reluctant approval to this act; but the difference in the conduct of the officers was immediately perceptible, displaying a confidence in Beiram Khan which was in the last degree important. The Moghul army had gradually assembled at Nowshéhra, and now advanced upon Dehly. Hémoo, who had assumed the title of Raja Vikram Ajeet, was at Dehly, and marched out his army to Paniput, the old battle-field since the age of the Máhábhárut, and took up his position; but he had already lost his advance guard with its guns, which had been captured by Beiram Khan in a skirmish. The action commenced on the morning of November 5, 1556, by Hémoo's advance with his elephants, which he hoped would terrify the Moghul cavalry; but, galled by flights of arrows and javelins, they became furious, and ran back upon their own army, causing vast confusion, of which full advantage was taken. Hémoo himself, mounted upon a huge elephant, and accompanied by 4,000 Patán cavalry, continued the fight in the centre, when he was wounded in the eye by an arrow; and sinking back from the pain, his troops considered he was killed, and fled; but drawing the arrow from his eye he still fought on, and endeavoured to break his way to the rear, till he was surrounded by a body of horse, who conducted him to the emperor, then at a short distance. Here Beiram Khan prayed Akbur to kill the 'infidel captive,' with his own hand, and so become entitled to the proud title of 'Ghazy,' or Champion of the Faith. The boy burst into tears; but drawing his sword, touched the head of his captive with it, when Beiram Khan, observing his emotion and natural reluctance to strike, at one blow with his sabre severed the captive's head from his body. Thus perished one who, raised from the lowest ranks of society, to be the minister and general-in-chief of a powerful Patán monarchy, had not only conciliated the proud people he had to control, but exhibited a clearness of judgment in military as well as in civil affairs, which had not only prolonged the existence of his master's kingdom, but had enabled him to contest the empire of India with the bravest and most successful of the Moghul generals. He was the first Hindoo who had ever risen to distinction among the Mahomedans; and the high talent and devotion he had displayed, were worthy of a better fate.

The emperor's triumph was complete: 1,500 elephants were captured, the Patán host dispersed, and Akbur entered Dehly in triumph. Blood-stained, and of evil reputation as the capital was, it was yet the throne of India; and the young conqueror may be forgiven the emotion he displayed, as he ascended the royal seat of his revered father. Akbur did not remain there long. News reached him from Kabool that Kandahar had fallen to the Persians, and that his general, Khizr Khan, had been defeated by Sikunder Shah Soor in the Punjâb. The former misfortune was for the present irremediable; but the latter must be looked to without delay. Sikunder Shah advanced to meet the emperor, but finding himself too weak to encounter him in the field, retired to the fort of Mánkote, which he defended, with much gallantry, for six months. When suffering from his wounds, he asked for terms of surrender, which were granted; and leaving his son Sheikh Abdool Rahman in the emperor's service as a hostage, he was allowed to retire to Bengal. This event occurred in July 1557, and left Akbur the undisputed possessor of the whole of North-Western India.

Sikunder Shah Soor retires to Bengal.

CHAPTER VIII.

OF THE REIGN OF THE EMPEROR AKBUR (*continued*), 1559 TO 1567.

It may be doubted, from the records of the period, whether the young emperor's relations with Beiram Khan continued to be as cordial as usual. Akbur of late had had many great questions to decide, and many new and serious responsibilities to assume, which had given strength and decision to his character; and he had rewarded independently, those who had done him good service. Beiram Khan does not always appear to have been present on these occasions, and the boy was thus thrown on his own resources. It is evident also, that acts of Beiram Khan had been of a violent, and perhaps revengeful, character; and though, as a State necessity, Akbur had openly acquiesced in the policy of the execution of Tardy Beg Khan, yet that officer had been one of his father's earliest and most devoted friends and companions: no taint had ever fallen upon his reputation for bravery; and a general sympathy for his fate prevailed, which was shared by Akbur himself. When Beiram Khan heard that Akbur had rewarded persons without referring them to him, he took offence, and withdrew himself for some days. One day afterwards, during an elephant fight, which the emperor was witnessing, one of the beasts engaged ran through the ropes of the minister's tent, who took the accident as a personal affront, and remonstrated against it; but was apparently satisfied with his ward's protestations that no indignity was intended. Several other occurrences served to excite mutual suspicion. The summary execution by Beiram Khan of a person of some rank, who had given him offence, aroused the anger of the Choghtay Tartar nobles of the court, to whose tribe he had belonged; and Moolla Peer Mahomed, the emperor's preceptor, who had also given offence to the minister, was summarily removed from office, banished from court, and replaced by a person in the minister's interest. Other events of the same character followed; and on one occasion, the courtiers gave vent to their feelings, and remonstrated with the emperor against the minister's now frequent acts of violence. The breach between them was now evidently widening, when at Agra one of the royal elephants attacked and killed another belonging to the minister, who ordered the driver of the emperor's elephant to be put to death; and on another occasion, an elephant ran against a boat in the river in which the minister was seated, and almost upset it. Beiram Khan, considering this act as a plot against his life, demanded the punishment of the driver, and Akbur sent him to the minister to be dealt with as necessary. He also was put to death—an act of cruelty which caused the emperor deep pain and offence. Perceiving himself out of favour, Beiram Khan undertook a campaign against Byana, but was unable to continue it unsupported, and released Shah Abdool Maaly, a nobleman who had been imprisoned for revolt, and seems with his aid to have contemplated an expedition against the Afghans of Bengal, with a view of establishing his own independence in that direction. All these acts combined to bring on a total estrangement between the emperor and Beiram Khan: and Akbur resolved upon asserting his right to carry on the government himself. He, therefore, sent his preceptor to the minister, with the following characteristic message. 'Till now,' he wrote, 'our mind has been taken up with our education, and the amusements of youth, and it was our royal will that you should regulate the affairs of our empire; but it being our intention to govern our people by our own judgment, let our well-wisher withdraw from all worldly concerns, and retiring to Mecca, far removed from the toils of public life, spend the rest of his days in prayer.'

Beiram Khan did not resist; he sent the insignia of his rank and public establishments to the emperor, and proceeded as far as Bhikanere, in Rajpootana, on his way to Mecca. Here he seems to have changed his pacific submission for an attitude of defiance and rebellion, and in 1559 began to raise troops. A force was sent against him, which he evaded by marching into the Punjab; but he was eventually brought to action, and defeated at Machywara, with heavy loss. Thence he fled into the mountains, where the people protected him for a time; but weary of such an existence, he sent a favourite servant to the emperor, imploring forgiveness, and an officer was dispatched to bring him safely to court. In December 1560, he was met near the royal camp by a deputation of officers from the emperor, and conducted honourably to his presence; where he hung his turban about his neck, and threw himself weeping at the foot of the throne. Akbur, much affected, stretched forth his hand and raised him, invested him with an honorary dress, and placed him in his old position, as head of the nobles. The emperor then offered him the government of Kalpy and Chundery, or, should he prefer to remain at court, his favour and protection; or otherwise, an honourable escort to Mecca. But it was evident to Beiram Khan that his former position could not be re-attained, and the great general accepted the retirement offered. 'The royal confidence once broken,' he said, 'how can I wish to remain in thy presence.

The clemency of the king is enough, and his forgiveness is more than a reward for my former services.' A pension of 50,000 rupees (5,000*l.*) a year was settled upon him, and Beiram Khan proceeded to Guzerat, on his way to Mecca. His fate was a sad one. He had been enjoying a boating excursion on a lake near the temples of Sahasnuk, and on his return to shore with his friends, was accosted by a Patán, Moobarik Khan, whose father he had slain in battle; and when in the act of receiving the embrace of this man, was stabbed to the heart by him, and died instantly. The event occurred in January 1561. His widow and infant son were sent with a suitable escort to Agra, where they were amply provided for by the emperor; and to the last the early services of Beiram Khan, his great bravery, and his spirited conduct at a very critical moment, continued to be Akbur's constant subjects of eulogium. It must be admitted, indeed, that Beiram Khan was a gallant soldier, and a character eminently suited to guide the rough men with whom he was associated. But for him, the Moghuls would have turned back from Nowshéhra. Under his leading they won a magnificent victory over five times their number. As the head, however, of a military aristocracy, the minister's presumption led him beyond bounds of endurance; and in no act of his life did the emperor display more acute judgment and fine temper, than in the graceful dismissal of his great minister. Henceforth Akbur was to rule alone. He was now eighteen years of age, and at the head of a body of chieftains who were but too ready to overrate the services they had performed. They looked more to such present advantages as they might be able to attain or extort by intimidation, or haughty bearing, than to their real bond of union and strength in the security of their emperor's position, which many of them were ready to dispute.

Beiram Khan assassinated, 1561.

Mr. Elphinstone well observes, 'Of all the dynasties that had yet ruled in India, that of Tamerlane was the weakest and most insecure in its foundations.' It had as yet obtained no real hold of the country, and its enemies were powerful and numerous. Its civil government had never been properly organized, and the short reign of Hoomayoon had proved its military weakness. Numerically speaking, the troops of Akbur were even less powerful than those of his father, and certainly less than those of his adversaries; his chances of obtaining aid from Afghanistan or Central Asia were fewer, while the native soldiery of India were untried, and from their local attachment to former dynasties, as yet impossible to be trusted. The first employment of his own means of conquest was little calculated to inspire Akbur with confidence in his project for the subjection of the whole of India to his own rule. One of his most trusted generals, Khan Zumán, was dispatched to Bengal against Shére Shah II., the successor of Mahomed Shah Adily, in 1560. Shére Shah had advanced with 40,000 Afghans to Joonpoor, and the events of Hoomayoon's reign might be renewed. Zumán Khan was, however, entirely successful, and with only 12,000 Moghul cavalry he and his brother overthrew the Afghans; but they retained the spoils of conquest, and behaved in so haughty a manner, that the emperor was obliged to proceed to the spot to assert his authority. He used no force; but, as Ferishta records, 'giving them a gentle reproof, he secured their attachment by his princely behaviour and courtesy.' A second instance was that of Adam Khan, an equally trusted officer, who, in the following year, was employed to reduce Báz Bahadur, a Patán, who had gained possession of the kingdom of Malwah. Adam Khan obtained a brilliant success, captured his opponent's family and property, and, as Ferishta writes, 'sent him with streaming eyes and a broken heart towards Boorhanpoor.' But, as had been done by Zumán Khan, Adam Khan retained the spoil, and the ladies of Báz Bahadur's court. The latter was the occasion of an affecting incident. One of them, the beautiful Hindoo mistress of the Malwah king, was required by Adam Khan to receive him; and, unable to resist, appointed an hour for the purpose. Dressing herself in her richest apparel, she lay down on a couch; but, as her attendants tried to rouse her on the Khan's approach, they found her dead. She had poisoned herself rather than submit to be disgraced. Here again Akbur displayed that decision and promptitude of action which alone prevented a rebellion. Marching at once from Agra on his general's camp, he recalled him to his allegiance, received the spoils of Malwah, which he was told had been retained in order to be presented in person, and returning to Agra, removed Adam Khan from his government. The king's choice of a successor was, perhaps, unfortunate; for he appointed his own preceptor to the post, who, being more a man of letters than of war, was defeated by Báz Bahadur, who, for a time, regained the whole of his dominions; but the loss was quickly redeemed, and Báz Bahadur, finding resistance useless, and after many fruitless wanderings from place to place, eventually threw himself upon Akbur's clemency, and was honourably entertained in his service.

Adam Khan murders the minister, and is executed.

Adam Khan's fate was very different. Smarting under the loss of his government, and prospect of independence, he stabbed the emperor's minister to the heart; and as he stood with the bloody dagger in his hand, was, by the emperor's orders, seized and thrown from the terrace of the building in which the murder had been done. The defection of the new governor of Malwah followed in 1563. He was an Uzbek—a tribe which had furnished many officers and men to the emperor's army. All these formed a confederation which, at one time, assumed very formidable dimensions, and will be noticed hereafter.

The emperor marries an Hindoo princess of Sumbhul, 1561.

In the year 1561, the emperor being in Rajpootana, visited Sumbhul, the rajah of which territory gave him his daughter in marriage, and, with his son, was enrolled among the nobles of Akbur's court. It is evident from this act, what turn the emperor's policy was taking. No fanatical attacks upon Hindoo States are perceptible; no wanton destruction of Hindoo temples and idols; but, on the contrary, a policy of conciliation and regard, which, to the Hindoo princes, was perhaps at first incomprehensible, but which, in the sequel, secured the attachment of the greater part of them. Some, however, of the Hindoo princes did not submit; and while the emperor, with six attendants, rode from Ajmere to Agra, a distance of 200 miles, in three days, an officer was sent against the fort of Mairta, which was captured, but not till after a long siege. Soon after his return from Rajpootana, the emperor had a narrow escape from assassination—an arrow shot at him by a slave penetrated his shoulder deeply; but he bore its extraction without a murmur. In the year 1564 Asof Khan Uzbek had been employed against the Hindoo principality of Guna. He had defeated the Ranee, who had stabbed herself on the field of battle rather than be captured, and following up his success, had obtained a vast booty in jewels, gold and silver coin, and bullion. A few indifferent elephants were alone sent to the emperor, and Asof Khan retained the rest for his own purposes. For this he was called to account; and immediately rebelled, in concert with the other Uzbek officers of his tribe. The first force sent against the Uzbek confederates in Bengal was defeated: a second was dispatched, which made no impression on them; and the emperor followed in person, in April 1566, when some of the rebel chiefs submitted. But the rebellion was by no means at an end, when the emperor was obliged to proceed to the Punjâb, to check a formidable combination in favour of his half-brother, Mahomed Hakeem Mirza, who, expelled from Kabool, sought to establish himself in the Punjâb, and was encouraged by several of the local commanders. On this occasion, however, Akbur's energy averted serious consequences. In the course of a few days he was in the Punjâb, whence his brother fled to Kabool, and local tranquillity ensued. The emperor now turned once more against his rebellious Uzbek chiefs, who, during his absence, had made much progress, and had gained the greater part of Oude. He crossed the Ganges, though much swollen, on his elephant, at night, and with only his body-guard attacked the insurgents on the morning of June 6, 1566. Khan Zumán, one of the chief rebels, was killed; Bahadur Khan was taken prisoner, and the rest dispersed, most of them being afterwards taken prisoners, and executed. The rebellion had lasted for more than two years, had resisted some of the emperor's best generals, and was put an end to only by the personal energy and bravery of Akbur himself; and it is evident from its details, which are amply given by Ferishta and other writers, that the Uzbeks were not only strengthening themselves in the eastern provinces, but were identifying themselves with the former Mahomedan parties there—an obviously appropriate course for them, and which added much strength and importance to their rebellion. The slight hold which the emperor possessed upon his Moghul chiefs will also have been apparent to the reader from the rebellions of his officers in Malwah, Guna, the Punjâb, and Bengal, the danger of which was increased by the transactions in Afghanistan and Mooltan; and it is impossible to withhold a tribute of high admiration of the ability, firmness, and personal activity which Akbur displayed. Never during these exciting occurrences does he appear to have hesitated as to his mode of action, and never to have thrown away a chance of success. He had now subdued his military aristocracy, and had defeated their formidable combinations. He had checked, if not entirely broken up, the Afghan party in Bengal; he had annexed a large portion of that country to his dominions, and had extended them to Malwah, and the frontiers of Khandésh and the Deccan. Yet it does not appear that his original means as to troops had been augmented. Kabool and Budukshán were too unstable and precarious to afford supplies of men; and admiration for his character is increased by the consideration of the accurate judgment by which his military operations must have been directed, in the employment of such troops as he possessed, amidst such serious distractions, and in so widely divided provinces.

Defeat of the Uzbek chiefs.

CHAPTER IX.

OF THE REIGN OF THE EMPEROR AKBUR (*continued*), 1567 TO 1586.

IN July 1567, after arranging the government of the provinces which had been held by the rebel Uzbek chiefs, the emperor returned to Agra, and thence proceeded on a tour through Malwah—of which province he changed the governor—to Chittore, the rajah of which had refused to acknowledge him. This place was the stronghold of Hindoo independence; Rana Oody Singh was the head of the Rajpoot clans, and must be subdued before he could expect a general acknowledgment of his authority as emperor. The Rana left 8,000 picked men as its garrison, and retired to an inaccessible part of the country to wait the issue, and the fort was regularly invested. Ferishta gives a minute and spirited account of the siege; but what is especially noticeable in the detail, is the scientific mode of approach and attack, which, it is questionable, could have been exceeded in Europe at the period. Akbur does not appear at this time to have possessed, or to have in any form used, artillery. No mention is as yet made of it in his battles. A fort was to be taken by sabats, or zigzag approaches formed by gabions and trenches, thrown up to reach a part of the wall selected to be breached, by mining. In the case of Chittore, there were two principal sabats, carried under two separate bastions, ending in mines. Both were loaded with gunpowder, and were to have exploded simultaneously; but while one succeeded, the other hung fire till the storming party was near it, and blew up, causing much loss to the besieged as well as to the storming party. This attack, therefore, failed; and another one was in progress, when the emperor chancing to see Jugmul, the governor of the place, directing the repair of one of the breaches by torchlight, seized a matchlock from an attendant and shot him in the forehead. The Rajpoots now became desperate; they performed the ceremony of Jowhur—put their women and children to death, and burned them with their leader's body; they then retired to their temples, and awaited the Mahomedans' approach. The emperor, seeing the walls deserted, entered the place at daylight; the temples were stormed, and the brave garrison, rejecting his offers of quarter, perished to a man. The capture of Chittore conduced in a great degree to the pacification of Rajpootana, and to the eventual co-operation of the Hindoo princes, which was a leading feature in the emperor's policy; and it does not appear that the Rajpoots, on any other occasion afterwards, repeated their rebellion.

Chittore captured, 1567.

In the year 1569, the strong fort of Runtunbhore, so frequently in the alternate possession of the Hindoos and Mahomedans, was taken; and on September 2 the emperor's first child was born, and named Selim. Kalinjer, which had lapsed again into Hindoo possession, was surrendered; and in 1570 a second son was born, who was named Moorád. In this year also the emperor married the daughter of Rajah Kullian Mul, of Bhikanere, and enrolled him with high rank among the nobility. Both his sons having been born in the town of Sikry,

Runtunbhore taken, 1569.

the emperor laid the foundation of a city, to be called Futtehpoor —a name which the town still bears. The year afterwards, the affairs of Guzerat, as will be elsewhere related, having fallen into confusion, the emperor marched thither, and on the road received the intelligence of the birth of his third son, the Prince Daniel; and as he approached Ahmedabad, the capital, Mozuffer Shah, the king, came out to meet him, and submitted, laying down his crown and being enrolled among the nobility. The emperor's cousins, however, sons of Soliman Mirza of Budukshán, were at the head of considerable forces in Guzerat, where they had retreated from Malwah, and their reduction occupied some time. One affair with them is remarkable as showing Akbur's personal bravery. A body of the rebels, under his cousin Ibrahim Mirza, intending to march into the Punjâb and continue their insurrection there, was endeavouring to pass the royal forces, when the emperor heard of its position, and marched upon it at once with a slight escort. At Surtál he found he had but forty troopers with him; but a reinforcement arrived of seventy men under Rajah Mán Singh, Soorjun Rái, Bhugwundas, and some other officers. The whole party amounted to only 156 men in all. With these, the emperor determined to attack his cousin's force, which was dispersed after a sharp skirmish, in which his cousin escaped. This affair shows what trust the emperor now placed in his Rajpoot friends, and how heartily it was reciprocated; for the Rajpoot chiefs fought side by side with him in the affray, and one of them lost his life; nor, though otherwise blamable for the reckless exposure of his person, could such events fail to cement a personal affection and respect. Akbur left Guzerat before the monsoon set in, and reached Agra on June 4, 1573. His cousin, Ibrahim Hoosein Mirza, who had escaped from him at Surtál, had proceeded to Sumbhul, in the Punjâb, but was pursued and killed; and his head sent to the emperor by the governor of Mooltan.

Futtehpoor Sikry founded, 1571.

Guzerat campaign, 1572.

Affair of Surtál.

The emperor had little time to rest. In July he received advice by express from Guzerat, that the officers of the Guzerat kingdom had united in a formidable insurrection, taken several districts, and were then besieging Ahmedabad. The rainy season had set in, and the transport of a large force was impossible. Two thousand picked horsemen were therefore pushed on, and the emperor and his retinue, about 300 persons, followed by double marches on camels. When he reached his advanced troops at Paitun, the whole, Ferishta states, did not exceed 3,000 men. They had marched 450 miles in nine days. With this small force the emperor marched direct on Ahmedabad, ordering the

Rebellion in Guzerat, July 1573.

Akbur's march from Agra to Guzerat.

royal kettledrums to beat as he approached the enemy's camp. Mahomed Hoosein Mirza, the king's cousin, and brother of Ibrahim, rode out to the river to reconnoitre, and perceiving one of the emperor's officers examining the ford, asked whose army was approaching, and was told it was Akbur in person. 'Impossible!' he exclaimed; 'it is only fourteen days since one of my spies saw him at Agra.' 'It is only nine days since he marched,' was the reply. In the battle which followed outside the walls of the city, the emperor led several charges in person; and in one of these directed his own body-guard against his cousin, broke through his troops, and Mahomed Hoosein Mirza was captured. The beleaguered governor was now able to sally from the city, and the enemy's rout was completed.

Attack on the insurgents before Ahmedabad.

Who are defeated.

Akbur did not stay in Guzerat. Bengal required his immediate attention; Dáwood Khan Kirany had taken up arms, and the whole of the eastern part of the province was yet unsubdued. The emperor loaded a thousand boats with soldiers, and sailed down the river in the heaviest part of the monsoon. Hajypoor was occupied without resistance. Dáwood Khan wished to treat, but the emperor insisted on his unconditional submission. 'Tell Dáwood Khan,' Ferishta records of him, 'I have a thousand men as good as he, and if disposed to put the point to an issue in single combat, I will myself meet him.' But Dáwood Khan fled: and the emperor, perhaps despising his antagonist, left the war to be finished, as was his custom, by his commander, Moonjim Khan. Rajah Toder Mul, subsequently the famous minister of finance, pursued Dáwood Khan into Orissa, and was defeated by him; but reinforcements arriving under Moonjim Khan, the war was renewed, and Dáwood Khan, in a final arrangement, being permitted to retain Orissa and Kuttack, surrendered all pretensions to Bengal and Behar, which, in the year 1575, became incorporated with the empire. It was after the conclusion of this campaign, that the emperor lost his faithful servant and able commander, Moonjim Khan. He had endeavoured to establish Gour as the metropolis of Bengal, but died there of its unhealthy climate, on October 12, 1575. On hearing of this event, Dáwood Khan endeavoured to repossess himself of Bengal; but in an action fought on July 23, 1575, he was defeated, taken prisoner, and executed after the battle. His son, Jooneed Khan, died of the wounds he had received, and thus the last of the Patán dynasties of Bengal became extinct, while Orissa and Kuttack reverted to the emperor. Several subsequent revolutions nevertheless followed, which will be hereafter noticed.

Dáwood Khan rebels in Bengal.

Akbur proceeds thither.

Bengal and Behar annexed, 1575.

Death of Moonjim Khan at Gour, 1575.

Dáwood Khan taken and executed.

From 1575–6 to 1579 seems to have been a brief interval of peace, employed by the emperor in civil affairs, and the construction of the splendid mosque and other buildings at Futtehpoor Sikry and Agra (he habitually avoided Dehly); and in the latter year, his brother, Mahomed Hakeem Mirza, ruler of Kabool, invaded the Punjâb, and defeated Rajah Mán Singh, the governor of the province. It is thus evident, that Hindoos of rank now shared the highest offices with the Moghuls. The Punjâb was one of the most important provinces of the empire, and the emperor would not have appointed Rajah Mán Singh to the charge of it without full confidence in his ability, both as a soldier and an administrator. Prince Hakeem Mirza invaded Lahore; and on the urgent request of his commanders, who were defending the place, Akbur marched to the scene of action, and his brother retreated to Kabool, in February; but, following up his success, the emperor deputed his son, the Prince Moorád, to pursue him. This division was, however, defeated near Kabool; but on March 6, 1579, a victory was gained, on which the Prince Hakeem Mirza fled to the mountains, and the emperor entered Kabool, but on his brother's submission forgave him, and restored his territories to him. Nevertheless, in October of the same year, Rajah Bhugwundas, of Jeypoor, was appointed to the charge of the city—perhaps as a check upon his brother's actions. In this year the fort of Attock on the Indus was rebuilt; and about the same time the fortifications of Allahabad, one of the most splendid memorials of the emperor's reign, were commenced.

Hakeem Mirza invades the Punjâb, 1579.

Akbur proceeds to the Punjâb, and his brother flies to Kabool.

Akbur enters Kabool.

Mozuffer Shah, the king of Guzerat, who had abdicated on the emperor's first expedition into that province, had remained at court, and had been granted an estate for his maintenance; but he had kept up his connection with his former dependants, and in 1581 an insurrection was commenced in his favour, which was for the time highly successful. Mozuffer Shah now proceeded to join his friends, and regained possession of Ahmedabad and the southern districts without difficulty. After desultory operations and struggles on both sides, which continued for three years with varied success, Mirza Khan, the imperial general, brought the king to action on January 29, 1584, near Ahmedabad, and completely defeated him. He fled to the vicinity of Joonagurh, and there assembled another force, and with the Jám of Joonagurh, advanced towards the capital; but did not await the attack of Mirza Khan, and again fled. He renewed his efforts a third time, when he was equally unsuccessful, and continued to reside in Kattywar, until, in 1586, he again plundered the country, but without any

Insurrection in favour of the King of Guzerat, 1581.

Joined by Mozuffer Shah

The king defeated, 1584.

decisive result. About this period, the emperor was drawn into the disputes in the Deccan, which were in progress at the court of Ahmednugger in 1585. Shah Futteh Oolla Shirazy, a holy person who had arrived from the Deccan, received an office near the emperor's person, and was succeeded by two officers of the Ahmednugger court who had been defeated by Sulabut Khan. Other refugees followed, and were hospitably received. There can be little doubt that the accounts given by those persons of the political state of the Deccan, the constant wars between the rival sovereigns, as well as of its fertility and fine climate, acted gradually upon the emperor's mind, and induced an eventual interference in its affairs. For the present, however, the emperor was fully employed, and the most he could do was to direct Mirza Azeez Koka, the governor of Malwah, to take advantage of circumstances. In 1586 the emperor married his eldest son, the Prince Selim, to the daughter of Rajah Bhugwundas, which still further strengthened his Rajpoot connection; and as his brother, Hakeem Mirza, ruler of Kabool, had died, Akbur proceeded thither, sending Mán Singh, the son of Rajah Bhugwundas, to bring the children of the Prince Hakeem Mirza to Lahore; and the son of Mán Singh was afterwards appointed to the charge of Kabool on the part of the emperor. No objection seems to have been made by Hindoos of any grade to cross the Indus, or to serve in Afghanistan during the emperor's reign; yet it is worthy of remark that, in after times, the Hindoo Sepoys of the British army were held to have violated caste by proceeding beyond Attock. During his residence at Attock, in 1586, the emperor dispatched a force into Kashmere, which was distracted by family disputes, and another against the Afghans of Swát and Bijour, who had been uniformly rebellious.

Refugees from the Deccan received at court.

CHAPTER X.

OF THE REIGN OF THE EMPEROR AKBUR (*continued*), 1586 TO 1605.

THE operations against the Afghans were more unsuccessful than any of the emperor's previous warlike undertakings. Zein Khan Koka, the emperor's foster-brother, commanded the army, being assisted by Rajah Beerbul Singh, and other distinguished officers. The rajah was an especial favourite of Akbur; witty, brave and accomplished, he was one of his habitual comrades and companions, and many of his *bons mots* have survived him. The Moghul forces were no match for the Eusufzyes on their own ground. The latter had been easily beaten in the plains; and pursued to their mountain valleys and fastnesses. They drew on the Moghuls, till extrication was impossible; and Rajah Beerbul Singh and 8,000 men perished in one of the rugged defiles. On the other hand, Rajah Mán Singh, who had been dispatched against the Afghans of the Khyber Pass, when it had been closed by them between Kabool and Peshawur, gained a complete victory. The expedition against Kashmere, under Shah Rokh Mirza and Rajah Bhugwundas, suffered severely from snow in the passes, and did not succeed in entering the country. They were met by the King Yoosuf Shah Chuk, with whom they entered into a convention, by which a small tribute and some minor advantages were secured to the emperor; and on their return to Lahore, the king accompanied them. Akbur, however, refused to ratify the convention, detained Yoosuf Shah Chuk, and sent another force, under Mahomed Kassim Khan, who bore the title of Ameer-al-Behr, or admiral. This officer penetrated to the capital, Sirinugger; and though Yakoob, the son of Yoosuf Shah, maintained a desultory warfare for some time, and even gained some temporary advantages, he was eventually obliged to surrender, when he and his father received estates in Behar, and were enrolled among the Moghul nobility. In 1589 the emperor proceeded on a tour through his new dominions, and made arrangements for their proper government; travelling thence to Kabool, where he stayed for two months. Here he received intelligence of the death of Rajah Toder Mul, his great finance minister, which caused him sincere distress; and he returned to Lahore, where he continued to reside for some years.

Rajah Beerbul Singh and 8,000 men killed by the Eusufzye Afghans, 1586.

Kashmere annexed, 1587.

Akbur visits Kashmere and Kabool, 1589.

Death of Rajah Toder Mul, 1589.

It does not appear that the imperial authority had ever been extended to Kattywar, where, with the Jám rajah of that province, Mozuffer Shah had taken refuge. In 1589 Mirza Azeez Koka, governor of Guzerat, attempted to annex the province. He was met by the Jám with 20,000 horse, and a severe action was the result, in which both sides lost heavily; and, as no further attempt was made by Mirza Azeez, he had probably found the Jahreja Rajpoots, the descendants of the proud Saurashtra dynasties, too powerful to be interfered with for the present; but, watching his opportunity, he took advantage of the death of the Jám in the succeeding year, and captured Joonagurh, after a siege of several months duration, when the rest of the province submitted. Sinde still remained independent. The Arghoon family had been succeeded by one of Persian extraction;

among which arose continuous disputes; and the harbouring of malcontents, and other frontier troubles, gave a pretext for interference, which probably amounted to necessity. In 1590 Mirza Khan attacked Sehwán by sea, but the Prince of Sinde defended himself bravely, and the Moghuls were reduced to some straits; when a detachment from another force sent from Lahore into the north of Sinde, by a rapid march into the province, induced its ruler to submit; and in 1592 he proceeded to court, where he was favourably received; and, as was the case with all conquered princes who submitted, enrolled among the nobles of the empire. In the same year, the Prince Moorád, now twenty years old, was employed in the public service, and made governor of Malwah.

The year 1593 was very productive of incidents. Mozuffer Khan, the ex-king of Guzerat, was given up by his protectors to Mirza Azeez Koka, the viceroy of Guzerat, and on his way to Ahmedabad committed suicide. In Bengal, Rajah Mán Singh, the governor, overthrew Kootloogh Khan, who had raised an insurrection of the old Afghan families, and occupied part of Orissa. The emperor, in 1590, had dispatched ambassadors to the four Kings of the Deccan, with, as it may be believed, demands to acknowledge his supremacy. They all returned in this year (1593), with the same result. The four Mahomedan kings evaded or refused the emperor's demand; and this increased his desire to bring to subjection territories which he considered belonged to the empire of Dehly. About the same period, also, Kandahar and its dependencies were made over to the emperor by Prince Roostum Mirza, whose family had occupied them independently since their possession by Persia. The Kandahar chief was created a noble of the empire, and appointed to the government of Mooltan. By the occupation of Kandahar, Akbur had thus regained the western portion of the ancient empire of India; and the whole of India itself, as far south as the Nerbudda, was now in his possession.

If the reader have followed the course of events and conquests since Akbur's accession in 1556 to the present period, it will have been evident how, in the course of thirty-seven years, province after province, at different intervals, was conquered or submitted to his rule. His empire now included Afghanistan on the west, Kashmere and the Punjâb on the north, and the whole of the north-western provinces; on the east, Oude and Bengal, with Orissa and Kuttack; while on the south, Malwah and Guzerat, with Sinde, formed the southern frontier. The Rajpoot provinces remained under the direct government of their own chiefs; but most of these were connected to the empire by marriages, or by political alliances, and furnished not only some of its best troops, but many of its most able commanders and civil governors. Over the whole of the rest of Northern India the emperor's administration was firmly established, and maintained in a spirit of tolerance and general advancement, which secured tranquillity and the good-will and affection of his subjects. The emperor was, however, deeply mortified by the conduct of the Deccan sovereigns in the absolute rejection of his authority, and prepared to enforce it. An army was ordered to march southwards under the command of the Prince Daniel; but the emperor revoking the order, recalled his son, and conferred the command upon his general, Mirza Khan.

The kingdom of Ahmednugger, which, as the reader will remember, adjoined Guzerat, had fallen into confusion, the particulars of which will be reviewed hereafter. A boy had been raised to the throne by the vizier of Ibrahim Adil Shah II., Meean Munjoo, to whom the nobles objected; and the vizier, besieged by them in Ahmednugger, besought the aid of the Prince Moorád Mirza, now viceroy of Guzerat. Any legitimate pretence for interference in Deccan affairs was most opportune; and the prince, with his father's permission, moved with his army towards the scene of action. Meanwhile Mirza Khan had arrived in Malwah, and at Mandoo had received the submission of Rajah Ally Khan, the ruler of Khandésh, who joined him with 6,000 horse. With these, and his own forces, he marched to join Prince Moorád, and formed a junction with him at Galna, whence the united armies marched upon Ahmednugger. Here, however, they found that the vizier, who had called upon the Moghuls for support, had been obliged to return to his master at Beejapoor, and that Ahmednugger was defended by Chánd Beebee, the widow of Ally Adil Shah of Beejapoor, a princess of Ahmednugger, who now acted as regent on behalf of her nephew. The fort was invested by the Moghul army in November 1595, and its memorable siege will be detailed in its proper place, in connection with the history of the kingdom.

The siege of Ahmednugger, 1595.

Several desperate assaults having failed, and an army from Beejapoor being on its way to relieve the garrison, the Prince Moorád accepted the terms offered by the queen-dowager, which included the cession of Berar; and raising the siege, marched thither to take possession of that rich and fertile province. Shortly after his departure, however, a revolution occurred at Ahmednugger, and Chánd Beebee was deprived of power. Her treaty with the Moghuls was set aside, and the chiefs of Ahmednugger and Beejapoor, at the head of 50,000 horse, marched to expel the Moghuls from the province. The armies met at Soopa, on the banks of the Godavery river, on December 27, 1596. The Moghuls were commanded by Mirza Khan, who was now better known under his title of Khan Khanán, with Rajah Ally Khan of Khandésh, and Rajah Ram Chundur; the Deccanies by Soheil Khan, who assumed charge of the confederate troops of Ahmednugger, Beejapoor and Golcondah. The action was well fought on both sides; it was, in fact, a national contest for superiority, which both parties, nearly equal perhaps in numbers, maintained with appropriate vigour and bravery. Rajah Ally Khan of Khandésh and Rajah Ram Chundur were killed in the first onset, and by nightfall the action was still undecided. Over the field of battle, parties of Moghuls and Deccanies, separated from their main bodies, wandered in the darkness, through heaps of dead and dying, and frequent collisions and skirmishes ensued, which increased the general confusion and added horror to the scene. As day broke, Soheil Khan, who had contrived to collect 12,000 horse, advanced upon the Moghuls, who were now much inferior in numbers, and the contest was renewed with fury; but he had been badly wounded the day before, and was again wounded; and worn out by loss of blood and fatigue, fell from his horse. He was borne off the field; and his troops, believing him dead, followed. The Moghuls thus kept possession of the field of battle: but were unable to pursue any advantage they had thus gained, and returned to the Prince Moorád, who was at Shahpoor, his cantonment, in Berar. As Khan Khanán and the Prince Moorád could not agree, the emperor recalled the former in 1597, and the prince occupied his troops for the present in reducing Narnalla, Gawilgurh, and other mountain forts of the province. He had married also the daughter of Bahadur Khan Farooky of Khandésh, and established a local court in the new province. The climate of Berar did not, however, suit him, and he fell ill, and died at Shahpoor, in May 1599, to the great grief of his father, who, perceiving that his best troops had made little impression on those of the Deccan, determined upon proceeding to the south himself. He appointed his eldest son, Prince Selim Mirza, to conduct the affairs of government, and having dispatched a fresh army under the command of the Prince Daniel and Khan Khanán, he followed them by easy stages to the Deccan.

Battle of Soopa, December 26, 1596.

Death of Prince Moorád, 1599.

The emperor proceeds to the Deccan, 1599.

The affairs of Ahmednugger were found to be in a worse state if possible than before; and the queen-dowager, Chánd Beebee, was for a second time obliged to defend her capital against the Moghuls. These events will be detailed in the history of that State; but after the queen's murder, the fort was taken by assault, and the young king was sent to

Second siege and capture of Ahmednugger, 1600.

reside at Gwalior, as a State prisoner. Meanwhile the ruler of Khandésh, Meerun Bahadur Khan, had evinced a rebellious spirit, and the emperor himself proceeded to Boorhanpoor, whence he directed the siege of Aseergurh: and the fort was eventually surrendered to him, with the accumulated wealth of the ancient Hindoo as well as the Mahomedan dynasties. Khandésh was now finally annexed to the empire; but Ahmednugger continued to resist, and to occupy the exertions of the imperial forces for some years. While the emperor was at Boorhanpoor, he received an embassy from Ibrahim Adil Shah II. of Beejapoor, offering his daughter in marriage to the Prince Daniel, and an escort was dispatched for the bride. Before her arrival, however, the emperor, in 1602, was obliged to return to Agra; and having consolidated the new provinces of Ahmednugger, Berar and Khandésh into one government, he appointed the Prince Daniel as viceroy. The Beejapoor princess arrived shortly afterwards, and the marriage was solemnised in the camp at Paitun, on the Godavery, with great splendour, in June 1604; but the prince did not long survive it. He died at Boorhanpoor on April 8, 1605, of the effects of excessive drinking, from which no one could restrain him.

Death of Prince Daniel, 1605.

The cause of the emperor's sudden return to Agra was the conduct of his eldest son Selim, whom he had left in charge of the government. He had been ordered to carry on the war against the Rana of Oodypoor, and Rajah Mán Singh, the viceroy of Bengal, was appointed his coadjutor. The prince had hardly commenced the campaign in Rajpootana, when an Afghan insurrection in Bengal broke out, and the rajah was obliged to proceed to his own government. The prince, freed from restraint, now seems to have formed the idea of asserting his own independence. He first tried to secure Agra, but the governor was faithful to the emperor, and refused to give up the fort. The prince then proceeded to Allahabad, seized the local treasury, which contained 300,000*l.*, and proclaimed himself king. The grief caused to the emperor by this unlooked for conduct, was aggravated by the news of the murder of his minister and intimate friend, Abool Fuzl, the author of his biography, and one of the most remarkable characters of the period, at or near Oorcha, as he was travelling to join the emperor, from the Deccan. It was a happy circumstance that Akbur never knew whose hand had directed that crime; but the prince himself, in his Memoirs, as the Emperor Jehangeer, not only acknowledges that he had directed the Rajah of Oorcha to kill Abool Fuzl, but justifies the act, as well as his own rebellion, by asserting that the minister had persuaded his

Rebellion of Prince Selim, 1600.

Murder of Abool Fuzl, 1602.

father to renounce Mahomedanism. In regard to his son's conduct, Akbur displayed his usual consideration and fine temper. Had he proceeded against him in person, or dispatched an army to Oude, there can be little doubt that a civil war would have commenced, and with it the scenes of the Afghan monarchies would have been renewed. Instead of this, the emperor wrote a kindly and impressive remonstrance, at the same time offering his son reconciliation and forgiveness if he would return. The prince seems to have hesitated at first, and even collected troops, with which he advanced towards his father's camp; but being requested to come slightly attended, returned to Allahabad; and it was during this interval of indecision, that he directed the assassination of the minister. The emperor, however, still pursued his policy of reconciliation. He conferred Bengal and Orissa on his son, and sent to him one of his queens, who, on the death of his own mother, had adopted him; and it was probably owing to her good offices that the prince returned to his father's court and made his submission. After a while, he was requested to resume his campaign against Oodypoor; but his conduct continued to be so far from satisfactory, that he was directed to return to Allahabad. The prince had been long addicted to drinking profusely; and this vice increased upon him so rapidly and materially, that not only may much of his wild and rebellious conduct be attributed to it, but the cruelties he now practised, which, to his humane father, were peculiarly abhorrent. Remonstrance was of no avail; but the emperor's affection could not be restrained, and had in the end some effect upon his son, who repaired to Agra, and for a time submitted to restraint. Here his sons Khoosroo and Khurrám quarrelled, both being still boys, and separate parties were formed for each; thus the condition of the imperial family was productive of many sad anticipations for the future. In the midst of these trying scenes, the news of the death of the Prince Daniel reached the emperor, and the grief he felt seems to have stricken him down. Daniel was perhaps his favourite son, and was possessed of much real ability; but the vice he was addicted to, though it had produced no bad effect like that of his brother, was even more ineradicable; and in regard to any reformation, as was proved by his sudden and untimely death, the emperor's continuous remonstrances, and the prince's oaths to his father, were alike useless.

Akbur's illness commences.

From the time he heard of the event, the emperor, it may be said, never completely rallied, nor was the conduct of those around him calculated to soothe his last days; for there was, for a time, every prospect of a contest between the Prince Selim and his sons for the throne. In September 1605 Akbur grew worse. Finding his end approaching, and true to his promises to his son Selim, he assembled the nobles of his court to hear his dying declaration that he was to succeed him. Mr. Elphinstone, from Price's 'Memoirs of Jehángeer,' thus describes the final scene. 'When they were assembled, he (the emperor) made a suitable address to them, and after wistfully regarding them all round, he desired them to forgive any offences of which he might have been guilty towards any of them. Selim now threw himself at his feet, and burst into a passion of tears; but Akbur pointed to his favourite scimitar, and made signs to his son to bind it on in his presence. He seems afterwards to have recovered from this exhaustion; he addressed himself to Selim, and earnestly conjured him to look to the comfort of the ladies of his family, and not to forget or forsake his old friends and dependants. After this he permitted one of the chief Moollahs, who was a personal friend of Selim's, to be brought to him, and in his presence he repeated the confession of faith, and died in all the forms of a good Mussulman ('Hist.' vol. ii. book ix. p. 276). The event occurred at Agra, on October 13, 1605.

Death of the Emperor Akbur, 1605.

The emperor was born on October 14, 1542, and had thus completed his sixty-third year, all but a day. Of that period he had reigned, in all the success and glory which have been detailed, for fifty-one years and some months. He was buried in a splendid mausoleum, near Agra, erected by his son Selim, who, as the Emperor Jehángeer, succeeded him, which is well described by Bishop Heber in his 'Travels,' and is still perfect.

CHAPTER XI.

OF THE CHARACTER AND ADMINISTRATION OF AKBUR.

But little romance has ever attached itself to the characters of Indian history: and in this respect the difference between the actions of the Moors of Spain, and the early Mahomedans of India, is very remarkable. During the cruel and gloomy reigns, with few exceptions, of the Afghan dynasties of India, there was little scope for romantic incident, or the development of any free or chivalrous spirit among the people; and it is to the research of Colonel Tod, the Froissart of the Rajpoot clans and States, that the history of all that existed among them, exceptional as it was, is due. The Mahomedans of the same period may be considered too cruel and too savage to allow of the existence of any chivalry. Where they predominated, whatever had hitherto existed was crushed out; their conquests were massacres of the people, or captures of them for sale into slavery. Any idea of equality or sympathy with Hindoos and infidels was utterly foreign to their morose and gloomy fanaticism; and consequently there was no birth of that free social intercourse and mutual respect which sprang up afterwards under Shére Khan Soor, and was perfected by Akbur. This, in some respects, may be compared to the relative situation of the Moors and Christians of Spain; hereditary enemies and religious opponents, yet becoming fused together, as it were, under the influence of a common and beneficent civilisation.

In Akbur's character, romance prevails from the earliest dawn of its development, through its constant exercise, down to his last sad moments in the forgiveness of his son's rebellion. In his wars, in his hunting exploits and expeditions, in his State policy, in the generous and tolerant spirit of his religious principles, and their application to the necessities of the varied classes of his people — instances are so numerous, that nothing short of an entire biography would suffice to exemplify them. Romance may be of two kinds: healthy and vigorous; or, on the other hand, mawkish and sentimental; devoted to public benefits, or confined to private gratifications. In Akbur, it was emphatically the former. It made him humane and merciful in conquest, just and considerate; yet, in all cases, firm and decided in action; and while he permitted no scope for the exercise of national fanaticism, he yet secured the high respect, and often the affection, of his opponents. In former times, the rulers of conquered States in India were either trampled to death by elephants, hewn to pieces, or blinded and consigned to State prisons for life; and there were occasions in Akbur's reign when similar courses would have been applauded by his countrymen and courtiers. Yet they were never followed; and when a foe submitted, he was, in the highest spirit of romance, promoted to dignity, and provided with estates, while very rarely was there any instance of subsequent defection.

As one of the first instances of this generous spirit, the case of Báz Bahadur may be stated, who, an usurper of the throne of Malwah himself, and a military adventurer, had no claim but that of his sword to that portion of the imperial dominions. Indolent and voluptuous, he fought badly at first; but he redeemed his character as a soldier, and in the second campaign against him, slew the young emperor's preceptor and friend, and hunted his army nearly to Agra. Continuing afterwards a predatory life, he became unable to bear its privations, and at last threw himself on the emperor's mercy. By any former sovereign of India, his conduct would have provoked, if it did not deserve, instant execution; but Akbur respected the man who had fought bravely for his territory, and of whose prowess in love and war romantic tales were in the mouths of singers and minstrels; and he was not only forgiven, but raised to the highest rank of local nobility. It was the same with all other cases of which accounts can be found in his history or his memoirs. It might even be supposed he had modelled his conduct upon the laws of Menu in regard to kingcraft. 'When a rajah has conquered a country,' writes Menu, 'he should respect the deities which are worshipped . . . distribute largesses . . . and reassure the people by loud proclamations. . . . He should respect the laws of the country: or he may form an alliance with the rajah whom he has conquered, and act in union with him . . . by securing a firm ally, a rajah obtains greater strength than by gaining wealth and territory.' Yet, though the emperor's acquaintance with Hindoo moral codes, from Feizi's translations, may have influenced his decision in later times, his earlier instances of generosity proceeded from the spontaneous romance of his character. When the captive Hémoo was brought before him after the battle of Paniput, and he was asked to slay him, he burst into tears, and refused to strike a wounded and helpless enemy. In this case, too, the difference between the old merciless cruelty, and the new tolerance that was to follow, was exemplified in a marked degree. As Akbur wept, Beiram Khan, his uncle and general, struck the 'infidel's' head from his body. Had Akbur obeyed his uncle's desire, the bloody act might have influenced his whole life.

This gentleness, the truest test of chivalrous valour, followed Akbur through his life. With a rare perception of its value, both to himself and to his posterity, he forbade, under heavy penalties, the practice of making slaves of persons captured in war, or selling captives as slaves. In former times, while thousands of male Hindoo prisoners were massacred in cold blood, women and children were openly sold into slavery. They were not only sold in India, but dispatched to foreign markets—Arabia, Afghanistan, and Central Asia; but this was now rendered impossible. In regard to the practices of Hindoos also, Akbur's perceptions for the necessity of reform were very deep; yet he did not carry them out with any show of fanatical zeal—they were reforms, not persecutions. He prohibited suttee, except when the act should be entirely voluntary, and on one occasion rode a long distance to prevent the sacrifice of a princely Rajpoot lady, by her family. He allowed, and even provided for, the re-marriage of Hindoo widows; made trial by ordeal a crime; prohibited the sacrifice of living animals, and forbade marriage before the age of puberty.

All these were serious innovations upon Hindoo faith and usage, and might have been considered dangerous experiments by another; but Akbur knew no fear: his designs were benevolent, and in the ordinary practices of their religion, the Hindoos were not only unmolested, but all previous restrictions, in the taxation of temples and places of pilgrimage, of sacred bathing-places, with the odious capitation tax, were removed.

Considering the emperor's toleration of 'infidels,' his refusals of fanatical persecution, his abolition of slavery and of the poll-tax, his non-interference with temples; his protection of his Hindoo subjects, their priests and wealth—all the opposite of which had been avowed, and heretofore jealously maintained, as tokens of Mahomedan supremacy; and considering also his own unconcealed doubts upon many points of Mahomedan faith, and law as part of that faith; his rejection of any religious opinion promulgated by man, as an article of faith; his rejection of Mahomedan forms of prayer and ceremonial; his encouragement of Christians, his veneration for Christian symbols, his reverence for the sacred Scriptures, and his permission for the establishment of Christian schools, missions, and colleges—it is only wonderful how he escaped, or repressed, solely by his indomitable will, any outbreak of intolerant zeal, to which he would probably have been the first victim. If Mahomedans hated Hindoos, they hated Christians even more; yet the emperor's patient and constant discussion of points of faith with them, and his encouragement of theological controversies between the Christian and Mahomedan priests, were regarded by his powerful nobles, priests, and courtiers without remonstrance.

It is easy to perceive how deeply Akbur's religious tolerance affected his State policy. He had induced the proudest and most exclusive of the hitherto inaccessible Rajpoot chiefs to bestow daughters in marriage upon himself, his sons, and his grandsons. He employed Rajpoot princes as generals and civil administrators, and his great finance minister, Rajah Toder Mul, brought, by his measures of reform, thousands of Hindoos into the imperial service. They shared the details of all ordinary business with Mahomedans; were collectors, treasurers, surveyors, assessors, everything indeed but judges; for their administration of Mahomedan law would have been impossible. Hindoos, however, enjoyed the protection of their own laws, which were now recognised and explained in the courts of the Mahomedan judges. When all these reforms are considered, it becomes difficult to realise how they not only emanated from, but were carried out in all their details by, one mind; and that too under frequent interruptions by war, and other political events. One material circumstance, however, in the emperor's proceedings, will not have escaped the reader's observation. He seems to have had no abstract passion for war, nor ever employed much of his time in it. If necessary, he opened a campaign in person; and after giving general instructions to his commanders, in regard to its prosecution, he returned to his seat of government, and devoted himself to civil affairs. But his opponents well knew that, though absent in person, he was yet present in spirit, and in case of any reverse to his troops, that he would join them as rapidly, and fight in person with the same fiery valour he had displayed at Surtál, and from his youth upwards.

When everything he directed for the relief of his people was important and progressive, Akbur's system of the assessment of the land revenue of his kingdom was perhaps the most perfect and most elaborate of his reforms. The measure was devised in conjunction with Rajah Toder Mul, and possibly other ministers; but the clear decision of the emperor himself can be traced throughout. The merit of entire originality may be denied him, for he took up what Shére Shah Soor had partly begun; but the recognition and perfection of so grand a reform, is not much below that of original discovery. The land—that is, every field of every village—was measured by an imperial standard. Fields and part of fields might each contain soils of various qualities, and these were calculated in three classes. The averages of value of produce were then decided upon an average of the prices for nineteen years. Of the product, the Government share was fixed at one-third, which was a greater proportion than that of Shére Shah Soor; but, on the other hand, it was now the only rate or tax levied on the agricultural classes. All minor petty taxes, many of which had been very vexatious, were abolished; extra fees and considerations to officers of Government were removed, and the system of farming out districts to individuals, and contractors for revenue, which had given rise to much abuse and oppression, was entirely discontinued. In its main features, Akbur's system bears a very close resemblance to that of the recent revenue survey and assessment of the Bombay Presidency. The groundwork in the measurement of the land, the record of proprietors and occupants, the classification of soils, and the calculation of the value of produce, is as nearly as possible identical in both, and served the same great national purpose and need—the prosperity and contentment of the people. Under Akbur's settlement, no land tenures were altered, or interfered with, in any way. They were accepted as they were found to exist among the people; and so long as an hereditary occupant paid the Government assessment, either in commuted money payments or produce, as he pleased, he could not be outbid, or removed from his possession. It is not to be considered that the emperor's system was perfect; its first provisions were found to be too minute, and involved yearly settlements, which were altered to terms of ten years; but it was an immense and liberal concession to the people, and that it formed the foundation of subsequent revenue settlements in India by native powers, and even English administrators, vouches for its excellence, after an experience of three hundred years.

It is impossible to review thoroughly the emperor's various reforms—of the army, of justice, of police, and of general State policy—which are contained in the 'Ayeen Akburi,' which Mr. Gladwin's translation has placed at the command of all students of Indian subjects. Taking the code as a whole, it displays an amount of careful consideration and practical ability before unknown in India, combined with a rare benevolence and philanthropy highly characteristic of its author. Although it is impossible that the whole can have emanated from Akbur himself, yet there can be no doubt that it was compiled under his own immediate direction, and that he watched its execution very carefully. A proof of this is afforded by the emperor's letter to the Viceroy of Guzerat, given entire in Mr. Bird's history of that province, and quoted by Mr. Elphinstone. While it specifies the limited punishments he was authorised to award, he is enjoined to be sparing in capital punishment; and, unless in dangerous sedition, to inflict none, until he has sent the proceedings to court, and received the emperor's confirmation—nor was execution to be accompanied with mutilation or other cruelty. Thus, throughout the whole, the evidences of order, and systematic regularity, extend from the highest to the lowest branches of State policy and executive detail of administration.

Akbur's court was perhaps the most magnificent in the world. It was the most gorgeous that even India had ever seen; and when the details of it, as given by Sir T. Roe, Hawkins, Bernier, and the Portuguese priests, which cannot be questioned as to accuracy or truth, are considered, it must be admitted that splendour—whether in jewels and ornaments, in costume and decoration, in cloth of gold and velvet, and the gorgeous manufactures of the country; in camp and hunting equipage, elephants, horses, and general equipment of the nobility and the army—could go no further. Akbur had a revenue of 30,000,000*l.* sterling a-year, which, without any reckless extravagance, was royally expended; as was proved by the State treasury at his death, which contained only 10,000,000*l.* sterling, with some bullion. He was never in debt, and the stipends of his civil establishments of all kinds, as well as the pay of his army, were disbursed with the utmost regularity. The emperor's personal application to business was immense. He took but little sleep; three to four hours a day being sufficient for him. He had used to indulge in wine, though not to excess, in his youth, but he gave it up entirely; and he ate moderately of plain food, abstaining from meat two days in every week. Every day he sat in public, transacting business, and receiving petitions even from the most humble. As Purchas describes him, he was 'affable and majestical, merciful and severe; loved and feared of his own, terrible to his enemies.' In all professions of handicraft he took the greatest interest, especially in cannon founding, the manufacture of arms, and architecture, which, of his reign, is at once grand and beautiful. The town of Futtehpoor Sikry, one of his favourite places of residence, was especially decorated with public buildings, and the palaces and mosques at Agra remain exquisite specimens of his pure taste and costly expenditure.

Such a man may have had private vices, yet they do not appear; and had any existed as prominent points in his character, they must, more or less, have influenced his public conduct. Faults, indeed, he humbly acknowledged to all. Of other Indian monarchs, the native historians of their times have not been sparing in comment or record when vices, meanness, or cruelty appeared; and there is no reason to suppose that Akbur would have escaped had there been necessity for animadversion. His public and private character display a vivid sense of true honour, rare perhaps in royal life. He had no deceits, no falsehood, no shifts, no intrigues. He could find, he once said, 'but one road to the attainment of his purposes, and that was the straight one,—after all the easiest and best.' In his private friendships, who more sincere and constant? The men he raised to that honour were of the people, and so far inferior in rank to himself; yet he was true and faithful to all, lamenting their deaths with a passionate grief which could hardly be pacified or consoled. Enough, however, of the great emperor. There is no character of the period with whom he can be compared, nor indeed with any other who, like himself, created an empire and ruled over it. At his death, the population of his empire can hardly have been less than 150,000,000, and may have been more; and there is no instance in the world's history, of such a kingdom having been won, not only with so small an amount of human suffering, but with so positive a relief from oppression; and the more his acts, his policy, and his disposition, in all their generosity and humanity, are studied and understood, the stronger will be the conviction that Akbur stands alone. Of his personal appearance there are few very particular accounts. His manly vigour of body was a fit accompaniment for so large a mind; and of his feats in riding great distances, of walking sometimes forty miles a day, of slaying wild animals, and of his valour in battle, there are many interesting details in his Memoirs. The Jesuits record that he was white like a European; but his son Selim's picture may be nearer the truth, when he describes him as tall of stature, of a ruddy brown complexion, his eyes full and dark, and his eyebrows meeting; while his great breadth of chest, and long sinewy arms, gave him the strength of a lion.

CHAPTER XII.

OF THE PROGRESS OF THE PORTUGUESE IN INDIA, 1527 TO 1612 (*continued from Chapter XXIII., Book III.*).

ENCOURAGED by the success of his fleet, the King of Guzerat, in 1527, sent it again against the Portuguese, who were at their naval station of Choule; but on this occasion the Portuguese were entirely victorious, and of eighty-three Guzerat vessels, seventy-three were either sunk or driven on shore and burned; and the Portuguese followed up their success by an advance by land under Hector di Silviera, in which Tannah, Salsette, and other towns were made tributary. On this occasion, and subsequently, the Portuguese co-operated with the troops of Ahmednugger. In 1530, Antonio di Silviera sacked the rich city of Surat, and burned Damaun; but their greatest expedition was directed against Diu, in 1531. Four hundred vessels of all sizes were assembled in the present harbour of Bombay, under the command of Nuño da Cuerpa, governor-general in India; and conveyed 22,000 men, of whom no less than 3,600 were Europeans. On February 7, the island of Beyt, in the Gulf of Cutch, a strongly fortified position, was carried by assault, with heavy loss to the enemy in men, and sixty pieces of cannon; but the brave Hector di Silviera fell in the attack. The expedition then proceeded to Diu, but was eventually repulsed with heavy loss by its defender, Moostafa Khan, a Turk, and the Portuguese returned to Goa, burning and destroying several towns by the way. But they had by no means given up the idea of possessing Diu. They were joined by the Prince Chánd of Guzerat, who promised them extensive privileges for their assistance; and, ostensibly on his behalf, nearly the whole of the Northern Koncan, including Bombay, was annexed. When the prince's rebellion failed, the governor-general made overtures to the Emperor Hoomayoon, who had invaded Guzerat; but this policy was abandoned for an alliance with Bahadur Shah, the King of Guzerat, who, in his extremity, ceded to them Bassein, and the long-coveted Diu. Bahadur Shah took Portuguese into his pay, and in his contests with Hoomayoon was latterly assisted by a corps of 450 Europeans. On a subsequent visit to the Portuguese at Diu, he was killed, as is elsewhere related. In 1537, after the representations and petitions for assistance of Bahadur Shah had reached Constantinople, the sooltan determined upon an expedition against Diu, and seventy-six vessels were fitted out at Suez, carrying 7,000 men. This fleet arrived off Diu in September, at a time when the garrison had been reduced to 600 men, and was straitened for provisions. The Egyptian fleet was supported by a Guzerat land army of 20,000 men. The commander of Diu, Antonio di Silviera, made a noble defence in a close siege of eight months' duration, during which the garrison suffered the extremities of hunger—a crow shot on the dead bodies was a luxury for the sick, and nauseous vermin were used as food. The Portuguese ladies took a noble part in the defence, and the details, as given by Faria y Souza, exhibit the highest qualities of heroism. The siege was raised by a fleet under the command of the viceroy, John de Castro, carrying 1,000 pieces of cannon and 5,000 men. Of the fleet, 93 vessels safely reached Diu, and their progress up the coast had been marked by horrible outrages on the inhabitants of many of the large towns; not only were they pillaged and burned, but men, women and children massacred without distinction, while several thousands of the people were sold into slavery. When the relief arrived, the garrison sallied out and routed the besiegers; and on his return to Goa, the viceroy made a triumphal entry, the particulars of which excited astonishment, even in Portugal.

In 1543 Garcia de Noronha being viceroy, the Prince Abdoolla, or Mulloo Khan, of Beejapoor, took refuge at Goa. Assud Khan, the minister, according to the Portuguese historian, offered the whole of the Koncan to him, if the prince should be given up; but the offer was refused. On the death of Assud Khan, it is recorded that they agreed to the demand of Ibrahim Adil Shah, for the delivery of his brother, on condition of receiving the whole of Assud Khan's wealth, and acknowledge to have received ten millions of ducats; but the prince was not surrendered. In 1545, Diu was attacked unsuccessfully by Mahmood Shah of Guzerat, and the siege was renewed in 1548; but the place was relieved by Dom John de Castro, who obtained a great victory, both by sea and land. The King of Beejapoor also renewed his negotiations for the surrender of his brother, which was again refused; and in 1554 the Portuguese assisted him with a force of 3,000 European infantry, with which he took possession of the Poonda ghaut and fort, the pass leading from Goa to the Deccan. Here, however, the intervention seems to have ended; and whether the Portuguese had any political objection, as may have been the case, to entering upon the continent of India, or whether they found Mulloo or Abdoolla's party less powerful than they had supposed, does not appear; but they at once abandoned his cause, and the prince, persisting in his rebellion, was defeated, taken and executed. Had the Portuguese advanced with him, his expedition against his brother, then in the last degree unpopular, would, most probably, have been successful. Ibrahim Adil Shah retaliated by sending a large army to invade the Goa territory; but it was repulsed, though some of the Koncan was lost. In 1570, however, a serious combination was made against the Portuguese by the Kings of Beejapoor and Ahmednugger, assisted by the Zamorin of Calicut. Ally Adil Shah of Beejapoor invested Goa with an immense army, and 350 pieces of cannon of all sizes. The siege continued for ten months, and was ultimately abandoned by the king, who had lost 12,000 men, 300 elephants, 4,000 horses, and 6,000 head of oxen, partly by casualties of the siege, and partly from the effects of climate. The attack upon Goa by the King of Beejapoor was seconded by one on Choule by the King of Ahmednugger, of almost equal magnitude; but it suffered a very severe defeat. At the same time, however, the Zamorin's attack upon Châle, near Calicut, was successful. The fort was surrendered by Don George de Castro, who was afterwards beheaded for imputed cowardice. These efforts on the part of the Portuguese appear to have inspired their enemies with respect, for peace ensued on favourable terms with the Deccan kings. In 1592, Boorhan Nizam Shah of Ahmednugger renewed his attack upon Choule; but this expedition was even more disastrous than the first. Its commander, Furhâd Khan, was taken prisoner with his family. Seventy-five pieces of large cannon were captured, and the Mahomedan historian acknowledges the loss of 12,000 men. Furhâd Khan and his daughters became Christians, and went ultimately to Lisbon. The year 1595 brought the first real interruption to the trade of the Portuguese. The Dutch, their first rivals, had sent two ships to the Indian Archipelago, which were, however, intercepted on their return in 1597. They were followed by a fleet of eight ships, which returned to Holland safely, and henceforth the maritime supremacy of the Portuguese was not only disputed, but afterwards destroyed in the East, by the Dutch and by the English. In 1604 they were expelled from Amboyna, and in 1612 they suffered their first defeat in Indian waters from an English fleet. The Portuguese never aspired to be more than a maritime and trading power in India, and this continued only so long as they preserved a monopoly. They might have used their opportunity both in Guzerat and in the Deccan to acquire political and territorial influence; but they had apparently no desire for any possessions but what could be guarded by sea. They were excellent sailors: but their never attempting military operations by land, except in the defence of their own seaports, either marks timidity or disinclination, amidst opportunities which few other adventurers would have neglected during a career of more than 100 years. Of their actions, some rise to heroism; but they are deplorably tarnished by cruelty and vindictiveness, which surpassed the acts of their Mahomedan contemporaries, and combined with their unscrupulous avarice, made them in the end detestable. Their history in detail, however revolting in many respects, is extremely curious and interesting, and well repays the perusal of the student from its outset to its close. The acts of the horrible Inquisition of Goa need no exemplification, and the nominal conversion of 'infidels' to Portuguese Christianity, gave pretexts of persecution and vengeance to this horrible tribunal, at which humanity shudders.

CHAPTER XIII.

OF THE EARLY ENGLISH VOYAGES TO INDIA, 1553 TO 1613.

Robert Thorne's petition.

IN the reign of Henry VIII., Robert Thorne, a merchant, who had resided in Spain, addressed a memorial to the king, setting forth the benefit of direct trade with China. The text of this document is extremely curious, as exhibiting the ideas then prevalent, of a passage to India by the north-west, and the information possessed regarding India; and it became the foundation of subsequent expeditions. In 1553, three ships, under the command of Sir Hugh Willoughby, with instructions from Sebastian Cabot, sailed from Greenwich on May 10, bearing letters from Edward VI., addressed to all the potentates of the earth, in furtherance of the designs of the expedition. The little fleet was separated in the White Sea. Willoughby's two ships were frozen in, their crews perished during the winter, and one only returned to England. Several other attempts followed, the last by Henry Hudson, in 1597, serving to satisfy even the most sanguine, that a north-west passage to the East was impracticable.

Sir Hugh Willoughby's expedition, 1553.

Henry Hudson's voyage, 1597.

Failure to the northward of the American continent induced attempts to the south; and the route of Magellan, in 1519-22, whose expedition had circumnavigated the globe for the first time, was followed by Sir Francis Drake in 1577, who, with five small vessels, the largest of which was barely 100 tons burden, left Plymouth on December 13, and on September 26, 1580, again reached that port. He had crossed the Atlantic and Pacific, had sailed through the Eastern Archipelago, and touching at Ternate, had doubled the Cape of Good Hope from the east; but he had not seen India. Nor was it till his subsequent capture of a Portuguese ship from India, that particulars of trade with, and access to, that country were understood. Drake's voyage was followed by that of Cavendish, 1586–88, which was perfectly successful, and returned with a large booty from ships and countries of all nations, which he seems to have considered lawful prize; and in his report of his voyage to Lord Hunsden, chamberlain to Queen Elizabeth, he expressly states that he had been well treated by the heathen inhabitants of 'Malucoes,' and where 'our countrymen may trade as freely as the Portugals if they will themselves.'

Magellan's voyage round the globe, 1519–22.

Sir Francis Drake follows, 1597.

Cavendish's voyage, 1586.

The supplies of eastern produce to England had hitherto been obtained through the Mediterranean Sea, by means of Venice and Genoa, as also directly from the Levant; and a company was chartered by the queen in 1581, which traded direct with the Levant and Turkey; but the eastern trade had already turned into a different channel, of which, as will have been understood, the Portuguese had the monopoly, and the supplies obtained by the Levant Company were entirely insufficient to meet the demand for eastern produce now rapidly increasing in England. There had been a remonstrance from Spain against Drake's passage through the Eastern Archipelago and Indian Ocean, which the queen treated with characteristic contempt. She declared the sea, as the air, common to all men; and that her subjects had as good a right as the Spaniards to sail where they pleased. An expedition to India direct was therefore projected, and instructions issued to Mr. Edward Fenton for its fulfilment, which may be read at length in 'Hakluyt,' vol. iii., and were admirably adapted for the purpose. Four ships sailed on May 1, 1582; but the expedition failed signally, only reaching the Brazils, and returning with but one ship out of the four. No attempt whatever appears to have been made to double the Cape of Good Hope; and the failure may be attributed to the ill-conduct and want of enterprise of the commanders. No further attempt was made for several years to renew English enterprise to the east; but after the failure

Levant Company, 1581.

Remonstrance by Spain against Drake's voyage.

Queen Elizabeth's reply.

Fenton's expedition to India, 1582.

Its failure.

of the Spanish Armada, a body of merchants of London petitioned the queen to allow them to despatch three ships to the east by way of the Cape of Good Hope; and, after some delay, the expedition sailed from Plymouth on April 10, 1591. On July 28 the Cape was seen, and on August 1 the three ships anchored in Saldanha Bay. They had lost a great proportion of their crews from scurvy. One of the ships, the 'Royal Edward,' was despatched home with the sick; and with the 'Penelope' and the 'Edward' the voyage was continued. Of these, the 'Penelope' was lost, and is supposed to have foundered; but Lancaster held on his course with the 'Edward,' and continued a desultory cruise by the Nicobar Islands into the Eastern Archipelago, capturing two large Portuguese ships in the Straits of Malacca. Thence the ship returned to Ceylon, where the crew being mutinous, obliged Lancaster to proceed homewards. The close of the voyage was most disastrous. While on the coast of Brazil, nearly all the crew being on shore, the carpenter cut the ship's cable, and it drifted out to sea. Lancaster, and six men, were eventually taken to St. Domingo by a French ship, and he finally reached England alone, on May 24, 1594. Thus a second expedition to India had failed in its object. The Dutch, however, took up the project, and under the command of Cornelius Houtmann, sent out four powerful vessels, in 1595, which sailed on April 2. On June 1, 1596, after many delays, they arrived on the coast of Sumatra, and finally reached Bantam, a Portuguese factory in Java. Here his attempts to open trade were met with the utmost jealousy by the Portuguese; Houtmann and some of his countrymen were imprisoned; and they escaped finally, having undergone much danger of their lives, but having, nevertheless, obtained recompense for their maltreatment. On the coast of Java one of the ships was abandoned as unseaworthy, and with the other three, the united crews being reduced to only eighty-three men, Houtmann arrived in Holland on August 14, 1598. He was honourably welcomed, and a fresh expedition immediately fitted out of eight ships, four of which returned in fifteen months with rich cargoes. Thus the eastern trade of Holland became established, and in 1602 the several companies which had engaged in it were incorporated as one, under a charter.

The merchants of London despatch three ships, 1591.

Disastrous ending of the enterprise.

Dutch voyage under Houtmann, 1595.

Second expedition of the Dutch, 1598.

This example was followed in England. A company was established with a subscribed capital of 30,000*l.*, and in a petition to Queen Elizabeth, set forth its objects in a clear and business-like manner, embodying the results of Portuguese and Dutch successes. The petition

English company established under charter by Queen Elizabeth, 1600.

was accepted by the queen, and the company was finally embodied by charter in 1600, under the title of 'The Governor and Company of the Merchants of London, trading to the East Indies.' It was provided with rules expressed in the charter, which embraced all possible contingencies, and a letter was drawn up by the queen, recommending the expedition and its objects to the care and hospitality of all monarchs and peoples whose countries it might visit. Finally five ships left the English coast on April 22, 1601; but the 'Guest,' of 130 tons, was unloaded at sea and abandoned. On November 1, the Cape of Good Hope was doubled, and the fleet, after much terrible suffering from scurvy, reached Acheen, in Sumatra, on June 6. Here Lancaster, who was the commander, delivered the queen's letter, and trade was opened with much spirit. Lancaster did not, however, confine his operations to trade; he captured a Portuguese ship of 900 tons with a valuable cargo of Indian produce and manufactures, by which, and with pepper and spices, his ships were completely laden; and having established a factory at Bantam, where he traded very profitably, he set sail homewards with the 'Dragon' and the 'Hector,' leaving the 'Susan' to follow when her cargo should be completed. On the voyage, his ship, the 'Hector,' lost her rudder, and Lancaster writing a very noble letter to the company, advised the commander of the 'Hector' to abandon him to his fate; but, eventually, both ships reached England together, finding their consorts had arrived before them.

Dispatch of five ships, 1601.

Captain Lancaster's proceedings.

Factory at Bantam established.

Before the return of these ships, the queen had endeavoured to prevail upon the company to dispatch another expedition; but her energetic, and even reproachful, language had no effect, and she died before the first reached England. The enterprise had, however, been eminently successful, and the same ships were again fitted out for a second. The commander received the honorary title of admiral and vice-admiral; and Captain, or Admiral, Middleton, was placed in command of all. This fleet sailed on March 25, 1604, and had a prosperous voyage to Bantam, where it arrived on December 20, and was at first hospitably received by the Dutch; but jealousies afterwards broke out, and it was evident that they aspired to a monopoly of the spice trade. Nevertheless, by trading at Ternate, Banda, and other islands where the Dutch had no pretext for interference, the cargoes were completed. The 'Susan' was the first to leave for England, but is supposed to have foundered at sea. The other three ships reached England

The same ships again dispatched under Middleton, 1604.

on May 6, 1606. As yet, therefore, India Proper had not been visited by any English vessel.

The third expedition, 1607.

In the third eastern venture, three ships were employed: the 'Dragon,' the 'Hector,' and the 'Consent,' a small vessel of 150 tons burden only, which, under the command of David Middleton, sailed alone on March 12, 1607; and it can only now be marvelled at, as in the case also of Drake, how such small ships contrived to escape the perils of their long voyages. The project was, however, perfectly successful. The 'Consent' reached Bantam on November 14, and having taken in pepper, was on a cruise, when she met with a Java junk, from which Middleton purchased cloves to the value of 3,000*l*., which realised in England 36,287*l*. He now returned to England, which he reached in December 1608. The other two ships sailed on April 1, 1607, and after doubling the Cape, proceeded along the coast of Africa to Socotra. Here they separated, the 'Hector,' under the command of Captain Hawkins, sailing to Surat, and thus being the first English ship which had reached India. But he does not appear to have effected anything in regard to trade, and in hope of making arrangements for the establishment of a factory remained on shore, sending his ship to Bantam to rejoin her consort. Captain Hawkins's subsequent proceedings will be hereafter noticed. From Bantam, both ships returned to England with full cargoes. Two vessels, dispatched during their absence, were wrecked with heavy loss to the company; but the next expedition, under Middleton's command, which sailed on April 24, 1609, for Bantam, returned to England in safety. The profit on the whole undertaking proved to be enormous, and fully justified further proceedings; and on the petition of the company, King James I. granted a new charter in 1610, which confirmed all existing privileges of the former. Upon this, and a new subscription for trade, three ships were dispatched under Sir Henry Middleton, one of them, 'The Trade's Increase,' being of 1,000 tons burden. Leaving one ship at Aden, Middleton sailed for Mocha; but, when within sight of the port, his Arab pilots ran the ship on a bank, and he, with many of his crew, were imprisoned. 'The Trade's Increase' was however floated, and he was eventually released, when he proceeded to Surat.

Middleton's second voyage, 1609.

The company obtains a new charter from James I., 1610.

Sir Henry Middleton's voyage, 1610.

Hindrances of the Portuguese at Surat.

The Portuguese were fully aware of the transactions of English vessels in the Red Sea, and Middleton found a fleet of considerable strength waiting to oppose him. The Portuguese pleaded their monopoly of trade, recognised by the West Indian authorities, as superior to any pretensions on the part of the English; but Sir Henry Middleton, while he could not dispute the right of the Portuguese to trade, denied their establishment of monopoly, and gave them to understand that, as he considered India a free and independent country, he should persevere, by force if necessary, and in pursuance of the royal charter, to trade as he pleased. The native authorities were, however, so fearful of the Portuguese, that Middleton found trade impossible at Surat, and was advised to proceed to Gôgo, not far distant, where he would not be interfered with. This advice he adopted, taking on board, as passengers, Captain Hawkins and his wife, who had recently arrived from Agra. Hawkins's adventures had been of a very romantic character in those early days of English intercourse with India. When he had remained at Surat, in 1608, and sent his ship, the 'Hector,' to the eastern settlements, he soon found that without an imperial deed of permission, he would be unable to establish a factory or to enter into mercantile transactions with the native traders; and having the king's letter to 'the Great Moghul' in his possession, determined, in absence of other credentials as ambassador, to proceed to Agra and present it in person. He was received honourably by the Emperor Jehángeer, promised a handsome salary, and became a personal favourite. According to the emperor's desire also, he married an Armenian lady, who appears to have made him a faithful wife. But, as far as the object of his mission went, he was unsuccessful; the intrigues of the Portuguese Jesuit missionaries frustrated all his efforts to obtain a firman—his salary remained unpaid —he was in continual dread of being poisoned, or otherwise made away with by Portuguese emissaries; and failing to receive assistance from Jehángeer, he returned with some difficulty to Surat, in turn to be taken on board Sir Henry Middleton's ship.

Middleton proceeds to Gôgo.

Captain Hawkins arrives from Agra.

His previous proceedings, and journey to Agra.

Intrigues of the Jesuits against him.

Middleton and his council now came to the determination of taking by sea what could not be obtained by land; and he stationed himself near the Straits of Babel Mandeb, intercepting vessels from India, from which he took Indian products, giving their masters portions of his own cargoes in payment. These transactions, it is evident, were little better than rank piracy; but they were continued till the arrival of three ships, the 'Thomas,' 'Hector,' and 'Clove,' which had left England under the command of Captain Saris, and had proceeded direct to Mocha: but the former jealousies of the people still existed, and on his return he found Sir Henry Middleton engaged as has been related. Saris appears to have seen nothing objectionable in Sir Henry's proceedings; and joined

Middleton's proceedings.

Is joined by three ships under Captain Saris.

him, receiving on each transaction of forced barter, a proportion for his three ships. In the course of a short time, the ships, having obtained cargoes for the eastern market, and disposed of their own, all set sail for Bantam. The finest of these ships, 'The Trade's Increase,' was lost on the voyage, and Sir Henry Middleton died; but Captain Saris proceeded to Japan, in order to establish a factory there, and, notwithstanding the jealousy of the Dutch, was favourably received. The produce of this voyage proved very remunerative to the company. Captain Hippon's voyage in the 'Globe' about the same time possesses a peculiar interest; for, instead of following the usual track, he sailed up the eastern coast of India, touching at several native ports, where he found the Dutch established under grants from the King of Golcondah. At these stations trade was impossible; but he succeeded in establishing a small factory near Masulipatam, and these comparatively insignificant proceedings laid the foundation of the extensive trade subsequently developed.

The fleet proceeds to Bantam.

Captain Hippon's voyage.

Factory established near Masulipatam.

It had now become sufficiently evident in England, that small enterprises, in weakly manned and nearly unarmed vessels, could have no chance of establishing trade in India, in the face of the superior strength possessed by the Portuguese; and that means must be adopted to repel force by force, if necessary. Accordingly, four ships, the 'Dragon,' 'Osiander,' 'Solomon,' and 'James,' sailed from England on February 1, 1612, under the command of Captain Thomas Best. These ships were fully armed as vessels of war, and made direct for Surat, where they anchored early in September. Mr. Kerridge, the factor of the 'Osiander,' who had before resided at Surat, soon obtained an official permission for trade, and it was about to open, when a Portuguese fleet of four galleons, convoying a large number of trading vessels, entered the harbour. These Best immediately attacked, and three of the Portuguese ships were driven ashore. They were got off, and the fight renewed, but with even more certain and disastrous results. Up to this time, perhaps, the English had been looked upon as mere traders, and as such with a certain degree of contempt, which, artfully fomented by the Portuguese at Agra, had tended to Hawkins's discomfiture; but the position was now changed: the hitherto irresistible Portuguese had been beaten on their own element, as it were; the English had established a reputation for valour, and its effect was soon practically and beneficially apparent. The Emperor Jehángeer concluded a treaty, by which

Armed fleet sent out under Best, 1612.

Naval engagement with Portuguese at Surat, who are defeated.

Treaty of the Emperor Jehángeer with the English, 1613.

English settlers or traders at Surat should be protected. An ambassador from England should reside at his court, and customs dues on imports should amount to no more than 3½ per cent. This treaty, which contained many other privileges, was received by Captain Best at Surat, on February 6, 1613, and necessarily becomes a famous incident in the progress of the English in India. They may be considered as established from that period, and their heretofore desultory proceedings to be at an end.

CHAPTER XIV.

OF THE MAHOMEDAN KINGS OF GUZERAT (*continued from Chapter III., Book III.*), 1526 TO 1584.

WHEN Sikunder, who succeeded his father Mozuffer Shah II., ascended the throne, there were two parties in the State—one his own, which was the weakest; the other that of his brother, Bahadur. Imád-ool-Moolk, the minister, secretly favouring the latter, and believing that the king intended to put him to death, watched his opportunity, and caused him to be assassinated on May 31, 1526, after a brief reign of three months. At this time, Bahadur was absent at Dehly, where he had taken refuge; but, when his younger brother, Nusseer Khan, was elevated to the throne, under the title of Mahmood Shah II., and letters reached him from many of the nobility offering him assistance to attain his rightful position, he set out for Guzerat. He had, however, been offered the kingdom of Joonpoor, in Bengal, by the Afghans; and, undecided as to whether he should accept this offer, or proceed to Guzerat, determined to leave the matter to chance or fate, and to take whatever direction his horse should proceed in. Casting the reins on its neck, the animal took the southern road; and Bahadur, believing in the omen, proceeded. He was joined on the frontier by parties of the nobility, and proceeded to Nehrwalla Puttun, where he was formally crowned on August 3, 1526, and reached Ahmedabad on the 28th, when his brother was deposed. In 1528 the king entered upon a campaign against Boorhan Nizam Shah of Ahmednugger, on behalf of Imád Shah, king of Berar, and marched as far as Mahore; but the expedition was fruitless of result, except the nominal submission of the Ahmednugger king, and his acknowledgment of the sovereignty of Bahadur over his dominions. In 1531, however, when visited by Boorhan Nizam Shah in

Sikunder Shah assassinated, 1526.

Mahmood Shah II. succeeds, 1526.

Bahadur Shah crowned, 1526.

Khandêsh, he withdrew his pretensions, and even conferred royal honours and insignia upon him, as is related in the history of Ahmednugger. During this campaign, the fortress of Raiseen was surrendered by Lôkman, the brother of Rajah Silhuddy, its owner, who had been taken prisoner, on condition of his brother's release, and became the scene of a terrible and memorable tragedy. Wishing to remove the females of his family before the Mahomedan garrison should take possession, Lôkman proceeded to the private apartments, where he was received with indignation by Doorgawutty, his brother's wife, who upbraided him with cowardice in not defending the fort, hitherto deemed impregnable; and having previously filled the palace with combustibles, she set fire to the place, and with 700 other women perished in the conflagration. This event so affected the brothers, Silhuddy and Lôkman, that, at the head of a few adherents, they attacked their guards, and perished to a man. The Portuguese armament for the reduction of Diu arrived after the king's return to his capital, and its defeat is only slightly alluded to by the Guzerat historian, though it was in reality a great victory against an immense expedition. One of the guns taken from the Portuguese was the largest ever then seen, and was taken to the fort of Champanair.

In 1533 Mahomed Zumán Mirza, a relative of the Emperor Hoomayoon, fled to Guzerat, and the king contemptuously refused all demands to give him up. Not content with protecting this prince, Bahadur Shah, over confident of his strength, conferred the highest honours upon him. About the same time also, Tartar Khan, the son of the late Emperor Bheilole Lody of Dehly, also a fugitive, received a warm reception; and Bahadur Shah appears to have contemplated the possibility of becoming emperor. Tartar Khan was furnished with an army of 40,000 men; but he was utterly defeated by the Prince Hindál Mirza; and the Emperor Hoomayoon, who had been waiting a suitable opportunity, now declared war against Bahadur Shah, and marched upon Guzerat; but purposely delayed by the way, till its king had finished the siege of Chittore. After some desultory movements, Bahadur Shah, depending upon his artillery, and against the advice of his best officers, intrenched himself. By this act he left the country open to the Moghuls, who cut off all his supplies, and the army became reduced to such straits, that Bahadur Shah fled secretly at night to Mandoo; but he was pursued, and sending his jewels and treasures to Diu, took refuge at Cambay. The siege of Champanair and occupation of Guzerat followed, as has been related in the history of the first reign of Hoomayoon. No sooner had the emperor left the province, than an insurrection against the

Moghuls broke out, and they retired, after a few feeble and ineffectual struggles.

During the war with Hoomayoon, and while the king was at Cambay, he had concluded a treaty with the Portuguese, in the hope of receiving their assistance: by which, with other stipulations, permission to erect a fort at Diu was granted. This treaty was executed in 1534, and the Portuguese seem to have lost no time in constructing a very strong fortification. When the Moghuls withdrew, Bahadur Shah evidently repented of what he had done; and, as the Portuguese historian, Faria de Souza, and the Mahomedan, in the 'Mirat Iskunderi,' both relate, was endeavouring to get the fort into his possession. The Portuguese general and viceroy, Nuño de Cuerpa, was invited to a conference, which he declined: and the king was proceeding to the viceroy's ship, according to the Portuguese account, when a sudden brawl arose between some Portuguese officers and the king's attendants, during which the king, falling into the sea, was struck with a pike, and killed. The Mahomedan account is somewhat different, and attributes the act to deliberate previous arrangement; nor is it at all improbable that treachery was intended on both sides. The event happened on February 14, 1537, in the thirty-first year of the king's life, and eleventh of his reign. The gorgeous jewels and treasures he had sent to Diu—the spoils of Hindoo princes of Guzerat—had been forwarded to Medina for greater security, and fell into the hands of Soliman, the sooltan of Constantinople, by whom they were appropriated.

Bahadur Shah killed by the Portuguese, 1537.

Bahadur Shah having left no offspring, the throne was conferred by the nobles of the State upon Meerun Mahomed Farooky of Khandésh, the late king's nephew; but he died suddenly, after a brief reign of hardly two months, and the only representative of the royal line that remained was Mahmood, the son of the late king's brother, Lutteef, who was residing at Boorhanpoor. He was now sent for, and crowned at Ahmedabad, on April 5, 1538. Mahmood appears to have been a moderate man, of simple habits, fond of erecting palaces and ornamenting parks, but in public affairs a mere cipher. His deer-park was walled round, and was fourteen miles in circumference; and in his reign, also, Surat was strongly fortified to repel the frequent incursions of the Portuguese. Having incurred the deadly enmity of his private chaplain Boorhan, whom on one occasion he had built up to his neck in a mud wall, he was assassinated at his instigation in the year 1553, after a reign of fifteen years. On this occasion Boorhan succeeded in destroying several of the ministers by armed men, whom he had

Meerun Mahomed Farooky succeeds, 1537; and dies.

Mahmood Shah III. succeeds, 1538.

Mahmood Shah assassinated, 1553.

stationed in the king's chamber, and even assumed the crown; but he and his accomplices were all put to death as soon as they appeared in public. Mahmood left no heir, and a youth named Ahmed, declared to be a son of the Prince Ahmed, was crowned; but during his inglorious reign of eight years he was admitted to no exercise of power, and the affairs of State were managed by the nobles, who seem, for the most part, to have divided the kingdom among them. In the year 1561, the king was found dead of wounds, lying under the wall of a nobleman's house, where it was supposed he had been carrying on an intrigue. He had left no heir, and a boy named Hubeeb, declared to be a son of Mahmood Shah II., was produced and crowned under the title of Mozuffer Shah III. Etimád Khan became regent and minister, but was a weak character, afraid of his colleagues, among whom he divided the kingdom into five districts (reserving one for himself), over which they were virtually supreme. In the year 1566 Chungiz Khan, the most active and ambitious among them, declared independence at Talnair, of which he had gained possession; and proceeding towards the capital, defeated Etimád Khan and the king, and took possession of it. He now allotted estates to the five sons of Mahomed Sooltan Mirza, who had fled before the Emperor Akbur; but these persons in the sequel disputed his authority, and even defeated him in a general action. Chungiz Khan was afterwards killed while playing at choughan, by an Abyssinian—an event which gave some relief to Etimád Khan; but it was of short duration. Quarrels ensued between him and the other powerful chiefs, and eventually he wrote to the Emperor Akbur, requesting him to come and take possession of the kingdom. The emperor proceeded at once to Guzerat, where he was received without opposition, and the kingdom was annexed to the empire on November 20, 1572. The king abdicated, and was provided with an estate; but nine years afterwards he escaped from surveillance, and in his last efforts to regain his kingdom, Mozuffer Shah III. displayed more spirit and energy than when he was its real sovereign. After his final struggle, in 1584, he retreated into Kattywar, where, until his death, he lived under the protection of Rajah Rái Singh. Thus ended the royal dynasty of Guzerat, which had reigned, for the most part in great splendour, from 1396 to 1572, or 176 years.

Ahmed Shah succeeds, 1553.

Is killed, 1561.

Mozuffer Shah III. succeeds, 1561.

CHAPTER XV

OF THE ADIL SHAHY DYNASTY OF BEEJAPOOR (*continued from Chapter XX., Book III.*), A.D. 1534 TO 1579.

THE long reign of the Emperor Akbur, and the occurrences which preceded it after the first reign of Hoomayoon, have brought the history of the Moghul dynasty down to the period of his death, in 1605; and it becomes necessary to revert to the progress of the other kingdoms of India, to make the general history of the period as complete as possible. Up to the death of the emperor, no interference with any of the Deccan kingdoms, except Ahmednugger, had taken place; and their power, and the interests attached to their progress, entitles them to more consideration than has hitherto been bestowed upon them by writers of Indian history.

A.D. 1534.

Reformation in England.

Ibrahim Adil Shah restores the Soony faith in Beejapoor.

As has been already related in Chapter XX., Book III., Ibrahim Adil Shah succeeded to the crown on the dethronement of his brother Mulloo, in 1534. His first act was to abolish the profession of the Sheea faith, and to restore the Soony, and also to exchange Persian for Mahratta, as the language of accounts and current business in the State. This involved the introduction of many Brahmins into the royal service, and was a concession to Hindoo influence which had a marked effect. The foreign troops, the majority of whom were Persians and therefore Sheeas, were discharged, and their places supplied by Deccanies and Abyssinians. The new army consisted of 30,000 cavalry, the horses of which, for the most part, belonged to the State; and it does not appear that infantry or artillery formed any considerable part of the Beejapoor equipment. Of the foreign cavalry discharged, 3,000 were taken into the service of Ramraj, the Hindoo prince of Beejanugger; and as they refused to salute an infidel, a Korán was placed before the rajah's throne, to which the usual reverence was paid. The year after Ibrahim Adil Shah's accession, a revolution occurred at Beejanugger, and the aid of the Beejapoor king was sought by the rajah for his own support. This proceeding, involving Mahomedan intervention, caused vast alarm throughout the Hindoo kingdom, and for the present arrested mutual differences. Ibrahim, who had proceeded to Beejanugger, was royally enter-

Mahomedan cavalry entertained by the Rajah of Beejanugger.

Ibrahim Adil Shah assists the Rajah of Beejanugger.

tained, and dismissed with the payment of fifty lacs of hoons—1,750,000*l.*—for his own and his army's expenses. In consequence, however, of a fresh revolution, in which the rajah had perished, Ibrahim became involved in hostilities with his successor; but these were of short duration, and the king returned to his capital. A period of tranquillity followed; but, jealousy of his minister, Assud Khan, induced that able person to retire to his estates; and the quarrel was taken advantage of by Boorhan Nizam Shah, of Ahmednugger, and Ameer Bereed, of Beeder, who coalesced, and reduced King Ibrahim to such straits, that he was obliged to retire to Goolburgah. From this difficulty he was released by the instrumentality of the man he had suspected. Assud Khan wrote to the King of Berar, the uncle by marriage of the king, beseeching him to render assistance; and he marched with a large force, which had the desired effect. Ibrahim's own army, too, rallied about him, and the losses by the invasion were soon redeemed; while Ameer Bereed's death broke up the confederacy. This peace was not, however, of long duration. Boorhan Nizam Shah was smarting under his defeat, and in 1543, assisted by Jumsheed Kootub Shah of Golcondah, and Rajah Ramraj of Beejanugger, declared war against Beejapoor. The kingdom was now invaded on three points simultaneously; and its destruction and division among the confederates seemed inevitable. Assud Khan was again called into council: who advised, that, at some small sacrifices, peace should be made with the King of Ahmednugger and the Rajah of Beejanugger. This having been effected, Assud Khan led the Beejapoor army against the King of Golcondah, who was defeated, and followed up to his capital, receiving so severe a wound in the face from Assud Khan's hand, that he never recovered its effects.

Coalition of the King of Ahmednugger and Ameer Bereed.

Renewed coalition against Beejapoor.

The King of Golcondah defeated.

But it seems to have been impossible to restrain the quarrelsome disposition of the Ahmednugger king, who, soon afterwards, again marched with a large army against Goolburgah. He was met near the town of Oorchán, on the Bheema river, by Ibrahim and Assud Khan, who gained a memorable victory; Boorhan Nizam Shah leaving 250 elephants, 570 pieces of cannon, with all the royal insignia and camp-equipage, on the field of battle. Ibrahim fought bravely in this action, slaying three antagonists in single combat. Here, however, the quarrel did not rest; and in the next campaign, Boorhan Nizam Shah not only redeemed his losses, but reduced Ibrahim to serious extremities. These fluctuations of fortune seem to have affected the king's disposition

Ahmednugger renews the war.

And is defeated.

very materially; and he became morose, and suspicious of his officers. In the course of two months he put forty Hindoos and seventy Mahomedans of rank to death; and a plot was formed to dethrone him, and elevate his brother Abdoolla to the throne. On the discovery of this conspiracy by the king, Abdoolla fled to the Portuguese at Goa, and endeavoured to persuade the viceroy to assist him with troops, proffering large concessions of territory. Had the Portuguese yielded to his solicitations, there is no doubt, under the prevailing discontent, that they would have succeeded, and might have laid the foundation of local power in the Deccan; but they declined all offers, and the prince, finding them impracticable, addressed himself to the Kings of Ahmednugger and Golcondah. The Portuguese, in their history, declare that Assud Khan was the prime mover in Prince Abdoolla's rebellion; but this is contradicted by the fact that Assud Khan repelled with scorn the overtures of the King of Ahmednugger to support the pretensions of the prince. Had Assud Khan indeed been disloyal, there can be no question that Ibrahim would have been deposed. While these events were pending, the great minister died, in January 1549, and left a reputation little less, in general estimation, than that of Mahmood Gáwan, the regent and minister of the Bahmuny kingdom.

Ibrahim Adil Shah's cruelties.

The Portuguese refuse to take part in native struggles.

The remainder of the reign of Ibrahim was occupied with almost perpetual wars and struggles with Ahmednugger, in which Ramraj of Beejanugger appears as the active ally of the latter. Boorhan Nizam Shah had died; but his successor Hoosein followed the same policy, and defeated Ibrahim in a severe action near Sholapoor. This, with the rebellion of his great general, Seif Ein-ool-Moolk, whom his harsh conduct had driven into insurrection, reduced the king's fortunes to the lowest ebb; and though, by the payment of twelve lacs of hoons—420,000*l.*—he obtained temporary relief from the Rajah of Beejanugger, he was unable to take the field. Latterly he had become afflicted with a complication of disorders, and as he put to death, one after another, physicians who failed to relieve him, he was deserted by all, and died miserably in the year 1557. Ibrahim Adil Shah I. had reigned twenty-four years, and was buried near his father and grandfather, at Gógy. He left two sons and two daughters, and was succeeded by his eldest son Ally without opposition.

The struggle with Ahmednugger continued.

Ibrahim Adil Shah dies, 1557.

Philip II. of Spain defeats the French at St. Quintin.

Ally Adil Shah succeeds, 1557.

The first act of Ally Adil Shah was to restore the public profession of the Sheea faith, which had been

Restores the Sheea faith.

set aside by his father. These changes of State religion, accompanied, as they were, with changes of offices in almost every department, produced the worst effects in the State of Beejapoor, and were a fertile source of disaffection, as well as of party intrigues; for the present, however, the young king's cause was not impeded. His negotiations with Hoosein Nizam Shah, in regard to restoration of Beejapoor territory, having failed, he made an alliance with Ramraj of Beejanugger; and in 1558 their combined armies invaded the Ahmednugger territory, and completely overran it. The Hindoos, revenging themselves for all the outrages they had suffered from Mahomedans from the earliest times, behaved with shocking barbarity in the first campaign, which was exceeded, if possible, in the second. But the combined forces failed to take the fort of Ahmednugger, and the monsoon breaking upon the besiegers, they were eventually obliged to raise the siege. The allies returning southwards, separated at the fort of Nuldroog, the fortifications of which were renewed by Ally Adil Shah.

Ahmednugger invaded.

The siege of Ahmednugger raised.

This campaign and its consequences, brought about the memorable quadruple treaty of alliance against Ramraj, whose power was now thoroughly comprehended, and felt to be dangerous to the Mahomedan interests. No single Mahomedan kingdom could pretend to oppose the Hindoos of Beejanugger in the field: and after mature deliberation with his counsellors, Ally Adil Shah determined to sound the intentions of the Deccan monarchs on the subject of a crusade against them. His minister, Kishwur Khan, was therefore despatched to Golcondah, where the project was well received; and an envoy from that State proceeding from Beejapoor to Ahmednugger, found Hoosein Nizam Shah willing to sink all differences with Beejapoor in the common alliance. To cement this, he gave his daughter, the afterwards famous Chánd Beebee, in marriage to Ally Adil Shah, with the long disputed frontier fortress of Sholapoor as her dowry; and received Ally's sister, Huddeea Sooltana, as the bride of his eldest son, Moortuza. With Ally Bereed Shah of Beeder there was no difficulty: and the treaties were exchanged and confirmed by solemn oaths. Early in the month of December 1564, the confederate armies had assembled at or near Beejapoor, and the kings and their whole forces marched leisurely southwards on December 26, by the route of Talikote. It is only a short march from Talikote to the river Krishna, and on arrival there, the confederates found the right bank occupied by the enemy's out-

Combination against Beejanugger.

League of the Mahomedan Kings of the Deccan against Beejanugger.

Maximilian emperor of Germany.

The combined armies unite near Beejapoor.

posts, while the main body of his army was encamped at a little distance beyond. Ramraj had, for this great need, assembled all the available forces of his dominions. He had dispatched his younger brother, Yeltum-raj, with 20,000 cavalry, 500 elephants, and 100,000 foot, to secure the river; his second brother, Venket-Adry, with an equal force, to support him; and he himself followed with the flower of the army. The numbers of this host, as given by Ferishta, are beyond belief; but unquestionably they were very numerous. Finding the fords guarded by heavy masses of men, that on the extreme right of the Hindoo position, which was defended by a field-work, the traces of which are still visible, was esteemed the most assailable; and the allies, making a feint of marching up the river, returned suddenly on the night of the third day and carried the ford by storm. The Hindoos fell back upon their supports and main bodies, and the Mahomedans crossing the river, advanced for about twelve miles to the south-west, where they found the whole Hindoo army in position. The Mahomedans now formed in line of battle, Ally Adil Shah commanding the right wing, Ally Bereed Shah and Ibrahim Kootub Shah the left, while Hoosein Nizam Shah, with his famous artillery, took post in the centre. On the other side, Yeltum-raj commanded the right wing of the Hindoos, Venket-Adry the left, and Ramraj himself the centre. There were 2,000 elephants in the Hindoo army, and these and the artillery were posted along the line. It was a memorable battle —to decide, as each party knew, the final supremacy of Hindoo or Moslem in Southern India—and was well fought on both sides. In the first attack by the Hindoo cavalry on the wings of the Mahomedan army, both fell into confusion from the showers of rockets, and were even retreating; but Hoosein Nizam Shah, with his artillery, was not to be denied. He had brought 600 pieces of all calibres into action, commanded by Chuleby Roomy Khan, a Turk of great ability; and these preserving order, advanced in three lines, supported and assisted by the elephants. Seeing the danger, Ramraj directed them to be charged by his best infantry in a mass. As it approached it was met by a withering fire from the large guns, of shot, and copper money enclosed in strong canvas bags, which did vast execution: 5,000 of the Hindoos were left in heaps before the guns, and Kishwur Khan Lary, an intelligent Beejapoor general, fell on the flank of the retiring column with 5,000 of the Beejapoor cavalry, and completed the rout. Ramraj had witnessed the defeat of his infantry from a singhasun, or lofty royal litter, whence he had been distributing rewards; and his attendants

The invasion resisted by Beejanugger.

The allies cross the Krishna river.

A great battle ensues.

placed him on horseback as the Ahmednugger elephants came up. He was then taken prisoner, and conducted to Chuleby Roomy Khan, who sent him to Hoosein Nizam Shah. On ascertaining who he was, the king ordered him to be beheaded; and his head, stuck on a long spear, was displayed to the army. The ghastly trophy was preserved, and for many years afterwards was annually displayed at Ahmednugger on the anniversary of the victory. The rout of the Hindoo army was quickly completed: 100,000 men are stated to have perished on the field and in the pursuit. Yeltum-raj was killed, and the whole of the treasures of Ramraj, an immense booty, were captured. Venket-Adry escaped to Penkóndah, and the allies continued their march to Beejanugger, which was completely plundered, and for the most part destroyed, and henceforth became almost deserted. By this great battle, which is usually called that of Talikote, though in reality fought nearly thirty miles to the south-west of that town, the Hindoo power of Southern India was destroyed. The dynasty of Beejanugger, represented by the Prince Venket-Adry, settled for a time at Penkóndah, but afterwards withdrew, under the encroachments of the Mahomedans, to Chundergiry, and its great dominions became parcelled out among its feudal chieftains.

Ramraj is taken prisoner.

And is beheaded.

The Hindoo army is routed.

The allies advance to Beejanugger, and plunder the city.

The Hindoo power of Southern India broken.

Beejanugger abandoned.

It is curious, perhaps, that Ferishta, generally so ample in the detail of wars, should have omitted, in his history of Ally Adil Shah's reign, any account of the alliance between the Kings of Beejapoor and Ahmednugger, for the reduction of the Portuguese. This occurred, however, in 1571, when Ally Adil Shah besieged Goa; but was repulsed with severe loss, and at the same time their other factory, Choule, or Revadunda, in charge of Dom Luis de Andrada, was attacked by Moortuza Nizam Shah, with a like result. This event is slightly noticed in Ferishta's history of the reign of Moortuza Nizam Shah of Ahmednugger, but there is no indication of the combination of the two powerful monarchies against the Portuguese, and their failure. In the year 1573, part of the intermediate period having passed in a desultory campaign with Ahmednugger, founded upon the jealousy of its king in regard to territorial acquisitions from Beejanugger, Ally Adil Shah marched to the south-west, captured Bunkapoor and Dharwar, and attached their dependencies, with the country nearly as far as Penkóndah, to his dominions; but the subjection of the petty chieftains proved to be no easy task; it occupied several years, and was in the end only partially

Attack on the Portuguese, 1571.

The Turks defeated at Lepanto.

Haarlem taken by the Spaniards.

effected by confirming them in their estates as feudal vassals. In 1579 the king, who, on the termination of these operations, had returned to Beejapoor, was assassinated by a favourite eunuch, to whom he had given offence. Having no male issue, he had previously appointed his nephew Ibrahim, son of his brother Shah Thamasp, to succeed him. During his life, Ally Adil Shah had commenced a noble mausoleum for himself, which remains as it was left by him, unfinished, and in the centre of its precincts he was buried. He had also erected the spacious Jooma mosque, which would accommodate 5,000 persons at prayer—a grand edifice, which is still perfect. Aqueducts for the supply of water to all parts of the city were constructed, and the city walls and fortifications, which were six miles in circuit, were completely finished. Ally Adil Shah had reigned twenty-two years.

Ally Adil Shah assassinated, 1579.

Republic of Holland.

The public works of Ally Adil Shah.

CHAPTER XVI.

OF THE ADIL SHAHY DYNASTY OF BEEJAPOOR (*continued*), 1579 TO 1626.

At the period of his accession to the throne, Ibrahim Adil Shah II. was nine years old. The queen-dowager, Chând Beebee, took charge of him, and the affairs of State were managed by the minister, Kamil Khan. As had been frequently the case in similar circumstances, the minister endeavoured to usurp the chief authority, but had little counted on the cost of deceiving such a woman. The queen resolved on his deposition, and directed Kishwur Khan to remove him from office. Fearing for his life, Kamil Khan fled, but was pursued, overtaken, and killed ere he had proceeded more than a few miles from the capital, and Kishwur Khan succeeded him. But the queen had not delivered herself from thraldom; on the contrary, she had increased it. One of the new regent's first acts was to procure the assassination of Moostafa Khan, the ablest officer of the State, who had been employed in the government and pacification of the territory acquired from Beejanugger, and was a person on whom the queen could thoroughly depend. Freed from his influence, Kishwur Khan now removed the queen from Beejapoor, and confined her in the fort of Sattara. This, with other acts of violence and oppression, rendered the regent highly unpopular. Plots were made

Ibrahim Adil Shah succeeds Ally Adil Shah, 1579.

Kamil Khan, regent, killed.

Kishwur Khan succeeds.

Moostafa Khan Ardistany assassinated.

The queen-dowager confined in Sattara.

against his life; he was even hooted by the populace of the city, and would probably have fallen a victim to its fury; but he escaped to Ahmednugger, where, receiving only a cool reception, he proceeded to Golcondah, and was killed there by a relation of Moostafa Khan, who had pursued him.

Kishwur Khan escapes to Ahmednugger.

Is killed at Golcondah.

Meanwhile an insurrection was in progress in the queen's favour, headed by Yekhlas Khan and other Abyssinian chiefs, who, at the head of a large army, proceeded to the capital. The queen was released, and placed in her former position, and Yekhlas Khan created minister. The parties of Deccanies and Abyssinians had frequently been in opposition to each other, and their feuds and jealousies now broke out with great violence; the streets of the capital were frequently the scene of bloody conflicts between them, and duels were of ordinary daily occurrence. These disturbances afforded a pretext for the interference of the Kings of Golcondah and Ahmednugger, who, in concert, besieged Nuldroog or Shahdroog, one of the strongest forts of the kingdom; but it was bravely and loyally defended, and being unable to take it, the combined forces marched upon Beejapoor. At this crisis there were not more than 3,000 troops in the city; but two generals, Ankoos Khan and Ein-ool-Moolk, arrived with 8,000 cavalry, and kept the enemy in check. Between them, however, and the Abyssinian chieftains in the city, disagreements reached such a pass, that the generals went over to the enemy, declaring that it was impossible to save the State. At this time also, a large portion of the city wall fell down, owing to heavy rain, and its capture appeared imminent. The breach was, however, repaired; and under the intervention of the general of the Berar contingent, who was unwilling to witness the success of the allies, the Beejapoor generals were induced to return to the city and offer their services to the queen-dowager. The office of minister had been conferred upon Syed Abool Hussun, an able man, who rendered essential service. All differences between the parties of the State were accommodated, and in six months he had raised an army of 20,000 horse. Beejapoor had been besieged for twelve months, and its suburbs for the most part destroyed; but before a reunited kingdom the allies could effect nothing, and abandoning further efforts, returned to their dominions; Dilawur Khan, the Beejapoor general, pursuing the King of Golcondah to the gates of his capital, and returning laden with booty. But the efforts of Abool Hussun were ill-rewarded. Dilawur Khan, on his return, conspired against him

The queen is released.

Kings of Golcondah and Ahmednugger besiege Beejapoor.

Danger of the city.

Syed Abool Hussun minister.

The siege of Beejapoor abandoned.

seized and blinded him, and afterwards put him to death; nor could the queen prevent his assumption of the regency, for she was now confined to the palace, and deprived of authority. Dilawur Khan, however, proved in the sequel to be both able and loyal, and in the course of the six years of his regency, the affairs of the kingdom were completely retrieved. There had been no further quarrel with Ahmednugger, and in 1584 the king's sister, Khodeija Sooltana, was betrothed to the son of its sovereign, Moortuza Nizam Shah. On the occasion of the journey of the bride to Ahmednugger, the queen-dowager, her aunt, accompanied her on a visit to her brother Moortuza, and never afterwards returned to Beejapoor.

Abool Hussun blinded by Dilawur Khan.

Chánd Beebee, the queen-dowager, returns to Ahmednugger, 1584.

In 1586, Mullika Jehán, the daughter of the King of Golcondah, was asked in marriage for the young king—a transaction which gave great offence to the King of Ahmednugger, and had well-nigh produced a fresh war; but the difficulties were overcome, and the marriage took place at Shahdroog, with great pomp, though not without the cover, as it were, of an army of observation from Beejapoor. The king, who displayed great aptitude for public business, now desired to be freed from the trammels of his minister, whose conduct had become offensive, not only to the king, but to others. Buleel Khan, an officer of great ability and distinction, who had been employed as viceroy in Malabar, arrived at court when the Beejapoor army was in the field against Ahmednugger, and was received with honour by the king; but the minister, jealous of the distinction that had been shown him, caused him to be seized and blinded—an act which the king would have resented at once had he been able. He, however, watched his opportunity, and soon afterwards escaping from his guards, proceeded at night to the camp of Ein-ool-Moolk. Dilawur Khan followed him at daylight, and a slight skirmish ensued, when the minister, seeing that he had no further chance, fled to Ahmednugger, and the revolution was complete. In his history, Ferishta, who was a spectator and actor in the whole scene, gives a graphic account of it, which is highly interesting (Briggs's Trans. vol. iii. pp. 163–170). Ibrahim now returned to Beejapoor, and entered on the administration of public affairs with great ability and success; but his character is tarnished by his conduct to Dilawur Khan, now upwards of eighty years old, whom he induced to return to Beejapoor under promises of favour; and on his arrival, caused to be blinded and imprisoned in the fort of Sattara, where he died.

The king's marriage.

Case of Buleel Khan.

The king declares his independence, 1587.

Mary queen of Scots beheaded.

Dilawur Khan flies to Ahmednugger.

Dilawur Khan blinded and imprisoned.

Rebellion of Prince Ismail, 1593.

In 1593, the king's brother, Ismail, who resided at Belgaum, rebelled, and the insurrection grew formidable. Ein-ool-Moolk, who was sent to quell it, joined the prince, and proclaimed him king; but, in an action which followed, he was defeated and slain; his head was sent to the king, who caused it to be fired from a cannon on the walls, and the prince was executed. These events were hardly at an end before the ever-restless King of Ahmednugger entered into an alliance with the Rajah of Penkóndah, and invaded the Beejapoor territory. During the campaign, he fell ill and died; but the war was continued by his son, or rather by the regent, as he was a minor, and in a severe general action, the young king was killed. Ibrahim Adil Shah, who had acted only on the defensive, returned to his capital on September 9, 1596, making a triumphal entry amidst the rejoicings of his people. This proved to be the last war with Ahmednugger; and the conclusion of those frequent and desperate struggles for superiority which had lasted throughout their existence, which treaties and intermarriages did not prevent, and which weakened and at times exhausted both.

He is executed.

New war with Ahmednugger.

Cadiz taken by the English.

Separate history of Beejapoor ceases.

From this period henceforth the kingdom of Beejapoor had no special historian, and its progress and final extinction by the Emperor Aurungzebe, form events of general history which supplies only great occurrences; but it can be gathered, that the last portion of the reign of Ibrahim Adil Shah was prosperous and splendid. In the first attack by the Moghuls upon Ahmednugger his forces were too late to relieve the city, and in the attempt, conjointly with Golcondah and the Ahmednugger army, to drive them from Berar, his best troops were defeated in the battle of Soopa, as already related in Chapter X. of this Book, and the contest was never renewed. On the arrival of the Emperor Akbur at Boorhanpoor, in 1603, Ibrahim Adil Shah sent an embassy to him with costly presents, and overtures of alliance. It is believed that a secret treaty was then executed, which, while it protected Beejapoor, left the emperor free as regarded Ahmednugger; the marriage of Ibrahim's daughter to the Prince Daniel followed, and his subsequent neutralility saved his kingdom from any attempt at subjugation by the Moghuls, during the reign of his son. Ibrahim Adil Shah died in 1626, in the fifty-sixth year of his age. He was the greatest of all the Adil Shahy dynasty, and in most respects, except its founder, the most able and popular. Without the distraction of war, he applied himself to civil affairs with much

Death of Ibrahim Adil Shah.

His character and acts.

care; and the land settlements of the provinces of his kingdom, many of which are still extant among district records, show an admirable and efficient system of registration of property, and its valuation. In this respect, the system of Toder Mul, introduced by the Emperor Akbur, seems to have been followed with the necessary local modifications. Although he changed the profession of the State religion immediately upon assuming the direction of State affairs from Sheea to Soony, Ibrahim was yet extremely tolerant of all creeds and faiths. Hindoos not only suffered no persecution at his hands, but many of his chief civil and military officers were Brahmins and Mahrattas. With the Portuguese of Goa he seems to have kept up a friendly intercourse. Portuguese painters decorated his palaces, and their merchants traded freely in his dominions. To their missionaries, also, he extended his protection; and there are many anecdotes current in the country that his tolerance of Christians equalled, if it did not exceed, that of his contemporary Akbur. He allowed the preaching of Christianity freely among his people, and there are still existent several Catholic churches, one at Cheetapoor, one at Moodgul, one at Raichore, and others, endowed by the king with lands, and other sources of revenue, which have survived the changes and revolutions of more than 300 years. Each of these churches now consist of several hundred members, and remain under the spiritual jurisdiction of the Archbishop of Goa.

Catholic churches endowed.

Ibrahim Adil Shah was fond of architecture, and during his long reign, and its peaceful close, embellished his now splendid capital with many noble buildings. His own mausoleum, which is still perfect, and kept in repair by the British Government, is one of the most elaborate specimens of Indo-Gothic architecture in India; and both of the tomb, and the fine mosque and terrace attached to it, the basalt of which they have been constructed has been worked with admirable skill and grace of design, and much of it is polished like marble. These buildings were not quite finished at the king's death: and the inscription records their completion in the reign of his son Mahmood, at a total cost of 528,150*l.* at the present value of gold coinage, which was perhaps greater at the period. The work occupied thirty-six years. The noble palaces at Toorwah, three miles west of the city, which were entire till unroofed by the Mahrattas, with their gardens, were constructed by the king in 1604, and were connected with the fort by a broad street, three miles long, and perfectly straight, which can be traced by its ruins: while to the right and left the extent of the old city can be followed for several miles.

Architecture.

At his death the king left a full treasury, a large and well-paid army of 80,000 horse, and his dominions extended to the borders of Mysore. He was succeeded by his son Mahmood, then in his sixteenth year, and the history of his reign and that of his successors, in the absence of any local record, must be traced in connection with the general history of India.

CHAPTER XVII.

OF THE NIZAM SHAHY DYNASTY OF AHMEDNUGGER (*continued from Chapter XVIII., Book III.*), 1532 TO 1586.

BOORHAN NIZAM SHAH, after the death of Ismail Adil Shah of Beejapoor, in 1532, enjoyed a period of peace until 1542, when he endeavoured to take advantage of the quarrel between Ibrahim Adil Shah and his minister, Assud Khan. The real object of the attack seems to have been the acquisition of the districts of Purainda and Sholapoor, always in dispute between the States; and having taken possession of them, he marched to Belgaum. Here there appears some inconsistency in Ferishta's history, for Boorhan Nizam Shah is represented as having induced Assud Khan to join him in attacking Beejapoor; whereas, as is most probable from the general loyalty of Assud Khan's conduct, the history of the events as given in the account of Ibrahim's reign, is much more probable. The result of the attack on Beejapoor was unfortunate: and the king was not only obliged to surrender what he had taken, but to retreat to Dowlatabad. His restless disposition, however, impelled him into a fresh war in 1546, when he was defeated at Oorchán, as has been related in Chapter XV. of this Book, with the loss of his artillery, elephants, and camp-equipage. Failing against Beejapoor, the king now attacked the Beeder State, in revenge for having denied him assistance against Beejapoor; defeated the Beeder troops, and took Owsa, Kandhar, and other forts, which occupied him till 1545, when the rebellion of the Prince Abdoolla of Beejapoor, and his flight to Goa, occurred. In this matter he was able to effect nothing; Assud Khan rejected his overtures, and the Portuguese would not join the confederacy against Beejapoor. The king now invited the cooperation of Ramraj of Beejanugger, and advanced as far as Kulliany to meet him. Near this town he defeated Ibrahim Adil Shah, with severe loss, and returning by Purainda, again took possession of it. This war

The king is defeated at Oorchán.

Defeats the troops of Beeder.

The king invites the co-operation of the Rajah of Beejanugger.

continued till 1549, in which year the king proceeded into the Raichore Dooáb, and had a conference with the Prince of Beejanugger; the result of which was, that each was left to pursue the conquest of such portions of the Beejapoor territory as he could effect. Ramraj, therefore, occupied Moodgul and Raichore, while Boorhan Nizam Shah besieged Sholapoor, which was taken by assault. In the year 1553, the affairs of Beejapoor being in a distracted condition, Boorhan Nizam Shah again commenced operations against its dominions, and besieged Beejapoor; but being taken ill of dysentery, the siege was raised, and he returned to his capital, where he died at the age of fifty-four, having reigned forty-seven years. He left two sons, Hoosein and Abdool Khadur, by his wife Ameena, and two by Beebee Muryam, the daughter of Yoosuf Adil Shah. Of these Hoosein was the eldest, and at thirteen years of age succeeded him.

Mary queen of England.

Death of Boorhan Nizam Shah, 1553.

Hoosein Nizam Shah succeeds, 1553.

Notwithstanding his youth, Hoosein Nizam Shah entered upon the conduct of public affairs with much spirit. A rebellion by his brother Abdool Khadur, supported by the Deccany party, was quickly suppressed, while his half-brothers took refuge with their uncle at Beejapoor. These desultory contests, as has been already related, continued to the last with Ibrahim, and were revived after Ally Adil Shah's succession. They eventually provoked the invasion of the Ahmednugger dominions by Ally Adil Shah and Ramraj conjointly, with, according to Ferishta's account, 100,000 horse and 900,000 infantry, by whom the country was overrun and plundered. But Ahmednugger, though besieged, was not taken; provisions were supplied to the garrison from without; the allies seem to have been unprovided with artillery, by which alone the fort of Ahmednugger could be attacked, and the monsoon compelled them to retire. The danger, however, was imminent, and Hoosein Nizam Shah begged for peace, when it was offered on the condition of giving up Kulliany to Ally Adil Shah; putting Jehángeer Khan, the Berar general, to death, and accepting a pâu, or betel, from Ramraj. These terms were accepted, and the brave Jehángeer was murdered by a band of assassins, an act which, done at the desire of 'an infidel,' produced universal execration, and the king afterwards proceeded to the camp of Ramraj. Ferishta's account of the scene which ensued is too characteristic to be omitted. 'Ramraj rose on his entering the tent, and took him by the hand. Hoosein Nizam Shah, who possessed great pride, called for a basin and ewer, and washed his hands, as if they had been polluted by the touch of Ramraj, who said in his own language, "If he were not my guest, I

Invasion of Ally Adil Shah.

would cut off his hands, and tie them round his neck;" then calling for water, he also washed; and such were the bad feelings which prevailed, that a tumult nearly occurred on the spot.' On giving the keys of Kulliany to Ramraj, the king said, 'I give them to you as a present.' But the peace did not last.

War with Beejapoor renewed.

Battle of Dreux.

In 1562 Hoosein Nizam Shah made an attempt to recover Kulliany, but failed; and was attacked in turn by Ally Adil Shah and Ramraj, when he lost all his artillery—which numbered 700 pieces—except forty. Colonel Briggs, the translator of Ferishta, supposes that the great gun of Beejapoor, the largest piece of ordnance in the world, weighing forty tons, cast at Ahmednugger by Chuleby Roomy Khan, in the reign of Boorhan Nizam Shah, was taken on this occasion; but this was not the case: the gun was first mounted on the walls of Purainda, and was removed from thence during a temporary occupation of that fort by Beejapoor. Ahmednugger was again besieged; but in the meantime the ditch had been enlarged, the bastions built of stone, and much strengthened; and the allies, whose forces had pillaged the country, were obliged by a pestilence that broke out among them, and by a sudden rise of the river Seena—which Ferishta states swept away 25,000 men at night from their crowded camp—to retire.

The great gun at Beejapoor.

Confederacy against Beejanugger, 1564.

No greater example of revulsion of feeling can well be imagined, amidst these perpetual broils, than the sudden alliance of the five Kings of the Deccan against Beejanugger, in the ensuing year, 1564. While Ally Adil Shah had called in the aid of Ramraj to avenge himself upon Hoosein Nizam Shah, the Kings of Golcondah, Beeder, and Berar had aided the latter with all their forces against the 'infidel.' Now, all alike were excited by the same religious zeal to sink their mutual differences, and the war with the Hindoos of Beejanugger became a national crusade. How it was carried out has already been related (Chapter XV. of this Book), and it is perhaps strange that no mutual jealousies prevented its fulfilment.

Hoosein Nizam Shah dies, 1565.

Under their influence, however, no partition of territory took place till long afterwards. Hoosein Nizam Shah, who had had the satisfaction of witnessing his artillery win the battle, only lived till he returned to his capital, where he was taken ill, and died on June 7, 1565. He was only twenty-four years old, and had reigned fifteen years, amidst constant war and turmoil. He was succeeded by his son Moortuza, then a minor, whose mother, Khoonza Sooltana, undertook the regency, assisted by her brothers.

Moortuza Nizam Shah, his son, succeeds, 1565.

The jealousy of Hoosein Nizam Shah had prevented any occupation of the territory of Beejanugger by Ally Adil Shah; and on his death, the King of Beejapoor proceeded against the southern provinces. But, true to the preceding policy of her kingdom, the queen-dowager took the field in person, and Ally Adil Shah was, for the present, forced to postpone his intentions of annexation. A desultory war continued between the kingdoms till 1569, when the king released himself from his mother's regency, and assumed charge of his own affairs, behaving with so mnch spirit in the continuance of the war against Beejapoor, that peace was concluded on the understanding that, while Beejapoor should not be molested in annexing the province of Beejanugger, Ahmednugger should be at liberty to conquer Berar. In 1572, therefore, Moortuza Nizam Shah marched against Toofál Khan, the minister of the Imád Shahy dynasty of Berar, who had usurped the local power, and defeated him. Toofál Khan would have been taken prisoner, but for a devotee, who stood up in the path of the king and his army, in a narrow defile, and forbade him to proceed till he had paid down to him 12,000 hoons, or 4,800*l*. The anecdote is given by Ferishta, and affords a specimen both of the extortions of religious devotees, and the strong superstition of the period. Toofál Khan afterwards took refuge in the fort of Narnalla, and wrote to the Emperor Akbur, placing himself and the Imád Shahy dominions under his protection; when the emperor issued a mandate to Moortuza Nizam Shah, forbidding him to molest Toofál Khan or the Berar territory. To this, however, the young king paid no attention. He captured Toofál Khan, with his sovereign, Boorhan Imád Shah, and confined them. Boorhan Imád Shah died soon afterwards; but meanwhile Moortuza had annexed Berar to his dominions—an act which the Emperor Akbur deeply resented. The ruler of Khandésh made an attempt to recover Berar for a relative of its deceased king, but it failed, and he was pursued to Boorhanpoor.

War with Berar.

Pope Gregory XIII.

Toofál Khan captured.

Berar annexed to Ahmednugger.

Moortuza Nizam Shah was now advised by his minister, Chungiz Khan, to reduce Beeder, as a balance against Ally Adil Shah's southern annexations; but the minister's enemies persuaded the king that this was only a ruse to draw him away from Berar, of which Chungiz Khan desired to take possession. The king, becoming impressed with the truth of the accusation, which, however, had no real foundation, sent a cup of poison to his minister, who, seeing he could not escape death, drank it and died, leaving an affecting letter to the king, quoted by Ferishta, which produced such

Chungiz Khan poisoned.

The king abdicates.

an effect upon his mind, that he abdicated the throne, and gave up the conduct of affairs to his ministers, Sahib Khan and Salabut Khan. The former now pursued a course of unbridled profligacy and licentiousness, and eventually fled, but was pursued, and put to death by the nobles whom he had provoked. Salabut Khan, however, continued in office, and directed the affairs of State with great ability, for a long period. The king's mind had now become completely disordered; and in a moment of anger, Salabut Khan was imprisoned. After this the State affairs fell into great confusion. Mirza Khan, one of the chief nobles, marched with a force to Dowlatabad, and released the Prince Meerun Hoosein, who was confined there. The king, in his extremity, now released Salabut Khan; but it was too late: Meerun Hoosein hastened to Ahmednugger, surprised the fort, and after grossly insulting his wretched father, shut him up in a hot bath-room, where he died of suffocation. This event took place in the year 1586, in the twenty-fifth year of his reign, and he was succeeded by the parricide. The king's body was taken to Roza, near Dowlatabad, and interred in a fine mausoleum he had erected there; but was afterwards disinterred and sent to Kerbela.

Moortuza Nizam Shah put to death, 1586.

CHAPTER XVIII.

OF THE NIZAM SHAHY DYNASTY OF AHMEDNUGGER (*continued*), 1586 TO 1607.

MEERUN HOOSEIN, NIZAM SHAH ascended the throne immediately on his father's death, and created Mirza Khan, who had released him from confinement, minister. The king now gave way to excess of all kinds; he was rarely sober, and one of his amusements was to ride through the city, with his drunken companions, and hunt to death any one who might cross his path. To avert the chance of rebellion, he destroyed all the male representatives of his family then present—fifteen persons—in one day. Becoming suspicious of Mirza Khan, he endeavoured to get him into his power; but the minister was wary, and succeeded, on the other hand, in seizing and imprisoning the king, on March 15, 1588. He then dispatched an escort to Lohgurh, where the sons of the king's paternal uncle, Boorhan, were confined: and brought from thence Ismail, then in his twelfth year, and placed him on the throne. This act, however, produced

Accession of Meerun Hoosein, 1586.

Who is dethroned, 1588.

Destruction of the Spanish armada.

Ismail Nizam Shah succeeds, 1588.

a great commotion among the troops, and Jumál Khan, the leader of the Deccanies and Abyssinians, protested against it with much violence. Mirza Khan, believing the tumult would subside if the king were dead, caused him to be beheaded; and his head, stuck upon a long pole, was exhibited from one of the bastions. But this murder exasperated the mob still more; and Jumál Khan and his party set fire to the gates. During the night, Mirza Khan and his friends escaped; but Jumál Khan, at the head of the mob of soldiers and townspeople, plundered the houses of all foreigners, and slew all they could find, under circumstances of great barbarity and cruelty. On the fourth day, Mirza Khan, who had been seized in his flight, was brought to Jumál Khan, who, after having him led about the city on an ass, caused him to be hewn in pieces, and his members affixed to different public edifices. Others were blown from guns, and the Deccan party remained triumphant. Thus, too, the murder of Moortuza Nizam Shah was avenged.

Meerun Hoosein beheaded.

Mirza Khan executed.

This revolution did not, however, affect the young king's position, and Jumál Khan was prepared to support him. Ismail Nizam Shah was the son of Boorhan, who had fled from the Deccan to the court of the Emperor Akbur, and still remained there; and it was considered by many that his was the best right to succeed. But Jumál Khan was an able man, and a brave soldier, and having given his allegiance to the young king, was now prepared to do his duty by him. Salabut Khan, who was employed in Berar, was the first to take the field in the interests of Boorhan; but he was defeated by Jumál Khan, who now turned against the army of Beejapoor, which had advanced from the south. No action ensued, and its retreat was effected by the payment of 270,000 hoons, or 108,000*l.*, for the expense of the campaign.

Salabut Khan, now an aged man, was afterwards allowed to return to Ahmednugger, and died in the same year. His noble mausoleum, erected on a lofty hill south of the city, is still in perfect repair, and is used by pleasure parties from Ahmednugger. It commands a grand view over the mountains to the south and east, and over the broad valley of the Godavery river.

The Emperor Akbur, who greatly desired a pretext for interference in Deccan affairs, and who had kept himself fully advised of the political state of Ahmednugger, now offered Boorhan an army to reinstate himself; but he declined the attempt, and for the present stationed himself near the frontier, in the province of Hundia, which was allotted for his support; and thence, having made a desultory effort to

The Emperor Akbur's interference.

invade Ahmednugger, was defeated. The war with Beejapoor, however, continued. Boorhan's cause was espoused by Ibrahim Adil Shah; and, in a general action, Jumál Khan was slain, when Boorhan, advancing from the north, deposed his son Ismail, after a nominal reign of two years.

Ismail Nizam Shah deposed, 1591.

Boorhan Nizam Shah was of somewhat advanced age when he ascended the throne. He was the brother of Moortuza Nizam Shah, and had been allotted an ample estate at Lohgurh; but, on the king's displaying symptoms of madness, had rebelled, been defeated by him, and forced to fly, first to Beeder, and thence to Beejapoor, and eventually received protection from the Emperor Akbur. Boorhan Nizam Shah's espousal of the cause of Dilawur Khan, ex-regent of Beejapoor, led to a war with Ibrahim Adil Shah; and this concluded, he dispatched an army against the Portuguese, in 1592, which besieged Revadunda; but it suffered a severe reverse. The garrison, reinforced, attacked the Mahomedans, took seventy-five pieces of cannon, and killed, according to the Mahomedan historian, 12,000 men, while the Portuguese claim 10,000. 1,500 Europeans, and about the same number of native soldiers, composed the Portuguese force. The Mahomedan commander, Furhád Khan, with his family, were taken prisoners, and having become Christians, went to Portugal. In 1594, while engaged in a campaign in support of the Prince Ismail of Beejapoor against his brother Ibrahim Adil Shah, the king fell ill; and declaring his son Ibrahim to be his successor, and passing over Ismail, on account of his religious opinions, died on May 15, 1594.

Boorhan Nizam Shah II. succeeds, 1591.

University of Dublin erected.

Expeditio against the Portuguese defeated.

Boorhan Nizam Shah II. dies, 1594.

Immediately before the late king's death, an attempt had been made by Yekhlas Khan to create a revolution in favour of his eldest son Ismail; but it had failed, and Ibrahim ascended the throne without further opposition. He appointed Meean Munjoo Deccany to be his minister, and Yekhlas Khan was allowed to return to court; but a rivalry immediately commenced between them, which, in the end, proved disastrous. In the confusion which prevailed, the ambassador of Ibrahim Adil Shah was insulted, and left the court, and Ibrahim himself moved with an army to support him. It was in vain that the moderate Meean Munjoo urged the prospective interference of the Emperor Akbur as a reason for peace between the two States. Yekhlas Khan was for war, and the young king, under the influence of almost habitual intoxication, marched with his army. Still Meean Munjoo persisted in his endeavours to prevent bloodshed, and had influence enough with the Beejapoor commander, Humeed Khan, to prevent his being the assailant. When the

Ibrahim Nizam Shah succeeds, 1594.

armies were encamped near each other, and, after a night of debauch, the king ordered out his forces and attacked the Beejapoor troops; but, as he was leading the centre of his army, was shot in the forehead, and died instantly. His reign had only lasted four months. His body was taken to Ahmednugger, and a boy named Ahmed, supposed to be a descendant of the royal family, and who had been confined at Dowlatabad, was sent for by Meean Munjoo, and proclaimed king, while the late king's son, Bahadur, then an infant in arms, was despatched to a distant fortress.

Ibrahim Nizam Shah killed in action, 1594.

Ahmed proclaimed king, and crowned, 1594.

Ahmed was crowned with great pomp on August 6, 1594, but it was shortly afterwards discovered that he had no pretensions to royal descent; and Yekhlas Khan, with his Abyssinians, disputed the succession, raising an insurrection, and proclaiming another boy as king. In his despair, Meean Munjoo now took the desperate resolution of inviting the Prince Moorád Mirza from Guzerat, and the prince, already in possession of his father's instructions to advance into the Deccan on any reasonable pretext, marched at once for Ahmednugger. Meanwhile Meean Munjoo had retrieved his position, and had defeated Yekhlas Khan and his party; but it was too late: nothing could stay the prince's progress, and leaving the dowager-queen, Chánd Beebee, as regent, and the fort of Ahmednugger well provided for defence, Meean Munjoo departed to implore the assistance of the Kings of Golcondah and Beejapoor against the common enemy, the Moghuls. The queen had, from the first, been opposed to the election of Ahmed as king. She considered the infant Bahadur the rightful heir, as in truth he was; and collecting a strong party around her, prepared to defend the fort to the last. There were now four competitors for the throne; 1, the infant son of the late king; 2, the boy Ahmed, already crowned; 3, the boy selected by Yekhlas Khan, who was at the head of his own party for his support; and, 4, Shah Ally, the son of Boorhan Nizam Shah I., an old man, seventy years of age, who had lived in retirement at Beejapoor, and whose pretensions were supported by Nehung Khan, another powerful Abyssinian chief. Of these parties, Yekhlas Khan's was defeated near the Godavery by a Moghul detachment, and dispersed. Nehung Khan cut his way through the Moghul army, and joined the queen in the fort; but Shah Ally and his followers were cut off, and perished. On hearing of the Moghul invasion, Ibrahim Adil Shah despatched his able general, Soheil Khan, to Nuldroog, with 25,000 horse, where he was joined by Yekhlas Khan with the wreck of his force, and by

The succession disputed.

Prince Moorád Mirza invited to the Deccan.

Claimants of the throne.

a contingent of 6,000 horse from Golcondah; and had this force marched on Ahmednugger at once, the present crisis might possibly have been averted.

Hearing of the assembling of these forces, the Prince Moorád Mirza now pressed the siege with ardour. Mines were laid under the two principal bastions, and charged ready for explosion. Respecting the bravery of the garrison, the Moghul officer in charge of the trenches made his way to the walls, and informing them of their danger, called upon them to surrender. The queen-dowager would, however, hear of no terms. She began counter-mines, herself working with the men, and by daylight two mines had been discovered and destroyed. In the act of removing the powder from a third, the train was fired, and some of the wall fell. Several of the officers now prepared for flight, and urged the queen to escape; but the heroic woman put on armour, and with a veil over her face, and a naked sword in her hand, took up her post in the breach, while her example caused the utmost enthusiasm to prevail among all ranks. In the afternoon, the Moghuls advanced to storm, but were beaten back with immense loss; the ditch was nearly filled with the dead. Again and again the attack was renewed, but the queen in person repulsed them all, and without quitting her post all night, caused the breach to be built up. But the danger was imminent; another such crisis could hardly be endured, and she therefore wrote to Soheil Khan, urging him to advance. This despatch was, however, intercepted by the Prince Moorád, who read it, and adding, 'the sooner you come the better, I am most anxious to meet you,' forwarded it to its destination. As the relieving forces advanced, they cut off the supplies of provisions to the Moghul camp, whereupon Prince Moorád made overtures to the queen, offering to quit the country if Berar were ceded to him. This, at first, she refused; but her allies were still distant, and even did they arrive, the result of an engagement between them and the Moghul veterans was very doubtful. She, therefore, signed the treaty, and Prince Moorád Mirza marched, unmolested, to take possession of Berar. Three days afterwards, the allies reached Ahmednugger, and Meean Munjoo pressed the recognition of Ahmed upon the queen. She, however, was firm in her support of the infant king, whom she sent for, and caused to be crowned, while Ahmed was provided with an estate by the King of Beejapoor, and resigned all pretensions to the kingdom.

Ahmednugger besieged by Prince Moorád Mirza.

Valour of the queen-dowager.

Repulse of the Moghuls.

Prince Moorád negotiates with the queen-dowager.

She cedes Berar.

The infant son of the king is crowned.

But the State was doomed. The queen appointed Mahomed

Khan as minister, who soon set her at defiance, appointed his own creatures to offices of trust, and obliged her to apply to Beejapoor for aid, which was promptly given. Ibrahim Adil Shah despatched Soheil Khan with 25,000 cavalry, to remain under her orders, and he arrived in 1596; when Mahomed Khan, finding his power at an end, wrote to Khan Khanán, the Moghul commander in Berar, offering his own assistance to subdue the whole of the Ahmednugger kingdom. When this became known, the garrison of Ahmednugger seized the traitor, and made him over to the queen, who, by this step, was reinstated in her authority. Soheil Khan now set out on his return to Beejapoor; but having received intelligence of the annexation, by the Moghuls, of other districts not included in the cession of Berar, halted for instructions, and received orders to defend the northern frontier. He, therefore, advanced with his own army and the contingents of Golcondah and Ahmednugger, to Soneput or Soopa, on the Godavery, when the general action which eventually decided the fate of Ahmednugger was fought, on January 26, 1597, as described in Chapter X. of this Book. The Moghuls did not immediately advance upon Ahmednugger; but the local disputes were by no means at an end. Nehung Khan, who had been appointed minister after Mahomed Khan, resisted the queen and revolted: and affairs continued in the same distracted state until the arrival of the Emperor Akbur at Boorhanpoor, in 1599. On the Moghuls' advance from Berar, Nehung Khan made an ineffectual attempt to oppose them, and fled to Joonair, and Ahmednugger was again invested. The queen once more defended it bravely, but she had now no dependence upon the garrison, and openly gave her opinion that it would be better to accept terms, and carry the young king to Joonair. As this opinion was uttered, Humeed Khan, a eunuch, to whom it had been expressed, ran out of the palace into the parade-ground of the fort, crying that the queen was about to give up the fort to the Moghuls; and the ungrateful Deccany troops, led by him, rushed into the private apartments and put the royal lady to death. Thus perished one of the noblest characters that the Deccan had ever produced. Beautiful in person, and at an early age a widow, there is yet no stain upon her honour. The trying scenes of her early life at Beejapoor were often repeated; yet, with a devotion rarely excelled, she never hesitated to do her duty in the great political emergencies which occurred, both in Beejapoor and Ahmednugger. Her valour was unquestionable, and was put to the severest proof on many occasions; and her sad fate excited

The King of Beejapoor assists the queen-dowager.

Battle of Soopa.

Second siege of Ahmednugger by the Moghuls.

The queen-dowager is murdered.

Her character.

a feeling of universal commiseration, which has survived to the present time—among her old people.

After the queen's death, the Moghuls pressed the siege more rapidly. Their mines were sprung, and in the storm which followed, the garrison was put to the sword, for the Moghuls gave no quarter. The infant king, with all the members of the royal family, were sent to the Emperor Akbur, and were confined in the fort of Gwalior. But there was still some vitality in the State. Moortuza, the son of Shah Ally, who was the son of Boorhan Nizam Shah I., proclaimed himself king, under the title of Moortuza Nizam Shah II., and was supported by the famous Mullik Umbur, who, as minister-in-chief, and viceroy of the province of Dowlatabad, long preserved what remained of the old kingdom, and carried out in detail those surveys of village lands, registrations of property, and revised assessments which have rendered him ever since famous throughout a large portion of the Deccan. Mullik Umbur was one of those Abyssinians who, little better than savages in their own country, displayed in the Deccan abilities as statesmen and generals which were hardly exceeded by the more civilised Persians. The king continued to reside at Owsa for some time, but was afterwards removed to Purainda, which became for a brief period the capital of the kingdom; but Mullik Umbur, in 1607, having overcome his rival, Meean Rajoo, who had held nearly half the Nizam Shahy dominions, removed the king to Joonair. The power of the Moghuls was, however, progressing rapidly, and the details of the final extinction of the Nizam Shahy dynasty belong more particularly to the general history of the succeeding period.

Capture of Ahmednugger by the Moghuls.

The infant king sent to the Emperor Akbur.

Moortuza Nizam Shah succeeds.

Mullik Umbur's administration.

His character.

CHAPTER XIX.

OF THE KOOTUB SHAHY DYNASTY OF GOLCONDAH (*continued from Chapter XXI., Book III.*), 1550 TO 1611.

THE principal incidents of Ibrahim Kootub Shah's reign have connection with the kingdoms of Beejapoor and Ahmednugger, into whose constant disputes he was frequently drawn; but these need not be repeated here. He formed one of the confederate allies for the reduction of Ramraj, and in the act displayed, it may be thought, a bad return for the refuge and hospitality he had experienced for many years at Beejanugger; but the events of the intervening years had been productive of many disagreements, and a remonstrance addressed by Ramraj to the king, on the occasion of his attack on Beejapoor in concert with the King of Ahmednugger, deserves to be quoted as a good specimen of the political correspondence of the period. 'Be it known to your Majesty,' writes Ramraj, 'that it is now many years since the two courts of Beejapoor and Ahmednugger have been in a constant state of warfare, and that the balance of power between them was so equal, that although every year each of these sovereigns had been in the habit of making a campaign on each other's frontiers, yet no advantage accrued to either. It now appears that your Majesty, whose ancestors never interfered in these disputes, has marched an army to turn the scale in favour of Hoosein Nizam Shah, without having any cause of enmity against Ibrahim Adil Shah of Beejapoor, who has sought our alliance. As a friendship has long subsisted between our court and your Majesty, we have thought fit to lay these arguments before you, to induce you to relinquish the offensive alliance which your Majesty has formed, and by returning peaceably to your capital, show a friendly disposition to both parties, who will afterwards conclude a peace, and put an end to this long-protracted war.' This dignified letter had, for the moment, a good effect; but the subsequent conduct of Ramraj in the campaign against Ahmednugger, with other transactions and frontier disputes, seemed to have obliterated all good-feeling between them. The Golcondah historian records, that the suggestion to the Kings of the Deccan to undertake a crusade against Ramraj proceeded from Ibrahim Kootub Shah; but there is greater probability, perhaps, in Ferishta's account of the opening embassy to Golcondah from Beejapoor, by which the measure was first mooted. There is no doubt that Ibrahim cordially engaged in the war, and that by his ambassador, Moostufa Khan, the details of the confederacy were finally arranged; and the results of the great battle fought on January 25, 1565, have been elsewhere related. By this event, the king recovered all the territory which he had lost during his latter disputes with Ramraj, and was left at liberty to pursue his conquests to the south.

Remarkable letter from the Rajah of Beejanugger.

League against Beejanugger.

In the year 1567, Ruffat Khan, an able commander, undertook a campaign against the Hindoo Prince of Rajahmundry, which was entirely successful, and the whole of his territory was annexed to the kingdom; and before the close of the king's reign, many of the Hindoo rajahs whose territories lay immediately south of the Krishna river were in succession overcome, though not without prolonged

King Henry Darnley murdered.

James VI. king of Scotland.

resistance, and in many instances very obstinate combats. On June 2, 1580, the king died, in the thirty-first year of his reign and fifty-first of his age. During his life he had been constantly in the field, and had behaved with much personal bravery on many occasions. His civil government was also good; and, under his tolerance, Hindoos were freely employed in State affairs, attaining, in some instances, the very highest rank. Many of his great public works survive him: the fortifications of Golcondah; the almshouses, and the embankments of the great lake-reservoirs of Hoosein Ságor and Ibrahimputtun. He encouraged trade, and Golcondah became a mart for the sale of the produce and manufactures both of Europe and all parts of Asia. The king was succeeded by Mahomed Koolly, his third son, the two elder having died previously.

Ibrahim Kootub Shah dies, 1580.

His acts and character.

Mahomed Koolly Kootub Shah succeeds, 1580.

Philip II. takes Portugal.

For some years after the king's accession, a constant war was maintained with the Rajah of Penkóndah, the representative of the Beejanugger family, and with other Hindoo princes south of the Krishna; but it does not appear that the Mahomedans made much progress to the south or south-east, and their possession of the Province of Condbeer, or Guntoor, was fiercely disputed. In 1589, as Golcondah had become overcrowded and unhealthy, and the supply of water was scanty, the king laid the foundation of the present city of Hyderabad, on the right bank of the Moosy river, about eight miles from the fort. He named it Bhágnugger, after his beautiful Hindoo mistress Bhágmutty (a title still used by all Hindoo bankers); but after her death it was changed to Hyderabad, after his son Hyder. The city was well laid out with broad streets, then sheltered by rows of trees, and the supply of water from a dam in the river above Golcondah was, and continues to be, abundant. The king adorned the city with many fine buildings, which are still perfect; and among them the noble Jooma mosque, and the Char Minar, or four minarets, hospitals, almshouses, and palaces, attest the splendour of his reign. Mahomed Koolly, although, during the whole or greater part of his reign, there was a perpetual frontier war in progress with the Hindoos, never appears to have taken part in it; and continued to reside at his new capital, employing himself with much ability in the civil affairs of his government, and in public works. During his reign three millions sterling had been expended by the king, and the noble irrigation works throughout the provinces were kept in perfect repair. The king's example was followed by his nobility;

Hyderabad founded, 1589.

Henry III. of France murdered.

Public edifices of Hyderabad.

Munificence of the king in public works.

and not only at Hyderabad, but throughout the dominions of the Kootub Shahy dynasty, the number of handsome mosques, palaces, and other edifices, is not surpassed, if indeed it is equalled, in any other of the Mahomedan kingdoms of the Deccan. In December 1611, the king was suddenly taken ill, and died on the 17th of that month, after a reign of thirty-four years, much regretted by his subjects.

Mahomed Koolly Kootub Shah dies, 1611.

During his life 24,000*l.* sterling was annually distributed to the poor, besides a munificent support and endowment of colleges, schools, hospitals, and almshouses throughout his dominions.

His private and public charities.

He was succeeded by his son Abdoolla, under the title of Sooltan Abdoolla Kootub Shah; but the separate history of the dynasty ceased with his father's reign, and subsequent events, till the subversion of the Kootub Shahy kingdom by Aurungzebe, are only to be traced in the account of Moghul progress in the Deccan. It is evident from the record of the local historian of Golcondah, that little substantial impression had been made on the Hindoos of the southern States. Their armies were numerous, and though often defeated, yet resisted bravely and defiantly any annexation of territory; and beyond a portion of the present Guntoor Sircar, the Kootub Shahy dynasty made no conquests south of the Krishna river.

Abdoolla Kootub Shah succeeds, 1611.

Baronets created.

CHAPTER XX.

OF THE REIGN OF THE EMPEROR JEHÁNGEER, 1605 TO 1627.

UNDER the proud title of Jehángeer, or 'Conqueror of the World,' the Prince Selim was crowned at Agra soon after his father Akbur's death. His sullen temper, and habitual excess in drinking, afforded little prospect of a happy reign; nevertheless, his first acts gave promise of amendment. Many of his reforms exceeded those of his father in practical utility, particularly in regard to the abuses in levying customs duties, and in respect to the admission of complainants to his presence. He also affected a stricter observance of the forms of the Mahomedan faith, and issued a prohibitory edict against the use of wine or spirits, opium, and other intoxicating drugs and compounds.

The Prince Selim, as Jehángeer, succeeds Akbur as emperor of Dehly, 1605.

Gunpowder plot.

The first acts of the emperor's reign.

The breach between the emperor and his eldest son Khoosroo had however become wider: and in March 1606, the young prince left Agra in open rebellion. He was pursued by his father into

Rebellion of his eldest son, who is defeated and captured.

the Punjâb, by which time he had collected 10,000 men, was defeated, and again fled westward, in the hope of reaching Kabool; but the ferry-boat in which he was crossing the Ravee or Hydaspes, ran on a sand-bank, and the prince was taken in chains to his father. Now followed one of the most horrible scenes of cruelty ever perhaps witnessed in the world. No less than 700 of the prince's followers were impaled on stakes in a line from the gate of Lahore, and while most were still living, and writhing and shrieking in agony, the emperor directed his son, placed on an elephant, to be carried down the line. The account, as written by himself, in his Memoirs, is too revolting to be quoted; and had it not been confirmed by his own journal, it is probable such an event would have been hardly credible. The prince remained in chains, but was not sent into a distant imprisonment: he accompanied his father to Kabool, where, in 1607, a conspiracy to assassinate the emperor and raise Khoosroo to the throne was discovered and defeated.

The emperor's cruelty.

With the exception of a campaign against the Rana of Oodypoor, no great event marks the period between 1607 and 1610. The emperor had returned from Kabool to Agra, where he had been visited by Captain Hawkins, the commander of the English ship 'Hector;' and had promised him extensive privileges of trade, with the results already detailed; and by Hawkins's account of his life at court, it does not seem that the emperor's habits of drinking had been overcome, though they were in some measure regulated. In 1610, affairs in the Deccan took an unfavourable turn. Khan Khanán, the general in command, had been defeated by Mullik Umbur, the great Ahmednugger minister and general. Ahmednugger had been recaptured, and the imperial forces had been obliged to retreat on Boorhanpoor, and for the present to abandon their most southern conquests. Mullik Umbur had taken advantage of the rebellion of the Prince Khoosroo to attack the imperial forces, and to consolidate his own power. As the Moghuls held Ahmednugger, he had founded a new capital near Dowlatabad; and while the King Moortuza III. resided at Owsa, near the southern frontier of the kingdom, governed the northern portion of the dominions; nominally in his behalf, but in reality in an almost independent position, during which period he carried out his great revenue reforms. He had also rallied around him many of the Mahratta chiefs, who had gradually risen into military consequence, and were becoming a new, but powerful, element in the affairs of the Deccan. For the present the emperor contented himself with transferring the command of the southern armies from Khan Khanán to Khan

Henry IV. of France murdered, 1610.

Events in the Deccan.

Mullik Umbur's independent position.

Jehán, and no new operations against Mullik Umbur were undertaken.

In the ensuing year, 1611, the emperor married the celebrated Noor Jehán, whose beauty and abilities rendered his reign famous. She was born of Persian parents, who had emigrated from Persia to India, under circumstances of great privation. Her father had entered the service of the Emperor Akbur, who had promoted him; and his wife, with her daughter, was in the habit of visiting the emperor's harem. Here Noor Jehán used to be seen by the Prince Selim (Jehángeer), who conceived a violent passion for her, and demanded her of his father in marriage. The Emperor Akbur did not however approve of the alliance, and caused her to be married to a young Persian nobleman, Shére Afghan Khan, whom Akbur settled on an estate in Bengal. Whether the Prince Selim had authorised the Viceroy of Bengal to propose that Shére Afghan should relinquish his wife, or whether any other reason for the act existed, can never be known; but on the occasion of a visit to the viceroy, Shére Afghan Khan stabbed him to the heart, and was immediately dispatched by the attendants. Noor Jehán was sent to Agra as an accomplice in the act, but was not prosecuted. She refused many offers of marriage from the emperor, but at last consenting, they were united. No empress of India had ever before received such high honours, or been so openly recognised as an element of the State, as was Noor Jehán. A new coinage was struck in her name, which was inscribed on it. She was supreme in the palace; her father became prime minister, and she may be said to have virtually ruled the State. The empress soon obliged her husband to comport himself with dignity, and to abstain from excess, at least in public; and the court, under her admirable management, became not only more magnificent and decorous, but its expenses were considerably reduced.

The emperor's marriage with Noor Jehán.

Her origin.

The Deccan, however, continued to be a subject of vexation. To assist the operations of Khan Jehán Lody, an army was directed to proceed to his support from Guzerat, in 1612. This movement was met by Mullik Umbur in a spirited manner, and defeated; the retreat of the Imperial forces was sorely harassed by his Mahratta cavalry, and the Prince Purviz and Khan Jehán Lody did not venture to attack him again. The campaign of the Prince Khurrám (Shah Jehán) in Oodypoor was more successful, and finally triumphant. The Rana submitted to him, and was not only restored to his dominions by the emperor, but received into the highest rank of the nobility of the empire. In the year 1613, the emperor, on the representations

Troops dispatched to the Deccan.

Matthias emperor of Germany.

Campaign in Rajpootana.

Permission to trade given to the English.

of the authorities at Surat and Ahmedabad, had conferred privileges of trade upon the English, and had granted permission for the establishment of four factories, at Surat, Cambay, Gôgo, and Ahmedabad. He had also invited an ambassador from the English court, which was an act of courtesy too valuable to be neglected; and Sir Thomas Roe, already experienced in Oriental character and manners by a residence at Constantinople, and acquainted with the Turkish language, was dispatched by King James I. to Jehángeer's court in 1615. His journal is extremely curious and interesting; and contains much valuable information upon the actual state of the country, the condition of the people, and the court life of Jehángeer, which excited the utmost astonishment in England, where the Great Moghul was probably considered little more than a painted savage, and the civilised character of his country was entirely unknown. The paltry presents brought by the ambassador, though courteously received, yet caused pain in presentation, as the offerings of a poor nation; for all the jewels of the British crown would have been of no account before those of the throne of Jehángeer, and the precious stones with which he was covered. Sir Thomas Roe resided at Jehángeer's court for nearly three years. He was admitted, as Hawkins had been, to intimate association with the emperor, and attended him in his private chamber, being present at his drinking bouts, and accompanying him in his marches, wars, and excursions. He describes the royal princes; the pity for Khoosroo; the gravity and self-esteem of Khurrám or Shah Jehán, and the glory of the empress. But it is impossible to follow any portion of these interesting details with the particularity they deserve; they should be read by the student of Indian history in their entirety, not only for the remarks upon court and political affairs, but as regards the state of government, and its effects on the people; the latter were not favourable, and it may be presumed that the strict administration of Akbur had relaxed.

Four factories are established.

Sir Thomas Roe arrives as English ambassador, 1615.

Sir Thomas Roe's narrative.

In the year 1616, the Prince Khurrám received the title of Shah Jehán, or 'King of the World,' and was nominated successor to the emperor, as well as commander-in-chief of the army of the Deccan; and Jehángeer moved with his son southwards as far as Mandoo, accompanied by his court. The emperor's proximity to the scene of the Deccan campaign infused energy into the proceedings of the imperial commanders. Mullik Umbur was defeated, and obliged to relinquish Ahmednugger. Ibrahim Adil Shah of Beejapoor became an ally, and the previous conquests of the

Settlement of Virginia.

Mullik Umbur defeated.

empire were re-established. In this campaign the Prince Shah Jehán distinguished himself on many occasions, and the success of the Moghul operations may, in a great measure, be attributed to his military skill. The emperor now proceeded (1617) to Guzerat, which was added to his son's viceroyalty, and thence returned to Agra, in 1618. Peace in the Deccan was, however, of no long continuance. Mullik Umbur, in 1620, had again defeated the imperial commanders, and his army had penetrated northwards as far as Mandoo. Shah Jehán was, therefore, again dispatched to the scene of conflict, where the imperial affairs were gradually retrieved; and Mullik Umbur, defeated in a general action, submitted to the terms imposed on him. On the occasion of proceeding on this service, Shah Jehán had requested that Prince Khoosroo might be allowed to accompany him, which was granted; but he did not long survive his release, and died in the Deccan.

The emperor visits Guzerat.

Mullik Umbur's successes in 1620.

But he is defeated, and submits to Prince Shah Jehán.

Death of Prince Khoosroo.

Hitherto the empress had been the active friend and partisan of Shah Jehán; but her father's death, which happened in 1621, caused her to change her policy. She had married her daughter, by her first husband, to the Prince Shahriar, the emperor's younger son, and now determined that he should succeed the emperor, who had already declared Shah Jehán to be his successor. Meanwhile, Kandahar had been invaded and taken by the Persians, and Shah Jehán, to whom the service of recovering it had been first proposed, advanced from the Deccan northwards with a part of his army, for the purpose of proceeding into Afghanistan; but, under the appearance of affairs at court, he conceived that the service was only a pretext for removing him from India, and declined to proceed without special assurances from his father. In reply to this application, he was now ordered to send large portions of his army to be placed under Shahriar, who had been nominated in his stead. With this order Shah Jehán declined to comply, and marched upon Agra. The emperor, who had been at Lahore, now set out, in February 1623, to oppose him; and the armies met on the borders of Rajpootana, where some partial engagements took place; but Shah Jehán, having probably no desire to press his father to extremity, retreated southwards to Mandoo. He was followed by the emperor to Ajmere, and thence an army, under the joint command of the Prince Purviz and Mohubut Khan, was dispatched to reduce him. Shah Jehán was now deserted by the governor of Guzerat, and

Intrigues of the empress.

Kandahar taken by the Persians. Shah Jehán proceeds against them.

But is superseded by Shahriar.

The emperor attacks Shah Jehán's army.

Shah Jehán withdraws.

Retires to Boorhanpoor.

retired to Boorhanpoor; where the imperial general, Khan Khanán, also declared against him, and obliged him to retreat into Telingána, whence he proceeded by the coast route into Bengal, in 1624. Here his cause was warmly espoused by the local authorities, and he defeated the governor of Raj Mahál. He had now obtained possession of Bengal and Bahar, and further successes seemed possible; but the Prince Purviz and Mohubut Khan marched from Boorhanpoor direct upon Allahabad, and in an action which ensued with the prince, completely defeated him, and obliged him to retrace his steps into the Deccan. Here he hoped to enlist the Kings of Golcondah and Beejapoor in his cause; but they were faithful to the emperor. Mullik Umbur, however, received him gladly; but he soon found himself helpless, and wrote a humble submission to his father: who, requiring him to give up the forts in his possession, and to send his sons Dára and Aurungzebe to court, as hostages, was prepared to forgive the past.

And thence into Telingána and Bengal.

He possesses himself of Bengal and Bahar.

He is defeated by Prince Purviz,

and retires to the Deccan.

Shah Jehán submits to the emperor.

The emperor was then in progress on his annual journey to Kashmere and return to Dehly, in company with the empress. She had become jealous of Mohubut Khan, whom she herself had selected to act against Shah Jehán, and he had been summoned to court. Mohubut Khan was at that time the most eminent of the State servants; but he was charged with malpractices in Bengal, and though for a time he delayed to appear to answer them, he eventually proceeded to court under the escort of 5,000 Rajpoots, whom he had attached to himself. When he reached the emperor's camp, he understood that his disgrace had been already determined upon, and he resolved to get possession of the emperor's person, and make his own terms. With this view he occupied the bridge of boats by which the emperor was to cross the Hydaspes with a portion of his troops, and dashing into the emperor's camp with the rest, surrounded his tents, and took him prisoner. The emperor, who had been in a heavy sleep, awoke when his bed was surrounded with armed men, and recognising Mohubut Khan, reproached him with treachery; but he did not resist, and mounted upon an elephant, was conducted, with every mark of respect, to his general's tents. Meanwhile the empress was not idle. Putting on mean attire, she directed herself to be conveyed to the camp of the army on the other side of the river, where she made preparations for an attack upon Mohubut Khan's camp, and the rescue of the emperor; and early next morning she moved in

The empress's jealousy of Mohubut Khan.

His conduct.

Seizes the emperor's person.

The empress attacks Mohubut Khan's camp.

person to the attack at the head of the whole of the royal forces. The bridge had been destroyed, and she attempted to cross by a dangerous ford below. After a fruitless struggle, in which many were carried away by the stream, and others shot by the Rajpoots, who held the opposite bank, it was found impossible to carry their position, and a furious conflict now raged round the elephant of the empress, which was the special object of capture by the Rajpoots. The driver was killed, and the infant daughter of Shahriar, sitting in the empress's lap, was wounded by an arrow, while the empress's escape was wonderful. The elephant, now beyond control, and wounded badly, rushed back into the river, and plunging into deep water, reached the bank safely. Another attack by Fidái Khan had also failed, and Noor Jehán, seeing that there was no hope of rescuing the emperor, voluntarily joined him.

Her valour and great peril.

She joins the emperor.

The army now commanded by Mohubut Khan proceeded to Kabool, and the strict confinement of the emperor was considerably relaxed. The Rajpoots, on whom Mohubut depended, were here in a foreign land, the people of which had more sympathy for the emperor than for his general; and Noor Jehán, on pretence of summoning all feudal contingents for muster, increased her own, and contrived the support of others. Finally she proposed a review of her own troops: and on this occasion they moved so as to separate the emperor from the Rajpoot guard by which he was attended, and to close around him. From that moment he was free. Noor Jehán would now have dealt severely with Mohubut Khan; but her brother was his prisoner, and he was too powerful to be attacked; so setting his pardon on the condition of her brother's release and Mohubut's immediately proceeding against Shah Jehán, he accepted the conditions, and marched to meet the prince. But Shah Jehán was in no condition for rebellion; he was, in fact, very helpless. He was residing at Ajmere with only 1,000 men, and his friend, Rajah Kishn Singh, had died. This was the crisis of his fortunes; and had he been able, he would have fled to Persia. While in this distress, he heard of his brother Purviz's death, and trusting now to recover his position in the Deccan, he proceeded thither, followed by Mohubut Khan, to whom he quickly became reconciled. Before they could decide upon any plan of future proceedings, news of the emperor's death reached them. He had found the climate of Kashmere too severe, and had died of asthma, his old complaint, as he was being taken to Lahore. Jehángeer expired

The army proceeds to Kabool.

The empress's plot to release the emperor.

Which succeeds.

She sends Mohubut Khan against Prince Shah Jehán.

Who proceeds to the Deccan, followed by Mohubut Khan, to whom he is reconciled.

Death of the Emperor Jehángeer.

on October 28, 1627, in the sixtieth year of his age, and the twenty-second of his reign, and was interred in the mausoleum he had prepared for himself at Lahore.

CHAPTER XXI.

OF THE REIGN OF THE EMPEROR SHAH JEHÁN, 1627 TO 1655.

IMMEDIATELY on the receipt of the news of his father's death, Shah Jehán proceeded to Agra, and ascended the throne on January 26, 1628. Between that period and the death of Jehángeer there had been an attempt by Prince Shahriar to gain the throne; but it had been suppressed by Asof Khan, the prime minister, who defeated and imprisoned him. And the empress, after this event, retired into privacy, from which she never again emerged. She was allowed a pension of 250,000*l.* a year; and, according to Khafie Khan, the historian of the period, abstained from all entertainments, became profuse in her charities, and wore no colour but white, to the period of her death. The emperor's accession was the occasion of splendid rejoicings at Agra; and there being no war in progress, in any part of his dominions, he devoted himself to his favourite pursuit—architecture—and commenced those famous buildings by which his name is perpetuated. An invasion of the Uzbeks, and the insurrection of Rajah Nursing Déo of Bunkelkund, gave employment to portions of the army; but the rebellion of Khan Jehán Lody, the commander-in-chief and viceroy of the Deccan, was of more moment, and became ultimately the foundation of a greater interference in, and control over Deccan affairs, than had ever yet been exercised. It may be presumed that, from the first, Khan Jehán Lody had determined upon achieving independence. He was originally an Afghan adventurer, and had risen by his personal valour and skill to the highest rank. He declined to accompany the emperor to Agra; but was invited to court after his accession to the throne, and treated with the utmost consideration. So far, however, from receiving these attentions in a pleasant spirit, Khan Jehán viewed them with the utmost jealousy and alarm; and suddenly quitting his palace at Agra, with all his family, escorted by 2,000 of his veteran retainers, marched southwards. He was pursued and overtaken at the Chumbul river; but he checked the advancing force in a sharp skirmish,

Shah Jehán crowned at Agra, 1628.

The empress pensioned.

Rebellion of Khan Jehán Lody, 1628.

His antecedents.

Escapes from Agra to the Deccan.

crossed the river, and plunging into the woody country of Bundelkund and Góndwana, made his way into the Deccan. As soon as his position was ascertained, a Moghul force from the army of the Deccan was sent against him; but Lody had made friends of the local Mahratta authorities, who rose in his defence, and repulsed the Moghuls with severe loss.

Defeats the Moghul troops.

The position and character of Khan Jehán Lody were now a subject of much anxiety to the emperor, whose experience of Deccan politics led him to fear the effect which a powerful character like his general's might have upon the Kings of the Deccan. If they could be brought into a confederacy, and their united armies led by Khan Jehán Lody, it would be difficult to oppose them; for the contest with Ahmednugger alone had already required all the power of the empire, and that State was still powerful, while Beejapoor and Golcondah were both in a high condition of prosperity. In this state of affairs, Shah Jehán trusted the Deccan to no one; he proceeded to that country in 1629, and dividing his army into three portions, remained himself at Boorhanpoor, to direct the general policy of the campaign. Of the three officers employed, Azim Khan proved the most efficient. He drove Khan Jehán Lody from place to place, and forced him to retreat to the south, while Lody's cause was much weakened by the defection of his hitherto friend and ally, Shahjee Bhóslay, a Mahratta chieftain of much power and influence, who had been in possession of a great portion of the western dominions of the Ahmednugger State since the death of Mullik Umbur in 1626. It was evident to Shahjee that, in the present condition of the Deccan, Khan Jehán had no chance of success; and he accordingly proceeded to Boorhanpoor, paid his respects to the emperor at the head of 2,000 of his retainers, and was taken into the service as a commander of 5,000, which involved a patent of nobility, and the confirmation of the estates he possessed. This example was followed by his cousin Kelloojee and other Mahratta chiefs, and it is evident that, by this conciliatory and practically useful policy, Shah Jehán not only materially strengthened his own position, but weakened that of his opponents.

The emperor's anxiety.

The emperor proceeds to the Deccan, 1629.

Campaign against Khan Jehán Lody.

Shahjee Bhóslay joins the emperor.

Khan Jehán Lody, driven southwards, took refuge at Beejapoor, where he endeavoured to incite the king, Mahmood Adil Shah, on pretence of checking the Moghul progress, to assist him. But Mahmood could not be induced to do so. He was a peaceful monarch, who devoted himself to civil affairs, and to architecture, in

Khan Jehán proceeds to Beejapoor.

King Mahmood Shah declines to interfere.

which he was a scientific proficient; and all that he could hope for was to preserve what he already possessed, which he considered would be impossible under a Moghul attack. This was perhaps a shortsighted policy, and indeed proved to be so in the end; but Khan Jehán Lody had nothing to offer to induce Mahmood Adil Shah to break his already existing engagements with the emperor based upon the previous treaties, and Lody was dismissed. He returned to Moortuza Nizam Shah III., then defending himself against the emperor's attacks; and finding no chance of assistance, endeavoured to break through the imperial posts and reach Bundelkund, and incite its ever lawless chiefs to rebellion. Here, however, he was disappointed; so far from assisting him, the local chiefs opposed his progress, and he was finally slain, fighting bravely to the last, near the fort of Kalinjer. The imperial operations were delayed for nearly a year, owing to famine, which followed a scarcity of rain; but in 1630, when forage was once more available to some extent, Azim Khan marched upon Dowlatabad. Here he was encountered by Moortuza Nizam Shah III. and his army: but the king was defeated in a general action fought near the fort, and the Moghuls following up their advantage, took possession of the country as far as Dharoor. Moortuza III. now dismissed his minister, Tukurrib Khan, who immediately joined Azim Khan, and released Futteh Khan, the son of Mullik Umbur, who had been confined. The defeat of Moortuza III. by the Moghuls, and their occupation of Dharoor, now alarmed Mahmood Adil Shah, and an alliance between him and Moortuza followed, Moortuza ceding to him the fort of Sholapoor and its dependencies, with some districts in the Koncan. This alliance, however, came too late. Moortuza Nizam Shah was put to death by his minister, who then proffered his allegiance to the emperor; and the army of Beejapoor, before it could effect a junction with that of Ahmednugger, was defeated by Azim Khan.

Lody is dismissed.

Khan Jehán Lody killed, 1630.

The Moghul forces advance on Dowlatabad, and defeat Moortuza Nizam Shah III.

They occupy Dharoor.

Alliance between Beejapoor and Ahmednugger, 1632.

The Beejapoor army defeated.

His open defiance of the Moghuls now drew upon Mahmood Adil Shah the whole brunt of their power; and he was besieged in his capital by Asof Khan. Beejapoor was bravely defended, and the light troops of the State cut off all the supplies of grain and forage from the Moghul army, which was eventually obliged to abandon the siege. These operations had prolonged the emperor's residence in the Deccan, and he was now (1632) obliged to return to Agra. Mohubut Khan was left as viceroy and

Beejapoor besieged, 1632.

But without result.

The emperor returns to Agra, 1632.

commander of the forces, and the war was prosecuted with vigour. When Futteh Khan of Ahmednugger made overtures to the emperor, he had been required to give up the State elephants and jewels of the Nizam Shahy kingdom. This, however, he had evaded, and shut himself up in the fort of Dowlatabad. Here he was eventually confirmed as regent of the State; a proceeding which disgusted Shahjee Bhóslay, who made overtures to Beejapoor through Morar Punt, a Mahratta Brahmin, who was the chief minister, and he joined the Beejapoor army in an advance upon Dowlatabad, while Mohubut Khan proceeded to its relief. Meanwhile, Futteh Khan had again changed sides, and refused to give up the fortress. Mohubut Khan now invested it, and the place was surrendered after a siege of fifty-eight days. He also defeated the Beejapoor army, which was weak, and followed it for some distance; but it eluded him. After this, Futteh Khan entered the Moghul service; and the boy whom he had created king was sent as a State prisoner to Gwalior, in February 1633. Thus ended the Ahmednugger kingdom; but the Deccan was by no means pacified. The King of Beejapoor could not be subdued. Mohubut Khan failed in the siege of Purainda, which he had undertaken with the Prince Shujah, who had been sent as his coadjutor; and the Moghul army having retired to Boorhanpoor, both were superseded in their command, and returned to court. Taking advantage of their discomfiture, Shahjee Bhóslay now set up another prince of the Ahmednugger house, and in his name re-occupied the whole of the western portion of the old dominions, as far as the sea.

Mohubut Khan viceroy of the Deccan.

Dowlatabad taken by the Moghuls.

End of the Nizam Shahy kingdom.

These events necessitated the return of the emperor to the Deccan in 1635. He now divided the army into two portions; one to act against Shahjee—the other, under the command of Khan Dowrán, was directed against Beejapoor, which was again besieged; but the mode of defence which had been successful before was again resorted to: the districts around the capital were deserted, the reservoirs of water beyond the fort emptied, and the wells poisoned; while Rendoolla Khan, at the head of the cavalry, harassed the imperial army. He could not, however, save the country, which was mercilessly plundered; and in 1636, Mahmood Adil Shah sued for peace. By the treaty which ensued, he received a considerable portion of the Ahmednugger dominions, including Sholapoor, Purainda, part of the Koncan, and the country on the banks of the Bheema and Neera; and in return engaged

The emperor returns to the Deccan, 1635.

Second siege of Beejapoor fails.

Peace with Beejapoor, 1636.

And its provisions.

to pay twenty lacs of pagodas, or 800,000*l.*, per annum. Shahjee was also to be reduced; but seeing the futility of resistance, he submitted to the emperor, and in 1637 was pardoned, and re-admitted into the imperial service.

The emperor returns to Agra, 1637.

Ferdinand III. emperor of Germany.

Kandahar regained.

The Deccan being thus pacified for the time, the emperor returned to Agra in 1637. Several minor affairs had occurred during his absence, in which his troops had been successful; but the most important news he received was the recovery of Kandahar, which had been given up to him by Ally Merdan Khan, its governor, who, having come to court, was taken into the imperial employ, and rendered excellent service in many capacities. A canal which supplies Dehly with water still bears his name. In 1644, in concert with Rajah Jugut Singh, who brought 14,000 Rajpoots of his own clan, Ally Merdan Khan invaded Balkh; and despite of the severe climate, and stupendous mountain-passes, these brave Indian warriors achieved splendid successes. The service was, however, so arduous, that the emperor moved to Kabool in support, and despatched his son Moorád to operate with his general. The campaign was crowned with success, but tranquillity did not ensue. The Prince Moorád returned without leave, and was disgraced, and his brother Aurungzebe sent to replace him; the emperor, who had returned to India, again proceeding to Kabool. Aurungzebe was at first triumphant; but reverses ensued, and he was obliged to take up his position in Balkh. The emperor, perceiving the waste of life and means which these campaigns involved, made over the province to Nuzzur Mahomed, who had originally tempted him to undertake the war, and Aurungzebe was directed to withdraw from Balkh; but his retreat was very disastrous: many of his troops perished in the snow, and by the unceasing attacks of the mountaineers, and the remnant of the army reached Kabool about the end of 1647, in a pitiable condition.

Expedition against Balkh, 1644.

Prince Moorád's bad conduct.

Aurungzebe replaces him.

The emperor transfers Balkh to Nuzzur Mahomed.

Disastrous retreat of Aurungzebe.

In the year 1648, Kandahar was retaken by the Persians. Aurungzebe had been dispatched to relieve it, but arrived too late; and the siege of the place was undertaken in 1649. The Persian king sent a force for its relief, and the prince was ultimately obliged to raise the siege; but it was renewed in 1652, with a similar result. The artillery employed was in fact insufficient, and Aurungzebe returned to Kabool, to be sent as viceroy to the Deccan. The Prince Dára Shekoh, the emperor's eldest son, now besought his father to allow him to attempt what had resulted in such signal failures, and a splendid army was

Kandahar retaken by the Persians.

Is besieged by Aurungzebe without effect.

Prince Dára's attempt.

placed under his command. With this, in 1653, he invested the fort, and the siege was prosecuted with great vigour; but the result was in nowise more fortunate than the former. Kandahar was bravely and desperately defended by the Persians; and, after losing the best of his troops in ineffectual assaults, Dára was obliged to raise the siege and return. This proved to be the last effort of the Moghul dynasty to repossess Kandahar, and the imperial dominions in Afghanistan were confined to Kabool and its dependencies. The years 1654-55 were an interval of peace, during which the revenue system of Toder Mul was introduced into Berar and other possessions in the Deccan; but the emperor had the misfortune to lose his great and able minister, Sääd Ullah Khan, who, had he lived, might probably have averted the further entanglement in Deccan affairs which, in the sequel, proved so disastrous to the empire, and those contentions among the emperor's sons which resulted in rebellion and usurpation.

The Dutch fleet defeated by Monk.

The siege of Kandahar is raised.

Death of the minister Sääd Ullah Khan, 1655.

CHAPTER XXII.

THE REIGN OF THE EMPEROR SHAH JEHÁN (*concluded*), 1655 TO 1658.

ALTHOUGH Shahjee Bhóslay had been pardoned, and nominally re-admitted into the imperial service in 1637, it did not prevent his being employed by Beejapoor; and for a time he was placed in charge of the greater part of the new cessions. But he was afterwards appointed to a command on the southern frontier; and a large territory, which included part of Mysore, was conferred on him as an estate. It will be observed by this, that the conquests of the Beejapoor State had now extended materially to the southward; and by this time, that the descendants of the Beejanugger family had been deprived of all the northern portions of their already reduced dominions. In 1630, Shahjee had married a second wife of the family of Mohitcy, which gave offence to his first wife, who belonged to the higher family of Jadow, and she separated from him. She had borne him two sons: Sumbhajee, the eldest, who remained with his father; and Sivajee, the youngest, who was afterwards destined to take so great a part in the political affairs of the Deccan and of India.

Shahjee Bhóslay employed by Beejapoor.

His second marriage.

Sivajee was born at Joonair in May 1627; and after his father's departure for the Carnatic, in 1636, remained with his mother at Poona, under the protection of his

Birth of Sivajee, 1627.

father's agent, Dadajee Konedeo, who managed his patron's estates with much skill. Many of them lay among the wild valleys of the western Ghauts; and as he grew up, Sivajee made friends of the sons of several of the smaller proprietors, who, for the most part, led lawless lives, resisting the Mahomedans, and occasionally plundering the open country. He became skilled in all martial exercises, but would never learn to read or write, considering such acquisitions as beneath notice; and, with his companions, conceived the project of becoming independent of Mahomedan control. In 1646 he obtained possession of the strong hill-fort of Torna; and as this act might be resented by the government of Beejapoor, he dispatched agents to the capital to negotiate possession of the district in which it was situated, on payment of a high rent. The discovery of a large amount of gold among the ruins of the fort, which was attributed to a miracle, enabled him not only to put it in complete repair, but, in 1647, to fortify another mountain-top near it, which he named Rajgurh. These proceedings seem to have excited some uneasiness at Beejapoor; but, beyond a remonstrance to his father, and warnings to himself, which were received with apparent submission, no further proceedings were taken against him. For a time Dadajee endeavoured to turn Sivajee from his designs; but, failing in this, he seems to have acquired faith in them, and on his death-bed encouraged him to persevere.

His education.

Torna taken.

Rajgurh fortified.

The main spring of Sivajee's actions from the first, however, appears to have been his mother, to whom he confided his plans. She was an enthusiast in religion, and, as is not uncommon among Mahratta women, conceived that divine revelations were made to her by the Goddess Bhowanee, the tutelary divinity of her family, shadowing forth the future greatness of her son, and the delivery of the Hindoo faith from its subjection by the Mahomedans. There is no doubt that in these visions and declarations of his mother's, Sivajee implicitly believed; and the death of Dadajee, and the management of the family estates by himself, gave him local means and authority, which he used in the prosecution of his designs. Gradually, too, the rude but warlike population of the mountain glens grew to have faith in him, they were at his call on every occasion on which he required them, and by their assistance, Sivajee became possessed of other hill-forts, and thus gradually acquired a position of immense natural strength; while, by avoiding collisions with the Mahomedan agents and commanders, his proceedings up to 1648 attracted no notice. In that year, however, his actions grew bolder; he intercepted a

Influence of his mother.

Her character.

large remittance of treasures by the governor of Kullian, in the Koncan, and the place itself was surprised, and taken with its governor, who, on being courteously released by Sivajee, proceeded to Beejapoor, where his accounts of the young rebel's position at last excited alarm. In 1649, Shahjee was arrested and brought to court, and charged with complicity in his son's designs. It was in vain that he denied them; he was placed in a cell, the door of which was nearly built up, and he was threatened with its being closed, and a horrible death by starvation, if he did not procure his son's submission. Sivajee, now in extremity, applied to the Emperor Shah Jehán, on his own and his father's behalf. His application was favourably received, and he was admitted to the imperial service as a commander of 5,000. His father's desertion of the emperor's service also was overlooked; and, probably under an order from the emperor, he was released from his horrible dungeon, but retained at Beejapoor for four years—that is, till 1653—when, in the repression of disorders on his estate, his son Sumbhajee was killed, and Sivajee became heir to the family property. By his father's release and re-employment, and his own admission to the imperial service, Sivajee's position had been much strengthened, and his actions assumed a bolder character. Fort after fort among the mountains fell into his hands, and in 1656 he selected an almost impregnable position on a mountain near the source of the Krishna river, which he fortified, and, under the name of Pertábgurh, it became the capital of his possessions.

Shahjee's arrest, 1649.

And cruel imprisonment at Beejapoor.

Is released.

Death of Sumbhajee.

Pertábgurh fortified.

It has been already related in the last chapter, that the Prince Aurungzebe, after his failure at Kandahar, in 1653, was appointed viceroy of the Deccan. He took up his abode at Kirkee, the city near Dowlatabad, founded by Mullik Umbur, and changed its name to Aurungabad. Here, until 1656, he remained in peace, carrying out the settlement of the imperial provinces of the Deccan under the system of Toder Mul, according to the emperor's design, with great assiduity and success. With Golcondah and Beejapoor the relations continued friendly, both States paying their quotas of tribute, and to all appearance avoiding any cause of quarrel. At this period, the minister at Golcondah was the celebrated Meer Joomla, formerly a diamond merchant, who had raised himself to his present office by his great abilities. He had cultivated the friendship of Aurungzebe, and was much respected by him, as well as by the emperor. While he was absent on a local campaign in eastern Telingána, his son, Mahomed Ameen, had given offence to Sooltan

Aurungzebe viceroy of the Deccan, 1653.

Abdoolla Kootub Shah, and was imprisoned by him. Failing to obtain his son's release, Meer Joomla appealed to Aurungzebe, who forwarded the application to his father with his support; and an order was issued by the emperor for the young man's release. This mandate was, however, resented by Sooltan Abdoolla, who now confined Mahomed Ameen with more strictness, and attached the property of his father, the minister. Shah Jehán now ordered Aurungzebe to carry out his instructions by force; and, under pretence of visiting his brother in Bengal, the prince proceeded with an army towards Masulipatam; but, turning suddenly upon Hyderabad, surprised the city, which was mercilessly plundered, while the king had only time to escape to the fort of Golcondah. Here he was besieged by Aurungzebe, to whom large reinforcements had arrived. The minister's son and all his property were released; but this did not satisfy Aurungzebe, who obliged the king to agree to pay a fine of 1,000,000*l.* sterling, and to give his daughter in marriage to his son Mahomed, with an appropriate dowry. These heavy impositions were relaxed by the emperor; but Meer Joomla had now joined Aurungzebe, and his counsels, there is little doubt, led to further aggressions upon the Deccan kingdoms.

Interference at Golcondah.

Hyderabad sacked by Aurungzebe.

At this crisis, Mahmood Adil Shah, king of Beejapoor, died, on November 4, 1656, and was succeeded by his son, Ally Adil Shah II., then in his nineteenth year. Many noble monuments of Mahmood's reign survive him. His palaces are in ruins; but his mausoleum has the grandest dome in the world, and the scientific principles upon which it was constructed, according to Mr. Fergusson, are superior to any practised in Europe. During the period of his reign, Beejapoor was probably the finest and most populous city of India. Ally Adil Shah II. had scarcely ascended the throne, when his right to it was questioned by Aurungzebe, on the ground that he was not a son of the late king, and the right of selection lay with the emperor. There was no pretext, whatever, for the statement; but it afforded an excuse for war, which in this case was utterly unprovoked and unjustifiable. The Moghul army advanced from Aurungabad, under the nominal command of Meer Joomla, who had been sent from court, but in reality of Aurungzebe himself, by way of Beeder, which was captured from a descendant of Ameer Bereed, who still held it; and on this occasion the magnificent college, erected by Mahmood Gáwan in 1478, which was used for a powder-magazine, was blown up. The young King of Beejapoor could assemble no troops to check the Moghuls, as the bulk of his army was employed in

Death of Mahmood Adil Shah, 1656.

Ally Adil Shah II. succeeds.

War with Beejapoor.

Beeder captured.

The college destroyed by an explosion.

the Carnatic; and in February, 1657, the city was invested. The king offered to pay 1,000,000*l.* sterling, and to accede to any other terms demanded; but Aurungzebe had determined to reduce and annex the kingdom; and the capture of the city was only a question of time, when news of the supposed mortal illness of the emperor reached him from his sister; and accepting the overtures of Ally Adil Shah II., he concluded a hasty peace, and marched northwards, to contend with his brother Dára Shekoh, for the throne. Sooltan Mauzum, his second son, was left in charge of the Deccan provinces, and his family, and Meer Joomla, who had affected loyalty to Dára, though secretly favouring Aurungzebe, were confined in Dowlatabad.

Beejapoor besieged.

Illness of the emperor.

Peace with Beejapoor.

Aurungzebe proceeds to Hindostan.

For some time past, owing to his father's infirm state of health, the government of the empire had been carried on by Dára. He was a high-spirited, liberal prince, but lax, according to Mahomedan estimation, in his religious opinions, leaning more to those of the Emperor Akbur than to the rigid fanaticism professed and practised by Aurungzebe, who was looked to by the Mahomedans of the period as the ultimate regenerator of the faith in India. In this respect, Aurungzebe held a great advantage over his brother; and his unscrupulous ambition, and implacable policy, combined with unfailing daring and resolution, completed his remarkable character. The Prince Shujah, viceroy of Bengal, an habitual drunkard, professed the Sheea faith, and was even more unpopular among the orthodox than Dára. Moorád, viceroy of Guzerat, was a man of no ability, and also addicted to drinking; but he was brave and generous. He was the youngest of the four, and had least influence. Shujah and Moorád forthwith assumed royal titles, and marched from their respective governments at the head of their forces; and Aurungzebe, advancing from Boorhanpoor into Malwah, addressed himself to Moorád, professing himself ready to act in his interest, to place him on the throne, and then to return to Mecca. It is difficult to conceive how Moorád could have been cajoled by such hollow and hypocritical professions; but they succeeded, and the armies of the two brothers made a junction in Malwah.

Character of Prince Dára Shekoh and his brothers.

Aurungzebe joins his brother Moorád.

Meanwhile Dára was not indifferent to the progress of events: he dispatched an army under his son Soliman against Shujah, who was defeated near Benares, and returned to Bengal; and Rajah Jey Singh, who was nominated to the command of another to oppose Aurungzebe and Moorád, took up a position near Oojeyn, and was defeated in the month of April, 1658. The princes now advanced to

Prince Shujah defeated.

Rajah Jey Singh defeated.

the Chumbul; and the emperor, who was proceeding to Dehly, would have turned to meet them; but he was prevented by his brother-in-law, and Dára, who would not wait the arrival of the army he had sent against Shujah, could not be restrained by his father. His army, at the least computation, was treble in number to the combined forces of Aurungzebe and Moorád; but its sympathies were perhaps more with Aurungzebe than himself, and in the battle which ensued, he was totally defeated and fled. On the third day after the battle, Aurungzebe arrived at Agra, and endeavoured to conciliate his father; but his efforts were fruitless, and the emperor was confined to the palace and deposed. Shah Jehán lived till December 1666, in the strict seclusion imposed upon him; but his reign virtually ceased after the victory over Dára. Aurungzebe now usurped the government, though he was not formally crowned till a year afterwards; and Moorád was seized, while intoxicated, after a supper with his brother, and imprisoned, first in the citadel of Dehly, and afterwards in the fort of Gwalior.

Prince Dára defeated.

The emperor deposed by Aurungzebe.

Aurungzebe usurps the government, and imprisons Moorád.

The character of the Emperor Shah Jehán and of his government are freely given by Bernier, who resided at his court, and frequently accompanied him in his excursions; by Tavernier, by Mandelsloe, and other European travellers in India, whose accounts are beyond suspicion of correctness or of adulation. He was magnificent beyond all former emperors of India, not only in his court, but in the noble works which have survived him in the city of Dehly, and the most beautiful of Indian buildings, the Táj Mahál of Agra. If he was expensive in his tastes, he had at least a noble revenue, and supported well-paid civil establishments and a numerous army: and when he was dethroned by his ungrateful son, the treasury of the State, containing 24,000,000*l.* sterling, besides bullion and jewels, was rich beyond precedent. Throughout his reign of thirty years, there had been no public calamity, and he had governed his immense dominions—for it must be remembered that they extended from Bengal to the borders of Persia—with the ability of a great statesman, and with humanity and consideration rare among Oriental monarchs.

Character of Shah Jehán and of his government.

CHAPTER XXIII.

OF THE REIGN OF THE EMPEROR AURUNGZEBE, 1658 TO 1672.

FOR some time before Aurungzebe's attack upon Beejapoor, he had kept up a constant correspondence with Sivajee. He had approved of his retaining all he could wrest from Beejapoor, and even desired a personal interview with him, to arrange, as he wrote, plans of mutual aggrandisement; but Sivajee was too wary: and while he forwarded submissive letters, continued to act boldly on his own behalf. In May 1657, he even attacked Joonair, and carried off specie belonging to the revenue collections of the Moghul provinces, to the value of 120,000*l.*, which was sent to Rajgurh: and next assaulted Ahmednugger; but was less successful, though he secured 700 horses and four elephants. The sudden war with Beejapoor, however, alarmed him. When the fort of Beeder was captured, Aurungzebe wrote to him the following characteristic letter, which is quoted by Grant Duff, in his 'History of the Mahrattas':—'The fort of Beeder, which is accounted impregnable, and which is the key to the conquest of the Deccan and Carnatic, has been captured by me in one day—both fort and town—which was hardly to be expected without one year's fighting.' Sivajee, perhaps, considered that Beejapoor would also fall; but its escape, under the circumstances already detailed, was a relief to him. Considering, therefore, that Aurungzebe was fully occupied with the public affairs in Hindostan, he now pressed demands upon various counts, with which Aurungzebe for the present complied, rather than risk collision with him during his own absence. Meanwhile Sivajee continued his aggressions upon the Beejapoor territory in the Koncan; and it was impossible for that State to delay proceedings against him.

Aurungzebe's intercourse with Sivajee.

Sivajee's exploits.

Letter from Aurungzebe to Sivajee.

Sivajee's aggressions on Beejapoor.

Afzool Khan, an experienced officer, volunteered for the service, and was placed in command of an army of 12,000 horse and foot, with a train of artillery. Sivajee had no means by which such a force could be encountered in the field, and his object was to draw it into the narrow mountain-defiles, where it could be attacked at a disadvantage; and, if Afzool Khan could be induced to come to a conference, to destroy him. In these projects Sivajee was perfectly successful. Receiving con-

Afzool Khan volunteers to act against him.

Sivajee's plot to destroy Afzool Khan

tinuous messages of the most profound humility and submission, the Beejapoor general advanced nearly to Pertábgurh, and having encamped his army in a defile, proceeded with a slight escort to Sivajee's capital. A small pavilion or shed had been erected on the mountain-side for the conference, and Afzool Khan here awaited the arrival of Sivajee, who, having received his mother's blessing, descended from the fort, accompanied by his friend, Tannajee Maloosray. As he embraced Afzool Khan, he struck him in the bowels with a crooked dagger, concealed in his hand, and his blow was immediately followed up by Tannajee. By a preconcerted signal, the Beejapoor army in camp, completely off its guard, was attacked on all sides by parties which had been stationed in ambuscade in the woods, and very few escaped the massacre; while four thousand horses, with all the elephants and field-train, fell into Sivajee's hands. He now pressed Beejapoor severely, and plundered up to the gates of the capital. Several districts bordering upon his own possessions were annexed, and it became necessary for the king, Ally Adil Shah II., to take the field in person. He recovered most of the lost territory; but at the close of the struggle, in 1662, Sivajee retained nearly 300 miles of the coast territory, with a breadth of 100 miles, and his army consisted of 50,000 foot and 7,000 horse.

Murder of Afzool Khan.

Destruction of the Beejapoor force.

Final results of Sivajee's plans.

Meanwhile Aurungzebe, now emperor, had assumed the title of Alumgeer, on April 6, 1659, had consolidated his government, and overcome all opposition on the part of his brothers. The melancholy fate of Dára forms part of the graphic narrations of Bernier and Dow, where, and in Mr. Elphinstone's admirable history of the period, it will be read with the highest interest. Defeated near Jeypoor, and afterwards pursued from place to place, Dára was at last arrested by the Prince of Ján, in Sinde, when on his way to Kandahar. Here his wife died of fatigue, and the prince was sent to the emperor, who, fearing the sympathy of the people, which was unequivocally exhibited on his behalf at Dehly, had him tried, by a mock tribunal, as an apostate from the faith—the only charge against him. He was condemned to death, and was beheaded in prison, in August 1659, though not without making a stout resistance. The Prince Shujah had previously advanced from Bengal, and was defeated at Cujwa, on January 3, 1659. He was followed by the emperor's son, Prince Sooltan, and Meer Joomla, at the head of a large army; and though Sooltan deserted to him, and his cause was thereby sustained for a brief period, he

The fate of Prince Dára Shekoh.

Dára beheaded in prison.

Prince Shujah defeated.

Disappears in Arracan.

was again abandoned by the prince; and, after an ineffectual resistance, fled to Arracan, where he is supposed to have perished. Soliman and Sepéhr Shekoh, the sons of Dára, were successively imprisoned in Gwalior, and, with a son of Moorád, died, as was believed, of poison in a short period; and the unfortunate Moorád, detected in an attempt at escape, was, with a detestable hypocrisy, tried on a charge of having arbitrarily put to death a person in Guzerat, condemned to death, and executed in his prison. None of his brothers, or their offspring, now remained alive, and in 1661 the emperor at last believed himself secure. He had employed Meer Joomla, his great minister and general, first in the government of Bengal, and afterwards in the reduction of Assam; but, worn out by the effects of climate and privation, he too died, on March 31, 1653. The emperor's own serious illness followed, and for some days his life was despaired of; but he recovered, and proceeded to Kashmere for the re-establishment of his health.

Fate of other members of the family.

Death of Meer Joomla, 1653.

This success in the murder of Afzool Khan, and the destruction of his army, established Sivajee's fame among the Mahrattas on a firmer basis than ever. No one doubted but that his mother's dreams and visions, which became current among the people, were in reality divine revelations; and Sivajee made use of his great popularity, his reputed assistance by the gods, and the means he had obtained, in now attacking the Moghul possessions in the Deccan. At this period, Shaisteh Khan, the maternal uncle of the emperor, was acting as viceroy, and did his utmost to check the Mahratta incursions; but he could make no impression on their strongholds, and the emperor becoming alarmed, recalled his uncle, and dispatched his son, the Sooltan Mauzum, to the Deccan, with Rajah Jey Singh, as his military commander. Meanwhile Sivajee had plundered Surat, made exactions from the English and Dutch factories, and was prosecuting his predatory excursions with great rapidity and effect. In the year 1664, his father Shahjee died. He had extended the Beejapoor conquests considerably to the south, and had become possessed of the territory of Tanjore, which the King of Beejapoor allowed him to retain. Sivajee did not, for the present, press his claim on the Tanjore estate; but he now assumed the title of rajah, and struck coins in his own name. In this year his exertions almost exceed belief, and by sea as far as Barcelore, 150 miles south of Goa, he had levied contributions with his fleet from every port; he had defeated the Beejapoor troops by land, and again plundered the Moghul districts as far Dowlatabad.

Sivajee's proceedings.

Surat plundered.

Sivajee assumes the title of rajah.

His predatory warfare.

If the emperor had put forth his strength at this period, it is probable he would have crushed Sivajee; but he seems to have considered it advisable to allow him to weaken Beejapoor, and perhaps Golcondah also, so that they could be overwhelmed by him at any time. The plunder of some pilgrim ships by Sivajee's fleet was not, however, to be borne; and Rajah Jey Singh and Dilére Khan, two of the most efficient of the imperial generals, were sent to the Deccan. Their combined efforts evinced more vigour than the Moghuls had lately shown; and several strong forts having fallen, Sivajee—partly, it is believed, from a superstitious objection to fighting against a Hindoo prince, as Rajah Jey Singh was, but more probably to secure a position for acting with more effect against Beejapoor (for the conquest of which Jey Singh had received the emperor's commission)—joined the rajah with 2,000 horse and 8,000 infantry, and was confirmed in his acquisitions, except those portions which he had taken from the Moghuls. Rajah Jey Singh now marched upon Beejapoor; but there does not appear to have been the smallest pretext for the invasion, and as the Beejapoor State had had ample time for preparation, and its troops fought bravely, the Moghul army was obliged to retreat. Sivajee had, however, behaved with much valour in several actions, and was invited to court; and he set out for Dehly, accompanied by his eldest son Sumbhajee, in March 1666, under the assurance of Rajah Jey Singh as to his honourable reception. In this, however, he was disappointed. The emperor took little notice of him, and by the proud nobility he was probably accounted little more than an infidel barbarian. His miserable reception caused him to faint in the emperor's court, and he soon after confined himself to his residence, on plea of serious illness. He now obtained passports for his escort, and sent them away, retaining only a few personal attendants; and finally, and after the emperor had shown his ultimate design by subjecting his guest to a strict surveillance, Sivajee and his son escaped, being carried out in large baskets to a place where a horse had been posted for them, when, taking up his son before him, he proceeded southwards, by unfrequented routes, and in various disguises, to the Deccan, and finally reached Rajgurh in December 1666, after an absence of nine months.

The emperor's motive in regard to Sivajee.

Sivajee joins the Moghul general.

Beejapoor attacked.

Sivajee invited to Dehly.

He is slighted there.

And escapes to the Deccan in disguise.

Meanwhile Rajah Jey Singh had renewed the war against Beejapoor, and even invested the city; but the army of the State, assisted from Golcondah, cut off his supplies, and he was obliged to retreat, with serious loss, to

Beejapoor again attacked, but is relieved.

Aurungabad. Sivajee's officers were not slow to avail themselves of this opportunity. They had already recovered several of the relinquished forts, and on Sivajee's return he re-possessed himself of the northern Koncan. Jey Singh was recalled, but died on the road, and was replaced by Sooltan Mauzum, with Jeswunt Singh as his coadjutor. Treaties were soon afterwards concluded between the emperor and the courts of Beejapoor and Golcondah, and Sivajee also obtained payment of tribute from both, on condition of abstaining from the forcible collection of the demands which he had threatened to enforce. The Deccan, therefore, was at peace; and Sivajee employed the years 1668 and 1669 in perfecting the arrangements for his civil government, and the regulation of his army, which were not only admirably conceived, but carried out to the minutest details, with wonderful ability and regularity. They are given in full in Grant Duff's 'History of the Mahrattas,' and will amply repay the perusal of all students of Sivajee's strangely eventful and successful career.

Rajah Jey Singh recalled.

Treaties with Beejapoor and Golcondah.

Peace of Aix-la-Chapelle.

Civil administration of Sivajee.

The emperor, who had viewed Sivajee's escape with alarm, and his subsequent progress, as well as the well-founded reports that his son and Jeswunt Singh were receiving large sums of money from him, with real uneasiness, now ordered them to effect his apprehension. Of this design Sivajee was privately informed by the prince; and, with his wonted energy, he recommenced the war by capturing the strong fort of Singurh, held by a picked garrison of Rajpoots. On this occasion, Tannajee Maloosray, his tried friend and commander, was slain; but the success was great, and covered Maloosray's name with a glory which has never diminished among his countrymen. Sivajee then again plundered Surat, and sent his general, Pertáb Rao, into Khandésh, who imposed on that province, for the first time, a demand for chouth, or one-fourth of the revenues. Jinjeera was also besieged, but without effect, and after a revolution in the place, the successful party threw themselves on the protection of the Moghuls. The emperor now sent an army of 40,000 men to the Deccan, under the command of Mohubut Khan, which arrived in 1672; but a large portion of it was totally defeated by Sivajee's general, Pertáb Rao Goozur, in a general action, and the rest, after forming a junction with the imperial troops at Aurungabad, remained inactive. The emperor shortly afterwards recalled his son Muázzim, of whom he had long been suspicious, and also Mohubut Khan,

The emperor's anxiety in regard to Sivajee.

Orders him to be apprehended.

Singurh taken by Sivajee.

Death of Tannajee Maloosray.

Surat plundered.

The demand for chouth established.

The Deccan reinforced by the emperor.

The troops are defeated by Sivajee.

and replaced them by the viceroy of Guzerat, Khan Jehán; but the struggle in the Deccan was not renewed for several years, nor until undertaken by himself.

CHAPTER XXIV.

OF THE REIGN OF THE EMPEROR AURUNGZEBE (*continued*), 1672 TO 1680.

THE circumstances which prevented the emperor's further interference in the affairs of the Deccan in 1672 were connected with the government of Kabool. The Afghans who held the passes had rebelled, and defeated Ameer Khan, the son of Meer Joomla, who was viceroy of the province, and had even set up a king of their own. In 1673, therefore, the emperor proceeded to the seat of war, and some successes were obtained by his son, the Prince Sooltan; but they were of small moment, as the mountain tribes were never thoroughly reduced or otherwise pacified. While engaged in directing operations against them, disturbances of a serious nature occurred near Dehly, which obliged the emperor to return. A sect of Hindoo devotees, who styled themselves Sátnaramiés, had risen in rebellion, and committed many excesses. Several detachments sent against them had been successively defeated, and a belief ensued that they were magicians, upon whom weapons or bullets had no effect. To restore confidence, therefore, the emperor took the field in person, and even wrote sentences of the Korán with his own hand, to be tied upon the standards to avert malign influences. The result was the complete dispersion of these rebels; but the manner in which their cause had been aided by the Hindoos of the localities of the insurrection, so irritated the emperor, that, yielding to his own bigoted and fanatical feelings, he encouraged the massacre of the male inhabitants by his troops, while women and children were seized and sold as slaves. Above all, he reimposed the detested jezia or capitation-tax upon Hindoos, which had been abolished twice before the establishment of the Moghul dynasty—an act which excited the utmost unpopularity and discontent in all portions of the empire, and proved the means of detaching from him not only many friends, but the goodwill of the entire Hindoo population of his dominions, which

Louis XIV.'s conquests in Holland.

Rebellion of the Afghans.

Aurungzebe proceeds to the frontier.

Disturbances at Dehly.

Massacre of Hindoos.

Capitation-tax reimposed.

Its bad effect.

the tolerance of preceding reigns had so satisfactorily secured. On the promulgation of the imperial edict, his palace was besieged by masses of clamorous petitioners; and on the occasion of a State visit to the great mosque, many of the people, who had blocked up the streets in crowds in order to beg remission of the tax, were trampled to death by his elephants.

Development of the emperor's austere character.

The innate austerity and fanaticism of the emperor's character were beginning to develope themselves in other strange forms. Poets and authors, with all the musicians, singers, and dancers, were forbidden the court, and discharged. Public edicts were issued against the practice of their professions; and the record of the history of his reign, which had been hitherto an official transaction, by a specially appointed officer, was discontinued. Half the customs dues were remitted to Mahomedans, while their collection from Hindoos was rendered vexatious and oppressive; and whereas Hindoos and Mahomedans, since the reigns of Shére Shah Soor and Akbur, or for a century, had shared in government employment and offices, it was now directed that no more of that religion were to be allowed to hold them. The wise measures of his predecessors had been specially directed to an amalgamation of the people; and the imperial marriages with Rajpoot princesses had been means to this end. The emperor himself was a descendant of one of these marriages; but he now repudiated all connection with Hindoos, and throughout Rajpootana and the Deccan his policy created undisguised discontent. In Orme's 'Fragments,' page 252, a translation of an anonymous letter of the period is given, the authorship of which has been attributed to many distinguished persons, and should be consulted in order to understand the tone of popular feeling at the time.

Discontent of the Rajpoots. They rebel.

In 1677, Rajah Jeswunt Singh died at Kabool, and on their return home, the emperor was desirous of securing his widow and children. They escaped, however, owing to the bravery and fidelity of Doorga Das, the commander of the late rajah's troops, and reached Jondhpoor in safety. Several of the Rajpoot chieftains now combined to obtain satisfaction for the wanton and unprovoked insult to the widow of Jeswunt Singh; and also to oppose the exaction of the poll-tax. Over this combination the emperor obtained some success, and returned to Dehly in 1679; but the truce with the Rajpoots was soon broken, and the new operations were carried on with all the bitter animosity, savagery, and fanaticism of the old Mahomedan wars. Whole districts were desolated, and the women and children sold into slavery.

Cruel character of the war.

Doorga Das, who continued the defence of Rajpootana, now offered the crown to the emperor's son, the Prince Muázzim; but he rejected the overtures. They were, however, accepted by the Prince Akbur, his father's favourite, who joined Doorga Das, assumed the ensigns of royalty, and, with a force of no less than 70,000 men, seemed likely to effect a revolution. One of the Mahomedan leaders, however, rejoined the emperor with his forces, and the whole confederacy shortly afterwards fell to pieces. The Prince Akbur, with Doorga Das, retreated to the Deccan, and received protection from the Mahrattas. These proceedings had the effect of aggravating the animosity between the Moghuls and the Rajpoots; and though the emperor concluded an inconsequent peace with the Rana of Jondhpoor, the former good understanding was never restored, and reprisals on either side were still continued; but the emperor was left at liberty to draw off his forces to the Deccan, where his presence had now become an urgent necessity.

Rebellion of Prince Akbur.

Rajpoot confederacy disolved.

On December 15, 1672, Ally Adil Shah II., of Beejapoor, was attacked by paralysis, and died a few days afterwards. He had one son, the Prince Sikunder, who was five years old, and a daughter, Padshah Beebee, unmarried. Abdool Mahomed, the chief minister, was a timid character, unfit to meet the emergency, and before the king's death, he obtained his unwilling consent to an arrangement by which Khowas Khan, one of the chief nobles, was constituted regent, while he, with other officers, should undertake the government of the provinces. But the State was distracted by factions, and had now little chance of surviving the encroachments of Sivajee on the one hand, and the power of the Moghul empire on the other. The first attack upon it was made by Sivajee, in 1673, who rapidly gained possession of many important places in the Koncan; while his general, Pertáb Rao, plundered the open country up to the gates of Beejapoor. A truce made with him enabled the regent of Beejapoor to refit his army; but the engagement was repudiated by Sivajee, who, in 1674, reproaching Pertáb Rao with his conduct, sent him again against the Beejapoor army, which had advanced as far as Panalla. Here a general action ensued, in which Pertáb Rao was killed: and for a time the Beejapoor troops were successful; but on the arrival of reinforcements to the Mahrattas, the brief victory was changed to defeat. Soon after this, Sivajee was enthroned for the second time, on June 3, 1674, with great formality and splendour. On this occasion, he openly declared his independence; the designations of his officials were

Death of Ally Adil Shah II., 1672.

Sikunder Adil Shah, a minor, succeeds.

Danger of the State.

Sivajee's attack.

Sivajee, enthroned a second time, declares independence.

changed from Persian to Sanscrit, and the establishment of the Mahratta, as a Hindoo nationality, may be said to have commenced. Mr. Oxenden was present at the enthronement as an ambassador from the English, and received permission to trade throughout Sivajee's dominions: import duties were fixed at 2½ per cent., *ad valorem*, and all wrecks were to be restored.

The Moghuls could not be indifferent to these proceedings; and in 1675, Dilére Khan, the imperial commander in the Deccan, resumed the war against Sivajee. This was what Sivajee no doubt desired, as it cancelled former obligations; and contriving to occupy the imperial forces in attacks upon petty hill-forts, his cavalry, under Humbeer Rao, crossed the Nerbudda, plundered Khandésh and Berar, and though now pursued by Dilére Khan, reached home safe with a large booty. In this year, also, Khowas Khan, the regent of Beejapoor, was assassinated. He had opened negotiations with the Moghul viceroy, by which he had agreed to hold Beejapoor as a province of the empire, and to give the king's sister in marriage to one of the emperor's sons; these overtures were considered traitorous, and brought on the conspiracy which ended in his death. He was succeeded by Abdool Kurreem Khan, who was popular and faithful.

The Moghuls make war on Sivajee.

Carolina planted.

Sivajee's operations.

Regent of Beejapoor assassinated.

Sivajee had little fear of the Moghuls in the Deccan. Their forces were comparatively small, and could be effectually checked by his own. The viceroy was accessible to flattery and to the receipt of money; and the emperor was as yet far distant, and professing, if no more, a contempt for Sivajee and his proceedings. The opportunity for a southern expedition, long meditated by Sivajee, was not now to be neglected, and at the head of 30,000 horse, and 40,000 lightly-equipped infantry, he marched direct upon Golcondah, respecting the territories both of Golcondah and Beejapoor as he moved. At Golcondah he halted for a month, obtaining a train of artillery, with a considerable sum of money; and having engaged, as is believed, to divide the southern provinces of Beejapoor with that State. By the end of September he had reduced the fortress of Vellore, and though he did not then succeed in inducing his half-brother, Venkajee, to give up half of Tanjore, he nevertheless possessed himself of Bangalore and other portions of his father's conquests; while the districts of the Carnatic, which belonged to Beejapoor, were overrun and plundered under pretence of collection of his hereditary claims of chouth, and a foundation laid for their further enforcement.

Reasons for Sivajee's confidence.

His expedition southwards.

His proceedings in the Carnatic.

During his absence, Khan Jehán, the viceroy, was removed

from office by the emperor, and Dilére Khan appointed in his room. Dilére Khan was by no means disposed to weaken his strength in attacks upon Sivajee officers, and considering that Sivajee's reception at, and treaty with, Golcondah was an offence to the emperor and Beejapoor, and afforded pretext for a war with that State, he induced Abdool Kurreem, the regent of Beejapoor, to join him in an expedition against Golcondah. The invasion

Golcondah invaded by the Moghuls, who are defeated.

was, however, resisted and defeated by Mahdana Punt, the Brahmin minister of the kingdom; and Abdool Kurreem dying soon afterwards, in January 1675, the regency of Beejapoor was conferred upon Musaood Khan, a wealthy Abyssinian, who undertook to pay the arrears of the army, and to reform the financial affairs of the State, which had fallen into great disorder.

Sivajee returns.

Sivajee now returned to the Deccan, by way of Bellary, of which he took possession, and also of Kopál Bundur, both very important forts; and while thus employed, came to an understanding, through the officer he had left in the south, with his brother Venkajee, by which he obtained his half share of the southern estates.

Annexes the southern districts of Beejapoor.

The regent of Beejapoor was unable to check Sivajee in his annexation of the territory west and south of the Krishna, and the Moghuls viewed his proceedings with undisguised alarm. The emperor had disapproved of the appointment of Musaood Khan as regent, and had censured Dilére Khan for not having made a better use of his opportunity to get possession of the administration of the kingdom of Beejapoor.

Dispute in regard to the Princess of Beejapoor.

Sooltan Mauzum was, therefore, appointed viceroy; but Dilére Khan was allowed to retain his command, and seeking for occasion of war with Beejapoor, now demanded the young princess, in virtue of the former agreement. This, however, Musaood Khan refused, and serious contentions were about to ensue at the capital between the parties for and against the marriage, when the princess herself,

Her noble conduct: she proceeds to the Moghul camp.

mounting an elephant, proceeded to the scene, and declared her intention, in order to save her brother and the State, of proceeding to the Moghul camp. She was allowed to do so, and the devotion of the last princess of the royal race is still fondly remembered.

This act did not, however, prevent war. In his extremity—for the Moghuls had invested Beejapoor—Musaood Khan

Beejapoor besieged.

applied to Sivajee, who advanced to raise the siege; but finding the besiegers too strong for him, turned northwards, plundering the Moghul districts without mercy, up to Aurungabad. He was, however, attacked by a superior force of cavalry, and escaped with difficulty. Meanwhile Dilére Khan was pressing his attack upon Beejapoor with vigour; and Musaood Khan besought Sivajee to turn southwards and raise the siege; but at this crisis Sumbhajee, the eldest son of Sivajee, who had been for some time at variance with his father, suddenly joined Dilére Khan. Great expectations had been formed by the Moghuls that the Mahrattas would be divided and weakened by this act of rebellion; but nothing of moment occurred. Beejapoor still held out resolutely, and Sivajee's troops, now acting in the open country, cut off the supplies to Dilére Khan's camp, and obliged him to raise the siege and retreat. In this movement he was severely defeated by Jenardin Punt, one of Sivajee's generals.

Sivajee's son joins the Moghuls.

The siege of Beejapoor is raised.

The events of the year 1679 in the Deccan were, as may be imagined, very unsatisfactory to the emperor, who recalled his son Sooltan Mauzum and Dilére Khan, and re-appointed Khan Jehán. Sumbhajee was directed to be sent to Dehly; but escaped, as was believed, under the connivance of Dilére Khan. Before any new combination on the part of the Moghuls could be made, Sivajee had proceeded to Beejapoor in the beginning of 1680, where he concluded a treaty with Musaood Khan, obtaining a formal cession of the recently annexed districts, and relinquishment of all claims to sovereignty over the family estate in the south. He then returned to Rajgurh, where he was attacked by a white swelling in his knee, and died on April 5, 1680, in the fifty-third year of his reign.

The emperor recalls his son, Sooltan Mauzum.

Sivajee's treaty with Beejapoor.

Sivajee's death.

For an admirable summary of the character and acts of this remarkable man, the student should consult Grant Duff's 'History of the Mahrattas,' vol. i. pp. 296-300. 'His own nation considered him an incarnation of the Divinity, setting an example of wisdom, fortitude and piety.' From an unknown petty chieftain he had become sovereign of a great portion of Western India, besides his possessions in the south. He had successfully braved the whole power of the Moghul empire, and had taught his countrymen the secret of success in those sudden predatory movements which, from the first blow struck against Mahomedan power in the destruction of Afzool Khan and the army of Beejapoor, were, in a hundred years, to effect the total subversion of their empire.

His character.

CHAPTER XXV.

OF THE REIGN OF THE EMPEROR AURUNGZEBE (*continued*), 1680 TO 1698.

Sivajee's death was kept secret for a while, when a plot was formed to imprison Sumbhajee, and place Rajah Rám, his half-brother, by Soyéra Bye, the second wife of Sivajee, on the throne, which was for a time successful. Rajah Rám was actually invested in May 1680; but in June Sumbhajee gained possession of the capital, Rajgurh, and received the submission of all the State authorities. He now commenced a series of barbarous executions. Among the first was that of Soyéra Bye, who suffered a cruel and lingering death; and the savage temper displayed by the new sovereign gave but little hope of a peaceful reign. After some desultory affairs with the Seedees of Jinjeera, who had defied his father, Sumbhajee's attention was occupied by the arrival of the Prince Akbur, who sought refuge with him, against his father the emperor; and by a new conspiracy in favour of Rajah Rám, the detection of which was followed by other executions. Against these proceedings, and the destruction of several Brahmin officers of high rank, his Péshwah, or chief minister, Moro Pingley, protested; and at the suggestion of an unworthy favourite, Kuloosha, a northern Brahmin, was imprisoned. Henceforward Kuloosha's influence became paramount, and the source of much eventual mischief and misery. In 1682, the attack upon Jinjeera was renewed; the place was besieged, but without effect; and Sumbhajee's fleet was defeated by the Seedees in the harbour of Bombay. His movements and threats against the English produced much uneasiness in Bombay; but his operations were confined to attacks on the Portuguese, over whom he obtained considerable advantages, especially on one occasion, in which he behaved with distinguished bravery. Propositions for peace ensued from the viceroy of Goa, but the demands of Sumbhajee were so exorbitant, that they were rejected. These operations were, however, brought to a close by the arrival of the emperor in the Deccan, in 1683.

Rajah Rám succeeds, but is deposed by Sumbhajee.

Jinjeera attacked.

War with the Portuguese.

Siege of Vienna.

Aurungzebe's policy is sufficiently intelligible from his subsequent operations. He believed that if Sumbhajee could be first checked, or driven from his strongholds, the conquest of Beejapoor and Golcondah was only a question of

Policy of the emperor.

time; and he considered, with reason, that neither kingdom would move in defence of a common predatory enemy. When, therefore, he reached Boorhanpoor, he detached Prince Azim to reduce the Mahratta forts in the northern range of mountains, and Prince Muázzim to invade the Koncan. Both failed in their object. Sumbhajee well knew the impossibility of anything being effected by the Moghul cavalry in the Koncan, or against the northern line of forts; and after losing most of his horses and many men in the Koncan, the Prince Muázzim ascended the Ghauts at the close of the hot season, and encamped in the open country, near Meerich, on the Krishna. The Prince Azim, on the other hand, being equally unsuccessful, marched into the Deccan, and having taken Sholapoor, would have advanced upon Beejapoor; but, being opposed by a superior force, was obliged to retreat. The emperor, with a powerful reserve, took up a position at Ahmednugger, prepared to support either or both his sons, as might be necessary. Sumbhajee did not attempt to meet the regular armies of the Moghuls in the open field; but, relying upon the predatory system of warfare organised by his father, he now despatched a force under Humbeer Rao, which rapidly traversed the provinces in the Moghul rear, plundered Boorhanpoor and Khandésh, and threatened Berar. Khan Jehán, who had been stationed at Aurungabad, moved in pursuit; but was unable to bring the Mahrattas to action. As soon as the season permitted, the army of the Prince Muázzim was put in motion against the districts which had been taken from Beejapoor by Sivajee, and Dharwar, with several other forts, was captured; but his army had already suffered so terribly from sickness and privation, that it was unable to resist a small army from Beejapoor, and the wreck of the whole finally retreated to Ahmednugger, covered by a Moghul force, specially dispatched by the emperor for the purpose.

His campaign.

Its failure.

Position of the emperor.

Sumbhajee's measures.

The Moghuls renew the campaign.

They retreat.

Meanwhile the emperor, with the flower of his army, composed of men of all the northern nations of the empire, a magnificent train of artillery, and the most gorgeous camp-equipage that had ever been seen in the Deccan, advanced southwards from Ahmednugger, and having formed a junction with his son Azim, proceeded in person to invest Beejapoor. Sumbhajee having meanwhile made a treaty with Golcondah, now attacked Guzerat, and plundered its cities without check; but these proceedings do not appear to have altered the emperor's plans in any degree, except that instead of deferring operations against Golcondah, he resented the treaty with Sumbhajee, which had come to his knowledge, and sent an army against it, under Khan Jehán, continuing his march to Beejapoor. There was no army at the

The emperor invades Beejapoor.

disposal of the Beejapoor State to contend with the Moghuls in the field, or to check the investment of the city; batteries were erected by them near the south-west angle of the outer fortifications, and a practicable breach was soon effected. The garrison fought bravely, and the defence of the citadel might have been protracted; but, falling short of provisions, the city capitulated on October 15, 1686, when the emperor was carried in triumph through the breach, and conducted into the citadel, where the young king, Sikunder Adil Shah, and the officers of State mournfully submitted themselves to him, amid the wailings of their people. Sikunder Adil Shah was at once transferred to the Moghul camp as a prisoner, and lived for three years afterwards, when he died suddenly, as was believed of poison, administered by the emperor's orders, owing to some popular demonstration on his behalf. Thus closed the illustrious dynasty of the Adil Shahy kings, which had reigned, for the most part in great splendour and prosperity, for 197 years.

The city is besieged.
The garrison capitulates.
League of Augsburg.
The King of Beejapoor submits to the emperor.
And subsequently dies.
End of the Adil Shahy dynasty.

The emperor would probably have turned his arms at once against Golcondah, but was prevented by a convention made by the Prince Muázzim. When Khan Jehán was detached against that State, he had been met by the Golcondah army under Ibrahim Khan, and being unable to oppose it, intrenched himself and wrote urgently for reinforcements. The Prince Muázzim was, therefore, dispatched to his assistance; but had Ibrahim Khan been faithful to his State, Khan Jehán's army might have been destroyed before the prince's arrival. Instead of this, he kept aloof, and allowed the united forces to proceed to Hyderabad unmolested, where he joined the Moghuls with the greater part of his troops. The king, Aboo Hussun Kootub Shah, shut himself up in the fort of Golcondah, and Hyderabad was left open to plunder. His minister, Mahdhana Punt, was killed in a popular tumult, and having now neither army nor adviser, the king accepted such terms as he could obtain. These were the payment of two millions sterling in money and jewels, and Sooltan Muázzim was left to collect the tribute.

Prince Muazzim's convention with Golcondah.
The Moghuls under Prince Muazzim reach Golcondah.
Terms obtained by the king.

By this treaty, however, Golcondah obtained only a very brief respite. In 1687, the emperor proceeded to Goolburgah, to pay his devotions at the tomb of Syed Geesoo Duráz, a celebrated Deccan saint, detailing at the same time a heavy force of cavalry to the south of Golcondah, to cut off any succour from that quarter. From

Soliman emperor of the Turks.
The emperor declares war against Golcondah.

Goolburgah he despatched a formal declaration of war against the king, the principal articles of which were accusations of perpetual profligacy, the employment of a Brahmin minister, and alliance with an 'infidel'—Sumbhajee. The provisions of Sooltan Muázzim's treaty of the previous year were altogether ignored, and the unprovoked attack sought to be rendered justifiable by the detestable hypocrisy and religious bigotry under which Aurungzebe endeavoured to cover and justify the worst events of his life. While he was proceeding to Golcondah, his emissaries were corrupting the troops and officers of the State; but the king bravely defended the fort for seven months, and lost it at last by treachery. Aboo Hussun had been a popular monarch. A minstrel himself, his ballads and amatory poems have survived him, and the regret at his deposition was deeply and universally felt by his subjects. But for treachery within, Golcondah would have been more defensible than Beejapoor; but its reduction could not have been long delayed. Golcondah fell in September 1687, hardly a year after Beejapoor, and the king was sent a prisoner to the fort of Dowlatabad, where he resided till his death, and where, as in the Deccan generally, many anecdotes of him, as the good and brave King Tanah Shah, are still current. The Kootub Shahy dynasty had lasted from 1512 to 1687, or 175 years, and left more memorials of its greatness in works of public utility than any other of the Deccan kingdoms.

Prince Muázzim's treaty ignored.

Golcondah taken by treachery.

Character of the king.

The king imprisoned for life.

The Kootub Shahy dynasty ends.

Although the emperor had destroyed two great monarchies within a year, he had by no means obtained possession of the country. The people had been attached to their respective dynasties, and were not disposed to welcome foreign conquerors. The subjugation of the Deccan and Carnatic had therefore to commence. For a short period, all appeared stunned by the emperor's unscrupulous proceedings and rapid successes; but gradually on every side rebellions sprang up, headed by disbanded officers and troops, and encouraged by local Hindoo authorities; while the attempt to collect the poll-tax only caused greater exasperation. And while the country, even to the most southern possessions of Golcondah, including Sumbhajee's estates in Tanjore, was held by large forces, the details of these large provinces were, in many places, unaffected by the change, and were occupied by a lawless population.

The subjugation of the Deccan commences.

If, during this period, Sumbhajee had continued in the field, he might have saved Beejapoor or Golcondah, or both. But he was entirely inactive; he had wasted his father's

Sumbhajee's inaction.

treasures, and given himself up to perpetual debauchery and profligacy; and his people, who could not understand his want of enterprise, attributed his condition to the effects of spells cast upon him by his favourite Kuloosha. While in this condition, and residing at the town of Sungméshwur, he was surprised by Ikhlas Khan, an active Moghul officer, and taken direct to the emperor, then at Tolapoor, near Beejapoor. Mounted upon camels, and attended by jeering crowds of the Moghul soldiery, he and his favourite Kuloosha were led through the imperial camp, and confined. Sumbhajee was promised his life by the emperor if he would become a Mahomedan; but spurning the offer by a message as brutal and violent as it was indecent, he was executed with barbarous torture, in company with his friend. This event occurred in August 1689. Sumbhajee had left one son, Sivajee, six years of age, who, with his mother, were at Rajgurh. He was recognised as successor, and his uncle, Rajah Rám, declared regent; but shortly afterwards, Rajgurh was besieged by the Moghuls, and upon its capture, in 1690, though Rajah Rám escaped, the young rajah and his mother were made prisoners and dispatched to the emperor's camp. The capture of other forts followed, and such was then the weakness and poverty of the Mahratta State, that it was unable to make any effort to check the Moghuls.

He is captured and taken to the emperor.

And is executed.

William and Mary king and queen of England.

Sumbhajee is succeeded by his son.

He is taken prisoner.

Weakness of the Mahrattas.

Under these circumstances, Rajah Rám strengthened every retainable fort as much as possible, and committing the charge of local affairs to the best men he could select, proceeded in disguise with a few followers to Ginjee, in the southern province of Tanjore, and there publicly established his court. The emperor no sooner heard of this proceeding, than he dispatched Zoolficar Khan, in 1691, with an army for its reduction; but Ginjee was one of the strongest forts in Southern India, and defied his efforts. He applied for reinforcements, but the emperor was in no condition to grant any; his large army was split up into small portions, and for these the localities in which they were stationed found ample occupation. In particular, the Näik of Wakingérah, a Beydur chieftain of the Beejapoor kingdom, defied the Moghuls, and an army under the Prince Kámbuksh was sent against him, in 1692. His fort, Wakingérah, was in reality an insignificant place; but the Beydurs defended it valiantly, and the prince was obliged to retreat with heavy loss.

Rajah Rám proceeds to Ginjee.

Which is besieged ineffectually.

The Beydur Näik of Wakingérah rebels.

An attack upon it repulsed.

Meanwhile Rajah Rám was not idle. Dispatching Suntajee Gorepuray and Dunnajee Jadow, two of the companions of his flight, and excellent partisan officers, in 1692, to the Deccan, they at once engaged in the predatory warfare peculiar to the Mahrattas, and occupied themselves very successfully in cutting off the Moghul convoys from the north, plundering and devastating their districts, and spreading terror and confusion everywhere. It was in vain that the emperor sent or led unwieldly hosts against them: as he advanced, they retired, again following him and acting against his convoys. The siege of Ginjee had not been concluded, for the emperor would not hear of its being abandoned, and had recalled Zoolficar Khan, sending (in 1694) the Prince Kámbuksh, with Assud Khan, in his stead, who, however, fared no better. In 1696, Suntajee and Dunnajee, in order to relieve Ginjee, changed their field of operations to the south, ravaged the Moghul districts, and on several occasions defeated the imperial troops in the field. It was impossible that the siege of Ginjee could progress, and finally Prince Kámbuksh blew up his cannon, and abandoned the attack, being permitted, under a convention, to withdraw his troops to Wandiwash, in Tanjore. Nor did Kassim Khan, the governor of the districts west of the Krishna, fare better. He was attacked in turn, and defeated by Suntajee Gorepuray; being pursued with such pertinacity, that the survivors surrendered, were stripped of their arms and clothes, and in this condition sent in derision to the emperor. Kassim Khan, a gallant officer, unable to support the disgrace, took poison and died. Zoolficar Khan, the only general upon whom the emperor could rely, was now again dispatched to Ginjee in 1697: the siege was resumed, and the place was finally taken by escalade in January 1698. Rajah Rám, however, escaped, with all his family and chief officers, under the connivance, of which there was little doubt, of Zoolficar Khan; and the prolonged defence of Ginjee may be attributed to his secret sympathy with the Mahrattas.

Rajah Rám's measures.

The emperor is foiled.

Siege of Ginjee raised.

Siege of Ginjee renewed, and it is captured.

Rajah Rám escapes.

CHAPTER XXVI.

OF THE REIGN OF THE EMPEROR AURUNGZEBE (*concluded*), 1698 TO 1707.

AFTER the capture of Ginjee, and the withdrawal of the Mahratta court from the south, as well as the absence of any local authority from which any material resistance was to be apprehended, the emperor was enabled to concentrate his forces in the Northern

Deccan, and resume the war with the Mahrattas. Rajah Rám had now settled at Sattara, and assembled a considerable army. He had lost, however, one of his best officers, Suntajee Gorepuray, who, in consequence of a quarrel with Dunnajee Jadow, had been deserted by his adherents, and was hunted down and murdered by a man whom he had offended. Dunnajee had been unable to oppose Zoolficar Khan in the field, and it did not appear probable that the Mahrattas could resist the now overwhelming force of the emperor. In the year 1699, Aurungzebe, who had established a cantonment at Brumhapooree, on the Bheema, a very central position, made his disposals for a new campaign. He proposed to lead a part of the army against the fortified strongholds of the Mahrattas, while the other, under Zoolficar Khan, should act in the open country against Rajah Rám, Dunnajee, and other leaders. In April 1699, the fort of Sattara capitulated, after a resolute defence. Previous to its fall, Rajah Rám, who had been occupied to the northward, had been beaten by Zoolficar Khan, who pursued him to Singurh, where he died of exhaustion and inflammation of the lungs, in the month of March. This did not, however, affect the Mahratta State. Rajah Rám had left two sons, Sivajee, who was ten years old, and Sumbhajee, who was three years old; and Tara Bye, the mother of the former, undertook the regency.

War with the Mahrattas resumed.

The emperor's plans of campaign.

Sattara capitulates.

Death of Rajah Rám.

Regency of Tara Bye.

As the emperor continued his operations against the fortresses, and the establishment of a court would have at once invited his attack, Tara Bye, with the principal chiefs and officers of the State, led a wandering life; while the various leaders were occupied by the levy of the national demands of chouth, or one-fourth the revenue of all foreign provinces; ghás-dána, or grass and corn dues, and sur-déshmookhee, a claim difficult to define, but which rested upon assumed rights over the collections of revenue. Wherever these claims were paid to the revenue officers, the people were not plundered; when they were resisted or evaded, towns or villages were laid under contribution or openly plundered, and often burned. No Moghul force could overtake or intercept the lightly equipped Mahratta horsemen, and they became daily more persevering and more dangerous. It must be remembered, too, that much of the Golcondah and Beejapoor cavalry had joined the Mahrattas, or supported themselves by independent plunder. Thus, during the years 1700 to 1702, little variation occurred in the position of the contending parties. The emperor had succeeded in capturing six of the main forts of the outer line of the Mahratta defences; but behind them lay many others, equally strong and more inaccessible.

Claims for chouth and ghás-dána, &c. levied.

Activity of the Mahratta horse.

In 1702, the Mahrattas had again plundered portions of Guzerat and Khandésh; and by 1705 they had crossed the Nerbudda into Malwah, routed the imperial troops, and devastated the country. No armies could check these predatory movements; none could follow the Mahrattas when they retreated. They assembled on particular points with secrecy and celerity, made long and rapid forays, and again dispersed to form a fresh combination and attack.

Mahrattas plunder Guzerat, Khandésh, and Malwah.

In his history of this period, Grant Duff is of opinion that though the Mahrattas were excited, the war had not created patriotism. This, however, may be doubted. The success of Sivajee can only be attributed to the creation of a national spirit before unknown, and to his constant and passionate appeals to all classes and grades, to throw off the hated Mahomedan yoke, and to establish a pure Hindoo rule, when the Hindoo faith could be professed without check or oppression, and its sacred kine and temples preserved from outrage. These were his messages to the people; and, as he had established a belief in his Divine mission, was the surest method of exciting them. He and his mother had passed away, but their dreams and visions were not forgotten; they had rested in the hearts of the nation, and were bearing fruit. From a rude unwarlike peasantry, the Mahrattas had become warriors; in many instances their best generals were Brahmins, and the experience of thirty years had only proved the more distinctly, by what manner of warfare the Moghuls could alone be defied, and eventually wearied out. When, therefore, to national religious excitement that of plunder was added, it is not surprising that the war became more than ever popular and successful. From Aurungzebe's entry into the Deccan, up to the period of his commencing his last struggle with the Mahrattas, sixteen years had passed of almost constant strife. They had bowed to the storm, but were never broken, and in the now declining years of the emperor's life, they met his greatest efforts with renewed vitality.

National spirit of the Mahrattas.

Popularity of the war with the Moghuls.

Meanwhile, disorders progressed in other quarters. The Rajpoots had grown bolder; the Játs were in rebellion about Agra, Mooltan was disturbed, and all required the employment of heavy masses of troops. The real weakness of the emperor in the Deccan may be estimated by the second rebellion of the Beydur chief, Pám Naïk of Wakingérah. The Prince Kámbuksh and the emperor had invited him to court, and he had been admitted to the rank of a commander of 5,000; the Order of the Fish had been conferred upon him, and his dues of black-mail had been

Rebellion of the Rajpoots and Játs.

Second Beydur rebellion.

confirmed by royal decrees. But the rude Beydur baron felt himself jeered at and insulted by the imperial courtiers; and, in 1705, he suddenly broke all his engagements, and took to his old courses. It was in vain that the emperor addressed cajoling letters to him, impressed with the mark of his own hand, dipped in ground sandal-wood. In vain that in one of these he wrote, 'Alas! that you are not a Mahomedan, you would then be to me as a brother.' Pám Näik was at the head of 20,000 militia of his own clan—incorrigible banditti, but brave and resolute soldiers, and was assisted by Dunnajee Jadow; and when the emperor in person besieged Wakingérah, they plundered his camp, and vexed him by night attacks, while all attempts to storm the defile of Wakingérah proved fruitless. After seven months of constant attacks and repulses, and the efforts of the emperor, the Prince Kámbuksh, Zoolficar Khan, and Dáood Khan Punnee, had alike failed on many occasions, the position was stormed by the two latter generals, with heavy loss on both sides—a fruitless result, for the Beydur chief retreated to a stronger position in the hills, which, under the name of Soorpoor, or Shorapoor, is still the capital of the district.[1] The case of Wakingérah is merely an example of the times. Nor was it long before the Mahrattas began to recover the forts they had lost. Their cavalry, emboldened as well by success as by the real weakness of the emperor's army, gradually drew a cordon around it, and plundered convoys and detachments up to the skirts of the camp. The young Mahratta Prince Shao was still under detention, and in 1706, the emperor, in his distress, opened a negotiation for his release; but the exorbitant demands of the Mahratta chiefs prevented any conclusion. Soon afterwards, the imperial forces, no longer able to keep the field, retreated upon Ahmednugger, where, on account of the strength of its fort, the emperor proposed to establish his principal camp. On its way thither, the army was attacked by Dunnajee Jadow and other chiefs, and very sorely handled, the whole narrowly escaping a complete defeat. The emperor did not long survive this event; and died at Ahmednugger on February 13, 1707, in the

The emperor besieges Wakingérah.

But without success.

Mahratta successes.

Battle of Ramillies.

The emperor opens negotiations.

But is obliged to retreat with loss.

Death of the Emperor Aurungzebe.

Battle of Almanza.

[1] The records of Shorapoor were very valuable and interesting, as containing original correspondence between the Beydur chiefs in succession, the Rajahs of Beejanugger, the Kings of Beejapoor, the Emperor Aurungzebe, and the Mahratta leaders. They had been classed and arranged by me when in political charge of the State, with a view to complete translation; but on the capture of Shorapoor, after the rajah's rebellion in 1858, they were destroyed by the English troops in possession of the place.—*M.T.*

fiftieth year of his reign, and eighty-ninth or ninetieth year of his age.

The public acts of his reign are the best index to his character. To an insatiable ambition, and unscrupulous employment of means to attain his ends, he added a detestable hypocrisy, and indulgence in the worst characteristics of the gloomy bigotry and fanaticism of his faith. Of all about him, and most perhaps of his sons, he was habitually suspicious; and it is difficult to conceive how those employed by him, knowing themselves to be surrounded by unscrupulous spies and informers, could serve him faithfully or freely. The mistakes of his political conduct are sufficiently evident by the sequel. Strengthened by him, Beejapoor and Golcondah might have circumscribed, and perhaps destroyed, the Mahratta power, which, freed from these checks, now rose superior to all; while the delusion of universal authority in India, and the alienation of the affections of the Hindoos, carried with them their own elements of destruction. But with all his hideous defects of character, it is impossible not to admire the vast ability, the patience, the courage and energy with which, to the very last, Aurungzebe conducted the affairs of his government, in person. No detail, however insignificant, in all his widely-extended dominions ever escaped him, and all the great measures of his reign were exclusively his own. It is questionable whether he ever sought or accepted advice, and equally whether he ever admitted anyone to his perfect confidence; yet, in spite of his suspicions, his natural love for his children was great, and the beautiful mausoleum erected over his daughter at Aurungabad remains a memorial alike of his affection for her and his munificence. His remains were carried to Roza, near Dowlatabad, and interred in the precincts of the tomb of the celebrated saint, Boorhan-ood-deen. His grave is an open one, covered with a trellis-work of wood, over which a jessamine has been trained. He desired in his will that his funeral expenses should be defrayed from the proceeds of caps which he had quilted and sold, and this amount did not exceed ten shillings, while the sale of his copies of the Kóran—eight hundred and five rupees—were distributed to the poor. By another will he left the northern and eastern provinces to be divided between his sons, Muázzim and Azim, and Golcondah and Beejapoor to Kámbuksh; an arrangement which, virtually impossible of execution, laid the foundation of civil war.

His character.

The bad effects of his policy.

CHAPTER XXVII.

OF THE REIGN OF THE EMPEROR BAHADUR SHAH, 1707 TO 1712.

Contention of the emperor's sons.

AURUNGZEBE had provided by will for the division of India among his sons, but it proved to be an arrangement, though just in the abstract, impossible of execution. At the period of his death, Muázzim, the eldest, was viceroy of Kabool. Azim was encamped near his father, and Kámbuksh had been dispatched to his government of Beejapoor. Under the support of the forces present, Azim, in defiance of his father's will, proclaimed himself emperor of all India, and proceeded at once to the northward. Muázzim, who was advancing from the north-westward, had called up his eldest son Moiz-ood-deen from Mooltan, and his second son Azim-ush Shán from Bengal; and they joined him with their respective quotas of troops, before the arrival of Prince Azim from the Deccan. The prince had hurried on by forced marches, and when he reached Gwalior, nearly all his artillery, and most of his infantry, were in the rear; but, hearing that his brother had taken up a position near Agra, he could not be restrained, and proceeded at once to attack him. The armies met on May 31, 1707, and at the outset of the engagement, Azim's impetuosity gained him some advantage, for Muázzim was absent hunting, and the attack was evidently a surprise. He returned, however, immediately, and his veteran troops were soon able to redeem their loss and to attack in turn. When the battle was thus raging, a violent storm of wind and dust arose, which darkened the air, and blowing furiously in the faces of Azim's troops, threw them into confusion. It was in vain that the experienced Zoolficar Khan now besought Prince Azim to draw off his army and await the arrival of troops from Gwalior; but this advice was disregarded, and Zoolficar left the field. At this juncture, news was brought to Azim that his sons, Bedár Bukht and Wallajah, whom he had placed in command of the right and left wings, had been slain, and that most of his best officers had also fallen; he then caused his elephant to be urged into the thickest of the fight, where he was wounded by several musket-shots, and was finally beheaded by a soldier, who climbed up into his howdah. His youngest son, Ally Tebár, had accompanied him, and being found unhurt, was taken to his uncle, who received him with the utmost affection

Action between the Princes Muázzim and Azim.

Azim is defeated and slain.

and adopted him as his own. After this battle the Prince Muázzim was formally crowned emperor, under the title of Bahadur Shah, and the whole of the Prince Azim's adherents, including Zoolficar Khan and his father, Assud Khan, submitted to him, and were pardoned.

Prince Muázzim crowned emperor.

The Prince Kámbuksh, who had taken charge of Beejapoor, had acknowledged the superiority of Prince Azim, but he refused to recognise that of the emperor: and after a fruitless negotiation with him, Bahadur Shah, as soon as the season permitted, marched, on October 5, to the Deccan, and encountered his brother's army on February 14, 1708, near Hyderabad. On this occasion, Kámbuksh died of wounds received in the action, and the submission of all the provinces of the Deccan and Southern India to the emperor followed.

Prince Kámbuksh resists, and is killed in action.

Battle of Oudenarde.

It will be remembered, that Shao, son of Sumbhajee, the real Rajah of the Mahrattas, had remained a nominal prisoner in the hands of the Emperor Aurungzebe. He had been kindly treated; his mother had become a personal friend of the emperor's daughter, and the boy a favourite of the emperor himself, who had given him the familiar appellation of Shao, by which, instead of his proper name of Sivajee, he was afterwards known. After the emperor's death Shao accompanied Prince Azim for a considerable distance on the way to Agra: and would probably have been carried on, but for the advice of Zoolficar Khan, who recommended his release. The Mahrattas of Tara Bye's party had immediately taken advantage of the withdrawal of the greater part of the Moghul army from the Deccan, and had already retaken several forts, and were plundering the Moghul districts. Zoolficar Khan, who was thoroughly acquainted with the state of parties among them, considered that Tara Bye would oppose Shao, and that a contest for superiority would ensue between them, which, for the present, at least would prevent further aggressions. At his release, Shao agreed to preserve his allegiance to the throne of Dehly, and in return was promised the districts conquered from Beejapoor by Sivajee, should he prove successful. Among the Mahratta chiefs there were many who were discontented with Tara Bye's administration, and Shao found himself in a short time at the head of 15,000 men. By Tara Bye he was denounced as an impostor; but this had little effect, in the face of his well-known identity. As he advanced upon Poonah, he was joined by Dunnajee Jadow, and Tara Bye's forces were defeated in an action at the village of Kheir. Thence he

Aurungzebe's kind treatment of Rajah Shao.

He is released by Prince Azim.

He is joined by several chiefs.

And defeats Tara Bye.

pressed on to Sattara, which was given up to him, and he was enthroned there in March 1708. He had sent a contingent of Mahratta cavalry to the emperor, which did good service against Kámbuksh in the action near Hyderabad, and had therefore fulfilled his promises of allegiance.

Then enthroned at Sattara.

The emperor did not remain in the Deccan, but marched northwards to Dehly. He had created Zoolficar Khan viceroy of the Deccan; but as he could not be spared from court, Dáood Khan Punnee, an officer of great distinction, ability, and bravery, intimately acquainted with Mahratta politics, was left as his substitute. With him Shao opened negotiations for the payment of the national claims of chouth and sur-déshmookhee; but, while these were fully admitted, Dáood Khan reserved the right of paying them himself, as a check, not only on the habitual plunder of the Mahrattas, but as security for their allegiance. This system proved perfectly successful; and while Dáood Khan remained in the Deccan, was observed with scrupulous good faith by both parties. Tara Bye continued a fruitless and desultory struggle till 1712, when her son, on whose behalf her claims as regent existed, and who was, in fact, an idiot, died. She was soon afterwards placed under restraint, and her party ceased to exist.

The emperor leaves the Deccan.

Dáood Khan becomes viceroy.

Tara Bye confined.

Meanwhile the emperor, freed from apprehension in regard to the Deccan, proceeded towards Rajpootana, in order to adjust existing differences with the several States. It is possible that these arrangements might have been protracted; but the Sikhs had risen in the Punjâb, and had captured Sirhind; and the alarm which they had created required the presence of the emperor for their suppression. As he passed through Rajpootana, therefore, in 1709, the several chieftains met the emperor in turn, and the existing differences seem to have been amicably adjusted. The Sikhs were as easily disposed of. They had suffered bitter persecutions from the Mahomedans for nearly a hundred years; but their numbers, so far from diminishing, had materially increased; and from a sect of harmless religious devotees, they had become an association of warriors, stimulated as well by the memories of former persecution, as by revenge and plunder. Gooroo Govind, the tenth high-priest in succession from their founder, had first led them in force against the Mahomedans, in 1675; but he was beaten back, his forces dispersed, his mother and children put to death, and he wandered, at times bereft of reason, to Nandair, in the Deccan, where he founded a Sikh monastery, and was after-

The emperor proceeds to Rajpootana.

Insurrection of the Sikhs.

Condition of the Sikhs.

wards assassinated. In the Punjâb, however, the Sikhs still continued their resistance, and their reprisals upon the Mahomedans were accompanied by the most shocking cruelties. Their present chief-priest, Bandoo, was a furious fanatic, but an enterprising leader, and he carried fire and sword into the Moghul territories, even as far as Dehly.

Charles VI. emperor of Germany.

Death of the Emperor Bahadur Shah.

His character.

By the end of the year 1711, the Sikhs had been driven into the hills north of the Punjâb, and were, for the present, in some degree restrained; but the campaign against them was the last act of the emperor's brief reign. On February 16, 1712, he died suddenly at Lahore, in the fifth year of his reign, and the seventieth of his age, leaving his dominions, except from occasional disturbances by the Sikhs, in perfect peace. He was a merciful and considerate monarch, and though his brothers had wantonly rebelled and perished in arms against him, he had adopted their children and provided for them. These acts form a key to his whole character, which, if somewhat deficient in energy, was yet unstained by crime. As he had made no will, a contest at once ensued between his sons. Azim-ush-Shán, the second, who had been most in his father's confidence, and had the royal treasures in his power, assumed the title of emperor, and intrenched his camp. Zoolficar Khan, who was present, now incited the three other brothers to action, and the camp of Azim-ush-Shán was cannonaded for several days, when, abandoned by most of his adherents, he attempted a sally, and perished in the river Ravee. During a division of the treasure in camp, a contest followed between the three surviving brothers. Khujista Akhir was killed in the first battle, when Moiz-ood-deen ascended the throne, under the title of Jehándár Shah. No sooner had this event taken place, than on the day following Rufy-ool-Kudr, the youngest, suddenly rebelled and attacked his brother, but was defeated and killed in action. Jehándár Shah, therefore, remained emperor without a rival, and marching at once on Dehly, made a triumphant entry into the city on June 9, 1712.

CHAPTER XXVIII.

OF THE REIGNS OF THE EMPEROR JEHÁNDÁR SHAH AND FEROKSIÁR, RUFY-OOD-DERJÁT AND RUFY-OOD-DOWLAH, 1712 TO 1720.

The new emperor was little fitted for his position, and soon gave evidences of cruelty and weakness of character which have hardly a parallel in the histories of the older dynasties of Dehly. He put to death, in cold blood, all the male children of his brothers and of his uncles whom his father had spared, an act which caused the utmost indignation and horror among all classes of the people. Assud Khan and Zoolficar Khan were promoted to the highest offices of the State; and upon the relations of his mistress, Lall Koor, were showered honours and employments for which they were not only notoriously unfit as they were only professional singers and musicians, but which exasperated the nobility and courtiers, who were obliged to acknowledge them. An anecdote is related by the author of the 'Syr-ool-Mutakherin,' of Zoolficar Khan, who, as vizier, had to affix his seal to, and settle the fees of, all deeds of appointment to office; that, in fixing the dues of the patent of the brother of Lall Koor, he had written them as 5,000 guitars and 7,000 timbrels. Lall Koor complained bitterly to the emperor of this insult; and Zoolficar Khan was called to answer for his conduct. 'It is no joke at all,' he said seriously. 'If the dancers and singers take to the professions of the nobility, *they* at least must live. When, therefore, I asked so many thousands of guitars and timbrels from this gentleman, it was with a view of distributing them to your Majesty's dispossessed governors and generals, who certainly have a right to earn their bread as well as others.' Zoolficar Khan, indeed, does not appear to have spared either the emperor or his unworthy favourites on any occasion, and the estrangement between them was increasing, when news arrived from Bengal which caused great consternation.

Murder of members of the royal family.

Unworthy favourites of the emperor.

Anecdote of Zoolficar Khan.

Before he had joined his father, Bahadur Shah, Prince Azim-ush-Shán had been viceroy of Bengal, and had left his family at Ráj Mahál. He had only one son, Feroksiár, who was in some danger after the destruction of the other princes of the blood; but his cause was espoused by the

Rebellion of Prince Feroksiár.

governor of Behar, Syed Hoosein Ally, who, with his brother, Syed Abdoolla, governor of Allahabad, assembled a considerable force, and defeated the first army sent by the emperor against them, under the command of his son, capturing not only their field-artillery, but their treasure in camp. The emperor now left Dehly on November 30, 1712, with an immense army, under the command of Zoolficar Khan; and the rivals met in the neighbourhood of Agra, on December 28. After a desperately fought battle, the imperial troops retreated in confusion; and though Zoolficar Khan, at the head of his veterans, tried to retrieve the day, it was impossible to do so. The emperor, with his mistress, Lall Koor, had fled from the field; and covering the retreat of the disorganised army, Zoolficar Khan returned to Dehly. He found the king had preceded him in disguise, and was under the protection of his father, Assud Khan. He would have preferred making cause with him, or at least carrying him off to the Deccan: but the timid counsels of his father, and the fact that the principal members of the nobility had already done homage to Feroksiár, prevented any movement.

The emperor's forces defeated.

The emperor's campaign.

He is defeated.

The emperor deposed.

On January 1, 1713, Feroksiár ascended the throne, and conferred dignities upon all who had joined him. Among others was Chin-Khilich Khan, a noble of high rank, already much distinguished as a statesman and a general, to whom the title of Nizam-ool-Moolk Asof Jáh was allotted, under which he became afterwards one of the most celebrated characters of the time. The emperor then marched leisurely towards the capital, and was met, on January 30, at Bara Palla, by Assud Khan and his son Zoolficar, who were presented to him, and received honorary dresses and assurances of favour and protection. A party at court was, however, inimical to them. The new vizier, Meer Joomla, an obscure person, had no tolerance for the old nobility; and as the father and son withdrew from the emperor's presence, they were separated. Zoolficar Khan was shown into an adjoining tent, where he was immediately surrounded with persons who taunted him with the death of the emperor's father, Azim-ush-Shán, and he was partly strangled and then dispatched by their daggers. A similar fate awaited the ex-emperor, Jehándár Shah; while a few days afterwards, on February 4, as the emperor entered Dehly, the venerable Assud Khan was forced to behold the two bodies dragged by an elephant about the city, and denied burial. Other cruel executions and mutilations followed, and the new reign, like the preceding, commenced with bloodshed.

Feroksiár succeeds.

Peace of Utrecht.

Zoolficar Khan is put to death.

Jehándár Shah strangled.

The ex-emperor could not be regretted; but the fate of Zoolficar Khan, the bravest and the noblest of the great generals of Aurungzebe, excited universal pity.

Syed Abdoolla created vizier.

Feroksiár had owed his elevation entirely to the bravery and devotion of the brother Syeds, Hoosein Ally and Abdoolla, and had advanced the latter to the office of vizier, the former to be commander of the forces. But he had already become jealous of them, and sought their ruin; and to this he was urged by the insidious counsels of his favourite, the Meer Joomla, who felt in them an opposition to his designs which he could not overcome. Hoosein Ally was, therefore, dispatched with an army against Ajeet Singh, the rana of Jondhpoor; but, receiving intelligence of the intrigues in progress at the capital, concluded a peace, by which the rana sent his son to make submission to the emperor, and agreed to give his daughter in marriage to him. On his return to Dehly, it was evident to the brothers that nothing could be effected without the separation of Meer Joomla from the emperor; and under pretence of apprehensions for their own safety, they fortified their palaces and filled them with troops. These proceedings excited the utmost alarm in the emperor's mind, and after an interview with them, Meer Joomla was created viceroy of Behar, and despatched to his seat of government. Abdoolla Khan was now reappointed vizier, and his brother Hoosein Ally nominated to the viceroyalty of the Deccan.

Measures of the Syed brothers.

Syed Abdoolla Khan re-appointed vizier.

Arrival of an English embassy.

Louis XV. king of France.

The emperor had been long ill, and in the year 1715 an embassy arrived from the English of Calcutta, with complaints against Meer Jaffier, the governor of Bengal. In so corrupt a court as the emperor's, it was probable they would have received little notice; but the emperor's physician having failed to relieve him, Mr. Hamilton, the surgeon of the embassy, was applied to, and was fortunate enough to effect a cure in a short period. Feroksiár was grateful, and would have bestowed high rewards for the service done him; but Mr. Hamilton declined all personal remuneration, and, as Mr. Boughton had done on a former occasion, begged as his recompense that the justice sought by his countrymen might be granted. The terms demanded were important; but they were conceded, and secured by imperial patent. The English were allowed to purchase the proprietary rights over thirty-eight villages near Calcutta, and the President was to have the power of granting passes which would exempt goods from examination by the customs officers. Money was

The emperor is cured by Mr. Hamilton.

Whose noble conduct secures a patent for the English.

Particulars of the patent.

to be coined for them in the mint; and all persons indebted to the company were to be made over to them. These terms were opposed by the viceroy; but they neverthless formed the basis of a far higher authority in Bengal than the East India Company had ever before possessed. The marriage of the emperor to the Rajpoot princess followed his recovery, and was performed with unusual splendour at Dehly.

On the conclusion of the nuptial festivities at Dehly, Hoosein Ally set out with his forces to assume charge of his government of the Deccan. On taking leave of the emperor, he gave him distinctly to understand that if his brother's position were in any way affected or threatened, he would return instantly at the head of his army; and this haughty communication probably increased the emperor's desire to rid himself of his powerful subject. He, therefore, wrote to Dáood Khan Punnee, promising him the viceroyalty if he would attack Hoosein Ally on his arrival in the Deccan, and destroy him. It will be remembered that Dáood Khan had been left by Zoolficar Khan in charge of his government. He was a brave and skilful officer, and through his exertions the Mahrattas had been hitherto restrained from their accustomed predatory excursions and violence. No more acceptable commission could have been offered to him than to revenge the death of his earliest friend and patron; and taking up a position at Boorhanpoor, he proclaimed himself viceroy, and awaited Hoosein Ally's arrival. On August 25, 1715, the rivals met; when a severe battle was fought near the city of Boorhanpoor, in which Dáood Khan was on the point of victory, when he received a matchlock ball in his forehead, and died instantly. Upon this becoming known, his troops scattered and fled, except some bodies of Mahratta horse, which had hovered around the combatants, without taking any decided part in the action, and now tendered their allegiance to the viceroy. Dáood Khan's wife, who had been a Hindoo lady, on receiving news of his death, put an end to her existence.

The emperor's plot against Hoosein Ally.

Action between Hoosein Ally and Dáood Khan.

Dáood Khan is killed.

Some time previous to his encounter with Hoosein Ally, Dáood Khan had been removed from the Deccan to the viceroyalty of Guzerat; and the affairs of the Deccan had been conducted by Asof Jáh Nizam-ool-Moolk, who had formerly been employed by the Emperor Aurungzebe as governor of Beejapoor and its dependencies. His part in the revolution by which Feroksiár was placed on the throne has already been detailed; and it was shortly after that event that he had proceeded to the Deccan. During his incumbency, the southern provinces had been governed with skill: and although the Mahrattas

Government of Nizam-ool-Moolk.

affected to consider that the arrangements with Dáood Khan had ceased with his transfer to Guzerat, they were, nevertheless, kept under a general control. But their internal distractions had not ceased; and though Tara Bye was under restraint, the members of her party continued to oppose Shao, with varying success, acting on behalf of Sumbhajee, the son of Rajah Rám by his youngest wife, who had been elected to succeed Sivajee, the son of Tara Bye. Thus two parties had arisen in the Mahratta States; one that of Shao, who resided at Sattara; the other of Sumbhajee. The latter was called the Kolapoor faction, and each had the support of numerous partisan chieftains and officers. During Dáood Khan's administration, he had maintained the supremacy of Shao; but Nizam-ool-Moolk, who had been joined by some disaffected chiefs, was led to favour the party of Kolapoor. His policy was evidently directed to perpetuating the existing strife, hoping that the contending factions might exhaust each other; but he did not remain long enough to watch its progress, for he was removed to the government of Moorádabad, when Hoosein Ally was appointed viceroy of the Deccan.

Condition of the Mahrattas. *Mahratta factions.* *Nizam-ool-Moolk transferred to Moorádabad.*

The new viceroy found both parties of Mahrattas sufficiently powerful to protect their own interests, and equally disposed to plunder the Moghul districts for the nominal collection of the national demands. The emperor, too, with a singular refinement of treachery, had secretly instigated the Mahratta chieftains to oppose the viceroy; and in an attempt to suppress the forays of Dhabáry, a semi-independent chieftain, who occupied part of the country between Khandésh and Guzerat, his troops met with a severe defeat. After weighing the comparative advantages to be derived from each party, the viceroy was induced to support Shao, who had at least displayed a consistent attachment to the Moghuls, and opened negotiations with him. The Péshwah, or chief minister of Shao, was now Ballajee Wishwanáth, a Brahmin of humble origin, but who had risen by his character and great ability to the rank he now occupied. Under his advice, Shao demanded all the territory which had belonged to Sivajee, both in the Deccan and Southern India; and the collection of the national demands. The pretensions of Sumbhajee as rajah of the Mahrattas were to be ignored altogether; and his recognition as Rajah of Kolapoor only to be admitted. For these privileges, Shao promised to pay a tribute of 100,000*l.* a year, to maintain a body of 15,000 horse for the emperor's service, and to clear the country of all depredators, making good to the people any losses they might sustain. These terms were at once accepted by the viceroy; and although the considerations granted were enormous, yet

Treachery of the emperor. *Demands of Shao.* *His terms are accepted.*

they had the effect of consolidating the power which had shown most desire to aid the imperial interests, and possessed the greatest amount of means to maintain them.

The emperor's intrigues.

Meanwhile the emperor, whose schemes for the destruction of Hoosein Ally had been abortive, chafed under the restraint of his brother Abdoolla; and having reopened communications with the Ameer Joomla, commenced other intrigues with nobles of the court, who were jealous of the influence possessed by the Syed brothers. These proceedings alarmed the vizier, who increased his own forces to 25,000 men, and wrote to his brother to return with the least possible delay. Accordingly, Hoosein Ally, having completed his arrangements with Shao, left Boorhanpoor in November 1719, at the head of his forces, which were materially increased by a contingent of Mahratta cavalry, under the charge of Ballajee Wishwanáth, and reached Dehly on December 31, with an immense retinue, and the pomp of an emperor. The brothers, now united, had forces at their command which probably exceeded those of the emperor in number, and were infinitely more united and efficient. It was in vain that Rajah Jey Singh besought the emperor to put himself at the head of his troops, to denounce the brother Syeds as rebels, and to appeal to the loyalty of the army at large; but he was not to be moved to action. Either from cowardice, or from an impression that resistance was useless, he submitted to the demands of the brothers, which increased in exorbitancy from day to day, and ended in their obtaining possession of the royal citadel and palace, which were occupied by their troops. This having been accomplished, Hoosein Ally marched in battle array with all his forces to the palace on February 3, 1720, and paid a short visit to the emperor, who made no remonstrance, and appeared to submit. A few days afterwards, the vizier, having obtained the keys of all the private apartments, repaired to the emperor, and producing the letter he had written to Dáood Khan Punnee, in regard to the destruction of his brother the viceroy, upbraided him with his treachery, at the same time demanding that other high offices should be conferred upon them both. These arrogant demands seem to have driven the emperor to despair. He retorted in violent language, and rising suddenly, retired unceremoniously to the women's apartments. Meanwhile the city was filled with tumult. A body of Mahratta cavalry, 1,500 in number, under Suntajee Kudum, proceeding to the viceroy's camp, were attacked by troops in the interest of the emperor and the populace, and, cut off in the streets from all aid, perished to a man. Other

The vizier is alarmed.

Hoosein Ally returns to Dehly.

The emperor submits to the Syeds' demands.

He is confined by the vizier.

Tumults in Dehly.

desultory combats were in progress, with much bloodshed, when a proclamation was suddenly made that the emperor had ceased to reign, and that the Prince Rufy-ood-Derját had been called to the throne in his stead.

The emperor deposed.

The vizier had not quitted the palace. He had sent message after message to his brother to enter the city in force, and put an end to the increasing riot; but before any movement could be made, some Afghan soldiers in his service contrived to enter the private court of the palace from the terrace of an adjoining house, and the terrified women, under threats and tortures, disclosed the place where the emperor had concealed himself. His mother, and the ladies of his seraglio, endeavoured to defend him; but he was dragged away from them, and placed in strict confinement. Thus ended the revolution. The prince selected to be emperor, was the nephew of the late Bahadur Shah, and was twenty years old. Next day he ascended the throne in public, and on the petition of the Hindoo officers, issued an edict for the abolition of the poll-tax. Two months afterwards, the wretched Feroksiár, who had resorted to every possible contrivance to procure his escape, or liberty on any terms, was first blinded by order of the brother Syeds, and had then poison administered to him. While he lay in his last agony, he was visited by them, and as he bitterly reviled them for their treachery, they ordered him to be strangled, and stood by till he was dead. Guilty and treacherous as he had been during his life, his murder excited public horror; and as his body was carried to the grave, it was followed by thousands of the people, invoking curses on his destroyers.

The emperor is confined.

Rufy-ood-Derját succeeds

The poll-tax abolished.

Feroksiár is blinded, poisoned, and then strangled.

The selection of the new emperor was in one sense unfortunate. He was then ill, and died of consumption on June 16, 1720. His younger brother, Rufy-ood-Dowlah, was then placed on the throne; but his elevation was contested by the officers in charge of Agra, who declared in favour of Nikosiár, the younger son of the late Prince Akbur. This rebellion was quickly suppressed; but the young emperor, who, like his brother, was consumptive, died soon afterwards. The choice of the Syed brothers now fell upon Roshun Akhter, a grandson of the Emperor Bahadur Shah, who had hitherto lived in retirement at Dehly. He had, however, been well educated, and his mother, a woman of great strength of character and ability, was much respected. Roshun Akhter was in his eighteenth year, and ascended the throne under the title of Mahomed Shah. The date of his accession was, however, fixed from the deposition of Feroksiár, or September 1719.

The young emperor dies.

Is succeeded by his brother Rufy-ood-Dowlah.

Who also dies.

Roshun Akhter succeeds as Mahomed Shah.

CHAPTER XXIX.

OF THE REIGN OF THE EMPEROR MAHOMED SHAH, 1720 TO 1723.

AFTER his accession, the young emperor continued under the strict control of the brother Syeds, who carried on the government of the empire in his name. His mother enjoined upon him the most careful observance of their wishes, at least for the present; for it was evident that any attempt on his part to attain independence, would be attended with nothing short of destruction. One of the first acts of his reign was the dismissal of Ballajee Wishwanáth, and the Mahratta forces which had accompanied the viceroy, Hoosein Ally, to Dehly. It was by no means consonant with the policy of the viceroy to behave to them with ill-faith. He had not only been assisted very materially by them, but without the fulfilment of his engagements, he well knew that the Deccan would relapse into the disorder in which he had found it. The Mahratta forces were, therefore, fully paid. Shao's mother and family, who had been hitherto detained at Dehly, were given over to the care of Ballajee Wishwanáth; and imperial patents for the collection of the chouth and sur-déshmookhee dues, in confirmation of the engagements between the viceroy and Shao, were duly executed and delivered during the year 1719–20. Nothing so formal or complete in character had ever before been obtained by the Mahrattas; and their hitherto desultory claims, enforced at the point of the sword, were now placed upon a national footing, acknowledged and confirmed by the imperial government. The student will find them detailed with great precision, from the original documents, in chapter 13, vol. i. of Grant Duff's 'History of the Mahrattas,' pp. 445–462.

The Syeds' position.

Settlement of the Mahratta claims.

So far, therefore, the Mahrattas were safe for the present; but elements of trouble were thickly strewn in the empire, which were not long in assuming decided forms. Several formidable insurrections broke out in different quarters; that in Kashmere, assuming the aspect of a religious war, was with difficulty suppressed. These, however, were minor occurrences in comparison with the proceedings of Nizam-ool-Moolk. He had been relieved from his government of Moorádabad, and sent for to the capital, where the Syeds had hoped to make him subservient to their

Insurrections

Nizam-ool-Moolk appointed governor of Malwah.

views; but, finding him impracticable, appointed him governor of Malwah. Under his vigorous administration, the local disorders were soon suppressed, and he began to turn his attention to the Deccan, then scantily garrisoned by imperial troops. Among these he had many friends; the people were favourable to him, and the position of the brother Syeds at Dehly rendered it improbable that they could dispatch any considerable force against him. They were not, however, without apprehension; and after remonstrances, which proved to be of no avail whatever, an army of observation was stationed by them on the northern frontier of Malwah.

His vigour in regard to the Deccan.

The latter measure seems to have decided Nizam-ool-Moolk as to his course of action. He marched suddenly southwards from Seronje in the month of April 1721, and after passing the Nerbudda, the great fortress of Aseergurh was given up to him by its commander. Boorhanpoor followed; and Ghous Khan, the governor of Berar, joined him with all his troops and a train of artillery, as did also several Mahratta chiefs, who were at variance with Shao, with their forces. Dilawur Ally Khan, the general who was in command of the army to the north of Malwah, saw that no time was to be lost; and following Nizam-ool-Moolk across the Nerbudda, found him in a position near Boorhanpoor, and attacked him furiously on June 20; but he was killed in the action, and the whole of his artillery, camp-equipage and treasure captured. This victory secured Nizam-ool-Moolk in his position, and the news of it gave secret satisfaction to the emperor and his party, while to the Syeds it was a subject of profound disquiet; and after much consultation, it was determined that Hoosein Ally should take the field against the conqueror.

Nizam-ool-Moolk advances into that province.

Pope Innocent XIII.

Nizam-ool-Moolk attacked by the imperial forces, which are defeated.

Meanwhile the defeated troops of Dilawur Ally Khan had formed a junction with Alum Ally, the imperial commander-in-chief in the Deccan, who advanced into Berar at the head of a very powerful army. On the other hand, Nizam-ool-Moolk had been able to equip his artillery from the imperial magazines in Boorhanpoor and Aseergurh, and his forces were now little, if at all, inferior to those of the imperialists. The armies met near the town of Balapoor, in Berar, on August 8, 1721. Nizam-ool-Moolk had posted his artillery under cover of some brushwood, and Alum Ally, believing that the troops opposed to him were flying from the field, pressed ardently in pursuit, when the masked guns opened upon him with deadly effect in showers of grape. It was impossible to withdraw, and, fighting

The imperial troops again attack Nizam-ool-Moolk.

By whom they are again defeated.

Alum Ally is killed.

bravely to the last, he perished on the field with several of his best officers. This victory was as complete as that over Dilawur Ally Khan; and Nizam-ool-Moolk was afterwards joined by several of the commanders who had been opposed to him.

Effects of the victory.

No troops in the imperial interest now remained in the Deccan by whom the progress of Nizam-ool-Moolk could be opposed; and, on the news of the defeat of Alum Ally reaching the capital, Hoosein Ally prepared to march to the Deccan and to take the emperor with him, leaving his brother, the vizier, in charge of the government. For some time past, a private understanding had existed between the emperor and Mahomed Ameen Khan, a noble of the court attached to his person, in opposition to the Syeds; but it does not seem to have taken any definitive form till the march to the Deccan was commenced. On August 24, the emperor joined the camp, and by September 14, it had reached a point about 100 miles to the south of Agra. Meanwhile the conspirators had decided on putting Hoosein Ally to death, and drew lots for the purpose. The execution of the act fell upon a Kalmuk Tartar, named Meer Hyder, a savage fanatic, who, as the minister entered camp, approached his palankeen with a petition, and as he was reading it, stabbed him to the heart. The assassin was instantly cut to pieces; but the camp was filled with tumult and bloodshed, and it is probable the emperor would have perished in his tent but for the presence of mind of some of the officers of his guards, who seated him on an elephant and rallied the guards around him. Mahomed Shah seems to have been by no means deficient in the courage of his race, for he took an active part in the furious conflict which followed, exposing himself freely in the thickest of the fight. The attack on the emperor's camp had been made by the nephew of Hoosein Ally, who was killed; and upon the event becoming known, the rest of the troops submitted.

The emperor and Hoosein Ally march for the Deccan.

Conspiracy against Hoosein Ally,

who is assassinated.

A great tumult and conflict follows.

The news of Hoosein Ally's death, and the revolution in camp, reached the vizier on September 16, who at once prepared to resist; and on the 19th Rufy-ool-Kudr, a grandson of Bahadur Shah, was brought out of the palace and placed on the throne. The vizier also attempted to conciliate the troops by largesses and increased rates of pay, and to attach the old nobility to him by grants of offices and estates. On October 1, the new emperor and the vizier took the field; and their army moved in the direction of Mahomed Shah's camp, being much strengthened by the junction of many of Hoosein Ally's veterans. After some changes of position on

Rufy-ool-Kudr placed on the throne by the vizier.

The rival forces meet.

both sides, the armies met in battle on October 20. Partial contests ensued, with varying advantage, from that day till the 24th, when, in a charge on foot at the head of a body of Syeds of his own clan, the vizier was severely wounded, and with his younger brother taken prisoner and carried to the emperor, whose victory was now complete; and on November 2 he entered Dehly in triumph. Mahomed Ameen Khan had been created vizier, and his predecessor, though kindly treated, was for the present confined to his palace. The power of the family, so long dominant in the State, was, however, completely broken, and was never afterwards restored. The emperor received letters of congratulation from all the viceroys of the empire, including Nizam-ool-Moolk, and from all the inferior officers, as well as from the chiefs of the European factories, and for a time it appeared that the revolution had been the precursor of a long and peaceful reign; nor at this period of profound tranquillity did it seem as if any element of serious danger or apprehension existed.

The vizier wounded and taken prisoner.

Victory of the Emperor Mahomed Shah.

He receives public congratulations.

On January 10, 1721, Mahomed Ameen Khan died; and Nizam ool-Moolk, whose resistance to the Syed brothers had laid the foundation of the successful revolution, was created vizier in his stead. He was not for the present, however, able to leave the Deccan in order to assume office; and it soon became evident that the appearances of peace in the empire were delusive. Ajeet Singh, rana of Jondhpoor, had been a partisan of the Syeds, and watching his opportunity, possessed himself of Ajmere. No offensive movement against him was undertaken, and he was pacified or restrained by being allowed to retain it, and being made governor of Agra.

Nizam-ool-Moolk becomes vizier.

Rebellion of Ajeet Singh.

This weakness in the executive power was temporarily redeemed by the arrival of Nizam-ool-Moolk at Dehly, on January 18, 1722. He found the emperor given up to sensual pleasures, surrounded by favourites, whose only care was to gratify him; and, as might be supposed, little attention being paid to the affairs of State. Nizam-ool-Moolk was of too proud a disposition to conciliate the emperor, and was probably meditating his final proceedings; for the emperor and his courtiers were already supporting a rival against him in Hyder Kooly Khan, the late governor of Guzerat. The vizier was too astute a statesman to hesitate between preserving a difficult and distasteful office at court, and taking up an entirely independent position. On October 9, 1722, having been appointed to the viceroyalty of

Nizam-ool-Moolk arrives at Dehly.

Intrigues.

Nizam-ool-Moolk marches to Guzerat.

Guzerat, in addition to that of the Deccan, he marched southwards. In Guzerat he encountered a show of opposition from the troops of Hyder Kooly Khan, the late viceroy; but this having been overcome, he left his maternal uncle in charge of the province, and returned to Dehly, after a comparatively brief absence, in July 1723.

And returns to Dehly.

At the court of Shao some important changes had taken place. Ballajee Wishwanáth had died soon after his return from Dehly, and had been succeeded as Péshwah by his son, Bajee Ráo, who, possessing all his father's qualities as a statesman, was superior to him in ambitious design, and efficiency as a predatory commander in the field. Bajee Ráo at once appreciated the profound sagacity of his father's arrangements with Nizam-ool-Moolk, and the value of the confirmation by the emperor of the Mahratta national rights, and he soon succeeded in animating Shao, and with him the chief leaders of the Mahratta State, to a prosecution of similar demands upon the whole of the imperial provinces. He did not fail to see in Nizam-ool-Moolk's return to the Deccan, the future, and perhaps speedy, dismemberment of the Moghul empire. The Mahratta rights over the Deccan and Carnatic were secured; why should they not be spread to Hindostan? 'Let us strike,' he said to Shao, 'at the trunk of the withering tree; the branches must fall of themselves.' This policy was adopted with enthusiasm by Shao and by the Mahratta leaders, and the attempt was only delayed till a fitting opportunity should present itself.

Mahratta court: death of Ballajee Wishwanáth.

His son, Bajee Ráo, succeeds as Péshwah.

His measures.

The speedy success of Nizam-ool-Moolk in securing the government of Guzerat, surprised and mortified the emperor and his party at Dehly. It was an undertaking which they had supposed would have occupied much time, and might, as they hoped, have procured the vizier's destruction. His return to Dehly and resumption of office were least of all contemplated, and his presence became more than ever insupportable. His austere manners and habits, his attempts to wean the emperor from the debasing influences by which he was surrounded, were passively resisted; but the demeanour of the courtiers, and indeed of the emperor himself, was so unmistakably adverse, that, finding his situation daily more difficult to endure, he feigned sickness, and shortly afterwards tendered his resignation of the ministry. This was accepted with seeming regret, and he was permitted to depart to his viceroyalty of the Deccan on October 21, 1723, having received the new title of Asof Jáh, and a patent as lieutenant of the empire.

Effects of Nizam-ool-Moolk's return to Dehly.

He resigns office as vizier, and returns to the Deccan.

CHAPTER XXX.

OF THE REIGN OF THE EMPEROR MAHOMED SHAH (*continued*), 1723 TO 1738.

Plot against Nizam-ool-Moolk.

NIZAM-OOL-MOOLK had no sooner departed from Dehly, than a plot was formed against him by the emperor and his courtiers, which was of serious import; and the leisurely manner in which he moved through Malwah, allowed ample time for its preparation. Moobariz Khan, a brave and ambitious officer, well known to be inimical to Nizam-ool-Moolk, was the governor of Hyderabad and the Carnatic, with a fine army at his disposal; and the emperor wrote to him with his own hand, denouncing Nizam-ool-Moolk as a traitor who contemplated establishing his own independence, and urging him to attack and kill the viceroy by any means in his power, transmitting at the same time a new patent as viceroy of the Deccan for himself, to be used in case of success. Nizam-ool-Moolk did not reach Aurungabad till July 1724, by which time Moobariz Khan had made his preparations. Some correspondence passed between the parties, which led to no result, and finally he marched upon Aurungabad, near which, at the village of Shukur Khéra, between the city and the fort of Dowlatabad, a bloody battle was fought on October 2. In this action Moobariz Khan was slain with two of his sons, and his troops, for the most part, submitted to the conqueror. The victory was duly reported to the emperor by Nizam-ool-Moolk, who sent his adversary's head as that of a rebel who had conspired against the State, and had suffered a rebel's death; but there can be little doubt that Nizam-ool-Moolk was, at the time, fully aware of the emperor's treachery, and held himself virtually absolved from his allegiance. Marching southwards, he gained possession of Golcondah and Hyderabad, and the whole of the southern provinces submitted without a blow.

Moobariz Khan advances to attack Nizam-ool-Moolk.

Battle of Shukur Khéra.

Moobariz Khan is killed in action.

Submission of the southern provinces.

On receiving news of his success against Moobariz Khan, the emperor had deprived Nizam-ool-Moolk of the viceroyalty of Guzerat and Malwah, to which other officers were appointed; but Hamed Khan, the uncle of the viceroy, who had been left in charge of the province, although recommended by his nephew to give up his office, declined to do so, and was for a while successful, being aided by two Mahratta chieftains, at the head of a large body of cavalry. Sur Boolund Khan, however, who had been viceroy of Kabool, and was now transferred to Guzerat, was a skilful general, and Hamed Khan and his Mahratta allies were ultimately defeated, and driven out of the province; but, as the price of the Mahratta assistance, Hamed Khan had assigned to his allies the chouth and sur-déshmookhee of Guzerat, which had been only partially levied by marauding parties before. This became a new charge upon the revenue, and one which Sur Boolund Khan, his successor, was ultimately obliged to admit. The grants of chouth, &c. obtained by the Péshwah from Sur Boolund Khan, were made over to Peelajee Gáikwar, one of the Mahratta commanders, for collection as an hereditary right, and hence acquired a power unknown before. It was thus that the national Mahratta rights, the collection of which was confided to different chieftains, as they progressed, became, as it were, private as well as national property; for a portion of the collections was assigned to them for the maintenance of their troops, and a means of collection ensured which was never relaxed. These parties, instead of visiting the provinces over which their rights extended, at particular periods only, now settled in them; spread their agents over them, and thus gradually and insidiously extended the Mahratta influence far beyond its original bounds.

Hamed Khan defeated in Guzerat.

Peelajee Gáikwar obtains the grant of chouth of Guzerat.

Extension of Mahratta power.

Meantime Nizam-ool-Moolk endeavoured to pursue his old policy of sowing dissension among the Mahrattas, and securing himself thereby; but in Bajee Ráo, the Péshwah or chief minister of Shao, he had found a wily and successful opponent. Nizam-ool-Moolk's intrigues for the payment of a fixed sum, instead of the indefinite claims of chouth, which had been almost successful at the court of Shao, during the Péshwah's absence, were completely foiled on his return; and as Nizam-ool-Moolk had accepted the aid of the Kolapoor party, the Péshwah retaliated by pressing the claims on Guzerat, and distressing Nizam-ool-Moolk so effectively in the field in 1729, that he was able to make his own terms. While engaged in these operations, the forces of Sumbhajee, of Kolapoor, were defeated by those of Shao, and he was obliged to resign his pretensions to the Mahratta throne, and content himself with Kolapoor and the territory assigned to it. In 1730, Dhabáry, a Mahratta chieftain of much power, had been excited by Nizam-ool-Moolk to oppose the Péshwah in Malwah and Guzerat; but Bajee Ráo did not give him time to advance into the Deccan, or to effect a junction with Nizam-ool-Moolk: he met him near Baroda, and in the action fought on April 1,

Nizam-ool-Moolk's intrigues are unsuccessful.

Dhabáry defeated by the Péshwah, and killed in action.

1731, completely defeated him; Dhabáry was killed in the action. By this victory not only were the plans of Nizam-ool-Moolk completely overthrown, but Bajee Ráo became, without a rival, the supreme minister of the Mahratta State. At this juncture, Nizam-ool-Moolk probably expected that the arms of Rajah Ráo would have been directed against himself; but the Péshwah's policy was not so much directed to the humiliation of his rival, as to the extension of the Mahratta predatory system; and at an interview which was brought about between them, Nizam-ool-Moolk received assurances of good-will on the part of the Péshwah while he did not interrupt the Mahratta designs on Northern India. It is questionable whether this nefarious agreement was ever committed to writing, in the form of a treaty; but the historians of the period are unanimous in declaring it was made, and the conduct of Nizam-ool-Moolk justifies the belief. Up to 1732, many portions of Malwah had been laid under contribution by the Mahratta leaders, and the families of Powár, Sindia and Holkar had, like that of the Gáikwar, received allotments of the national rights of collection. The son of Dhabáry was confirmed in the rights of Guzerat, having Peelajee Gáikwar as his hereditary deputy; and thus four powerful Mahratta chieftains were established on the southern frontier of the imperial dominions north of the Nerbudda, prepared to extend their claims even to the capital.

Agreement between Nizam-ool-Moolk and the Péshwah.

After the agreement with Nizam-ool-Moolk, the Péshwah did not long delay the commencement of his movements. Sur Boolund Khan, in consequence of his assignment of the chouth, had been superseded in Guzerat by Rajah Abhy Singh; but this person—a mere court-favourite—proved less able to check the Mahrattas than his predecessor; and his having procured the assassination of Peelajee Gáikwar only served to exasperate the rest of the Mahrattas in the province more strongly against him. They not only aroused the predatory tribes of the province to rebellion, but invaded Rajah Abhy Singh's own territory, obliging him to return to it, and abandon Guzerat to themselves. In Malwah, Mahomed Khan Bungush was the imperial viceroy, and the Péshwah's first movement was against him. Bungush was then conducting a campaign against the Rajah of Bundelkund; and was surprised and driven into a small fort by the Péshwah, whence he was only rescued by the bravery of a body of his own Rohilla clansmen. For the service rendered to him by the Péshwah, the rajah conferred upon him the territory of Jhansee and some estates in Kalpee, which are memorable as the first possessions obtained by the Mahrattas in Hindostan.

The Péshwah's measures.

The court at Dehly was too weak to offer any resistance, and Bajee Ráo's claims grew in proportion. They would probably have been pressed in force, but for the appointment of Rajah Jey Singh as viceroy of Malwah, who induced the Péshwah to agree to be content with the executive government of Malwah—an arrangement which was confirmed by the emperor. This, however, was a material step gained in Bajee Ráo's policy; he had not only established the national claims over Malwah, and left four powerful chiefs to collect them, but had obtained the actual administration of the province. Contented with this arrangement for the present, Bajee Ráo returned to the Deccan, having directed Holkar to continue the predatory invasion of the imperial territory during his absence. This service was performed with alacrity. Not only did the Mahratta horse penetrate as far as Agra, but levied contributions in Northern Guzerat, which had been hitherto exempt from their presence. A great expedition under Mozuffer Khan was sent from Dehly against him, but eluding, yet constantly harassing, the Moghul army, Holkar pursued his own course, and Mozuffer Khan eventually returned to the capital.

Weakness of the Dehly court.

The Péshwah obtains the government of Malwah.

Mahratta predatory operations.

Bajee Ráo, having completed his arrangements in the Deccan, recommenced his proceedings against the imperial government in 1736, by pressing his demands for patents confirming the Mahratta dues on Malwah and Guzerat. It is probable the emperor would have granted them; but the Moghul nobility at court protested against the humiliation, and the measure was delayed. This, as might have been foreseen—if the Mahratta character had been understood—only produced higher demands, and they assumed very formidable dimensions. Malwah was to be given up, with many other forts and cities, and the chouth, &c. of the north-west provinces. With these terms it was impossible to comply: and a compromise was made by which Bajee Ráo obtained an additional right of two per cent. on the revenues of the Deccan, with some other minor privileges. This new grant might, it was supposed, and perhaps hoped at court, either lead Bajee Ráo into war with Nizam-ool-Moolk, on whose territory the new tax was imposed, or become the means of the viceroy's reconciliation with the emperor. Bajee Ráo, however, made no attempt to carry out the collection of the new grants, and still preserved his original claims. Holkar was levying contributions in Bundelkund, and as far as the borders of Oude; and the court of Dehly, finding Bajee Ráo impracticable, determined, if possible, to expel him from Malwah by force, and drive the Mahrattas across the

Mahratta demands on Malwah and Guzerat.

The imperial forces attack the Péshwah and Holkar.

Nerbudda. With this view, Khan Dowrán, and Kummur-ood-deen Khan, two of the best imperial generals, marched against Bajee Ráo from Dehly. Just at this juncture, Holkar, who had been plundering on the Jumna, was sharply attacked by Saadut Khan, the viceroy of Oude, and forced to retreat, and the viceroy moved on to Agra, writing a magniloquent despatch to the emperor of his successes. He then effected a junction with Khan Dowrán's army, which was near Muttra. Bajee Ráo, in no degree dismayed by these events, eluded the grand armies before their junction, and marching directly upon Dehly, at the rate of forty miles a day, pitched his camp near the suburbs. The emperor and his court, in the absence of the army, were naturally alarmed; but a force of 8,000 horse was sent out under Mozuffer Khan, which was defeated by the Mahrattas with heavy loss. The main army had meanwhile advanced; and after a brief and unimportant skirmish with a portion of it, Bajee Ráo drew off his forces to the southward, obtaining, however, from Khan Dowrán, a renewal of the promise of the government of Malwah, and of the payment of thirteen lacs of rupees, or 130,000*l.*, for his expenses.

Bajee Ráo Péshwah reaches Dehly.

The imperial cavalry defeated.

Bajee Ráo retires on payment of his expenses.

During this campaign the emperor had made profuse promises to Nizam-ool-Moolk, in order to induce him to come to court, and to secure his assistance; for it was more than ever apparent that the empire was seriously menaced by the Mahrattas; and leaving his son in charge of the Deccan, Nizam-ool-Moolk arrived at Dehly on June 22, 1737. His great age and some consequent infirmity, induced him to request that other commanders should be employed against the Mahrattas, whose operations he could direct; but the faction of Khan Dowrán was inimical to his remaining in authority at the capital: and an army having been assembled, he assumed the command, and towards the end of 1737, advanced into Malwah at the head of the imperial forces, and numerous contingents of feudatories. No sooner was the news of this movement known at Sattara, than Bajee Ráo prepared to meet it. He assembled an army of 80,000 men, chiefly cavalry: and rapidly crossing the Nerbudda, found his adversary in a strong position near Bhopál. A partial action ensued, with little advantage to either side; but Bajee Ráo, perceiving no indication of active movement on the part of the Moghuls, now succeeded in surrounding and establishing a complete blockade of their camp. If the Péshwah's earnest call upon other officers of the Mahratta State had been responded to in

The emperor negotiates with Nizam-ool-Moolk,

who returns to Dehly.

War between the emperor of Germany and the Turks

Nizam-ool-Moolk takes command of the army.

Bajee Ráo advances to meet him.

The Moghul camp at Bhopál is surrounded.

the spirit he made them—'that now was the time for all to unite and to deliver one effectual blow for the mastery of the Deccan'—there can be little doubt that Nizam-ool-Moolk's army must have been annihilated, or have surrendered at discretion; for there was no hope of relief either from Dehly or the south. As it was, Nizam-ool-Moolk made an attempt to retreat; but he could only move three miles a day, and having endured constant harassing attacks for twenty-four days, he halted at Duraee Suraee, near Seronje, and on February 11, 1738, entered into a convention with the Péshwah, by which the whole of Malwah and the territory between the Nerbudda and the Chumbul rivers were to be ceded to the Mahratta State in perpetual sovereignty; and a sum of fifty lacs of rupees—500,000*l.*—paid as the expenses of the war from the imperial treasury. At this price Nizam-ool-Moolk purchased exemption from further molestation, and was suffered to return to Dehly, where another danger, more imminent and more terrible than the Mahrattas, was to be endured.

Nizam-ool-Moolk retreats.

Convention of Seronje.

The Russians invade the Crimea.

CHAPTER XXXI.

OF THE REIGN OF THE EMPEROR MAHOMED SHAH (*concluded*), 1738 TO 1748.

THE new danger which threatened the empire at this crisis was the invasion of Nadir Shah, king of Persia. It is beyond the province of this work to detail the origin or the progress of this most remarkable man; but at the period under illustration—1737-38—he had been engaged in a campaign against Kandahar and Kabool. The latter city had fallen easily before the conqueror of Kandahar; and occupied by the affairs of the Mahrattas, the emperor had paid no attention to those of his Afghan provinces—a distant, and perhaps then considered an unimportant, dependency. Suddenly, however, news reached Dehly that the Persian army had descended the passes, had thrown a bridge of boats across the Indus, and was in full march upon the capital. Various reasons are given by the native historians of the period for this invasion by Nadir Shah. He had written letters to the emperor, which were not noticed; his messengers had been put to death, and the like: but the true cause, there can be little doubt, was the condition of India at that period. Even before the Mahrattas, the spirit of the old Moghul chivalry had declined; the court was corrupt and

Invasion of Nadir Shah.

effeminate; and to a successful general like Nadir Shah, there would have appeared no obstacle which could weigh in comparison with the chances of success. There was little resistance offered in the Punjâb: some of the troops stationed there fell back upon the capital, where the emperor assembled an army, to which Nizam-ool-Moolk contributed his forces; Saadut Khan was called up from Oude, and a camp was formed at Kurnaul, which was intrenched.

Preparations to oppose him.

Nadir Shah advanced leisurely. He had crossed the Indus in November 1738, and did not reach Kurnaul till February 1739, when he immediately attacked the imperial army, and easily defeated it, with the loss of a mere handful of men. The emperor immediately submitted, and through the instrumentality of Nizam-ool-Moolk, was conducted to the tent of the conqueror, and received with courtesy. Negotiations ensued, and Nadir was apparently content with the promise of two millions sterling, when Saadut Khan, jealous of Nizam-ool-Moolk, declared he could pay more himself, and that the treasures of the kingdom were beyond computation. Nadir Shah marched with the emperor very leisurely to Dehly, where they arrived in March, and occupied the city with a portion of his troops. Two days afterwards, a report was circulated that Nadir Shah was dead, whereupon the people attacked the Persians furiously, and many of them were killed. As he could not stop the tumult, Nadir Shah, enraged by the continued slaughter of his men, gave orders for a general massacre, which continued for some time, and was attended by a lamentable and indiscriminate destruction of all classes of the people. Quiet being at length restored, the work of plunder was deliberately commenced, and was continued for fifty-eight days. It extended from the emperor's palace and the nobility, to the lowest ranks of the people. The amount of booty carried off by the Persians is variously estimated at from 9,000,000*l.* to 30,000,000*l.* sterling, besides the celebrated peacock-throne, which Tavernier valued at 6,000,000*l.*, but which, according to the 'Life of Nadir Shah,' does not appear to have been worth more than 2,000,000*l.* The king's share, according to the author of his Memoirs, was 15,000,000*l.* sterling, and perhaps a similar sum was secured by his officers and men. On leaving Dehly, Nadir Shah presented Mahomed Shah with his crown as emperor of India, and seated him on his throne; but he annexed to his own dominions all the western provinces of the empire beyond the passes, with Mooltan and Sinde. Nadir Shah did not forget the assertion of

Nadir Shah defeats the imperial forces.

Submission of the emperor.

Nadir Shah proceeds to Dehly.

The Persians are attacked.

Massacre by Nadir Shah, and subsequent plunder.

Saadut Khan, that it would be a trifle to him to pay 2,000,000*l.* sterling. He was obliged to send for it, and shortly afterwards, in dread, as was reported, of torture and indignity, took poison and died. On May 15, 1739, Nadir Shah left Dehly by the route he had come: but it was long before the city recovered from the desolation he had caused.

If Bajee Ráo had been near Dehly when Nadir Shah arrived, it is not improbable that he would have joined the emperor in the defence of the empire; and could he have done so, or the Mahratta troops have been employed as auxiliaries, Nadir Shah's invasion would probably have had a very different conclusion. Bajee Ráo was very sensible of a common danger to all; but as soon as he felt assured that the Persians were really departed, he again commenced his demands, and although he had not received the imperial patent for Malwah, he strengthened himself, by making alliances with all the Hindoo princes, both in Rajpootana and Bundelkund. Nizam-ool-Moolk, finding his position irksome at Dehly, left his son, Gheias-ood-deen, in charge of his offices, and returned to the Deccan, where the conduct of his second son, Nasir Jung, had been for some time of a suspicious nature. Before his arrival, Bajee Ráo had had to encounter opposition from two of his own officers—Bhóslay, who held Berar, and Dhabáry of Guzerat. Bhóslay had demanded as his right the collections of chouth, or, in other words, the plunder, of Allahabad and Oudh; but this Bajee Ráo reserved for himself, and induced Bhóslay to undertake an expedition to the Carnatic. When he was gone, the Péshwah attacked Nasir Jung, the son of Nizam-ool-Moolk; but he gained no advantage, and a peace was ultimately concluded between them. Bajee Ráo was now discontented; he had powerful enemies at Shao's court, he was deeply in debt, and looked to plunder to reimburse himself. Under these circumstances he had contemplated a new campaign in Hindostan, and was proceeding thither, when he died in his camp, on the Nerbudda, on April 28, 1740. If his father had thoroughly comprehended and laid the foundation of the Mahratta predatory power, Bajee Ráo had carefully worked out his policy. He would accept of no commutations in money or in territory for the national demands, and he had enormously increased them; while on all sides the predatory system had spread from province to province, till it already included the greater part of the empire. Ballajee Ráo, his eldest son, succeeded to his office as Péshwah, in August 1740; his second son, Rugonath Ráo, afterwards

Bajee Ráo renews his demands.

Nizam-ool-Moolk returns to the Deccan.

Mahratta parties.

Bajee Ráo's position.

His death.

Frederick III. king of Prussia.

Character and acts of Bajee Ráo.

Ballajee Ráo succeeds as Péshwah.

received the support of the English, and an illegitimate son, Shumshére Bahadur, who was brought up as a Mahomedan, was provided for by the estates in Bundelkund.

Rughoojee Bhóslay, who had been diverted from his purpose of a campaign against Bengal by the late Péshwah, had proceeded to the south, and was besieging Trichinopoly when he heard the news of Bajee Ráo's death. As it was his object to oppose the election of Ballajee, he proceeded to Sattara; but the appointment took place notwithstanding, and he returned to Trichinopoly, which surrendered on March 26, 1741; and Chunda Sahib, in whose possession it had been, was sent as a prisoner to Sattara. But Rughoojee was by no means disposed to forego his designs upon Bengal and Bahar, and directed his minister, Bhaskur Punt, to attack those provinces from Berar. On the other hand, Bhaskur Punt had been invited by Meer Hubeeb, the minister of Moorshid Kooly Khan, who had been defeated in Bengal by Aliverdy Khan, to attack the province in his master's interests: and taking advantage of the Péshwah's absence from Malwah, he invaded Bahar in 1742, defeated Aliverdy Khan, whom he reduced to sore straits, and would have retreated, satisfied with the plunder he had obtained, but for the representations of Meer Hubeeb, who had escaped from Aliverdy's camp and joined him. As a proof of what might be obtained by plunder in Bengal, Meer Hubeeb, taking with him a detachment of Mahratta horse, marched rapidly upon the city of Moorshidabad, extorted two millions and a half sterling from the banking-house of Juggut Sett, and returned with his booty to the Mahratta camp. Thus stimulated, Bhaskur Punt remained during the monsoon at Cutwah and Hooghly, levying contributions, though unable to cross the Ganges. But Aliverdy Khan was not idle. Collecting all the troops he could obtain, he crossed the Hooghly, and attacking the Mahrattas with vigour, drove them out of the province into the forests of Orissa, whence they returned to Berar. Rughoojee Bhóslay had by this time returned from the Carnatic with his army, and at once proceeded to the succour of his minister; and a second Mahratta invasion of Bahar and Bengal was thus imminent.

Proceedings of Rughoojee Bhóslay.

He attacks Bengal.

Charles VII. emperor of Germany.

Bhaskur Punt invades Bahar.

Plunder of Moorshidabad.

Aliverdy Khan attacks the Mahrattas.

In 1741 Ballajee Ráo renewed his father's demands upon Malwah, claiming the execution of the emperor's promises, made upon the treaty with Nizam-ool-Moolk; and as soon as he could be spared from his civil duties at Sattara, proceeded into Malwah, and encamped near the Nerbudda. Before his arrival, Dunnajee Gáikwar, instigated by

Ballajee Ráo advances into Malwah.

Rughoojee Bhóslay, had entered Malwah from Guzerat, in order to divert the Péshwah's attention from his proposed expedition to the eastward; but, being unable to effect anything, retired into his own province. The Péshwah, now at liberty, renewed his negotiations at court, supported by Nizam-ool-Moolk and Rajah Jey Singh; but beyond doubtful promises in regard to Malwah, and an honorary present of a magnificent character from the emperor, the settlement of his claims made no progress. It was at this juncture that Bhaskur Punt, on behalf of Rughoojee Bhóslay, made his irruption into Bengal, and the emperor and his councillors turned to the Péshwah to assist them in the emergency. He promptly accepted the commission, and marched for Bahar, where he joined Aliverdy Khan in time to oppose Rughoojee, who had advanced from Orissa, and was already in Bengal. Rughoojee at once retreated before the Péshwah, but was pursued and severely defeated. There could be no question that the Péshwah had saved Bengal; and having returned to Malwah, he received the long-desired patent of appointment—not, however, as an independent ruler, but as the deputy of the prince imperial. This point having been gained, the Péshwah returned to Sattara, where a new difficulty awaited him. Rughoojee Bhóslay's party at court was strong; and it became a question whether it should be reduced by force, or attached by conciliatory measures. Rughoojee professed humble submission to Shao; but it was clear that he aimed at possessing the national rights, as claimed and levied in Bengal, and would be content with nothing less. The Péshwah therefore submitted, reserving to himself the rights of collection over the territories north of the Nerbudda and Mahanuddee rivers. It will be understood, therefore, that the collections of the national chouth and other dues were now divided as follows: the Péshwah held Malwah and the central and northern provinces; the Gáikwar, Guzerat; Bhóslay, Berar and Bengal. No change was made in the southern provinces, which had already been portioned out to other officers.

And renews his negotiations at court.

Ballajee Ráo opposes Rughoojee Bhóslay,

who is defeated.

The Péshwah's reward.

The right of chouth in Bengal assigned to Rughoojee.

Distribution of the right of collection of chouth.

It has already been stated that Nizam-ool-Moolk had left his son, Nasir Jung, in charge of his government of the Deccan; and for some time his conduct was all that could be desired. He had exchanged a sharp passage of arms with the redoubtable Bajee Ráo Péshwah with credit, and had preserved his father's dominions from Mahratta encroachments; but he was not superior to temptation, and his father's great age induced his companions to reckon upon his speedy demise

Rebellion of Nasir Jung in the Deccan.

and to advise him to secure his own position. Nizam-ool-Moolk, however, though aged, was yet vigorous in body and mind, and when written remonstrances had ceased to have effect, repaired to the Deccan. He arrived in 1741, and received his son's submission, to all appearances sincerely given; but the stern character of the old statesman induced his son to keep apart from him, and he was persuaded by Futteh Yáb Khan, one of his companions, to resort to arms, in order to extort from his father what could not apparently be won by moderation. Having surprised the fort of Malkhair, Futteh Yáb Khan was joined by Nasir Jung, and they proceeded to Aurungabad, where Nizam-ool-Moolk, though in some degree taken at disadvantage, was yet able to oppose them. Nasir Jung's troops were defeated on July 23, 1742, and he himself taken prisoner, and the scene, as characteristic of the times, and the persons engaged, is thus described by the Mahratta historian:—'Finding his troops give way, Nasir Jung impetuously charged his father's standard, pushed onwards towards his elephant, and slew three of his bravest attendants one after the other. The driver of his own elephant being killed, Nasir Jung sprang into his place; when his brother-in-law, Mutawussil Khan, approaching him, drew an arrow to the head, which must have transfixed him, had not his son, who sat on the same elephant, stayed his hand and saved his uncle's life. At that moment, Syed Lushkur Khan, an officer of experience, who knew Nasir Jung, and the pride as well as the generosity of his disposition, pushed his elephant close by the side of his, saluted him, and respectfully made room for him; when, overcome by the act of courtesy, Nasir Jung took the place, and was thus carried prisoner into Aurungabad.' But he was received affectionately by his father, who, as a precautionary measure, kept him confined to the fort of Kandhar, near Beeder, for some time afterwards. Having restored tranquillity, Nizam-ool-Moolk proceeded to Hyderabad, and thence to the Carnatic, the affairs of which had become much disordered; and in August 1743 Moorary Ráo, who had occupied the greater part of the territory on the part of the Mahrattas, was confirmed as chief of Gooty, and withdrew his troops from other districts. Anwur-ood-deen was established as governor of the southern provinces at Arcot, and Mozuffer Jung, Nizam-ool-Moolk's grandson, was appointed to the charge of the northern Carnatic, with his head-quarters at Adony and Beejapoor.

Arrangements in the Carnatic.

Freed from apprehension from Nizam-ool-Moolk, the Mahrattas were soon in active movement. Rughoojee Bhóslay dispatched Bhaskur Punt with 20,000 horse, in the close of 1744, again to Bengal, where, soon after his arrival he was,

Mahratta movements.

invited to an entertainment by Aliverdy Khan, and, with a number of his officers, basely and treacherously murdered; one only, Rughoojee Gáikwar, escaped; who, assuming command, led the remainder of the army back to Berar. Rughoojee himself, encouraged by the intelligence of a serious revolt against Aliverdy Khan, now invaded Bengal, and demanded 30,000,000 rupees, or 3,000,000*l.* sterling, as compensation for the murder of Bhaskur Punt, and as his price for sparing the country; but when the rains had ceased, Aliverdy Khan resumed the offensive, defeated the Mahratta army, and obliged them to retire. While these transactions were in progress, the Péshwah visited Malwah, and renewed his communications with the emperor; but was met with censure for not having interfered to check Rughoojee; and finding nothing was to be gained for the present, he returned to Sattara, and continued those reforms in the civil administration of the country, which, most urgently needed, were the measures on which his best fame rests.

Murder of Bhaskur Punt.

Rughoojee Bhóslay invades Bengal.

Is defeated by Aliverdy Khan.

A new danger was now threatening India from the west. After the death of Nadir Shah, the Afghan States had been united as a monarchy by Ahmed Khan, the chief of the Abdallies, who, young, ambitious, and fond of war, at once turned his attention to India as the best field for plunder and conquest. In 1747 he advanced into the Punjâb, and laid it under contribution; and, assisted by the Moghul viceroy in charge of the province, who had rebelled against the emperor, gained possession of Lahore and Mooltan. In this emergency, the emperor despatched his eldest son, the Prince Ahmed, with all the troops that could be collected, about 12,000 men: and, unable to oppose the Afghans in the field, he entrenched himself near Sirhind. Here he was attacked by the invaders in March 1748, who, repulsed in several desperate attempts to storm the camp, were finally defeated and pursued with heavy slaughter on their way back to the passes. The emperor, meanwhile, had been taken seriously ill, and expired at Dehly about a month after the victory of Sirhind, that is, in April 1748. He had reigned twenty-eight years, and was succeeded by his son Ahmed, under the title of Ahmed Shah. Taking advantage of the confusion inseparable from the event, Ahmed Shah Abdallee had meanwhile returned, and exacted from the Moghul viceroy of the Punjâb an engagement to pay him tribute for the future. Very shortly after the emperor's death, that is, on June

Danger of an Afghan invasion.

Ahmed Shah Abdalee advances into the Punjâb.

Admiral Hawke's victory.

The Afghans are defeated by the Imperial troops.

Death of the Emperor Mahomed Shah.

His son Ahmed succeeds.

Death of Nizam-ool-Moolk.

19, the great Nizam-ool-Moolk, Asof Jáh, died at Boorhanpoor, on his way, as he purposed, to Dehly, having attained the wonderful age of 104 years. He had been nominated to the office of vizier by the new emperor, but his age and his distance from Dehly, induced him to decline the offer.

BOOK V.

CHAPTER I.

THE PROGRESS OF THE ENGLISH (*continued from Chapter XIII., Book IV.*), 1613 TO 1674.

THE permission to trade at Surat, given to Captain Best in 1613, was followed up by the embassy of Sir Thomas Roe, sent by James I. in 1615 to the Emperor Jehángeer, by whom the first permission was extended to all India. Not long before his arrival at Surat, another naval engagement had occurred with the Portuguese, in which they had been defeated; and they had declared war against the emperor, which rendered an alliance with the English of more account.

Embassy of Sir Thomas Roe to the Moghul court.

While Sir Thomas was at the Moghul court, a new joint-stock capital was subscribed for in England, the largest which had been collected. It amounted to 1,600,000*l.*, with thirty-six ships. This armament, as well as the wealth of the company, excited much apprehension among the Dutch, both in Holland and in the eastern settlements, and was productive of many jealousies and negotiations between the governments. They were, however, smoothed over, and arrangements were made by which the English were to receive at Bantam a certain portion of the local produce of spices. The convention, however promising it might be in Europe, and upon paper, did not act well in practical application. On the contrary, matters grew worse, till they came to a climax at Amboyna, in 1623, when, on February 27, twelve Englishmen were executed for an alleged conspiracy to take possession of the castle. The indignation with which the news was received in England was immense; but James I. did little to repair the mischief or obtain satisfaction, and the trade of the company with the eastern settlements was much interrupted. In India, however, they were more successful. In 1628, a factory was established at

New capital subscribed in England.

Apprehensions of the Dutch.

Execution of English at Amboyna.

Factory established at Armegoor, near Madras.

Armegoor, about seventy miles north of Madras, but it was not well suited for trade, and Masulipatam was preferred, as more immediately adjacent to the seat of native manufacture. The establishment of Armegoor is, however, memorable as the first place fortified by the English in India.

Opposition of Charles I. to the company.

King Charles I. proved inimical to the affairs of the company. He was not only indifferent to any settlements with the Dutch, but he questioned the charter privileges of the company to such an extent, that they were compelled to bring their case under the immediate notice of Parliament.

Accusations.

The accusations of the king against the company were not, however, without foundation. It was notorious that their payment of their servants was insufficient; and that the amount of illicit private trade, at which it was believed the company connived, was enormous; and it is questionable whether the permission to increase the amount of tonnage granted for lawful private trade, was not in effect a direct increase of the evil. Nor were other elements of loss without effect.

The company's trade with Persia established.

The Dutch had entered into a spirited competition at Surat, and they had nearly extinguished the eastern trade of the English. In 1632, however, the company obtained important privileges from the King of Persia, Shah Sofy, for trade at Gambroon in the Persian Gulf, and the factory at Masulipatam was re-established under a treaty with the King of Golcondah.

Treaty with Golcondah.

Trade of Bengal opened.

In 1634, the Emperor Shah Jehán granted a firman, by which the trade of the whole of Bengal was opened to the English, and a factory was founded at Piply, near the mouth of the Hooghly. Under these successes, the factory at Bantam was once more established as a presidency. Charles I. had, however, by no means forgiven the company for its attempt at independence of royal control; and in 1634, just as the Portuguese and the Dutch had come to terms, he granted a new charter to a new company.

A new company obtains a charter from Charles I.

Many charges were brought against the old; the most material of which perhaps, was, that in all their trade they had never established permanent stations or forts, and could not be depended upon for augmenting the glory of the kingdom, or extending its trade. This shallow accusation proved, however, sufficiently transparent; the truth was, that the king, in the midst of his difficulties, needed money; that a new company was willing to supply it; and that he had obtained funds from Sir Thomas Courten, the projector of the new association. No time was lost by the new company, and before the factory of Surat could be informed of the transaction that had taken place in England, they found their rivals at their doors.

In 1637, before Shah Jehán had returned to Dehly, one of the princesses was severely burned, by an accident, and her life being despaired of, an English physician was sent for from Surat, and Mr. Gabriel Boughton, the surgeon of an Indiaman, was despatched to the emperor's camp. His cure of the princess was successful, and he was desired to name his reward; when, in a noble and disinterested spirit, he would accept nothing for himself, but asked for extended privileges of trade in Bengal for his countrymen; and having obtained them, was sent across India, at the emperor's charge, to carry them out. While engaged there, he visited Ráj Mahál, where the emperor's son, Prince Shujah, had established his court; and was fortunate enough to render a second medical service of high value, and obtained permission to establish English factories at Balasore and Hooghly. Though the rival companies continued to struggle from 1635 to 1646, the establishment of the elder company in Bengal gave it considerable advantage, and in the latter year a new factory was established at Chenna-Putnum (the little city) in Madras, under permission of the Rajah, or Näik, of Chundergiri, the descendant of the Hindoo sovereigns of Beejanugger, who constructed a fort for the protection of the English traders, which mounted twelve guns, and was named by them Fort St. George.

Mr. Surgeon Boughton obtains privileges for the company's trade.

Factories at Balasore and Hooghly.

Factory at Madras.

Though the first success of the new, or Courten company, had been brilliant, it was not continued. Its proceedings became more desultory than the old, and the establishment of a mint, and use of a debased, or counterfeit coinage, gave it an evil reputation. The civil war in England, however, affected the prosperity of both companies, and both petitioned Parliament — the old for the abolition of the new; the new for free trade; but the decision of the House was very vague, and by a resolution of January 1650, one company only was to carry on the trade, though any means for the amalgamation of the Courten company does not appear to have been suggested. In the same year the company renewed their complaint against the Dutch; but war was on the point of breaking out, and its actual occurrence caused all settlement to be postponed. During its continuance, however, the Dutch obtained some important advantages over the company in India. Three ships were captured at Gambroon, in the Persian Gulf, and the trade at Surat was seriously checked; but no further mischief seems to have been done, and after the conclusion of peace in 1654, the long-pending claims of the company were submitted, with those of

The rival companies petition Parliament.

War with the Dutch.

Arbitration of the Swiss cantons.

the Dutch, to the arbitration of the Swiss cantons. The company had claimed 2,600,000*l.*, but the final award in their favour only amounted to 88,600*l.* A very keen struggle now ensued between the rival traders, which lasted several years; but being finally considered in council, it was determined that the company and the 'Merchant Adventurers' should form one joint-stock company. This decision was ratified by Cromwell, and a charter issued, which, however, has never been discovered. It was probably evident, at last, that a friendly settlement of mutual differences would be most beneficial to all parties, and no difficulty seems to have attended the adjustment of accounts. Surat was maintained as a presidency, with control over the Persian Gulf and the factories on the western coast of India. Madras, or Fort St. George, became also a presidency, with authority over the factories at Hooghly, Patna, Cossimbazar, and Balasore.

The rival companies are united under a charter.

Cromwell died in 1658, and on the restoration of Charles II. the company's affairs were improved. In 1661 they obtained a new charter, which, in addition to trading privileges, conferred upon them important political and judicial authority, with power to appoint governors; and for them to exercise British laws within their jurisdiction. They were also empowered to make war with any power not Christian; to make reprisals for losses; to build fortifications, and the like; while suppression of the trade of unauthorised persons, or interlopers, was also committed to them. Under these arrangements, the power of the company became more respected in India; and their local position, especially at Surat, considerably improved. A slight check, owing to the indiscretion of an agent in Bengal, hindered affairs there for a brief period, but was soon adjusted. By the marriage of Charles II. with the Infanta of Portugal, in June 1661, the island of Bombay was ceded to the English crown, and an expedition under the Earl of Marlborough was sent, in March 1662, to take possession of it. This was unsuccessful, inasmuch as an excess of demand of territory was made, over that named in the cession; and while the earl returned to England, the troops, under Sir Abraham Shipman, were encamped on the island of Anjedéva, the climate of which proved fatal to many soldiers and to their commanders; but Bombay was eventually taken possession of in 1664, and transferred to the East India Company in 1688, with all the powers of local government. The fortifications were then enlarged and strengthened, and the population soon rapidly increased; the admirable situation of the fort and harbour, and the strength of the place,

Charter of Charles II. extends the company's powers.

Cession of Bombay.

Bombay transferred to the company.

attracting persons of all nations, European and Asiatic. The transactions of the period, however, are singularly deficient in incidents of history; and although the French, as well as the Dutch, the Portuguese, and the Danes, held factories in India as well as the English, it does not appear that local rivalry led to any bad consequences.

In 1664, when Sivajee attacked the city of Surat, the English not only defended their own premises, but protected the property of their neighbours, and set Sivajee at defiance; and the emperor was so struck with the valour displayed, that he remitted, by a special order, one per cent. of the duties levied at the port, with exemption from transit duties. In 1670, when Sivajee renewed his predatory expedition against Surat, he did not molest the English; but, on the contrary, sought to conciliate them. In the outset of his career, he had plundered the factory of Rajapoor, in the Koncan, and committed other acts of oppression against the English; but he now respected them, and in 1674, on the occasion of his second and more formal enthronement, invited the presence of an English ambassador. Mr. Oxenden was despatched for the purpose, with whom he made a treaty by which the amount of loss was compensated, and other privileges granted.

Gallant defence of Surat.

Sivajee respects the English.

In 1673, a powerful Dutch fleet of twenty-two ships made its appearance on the western coast of India, and seriously threatened Bombay; but President Aungier, aided by a squadron of French ships, made so strong a show of defence, that the attempt to attack the place was abandoned; the Dutch succeeded, however, in intercepting the company's ships from Bengal, off Masulipatam, on August 22 of the same year, and a partial action ensued, in which one ship was sunk and two captured; the rest escaped to Madras, where they found protection. The peace of 1674 afterwards prevented further molestation, and the trade of the East India Company became extended to China about the same period.

The Dutch fleet in India.

CHAPTER II.

THE PROGRESS OF THE ENGLISH (*continued*), 1674 TO 1708.

THE struggles between Sivajee and the Seedees of Jinjeera created considerable uneasiness in Bombay in 1674. The harbour was the scene of several engagements by sea, and the neighbourhood of Salsette by land. In this

Neutrality in Mahratta affairs.

contest, the English interfered on one occasion only, when the Mahratta fleet was dislodged from their position near the island of Kenery, at the entrance to Bombay harbour; in other respects, a perfect neutrality was observed. Bombay was now much strengthened by fortifications, on which 100 pieces of cannon were mounted, and a respectable garrison of European soldiers was maintained; but they were difficult to manage in the absence of regular military law, and a mutiny occurred in 1674, which was only repressed by the firmness of the president, M. Aungier, who, blamed by some authorities for an undue exercise of power in the execution of one of the soldiers condemned to death, yet appears justified by the necessity of the case, and the importance of enforcing military discipline. In 1676, the company separated their officers into four classes. The junior class were 'writers,' who received 10*l.* sterling after the third year of their employment, and rose, after further periods of service, to be factors, junior merchants, and senior merchants; and these designations continued to the last. The retrenchments ordered at Bombay between the years 1676 and 1683, proved a source of much disquiet and danger; and it is difficult to understand upon what ground of policy they could have been persevered in. By them the garrison was reduced to an entirely inadequate number; the pay was insufficient, and the armaments and fortifications were still incomplete. Sivajee was dead, but his son, Sumbhajee, was aggressive, and engaged in war with the Moghuls. Bombay was then perpetually threatened by both parties, and must have fallen had any real attack been made on it. In 1653, Captain Keigwin, the commandant of the garrison, which consisted of only 150 European and 200 native soldiers, imprisoned Mr. John Child, the governor, and proclaimed the authority of the crown. He afterwards obtained some important privileges from Sumbhajee, and his energetic conduct and character prevented any further encroachment by the contending powers; but his proceedings were the cause of much disagreement in England, where party spirit ran high, and he was saved, perhaps by his surrender of the island to Sir Thomas Grantham, on November 19, 1684, on condition of a free pardon.

Mutiny of Bombay garrison.

Separation of civil officers into classes.

Danger of the retrenchments of expenditure.

Imprisonment of the governor by Captain Keigwin,

who surrenders to Admiral Grantham.

At this juncture, Sir Josiah Child was the head of the company in England, and became the author and director of a new policy. The presidency of Surat, a defenceless position, was removed to Bombay; his brother, Mr., now Sir John Child, was appointed to the chief command

Sir Josiah Child's policy.

by land and sea in India; and measures of retaliation were to be carried out against native powers who interfered with, or otherwise oppressed, the existing trade. Hitherto, the transactions of the company in India had been uniformly conciliatory, if not unduly submissive. Exactions of any and every description had been patiently endured from the native powers, and though a retaliative policy might easily merge into one of aggression, such consequences do not seem to have been apprehended.

Transmission of forces to India.

The company's new expedition consisted of ten ships, mounting from twelve to seventy guns; with six companies of soldiers, and one company of regular infantry, altogether about 1,000 Europeans: and the point selected for the first operations was Bengal. Chittagong was to be taken possession of, and hostilities commenced against the imperial governor of Bengal.

Captain Nicholson's proceedings.

In October 1686, Captain Nicholson, with part of the fleet, had reached the Hooghly, when the town of Hooghly was cannonaded and partly burnt. The Moghul viceroy, a timid character, struck with amazement at these proceedings, would have made peace; but the exorbitancy of the British demands rendered this impossible. The company's agent in Bengal, Mr. Job Charnock, also repulsed the viceroy's attack upon the English factory, and retaliated with considerable advantage.

Transactions in Western India; attacks on Moghul possessions.

In Western India, appearances had been kept up with the Moghul viceroy of Surat, until the result of the attack in Bengal should be known; and on receiving intelligence of the successes, Sir John Child threw off the mask. Being disappointed in his endeavour to bring off the agents at Surat, and the property in the factory, he seized a fleet of Moghul vessels in Bombay harbour, and forwarded to Surat demands upon various counts of exactions. By vessels sent from Bombay, several 'interloper' ships were captured, as well as the emperor's own vessels, conveying pilgrims to Mecca, and therefore accounted holy. It is strange now to contemplate these proceedings, and the feeble irritation of a vast power, on whose forbearance the very existence of the company depended. They were not the avowed acts of the company, or those of the English Government. The war was actually on the part of the Childs, and professed to be undertaken by the younger, on his own responsibility. Had it succeeded, Sir Josiah Child, and even the government of England, might have acknowledged it; and on receipt of the first news of success, a thousand guineas was voted to Sir John Child. But the project did not succeed.

The Emperor Aurungzebe retaliates.

The Emperor Aurungzebe was enraged at the seizure of his pilgrim ships; and, in connection with the other proceedings of the English, ordered them to be expelled from India. Attacks upon their factories followed. Mr. Charnock was forced to retire to an island named Ijellee, at the mouth of the Hooghly, where many gentlemen and soldiers perished from the insalubrity of the climate. Masulipatam and Vizagapatam were taken with some loss. The factory at Surat was seized, and the goods and stores sold; and the Seedee of Jinjeera, directed by the emperor to attack Bombay, had occupied a portion of the island, to the great annoyance and loss of the garrison. After Mr. Charnock's retreat to Ijellee, the Moghul viceroy in Bengal had opened negotiations with him and induced him to return to Chutanuttee, where a treaty was in progress; but on the arrival of Captain Heath from England with orders to persevere in the war, communication with the viceroy was suspended; all the officers of the Bengal factories were embarked on board his ships, and after cannonading Balasore, and reconnoitring Chittagong, the fleet sailed for Madras. Thus, Bengal was abandoned for the present, and the company's stations virtually reduced to Madras and Bombay.

Mr. Charnock retreats to Ijellee.

Other factories captured.

Bengal is abandoned by the English.

In fine, it became evident that the foolish policy of war, which had been so rashly commenced, could not be maintained; and the President of Bombay, in a humble petition, sued for peace, despatching two envoys to the emperor's camp at Beejapoor for the purpose. The submission of the English was gladly received by the emperor, and in 1690 another firman or edict was issued, by which, on payment of 150,000 rupees (15,000*l.*), and promises of good behaviour for the future, the former privileges of trade with all the factories were restored to them. The emperor demanded the dismissal of Sir John Child, but he had died in Bombay while the negotiations were pending.

The English sue for peace,

which is granted by the emperor.

Death of Sir John Child.

The English company, at this period, were, however, by no means the only traders from Europe. The Portuguese, notwithstanding their present obscurity, continued their traffic from Goa and Bengal. In 1664, the French had established an East India company, and about 1676, had formed a settlement at Chándernagore, on the Hooghly river. They were followed by the Dutch and the Danes, who settled at Chinsura, near Chándernagore; and on the eastern coast of India, the French had formed a powerful settlement at Pondicherry. These various trading interests no doubt interfered considerably with the company's monopoly; but they could not be resisted, and as their trade was with foreign countries, it did not affect that

Other traders to India.

The French, Dutch, and Danes establish factories.

Trade by 'interlopers.'

of the company with England. The presence of other English traders, who were supported by parties in England, and who had paid heavily to the crown for their licenses, was productive of much more embarrassment. They were called 'interlopers,' and it was as much against their proceedings, as against the native authorities of the country, that the aggressions just detailed were directed. In 1698, they had applied for a charter, and had made offers of loans to the crown on moderate interest. In India their presence was in the last degree embarrassing; and on one occasion they seized, at Surat, the officers of the factory, and made them over to the Moghul governor, while they overbid and undersold the company in the chief markets.

They apply for a charter.

A new element of discord, too, appeared in the Scotch East India Company, which had been embodied in 1617 by King James I., and now issued its licenses for free trade. The result, as might have been foreseen, was great over-trading between the rivals; the English markets were glutted with Indian produce: calicoes, chintzes and silks, and the English manufacturers, feeling the effects of the excessive importation of these goods, petitioned for their prohibition, and obtained some relief in enhanced duties. All these circumstances caused alarm, both to the interlopers and to the company; and in 1702 brought about the eventual amalgamation of all traders to India, under the appellation of the United East India Company, which was established under Queen Anne's charter.

Scotch East India Company.

Great over-trade with India follows.

Establishment of the United East India Company.

By the inventory of the company's possessions at that period, the various localities in India are more clearly detailed than elsewhere, and may be enumerated as follows: In Western India, the factories of Surat, Baroche, Ahmedabad and Swally, with Bombay and its dependencies—Anjengo, Carwar, Tellicherry and Calicut. In Persia, factories at Ispahan, Shiraz, and Gambroon. On the Coromandel coast, Fort St. George or Madras, Fort St. David, with three square miles of territory, and the factories of Cuddalore, Masulipatam, Porto Novo, Madapollam, and Vizagapatam. In Bengal, Fort William, and Chutanuttee or Calcutta, and its territory; with factories at Patna, Maldah, Dacca, Balasore, Ráj Mahál, and Cossimbazar. Six years was allowed for mutual arrangements, and the final adjustment of the financial affairs of both societies was made under an award by Earl Godolphin, dated September 29, 1708. The previous proceedings had at least checked local irregularities, and the amalgamation of interests and capital no doubt strengthened the English connection with India in a

Enumeration of the company's possessions.

Earl Godolphin's award.

The English position strengthened by the new arrangement.

very remarkable degree, at a period when continued rivalry and dissension would have been attended with most disastrous results. Aurungzebe was dead, and his empire was about to experience the convulsions of a great, but expiring dynasty.

Details of factories.

It will be evident that the position of the English had now materially increased in local as well as general power. In Western India, Bombay formed an impregnable position, highly favourable to trade; and the older factories subordinate to it were flourishing. On the Coromandel coast, Madras had grown to be a large city with a strong fort; and Negapatam, or Nág Puttun, with three square miles of territory, had been purchased from Rajah Rám, regent of the Mahrattas, and Fort St. David built on it; while the older settlements at Vizagapatam and Masulipatam, which had prospered under the protection of the kings of Golcondah, were now secured by grants from the imperial government. In Bengal, after the peace with Aurungzebe of 1690, Mr. Job Charnock had returned from Madras, and established the English factory at Chutanuttee, on the left bank of the Hooghly, which, with several adjacent villages, he was allowed to purchase. In 1698, Rahim Khan, the last of the once powerful Afghan chiefs of Bengal, rebelled, and for a time set the viceroy at defiance. The unprotected European settlements could not be assisted, and were told to make provision for their own safety; and thus the jealousy which had hitherto existed against all defences was relaxed. The French, the Dutch, and the Danes fortified their respective factories, and after the defeat of Rahim Khan by a Moghul army under the Prince Azim, and his death in the action, the English were permitted to complete the fortifications of their settlement, now called Calcutta, by the erection of Fort William, named after the reigning king of England.[1]

Calcutta established by Mr. Charnock.

Fortification of European factories in Bengal.

Fort William built.

CHAPTER III.

THE PROGRESS OF THE ENGLISH (*continued*), 1708 TO 1746.

THE events connected with the decline of the Moghul empire had little effect upon the English, and their prosperity as traders continued unimpaired. Bombay was affected for a while by the piracies of Kanhojee Angria, a Mahratta chief, who, possessed

[1] *Note.*—The student is referred to Grant's 'History of the East India Company,' Bruce's 'Annals,' Mill's 'History of India,' Orme's 'Historical Fragments,' Anderson's 'Origin of Commerce,' Stewart's 'History of Bengal,' Beveridge's 'History of India,' for details of the events of the period embraced in this chapter.—*M. T.*

of strong fortresses upon the coast, claimed tribute by sea, as his fellow-chieftains exacted it by land. He respected no flag or nation, and defied alike the English and the Portuguese. In 1722, an expedition against his fort of Colaba was undertaken by the authorities of Goa and Bombay in concert; on which occasion Commodore Matthews commanded three vessels; but the attack failed, and was not renewed, and the Mahratta piracies continued. In 1727, a fine English ship, laden with a valuable cargo, was cut off by Angria, and his death, which occurred in 1728, was esteemed a relief, especially as his sons contested his possessions. In addition to the wars occasioned by their differences, the Seedee of Jinjeera was in perpetual strife with the Péshwah, and the neighbourhood of the Bombay harbour became the scene of frequent contentions. The authorities of Bombay, however, wisely preserved their neutrality, and the settlement flourished almost beyond expectation. In 1737, the Portuguese formally espoused the cause of Sumbhajee Angria, against his brother Manajee, who was supported by the Péshwah, and this led to a war between them and the Péshwah, and to an attack by his forces upon the island of Salsette, contiguous to Bombay, which the Portuguese still retained. On that occasion, the Fort of Tannah was captured by the Mahrattas, and the war continued during the ensuing year and 1739, under the direction of Chimnajee Appa, the Péshwah's brother, who carried on his operations with much skill and vigour. The Portuguese were expelled from Salsette, and on May 16, 1739, the fort of Bassein capitulated to the Mahrattas, after a close siege which had lasted from February 17. The siege and defence of this important place were alike creditable to the bravery of both parties. The loss of the Portuguese in killed and wounded was admitted to be 800 men, while that of the besiegers was acknowledged to be upwards of 5,000. During the war, the Portuguese accused the English of assisting the Mahrattas; and there is no doubt that some shells and shot had been sold to them In other respects, they maintained a strict neutrality: though the fact of a new commercial treaty having been executed with Chimnajee Appa after the siege of Bassein was concluded, that is, in July 1739, has at best a suspicious appearance.

Piracies of Kanhojee Angria.

Death of Angria.

War between the Portuguese and Mahrattas.

Bassein taken by the Mahrattas

In Bengal, the settlement at Calcutta also continued to prosper, in spite of the convulsions of the province. Under the government of the celebrated viceroy, Moorshid Kooly Khan, the country had attained a high degree of prosperity; and upwards of a million sterling, after paying the cost of troops and management, were annually remitted to Dehly. Moorshid Kooly

Prosperity of Bengal.

died in the year 1725, and his son-in-law, Shujah-ood-deen, was nominated in his stead—but to Bengal and Orissa only, Behar being separated from the viceroyalty. During his administration, the settlement of the Ostend India Company at Bunkipoor—against which the English and Dutch had protested—was attacked by a force sent by the viceroy under the orders of the emperor, and the company's representatives obliged to withdraw permanently from Bengal. On the death of Shujah-ood-deen, who had governed Bengal with considerable ability for fourteen years, he was succeeded by his son, Serefraz Khan; but his government was weak and of short duration. Aliverdy Khan, an Afghan officer, commander of his father's troops, intrigued against him at Dehly, outbid him with the emperor, and finally secured a patent of appointment for himself. Under these circumstances, both parties resorted to war, and in an action which ensued in the month of May 1740, Serefraz Khan was totally defeated and killed. Two days afterwards the conqueror entered Moorshidabad in triumph, and took possession of the government without further opposition. He sequestered the property of the ex-viceroy's family, and, as was the custom of the period, remitted it to Dehly; and 1,000,000*l.* sterling in coin, and nearly that amount in jewels and other valuables, is evidence of the wealth which in those days was derivable from such an office as an imperial viceroyalty.

Ostend East India Company expelled.

Aliverdy Khan becomes viceroy of Bengal.

Serefraz Khan defeated and slain.

His wealth is confiscated.

Aliverdy's reign, for it can be called little else, was a vigorous one. He drove out of his territory all partizans of Serefraz Khan's party, and it has already been related how he dealt with the first Mahratta invasion; but their hold on Bengal was not a light one, and was materially assisted by the rebellion of Moostufa Khan and the Afghan troops in 1745, which they assisted. The defeat and death of Moostufa Khan for a time delayed their progress; but they returned year after year, and caused so much distress throughout Bengal, that Aliverdy Khan was eventually obliged, in 1751, to admit their demands—to cede to Rughoojee Bhóslay the province of Orissa, and to agree to pay thirteen lacs —130,000*l.*—personally as the chouth of Bengal. The English at Calcutta were perfectly neutral in all these contests—indeed, could barely defend themselves: and, often threatened by the Mahrattas, threw up around their settlement a ditch and rampart which, known under the appellation of the 'Mahratta ditch,' served for many years afterwards as the municipal boundary. The trade of the settlement seems to have been satisfactorily progressive, and the factories and other agencies

Vigour of Aliverdy Khan.

Mahratta demands admitted.

The Mahratta ditch of Calcutta.

throughout the province were unmolested; but no particular records of the period appear in any history, and it may be inferred that no events of any remarkable moment occurred.

In Madras, however, it was very different. In the year 1744, war was declared mutually between the English and French, which was destined to affect the Carnatic in a greater degree than might at first view be deemed possible. It is, however, necessary to take a brief retrospective view of Carnatic affairs, in order to understand the condition in which they stood at the period alluded to. The campaigns of Zoolficar Khan in the Carnatic, during the reign of Aurungzebe, have been already detailed. He was succeeded, on his transfer to Dehly and the northern provinces, by Dáood Khan Punnee, who made personal friends of the English at Madras, and sometimes visited them, and joined the deep carousals which were features of the period. He was removed, as had already been related, to Guzerat, and killed in the action with Hoosein Ally near Boorhanpoor, in 1715. On leaving the Carnatic, he had appointed Saadut Oolla as his deputy, who governed the provinces from 1710, to his death in 1732, with much moderation and ability. On his demise, his nephew, Dost Ally Khan, assumed the government, as it were independently; for it does not appear that the emperor, the nominal, or Nizam-ool-Moolk, the real superior, were consulted at all. The latter, however, was too deeply engaged in the political events of Dehly and the Mahrattas, to alter the succession, and had he been even disposed to interfere, it would have given rise to a remarkable contest. Dost Ally had one son, Sufdur Ally, and had married two daughters, one to Moortuza Ally Khan, the other to Chunda Sahib; and a struggle ensued for the government. While this was in progress, the Mahrattas under Rughoojee Bhóslay invaded the Carnatic, and in an action with them, Dost Ally was slain. Sufdur Ally now made terms with Rughoojee, and on condition of the payment of 1,000,000*l.* sterling, was recognised as Nawáb of the Carnatic.

Events at Madras. War between the English and French.

Administration of Zoolficar Khan.

Saadut Oolla acts as viceroy.

Dost Ally Khan succeeds.

Local contentions.

But meanwhile, Chunda Sahib, on pretext of assisting the widowed Ranee, had obtained, by treachery, possession of Trichinopoly; and Sufdur Ally was too weak to attack him. Rughoojee, therefore, returned to the Carnatic after his visit to Sattara in 1741, and renewed the siege, when Chunda Sahib was obliged to capitulate, and, as a measure of safety, was sent to Sattara. During these transactions, however, he had placed his wife and family in the French settlement of Pondicherry, under the charge of Monsieur Dupleix,

Trichinopoly capitulates to Rughoojee.

the governor; and this act led subsequently to many strange and important events. In a year after his assumption of the government, Sufdur Ally was assassinated by Moortuza Ally, who was proclaimed Nawáb; but the family of Sufdur Ally had obtained protection in the English factory of Madras, and his son, a minor, was also proclaimed as successor to his father. To put an end to these convulsions, Nizam-ool-Moolk, as has been already related, marched from Hyderabad in 1743, at the head of an overwhelming force, and, setting aside the claims of Chunda Sahib, and Moortuza Ally, appointed Anwur-ood-deen, or Anwur Sahib, to the government of the province during the minority of the son of Sufdur Ally. The young Nawáb was, however, assassinated a few years later, and Anwur-ood-deen became Nawáb, or Nabob, of the Carnatic, and was thus the founder of the family which still exists. The foregoing sketch has been introduced in order to explain the relations which existed between Anwur-ood-deen and Chunda Sahib. The former had attached himself to the English, the latter to the French; and at this juncture the war between the English and French commenced.

Sufdur Ally assassinated.

Nizam-ool-Moolk appoints Anwur Sahib to the Carnatic.

Before the declaration of war—indeed, as early as 1741—the French ministry sent an armament to India under M. Labourdonnais, who, already distinguished by his talents, and by his successful government of Bourbon and the Mauritius, was also intimately acquainted with the politics and resources of India. He was to watch the progress of events in Europe, and be ready to act against the English in case war should be declared. These preparations were known to the English ministry, who, in order to check them, sent a squadron of four ships to India under Commodore Barnet, which for some time cruised successfully in the Straits of Sunda, and after the declaration of war proceeded to the Coromandel coast. On June 25, 1746, they fell in with the fleet of Labourdonnais, and an indecisive action ensued off Negapatam, which ended in the retirement of the English squadron to Ceylon, the reason assigned for the act being the unseaworthy condition of the flagship, a vessel carrying 64 guns. The retreat of the English fleet left the coast open to Labourdonnais. He proceeded to Pondicherry, where he in vain endeavoured to excite Dupleix to co-operation; but Dupleix had other schemes of his own in view, and was not to be moved. Labourdonnais was, however, by no means without energy. He knew how helpless and de-

Labourdonnais despatched to India.

Precaution of the English ministry.

Naval engagement off Negapatam.

The English retreat.

Labourdonnais and Dupleix.

fenceless Madras really was; he had a fine force at his command, and, with nine ships and two mortar vessels, anchored in the Madras roads on September 14. He immediately landed his troops, and commenced the siege of the fort with 300 European sailors and soldiers, 400 Indians, and 400 Africans: and had as many in reserve, with ample stores, and ammunition for his guns. Against these forces the Madras factory could oppose barely 300 Europeans; many of them, the merchants and clerks of the factory, were non-combatants. In addition to the land attack, the fort was bombarded from the sea: and though the factory held out for some days in hope of a diversion by the English fleet, it surrendered on September 25, the Council promising to pay a moderate ransom. This was subsequently fixed at 44 lacs—440,000*l.*—irrespective of the merchandise, and after three months, the settlement was to be evacuated, and to remain unmolested during the war.

Madras besieged by Labourdonnais.

Madras surrenders to the French.

To this convention Dupleix gave his unqualified opposition, and declined to become a party to it. The fort of Madras, he said, should have been razed to the ground, and the English deported; and it was with dismay that the English found they were to remain at his mercy. Labourdonnais could not, or would not, stay in India; he sailed for the Mauritius, and on his arrival found he had been superseded, and had no resource but to return home. The vessel in which he sailed was captured, and he was taken to England, where he was honourably and hospitably received and entertained; but on his arrival in France, he was imprisoned in the Bastille, on March 2, 1748. Here he remained more than two years without a trial, and when it took place, was acquitted of all the charges made against him; but his sufferings had been great; he was reduced to poverty, and died, so to speak, of a broken heart.

Dupleix refuses to sanction the terms of surrender.

Labourdonnais superseded.

He is imprisoned and tried, but acquitted.

His death.

CHAPTER IV.

THE PROGRESS OF THE ENGLISH (*continued*), 1746 TO 1751—THE WAR IN THE CARNATIC.

ON the departure of Labourdonnais, Madras remained in possession of his troops, a member of the Council of Pondicherry being in charge of the local administration. If the English, under the expectation of an attack from the French, had previously made an arrangement with the Nawáb of the Carnatic to afford them assistance, and had paid liberally for the services of his troops, Madras might have been better defended; but the Council was irresolute, entirely unaccustomed to war, and the opportunity passed by. The Nawáb, however, irritated by an attack upon the settlement within his jurisdiction, and from which he had derived friendly assistance, now remonstrated with Dupleix; but being haughtily refused satisfaction by him, attempted to enforce his demands, and sent his son Mafooz Khan, at the head of 10,000 men, to drive the French from Madras. He attacked the place on October 21, but was defeated in a sally by the French troops, and took up a position at Maliapoorum, or St. Thomé, about four miles south of Madras, where he hoped to cut off succour from Pondicherry. Here he was assailed in front and rear, with great effect, by the French, and after considerable slaughter of his men, his army fled. Madras being now secure, Dupleix deliberately violated the convention made by Labourdonnais. On October 30, he summoned a meeting of the English, confiscated all their property, and offered them the alternative of remaining as prisoners of war on parole, or being sent to Pondicherry. Some escaped to Fort St. David: but the governor and most of the inhabitants were taken to Pondicherry, and publicly degraded by being marched through the streets.

Intervention of the Nawáb of the Carnatic.

His troops defeated before Madras.

And again at Maliapoorum.

Violation of the convention by Dupleix.

The English publicly degraded.

Dupleix's next operation was an attack upon Fort St. David, a strong work fourteen miles south of Pondicherry, but in this he was unsuccessful; a portion of the attacking party was severely handled by a force sent for the relief of the place by the Nawáb, under his sons Mafooz Khan and Mahomed Ally; and a siege being impracticable, the troops, which had been commanded by a Swiss officer, named Paradis, retreated. Disappointed in this, and in a subsequent attempt to surprise the place, Dupleix now commenced reprisals against the Nawáb's territory about Madras, which excited so much alarm, that the Nawáb, now believing, from Dupleix's representations, that the English had no real power, abandoned them, and sent his son Mafooz Khan to Pondicherry, where he was received with great pomp. The fort of St. David still, however, held out, and had received a supply of money and a reinforcement of twenty men from Ceylon. On March 2, 1747, another French force was seen approaching for a third time, and the garrison drew up to receive them.

Failure of attack on Fort St. David.

Dupleix attacks the Nawáb's territory.

Who abandons the English.

Fort St. David relieved by a fleet from England.

While the parties were interchanging distant cannon-shots, some ships were descried nearing the coast, which proved to be the long-looked for English fleet. Fort St. David was immediately reinforced, and the fleet passed on to Madras, where a French ship of sixty guns lying there was destroyed; but the approach of the monsoon rendered any operations against the place impossible, and the squadron returned to Ceylon.

The fleet returns to Ceylon.

Before another season opened, Major Stringer Lawrence, a distinguished officer, arrived at Fort St. David as commander of all the forces of the company in India, and some treacherous communications from natives were detected and punished, which events added to the security of the place. On June 7, the French fleet again attacked the settlement, but without effect. The enemy suffered heavy loss in an assault upon Cuddalore, the native town, and retreated precipitately; and on July 29, a large fleet from England made its appearance, and being joined by the squadron under Admiral Griffin, amounted to thirty sail of ships. The land forces at Fort St. David now amounted to 3,700 Europeans, and about 2,500 natives, partly disciplined.

Arrival of Major Lawrence.

Arrival of English fleet.

With this force, the siege of Pondicherry was decided upon, and the Nawáb, emboldened by the new exhibition of power and resources, promised co-operation. But the siege, from many causes—principally the unskilful direction of the engineer officers—proved an utter failure. It had lasted fifty days, the monsoon was commencing, and upwards of 1,000 Europeans had died from casualties and the effects of climate. It was therefore raised, and the troops returned to Fort St. David. Dupleix made the most of his success: writing to every native court in India, including that of the emperor, that the English were cowards, who, with overwhelming forces, had been unable to recover their losses, or retrieve their honour. Another campaign would, there is little doubt, have had a far different termination. The English were all powerful at sea; succours to the French could not approach them, and Madras would have been recovered. Meanwhile peace had been concluded between the nations of Europe, and Madras was given up.

Siege of Pondicherry fails.

Peace between England and France.

It was now that the real ambition of Dupleix began to show itself. The war with the English had been confined to purely local affairs; but during its continuance he had already witnessed the ease with which his handful of Europeans had overthrown a host of Moghul soldiers; he had already made some progress in disciplining natives; and if

Policy and aims of Dupleix.

he cast his military means into any of the disputes between native authorities, there could be no question of success, and of the foundation of a military power in India, far transcending in national glory and advantage anything to be derived from trade. The same thoughts, at the same time, seem to have influenced the English, who, with a fine force at their command, were lying inactive at Fort St. David. Sanhojee, a relative of the Mahratta Rajah of Tanjore, made offers, as a claimant to the throne—of which he had been dispossessed by an illegitimate brother—of immense sums and territorial cessions, if he were assisted by a force; and his offers were accepted. The first expedition, under Captain Cope, set out in March 1749; but a furious storm, which overtook it in April, so completely disorganised the equipments, causing also the loss of a ship of sixty guns, that it was abandoned. It was renewed under Major Lawrence, who captured Dévicotta, an operation rendered memorable by the conduct of Clive, who had recently joined the army, and whose brilliant services will be hereafter detailed. Sanhojee gained a pension by the movement, and the further progress of the English was stayed by the cession of Dévicotta by the Rajah of Tanjore, with a small territory, and payment of the expenses of the war. Thus concluded the first insignificant attempt, in India, of English interference in native affairs; but that of Dupleix was of a far different character.

Proposals of Sanhojee of Tanjore to the English.

Expedition of Captain Cope.

Major Lawrence takes the field.

Adjustment of the dispute.

It will be remembered that Chunda Sahib, on his surrender of the fort of Trichinopoly to the Mahrattas in 1741, had been sent prisoner to Sattara, and that his wife and family had been committed by him to the charge of Dupleix, who had afforded them a secure retreat in Pondicherry. Madame Dupleix, though of pure French parentage, had been born and educated in Pondicherry, and consequently spoke the vernacular languages as her mother-tongue. She appears also to have been of an intriguing spirit; for it was she who managed the traitorous correspondence with the native troops of the English at Fort St. David, which was detected and punished. Madame Dupleix grew to be on terms of intimacy with the wife of Chunda Sahib, and readily listened to her schemes for obtaining her husband's liberty, to which want of money to bribe the court at Sattara seemed to be the only obstacle. Could he be released, there was no doubt, as he was a popular prince, and Anwur-ood-deen, the Nawáb, was much the reverse, that the people would declare for him; and, supported by Dupleix's army—now idle — would quickly give him the ascendant in the

Madame Dupleix's political intrigue.

Carnatic. This was the opportunity for establishing the political influence of his nation, for which Dupleix had long thirsted, and he eagerly embraced it. Seven lacs of rupees—70,000*l.*—were advanced by Dupleix, and remitted by Chunda Sahib's wife secretly to her husband, and he was at once set at liberty.

Dupleix enters into the transaction.

Early in 1748 Chunda Sahib left Sattara, accompanied by a few tried friends, and being a well-known leader, was engaged by the Rajah of Chittledroog, then at war with Bednore. In an action which ensued, however, he was taken prisoner and thus delayed; but at this juncture Nizam-ool-Moolk died, and Anwur-ood-deen, deprived of the aid of his master and patron, might not be able to resist. Consequent on Nizam-ool-Moolk's death, a contest now ensued between his second son, Nasir Jung, and his nephew, Mozuffer Jung, the son of Nizam-ool-Moolk's daughter. Mozuffer Jung was in no position to contest the Deccan, but he was joined by Chunda Sahib, who disclosed to him his connection with the French; and at the head of a respectable force they marched towards the Carnatic, being joined by a French detachment of 400 Europeans and 2,000 disciplined Sepoys, under M. d'Auteuil. Anwur-ood-deen prepared to meet the invasion with spirit; but it is somewhat unaccountable why he did not apply for assistance from the English. It is probable, perhaps, that their ill-success in the Tanjore affair had caused them to fall in his estimation as soldiers, or he may have deprecated any assistance from foreigners, which could only be obtained by great sacrifices. Be this as it may, he met the invaders at Amboor, where he had posted his army, and was defeated and slain in the combat. His two sons, however, escaped. The war was, for the present, at an end; the conquerors entered Arcot with great pomp; Mozuffer Jung was proclaimed Soobahdar of the Deccan, and Chunda Sahib Nawáb of the Carnatic. Thence the allies proceeded to Pondicherry, where Dupleix entertained his guests with regal magnificence, and received from them a grant of eighty-one villages near the town. Dupleix now urged his allies to complete their conquest of the province; but Chunda Sahib turned into Tanjore, from the rajah of which he hoped to exact a heavy sum of money, if not to dispossess him of his kingdom. The rajah made little resistance, and engaged ultimately to pay seventy lacs of rupees —700,000*l.*—by instalments. While the allies were occupied in these inconsequent operations, they received news from

Chunda Sahib released.

Nizam-ool-Moolk's death.

Chunda Sahib joins Mozuffer Jung.

A French detachment co-operates.

Anwur-ood-deen prepares to meet the invasion.

He is defeated and slain.

The allies at Pondicherry.

Grant of villages to the French.

Dupleix that Nasir Jung had arrived from the Deccan with an immense army, and was already in possession of Arcot. Thereupon they retired at once to Pondicherry.

Meanwhile the Council of Madras had fallen into great perplexity as to what course they should pursue. Was it preferable to remain neutral, or to take a part in the war? This question was in some degree decided by the impetuosity of Mahomed Ally, son of Anwur-ood-deen, who, after his father's death, had fled to Trichinopoly, where the family and treasure were deposited, and urgently besought assistance; 120 European soldiers were sent to him, but at the same time, by a strange inconsistency, the fleet of Admiral Boscawen was permitted to depart for England. The Council were, however, committed in their policy by the succour of Mahomed Ally; and as Nasir Jung, with his huge army of 300,000 men, advanced upon Pondicherry, they sent to his camp 600 Europeans under Major Lawrence, and Mahomed Ally also joined it with 6,000 horse. On the other hand, Dupleix augmented his force, with his allies, to 2,000 Europeans; but some disagreement, the cause of which has never transpired, existed between the French officers and Dupleix; they refused to fight, and with their men were sent to Pondicherry. On this, Mozuffer Jung surrendered himself to his uncle; but Chunda Sahib, fighting bravely, escaped. It might be supposed that the French combination was now broken up. Nasir Jung returned to Arcot, and Major Lawrence, unable to effect any object favourable to the English interests, returned to Madras.

Perplexity at Madras.

The Council assists the son of Anwur-ood-deen.

Advance of Nasir Jung.

Dupleix, however, was as active in intrigue as ever. He discovered, through an agent, that there was great discontent in the camp of Nasir Jung, and that the Patán chiefs of Kurnool, Cuddapa, and Savanoor, were in secret mutiny. He now sent an expedition by sea to Masulipatam, which was carried by assault. Mahomed Ally, with whom was an English detachment under Captain Cope, after some desultory movements, refused to pay its expenses, and it was withdrawn to Madras; upon which the French, in company with Chunda Sahib, attacked and routed him with great slaughter, and the reduction of Ginjee followed. Nasir Jung, now alarmed by these active movements and successes, sought to treat with Dupleix; but the French were now again masters of the situation, and Dupleix's demands rose in proportion. Mozuffer Jung was to be set at liberty, Masulipatam and its dependencies ceded to the French, and Chunda Sahib invested as Nawáb of the Carnatic. Nasir Jung would have resisted

Dupleix's intrigues.

He attacks Masulipatam.

The French and allies defeat Mahomed Ally.

Nasir Jung negotiates with Dupleix.

His demands

these hard terms, and ordered his army to fight; but it was one thing to order and another to execute. The army was well-nigh immovable, and Nasir Jung, having in vain tried to advance for the recovery of Ginjee, was obliged to accept the demands, heavy as they were, and to draw up the treaty. But there had been delay: and delay was intolerable to M. Dupleix. He had no assurance that the treaty would be executed, and he ordered an advance of his forces at Ginjee to enforce it; they amounted only to 800 Europeans and 3,000 Sepoys, who marched from Ginjee on December 4, to the attack of an army believed to be upwards of 300,000 strong, with 100 guns. When they neared the camp, which extended for eighteen miles, they were led, by a guide from their confederates, to the division occupied by Nasir Jung, and attacked it at night. Early in the morning Nasir Jung mounted his elephant to ascertain the progress of the fight, and soon discovered he was betrayed. Upbraiding the Nawáb of Kurnool with his treachery, he was shot dead by that chieftain as he spoke, and the conflict was at an end.

Dupleix's demands accepted.

Dupleix attacks the army of Nasir Jung.

Nasir Jung shot.

Mozuffer Jung was at once proclaimed Soobahdar of the Deccan; and accompanied by M. de la Touche, the French commander, proceeded to Pondicherry, where M. Dupleix, more than ever triumphant, and Chunda Sahib, gav him a magnificent reception. While it lasted, indeed, the result of his policy was more magnificent than Dupleix, in his wildest dreams, had ever perhaps contemplated. He had not only created a Nawáb of the Carnatic, but a Soobahdar of the Deccan. He was appointed governor of all the Moghul territory south of the Krishna; Chunda Sahib was to be subject to him; the coinage was to be struck at Pondicherry, and to the French nation was ceded Masulipatam and its dependencies, with other portions, yielding probably five lacs, or 50,000*l*., per year. For his own share of Nasir Jung's treasure he was to receive twenty lacs, or 200,000*l*., and the expenses of the war; and gratuities to the officers were provided for on equally liberal terms. But these were not the only claims which Mozuffer Jung had to satisfy. The three traitor Nawábs made their own demands. The territories they had usurped were to be confirmed; they were to be exempt from payment of tribute, and half the treasury of Nasir Jung was to be bestowed upon them. Mozuffer Jung, as well he might be, was afraid of these turbulent feudatories, and would not trust himself with them without a French escort. M. Bussy, therefore, the ablest officer at Dupleix's disposal, was detached with him in command of 300

Dupleix's success.

Is appointed governor of Southern India.

Demands of the Patan Nawábs.

M. Bussy detached with Mozuffer Jung.

Europeans and 2,000 Sepoys, and Mozuffer Jung marched for Hyderabad on January 4, 1751. On entering the territory of the Nawáb of Kurnool, an ambuscade was discovered; the French troops attacked and carried the defile, but in pursuing the Patáns, the Nawáb of Kurnool, finding escape impossible, turned upon Mozuffer Jung, whom Bussy had been unable to restrain, and slew him, himself being immediately killed. Instant action was necessary: and Bussy, without hesitation, sent for Salabut Jung, the third son of Nizam-ool-Moolk, and caused him, with the consent of the army, to be proclaimed Soobahdar of the Deccan. By this measure, tranquillity was at once restored; and it is impossible not to award to M. Bussy the highest meed of honour for his ready presence of mind, and great ability and vigour of conduct. He was not exacting in his demands on the new soobahdar. He might have required and exacted many additional concessions to his nation, and no opposition would have been made to them; but he was content with the confirmation of what had already been confirmed by Mozuffer Jung, and with this even M. Dupleix was satisfied.

The Nawáb of Kurnool kills Mozuffer Jung.

Admirable conduct of Bussy.

Mozuffer Jung's agreements are confirmed.

CHAPTER V.

THE PROGRESS OF THE ENGLISH AND WAR IN THE CARNATIC (*concluded*), 1751 TO 1754.

A STRANGE complication of affairs had now ensued. The English and French in the Carnatic, though their nations were at peace, had taken up different sides of native politics; and the real question at issue, the eventual local superiority, was to be fought out under cover of them. After the departure of Mozuffer Jung, the English would probably have acknowledged Chunda Sahib as Nawáb, if their ally, Mahomed Ally, were secured in Trichinopoly; but to this Dupleix would by no means consent: and Chunda Sahib's first act, after taking possession of Arcot, in February 1751, was to advance to the siege of Trichinopoly with his own forces and 800 French auxiliaries. The former weak garrison of English soldiers sent to the aid of Mahomed Ally from Madras, has been already mentioned: and Lieutenant Clive was now despatched with a further reinforcement; but Mahomed Ally, perhaps distrustful of them, and under apprehension from the superior forces of his rival, called in the aid of the Mahratta chief, Moorary Ráo of

Complication of Carnatic affairs.

Siege of Trichinopoly by Chunda Sahib.

Gooty, Nunjeráj, the regent of Mysore, and the troops of Tanjore. Meanwhile Clive, whose daring spirit and military talent were becoming more and more developed, conceived the bold design of seizing Arcot while the troops of Chunda Sahib were drawn off for the siege of Trichinopoly; and, on his return to Fort St. David, laid his plan before Mr. Saunders, the governor of Madras, who at once appreciated the boldness and strategetic utility of the measure. 200 European soldiers, 300 Sepoys, and ten field-pieces, were all that could be spared; and with these Clive marched directly upon Arcot, through a tremendous storm of wind and rain, reached it on August 31, and took possession of it, unopposed by the garrison, who had fled. It was almost an open town; but the fort was tenable, and by strengthening the defences, and scouring the country around for supplies, he made the position very formidable.

Clive's expedition to Arcot.

He takes possession of the city.

As he had supposed, his movement at once attracted the attention of Chunda Sahib, and a force was detached from Trichinopoly for the siege of Arcot. It is impossible to follow the details of this siege, which forms one of the noblest exploits of Clive's remarkable life; but for seven weeks, relief from Madras having failed to reach him, he bravely withstood the efforts of 10,000 native troops and 150 French. The fort was breached in several places; the scarcity was so great that the native troops drank the water in which rice was boiled, while they gave the rice to the Europeans; and the danger of capture seemed so imminent, that Clive despatched a messenger to Moorary Ráo, whose camp was about thirty miles distant, to come to his assistance. On November 14, however, the troops of Chunda Sahib, under their commander Rajah Sahib, advanced to the storm. There were two practicable breaches, and the defenders were reduced to eighty Europeans and 120 Sepoys; nevertheless the assailants were beaten back with great loss, and during the night evacuated the town. In the evening a reinforcement, under Captain Kilpatrick, arrived from Madras, and any further attack by the enemy was impossible. Clive now assumed the offensive, and was joined by about 600 Mahratta horse, his own force being 200 Europeans and 700 Sepoys. With this, however, he defeated a combined French and native army under Rajah Sahib, at Arnee, and following up his advantage, gave them another severe defeat at Caverypauk, where he captured twelve pieces of artillery. He would now have advanced to the relief of Trichinopoly, on which the strength of the French was concentrated; but the arrival of Major Lawrence

Arcot besieged.

Clive's noble defence.

The assailants are beaten and evacuate the town.

Clive takes the field.

His successes.

from England placed him in a subordinate position. Never before, however, in India, had British troops fought as they had under Clive, and never had native Sepoys so bravely emulated them. They had beaten the French in every encounter, and had risen immensely in native estimation.

Military operations at Trichinopoly.

The operations begun under Clive were successfully continued under Lawrence, who advanced to the relief of Trichinopoly, against which the French and Chunda Sahib had effected very little. Mahomed Ally's allies from Mysore and Tanjore, with those of Moorary Ráo, augmented his forces to an equality with those of Chunda Sahib, and in addition there were the English under Lawrence. After a series of operations, which are interesting and well repay the perusal of the student,[1] the French and Chunda Sahib were shut up in the fortified pagoda of Seringham on an island in the Cavery, opposite to Trichinopoly. Here they were summoned to surrender at discretion, and M. Law, their commander, agreed to the terms offered. 600 Europeans with 300 Sepoys laid down their arms, and became prisoners of war, and thirty pieces of cannon with a large quantity of military stores were taken possession of. Chunda Sahib had previously obtained permission to depart, and had fallen into the hands of Monajee, the Tanjore general. His fate is thus related by Major Lawrence, who states in his narrative that at a council on the subject, at which the native chieftains could not agree, 'I proposed that we should have the charge of him, and keep him confined in one of our settlements; this was by no means approved, and we parted without coming to any resolution; but some of Monajee's people put an end to the dispute by cutting off his head, which was done on June 3, 1752,' and it may be added that Major Lawrence was in no position to prevent the act. The war did not, however, end with the death of Chunda Sahib. The Mysore and Mahratta troops joined the French, for Mahomed Ally had failed in all his agreements with his allies, and most notably in respect of surrendering Trichinopoly to the Mysore troops, as he had promised to do. Lawrence urged that the whole of the Carnatic should be first cleared of the enemy; but this opinion was overruled by Mr. Saunders, who sent a totally inadequate force against the great fort of Ginjee, which proved a miserable failure. This raised Dupleix's hopes for a time, and his troops took the field; but they were encountered at Bahoor, near Fort St. David, on August 27, and totally defeated by Lawrence

The French in Seringham surrender to Lawrence.

Chunda Sahib is beheaded.

Continuation of the war, 1752.

The French defeated at Bahoor.

[1] *Vide* 'War in the Carnatic, 1761,' Orme's 'History,' Mill's 'History,' vol. iii.; Beveridge's 'History,' vol. i. &c.

with the loss of eight guns, and all their military stores: the officer in command, M. Kirjean, with 100 Europeans, being taken prisoner. This action, with the capture of Covelong and Chingleput by Clive, which were in reality two very desperate enterprises, closed the campaign of 1752.

In 1753, as soon as the monsoon closed, the Mahrattas and Mysoreans having meanwhile gone over to the French, the war was opened by an attack by the allies upon Trichinopoly, in which an English garrison had been left under Captain Dalton. It had been occupied in perpetual checks of the Mysore troops, which sought to gain possession, and at length endeavoured to reduce the garrison by famine. Dalton's provisions were nearly at an end, when he apprised Lawrence of the fact, who marched at once to his relief; and by a curious coincidence, arrived on the same day as a French detachment, which reinforced the troops already in possession of the Seringham pagoda. After a series of minor operations, an action ensued near the fort, on September 20, 1753, in which the French, in a spirited charge with the bayonet, were defeated, and their commander, M. d'Autuc, taken prisoner. The forces of the allies were still, however, very numerous, and Major Lawrence and a considerable number of the troops being temporarily absent, the fort was assaulted on the night of November 27; but the attempt failed, and the loss of the French was very severe. The repulse was, however, followed by a success, in which a convoy from Madras was surprised and cut off by the allied Mahrattas and Tanjoreans, assisted by the French, and in this manner the war continued till October 1754, the one party at times pressing the siege, and the other endeavouring to raise it, which occasioned many interesting and varied achievements.

Campaign of 1753.

Action at Trichinopoly, and the French defeated.

The French repulsed from the fort.

At this crisis, M. Dupleix found himself superseded by M. Godeheu, who had been specially sent from France to put an end to the war, and who reached India on August 2, 1754; and on October 10, a suspension of hostilities was agreed upon between the French commissioner and Mr. Saunders, governor of Madras, which was continued for three months in anticipation of a general treaty. On December 26 the more formal treaty was executed, the first article of which specifies that the companies should renounce all 'Moorish dignities,' and refrain from further interference with native powers. The possessions of each were to be equalised, and are specified in the articles; and the treaty was to continue in force as made, pending the confirmation or otherwise of the respective authorities in Europe. At first sight there undoubtedly appears a decided sacrifice of interests by

Arrival of Commissioner Godeheu.

Suspension of hostilities.

Treaty between the English and French.

the French; and if the relinquishment of the Northern Circars had been actually included, no doubt would have been so. These territories, however, had been assigned by Salabut Jung to Bussy, in payment of his troops; and so fell out of the general category.

Failure of M. Dupleix's schemes.

But M. Dupleix's masterly policy for the sway of the Carnatic had been unduly broken up, his ally Chunda Sahib was dead; and though his son, a minor, survived, and was even put forward by Dupleix, the opposite party, strengthened by the English, had become too powerful. Dupleix's fate was a melancholy termination to his ambitious schemes. When he went back to France, his accounts proved his large claims on the Government: for, in support of his policy, he had not only used his own private funds to the extent of 300,000*l.*, but had borrowed largely. These debts were, however, repudiated by the French Government; and though a letter of protection was granted to him against his creditors, he died of anxiety and vexation, and in poverty—a second victim to the short-sighted policy and ignorance of the French nation. Nor can the eminent services of Mr. Saunders be passed over without remark. It is questionable whether they were ever recognised; certain at least, that they were never rewarded as they should have been. But for his undaunted resolution, and perseverance under all difficulties, Mahomed Ally, unworthy as he was, would never have been adequately supported. Mr. Saunders, with true good faith which never swerved, was determined that the French should not possess a governor of the Carnatic wholly dependent upon them; and, amidst all difficulties and perplexities, calmly and perseveringly worked out his purpose till the arrival of M. Godeheu placed the question beyond issue, in the treaty which was obtained from him, which, more than success against them in the field, humiliated the French in the opinion of the natives of India, and laid the foundation of British ascendency.

Fate of Dupleix.

Services of Mr. Saunders.

Proceedings of Bussy.

Meanwhile M. Bussy had accompanied Salabut Jung, and the army had advanced as far as the Krishna river, when it was met by that of the Péshwah, who, instructed from Dehly, was acting in the interest of Ghazee-ood-deen, the late Nizam-ool-Moolk's eldest son, and therefore the real successor to his dominions. An action was imminent, when the Péshwah received news from Sattara which obliged him to return. Shao had died in 1751; but before his demise, having no male offspring, he was induced to adopt Ráma, or Rám Rajah, the son, as was alleged, of the second Sivajee, whose existence had hitherto been concealed; but before Shao's death the Péshwah had contrived to obtain an instrument from him, in which he and his descendants were created the executive rulers of the Mahratta State, on condition of governing it in the name and on the behalf of the great Sivajee's posterity. Sukwar Bye, the widow of Shao, would no doubt have opposed this arrangement, but under the effect of a taunting message from the Péshwah, who had discovered her conspiracy against him, she burned herself with her husband's body. It was a base and cruel alternative, and was assisted by the unhappy lady's brother; but it secured the Péshwah's present power, and its hereditary descent to his successors. The news received by the Péshwah now was that Tara Bye, the grandmother of Rám Rajah, had, with the assistance of several great chiefs, made a revolution at Sattara, by which Rám Rajah was to be delivered from the power of the Péshwah; but the attempt proved abortive: the Rajah was kept in close confinement by Tara Bye herself, and the Gáikwar, who had aided her movement, was secured and imprisoned.

The Péshwah's office confirmed hereditarily.

The Péshwah was now at liberty to proceed against Salabut Jung, who, with M. Bussy, had reached Ahmednugger. Thence they advanced upon Poona, and the Mahratta army was defeated by a night attack on November 22, 1751. On the 27th, Salabut Jung was attacked in turn, and was saved only by the gallantry of the French; and the campaign continued, with occasional advantages, now to one side and now to the other, till Salabut Jung's troops, already discontented by arrears of pay, threatened to mutiny. Under Bussy's advice, therefore, the Péshwah's overtures were accepted, and an armistice ensued. Although the terms of these overtures did not transpire, they may be readily imagined. The Péshwah had been in treaty with Ghazee-ood-deen, now on his way to the Deccan, and had been promised extensive territorial cessions for his assistance in the inevitable contest with Salabut Jung; and it is therefore probable, that these cessions were also promised by Salabut Jung should he succeed. Thus the Péshwah's neutrality was, for the present, apparently secured; while he evidently perceived that the side he should support in the contest must eventually prove victorious. Meanwhile, Rughoojee Bhóslay, during the campaign between Salabut Jung and the Péshwah, had invaded Western Berar, taken Gawilgurh and Narnalla, and occupied the country as far south as the Godavery. Ghazee-ood-deen was not opposed by his brother on his entry into the Deccan, and he was joined by the Péshwah, who, abandoning his promised neutrality, accompanied him to Aurungabad, and obtained from him the cession of the whole of the territory

War between the Péshwah and Salabut Jung.

Defeat of the Mahrattas.

An armistice ensues.

between the Tapty and the Godavery, which included Western Berar. While encamped near the city, Ghazee-ood-deen accepted an invitation from the mother of Nizam Ally, one of his father's widows who resided at Aurungabad, and partook of a poisoned dish, from the effects of which he almost directly expired. Whether the crime was instigated by Salabut Jung, or was one of the harem intrigues then only too common in great Mahomedan families, is nowhere explained; but no odium seems to have attached itself to Salabut Jung, now without a rival in the Deccan. As to confirmation from Dehly, it was not now needed as a matter of security, and would be acknowledged only as an honorary compliment. No opposition to Salabut Jung was offered, and under Bussy's advice, though unwillingly, he confirmed the grants to the Péshwah, already made by his brother, by which the Peyn Gunga became the southern boundary of the Mahratta possessions of Berar, the posts taken up by Rughoojee as far south as the Godavery being entirely withdrawn.

Ghazee-ood-deen poisoned, 1752.

Salabut Jung viceroy of the Deccan.

Bussy's conduct throughout these events is entitled to the highest praise. It will be readily imagined that a foreigner, entirely unsupported, and dependent only upon a prince's precarious favour, would become a mark for jealousy and conspiracy. He had no private means of his own, and must depend upon what he could locally obtain for the pay of his troops. After some struggles with the executive minister, Syed Lushkur Khan, who desired the dismissal of the Europeans, Bussy, who had been obliged to go to Masulipatam for change of air, suddenly returned to Hyderabad, and marched to Aurungabad, where the court then was. His presence once more secured Salabut Jung, who dismissed his enemy; and, as a provision for the French auxiliaries, assigned to M. Bussy the whole of the eastern provinces, called the Northern Circars, the revenue of which amounted to fifty lacs, or 500,000*l.*, per annum. No European power in India had ever acquired such a possession. It was fertile and productive; its coast was open for 600 miles, and communication with Hyderabad was easy and rapid. Nor did the convention of Pondicherry affect this possession, so long as M. Bussy remained the servant only of a native power. The country was well and moderately managed, and Bussy became as much distinguished by his civil administration as by his military talent.

Bussy's conduct.

CHAPTER VI.

THE PROGRESS OF THE ENGLISH AND FRENCH (*continued*), 1754 TO 1756.

ALTHOUGH the treaty of Pondicherry put an end to the actual war in the Carnatic between the French and English, it did not prevent further undertakings in concert with native powers; while, on the other hand, the late allies could not understand why they should be debarred from action by its provisions. Nunjeráj, the regent of Mysore, declared he would not depart till he had obtained Trichinopoly; while Mahomed Ally, the nawáb, considering he had a right to tribute from Madura and Tinnevelly, two small States to the southward, called upon the English for assistance. The Mysoreans were obliged to abandon their pretensions under an invasion of their dominions by the Péshwah; but the Madura expedition, which may be considered the first deliberate breach of the treaty, continued, and was prolonged by various circumstances for several years. In 1754, the Péshwah proceeded to the Carnatic to levy the national tribute, and Salabut Jung, accompanied by Bussy, also marched in the same direction. While Salabut Jung protected Mysore from the Mahrattas, he was bent upon exacting his tribute from that State, already impoverished by the expenses of the Carnatic campaign; and under these separate interests Bussy was placed in a delicate position, as his nation was in alliance with Mysore; but he contrived to extricate himself from it with his usual address, claiming to Mysore that his presence alone had prevented the Péshwah from plundering the country—which, indeed, was true.

Situation of the English and French and their native allies.

The Péshwah and Salabut Jung visit the Carnatic.

Bussy's position.

Colonel Clive, who had been absent on leave in England, returned to India in 1755; being sent out to Bombay in command of a large detachment of troops. While in England, he had afforded much information in regard to the effects of the treaty of Pondicherry, and the real strength and position of M. Bussy in the Deccan; and had shown clearly that, as he said, 'so long as there was one Frenchman in arms in the Deccan, or in India, there could be no peace. For his own part, he desired nothing better than to dispute the mastery of the Deccan with M. Bussy;' and it was perhaps then as privately clear to his

Clive returns to India.

His statements in England.

mind as it was avowedly so afterwards, that the whole of India must belong to the conqueror. At this time, the character of the English was fast rising in popular estimation in India. The faithful manner in which they had supported the Nawáb of the Carnatic, in spite of their own weakness; the manner in which they had been reinforced, and their superiority by sea, were becoming gradually observed.

The English character begins to be estimated in India.

In Bombay, their neighbour the Péshwah was not a person to neglect his own interests: and though he had not been able to avail himself of English aid in reducing Surat, another opportunity now presented itself. Toolajee Angria, who held possession of the coast between Bancoote and Sawunt-warree, south of Bombay, had defied the Péshwah's authority, whereas his brother Manajee acknowledged it. Toolajee's piracies were very active and mischievous: and the Péshwah, as also the English at Bombay, had severely suffered from them. Independent of Toolajee Angria, the chief of Sawunt-warree and the Rajah of Kolapore employed piratical vessels; and by these means the coast had become extremely unsafe. In March 1755, the Péshwah prepared to co-operate with the English officers at Bombay for the reduction of these piratical forts; and though there were none of the king's ships present, they sent Commodore James on March 27, with a vessel of forty-four guns, and a bomb-ketch, to be supported by the Mahratta fleet, against Severndroog, which was gallantly attacked and captured. It was made over to the Péshwah, according to stipulation; and the English obtained from him Bancoote, which was their first territorial possession, except Bombay, on the western coast. The season was too far advanced for further operations, and the Bombay Council, as well on that account as their paucity of means, deferred them till the arrival of Colonel Clive's force, and the fleet under Admiral Watson. Even, then, the question of employing Clive against Bussy in the Deccan, in which the Péshwah would no doubt have joined, instead of against Angria, was some time under consideration. The Madras Council would have preferred action by land, and strenuously urged this measure, but the authorities of Bombay were doubtful whether, under the treaty of Pondicherry, they could enter on such a campaign against Salabut Jung and Bussy, and it was finally decided to reduce Angria.

The Péshwah and Bombay Government coalesce to repress piracy.

Severndroog captured.

The Peshwah cedes Bancoote.

The armament was prepared and dispatched in February 1756. It consisted of fourteen vessels, three of which were ships of the line, and carried 800 Europeans and 1,000 native soldiers. Before the fleet sailed, the chief officers

Expedition of Admiral Watson and Clive against Gheriah.

had met and determined to divide the prize-money without reference to the Mahrattas, who, independently of the English, had already taken several of Angria's forts; but they had not succeeded against Gheriah, which they had only invested by land. On February 12, Admiral Watson opened fire against the fort, and Colonel Clive, landing the troops, took up a position between the fort and the Mahratta army. There was an attempt on the part of the Mahratta commander to prevent the English getting possession of the place, by asserting that Toolajee Angria was already negotiating with him for its surrender; but this was disregarded, and next day Angria's fleet was burned, and the fort surrendered. About ten lacs of rupees—100,000*l.*—was divided among the captors as prize-money, and for the present Gheriah was retained. Bancoote was offered in exchange for it: but this was refused by the Péshwah, and the settlement of the question remained in abeyance. Colonel Clive now proceeded to assume command of Fort St. David, to which he had been appointed in England, and all schemes against M. Bussy, on the part of the English, were for the present necessarily postponed.

Gheriah surrenders.

Clive proceeds to Fort St. David.

But there were other intrigues against Bussy in progress which were more important than the remote chance of a conflict with Clive. If the Bombay Government had consented to allow Clive to join the Mahrattas, Bussy, as well as his master, Salabut Jung, would have been attacked by the Péshwah, in 1755. Disappointed at their determination not to assist him, the Péshwah applied to the Council of Madras for artillery and gunners; and on April 14, 1756, they wrote, that if he would send troops to meet them they would be forwarded. This, however, did not happen. The Péshwah was employed against the Nawáb of Savanoor, who had defied both himself and Salabut Jung: and for the present they had united their forces in order to reduce him. During the siege of Savanoor, the success of Bussy's magnificent artillery won the admiration of the combined armies: and it is evident that he was thought too powerful for hostile influences to succeed presently against him. Certainly, so long as he was connected with Salabut Jung, it was clear to the Péshwah that he would have no chance of superiority, and Bussy was therefore, if possible, to be removed. Salabut Jung's minister, Shah Nuwáz Khan, had probably made his own terms with the Péshwah in this matter; but it is not clear how they combined to act upon Salabut Khan himself. Be this as it may, no sooner was Savanoor taken, than Bussy was informed that his services were no longer required, and he must retire with his European troops. Some of his Sepoys had

Intrigues against M. Bussy.

Siege of Savanoor.

Bussy is dismissed by Salabut Jung.

already been corrupted, and were disaffected towards him; but others were still faithful, and with these, 200 European cavalry, and 600 infantry, he obtained passports to Masulipatam, and marched from the camp on May 25, upon Hyderabad, which lay in his route to Masulipatam. Directly after he had set out, he received a communication from the Péshwah, offering him the same position with himself as he had held with Salabut Jung, as well as an escort of 6,000 horse. The latter he accepted for a few days, till he should have crossed the Krishna and Bheema rivers; but the offer of service he distinctly, though courteously, refused. Had he accepted it, as he might have done, under feelings of irritation at his sudden dismissal by Salabut Jung, and as he was now at liberty to do, there can be little doubt that the Péshwah would at once have attacked the army of Salabut Jung and shattered his power; but Bussy saw his best interests lay in regaining his position with Salabut Jung; and he probably confided the means of doing so to no one. The Krishna and Bheema proved fordable, and Bussy pursued his march to Hyderabad without opposition; but they swelled immediately afterwards, and hindered the return of Salabut Jung's army for some days.

He marches on Hyderabad.

The Péshwah offers him service,

which he refuses.

His measures.

On reaching the city, Bussy marched directly into it, and took possession of the Char Minár, and the buildings near it, with some of which were connected one of the viceroy's gardens. It was amply supplied with water, and afforded accommodation for all his troops. The Char Minár, a noble edifice of the Kootub Shahy period, consisted of four open arches of great size, with a lofty minaret at each corner, and formed a conspicuous object from all points of view. The roof was a large terrace, and was nearly a hundred feet from the ground. The place commanded the whole of the city within gun-shot, and was entirely unassailable; and, manned by guns on the terrace above as well as below, was quite impregnable. Having laid in provisions, Bussy permanently occupied it on July 5. A few days afterwards, the advanced portion of Salabut Jung's army reached Hyderabad. Salabut Jung himself arrived on August 1, and Bussy's position was closely invested.

He arrives at Hyderabad, and takes up a position in the city.

The Char Minár.

Salabut Jung arrives with his army.

Meanwhile, the French officers at Pondicherry and Masulipatam, on receiving news of Bussy's difficulties, made strenuous efforts to reinforce him. M. de Leyrit dispatched 320 Europeans and 400 Sepoys, with six guns, from Pondicherry to Masulipatam, and before their arrival there 160 Europeans and 700 Sepoys had marched for Hyderabad, under M. Law.

Efforts of the French officers.

Stress of weather had forced him to halt at Bézwarra, on the Hyderabad road, for a few days, and when the reinforcement from Pondicherry arrived, it was enabled to join him. For some marches he was not molested; but as he neared Hyderabad, he was attacked by troops sent from the city, and in a strange mood of despair, took up a position in the small fort of Mulkapoor, within a march of the capital, and wrote to Bussy that he could advance no further. Now Bussy had already gained over to his side the Mahratta officers, who were employed against Law's detachment, and who had agreed not to attack him, though they should appear to do so. There was, therefore, no danger which might not be overcome. He, therefore, wrote to Law to advance at all hazards, at the same time causing his own tent to be pitched outside the walls, as if about to march to attack Salabut Jung's troops. This ruse had the effect he had anticipated; no additional forces were sent against Law, who, after a night of sharp fighting in the Mulkapoor defile, reached Hyátnugger, in an open country. Bussy now sent a party of 140 Europeans with 1,000 of his best Sepoys, with conveyances for the wounded, to escort Law to Hyderabad. The march of both parties was unopposed, and on the morning of August 15, all reached Bussy's position in safety. Law had twenty-five Europeans killed, and sixty-five wounded; but the enemy acknowledged a loss of 2,000 men, chiefly from the field-pieces and the French musketry.

Law marches on Hyderabad.

Bussy secures the Mahratta officers.

Bussy reinforces Law,

who finally reaches Hyderabad.

Law had no sooner arrived than a letter was received from Salabut Jung, who became almost abject in his submission, and Bussy was enabled to make his own terms, which, under the treachery he had endured, were wonderfully moderate. He imposed no new conditions, receiving only confirmation of his districts and his command; and having thus overcome intrigue and violence by his bravery and dignified conduct, he was more than ever respected by the people. His greatest apprehension during the siege of the Char Minár was, that the Madras Government, to whom he knew Salabut Jung had applied for assistance, might dispatch troops before succour could reach him from Pondicherry or Madras; but the efforts of his countrymen at both places had been energetically directed, and had proved successful. The Council of Madras would, there is little doubt, have embraced the opportunity of employing Clive in the service against Bussy, in which he had been disappointed at Bombay; but events in Bengal, which have now to be noticed, had put it out of their power to send a single

Salabut Jung's submission.

Bussy's moderation.

man. Bussy, therefore, became stronger than ever; but he held a position which depended solely upon his own indomitable will and energy, and which his country had neither the means, nor perhaps the inclination, to strengthen.

CHAPTER VII.

OF THE REIGNS OF THE EMPERORS AHMED SHAH AND ALUMGEER II., WITH EVENTS IN BENGAL, 1748 TO 1756.

Prince Ahmed succeeds his father, the Emperor Mahomed Shah.

It will be remembered, that when the Prince Royal, Ahmed of Dehly, had repulsed the Afghan king, Ahmed Shah Abdally, in an attack on his camp at Sirhind, he had received intelligence of the death of his father, the Emperor Mahomed Shah; and returning to Dehly, was crowned under the title of Ahmed Shah. Kummur-ood-deen Khan, the vizier, had been killed at Sirhind; and Sufdur Jung, the son of Saadut Khan, the late viceroy of Oudh, was appointed in his room. An attempt was then made to suppress the Rohillas, the descendants of the old Afghans who had settled in the country near Dehly, and who had grown very powerful; but it proved abortive, and it was not until the Mahrattas, under Sindia and Holkar, and Sooruj Mul, rajah of the Játs, were called in to assist, that they were defeated; but the Mahrattas, as the price of their assistance, were allowed to plunder the country, and it was desolated. A defeat of the imperial troops in Marwar followed at a short interval, and was not redeemed; and after these examples of the growing weakness of the imperial government, a second invasion of Ahmed Shah Abdally ensued. His present demand was the cession of the whole of the Punjâb, which, being unable to oppose it, was granted by the emperor. Sufdur Jung, the vizier, during whose absence this cession had been made, was discontented with the humiliation: and resented it by causing a eunuch, the emperor's favourite attendant, whom he believed adverse to himself, and the adviser of the Punjâb cession, to be assassinated. This act precipitated matters between the emperor and Sufdur Jung, and he was superseded by Shahâb-ood-deen, the son of the late Ghazee-ood-deen, viceroy of the Deccan, who, though only a youth, was promoted to the office of commander of the forces. This event produced a civil war, which deluged the streets of Dehly with blood,

Rebellion of the Rohillas.

The second invasion of Ahmed Shah Abdally.

The Punjâb ceded to him.

Civil war in Dehly.

and was stayed only on the approach of the Mahrattas, whom Ghazee-ood-deen had called up from the Deccan; and Sufdur Jung, secure in his possession of Oudh, removed thither, and thenceforth became virtually independent. Shaháb-ood-deen, who succeeded to the office of vizier, in concert with his Mahratta allies, now entered upon a campaign against the Játs, and was occupied in besieging their strong forts, when the emperor moved from Dehly, possibly with a view of conciliating Sufdur Jung. This unlooked-for independent action it was necessary to check; and a Mahratta force was sent against him, by which he was defeated, and, with his mother, imprisoned. Shaháb-ood-deen then repaired to the camp, deposed the emperor, and having blinded him and his mother, created another of the princes emperor, who was crowned under the title of Alumgeer II., in July 1754.

The Mahrattas assist the emperor.

Campaign against the Játs.

The emperor is deposed.

Alumgeer II. succeeds.

In September of the same year, Sufdur Jung, viceroy of Oudh, died, and was succeeded by his son, Shujah-ood-Dowlah, when Sháhab-ood-deen made an attempt to assert the authority of the empire over the province, but could effect nothing. He afterwards proceeded towards the Punjâb, and in March 1755 had a narrow escape from death in a mutiny of a portion of his troops; but he reached the Punjâb safely. Lahore was then held on the part of Ahmed Shah Abdally, by the widow of Meer Munnoo, the late viceroy, acting on behalf of her son, who, though a minor, had been confirmed in the government. Shaháb-ood-deen was betrothed to a daughter of this lady; and having completely lulled her suspicions, surprised Lahore and carried her off to his camp. This insult to his authority was promptly resented by Ahmed Shah, who, marching rapidly from Kandahar, reached the vicinity of Dehly without opposition. Here he pardoned the vizier, who submitted to him; but Shaháb-ood-deen was too weak to prevent the king from proceeding to Dehly, and extorting a vast sum of money from the people by torture and massacre. Nor did his violence rest here. He deliberately attacked the rich city of Muttra, on the occasion of a religious festival, when thousands of Hindoo worshippers were slaughtered without mercy by the Afghans. Ahmed Shah also attempted to levy exactions upon the Viceroy of Oudh and the Játs; but they proved strong enough to resist him, and finding it impossible to delay longer in India, in consequence of the heat, he was about to proceed to Kandahar, in June 1757, when the emperor unexpectedly appealed to him for protection against the vizier, whose

The vizier attempts to regain Oudh

and the Punjâb.

Ahmed Shah Abdally resents the attack,

and plunders Dehly.

Plunder and massacre of Muttra.

perfidy he had so much reason to dread. Ahmed Shah therefore appointed Nujeeb-ood-Dowlah, a Rohilla nobleman of ability and good repute, to be commander of the army, a nomination he hoped would be respected by the vizier; but no sooner had the king departed, than the vizier superseded his nominee, replacing him by a creature of his own, and calling in the Mahrattas to support his measures. The consequences of this step will be detailed hereafter, for it now becomes necessary to revert to the affairs of Bengal.

The emperor appeals to Ahmed Shah for assistance.

Mahratta intervention.

On April 9, 1756, Aliverdy Khan, the gallant and persevering defender of Bengal against the Mahrattas, died at the age of eighty, much regretted by the people, and by the European settlers. He had behaved well to them; had made fewer exactions than he might have done; and he had been able to appreciate the effects of their trade in advancing the prosperity of the great province. At his death, Bengal was virtually an independent kingdom, though its ruler professed a nominal attachment to, and dependence upon, the throne of Dehly: and the successor assumed his position without more reference to the court than etiquette, and the payment of fees and presents to the courtiers, required. Aliverdy Khan had no son; but he had three daughters, who were married to the three sons of his brothers, and he fixed upon Suráj-ood-Dowlah, one of his grandsons, and his especial favourite, to inherit his dominions, an arrangement which was publicly made known, and continued till Aliverdy's death. No opposition was therefore made to this bequest, and Suráj-ood-Dowlah took quiet possession of his grandfather's dominions; but his uncle, who had married the eldest daughter of his grandfather, and who had been in charge of the government of Purneah, had left a son, Shoukut Jung, who, having great wealth at his disposal, was now intriguing at Dehly for the viceroyalty: and Suráj-ood-Dowlah marched against him. Before he could reach the place, he received news that Kishen Das, the son of Rajah Ráj Bullub, the late governor of Dacca, had proceeded to Calcutta with a letter of introduction to Mr. Drake, the governor, from Mr. Watts of Cossimbazar, and that he had taken all his wealth with him. To get possession of this wealth had been the desire of Suráj-ood-Dowlah for some time past: and the manner in which Kishen Das had evaded him, and thrown himself upon the protection of the English, excited his anger to a furious degree. He wrote first to Mr. Drake, demanding that the fugitive should be given up with all his property; and again, that the new fortifications

Affairs in Bengal.

Death of Aliverdy Khan.

Suráj-ood-Dowlah succeeds.

Shoukut Jung disputes the succession.

Kishen Das is protected by the English.

Suráj-ood-Dowlah's demands.

of Calcutta should be destroyed. It was in vain that Mr. Drake, who evaded the subject of Kishen Das, protested that the fortifications had only been partially repaired in case they should be attacked by the French; the Nawáb would hear of no excuses, and marched with his whole army, 50,000 strong, upon Calcutta, in the month of June, and reached the city on the 17th of that month.

He marches on Calcutta.

Calcutta was entirely unprepared for defence. The fortifications had been only partially repaired by Colonel Scott, and at his death, in the preceding year, the works had been suspended. The gunpowder was bad, and only 174 men composed the garrison. There was no soldier-like feeling among the officers, and discipline had been neglected. The English outposts were quickly driven in, and some of their guns captured: and by the evening of the 18th, the factory was closely invested. During that night a council of war decided that the place was not tenable, and that the women and children should be sent on board the ships. This was immediately done, amidst much confusion, and the ships' commanders, alarmed by a sudden discharge of fire-arrows, weighed anchor, and dropped two miles down the river. In the morning Mr. Drake, the chief, and Captain Minchin, the commandant of the factory, followed them. Mr. Holwell, however, was not dismayed, and preparations were made for defence. If the ships, or a portion of their crews, had returned, there can be little question that the place could have been held; and there were many on board the fleet who would have cheerfully taken part in the defence; but to the last, the signals of distress from the fort, though perfectly visible in the ships, were not answered, and on the 21st, the enemy, seeing the helpless situation of the defenders, assaulted the place with much vigour. Finding further resistance hopeless, and as some lodgments on the walls had been made, Mr. Holwell admitted a flag of truce sent by the Nawáb, and taking advantage of it, a rush was made by the enemy, and the officers and soldiers, most of the latter being intoxicated, were disarmed.

Weak condition of Calcutta.

The factory is invested.

Women and children removed.

Mr. Drake abandons his post.

Mr. Holwell's defence.

The factory assaulted.

Mr. Holwell admits a flag of truce.

The English are disarmed.

In the afternoon, the Nawáb visited the fort in state; and after expressing his disappointment that there was no more than five lacs of rupees—50,000*l.*—in the treasury, and receiving Kishen Das with courtesy, took his departure. No one seems to have apprehended danger, and so far as the Nawáb himself was concerned, there perhaps was none; but in the evening, no other place being considered secure by the native officer in

The Nawáb's visit.

charge of the fort, the whole of the prisoners, without distinction —146 persons—were thrust into a room barely twenty feet square, without proper ventilation, which went by the name of 'the black hole,' and had been ordinarily used as a lock-up place for disorderly soldiers. The result is too well-known by the narratives of Mr. Holwell and others, and need not be repeated here. It was in vain that the prisoners, in their agonies of thirst and suffocation, implored the guards to have the Nawáb informed of their condition; they were told he was gone to rest, and could not be disturbed, and in the morning twenty-three ghastly figures emerged from the place—the rest lay dead within. Mr. Holwell was now sent to Moorshidabad in confinement, the property of all the English factories in Bengal was confiscated, and the company's servants imprisoned; and before the end of June, the English had not, so to speak, a single possession in Bengal remaining to them. The ships, one and all, dropped down to Fuldah, a town near the mouth of the river Hooghly, and sending news of their disasters to Madras, those on board of them awaited the result.

The garrison confined in the 'black hole.'

CHAPTER VIII.

OF EVENTS IN BENGAL (*continued*), 1756 TO 1757.

NEWS of the disastrous state of affairs in Bengal did not reach Madras till July 15, and caused some alarm, though by no means as much as might have been expected. A ship, the 'Delawarr,' was, however, dispatched to the Hooghly with 250 men on July 20, which, arriving on August 2, found the fugitives from Calcutta unable to act in concert with them; and about the same time, the full extent of the Bengal loss became known at Madras. It is, however, now strange to consider, that, even under the pressure of this great national calamity, there were some there who would have preferred immediate action against M. Bussy on the requisition of Salabut Jung, to regaining a footing in Bengal; but it was at last wisely determined to act against Bengal, and Clive, chafing at his inaction in his subordinate post at Fort St. David, was appointed to command the expedition. There were 2,000 English soldiers then at Madras; but 900 were considered sufficient, and with 1,500 Sepoys, and artillery, made up the force to be employed. Much time was lost by unseemly discussions and jealousies in the Council; but eventually five ships of the Royal Navy, under the command of Admiral Watson, with five of the company's fleet, sailed from Madras on October 16.

Assistance sent from Madras.

Clive appointed to command the troops.

The expedition sails from Madras.

They made a long passage to Bengal, for the monsoon was now adverse, and did not arrive till December 20; even then two were wanting. Clive began his operations at once; and as the ships, carrying nearly 400 guns, ascended the river with the semblance of a triumphal procession, such an armament had never before been witnessed by the people. At the first fort attacked—Buj-Buj—Clive narrowly escaped destruction by careless over-confidence; but broadsides from the fleet destroyed the fortifications, and a large force under the native governor of Calcutta fled in dismay. On January 2, 1757, the English fleet reached Calcutta, and cannonaded the fort; but the garrison almost immediately disappeared, and it was occupied without opposition by Captain Eyre Coote, who had landed from the fleet. Clive, who had marched with the troops by land, claimed possession, and disputed Admiral Watson's power to appoint Coote. He even bitterly regretted that he had ever assumed the command of the expedition; but he afterwards withdrew his opposition, and the quarrel was adjusted: it proved, however, the foundation of many subsequent disputes between king's and company's officers, which were never perfectly overcome.

Clive's progress up the Hooghly.

Calcutta attacked by the English, and re-captured.

Disputes of the English commanders.

Clive was now determined to show the Nawáb that he could do more than retake what had been lost; and on January 10, the town of Hooghly, some distance up the river, was cannonaded, breached, and stormed with but very slight resistance. The interval of rest which followed was marked by serious dissensions and bickerings between the members of Council and Clive. They protested against his independent exercise of power, and Clive has recorded a very mean opinion of them. They claimed his obedience, which he flatly refused, and he continued to maintain the authority conferred on him at Madras in spite of vexatious opposition, though with much distress of mind.

Hooghly captured.

Disputes between Clive and the Council.

Meanwhile the success of the English had irritated Suráj-ood-Dowlah to the highest degree. He not only prepared his own army, but he called upon the French, between whom and the English war had been declared in Europe, and who had 300 European soldiers at Chándernagore, to join him; but the French governor, anxious to avoid a local rupture with the English, declined to do so, and remained neutral. Even as it was, the strength of the Nawáb's army caused Clive some misgivings; and he was at this time reminded strongly from Madras, that he must return by the period allotted to him—that is, April. He did not, therefore, oppose the negotiations of the Committee for peace, which was conducted by

Proceedings of Suráj-ood-Dowlah.

Negotiations for peace.

Juggut Sett and Omichund, through whom the principal trade had been heretofore carried on. The Nawáb, however, marched from Moorshidabad; and on February 2, his army was near Calcutta, his outposts locating themselves even within the Mahratta ditch. He was not opposed, though Clive had formed a camp on the outskirts of the settlement; but the reception given to the deputies from the Council, and the disposition of the Nawáb's troops, left little doubt of his hostile intentions, and Clive determined to attack his camp in the morning. He had 650 European infantry, 600 sailors, 800 Sepoys, and 100 artillerymen, with six field-guns; and the Nawáb's army was 40,000 strong. Unfortunately a thick fog prevented the success anticipated, and Clive's loss was severe; but he inflicted a serious injury upon the enemy, and the Nawáb retired with his army for more than three miles, and again opened his negotiations with the Committee. The result of these was a treaty executed on February 9. It was highly favourable to the company: all their possessions were to be restored, they might fortify Calcutta as they pleased, and all their privileges were to be continued; but there were many who thought that the treaty did not go far enough—that public and private losses were not sufficiently provided for; and Admiral Watson was of opinion, as he bluntly expressed it, that 'till the Nawáb was well thrashed, he could not be depended upon.' Very probably Clive thought the same; for, whether by design or oversight, he had obtained no guarantee for the execution of the several provisions, which were left to such good faith as might hereafter be displayed.

The Nawáb marches on Calcutta.

Clive attacks the camp.

The Nawáb retreats.

A treaty of peace is concluded with the Nawáb.

At this juncture, Clive appears to have been most anxious to prevent the Nawáb from making any coalition with the French, which indeed the faithful execution of the treaty would not leave him a pretence of doing; for, in addition to the first articles, others had been subsequently added, of offensive and defensive alliance. This secured, Clive considered he was at liberty to proceed against the French factory of Chándernagore, and caused the Nawáb to be sounded as to his willingness to assist, on the basis of the treaty; but on this point he could obtain no decided promise, or indeed encouragement, and determined, therefore, to act on his own judgment. On February 18, he crossed the river, at the head of the troops, and his design became evident to the French, who at once claimed the Nawáb's protection. Suráj-ood-Dolwah was perplexed by the situation of affairs. He was threatened himself by an invasion from Ahmed Shah Abdally who was plundering Dehly, and needed aid.

Clive's operations against the French.

Advances on Chándernagore.

Perplexity of Suráj-ood-Dowlah.

On the one hand were the English, flushed with victory; but, as appeared to him, in no great strength. On the other, the French, at Chándernagore, strong enough, he considered, to hold the place, would be reinforced by M. Bussy, who was already in the Northern Circars, at the head of a powerful army. Of the two, he deemed the French the most formidable, and the protection they claimed was granted. He sent them money, forbade the English to advance, and prepared a large body of troops to proceed to Chándernagore. This produced some delay, and negotiations with the French were carried on through Omichund, the great banker; but the French commissioners were obliged to admit, that though they might promise neutrality, they could not influence the decision of the chief authorities at Pondicherry, and the negotiations broke down. The possible junction of M. Bussy was a danger of which both Clive and Admiral Watson were fully aware. They also knew of the Nawáb's continued secret intrigues with the French, which were proved by his own letters, subsequently discovered; and Admiral Watson wrote to him, in plain terms, that the capture of Chándernagore was the only course upon which any future assistance could be founded, and pointed out to him how impossible it would be for the English to leave an enemy in their rear, if he required their services. Again he wrote, more sternly, that without he came to a speedy determination, 'such a war would be kindled in his country as all the waters of the Ganges should not be able to extinguish.' In reply, the Nawáb wrote two evasive letters, which are quoted by Orme; and finding delay as dangerous as it was useless, the commanders put their own interpretation on them, and determined to attack Chándernagore at all risks: a reinforcement had arrived from Bombay, and all the means which could be hoped for were now at their disposal.

The Nawáb assists the French.

M. Bussy's position in Orissa.

Admiral Watson remonstrates with the Nawáb.

His evasive replies.

The garrison at Chándernagore had not meanwhile been idle. The defences of the place had been improved and strengthened, and some vessels had been sunk in the channel of the river which led past the town. On March 14, Clive invested the fort by land, and the siege operations were carried on till the 24th, when the ships could be moved up by a new channel, which had been shown by a deserter. At sunrise on that day, the land batteries opened fire, and at seven o'clock, three ships, the 'Kent,' 'Salisbury,' and 'Tiger,' sailed up and anchored near the fort. By an accident to her cable, the 'Kent' did not retain her proper position, and suffered very severely, receiving no less than 142 shots in her

Siege of Chándernagore.

Attack by the ships of war.

hull, and the 'Salisbury' was altogether thrown out of fire; but the result was speedily manifest. Two hours afterwards, the garrison hung out a flag of truce, and by the afternoon terms of capitulation were agreed on; but the defence for nine days had been a noble one. The capture of Chándernagore was a severe disappointment and mortification to the Nawáb. He had expected to see it make a prolonged defence, and trusted that Bussy would be able to raise the siege, and co-operate with him for the destruction of the English; instead of which, he found Bussy had not moved, and Clive in no humour to retire, while to attack him was hopeless. Once, during the siege, a large portion of his army had approached the British camp; but dread of collision, or, as some assert, the bribery of its commander by Omichund, caused it to withdraw. The Nawáb now formed a camp at Plassy, on the river, about forty miles south of Moorshidabad, while Clive took up a position near Hooghly, and his letter to Mr. Pigott[1] explains the situation. The infatuated prince was still intriguing with the French; had not resolution enough to cast in his lot with the English, whom he detested; and was perpetrating acts of horrible cruelty and oppression among his own subjects, which induced his principal officers to enter into a conspiracy to dethrone him. He had secured the interest of Omichund, the banker, who was now his prime adviser, and by this step he increased the animosity of his own servants. It is impossible, within the limits of this work, to follow out the full course of this conspiracy, in regard to which volumes have been written; but the main facts are these. Meer Jaffier, the commander of the Nawáb's army, was the brother-in-law of the late viceroy, Aliverdy Khan. He had been employed in many capacities; but his character was weak and treacherous, and he became a ready tool in the hands of able and unscrupulous conspirators. He could hope for no success except through the intervention of the English, and the English officers, who justified their conduct by the treachery of Suráj-ood-Dowlah, made no scruple of allying themselves by solemn treaty with him, and dictating their own terms. As he advanced upon Chándernagore, Clive had said, as it were prophetically, 'We cannot stop here;' and the future seemed even then to be dimly shadowed out to his mind. On the part of the English, Clive, Watson, Drake, Watts, and other chief authorities, swore 'on the holy Gospels,' that they would assist Meer Jaffier to be Soobah of Bengal, Bahar, and Orissa, with all

Capitulation of Chándernagore.

The Nawáb's hopes disappointed.

He encamps at Plassy.

Conspiracy against him.

Details of the conspiracy.

[1] Malcolm's 'Life of Clive,' vol. i. p. 199.

their troops. It would, however, have been more dignified and honourable to have done at first what was done at last, and, under the proofs of the Nawáb's treachery, to have openly declared war against him, and attacked him; but the English were not aware then of their own strength—the consciousness of it had to ensue, and the conspiracy proceeded.

Clive's proceedings.

After the treaty with Meer Jaffier had been executed, Clive threw off the mask. He summoned the troops he had dispatched to Calcutta, and set out from Chándernagore at the head of 900 Europeans, among whom were the 39th regiment of foot—who still carry on their colours 'Primus in Indis,' and 'Plassy'—and about 2,100 native soldiers; and after enumerating all the causes of grievance, declared that he was marching to Moorshidabad to have them settled in open council. He might have called in the assistance of the Mahrattas, for the Péshwah had written to him shortly before, offering higher terms of compensation and privilege than Meer Jaffier's treaty contained; but Clive knew that the price of the Mahratta assistance would be the plunder of Bengal, and declined it. What was to be done must be done alone, or not at all. At Cutwah, where he halted, the memorable council of war was held on June 21, and Clive himself even voted against an advance, on what at first sight appeared an hopeless enterprise. With 3,000 men he must attack 50,000 infantry and 18,000 cavalry, with a numerous artillery, posted in a strong position, from which his own escape, in case of defeat, would be impossible, while the amount of dependence he could place upon Meer Jaffier was even then doubtful; but, in the face of these doubts and dangers, Clive's bold mind recovered its wonted firmness during the night, and by sunrise on the morning of June 22, the whole army was crossing the Ganges. The rainy season had set in, with a violent storm at Cutwah, on the 19th; but this had cleared away, and the fresh bright morning gave a cheerful tone to the operation.

He refuses Mahratta assistance.

Council of war.

He votes against an attack,

but eventually advances on Plassy.

In many wonderful scenes have British troops been engaged; but it is questionable, considering the daring nature of the service, its importance in the world's history, or the beauty of its surroundings, whether any equals that crossing of the Ganges by the combined English and native troops, under Colonel Clive. That evening the little army, dragging its eight small field-pieces by hand, had marched to the grove of Plassy, fifteen miles distant, and about 1 A.M. took up a position in it. Clive discovered that the army of the Nawáb was not a mile distant from him, and the drums and trumpets of the night-watches and patrols sounded close at hand. In the morning, early, the Nawáb directed the English to be attacked. A coward by nature, he took no part in the action, and when his commander-in-chief, Meer Mudun, was wounded, and died on being carried to his tent, he lost all hope, and mounting a swift camel, fled to Moorshidabad. The army dispersed at once, and on Clive's advance, about noon, he saw little except a few Frenchmen to resist him; the remainder were a flying rabble, whom he disdained to pursue. Everything in camp had fallen into his hands, and his own singularly modest and graphic account of the battle,[1] possesses even more interest now that the results of the victory can be estimated, than it did when it first excited the wonder and admiration of the people of England.

The English are attacked by the Nawáb's army.

The Nawáb flies to Moorshidabad.

The Nawáb's army, being defeated, disperses.

CHAPTER IX.

OF EVENTS IN BENGAL AND THE CARNATIC (*continued*), 1757 TO 1759.

IT is trite to say that the victory of Plassy was the foundation of the British empire in India, but it is no less true, as will appear from subsequent events. It had been gained with the trifling loss to the victors of seventy-two killed and wounded, while that of the Nawáb's army was barely 300 of all ranks. As nearly as possible, 100 years before, the first great blow dealt against the Mahomedan power in India, was the slaughter of the army of Beejapoor by Sivajee in the wilds of the Western Ghauts; the direct result of which was the rise of the Mahratta power. That power had already broken down the Mahomedan empire, and now another was to rise upon the battle of Plassy, which was to subdue and extinguish both. The day after the victory, Clive was joined by Meer Jaffier, who had appeared with some cavalry on the outskirts of the combat, and had retired. Though he had taken no active part in the battle, he had done what had been expected from him, and was to receive his reward. Next day he proceeded in advance to Moorshidabad, followed leisurely by Clive, who, entering the city in triumph, on June 29, repaired at once to the hall of audience, where he placed Meer Jaffier on the throne, and declared him Soobah of Bengal, Behar, and Orissa.

Effect of the victory of Plassy.

Clive proceeds to Moorshidabad,

and enthrones Meer Jaffier.

[1] Malcolm's 'Memoirs,' Dispatch to Secret Committee, vol. i. pp. 263-272; Orme, vol. ii. &c.; Mill's 'History,' vol. iii. book iv. chap. iii. &c.

When Meer Jaffier arrived in the city, Suráj-ood-Dowlah was still in the palace, preparing for flight; and taking with him one of his mistresses, a menial, and a casket of jewels, he escaped at night from a window of the palace into a boat, which had been prepared, and was rowed rapidly up the river, in the hope of meeting with M. Law, who, with 200 Frenchmen, had been coming to his assistance from Behar. But in this he was disappointed; and having landed near Ráj Mahál, in order to have a meal cooked in a lonely fakeer's hut by the river-side, found it tenanted by a man whose ears he had caused to be cut off a year before, and by whom he was instantly recognised and seized. Escape was impossible, for his flight was known to all, and the pursuit by land was close; and he was conducted back to Moorshidabad, amidst the execrations of the people. The night he arrived, he was put to death by Meer Jaffier's son, and his body, after being publicly carried about the city, was buried in his grandfather's tomb. He was twenty-five years old, and had reigned fifteen months. Clive is blamed by some for not having saved or protected him; but he was not informed of his capture, and to prevent his death was, therefore, impossible.

Suráj-ood-Dowlah escapes.

He is seized near Raj Mahal.

and put to death at Moorshidabad.

Another tragedy, for so it proved in effect, resulted from the conspiracy and revolution. The name of Omichund has been already mentioned in connection with the intrigues in progress, in which he took a prominent part. Sometimes he favoured one party, sometimes another, and appears to have been equally ready to encourage Suráj-ood-Dowlah in his plots against the English, as he was to enter into the conspiracy against him; but, on the whole, he seems to have done more for the English than against them; and his losses in the capture of Calcutta had been severe. When the plot was ripe, he communicated his knowledge of it to the confederates, and made his own terms. They were heavy, and he agreed to receive thirty lacs of rupees, or 300,000*l*., as his share of Suráj-ood-Dowlah's treasures, or five per cent. on their amount, for his silence. He did not betray the plot. If he had done so, none could have escaped the Nawáb's vengeance. Meer Jaffier, his family, the Sett bankers, all in fact at Moorshidabad, whom the conspiracy involved, must inevitably have perished. Yet it was nevertheless determined to balk his avarice, as it was called; to cheat the man who, had he pleased, could have cheated all. Clive, and the members of Council, were determined he should get nothing; yet no one dared openly refuse his demand, and it was ratified

Omichund's part in the conspiracy.

His stipulation with the confederates.

The false treaty.

by a clause granting him twenty lacs of rupees—200,000*l.*—inserted, not in the real treaty with Meer Jaffier, but in a counterpart written on red paper, which was signed by all but Admiral Watson, who refused to be avowedly a party to it, though he allowed, as subsequently recorded in evidence, his name to be written by another. In the certainty that he was to receive enormous wealth, Omichund rested till the drama was played out, and the treasures were being divided at Moorshidabad. He seems to have been gloating over the idea of his coming riches, when, as he sat apart, Clive and Mr. Scrafton went to him, and told him the red treaty was a trick, and that he was to have nothing. The revulsion of feeling proved too much for his mind—he fainted, and was carried away to his palankeen, and so to his house; but he never recovered his reason, and died, a drivelling idiot, in about a year afterwards. No act of Clive's life has been more commented upon than this. His own opinion was, that in this case it was necessary to meet fraud by fraud, that the end justified the means, and that he 'would do it over again a hundred times.' The act was one, however, of deliberate and unworthy treachery. The great object seems to have been to save the sum of 200,000*l.* for the Nawáb's treasury; and the question, like many others of equally doubtful character in history, will probably never be settled, whether, under the peculiar circumstances of the case, and with the lives of so many persons hanging upon the chances of Omichund's silence, the act of deceit was not justified by necessity. At best it has a revolting circumstantiality, and is thus on a par with the general conspiracy, which, though successful, seems equally unjustifiable. It is at least certain that the subsequent history of India happily furnishes no parallel to either.

The truth is told him, and he becomes insane.

Comments on the proceeding.

A remarkable episode of the war, the details of which are of extreme interest, was the chase of M. Law and his party, by a small detachment under Captain Eyre Coote, who proved, on this occasion, an excellent partisan officer; and although Law escaped, yet the indomitable perseverance by which European soldiers were marched literally hundreds of miles through an unknown country, and in the rainy season, had an effect upon people who had never before seen a European, which was never effaced.

Coote's pursuit of M. Law.

It need hardly be recorded that the full amount of loss, public and private, was paid from the Nawáb's treasury. In addition to the sums specified in the treaty, Meer Jaffier made a present of 500,000*l.*—fifty lacs of rupees—to the army and navy; to each member of the Committee of Calcutta,

Compensation for losses and gratuities.

24,000*l.*; to Clive in that capacity, 28,000*l.*; while, on other heads, his total gain was, by his own account, 160,000*l.*, and in all, cannot have been less than 230,000*l.* Of the general funds, the first instalment of 800,000*l.*, or eighty lacs, was brought to Calcutta in a triumphal procession of boats from Moorshidabad, and the total amount of payment was 2,200,000*l.* sterling. The division of the money among the various claimants gave rise to fierce disputes and heartburnings, which are of little value in detail, in the presence of the great fact, that the Nawáb, or Nabob, as he was called, of Bengal, had been seated on his throne by the company's power, that all their losses had been redeemed, that no impediment whatever existed to their trade, and that the French power in Bengal was utterly crushed. The local revolution was more complete than that in the Carnatic conducted by Dupleix; for no one remained to dispute it, and the English remained masters of the situation. Clive had been ordered by the Madras Government to return by April 1757, but that had been impossible. He was now in a position from which he could not withdraw, for he had been appointed President of Bengal.

Their total amount.

During Clive's absence an attempt had been made to gain possession of Madura, which was unsuccessfully attacked in April 1757, by Captain Calliaud, the commandant of Trichinopoly. While thus engaged, the French dispatched a force to Trichinopoly, which invested the fort; hearing of which, Calliaud left Madura, and by a memorable march, succeeded in evading the enemy's positions and regaining his post, and the French commander retired. Wandiwash, the chief of which refused to pay tribute, was next attacked by Colonel Aldercron; but, on the French advancing, he was forced to raise the siege. Meanwhile, the Mahrattas had arrived, and demanded an arrear of chouth of forty lacs of rupees—400,000*l.*—which it was impossible for the Nawáb to pay; but their claim was eventually compromised for four and a half lacs. The Patán Nawábs, who were now independent of the Soobahdar of the Deccan, and Moorary Ráo, offered to join the English against the Mahrattas; but the Council had the wisdom to decline so irregular an alliance, and for the present the Mahrattas were content. In June, Calliaud renewed his attack upon Madura, and having breached the fort, attempted to storm it, but was repulsed with severe loss. As the investment continued, the garrison capitulated; and on August 8 he entered the town, receiving 17,000*l.* as arrears of tribute. Many other desultory movements and attacks of forts of a minor character followed, both by the French and the English, without any decided result on either side; their forces were nearly balanced in amount, and

Events in the Carnatic.

Calliaud repulsed at Madura,

which afterwards capitulates.

neither possessed the power of striking a decisive blow. This state of affairs was, however, soon to alter.

Soon after the declaration of war in Europe, the French Government dispatched the Count de Lally as commander of the French forces in India, with a fine fleet, in May 1757. Lally had already highly distinguished himself as a soldier, and great expectations arose as to his future success.

Arrival of the Count de Lally.

He took with him his own regiment of Irish, upwards of 1,000 strong; but the troops suffered severely from fever on the voyage, and the fleet did not reach Pondicherry till April 1758. He had no sooner landed than he marched for Fort St. David, which he invested. An English fleet, under Admiral Stevens, had, however, arrived at Madras, and joined some ships under Mr. Pococke; and the combined fleet, on April 29, fought an indecisive action with the French, which did not, however, prevent the French from landing troops and stores at Pondicherry, and the siege of Fort St. David was pressed with vigour. It was not well defended, and the ammunition running short, it capitulated on June 1. The Council of Madras now expected that the settlement would be attacked; but it escaped for the present. All the outlying garrisons were, however, as far as possible, called in. If Lally had had funds at his command, he would probably have attacked Madras at once; but he had brought none, and Pondicherry could supply none. An attempt was now made to enforce payment of a bond for fifty-six lacs of rupees—560,000*l.*—given by the Rajah of Tanjore to Dupleix in 1751; but it failed of effect, as, partly from assistance the rajah received from the English garrison at Trichinopoly, and partly from the arrival of an English fleet off the coast, Lally was obliged to raise the siege and retire. His reputation with the natives had, however, suffered severely, not only from his ill success, but from his cruelty. He had plundered a Hindoo temple of great antiquity and sanctity at Kiveloor, and had blown away some of the Brahmins attached to it from his guns; he had threatened to send the Rajah of Tanjore and family into slavery, and he had forced the people of the country, without distinction, to carry the burdens of his army. The moderation and courtliness of Dupleix were well remembered, and the contrast with these qualities displayed by Lally, had the worst effect among the people.

His Irish regiment.

Fort St. David invested,

and capitulates.

Lally's efforts to obtain money.

His violence and cruelty.

If these were not errors sufficient to bring about disastrous results to the French, Lally now committed a greater in recalling Bussy, of whom he was intensely jealous. After recovering his position at Hyderabad, as has been previously

Lally recalls M. Bussy.

narrated, Bussy, at the close of 1756, proceeded, with 500 Europeans and 4,000 Sepoys, into the Northern Circars. Here he received pressing letters from Suráj-ood-Dowlah, to advance into Bengal against the English, and he moved up to the north-eastern frontier, to be ready to take advantage of circumstances; and, on receipt of the news of the fate of Chándernagore, he attacked Vizagapatam, the most important of the English factories on that coast, on June 24. The place was not capable of defence, and it capitulated; but before Bussy could enter upon further operations, he was suddenly obliged to marched rapidly upon Aurungabad, where Salabut Jung had been driven to extremity by his brothers, Nizam Ally and Basalut Jung, who had usurped the whole power of the State. In twenty-one days, and by a route little known, Bussy reached Aurungabad, where he found not only the armies of the usurpers, but a Mahratta force, prepared to act as circumstances might require. The French troops with the Soobahdar had protected him from violence, and Bussy's presence restored order. Nizam Ally was induced to moderate his pretensions, to give up the great seal, which was now entrusted to Basalut Jung, and to accept of the government of Hyderabad instead of Berar. But further precaution was necessary; and Bussy, by the assistance of the deputy-governor of Dowlatabad, obtained possession of that fort, one of the strongest in India. A plot was now laid for the assassination of Salabut Jung; but it was defeated, and in a tumult which ensued, the prime minister, who had been the most active in Nizam Ally's interest, and Nizam Ally himself, at once fled to Boorhanpoor. By these masterly operations, Bussy's power was rendered, to all appearance, more secure than ever; but at this juncture the order of recall from Lally reached him, and was the direct cause of his ruin. He might have disobeyed the order, for he was the servant of a native prince, who was in sore need of his services; but, a true soldier at heart, obedience was his first care, and leaving his troops under the command of M. Conflans, he proceeded direct to Pondicherry, and joined Lally in the month of September, just before his expedition to Arcot.

Bussy's proceedings in the Deccan.

His march on Aurungabad.

Events at the Nizam's court.

Immediate advantage was taken of M. Bussy's absence from the Northern Circars, by Anundráj, chief or Rajah of Vizagapatam, who made an insurrection on his own account against the French garrison, with some success, as he gained possession of the place; but he was unable to prosecute this advantage, and was fearful of reinforcements to the French arriving. He therefore applied to Clive, who, now at rest in Bengal, was enabled to assist

Effects of Bussy's absence.

Clive assists the Raja of Vizagapatam.

him. It was not only possible, he thought, to assist Anundráj, but to drive the French out of the Northern Circars. Bussy had delegated his authority in the Circars to M. Moraçin, the governor of Masulipatam; but he had been summoned to Pondicherry as well as himself, and Lally appointed the Marquis de Conflans to the vacant post. The proposal of Anundráj reached Calcutta in July 1758, but it was not before September that the expedition could be prepared, and it did not reach Vizagapatam till October 20 of that year. It was under the command of Colonel Forde, whom Clive had selected for his especial fitness, and consisted of 500 Europeans, 2,000 Sepoys, and six field-pieces. After making a treaty with the rajah, and preparations for a march, the allies set out towards Rajahmundry; and on December 3, encountered Conflans, who had with him 500 Europeans, 2,000 Sepoys, with a large park of artillery, and gave him a severe defeat, taking all his guns. Forde followed him up by a forced march to Rajahmundry, but found the place evacuated. On January 28, 1759, the army marched for Masulipatam, but its progress was delayed by Anundráj on various pretexts, and Colonel Forde did not reach Masulipatam till March 6. Meanwhile Conflans had summoned Salabut Jung, the Nizam, to his aid, by representing to him that both the English and Anundráj might be easily defeated. The war, therefore, had assumed a very complicated character, for the aid of Salabut Jung was, doubtless, of a very formidable character. Forde did not, however, lose heart, but opened trenches against the fort. Hardly had this been effected, when his Europeans broke into open mutiny, demanding not only arrears of pay, but the plunder of Musulipatam should they take it. But on news arriving that the Nizam was only forty miles distant, they set to work in earnest, completed the batteries, and by April 7 had made two breaches in the works. That day the fort was stormed by 346 Europeans and 1,400 native soldiers. There were 500 Europeans in the fort, with 120 pieces of cannon; but the defence had been miserable, and at its capture there were more European prisoners than assailants. Salabut Jung, after waiting at a respectable distance for assistance from Pondicherry, and on finding the French ships had arrived, but had again departed without landing the troops on board, gave up all hope from the French, and turned his attention to the English, in the hope of obtaining their assistance in his contest with Nizam Ally. On the basis of the negotiation which now ensued, a treaty was concluded, which in

Clive sends Colonel Forde into the Northern Circars.

Forde defeats the Marquis de Conflans.

Salabut Jung advances to assist the French.

Masulipatam besieged,

and taken by storm.

Colonel Forde's treaty with Salabut Jung.

all respects was most important for the interests of the English. Masulipatam, with a large tract of country, yielding four lacs—40,000*l.*—per year, was ceded in perpetuity. The French were to possess no settlements or factories north of the Krishna river, and the Soobahdar engaged not to employ any of them in his dominions for the future. Thus had the power established by Bussy in the Deccan crumbled away, as it were, in the course of a few months; and in a manner which, though arising from the incapacity of M. de Conflans, almost justified Lally's opinion, that it was delusive and unsubstantial.

Masulipatam ceded to the English.

Bussy's power destroyed.

CHAPTER X.

OF EVENTS IN BENGAL, FROM THE BATTLE OF PLASSY TO THE DEPARTURE OF CLIVE, 1757 TO 1760.

Difficulties with Meer Jaffier.

IT was one thing to set up a Nawáb of Bengal in the English interest, and quite another to control his actions, and to induce him to maintain a tranquil and respectable government. Meer Jaffier's treasury was utterly exhausted by his payments to the English; and he desired to resort to the usual Mahomedan practice of confiscation and extortion to supply his wants. The persons against whom he had begun these demands were his finance minister, Rái Doolub; the Hindoo governor of Midnapore, the Rajah of Purneah, and Rám Narráin, governor of Patna: and as many rebellions were the consequence. Unable either to effect his purpose, or to check these outbreaks, which it must be confessed had the sympathy of the people, the Nawáb applied to Clive, who, on November 25, 1757, arrived at Moorshidabad at the head of a small force, and a beneficial result was immediately apparent in a reconciliation between the Nawáb and his minister, who joined his master with 10,000 men. The Nawáb and Clive then proceeded to Patna, where a similar result with Rám Narráin followed, and Clive obtained from the Nawáb a monopoly of the saltpetre of the province, on fair terms, but not less than could have been obtained from other parties. Thus all the troubles passed off; but there were still apprehensions that Bengal might be invaded by the Soobahdar of Oudh, with whom was a party of French, under M. Law; and the Mahrattas had sent an officer to demand

Clive proceeds to Moorshidabad.

His measures there.

24 lacs—240,000*l.*—as the arrears of chouth. The principal elements of local disturbance had, however, been disposed of, and Clive was able to leave Moorshidabad for Calcutta on May 24. About a month later, a commission for the new government of the Bengal possessions arrived from England, which was strangely devised. There were to be ten counsellors, of whom the four seniors were to act as governors for three months each, in rotation; but no provision was made for Clive, and the Council at once elected him president. The fact is, that on the dispatch of the commission, Clive was supposed, in England, to have returned to Madras; and his appointment as President of Bengal was afterwards confirmed.

Commission for the government of Bengal.

Although Clive had temporarily adjusted the differences at Moorshidabad, affairs did not continue in a satisfactory state. The Nawáb's son, Meerun, proved vicious and intractable; and would have sacrificed Rái Doolub, but for Mr. Scrafton's interference. Even with his aid it became impossible for the minister to remain; and he succeeded in obtaining an asylum in Calcutta, and in saving his property, of which the Nawáb and his son had designed to deprive him. The excitement of this event had barely subsided, when a new, and to some extent a formidable, danger appeared. The Prince Royal of Dehly, Ally Johur, wearied of inaction, and of the tyranny of his father's vizier, escaped to the Rohilla chief, Nujeeb-ood-Dowlah, who, having been superseded in his office as commander of the forces, as already related in Chapter VII. of this Book, was the vizier's declared enemy. The emperor had conferred on his son the vice-royalty of Bengal, and a league was formed by the prince with the Soobahdar of Allahabad, the Nawáb of Oudh, and two powerful Hindoo rajahs, Bulwunt Singh and Soonder Singh, to carry out the invasion of the country. At the close of 1758, their preparations were completed; and the prince entered Behar at the head of 40,000 men, and invested Patna, which was well defended by Rám Narráin, the governor. Meer Jaffier alone would have been totally unable either to relieve Patna, or to oppose the invasion; and but for Clive, the results to him must have been in the last degree disastrous. It does not appear that Clive was distracted by the thought that the province had been really independent of the emperor, and that, as Mr. Mill justly observes, 'he had undoubted right to appoint his eldest son to be his deputy in the government.' Clive had pledged his faith to Meer Jaffier, and did not hesitate to move forward in his behalf.

Fresh difficulties at Moorshidabad.

The Prince Royal of Dehly takes the field.

The prince advances into Behar.

Meer Jaffier is unable to oppose him.

Clive advances in aid of Meer Jaffier.

Effects of Clive's advance.

The prince assisted by Clive.

Clive obtains a jahgeer, or estate, from the emperor.

It was in vain that the prince, when he heard of Clive's march, sent him letters, promising him large territorial cessions for his assistance; for, on the other hand, Meer Jaffier had received orders from the emperor, written, no doubt, by the vizier, to oppose his son, and if possible, to take him prisoner. Clive, therefore, continued his march at the head of 450 Europeans and 2,500 Sepoys, and passing Moorshidabad, sent forward a light detachment under Ensign Matthews, on the arrival of which at Patna, the confederates abandoned the siege and decamped. The Soobahdar of Allahabad had indeed preceded the general flight; for the Nawáb of Oudh, during his absence, had treacherously seized the fortress of Allahabad, and its recovery was doubtful. Forsaken by his allies, the prince would have thrown himself upon Clive's generosity; but as this would have been embarrassing, Clive dismissed him with a sufficient sum for his expenses. Meer Jaffier's gratitude for this service was, for the present, sincere. He obtained for Clive a patent of nobility from the emperor, with the title of Shoukut Jung, who conferred upon him an appanage, or jahgeer, of the value of three lacs, or 30,000*l.*, per year for its support. This consisted of the quit rent of the lands held by the company, which had hitherto formed part of the general revenues of the province of Bengal.

He returns to Calcutta.

The Nawáb's intrigue with the Dutch.

A Dutch fleet arrives in the Hooghly.

The Dutch commence hostilities.

Clive reached Calcutta in June, and the troops under Colonel Forde, or such portion of them as could be spared from the Northern Circars, arrived soon afterwards, in time to check a combination, as some assert, between the Nawáb, or his son Meerun, with the Dutch, who had a settlement at Chinsurah; or, according to other opinions, an effort of the Dutch government of Batavia to establish a counterpoise to the English power in Bengal. The latter supposition is hardly tenable, and, therefore, the probability of an intrigue with the Nawáb becomes the more possible. Meer Jaffier was Clive's guest at Calcutta in October 1759, when the Dutch fleet of seven ships, crowded with European soldiers, arrived in the river, and he took his departure somewhat abruptly, writing afterwards to Clive that he had granted some additional privileges to the Dutch. Holland and England were at peace; but Clive was by no means disposed to admit the presence of any rival European force, and he made preparations to resist the Dutch fleet as an enemy's. The Dutch were the first to commence hostilities, by seizing some of the company's vessels and grain-boats, hoisting their own colours upon them, and burning the storehouses at Fulta. These acts freed Clive from embarrassment.

Their fleet is defeated.

The Dutch fleet was attacked by Commodore Wilson, on November 3, and defeated, six of the ships striking their flags, and one being taken in endeavouring to escape. They had, however, landed 700 Europeans and 800 Malays above Calcutta, and these, after a skirmish with Colonel Forde, formed a junction with their countrymen in Chinsurah, to which place Forde had pursued them. He was doubtful what to do, when Clive's memorable note, written on one of the cards with which he was playing when Forde's dispatch reached him—'Dear Forde, fight them immediately, I will send you the order in council to-morrow'—decided the question. Forde had only 330 Europeans and 800 Sepoys; but he attacked the Dutch, who, far superior to him in force, were posted in the plain without Chinsurah, and severely defeated them, the European Dutch soldiers being nearly all killed or wounded. The complicity of the Nawáb's son, Meerun, was afterwards apparent; for he suddenly appeared after the action, without cause, at the head of 7,000 cavalry, and there is little doubt, had been prepared to act against the English if the Dutch had proved victorious.

Colonel Forde attacks the Dutch troops,

and defeats them.

Clive restores the Dutch ships.

The contest and temporary alarm were, however, at an end; Clive restored the ships, and a covenant was made that the Dutch should maintain only 125 Europeans for the protection of their factories; send away all other troops, and that they should pay for the damage and loss they had caused; and under their compliance with these stipulations, the affair ended.

Clive returns to England.

The government of Madras was still in warfare with the French, as has been already related; but it was strong enough to relieve any apprehension of danger; none was evident in Bengal, and Clive determined to proceed to England. He had already written his views of the English position in Bengal to Mr. Pitt,[1] and had sketched, with a bold, but true, hand, the probabilities of the company obtaining the whole of Bengal, and extending the British power into India; and it is probable, believing from the political aspect of affairs among native States, that such a contingency might be near at hand, that he considered it his best course to explain these subjects personally to the minister, as well as to the Court of Directors. He, therefore, sailed for England on February 25, 1760.

---

[1] *Vide* Malcolm's 'Memoirs,' vol. ii. pp. 119-125.

CHAPTER XI.

OF EVENTS IN THE CARNATIC (*continued from Ch. IX.*), 1759 TO 1760.

AT this period, two fleets, nearly equal in force—one English, of seven sail, under Admiral Pococke; the other French, under the Count d'Aché, consisting of eight ships—were on the coast of Coromandel. Admiral Pococke had been too late to relieve Fort St. David; but he attacked the French squadron on two occasions, and on the last having gained some indecisive advantage, the French admiral escaped to Pondicherry, whence, notwithstanding Lally's earnest remonstrances, he sailed for the Mauritius. The actual, as well as the moral force of Lally's position, were both much weakened by this event; but it was necessary for him to do something to establish Rajah Sahib, the eldest son of Chunda Sahib, whom the French had proclaimed Nabob of the Carnatic: and having entered into an intrigue with the native commandant of Arcot, which belonged to Mahomed Ally, he agreed to deliver up the place for 10,000 rupees; and Lally having marched thither, received a mock capitulation, and entered the town in triumph on October 4, 1758. He had hoped to capture Chingliput; but the authorities of Madras, fully alive to its importance, threw a strong garrison into the fort, and saved it. Arcot itself was of little value; and Lally's only hope appeared to be a successful siege of Madras. His own officers were, however, despairing. There was no money to be had at Pondicherry. Bussy, who had just arrived, could supply none, and all that could be collected was 94,000 rupees, of which Lally supplied 60,000 from his own funds; but, as the Count d'Estaign expressed himself, 'it was better to die by a musket-shot under the walls of Madras, than to starve at Pondicherry,' and under these circumstances the French marched for the siege of Madras in December.

Naval action on the Coromandel coast.

Lally's position.

Madras was fully prepared for the attack, but the forces were not sufficient to check the French advance, and after the occupation of the native town by the enemy, the fort was closely invested. The siege continued for nine weeks, with considerable loss to both sides, and a breach was effected, which

Siege of Madras.

would have been stormed on February 16, 1759, when, on that day, a fleet of English ships, with a reinforcement of 600 King's troops, arrived in the roads. For some time past the French army had been without pay, and were short of provisions, as well as of powder and shot; further prosecution of the siege was, therefore, hopeless, and the French retired on February 17. The English loss on all heads had been 579 Europeans and 762 Sepoys, and that of the French was probably much greater. If Lally had retired upon Pondicherry, it would have been tantamount to a relinquishment of the struggle; but he moved to Arcot, and after come desultory operations by both armies, the English having also taken the field, they went into quarters early in May. To the English the sea was open, and they continued to receive troops and supplies; but the hopes of the French that their long looked-for fleet would arrive with money and stores was disappointed. On September 10, it was attacked by Admiral Pococke off Trincomalee, and dispersed: but a portion of it subsequently reached Pondicherry, and M. d'Aché having landed about 40,000*l.* in money and diamonds, with 500 Europeans, marines and sailors, could neither be induced nor commanded to remain, and again left India. Meanwhile, Wandiwash had been attacked by the English, who were repulsed with severe loss; and M. Bussy, who had obtained permission to return to the Deccan, to meet Basalut Jung, left that place with the troops which had been made over to him. He had no sooner departed, than the whole French army broke out into mutiny, and he was obliged to halt at Arcot for some days. This delayed his junction with Basalut Jung, who had approached the frontier of the Carnatic; but they met finally on November 10. Basalut Jung, instead of giving money, demanded it, and wished to be made sovereign of the whole Carnatic; all which being impossible, Bussy returned from an expedition which seems to have had no practical object from the first.

Arrival of English ships.

The French retire.

The French fleet reaches India.

Before he could rejoin, Lally, who was unable, for want of funds, to keep the whole of his army together, now sent half of it to the south; and Coote, who had arrived at Madras, and who saw his error, determined to take advantage of it. His first operation was the capture of Wandiwash, which surrendered on November 29, and was followed by the fall of Canangooty, on December 10. After this, the movements of both armies continued till January 22, 1760, when they encountered each other near Wandiwash, which Lally was again besieging. The English had 1,900 Europeans and 2,100 native infantry, with 1,250 native cavalry and sixteen field-pieces; the French, 2,250 Europeans and 1,300 Sepoys, besides

Coote takes Wandiwash.

General action.

their Mahratta horse, with twenty field-pieces. The forces, therefore, seem to have been pretty nearly equal on both sides. After a brilliant combat, the French, who had suffered very severely, as well by the fire of Coote's own regiment as from the bayonet, retreated. They had lost 600 Europeans in killed and wounded, that of the English being about 200. Bussy, who had led one of the charges, had his horse shot under him, and was taken prisoner; and if the English native cavalry had done their duty, the retreat of the French might have been severely harassed.

The French defeated.

Coote now proceeded to attack Arcot; and on February 5 his batteries opened against the fort; and by the 9th a breach had been partly effected, when the garrison surrendered. Other minor operations succeeded, and by the middle of March, with the exception of Pondicherry itself, Calicut was the only possession on the coast which remained to the French. This place fell to a detachment from Trichinopoly on April 5, and by May 1, the French were confined to Pondicherry by the English army, which was preparing to invest it. The condition of the French affairs in the Carnatic now appeared desperate. No fleet had arrived with supplies or money: and it was questionable, if any ships should reach India, whether they could approach the coast, as no less than eleven ships of the line of the English fleet were now present, and the English had secured further reinforcements of troops. In his despair—for it can be called little else—Lally now applied to Hyder Ally of Mysore, who had risen into power, and was believed capable of rendering material assistance; but the negotiation was productive of no result. Hyder Ally was obliged to return suddenly to Mysore, and was followed as suddenly by his troops. Meanwhile Madras had received further reinforcements of King's troops, and the fleet was increased to seventeen sail of the line, besides the company's armed vessels. Ample means, therefore, existed for the siege of Pondicherry, and operations against it were commenced without delay. The recently arrived fleet had, however, brought out a commission for Major Monson, who, as colonel, now virtually superseded Coote on the eve of the final triumph of the war he had so admirably conducted, and he prepared to depart from Bengal with his regiment; but, under the necessity of the situation, he allowed it to remain, and stayed also himself, at the request of the Madras Council; but for the present without command. The first operations, therefore, were commenced by Monson. After a partial attack upon the English camp by Lally, on September 4, which failed, the investment of the place was commenced; and in the first attack on the outposts and redoubts,

Coote's proceedings.

Lally applies to Hyder.

Siege of Pondicherry.

Monson was severely wounded. Coote, however, had not sailed, and now resumed his command; and the confidence of the army, which had been somewhat weakened, was fully restored.

Distress of the native population.

At this period, Pondicherry was sorely straitened for provisions, and the expulsion of the entire native population was urged by Lally; but for the present it was not carried out. A gleam of hope presented itself in the arrival of the Mahrattas, who had returned to the Carnatic; but the negotiation with Ballajee Ráo Péshwah proved delusive. On November 16, the stores for the siege operations arrived from Madras, and Lally seeing that it would be no longer delayed, expelled 1,400 of the natives, who, of all sexes and ages, without provisions, wandered for seven days between the fort and the bound hedge now held by the British, subsisting upon roots of grass, or whatever they could pick up. Coote's desire was to drive them back into the fort, but they were fired upon from thence, and he at last allowed them to pass into the open country. On the 30th, a furious storm wrecked several of the blockading fleet, and damaged the trenches very seriously; but Lally was unable to take advantage of the disaster. The damages were soon repaired, and on January 12, 1761, the trenches were opened. On the 15th, about sunset, a party from the fort approached with a flag of truce, bearing letters from Lally and the Council. Both letters contained stipulations, some of which were acceded to; but in regard to the garrison, Coote replied that he would only accept terms of unconditional surrender, and these terms were agreed to. On the 16th, the Villenore gate was occupied by Coote's grenadiers, and the surrender of the citadel followed in the evening. There were only two days' provisions remaining, and to have protracted the defence would have been impossible. The troops in the town amounted to 2,072, and there were 500 pieces of cannon, with 100 mortars and howitzers, with small-arms, ammunition, and stores, in great quantities. At sunrise on the following morning, the British flag was hoisted, amidst the thunder of cannon from the ships in the roads and the artillery in camp.

Lally expels the natives from the fort.

Progress of the siege.

The fort is surrendered.

Strange dispute as to the possession of the fort.

Lally, hooted out of the fort by his ungrateful countrymen, went to Madras, where the wife and family of Rajah Sahib also received an asylum. After the fall of Pondicherry, a question arose as to whom it should belong. It had been surrendered to His Britannic Majesty, and a council of war decided it should belong to the King; but Mr. Pigott, the governor of Madras, not only claimed it, but resolutely declared he would neither pay the troops, nor subsist the prisoners, unless it were made over to him; and the objection was speedily withdrawn. Thus the capture of Madras was more than revenged; for the French power in India, after a vast expenditure of blood and treasure, was now completely overthrown. Three places alone remained to them in India. Tiagar and Ginjee in the Carnatic, which were soon reduced, and Mahé on the western coast, which capitulated in February, to Colonel Monson. With all his faults, Lally was deserving of a better fate than he experienced. His enemies in India and in France had exaggerated his losses, and the weak points of his character, and all the odium of the defeat in India was thrown upon him. On his arrival in France he was imprisoned for eighteen months, tried, and condemned to death; and was executed by the guillotine on the day his sentence was known, being conveyed to the scaffold with a large gag in his mouth to prevent his speaking to the people. Thus perished the last of three victims to French policy in India, at the hands of their own ungrateful nation, and the fortifications of Pondicherry, constructed at immense cost, being afterwards razed to the ground by the Madras authorities, the humiliation of the French in India was completed.

Extinction of the French power.

Fate of Lally.

CHAPTER XII.

MAHRATTA PROGRESS, TO THE BATTLE OF PANIPUT, 1757 TO 1761.

THE main object of Salabut Jung the Nizam's treaty with Colonel Forde at Masulipatam, was to engage the services of the English against his brother Nizam Ally, who, since his flight from Aurungabad, and the departure of M. Bussy, had become again powerful. He had raised troops at Boorhanpoor, and had been joined by Ibrahim Khan Gardee, an officer who had been educated in his profession in the French corps, and who understood the management of artillery. Basalut Jung, who had been created minister under Bussy's advice, sent Janoojee Bhóslay with his Mahratta forces against Nizam Ally, and he was forced to retire; but his artillery being now completed, Nizam Ally again took the field, and defeated Janoojee with great loss. Salabut Jung had proceeded to Hyderabad, and when he marched for Masulipatum, to the assistance of M. de Conflans, Nizam Ally not only took possession of Aurungabad, but proceeded to Hyderabad. From these circumstances, the desire of Salabut Jung to obtain the assistance of the English will be fully apparent; but, as has been already explained, Colonel Forde

Contest between Salabut Jung and his brother.

was in no position, even had he been free to do so, to engage in Deccan politics, and Salabut Jung returned to Hyderabad. Here, after much discussion between the three brothers, the office of minister was conferred upon Nizam Ally, and Basalut Jung departed to his province of Adony.

Mahratta affairs.

The Péshwah invades Mysore.

In the year 1757, the Péshwah had proceeded into the Carnatic for the purpose of levying the usual chouth, which had fallen considerably into arrears; and in March of that year, he appeared before Seringapatam with an army of 60,000 men, and canonnaded the town; but after negotiation with the minister and regent Nunjeráj, the Mahratta demand was compromised for thirty-two lacs of rupees—320,000*l.* The Péshwah had contemplated further operations for regaining possession of Shahjee's districts; but the approach of the monsoon rendered these impossible, and he returned to Poona, leaving a force under Bulwunt Ráo Méndlee, to resume the campaign in the ensuing season. Bulwunt Ráo was an active and enterprising officer. He defeated the Patán Nawáb of Kurpa and Kurnool on September 24; but he was unable to attack Hyder Ally, who was in the field on behalf of the Mysore Government, which now refused to make the payments that had been agreed on. At this time, the events in the Deccan obliged the Péshwah to concentrate his forces, and instead of being able to reinforce the army in Mysore, he was obliged to recall it. Hyder thus obtained leisure to mature his own plans, of which he took full advantage.

The Nizam and Mahrattas.

War in the Deccan.

For some time past, the relations between the Péshwah and the Nizam had been in an unsatisfactory state. On the one hand, the chouth had fallen into arrears; and, on the other, the surrender of the important fort of Ahmednugger to the Mahrattas by its governor, was an insult which could not be endured by the Nizam, who declared war, and moved his army northwards, with the intention of its recovery. The Péshwah was not slow to meet him. Taking command of a portion of the army himself, he moved towards Ahmednugger, while he detached another and larger portion, under Sudasheo Ráo Bhow, to operate upon the Moghul left flank. Sudasheo Ráo had taken into the service the corps of Ibrahim Khan Gardee, which Nizam Ally had, in deference to his brother, dismissed; and his army was both complete and numerous. Salabut Jung and Nizam Ally had proceeded together northward by the usual road to Aurungabad, where the great army was to assemble, and had nearly reached Oodgeer, when Sudasheo Ráo, whose scouts had been watching their movements, now hurried on to attack them. Some light troops, sent in advance, were sufficient to interrupt the progress of the brothers, who, with their comparatively small force of 7,000 cavalry, occupied the town and fort of Oodgeer, hoping for and awaiting reinforcements. These, however, did not reach them; and on the approach of Sudasheo Ráo, with 40,000 horse, they made an attempt to pursue their march, but with great loss. The old Moghul spirit was not entirely extinct: Sudasheo Ráo's proposal for them to surrender was met with a refusal, and an attack on Ibrahim Khan's brigade, which was nearly destroyed, followed; but the Mahratta cavalry charged the right wing of the Nizam's army in turn, and almost annihilated it, nearly 3,000 Moghuls being slain. Escape was now hopeless, and Nizam Ally sent his seal to Sudasheo Ráo, thus submitting to his generosity; but the terms, though less than might have been exacted, were yet very heavy. Dowlatabad, Beejapoor, and Aseergurh, including the province of Beejapoor and much of Aurungabad, yielding a revenue of sixty-two lacs of rupees a year—620,000*l.*—were ceded in perpetuity, and the Moghul possessions in the Deccan were thus circumscribed to a comparatively small space, which would be difficult of defence.

Defeat of the Nizam.

Terms of peace.

Sudasheo Ráo's success met with the warm approval of his cousin, the Péshwah; but other events were in progress in Hindostan, which were not of so favourable a character. Shaháb-ood-deen, who is styled by some authorities Ghazee-ood-deen, the vizier of Alumgeer II., had called in the aid of the Mahrattas to support his authority against Nujeeb-ood-Dowlah, who had been nominated commander-in-chief of the imperial forces, by Ahmed Shah Abdally, and who was in possession of Dehly. Rughonath Ráo, who is better known under his familiar appellation of Rughoba, was in Malwah; but he at once obeyed the summons, and repaired to Dehly. The royal fort stood a siege of a month's duration, but was taken, and Nujeeb-ood-Dowlah escaped. The emperor had thus fallen a second time under his vizier's control. It is very possible that Shaháb-ood-deen was at a loss how to employ his Mahratta allies; but the Punjâb was perhaps recoverable, and if they could be engaged there, he would at least be relieved of them for the present. At this juncture, Rughoba was invited by Adina Beg, who was himself in rebellion against the Prince Timoor, viceroy of Lahore, on behalf of his father, Ahmed Shah, to join him, and he at once accepted the proposal. In May 1758, he defeated the local governor, and entered Lahore a conqueror. The Mahrattas had thus fulfilled the prophecy of Sivajee, that they should water their horses in the Indus and in the Hooghly; but their new acquisi-

Events in Hindostan.

The Mahrattas at Lahore.

tion proved only delusive. Rughoba returned to Poona, where he was severely taken to task by Sudasheo Ráo Bhow, for a conquest which yielded nothing, and had already cost a million sterling. It was in vain that he pleaded the value of the Punjâb, and the necessity of its retention; and the dispute ended by Rughoba's resigning the command of the army of the north, which was assumed by Sudasheo Ráo, under the Péshwah's sanction.

On leaving Hindostan, Rughoba had divided his forces into two portions, one of which was at Lahore, the other at Dehly, under Duttajee Sindia. The latter was induced by Shaháb-ood-deen to undertake a campaign against Nujeeb-ood-Dowlah and the Rohillas; but, after some success, and the plunder of 1,300 villages, the force under Govind Punt was routed, and driven across the Ganges. Meanwhile Ahmed Shah Abdally was advancing, in September 1759, to recover the Punjâb. On his arrival in the province, the Mahratta commander at Lahore was defeated with serious loss, and fell back upon Dehly. Nujeeb-ood-Dowlah, who had formed a junction with Ahmed Shah, assisted him with supplies, and under his guidance, Duttajee Sindia was surprised, and totally overthrown, with immense loss in men. Holkar, who at first obtained some advantages over the Afghans, was in turn pursued, defeated, and his army utterly routed; but the unfortunate emperor did not escape: before he could be rescued by Ahmed Shah and Nujeeb-ood-Dowlah, Shaháb-ood-deen, dreading the effect of his restoration to power, caused him to be murdered, in November, and raised to the nominal throne a son of the Prince Kámbuksh, who, however, was never acknowledged. At this period, Ally Johur, the real prince imperial, was a fugitive in Bengal, and thus the Moghul empire was virtually extinct. The perfidious vizier, who dared not trust himself at Dehly, betook himself to the protection of the Rajah of the Játs; and there can be little doubt, had the Mahrattas defeated Ahmed Shah, that Duttajee Sindia would have proclaimed the Péshwah emperor of India.

Ahmed Shah Abdally enters the Punjâb and defeats the Mahrattas.

The Emperor Alumgeer II. is murdered by the vizier, November 1759.

News of these disasters reached the Péshwah after his victory over Salabut Jung and Nizam Ally, and produced much excitement. Sudasheo Ráo Bhow at once volunteered to lead the Mahrattas to conquest, and boasted that he would drive the Afghans across the Indus. The army which set out from the Deccan was the most complete and magnificent that had ever taken the field. In addition to 20,000 chosen cavalry, the corps of Ibrahim Khan Gardee, composed of disciplined infantry and artillery, was 10,000

The Mahratta army marches for Hindostan.

strong; and these forces were augmented by the various contingents of the Mahratta chieftain. Wiswas Ráo, the son and heir of the Péshwah, accompanied Sudasheo Ráo, who proceeded direct to Dehly, of which he took possession; and having plundered the royal palace of all its valuables, and stripped the hall of audience of its ceiling of silver, which, when coined, produced no less than seventeen lacs of rupees, or 170,000*l.*, took up a position for the monsoon. These acts of spoliation, with others of destruction, coupled with the peevish rejection of his advice, so disgusted Sooruj Mul, the able leader of the Játs, that he left Sudasheo Ráo, and retired into his own territory. His advice had been, that the Mahrattas should trust to their ancient method of warfare, and cut off all supplies to Ahmed Shah; and that their heavy artillery should not be used in the contest. Sudasheo Ráo, however, had placed more than ordinary confidence in Ibrahim Khan's corps, and treated Sooruj Mul's advice, with similar counsel from many of his own most experienced officers, with scorn. As the monsoon declined, he raised Mirza Juwán Bukht, the son of the prince imperial, Ally Johur, to the throne, and appointed Shujah-ood-Dowlah, viceroy of Oudh, to the office of vizier. He then moved into the field, and about the same time Ahmed Shah crossed the Jumna above Dehly, and skirmishes between the armies commenced.

Sudasheo Ráo plunders Dehly.

Sooruj Mul Ját recedes from the Mahrattas.

Prince Mirza Juwán Bukht created emperor.

The Mahrattas had 55,000 horse, 15,000 foot, and 300 pieces of cannon; the Mahomedans, 41,800 horse, 38,000 foot, and 70 pieces of cannon; the irregular troops on both sides were also very numerous. On October 25, Sudasheo Ráo moved with his whole army to Paniput, the great battle-field of India since the age of the Máhábhárut, and where its fate had frequently been decided; and threw a wide ditch and rampart round the camp, the town being in the centre of his position. Ahmed Shah also entrenched himself at a short distance; and thus the parties lay, watching each other for two months, scarcely a day passing without severe conflicts, with varied advantage. But provisions ran short in the Mahratta camp; and as no supplies arrived, the army, both officers and men, could endure the privation no longer. On January 6, 1761, they implored to be led against the enemy, and Sudasheo Ráo, having no other resource, gave orders for battle. Next morning, before break of day, the Mahrattas were in motion, and formed their line regularly. Ahmed Shah, whose personal activity had been surprising, had just fallen asleep in his tent, but he was already dressed, and,

Relative forces in the field.

Entrenched position of Paniput.

Battle of Paniput.

mounting his horse, proceeded to reconnoitre. A glance showed him that an action must be fought, and his army took up their several positions. The details of the great battle, given at length by Elphinstone, vol. ii. pp. 642–652, and Grant Duff, vol. ii. pp. 143–156, are more than usually interesting, but need not be repeated here; suffice it to say, that after an obstinate combat, and varying fortune, King Ahmed at length, watching his opportunity, directed charges of bodies of 10,000 cavalry to be made in succession at a gallop on the Mahratta centre. They proved successful, and the Mahrattas, fighting desperately, finally broke and fled, being pursued with a vast carnage. Of all that were taken in the camp, women and children became slaves, and next morning the males were cruelly butchered in cold blood. Wiswas Ráo and many other chiefs were slain, and a body, believed to be that of Sudasheo Ráo, was afterwards found.

Defeat of the Mahrattas.

Thus, at the zenith of their power in Northern India, the Mahratta forces were destroyed so completely that any junction or re-formation of them became impossible. The Péshwah had moved up to the Nerbudda in support, in November; and when, in his anxiety for news, and fears that disaster must have occurred, he was crossing the river in January, he received advice of the national defeat, which had been written by a banker to his correspondent in the following terms:—'Two pearls have been dissolved, twenty-seven gold mohurs have been lost, and of the silver and copper, the total cannot be cast up.'[1] The details soon followed, and the Péshwah never recovered the shock caused by them. His mind became affected, and he returned to Poona, where he lingered till June; and about the end of September, Mahdoo Ráo, his second son, then about seventeen years of age, was invested in his room.

Consequences.

CHAPTER XIII.

OF THE POLITICAL CONDITION OF INDIA, 1761.

The various revolutions which had already altered the territorial divisions of India will have been traceable from the narrative of its history; but a brief definition of them, as they existed at the battle of Paniput, may be found useful to the student, and may serve as an introduction to the further changes which were to ensue.

[1] Grant Duff.

I. The great empire of Dehly had virtually ceased to exist; and with the murder of Alumgeer II., in 1760, the last of the emperors had passed away. His son, Ally Johur, a fugitive in Bengal at the period of his father's death, subsequently ascended the throne, under the proud title of Shah Allum, or king of the world, when, in fact, all that actually remained to him were a few small districts in the immediate neighbourhood of Dehly. All else had been alienated and usurped, either by the viceroys or foreign powers, and was totally irrecoverable.

Final disruption of the empire of Dehly.

Commencing from the north-west, the whole of the former Afghan territory of Dehly had been conquered, and was now possessed, by Ahmed Shah Abdally. It included Kandahar and Kabool, some of the north-western portions of both having been gained by the Persians. Ahmed Shah had received from Dehly the cession of the whole of the Punjâb; and to this had added Mooltan, which could not be defended. He was not so successful in Scinde, where the Tálpoor chiefs had asserted their independence, and were maintaining it; but his dominions were of great extent, and, as the result of the battle of Paniput proved, he was at once powerful and popular among his subjects.

Details of the former empire.

Afghanistan and Punjâb.

II. Omitting the few districts on the Upper Ganges and Jumna which remained to Dehly, the Rohillas, who were descended from the former Afghan troops and settlers at Dehly, had become very powerful, and were actually independent under their chief Nujeeb-ood-Dowlah; but to the period of the Emperor Alumgeer II.'s death, they had assisted him against his treacherous vizier, Shaháb-ood-deen, and were the active allies of Ahmed Shah Abdally in the campaign of Paniput. Their territory was called Rohilkhund, and occupied a position between Dehly and the lower range of the Himalayas, with the city of Bareilly as its capital.

Rohillas.

III. On the south-east of Rohilkhund lay the great province of Oudh, heretofore a viceroyalty of the empire, and still preserving that designation; but now, to all intents, independent. Shujah-ood-Dowlah had succeeded his father Sufdur Jung, and for a time became the nominal vizier of the empire; but his interests lay completely apart from those of the nominal emperor, and his great power and wealth enabled him to preserve the independence he had assumed.

Oudh.

IV. Bengal, Behar, and Orissa were united under the government of Meer Jaffier, who, upon the support of the English, had become Nabob, or, more properly, Nawáb. His position was an anomalous one, in contrast with that of other

Bengal, Behar, and Orissa.

nominal viceroys; for he was perfectly independent of Dehly, and, though he may have kept up communication with officers at the court, it is certain that he rendered it no assistance; and, as has been related, resisted the prince imperial when he attempted, in 1759, to assume the viceroyalty. These provinces were therefore, in all respects, completely alienated from the empire.

V. The Rajpoot States had become perfectly isolated. It is uncertain how long their annual tribute was paid; but it is questionable whether they had contributed anything to the imperial exchequer for some time previous to the invasion of Ahmed Shah, and it is certain that the emperor and his vizier had, for many years, been too weak to attempt to enforce payment. The principal states were Jeypoor, Joudhpoor, and Oodypoor, and there were others of minor extent and consequence, whose chiefs belonged to the Rajpoot confederation, but whose condition does not need particular specification. Over the whole of Rajpootana, the Mahrattas had imposed their demands of chouth; but they were irregularly paid, and their enforcement was by no means easy. The Rajpoots took part with the Mahrattas in the contest at Paniput, and their independence was absolute.

The Rajpoot States.

VI. The Mahrattas had possessed themselves of the whole of Guzerat and Malwah, having gradually driven out the imperial viceroys and garrisons. They also occupied Khandésh, and Berar, with Kuttack; and the recent cessions by the Nizam had given them the province of Beejapoor and most part of Aurungabad. The province of Malwah had been divided between Sindia and Holkar; the Gáikwar possessed Guzerat; the Péshwah's estate of Kalpy and Jhansy extended their territories to the Jumna on the north, while south-westwards they reached unbroken as far as the northern boundary of Mysore; and they possessed, in the extreme south, the principality of Tanjore, the remains of one of the most ancient Hindoo kingdoms. Such had been their growth in territorial acquisition during a hundred years, while their demands for the national chouth and sur-déshmookhee now extended all over India.

Mahrattas.

VII. Between Agra and Jeypore, the Játs, a tribe of martial cultivators from the banks of the Indus, had established themselves about the close of the reign of Aurungzebe. They were now, under their famous chieftain, Sooruj Mul, exceedingly powerful, and his capital, Bhurtpoor, was undoubtedly the strongest fortress in Northern India. South-eastward from the Bhurtpoor State, lay the province of Bundelkund, divided into several minor principalities, the chief of which was Rewah; and on the borders of Malwah a small tract of country had become

The Játs, and Central India.

independent under its Mahomedan governor, the capital of which was Bhopál. All these had been overrun by the Mahrattas, and were, in essential respects, subject to them, as well as tributary.

The Soobahdar of the Deccan.

VIII. The progress of the Soobahdar of the Deccan, Nizam-ool-Moolk, and his descendants, has been sufficiently illustrated to make the position of Salabut Jung, or the Nizam, as he may be called—the title by which he was best known—sufficiently intelligible. But the territory of the viceroyalty had become seriously circumscribed by the recent cession to the Mahrattas; and in the maintenance, by the English, of Mahomed Ally, as ruler of the Carnatic, the Nizam had lost all the southern portion of the dominions over which Nizam-ool-Moolk, his father, had ruled. The Patán Nawábs of Savanoor, on the borders of Mysore, of Kurpa and Kurnool, on the southern bank of the Krishna river, had also become independent, and had alienated a considerable portion of the former dominions. The territories of the Nizam now consisted of the southern portion of the Deccan; with the Krishna river as its southern boundary, and the whole of Telingána to the sea, between the rivers Pennaar and Godavery, north of the latter, as far as the frontier of Orissa, the Rajah of Vizagapatam, or Vizianagram, had re-established an independent principality under the protection of the English; but it was of limited extent, and of inconsiderable political importance.

Mysore.

IX. Mysore.—The traditions of this state attribute its foundation at a very remote period, about the 12th century, to two brothers of the Yádává family of Guzerat, one of whom married the daughter of a petty chieftain, and settled in the country. His descendants gradually acquired territory, and, in 1507, became possessed of Mysore, where a fort was built. The kingdom of Beejanugger was conquered by the Mahomedans in 1575, and its representatives, after many vicissitudes, and the loss of Penkóndah, their second capital, established themselves at Chundergiry, whence they endeavoured to regain Mysore; but, failing in this, dwindled into insignificant chieftains, and disappeared from the history of the period. During these struggles, Mysore had gradually increased in power and extent; and, in 1667, occupied not only the whole of the plateau of Mysore, but had extended its dominion to the Bárá Mahál, lying below the plateau to the south. The Emperor Aurungzebe's armies had invaded Mysore, and an agreement to pay tribute had been exacted by his officers from the reigning prince; but it does not appear that this was ever regularly levied, if indeed at all. In 1724 the rajah was obliged to pay a million sterling to the Patán Nawábs of Savanoor, Kurpa and Kurnool, who were in alliance with Moorary Ráo of Gooty; and the Mahrattas also claimed chouth and other dues as mposed by Sivajee; but, on the whole, the state was singularly exempt from the convulsions and struggles of the period, and was governed by a succession of able ministers.

Affairs of Mysore continued.

In 1757, the Mahrattas, under Balajee Ráo Péshwah, had exacted an agreement from Mysore to pay thirty-two lacs, or 320,000*l.*, as arrears of chouth; and the revenue of fifteen districts had been pledged to them in liquidation; but Hyder Ally, who had risen from a low position to be general-in-chief of the troops of the state, had expelled them. In 1759, they had reinvaded the country, and Hyder Ally, after a brilliant campaign, had proved so successful, that the Mahrattas, on payment of the stipulated sum, surrendered their claim to the assigned territory. Thenceforward Hyder Ally became supreme in Mysore; and not only pursued the predatory system he had organised, but reduced in succession Bednore, Chittledroog, Hurpunhully, and other small states lying to the north and west of Mysore, and, extending his conquests considerably to the south, increased the dominions of Mysore to a very considerable extent. The legitimate rajah of the country was eventually deposed by him, as will be hereafter related; but at the period now under record, 1761, Hyder Ally was the supreme executive authority in Mysore. He had formed no political alliances or connections, and was alike opposed to the Mahrattas, the Nizam, the Nawáb of the Carnatic, and the English. The overtures made to him by M. de Lally had been interrupted; but he retained an esteem for, and sympathy with, the French, which afterwards became more fully developed.

Hyder Ally.

He deposes the rajah.

The Nawáb of the Carnatic.

X. Mahomed Ally, protected by the English, was now secure in his possession of the Carnatic, and was independent alike of the Nizam and of Dehly. His dominions were considerable. To the north they extended to the Pennaar river; to the west they were bounded by Mysore, and on the south by Tanjore; but they contained many small Hindoo principalities, which were portions of the original dominions of the great Beejanugger and Chôla kingdoms, and over these his authority was doubtful. These petty states, however, possessed no political significance.

Tanjore.

XI. Tanjore had been established by Sivajee, on the ruins of the ancient Hindoo kingdom, and his brother, Venkajee, had been created its rajah. It still remained to his descendants; but it was weak, and lay at the mercy of the stronger powers in its neighbourhood, though for the present it was not seriously molested. The English and French transactions with it have already been detailed.

XII. Travancore and Cochin complete the southern states of

India; but at the period under notice they possessed no importance whatever; and the same may be said of the smaller states of Coorg and Bednore, which lay west of Mysore, and were dependent upon it.

Tarvancore and Cochin.

XIII. The Portuguese, since their unsuccessful war with the Péshwah, had shrunk into insignificance. They still possessed Goa and its dependencies, with a few other factories; but they took no active part in the political affairs of India.

The Portuguese.

XIV. The French power in India had been broken by the result of the capture of Chándernagore and Pondicherry, and by the departure of M. Bussy from Hyderabad. The attempts to regain it have to be recorded hereafter.

The French.

XV. The English, by the results of their policy in Bengal and in the Carnatic, had established the basis of their political authority; but, as yet, their territorial acquisitions were very insignificant. The thirty-eight villages they had acquired round Calcutta, the grant made by Salabut Jung near Masulipatam, in the Northern Circars, small strips of land near Madras, Fort St. David, and Negapatam, constituted their only possessions on the eastern and southern sides of the continent. On the western coast, they occupied the island of Bombay, and they had not relinquished their conquest of Gheriah to the Péshwah. They had also captured the fort of Surat from the Moghul governor, which they held independently of the Gáikwar of Guzerat.

The English.

CHAPTER XIV.

OF EVENTS IN BENGAL, FROM THE BATTLE OF PANIPUT TO THE BATTLE OF BUXAR, 1761 TO 1764.

AHMED SHAH ABDALLY was not tempted by his victory over the Mahrattas to assume the government of India, or even to delay his departure for his own dominions, to which he immediately returned; and the Mahrattas, humbled for the time by their defeat, retired into Malwah and the Deccan.

Ahmed Shah returns from India.

In Bengal, after Clive's departure, Mr. Holwell assumed charge of the presidency, pending the arrival of Mr. Vansittart, a Madras civilian, who had been selected by Clive, and received his nomination from England. Mr. Holwell had always been opposed to Meer Jaffier; and the members of council, influenced by him, prepared a scheme for a new revolution, by which Meer Jaffier was to be super-

Changes in Calcutta.

Proposed revolution at Moorshidabad.

seded in the executive government by his son-in-law, Meer Cassim, whose ability, and, it was then believed, attachment to the English, promised the best results. Mr. Vansittart, who was totally ignorant of Bengal affairs, fell into the views of his council; but action upon their resolution was delayed by the advance of the Prince Royal of Dehly, who, after his father's murder, had assumed the title of Shah Allum, and, as emperor, determined to attempt the recovery of Bengal. At the head of an inconsiderable body of troops, he advanced into Behar early in 1760, and was joined by Shujah-ood-Dowlah, viceroy of Oudh, who, it will be remembered, had been appointed vizier of the empire by Sudasheo Ráo Bhow, before the battle of Paniput.

The Prince Royal of Dehly, now emperor, endeavours to regain Bengal.

The possibility of this invasion had been apparent to Clive before his departure, and he had made provision to meet it at Moorshidabad. Colonel Calliaud, who now commanded the forces, had marched from Calcutta at the head of 350 Europeans and 1,000 Sepoys, with six field guns; and 15,000 horse, under the Nawáb's son, Meerun, had been prepared to accompany him. While the emperor and the vizier advanced on Patna from the west, Calliaud and his ally approached the city from the east; but before they could arrive, Rám Narráin, the governor, had met the emperor in the field, and suffered a sharp defeat; and but for Calliaud's energy, Patna might have been captured. On his near approach, the emperor fled; but, in the hope of evading the English, entered Bengal, pursued by Calliaud, who came up with him on February 20, 1760, and routed his forces. Hoping to receive a reinforcement from the Mahrattas, whom he had invited to his assistance, the emperor now turned towards Moorshidabad; but he was again pursued and checked by the indefatigable Calliaud, and finding he had no chance of success in that direction, appeared suddenly again before Patna, and laid close siege to it, assisted by the French party, under M. Law, who had joined him, as well as the Nawáb of Purneah, with 30,000 men. A reinforcement to Calliaud, consisting of 200 Europeans and a battalion of Sepoys, with 300 horse, under Captain Knox, had been advancing from Bengal, and now hurried on. On its arrival at the scene of action, Knox did not hesitate; but with the utmost gallantry crossed the river, and in sight of the inhabitants of Patna, who crowded the walls to witness this extraordinary and astonishing combat, completely defeated the emperor and his allies, who precipitately retreated, and were followed up by Colonel Calliaud and Meerun, who captured their baggage and artillery, and their forces dispersed. On July 2,

Colonel Calliaud's successful campaign.

Exploit of Captain Knox.

1760, Meerun's tent was struck by lightning at night, and he, with three attendants, perished.

Meerun's conduct had from the first been cruel and licentious; but whatever vigour the Government of Bengal possessed, belonged to him, both as a soldier and administrator. On the arrival of the news of his death at Moorshidabad, Meer Jaffier, afflicted by leprosy, became imbecile, the troops broke into mutiny, and, but for the presence of Meer Cassim, might have put the Nawáb to death; but from this fate he was preserved by his son-in-law, who quieted the troops by an advance from his private funds. The state of the administration now became intolerable, and the Council of Calcutta determined upon requiring Meer Jaffier to abdicate. On sounding Meer Cassim on the subject, he deliberately proposed to Mr. Holwell to have Meer Jaffier put to death after the usual fashion of Indian revolutions; but Mr. Vansittart advanced from Calcutta with 200 Europeans and a battalion of Sepoys, and the old Nawáb reluctantly submitted, protesting violently against the deliberate breach of faith, and only requiring an asylum in Calcutta.

Events at Moorshidabad.

Meer Jaffier is forced to abdicate.

As far as financial results were concerned, the new revolution was profitable. In payment of the sum due to the company, the large districts of Burdwán, Midnapoor, and Chittagong were assigned to them; and five lacs were contributed for the war in the Carnatic. For the services of the Council, twenty lacs, or 200,000*l.*, were allotted, of which 30,000*l.* to Mr. Holwell, and about 60,000*l.* to Mr. Vansittart, besides smaller donations, were actually paid. But the whole transaction had been faithless and dishonourable. It was not even justified by the pecuniary embarrassments of the company. The viceroyalty of Bengal, at a time when its lawful sovereign was endeavouring to assert his rights, was, as it were, sold to one who had no claim to it whatever, except the assumed security of the company's interests, by men who used them as a cloak for their own avarice. As an immediate consequence, the most acrimonious discussions ensued in Council between those who had, and those who had not, received shares of booty; but there were other and worse events to come which cast these into the shade. If the question be considered calmly, after the lapse of a hundred years, it seems only surprising, if the Council desired a change, that they did not espouse the just cause of the emperor, with whom they might have made their own terms, and obtained more favourable and more extensive grants than they exacted from Meer Cassim.

Dishonourable character of the transaction.

The new Nawáb possessed great vigour, and the effect of his

reforms and retrenchments was soon apparent in the flourishing condition of his treasury; but the emperor, who dare not proceed to Dehly, and had not foregone his intentions upon Bengal, had remained near its northern frontier. Major Carnac, who had succeeded Calliaud in the command of the forces, was deputed to watch his movements; and in January, 1761, advanced on the emperor's camp, and defeated him. On this occasion, M. Law and his French party were taken prisoners; and Carnac, who had received instructions from Mr. Vansittart, visited the emperor, and invited him to Patna, whither he accompanied him. The fact of his sovereign being an honoured guest in the English camp, excited the alarm and jealousy of Meer Cassim in no ordinary degree; but his own plans were not matured, and he sullenly submitted to be created Viceroy of Bengal, at the same time agreeing to pay twenty-four lacs of rupees per year to the emperor—a miserable sum, if it be remembered that Aliverdy Khan, after providing for all local expenditure, used to remit upwards of a million sterling, year by year, to the imperial treasury. There was now no pretence for detaining the emperor, who, accompanied by Carnac as far as the frontier of Behar, proceeded towards Dehly; but before his final departure, he had offered to the English company the dewany, or financial management of Bengal.

Position of the emperor. *He is defeated by Major Carnac.* *The emperor joins Carnac.* *Visits Meer Cassim.* *The emperor offers the dewany of Bengal to the English.*

Meer Cassim was now secure in his office; and, as Meer Jaffier had attempted, began exactions from the principal officers, who, under his father-in-law's lax administration, were reputed to have amassed wealth. Carnac and Coote would have protected Rám Narráin of Patna, who had so often proved faithful; but his English friends were withdrawn, and he was shamefully abandoned to the Nawáb by Mr. Vansittart, and mercilessly despoiled. Meer Cassim, however subservient he might find his English friends at times, yet heartily desired freedom from interference. With the emperor he was fully able to cope; but he dreaded the English, was powerless to do anything at Moorshidabad, and he therefore removed his residence to Mongheer, 320 miles from Calcutta. There he believed himself secure; and, with the aid of one Petrus, an Armenian, and other adventurers, he began secretly to cast cannon, and to make muskets and accoutrements for a native army. In 1762, the famous dispute in regard to transit duties, and the dustuks or passes which could be granted by the company's officers and which exempted merchants from payment of Custom dues, had reached a high pitch; and there was no doubt the privilege had

Meer Cassim's exactions. *Meer Cassim removes to Mongheer.* *Peter III., emperor of Russia.* *Disputes with the English regarding Custom duties.*

been shamefully abused. Mr. Vansittart even visited the Nawáb at Mongheer, who, so far from supporting his view of the subject, abolished all transit duty whatever, and threw open the trade. This was considered, if possible, a more unjustifiable act than his interference with the dustuks; and at this juncture, a boat or boats, which had some arms for the garrison of the factory at Patna on board, was seized by the Nawáb's officers. Two gentlemen of the factory, Messrs. Hay and Amyatt, were deputed to require their release; but the Nawáb refused the request unless Mr. Ellis, the chief of the factory, was removed. Mr. Hay was detained as a hostage, but Mr. Amyatt was allowed to return. Mr. Ellis, a violent man, considering the Nawáb's demeanour to be unequivocally hostile, now seized upon the city of Patna. He could not however maintain his position, and proceeded up the river; but was intercepted and brought back. Meer Cassim now threw off the mask, and issued orders for all the English to be apprehended. Mr. Amyatt, who was travelling, resisted the order, and was killed.

Their consequences.

Mr. Amyatt is killed.

Both parties prepared for war; and the English, as if unable to act except under the authority of a native prince, withdrew the aged Meer Jaffier from his obscurity in Calcutta, and, in spite of his inveterate leprosy, on July 7, 1763, proclaimed him Nawáb, and having secured from him a grant of the three districts, and the other agreements of Meer Cassim, marched with him to Moorshidabad. Meanwhile, Meer Cassim had set out with a powerful force to meet the English. His troops had been disciplined by a Swiss of the name of Sumroo, who had been a sergeant in Law's corps, and his artillery and small arms were excellent. On July 19, the English force, which consisted of 650 Europeans and 1,200 Sepoys, met the Nawáb's army at Cutwah, and defeated it; but it rallied and gave battle again at Gheriah, on August 2, when the Nawáb's troops fought with unusual resolution, but were again routed and lost all their guns. The double defeat enraged the Nawáb beyond endurance, and he gave full rein to his passion and ferocity. Rám Narráin was cast into the Ganges, as were also the great Sett bankers of Moorshidabad, then at Mongheer; and Rajah Ráj Bullub, another friend of the English, was put to death, with all his family. On the Nawáb's arrival at Patna, he directed the English prisoners to be slaughtered, and the bloody work was done by Sumroo, who fired volleys into their prison rooms till all, upwards of 200 souls, were dead. The English were, however, advancing to revenge their countrymen; the Nawáb's army, which had again rallied

Meer Jaffier again proclaimed Nawáb.

Peace of Paris.

Catherine II., empress of Russia.

War with Meer Cassim,

who is defeated at Cutwah, and again at Gheriah.

Murders and executions by Meer Cassim.

The English prisoners put to death.

at Owda-Nulla, near Mongheer, was 60,000 in number, and had placed 100 guns in position; but the English, though only 3,000 strong, Europeans and natives, stormed the position, captured the guns, and the Fort of Mongheer was taken after a short siege.

The Nawáb defeated at Owda-Nulla. Mongheer taken.

The Nawáb had fled to the vizier of Oudh, and formed a league with him. Early in 1764, these confederates, who had been joined by the emperor, marched upon Patna, which was assaulted on May 3, 1764; but it was defended by English troops, and the vizier's army retired to Buxar, where it encamped during the rains. Before a new campaign could open, Major Hector Munro had taken command of the army; but the native portion of it, which was very considerable, and was flushed by victory, was in a condition of serious mutiny, demanding large donations and increased rates of pay. One regiment of Sepoys marched off with their arms to join the enemy, but were pursued and brought back. Major Munro's conduct at this trying period is beyond praise; but it was not till the ringleaders had been tried, and many of them executed, that the Sepoys returned to their obedience, and, to prove their faith, demanded to be led against the enemy. The confederates had an army of 30,000 men. Munro's forces consisted of 857 Europeans, 5,297 Sepoys, and 918 native cavalry, with 20 field pieces; in all 7,072 men—the largest English force which had as yet assembled in India. On October 22, he arrived at Buxar, and was met by the enemy, whom he completely defeated. 130 pieces of cannon were taken, and only that a bridge, over which the enemy passed, had been broken down by them, the whole of their treasure and jewels, which were estimated at 3,000,000*l.* sterling in value, must have fallen into the victors' hands. 4,000 of the enemy perished, and Major Munro lost 847 in killed and wounded. The consequences of this victory were immense; the whole of Bengal lay at the disposal of the company. The vizier of Oudh had irretrievably lost both prestige and power, and the emperor had no resource but to place himself under English protection.

Alliance between Meer Cassim and the vizier of Oude. Mutiny of the English army. Is suppressed by Major Hector Munro. Victory of Buxar. Its consequences.

CHAPTER XV.

EVENTS IN BENGAL (*continued*), FROM THE BATTLE OF BERAR TO THE DEPARTURE OF LORD CLIVE, 1764 TO 1767.

AFTER the defeat of his allies at Buxar, the emperor voluntarily joined the English, and opened negotiations with the Council at Calcutta in regard to the disposition of the Oudh territory, which was declared to be forfeit. The Council proposed to divide it with the emperor, retaining the southern portion; but the negotiation was ultimately broken off, and was not resumed. On the other hand, the vizier was also negotiating; but he evaded Munro's demand for the surrender of Meer Cassim, whom, after despoiling of much of his wealth, he allowed to escape, and of Sumroo, whom, however, he coolly proposed to assassinate. The army, therefore, advanced towards Allahabad, and invested Chunargurh; but it was inactive, and as, for want of money, no extensive operations could be carried on, Munro resigned his command. In the hope of recruiting their now exhausted finances, the Council sent for Meer Jaffier Not only was the public service to be provided for, but the shameless demands for private presents and losses were pursued with even more than usually stringent rapacity, even to the neglect of the public interests, which, indeed, seem to have been of very secondary consideration. The finances of the Nawáb, were, however, as low as those of his friends; and, already worn out by anxieties, disease, and age, he died at Moorshidabad soon after his return there in January 1765, but not before he had disbursed the enormous sum of fifty-three lacs—530,000*l.*—to the private claimants.

The emperor joins the English. Negotiations.

Pecuniary difficulties of the Council: their rapacity.

Death of Meer Jaffier.

Meer Jaffier's death rendered a new appointment necessary, and Nujm-ood-Dowlah, his second son, was elected to succeed him. This event, as might have been expected, was too tempting, in regard to demands for presents, to be resisted; and in these days we read, with as much amazement as indignation, the sums which were demanded almost as rights, and received without the least compunction, by the senior officers of the Calcutta Council. Among them, in various shares, was paid away no less than 138,355*l.* While by Mr. Mill's accounts ('Hist.' vol. iii. pp. 326-329) the totals of private donations received by individuals from the Moorshidabad treasury up to this period were 2,169,655*l.*, the payments on account of

Nujm-ood-Dowlah.

Fresh exactions by the Council.

'restitutions,' had reached 3,770,833*l.*, making a sum total of no less than 5,940,498*l.* Private individuals were indeed enriched beyond conception; but the public finances of the company were impoverished, notwithstanding their enormous extra receipts. By the treaty with the new Nawáb, the military defence of the country was undertaken by the company, and a deputy, Mahomed Reza Khan, was appointed as the Nawáb's representative and executive minister. Mr. Vansittart had returned to England, and Mr. Spencer, a civilian from Bombay, occupied his place.

The Council undertakes the military defence of Bengal.

The Court of Directors were not, however, satisfied with the progress of affairs in Bengal. It was impossible for them to defend their servants from the imputations of scandalous rapacity which were becoming notorious, and it was even more unendurable that the public trade of the company should have been well-nigh extinguished by the private trade of its own servants. Clive was, therefore, requested to proceed again to Bengal. During his residence in England, he had been elected an Irish peer; he was a member of Parliament, and aspired to be a director of the East India Company; but in this he had failed. There was a party in the court who virulently opposed him, and who had ordered a resumption of the payment of the revenue of his jahgeer, or estate, which obliged him to resort to an action at law; and it is probable these contentions would have continued, but for the dangers and embarrassments of Bengal, which he alone was considered capable of removing. In regard to the jahgeer, he agreed to relinquish it to the company after ten years, if he lived so long, and this closed the discussion. Lord Clive landed in Calcutta on May 3, 1765, and on the same day the Vizier of Oudh, with his Mahratta and Rohilla allies, was again defeated at Corah by General Carnac, and threw himself on the generosity of the English. It was a strange sight for the people of India to behold. Their emperor, and his most powerful subject, were alike suppliants for assistance and for consideration, at the hands of those who, not ten years before, were no more than humble merchants, and had been ignominiously expelled from Bengal. It was a situationwhich required the solution and direction of a master mind; and Lord Clive, after a brief survey of affairs in Calcutta, which disclosed to him unbounded rapacity and vice—and having declared that he would summarily dismiss from the service any servant of the company who refused to sign the new covenants which had been prepared in England—left Calcutta on June 25, and proceeded to

Dissatisfaction of the Court of Directors.

Clive is requested to proceed to Bengal.

Clive reaches Calcutta.

Joseph II., emperor of Germany.

Vizier of Oudh defeated.

Clive proclaims the new government;

and joins the army.

join the army. As he passed Moorshidabad, the arrangements for the military defence of the country were definitively settled. Fifty-three lacs of rupees—530,000*l.*—were assigned for the purpose, and in order to preserve a check upon Mahomed Reza Khan, two Hindoo gentlemen of rank, Rái Doolub and Jugget Sett, the banker, were associated with him. Clive now proceeded to the camp; and, on August 2, the affairs of the vizier were considered and decided. His dominions, which he had forfeited by an unprovoked war, were restored to him, except two districts, Corah and Allahabad, which were reserved for the emperor; he was to pay fifty lacs for the expenses of the war, and Rajah Bulwunt Sing, who had rendered material assistance to the English, was confirmed in his possession of Benares and Ghazipoor.

Settlement with the vizier of Oudh.

The emperor only remained. On him were settled the two reserved districts of Oudh, and twenty-six lacs—260,000*l.*—of the annual revenue of Bengal, Behar, and Orissa; but he was required to relinquish his claims to the arrears which had accumulated. He had already twice offered the dewany, or revenue management of Bengal, to the English, once to Clive and once to General Carnac; and on Clive again proposing the arrangement, he readily acquiesced in it. On August 12, the emperor took his seat on a throne, constructed of the dining-tables and an arm-chair, in Lord Clive's tent, covered with rich cloths, and the imperial firman was executed and formally delivered to the representative of the English nation. It conferred upon them in perpetuity the three provinces, which possessed a population of 25,000,000, and a revenue of 4,000,000*l.* sterling, the only alienation being the twenty-six lacs—260,000*l.*—guaranteed to the emperor, and fifty lacs, the pension of the Nawáb of Moorshidabad. At the same time, Clive obtained from the emperor a formal grant of the whole of the Northern Circars, at present in the possession of the Nizam, to be used when the English might be in a position to enforce their surrender.

Transactions with the emperor.

Cession of the dewany of Bengal.

Particulars of the cession

On Lord Clive's return to Calcutta, he resumed the question of the check of private trade, and in this had to oppose his resolute will to the interests of the whole English community, who, in the unbridled exercise of privilege and power, had become alike insolent and reckless. The salaries of the civil officers had hitherto been nominal, and were on a scale so paltry that to live on them would be impossible. To raise them in a sufficient degree would be difficult, and he therefore arranged that the proceeds of the monopoly of salt, which had hitherto been considered one of the

Clive's measures at Calcutta.

Duties on salt assigned in lieu of civil salaries

Nawáb's private perquisites, should be collected into a joint-stock sum, to be divided in proportion to their rank among all grades. It amounted to about thirty-two lacs of rupees, and the proper division was to be made by a committee formed out of the whole body.

So far everything had been settled on comparatively easy terms; but the turn of the army was now to ensue, and the risk was much more formidable; extra allowances, called batta, had been granted to it, with other special augmentations: and the whole was to be reduced to one system by which the receipts of pay would be greatly diminished. Notwithstanding the danger, it was proclaimed that after January 1, 1765, all these extra perquisites were to cease. The consequence was an immediate mutiny of the officers; but their proceedings were kept secret till March, when Clive, who had gone to Moorshidabad, received the first 'round robin' remonstrance. The officers had threatened, as they had bound themselves to each other, to resign; and Clive directed Sir Robert Fletcher, who commanded one of the three divisions, to receive any resignation offered, and dispatch the individuals at once to Calcutta, while he wrote to Madras to send up every officer that could be spared. At Mongheer, on March 13, the European soldiers assembled in arms to support their officers; but were overawed by the Sepoy regiments. In the camp at Serájpoor, similar scenes took place; but there was no actual outbreak, and the sudden arrival of a regiment of Sepoys, who had marched 104 miles in fifty-four hours, prevented what had been contemplated. By these resolute means had Lord Clive again obtained the mastery of a position from which most men would perhaps have receded by compromise, and it was a strange element of his success, that the Sepoy battalions, led by a few faithful and devoted officers, should have overawed and controlled the Europeans. Sir Robert Fletcher, who was the instigator and ringleader of the whole, was tried and cashiered, and others were similarly sentenced; but the whole was settled more by firmness and resolution than by severity, and the majority of the officers expressing their contrition, were restored to their rank in the service. During the progress of this mutiny, the young Nawáb died at Moorshidabad on May 8. The event was of no political importance, and his brother, Syf-ood-Dowlah, a youth of sixteen years old, was invested with his dignity.

Difficulties with the army. — *Mutiny of the officers.* — *Mutiny of the European soldiers, checked by the native regiments.* — *Clive's eventual success.* — *Death of the young Nawáb of Moorshidabad,* — *who is succeeded by his brother.*

If the state of Lord Clive's health had permitted him to remain in India, it is probable that he would have stayed to watch, for a time, the progress of the revolution he had directed: but he was unable to bear the effects of the climate, and in January 1767 intimated to the Council his intention of proceeding to England. His second administration had lasted only twenty-two months, and yet was crowded with events which had added greater lustre to his reputation than his first. The objects he had most deeply at heart, the possession of the three great provinces of Bengal, had been secured with marvellous ease; he had treated the enemies of his nation with singular courtesy and favour; and as he left India, he recorded that any further extension of territory in India would be 'a scheme so extravagantly ambitious, that no government in its senses would ever dream of it.' In his latter acts none of the greed of money which he had at first displayed was evident, else he might have obtained any sum he chose to demand from the Vizier of Oudh, whose dominions he restored to him, and from the Rajah of Benares, for the confirmation of his possessions; and in regard to the Nawáb, his declaration of defence before his peers, that, when piles of money and jewels lay before him in the treasury of Moorshidabad, he only 'marvelled that he had taken so little,' has been accepted by posterity. One of his last acts in India was to refuse a legacy of 50,000*l.* which had been left him by the Nawáb, and cause the sum to be applied to the maintenance of the Invalid Poplar Hospital. In regard to the application of the salt duties to the pay of the civil officers, the directors and proprietors of East India stock, eager for increased dividends, disapproved of the measure, and ordered the salt duties to be incorporated with the general revenue of Bengal; but as no provision was made for the pay of these officers, Lord Clive took upon himself to order the continuance of his own plan, until proper gradations of salary could be decided in England. He left India finally on January 29, 1767, being succeeded in office by Mr. Verelst.

Lord Clive returns to England.

Review of his policy.

CHAPTER XVI.

OF EVENTS AT MADRAS, 1761 TO 1768.

THE capture of Pondicherry had raised the English in the Carnatic to the highest rank of local power. The difference between their positions in Bengal and Madras was this; that, whereas in the former the English had created their own Nawáb, who was solely dependent on them, in the

Position of the English in Madras.

Carnatic they had assisted a Nawáb already established under hereditary grant from his sovereign, who, to some extent, still exercised independent action; but, as in Bengal, the military defence of Mahomed Ally's territory had devolved upon them, and they had no means of supporting an army, except from the Nawáb's revenues. The Nawáb, however, being wasteful and extravagant, was deeply in debt; and on application being made to him for money, he proposed the spoliation of several persons as a resource. Of these the Rajah of Tanjore was the most considerable; but a settlement was arrived at with him without war, by which he agreed to pay twenty-four lacs, in four instalments, and four lacs as a yearly tribute. This, however, gave very little real relief to the Madras finances; and Moortiz Ally of Vellore, and Mahomed Issoof of Madura and Tinnevelly, who refused to negotiate, were in turn attacked; but with no pecuniary advantage; what was obtained from them being in small proportion to the expenses of the war. Of the latter chiefs, Mahomed Issoof was subsequently betrayed to the Nawáb by a Frenchman named Marchand, and put to death. The weakness of the Nawáb, in a military sense, had become more than ever apparent, and the necessity for his support by the company equally unavoidable; under a mutual combination of interests, therefore, the connection continued, and the available revenues of the Carnatic gradually passed into the hands of the Council.

Financial difficulties.

Failure of attempt to exact money.

Results.

Peace between France and England was concluded on February 10, 1763: under the articles of which, restoration was made to the French of their original Indian possessions. Had Clive been consulted in the matter, he would probably have given ample reasons against the readmission to India of the French on any terms; but the interests of the English were in a great measure already secured by the agreements of the French not to erect forts or keep troops in Bengal, and not to dispute the authority of Mahomed Ally in the Carnatic; thus the provisions of the treaty were carried out. Both parties had also agreed to acknowledge Salabut Jung as Soobahdar of the Deccan; but he was now dead. Shortly after the news of the battle of Paniput had reached the Deccan, Salabut Jung and his brother, Nizam Ally, invaded the Mahratta dominions, in the hope of wresting from them the territories ceded by the treaty of Oodgeer. They penetrated as far as Poona, which they plundered and partly burned; and Nizam Ally actually obtained re-cessions of the value of twenty-seven lacs of rupees. After this, the brothers returned to Beeder, where, in the month of July, 1762, Nizam Ally dethroned and imprisoned

Transactions in the Deccan.

Salabut Jung dethroned and put to death by Nizam Ally.

Salabut Jung, whom he afterwards put to death, and became Soobahdar of the Deccan.

In the following year, Nizam Ally was drawn into further disputes with the Mahrattas by his minister, Rajah Pertábwunt, who supported an intrigue for depriving the Péshwah of his power, and the elevation of Janoojee Bhóslay to the regency. In this campaign, the main body of Mahratta horse, evading Nizam Ally, plundered the Moghul territories as far as Berar; but Nizam Ally, unable to overtake them, marched back upon Poona, which was again plundered, and many of the best houses burned. On the return, however, of Nizam Ally to Aurungabad, part of his army being on the left bank, and part on the right bank, of the Godavery, it was attacked in this position by the Mahrattas, and the latter portion cut to pieces. The Moghuls are said to have lost 10,000 men on this occasion, and the Mahrattas followed them to Aurungabad, where a fresh treaty was concluded, in October 1763.

War between the Nizam and the Mahrattas.

Defeat of the Nizam.

In the year 1765, the Mahrattas, under the command of the young Péshwah, Mahdoo Ráo, attacked Hyder Ally, of whose rise to power they were extremely jealous. The campaign was an active one on both sides; but in the end Hyder was defeated, with very severe loss; was obliged to pay thirty-two lacs to the Péshwah, and relinquish all the Mahratta districts he had occupied. About the same time, Nizam Ally had made an irruption into the Carnatic, but was unable to prosecute his designs against the Nawáb, owing to the attitude of the English, who advanced a force to meet him, under Colonel Campbell, as far as the frontier; but he had succeeded in reducing the power of Basalut Jung, who had evidently been disposed to make league with Hyder Ally against his brother and the Mahrattas. No sooner were they respectively at liberty, than the Mahrattas and Nizam Ally coalesced against Janoojee Bhóslay, of Berar, who had in turn deceived them both, and forced him to restore the districts he had usurped, of which the Nizam's share was fifteen lacs per year. From this campaign in Berar, Nizam Ally was recalled to Hyderabad, by a movement on the part of the English, which it is necessary to explain.

War between the Mahrattas and Mysore.

The Nizam and the Mahrattas unite against Berar.

The Northern Circars had been bestowed upon the English by the emperor, as has been already stated, on August 12, 1765, in free gift, in the words of the deed—'To their heirs and descendants, for ever and ever; free, exempt, and safe from all removal, and from all demands of the Dewany Office, or the Imperial Court;' and execution of the grant was charged upon 'our sons, oomras, viziers, governors, &c.'

English movement to obtain possession of the Circars.

But the Circars were in possession of the Nizam; and his voluntary acquiescence in the terms of the grant was not to be hoped for. Clive had urged an immediate movement by the Madras Government, to effect their occupation; but Mr. Pigott was no longer at the head of affairs; and the new president, Mr. Palk, and his Council, hesitated until the opportunity had passed by. Their own necessities, however, impelled them at last into action; and on March 3, 1766, proclamation was made at Masulipatam, on the terms of the emperor's grant, and on the 7th, General Calliaud stormed the fort of Condapilly; the process of assuming charge of the country being simultaneously carried on by the civil officers. It was to resent this assumption of authority and territory, that Nizam Ally marched from Berar; and it is probable, that had the Council of Madras boldly asserted their right to the districts, and intention of maintaining them by force of arms, if necessary, the Nizam would not have dared to attack them; but they again hesitated, and, as usual in India, their opponent blustered the more. Finally, General Calliaud was deputed hastily to Hyderabad, and concluded a treaty with the Nizam, by which five lacs per annum was engaged to be paid by the company for Ellore, Moostufa Nugger, and Rajamundry, and four lacs in addition whenever the district of Guntoor, then held in jahgeer by Basalut Jung, should be made over to them. The English and the Nizam were further to assist each other with troops, when necessary; and for the present, two battalions of infantry, with six guns, joined the Nizam's forces, and assisted him in capturing Bangalore, and in reducing refractory Poligars, in the Carnatic.

Treaty with the Nizam in regard to the Circars.

But the ever fickle and restless Nizam Ally did not long abide by this engagement. While Colonel Smith, the officer in command of the British contingent, was employed in Eastern Mysore, he discovered that the Nizam was intriguing with Hyder Ally, and warned the Madras Council to be on their guard. He then, in May 1767, retired to the frontier of the Carnatic, leaving only a detachment with the Nizam's forces. Meanwhile the Nizam was negotiating with Nunjeráj, the minister of Mysore, for the destruction of Hyder Ally: and on this being discovered by Hyder, he seized and imprisoned the minister. After this event the Nizam made overtures to Hyder, who had become supreme in Mysore, and promised to assist him against the English, on receiving payment of twenty lacs, and an engagement by him to pay a tribute of six lacs of rupees a year. This being concluded, the Nizam threw off the mask; and having joined Hyder, their united forces advanced against Colonel Smith, whose detachment with the Nizam

Intrigues of Nizam Ally.

Nizam Ally and Hyder unite against the English.

had been allowed to depart. The Council of Madras, on the first warning by Colonel Smith, had dispatched one of their members, Mr. Bourchier, to negotiate; but it is almost unnecessary to record, that the object of the mission entirely failed.

The combined armies of the Nizam and Hyder amounted to 42,860 cavalry, 28,000 infantry, and 109 guns. Colonel Smith's force consisted of 1,030 cavalry, 30 of whom were Europeans, 5,800 infantry, of which only 800 were Europeans, with 16 guns. He had taken up a position in a hilly country, where he was attacked on August 25, 1767, and suffered a trifling loss. Finding the hilly tract untenable, he retired into a more open locality, where he was followed by the enemy, who attacked him again at Changama, but suffered a sharp defeat. Colonel Smith's condition was, however, precarious, on account of scarcity of provisions: and he made a bold and rapid march upon Trincomalee, which he reached on September 4, hoping to find stores of rice laid in; but in this he was disappointed. He was joined shortly afterwards by a brigade under Colonel Wood, and he now determined to attack the allies. His force had meanwhile been increased to 10,000 infantry and 34 guns, the cavalry remaining as before. On September 26, the allies moved to attack the English, and endeavoured to turn their flank. Colonel Smith, who saw their design, advanced to meet them, and the movements of both being concealed by an isolated hill, they came upon each other unawares. The result was not long doubtful. The allies were defeated, with the loss of 4,000 men and 64 guns, and next morning they were pursued, with some effect. While these operations were going on, Tippoo, Hyder's son, had advanced to Madras, and had attacked the suburbs; when the news of his father's defeat caused him to withdraw precipitately. The monsoon had now set in, and for a time both sides were inactive; but when operations again commenced, the allies sustained several sharp reverses in succession, and the Nizam, already weary of a war by which he had at first hoped the English might be crushed, and the Carnatic recovered, but had gained nothing, now entered into secret negotiations with Colonel Smith; and when Hyder Ally began to send back his guns and stores to Mysore, and was evidently bent on abandoning the alliance, Nizam Ally entered, avowedly, into negotiations with Madras.

Nizam Ally and Hyder attack Colonel Smith,

who retires.

Defeat of the allies.

Tippoo attacks Madras.

The Nizam negotiates with Smith and Madras.

To this he was impelled by what he considered a very serious danger. The Bengal Government had already dispatched a force, commanded by Colonel Peach, into the Northern Circars, which had advanced without

Movement of Bengal troops into the Nizam's dominions.

check, as far as Wurungul, the ancient capital of Telingána, only eighty miles from Hyderabad, and the Circars were therefore completely subdued, while the very capital of his dominions was menaced. At this juncture the Council of Madras, had they possessed only ordinary firmness and ability, might have considered—as they had a right to do from the Nizam's treachery—the former treaty annulled; and while dictating their own terms, as to the Carnatic and the expenses of the war, have occupied the Circars in virtue of the emperor's free gift. But they did neither, and the treaty of February 23, 1768, done at Madras, contained, with some advantages, conditions so absurd and impracticable, that it is strange how they ever came to be entertained. Mahomed Ally, the Nawáb of the Carnatic, was now, for the first time, recognised by the Nizam as one of the contracting powers. The company's right to the Northern Circars upon the emperor's grant was conceded, and the peshcush, or tribute, reduced from five lacs to two, the other three lacs being deducted as expenses of the war, the stipulations as to Guntoor remaining as before. So far, the provisions of the new treaty were moderately advantageous; but, between the Nizam and Mahomed Ally, the company were drawn into action against Hyder, who was rudely denounced as an usurper and freebooter; and the Council actually agreed to recover the tableland of Mysore, or the Carnatic 'Bála Ghát,' from him, on behalf of the Nizam, and to pay seven lacs of rupees a year for it and the Northern Circars combined, if Mysore could be conquered. This was, in fact, a feeble imitation of the policy of Clive in regard to the dewany of Bengal; but it made a bitter enemy of Hyder Ally, whose power was now at its zenith. The court of directors commented most severely upon the provisions of this treaty, and its weakness and absurdity were set forth with unsparing censure; but it was too late: the treaty could not be revoked, and its disastrous consequences have to be recorded. One passage of this memorable dispatch is, however, worth quoting. After enumerating their present possessions in India, the directors wrote:—'The protection of these is easily within the reach of our power, and may mutually support each other without any country alliance whatever. If we pass these bounds, we shall be led on from one acquisition to another, till we shall find no security but in the subjection of the whole, which, by dividing our force, would lose us the whole, and end in our extirpation from Hindostan.'

Inefficiency of the Madras Council.

Treaty with the Nizam.

Its unwise provisions.

CHAPTER XVII.

FROM THE RENEWAL OF THE WAR WITH HYDER, TO THE PEACE OF MADRAS; AND THE WAR BETWEEN HYDER AND THE MAHRATTAS, 1768 TO 1771.

In a subsequent dispatch on the same subject, the directors thus wrote to the Madras Council:—'Instead of pursuing pacific measures with Hyder Ally, as we think you ought to have done, knowing, as you did, our sentiments with respect to extending our territories—you have brought us into such a labyrinth of difficulties, that we do not know how we shall be extricated from them. If, however, Hyder Ally be extirpated'—then the directors recommended restoration of rajahs and others whom he may have dispossessed. But Hyder was quite the reverse of 'extirpated;' his separation from the Nizam had added to his freedom of action, and he undertook the continuance of the war with more than usual spirit and effect. While he had been engaged in the Carnatic, several of the small powers on the western coast had made an attempt to recover independence, and were assisted by the Bombay Government, whose ships destroyed a small fleet, which Hyder had commenced to establish, and landed a force at Bangalore. In May 1768, Hyder suddenly attacked this town, which the English commander precipitately abandoned, leaving even his sick and wounded, with the artillery. Freed from the presence of the English, Hyder now held all the native princes to ransom, and by these means obtained funds for his prosecution of the war against Madras.

Hyder continues the war.

If the Council had attended to the admirable advice given to them by the directors, they would have met Hyder 'half way:' and a treaty for the mutual advantage of both might have been concluded without further war; but the Council were inflated by the prospect of a speedy conquest and possession of Mysore, and were urged on by Mahomed Ally to undertake it. On the other hand, Hyder saw clearly that he had no resource but to fight for political and territorial existence; and that the chances of accommodation with the English had altogether disappeared. The campaign opened in June 1768. Colonel Smith, accompanied by the Nawáb and two members of Council, commenced operations against Eastern Mysore, and Colonel Wood against the Báráh Mahál—

Views of the Madras Council.

Campaign against Hyder opened.

the country lying below the tableland to the south. Owing to the absence of cavalry, in which arm Hyder Ally was very powerful, Moorary Ráo, the Mahratta chieftain of Gooty, was engaged by the Council of Madras, and joined Colonel Smith on August 4. The movements on both sides are full of military interest, and the results were at first in favour of the English; for Colonel Smith had invested Bangalore, and Colonel Wood had overrun the Báráh Mahál, driving out Hyder's garrisons: but, as well as from the English, Hyder was in perpetual dread of an attack from the Mahrattas, or from a coalition of the English with them. He had only just suppressed an insurrection on the part of his brother-in-law, Mukhdoom Sahib, who had been recognised as the independent Nawáb of Séra, in Northern Mysore, by the Péshwah; and this act might be considered a course of war. In this perplexity Hyder Ally now proposed terms of peace to the Madras Council, offering to cede the Báráh Mahál and to pay ten lacs—100,000*l.*—as the expenses of the war. This offer was rejected by the Council, who, believing Hyder's actual weakness to be the sole cause of his advances, now sought to take advantage of it by proposing, not only an enormous sum for the expenses of the war, but the payment of tribute to the Nizam, with cessions of territory to Moorary Ráo, and a materially enlarged frontier to themselves, including a portion of the Malabar coast. These inflated propositions were in turn refused by Hyder Ally, and active operations again began. Colonel Smith now remonstrated with the Council on various points, and was ordered to Madras to account for them, as well as to explain his intentions in regard to the campaign.

English successes.

Hyder's difficulties.

Hyder proposes peace.

The terms are refused.

English demands.

Refused by Hyder.

Colonel Smith proceeds to Madras.

During his absence, Colonel Wood, who had been the favourite with the Council and the Nawáb, was not only out-manœuvred by Hyder, but, on November 16, at Oossoor, was defeated by him, losing 2,000 draught cattle, with his stores, and two eighteen-pounder guns; and on the 23rd was again severely handled, and escaped only by the timely arrival of a reinforcement under Major Fitzgerald. Colonel Wood was now superseded by Colonel Lang; but the English army was much crippled and weakened; the siege of Bangalore had been raised; and Hyder Ally, taking advantage of their position, at once descended into the Báráh Mahál. Here, with surprising energy and rapidity, he recovered all the forts which had been taken by Colonel Wood, and then marched southwards upon Tanjore; but, after receiving four lacs of rupees from the rajah, he suddenly turned northwards

Hyder defeats Colonel Wood.

The siege of Bangalore raised.

Hyder's successes.

towards Madras, the road to which was now open. The consternation of the Council was extreme; and an officer—Captain Brooke—was dispatched to negotiate. Hyder's proposals were those of a dignified statesman, as well as an able general. He pointed out how often his peaceable overtures had been rejected; explained how he was, in fact, the only barrier between the English and the Mahrattas, and that it was open to him either to join them, or the English; and as it was impossible to oppose both, he would join the English in preference. The Council were, as before, irresolute and incapable. They sent Mr. Andrews, a member, to Hyder on February 14, 1769, while they again placed Colonel Smith at the head of the army at Chittapet. The Council proposed an armistice for forty days, of which Hyder would accept only twelve: and at the expiration of this period he again moved southwards, followed by Colonel Smith.

He approaches Madras, and negotiates with the Council.

The negotiations broken off.

Hyder departs southwards.

Meanwhile Hyder had entered into communication with M. Law, now chief of Pondicherry. He detailed the victories he had gained over their mutual enemies, the English, and invited an envoy to his camp; and while Mr. Andrews had returned to Madras for instructions, received a deputation from the French, which was sent with all the pomp they could contrive to exhibit. This was possibly intended by Hyder as a ruse to alarm the English Council; but, not depending on its effect, and having succeeded in inducing Colonel Smith to follow him to a distance of 140 miles from Madras, he suddenly left his camp at the head of 6,000 chosen cavalry, and, marching 130 miles in three days and a half, arrived at St. Thomé, five miles south of Madras, on March 29. Thence he wrote temperately to the Council, that he had respected their country; that he had preferred to negotiate with them instead of fighting Colonel Smith, and requested Mr. Du Pré might be sent to him.

Opens negotiations with the French.

Evades Colonel Smith and marches rapidly on Madras.

Hyder was master of the situation, and dictated his own terms. His overtures were strenuously opposed by Colonel Smith, who declared he could turn Hyder's position to his disadvantage, as indeed was quite possible; but the Council were full of fear, and on April 3, 1769, a treaty was executed. Its principal terms were that mutual conquests were to be restored; that, in case the dominions of either party were attacked, the other should aid in driving out the enemy—which, in fact, amounted to an article of offensive and defensive alliance; but by the treaty the English became saddled with the whole expense of the war, had been obliged to abandon all that had been gained, and by the dominant position

Hyder dictates the terms of a treaty.

Its unfavourable terms in regard to the English.

of Hyder at the gate of Madras, had, for the present, lost what prestige they had won. As to Mahomed Ally, who refused to be a party to the treaty, and Hyder, who objected to his being considered at all, they thus mutually ignored and defied each other; and it added not a little to the estimation of Hyder's power by the people of the country, that he insisted upon the families of Chunda Sahib and other persons of rank, hitherto kept under surveillance by Mahomed Ally, being released and made over to his protection. Thus ended the second war with Hyder Ally, which had assumed an aspect of long, difficult, and costly prolongation.

Defence of the Council.

The best and only excuse perhaps that could be made for the hasty treaty, was given by the Council of Madras, who, in their defence, declared that they had made peace, because they had no money to make war.

Hyder at war with the Mahrattas.

Hyder was no sooner at peace with the English, than he entered on a contest with the Mahrattas. He not only refused payment of their chouth, but his troops made incursions into the southern districts of the Mahratta dominions. This was not to be endured; and having dispatched a large body of horse under Putwurdhun, Rastia, and other leaders, in November 1761, Mahdoo Ráo Péshwah followed at the head of 20,000 horse and 15,000 infantry. With these forces, the whole of Northern and Eastern Mysore, as far as Nundidroog, were quickly overrun and plundered. Hyder, who could not oppose the invaders, hoped they would retire on the approach of the monsoon; but Mahdoo Ráo, who was obliged to return to Poona in June, on account of his health, was bent on a prosecution of the war, and left Trimbuk Ráo Máma in Mysore, in command of 30,000 men.

Second campaign.

After some inconsequent negotiation, the campaign was opened after the monsoon by the Mahrattas, under the command of Appa Bulwunt. Their army having been reinforced, amounted to 40,000 horse and 10,000 infantry, but their artillery was weak. Hyder brought into the field 12,000 horse, 25,000 infantry, and forty guns; but, under the Mahratta superiority in cavalry, he could undertake no offensive operation.

Hyder defeated at Mailgóta, and Seringapatam is besieged.

As the Mahrattas pressed him back upon Seringapatam, he attempted to defend the pass of Mailgóta; but he was defeated, with terrible slaughter, on March 5. He fled to Seringapatam, followed by the wreck of the army, where he was besieged by the Mahrattas; but, deficient as they were in siege guns, they were unable to make any impression upon it.

Hyder appeals to the English for assistance.

Meanwhile Hyder had besought the Council of Madras to afford him assistance; but it was in vain that he appealed to the terms of the treaty, offered twenty lacs for an English brigade, to cede the Báráh Mahál, or, as his only alternative, to call in the aid of the French. The Council would willingly have observed the engagements of the treaty, and assisted him; but they were overruled by Sir John Lindsay, who had been sent out by the ministry of England, to the Nawáb, as ambassador-plenipotentiary, and they feared him. The Nawáb, who detested the 'upstart,' would not hear of Hyder's being assisted; and, on the contrary, demanded a junction with the Mahrattas against him; and as Sir John Lindsay supported the Nawáb, Hyder was abandoned and compelled to make the best terms he could with his foes. If the Council was unable, under the circumstances, to assist Hyder, they did not at least disgrace themselves by joining the Mahrattas against him. The terms to which Hyder was eventually obliged to submit were very stringent. He had to pay, at once, thirty-six lacs of rupees—360,000*l.*—as arrears of chouth and expenses of the war; and to promise for the future an annual tribute of fourteen lacs; as also to surrender Kolhar, Bangalore, Ooscotta, Balapoor, and Séra, which had formerly been held by Shahjee, the father of Sivajee; and by this cession his dominions were materially contracted. Hyder never forgot or forgave the treacherous and cowardly, as he termed it, abandonment of him by the English on this occasion; and by the cession of territory forced from him, the Mahratta outposts in 1771 had advanced to the north-western frontier of the Nawáb's territories.

The terms of the treaty are not observed.

Hyder abandoned.

CHAPTER XVIII.

OF THE PROGRESS OF THE MAHRATTAS IN HINDOSTAN, 1769 TO 1772.

After the close of the Péshwah's campaign against Janoojee Bhóslay, in Berar, in 1769, an army was sent into Malwah, under the command of Visajee Kishen, which was the first effort the Mahrattas had made in that direction since the fatal battle of Paniput. On the junction of the contingents of Holkar and Sindia, the cavalry amounted to about 50,000 strong, and the infantry, composed, for the most part, of Arabs, Abyssinians, and other foreign mercenaries, was numerous and effective. The Mahrattas had not only to collect the arrears of chouth, but to recover the prestige they had lost. On the part of the Emperor of Dehly, there was nothing to oppose them. The Prince Juwán Bukht, with Nujeeb-ood-Dowlah, the Rohilla chief, maintained Dehly, and Sooruj Mul, the Ját, having

The Mahrattas advance into Malwah.

threatened it, was killed in action in 1769. His son afterwards laid siege to the city in conjunction with Holkar; but the influence of Nujeeb-ood-Dowlah over Holkar, induced him to retire into Malwah, and the siege was abandoned. The first act of the Mahratta general was to require the Rajpoot chiefs to pay arrears of tribute; and Visajee Kishen next turned upon the Játs, who, after a defeat, were compelled to agree to pay sixty-five lacs of rupees—650,000*l.*—partly in cash, and partly by instalments. It now became a question whether the Rohillas should be attacked or not: and eventually, though not without much discussion among the leaders of the army, the Mahratta forces, after the death of Nujeeb-ood-Dowlah, in October 1770, moved into Rohilkhund, and completely overran it, at the same time threatening Shujah-ood-Dowlah of Oudh, who was, nominally at least, under the protection of the English. The vizier, however, temporized.

Their proceedings.

Rohilkhund overrun.

The young emperor, Shah Allum, had found his English allies averse to proceeding to Dehly and seating him on the throne; and he now turned to the Mahrattas for that purpose, who readily met his advances. After the plunder of Rohilkhund, they had proceeded to Dehly, and were prepared to receive him, whenever it suited him to come. The emperor, therefore, though warned of the consequences by the Council of Calcutta, was met by Sindia, who escorted him to the camp of Visajee Kishen, and on December 25, 1771, he was placed on the throne of his ancestors with much pomp. Although Rohilkhund had been for the most part already laid under contribution, yet Visajee Kishen had protected Nujeeb-ood-Dowlah and his family; and Sindia now urged the spoliation of his son, a course to which the emperor gave a ready consent. Early in 1772, therefore, the Mahrattas attacked Zabita Khan, and plundered him of all the wealth accumulated by his father. Of this the emperor had hoped to get a share, but he gained nothing, and the condition into which he was sinking, from the intolerable behaviour of the Mahratta leaders, was becoming more and more insupportable.

The emperor joins the Mahrattas.

The emperor is crowned as Shah Allum.

Zabita Khan plundered.

There were three parties now in active intrigue: the Rohillas, wishing to get rid of the Mahrattas on any terms, and willing to assist the Vizier of Oudh; the vizier, detesting and fearing both, was temporizing with each alternately; and the Mahrattas, desiring to plunder both Oudh and Rohilkhund, or willing to be bought off by either or both. The vizier's policy was, however, detestably treacherous, for he would willingly have sacrificed the Rohillas to the Mahrattas, in order

Position of parties in Hindostan.

that he might follow up their ravages and annex the country; but, on the other hand, he dreaded the occupation of Rohilkhund by them, a step which he was assured would be followed by an attack upon his own dominions. In June 1772, a convention was made, by which the Mahrattas agreed, on the payment of forty lacs of rupees, to spare Rohilkhund; but would not accept the bond of Hafiz Rehmut, the Rohilla chief, unless it was guaranteed by the vizier. On this being effected, Hafiz Rehmut actually paid five lacs to the vizier as his share; but of this sum nothing was paid to the Mahrattas. As the monsoon was at hand, the Mahrattas having received no money, would delay no longer; and crossing the Ganges by the fords, attacked the Rohillas, and routed them with great slaughter, plundering Nujeeb Khan, one of their chiefs, of all his wealth, and committing vast devastation. The consequences of these attacks were, that the Rohillas threw themselves on the protection of the vizier, and fell completely into his hands. Contrary to the expectations of the emperor and all other parties, the Mahrattas did not leave the vicinity of Dehly, but cantoned themselves in the Dooáb for the rains, during which period, the emperor, weary of their insolence and rapacity, endeavoured to resist them by force; but his general, Nujeeb Khan, was defeated, Dehly was occupied by them, and he was obliged to purchase their forbearance by the cession of Allahabad and Corah, two of the districts of Oudh, which had been reserved for him by the English after the battle of Buxar. These were, however, protected by a British force under Sir Robert Barker, which the Mahrattas hesitated to attack; and they now offered to forego their demands on the Rohillas, if they would join them in an invasion of Oudh. Hafiz Rehmut Khan, however, refused to comply, and cast in his lot with the vizier and the English, by whose combined forces, with his own, the Mahrattas were held in check. While the parties were thus occupied, news reached the Mahratta camp of the death of Mahdoo Ráo Péshwah, on November 18, and Visajee Kishen, taking the whole of the army with him, retired southwards, and crossed the Nerbudda, laden with plunder, in the month of May of the ensuing year, 1772.

Convention with the Rohillas.

Transactions in Rohilkhund.

The Mahrattas defeat the emperor's forces.

Poland dismembered.

CHAPTER XIX.

OF TRANSACTIONS IN ENGLAND, 1769 TO 1773.

The rapid progress of the English power in India, coupled with the possession of immense wealth by the servants of the company, which was ostentatiously displayed in England, not only excited public envy, but reports of the oppression of the natives, and malversation of public funds, became at length so prevalent, and were to all appearance so well supported by facts, that the utmost indignation prevailed, and an investigation by a parliamentary commission was loudly demanded. On Lord Clive's return from India, he had been attacked virulently by his old enemy, Mr. Sullivan, and the corruption prevailing in the court of proprietors, in which, by investments in India stock, numbers of additional votes were provided, enabled his adversaries, who had been in India, to assist materially the combination against him, and eventually to bring his transactions before Parliament.

Ministerial transactions with the East India Company.

During these proceedings, the magnitude and importance of the imperial grant of the dewany of Bengal, which Lord Clive, it was admitted, had obtained, became better comprehended than before; and his own estimate of the surplus revenues of the three provinces was a million sterling. In 1767 the amount of dividend on stock had been limited to ten per cent, until February 1, 1769; but the anticipation of heavy remittances from India induced the ministry to demand a payment of 400,000*l.* per annum, for five years, while permission to raise the dividends on stock to twelve and a-half per cent. was conceded; but should the rate of dividend fall below ten per cent., a proportional reduction of the payment to the public exchequer was to ensue. At the same time, Mr. Vansittart, Mr. Scrafton, and Colonel Forde, were appointed as supervisors of financial affairs in Bengal, and sailed together in the 'Aurora,' a frigate of the Royal Navy; but the ship never reached her destination, and is believed to have foundered at sea.

Condition of finances in India.

Financial affairs in India, so far from furnishing any prospect of payment to the exchequer, or increased dividend, were in reality labouring under a condition of chronic deficit in all the presidencies. The magnificent revenues of Bengal were badly collected, and the peculations made from them were immense. In Madras, the Carnatic war had not only drained the local treasury, but the Nawáb had been obliged to borrow at heavy interest: and these were the main sources from which the surplus revenue had been expected. Instead of receiving remittances, therefore, the directors had to meet heavy bills drawn upon them in Calcutta and Madras. Notwithstanding these impending difficulties, dividends of six and a quarter per cent. in March and September 1771 were declared, by an immense majority in the court, which indeed was all but unanimous on the subject, and proposals for the dividends of 1772 were made at the same rate.

Deficiency in England.

It was impossible, however, to meet the future engagements. Instead of a surplus, a deficiency of 1,293,000*l.* appeared in England, and there was even a greater one in Calcutta. Loans were applied for to the Bank, for 400,000*l.* and 300,000*l.* respectively; and these proving insufficient, an application was made to the ministry for the loan of 1,000,000*l.* sterling. The request was not immediately responded to by Lord North, but Parliament was convened earlier than usual, and its proceedings, which are memorable in English history, were carried on amidst much excitement on both sides.

Proceedings of the Select Committee.

The Select Committee did its duty fearlessly, and the exposure made of fraud, peculation, and mismanagement by the company's servants, determined the ministry to make an entire renovation in the conduct of affairs in India, until at least the expiration of the company's charter, which had yet six years to run. It was in vain that the company denounced the proceedings in Parliament as an infringement of their rights, and violation of their property; the English public was thoroughly aroused, and would be content with nothing short of a searching enquiry. After a further protest by the directors against the minister's proposal in regard to regulation of dividend and payment of debt, which had no effect, he introduced a Bill for a new constitution of the company, which struck fairly and decisively against the prevailing corruption. The qualifications for voting were enhanced; directors were to be changed in rotation. A governor-general for Bengal, Bahar, and Orissa, with a salary of 25,000*l.* a year, with four counsellers at 8,000*l.* each, were to be appointed; and a chief justice, and three puisne judges were to form a royal court. All correspondence was to be submitted to the ministry; and no person whatever, either king's or company's servants, should be allowed to receive presents, or engage in commercial affairs. 'If,' says Mr. Mill, 'the alarm and indignation of the company, directors, and proprietors were excited before, that body was now struck with the highest terror and resentment.' They carried on their agitation both in Parliament and in the City of London—indeed, throughout

Bill for the future constitution of the company.

Resistance by the company.

England, with unsparing assiduity and vigour. They made long, ingenious and severe protests; they were defended before both Houses by eminent counsel, and they left nothing untried by which a verdict in their favour could be obtained; but Parliament was obdurate: and the ministerial measures were carried by large majorities in both Houses. It cannot be admitted they were perfect; for the real founders of the management of Indian affairs had yet to gain experience, and of that even the company's servants possessed none beyond trade, to which they had been accustomed; nor could even the Select Committee elicit information on which they could have formed particular measures; but the conviction that a new constitution was needed, apart from the fiery denunciations of Burke on the one hand, and the special pleading of the company on the other, was clear to moderate men of all shades of politics, and the Bills received the royal assent on June 21, and July 1, 1773. It was at this time that the final and specific accusations against Lord Clive, which had long been impending over him, were brought forward by the chairman of the Select Committee, in the shape of a demand for enquiry into the death and deposition of Suráj-ood-Dowlah, and the fictitious treaty. On Clive's part nothing was denied: he gloried in every act he had done, and the sympathy of both Houses, representing the English nation, ultimately went with him; but the strain upon his mind, coupled with a painful chronic disorder, produced aberration of intellect, and he died, by his own hand, on November 2, 1774.

The Bill receives the royal assent.

Proceedings against Clive.

Clive commits suicide.

Louis XVI. king of France.

The first appointments made under the new constitution were Mr. Warren Hastings, an experienced company's servant, then in Bengal, to be governor-general, with General Clavering, Colonel Monson, Mr. Francis, and Mr. Barwell, a civil servant, as members of Council. Of the new court, Sir Elijah Turpey was chief justice, and Le Maistre, Hyde, and Chambers the puisne judges. On October 14, 1774, the three members of Council, Clavering, Monson, and Francis, who had sailed from England, landed in Calcutta, and on the next day the royal commission was read.

Appointment of Warren Hastings as governor-general.

CHAPTER XX.

OF EVENTS IN BENGAL, 1767 TO 1775.

ON the departure of Lord Clive, in 1767, he was succeeded by Mr. Verelst; but the genius and decision of the administration had departed with him, and the old malpractices were quickly resumed by all grades of the local civil servants. It is questionable whether their individual rapacity or incapacity were ever more signally displayed than at this period. The local executive administration was carried on by Mahomed Reza Khan, as deputy of the Nawáb, and Rajah Shitáb Rái; but it was corrupt, extravagant, and wholly without check or control. Immense grants of lands were made to their creatures, both Hindoo and Mahomedan, with a corresponding alienation of the revenue: and together with the local charges, not only absorbed the whole of the funds, but created ultimately a deficit of more than a million and a half sterling. Lord Clive's plan of a double government was gradually breaking down; for, with all his genius as a politician, and as a military commander, he had failed to estimate the difference between the detail of a government carried on according to the native system, and one which released native authorities from responsibility, and left them to unrestrained malversation of the revenues, and oppression of the people.

Maladministration of Bengal.

Evils of the double government.

There were, however, some officers who saw the danger, and among them Mr. Holwell, who wrote boldly to the Council as early as 1761:—'We have nibbled at these provinces for eight years, and notwithstanding the immense acquisition of territory and revenue, what benefit has resulted from our successes to the company? Shall we go on nibbling and nibbling at the bait until the trap falls and crushes us? Let us boldly dare to be soobahs ourselves.' So decisive a policy, however, even Clive rejected; and it was not till 1769 that supervisors were appointed to each of the provinces, to act as checks upon the native governors, and to collect information regarding the revenue settlements and the land tenures. They had hardly begun their work when the whole of Bengal was visited by a terrible famine, the results and effects of which have been passed over, almost with silence, by most of the English historians of India, but which have risen into new and prominent interest by the publica-

Mr. Holwell's remonstrance and advice.

Supervisors appointed.

Terrible famine in Bengal.

tion, in 1868, of Mr. W. Hunter's 'Annals of Rural Bengal,' a work full of most interesting details to the student of the history of this period. Mr. Verelst left India soon after it began, and was succeeded by Mr. Cartier, who had been one of the supervisors, and who made a faithful report to the Court of Directors; but it was coupled by an assurance that not only would the revenue be safe, but that ten per cent. would be added to it. The famine and its horrible accompaniment of destruction of human life continued; and in the summer of 1770, as Mr. Hunter writes: 'The people went on dying, the husbandmen sold their cattle, they sold their implements of agriculture, they devoured their seed-grain; they sold their sons and daughters, till at length no buyer of children could be found; they ate the leaves of trees and the grass of the field, and in June 1770, the Residents at the Durbar affirmed that the living were feeding on the dead. Day and night a torrent of famished wretches poured into the great cities. At an early period of the year pestilence had broken out. In March, we find small-pox at Moorshidabad, where it glided through the viceroyal mutes, and cut off the Prince Syfut in his palace. The streets were blocked up with promiscuous heaps of the dying and the dead' (p. 26). The famine ceased by the close of 1770, and a plentiful harvest ensued; but the desolation it had caused was frightful. More than one-third—thirty-five per cent.—of the general population, and fifty per cent. of the cultivators, had perished, and 'notwithstanding the abundant crops of 1771, the country continued to fall out of tillage; and the commissioners appointed in 1772 to visit the different districts, found the finest part of the province desolated by famine, the lands abandoned, and the revenue falling to decay' (p. 33).[1]

Effects of the famine.

The mischiefs of the double government, coupled with the famine, roused the directors to action; and, almost in the words of Mr. Holwell, they wrote to Bengal, that they had resolved 'to stand forth as dewán, and to take on themselves the entire care and management of the revenues, through the agency of their own servants.' On April 13, 1772, Mr. Warren Hastings assumed charge of the new administration. He had originally belonged to Bengal, where his eminent talents having attracted the notice of Clive, he was employed in political duty at Moorshidabad; and having subsequently visited England on leave, his evidence before the Select Committee proved so valuable, that he was appointed to the Council of Madras; and thence being, it was considered, the only civil officer

Warren Hastings assumes the government.

[1] 'Annals of Bengal.'

capable of carrying out the new measures in Bengal, was appointed President of the Council in 1772. After deciding upon the best means for the revenue management, which was a lease of all lands for a term of five years, and providing courts for the administration of civil and criminal justice, Mahomed Reza Khan and Rajah Shitáb Rái, who had been chiefs of the prior administration, were brought to trial on various charges of malversation, but were acquitted. They were not, however, re-employed.

Political events and financial affairs.

Mr. Hastings' attention was now drawn to the political events in the neighbourhood of Dehly, and he met the Vizier of Oudh at Benares by appointment, in the month of September. The financial condition of affairs in Bengal at this time, was as distressing as that of the directors in England: and a debt of 160 lacs—1,600,000*l.*—had accumulated. There were two questions for discussion: first, the emperor's pension of twenty-six lacs from Bengal, to which, as he had become dependent on the Mahrattas, the directors had already decided as early as 1768 he would be no longer entitled; the second, that as he had assigned Corah and Allahabad to the Mahrattas, such an arrangement could not be permitted, and the original grant to him should be revoked. In both of these measures the vizier concurred; and as the cost of the maintenance of the two districts had proved extremely heavy, amounting to nearly two millions sterling in five years, they were assigned to the vizier for an additional payment of fifty lacs.

The vizier's offer for possession of Rohilkhund.

On the other hand, the object of the vizier was to obtain possession of Rohilkhund, for which, as already explained, he had long been intriguing: and he offered to Mr. Hastings forty lacs of rupees—400,000*l.*—the amount of the bond he had obtained from Hafiz Rehmut Khan, if he were put in possession of the province, besides paying the costs of the troops employed. Mr. Hastings closed with the offer; but, although the Court of Directors, on March 3, 1775, wrote to Bengal, 'We, upon the maturest deliberation, confirm the treaty of Benares,' there is no act of his brilliant career which has been deemed more questionable.

Accepted by Hastings.

Objections to the treaty.

It was, in the first place, the deliberate hiring of English troops to perform an act of spoliation: for the Nawáb had no real cause of war with the Rohillas, their bond being untenable; and it was dangerous, because, as Mr. Hastings admitted, it was evident that the Nawáb, who could not defend his own dominions without English aid, coud not hope to defend, in addition, the Rohilla province. Moreover it was treacherous, because the Rohillas had already professed their attachment to the English, and high trust in their good faith. On the other hand were questions of expediency, which Hastings afterwards urged; the danger of the Rohillas coalescing with the Mahrattas and the emperor against Oudh—their power and restless character, and the necessity of strengthening the vizier against all. But the measure had already been decided by the treaty of Benares, and action upon it was not delayed. Before it took place, the vizier had made advances to the emperor. He had assisted him with money, and troops which were employed against the Játs; and had engaged him to assist in the reduction of Rohilkhund, receiving one-half of the plunder and one-half of the territory. Whether this secret agreement was known to Mr. Hastings or not, seems doubtful. If it were, he would have had ample excuse for withdrawing from his engagement as regarded the Rohillas; but early in November 1773 he was applied to by the vizier to furnish troops for the Rohilkhund service, and in January 1774 the necessary orders were issued. Colonel Champion assumed the command, and, in February, the troops arrived in the vizier's territory.

Troops are furnished for the invasion of Rohilkhund.

The vizier now called upon Hafiz Rehmut Khan, the Rohilla chief, for payment of the bond of forty lacs of rupees, intimating that his refusal would be considered a 'casus belli.' In reply, the chief stated that he would pay anything that the vizier might have paid to the Mahrattas, but nothing more; and a subsequent offer of compromise was met by a demand of two crores, or two millions sterling. As this was necessarily refused, the British troops advanced on April 17, and on the 23rd attacked the Rohillas in position, and defeated them. They lost 2,000 men, and their brave chieftain, Hafiz Rehmut, and one of his sons, but not their honour; and Colonel Champion, while he wrote in admiration of their valour, did not spare the vizier's exceeding cowardice. The Rohillas rallied under Fyzoolla Khan, and took up a strong position, under the hills, which was invested; but the vizier had already opened negotiations with him, and on his agreement to receive a jahgeer or estate, yielding nearly fifteen lacs—150,000*l.*—a year, the Rohilla war ended.

The vizier's demands on Hafiz Rehmut Khan.

His reply.

The British troops defeat the Rohillas.

Hafiz Rehmut Khan is slain.

Conclusion of the war.

These events had occurred previous to the arrival of the members of Council; and, important as they were, had been thrown into the shade by the success of Hastings' financial arrangements. 'In less than two years,' as he afterwards recorded in his 'Memoirs relative to the State of India,' 'I saw the debt completely discharged, and a sum in ready cash, of the same amount, actually accumulated in store in the public treasuries;' and if this assertion is not borne out by the figures

Prosperity of the finances.

quoted by Mr. Mill (vol. iii. p. 516), there can at least be no question that the English credit in Bengal was restored, and that the finances were easy. These circumstances were, however, overlooked; and from the first day of their sitting, the new members, as if they had arranged a plan on the voyage, as they most likely had done, evinced a decidedly hostile attitude to Hastings. They first attacked his political transactions; and, on the death of Shujah-ood-Dowlah, the vizier of Oudh, early in 1775, and the accession of his son, Asof-ood-Dowlah, they, forming a majority in the Council, abrogated all former treaties, and arbitrarily forced the vizier into the conclusion of new engagements. They confirmed the cession or sale of Corah and Allahabad; but required, as equivalent, the district of Benares, which belonged to Rajah Cheyt Singh, and yielded a revenue of twenty-two lacs. The allowance for the English troops was to be raised to 266,000 rupees per month, and all balances due were to be paid up. This new treaty was executed on May 21; but Mr. Hastings had no part in it; he considered the terms too exacting, and more than could be fulfilled. The directors afterwards signified their approval; but the Council deprived the Nawáb of means of fulfilling the obligations they had imposed upon him, by supporting the claims of the Bégums, the mother and widow of Shujah-ood-Dowlah, to the whole of the treasure amassed by him, which was about two millions sterling. Nor did the mischief of the interference end here. With an empty treasury the new Nawáb had no means of paying his army, which was twelve months in arrears, and it broke into violent mutiny, which was not quelled without the slaughter of many thousands.

The Council oppose Hastings.

and abrogate the Oudh treaties.

A new treaty is executed.

The Council supports the Bégums' claims.

The opposition to Mr. Hastings was not confined to transactions in Council. It was openly understood, if not proclaimed, that accusations against him would be acceptable: and petitions, as might be expected, poured in not only publicly, but were received at the private residences of Clavering, Monson, and Francis. The most important of them, however, that of the Ranee of Burdwan, broke down; others succeeded, and the personal animosity displayed against Hastings was so evident, that he threatened to dissolve the Council in case any enquiry in relation to himself should be commenced. On the other hand, Francis and his friends placed on record, 'that there appeared no species of peculation from which the Honorable Governor-General has thought it reasonable to abstain.' These miserable proceedings culminated in the famous case of Nundkoomar, a man whose treachery and deceit had frequently been established. He

Petitions against Warren Hastings encouraged.

Accusations by Nundkoomar.

issued specific charges against Hastings for having received a bribe of three and a half lacs of rupees from the widow of Meer Jaffier, which the Council proceeded to investigate; but Hastings withdrew from the proceedings, refusing to sit in Council while criminal accusations were made against him. Nundkoomar produced a letter of the Bégum's in support of his charge, of which the seal appeared genuine. The lady herself denied the transaction; but the Council considered the charge proved, and it was not discovered till after Nundkoomar's execution, that the Bégum's seal, with many others that had been in his possession, were counterfeits.

Proceedings by the Council.

Hastings now brought forward a charge against Nundkoomar in the supreme court for forgery; and a native merchant, Mohun Prusád, also prosecuted him on a separate accusation of a similar nature, which had been partially tried in a local court, but was transferred to the supreme court on its establishment. On this charge, Nundkoomar was tried, found guilty, and condemned to death. No one, perhaps, expected that the sentence would be carried out; but the judge, Sir Elijah Impey, was inflexible. Hastings did not interfere, and on August 5 Nundkoomar was hanged. It was quite possible for the majority in Council, if not to have forbidden the execution, at least to have suspended it; but they were silent, hoping, perhaps, that the act would infallibly sacrifice Hastings; and it afterwards formed one of the articles of his impeachment. The question of the legality or illegality of the act has often been discussed. If forgery by the English law was felony, it was considered only as fraud by natives of India. This act of forgery had been committed before the introduction of English laws, and might therefore be considered as unaffected by them; but the judge argued that he saw the necessity of a severe example among a people of lax morality, and whether influenced by his friendship for Hastings or not, stood firm upon the legal aspect of the case, and acted upon it. Hastings gained, for the present, the re-establishment of his authority and immunity from petty charges; but the recoil was, in the end, worse to himself than the endurance of them could have been: it entailed years of anxious suffering, in the thought that by many, perhaps most, of his countrymen he was held morally guilty of having used Sir Elijah Impey for the destruction of his enemy.

Counter accusations of forgery against Nundkoomar,

who is found guilty, and sentenced to death, and executed.

Considerations on the event.

CHAPTER XXI.

THE ADMINISTRATION OF WARREN HASTINGS—THE FIRST MAHRATTA WAR, 1772 TO 1779.

AFTER the death of Mahdoo Ráo Péshwah in 1771, his brother, Narráin Ráo, was invested as Péshwah: and Rughonath Ráo, or Rughoba, his uncle, who had previously been confined by Mahdoo Ráo, but released before his death, was now again arrested, and confined in a part of the Péshwah's palace. On August 30, 1773, the regular infantry, who were deeply in arrears in pay, broke into mutiny, and a party of them entering the palace, the Péshwah was put to death during the confusion by a servant of Rughoba's. The odium of the act rested upon Rughoba for a time, but it was discovered afterwards that an order to 'seize' Narráin Ráo had been altered to 'kill' him, and the Mahratta nation acquitted Rughoba of the murder. There was now no heir to the Péshwahship, and Rughoba assumed the office as nearest of kin to the deceased. His first proceeding, after having received official investiture, was to lead the army against Nizam Ally, whom he forced to return to Beeder, and obliged to make a further cession of territory, to the amount of twenty lacs of rupees a year; but the wily Nizam, at a subsequent friendly interview, so worked upon him by flattery and cajolery, that the cession was not enforced, and the effect of this act was to weaken Rughoba's power with his countrymen. Shortly afterwards it was discovered that the widow of the late Péshwah, Narráin Ráo, was pregnant; and the party of Rughoba was gradually weakened by defections. He had advanced into Mysore, but his transactions with Hyder Ally, which were intended to obtain Hyder's support, were, in proportion to the national demands, much reduced, and increased the dissatisfaction against him. His defeat of a portion of the army in the interest of the rival party had the effect of strengthening him for a short period: but he was unable to enter Poona, and on April 18, 1774, the widow of Narráin Ráo was delivered of a son, who was called Mahdoo Narráin, and who was formally installed as Péshwah when he was forty days old. Meanwhile Rughoba had proceeded to Malwah, where he hoped to obtain the co-operation of Sindia and Holkar; and at the head of their forces moved from Indoor to the Tapty river, and entered into negotiations with the English at Bombay. During the division between the great Mahratta

Mahratta affairs.

Transactions with the Nizam.

parties, and while the rival factions were watching each other, Hyder Ally overran all the Mahratta districts south of the Toongboodra river, while Basalut Jung, advancing from Adony, plundered the Southern Mahratta provinces unchecked.

In 1772, under the orders of the Court of Directors, an envoy from Bombay had been established at Poona; the great object of the mission being to secure the island of Salsette, with other islands in the harbour of Bombay. In the same year, in consequence of claims on the Nawáb of Baróch, that city had been taken by storm on November 18, and the Bombay Council desired to exchange it for Salsette: but unexpected events at Poona had nearly determined them to occupy the island by force of arms, when they received overtures from Rughoba for assistance in troops and money, in order to establish himself in his government. In reply, the Council, on September 6, promised to assist him with about 2,500 men, if he would advance twenty lacs of rupees, and, on his re-establishment in his government, cede to the company Salsette, with Bassein and its dependencies. But Rughoba refused to engage to make these cessions, offering other districts in Guzerat, of the value of eleven lacs, with six lacs in cash and one and a half lacs per month, for the services of 1,000 Europeans, 2,000 Sepoys, and 15 guns.

Embassy from Bombay to Poona.

Overtures from Rughoba.

While these negotiations were in progress, news reached the Council that the Portuguese, reinforced from Europe, were about to attempt the recovery of Salsette and Bassein; and to anticipate their operations, it was determined to attack Salsette. The fort of Tannah, in spite of protestations by the Portuguese, who had sent a fleet to Bombay, was besieged and taken by assault on December 28, 1774, and by the close of the month the whole of that island, as well as Carinjah, were occupied. Rughoba by this time had fallen into a difficult position. He had been deserted by Sindia and Holkar, and retreating on Guzerat, reached Baroda on January 3, 1775. Here he hoped to engage the aid of the Gáikwar, and perhaps of the English; and he renewed his negotiations, which were closed on March 6. The Bombay Government agreed to furnish 3,000 men, and Rughoba ceded Salsette and Bassein in perpetuity, with Jumboseer and Oolpur, in Guzerat, which, together with assignments of revenue, amounted to a yearly value of nineteen and a quarter lacs per year.

The English take Salsette.

Cession of Salsette and Bassein by Rughoba.

In anticipation of the execution of this treaty, the Bombay Government had dispatched a force under Colonel Keating to Guzerat, where Rughoba had already been defeated by the Mahratta ministerial army; and

Dispatch of troops to Guzerat.

having formed a junction with what remained of his troops, the united forces on April 19 moved towards Ahmedabad; but the Bombay Council were urgent in their desire for Rughoba to proceed to Poona, and the allies turned towards the river Myhie. On the morning of May 18, as the British force was marching through a narrow road with high banks, it was attacked by the Mahrattas, and, after considerable loss and much confusion, defeated their assailants. A renewed attack on June 10 would have been more successful; but, owing to the misconduct of some of Rughoba's horse, Colonel Keating's advance was perceived and the enemy escaped, not however without throwing their guns into the Nerbudda. It was too late now to proceed to Poona, as the monsoon had set in; and the forces were cantoned during the rains. Guzerat had at least been freed of the enemy, whose fleet also was defeated by sea; and Rughoba presented to the company the districts of Hansóte and Amód, of the yearly value of three lacs of rupees, making up the total of acquisition to upwards of twenty-four lacs per year.

The Mahratta army attacks the English, and is repulsed.

The Mahrattas retreat to Poona.

Rughoba's further cessions.

The assistance of, and treaties with, Rughoba, notwithstanding their individual disagreements, found no favour with the Bengal Council. They unanimously decided that the treaty was 'impolitic, dangerous, unauthorised, and unjust,' and ordered all the troops to be recalled. The Bombay Council defended themselves by the plea that the Supreme Council of Bengal was not in existence when the treaty with Rughoba was made; and they dispatched Mr. Taylor, an able member, to Bengal, whose explanations in regard to Mahratta offices proved very valuable. The governor-general, nevertheless, directed a suspension of hostilities, sent Colonel Upton as envoy to Poona, and gave the Bombay authorities to understand in distinct terms, that he was the only English authority in India who could make war or peace.

The Council of Bengal disapprove of the treaty with Rughoba.

Colonel Upton did not at first understand Mahratta Brahmins; and in Succaram Bapoo, the acting agent, and Nana Furnawees, the minister for political affairs, he had to encounter two of the ablest men that had ever been in office. Had he, as Grant Duff assumes, at once taken the highest ground and 'dictated a peace,' in all probability, he would have prevented war; but, in proportion as his demeanour assumed a tone of remonstrance, instead of decision, the Mahratta demands increased; and with the surrender of all Rughoba's cessions, they required that of Rughoba himself, engaging to pay the English twelve lacs for their losses. Colonel Upton's report produced an immediate

Negotiations.

change in the opinion of the Calcutta Council, and they made preparations to support Rughoba. Meanwhile, the Mahratta ministers had lowered their tone: they found Colonel Upton had not been deceived by their demeanour, and before a reply could arrive from Calcutta, they had executed the treaty of Poorundhur, by which most of the cessions to the English were confirmed, with a payment to them of twelve lacs of rupees; but the treaty with Rughoba was annulled, his army was to be disbanded, the British troops withdrawn, and he was to reside at a place pointed out, with a pension of 25,000 rupees a month and a suitable retinue. By this treaty the Bombay Government was placed in a serious dilemma; and Rughoba declared, rather than submit to be degraded, he would continue the war on his own resources. It was in vain that Colonel Upton protested against the Bombay opinions and hindrances to the new treaty; and equally vain that the Mahratta ministers threatened to carry fire and sword into the English possessions if it were broken. Mr. Hastings did not, in reality, approve of the new treaty: a dispatch from the Court of Directors confirmed that of Surat with Rughoba; and Colonel Upton was recalled to Bengal. The Bombay Government then sent Mr. Mostyn to Poona, who entered upon negotiations with the ministry.

The Mahratta ministers confirm the treaty of Poorundhur.

This was making slow progress, when a French adventurer, named St. Lubin, having landed at Choule, arrived at Poona, and gave himself out as an ambassador from the King of France. He offered to the Mahratta ministers a treaty of offensive and defensive alliance, to be supported by 2,500 Europeans and 10,000 Sepoys, and denounced the war with Rughoba, and the perfidious conduct of the English; but though the astute Nana Furnawees was not deceived, he yet imagined he could use this new element to serve his purposes with the English. The directors had, however, again signified their approval of the treaty with Rughoba; and the Bombay Government were not only more than ever confident, but set forth the encouragement of the French at Poona as a ground for at once breaking with the Poona ministry and putting Rughoba in possession of his office.

M. St. Lubin reaches India.

His proposal.

At this period, also, the Mahratta ministry became divided. Moraba had gained over Holkar, and Succaram Bapoo, the nominal head of all, to the party of Rughoba, and they united in requesting the Council of Bombay to send Rughoba to Poona at once. Meanwhile, the whole question had been reconsidered in Calcutta, and Mr. Hastings had decided that it would be most advisable to support the Bombay

Mr. Hastings supports the Government of Bombay.

Government with a large force. Six native regiments, therefore, with a proportion of artillery and cavalry, were directed to assemble at Kalpy on the Jumna, under Colonel Leslie, and the first attempt of British troops to march across India was decided on. In Moraba, however, the Bombay Government found a weak ally. Nana Furnawees had temporarily retired from office; but his counsels prevailed, and there seemed so little encouragement from Poona, that the Council had nearly committed themselves to the step of forbidding Colonel Leslie's advance, when, by a new revolution at Poona, Moraba was seized, on July 11, deposed from office, and confined by Sindia; Holkar again changed sides, and Nana Furnawees was raised to the highest rank in the ministry. At this juncture, news of a renewal of war between England and France arrived; and considering the proceedings of Nana Furnawees and his party as an actual breach of the treaty of Poorundhur, the Bombay Council determined to seat Rughoba in the regency. Nor did the destruction of his party affect their decision. The Council had already frittered away time and opportunity; for, during the dissensions at Poona, a decisive blow could have been struck; and had Rughoba been placed in office, supported by the English, all the chiefs would have submitted to him. Now Nana, the ablest of all the former ministry, was supreme; and he prepared himself for the conflict. On November 22, 1778, the first detail of English troops embarked at Bombay and crossed the harbour to the continent; and in a month, the army, about 2,500 strong, had assembled at Khundalla, the head of the Bhore Ghaut on the Poona road, when Rughoba joined it with his followers, and Mr. Carnac, on the part of the Council, accompanied him. Colonel Egerton had been placed in command, and his advance was never more than two miles, often as little as three-quarters of a mile a day. The march was harassed by clouds of Mahratta horse, and the main body of their army, 50,000 strong by the lowest computation, assembled at Tullegaon, sixteen miles from Poona, to dispute further advance. Here the British force arrived on January 9, 1779; they had eighteen days' provision in camp, and the Mahratta forces would not risk a general action; nevertheless, almost with the prize within their grasp, the hearts of the committee failed them. Mr. Carnac proposed a retreat, and on the night of the 11th the heavy guns were thrown into a tank, and the army began to retrace its steps. On the 13th, the village of Wurgaom was reached, but by this time, the force was entirely surrounded, and the committee began to negotiate. Rughoba had already given himself up to

Troops assemble at Kalpy.

Revolution at Poona.

The Bombay Government determine to establish Rughoba at Poona.

The English troops reach Khundalla,

but advance slowly.

The British forces retreat from Tullegaon.

Sindia, and the English alone remained to be dealt with. The army was allowed to depart; but an unconditional surrender was made of all acquisitions, and the English and Mahrattas returned to their mutual positions of 1773. This disgraceful convention was followed by the subsequent dismissal of Mr. Carnac and Colonels Egerton and Cockburn, nor was it till the conclusion of the long and difficult campaign which ensued, that the English, in the west of India, recovered the prestige they had lost.

Negotiations with the Mahrattas.

CHAPTER XXII.

THE FIRST MAHRATTA WAR (*continued*), FROM 1779 TO TREATY OF SALBYE, 1782.

MR. HORNBY, the President in Council at Bombay, altogether ignored the convention of Wurgaom. Mr. Carnac had had no authority for making any new, or abrogating any old treaty; and the spirit displayed by their president now animated the whole of the members. Colonel Leslie, though he had crossed the Jumna in May 1778, made no material advance, and had entered into some petty local contests. He was, therefore, recalled; but died before the order reached him, and Colonel Goddard was appointed in his room. He did not delay his important and interesting march. He pressed on through Bundelkhund and Malwah, in spite of the threatening appearance of the Mahrattas; was heartily welcomed, and materially assisted at Bhopál by its Nawáb; and on December 2, had crossed the Nerbudda. By the strict discipline he preserved, he obtained ample supplies, and this memorable march raised the reputation of the English in a very material degree throughout India.

Colonel Goddard's march across India.

Hastings had been for some time in negotiation with Moodajee Bhóslay of Berar, offering to support him against the ministry of Poona: but Moodajee had kept aloof from the existing contest, and the negotiation, renewed by Colonel Goddard, broke down. He, therefore, pursued his march, and reached Boorhanpoor on January 30, 1779, proceeding thence to Surat, where he arrived on February 26. It need hardly be recorded that he was heartily welcomed by the Bombay authorities, and was unanimously elected a member of their Council. Mr. Hornby would have once proceeded to make the Gáikwar independent of the

Warren Hastings negotiates with Moodajee Bhóslay.

Goddard reaches Surat.

Poona ministry, and have taken forcible possession of the Péshwah's districts in Guzerat; but he could adopt no decisive measure without the permission of the governor-general.

Mr. Hastings also rejected the convention of Wurgaom; and, on April 15, instructed Colonel, now General, Goddard, to negotiate a new treaty with the Mahrattas, on the basis of that of Poorundhur, with a proviso against the admission of the French; and if this failed, Mr. Hornby's plan in regard to Guzerat might be followed. Nana Furnawees dallied with the new proposals; and it was not till October, when reports of a coalition between the Nizam, Hyder Ally, and the Mahrattas began to arise, that, being pressed for a reply, he declared that the surrender of Rughoba, who had escaped from Sindia, and again thrown himself on British protection, and of Salsette—were the only terms on which any new negotiation could be based or admitted. These were necessarily inadmissible; and the Council and General Goddard prepared for war. On proposing their plan to Futteh Singh Gáikwar, they found him indisposed to commit himself with the Mahratta ministry, and General Goddard proceeded to occupy the Péshwah's districts in Guzerat. These were overcome without material resistance, and on February 15, 1780, Ahmedabad, the capital of the province, was taken by assault.

Mr. Hastings proposes a new treaty.

Nana Furnawees' proposal.

The Péshwah's districts in Guzerat taken.

Ahmedabad captured.

Mahadajee Sindia and Holkar now advanced with about 20,000 horse. They crossed the Nerbudda on February 29, and avoided the English, with whom Sindia always professed great friendship; and he now released Mr. Farmer and Lieutenant Stewart, who had remained with him as hostages of the Wurgaom convention, and whom he had most hospitably entertained. General Goddard was not, however, to be deceived by indefinite negotiations which would have sacrificed the fair season, and pressed for Sindia's decision; but finding his terms inadmissible, they were rejected, and the campaign continued. On April 2, General Goddard attacked the Mahratta camp, and again on the 14th; but beyond forcing the leaders to take up new positions, no other advantage was gained. On May 8, Colonel Hartley was detached into the Koncan, where the Mahratta forces had been very active, with good effect; but General Goddard was unable to leave Guzerat in the presence of the Mahratta cavalry, which evaded all his attempts to bring them to a decisive action, and he advised the governor-general to make a diversion in Bundelkhund and Malwah, in order to draw off Sindia, or Holkar, or both from Guzerat.

Proceedings of Sindia and Holkar.

Goddard advises a diversion in the north.

His suggestion was at once adopted by Mr. Hastings, and a

force, which consisted of drafts of men from Goddard's army, was employed for the purpose under Captain Popham. The whole force consisted of 2,400 men, with a small detachment of European artillery. Popham crossed the Jumna in February 1780, defeated a Mahratta force which was levying contributions, and took the fort of Lahar by storm. He then effected, on August 4, with admirable intelligence and great valour, the capture of the celebrated fortress of Gwalior, always heretofore deemed impregnable, which closed his operations for the season. His diversion had proved most effective, and was gallantly and judiciously conducted from first to last.

Mr. Hastings dispatches a force for the purpose.

Captain Popham's proceedings.

Gwalior surprised and taken.

The Bombay forces resumed the campaign after the close of the monsoon of 1780, and their first operation was the siege of Bassein, which, fortified by the Portuguese, was unusually strong; but it surrendered on December 11, on which day also, Colonel Hartley, who had been covering the siege operations, and engaged in almost incessant fighting for six weeks, defeated a spirited attack made on him by Ramchunder Gunnésh, at the head of a division of the Mahratta army, of 20,000 men, and who was killed in the action. The whole British army now united. The Bengal Government had written to Bombay that they intended to make peace with the Péshwah; but until a truce was demanded by the Mahratta ministry, the war was to be carried on with vigour. A peace with the Mahrattas was the more desirable, as war had broken out between Hyder Ally and the Presidency of Madras, and Nizam Ally's reputed league with him and the Mahrattas was now considered more probable than before.

Bassein besieged,

and captured.

General Goddard, as the Mahratta troops had retreated from the Koncan, now prepared to advance on Poona; and the Bhore Ghaut was carried on February 8, 1781. But Nana Furnawees dispatched a force of 12,000 men, under Puréshrám Bhow Putwurdhun, by another pass, to act upon General Goddard's rear, and intercept convoys from Bombay; and on March 15, a sharp affair occurred between him and Captain Mackay with two battalions of Sepoys, in which the Bhow was fairly beaten off with heavy loss. But there seemed no prospect of a successful advance above the Ghauts, so long as the Mahratta army occupied positions on the flank and rear. Nana Furnawees was by no means alarmed. He had every confidence in Puréshrám Bhow, who occupied the road to Panwell and had been largely reinforced, till his army amounted to 15,000 horse. In addition to this force, Holkar was at the foot of the Kussoor pass with 15,000 horse, while above the

Goddard advances towards Poona.

Positions and numbers of the Mahratta forces.

Ghauts, in Goddard's immediate front, Hurry Punt was posted with 25,000 horse, 4,000 infantry, and some artillery. The Mahrattas had, in fact, put forth their utmost power to destroy Goddard's troops, if possible; and their whole army was over 60,000 strong.

On April 15, a convoy under Colonel Browne, which had fought its way from Panwell with great bravery and credit, reached Goddard's camp, and he prepared to retreat. During his march to Panwell he was pertinaciously attacked by the several Mahratta corps in succession; but he finally reached his destination on April 23, with a loss of 466 in killed and wounded, with some baggage and stores, which it was impossible to save. Considering the rugged nature of the country and the roads, and the immense superiority of the Mahratta forces, the retreat had been conducted with masterly skill; but the Mahrattas, nevertheless, claimed it as a victory. The season was now too far advanced for further operations, and the English troops were cantoned near Kullian.

General Goddard's retreat.

Mr. Hastings' diversion against the Mahrattas in Malwah and Bundelkhund had produced the desired effect, for Sindia had been obliged to leave the Deccan, and proceed to the defence of his territories. He met Colonel Carnac on March 7, 1780, who retreated carefully for some days, and, on the 24th, attacked his camp at night, and routed his force. On April 4, Colonel Carnac was joined by Colonel Muir; but Sindia eluded further collision, and it was impossible to bring him to action. About this period considerable anxiety prevailed as to the part Moodajee Bhóslay of Berar would take in the existing contest. Mr. Hastings had hoped to secure his active co-operation against Hyder Ally, the Nizam, or the Poona ministry; but he did not commit himself to an open rupture with any, and his neutrality, when, with a force of 30,000 horse at his disposal, he might have attacked and overrun Bengal, was purchased by Mr. Hastings for thirteen lacs of rupees. Peace with the Mahrattas was, however, Mr. Hastings' grand object, provided it could be obtained without any material sacrifice; and, on October 13, 1781, Sindia, who was unable to prosecute the war against Colonel Carnac, had made the first advance to it, by a treaty with Colonel Muir; by which, on engaging to remain neutral, and to further a general arrangement, his districts near the Jumna were restored to him. Moodajee also had offered his mediation: and on September 11, 1781, the Council of Madras wrote to the Péshwah their desire for a general accommodation. Mr. Anderson, who had previously distinguished himself in the negotiations with

Success of Mr. Hastings' diversion.

Sindia defeated by Colonel Carnac.

Neutrality of Moodajee Bhóslay.

Sindia's overtures for peace.

Moodajee Bhóslay, was now dispatched by Mr. Hastings to Sindia's camp. His neutral position enabled Sindia, under the authority of the Poona ministry, to act as plenipotentiary on the part of the Mahratta nation; and a treaty was finally concluded with him at Salbye, on May 17, 1782. It consisted of seventeen articles. All conquests made since the treaty of Poorundhur were to be restored; the Gáikwar's territories were to remain inviolate, and Rughnonath Ráo was to be allowed 25,000 rupees a month, and permitted to reside where he wished; Hyder Ally should be obliged to surrender his conquests from the English and the Nawáb of Arcot; and, in consideration of Sindia's hospitality to the English hostages, and his humane behaviour at Wurgaom, the district of Baróch was bestowed upon him. This treaty was ratified by the governor-general; and afterwards, but not before he had heard of Hyder's death, by Nana Furnawees. The Mahrattas had gained the rejection of Rughoba as regent, and recovered Bassein and the districts in Guzerat: on the other hand, the English retained Salsette, and had secured the independence of the Gáikwar's state; and, with comparatively slender means and resources, had maintained the war with credit, against the whole power of the Mahratta nation, for a period of nearly seven years.

Treaty of Salbye concluded with Sindia.

CHAPTER XXIII.

OF EVENTS AT MADRAS, AND THE SECOND MYSORE WAR, 1771 TO 1780.

It will be remembered that in the treaty with Hyder Ally, executed at Madras, detailed in Chap. XV. of this Book, a clause of offensive and defensive alliance had been introduced by him; and that, in his subsequent struggle with the Mahrattas, the Council of Madras, from whom he had almost implored aid, had evaded compliance with it. They would probably have assisted him, for the dread of the Mahrattas in Madras was very great, and Hyder was a powerful barrier between Mahratta encreachment and the Carnatic; but they had found it impossible to do so in the face of Sir John Lindsay's coalition with the Nawáb, and their endeavours in favour of a Mahratta alliance against Hyder Khan. Sir John was removed. His successor, Sir Robert Harland, proved even more intractable; and by the end of 1772, Hyder, reduced to extremity, was obliged to satisfy the Mahrattas by large sacrifices.

Excited by the comparatively helpless position of Hyder Ally, the Nawáb of the Carnatic, in 1773, called upon the Council of Madras to assist him against the Rajah of Tanjore, who had been already attacked, in 1771, by the combined forces of the English and the Nawáb, and forced to pay a sum of fifty lacs of rupees. He was now accused of intriguing with Hyder and the Mahrattas, which the Council affected to believe; or in any case, 'as he might join the French or some native power, he were better disposed of.' Tanjore was therefore attacked and captured in August 1773, and the rajah, who was taken prisoner, was made over to the Nawáb, who annexed Tanjore to his own dominions. This disgraceful proceeding did not escape notice in England. In April 1775, the directors declared the act to have been violent and unjust; and they removed the president, Mr. Wynch, from office, and appointed Lord, formerly Mr., Pigott, in his room, who, in April 1776, proceeded to Tanjore and restored his dominions to the rajah, fixing his annual tribute at fourteen lacs of rupees.

The Nawáb of the Carnatic requires the coercion of Tanjore.

Tanjore attacked and captured, and the territory annexed.

The proceeding is denounced in England.

American War.

The rajah is restored.

This restoration brought about the strange episode of Mr. Paul Benfield's transactions with the Nawáb: and though only a junior civilian, he claimed about 240,000*l.*, for instalments of which he asserted he had received assignments on the revenue of Tanjore. There was little doubt that members of the Council were personally interested in the claims, and, therefore, in the support of Mr. Benfield; and on Lord Pigott's opposition to him, the proceedings in Council grew very violent, and culminated in the arrest of the governor, and his confinement for eight months. Mr. Hastings had approved the conduct of the majority in Council; but, on its proceedings becoming known in England, the directors reversed them, and directed Lord Pigott, with the majority who had acted against him, to return to England. Mr. Rumbold was appointed governor of Madras, and Sir Hector Munro to be commander-in-chief; but before he could embark for England, Lord Pigott had died at Madras.

Mr. Paul Benfield's proceedings.

Violent proceedings in Council.

Disapproved in England.

In the year 1778, war was renewed between England and France; and the Carnatic became again the scene of active operations. Sir Hector Munro laid siege to Pondicherry, and an attempt to relieve it was made by a French fleet; but this was defeated by Sir Edward Vernon, and the place surrendered in October, when the garrison was allowed to march out with the honours of war. The fortifications, which had been renewed, were

War between French and English.

Pondicherry taken.

The fortifications destroyed.

now destroyed. Chándernagore, Carical, and Masulipatam had already submitted, and there was no French possession left in India except Mahé, on the western coast. Mr., now Sir Thomas, Rumbold intimated to Hyder the necessity for reducing Mahé, and offered to send an ambassador to reside at his court; but Hyder declined this arrangement, and he protested against any attack upon Mahé. It was well known that through this fort, and the agency of the French, Hyder had been regularly supplied with European articles, including munitions of war; and its capture, therefore, was of the more importance to the English. Mahé was therefore invested by Colonel Braithwaite, on March 19, 1779, but surrendered without resistance. Hyder's interest in the place was proved by the presence of his troops, and his colours were hoisted with those of the French.

Hyder objects to an attack on Mahé.

Mahé taken by Colonel Braithwaite.

During this year Hyder had been very active. He had extended his northern boundary to the Krishna river, driving back the Mahratta forces; and he had previously recovered all he had been obliged to cede to them during the former war. The Mahratta ministry had endeavoured to check him; but, under the pressure of the English war, had not been able to effect anything, and finally retired. Hyder then turned upon the Patán Nawáb of Kurpah, defeated him, and annexed his territory. During these operations, the Nizam was inactive; but he was nominally in alliance with the Mahrattas, a report being very prevalent that Hyder had obtained, or was to be granted, by the emperor, a deed for the possession of the whole of the Deccan. It does not appear that any such deed was at that time applied for, much less obtained; but the report was of much significance in the political transactions of the times.

Hyder's active proceedings.

Immediately after the capture of Mahé, a new cause of offence to Hyder occurred in the march of a British detachment through a portion of the country formerly possessed by the Nawáb of Kurpah towards Guntoor, the reason of which it is necessary to explain. The treaty of Masulipatam with the Nizam contained an article by which no French were to be permitted to remain in the Deccan; but Basalut Jung, the Nizam's brother, had a small corps of French in his service: and against this breach of treaty the Madras Government had repeatedly remonstrated, both to Basalut Jung and to the Nizam; but without effect. Basalut Jung, however, had been roughly handled by Hyder, and forced to pay four lacs of rupees; and had found his French corps to be no protection. He therefore made overtures to Sir T. Rumbold to give him the support of an English force, when he would assign the dis-

Hyder takes offence at a treaty with Basalut Jung.

Explanation of the treaty.

trict of Guntoor, already allotted to the English after his death, in payment of it. This mischievous treaty was concluded; but it gave deep offence both to Hyder and the Nizam. The former protested against the occupation of the Guntoor Sircar under any terms by the English; the Nizam resented any interference with members of his family, took into his own service the French corps which his brother had discharged, and would, there is little doubt, notwithstanding the assurances of the governor-general, have joined Hyder, had not the report of Hyder's having actually received a deed from Dehly—which included the territories of Hyderabad—been confirmed. Sir T. Rumbold remonstrated against the governor-general's interference against his treaty with Basalut Jung, but necessarily without effect; and he was shortly afterwards dismissed by a resolution of the directors, which, however, he had anticipated by leaving Madras without permission.

Its effect on Hyder and the Nizam.

At his own request, the English force did not proceed to Basalut Jung; but the Madras Council did not restore the Guntoor Sircar, and at this juncture an envoy from the Mahratta ministry reached Hyder. Nana Furnawees had delayed his reply to General Goddard's requests in regard to definite terms of treaty, for he had hoped to stir up Hyder, whom he knew to be watching his opportunity, into action against the English. The Mahratta envoy to Hyder promised freely. Not only were all claims for arrears of chouth to be resigned, and future payments limited to eleven lacs, but the Krishna was to be recognised as the northern boundary. This, it is evident, was the price at which Hyder agreed to engage the English; while, secure of Hyder's diversion, Nana Furnawees had little hesitation in rejecting overtures from General Goddard, and continuing the war.

Negotiations between the Mahrattas and Hyder.

Hyder was better prepared for war than the Mahrattas. He had a well-organised army little short of 100,000 men, of which the greater part of the infantry, and some of his cavalry, had been disciplined by French officers. His artillery also—which amounted to 100 guns—had been organised by them, and was thoroughly effective. This war had been his darling project since the peace he had dictated at Madras; and though now seventy-eight years old, his ambition impelled him to attempt the destruction of the English power of Madras, in order that, with no enemy in his rear, he should be free to advance to the conquest of the Deccan—Nizam and Mahrattas alike—and even to that of Hindostan. He seems to have had no misgiving as to the result. The war against the 'infidel' English was proclaimed as a jehád, or holy crusade, in all the mosques, and even

Hyder's preparations for war.

in the Hindoo temples of Mysore; and on July 20, 1780, while the Council of Madras could neither see, nor be brought to see, the danger by which they were threatened, Hyder Ally burst through the passes from Mysore, and burning and plundering the villages, and mutilating the people as it poured on, his army invested Arcot, while detachments advanced to within nine miles of Madras, whence the smoke of the burning villages was clearly discernible.

He suddenly advances on Madras.

The forces of the Madras presidency did not amount to more than 8,000 men, of whom 2,500 were in Guntoor, under Colonel Baillie, and were directed to form a junction with Sir Hector Munro, who advanced to Conjeveram. Hyder, without attacking Munro's force, sent his son Tippoo, with a select division of his army, to prevent Colonel Baillie's progress, which had been delayed by a flood in the river Cortella; and on September 6, Tippoo attacked Baillie, but with no result; and as Baillie saw no means of advancing, he requested Sir Hector Munro to march with his whole force to his assistance. Instead of this, however, Munro dispatched Colonel Fletcher with 1,100 men to join Baillie, and he succeeded in doing so with some difficulty. The united brigades now advanced on the 9th, but Hyder suddenly surrounded them with his whole army, as they bivouacked during the night of that day, and further progress was impossible. After fighting for most part of the 10th with untiring resolution and valour, Baillie, having only 300 Europeans left, and despairing of assistance from Munro's army, then only two miles distant, surrendered, and the troops laid down their arms. In this helpless condition, they were savagely attacked, and would all have been put to death, but for the intervention of the French officers. Had Munro moved up as he heard the cannonade, the army of Hyder must have suffered a terrible defeat; instead of which, with a scandalous incapacity, if it does not deserve a severer designation, Munro threw his heavy guns into a tank, sacrificed most of his stores, and retreated in precipitate confusion upon Madras. Thus perished a reputation which had risen high at the battle of Buxar and in the mutiny of the Bengal Sepoys, in the conclusion of a campaign which had only lasted three weeks, but which had already lost the whole of the Western Carnatic. The victory was a glorious triumph to Hyder, and the bloody scenes of Baillie's defeat were painted on the walls of his palace at Seringapatam, as may yet be seen, with every exaggeration of insulting detail that could be devised.

Colonel Baillie's detachment attacked by Tippoo.

Baillie surrenders; many of his troops are massacred.

Retreat of Munro.

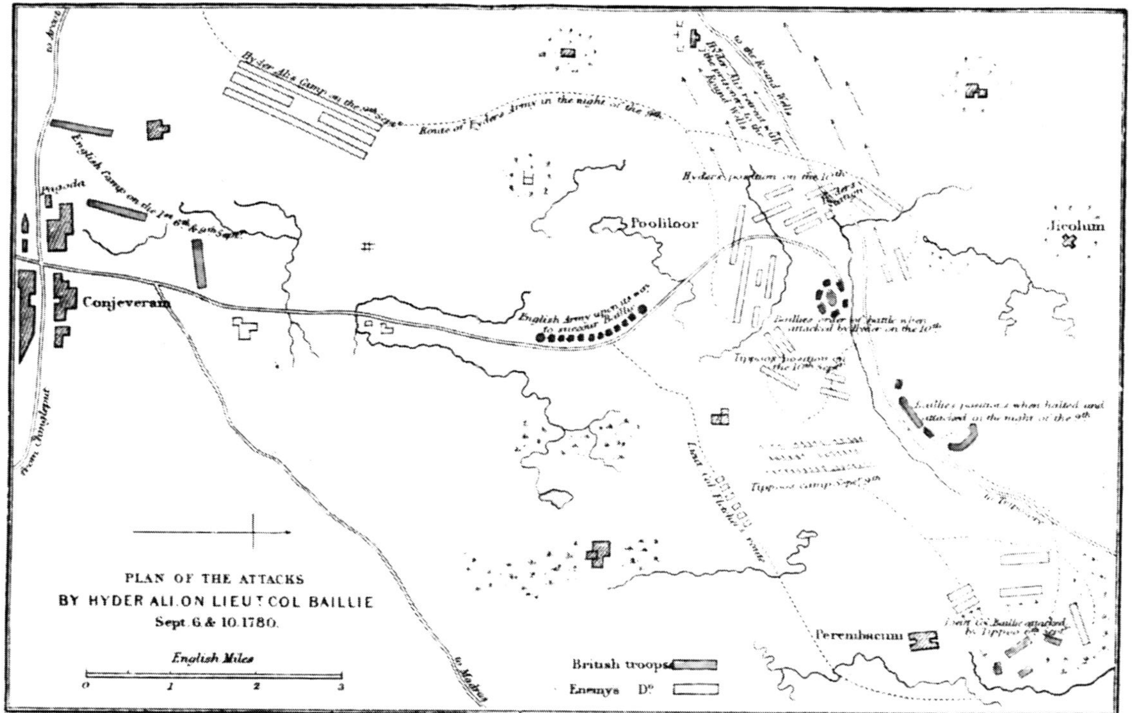

London, Longmans & Co.

Edwd Weller

CHAPTER XXIV.

THE SECOND MYSORE WAR (*concluded*), 1780 TO 1784.

ENGAGED as he was in a war with the Mahrattas, which had every appearance of being long protracted, and which demanded all his resources in men and money, Mr. Hastings received the news of Hyder's sudden attack, and the miserable catastrophe which had followed it, with undaunted resolution. In little more than a fortnight he had dispatched the veteran, Sir Eyre Coote, to the scene of his former triumphs, with all the forces that could be collected, and fifteen lacs of rupees; and he boldly stopped the company's remittances, and applied them to the use of the war. He also removed Mr. Whitehill, the acting-president of Madras, from office; for having, notwithstanding his instructions for its release, delayed to give up Guntoor. More could not have been undertaken under the circumstances, and the effect was at once perceptible. Instead of driving the English into the sea, as he boasted he would do, Hyder now found his old opponent Coote in the field against him. Arcot had capitulated after a long siege, in which the native troops of the garrison had been corrupted by Hyder's officers, and Hyder himself was engaged in besieging Wandiwash—which, under the brave Lieutenant Flint, held out gallantly—and other forts in the Carnatic. Sir Eyre Coote, in order to obtain supplies by sea, had moved, in January 1781, towards Cuddalore. On the 19th, he reached Chingliput, and thence a detachment, under Captain Davis, took Caráugooty by a *coup de main*, where a good deal of rice was obtained. On the 23rd, he reached Wandiwash, where he found Lieutenant Flint with only one day's ammunition remaining for the hundred men who composed the garrison, and thence he marched to Porto Novo; but he was sorely distressed for provisions, and lay there inactive for nearly four months, when he attacked the fortified temple of Chillumbrum, but was repulsed on June 18.

Energetic proceeding of the governor-general.

Sir Eyre Coote's movements.

Relief of Wandiwash.

Hyder now deemed his enemy weak, and advancing suddenly upon Cuddalore with 80,000 men, took up a position in the English front on the road to Cuddalore, and threw up extensive fieldworks for its defence. Coote, who had been vainly endeavouring to bring Hyder to action, and for want of supplies had been nearly inactive, was now on his march from Porto Novo to Cuddalore, on July 1, with about 8,000 men, when

Hyder's movements.

he discovered the enemy. The troops had only four days' provisions, which they carried on their backs, and Hyder's position was a very strong one. Nevertheless, Coote did not hesitate to attack him. A road which had been cut through the jungle and sand-hills, intended for a flank attack upon the English, was happily discovered, and by this a part of Coote's army advanced, while two other divisions in line passed the sand-hills in front. The battle was hotly contested for six hours, but ended in a complete victory over Hyder's forces, by which he lost 10,000 men; and Coote, in killed and wounded, not more than 300. The English artillery had been excellently served, and had been dragged into action by the Sepoys. His father's defeat caused Tippoo to raise the siege of Wandiwash, and to retire to Arcot.

Coote attacks Hyder's army.

And defeats it.

On August 27, Coote's army was attacked by Hyder near Tripasore, but without any result, though the losses on each side were serious. Coote, worn out by the service, and constant anxiety in regard to supplies and provisions, would have resigned the command, but for Lord Macartney's entreaties to the contrary; and taking charge of a convoy for the relief of Vellore, he defeated Hyder severely, at the pass of Sholinghur, on September 27; not less than 5,000 of Hyder's cavalry being destroyed in their charges upon the English guns. With the relief of Vellore and capture of Chittore, the season's campaign against Hyder was brought to a close with good effect.

Incidents of the campaign.

The English and Dutch were now at war; and Lord Macartney urged Coote to attack their principal settlement, Negapatam. This Coote declined to do in the face of Hyder's positions; but Lord Macartney dispatched Sir Hector Munro, with a force made up of seamen, marines, and other detached parties, and the place was invested, and the siege commenced, on October 21. On November 12, the garrison, which numbered upwards of 6,500 men, and far exceeded the besieging force, capitulated: and the military stores and goods found in the fort were numerous and valuable.

War with the Dutch.

Siege of Negapatam.

The garrison capitulates.

The year 1782 was opened by an advance to relieve Vellore, by Sir Eyre Coote, on January 2, which was successful and well-timed, as the place could not have held out much longer; but the English sustained a reverse on February 18, in the defeat of a detachment of about 2,000 men, under Colonel Braithwaite, in Tanjore, by the army of Tippoo, consisting of Lally's corps of Europeans, with 20,000 horse and 20,000 infantry. Colonel Braithwaite's small force—nearly all Sepoys—defended itself desperately for two days, and inflicted great loss on the enemy; but it was in the end over-

Campaign of 1782.

Defeat of Colonel Braithwaite.

whelmed. The details of this gallant but unequal combat are given at length by Mr. Mill, vol. iv. pp. 212-3, and he records a deservedly high tribute to its conduct. 'The annals of war,' he writes, 'can seldom exhibit a parallel to the firmness and perseverance' of this little army. This loss was, however, counterbalanced by the spirited conduct of the garrison of Tellicherry, in Malabar, under Major Abingdon, who had been besieged for eighteen months by a Mysore army. Being, however, reinforced from Bombay, he sallied on the enemy's camp on the night of January 7, routed his forces, and took 1,200 prisoners, with sixty guns. The reduction of Calicut followed; and Colonel Humberstone, who arrived from England with 1,000 men, rallied the chiefs of the country about him, and created a formidable division against Hyder's authority in the western portion of his dominions.

Gallant defence of Tellicherry.

To Hyder's perception, the western was by far the weakest portion of his territory: open to attack from the English by sea, and by the Mahrattas, with whom he now perceived the English were making peace. He dreaded their power, which, in concert with that of the English, might overwhelm him; and the governor-general had already secured the Nizam's neutrality, even could his co-operation have been obtained at any price. Still, the French remained; and for a time Hyder was encouraged by the arrival of a powerful fleet under Admiral Suffrein. Early in January that fleet had reached the coast; and though partially crippled by an action with Admiral Hughes, the French admiral succeeded in landing 2,000 infantry and 1,000 Africans at Porto Novo. Cuddalore, which had been weakly garrisoned, was taken, and Hyder's hopes again rose. Various other affairs followed; but with little result to either side, except the loss by the English of a party of European cavalry, which was drawn into an ambuscade, and almost destroyed. The real interest of the warfare at this period lay in the naval engagements between the fleets; but though superior in ships, Suffrein was unable to obtain any advantage over Hughes, and the last action fought off Trincomalee was severe, though without result. Soon afterwards, Admiral Hughes was obliged to proceed to Bombay to refit; but his place was in no degree supplied, as was hoped, by Admiral Bickerton, who, after landing 4,000 men whom he had brought from England, also sailed for Bombay.

Arrival of a French fleet under Admiral Suffrein.

Indecisive naval actions.

The close of the season had in all respects a gloomy aspect, for Madras was suffering from famine; the Carnatic was desolated by the war; the renowned Bussy was expected with reinforcements for the French; and there

Gloomy prospects at Madras.

was a recurrence of hurricanes, which caused great loss and damage. Sir Eyre Coote, too, was obliged by his shattered health to return to Bengal. In the west, Colonel Humberstone had made progress as far as Pálghautchery, but he was recalled by the Bombay government, who were not prepared to support him, and in his retreat was harassed by Tippoo, whom his father had dispatched for the purpose. He had attacked Colonel Humberstone on November 29, but without effect, and was waiting for heavy guns, when news reached him of his father's death in camp on December 7. Hyder had been long ill, and his last moments are thus described by Meer Hussein Ally, his faithful biographer. 'He had directed that water might be made ready for him to bathe, and although the physicians objected to his bathing, the servants turned them out of the tent, and the Nawáb bathed. Then, having put on clean clothes, he repeated some prayer or invocation on his fingers, rubbing his face; and at the same time dispatched 2,000 horse to ravage the country of the Poligars, and 5,000 horse to Madras for the same purpose. Then he took a little broth, and lay down to rest. That same night his ever-victorious spirit took its flight to Paradise.' He was eighty years old, and during his last eventful campaign had been as active almost, as ever; yet he had been suffering from a virulent carbuncle or cancer in the back, which, in the end, caused his death. The student is referred to Colonel Wilks's 'History of Mysore' for details of his strange character and the romantic events of his career, which possess varied interest. Nor, except Sivajee, is there one of the great adventurers of India who can be compared with Hyder, whether as to ability or success. Hyder was however, according to his native biographer, a cold-hearted, cruel man, possessing and evincing no affection, except to his son Tippoo, who he believed would lose all that he had gained. He never made a friend, even of his wife, of whom he was afraid; and every one around him, to the very last, was watched by his spies. On the other hand, the naturally affectionate disposition of Sivajee was displayed in many engaging forms, and continued unchanged to his death. Hyder's death was kept secret in camp—though his remains were dispatched to Mysore—until the arrival of his son Tippoo, who, by a liberal donation to his army, and payment of arrears, succeeded to his father's great possessions without opposition.

Death of Hyder.

His character.

Had the Madras army possessed a fit commander at this critical period, a possibly fatal blow could have been struck against the Mysore army before Tippoo's arrival; but General Stuart was perverse, disobedient, and incapable, and allowed the opportunity to pass without attempting a single movement. On the other hand, Tippoo, instead of prosecuting the war in the Carnatic, withdrew his army, reinforced by a detachment of French troops, to the west. Sir Eyre Coote had been again dispatched to Madras by Mr. Hastings; but the gallant veteran, worn out by disease, and exposure during the voyage, in which the ship was chased for several days by French vessels, expired two days after he had landed at Madras. Bussy had now reached India, and assumed command of the French forces at Cuddalore on April 10, 1783. He had an army of 2,300 Europeans and 5,000 Sepoys, and could he have co-operated with Tippoo, the results to the English would have been very embarrassing. As it was, engagements between the French fleet and Admiral Hughes had the effect of driving Admiral Suffrein from the coast, and Bussy was reduced to his own resources. General Stuart now marched on Cuddalore with 3,000 Europeans and 11,500 Sepoys, and invested it on June 7. On the 13th, Bussy made a sally, which resulted in a general action, in which he was defeated, with the capture of thirteen guns, though not without inflicting the severe loss of 920 Europeans in killed and wounded upon General Stuart's army. While the battle was in progress, Admiral Suffrein's fleet appeared off the town; but he was brought to action by Admiral Hughes, who came up from Porto Novo, though again without decisive result. Hughes, however, whose crews were disabled by scurvy, was obliged to proceed to Madras to refit, and Suffrein, availing himself of the opportunity, reinforced Bussy with 2,300 marines and sailors. With these and his garrison, Bussy attacked General Stuart's camp on June 25, at night: but he was repulsed with heavy loss, and Bernadotte, then a sergeant, and afterwards King of Sweden, was taken prisoner. Nothing, however, had been effected in regard to siege operations by General Stuart, and it is probable he might have been altogether repulsed, for his fine army was much weakened by losses and sickness; but the arrival of news of peace between England and France prevented further collision, and by the convention which ensued, Bussy engaged to withdraw the French troops in Tippoo's service.

Death of Sir Eyre Coote.

M. Bussy returns to India.

Cuddalore invaded by General Stuart,

who defeats Bussy.

Bussy reinforced by Suffrein, but defeated by Stuart.

Peace between England and France.

Meanwhile, Tippoo had proceeded to the western coast to oppose an invasion by General Matthews, who had been dispatched from Bombay, and after some successes was directed by the Bombay government to attack Bednore, on the tableland of Mysore. The path which led up to it was almost impregnable; but the 42nd Highlanders, led by Colonel Macleod, bravely carried all the defences, and the town and districts were

Proceedings of Tippoo.

surrendered by the native officer in command. To this point of danger Tippoo now proceeded by forced marches, and invested the fort on April 9. It was gallantly defended for five months; but with no hope of relief the garrison was obliged to capitulate, and their defence forms one of the most interesting and wonderful episodes of Indian war. The terms of the capitulation were shamefully violated by Tippoo, on the ground that treasure had been carried away; and the survivors of the brave garrison, instead of being sent to the coast, as Tippoo had engaged, were immured in the fortresses of Mysore.

Bednore capitulates.

Tippoo violates the convention.

From Bednore, Tippoo proceeded to Mangalore with his whole army, at least 100,000 strong. The place was garrisoned by 700 English and 2,800 native soldiers, under Colonel Campbell, and made a noble defence, until August 2, when an armistice ensued, and continued till January 30, when the garrison—unable to obtain provisions, either according to agreement from Tippoo, or from Bombay or Madras, and reduced to the last extremities by famine—marched out with the honours of war to Tellicherry. Another diversion had, however, been made against Tippoo by Colonel Fullerton, who, with 13,500 men, had reduced Dindigul, Pálgautchery, and Coimbatoor, and was now on the confines of Mysore, ready and able to advance against the capital. Another army was employed in the Kurpa territory, on the north-east of Mysore, and, owing to Tippoo's cruelties, the Hindoos of his dominions were known to be disaffected. By a bold venture, therefore, the Rajah of Mysore might have been released, and restored under British intervention. This, which afterwards occurred, was not then however to happen; for Lord Macartney, in defiance of the governor-general's instructions, had opened negotiations with Tippoo and agreed to a truce; and it is now impossible to read, without a sense of humiliation, the absurd proceedings of the ever-incapable Council of Madras. It appears, indeed, that although Bengal had its Clive, Hastings, and even meritorious subordinate officers, and Governor Hornby and a stout-hearted Council had guided Bombay through a momentous crisis with the Mahrattas, Madras, except Mr. Saunders, had never possessed a chief of political capability or resolution. The Council sent commissioners to Tippoo, whom another campaign must have compelled to become their suppliant, to ask peace; and he detained them haughtily for three months. He then sent them back to Madras with an agent of his own. It was in vain Mr. Hastings protested that the only course for peace was to dictate it, as Hyder had done to Madras, at the gates

Defence of Mangalore.

Proceedings of Colonel Fullerton.

Lord Macartney negotiates with Tippoo.

Humiliating proceedings of the Council of Madras.

of the Mysore capital. 'How will you manage the beast,' said Missionary Swartz to Colonel Fullerton, 'now you quit the reins?' How indeed! Lord Macartney was beyond control, and managed matters after his own fashion. He sent back his commissioners with Tippoo's envoy, and as they proceeded, they were mocked and insulted at every stage. At Mangalore, gibbets were erected opposite to their tents: and such was the dread they were in, that they had planned to escape to the English ships in the roads. Nor was it till Tippoo was actually in possession of Mangalore, that he would condescend to notice the matter at all. At last, on March 11, 1784, as Tippoo caused it to be recorded, 'the English commissioners stood with their heads uncovered, and the treaty in their hands, for two hours, using every form of flattery and supplication to induce compliance. The Vakeels of Poona and Hyderabad united in the most abject entreaties, and His Majesty, the Shadow of God, was at length softened into assent.' The basis of the treaty was the restitution of mutual conquests; and, after its execution, the English commissioners hurried back to Madras, leaving the release of the prisoners to be effected by the officer who commanded their escort. This difficult duty was bravely executed. 180 officers of all grades, 900 English, and 1,600 native soldiers were rescued from captivity, and their accounts of their barbarous treatment, and the cold-blooded murders of General Matthews and many others, cannot be read without mingled feelings of execration and compassion. Like every peace concluded by Madras, this was no more than an inconsequent makeshift, and with a man of Tippoo's haughty and arrogant character, there was no hope of its being observed longer than suited his convenience.

Insults to the British commission.

Tippoo's record.

BOOK VI.

CHAPTER I.

OF THE PROGRESS OF EVENTS IN HINDOSTAN, 1773 TO 1787.

AFTER the retirement of the Mahratta forces in 1773, Nujuf Khan resumed his office, as minister, at Dehly; and, assisted by the Vizier of Oudh, expelled their garrisons from the provinces yet possessed by the emperor; and he was successful also against the Játs. His efforts were neutralised, in a great measure, for several years, by the acts of his deputy at Dehly; but he ultimately overcame his difficulties, and, as the last of the imperial ministers and generals, conducted the affairs of the state with great fidelity, judgment, and ability, until his death, which occurred in 1782. His adopted son, Afrasiab Khan, succeeded to his office; but factions arose in the court, to which he was obliged to submit, and it was not until the assassination of the principal conspirator by a member of his own faction, that Afrasiab Khan in some respects regained his authority. Sindia meanwhile was a close observer of local events. Before the re-consolidated power of Nujuf Khan, he would, perhaps, have had small chances of success; but by the division of Dehly into factions, the imperial resources had been greatly weakened; the English, as he was assured by Mr. Hastings, had no desire to interfere with him; and from Poona he expected no opposition. In the year 1784, the Prince Mirza Juwán Bukht fled from Dehly to Lukhnow, and claimed for himself and his father the protection of Mr. Hastings; when Afrasiab Khan offered any terms that might be demanded for both, provided he was assisted by the English against the opposite faction, the chief of which, Mahomed Beg, was still in rebellion. But Mr. Hastings declined to interfere: and Afrasiab Khan, in his extremity, sought the assistance of Sindia, who gladly availed himself of an opportunity, which he had long desired, of obtaining authority at Dehly.

Affairs of Dehly. — *Death of Nujuf Khan.* — *Proceedings and designs of Sindia.* — *The minister's request for British assistance,* — *which is declined.*

On October 22, 1784, Sindia met the emperor and Afrasiab Khan at Agra; but before any arrangements could be effected, Afrasiab Khan was assassinated. Sindia now became master of the situation. Declining the high office of Umeer-ool-Oomra, or chief of the nobles, for himself, he obtained for the Péshwah the dignity of Vakeel-i-Mootluq, or supreme deputy of the empire; accepting, at the same time, the office of deputy executive minister, with the command of the imperial army. There was no one to dispute his authority, and the factious nobles, who had been in rebellion, submitted to him; but though the accession of dignity to the Péshwah gratified the Mahratta people at large, it augmented the jealousy of Nana Furnawees, Holkar, and other authorities, from whom no assistance could be looked for, at least for the present.

Death of Afrasiab Khan.

Sindia's power.

He becomes minister and commander-in-chief.

In 1786, Sindia demanded the arrears of tribute from the Rajpoots at the gates of Jeypore, and a portion of it was paid; but on a demand being sent for the balance, the Rajpoots rebelled. He had a powerful army, his infantry being commanded and disciplined by M. Benoit de Boigne, one of the ablest adventurers that ever appeared in India; but it was weakened by detachments employed against the Sikhs, and the army of the emperor was disaffected. Sindia, notwithstanding, fought an action with the Rajpoots, who had been joined by the discontented nobility: at the close of which the emperor's regular infantry, with eighty guns, went over to the enemy. This was a severe and unexpected blow; but Sindia met his misfortune with patience and ability. Withdrawing for a time to Gwalior, he wrote an eloquent appeal to Nana Furnawees for assistance, in which, after enumerating his own services, he besought him to banish suspicion and 'prevent our empire from being disunited and overthrown.' The Rajpoots had latterly kept aloof from the contest, which lay between Ismail Beg, the head of the adverse faction, and Gholám Khadir, a Rohilla chief, who for the present was plundering friends and foes alike. They had, however, united for the siege of Agra, when Sindia's forces advanced to raise the siege, aided by the Játs. An action was the consequence, in which, on April 24, 1785, Sindia's troops were defeated, and retreated to Bhurtpoor. Agra, however, still held out, and the Mahrattas and Játs having again advanced, defeated Ismail Beg in turn on June 18. They could not, however, save the unfortunate emperor. Gholám Khadir had gained possession of the palace, where a scene of shocking barbarity ensued, which hardly finds a parallel in the worst times of the elder

Rebellion of the Rajpoots.

Sindia is defeated and retires to Gwalior.

Battle near Agra.

Gholam Khadir gains possession of the emperor, and blinds him.

imperial dynasties: Gholám Khadir himself put out the emperor's eyes; and his whole family, males and females alike, were publicly exposed, and treated with horrible indignity. This conduct had the effect of inducing Ismail Beg to join Sindia, who, at last reinforced from Poona, was enabled to send his troops against Dehly, whence Gholám Khadir fled; but was afterwards discovered and taken to Sindia's camp, where he was executed.

Gholam Khadir executed by Sindia.

The emperor was now reseated on his throne with great pomp, but the actual power rested with Sindia, who continued steadily to consolidate his position. The whole of the imperial dominions in Hindostan now belonged to him, as the Péshwah's deputy; the blinded emperor existed only as a pageant. There were possible enemies in the Rajpoots, and in Mahomedan combinations against him; but these were distant contingencies, and to provide against them he strengthened and reformed his army in a remarkable degree. De Boigne's infantry now consisted of twenty-four regiments, with 200 excellent guns, of various calibre, and was in every respect well commanded by European officers; and the rest of his troops were more efficient than they had ever been before. Such, therefore, was Sindia's condition at the beginning of the administration of Lord Cornwallis; the positions of other great powers in India being intelligible from the current narrative. They may be thus summarised: In Hindostan, Sindia, and in the Deccan, the Mahrattas, with whom he was connected; the Nizam, Tippoo Sooltan of Mysore, and the English.

Sindia's power increases.

CHAPTER II.

EVENTS IN BENGAL, 1780 TO 1785.

There is no portion of the varied nature of Warren Hastings' administration as governor-general which more abounds with interesting detail than the establishment of courts of justice. In the appointment of a royal court, and the introduction to some extent of English law, the parliament of England had no doubt acted to the best of their judgment for the relief of the 'oppressed natives of Bengal,' as they were then designated; but it soon began to be experienced that the royal court could be used as an instrument of vexatious interference, and of greater practical oppression and suffering, than even the inefficient and notoriously corrupt courts of the former native administration. It need hardly be stated that English law, and the procedure of English

Warren Hastings' administration of justice.

The royal court.

courts, were entirely unknown to the people of Bengal; and when writs and processes began to issue from an hitherto unknown and mysterious power, which seemed to be backed by the whole authority of the government, universal terror and consternation were the result. The old local courts were utterly ignored by the judges of the crown; and the violent and actually lawless proceedings of the attorneys and their myrmidons, who, in many instances, resorted to actual force, raised a storm of discontent in the provinces which it became most difficult to appease. It was impossible also that the judges should not be brought into direct collision with the executive government; and the struggle—which is replete with interest, and is very fully detailed in the histories of Mr. Mill and Mr. Thornton—resulted, in 1780, in the separation of the ordinary civil procedure from that of the revenue, and the establishment of a new court of appeal, which was called the Sudder Dewány. To preside over this court the chief justice, Sir Elijah Impey, who still held that office, was appointed, and he drew up a strict code of laws for the regulation of the proceedings of the new provincial and district civil courts, admirably suited to the comprehension of the judges, as well as of the people. Thus the new system not only worked well, but was a boon, than which nothing more practically useful could have been devised. Mr. Hastings was afterwards violently attacked in England for the creation of the new court, and Sir Elijah Impey was recalled for having accepted the office of its judge; but though the chief justice was subsequently withdrawn from the court, and the crown and company's courts were separated, the arrangement and functions of the Sudder Dewány remained in force until a very late period.

Sudder Dewany court established.

If the expenses of three separate wars with the Mahrattas, the French and Dutch, and Hyder Ally, had not drained the Bengal treasury, it is certain that Mr. Hastings' financial administration would have proved most satisfactory to him and to the company. His early success, before he received the appointment of governor-general, has been already mentioned; and his improved systems of rental, and collections of revenue, had been at least as successful as could be expected in a commencement of reform. Still, the drain on his treasury had never ceased: Bombay afforded nothing that could be depended upon. The Carnatic had been wasted by fire, sword, and famine; and the administration of the Northern Circars had been corrupt and neglectful. Moreover, the demands for money in England were loud and incessant: and the debt in Bengal had now again reached upwards of a million sterling, while the credit of the government was not better than Hastings had found it. In his

Financial results.

extremity, therefore, he sought for extra sources of supply, and he called upon Rajah Cheyt Singh of Benares for a contribution to the public service of 2,000 horse and five lacs of rupees. The terms on which the rajah held his estate were the payment of twenty-two and a half lacs of rupees per year; but he can hardly be said to have been an independent tributary, so much as the renter of a property which was always subject to enhanced demand, or, according to native usage, to a requisition for contribution on any extraordinary occasion; and the governor-general's demand for a contingent of horse, and a really insignificant sum in excess of his ordinary payment to the public revenue, cannot be considered unjust or extortionate. The rajah, however, refused or evaded compliance; and the governor-general determined now to exact a heavy fine for contumacy, while he knew that the payment of it would by no means distress him. Cheyt Singh afterwards offered twenty lacs, which to the first instance might have sufficed; but the governor-general demanded fifty, and on his arrival at Benares, sent a guard to imprison the rajah in his palace. A disturbance ensued which occasioned loss of life, and Cheyt Singh escaped across the river.

Rajah Cheyt Singh.

For some time, during which he was calmly arranging the detail of the treaty with Sindia, the governor-general was in imminent peril of his life: and he was obliged, eventually, to escape to Chunar. Meanwhile, troops had collected, and Cheyt Singh, who still maintained negotiations for forgiveness, was defeated, and fled to Bidgeghur, and thence, with all the treasure he could find means to transport, into Bundelkhund. Bidgeghur surrendered to Colonel Popham, on November 9, 1781, and fifty lacs of rupees were captured, which, under the interpretation of an incautious letter from the governor-general to Colonel Popham, was immediately divided as prize money among the troops. Mr. Hastings thus lost all; when, had he admitted Cheyt Singh to terms, he might have gained a large proportion of what he had demanded, if not the entire sum of fifty lacs; for the capture of forty lacs in Bidgeghur, and the immense sum the rajah was known to have taken to Gwalior, where he afterwards resided, proved that his false plea of poverty was more calculated to irritate the governor-general than to induce him to relax his demand. Cheyt Singh never returned to Benares. His nephew was appointed to succeed him, and the annual payment for Benares was raised from twenty-two lacs to forty lacs.

Military operations against Rajah Cheyt Singh.

The Nawáb Vizier of Oudh owed at this time upwards of a million sterling to the Bengal Government; but he was entirely unable to pay this debt, or any part of it; and the proceedings which ensued are, perhaps of all, the

Transactions with the Vizier of Oudh.

least defensible of the several questionable acts of Warren Hastings's official career. In 1776 the Bégums, or princesses of Oudh, on the accession of the new Nawáb Vizier, had been allotted jahgeers or appanages, for their maintenance; and allowed to retain, it was supposed, nearly two millions of treasure, under the official guarantee of the English representative, Mr. Bristow, supported by the Council of Calcutta. This, at the time, was a very unnecessary act of interference in the domestic concerns of a native State independent of English laws and customs; and had the effect of crippling the Nawáb's finances at a critical period. Mr. Hastings too had protested earnestly against the arrangement: but had been overruled by his colleagues, and the guarantee was confirmed. The Nawáb Vizier, who, under other circumstances, and according to the practice of all native States, might at any time have resumed these jahgeers, or laid upon them a tax or demand in proportion to the general necessities of the State, now asked Mr. Hastings to allow him to attach them, and to take possession of the ladies' treasures, which were in fact State property, and as such, both according to Mahomedan laws and local custom, were alienable. Instead of boldly withdrawing the original guarantees, which, on the grounds of his original protest, might have been pronounced an unjustifiable interference with family affairs, in which the British had no pretence of jurisdiction, Hastings sought to cover the proceedings against the Bégums, by averring they had aided Cheyt Singh in his rebellion, with men and money; and it added not a little to the suspicions cast on this transaction, that Sir Elijah Impey was specially summoned from Calcutta to take affidavits in support of the accusations against the Bégums, which were afterwards found to be worthless. The Nawáb's proceedings were not only rigorous, but cruel; yet he contrived that the whole odium of the transaction should fall upon the English, as he paid a part, if not the whole, of his exactions—seventy-six lacs of rupees (760,000*l.*)—into the Bengal treasury.

Affairs of the Bégums.

Hastings's accusation against the Bégums.

A third questionable transaction was that in regard to Fyzoolla Khan, the Rohilla chief who, it will be remembered, had been settled in a jahgeer of fifteen lacs of rupees by the arrangement of 1774, with an agreement to furnish a contingent of 3,000 men to the Nawáb. In November 1780, Mr. Hastings applied to him, through the Nawáb, for 5,000 men, to supply the place of troops in Bahar, required for service in Madras. Fyzoolla Khan offered 2,000 horse and 1,000 foot. These Hastings refused, whereupon the Nawáb suggested his being altogether deprived of his jahgeer, and this was effected; but Mr. Hastings subsequently revoked his permission, and caused

Fyzoolla Khan Rohilla.

the Nawáb to restore the jahgeer, which was not done without an agreement on the part of Fyzoolla Khan to pay fifteen lacs of rupees.

When the news of these several proceedings reached England, a storm of indignation was raised against the governor-general, and he was ordered to reverse his acts against Cheyt Singh and the Bégums. He was even threatened with dismissal, and his Council rebelled against him. This was more than he could bear, and he wrote to the directors, declaring that while the degradation involved by their orders was known at every native court in India, he, responsible as he was for the well-being of their affairs, could no longer discharge his trust with credit or effect. On March 20, 1783, he formally tendered his resignation; but before he embarked for England, he visited Lukhnow, and caused the Nawáb to restore the greater portion of their jahgeers to the Bégums, at the same time withdrawing the Resident, or English agent, from the court. When he returned to Calcutta, he found his successor, Mr. Macpherson, had arrived; and after making over charge of the government to him, and writing farewell letters to all the native courts of India, he sailed for England on February 8, 1785.

The effect of these proceedings in England.

Censures.

Warren Hastings resigns office.

He sails for England.

Warren Hastings's administration of thirteen years is, on the whole, perhaps, the most important and interesting on record. It has been impossible, within the limits of this manual, and where events were crowded together, to relate any except those of most prominent importance in the history of India at large; but the miserable disputes with the members of his Council, the resolution with which they were met, and the undaunted spirit with which he raised and maintained the new position of England as a first-rate political power in India, cannot fail to be appreciated by the student of history. On the other hand, were many errors, many serious blemishes, and some suspicious transactions. Mr. Mill, after reviewing his career, is of opinion that 'there was not one of the chief rulers whom the company had employed, who would not have succumbed under the difficulties he had to encounter.' With the natives of India, princes and people alike, he was then as popular, and as respected, as his memory still remains; ballads, songs, and nursery rhymes, written in his honour, are still sung all over India, and in this will be recognised no small tribute of affection to a foreigner. Above all, it must be remembered, that amidst the constant distractions and local feuds with his Council; the anxieties attendant upon the separate wars and their progress; the keen encounters with astute native statesmen in diplomatic

Character of his administration.

affairs, and the depression arising out of inadequate finances —he was yet, with a calm thoughtful spirit, directing the new judicial and fiscal details of the whole of Bengal, and delivering it from the evils of a double government, which, if he had left no other memorial of his great mind, and indefatigable application, would have earned for him a high rank in the roll of Indian statesmen and legislators; and that he had succeeded moreover, as he desired to do, in making the English, for the future, controllers of political events in every part of the great continent.

Contrary to his expectations, Mr. Hastings was well and honourably received in England. He became a member of Parliament, where the proceedings of his memorable impeachment and trial form a grand episode in the history of England; which, with the events, the struggles, and the vicissitudes of his life, are nowhere more vividly or eloquently described than in the brilliant essay of Lord Macaulay. Warren Hastings died on August 22, 1818, in the eighty-sixth year of his age; and it may be said to his infinite credit—when, with the power at his disposal in India, his wealth might have rivalled that of Clive—in comparative poverty. The pension of 4,000*l.* a year granted him by the Court of Directors was nearly all he had left for his support.

His reception in England.

His death.

CHAPTER III.

CURRENT EVENTS, ENGLAND AND INDIA, 1780 TO 1787.

DURING the latter part of the administration of Warren Hastings, the affairs of India had received much discussion in England. The company's charter was to expire on three years notice from March 25, 1780; and the question was brought forward by Lord North, when it was decided that the extension was to commence from March 1, 1781; the company was to pay 400,000*l.* to the nation; and after a dividend of eight per cent., all surplus profits were to become national property. At this period, also, Mr. Burke's twelve celebrated reports upon the proceedings of the Supreme Court of Calcutta were submitted to Parliament, and should be read by every student of the history of this interesting period. These discussions were followed by Mr. Fox's Bill in 1783, which not only advocated Clive's and Hastings's proposals, that the government of India should be administered directly by the King instead of the company, but prescribed the form in

Indian affairs in England.

Mr. Burke's report.

Mr. Fox's Bill.

which the administration should be carried on by a board of seven commissioners. This Bill, in spite of the strenuous opposition of the directors and proprietors of the company, was carried in the Lower House by 208 to 102; but the King was afraid of it, and the Bill was thrown out in the House of Lords.

After the dismissal of Mr. Fox's coalition ministry, and the appointment of Mr. Pitt, a Bill was brought forward by him in 1784; and there was not, in truth, very much essential difference between it and that of Mr. Fox. If Mr. Fox's Bill altogether deprived the company of existence, Mr. Pitt's deprived them of power: and substituted the control of a minister of the crown, assisted by a board, which was to be termed the Board of Control. While, therefore, the company continued to exercise a nominal executive power, every act was to become known to, and regulated by, the new board. The authority of the Court of Proprietors was much circumscribed: and three only of the Court of Directors, out of twenty-four, were admitted to the privilege of association with the board in political affairs. As to the clauses and resolutions that conquests were repugnant to the British nation, and that governors-general should neither make wars, nor peace, nor treaties, without the concurrence of the home authorities, it will be seen hereafter that they gradually became dead letters. Mr. Dundas was chosen as the first President of the Board of Control. He was already experienced in Indian affairs and politics, and he proved both capable and useful.

Mr. Pitt's Bill.

Establishment of the Board of Control.

At that time, the open and unblushing corruption of Bengal had been checked by Clive and Hastings, roughly, yet to some extent effectively; but no one had interfered at Madras. Loans of an immense amount, of which Mr. Paul Benfield's transactions were a specimen, were claimed from the Nawáb of the Carnatic. Governor Rumbold had, it was alleged, received nearly 200,000*l.* in two years from the Zemindars of the Northern Circars and other corrupt sources, and remitted it to England; and many other scandals were notoriously prevalent. In 1785, this subject was debated in Parliament: and to the astonishment, perhaps, of Mr. Paul Benfield himself, he found that his claims, to the amount of nearly 600,000*l.*, had been admitted. If Mr. Hastings's proposal in 1781 to compromise the whole of the debts of the Nawáb for a million and a half sterling—as could have been effected—had been agreed to, an enormous eventual loss would have been prevented. As it was, a commissioner was appointed for their registry and investigation; but as no means were adopted for preventing the Nawáb from contracting fresh loans, or for the

Corruption at Madras.

Mr. Benfield's claims.

Commission upon Carnatic debts.

gentlemen of Madras for making them, the measure had little practical effect. In 1785 also, the revenues of the Carnatic, which had been well administered by a board of officers, were restored to the Nawáb, under an order of the Board of Control, which overruled the decision of Lord Macartney and the Court of Directors; and Mr. Dundas, on the basis that the war with Mysore had ceased, considered that no ground remained for their retention.

While the Council of Madras and the Nawáb of the Carnatic were engaged in disputes in 1767, Mr. Macpherson, the purser of one of the company's ships, son of a Scotch minister in the Isle of Skye, arrived at Madras, and entered the Nawáb's service, with whom he so contrived to ingratiate himself, that he was despatched to England to appeal to the ministry against the acts of the Madras Council. Mr. Macpherson contrived to get the ear of the Duke of Grafton: and pleaded the cause of his employer so successfully, and perhaps unscrupulously, that on the foundation of what they had heard from his agent, the ministry determined to recognise the Nawáb of the Carnatic as a royal personage, and depute an envoy to his court. This was the real foundation for the appointment, first of Sir John Lindsay, and afterwards of Sir Robert Harland, as ministers plenipotentiary, which led to the invasion of the Carnatic by Hyder Ally; and though the Nawáb may have had good cause of complaint, the course adopted proved, in the end, the worst and most injudicious means of obtaining justice for him. The Duke of Grafton nominated Mr. Macpherson to the civil service of Madras, which gave him local standing, and he subsequently obtained the office of military paymaster; but as he still maintained his connection with the Nawáb, he was removed from his situation, and again returned to England on his behalf, and entered Parliament, whence he was sent to Calcutta as second member of Council. On the departure of Mr. Hastings, therefore, he assumed the office of acting governor-general, and continued in that exalted post for twenty months. During this period the only political event of importance with which he was concerned, was the denial of obligation to pay chouth to the Mahrattas for Bengal, and the offer to send three battalions of infantry to assist in the protection of the Mahratta dominions, on the eve of their war with Tippoo; but Nana Furnawees rejected the latter proposal, which however gave deep offence to Tippoo, and was in fact a direct breach of treaty. Lord Macartney could have assumed the office of governor-general, in virtue of a commission sent from England, and he even went to Calcutta; but his health had failed, and he returned to England in 1786. Sir John Macpherson, therefore, continued in office, and

Proceedings of Mr. Macpherson.

Mr. Macpherson acts as governor-general.

applied himself to the reduction of expenditure, in which he had some success; though in other respects his administration was feeble and inconsequent. Lord Macartney, on his arrival in England, desired to have the appointment of governor-general renewed on his own terms; but these were declined by the ministry, and Lord Cornwallis, who had already distinguished himself in the American war as a soldier and diplomatist, was appointed governor-general, and reached Calcutta early in September 1786. Before entering, however, upon his eventful administration, it is necessary to revert to the position then occupied by the Mahrattas and Tippoo Sooltan.

Lord Cornwallis governor-general.

There is no doubt that the treaty of Salbye with Sindia on the part of the Mahratta nation, had been based on an understanding between Mr. Warren Hastings and Sindia, in regard to the power of Mysore, which was becoming, so to speak, a sharp thorn in the side of the Mahrattas; and Mr. Hastings, by an early understanding with Sindia, prevented him, courted as he was by Hyder, from joining him in an invasion of Bengal; while, by the treaty of Salbye, the whole Mahratta nation was removed from any possible coalition with Mysore against the English. Nana Furnawees, whose jealousy of Sindia's ascendency was extreme, would willingly have seen that chieftain seduced into an alliance with Hyder, and the English attacked by their combined forces: hence his delay in ratifying the treaty of Salbye; but, on the arrival of the news of Hyder's death, he submitted to necessity, and it was duly executed. On the continuance of the war by Tippoo, after his father's death, which Sindia did not expect, he concluded a new treaty with the governor-general, on October 28, 1783, under the terms of which he wrote to Tippoo threatening him with a combined attack. Whether this would have had any effect or not, could not be proved—it is most probable it would have had; but the Madras Government, unable perhaps to comprehend Mr. Hastings's masterly diplomacy, disobeyed his instructions, took the matter into their own hands, and concluded the treaty of Mangalore, as has been already related. That treaty was, there is little doubt, offensive to the Mahrattas, for it ignored their existence altogether; and had the proceedings of the Madras Government been boldly thrown over, and a new treaty demanded by Mr. Hastings in conjunction with the Mahrattas, or singly, on the basis of the treaty of Salbye, there can be little doubt they would have supported him in effecting it. This was not however done, and Nana Furnawees, having made demands on Tippoo for arrears of chouth, which, if refused, would be a

Effects of the treaty of Salbye.

Treaty with Sindia.

Nana Furnawees meets the Nizam at Yatgeer.

sufficient cause of war, went to meet the Nizam at Yátgeer, on the Bheema, in July 1784, avowedly to settle existing claims and disputes in a friendly manner, and secretly to arrange an offensive and defensive war against Mysore. Tippoo, who was better prepared for war than either, when he heard of the conference, claimed the province of Beejapoor from the Nizam, and demanded that the standards of weights and measures which he had established should be made current throughout the Nizam's dominions. These contemptuous and arrogant proposals were no doubt intended as an insult; but the Nizam was not prepared to resent it by war, and temporized, while various matters of domestic policy prevented Nana Furnawees from concluding the alliance resolved upon at Yátgeer.

Tippoo's demands on the Nizam.

Affairs did not, however, long continue in this uncertain position. Tippoo had crushed out all embers of revolt in his western provinces by forcible conversions of great numbers of Christians and Hindoos to Mahomedanism; had carried off the people of Coorg by thousands into slavery; and had thus established a rule of terror and cruelty, against which there was no prospect of resistance. In 1785 he turned his attention to the northern frontier of his dominions. His troops were not long in coming into collision with the Mahratta forces, and obtained some advantages over them, which, in addition to his forcible conversions of Hindoos on the very borders of the Mahratta territory, if not within its bounds, and the voluntary death of 2,000 Brahmins to escape the indignity, caused Nana Furnawees very grave alarm. He was doubtful of the ability of the Nizam to abide the result of a contest; he estimated the powerful aid which Tippoo had obtained from the French, and the admirable discipline of his army, and at last he turned to the English for assistance. This, however, though preferred through Sindia to the governor-general, Mr. Macpherson, and urged upon the basis of the treaty of Salbye, could not be granted. The treaty of Mangalore had, in fact, placed the English in the position of a neutral power; and Nana Furnawees had no resource but to conclude the alliance with the Nizam. For this purpose Nana moved with his army till he met the Nizam, and Moodajee Bhóslay of Berar, near Yátgeer, and a treaty was concluded for the conquest and partition of the whole of the Mysore dominions. The campaigns which ensued have little interest, and were feeble on both sides; but Tippoo, at the close of 1786, proposed peace, which was finally concluded in April 1787. The Mahrattas obtained some restitution of territory. Adony was restored to the

His cruelties in the western provinces.

He attacks the Mahrattas.

Nana Furnawees applies to the English.

Treaty between the Mahrattas and the Nizam.

Peace with Tippoo.

Nizam, and Tippoo agreed to pay forty-five lacs of tribute—thirty in cash, and the balance in a year. The reason of so sudden a proposal of peace by Tippoo has never been understood; but the appointment of an English envoy to the Mahratta court probably gave rise to an opinion, or indeed conviction, that the English were about to join the existing coalition against him.

CHAPTER IV.

OF THE ADMINISTRATION OF LORD CORNWALLIS, 1786 TO 1792.

Lord Cornwallis arrives at Calcutta.

LORD CORNWALLIS reached Calcutta in September 1786, bringing with him detailed instructions from the President of the Board of Control, and from the Court of Directors: and possessing not only their entire confidence, but that of the English nation at large. If he had no local experience of Indian affairs, he was as yet unfettered by local interests and prejudices: and it was felt that the presence of a man of rank, possessed of good abilities and sound judgment, would strengthen the position of the representatives of England. India, as far as the British were concerned, was fortunately at peace on Lord Cornwallis's arrival, and continued so for three years afterwards. He had ample time, therefore, to apply himself to correction of abuses, which he found to pervade every department of the service, and which as yet had been remedied only in a very partial degree. In all his acts he was not only just, but inexorably honourable and persistent. No solicitations from any quarter, however high or influential, caused him to swerve from the position he had assumed, and resolutely maintained. Private trade, contracts, false musters of soldiers, with every other source of official corruption and peculation, were searched out, and prevented; while salaries in proportion to the duties and responsibilities of every office were allotted.

Correction of abuses.

Affairs of Oudh.

During this period the affairs of Oudh were reviewed and settled to mutual advantage: and while the governor-general, in the present condition of the Dehly province, would not consent to withdraw the British brigades on the frontier, he reduced the payment for them from seventy-four to fifty lacs of rupees a year, and he relieved the vizier of many other pecuniary demands which had been imposed or accepted. All applications for interference on behalf of creditors were refused, and the vizier was made independent in his local government; but it was so corrupt and inefficient, that he received a sharp caution in regard to its management, and in regard to the waste of his resources.

The affairs of the Nizam were next in order: they involved questions of great importance. The Guntoor Sircar had not been surrendered, and on the conclusion of the Nizam's war with Tippoo, in 1788, the governor-general dispatched a demand for it by the hands of Captain Kennaway, an officer of his own personal staff. Some opposition had been apprehended, and troops had been collected to advance into the territory; but the Nizam made no objection whatever to its surrender, though on the other hand he called upon the English for the troops specified in the treaty of Masulipatam, and for the recovery of his districts seized by Hyder and Tippoo Sooltan. Not content with this, however, the Nizam at the same time sent an embassy to Tippoo, bearing a splendid copy of the Koran; warned him of the power of the English, and urged a mutual treaty of defence on the common grounds of religion and interest. Upon this invitation Tippoo proposed an alliance by marriage, as a preliminary; but this was haughtily rejected by the Nizam, who had no sympathy with an upstart family. The negotiation, therefore, had only the effect of increasing mutual resentment: and it was equally certain that action upon the treaty of Masulipatam would be considered an offence by Tippoo, the more especially as his name, either by design or accident, was omitted from the enumeration of the powers against whom the British brigade was not to be employed by the Nizam.

Negotiations with the Nizam.

The Nizam's embassy to Tippoo Sooltan.

Its effects.

It has already been detailed, that Tippoo had concluded a sudden peace with the Mahrattas and the Nizam; and he expected perhaps that, in ensuring their neutrality, he should be at liberty to break again with the English—with whom, as he assured the governor of Pondicherry, he should again go to war on the first opportunity. The English were, he always considered, as his father had done, the only obstacle in the way, not only of the conquest and possession of the whole of the south of India, but of the Nizam's dominions. In short, there was no bounds to the ambition of Tippoo, except the conquest of the whole of India, if indeed even that would suffice.

Views of Tippoo.

While these events were pending, and even the Government in England were rapidly coming to the conclusion that the English in India could not remain a neutral power, Tippoo had decided on war. The territory of Travancore, by the treaty of Mangalore, was declared to be under English protection; and the rajah had recently purchased two towns on the coast, Cranganore and Ayacotta, from the Dutch. These

Tippoo prepares for war.

Tippoo demanded, on the ground that the sale by the Dutch was invalid, and that they belonged to his ally, the Rajah of Cochin. Lord Cornwallis was prepared to support the Travancore purchase, and directed Mr. Holland, the president at Madras, to make the necessary communication to Tippoo; but he withheld it, and instead, tried to extort a sum of money from the Rajah of Travancore for himself. Notwithstanding the reforms in Bengal, the corruption of Madras does not appear to have been as yet affected, and carried with it corresponding weakness and irresolution.

Travancore attacked by Tippoo,

The Rajah of Travancore had thrown up lines of fortifications on his northern frontier, between the mountains and the sea; and Tippoo, whose forces had been for some time watching an opportunity, attacked them on the night of December 28, 1789. He was gallantly repulsed, with heavy loss, when he called up reinforcements, and a siege train, and prepared to carry on the war with vigour. Against this violent proceeding, the Government of Madras made no effort or protest: and Governor Holland even deserted his post, and sailed for England. But Lord Cornwallis, who was prepared to hear at any time of an outbreak on the part of Tippoo, hesitated no longer. On receiving news of the attack of Travancore, Nana Furnawees immediately offered an alliance with the English against Tippoo, which was accepted, and concluded in the month of March 1790; and specified the number of troops to be employed in the war, with many other necessary conditions. A treaty with the Nizam was also concluded, to the same purport, in July of the same year. The finances of Bengal were in a most flourishing condition, and a large surplus remained in the treasury; and General Medows, now governor, as well as commander-in-chief, of Madras, was appointed to the conduct of the war now declared. General Medows had been delayed longer than he anticipated in the equipment of his forces; but he opened the campaign by marching from Trichinopoly on May 26, 1790, at the head of 15,000 fine troops; and on July 21, the army reached Coimbatoor, having captured several forts during the march. By the end of September, Pálghautchery and Dindigul, both deemed impregnable, had surrendered. This completed the occupation of the low country: and the army was at the foot of the passes preparing to ascend into Mysore, when Tippoo, by a masterly movement, interposed between two portions of it, fought Colonel Floyd, and forced him to retreat. But it was impossible to bring the sooltan to action again, and the subsequent movements of both sides have little

who is repulsed.

Governor Holland deserts his post.

Treaties with the Mahrattas and the Nizam.

General Medows' campaign.

Incidents of the campaign.

interest. In Malabar, however, Colonel Hartley defeated the Mysore general, Hoosein Ally, and forced him to surrender, and General Abercrombie had reduced Cannanore, by which means the coast province was secured.

Mahratta movements. Captain Little's narrative.

Nor had the Mahrattas been idle. Joined by a detachment of Bombay troops, under Captain Little (the narrative of whose operations, written by Lieutenant Moore, is extremely interesting, and should be perused by the student), Puréshrám Bhow Putwurdhun opened the campaign on August 25, 1789. He was opposed by two Mysore officers, Budr-ool-Zemán Khan and Kootub-ood-deen; the former with 8,000 men occupied the strong fort of Dharwar, while the other operated in the field. Dharwar was invested on October 30, 1789, but owing to the inefficient Mahratta artillery, and the absence of English siege guns, the place held out till April 4, 1790, when Budr-ool-Zemán Khan and his garrison—who had defended the place valiantly—capitulated, and marched out with the honours of war. During the whole of this period, the Nizam's forces had been comparatively inactive: and their sieges of Kopuldroog, and Bahadur Bunda, had been ineffective.

Dharwar capitulates.

Lord Cornwallis conducts the second campaign.

The results of the first campaign had fallen short of Lord Cornwallis's anticipations, and he determined to conduct the second himself. He accordingly proceeded to Madras, where his first act was to re-attach the revenues of the Carnatic, which, it will be remembered, had been assigned to the Nawáb, but had been scandalously mismanaged by him. On January 29, 1791, Lord Cornwallis assumed the command of the army: and having amused Tippoo by feints in the direction of the former passes into Mysore, ascended the Móglee Ghát without opposition, and marched direct upon Bangalore, where the petta, or native town, was taken by assault, and an attempt to recover it by Tippoo was defeated with severe loss. The fort was afterwards breached, and carried by storm on the night of March 20. The Nizam's forces—about 10,000 cavalry—now took heart, and made a junction with Lord Cornwallis; but though eminently picturesque in appearance, they proved utterly useless in the campaign, and indeed became an inconvenience rather than assistance. The united forces then moved westwards upon Seringapatam, and at the same time General Abercrombie advanced from the west coast. Tippoo, who had hitherto consistently avoided general actions, drew up his army to protect his capital, and took up a strong position at Arikéra, on April 13, and awaited an attack; but Lord Cornwallis, by a masterly manœuvre, carried

Bangalore taken.

The army moves on Seringapatam.

out through a tremendous storm, contrived to turn part of the position during the night, and by daylight of the 14th a general action ensued, which resulted in Tippoo's defeat. The victory, however, proved useless: Lord Cornwallis's supplies were so scanty and defective, that he was obliged to retreat, after destroying the battering-train and heavy stores; and he was perhaps only saved from serious disaster by the opportune arrival of the well-supplied Mahratta forces under Puréshrám Ráo, with Captain Little, whose messengers, announcing their progress, had all been cut off by Tippoo's spies. Hurry Punt, with another Mahratta force, reached camp soon afterwards; but Lord Cornwallis was in no position to renew the operations, and took up a position at Bangalore. Thus ended the second campaign.

General action at Arikéra. Tippoo is defeated.

Want of supplies obliges Cornwallis to retreat.

For the third, a portion of the Mahratta army under Puréshrám Bhow, with Captain Little, was sent to the north-west. The Nizam's forces also, with an English detachment, were employed in reducing the country to the north-east, while the main army, with Lord Cornwallis, aided by Hurry Punt, remained for the central service. Before advancing again upon Seringapatam, and before the arrival of reinforcements, Lord Cornwallis directed the reduction of several of the stupendous mountain fortresses of Mysore: and the captures of Nundidroog, Savandroog, Ráyacotta, and other places were marked by a series of brilliant exploits, which gave a tone of confidence to the whole army. In the north-west also, the Mahrattas and Captain Little had been successful, defeating Tippoo's forces in a well-fought action near Simóga; but Coimbatoor was lost, after a long and valiant defence by Lieutenant Chalmers, and its capitulation shamefully violated. These operations, against which Tippoo took no part in the field, had occupied the whole of 1791. In January 1792, Lord Cornwallis had completed his preparations: and joined by a part of the Nizam's and Mahratta forces, advanced on Seringapatam, which he reached unopposed on February 5. He was joined on the 16th by General Abercrombie with the army of Bombay; but the fort had been previously invested, and was held by the sooltan in person at the head of the greater portion of his army. The operations of the Bombay army on the south side of the fort, and its now complete isolation, together with the rapid progress made by the besiegers, seemed to have combined to produce in Tippoo's mind a dread of British power which he had never before experienced. He had little thought when Lord Cornwallis retreated after the action of Arikéra, that the stores then destroyed could be replaced; but his second advance, at the

Third campaign.

The army advances on Seringapatam.

Siege of the fort.

head of a far more complete equipment, caused Tippoo to exclaim, 'It is not what I see of the English, that I fear; but what I do not see;' and it was true. On February 24, the sooltan sent Lieutenant Chalmers, a prisoner of war, to open negotiations for peace, which, after some interruption in regard to a stipulation in favour of the Rajah of Coorg, who had materially aided General Abercrombie, and dreaded Tippoo's vengeance, were concluded on the 24th; and on the 26th, the two sons of Tippoo, who were to remain as hostages for the fulfilment of the conditions, arrived in camp, and were very honourably welcomed. The terms of the treaty, which was not finally executed till March 19, were hard but necessary. The sooltan ceded half his dominions to the allies, of which the English portion was Malabar, Coorg, and the Báráh Mahál. To the Nizam and the Mahrattas, districts contiguous to their own territories, of proportionate value, were allotted; and a sum of 3,300,000*l*., sterling was to be paid as expenses of the war, half in cash and half within a year. Although the Nizam's and Mahratta troops had been treated with scrupulous good faith by Lord Cornwallis, yet it was nevertheless discovered, in 1799, that their leaders had been in traitorous correspondence with Tippoo, during the actual negotiation of the treaty: and that nothing short of Lord Cornwallis's energy, and ability in diplomacy, for which they were not prepared, had prevented their siding with Tippoo and attacking the English forces. This result was happily averted by the acceptance by the sooltan, after a long and anxious conference with his ministers and officers, of Lord Cornwallis's terms, and a determination to rely upon the good faith of the English commander alone. It may also be recorded, as a tribute to the memories of the two great commanders of the army, Lord Cornwallis and General Medows, that they refused any share of prize money, and gave up their portions to the forces.

Tippoo negotiates for peace.

Terms of the treaty.

CHAPTER V.

THE PROGRESS OF ADMINISTRATION, 1793.

THE Mysore war having thus been brought to a triumphant conclusion, Lord Cornwallis returned to Bengal to carry out the final measures of his administration, which had been in gradual progress. Of the consolidation of English power in India, after the result of the Mysore war, there could be no doubt. The Mahrattas and the Nizam had dwindled in influence, in proportion as the new power had risen, and there was no longer a question that, but for the English intervention, Tippoo Sooltan would inevitably have defeated both. Notwithstanding the just ground of the war and its necessity—as well to preserve the Carnatic and repress ambitious violence, as to maintain a balance of power among the native States of India—the conduct of Lord Cornwallis was severely arraigned in England, where the idea of territorial conquest was still foreign to the people, and the peculiar political conditions of the several native powers necessarily very imperfectly known. Could it have been understood, that all, with few exceptions, were, so to speak, political adventurers; that the most powerful had, within a comparatively short period, obtained their dominions by usurpation and violence; that each was striving, or prepared to strive, for a general mastery—the position of England might well have been recognised as a military power, prepared to strike in the general *mêlée* and win what it could. This however, could not be; and the national feeling against territorial acquisition, or aggression in any form, was sedulously maintained, and became modified only by necessities which could not be anticipated. No one had laboured more earnestly to impress upon Lord Cornwallis the necessity of avoiding war and conquest, than Mr. Pitt and Mr. Dundas, backed by the Court of Directors; and it was impossible for any one to have assented to their views more decidedly than Lord Cornwallis, when he accepted the office of governor-general; yet the violent ambition of one native power had rendered immediate action unavoidable, and in due time the war policy of Lord Cornwallis became thoroughly appreciated and approved by his country.

The triumph of the Mysore war was, however, only an episode of Lord Cornwallis's administration. It is on deeper foundations that his reputation as a statesman deserves to rest. Warren Hastings, whose efforts in reference to executive government have already been detailed, had in effect done little more than prepared the way; and the first three years of Lord Cornwallis's incumbency had been devoted to checking abuses, and placing the duties and responsibilities of public servants on a proper footing. These measures had been attended with very satisfactory results: and the field was open to the governor-general to proceed to further, and more enlarged, measures in relation to the collection of revenue, and the administration of justice. If Hastings had remedied some evils, by abolishing the double government, Lord Cornwallis was now to prescribe a future policy of more comprehensive executive administration.

Land tenure and revenue. It would be necessarily beyond the scope of this manual to enter upon the varied and intricate questions of the tenures of land in Bengal and the condition of its occupants. As in all other provinces of India, the Moghul settlements by survey and valuation of land in the time of the Emperor Akbur had decided the amount of revenue to be paid. So also in Bengal; but these settlements had become obsolete in most respects. Increase or decrease of population and cultivation, the value of produce and money, had affected all; and the hereditary position of the collectors of revenue, with whom the subsequent Moghul governments had not interfered, had given them those prescriptive rights of which they were found in possession. Such was the state of affairs when the English obtained the imperial grant of Bengal: and the subsequent regulations of affairs were a succession of temporary makeshifts to secure the largest amount of revenue from year to year. Inquiries had led to the collection of information; but it was ill-digested and only very partially understood in England. Nevertheless, on April 12, 1786, the directors wrote a long and evidently deeply considered dispatch on the subject, condemning many former practices, and recommending a settlement with the hereditary Talookdars, or revenue officers, for a period of ten years, to be made permanent, if it should work satisfactorily. This dispatch can hardly be termed the basis of Lord Cornwallis's proceedings, for his measure was founded upon independent sources of observation and inquiry; and he now proposed to bestow upon the Zemindars of Bengal the property of the soil, and to fix the revenue to be derived from it in perpetuity, as far as the demand of Government was concerned. The only reservation was in favour of the cultivators, who were to be protected by leases: but were not thereby defended from increase of demand. Mr. Shore, to whose abilities Lord Cornwallis owed his knowledge of detail, opposed a permanent settlement very strenuously: and the question being referred for the decision of the Home Government, which approved of the perpetual settlement, the measure was finally proclaimed in Bengal on March 22, 1793.

The Court of Directors recommend a land settlement.

The perpetual settlement.

Although it relieved present apprehensions, and certainly inspired confidence, it is very questionable whether the advantages have in any degree counterbalanced the disadvantages which have proceeded from this measure. It established a local aristocracy and created immense private wealth. On the other hand, it depressed the cultivators to an extent hardly realisable. It secured the existing demands of Government without fluctuation; but provided nothing against the possible necessities of the State, while it alienated the prospective advantages, which would have been enormous; and it required additional

Merits of the measure.

legislation for years, to prevent that very oppression of the people which it was desired to avert. As to the native aristocracy, it is very questionable, except in a few instances, whether it has raised itself above its original condition; but the national covenant has never been infringed, all temptations and necessities to the contrary notwithstanding.

Judicial questions.

The judicial reforms of Lord Cornwallis are in many respects open to objection; but were received, as was their due, with admiration for their advance upon existing institutions. He separated the office of judge from that of collector of revenue, and established separate civil courts in every district for the trial of native suits, with four general courts of appeal, and a final appeal from any one of them to the Sudder Dewány Court of Calcutta. The criminal courts were presided over by judges of the civil courts in rotation, who held sessions: and the Mahomedan law, as interpreted by native officers attached to them, became the basis of their decisions. Sir Elijah Impey's code was remodelled: but it is doubtful whether it was improved, and the appointment of native officers, called daróghas, who had minor jurisdictions, proved in the sequel unfortunate. It was equally to be regretted also that the service was closed to all natives, except in the most inferior positions; but reform, in this material respect and others, was only to ensue upon the bitter experience of years.

Lord Cornwallis returns to England.

Lord Cornwallis, having concluded his administrative acts in Bengal, proceeded to Madras, intending to take command of an army against the French, with whom a new war had begun; but he found that his intended operations against Pondicherry had been anticipated, in the surrender of the town to Colonel Braithwaite, and he embarked for England in October 1793, and was succeeded by Sir John Shore, a civil servant of Bengal, in connection with whom the great land settlement of Bengal had been effected, and who, in virtue of the commission sent to him from England, assumed charge of his office on October 28, 1793.

Sir John Shore succeeds.

Opposition to renewal of the company's monopoly.

Meanwhile, the expiration of the period of charter had brought about new discussions in England in regard to the continuance of the company's monopoly of trade with India, and its extension was opposed by the mercantile interests of England, with much ability. The ministry, however, supported the claims of the company; and the prosperous state of the Indian finances justified Mr. Dundas in pointing to them as a result of good management with which interference would be inexpedient. The merchants of England were not, however, satisfied: and free trade to the amount of 3,000 tons per year became a clause in the new charter,

A limited free trade established.

which was to continue for twenty years. Hitherto all applications for missionaries, schoolmasters, and other instructors in religion and knowledge, had been refused, on the ground that dangerous effects might be produced by their presence among the people of India; and MR. Wilberforce's motion for their admission to India, and recognition under the new charter, was rejected.

Christian missions are not permitted.

CHAPTER VI.

MAHRATTA AFFAIRS, 1793 TO 1795.

Sindia's proceedings in Hindostan.

SINDIA had not become a party to the treaty of Poona against Tippoo Sooltan. He had demanded the protection of his territory by the English during his absence at the war, and two battalions to be attached to his forces; and with these terms, which would have had the effect of neutralising the good feeling of Nana Furnawees, Lord Cornwallis did not comply. On June 20, 1790, Sindia's forces had defeated Ismail Beg, who was still in the field on his own account, in a bloody battle near Pátun, with the loss of all his artillery and ten battalions of infantry, who laid down their arms. In 1791 the Rajpoots again took the field; but were defeated on September 12, when peace ensued, on their promise to pay an annual tribute. Sindia's prosperity and the completeness of his army were now viewed with intense jealousy by Holkar, and he took the Chevalier Dudrenec into his service, for the purpose of raising a similar disciplined force to that of his rival. Holkar was, of the two, the favourite at Poona, and was employed by Nana Furnawees to operate as a check against Sindia's power; but Sindia, who was perhaps apprehensive that a too prolonged absence from Poona might operate to his disadvantage, set out for the Deccan, taking with him the insignia of the Péshwah's office, which he had obtained from the emperor. He reached Poona on June 11; and though opposed by Nana Furnawees, the permission of the Rajah of Sattara was obtained to the investiture of the young Péshwah with the honorary robes and jewels, and the ceremony was carried out with gorgeous pomp; but it was hardly questionable that the representatives of the ancient Mahratta families viewed the reception of honours from a pageant emperor with dissatisfaction and contempt. Mahdoo Ráo Péshwah, a high-spirited and generous youth, was delighted with Sindia, whom he found to be

Rivalry of Holkar.

Sindia proceeds to the Deccan.

Investiture of the Péshwah.

a frank, free soldier: and the intercourse with him was very different and far more agreeable than that with his guardian and minister, Nana. Sindia hoped to gain over the youth to his interests and policy; Nana's policy was to prevent his effecting this object.

While these intrigues were in action at Poona, Sindia's and Holkar's forces, which had been acting in concert in Hindostan for the collection of tribute, came into collision on a division of plunder, and one of the severest actions on Mahratta record was fought between them at Lukhairee, near Ajmere. Holkar's forces were routed, and his disciplined infantry, under Dudrenec, almost annihilated, with the loss of thirty-eight guns. On receipt of this news at Poona, Nana called up Puréshrám Bhow with 2,000 horse; and, on the other hand, Sindia sent for an infantry brigade to reinforce the detachment which had accompanied him. What might have been the result of these movements it is difficult to conjecture; but at a crisis when Nana, despairing of recovering his authority, had besought the Péshwah to allow him to retire to Benares, Mahadajee Sindia died of fever at Wurólee, near Poona, on February 12, 1794. He left no issue, but he had declared Dowlut Ráo, son of his youngest brother, Anund Ráo, to be his heir; and this election, though it had not been confirmed by formal adoption, was recognised by the whole of the confederate Mahratta chieftains. At that time, Dowlut Ráo was less than fifteen years of age, and it would necessarily be some time before he could take a part in public affairs. Nana Furnawees, therefore, continued to exercise, now without interruption, the whole authority of the Mahratta nation.

Holkar's forces routed by Sindia's.

Death of Mahadajee Sindia.

Dowlut Ráo succeeds him.

There had remained many questions for settlement between the Nizam and the Mahrattas, in which no progress had been made since the interview between him and Nana Furnawees at Yátgeer, before their brief war with Tippoo, and many of these were of old standing. On the other hand the Nizam preferred claims upon the Mahrattas; and it is probable, if both had agreed to submit them to Lord Cornwallis, they would have been amicably settled; but there can be little doubt that each party was jealous of the English success, though both had benefited by it, and the English was the last power to be resorted to, as from its decision there could be no appeal. But after the departure of Lord Cornwallis, the Nizam, pressed by the Mahrattas for a settlement, applied for a treaty of guarantee to Sir John Shore, who, foreseeing that the grant of it would cause offence to the Mahrattas, refused to consent. This transaction became known to Nana

Disputes between the Nizam and the Mahrattas.

The Nizam's application to Sir John Shore is refused.

Furnawees, who was emboldened by the non-interference of the English to press the adjustment of the national claims more decidedly. But correspondence and envoys were alike unable to make any impression on the Hyderabad court. The Nizam had materially increased his forces, and under the able management of M. Raymond, twenty-three battalions of disciplined infantry, with an excellent artillery, had been organised, and seemed to be a formidable addition to his ordinary army. The demands of the Mahratta envoy, which amounted to no less than 260 lacs of rupees, or 2,600,000*l.* sterling, were roughly and insultingly rejected, and both parties prepared for war. The armies which took the field in January 1795 were enormous. The Nizam at the head of 110,000 men advanced by way of Beeder and Oodgeer, and descended the Mohree pass, in the direction of Purainda, where he purposed to meet the Mahrattas; while Nana Furnawees, taking the young Péshwah with him, appointed Puréshrám Bhow to the command of the army, which consisted of 130,000 men, chiefly cavalry, with 130 guns.

Nana Furnawees presses his claims.

The Nizam rejects the Mahratta claims;

and war ensues.

The advanced guards of the armies met on March 11, 1795, a little to the westward of the town and small fort of Khurdlah, below the Mohree pass; and the first attack on the Mahratta horse was favourable to the Patán cavalry of the Nizam; but M. Perron, who commanded Sindia's troops, had, with great judgment, occupied some low eminences on the left of the road, with his artillery; and as the main body of the Nizam's cavalry advanced to M. Raymond's support, he turned upon them the concentrated fire of thirty-five field-guns, while at the same time they were assailed by flights of rockets. The whole of the Moghul cavalry then broke and fled; but Raymond held his ground well, and the cavalry might yet have been rallied, had not the Nizam at this crisis recalled Raymond for his protection, and that of the ladies of his family. Thus the battle was lost. In the morning the Nizam was found to have retreated into the fort of Khurdlah, where, for two days, protected by Raymond, he was cannonaded by the Mahrattas; but escape was impossible, and his great army, now become a total rout, had fled up the Mohree Ghát, being pursued down the banks of the Manjera, and as far as Oodgeer, by the light Mahratta horse, and plundered without mercy. The Nizam now sued for terms, which were prescribed by the Mahrattas, and were very humiliating. He was obliged to agree to pay three millions sterling on all accounts—one third in cash; to surrender frontier districts including Dowlatabad, of the annual revenue of thirty-five lacs —350,000*l.*—and as a hostage for the fulfilment of these condi-

Battle of Khurdlah.

Defeat of the Nizam.

The Nizam executes a humiliating treaty.

tions, to surrender his minister, Musheer-ool-Moolk, who, at the memorable Council at Hyderabad, had boastfully declared to the Mahratta envoy that he would bring Nana Furnawees to sue for terms at his master's feet. The treaty was finally concluded on March 13, 1795, and the minister was escorted to the Mahratta camp, where he was honourably received by the Péshwah. Barely 200 men had been lost by both parties in the battle, and the young Péshwah, as recorded by Grant Duff, grieved that so disgraceful a submission had been made by the Moghuls, and that his own soldiers vaunted of a victory obtained without an effort.

Neutrality of the English.

The Nizam dismisses the English brigade.

The British envoys at the courts of Poona and Hyderabad had accompanied the respective armies, but took no part in their proceedings. The Nizam was incensed by the absolute neutrality of the English: and on his arrival at Hyderabad, dismissed the English brigade which had been attached to him, and increased the forces of M. Raymond, assigning for their support the districts which he had acquired from the Mysore war. Soon afterwards, Ally Jáh, the Nizam's eldest son, rebelled against his father, and being joined by the troops who had been discharged after the battle of Khurdlah, his movement had assumed a dangerous aspect, when he was pursued and taken prisoner by M. Raymond; but, dreading his father's resentment, he poisoned himself before he could be brought to Hyderabad.

His son rebels, and poisons himself.

Sir John Shore's policy reviewed.

It is urged by some authorities, that Sir John Shore, in preserving absolute neutrality on the occasion of the war between the Nizam and the Mahrattas, had sacrificed the Nizam to an unworthy desire to maintain peace: and the case of the Rajah of Travancore has been cited as an instance where, to preserve the provisions of a treaty, Lord Cornwallis did not hesitate to declare war—a precedent which ought to have been followed in this instance. But the situations are widely different. Tippoo's attack upon Travancore was unjustifiable; whereas between the Nizam and the Mahrattas old unadjusted claims existed, which the Nizam had admitted, but with which he evaded compliance or settlement. Moreover, in discussing them, the Mahratta envoy had been grossly insulted. If Sir J. Shore had interfered in force to protect the Nizam against the equitable demands of the Mahrattas, it would undoubtedly have produced a new Mahratta war, for which there was no true ground, and most probably thrown them into alliance with Tippoo; and the elaborate minute recorded by him, in which the disadvantages of war with the Mahrattas and Tippoo Sooltan were discussed at great length, was perhaps unnecessary, except to bring his own actions into accordance with the Act of Parliament. Lord Cornwallis might—probably would—have taken a bolder course, and at all risks have not only maintained peace, but interposed as mediator between the contending parties; but it need hardly be said that Sir John Shore had neither the resolution nor the abilities of his great predecessor.

The Péshwah commits suicide.

The victory of Khurdlah was followed by a sad tragedy. Nana Furnawees had never relaxed the strict discipline in which he kept the young Péshwah; but soon after the return of the army to Poona, Bajee Ráo, the son of Rughonath Ráo, and, therefore the Péshwah's cousin, was allowed to visit him. Bajee Ráo was a gay libertine of seductive manners: and there is no doubt that his comparative freedom and pleasant life were contrasted by the Péshwah very bitterly with his own seclusion. Correspondence passed between the young men, which was discovered by Nana, and resented; and the effect of this harsh conduct upon the Péshwah produced despair. On the morning of October 25, 1793, he deliberately threw himself from a terrace of his palace at Poona, and was so injured, that he died on the second day, nominating his cousin, Bajee Ráo, as his successor. Nana Furnawees, who dreaded Bajee Ráo, and was convinced that his own power would cease on his accession, endeavoured to set him aside in favour of a successor to be adopted by the widow of the deceased Péshwah; but the intrigue, though for a while supported by Holkar and other chiefs, fell to the ground, and Nana became reconciled to Bajee Ráo. Further revolutions, however, were to follow, before the accession of Bajee Ráo was finally secured.

CHAPTER VII.

CURRENT EVENTS AND MAHRATTA AFFAIRS, 1795 TO 1798.

Mutiny of the officers of the Bengal army.

One of the most important events connected with Sir John Shore's administration was the mutiny of the officers of the Bengal army, which, at one period, assumed even a more dangerous aspect than a similar occurrence in the time of Lord Clive. A project for the amalgamation of the local armies with that of the Crown had been proposed by Mr. Dundas in 1794, and on his arrival in England, Lord Cornwallis supported the ministerial view of the subject; but the measure nevertheless was thrown out, both by the Board of Control and the Court of Directors. Whatever the final decision of the home authorities might be, and it was looked to with much anxiety, the officers of the company's army in Bengal had associated themselves together for the protection of their general interests. They opposed the idea of amalgamation, and demanded that all previous allowances, including double batta, should be re-established. Their attitude was so threatening, that the governor-general sent for troops from Madras and the Cape, assembled the naval squadron at Calcutta, and even applied to General de Boigne for the services of a regiment of cavalry. These precautions, and the presence of Sir Robert Abercrombie, the commander-in-chief at Cawnpore, for a while maintained order; but the arrival of the long-expected decision from England only created fresh confusion, with which Sir John Shore confessed himself incompetent to deal; and the local regulations were, therefore, modified to suit the crisis. By these, the army obtained even more than they had expected: the arrears of batta were distributed, and brevet rank conferred; but Sir John Shore's apparent weakness caused real alarm in England, and it was determined he should be superseded. Lord Cornwallis was solicited to take up the office of governor-general again, and agreed to do so; but the concessions made to the London committee of the Bengal officers alarmed him, and he refused to proceed to India. These concessions had, however, restored order in Bengal, and no further notice was taken of the late proceedings.

Settlement of the officers' claims.

If Sir John Shore be accused of weakness in some instances, yet in dealing with the affairs of Oudh he undoubtedly displayed courage of a very high order. The vizier died in 1797, and a reputed son, Vizier Ally, succeeded him; the accession being ratified by the governor-general. It transpired, however, that Vizier Ally was not the offspring of the late Nawáb Vizier, and the representations of the minister, Tufuzzul Hoosein, convinced Sir John that the only lawful successor to the throne was Saadut Ally, the brother of the late vizier. Negotiations were therefore commenced with him at Benares, where he resided: and a new treaty was concluded, by which the fort of Allahabad was given up to the English, and an annual payment of seventy-six lacs of rupees to be made for 10,000 English troops, to be stationed in the Oudh territories. When the arrangements were complete, Sir John Shore directed a British force to escort Saadut Ally to Lukhnow, where he himself had been encamped for some time, exposed to the constantly threatened attacks of the partisans of Vizier Ally, who were very numerous. Sir John, however, had firmly maintained his position, and the result showed the benefit of this course; for, on the approach of the legitimate prince, he was welcomed by the people, and the forces of Vizier Ally dispersed

Affairs of Oudh.

New treaty with Saadut Ally.

Saadut Ally proclaimed.

without firing a shot. Saadut Ally was proclaimed Nawáb Vizier on January 28, 1798, and seated on his throne; and Sir John Shore, now Lord Teignmouth, proceeding to Calcutta, sailed for England on March 25. Lord Teignmouth leaves India.

After the death of Mahdoo Ráo Péshwah, as described in the last chapter, the affairs of the court of Poona continued in much confusion. Nana Furnawees, being pressed by Mr. Malet, the British Resident, and equally by his own necessities, convened the officers of State, and prevailed on them to agree to the adoption, by the widow of Mahdoo Ráo, of Chimnajee Appa, the younger brother of Bajee Ráo, by which course his own power would have been secured. This was necessarily opposed by Bajee Ráo, who applied to Sindia and his minister, Balloba Tantia, for assistance. Of both these persons Nana was apprehensive. Of Sindia, because of his powerful position; and of Balloba, because he aspired to be chief minister of the nation. Nana, now reversing his policy, called up Puréshrám Bhow from Tasgaum, who, on this occasion, marched 120 miles in forty-eight hours with his cavalry; and they agreed, in order to neutralise Sindia's influence and that of Balloba, to proclaim Bajee Ráo themselves; and Puréshrám Ráo, proceeding to Sewnair, took a solemn oath that no deception was intended, and escorted Bajee Ráo to Poona. Balloba now advised Sindia to march on Poona, which was done; but Nana proceeded to Sattara, avowedly to avoid Balloba and Sindia, but actually to endeavour to rouse the rajah into action, and once more to proclaim his authority as the head of the Mahratta nation. On the other hand, Balloba, distrusting Bajee Ráo, now proposed to have Chimnajee Appa adopted as Nana Furnawees had arranged; and, strange to say, Nana, who had found his scheme in regard to the rajah impracticable, consented to this measure. On reflection, however, he considered that the proposed arrangement might only be a scheme to entrap him, and he went to Wáee on pretence of performing religious ceremonies; while Puréshrám Bhow, having carried off Chimnajee Appa to Poona, caused the ceremony of adoption to be performed, in spite of his protests against usurpation of his brother's rights, and his own oath to Bajee Ráo to protect them. Chimnajee Appa, therefore, was invested as Péshwah on May 20, 1796. Puréshrám Bhow, who was nominally at the head of the government, now proposed that Nana should come to Poona, and that a general reconciliation should take place; but Nana was in more alarm than ever, and retired into the Koncan, until he should be able to mature plans for his own defence. They were subtle, ingenious, and for the time effective. Sindia even espoused his

Events at Poona.

Intrigues for the Péshwahship.

Nana's policy.

cause; and Balloba, trembling for his own position, sent off Bajee Ráo to Hindostan. Bajee Ráo now intrigued with Ghátgay Shirzee Ráo, who commanded his escort: and persuaded him to marry his beautiful daughter to Sindia, who had become enamoured of her; and this being agreed to, Bajee Ráo feigned illness, and did not proceed.

Nana had meanwhile enlisted the Nizam in behalf of Bajee Ráo and himself, by making a treaty with Musheer-ool-Moolk, the Nizam's minister, who had been released by Puréshrám Bhow; the main object of which, the accession of Bajee Ráo, was secured by extensive advantages to the Nizam, which included the relinquishment of the balance of arrears, and of the districts assigned under the treaty of Khurdlah. This treaty was executed at Mhar, on October 8. Rughoojee Bhóslay of Berar had also been gained over, and the English had signified, through their representative, their recognition of the claims of Bajee Ráo. Nothing being now wanting to the new arrangement, and Nana's wonderful political combinations having been matured, Sindia made the first movement by confining Balloba Tantia on October 27. Puréshrám Bhow, foreseeing the conclusion, fled from Poona, taking Chimnajee Appa with him; and Bajee Ráo returned to Poona, where he was joined on November 25 by Nana Furnawees, and finally invested as Péshwah on December 4, 1796. The adoption of Chimnajee Appa, as within the bounds of consanguinity, was declared illegal, and revoked. Thus concluded the strange revolution which, from the variety of its intrigues, and curious involvements, is unparalleled, even in Mahratta history.

Treaty with the Nizam.

Bajee Ráo invested as Péshwah.

The provisions of the several agreements and treaties were not, however, carried out: and the most material of them, that with the Nizam, was ignored by Bajee Ráo, without considerable modifications. To these Musheer-ool-Moolk would not consent, and he quitted Poona in great indignation. The Péshwah was not long in revealing his really perfidious disposition. He wrought upon the young Sindia by complaints of the power of Nana, and by arguments to prove that their mutual interests required his deposition. Sindia would perhaps have declined association with this infamous conspiracy; but Ghátgay's influence was brought to bear upon him, and he consented. By December 31 all had been prepared, and on that day, on the occasion of a state visit paid by Nana to Sindia in his own camp, he was seized by Michael Filoze, one of Sindia's European commanders, who had previously guaranteed his safe return to Poona. Nana's escort had resisted, and was, for the most part, cut to pieces; and Poona became a

The Péshwah's intrigues.

Nana Furnawees treacherously seized and imprisoned.

shocking scene of riot and slaughter for several days. Nana was sent to Ahmednugger in close confinement, and all the most influential members of his party were imprisoned. In the month of March, 1798, the marriage of Sindia to Báiza Bye, the daughter of Ghátgay, took place. The expenses of the ceremony were enormous, and Sindia, urged by Ghátgay, now demanded two millions sterling, which had been promised by the Péshwah. A secret understanding had previously existed, that Bajee Ráo should procure the office of minister to Sindia for Ghátgay, which was in fact the price of Ghátgay's base seizure of Nana Furnawees; and the measure was pressed upon Sindia by the Péshwah, as a means for obtaining the money he required. Sindia did not hesitate, and on Ghátgay's appointment, the Péshwah proposed that the sum required should be levied by him from the bankers and other wealthy persons of Poona. The result was horrible. Tortures, which cannot be related, were invented by the miscreant, and Poona was literally given up to pillage. Sindia, however, did not depart; and the Péshwah proposed a joint attack upon the Nizam, which might have the effect of inducing him to march from Poona; but though the project was announced to the British Government as early as February 9, no movement was made.

Sindia marries the daughter of Ghátgay.

Extortion by torture from the bankers of Poona.

The Péshwah had created Amrut Ráo, his illegitimate brother, minister in succession to Nana Furnawees, and he, despairing of other means of getting rid of him, proposed the assassination of Sindia. The scene is graphically described in Grant Duff's 'History,' vol. iii. p. 155-6; but at the moment when the Péshwah should have given the signal for the deed, his heart failed him, and Sindia escaped. Other disorders, however, ensued. The widows of the late Mahadajee Sindia were brutally treated by Ghátgay, and he endeavoured to have them conveyed to Ahmednugger; but they were rescued on the way by a Patán officer, who carried them to the camp of Amrut Ráo, who protected them. Sindia made an attempt to rescue them, by attacking the camp of Amrut Ráo, on June 7; but his force was beaten off with severe loss. Bajee Ráo now requested the intervention of Colonel Palmer, the British Resident, with Sindia; but this was refused, and the quarrel culminated in a fresh attack on Amrut Ráo by Ghátgay with two brigades of infantry. As the rupture between the Péshwah and Sindia was now complete, the Mahratta chiefs ranged themselves on either side, and the Péshwah concluded a fresh treaty with the Nizam, confirming that of Mhar.

Proposed assassination of Sindia.

The treaty of Mhar confirmed.

On the other hand, Sindia was in much perplexity, and the

arrears to his army had greatly accumulated. He even professed himself disposed to follow the excellent advice of Colonel Palmer; but this nevertheless failed of effect. Tippoo had been applied to by both parties; and in the end Sindia considered that Nana Furnawees might be his best protector, and released him on the payment of ten lacs of rupees. The effect of this act upon the Péshwah was his revocation of the treaty with the Nizam, and overtures to Sindia and Nana. About the same time Sindia, grown weary of the cruelties and exactions of his minister Ghátgay, caused him to be arrested and confined; but he still remained at Poona, and the intrigues incident to the position of all the parties present there continued unabated, and led, in the sequel, to the second Mahratta war.

Nana Furnawees released.

CHAPTER VIII.

THE ADMINISTRATION OF THE EARL OF MORNINGTON, 1798.

THE successor to Lord Teignmouth, chosen in England, was the Earl of Mornington, whose remarkable talents were already developed by political experience, and whose acquaintance with Indian affairs, gained in the Board of Control, could not fail to be of the highest value in the office of governor-general. From the Cape of Good Hope he was accompanied by Major William Kirkpatrick, who, as Resident at the Nizam's and Sindia's courts, and otherwise actively engaged in political affairs, was enabled to supply Lord Mornington with the practical information he required as to the power and resources of the existing native States of India. This, no doubt, was of a very different character and purport to the knowledge possessed by the ministry or the Court of Directors, who, lulled by the non-interferent policy of Lord Teignmouth, considered that the peace of India would be maintained on the basis established by Lord Cornwallis. The current narrative of history will, however, have prepared the student for the possibility of future struggles, in the fact that no treaties could bind parties who made them and ignored them according to the results of local intrigues, or contemplated schemes of revenge, plunder, or aggrandisement. On these points Major Kirkpatrick's information must have combined, with other circumstances, to determine the policy of the governor-general: and it was more than ever evident that, sooner or later, the power of the English nation would be the only arbiter to all in India.

Appointment of the Earl of Mornington.

Condition of native States.

Lord Mornington reached Calcutta on May 17, 1798; and his attention was almost immediately directed to the designs of Tippoo Sooltan, whose intrigues with the Afghans, with the Nizam, and the Mahrattas, for operations against the English, had become notorious, though as yet abortive, and now took the form of alliance with the French Republic, then at war with England. Tippoo had entered into negotiations with General Malartic, governor of the Mauritius, for the aid of a fleet and 30,000 troops against the English, and these had been referred for the consideration of the French Government. He had already a considerable number of French officers in his pay, who had disciplined his troops; and although the results of the former war had crippled his resources, they were yet considerable, and the interval of peace had enabled him to refit his army with great efficiency. At Hyderabad, the forces of M. Raymond were 15,000 strong, with an efficient park of artillery; and the officers as Republicans were in close correspondence with those of Tippoo: both alike animated with the most hostile intentions against the English. De Boigne's forces with Sindia were at least 40,000 men, in the highest state of discipline and efficiency, with 450 guns. As yet these officers had not openly professed republicanism; but it was not beyond the bounds of probability that they might join the designs of their countrymen at Hyderabad and Mysore in a national effort against the British power. Lord Mornington was not deterred by these possible combinations; but wrote to General Harris, then governor and commander-in-chief at Madras, to march at once upon Seringapatam.

Intrigues of Tippoo Sooltan.

His negotiations with the French.

Condition of his army.

French troops at Hyderabad.

The governor-general's determination.

These orders, utterly unexpected as they were, created the utmost consternation at Madras. The army was not more than 8,000 strong, and was unprepared to take the field; it would indeed have been unequal to check an invasion by Tippoo, and the treasury was empty. These facts induced the governor-general to recall the order of immediate advance, while he urged the completion of the equipment of the forces with every possible diligence. He now turned his attention to Hyderabad, where the minister, Musheer-ool-Moolk, now Meer Allum, was a steady friend of the English, and had foreseen the weakness, as well as the danger, of the French connection. He was also thoroughly aware of the helpless condition of the Nizam's State, between the Mahrattas and Tippoo Sooltan; and his detention at Poona had opened his eyes as to the futility of reliance on either. The governor-general's offer therefore of a subsidiary treaty, an object Meer

Madras unprepared for war.

Subsidiary treaty with the Nizam.

Allum had had long at heart, was immediately accepted: and the negotiation and subsequent proceedings were conducted by the Resident, Captain Achilles Kirkpatrick, with a rare degree of decision and ability. The first object was the disbandment of the French disciplined battalions. Raymond had died early in 1798, and his successor, Piron, had fortunately less influence over the Sepoys. The minister had withdrawn the districts from which the forces had been paid, and they had fallen into arrears: and the men were disaffected, if not mutinous. On October 10, four Madras regiments, destined for the Nizam's service, reached Hyderabad: and for a few days the Nizam and his minister hesitated as to their course of action; but delay was impossible. The minister at last sent their dismissal to M. Piron and the officers under him, and the English brigade took up a commanding position near the French cantonments. M. Piron and his officers at once submitted, and claimed the protection of the Resident; but the Sepoys would not let them depart without the adjustment of their arrears: and it was perhaps owing to the address of Captain, afterwards Sir John, Malcolm, more than to any other cause, that bloodshed was averted. The Sepoys, satisfied by his assurances, laid down their arms, gave up the guns, and the French corps no longer existed.

Disbandment of the French battalions.

Another subject of anxiety had meanwhile occupied the governor-general. Zemán Shah, king of the Afghans, wrote to him, announcing his intention of invading Hindostan and attacking the Mahrattas, and claimed the assistance of the English, and he had now crossed the Indus and was at Lahore. Lord Mornington had applied to Sindia to conclude an alliance against Zemán Shah, or in any case to proceed to check him in Hindostan; but Sindia was as yet too much occupied by his intrigues and difficulties at Poona, and would do neither.

Threatened invasion by Zemán Shah.

But it was impossible to delay operations against Tippoo. Bonaparte had landed in Egypt, and the issue of that step was as yet uncertain. The directors had, however, approved of an immediate war with Tippoo, and so far, the policy of the governor-general was strengthened. The equipment of the coast army had been gradual, but complete; and the 33rd regiment of Foot, commanded by Colonel Arthur Wellesley, the future Duke of Wellington, brother of the governor-general, and 3,000 volunteer Sepoys, were sent to Madras. Finally, the governor-general himself proceeded to Madras, to meet a reply from Tippoo Sooltan to a despatch already sent to him by the hands of Colonel Doveton. In that letter, the governor-general desired earnestly to remain at peace;

Preparations for the Mysore war.

Lord Mornington proceeds to Madras.

but pointed out the French connection as a menace to the English Government which could not be permitted. Lord Mornington found the sooltan's reply awaiting his arrival. He had declined to see Colonel Doveton; and generally professing peaceful intentions, had evaded all other points of the governor-general's dispatch, appealing to the existence of the former treaties as the best means of future tranquillity. The governor-general was not a man to be satisfied with vague and plausible professions; and he again wrote in a friendly spirit, and with additional warning, but without effect. At that very time, Tippoo was urging the French Government to send him troops, and inviting Zemán Shah to advance and join him in a holy crusade against all infidels; he had confident expectations that the French would carry Egypt by a *coup de main*, and would speedily arrive in India; and a letter addressed to him by Bonaparte was afterwards intercepted. It was in vain that Lord Mornington advised him of the destruction of the French fleet at Aboukir, and sent him a letter from the Sooltan of Turkey to warn him against the French alliance. Nothing could affect him: and with the greatly augmented forces of his former enemies in his front, Tippoo was still defiant, or at least professing indifference.

Tippoo's evasions and intrigues.

The governor-general's remonstrances are futile.

Such a condition of affairs could have but one termination. Seringapatam could only be attacked while the Cauvery was low, and the sooltan's evident desire was to protract negotiation till the rains. The army, therefore, advanced from Vellore, on February 11, 1799. It consisted of about 21,000 English, European, and native troops, and 10,000 of the Nizam's contingent, nearly 4,000 of whom were the former Sepoys of Raymond, now commanded by their popular leader, Captain Malcolm. A corps of 6,000 men was advancing from the western coast, under General Stuart and the veteran General Hartley. General Harris reached Bangalore on March 15, unopposed; but on the 11th a sharp action was fought at Sedaseer, on the Coorg frontier, with Tippoo's forces, which retreated with a loss of 2,000 men. Tippoo now proceeded to meet the main army; but his movements evinced neither ability nor resolution. He acted as a man dazed and confounded by the magnitude of the effort made against him—the effect, not of what he could see, but of what he could not see. Only a few years had elapsed since the English were at his mercy, so to speak, in the Carnatic; and their strength now filled him with dismay. He drew up his army at Malavelly, where it was defeated on March 27, and the English forces, avoiding the country purposely desolated by Tippoo, moved southwards by

The English army advances from Vellore.

Action at Sedaseer.

Tippoo defeated at Malavelly.

a fertile district, and crossed the Cauvery, by the hitherto unknown ford of Sosillay. The last hope of the sooltan perished with this movement, and he retired at once into his capital.

Returns to Seringapatam.

Up to the time of Lord Harris's advance, Tippoo might have obtained peace on fair terms. Then, his arrogance prevented his consideration of it; now, his despair. On April 6, the fort of Seringapatam was invested, and it was evident to Lord Harris that the siege operations must be rapidly pushed on, not only on account of the near approach of the monsoon, which would flood the river, but because the supplies of the army were already short. On the third day there was a brief cessation of hostilities to receive Tippoo's proposals for peace; but the demands of General Harris were heavy: 2,000,000*l.* sterling, and one half his dominions. These he refused, declaring death as a soldier was preferable to ignominious submission; and the siege recommenced. On May 2 the breach was reported practicable. On the 3rd, at noon, 4,400 men were assembled in the trenches, and were led to the storm by General Baird, who, from his long captivity in the fort, knew the place well. The breach was bravely defended, the fortifications were yet strong and intricate, and the sooltan himself took part in the conflict; but nothing could repress the dour of the assault: the place was carried, and all its defenders had submitted before evening. It was with difficulty that the European soldiers were restrained from outrage, for they had heard of the murder in cold blood, only the previous night, of twelve of their comrades. The sooltan was not found in the palace, and on searching for him, his dead body was discovered by General Baird under a gateway. It was conveyed to the palace, and the next day buried with all the honour which could be conferred by a military funeral, added to the solemn rites of his own faith. The descriptions of the event have a weird sublimity, in the crashing peals of thunder which mingled with the roar of the English cannon saluting the dead. No achievement of English arms as yet in India had equalled the capture of Seringapatam, and the details of the siege, and indeed of the whole campaign, which have been described at length in many historical and military narratives, are of surpassing interest, as well to the student as to the general reader. For his conduct during this eventful year, Lord Mornington received the thanks of both Houses of Parliament, and was created Marquess Wellesley. General Harris was also raised to the peerage, and the siege of Seringapatam

Seringapatam invested.

Storm of the fort,

and capture.

Tippoo Sooltan killed in the assault.

Lord Mornington created Marquess Wellesley.

General Harris raised to the peerage.

became as much one of the most popular victories of the British army as General Baird was of its heroes. The British loss in killed and wounded in the siege was 1,164 men. 929 pieces of ordnance, brass and iron, 424,000 round shot, and 520,000 lbs. of gunpowder were found in the fort; and the amount available for prize-money was 1,100,000*l.*, which was at once distributed to the army; the Marquess Wellesley, however, refusing to accept his share.

CHAPTER IX.

CURRENT EVENTS AND MAHRATTA AFFAIRS, TO THE TREATY OF BASSEIN, 1799 TO 1802.

Character of Tippoo Sooltan.

THE character of Tippoo Sooltan was so strange, that it can hardly be passed without a few brief remarks. His cruelties to his own subjects, his forcible conversions of Hindoos, and the tenor of his administration, combined with his fierce religious bigotry and fanaticism, were sufficiently revolting to his people at large; while the murder in cold blood of many English prisoners, and his almost systematic ill-treatment of all, had produced a feeling of revenge against him personally, which had never before been excited in India, and pervaded all ranks of the invading army. There seemed to be no bound to his arrogance or his ambition in political questions, and treaties were made or repudiated as suited his convenience. His subjects even were weary of a reign which had lasted seventeen years in a succession of turmoil, cruelty, and oppression, which has been faithfully portrayed by the native historians of the period, and by Tippoo himself in his own diaries. Perhaps the best estimate of his character is given by Syed Hussein, one of his most confidential servants, whose memoirs of the sooltan are very interesting. He writes:—'There was nothing of permanency in his views, no solidity in his councils, and no confidence on the part of the government. All was innovation on his part, and the fear of further novelty on the part of others; the order of to-day was expected to be reversed by the invention of to-morrow. All the world was puzzled what distinct character should be assigned to a sovereign who was never the same. The most intelligent and sincere well-wishers of the house concurred in the opinion of his (Tippoo's) father, that his head and heart were both defective, however covered by a plausible and imposing flow of words; and that they were not always without symptoms of mental aberration.' Of no court or sovereign of India, are there more profuse records than those of Mysore, nor have any Indian monarchs, not even Babur or Hoomayoon, left more copious memoirs than Tippoo, in his own handwriting. French, English, and native accounts differ little in details of murder, torture, and mutilation, which marked the savage; while the strange records of visions and dreams, the contemplated construction of a new sect, of which he should be the prophet and teacher; the wild doctrines he propounded, and his horrible superstitions, mark indeed but too strongly the 'mental aberrations' noted by his biographer. His father prophesied he would lose the kingdom he had gained; and he lost it, dying bravely in defence of what he had made the strongest fortress in India. Mr. Mill, strange to say, takes a high view of Tippoo's character in many respects; but it is difficult to receive it in the face of his own admissions and records, and those of his servants and biographers, who were at least uninfluenced by foreign considerations.

Division of Mysore.

The Mysore territory was now to be divided. Portions were set aside on their several frontiers for the British, the Nizam, and the Péshwah; for though the latter had taken no part in the contest, he could not, in the face of the former tripartite treaty, be entirely ignored; and the remainder, which consisted of the ancient kingdom of Mysore, was made over to the real rajah of the country, a boy of five years old, who was found with his family in confinement. Lord Wellesley appointed English commissioners to arrange the details of administration during his minority; and Poornea, the able finance minister of the late kingdom, was associated with them in the executive detail. The family of Tippoo Sooltan was removed to Vellore, and an allowance of 240,000 pagodas, about 84,000*l.*, per annum assigned to them, payable from the revenues of the British portion of the conquest, the balance of which was indeed inferior to that allotted to the Nizam. The portion to be assigned to the Mahrattas brings the narrative of history again into connection with them.

The ancient kingdom of Mysore restored to its rajah.

Allowances to the family of Tippoo.

Mahratta affairs.

Sindia still, as has been related, remained at Poona; but he was really desirous of returning to his dominions, and a further advance of money by Nana Furnawees enabled him to do so. This aroused the fears of Bajee Ráo, who, so long as he could play off one against the other, conceived himself secure, and he now visited Nana secretly by night, reiterating his promises of good faith, and laying his head onthe feet of his minister—the most sacred oath he could take—swore to be true to him. Nana, therefore, retained his office; but shortly afterwards understood from Sindia himself that the Péshwah was faithless, and was trying to persuade him to arrest him. The Péshwah, upbraided by Nana, denied the accusation; but Nana's suspicions were not removed, and, to an unavoidable extent only, he continued the duties of his office. While these intrigues had been in progress, the Nizam had concluded the new subsidiary alliance with the governor-general; and a similar one was offered to the Péshwah, but declined, on the grounds that the former treaties were sufficient, and that he was ready to afford his aid in the war with Tippoo. The Péshwah was still uncertain whether his interests lay in a junction with Tippoo, whose agents were at his court, or with the English against him. The Mahratta force, therefore, which had been assembled avowedly to co-operate with the English and the Nizam, was kept inactive. After much irresolution, the Péshwah finally determined to side with Tippoo; and a scheme was prepared with Sindia to attack the Nizam, which must necessarily, they considered, cause a diversion of the British forces; they hoped, also, that Rughoojee Bhóslay of Berar would join their confederation. Of these intentions the governor-general was completely advised: and before any action could be taken by the Péshwah and Sindia, the death of Tippoo, and distribution of his territories, had occurred. On this event, the Péshwah and Sindia both tendered their congratulations to the governor-general, though Sindia, at the same time, had dispatched messengers into Mysore to stir up disaffection. The Péshwah agreed to receive the territory allotted to him, 'as an equivalent for the demands of chouth on the Mysore State;' but as he still distinctly refused to accede to the mediation of the English in regard to his claims on the Nizam, or to recognise the treaty of Mhar, the negotiations with him entirely broke down, and the reserved territory was ultimately divided between the English and the Nizam.

The Péshwah declines a subsidiary alliance.

Mahratta intrigues.

With his highness a new treaty was concluded on October 12, 1800, by which the subsidiary force was increased to eight battalions; and for their payment the districts obtained from Mysore were ceded by him in perpetuity. On their part, the English contracted to defend the Nizam's territories from all aggression. This treaty was necessarily the death-blow to the schemes of the Péshwah and Sindia, who, in the event of any movement on the Nizam, would be attacked by the British forces. On the other hand, the Nizam, by the cession of territory just acquired for the payment of the British forces, was in no worse pecuniary condition than before, was removed from all demands and liabilities for

New treaty with the Nizam.

Advantages gained by the Nizam.

money, and was protected from his hereditary enemies. The possession of the ceded districts brought up the British frontier to the Krishna river, which, with the exception of a small portion of the Mahratta territory in the west, formed a well-defined line of frontier.

Omitting details of a war between the Péshwah and the Rajah of Kolapoor, which desolated the Southern Mahratta provinces, and in which the gallant Puréshrám Bhow was killed, the death of Nana Furnawees must be mentioned, which occurred on March 12, 1800. 'With him,' wrote Colonel Palmer, the Resident at Poona, 'has departed all the wisdom and moderation of the Mahratta Government.' He had consistently been opposed to the political progress of the English as subversive of Mahratta power, and he objected to the employment of foreign troops under any conditions; but he was faithful to his political engagements, and his devotion to the maintenance of the honour of his own nation is attested by the respect of all his contemporaries. The faithless materials with which he had to deal at the close of his life threw him into intrigues and combinations for his own preservation, which would otherwise have been avoided, and left him at liberty to continue the able administration he had conducted for twenty-five years. Disorders soon became prevalent in the Deccan. Sindia took the lead in them, in an attempt to possess himself of the estates of Puréshrám Bhow; Ghátgay was released, and renewed his horrible barbarities; and the Rajah of Kolapoor was at war with the Péshwah; Dhoundia Wáug, who had passed from Tippoo's service to that of Kolapoor, left the latter, and commenced a career of plunder on his own account, which was cut short by a force under Colonel Arthur Wellesley, which pursued him for four months, and at last brought him to bay in an action, on September 10, in which he was killed. Sindia kept guard over the Péshwah, who probably, in order to be freed of him, would now have courted a more intimate English alliance; but, always wavering, and involved in petty intrigues and temporary expedients, he could decide upon no consistent course of policy.

Death of Nana Furnawees.

His character.

Disorders in the Deccan.

Dhoundia Waug pursued and slain in action.

Meanwhile, the Holkar family were again rising into notice and power. Jeswunt Ráo, though illegitimate, was bold and enterprising. He was joined by the Chevalier Dudrenec and his battalions, and he commenced to plunder Sindia's dominions in Malwah with so much pertinacity and success, that Sindia, at the close of 1800, was obliged to leave Poona, and advance into Malwah. Holkar was prepared to receive him, and in an obstinate battle near Oojein, in June 1801, Sindia's forces were defeated; but Holkar, who

Holkar's proceedings.

Sindia opposes him, and is defeated.

afterwards attacked Sindia's convoy of artillery, was in turn repulsed. The departure of Sindia left the Péshwah entirely at liberty; but, instead of consolidating his authority, he began deliberately to destroy and despoil all families whom he conceived had ever opposed him. Among others, Wittoojee, the brother of Jeswunt Ráo Holkar, was executed in his presence, by being dragged at the foot of an elephant. In Malwah, the war between Sindia and Jeswunt Ráo Holkar proceeded; and on October 14 the latter was defeated near Indoor, with the loss of ninety-eight pieces of cannon and the plunder of his capital. By this event, however, he was not discouraged. He soon afterwards attacked Sindia's possessions in Khandésh, and his operations had extended almost to Poona, when the Péshwah again besought aid from the British Government, but still refused the terms prescribed by the governor-general in regard to the Nizam, which were the only basis on which they could be obtained. After a variety of manœuvres, Jeswunt Ráo advanced close to Poona, professing allegiance to the Péshwah, but demanding his interference in regard to Sindia; and this having been refused, the Péshwah's and Sindia's united armies drew up for battle on October 25. The forces on both sides were nearly equal; but Holkar, displaying great energy and valour, led charge after charge against Sindia's disciplined battalions, broke and defeated them, and the rest of the army fled, leaving all their guns and stores to the victor. The consequence of this victory was, that the Péshwah fled immediately to the fort of Singurh, and transmitted an engagement to the British resident, Colonel Close, to conclude a subsidiary treaty for the maintenance of six battalions of Sepoys. From Singurh, the Péshwah proceeded to Mhar, and thence to Bassein, where he was joined by Colonel Close; and by December 31, the articles of a new treaty were completed. In substance, they comprised mutual defensive alliance, with the cantonment of six regiments of native infantry, and a proportion of European artillery, in the Péshwah's dominions; and districts yielding twenty-six lacs of rupees were to be assigned for their support. The Péshwah also confirmed the treaty of Mhar, and submitted his claims on the Nizam and the Gáikwar to English arbitration, and finally contracted to enter upon no hostilities, without consultation with the British Government. The treaty was a virtual surrender of independence; but it arose out of a position into which his own intrigues had driven him.

Holkar defeated by Sindia.

Holkar advances to Poona.

and defeats the Péshwah and Sindia.

The Péshwah executes the treaty of Bassein with the English.

CHAPTER X.

THE ADMINISTRATION OF THE MARQUESS WELLESLEY, 1800 TO 1803.

Affairs of Tanjore and Surat.

Before he left Madras, the governor-general placed the State of Tanjore under British administration. The rajah had died in 1787, and having no natural heir, had adopted a boy named Syfajee. This adoption was set aside by the deceased Rajah's half-brother, Ameer Singh, as illegal: and his own succession was confirmed by the Court of Directors, upon the representation of the Madras Government. It was discovered afterwards, however, that the adoption had been perfectly legal, according to Hindoo law: and the court having admitted the fact, Syfajee was declared rajah, with an allowance of 40,000*l.* a year, and a fifth of the net revenues in addition. It will be remembered that this State had been founded by Shahjee, the father of Sivajee, in the time of the Beejapoor monarchy.

Settlement of the Carnatic.

About the same time also, the governor-general directed that the small State of Surat, in which the authority was divided between the Nawâb, who was a descendant of the last imperial governor, and the English, should be managed on the same principle as Tanjore. The settlement of the affairs of the Carnatic followed. Suspicions had not been wanting that the present Nawâb, Oomdut-ool-Oomrah, as well as his father, had not been, at heart, well affected to the English; and a correspondence was found among Tippoo Sooltan's papers which confirmed the fact beyond question. Lord Wellesley did not hesitate to make this discovery the basis of a final settlement of the Carnatic affairs: and he wrote on May 28, 1801, to Lord Clive, the Governor of Madras, to proceed with it. Oomdut-ool-Oomrah, the Nawâb, was then on his death-bed, and expired on July 15. It was found that he had appointed his reputed son, Ally Hussein, as his successor, who was now informed that the illness of the late Nawâb had formed the only ground for action not having been taken upon the discovery of the traitorous correspondence with Tippoo, and that the only terms on which his succession could be recognised, would be his relinquishment of the administration, and acceptance of an allowance from the revenues of the country. The youth, acting under the influence of his advisers, rejected this; and there is hardly a doubt that he was counselled to resist by the clique of English and native money-lenders who still flourished at the court. Lord Wellesley's instructions, however, allowed of no modification; and setting aside Ally Hussein, application was made to Azeem-ood-Dowlah, son of the late Nawáb's brother, who accepted the terms offered without hesitation. A fifth of the net revenues of the Carnatic was assigned for his support, and the entire administration of the provinces was assumed by the Government of Madras, to the extinction of the double authority from which they had so long, and apparently so hopelessly, suffered.

In the north-west, the threatened progress of Zemán Shah had been stopped by the rebellion of his brother at Kabool; and by the effect of a native agent sent to the King of Persia by the governor-general—who, being a Sheea, contrived to excite the King of Persia against the Afghan Soonies—the diversion was caused which obliged Zemán Shah to leave India. The cordial reception of this agent encouraged Lord Wellesley to send a formal embassy to Persia in 1800, and Captain Malcolm made an admirable ambassador. The embassy was the first that had visited Tehrán since the period of Queen Elizabeth; it was magnificently equipped, and furnished with costly presents, and was so far successful, that it established commercial intercourse with Persia, bound the king not to permit the introduction of French influence, and to check the Afghans should they have designs upon India. Perhaps, however, the results of the previous native agency had had the most practical effect.

Malcolm's embassy to Persia.

It will be remembered that Vizier Ally, who had assumed the government of Oudh, had been displaced by Lord Teignmouth in favour of the now reigning prince, Saadut Ally. Vizier Ally took up his residence at Benares, where it was found he was in correspondence with Zemán Shah, and was a focus for many other traitorous intrigues. The local agent, Mr. Cherry, was directed to remonstrate with him, and to cause his removal to Calcutta, and Vizier Ally affected to comply; but on an occasion of an apparently friendly visit, on January 14, 1799, he attacked Mr. Cherry, killed him, Mr. Graham, and Captain Conway, then present, and endeavoured to murder Mr. Davis, the judge, who, however, defended himself valiantly in his house, and escaped. Vizier Ally's house was then attacked in turn by the British troops: but he contrived to escape, and after endeavouring to create a rebellion in Oudh, was given up by the Rajah of Jeynagurh, and confined for life in Calcutta.

Murder of Mr. Cherry by Vizier Ally.

He is imprisoned for life.

This melancholy episode preceded the adjustment of affairs with Saadut Ally, the Nawáb Vizier, which had fallen into a very unsatisfactory condition; and so far from

Affairs of Oudh.

Oudh being a barrier against Mahratta or other encroachment from the north-west, as it was hoped according to former policy it would be, the province had become a serious weakness, and subject of apprehension. Sir John Craig, who commanded the British forces in Oudh, had reported the utter uselessness and disorganisation of the Nawáb's forces, and considered them more a source of danger than advantage. On the other hand, the exactions of the Nawáb, and the effete character of his administration, had disgusted his people, and decreased the legitimate revenues of the State. Reform could not, therefore, be delayed, and the governor-general applied himself to effect it with his accustomed vigour. His right of interference had been established by former treaty; in short, the Vizier held the country only upon the sufferance of the English: there was more absolute right of control in Oudh than had existed in the Carnatic, and had that right been at once declared and exercised, the effect would have been better, perhaps, than the policy of expediency, as subsequently followed in the other case. The negotiations in the question were very protracted. They had commenced in 1799, on the apprehended danger from Zemán Shah. The Nawáb was asked to disband or reduce his useless forces, and to receive, in lieu of them, additional English troops, equal to the defence of his territories; but the increased expense would be fifty lacs of rupees a year, and to this he objected, and offered to abdicate. Lord Wellesley trusted that the abdication would be made, when, as he advised the home government, he should assume absolute charge of the Oudh territory; but this course had never been the real intention of the Nawáb, and he contrived to protract the negotiation by every means in his power.

Lord Wellesley's measures of reform.

It must be admitted that many of his representations have truth on their side; and that at first sight the policy of the governor-general appears harsh and exacting. On the other hand, that policy was exclusively directed to the defence of Oudh against the restless and unstable Mahrattas, which, as Lord Wellesley foresaw, was an unavoidable necessity, because it involved also the defence of Bengal; and though the Nawáb at one time showed indications of submission, in the discharge of some of his troops, yet he still pleaded inability to pay the new demands, or to make any arrangement for them. The governor-general was not disposed to relax these demands; he pointed out the districts of Corah, Allahabad, and Rohilkhund, as sufficient for the purpose; and dispatched his brother, the Hon. Henry Wellesley, afterwards Lord Cowley, to bring the affair to a conclusion. Mr. Wellesley found the Nawáb Vizier practically,

Mr. Wellesley is sent to Oudh.

though professing submission, as much opposed to the execution of a new treaty as ever; but he nevertheless induced him to conclude one on November 14, 1801; not, however, before orders had been issued to the revenue officers of the province to retain their collections on account of the British Government. The amount of these revenues was estimated at 135 lacs—1,350,000*l.*—per annum. The whole of the transaction has formed a subject of discussion which it is useless to revive; but it will at least be conceded that the defence of Oudh was completed, and the substitution of territorial revenue for continued demands for money, never before punctually paid, and the security of the Nawáb in the territory which remained to him, were at least effected; while it was evident that the release of the people from the baneful effects of a government which had never either been protective or efficient, was a corresponding advantage which can hardly be overrated. Some slight resistance was made by Zemindars, who had always been lawless and refractory: and by the Nawáb of Furrukabad, who had been a feudal tributary of Oudh; but these local affairs were soon adjusted by Mr. Wellesley, and the Nawáb of Furrukabad was pensioned.

and the Nawáb executes a new treaty.

Results of the treaty.

If the governor-general could have secured the co-operation of Admiral Rainier, he would have attacked the Mauritius in 1799, when French privateers committed great depredations; but the admiral could not be persuaded to enter upon such an enterprise without an order from the king, and the project was necessarily abandoned. The expedition to Egypt, however, in 1800, was fully carried out. Seven thousand English and native troops landed at Kosseir; made a memorable march across the Desert, and from Ghenneh descended the Nile to Rosetta. Peace with France prevented their having an opportunity of meeting the French troops in action, but the moral effect of the expedition made a deep impression throughout India.

Indian troops sent to Egypt.

During all his political negotiations, Lord Wellesley had devoted a full measure of his great talents to the improvement of the civil administration of India, and reforms of what he considered, and really were, existing abuses. In regard to the Sudder Court of Appeal, the head of which was the governor-general in council, he renounced his own authority: and in 1800 separated the court finally from the legislative and executive functions of the administration. New judges, selected from the ablest of the civil servants, were appointed, with a result which was hailed with satisfaction by the people, and proved as useful as it was necessary. For the education of the young civilians in duties and responsibilities now immensely extended, the college of Fort William was established

Reforms in the civil administration.

College of Fort William established.

in the same year. It was perhaps—though its use was unquestionable—founded on too magnificent a basis, and on January 22, 1802, the directors ordered its abolition. Many alterations had been made by the court in regard to officers in India, to which Lord Wellesley had appointed the ablest men he could select. They were displaced, and nominees of the court, in many instances totally inefficient, were appointed; but his greatest crime in the eyes of the court, was Lord Wellesley's encouragement of private Indian trade, by means of which, in India-built ships, he was creating a noble mercantile navy, with corresponding increase of trade. The company, under their narrow views of monopoly, could not follow the practically magnificent plans of their governor-general: and though he was supported by the ministry of the crown, the Court of Directors and Proprietors recorded severe resolutions of censure. Against these, and against the general policy of the court, in regard to vexatious interference with his acts and patronage, Lord Wellesley protested in vain. It was impossible for him to bring about any conception of the magnitude or effect of his general policy. It can be followed now, with full admiration and appreciation of the views and acts of a great statesman; but then it was simply alarming and incomprehensible to men of narrow minds, professing a policy jealously guarded and circumscribed by previous tradition and experience. Lord Wellesley, therefore, tendered his resignation, and awaited the reply, which arrived early in 1803, and in which, perhaps to his surprise, with a commendation of his great zeal and ability, he was requested to continue in office for another year.

Encouragement of private trade offends the Court of Directors.

Votes of censure passed.

The Marquess Wellesley resigns office, but retains it for a year.

CHAPTER XI.

THE ADMINISTRATION OF THE MARQUESS WELLESLEY (*continued*)—THE SECOND MAHRATTA WAR, 1803.

The treaty of Bassein was viewed with great alarm by the Mahratta chiefs. The policy which Nana Furnawees had continued for twenty-five years, to remain independent of foreign alliances, had been deliberately broken by the head of the nation; and it was evident that the English possessed not only the will, but the power, to resent and punish any breach of faith. Sindia, Holkar, and the Rajah of Berar, had neither been consulted in regard to it, nor

Alarm of the Mahrattas in regard to the treaty of Bassein.

were aware of its purport till its execution. After the battle of Poona, Holkar indeed tried to induce the Péshwah to return, in order to mediate between himself and Sindia; but, failing in this, he affected to consider Bajee Ráo's flight as a virtual abdication, and offered the office of Péshwah to his brother, Amrut Ráo, who accepted it; and a deed of investiture was obtained from the Rajah of Sattara. In order to supply themselves with funds, the unhappy inhabitants of Poona were again mercilessly plundered by Holkar and Amrut Ráo, and the country around devastated. Meanwhile, the Péshwah had no sooner signed the English treaty than he was prepared to ignore it; and he sent private letters to Sindia and the Rajah of Berar, urging them to march upon Poona, avowedly to punish Holkar, but in reality to support him against the English.

New intrigues by the Péshwah.

With Sindia, the governor-general had entered into negotiations, and offered a subsidiary treaty. Captain Collins, Lord Wellesley's agent, visited Sindia in his camp at Boorhanpoor, at the end of February 1803; but he found him impracticable on the subject of such an alliance. He professed himself hurt, that as in the case of the treaty of Salbye, that of Bassein should not have been conducted through his instrumentality; and he gave it to be understood that though he could not interfere with its provisions as regarded the Péshwah, he considered himself altogether independent of the transaction. The fact was, that he was then negotiating with the Rajah of Berar a joint confederacy of the whole of the Mahratta nation against the English—a course in which both he and the Rajah of Berar were secretly encouraged by the Péshwah. It is impossible within the scope of this work to review the various able papers to which this crisis gave rise; but the student should not fail to peruse the Marquess Wellesley's dispatches on the subject, and the opinion of Lord Castlereagh in his minute on the treaty of Bassein, which he condemned; but by far the most practical and correct of all, is the late Duke of Wellington's (then General Wellesley's) paper upon Mahratta affairs, which reviews the whole subject, with a clearness and precision which are truly admirable; and was continued, in the war which followed, by those numerous military and political dispatches, which form in themselves a complete illustration and history of the period. Holkar was as yet at Poona, and declined association with the league. His plans were, no doubt, then directed to his own aggrandisement in Hindostan; and he foresaw, should Sindia decide upon war with the English, that his possessions in Hindostan and Malwah would be defenceless.

Sindia refuses a subsidiary treaty.

His motives.

State papers, and review of Mahratta affairs.

These events were fully known to the governor-general; and,

whatever might be the result of the combination between Sindia and the Rajah of Berar, it was at least necessary to carry out the provisions of the treaty of Bassein, and place the Péshwah in his authority at Poona. This was an object in which the subsidiary force with the Nizam, as well as some of the Nizam's own troops, could be employed under the treaty; and on March 25, 1803, the Hyderabad subsidiary force, under Colonel Stevenson, with 9,000 horse and 6,000 foot of the Nizam's, reached Puraindа, on the Seena river, which formed the Péshwah's boundary. At the same time, General Wellesley, with 8,000 infantry, 1,700 cavalry, and 2,000 Mysore horse, was moving up from Mysore, through the Southern Mahratta provinces, whence he succeeded in carrying with him 10,000 Mahratta horse, contributed by the Péshwah's feudatories to assist in his restoration.

Military operations to support the Péshwah.

Holkar did not wait the arrival of the British troops, fearing, as was reported, that Poona would be burned by Amrut Ráo. General Wellesley made a forced march of sixty miles in thirty-two hours with the cavalry, and found the city evacuated. Holkar had retired northwards to Malwah, and Amrut Ráo towards Nassuk, where he was plundering the country. He made overtures, however, to General Wellesley, for reconciliation with his brother; but this being refused by the Péshwah, Amrut Ráo retired from the contest to Benares, on a pension of 80,000*l.* per year, paid by the British Government.

Holkar returns to Malwah.

On May 13, 1803, the Péshwah arrived at Poona under an escort of British troops, and took possession of his office. Holkar was invited to come to Poona, and the British Resident offered his intervention: but between thoughts of revenge for his brother's execution, and the chances of war in Hindostan, Jeswunt Ráo could not be prevailed upon to abandon his own independent designs. It was impossible, however, for the governor-general to be content with the attitude assumed by Sindia, and he was called upon for explanation of it. The answer was evasive and defiant: he could promise nothing, he replied, till he had seen the Rajah of Berar, when 'the Resident should be informed whether there would be peace or war.' To General Wellesley, as political agent, the governor-general now confided the negotiations to ensue, and a remarkable document was drawn up by him, proposing to the chiefs, who all as yet professed friendly intentions, to withdraw their armies within their own territories: while, on his own part, he promised a similar proceeding on behalf of the British forces. This straightforward proceeding had the effect anticipated. The

The Péshwah reaches Poona.

Defiant attitude of Sindia.

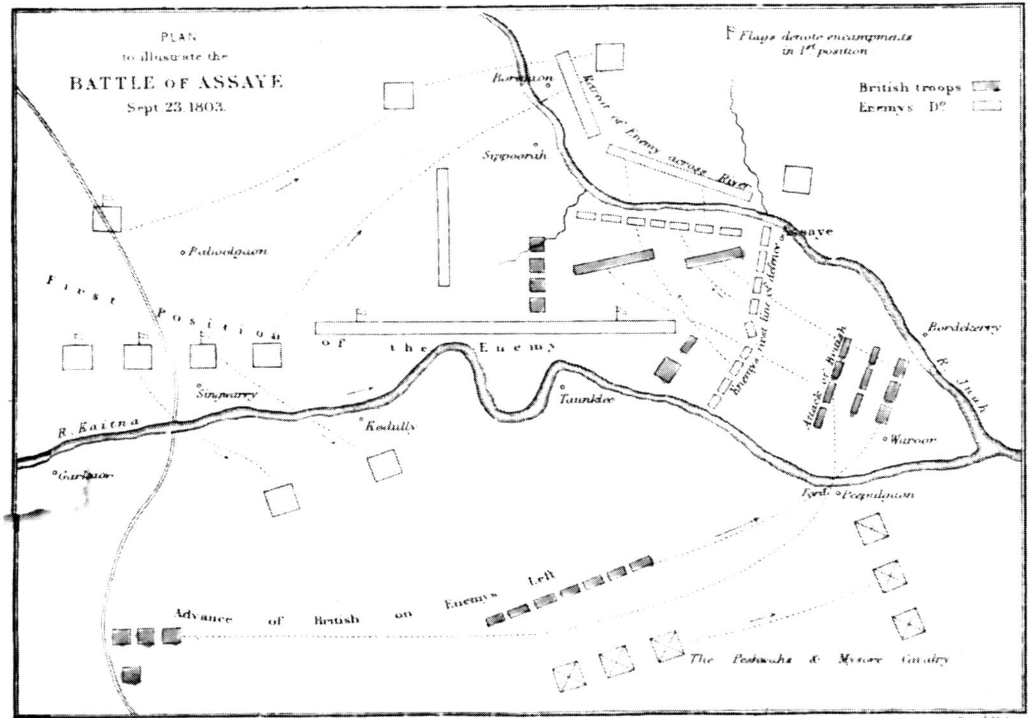

Edwd Weller

London, Longmans & Co

appeal to the confederate chiefs was rejected by them, and on the withdrawal of the envoys, on August 3, war was virtually declared. Lord Wellesley, it will not be doubted, had fully foreseen the contingency of war, and had made every preparation for it. In addition to the army in the Deccan, under General Wellesley, 8,000 men as a reserve were placed in the Southern Mahratta provinces, under General Stuart; a similar number in Guzerat, under Colonel Murray; in Hindostan, an army of 10,500 men, under General Lake; with a reserve force of 3,500 at Allahabad; and towards Cuttack, 5,000 men were prepared for the invasion of that province, held by Rughoojee Bhóslay of Berar. The whole amounted to upwards of 50,000 men, animated with the highest ardour, and in every respect complete in equipment. On no other occasion had the English displayed such force in the field, nor had they ever before encountered greater, because such efficient, adversaries.

War ensues.

Enumeration and positions of the British forces.

General Wellesley had with him an army of about 7,000 British troops, with which he opened the war by capturing the strong and important fort of Ahmednugger, on August 12, which formed a basis for his operations. Dowlut Ráo Sindia, to whom he was immediately opposed, had with him about 16,000 disciplined infantry, with a noble park of artillery and 20,000 cavalry, in addition to which were the more irregular troops of the Rajah of Berar. The capture of Ahmednugger was a severe blow to Sindia; but he advanced by ascending the Ajunta Ghát from Berar, on August 24, and took up a position at Jaulnah. Sindia's design seemed evidently to get in the rear of General Wellesley, and to plunder the Nizam's districts; but an advance made by General Wellesley from Aurungabad defeated this intention, and Sindia halted on the banks of the Kailnah river, between the villages of Assaye and Bokerdun. On the 23rd, General Wellesley found himself within six miles of Sindia's camp, and resolved, without waiting for Colonel Stevenson's junction with him, to attack the Mahratta army. He had not more than 4,500 men of all arms; but by sheer valour and hard fighting he won the most splendid victory that had ever been achieved in the field in India. Sindia's army was routed, with the loss of 98 pieces of cannon, and 12,000 men killed on the field; for the old battalions of De Boigne had fought desperately by their guns. On the other hand, General Wellesley's loss in killed and wounded exceeded a third of his whole force; but the combined Mahratta armies were irretrievably routed, and Sindia and Rughoojee Bhóslay had fled from the field early in the action, leaving their troops to their fate.

Ahmednugger captured.

Sindia advances from Berar.

Battle of Assaye.

Defeat and rout of Sindia's army.

On the 24th, Colonel Stevenson joined General Wellesley, and was immediately dispatched in pursuit of Sindia beyond the Tapty—a movement which, by October 21, resulted in the capture of the city of Boorhanpoor and the famous fortress of Aseergurh.

Pursuit of Sindia.

Boorhanpoor and Aseergurh captured.

Meanwhile, Sindia's possessions in Guzerat had been reduced, and Baróch, Pawángurh, and Champaneer captured; by September 17, Hindostan alone remained, and was the scene of a spirited campaign by General Lake. Sindia's forces were commanded by M. Perron, the successor of De Boigne, who had retired to Europe in 1796. They had not decreased in efficiency, and formed the best part of his army. In addition to his military command, M. Perron had been invested by Sindia with civil and political power over the whole of his northern territories, and during the events at Poona he had managed them with great ability. Now, however, local intrigue proved too strong for him, he was superseded in his civil office, and no doubt foreseeing the issue of the war with the British, he resigned Sindia's service, and retired to Calcutta, when the command of the disciplined troops devolved upon M. Louis Bourquin. General Lake found Sindia's forces, chiefly cavalry, encamped at Coel, near the fort of Allygurh, which was forthwith attacked and carried by storm, on August 29, by an extraordinary *coup de main*, on the almost impregnable gateways. This was followed up, on September 7, by an advance upon Dehly, where General Lake was met near the city by the Mahrattas, under M. Louis Bourquin, whom he defeated, after a bloody action, with the loss of his guns, and 3,000 killed and wounded, that of the British being proportionably severe. Dehly was then taken possession of, and the unfortunate sightless emperor found himself again under English protection. On October 10, Lord Lake, who had been joined by 5,000 horse, sent by the Ját Rajah of Bhurtpoor, defeated the enemy near Agra, taking 26 guns; and on the 18th, the celebrated imperial fortress capitulated, and the treasury, arsenal, and 162 pieces of cannon were captured. The last action of this campaign was fought at Laswaree, on November 1. Sindia's forces consisted of the battalions of Dudrenec, which had been sent up from the Deccan, joined to those of Bourquin. The engagement proved to be the most obstinate yet fought; the battalions of De Boigne in their last battle, though they lost 71 guns, covered themselves with glory, and for the most part died fighting to the last; but the British loss was proportionably severe in 824 killed and wounded.

Sindia's forces in Hindostan.

M. Perron resigns, and is succeeded by M. Bourquin.

Lake's first campaign.

Mahrattas defeated at Dehly.

Agra captured.

Victory of Laswaree.

In Cuttack, the resistance was comparatively feeble; and by October 10 Cuttack itself had fallen, and the capture of the fort of Barabuttee by storm, on October 14, completed the reduction of the province. The operations in Bundelkhund present no remarkable features. The Péshwah's possessions were occupied, and in consideration of the importance of their situation, they were retained under an engagement with him, by which the quota of troops he had contracted to supply was reduced in proportion to their value. The cession of territory of the value of twenty-six lacs of rupees per annum for the payment of the subsidiary force to be made in the Deccan, was also exchanged for the Péshwah's possessions in Bundelkhund. These, however, proved to be more nominal than real, and involved much subsequent difficulty.

Cuttack reduced.

Meanwhile, the movements in the Deccan and Berar had continued; but the details of them have comparatively little general interest. Rughoojee Bhóslay found that he had no chance of plundering the Nizam's districts, or of outmanœuvring General Wellesley, and turned towards his own dominions. In this movement he was followed by both corps of the British army: the capture of the great hill-fortresses of Narnalla and Gáwilgurh being a material object. Sindia, now thoroughly disheartened, sent an envoy for peace, and after the arrival of his proper credentials, a suspension of hostilities was granted, on November 22, by General Wellesley, on condition that Sindia's forces should move to the eastward: but the same terms could not be extended to the Rajah of Berar so long as his army was in the field. At this time Rughoojee Bhóslay's troops were encamped at Argaom, in West Berar, in order to cover Gáwilgurh and Narnalla. Some of the wreck of Sindia's infantry, with his own, and a park of artillery, were with them in this position, protected by a body of Sindia's cavalry stationed at a short distance. General Wellesley, as Sindia had not complied with the conditions of the armistice, determined to attack the whole; and, having been joined by Colonel Stevenson, advanced on November 28 and 29. At the close of a long march, on the afternoon of the 29th, intending to halt at Argaom, General Wellesley, on the arrival of the advanced guard, found himself in front of the army of the confederates. He immediately attacked them, and though a portion of their troops fought well, and a brilliant charge was made by Sindia's cavalry, they were defeated with severe loss in men and their guns. The capture of the stupendous mountain-fortress of Gáwilgurh followed—an operation of exceeding labour and skill, patiently and successfully achieved. On

Campaign in Berar.

Sindia proposes peace.

Battle of Argaom.

Gáwilgurh taken.

December 15, the outer or northern fort was breached, and the whole place stormed and captured; but the Rajpoot commander and his relatives were found to have put their families to death before they met the storming party by which they were killed.

Thus the last hope of the Mahratta confederates perished, and negotiations were now opened in earnest. The treaty with Rughoojee Bhósley, rajah of Berar, was first concluded on December 17. He was obliged to cede the province of Cuttack, the whole of Berar lying west of the Wurdah river, and to resign all claims on the Nizam. The negotiation for the treaty with Sindia was not so quickly accomplished, and as the principal aggressor and contriver of the confederacy, the terms insisted upon were more severe. Nor was it until he was assured that in case of a protraction of the war the whole of his dominions would be inevitably annexed by the governor-general, that he agreed to receive the conditions offered. The treaty was concluded at Sirjee Anjengaom on December 30, and by it he relinquished all his territory between the Jumna and Ganges called the Dooáb; all his districts in Rajpootana, except those between Jeypoor and Joudhpoor; all his possessions in the Deccan and Khandésh, except his private hereditary estates; and he resigned all claims upon the Nizam, the Péshwah, and the Gáikwar. There were also many other minor points, in regard to his own private estates in other localities and settlements with dependants, which need not be enumerated. He was offered a defensive alliance, which he accepted, on February 27, 1804, by a new article added at Boorhanpoor, and agreed to maintain a force of 6,000 infantry with artillery; but this portion of the treaty was never carried out.

Treaty with Rughoojee Bhóslay.

Treaty of Sirjee Anjengaom with Sindia; its provisions.

Thus concluded the Mahratta war of 1803. The whole of the operations, from the capture of Ahmednugger, on August 8 to 12, and that of Gáwilgurh on December 15, had occupied only four months and four days, and had been carried on simultaneously and with unvarying success in four quarters of India, separated from each other by many hundreds of miles, while the revenues of the provinces obtained amounted to nearly six millions sterling a year.

Conclusion of the first Mahratta war.

CHAPTER XII.

THE ADMINISTRATION OF THE MARQUESS WELLESLEY (*concluded*)—THE WAR WITH HOLKAR, AND SECOND ADMINISTRATION OF THE MARQUESS CORNWALLIS, FOLLOWED BY THAT OF SIR G. BARLOW, 1804 TO 1805.

THE great Nizam Ally had died at Hyderabad on August 6, 1803, and was succeeded by his eldest son, Sikunder Jáh. This event had no effect upon the result of the war, or the obligations of the subsidiary treaty; nor was the Nizam made answerable for the conduct of his district officers, who behaved traitorously, and were strongly suspected, and in many instances accused, of complicity with the enemy. The governor-general, notwithstanding, bestowed upon the Nizam the fine province of Berar lying west of the Wurdah river. Many other treaties of offensive and defensive alliance were concluded by General Lake, of which Bhurtpoor and the Játs, with several minor Rajpoot principalities, were rendered independent of Sindia and the Mahrattas. A subsidiary treaty, concluded with the Gáikwar, provided that five battalions of infantry should be received by him, and districts yielding twelve lacs of rupees were assigned for their payment. At this period, the Gáikwar's State was oppressed with debt, and the expenditure was far above the income; but, under the admirable management of Colonel Walker, the Resident, the turbulent local army, a great proportion of which were Arabs, was paid off and reduced, and the State affairs gradually recovered.

Death of Nizam Ally. Sikunder Jáh succeeds.

Other new treaties with native States.

Although the additional year of service requested by the Court of Directors and the Board of Control had expired, the Marquess Wellesley still remained in India, and the events recorded are among the most wonderful in the history of the country. In no portion of the political or military combinations had any weakness been displayed, or check appeared. Sindia's power was broken, that of the Rajah of Berar circumscribed, and the prestige of the capture of Dehly, and the protection of the aged emperor, belonged to the British, who, from Calcutta to Dehly, were now supreme. Holkar, however, remained; and it was evident that he could not be allowed to continue as he was, a nucleus for all the disbanded soldiery of the north-west, supporting them by indiscriminate plunder. He had already levied contribution in Sindia's territory

Effects of the Marquess Wellesley's policy.

Holkar's proceedings.

to a large extent, and, after his own violent fashion, devastated several of his provinces; and he was evidently watching an opportunity for further action. In the war with Sindia he took no part; and openly rejoiced at the complete humiliation of his rival.

His demands.

Early in 1804, he addressed demands to General Lake and General Wellesley, by letter and by his agents, for chouth, and in regard to certain districts in the Doośb, which he asserted had many years before belonged to his family; and they were made in such threatening terms, and with such arrogance, that it was impossible even to consider them. Holkar had indeed determined, as he expressed it, 'to fight Lake,' and to take the place of Sindia in Hindostan; and the governor-general was equally resolved to repress this fierce outbreak of predatory power.

Military movements against Holkar.

He therefore, on April 16, directed Generals Wellesley and Lake to attack Holkar's possessions. Owing to famine in the Deccan, General Wellesley was unable to move; but Colonel Murray advanced from Guzerat upon Indoor, and by General Lake's arrangements in the north, Holkar was soon driven south of the Chumbul river. Tonk Rámpoora was taken on May 16, after which the British army retired into cantonments, for the monsoon had commenced early.

Monson's injudicious advance.

Colonel Monson was, however, left in the field with a force of five Sepoy regiments and 2,000 horse, partly belonging to Sindia and partly to Jeypoor, as a corps of observation. Monson, wishing to form a junction with Colonel Murray, advanced into Holkar's territory without adequate caution, and without sufficient supplies for his camp. It was at the best a useless, and proved an unfortunate, movement. When he heard of Murray's retirement into position for the rains, he began to retreat himself on July 8, and Holkar followed him with his whole army.

Monson's disastrous retreat.

On the next three days the column was attacked during its march, and the surrender of the whole demanded. On the 12th, the force reached Kóta, where they had hoped to receive assistance in food, and, in any case, shelter; but the rajah refused both, and the retreat continued. The miserable hardships endured, the repeated attacks and the gallantry displayed by the whole force, are well described in General Monson's narrative of the event, and it was not till August 31 that the shattered remains of the troops reached Agra.

This defeat, as it was considered by Holkar, and by many of the native chiefs who were as yet neutral, excited him to fresh exertion.

Holkar continues the war.

At the head of 60,000 cavalry, 15,000 infantry, and 192 guns, he advanced to Muttra, whence the British force retreated, and he afterwards made an attempt to capture Dehly, which was gallantly and successfully defended by Colonel Ochterlony, from October 8 to the 14th, with a weak detachment of Sepoys under his command. No action of the war, indeed, deserves greater commendation than this very brave and skilful defence of an almost untenable position. Dehly was relieved on October 18 by General Lake; and Holkar, who avoided an action with him, retired into the Bhurtpore territory, where the rajah, doubtful, after Monson's retreat, of the English supremacy, had broken the treaty with General Lake, and leagued himself with Holkar. On his way, he burst into the Dooáb, burning villages, and plundering the people without mercy; indeed, since the outbreak of the war, Holkar's conduct towards all belonging to, or connected with, the English, had been shockingly cruel and vindictive. General Lake's pursuit of Holkar was persistent and effective; and on November 12, his forces, no longer able to pursue their march, were found to have taken up a very strong position at Deeg, with their right resting on the batteries of the fort. Here they were attacked by Major-General Fraser, on the 13th; who fell early in the action, which was conducted to the finish, with great bravery, by Colonel Monson. The enemy lost about 2,000 men and eighty-seven guns; and on the side of the British, 643 men were killed and wounded; but the victory was complete. General Lake meanwhile, with his cavalry, was pursuing Holkar's horse, which was moving eastwards with a vast celerity; but they were overtaken near Furrukabad, and routed with a loss of 3,000 men. Holkar fled towards Deeg to join the remains of his broken infantry, and General Lake undertook the siege of Deeg, which was commenced on December 13, and ended in the surrender of that important place, after the storm of the city and outworks, on the 23rd.

Defence of Dehly.

Holkar returns to Bhurtpore.

He is pursued by General Lake.

Battle of Deeg.

The fort of Deeg captured.

For the present Holkar escaped; and General Lake, instead of pursuing him, which would have been the better policy, commenced the siege of Bhurtpore, and with very inefficient means. Accustomed to the capture of fortresses by *coup de main*, and comparatively feeble resistance, he was not prepared, either for the real strength of Bhurtpore, or for the obstinate valour displayed in its defence. Holkar had thrown the whole of his remaining infantry into the fort, and the Játs themselves were brave soldiers. During the progress of the siege, Ameer Khan, on the part of Holkar, made efforts for its relief, but in vain. The Bombay divisions under Major-General Jones joined General Lake's army on February 10, 1805; and a previous assault having failed, another was made on the 20th, when two European regiments, one being the hitherto invincible 76th, the

First siege of Bhurtpore.

victors in many a desperate fight, refused to follow their officers; but the 12th Bengal Native Infantry took their place, and covered themselves with glory. The assault, however, failed; but was renewed next day by the 75th and 76th, though without result, and with terrible loss. Holkar continued to hover around the fort with his cavalry, and to endeavour to intercept convoys; but on one occasion he was routed by Lord Lake, losing a thousand men; and about the same time a detachment of his infantry, 3,000 strong, was attacked and defeated with some loss, by Captain Royal. The Rajah of Bhurtpore, finding no hope from Holkar's efforts, now made overtures for peace, which were accepted. He paid twenty lacs of rupees, and renounced the advantages of his former treaty with General Lake. This result, it must be confessed, was somewhat humiliating, for Bhurtpore remained unshaken; and till its final capture, held the proud distinction of being the only fortress of India which had defied the British arms; but the pursuit of Holkar was an imperative necessity, and it had become doubtful whether he would not be joined by Sindia. Two of Sindia's officers had already joined Holkar; his father-in-law, Ghátgay, who continued to possess much influence over him, urged him to do the same, and he had attacked and plundered Mr. Jenkins, the acting Resident, retaining him prisoner in his camp. This attitude was promptly checked by the advance of General Martindell's force from Bundelkhund, and Sindia's tone now moderated; but he was joined soon after by Holkar himself, and General, now Lord, Lake advanced upon them with his whole army. They did not wait to meet him; but retired upon Kotah, and afterwards to Ajmere, and as the monsoon was commencing, the British troops took up positions for the season.

Unsuccessful attack on the breach.

The Rajah of Bhurtpore sues for peace.

Movements of Holkar and Sindia.

So long as the Marquess Wellesley's combinations had been successful, his authority had not been interfered with; but on the first sign of difficulty, a strong opposition was organised against him in England; the Marquess Cornwallis was solicited to resume the office of governor-general, and he reached Calcutta on July 30. There can be no doubt that by this unfortunate act the war was ultimately protracted, and Lord Wellesley's plans for peace frustrated. He had become disposed to make some cessions to Sindia on which that chieftain had set his heart; and there is no question that he would have prevailed, as Sindia had no real desire for a renewal of war. Ghátgay had been set aside by Holkar, and Sindia was already experiencing in some degree what would have inevitably been his fate, had he irrevocably linked his destinies

Recal of the Marquess Wellesley.

Lord Cornwallis succeeds.

with those of his rival. But the chances of bringing his great policy to a triumphant conclusion were denied Lord Wellesley, and he returned to England to find his conduct condemned in the Court of Proprietors, by 928 to 195. It was only after a period of nearly thirty years that the verdict was reversed, by a record of his eminent services, 'in upholding the interest and honour of the British empire.' His statue was placed in the India House, and a grant of 20,000*l.* made to him.

Lord Wellesley's policy condemned in England,

but subsequently approved.

Lord Cornwallis arrived in India in very feeble health, and at the most trying period of the year; and he survived only till October 5, 1805. He was proceeding to the upper provinces, in order to carry out the policy which he had intimated to Lord Lake, and died at Ghazeepoor at the age of sixty-seven. His second administration had continued little more than two months. He had been sent to India to repress what was called the frenzy of conquest, which it was said had possessed not only Lord Wellesley, but all the company's servants in India; and as he thoroughly concurred in this policy, he made preparations to carry it out. On September 19, he wrote an elaborate despatch on the subject to Lord Lake. Sindia was to be conciliated by the restoration of Gohud and Gwalior. The possession of Dehly was deemed unfortunate; and the city should be given up to Sindia, the emperor being removed to Calcutta or some other city near it. The territory acquired west of the Jumna should also be relinquished. On the other hand, should Holkar prove reasonable, all his family dominions were to be restored to him. Lake was then in active negotiation with Sindia, and withheld communication of his instructions until their conclusion. He wrote a spirited remonstrance to Lord Cornwallis, but he had died before it reached him. Holkar, unable to restrain himself, and seeing he had little hope from Sindia, set out for the Punjâb at the head of about 15,000 men. He evaded detachments sent to intercept him; but Lord Lake was in his rear, and pursued him with five regiments of cavalry and four of infantry into the Punjâb. Sir George Barlow, the senior member of Council, had succeeded the Marquess Cornwallis; but this did not interfere with the conclusion of the treaty with Sindia, which was effected on November 22; and the particulars need not be enumerated, as, together with the confirmation of the treaty of Surjee Anjengaom, all minor subjects of dispute were amicably settled. Holkar had perhaps hoped for assistance from the Sikhs, and to excite their chief, Runjeet Singh, against the British Government; but they were immovable, only

Death of Lord Cornwallis.

Lord Cornwallis's project for peace.

Holkar invades the Punjâb.

Sir George Barlow succeeds Lord Cornwallis.

professing their willingness to mediate between him and Lord Lake, who had advanced to Amritsur; and Holkar, finding his own dominions closed against him, and being totally helpless, now sued for terms. Lord Lake had already in his possession Lord Cornwallis's instructions, and had no authority for modifying them, as Sir George Barlow had adopted the same policy. Holkar, therefore, obtained much easier terms than he expected, or indeed deserved. His own dominions were restored and secured to him, but he had to renounce all right to Boondee and Rampoor, and to accept the Chumbul as his northern boundary. The treaty was afterwards modified by Sir George Barlow, who restored Rampoor to Holkar, and in his declared policy of non-interference, left the Rajah of Boondee to his fate. Thus, for a period, the transactions with the Mahratta States came to a close. Each was left in possession of his own proper dominions, a strictly non-interferent policy had begun, and it remained with their several rulers to maintain this policy by their own good faith and moderation to the British Government, and to each other.

Holkar sues for peace.

Treaty of peace with Holkar.

CHAPTER XIII.

THE ADMINISTRATION OF SIR GEORGE BARLOW (*concluded*)—THE APPOINTMENT OF LORD MINTO, 1805 TO 1809.

THE policy of the Marquess Wellesley, and the tenor of all his acts, were directed as well to the preservation of the territories of the native powers of India as to that of general peace and amity to themselves. Accustomed, as the narrative of history shows, to make and unmake treaties as they pleased, to plunder each others' dominions on any or no provocation, they would be bound to one common superior power to observe mutual good faith. His policy was the very reverse of aggressive; and while a general peace on a sound footing was established, all native powers were left free and independent in the administration of their dominions, and only ensured condign punishment in the event of any deliberate breach of faith. When it is considered how deeply the peace of India affected the existence of millions of its people; how terribly the whole country had suffered, and was still enduring the ravages of war, which had hardly ceased for nearly a hundred years, it seems strange now, that so great and so humane a policy as Lord Wellesley's was not only unrecognised by the ministry of England, but directly

Character of Lord Wellesley's policy.

opposed, and another substituted, which, in the words of Sir George Barlow, allowed the national interests of England in India to rest upon 'the certain operation of contending and circumscribed interests among the States, whose independence will admit of their individual views of rapine, encroachment, and ambition.' Native States were, therefore, to be left to themselves, to fight with and plunder each other as they pleased; and all that would remain to the English was, that they should be passive witnesses of these conflicts so long as they were not attacked.

Its contrast with the policy adopted.

Nor was it to future contingencies alone that the new policy was directed. Had it been possible, every subsidiary alliance would have been cancelled, and the native powers of India left to the chances of lawless anarchy. Happily, however, this detestable course was impossible; and as it were as a premonitory example, Holkar soon displayed the effects of the liberty which the treaty had accorded to him As Lord Lake was obliged to return quickly from the Punjâb, he left Holkar to follow, who deliberately plundered the country as far as Jeypoor, where he extorted 18 lacs—180,000*l.*—from the rajah. The agents of this unfortunate prince in vain appealed to Lord Lake, and even upbraided him with inaction and want of faith: but his hands were now tied, and being unable to produce any effect on the governor-general, he resigned his political functions. Holkar next fell upon the Rajah of Boondee, who had been conspicuous for his loyalty to the English, and ravaged his country without any interference or remonstrance on the part of the governor-general. He put his own nephew Khundy Ráo and his brother Khassee Ráo to death; and it is impossible to conjecture to what extent his violent conduct might not have extended—for he continued to cast cannon, and increase his military preparations—when, partly from habitual intemperance, and partly from constitutional tendency, he became afflicted with furious mania, and was placed under restraint, in which condition he continued till he died, on October 20, 1811.

Holkar's extortion from Jeypoor

and Boondee.

Holkar becomes insane, and dies.

Although Malwah and Rajpootana, under the effect of this non-interferent policy, continued the arena for the struggles of Ameer Khan, Sindia, the Rajpoot chieftains, and many petty chiefs, by whom the country was desolated, yet it is probable that the affairs of Hyderabad were the first direct means of convincing Sir George Barlow of its inadvisability. The Nizam considered himself, like others, at liberty to prosecute new plans; and opened communications with Sindia, Holkar, and the Péshwah, the object of which, however,

Intrigues at Hyderabad.

did not appear certain, except a general desire to be rid of English control. This feeble attempt at the establishment of a new league was, however, instantly repressed by the governor-general. Meer Allum, the minister, who had been obliged to take refuge at the British Residency, was re-established in his authority, when Rajah Mohiput Rám, under whose advice the hostile combination had been planned, commenced plundering the country, but was quickly subdued. As peace had now ensued, Sir George Barlow had leisure to apply himself to the financial concerns of the State, and the reduction of expenditure soon placed them on an easy footing. The local administration of the new provinces of Cuttack, Bundelkhund and the Dooáb, was also well established, the previous experience of the governor-general giving him considerable advantage in questions of executive detail.

Finance.

The family of Tippoo Sooltan had, it will be remembered, been located in the fortress of Vellore, with a strong garrison of part of a European and two whole native regiments. On July 10, 1806, the native regiments mutinied; and at three in the morning, when the Europeans were asleep, attacked them, pouring volley after volley into their barrack-rooms, and shooting the officers as they came out of their houses. News of this rising was taken to Arcot, nine miles distant, and Colonel Gillespie, of the 19th Dragoons, at the head of a squadron and two field-guns, galloped to Vellore, blew open the gate, and with the assistance of the survivors of the 69th, the mutineers were soon shot down, sabred or captured—but they had killed 82 and wounded 91 of the 69th, and killed 13 officers. This movement, though it was traced to other causes—of new regulations regarding dress and caps—was not supposed to be without the complicity of the Mysore family, whose standard was hoisted by the mutineers, and they were removed to Calcutta. Subsequent inquiry proved that the movement had been an essentially military one, as the whole of the Madras native army was, at the time, disgusted by vexatious interference with established practices. On Lord W. Bentinck, then governor of Madras, however, the chief consequences fell, for he was recalled from his administration; but unjustly, for no time had been allowed him for explanation of the circumstances which had in reality led to the mutiny. No rising or other demonstration in favour of the Mysore family followed, and the apprehensions which had existed, particularly in England, in regard to general disaffection, subsided gradually. Sir George Barlow was transferred from Bengal to the government of Madras, in place of Lord W. Bentinck, and Lord Minto, who had been President of the Board of Control, arrived in Calcutta in July 1807.

Mutiny at Vellore.

Causes of the mutiny.

Sir George Barlow transferred to Madras.

Lord Minto arrives as governor-general.

Coinciding with the policy of his predecessors Lord Cornwallis and Sir G. Barlow, Lord Minto found India at peace, with the exception of Bundelkhund, the petty chiefs of which, continuing their hereditary lawless opposition to any superior government, had proved themselves as intractable as in the times of the Moghul emperors. Lord Lake, indeed, if his actions had been unfettered, would speedily have disposed of them, by the reduction of their strongholds; but Sir George Barlow refusing to second him, had temporized with the difficulty, and their resistance, accompanied with rapine and plunder, continued to be maintained. Lord Minto, however, at once reversed this policy, and declared that the British Government had no resource but to interfere for the 'suppression of intestine disorder.' All the great fortresses were therefore captured in succession by General Martindell, the most important operation being the reduction of Kalinjer, always supposed to be impregnable; and the banditti which had desolated the province, deprived of shelter and encouragement, were gradually suppressed.

Disorders in Bundelkhund,

which are suppressed.

In the year 1807, an embassy from the Emperor Napoleon to Persia, under General Gardanne, excited the apprehensions of the Governments at home and in India; and Lord Minto began to renew negotiations with the powers on the north-western frontier, the nearest to India being that of the Sikhs, now consolidated under Runjeet Singh. The Afghans, to whom the Punjáb had belonged, were broken into parties after the death of Ahmed Shah Dooránee; and no longer able to maintain themselves against the Sikhs, had evacuated the province as far as the Indus, while the Sikhs had gradually established a federation of their principal clans. This, at first, was in many respects weak and disunited. Churut Singh, the grandfather of Runjeet, was the first to take advantage of intestine disagreements, and his son Máha Singh followed his example with greater success; but it was not till Runjeet Singh, by his own ability and bravery, had overcome all opposition, that the confederacy attained its real strength. There were other Sikh States lying east of the Sutlej river, whose rulers had kept aloof from the Sikh confederation, and refused allegiance to Runjeet Singh. They had been obliged to submit to Sindia, but were now practically independent, and desired the protection of the British Government, with whom the chief of them had maintained friendly relations. Runjeet Singh, however, desired to extend his dominions to the Jumna river; and taking advantage of a quarrel between the Rajahs of Putialla and Nabha, in which the latter called for his interposition, crossed

The Sikhs gain the Punjáb.

Confederacy under Runjeet Singh.

Sikh States east of the Sutlej remain independent.

the Sutlej in 1807, and laid contributions upon the province of Sirhind.

They claim the protection of the British Government.

Fearing a repetition of the visit, and being unable to oppose an invasion if it were made, the chiefs sent agents to Dehly in 1808, imploring the protection of the British Government. On the other hand, Runjeet Singh asserted his authority over the whole of these Sikh States. It became, therefore, a question, the solution of which admitted of no delay, whether these Sikh States should be supported, and the river Sutlej declared the boundary between the British and the Sikhs, or whether Runjeet Singh should be allowed to advance to the Jumna. Under the apprehensions of French influence, combined with a real desire to protect States who were unmistakably friendly, Lord Minto set aside the non-interference policy, and determined to protect Sirhind. To this end, he dispatched a young Bengal civilian, Mr. Metcalfe, already distinguished for his political ability and firmness, as envoy to Runjeet Singh: preparing at the same time to maintain his demand by force of arms, should negotiation prove unavailing. Mr. Metcalfe's mission was conducted with profound ability and a patient courage and determination, which, even under threats and insults, never failed him; and on April 25, 1809, a treaty with Runjeet Singh was concluded at Amritsur, not however before General Ochterlony had advanced with an army to the banks of the Sutlej, and declared the chiefs of Sirhind to be under the protection of the British Government. It is due to the memory of Runjeet Singh, to state that this treaty was observed by him with absolute fidelity as long as he lived: and thus the British frontier was extended to Loodhiana, on the banks of the Sutlej, where a small force was stationed, with the full concurrence of all concerned.

and their request is granted.

Mr. Metcalfe's mission to Runjeet Singh.

Treaty of Amritsur.

The Sutlej becomes the frontier.

Embassy to Kabool under Mr. Elphinstone.

About the same time, an embassy under the Hon. Mountstuart Elphinstone was sent to the Afghan king, Shah Soojah, who resided at Peshâwur, also directed against the admission of French influence. The object was not well understood by the Afghan king, who was at the time helpless, in consequence of his brother's rebellion; and he applied for assistance in men or money, to recover Kabool and Kandahar, which had been wrested from him. This, however, was not granted by Lord Minto, though advised by Mr. Elphinstone, to the extent of ten lacs of rupees, and the embassy was withdrawn; its proceedings, however, proved most valuable, in the interesting record of them written by the young envoy, and in his accounts of a people, and their country, then comparatively unknown.

The embassy to Persia, where French influence was for the time in the ascendant, was very nearly the cause of a war with that power, which, in the sequel, was happily averted. Sir Harford Jones was appointed envoy by the ministry and the Court of Directors; but Lord Minto desired an embassy of his own, and dispatched Colonel Malcolm, who proceeded as far as Shiráz, where he was directed by the king to place himself in communication with his son. At this treatment Colonel Malcolm took offence and returned to Calcutta, advising a demonstration in force against Kurrack, an island in the Persian Gulf. In this view Lord Minto concurred, and the expedition was even determined upon; but Sir Harford Jones, who had proceeded to Persia from Bombay before Lord Minto had known of Colonel Malcolm's retirement, contrived to effect the object of the mission; the French alliance was abandoned by treaty, which was confirmed by Lord Minto, and in order to establish direct friendly relations with the government of India, Colonel Malcolm was dispatched again, with good effect, in 1809, and the king was reconciled as much by his ready wit as by the general tenor of the negotiations. Both ambassadors were, however, superseded in 1810, by the appointment, by the crown, of Sir Gore Ouseley, who continued to reside at the Persian court as permanent envoy.

Malcolm's embassy to Persia.

CHAPTER XIV.

THE ADMINISTRATION OF LORD MINTO (*concluded*), 1809 TO 1813.

As if it had been necessary to prove, by practical illustration, the mischiefs which would arise out of a strictly non-interferent policy, the case of Ameer Khan occurred in 1809. This chieftain had been an ally of Jeswunt Ráo Holkar in his predatory operations; and had taken an active part, now on one side and now on the other, in the wars and revolutions of Northern India. The Patáns, the descendants of the Afghan soldiers of the former empire, formed a numerous class in the country; and were not as yet in any way changed in character, being fierce, restless, and unwilling to adopt cultivation or other means of peaceful employment. Of them, Ameer Khan was recognised as the head: and he supported a large body of them from

Ameer Khan's predatory movements.

the revenues of districts which he had wrested from weaker powers than himself. He had also collected around him a large body of irregular horsemen, who, subsisting upon plunder alone, had gradually increased with every Mahratta army, and were called Pindhárees. In 1809, no longer able to support his increasing followers, Ameer Khan left Rajpootana at the head of 40,000 horse and 24,000 Pindhárees, and on pretence of a claim on the Rajah of Nagpoor for jewels said to have been deposited with him by Holkar, crossed the Nerbudda, and attacked his territory.

He attacks the Rajah of Nagpoor.

According to the strict letter of the non-interferent policy, Lord Minto would have had no pretence for noticing Ameer Khan so long as his ravages were confined to native States; but happily the governor-general had become sensible of the evils which would accompany these outrages: and without application from the Rajah of Berar, forces were ordered into the field, when Ameer Khan was directed to withdraw into his own territory. It was in vain that he remonstrated, and even pleaded the provisions of the treaty with Holkar, on whose behalf he professed himself to be acting: Lord Minto was resolved to repress the first efforts of predatory warfare in Central India, and the British forces continued to advance. It is only to be regretted that such intentions were not fully carried out, and that one severe example was not made. Ameer Khan was checked, but not suppressed. He retired upon Indoor, and his territories, which had been occupied, were restored to him; but no diminution of his forces was required, and in the sequel it will be admitted, with what bad effects such precaution, at least, had been overlooked. Lord Minto, in truth, was still afraid of the non-interferent edict of the Court of Directors: and yet it is curious to observe in the history of this transaction, that he was actually blamed by the court for the very moderation to which he had considered himself constrained.

Change in Lord Minto's policy.

Forces sent against Ameer Khan,

who is forced to retire.

In the year 1809 vigorous proceedings for the suppression of piracy were undertaken in India, and in the Persian Gulf. The pirates of the western coasts, issuing from the small ports of the Kolapoor and Sawuntwurree States, still preyed upon coasting vessels; the ports themselves were, therefore, occupied. In the Persian Gulf, the pirate stronghold of Rás-el-Khyma was attacked and captured, with several other places. The fleets, as they actually proved to be, of piratical vessels, were invariably burned, and though the Arabs defended themselves with great desperation, they were everywhere defeated.

Suppression of piracy.

In the same year all the Portuguese settlements in India were held by British detachments, in consequence of the occupation of Portugal by Napoleon; and a force was dispatched to Macáo, in China—the first occasion of British troops being employed in that country—for the same purpose. No resistance was made by the governor of Macáo, but the Viceroy of Canton protested against the location in any part of the country of a foreign force, and refused to allow trade to continue. The troops were therefore withdrawn, and the former good understanding re-established.

Occupation of Portuguese possessions.

On November 30, 1810, the important island of Mauritius was surrendered to the British Government. Lord Minto had fitted out this expedition with great care and efficiency. 6,300 European infantry, 2,000 seamen and marines, and 3,000 Sepoys, backed by one ship of the line and thirteen frigates, formed an overwhelming force, to which the French governor submitted without resistance. This measure had become imperative. Mauritius was the great French naval station in the Indian seas, and the effects of the depredations on Indian commerce by its frigates and privateers had become very serious indeed. In one year the company had lost six fine ships, valued at half a million sterling.

Expedition against the Mauritius.

Meanwhile, the administration of Sir George Barlow at Madras had been neither tranquil nor easy. In 1808, the payment of the subsidy by the Rajah of Travancore had fallen into arrears, and the Resident, Colonel Macaulay, attributing the neglect to the conduct of the rajah's minister, Vailoo Tumbee, requested his removal from office. This the minister resented, and resisted by actual insurrection. Colonel Macaulay was attacked in his house, and escaped with difficulty; and Colonel Chalmers, who commanded in Quilon, had not sufficient force to take the field against the rebels. On the arrival, however, of Colonel Picton, with H.M.'s 12th regiment, the minister's forces, though 30,000 strong, with eighteen guns, were resolutely attacked on January 15, 1809, and defeated with great loss. Troops were now poured into Travancore, and Vailoo Tumbee, whose followers had deserted him, was found dying of self-inflicted wounds in a pagoda where he had taken refuge. His insurrection had been marked by savage cruelty in the murder of twelve men of H.M.'s 12th regiment, who had fallen into his hands, and of Surgeon Hume, from whom he had previously received medical services; and he had put to death 2,000 native Christians in cold blood on account of their religion. The relations of the States of Travancore and Cochin continued, however, to be unsatisfactory. Their subsidies were irregularly paid, and the internal administration of both was unsound and inefficient.

Events at Madras.

Insurrection of Vailoo Tumbee. Travancore.

By the treaty of 1805, the British Government was authorised, in the event of irregularity, to assume the direct management of the local administrations, and this measure was carried out, as it already existed in the case of Tanjore.

Discontent of the Madras officers.

In the year 1809, the retrenchments in the military service, as had previously been the case in Bengal, excited much and deeply laid discontent among the European officers of the Madras army, and to a great extent they were sympathised with, if not actually encouraged, by General Macdowall, the commander-in-chief, who had his own special grievance in having been denied a seat in Council by the Court of Directors. He resigned his office, and embarked for England in 1809; but the vessel he had sailed in foundered at sea. He had left, however, abundant seeds of discord. Colonel Munro, quartermaster-general of the army, had been directed to report upon the contract of tents, which was lucrative to officers in command of regiments, and had been hitherto, like most others, much abused. Colonel Munro's report offended the officers of the army generally, and also General Macdowall, who placed him under arrest, for the purpose of being tried by court-martial; but he was released by the Government, and the commander-in-chief retorted, in an intemperate general order, which was promulgated to the army, in their official capacity, by Colonel Cuppage and Major Boles, the adjutant and deputy-adjutant-general. Colonel Cuppage sailed for England, but perished at sea. Major Boles remained, but was deprived of his appointment. His cause was now taken up by the whole of the European officers of the army, and those of several stations were in actual mutiny, which in several instances proceeded to outbreaks; the officers of the Hyderabad, Jaulnah, and Masulipatam forces had even determined to march their troops upon Madras. Colonel Malcolm was dispatched to Masulipatam to endeavour to restore order; but he failed, and reported that submission by Government would be the best measure. Sir George Barlow, however, was not to be intimidated. He satisfied the native officers and Sepoys, and they remained faithful. The only actual outbreak which occurred was at Seringapatam, where the European officers of the garrison shut the gates of the fort and cannonaded the detachment of royal troops sent against them; but they eventually submitted, as did all the other stations and garrisons, and the full authority of Government was confirmed by their penitential letter. Lord Minto, alarmed by the crisis, had proceeded to Madras in September 1809; but it was already past. Some of the ringleaders were punished by being cashiered, and

Case of Colonel Munro and of Major Boles.

Mutinous proceedings.

Sir George Barlow's measures.

The mutinous officers submit.

sixteen by dismissal, and the whole proceeding was closed by the recal of Sir George Barlow, who, though he had displayed equal firmness with Clive on a similar occasion—a merit which was fully accorded to him—had undoubtedly given provocation to the army in his conduct to Major Boles, and otherwise, before the discontent commenced.

Sir George Barlow is recalled.

As Holland had become a portion of the French empire, it was resolved to reduce the Dutch possessions in the East; and in 1810, Amboyna was captured, with Ternate and Banda; but the operations against Java, which had been reinforced from Europe, required a larger force than had hitherto been employed. As soon, therefore, as the Mauritius expedition was at liberty, it was directed by Lord Minto against the island. The troops, about 13,000 strong, European and native, assembled at Malacca on June 1, 1811, under the command of Sir Samuel Achmuty, and were accompanied by the governor-general himself, though only as a volunteer. The French army, European and native, in Java, amounted to 17,000 men. The English forces reached Batavia on August 4, and the city submitted on the 7th; but the main body of the French army had taken up a very strong position at Cornelis, which had been strengthened by field-works thrown up by General Jansaen and was believed impregnable. After several days' operations, the flank of the position was turned by a splendid attack made by General Gillespie, of Vellore celebrity, and by a simultaneous charge in front, the whole position was carried, and the enemy pursued for many miles; but the loss on both sides had been very severe. Eighty-five British officers and about 900 men were killed and wounded, and the French slain on the field were computed at 1,500; 6,000 soldiers were captured, with nearly 300 pieces of cannon. General Jansaen retired into the eastern part of the island; but was ultimately obliged to capitulate, and the Sooltan of Joje Kurta, who had assembled an army, and held his capital with 17,000 men, was attacked by General Gillespie, who carried the place by storm, capturing 100 guns with which the forts were manned, and inflicted some loss upon the sooltan's army. Java was now subdued, and the people submitted easily to their conquerors. General Gillespie was left in command of the army, and the administration was confided to Mr., afterwards Sir, Stamford Raffles, who justified the appointment by his ability in the management of his new and peculiar duties. The Court of Directors had indeed ordered the abandonment of the island, should it be captured; but in deliberately disobeying this order, the governor-general acted with wisdom

Action against the Dutch possessions.

Expedition against Java

accompanied by the governor-general.

Capture of Cornelis.

Java subdued.

and true humanity; and it is difficult to realise the heartless policy which had influenced the court in dictating the dispatch.

First measures against the Pindhárees.

When Lord Minto returned to Calcutta, he found it necessary to take measures against the Pindhárees, who, no longer able to follow native armies, had commenced indiscriminate plunder; and it is necessary to sketch briefly the antecedents of the principal leaders. In 1808, two persons, Hurrun and Burrun, who had been attached to Sindia, were employed by the Rajah of Nagpoor, to ravage the territories of the Nawáb of Bhopál, with whom he was at war; and the mischief they had created was incalculable. On their return to Nagpoor, the rajah, as was commonly the case, imprisoned Burrun, and extorted from him all he could of the plunder. Hurrun escaped, but died; and his two sons, Wasil Mahomed and Dost Mahomed, continued their father's profession and authority. The leadership of Burrun's band was conferred by the family and dependents upon Cheetoo, who had already attracted the notice of Dowlut Ráo Sindia, from whom he had received an estate and its appanage. These three men eventually became the most daring leaders of the whole of the Pindhárees of Central and Northern India; but there was still a fourth, Kureem Khan, a Patán, who was perhaps the most celebrated of all. Sindia, from his irrepressibly lawless disposition to plunder, and for outrages in his own territory, had at one time imprisoned Kureem Khan; but he eventually released him on payment of a heavy fine. Kureem now rose higher than before; and for a time was joined by Cheetoo; and he became so mischievous, that he was again imprisoned at Indore.

The Pindháree chiefs.

Depredations of the Pindhárees.

It is impossible to follow the depredations of the Pindhárees for four years, 1807 to 1811-12, in Central India, which were confined to native territories; but in 1812, emboldened by success, Dost Mahomed swept through Bundelkhund, plundering unresisted as far as Gya, and escaped free. Lord Minto might well now ask the Court of Directors, whose detestably selfish policy he was carrying out in only too obedient a spirit, whether he could longer observe a strict neutrality amidst these scenes of disorder and outrage, 'or refuse to listen to the calls of suffering humanity, and interfere to protect weak native States who called upon us for assistance.' For several years in succession, the Pindhárees had roamed over Central India, Rajpootana, Berar, and the Nizam's dominions, increasing in numbers, strength, and daring, year by year, and inflicting torture, misery, and desolation, on every province they mercilessly plundered. These acts had been correctly known in England; but not a line was written, or a

The non-interferent policy prevents their suppression.

soldier moved to prevent them. It cannot be doubted that had Lord Minto been free to act, they would have been summarily checked and suppressed. Now, indeed, the 'company' were touched to the quick by the invasion of one of their own provinces; but till the reply from England arrived, Lord Minto was as little a free agent as ever.

Character of Lord Minto's administration.

In other respects his administration was just, and, as far as his powers extended, comprehensive; and he was thoroughly respected by the native princes and people of India. In his civil administration, he was at once liberal and practical, and the measures applied for the suppression of dacoity, the normal crime of Bengal, were to a great extent effective; but the police administration still continued inefficient, and in many respects scandalous and oppressive to the people. He took much interest in the maintenance of native literature; but it is strange that at the same time he was neutralising, as far as possible, the efforts of Christian missionaries, and preventing their attempts to spread true knowledge among the people. It may be questionable whether he really approved of the orders he received from the Court of Directors on this subject, which, like those of the non-interference policy, he had not sufficient determination to set aside; and it still required many years of experience to induce the executive Government to manifest to the people of India that the English were neither ashamed of their religion, nor the promulgation of the knowledge they possessed. Lord Minto's financial administration had been very creditable. If he had not succeeded in reducing the debt, he had at least been able to pay off old loans raised at twelve per cent. per year, by others raised at six; which showed a healthier state of public credit than had previously existed, and carried with it a proportional diminution of expenditure. Before he left India, at the close of 1813, he was impressed with an opinion that there was not a cloud to dim the political atmosphere, except the Pindhárees, in regard to whose suppression he wrote fully and earnestly. As the reward of his eminent services he was created Earl Minto, a dignity which he did not long enjoy, as he died the year after his arrival in England. Earl Minto was succeeded as governor-general by the Earl of Moira, who had been nominated to the office nearly two years before, but whose departure had been delayed.

Lord Minto leaves India.

He is succeeded by the Earl of Moira.

BOOK VII.

CHAPTER I.

THE ADMINISTRATION OF THE MARQUESS OF HASTINGS, 1813 TO 1816—THE GOORKHA WAR.

Condition of the native States.

WHEN Lord Minto left Calcutta, political events had not been so tranquil as before, in all respects: and had he remained he would have had the several questions to deal with that speedily occupied the attention of Lord Moira, who wrote there were no less than seven of a pressing character, which he found he had to settle. The fact was at last proved, that the non-interferent policy had been misunderstood by the native powers: and in some instances they had become overbearing and intractable. In Central India, matters continued in the same state as before; but the armed classes of the country were augmenting the ranks of Sindia, Holkar, Ameer Khan, and the Pindhárees; and every petty chieftain was supporting levies as well for his own protection, as to strike in whenever a general *mêlée* should commence. Lord Moira was a man of mature age and experience, he had taken part against Lord Wellesley's policy in England, and had belonged ostensibly to the non-interference school of Eastern politicians; but on his arrival in India, affairs which admitted of no delay, and which had arisen out of the previous inaction of the English authorities, were early forced upon his attention, and gave that tone of decision to his political acts which continued, with such eventful results, throughout his administration.

Relations with Nipál.

Among the last political questions with which Lord Minto had been occupied before he left India, was that of relations with the Goorkha State of Nipál, whose dominions consisted of a broad fertile valley lying between the lower, or southern, range of the Himalayas and the northern. The frontier on the British side extended nearly from Dehly to

Bengal, and had never been properly defined. The Goorkha State had been established by an invasion of the valley, in the fourteenth century, by Rajpoots, who had gradually conquered the former Tibetan possessors; and of them, one family had gradually extended its authority over all. The inhabitants had become for the most part converts to Brahminical Hindooism; they were divided into classes, and of these, the military was brave and reliant. While they defended their own territory to the south, the Goorkhas had attempted conquests in China; but had been driven back, and forced to pay tribute. Foiled in their attempts northwards, they had made gradual encroachments upon the country lying south of their mountains, the whole of the northern frontier of Oudh became insecure, and they finally demanded and seized two districts of that province, Bootwul and Seoráj.

Antecedents of the Goorkhas.

Lord Minto's negotiations with the Goorkha court had been abortive, and he had been obliged to threaten the re-occupation of these districts by force of arms; but no reply had been received to his demand. The governor-general, therefore, directed immediate action upon the question, and the town of Bootwul was occupied by the police. It now became a question of peace or war among the Nipálese, and many of their Council declared for peace; but the majority were for war, which was entered upon with great enthusiasm. The prospect of driving back the 'cowards who had failed to take Bhurtpoor,' with the certainty of unlimited plunder, were temptations too strong to be resisted; but their whole army did not exceed 12,000 men, and they had no guns. On May 29, 1814, they attacked the police at Bootwul, and murdered the native officer and eighteen of his men in cold blood. This cruel act admitted of no hesitating policy. Lord Moira was then travelling in the upper provinces, and had visited Lukhnow, where his honourable and dignified treatment of the Nawáb so deeply impressed that prince, that he offered a loan of 1,000,000*l.* sterling for the war, which was accepted; and though more than half was unfortunately applied by the Council of Calcutta, in the absence of Lord Moira, to the liquidation of an old loan, the balance enabled him to enter upon vigorous proceedings. On the west of the Goorkha frontier, General Ochterlony took post with 6,000 men. General Gillespie having arrived from Java, advanced with 3,500 troops on the east; and the two central columns were one of 4,500 men under General J. S. Wood, and one of 8,000 under General Marley, which was to move direct upon Khatmandoo, the Goorkha capital. In all, therefore, 22,000 troops were employed for the campaign, with

The Nipálese declare war.

and murder an officer of police.

English troops take up positions.

60 guns; but never, in any war in which the English had been previously engaged, was more incapacity displayed.

Death of General Gillespie.

The first attack was made by General Gillespie, with his accustomed desperate valour, on the fort of Kalungah, which he endeavoured to carry by a *coup de main*, on October 3, 1814; but was shot through the heart in a vain attempt to rally the storming party, which had failed, after a loss of 20 officers and 220 men, killed and wounded. On the arrival of a battering-train from Dehly, the fort was breached, and Colonel Manbey attempted to storm it; but was repulsed, with a loss of 680 killed and wounded. The garrison had originally consisted of 600 Goorkhas, who had already inflicted a loss of nearly double their number on the invaders, and being reduced to only seventy men, their brave commander evacuated the now untenable fort and escaped. By this successful resistance, the Goorkhas had at once established a high reputation as soldiers, and were proporticnally dreaded by the Sepoys, who were utterly unaccustomed to mountain warfare.

Gallant defence of Kalungah.

General Martindell fails against Jythut, and General Ochterlony obtains only partial success.

General Martindell's operations against the fortified position of Jythuk were not more fortunate, for it proved so strong, that he was held at bay. General Ochterlony, after obtaining some success over the Goorkha officer opposed to him, Umur Singh Thapa, was unable to force the highest of the enemy's positions, and the winter coming on, prevented further operations in the upper ranges of the mountains.

General Marley's incompetency.

The central and largest force had no better success; and General Marley proved utterly incompetent for the enterprise of advancing upon the capital. He lost the whole of two important detachments, with their guns and stores, which he had sent to effect diversions from the main attack, and which were cut off by the Goorkhas. He then retired, as he professed, to guard the frontier, and was even reinforced by Lord Moira with two European regiments; but on February 10, 1815, he, as it were, deserted from the army, leaving it privately by night and proceeding to Dinapoor. General George Wood was appointed to succeed him, and in a skirmish with the enemy they lost 400 men, leaving the road to the capital open; but the general had neither the courage nor the capacity to avail himself of the circumstance. General J. S. Wood's operations were of a similar character. He advanced about the middle of December, and was conducted by a guide, in the interest of the enemy, to the stockaded position of

Who retires, and deserts his post.

General Wood succeeds, and fails.

General J. S. Wood also fails, and retreats.

Jeetpoor, which he failed to carry, and retreated within the frontier. Thus the first campaign of 1814–15 ended disastrously, with the exception of the division under General Ochterlony, which maintained the position it had won in the most stupendous country of all. His force continued to be animated with the highest ardour, and were impatient to be led on; but the other troops were disheartened, if not actually intimidated.

End of the campaign of 1814-15.

The crisis was indeed a momentous one; for the British operations had been watched with intense anxiety in every native State of India. Sindia, Holkar, Ameer Khan, and the Péshwah were known to be preparing a league against the English power; and some of their forces took up threatening positions. Sindia's army was advanced to the frontier. Ameer Khan, who represented Holkar, assembled an army of 25,000 men with 125 guns, and threatened Agra. Runjeet Singh, with 20,000 men, moved to the Sutlej, and the whole of the Pindháree chiefs were engaged by the Péshwah to assemble and act when called upon. To provide against this formidable combination, the Madras army was moved northwards, a Bombay force occupied Guzerat, and the Bengal army was increased to 80,000 men. While these arrangements were in progress, the threatening aspect of affairs moderated. Ameer Khan, who had been the most boastful, began to ravage Rajpootana; Sindia's army separated into two portions, and even the Pindhárees were inactive.

Threatening aspect of native States.

Precautionary measures.

Early in the spring of 1815, General Ochterlony's force had carried every Goorkha position in the west, as far as the fort of Malown. On April 15, this place was invested, and on the 16th a spirited attack by the enemy on the British positions was repulsed, with the heavy loss of 500 men. At this time, the central hill district of Almórah had been occupied by Colonel Gardner, who had been formerly in Sindia's service: and who, with some irregular forces raised in Bundelkhund, had already beaten the Goorkhas out of the Almórah district, and being assisted by Colonel Nicoll at the head of a division of British troops, the possession of Almórah itself was completed. Malown was now no longer tenable, and most of the Goorkha soldiery joined General Ochterlony. Ameer Singh would have continued to defend the fort; but, unwilling to sacrifice the remaining few men that stood by him, he surrendered, and marched out with the honours of war.

Second Goorkha campaign.

Malown surrenders.

With one flank of their territory open, the Goorkha Council now proposed terms of peace, and agreed to the governor-general's demands to cede all territory west of the Káty river, already occupied by General Ochterlony; to

The Goorkhas propose peace.

abandon their claims on the low country; to cede the district of Sikkim, and to receive a British envoy as permanent Resident. On these terms, the treaty was signed by the Goorkha agents on December 2, 1815, and by the governor-general at Calcutta; but peace was not yet to be established. Ameer Singh and his sons, the fiery defenders of Malown, arrived at Khatmandoo, upbraided the Council for cowardice, and urged them to continue the war. This advice prevailed, and the treaty was revoked. Remonstrance was evidently useless. The governor-general had no resource but to commence the war anew, and General, now Sir David, Ochterlony, was selected for the chief command and placed at the head of 17,000 men. With these, he opened the campaign on February 10, 1816, determining to advance on the capital by the Chowrea Ghát pass. This he found had been rendered impregnable; but by the intelligence of Captain Pickersgill and the guide department, another, though very rugged ascent, was discovered to the left, and by it, General Ochterlony, leading the third brigade, ascended in the night of February 14. As the morning dawned, he found he had completely turned the flank of the enemy's position, who fled to Mukwanpoor. Sir David, now joined by the fourth brigade, advanced on Mukwanpoor, within fifty miles of the capital. It was a strongly fortified position, but the outworks were carried, with a loss of upwards of 500 men by the enemy, and preparations were being made for the siege of the fort, when the Council at Khatmandoo, seeing further resistance hopeless, transmitted the treaty, duly executed, on March 2. No additional demands were made by Sir David Ochterlony, and the Goorkhas, notwithstanding many temptations to the contrary, have ever since maintained the peace of 1816 with perfect fidelity. Though they had fought valiantly, yet they had the good sense to perceive that the result of the campaign of 1815 had been the effect of chances which could never occur again, and that of 1816 was the true test of their possibility of resisting the English. For his masterly conduct of these affairs, Lord Moira was created Marquess of Hastings, and to Sir David Ochterlony and the army were voted the thanks of the Courts of Directors and Proprietors, with a pension of 1,000*l.* per annum to Sir David. The direct advantages gained by the British were the mountain provinces of Kumáon and Gurhwál, which strengthened the flank of the north-west provinces very materially; but the greatest benefit of all was the early and effectually permanent detachment of the Goorkhas from the machinations of the unstable and perfidious

Execution of a treaty.

The treaty is revoked by the Goorkhas.

The campaign renewed.

The Chowrea Ghát turned.

General Ochterlony advances on the capital.

The treaty executed; conclusion of the Nipál war.

Lord Moira created Marquess of Hastings.

princes of India. In reference to the details of the Nipál war, and in particular the stupendous operations of Sir David Ochterlony's force, the student is referred to Prinsep's most interesting narrative of the campaign.

CHAPTER II.

THE ADMINISTRATION OF THE MARQUESS OF HASTINGS (*continued*), 1816 TO 1817.

Non-intervention policy of the Court of Directors still prevails.

ALTHOUGH Lord Minto, and now the Marquess of Hastings, had laid before the Court of Directors, in the fullest manner, the necessity of suppressing the new predatory system established by the Pindhárees and Ameer Khan in Central India, and which, as regarded the Pindhárees, had already been extended to Mirzapore in Bengal, to Guzerat, and to the dominions of his highness the Nizam, they still adhered to their policy of non-intervention, and upheld the opinion of Sir George Barlow, that in the disorders of native States lay the true safety of the company's dominions. They replied to Lord Hastings's earnest dispatch of September 29, 1815, that he was not at liberty to engage in operations with the Pindhárees, 'either with a view to utter extirpation, or in anticipation of expected danger,' and they reiterated their orders in regard to the reduction of the army. But besides the Pindhárees, there were other causes at work, which rendered intervention imperative and immediate.

The Péshwah's intrigues.

The Péshwah, although he had been re-established in his authority by the English, had never ceased to intrigue against them with all the other Mahratta chieftains; and when news of the first reverses against Nipál reached him, his schemes became more actively propagated. From the period of his restoration up to 1814, he had been employed in endeavouring to reduce the power of his feudal chiefs in the Southern Mahratta provinces; principally by inciting quarrels among themselves, the result of which had been almost perpetual warfare, and corresponding desolation of the country. For his own immediate protection he proposed, in 1813, to raise a brigade of Sepoys, to be commanded by English officers, to which no objection was offered; and Captain Ford, of the Madras army, was selected to organise and command it. So far, his professions and outward acts bore the appearance of good faith; but they proved to be only a cloak to other and very perfidious designs. In 1813, Khooerojee Moodee, a Parsee, who had been employed as agent by the Péshwah with the Resident at Poona, was appointed to the charge of a province, and Trimbukjee Dainglia, originally a spy, who had raised himself to favour by pandering to the Péshwah's vices, was nominated in his room. Dainglia detested Europeans, and became his master's counsellor and adviser in all schemes for throwing off allegiance to them, and once more establishing the superiority of Mahratta domination. The purpose was excusable, if not indeed meritorious, considered as a national object; but the means employed, suggested by the narrow deceitful mind of the Péshwah, and the savage instinct of Dainglia, were detestable.

The Péshwah increases his army.

The Mahratta army, which had fallen below its usual footing, began to be gradually increased in numbers and efficiency; and distrusting his own subjects, the enlistment of Arabs and Gosains, and other foreign mercenaries, was carried on by the Péshwah under Trimbukjee's advice. The secret agencies at the courts of Sindia, Holkar, the Rajah of Berar and Ameer Khan, were also re-established. In 1814, the existing differences between the Gáikwar's State and the Péshwah, arising out of the Gáikwar's farm of the Péshwah's districts in Guzerat, and the counter-claims of the Gáikwar, required final adjustment: and Gunga Dhur Shastree was nominated agent on the part of the Gáikwar, to effect a settlement at Poona. In sending this envoy, the Gáikwar asked and obtained the guarantee of the British Government for his safety, and it was already understood that, according to the terms of the treaty of Bassein, a final arbitration should be made by the British in case the mutual negotiations broke down. The mission was not successful. The Péshwah, under Dainglia's advice, refused to continue the farm of the Guzerat districts, which were taken possession of by agents and troops sent for the purpose; and by means of these, local insurrections against the Gáikwar's authority were fomented. The Shastree now prepared to leave Poona; but this might bring on a collision with the English, and he was importuned to stay, and was invited to accompany the Péshwah on a pilgrimage to the annual great festival of Punderpoor, on the Bheema. Here, on the night of July 14, shortly after he had quitted the Péshwah's presence, who had been unusually familiar and courteous, the unfortunate Shastree was attacked in the street, and almost cut to pieces.

The Gáikwar sends an agent to Poona

under British guarantee;

but without effect.

Murder of Gunga Dhur Shastree.

There was no doubt that the act had been contrived by Trimbukjee Dainglia, and sanctioned by the Péshwah, for the complicity of both was proved afterwards by the clearest evidence. At the same time, the actual motive

at the instigation of the Péshwah and Dainglia.

for the crime, beyond a desire to be rid of a man who preserved an honest opinion on the subject of his embassy, is not apparent. There was but one course for the Bombay Government; and the person of Trimbukjee was demanded by Mr. Elphinstone, the Resident; but he was not surrendered till September 25, the intermediate time being occupied by considerations whether or no it would be possible to oppose the British demand by force. This, however, being impossible, Trimbukjee was apprehended, and imprisoned in the fort of Tannah; whence, on September 12, 1816, he effected his escape, in a somewhat romantic manner, retiring to the fastnesses of the mountains near Nassuk, where he was protected by their rude inhabitants.

Dainglia surrendered.

His escape.

The Péshwah, by his friendly demeanour, continued for a time to overcome the suspicion which had attached itself to him, in regard to the proceedings of Trimbukjee Dainglia; but in truth at no period had he been so active in his intrigues through him with the several Mahratta chiefs and the Pindhárees; and he was secretly supplying his favourite with large sums of money to raise troops. These levies soon appeared in considerable numbers, and their existence was noticed to the Péshwah by Mr. Elphinstone. Beyond affecting to consider them ordinary insurgents, and sending out a party of horse to disperse them, the Péshwah took no further measures for their suppression; but they were followed and routed by detachments of the subsidiary force—not, however, before one of their parties had murdered Lieutenant Warre of the Madras Artillery. These proceedings, and the now evident assistance Trimbukjee was receiving from the Péshwah, the repair of forts, and levies of new troops in all directions, duly reported by Mr. Elphinstone, induced the governor-general to demand the arrest of the person who was instigating the Péshwah to hostility, within a month: and as a pledge for the fulfilment of his demand, that three principal forts were to be placed in the hands of the English. The Péshwah at first absolutely refused compliance; but on May 8, 1816, he agreed to the demand—not, however, before Poona had been surrounded by British troops; sent orders for the delivery of the fortresses, and issued a proclamation offering two lacs of rupees for Trimbukjee Dainglia, dead or alive. After this, on May 10, a new treaty was executed, by which the Péshwah even admitted the guilt of Trimbukjee, and agreed to surrender his family as hostages till his apprehension, He also ceded districts yielding thirty-four lacs a year, as an equivalent for the contingent of 5,000 horse and 3,000 infantry which had formed an

The Péshwah's assistance to Dainglia.

Murder of Lieutenant Warre.

Mr. Elphinstone's reports.

Measures of the governor general.

A new treaty with the Péshwah.

article of the treaty of Bassein, with the fort of Ahmednugger, and his rights north of the Nerbudda river; and he admitted the Toombuddra to the south, and the Nerbudda to the north, to be the boundaries of his dominions. The disputes with the Gáikwar were also settled, and finally the Péshwah covenanted neither to send agents to, nor hold communication with, any foreign powers.

The terms of the treaty reviewed.

The foregoing embrace the principal items of the treaty, which also included many other minor points of which recapitulation is not needed. The terms were no doubt hard and stringent; and have been impugned as more calculated to drive the Péshwah to despair, than to secure, as they professed to do, his future peaceable possession of his real dominions. At the same time it must be remembered that they were dictated to one whom no treaties could bind, under a perfect acquaintance with his long career of deception, intrigue, and treachery, faithless alike to his own people and to the English; that his aim, from the first, had been to throw off the obligations of the treaty of Bassein into which he had entered with apparent good faith, and that, in the face of the guarantee of the English, an unprovoked and deliberate murder had been committed upon an envoy to his court, with his full approbation. The negotiations with him had been committed to Mountstuart Elphinstone, than whom, one more considerate and humane never filled high office in India; and whose name to this day is reverenced among the Mahratta people.

Proceedings of the Pindhárees.

Meanwhile, the Pindhárees had been unusually active. An extraordinarily large body of them, estimated at 25,000 men, under Cheetoo, assembled at Nimáur, in Central India, in the autumn of 1815, and, on October 14, 8,000 horsemen advanced into the Nizam's territories, plundering and devastating the country as far south as the Krishna river, returning safely to Nimáur, laden with an immense booty. This successful expedition was followed by another, upwards of 20,000 strong, in February 1816, a portion of which entered the Northern Circars, carried the English civil station of Guntoor, and returned plundering as they had come. They had destroyed 339 English villages, put 182 persons to death, wounded 500, and tortured 3,600; while they had carried off booty valued at fifty lacs of rupees—500,000*l*. Pursuit of Cheetoo was impossible. Spreading themselves over the country as the Pindhárees advanced rapidly from thirty to even fifty miles a day, not a town, village, or hamlet, escaped them. Wherever they stopped, their proceedings were immediate, and horribly cruel. The most ingeniously devised and agonising tortures were resorted to for the extortion of valuables, from men and women alike, and after collecting all they could, the town or village was set on fire, and the devastating horde passed on. They were men of all castes, creeds, and provinces, and in some instances well mounted; but the hardy small horses and ponies of the country were perhaps the most serviceable. They had no baggage or supplies of any kind, and the surprising rate at which their vast bodies moved, baffled pursuit.

It has been before mentioned, that the Pindhárees of Dost Mahomed had plundered the English districts in Behar, and that Lord Minto had applied to the Court for permission to punish them; but the reply, as has been already stated, which was received by Lord Hastings, was unfavourable. Now, however, a second and far more formidable irruption had taken place; it was quite uncertain in which direction the next blow would fall; and the absolute necessity of a reversion of the non-interferent policy could no longer be delayed or denied, even in England; but as yet no final decision had been made. Lord Hastings, however, commenced his plans by concluding a subsidiary treaty with the Rajah of Nagpoor. The old rajah, Rughoojee Bhóslay, who had refused all former offers of such an alliance, was dead; his successor was an idiot, and his nephew, Appa Sahib, who became regent, concluded a subsidiary treaty on March 22, 1816. In the same year Jeypoor had been attacked by Ameer Khan; but on the application of its rajah to Mr. Metcalfe, the Resident at Dehly, Lord Hastings, though opposed in Council, determined to assist the State and save it; and two separate forces were assembled for the purpose, backed by other combinations, which it would have been impossible for Ameer Khan to oppose. He therefore raised the siege, but the rajah, notwithstanding the aid afforded him, evaded making any alliance with the English.

Subsidiary treaties.

Mr. Canning was now at the head of the Board of Control, and the receipt of the news of the Pindháree irruption into the Northern Circars gave the final blow to the indecision which had prevailed in England. In a dispatch dated September 26, 1816, the governor-general was freed from his trammels. He was assured of the approbation of the Home Government in any measures he might have undertaken for 'repelling invasion and chastising the invaders,' and, added Mr. Canning with spirit, 'We can no longer abstain from a vigorous exertion of military power, in vindication of the British name, and in defence of subjects who look to us for protection.' Had this decision arrived a year earlier, the third Pindháree irruption might have been prevented; but the governor-general's military preparations were not as yet complete; and crossing the Nerbudda again, and breaking through

Mr. Canning's policy.

The third Pindháree movement.

the Nagpoor troops, one body plundered Kimedy and Ganjám, while the other, dashing through the Nizam's territories, repeated, and even exceeded, the enormities of their former visit. Even the stubborn Calcutta Council now yielded, and the already matured plans of the governor-general were suffered to proceed. 'Vigorous measures for the suppression of the Pindhárees,' as the Council unanimously resolved, 'had become an indispensable act of public duty!' What had been denied to justice, was now yielded to fear.

Lord Hastings takes the field. His military arrangements.

Towards the end of 1817, the military preparations of the governor-general were completed. He took command of the central division himself, which was at Cawnpore; and the other five divisions of the Bengal army were stationed at Agra, in Bundelkhund, and in Behar; with a reserve near Dehly under General Ochterlony. The whole numbered more than 60,000 men. In the south, the army of Madras was placed under the command of Sir Thomas Hislop, in five divisions, under Generals Doveton, Malcolm, Lionel Smith, and Colonel Adams. The forces of Guzerat were assembled under General Kerr; and the whole British army in the field was not less than 115,000 men, with 300 guns. Lord Hastings then intimated to Sindia, that the policy of non-interference had been renounced, and that he should proceed to contract alliance with all native States that desired connection with, or protection from, the British Government. He also required him to assist in the suppression of the Pindhárees.

Sindia's co-operation invited.

Sindia's acquiescence was not cordial; but he had sense enough to see that he had no alternative, and his neutrality, if not his active co-operation, was secured. The fact is, like others of the time, Sindia had been double-faced and treacherous. While he was treating with the governor-general, he was urging the Nipálese to attack the company's districts in the rear, and, to his great confusion, one of his intercepted letters to them was returned to him in open court by the English agent. It was equally well known that he was in treaty with the Péshwah, and had received as much as twenty-five lacs from him; but he had little time to consider, for Lord Hastings advancing across the Jumna, on October 16, marched directly upon Gwalior, supported by General Doveton's division from Agra; and resistance to those forces would have involved destruction. Ameer Khan alone remained to be secured or attacked. His army consisted of 52 battalions of disciplined infantry, 150 guns, and a heavy body of Patán cavalry.

His previous treachery detected and exposed.

Offer to Ameer Khan.

To him, Lord Hastings offered to guarantee the districts conferred upon him by Holkar, and to purchase all his artillery. He did not immediately acquiesce in this proposal; but the advantages were too solid to be declined, and he continued neutral, promising his best consideration of the terms offered.

CHAPTER III.

THE ADMINISTRATION OF THE MARQUESS OF HASTINGS (*continued*) —THE SECOND MAHRATTA WAR, 1817 TO 1818.

As the British armies were gradually converging upon the Pindhárees, who collected annually in the south-eastern portion of Malwah, a wild and rugged tract of country, the Péshwah suddenly broke into war, supposing that his example would be simultaneously followed by Sindia, Holkar, the Rajah of Berar, Ameer Khan, and the Pindhárees, and that in the contest with all these separate powers, the English forces would be distracted and overcome; but never in the many strange estimates of delusive strength in India had a greater mistake been made. After the conclusion of the new treaty, the Péshwah appeared actuated by candour; and while he deplored the humiliation of the new engagements, professed acquiescence in their provisions. He went on his usual annual pilgrimage to Punderpoor, and appeared to reduce his cavalry, though to each man pay for seven months was disbursed, under agreement for all to assemble when called upon. Instead of returning to Poona from Punderpoor, the Péshwah went to Mahóly, in order, as was alleged, to complete his religious observances; and was visited there by Sir John Malcolm, whom he satisfied as to his peaceful intentions; but Mr. Elphinstone's suspicions continued as strong as ever, and he viewed with apprehension the march of the subsidiary force from Seroor, on October 9, to its position in the general distribution of the grand army, a movement which left Poona entirely undefended. It had been arranged, however, that a regiment of European infantry should be sent up from Bombay.

War commenced by the Péshwah.

His peaceful professions.

His covert proceedings.

Apprehensions of Mr. Elphinstone.

Bappoo Gókla was now the adviser of the Péshwah in all political and military affairs, and the organisation of troops and the missions to the Mahratta courts were pushed forward with every possible expedition; but of all the Péshwah's wild schemes, that of corrupting the English officers and their Sepoys, coupled with the assassination of Mr. Elphinstone, seems to have been most at heart. It need hardly be recorded, that the Sepoys tampered with indignantly rejected the offers made to them, and that the corruption of their officers was never even attempted. Even his minister, Bappoo Gókla, refused to be concerned in any treacherous attack upon Mr. Elphinstone, from whom he had received many kindnesses.

The Dusséra at Poona.

The annual festival of the Dusséra was to take place on October 19, and is an occasion, in every Hindoo State, not only for a military display in commemoration of the capture of Ceylon by King Ráma, but for taking the annual muster of troops. The assembly on this occasion was greater than usual; while the only English troops at Poona were a weak brigade, partly composed of the battalions nominally belonging to the Péshwah. In noticing the unusual number of levies present, Mr. Elphinstone was informed that they were destined to operate against the Pindhárees; and to this no objection was open, as it was a point on which he had been already urgent. But in a few days the Péshwah's horse and foot began to crowd upon the British position very unpleasantly; and on November 4, Captain Ford was privately informed by Moro Dixit, a native friend, that the Péshwah intended to cut off the British troops, and recommended him to withdraw. There was no doubt, therefore, from every concurring circumstance, that an attack was imminent.

Threatening position of the Péshwah's troops.

Arrival of the European regiment.

The arrival of the European regiment was looked to with intense anxiety, for it had been already debated in the Péshwah's Council whether the British force should not be attacked before its arrival; and it was still believed to be at a considerable distance, when by forced marches it arrived on October 30. The whole force then, on November 1, took up an open position near the village of Kirkee; and on the 3rd, Mr. Elphinstone directed a battalion of light infantry, and a party of auxiliary horse, then at Seroor, to join him. On November 5, the Péshwah's plans were completed, and the whole army was ordered out, on pretence of escorting him to a temple in the suburbs of Poona. A last endeavour was made by him to remonstrate against the advance of the regiment from Bombay, and that of the battalion from Seroor, and to request their being returned; but Mr. Elphinstone resisted both demands firmly, and the Péshwah's officer had barely left him, when the great army was put in motion. No one knew the Mahrattas better than Mr. Elphinstone: and instead of allowing Colonel Burr, the officer in command of the brigade, to await attack, he directed him to move at once on the Mahratta forces. The effect of this act was a strange panic among the Mahratta troops; and an evil omen had occurred in the breaking of the staff of the Juree Putka, or national standard, as it left the

The Péshwah's army advances, and is met by the British troops.

city. Beyond one brilliant charge led by Gókla, which was successfully repulsed with heavy loss by Colonel Burr's own regiment, the 7th Bombay Native Infantry, the vast host of the Mahratta army did nothing; and as the British brigade still advanced, the whole took to flight. The strength of the forces engaged were—2,800 British, in the proportion of 2,000 natives to 800 Europeans; of the Mahrattas, 18,000 horse, 8,000 foot, with fourteen guns. In the night, the battalion from Seroor arrived, and the Mahratta attack was not renewed. This event was followed by the murder, in three instances, of English officers who were travelling; and Cornets Hunter and Morrison, of the Madras cavalry, were overpowered and confined in a hill-fort.

The Mahratta army abandon the field.

General Smith, who retraced his steps on hearing of the outbreak, arrived near Poona on November 13, and had made dispositions to attack the Péshwah's army, which was encamped west of the Moota river, on the morning of the 15th, at daylight; but this was prevented by the state of the ford. On the 16th the Mahratta army began to retreat. On the 17th no portion of their host was to be seen: the whole, with the Péshwah, had fled to Sattara. Poona was now taken possession of without resistance, and General Smith, after depositing his heavy guns and baggage at Seroor, commenced a pursuit of the Mahratta army. It is unnecessary to follow the movements of the several divisions of the British forces which were put in motion for the same purpose, and to avoid which the Péshwah adopted every expedient in his power; but an episode in the war occurred which cannot be passed by without record.

Arrival of General Smith's force.

The Péshwah flies to Sattara.

Poona occupied.

Pursuit of the Péshwah.

The second battalion of the 1st Bombay Native Infantry had been left at Seroor; and Colonel Burr, apprehending that the Péshwah might suddenly return to Poona, directed it to join him. It therefore set out on December 31, 1817, under the command of Captain Staunton, accompanied by two six-pounder guns of the Madras Artillery, and 300 of the newly-raised irregular cavalry. On the morning of January 1, 1818, having marched all night, the detachment reached the small village of Korygaom, on the Bheema, and Captain Staunton found the whole of the Péshwah's army, 25,000 strong, encamped before it. He did not halt, but passed on till he occupied the village. Here, throughout the whole of that day, he was attacked, by several bodies in succession, of Arabs, Gosains, and other foot soldiers; and every post of the village was desperately contested. The guns were taken and retaken; several of the few officers were killed and wounded; and the men, from whom water was cut off, were frantic with thirst, and faint with

Memorable defence of Korygaom by Captain Staunton.

hunger; but the defence was maintained with high valour, until nightfall, when the men obtained water, and the enemy gradually withdrew. At daylight, Captain Staunton opened his guns upon parties of horse which were careering about on the plain; but they had no disposition to renew the fight, and the whole Mahratta army gradually disappeared. Captain Staunton had lost 175 men in killed and wounded, with eight officers—three killed and five wounded—and only himself, Lieutenant Jones, and Assistant Surgeon Wyllie escaped; the Mahratta loss was between 500 and 600 men. The glory of the defence, with that of the battle of Seetabuldee, which had preceded it, are still sung by Mahratta minstrels, in every part of the Deccan; and a monument erected near the fort at Korygaom commemorates the names of every man who fell.

The Péshwah witnessed the fight all day from a distant eminence, and seeing the successive failures of those on whom he had most relied, bitterly upbraided them for having misled him. He had now no refuge but in flight, and the British divisions allowed him no rest. He proceeded to the south, being chased in turn by Generals Munro and Pritzler; and obliged to recross the Krishna, he turned northwards to Sholapoor, where General Smith took up the pursuit. On February 10, Sattara was taken possession of, and a manifesto issued to the people; and the Mahratta force, under Bappoo Gókla, was overtaken at Ashta, and routed by General Smith's cavalry, with the loss of their brave, but misguided commander, who was killed in the *mélée* by a dragoon. The action was important, however, as the Rajah of Sattara, who had been hitherto in confinement, was rescued, and assured of the good intentions of the governor-general, remained with Mr. Elphinstone. The Péshwah still fled northwards, intending, it was supposed, to make for Nagpoor.

The Péshwah pursues his flight.

Sattara occupied.

Combat of Ashta.

Release of the Rajah of Sattara.

Meanwhile, events of the highest interest had occurred there. Appa Sahib, the regent, had caused the idiot rajah to be strangled, and himself to be proclaimed successor, in February 1816. From that period he maintained an active correspondence with the Péshwah. Cheetoo, the Pindháree chief, visited him, and large levies of troops were made. This conduct was remonstrated against by the Resident; but protestations of loyalty to the English were received, perhaps, with too great reliance. So long as the Péshwah had made no direct movement, Appa Sahib was tranquil, and the Resident, Mr. Jenkins, saw no cause for apprehension; but on the news of the Péshwah's outbreak, he threw off the mask, and on the evening of November

Events at Nagpoor.

26, when he had drawn out his forces to witness his investiture with an honorary dress sent by the Péshwah, the British troops were suddenly attacked by the whole of his army. They had fortunately been able to occupy two eminences near the Residency, called Seetabuldee, and the possession of these was hotly contested during the whole of the 27th; but the enemy were at last repulsed, and the attack was not renewed. The disparity of numbers was even greater than at Poona. Appa Sahib's army was 18,000 strong, while the British force did not reach 1,400, who, with the exception of the artillerymen, were all Sepoys. Their loss was 333 in killed and wounded, with twelve officers. Appa Sahib endeavoured to lay the blame of the attack upon his Arabs, and other mercenaries; but the Resident, strengthened by reinforcements on November 29, and December 5th, 14th, and 19th, would listen to nothing short of unconditional submission; and the rajah came to the Residency and surrendered himself; but his army did not obey his orders in regard to the delivery of its guns, and they were taken in an action fought at once upon the spot. Mr. Jenkins dictated terms to the rajah, which involved a territorial cession of twenty-four lacs, equal to the pay of the subsidiary force, and included the military control of the country; and these terms were subsequently confirmed by the governor-general.

Remarkable battle and defence of Seetabuldee.

Battle of Nagpoor.

CHAPTER IV.

THE ADMINISTRATION OF THE MARQUESS HASTINGS (*continued*) —THE MAHRATTA AND PINDHÁREE WAR, 1818.

THE issue of events at Poona had placed the Mahratta dominions at the disposal of the governor-general, who, on hearing of the Péshwah's outbreak, resolved to annex them. Mr. Elphinstone was appointed commissioner for the whole of the Mahratta territories in the Deccan; but the public manifesto was not issued until Sattara had been taken possession of, when it was proclaimed that the authority of the Péshwah had ceased to exist, and that a portion of the territory had been set apart for the Rajah of Sattara. The dominant authority of the Péshwahs, from the recognition of Ballajee Wishwánath in 1717, by the Emperor Mahomed Shah, to the flight of his great-grandson, Bajee Ráo, in 1817, had been as nearly as possible a hundred years. Now, not only had the once vast power of the dynasty crumbled to pieces under the effects of mutual divi-

Annexation of the Mahratta dominions.

Proclamation at Sattara.

sions and contests for pre-eminence, but the dominions of one of the most important of the Mahratta confederacy, the Rajah of Berar, also lay at the mercy of the governor-general, and those of a third, Holkar, were speedily to follow.

Events at Holkar's court.

Regency of Toolsee Bye.

On the death of Jeswunt Ráo Holkar, in 1811, his favourite mistress, Toolsee Bye, a young and very beautiful woman, adopted Mulhar Ráo, an illegitimate son of her husband, and assumed the conduct of affairs as regent. Her government was profligate and ineffective; the army was mutinous and uncontrollable, and plundered the country at large for subsistence, and without opposition. Ameer Khan, whose Patáns formed the chief element of Holkar's military establishment, withdrew from Indoor soon after his death, to prosecute his operations in Rajpootana, leaving a relative, Ghufoor Khan, as his substitute. Before her own forces, Toolsee Bye was obliged in the sequel to fly to the protection of Rajah Zálim Singh of Kóta; but she could not long remain inactive, and entered into a contest with Ghufoor Khan, in an action with whom she displayed great valour at the head of her cavalry, but was obliged to fly from the field. The hereditary minister of the State was Gunput Ráo, who became her paramour; and there seemed little hope of a reconstruction of an efficient executive government, till Tantia Jógh, formerly a banker, was appointed minister, and rallied the Mahratta party about her. Ghufoor Khan, however, maintained his position, and for upwards of five years the scenes of contention and anarchy were but little, if at all, abated. Towards the close of 1817, the Péshwah's agents were again active at Indoor; and the support of the great military chiefs in his action against the English had been secured. Toolsee Bye's authority was little more than nominal; but it does not appear that she had entered into the schemes of the Péshwah, or the views of her military commanders; and on the proposal of a treaty by the governor-general, she had offered, though secretly, to place herself and the young prince, Mulhar Ráo, under the protection of the Resident at Dehly. It became, however, impossible for her to carry out this purpose, or to escape from the control of the army; and no sooner had the news of events at Poona become known at Indoor, than the commanders resolved to make common cause with the Péshwah; and the army, 20,000 strong, to whom liberal supplies of money were disbursed by the Péshwah's agents, marched at once for the Deccan. At this juncture, the divisions of Sir T. Hislop and Sir John Malcolm had united, and lay in their path. Nor was it possible for Holkar's forces to avoid them. Holkar's army, therefore, took up a strong position near Mehidpoor, on the Sipree river, in the

The Péshwah's intrigues at Indoor.

Holkar's army marches for the Deccan.

middle of December. Here, on the morning of December 20, a long existing plot for the destruction of Toolsee Bye and her paramour was carried out by Ghufoor Khan and others in his interest. The young Holkar, Mulhar Ráo, was first separated from them, when Gunput Ráo endeavoured to escape, but was brought back and imprisoned; and at night, Toolsee Bye was taken from her tent to the bank of the Sipree, beheaded, and her body cast into the stream.

Execution of Toolsee Bye.

Sir Thomas Hislop's force was then within ten miles of the Mahratta camp, and he had opened negotiations with the army; but they were haughtily rejected, and the commanders, reliant upon the strength of their position and their guns, decided to fight. The British force advanced upon them on the morning of December 21; and carried the artillery by storm, after a sharp contest, when the whole of Holkar's army dispersed and fled in confusion, except the horse, which, without an attempt to redeem the day, went off in a body unharmed. The brunt of the action had fallen upon the artillery, and disciplined infantry battalions, who had fought bravely, and suffered severely; and the loss on the part of the English was 778 in killed and wounded. The victory was, however, complete; and sixty-three guns, with all their stores and the camp-equipage, were captured. Holkar retreated with the wreck of his force to Mundisore, followed by Sir John Malcolm; but no further resistance was made, and on January 6, 1818, he concluded a treaty with the British Government, which provided for Ameer Khan and Ghufoor Khan, abandoned demands upon the Rajpoot States, which were transferred to the English, and agreed to maintain a contingent of 3,000 horse. On the other hand, the British Government guaranteed to protect his territories for the future.

Battle of Mehidpoor.

Defeat of Holkar's army.

Treaty of peace with Holkar.

The Pindhárees alone remain to be accounted for in this remarkable contest. Sindia's forces, closely watched by the governor-general's and other British divisions, had perforce remained neutral; but Jeswunt Ráo Bhow, one of his superior officers, harboured Cheetoo and other Pindháree chiefs, and so pertinaciously maintained his disobedience to Sindia's orders, that General Browne's division was sent against him, by which he was defeated at Jáwud, and his guns captured on January 28, and the districts he had usurped from the Rana of Oodipoor rescued from him, and restored to their lawful prince. As to the several divisions of Pindhárees, they had found themselves helpless from the first against Lord Hastings's combinations; and the events of the period, at Poona, Nagpoor, and Indoor, proved to them

The Pindhárees.

Jeswunt Ráo Bhow defeated.

Check of Pindháree movements.

that they could receive no help from the Mahrattas. Cheetoo, finding no refuge at Jáwud, had fled in a north-westerly direction, his followers deserting him at every march. He was hunted through Guzerat by General Keir, and afterwards by General Malcolm in Malwah; and on January 25, his camp was surprised and attacked by Captain Heath. This was the last appearance of his force; but for nearly a year he wandered among the fastnesses of the Vindhya and Sátpoora hills, and at last was killed by a tiger in the jungle between Aseergurh and the Tapty river, where his half-devoured remains were discovered by a shepherd, and recognised.

Flight of Cheetoo.

His death.

Kureem Khan and Wasil Mahomed were routed by a force under Colonel Adams, in January 1818, and their followers dispersed in every direction. Kureem sought protection from Jeswunt Ráo Bhow at Jáwud, whence he escaped when it was taken, and finally surrendered to Sir John Malcolm on February 15. He received a small estate for his support in the province of Gorukpoor, in Bengal, and his example was followed by his celebrated lieutenant, Námdar Khan. Wasil Mahomed betook himself to Sindia's camp at Gwalior, where he was surrendered, and sent to Ghazeepoor; he was not imprisoned, but he attempted to escape from thence, and was apprehended, when he committed suicide by poison. Thus ended that formidable combination of freebooters, which had wholly desolated large provinces, inflicted inconceivable torture and misery upon thousands of the people, was utterly without control or check, and if allowed to gain further organisation, would have carried fire and sword into every accessible province of India.

Other Pindháree chiefs.

Ameer Khan alone remained, and finding hopes from the Mahrattas futile, he dismissed the Péshwah's agents, and turned to Mr. Metcalfe and Sir David Ochterlony as his best friends. The offer before made to him by Lord Hastings was accepted; but it required all the address and firmness of Sir David to conclude a settlement with his Patán troops, and to obtain their artillery. This, however, was finally effected, and without bloodshed. Without entering into minute details of the alliances contracted with all the smaller chiefs of the central and northern provinces, which the non-interferent policy had before prevented, it will gratify the reader to learn that two especial instances of fidelity were amply rewarded. The Rajah of Boondee was freed from all demands on the part of Sindia; Holkar's and Sindia's usurpations were restored to him, and the State was established in the prosperity and independence which it still enjoys. The other was the

Settlement with Ameer Khan

and with minor States.

Nawáb of Bhopál, whose ancestor, it will be remembered, had rendered hospitality and material assistance to General Goddard, in his famous march across India. The Nawáb received a material addition to his small territory from the Mahratta possessions in Malwah, and the gratitude and good faith of the family have since been conspicuously displayed.

Bhopál.

The results of the campaign of 1817–18 may be very briefly summed up. In the middle of 1817, the Mahratta and Pindháree power, though divided, was unbroken, and has been estimated at nearly 200,000 men, with 500 guns. It was fast hastening to a combination of all interests, which the Péshwah, the Rajah of Berar, and Holkar had already joined, and which Sindia, Ameer Khan, and the Pindhárees would not have refused, had the British preparations been delayed. The whole was utterly shattered in a brief campaign of four months. The Péshwah's dominions had been annexed, and those of Sindia, Holkar, and the Rajah of Berar lay at the mercy of the governor-general, and were saved only by his exceeding and honourable moderation. There was at last, after sixty years from the battle of Plassy, no question of the supremacy of British power throughout India, now more perfectly established, and more effectively dominant, than that of Aurungzebe.

Summary.

With the fate of the Péshwah himself, this chapter may be appropriately closed. In the month of March, it was discovered that Appa Sahib, the rajah of Nagpoor, was still in active communication with the Péshwah, and assisting him by every means in his power to continue the war. Mr. Jenkins, therefore, arrested him, and kept him prisoner till Lord Hastings's pleasure should be known. The Péshwah, deprived of the promised succour, was still hunted from place to place by detachments from the several divisions, and his force was attacked and routed at Sewnee, by Colonel Adams, on April 18. The capture of Chandah followed, and he was driven northwards, all chances of aid from the south being cut off. During these wanderings, he had addressed himself successively to Mr. Jenkins, Mr. Elphinstone, and to the British commanders, offering terms; but as the only replies he received required his unconditional surrender, he pursued his route northwards, hoping to reach Sindia. This, however, was impossible: all the fords and passes were guarded; and abandoned by every adherent of importance, he reached Dhólkote, near Aseergurh, with about 8,000 men. Thence he dispatched an agent to Sir John Malcolm, who was at Indoor, who sent to him his two assistants, Lieutenants Low and McDonald, requiring him to renounce all

The Péshwah is assisted by Appa Sahib.

His force is routed.

He sues for terms.

The demands made on him.

claim to the sovereignty of the Deccan, to give up Trimbukjee Dainglia, and the murderers of the English officers. He was also to proceed to meet Sir John Malcolm. It is almost inconceivable why any negotiations whatever should have been opened, or anything short of unconditional submission accepted by Sir John Malcolm. It was quite impossible, either that Bajee Ráo could have escaped the forces which were rapidly closing round him, or have maintained himself in the rude tract of country into which he had been driven; but the negotiations with him nevertheless continued, and were even protracted. The best and only excuse for them lies in Sir John Malcolm's kindly disposition and generosity, and in spite of his treachery, sympathy with a prince so lately a monarch, and now a fugitive. His final agreement with the Péshwah provided him a pension for life, of eight lacs—80,000*l.*—per year: and it is due justice to Bajee Ráo to state that he was able also to secure estates, and other provisions, for those who had followed him to the last. These terms, though accompanied with some censure to Sir John Malcolm for exceeding instructions, were ratified by Lord Hastings, and Bithoor, near Cawnpoor, was selected by the Péshwah as his place of future residence. The surrender of Trimbukjee was evaded; but he was afterwards apprehended, and died at Chunar, in confinement.

The Péshwah pensioned.

Trimbukjee Dainglia arrested and imprisoned for life.

CHAPTER V.

THE ADMINISTRATION OF THE MARQUESS HASTINGS (*concluded*), 1818 TO 1823.

Closing operations of the campaign of 1818.

With an inconsiderable number of sieges and operations in the field, the campaign of 1818 closed. Aseergurh was surrendered to Sir John Malcolm on April 9: and as his justification for resistance and aid to the Péshwah, the commandant, Jeswunt Ráo, showed to Sir John, his master Sindia's instructions. It was not the only instance of Sindia's treachery which had been brought to light; but he had been effectually restrained and humbled, and the retention of Aseergurh, which was garrisoned by British troops, was thought sufficient punishment. Lord Hastings was, however, determined to make the treachery of the Rajah of Nagpoor an example to all, and ordered him to be transmitted to the fort of Allahabad as a state prisoner. On the road thither he contrived to seduce some of the Sepoys of his escort, and was allowed to escape. For a time, assisted by Cheetoo Pindháree, and at the head of a lawless rabble, he maintained a precarious existence in the Vindhya and Sátpoora mountains; but these bands were dispersed, and after wandering from court to court of the Hindoo princes, he received eventual protection, under the cognisance of the British Government, from the Rajah of Joudhpoor. In regard to the Nagpoor territories, the widow of Rughoojee Bhóslay was allowed to adopt a boy, who was duly proclaimed rajah, under the regency of his adoptress; but the authority was only nominal, as the whole of the administration was placed under the Resident, until the youth should attain his majority.

Escape of Appa Sahib.

British administration of Nagpoor.

In a comparatively few instances, resistance was offered to the British troops. Talnair, the former Patán capital of Khandésh, was extremely strong, and defended by a body of the Péshwah's Arabs. After a short resistance, the native officer in command submitted, and came out to Sir T. Hislop, who sent a party to take possession. It appeared, however, that the garrison had either not been consulted, or that it was an act of treachery: for the party, being allowed to pass several of the gates, were at last set upon by the Arabs, and the officer in command killed. On the news of this event reaching Sir Thomas, he ordered an assault, in which nearly the whole of the Arab garrison was killed, and the native commandant was hanged the next morning as an example. This act, which caused a good deal of subsequent discussion—especially in England—with the particulars of the attack on Talnair, will be found detailed at length in Prinsep's narrative, which, in regard to the final operations of this campaign, possesses extreme interest. Another somewhat memorable siege was that of Malligaom, in Khandésh, into which fort all the fugitive Arab mercenaries had collected. They defended the place very bravely, but from the first inefficient means had been employed in the attack; the garrison were in proportion confident, and they repulsed one assault. They eventually proposed terms, and were allowed to march out under promise of payment of their arrears of pay, and a free passage to Arabia. This generous treatment was, however, misunderstood. The Arabs considered they had had the best of the contest; and the result ever since then, has been held up as an instance of successful resistance by Arabs to English troops which could not be overcome, and at Hyderabad and elsewhere has produced many bad consequences.

Capture of Talnair.

Siege of Malligaom.

The garrison capitulates.

The hill forts in the Western Ghauts fell, one by one, to General

Pritzler's force, and in Wasota, Cornets Hunter and Morrison were found in good health, as also the wives and families of the Rajah of Sattara and his brother. It was then ascertained that the brave Bappoo Gókla had himself written to the commandant of Wasota, directing the two 'poor Europeans' to be well treated, and the order had been obeyed. The whole of the stupendous mountain fortresses having either submitted or been captured, the Rajah of Sattara was placed upon his throne with great pomp on April 11; the territory assigned to him, which yielded about fourteen lacs, or 140,000*l.*, was that of his ancestor Sivajee, and for the present an English officer, Captain Grant Duff, was placed with him to manage the affairs of his principality.

General Pritzler's operations.

The Rajah of Sattara enthroned.

At this period, General Munro's conduct was spirited and useful. Having no regular forces, he raised a levy of the armed people of Northern Mysore and adjacent districts, and with these he not only took possession of several of the strongest forts in the country, but followed up 4,500 of the Péshwah's infantry, with thirteen guns, to Sholapoor, where he routed them, with the loss of their guns; and the capture of the strong fort of Sholapoor followed.

General Munro's spirited conduct.

As far as military operations were concerned, the occupation of the Péshwah's territory was completed before the rainy season of 1818; the establishment of a civil administration necessarily occupied a longer period. The whole of the dominions were divided into four great portions. To the south-western, bordering on Mysore, Mr. Chaplin, an eminent Madras civilian, was nominated; Captain H. D. Robertson to the district and city of Poona; Captain Briggs to Khandésh, and Captain Pottinger to the central portion from the Bheema to Chandoor. To assist them, a number of native officers were selected from those of the late government, and it was surprising with what rapidity whole provinces and their people submitted to a new government. Here and there parties of the old soldiery, and of lawless characters, from time to time committed outrages and depredations, and some plots were discovered among the Brahmins; but these were unimportant in comparison with the great measures of pacification of the country, security of life and property, and guarantee of peace, which all well-affected classes desired, and which, up to the present time—upwards of fifty years—has continued unbroken; while the names of the four subordinate, and the chief commissioner, Mr. Elphinstone, live among the Mahrattas of all classes as household words. No portions of India had become more desolated from perpetual war, exactions, and misgovernment, than the Mahratta territories

Civil administration.

Cheerful submission of the people.

Effects of the British rule.

at the period of the war, and equally may be it declared that at the present time none is more content or prosperous. In place of widespread desolation, and thousands of deserted villages, there is not now a single ruined hamlet, or an acre of unoccupied land, except what is unculturable. The Péshwah's great feudatories, the Rajahs of Kolapoor and Akulkote, Appa Desaye Nepankur, the Putwurdhun, Rastia, and other great families, gave in their allegiance, and their possessions and estates were secured to them; and the hereditary rights of all district and village offices were continued. Any revaluation of the land, or change in the collection of revenue, would, necessarily, have been premature; and what had been the basis of the Péshwah's revenue system was continued. All hereditary pensions and allowances, rent-free lands, and charitable and religious endowments, were confirmed throughout the country. The great originator of these most judicious and benevolent measures, the Hon. Mountstuart Elphinstone, succeeded to the government of the Bombay Presidency on November 1, 1819, and was thus enabled to preside over the execution of details without interruption; and from first to last his liberal and generous settlements received the fullest approval of the Marquess of Hastings.

Security of property.

The final issue of the war, triumphant as it had been, was, to say the least of it, ill received in England: not indeed as regarded the military operations, which were beyond cavil; but as regarded the policy of the governor-general. Mr. Canning led the way in a speech to the House of Commons, in April 1819. The Court of Directors, while appreciating 'the promptitude and vigour with which Lord Hastings had dispersed the gathering elements of a hostile conspiracy,' denounced the extension of territory; but posterity has awarded ample recognition of his Lordship's great measures, by which Central and Western India had been delivered from a condition of never-ceasing anarchy, so long as the lawless armies of the rival powers were unconstrained. It was not only in regard to the issue of the war that the Court of Directors were hostile to Lord Hastings. He had undertaken the support of native education, and he followed it up with all the energy and generosity of his character. Vernacular schools began to be established, which were crowded by native scholars; and Lord Hastings himself became the patron of a society established for the education of native children in English literature and science. A native newspaper was issued by the missionaries at Serampoor, and the English press became virtually free. All these acts were directly opposed to the traditional policy of the Directors, which

Opinion on the war in England.

Hostility of the Court of Directors to Lord Hastings.

Native education.

The first native newspaper.

amounted in fact to the assumption that India could only be safe so long as its people were ignorant; and they afforded scope for irritating comments and censure upon the governor-general's conduct, which were as undeserved as they were illiberal; but he persevered notwithstanding, and laid the foundation of that great extension of education which is now in active progress.

Disapproval of the court.

The last years of Lord Hastings's administration were devoted by him, with a rare amount of labour, ability and comprehensiveness, to the duties of civil and financial administration: and though the details of Madras and Bombay were managed by their respective governments, his Lordship's supervision extended over all. His personal labour for nine years was enormous, and hardly credible; and wherever his intervention extended, it was on the side of liberal measures, and for the removal of oppressive or ill-suited laws: while at every turn he had to encounter the hardly-concealed enmity of members of his own Council, and their faction in the Court of Directors and Proprietors.

Lord Hastings's civil administration.

In 1819, the governor-general secured the cession and purchase of the island of Singapoor, which had become the great entrepôt of Eastern commerce; and an insurrection in the province of Kuttack, which had arisen from the rapacity of the subordinate government officials, was subdued and remedied. The financial results of this period of his tenure of office were more satisfactory, notwithstanding the expenses of the Nipâl and Mahratta wars, than those of any of his predecessors. There was an annual surplus of two millions sterling, with ample reserve in the treasury, and the national credit was established upon a more sound and enduring basis than it had ever before attained. During Lord Hastings's period, not the least reform was effected in the private and official conduct of the officers of government, civil and military, who were in every respect changed from the lawless times of Clive and Warren Hastings. Lord and Lady Hastings gave a high tone to the society of Calcutta; there was an honourable ambition to excel, induced by his patronage, and the new provinces and extended fields of labour excited efforts for distinction which were won by able servants of the period in all departments of the service. The servants of the company were no longer adventurers; on the contrary, it had become difficult to obtain India appointments by even the best families of England. Among all this glorious success, however, there arose a cloud which overshadowed the last days of Lord Hastings's administration, the story of which, though the details are immensely voluminous, must be told in a few words.

Singapoor purchased.

Successful financial results.

Reformation of government officials.

The Nizam's State, ravaged by Pindhárees and banditti, oppressed by its district administrators, and for the most part run to waste, was in an almost hopeless condition of insolvency. The Nizam, always weak and vacillating, had from the first no experience; and having secured private estates and sources of income, left the conduct of his affairs to his minister Moneer-ool-Moolk, and altogether retired from public life. Moneer-ool-Moolk had neither firmness nor capacity; and the executive administration fell into the hands of Rajah Chundoo Lall, whose ability could not indeed be questioned, but whose reckless financial conduct led to almost irretrievable results. The Resident at the court had no power to interfere, except by remonstrance, which was of little or no avail. It had been an object of the governor-general, in which he was supported by the court, to have the useless horse and foot of the Nizam's army reformed, as a measure of economy as well as efficiency; and, as regards a compact force of 10,000 men, artillery, cavalry, and infantry, the object was fully accomplished. No corresponding reduction was, however, made in the old or irregular troops, and the expenditure in the new force was established on a scale of liberality, hardly perhaps proportioned to the means available; but for the suppression of all local disorders, it was most efficient. The reckless extravagance of the minister continued, in spite of remonstrances; and as the revenue had fallen to a very low amount, Mr., afterwards Sir, Charles Metcalfe, in 1820, proceeded on a tour through the country, with a view to ascertaining its real condition. He then proposed, with the consent of the Nizam, to establish English officers in the several provinces, to make and guarantee the revenue settlements, and to act against the banditti; and the measure was carried out with good effect. Nor was it opposed by Chundoo Lall, whose ministerial revenues and credit were considerably enhanced. In the same year, Chundoo Lall solicited a loan of sixty lacs—600,000*l.*—from the banking-house of William Palmer & Co. of Hyderabad, and permission was granted for the transaction by the governor-general in Council on July 15.

Condition of the Nizam's State after the Mahratta War.

Supervision of the provinces by English officers.

Loan from Messrs. Wm. Palmer & Co.

The banking-house of Messrs. William Palmer & Co. had been established in 1814, under the license of the Supreme Government. The head of it, Mr. W. Palmer, was the son of General William Palmer, one of the ablest of the older school of diplomatists in India; he had entered the military service of the Nizam at an early age, and afterwards became a banker, in association with local native capitalists. In 1816, the Act 37 of Geo. III. c. 142, which prohibited pecuniary dealings with native powers by Europeans, was suspended in Messrs. Palmer's favour by an order in

Council, dated July 23, 1816, and the official instrument or deed which was transmitted to them, left them at liberty to carry on 'all acts within the territories of the Nizam, which are prohibited by the said Act of Parliament,' provided, that 'they communicate, when required to do so, the nature and objects of these transactions.' These transactions were manifold: the loan and other employment of capital, the opening of the trade of the country in cotton, timber, and other productions, and the import to a large extent of English manufactures; and it was by the punctual advances of the house alone, that the valuable reformed contingent was enabled to take and keep the field during the Mahratta war of 1817–18. Up to 1820, therefore, the same relations continued. The rates of interest were necessarily high, ranging from eighteen to twenty-four per cent.; but the Government of India had already borrowed at twelve per cent., and in the Nizam's and other native States the ordinary rates were from thirty-six, forty, and even more.

The house of Wm. Palmer & Co. suppressed.

The faction of the Calcutta Council which had consistently opposed Lord Hastings's measures was supported by a powerful party in England; and in 1820, the court withdrew the sanction of Council to the Hyderabad transactions. Messrs. Palmer's dealings with the minister were suddenly interdicted, and the sixty-lac loan paid off by the Resident. On his first arrival at Hyderabad, Mr. Metcalfe reported that, with the exception of a high rate of interest, he observed nothing in regard to the transactions of the house 'which required interference or restraint.' Again, 'that the house should be unfettered in its transactions,' and much more to the same purport. The change was sudden and overwhelming; and before the house could afford explanations, or draw up the documents which were afterwards so voluminously rendered, it had been irretrievably destroyed. Reasons for this strange issue appeared in time. Under the wealth and influence of the house, Sir Charles had considered himself slighted, and he recorded, perhaps on his convictions, however erroneous, that its further existence was dangerous. He saw also an opportunity for ridding the English Government of the annual payment of seven lacs—70,000*l.*—for the péshkush, or tribute for the Northern Circars, which had been punctually disbursed to the Nizam from year to year since their cession. This péshkush was, therefore, capitalised, to represent the sums due—78,70,670 rupees to Messrs. Palmer's, and 20,00,000 to the company; 98,70,670 rupees—987,000*l.*—or, in a fraction above, only twelve and a half years' purchase of the annual payment.

Capitalisation of the péshkush of the Northern Circars.

From this arbitrary course, two prominently important results ensued. First, the utmost offence was given to his Highness the Nizam, by the cessation of the péshkush under any circumstances—much more on a point connected with the financial affairs of his dominions, with which the British Government had no pretence whatever of interference. His protestations were in proportion bitter and vehement; but they were unheeded, and the act of spoliation has neither been forgiven nor forgotten to this day. It was considered a deliberate insult, and an arbitrary exercise of power over a helpless ally, and it was unquestionably both; while the sum allowed was quite inadequate to the value obtained. Secondly, to Chundoo Lall, or to the Nizam's government, the payment of the loan was of no practical benefit, but indeed much the contrary: for it loosed the minister's hands, and drove him into the power of Arabs, Patáns, Gosains, military chiefs, and local bankers, who, desperate as the credit of the State was, extorted the highest possible rates of usurious interest and bonuses for years afterwards, and brought it to the verge of extinction. 'So long,' said Chundoo Lall, 'as I can borrow three and pay one, I can go on.'

Offence to the Nizam.

Mischievous results of the transaction.

It was not, however, before the payment of the loan only that the house of William Palmer & Co. broke down. All their other dealings, of every kind, were at the same time proclaimed to be illegal, and the consequences were inevitable destruction. All outstanding debts, instalments, districts held in mortgage, district advances for timber and cotton, were forfeited. The house paid twenty-five per cent by way of instalment, but its further exertions were for the time utterly paralysed. The sequel to these transactions did not follow for several years, and will be related in its appropriate place; but the mortifications to which Lord Hastings had been exposed by the unworthy suspicions of the Court of Directors, and more than insinuations of corrupt motives in regard to Sir William Rumbold's connection with William Palmer & Co., were insupportable. He sent home his resignation in 1821, though he did not leave India till January 1, 1823: a great and good man, who, like Clive, Warren Hastings, and Lord Wellesley, was yet to experience the bitter effects of that clique by which his greatest acts, and most triumphant policy, had been persistently opposed.

Causes for the insolvency of Wm. Palmer & Co.

Mortification of Lord Hastings.

CHAPTER VI.

THE ADMINISTRATION OF LORD AMHERST—THE BURMESE WAR, 1823 TO 1825.

Mr. Adam acts as governor-general.

Lord Hastings was succeeded by Mr. Adam, the senior member of Council, who had uniformly opposed all his liberal measures, and who had assisted in, if not brought about, the ruin of Messrs. William Palmer & Co. Mr. Canning had been nominated to succeed the governor-general; but he preferred to remain in the English ministry, and of the two other candidates, Lord William Bentinck, and Lord Amherst who had recently conducted an embassy to China, the choice fell upon Lord Amherst; but it was seven months before he arrived in India. During this period, the narrow, despotic mind of Mr. Adam found congenial employment in ruining Mr. Silk Buckingham, the editor of one of the Calcutta newspapers, by deporting him from India, and prohibiting the issue of his paper. This was the only event of moment by which the interregnum was rendered memorable, and by which it attained an unenviable notoriety. Mr. Adam died at sea, on his passage home, and thus escaped the retaliation of Mr. Buckingham before the English people, and Mr. Buckingham was subsequently silenced by an annuity.

Lord Amherst appointed.

Disturbed relations with Burmah.

Lord Amherst reached Calcutta on August 1, 1823, and found the relations of the Government of India with the Burmese in an unsatisfactory and menacing position. During the administration of Lord Hastings, the Burmese, in 1818, had arrogantly demanded the cession of the whole of Eastern Bengal, and threatened to take it, if not given up. The governor-general, affecting to believe the letter a forgery, sent it back without comment; but it was not the less an authentic document. It proceeded out of the success which had attended the Burmese extension of their dominions, which, in 1822, had included Assam by conquest, and thus brought them, without any intervening power, to the frontiers of the British. Over the province of Assam the authority of the English had not been extended; and up to the date of its conquest, from a very early period, it had not only preserved its entire independence, but maintained its position against every attempt to subdue it by the Imperial viceroys of Bengal. Desirous as the Burmese were for war with the English, affairs were brought to a crisis by a claim made by the Burmese governor of Assam to the island

The Burmese occupy Shahpooree.

of Shahpooree, at the mouth of the Naaf river; and without attending to the governor-general's desire that the right to it should be decided by a mutual commission, forcibly occupied it by troops, which drove out the British detachment in charge, with some loss. The island was soon recovered, and a remonstrance addressed to the King of Ava; but this only produced a fresh ebullition of arrogance, and Máha Bundoola, the great Burmese general, was dispatched with an army, and a pair of golden fetters, to conquer Bengal, and send the governor-general, bound, to the 'golden feet' of the king.

The island recovered.

Remonstrance being useless, Lord Amherst, finding the Burmese general was preparing to invade Bengal on two points, issued a declaration of war on February 24, 1824. In regard to funds for the war, the situation of Government was one of unexampled prosperity. There was a surplus of two millions sterling a year, and ten millions sterling were in reserve in the public treasuries; and there was no apprehension felt as to the conduct of the native troops in a foreign country, who, at Java, the Mauritius, and in Egypt, had already proved their devotion. The greatest difficulty was in selecting a point for invasion. The eastern part of Bengal was a succession of forests, morasses, and deep unfordable streams; the climate was known to be most unhealthly, if not deadly, and the difficulty of transporting an army by land, with all its stores, was evidently insuperable. On the other hand, Captain Canning, who had been employed as envoy to the Burmese court, suggested an attack by sea on Rangoon, to be followed by an advance up the river Irrawaddy; and this plan was ultimately carried out.

Lord Amherst declares war.

Difficulty of attacking Burmah.

Captain Canning's project.

The Burmese had, in the meantime, been prompt in action. They had sent 20,000 men, under Bundoola, to the frontier of Bengal, where they drove in and destroyed a light detachment, under Captain Norton, on May 17; but their progress was checked by the advance of a regular force from Bengal. Meanwhile the army of invasion, consisting of 12,000 men, chiefly from Madras, had assembled at the Andaman Islands under the command of Sir Archibald Camp bell;and on May 11 the town of Rangoon, at the mouth of the Irrawaddy, was occupied, almost without resistance. Advance, however, proved impossible; the heavy continuous rain prevented movement for six months, and the army had to lie inactive, suffering from short supplies of bad unwholesome rations, and the climate. Some employment was found in minor operations on the Tenasserim coast, when its capital, Martaban, was taken possession of; and also in the capture of stockades near Rangoon,

Burmese proceedings.

Rangoon captured.

Martaban captured.

many of which were extremely strong, but in most instances ill defended.

Bundoola attacks Rangoon.

On December 1, Bundoola, abandoning his attack on Bengal, arrived near Rangoon with an army of 60,000 men, and the campaign opened in earnest. He commenced his operations by stockading the whole of his front, which was effected with great skill and rapidity. On the 6th these stockades were attacked by a combined force of infantry and gunboats, and partly destroyed; but Bundoola retaliated on the 7th by an assault on the English position at the great pagoda, which was repulsed with heavy loss to his forces, and followed up by four columns, which broke through the Burmese stockades and breastworks, and drove their whole army from the field. On the 15th the capture of the strong stockaded position of Kokein followed, and Bundoola retreated to Donabew with his whole army. On the side of Arracan, two expeditions proved failures, not from opposition by the enemy, for none was experienced, and Colonel Richards, with an insignificant force, had occupied the capital of Assam; but the impossibility of conveying troops through forests and morasses had forced Colonel Shuldham and his army of 7,000 men to return, and General Morrison, who marched from Chittagong with 10,000 men, lost most of them by the pestilential fever of Arracan, and the survivors were recalled. These movements gave rise to a deplorable episode of the war, in the disaffection of three Sepoy regiments, the 26th, 47th, and 62nd, which were under orders for Assam, and the actual mutiny of the 47th. The Burmese war had become a terror to men who had fought through the campaigns in Central India. The climate of the country, the magical arts of the Burmese, and their supposed invincibility, had possessed the minds of the Sepoys with a weird dread; and there was some discontent also about carriage. On November 1, the 47th was ordered to parade in marching order, for inspection. Some of the men obeyed, but the rest refused to attend the parade. On the 2nd the order was repeated, and two of H.M.'s regiments, with a detachment of artillery, were sent to the station—Barrackpoor—to enforce its execution. The three native regiments were paraded, and a solemn warning was conveyed to the 47th, after which their native officers left them. They were ordered to ground their arms, but they received the word with defiant shouts, on which the artillery present opened fire. The Sepoys broke, and fled, and eleven men were killed. The mutiny of the 47th was thus summarily repressed; the 26th and 62nd were not noticed, but the number of the 47th was struck out of the list of the army.

His defeat.

Difficulties in Assam.

Mutiny of three Sepoy regiments.

After the failures in Bengal, there remained only the route by the Irrawaddy; and in February, Sir Archibald Campbell was prepared to advance, in three columns, of which the central, by land, was under his own command; the second in boats under Brigadier Cotton, and the third, under Colonel Sale, having been first sent to take Bassein, which was easily effected, returned to Rangoon. Brigadier Cotton, whose force only amounted to 600 men, attacked the famous stockaded position of Donabew on March 7; but it was defended by 12,000 of the flower of the Burmese army, under the renowned Bundoola in person, and the assault was repulsed. On hearing of this event, Sir Archibald Campbell, whose force was considerably in advance, returned; and during a bombardment of the position on April 3, Bundoola was killed by a shell, whereupon the whole Burmese army retreated, leaving all their guns and stores, and the position was occupied without resistance. No further opposition was experienced, and on the 25th Prome, the capital of Lower Burmah, was occupied by the army, which took up quarters for the monsoon. Hence Sir Archibald Campbell gave it to be understood that he was empowered to negotiate for peace; and the Burmese, who had again assembled an army of 50,000 men, sent envoys to him for the purpose of negotiation. The terms proposed by the governor-general were, however, rejected by the king, and at the close of the rains the war was resumed.

Advance by the river Irrawaddy

Assault on Donabew repulsed.

Bundoola killed.

The Burmese retreat.

Proposals for peace.

At this time Sir A. Campbell had not more than 5,000 men with him; but they were in high health, and the real value of the Burmese in war had been already tested. The first expedition against the enemy, an attack on the position of Watigaon, on November 15, was repulsed with a loss of 200 men, and Brigadier MacDougall, who was in command. The enemy, as they had done at Rangoon, now gradually drew round Prome; and on December 1, Sir A. Campbell attacked their stockades on the Nawain river, and carried them in succession; and on January 19, the position of Mallown was similarly assaulted and captured, with a great number of guns, and much *matériel* of war.

The war proceeds.

Sir A. Campbell's successes.

The king, now really alarmed, dispatched Dr. Price, an American missionary, from Ava, to ascertain terms of peace; but before an answer could be obtained, the Burmese commander, Muring Phuring, had marched direct upon Prome, with 16,000 men—all that remained to him. Sir Archibald Campbell had only 1,300 men available, but he attacked the Burmese at once, on February 9, 1825, and drove

The king sues for peace.

them ignominiously from the field. The defeated general carried the news of his own loss to Ava, and begged for a new army; but he was beheaded the same evening, and the king set himself in earnest to obtain peace, sending Dr. Price and Mr. Jordan, American missionaries, with his own ministers, and a portion of the money before demanded, to Sir Archibald Campbell, who by this time had advanced to Yandaboo, within sixty miles of the capital. The terms of a treaty were soon arranged, and it was finally executed on February 24. By it the Burmese king ceded Tenasserim, Arracan, and Assam: and agreed to pay a million sterling, on account of the expenses of the war, of which twenty-five lacs—250,000*l*.—were forthwith delivered. An envoy from the governor-general was also to reside at Ava for the future.

The Burmese defeated.

The king's deputation to Sir A. Campbell.

Treaty of Yandaboo.

There was no doubt that this war had been mismanaged: but neither the country nor the climate, nor indeed the enemy, had been understood. The Burmese power and resources had been vastly overrated; and had the expedition been deferred to a proper season, when, as it did at last, it could have advanced at once by land, it would no doubt have carried all before it, and concluded a peace in one season. The war cost nearly 13,000,000*l*. sterling; but the provinces obtained have proved cheap at this cost, and are still improving. Assam produces tea equal to that of China, and the cultivation is fast increasing. Arracan is the most fertile rice district in India, and the Tenasserim coast boasts of the city and port of Moulmein, erst a small village, now an entrepôt for Eastern commerce, with a trade of nearly 1,000,000*l*. a year. The Court of Directors, who had hitherto been accustomed to value the issue of a war only by what it would yield, were astonished by the expenditure which had swept away all Lord Hastings's accumulations, and there was a loud cry for Lord Amherst's recal; but he was nevertheless suffered to remain.

Effects of the war.

CHAPTER VII.

THE ADMINISTRATION OF LORD AMHERST (*concluded*), 1825 TO 1828.

THE result of the English invasion of Burmah was watched with intense and extraordinary anxiety by all classes of the credulous and superstitious people of India; and to the strange magical acts of the Burmese, and their invinci-

Native opinion on the Burmese war.

ble prowess, were attributed the inaction of the army which had been sent. The truth, which lay in heavy continuous rain, bad food, and a country which became a flooded morass, was credited by none. The English, who had crushed Mahrattas, Patáns, and Pindhárees in a single campaign, lay, it was actually believed, helpless before an enemy who slew their soldiers by incantation, or prevented them from 'raising their feet,' and so confined them to a narrow strip of coast, where all must inevitably perish. No reports on this subject, however absurd, were too gross for credence, and by them many hopes were awakened among the military classes, now unemployed, with whom war and rapine had been the hereditary occupation of centuries. The English would, no doubt, persevere in the Burmese war; but they would sacrifice their army, and then—the old flags would be raised, and the result would not a second time be doubtful. Many strange crises of native feelings had from time to time arisen in India; but it is questionable whether any more universally experienced, or in which the truth was more hopelessly obscured and denied, was ever before encountered. There is always, however, a culminating point in such periods of excitement, and in this instance it appeared at Bhurtpoor.

Absurd credulity.

No disaffection had been manifested by the Játs since Lord Lake's peace with them in 1805; but their rajah was dead, his son had succeeded, and his heir, a boy of tender age, had been recognised by the government of India at his special request, and a political officer had assisted at the ceremony. Hardly a year had elapsed before the boy succeeded his father; but Doorjun Sál, his cousin, set him aside, and confined him, placing himself at the head of the troops, and proclaiming his own succession. Sir David Ochterlony—who held the office of political agent to the governor-general in Northern India, was perfectly aware of the existing feeling among the native military classes, and saw that any successful adventurer would draw tens of thousands of idle men to his standard for another struggle for dominion. He was prompt in action. He ordered an army of 16,000 men and 100 guns to support the nomination of the British Government, and would have attacked Bhurtpoor forthwith, but Lord Amherst prevented him. He was peremptorily ordered to recall the troops and the proclamation he had issued; and the veteran soldier and diplomatist, perceiving the animus of the order he had received, resigned his office, after writing an able protest, and retired to Meerut. He never recovered the indignity he had suffered, and died two months afterwards, as he said, of a broken heart. Sir Charles Metcalfe had been

Affairs of Bhurtpoor.

Doorjun Sál usurps the State.

Sir David Ochterlony's proceedings.

Death of Sir David Ochterlony.

summoned from Hyderabad in anticipation of Sir David's resignation, and eventually took charge of political affairs.

There can be no doubt that Sir David Ochterlony's policy was the true one, and his sacrifice to satisfy a Calcutta party was an act of weakness on the part of the governor-general which was welcomed with avidity by the disaffected. There ensued only one comment on the transaction throughout India,—the English are afraid to attack Bhurtpoor. Doorjun Sál, who would have yielded to a real show of force, would have submitted; the Ját chiefs would have rallied round their lawful prince; and the disaffected would have been overawed. As it was, they were encouraged: and in a short time 25,000 men had engaged themselves, 'to fight the company behind the walls which had defied Lord Lake, the conqueror of Hindostan.' And not only this, but the whole of the north-west, with its seething crowds of petty chiefs and military adventurers, the lawless chieftains of Bundelkhund and Malwah, the Mahrattas of Sindia and Holkar, were, it was evident on the best grounds, prepared to support the rising should any chance of success appear. Lord Amherst and his council were dismayed; nor was it till the arrival of Sir Charles Metcalfe from Hyderabad that the effects of the panic were redeemed. His minute on the subject is one of the finest of his state papers. He recorded that not only the interest, but the duty of the British Government to the people it had already rescued from anarchy, required the exercise of a bold, prompt, and uncompromising policy in regard to Bhurtpoor; and finally the governor-general and his council confirmed the opinion.

Native opinion in regard to English inaction;

its results.

Sir Charles Metcalfe's minute.

There was no delay; 20,000 troops of all arms, with 100 pieces of artillery, took the field and marched upon Bhurtpoor, under the command of Lord Combermere, the commander-in-chief. The army arrived on December 10, 1826, and the siege commenced. Sir Charles Metcalfe, who had joined Lord Combermere, again attempted to convince Doorjun Sál and the insurgents of their folly; but he could make no impression, they were too deeply compromised by intrigues at every native court in India to recede, and the siege operations progressed in earnest. Bhurtpoor had been much strengthened since the previous siege, which had exposed the weakness of some of the defences, and was impregnable before any ordinary attack. The heaviest artillery made no impression upon its immense walls and bastions, which were constructed of tenacious clay only: and at length mining was resorted to—a course advised from the first by Lieutenant Forbes, of the Engineers, but previously rejected. On January 18, a great mine containing 10,000 pounds

Preparations for the siege of Bhurtpoor.

Strength of the fort.

of gunpowder, laid under the principal bastion and counterscarp of the ditch, was exploded, and the fort was stormed and captured in a few hours; 6,000 of the enemy perished in its defence, but the loss of the British did not exceed 1,000 of all ranks. Doorjun Sál was apprehended in an attempt to escape, and the boy rajah was placed upon his throne on January 20, 1826, by Sir Charles Metcalfe and the commander-in-chief. The fortifications were thrown down into the ditch, and the whole levelled with the adjacent ground.

Bhurtpoor is stormed and taken.

So far the proceedings of the army had been glorious; but the public wealth and property of the family were seized as prize money by the forces, and, in the words of Sir Charles Metcalfe, 'our plundering, under the name of prize, has been very disgraceful, and has tarnished our well-earned honour.' The only alternative to save the property of the State would have been to grant a substantial donation to the troops as an equivalent; but this was not adopted, owing to the effects of severe financial pressure, and the 'prize money' of Bhurtpoor was subsequently divided among its captors. It is impossible to over-estimate the effect of the capture of Bhurtpoor combined with the destruction of its fortifications: and with this victory, and the conclusion of the Burmese war, the open disaffection of the armed classes of India passed away. Since Doorjun Sál, now a prisoner at Benares, had failed, no one else remained to lead a desperate enterprise: and the real power of the English, their inexhaustible resources, and their unfailing 'ikbál' or prestige, became perhaps more fully impressed upon the native mind than before.

Private property seized as prize-money.

Effects of the capture of Bhurtpoor.

Lord Amherst had been created an earl for his services, and had received the thanks of the Courts of Directors and Proprietors. His health had been indifferent in India, and he proceeded on a tour in the north-west provinces at the close of 1826, visiting the principal cities, receiving the homage of the chiefs, and finally retiring to Simlah in the Himalayas, for the hot weather, the first time it had been used as a vice-regal sanatorium. During his absence, the Council at Calcutta again signalised itself by an attack upon the press, one editor being summarily deported for a harmless squib; but during his residence in Calcutta, Lord Amherst had supported the press liberally, and relaxed many restrictions now re-imposed. The governor-general's progress through the provinces of Upper India was attended with excellent effect. He visited Lukhnow, where the Nawáb, now king, then in infirm health, died in the month of October 1827, and was succeeded by

Lord Amherst created an earl.

Simlah established as a vice-regal residence.

Beneficial effects of the governor-general's tour.

his son, Solimân Jáh. In a visit to the ex-emperor of Dehly, his future position was pointed out to him; and at Simlah, visits from agents of Runjeet Singh, Sindia, Holkar, and the princes of Rajpootana, with the various questions relating to each, fully occupied his lordship's attention. In March of 1827, the great Dowlut Ráo Sindia died of a chronic disease with which he had long been afflicted. He left no issue, male or female; but his wife, Báiza Bye, was allowed to adopt a successor, and a boy of eleven years old, Junkojee, was selected from among his relatives, and recognised by the governor-general. An old prediction exists in this family, that reigning Sindias leave no male heirs, which, up to the present day, has been strangely fulfilled.

Death of Dowlut Ráo Sindia.

The only other political event of importance which deserves record, is the attainment of his majority by the Rajah of Nagpoor: when his territories, which had been managed with admirable skill by Mr. Jenkins, from the period of his election to the sovereignty, in 1818, were delivered over to his charge. Material prosperity, and cultivation, had increased to an extent never before known in Berar; but the prosperity of the people only served to incite exaction, and in a comparatively short period the last memorials of Mr. Jenkins' benevolent administration had been utterly eradicated.

The Rajah of Berar attains his majority.

Lord Amherst's departure from India was accelerated by the intelligence of the dangerous illness of his daughter, and he left Calcutta in February 1828, having some time before sent home his resignation. For the present he was succeeded by Mr. Butterworth Bayley, the senior member of Council; but Lord William Bentinck had obtained the appointment of governor-general in 1827, and he arrived in Calcutta on July 4, 1828.

Lord Amherst leaves India.

Lord William Bentinck succeeds.

CHAPTER VIII.

PROGRESS IN MADRAS AND BOMBAY, 1813 TO 1828.

SINCE the termination of the war with Tippoo Sooltan, the progress of events in the southern presidency, Madras, had been very uneventful. No enemies remained to be overcome, and the whole of the ceded and conquered provinces remained tranquil. There was some difficulty, however, in establishing the demand for land revenue on an uniform basis, and it was not till Sir Thomas, then Colonel, Munro, who had

Sir Thomas Munro's land settlements.

been placed in charge of the ceded districts, struck out a plan for general settlements, that any decided measures were adopted. Like all parts of India in which the Mahomedans had not interfered with the original Hindoo system, it existed all over the new districts: not, perhaps, in so perfect a form as in the Deccan, but still sufficiently intact to preserve its distinctive existence, and to form a foundation for regular proceedings. The first attempts at settlement were made in imitation of Bengal with the few Zemindars, or landed proprietors, who were found to exist; but these classes were in no wise analogous to the Zemindars of Bengal. There the land had ceased to belong to the people. Their original rights, whatever they had been, had ceased to exist, and the land had passed into the possession of the Zemindars. In the Madras provinces, on the contrary, the land, according to immemorial custom, belonged to the people in right of occupancy, subject to the payment of the rulers' taxes; and the individual tenures were Meras, which involved hereditary occupation on payment of a fixed rent—with tenancies at will, in regard to lands which had originally been Meras, but had lapsed into the general village stock, and could be rented from year to year by payment in money, or by a proportion of the crop in kind. The so-called Zemindars, therefore, were not, in general, proprietors of the soil, though they possessed individual Meras rights; they were, with the exception of those who were hereditary princes or nobles of formerly existent Hindoo or Mahomedan dynasties, for the most part district or village officers: some of revenue, some of police, who held their position by hereditary rights of great antiquity. Any settlements with parties in such positions necessarily failed; and the people resented them, as conferring new rights upon the Zemindars, to which they were not entitled by ancient usage. The so-called Zemindars, therefore, became no more in fact than farmers of the revenue, which gave rise to many abuses, and was extremely unpopular.

Native system.

Settlements with Zemindars.

Local tenures.

Failure of the settlement with Zemindars.

These questions led Colonel Munro to consider the propriety and possibility of making settlements with the people themselves, or Ryots, as they are usually termed; and his measures, which had a semblance of possibility and even improvement upon the old native system, were put in operation. The lands of every village were surveyed after a rough fashion, and assessed; and a demand, equal to one-third of the produce of each crop or field, instituted. In the first place, the demand was too high, as the old Hindoo rate was from a seventh to a fifth: and, in the second, the proprietary rights of the people were not considered. It was a vast aggregation of tenants at will,

Ryotwary settlement.

Means adopted.

and was marked by many oppressive clauses. Lands were allotted to individuals which they might be unable or unwilling to cultivate, yet they could be punished by fine or even flogging for refusal. When the crops of certain fields failed, their rent could be assessed upon the village cultivation in general. Above all, the cultivator was taxed according to the crop he had sown, not according to the value of the land; and the duty of an officer of government was to visit every village, revise the record of cultivation, and assess the crop as it stood.

Severe penalties.

It will be understood how prolific such a system was in abuses of all kinds, and of oppression of the people; but it secured, for a time, a larger amount of revenue than had ever before been collected, and the system was therefore lauded and confirmed. When General Munro visited England in 1818, he was created a Knight Commander of the Bath for his services both in a military and civil capacity, and he returned to India as governor of the presidency in which he had so long served. Now, as administrator general over the whole of the provinces, he could calmly review the working of the land revenue system; and it is recorded to his credit, that he had no hesitation in undoing much of his own work, and relaxing the most stringent of the former crude and oppressive regulations. Cultivation was rendered voluntary; imprisonment and other punishment for refusals to cultivate, cesses for failure of crops, and, in general, all the objectionable provisions of the old system, were abolished; but even Sir Thomas could not get beyond a yearly settlement with each cultivator, and thus the yearly tenancies at will were continued. The ancient hereditary rights and practices fell into desuetude; while it was certain that the new system not only perpetuated the evils of the immediately preceding exactive native governments, but actually exceeded them. There were gross errors in regard to the land settlements in Bengal and in the north-western provinces; but it is questionable whether anything so universally depressing and demoralising as the Ryotwary system of Madras was ever attempted there. The old native proprietary of the north-western provinces, in many cases, disappeared under the action of the English laws, and of fraud, which it was impossible to check; but the people, even in such instances, were not reached as in Madras, and in the most material respects were not interfered with.

Abuses of the system.

Modification of the rules.

The relaxations in the revenue system of Madras, however, such had been the misery consequent upon its first establishment, rendered Sir Thomas Munro most popular among the people of the country; and over all hereditary rights and charitable endowments he had extended his protection. He

Sir Thomas Munro's popularity.

would have retired in 1824; but remained, especially to make provision for the Burmese war, until 1827, when, in a farewell visit to his old provinces and native friends, he sank under an attack of cholera at Puteechinta, near Gooty, to the great grief of the entire population he had governed and been intimately connected with for the whole period of his service.

His death.

In Bombay, the people had been more fortunate. Mr. Elphinstone, who was thoroughly acquainted with the existing institutions of the Mahratta country, very judiciously made no alteration in them. The Péshwah's territory had become so wasted by mal-administration, exaction, and plunder, that, added to the ravages of war and local banditti, much of it was lying waste; hamlets and villages had disappeared, villages had dwindled into hamlets, and once prosperous towns into half-deserted villages. To restore confidence and encourage the re-cultivation of the land was the first object. Easy settlements were made with villages on terms of five years; and though the principle has been called Ryotwar, and each cultivator's land and payments were entered in the village accounts, there was no interference with his proceedings; and on the old native system, the assessment lay not on the crop, as in Madras, but on the land itself. Nor was any change made in this proceeding until by enquiry and experience the government was enabled to carry out a more permanent and beneficial settlement. During his incumbency, Mr. Elphinstone completed the code of civil and criminal procedure which had been commenced by Governor Duncan and Sir James Mackintosh, and which, of all the older codes of India, has been found the most practical and most suited to the people, and has required less subsequent alteration. Luminous and simple, it provided for every existing want, and secured freedom and protection; and from first to last has contributed, in no small degree, to the social advancement of the country in which it was promulgated.

Bombay system.

Civil and criminal law.

After the Mahratta war, the noble province of Khandésh, which had been formerly a garden under its Mahomedan kings, was found to be, for the most part, a desert jungle. It had furnished the great plundering ground of Holkar and Sindia: and the Bheels, who had been repressed by the Mahomedans, had returned to it and increased its desolation. Forces were continually employed against them; but it was not till Lieutenant James, afterwards Sir James, Outram, of the 23rd Bombay Native Infantry, threw himself among them, visited their haunts at great personal risk, and made friends of their rude chiefs, that any impression was made on them. By degrees, also, a Bheel corps was raised by him: and by these and other means,

Khandésh.

Outram's success in reclamation of the Bheels.

the habits of this hitherto intractable aboriginal race were reformed. Sir James Outram afterwards attained high distinction; but it is doubtful whether any act of his life confers more honour on him than his reclamation of his wild hunting companions, the Bheels of Khandésh.

Ramoosee insurrection.

The only other disturbances of any moment which ruffled the tranquillity of Mr. Elphinstone's administration was the insurrection of the Ramoosees—another aboriginal tribe dispersed through the villages of the Deccan—under Oomajee Näik. It was, however, chiefly confined to the province of Ahmednugger, and directed principally against the Brahmins, of whom the Näik had a bitter hatred. Oomajee contrived, after the dispersion of his followers in 1827, to escape for some time; but he was eventually cleverly apprehended at Punderpoor, and suffered the penalty of his crimes. Mr. Elphinstone returned to England in 1827, and was succeeded by Sir John Malcolm.

Provincial administration of the Nizam's dominions by English officers.

After Sir Charles Metcalfe's departure, the office of Resident at Hyderabad was conferred upon Mr. W. Byam Martin, a Bengal civilian of large experience in 'regulation' judicial affairs. The European agency for the administration of the dominions of his Highness the Nizam, established by Sir Charles Metcalfe, was considerably enlarged, and with very beneficial results to the people. The first revenue settlements, like those in the Péshwah's late territories, had been made for terms of five years, and no interference had been exercised with the existent village administration. As these settlements expired, others were made on the same principle. The great object to which the employment of the English officers was directed, and, indeed, of the whole system, was to prevent exaction in excess of the rental by the native collectors; and the protection to the people ensured by these means resulted in an immense increase of cultivation, while the revenue, enhanced in proportion, was punctually realised. So long as the old Nizam, Sikundur Jáh, lived, no change was made; for he had thoroughly appreciated results which had indeed become self-evident, in the check which they imposed upon the rapacity of his minister, Chundoo Lall. But on his demise in 1829, and the succession of his son, Nasir-ood-Dowlah, a demand was somewhat rudely made by him at the instigation of Chundoo Lall, who had become impatient of control, for a sudden recall of all English officers employed in civil duties; and though those were allowed to remain who had concluded settlements, till the period of their expiration, their authority was circumscribed, and the people soon, and very bitterly, experienced the deplorable change which the measure involved.

The English officers are withdrawn.

These several transactions have, perhaps, comparatively little connection with the general history of India, but as they involved the well-being of many millions of its people, a brief notice of them is recorded.

CHAPTER IX.

THE ADMINISTRATION OF LORD WILLIAM BENTINCK, 1820 TO 1830.

THE results of Lord William Bentinck's government of India are so admirably summarised in the inscription on his statue at Calcutta, written by Lord Macaulay, that they form the most appropriate introduction to the variety of great means of advancement of which he was the author. This eloquent record has been, and will be in the future, read by thousands, with the conviction that it is not only literally true, but that his administration formed the basis of all the benevolent measures which have since arisen to redeem the English from those accusations of selfish and exclusive policy in regard to the natives of the country, with which they were charged. The inscription on the pedestal of the statue runs as follows:—'This statue is erected to William Cavendish Bentinck, who, during seven years, ruled India with eminent prudence, integrity, and benevolence; who, placed at the head of a great empire, never laid aside the simplicity and moderation of a private citizen; who infused into Oriental despotism the spirit of British freedom; who never forgot that the end of government is the welfare of the governed; who abolished cruel rites; who effaced humiliating distinctions; who allowed liberty to the expression of public opinion; whose constant study it was to elevate the moral and intellectual character of the government committed to his charge;—this monument was erected by men who, differing from each other in race, in manners, and in religion, cherish, with equal veneration and gratitude, the memory of his wise, upright, and paternal administration.' No such record exists of the services of any previous governor-general of India; and the brilliant triumphs of Clive, of Warren Hastings, of Lord Wellesley, and the Marquess of Hastings, are wanting in the peculiar and hitherto non-existent charm which is attached to the memory of Lord William Bentinck. During his incumbency, there were no glorious victories to be recorded, for no enemies remained to be overcome; but the successful development of moral force, and the

Inscription on the statue of Lord William Bentinck.

Character of his administration.

conversion of long-existing prejudices into a steady policy of improvement and advancement, is a triumph even more transcendent in the aggregate than that of successful war. Yet Lord William Bentinck had already been roughly dismissed from his government of Madras, and there were many who, from the early measures of his government of India, predicted even greater failure than, as was alleged, had attended his first Indian career.

His simple habits, the absence of State etiquette, which had been a distinctive feature of his predecessors, and, above all, the measures he had pledged himself to carry out, rendered him at first unpopular in a high degree, both with the civil service and the army. He had bound himself to effect reforms in the disbursements of the State, which the cost of the Burmese war had rendered imperative; but despite the opposition which he immediately encountered, he proceeded with them without delay. The allowances of the Civil Service were reduced, and as far as possible proportioned in regard to the various ranks and offices; but the measures of retrenchment as regarded the army involved more difficult considerations and no little danger. The Half Batta question, as it was termed, affected every officer and man in the army, and produced violent remonstrance and opposition. If the Court of Directors had given the governor-general a discretion to deal with the order they had sent to him according to circumstances, it is more than probable, from his recorded opinion, that the insignificant saving it finally accomplished, which did not exceed two lacs (20,000*l.*) a year, would have been abandoned; but in proportion as the demands of the army rose, the determination to exact absolute obedience from the officers continued, both by the Court and the governor-general; and in the end the measure was determined upon, though not as regarded the whole army. Stations within 400 miles from Calcutta only suffered, while all beyond were exempted. Having carried their points of obedience, it would have been an act of grace on the part of the directors to have acknowledged the faithful submission of their army by the abolition of the order; but, irritating and practically unnecessary as it was, it remained in force to the last. The magnanimity which would have directed its revision was absent.

Financial reforms.

Half Batta question.

The resumption of rent-free tenures was another unpopular measure as regarded the natives of Bengal; but had a real foundation in justice to the State. The alienations of land by Talookdars, Zemindars, and even petty village officers, under our own and former native governments, had been very large—in many instances they were without any sanction of superior authority, and the whole were revised.

Resumption of rent-free tenures in Bengal.

Those who could establish their rights to free lands were confirmed in them; from those who failed to do so they were resumed. The saving to Government was about thirty lacs (300,000*l.*) a year. The question had been first mooted in 1793, and additional powers were given to the English revenue officers on the subject in 1810. The measure had not, therefore, by any means originated with Lord William Bentinck; but the Act III. of 1828 brought the long-existing question to a final settlement, and all persons who failed to prove recent free tenure were allowed to retain their lands on payment of the regulated assessment.

The year 1829 was marked by one of the governor-general's most famous and most humane measures,—the abolition of Suttee throughout India. It was a subject to which he addressed himself with great earnestness directly he arrived in Calcutta. He applied for the opinions of military officers of experience as to the feeling of the native army on the subject; to civilians and other persons long resident in India as to those of the people at large. Here and there, as in the case of Mr. H. H. Wilson, he met with men who believed that the abolition of the rite would be attended with the highest degree of danger; and there were many also who, perpetuating the older traditions of the service, while they would fain have seen the cruel evil removed, yet lacked the nerve to make a step in advance of them, and pleaded the prescriptive right of the people to do as their forefathers had done for generations past. But Lord William Bentinck was deterred by no fears, and he had certainly no sympathy with the old service traditions. He saw no danger in India; and he was well aware that the whole of the public in England would welcome the abolition of the rite as one, perhaps the first, of England's great reforms of Hindoo abuse. On December 14, 1829, therefore, supported by Sir Charles Metcalfe and Mr. Bayley, the Act was passed, from which every governor-general, from Lord Cornwallis to Lord Minto, had shrunk with apprehensions, which they had recorded. Those implicated in the act of Suttee were now chargeable with wilful murder: those assisting at the rite with being accessaries. There were a few attempts to evade the law, but they were promptly suppressed, and the horrible rite ceased to exist.

Abolition of Suttee.

Success of the measure.

With 1830 came another deliverance from a great public danger, in the suppression of Thuggee. The word is derived from the Hindee verb 'Thugna,' to cheat or deceive; but in the sense it was used it meant the strangulation of travellers by Thugs, a fraternity which, from the earliest ages, had infested the roads of India, from the Himalayas

Operations against Thuggee.

to Cape Comorin, and from Guzerat to Assam. Occasionally gangs of these murderers had been apprehended; and in native States, and the Punjâb, punished by death or mutilation; but no knowledge of their peculiar association had been obtained.

Discovery of the crime.

One evening in 1829, as Major Sleeman, then the deputy commissioner of the Saugor district, was seated at his tent door, a man, advancing rapidly, threw himself at his feet, and begged to be allowed to make an important communication; but that Mrs. Sleeman should withdraw. He then proceeded to state that he was a leader of a gang of Thugs then not far off, and that the grove at Mundésur, in which Major Sleeman's camp was pitched, was full of corpses of travellers who had been murdered. Next day the hideous proof was given by exhumation of dead bodies where he pointed out their graves, and no time was lost in apprehending the gang to which the leader had belonged. Many of them became approvers, and by degrees circle after circle of information spread till they had covered all India. Hardly a province or district was found free from Thugs, and in their rites, proceedings, passwords and signs, there was little difference found anywhere.

Proceedings of the Thugs.

The system of the Thugs was to decoy travellers, single or in bodies, to join their gangs on pretence of mutual protection; to carry them on, sometimes for days in succession, to some spot decided upon, when, at a signal given by the leader, all were strangled and buried in graves already prepared for them. Major, afterwards Sir William, Sleeman, in a most interesting and effective report, laid the information he had obtained before Government; and Lord William Bentinck did not hesitate to put in force the strongest means at his disposal for the suppression of the crime. A new department was forthwith organised, and placed under the control of Major Sleeman, who applied all his great energy to the work, and was ably seconded. Its proceedings were extended into all native States as well as into every British province and district, and up to 1837, 3,266 persons had been apprehended and variously disposed of. The effect of these vigorous proceedings was, that every known Thug, or relation of a Thug, throughout India was apprehended; and as their numbers precluded the enforcement of severe penal measures, the least guilty were formed into a settlement, or school of industry, at Jubbulpoor, and instructed in various trades. Their descendants continue there, and carpets, tent-cloths and tents, with many other useful articles, are now manufactured with a rare skill and beauty. These artisans, as they may now be called, are, however, still kept under surveillance; and it may be

Special departments for the suppression of the crime.

Final suppression of the system.

hoped that in the course of a few generations, their traditions may become extinct, as for the last twenty years no case of Thuggee has appeared in any part of the continent of India.

Steam communication with India is now so familiar a subject, that allusion to its early commencement appears like a dream of the past. Yet forty years ago, only for the exertions of Lord William Bentinck, it might have been indefinitely delayed. In 1830, the first steamers, built at Calcutta, and fitted with engines from England, ascended the Ganges for 800 miles, and the success of the experiment amply justified its extension. So, also, the establishment of communication with England by steam vessels was taken up at the same time, with the same ardour, by the governor-general; but he was checked by the Court of Directors on the score of expense, and their inexplicable apathy can be traced perhaps to their own exclusive policy, and a dread that India might be brought too near to England. Thus the enterprise languished for nearly twelve years; but the merit of the first attempt rests with Lord William Bentinck's administration, and in the success of the Peninsular and Oriental Steam Navigation Company's first endeavours lie the admirable results enjoyed by the public of India and of England in the year 1870.

Steam communication with England.

With the regulation for the legalisation of Malwah opium, the record of the great measures of 1830 closes. By a system of licenses, it was enabled to be brought from the dominions of native princes in Malwah, where it was extensively produced, to Bombay, and by those means the former smuggling to the coast by way of Sindh and to the Portuguese ports was effectually prevented. The quality of the drug was tested in Bombay, and, under the official seal of Government, it was exported to China, on the same basis as that of Bengal, attended with a large corresponding increase to the public revenue.

Opium.

CHAPTER X.

THE ADMINISTRATION OF LORD WILLIAM BENTINCK (*continued*), 1831 TO 1832.

Up to the year 1831, it may be said, with truth, that the natives of India in the British provinces had been systematically denied all participation in the government of their country. Under the pressure of public necessity,

Advancement of natives.

a few offices had been created for the relief of the English functionaries; but the declared policy of the Government, both at home and in India, was against the measure of opening public employment to the people, on the ground that it was pregnant with danger to the existence of British authority. It therefore required no ordinary amount of resolution to break through these long existing, and, with few exceptions, persistently maintained, opinions; and, fortunately, the views of the governor-general were supported by the able and liberal members of his Council. The first reform was applied by the regulation of 1831 to the judicial department in the creation of native judges, and their primary jurisdiction over civil suits. This measure not only relieved the judicial department of a load of work which could never be completed, but it opened a way to official service which, during the last forty years, has been very materially enlarged in all departments of the administration, and in all parts of India, with singular success, and is still extending.

Native judges appointed.

Native Christians eligible for office.

The admission of natives of all castes and creeds, under the provisions of the enactment, included also native Christians, whose employment, under, as it were, a cruel refinement of prejudice and apprehension, had been before expressly prohibited—and they took their place with others, without prejudice. The recognition of the great principle was the first step gained: and since its wisdom and necessity were established the question has never retrograded; while the conduct of the native officials has amply justified the hope that their first real friend had formed of them.

Condition of Oudh.

In 1831, the condition of Oudh was brought under Lord William Bentinck's notice by the Resident, Mr. Maddock. The continuous history of this province shows that remonstrances against its misgovernment had been addressed by every governor-general in succession to the king; but at the present crisis local affairs were worse than ever. In order to judge for himself, the governor-general proceeded to Lukhnow, and the king was informed that the management of his country would be assumed unless reform ensued. This menace was followed by the reappointment, by the king, of the celebrated Hakeem Méndhy, as his minister, an able and fearless reformer, who effected some beneficial changes; but his honest advice was unwelcome to the king and his licentious court, and he was ultimately dismissed. The affairs of the kingdom thenceforward drifted into still greater confusion, which increased till its final extinction was determined on twenty-five years afterwards; but under the instruction of the Court of Directors, Lord William Bentinck, in 1831, was at liberty to have placed Oudh on the footing of the Carnatic, and the postponement of the measure only increased its difficulty.

Fanatical insurrection.

Mahomedan fanaticism, as if in proof that it would never be extinguished, caused an insurrection in the very vicinity of Calcutta in 1831. A Fakeer, named Teetoo Meer, of some local sanctity, had become a disciple of the famous Syud Ahmed of the Punjâb, and began to preach a holy war against all infidels. It was necessary, as their numbers increased, to employ force against his followers, for they burnt villages, defiled Hindoo temples, and their outrages became more daring and continuous. The insurgents were attacked and dispersed with severe loss, and the insurrection was crushed: but the fanatical sect has never been perfectly eradicated in Bengal, and several instances of sympathy with insurgents in the Punjâb have since been traced to members of the Wáhábee sect, many of them holding influential positions in the country.

The Kole war.

The small insurrection of Teetoo Meer in the Baraset district, was followed by a much more serious rising in 1832 by the Koles of Western Bengal, an aboriginal tribe, who, like the Santáls, described by Mr. W. Hunter, in the 'Annals of Rural Bengal,' had, at a very early period, been driven into the hills by the Aryan settlers. By degrees they had come under the operation of laws of which they had no conception, and of systematic encroachment by Bengal settlers, and the nominal Zemindars of their provinces; and against these they rebelled, and proceeded to acts of outrage which could not at first be suppressed. Many perished in a fruitless resistance against regular troops; but eventually the whole submitted. The regulations, unfitted, to as yet a savage people, were then withdrawn, and their province placed under a special commissioner. The Koles since then have gradually advanced in civilisation and prosperity: and at the present time many thousands of them have become Christians, and have established churches, where heretofore only the most debasing forms of a primitive idolatry existed.

The tribe is placed under special jurisdiction.

Conversions.

Law of inheritance modified.

In his remodelling of the laws, the stringency of the Hindoo law of inheritance did not escape the governor-general's perception. Under its provisions, no one who abandoned the Hindoo faith could inherit ancestral property, since the basis of inheritance consisted in performing certain ceremonies to the memory of his progenitors. This disability was, however, quickly removed. Other reforms in civil and criminal procedure were adopted; monthly jail deliveries were established; a new chief court was established in the north-

Other judicial reforms.

western provinces; and the cumbrous machinery of previous enactments swept away. These changes were accompanied by the great boon of directing the vernacular language of suitors or witnesses to be employed on all occasions instead of Persian, which, used by the Mahomedans, was as unintelligible to the people at large as English, and was indifferently comprehended, in most instances, by the judges.

Use of the vernacular languages.

In the year 1832, the affairs of Messrs. William Palmer & Co., of Hyderabad, again occupied the attention of the Government in England, and with so remarkable a result that, as an item in the history of the company's administration, it cannot be passed by. The Marquess of Hastings, chafing under the aspersions and insinuations of the Court of Directors, defended himself ably on his return in the House of Lords; and the whole question was re-opened in the Court of Proprietors, in a debate which lasted six days. Mr., afterwards Sir Henry, Russell, spoke at great length on the second day. He showed incontrovertibly, that the dealings of Messrs. Palmer & Co. with the Nizam, so far from being extortionate, had been liberal and fair; and that their rates of interest were greatly less than those prevailing in the country. He had been Sir Charles Metcalfe's predecessor at Hyderabad; and his statement of facts threw a flood of light on the whole of the loan transactions. As regarded William Palmer & Co., the revelation had indeed little immediate effect; but while Mr. Kinnaird moved that there was nothing in the Hyderabad papers which affected the character of the governor-general, the resolution was met by Mr. Astell with a counter motion, that while there was no ground for imputing corrupt motives to Lord Hastings, the dispatches sent to him should be confirmed. These very dispatches had covertly, if not indeed openly, attributed the basest motives to the governor-general; and their confirmation by these proceedings added insult to injury. At most, the Court's proceedings closed with a Scotch verdict of 'not proven,' leaving all the animus of the charges virtually increased. Soon afterwards, Lord Hastings accepted the humble post of governor of Malta; but the injury inflicted had been too deep and too wanton to be long endured, and he died on August 24, 1827, of a broken heart. Was the sum of 20,000*l.* voted afterwards to his son, then a minor, any reparation for the cruel injury? Yet had any concession been made to the noble marquess, it would have involved the reversion of the acts against William Palmer & Co., and against them the Court of Directors was as yet strong and virulent.

William Palmer & Co.

Sir H. Russell's speech.

Proceedings in the Court of Proprietors.

The question of justice to the firm was eventually agitated, both in England and in India, up to 1830; but it was in vain that the twelve judges of England recorded their opinion that there was no illegality in the rates of interest, or in the transactions of Messrs. Palmer & Co. Equally vain, that this opinion was confirmed by the most celebrated counsel of the day. The prohibition at Hyderabad continued in force; and its effects are best explained by a letter from Moneer-ool-Moolk, the prime minister, who was a large debtor, to the executive minister, Chundoo Lall. 'If,' he wrote, 'the order prohibiting any money transactions with them (W. P. & Co.), and the *proclamation describing the claims as void*, had not arrived, my debt to them would have been completely and fully paid; but how could I, in defiance of the prohibition, and of such a proclamation, pay them?' This was the situation in which not only Moneer-ool-Moolk, but many other large debtors to the house, were placed. They dared not pay.

Opinion of the twelve judges of England.

Situation of the debtors to the house.

In 1832 the President of the Board of Control took up the question in earnest, and required the directors to prepare a dispatch, by which the prohibition against the firm should be removed; but the court were still resolute not to disturb the policy on which they had acted for ten years; and a dispatch, which was in fact a repetition of former opinions, drawn up on March 20, 1832, was transmitted to the Board of Control for approval. It was not, however, approved. On the contrary, thirty-three out of thirty-seven paragraphs were rescinded, and a new draft sent to the court for adoption. The principle expressed was perfectly fair and open. It required the interposition of the Government of India, the authors of the wrong, to bring about a settlement with the Nizam, by means of a commission or an umpire. The amended dispatch was, however, rejected by the court; and after a tedious correspondence, which led to no result, the Board of Control applied for a writ of mandamus, to the King's Bench, to compel its adoption. On the issue of the writ, the dispatch was admitted under protest, by ten of the directors, who had maintained the most obstinate and inveterate opposition. As an event of historical importance, this memorable transaction, into which the court had been plunged by a prejudiced minority, was very momentous; for it proved, as might and ought to have been anticipated, its real inherent weakness in any struggle with the ministry of the Crown, and seriously impaired its power both in England and in India, which hitherto had been controlled, but never broken. The consequences were not immediately apparent; but they continued to progress in importance and magnitude, until the independence of the court had been weakened, if not

Measures of the Board of Control.

Writ of mandamus.

Effects of the struggle.

destroyed for all essential purposes of government, and resulted, after a hundred years' existence, in its final extinction.

As soon as the dispatch reached India, the governor-general appointed an umpire, Mr., now Sir, John Macleod, an able member of the Civil Service, who proceeded to Hyderabad, and, after a long investigation, made an award in favour of the principal private claim of Messrs. Palmer & Co., that against Moneer-ool-Moolk, which amounted to at least twenty-one lacs of rupees. The amount awarded was immediately paid, and enabled the house to discharge the new obligation it had entered into with its creditors. Here, however, the direct effect of the dispatch ceased. It was considered that a precedent had been established, under the provisions of which the remainder of the private claims, the most material being for loans to individuals granted by the house under the guarantee of the executive minister, could be now prosecuted in the local courts. The trustees of the house had little hope that these courts would exercise sufficient independence of character to investigate the claims; but they performed their duty fearlessly and conscientiously, and decrees were obtained on several suits for the aggregate sum of nine lacs, which were recognised by the executive minister, in the sequestration of the estates of the principal defendants. No other results, however, followed; the awards remained unpaid, and the courts being unable to enforce their awards or procure their enforcement, refused to entertain further suits. Equally fruitless were the efforts of the trustees to obtain satisfaction in any form from the government of the Nizam. It must be admitted, however, that it has never denied, though it has evaded, its responsibility; and perhaps, when time has obliterated the remains of original prejudices, it may be stimulated by the government of the Crown to a final act of satisfaction and justice, in favour of the descendants of those who were utterly ruined.

Measures taken on the dispatch in India.

Decree against Moneer-ool-Moolk.

Other claims referred to local civil courts.

In 1832, the management of the affairs of the State of Mysore was assumed by the Government of India. It will be remembered that, on the capture of Seringapatam, and death of Tippoo Sooltan, the rajah, then a boy, had been presented with the original dominions of his dynasty; and that Poornea, the able minister of Tippoo, assisted by English commissioners, had been appointed to their administration. In 1811, when the circumstances of the State were in the highest degree prosperous, and there were seven millions sterling in the treasury, the rajah, then only sixteen years old, was suffered to declare his majority and to assume the government. He proved to be intractable and wastefully extravagant; and by 1832,

Affairs of Mysore.

Wasteful extravagance of the rajah.

not only had his treasure been expended on profligate associates and in the wildest profusion, but the State had become deeply encumbered. He had been repeatedly warned; and most impressively by Sir Thomas Munro, in 1825; but without effect, and in 1830, the greater part of his dominions, unable to endure the perpetual extortion practised, broke into insurrection. It was quelled by a Madras force; but the conviction remained, that the British Government could not be identified with the rajah's malpractices, that the people had had just cause for revolt, that the employment of force against them was only justifiable by the excesses that had been committed, and that the enforcement of the provisions of the treaty were indispensable. It was notified, therefore, to the rajah, that for the future, a fifth part of the revenues, about 40,000*l.* per year, would be paid to him, and that the administration of his dominions, in all departments, would be carried on by English officers. Under these arrangements the country became tranquil and prosperous, and the benevolent measures of the chief commissioner, Sir Mark Cubbon, are remembered with gratitude and affection.

Insurrection of the people.

The rajah is pensioned.

In the same year—1832—the small principality of Cachár, on the north-east frontier of Bengal, was formally annexed to the British dominions, upon the spontaneous request of the people, whose rajah had been assassinated, and who had left no successor. The province is now the seat of extensive tea cultivation, and has been reclaimed, in a great degree, from its original wild character.

Cachár annexed.

CHAPTER XI.

THE ADMINISTRATION OF LORD WILLIAM BENTINCK (*concluded*), 1833 TO 1835.

THE year 1833 was marked by several great and beneficial measures, among which the land settlement of the north-west provinces takes a prominent place. Many previous attempts had been made towards a solution of the various questions regarding tenures and assessments, and Regulation VII. of 1822, the able work of Mr. Holt Mackenzie, laid the foundation of what was to follow. During his tour of the north-west provinces, the governor-general invited the freest discussion of the subject by all ranks of the civil service, and in March 1833, the new regulation was passed in Council, and the execution of it committed to Mr. Robert Mertins Bird. By the provisions of this

Land settlement of the north-west provinces.

Act, all village lands were surveyed, and every field, or portion of land, cultivated or waste, defined; all proprietary rights were registered, and all lands assessed, the rate to continue for thirty years. When it is considered that these operations concerned no less than 23,000,000 of people, and extended over nearly 50,000,000 of acres of land, and yet were completed with all the minuteness and care of the survey of a private estate in England—the momentous character of the whole may be estimated; with the amount of genius and perseverance necessary for its accomplishment. Yet it must be recorded, that Mr. Bird's great services passed away without reward, and without the public recognition which they had so eminently deserved.

Mr. Bird's services.

The supremacy of Oriental learning was still maintained in Calcutta, and was not overcome without a severe contention. Up to 1833, Sanscrit, Arabic, and Persian had been supported by the profound Orientalists of the period, in whose sight the obscure hymns of the Vedas, the graceful episodes and fables of the Máhábhárut and the Rámáyun, and the bygone sciences of Sanscrit and Arabic authors, possessed a charm far exceeding the extension of the true knowledge and brilliant and exact sciences of England. Able men argued on their respective sides with great pertinacity. Dr. H. H. Wilson led the van of the Orientalists, and was opposed by Sir Charles Trevelyan, Mr. Brian Hodgson, and Dr. Duff of the Scotch Church, with a host of others; and the question was finally debated in Council, where Mr. Macaulay gave pure Orientalism its death-blow. Then the English language, with its flood of light and truth, was opened to the people of India, as well by the recognition of the language itself in public educational establishments, as by its extension by translation into the vernacular of every province: but the school of the Scotch mission, with upwards of a thousand native day scholars, instructed in Christian doctrine as well as English literature, was of all the most effectual refutation of the abstract love of Sanscrit and Arabic, by which the interesting period of transition from old things to new is marked.

Education.

The charter to the company, extended, in 1813, for twenty years, expired in 1833, and with it, their monopoly of trade with China. It was impossible for Parliament to withstand the clamour of the English nation, which was directed against the continuance of that remnant of the company's exclusive privileges, in any form. The new charter was limited to the administration of India for a further period of twenty years; and henceforward the Court of Directors became an administrative body only, subject to the Board of Control, in many respects with greater stringency

The company's charter and monopoly.

The Government of India to continue for twenty years.

than before. The almost only remaining stronghold of former prejudices, the denial to Europeans of holding lands in India, was thrown down, while Lord William Bentinck's great measure of opening the public service to all natives without distinction of caste or creed, was confirmed by a special clause. A fourth presidency also was established at Agra, for the administration of the north-west provinces, and Sir Charles Metcalfe, in grateful recognition of his eminent services, was appointed its governor.

The public service opened to natives.

While occupied by the momentous reforms of his administration, the governor-general's attention was directed to the affairs of Coorg, in consequence of the outrageous proceedings of its rajah, Veer Rajendra, who had succeeded his father in 1820. He had committed a series of atrocious murders; and under the terror of his revenge, the particulars of his conduct were unknown, till his sister and her husband escaped, and threw themselves on the protection of the British authorities. The rajah was called to account for his acts of violence; but he proved utterly intractable and defiant, and finding the local disorders increasing, a proclamation was issued by the governor-general that he had ceased to reign. To take possession of the province, a force invaded it under the political direction of Major-General J. S. Fraser, which, though gallantly resisted in some attempts to penetrate the stupendous passes and defiles, was eventually successful, and the capital, Merkára, was occupied on April 6, 1834. The rajah, who surrendered to General Fraser, was removed to Benares, but ultimately died in England, where he resided for some years; and the affairs of the country were administered by a special commissioner, until incorporated with those of Mysore. Since then, Coorg has become celebrated as a coffee-growing district, and has proved proportionably valuable. Except Cachar, Coorg was the only territory annexed to the British dominions in India during the incumbency of Lord William Bentinck, and the proclamation expressed that the act 'was in consideration of the unanimous wish of the people.'

Coorg affairs.

The rajah is deposed.

Merkára occupied.

Death of the rajah.

Annexation of the country.

On a review of the political policy of Lord William Bentinck, it is found to have one uniform characteristic, non-interference; and every native State in India, for good or for evil, was made practically independent in its administration. As in the days of Sir John Shore, there were no great armies now to be checked, or princes who could inflict injury upon their own subjects, or those of others, by lawless plunder and internal commotion; yet it has always been charged against the governor-general, that the principle he professed, and

Review of policy in regard to native States.

literally observed, was carried too far, and served to weaken the paramount authority and prestige of British power in India. In Hyderabad, a wasteful minister was allowed to weary the people by exactions and want of faith, which seriously impaired the revenue, and created a horde of usurers, Arab chiefs, Patáns, and native bankers, whose extortions from the people of the districts assigned to them, in payment of loans and advances, are remembered with terror. As a relief to the State, an offer was made by the governor-general to disband the contingent, for a partial equivalent in money payment; but the services of this force were invaluable to the Nizam's Government, as a counterpoise to its own turbulent feudatories and military chiefs, and the offer, which had been accepted in Nagpoor, was declined. The pay and allowances of the contingent were, however, reduced to the standard of the company's forces, several staff appointments were abolished, and other reductions of expense followed. The Court of Directors were, however, by no means satisfied with the state of the Nizam's dominions; and on September 8, 1835, a remonstrance was written for communication to His Highness, in which they stated, 'that they could not remain indifferent spectators to the disorder and misrule which had so long prevailed in his territories,' and further signified that if the present minister, Rajah Chundoo Lall, could not provide remedies for them, he should be changed, or that other arrangements should be adopted, 'as might be advisable for the purpose of securing good government.' These remonstrances had, however, little practical effect, and the minister, taking courage from the prevailing non-interferent policy, made no change in his system.

Effects of non-interference in Hyderabad.

Reform of the Nizam's contingent.

Remonstrance with the Nizam.

In Bhopál, after the accidental death of the Nawáb, with whom a treaty had been made in 1818, his widow adopted his nephew, but retained the management of the State in her own hands. When the young man attained his majority, he was opposed by his aunt, and a struggle ensued, which involved much bloodshed in engagements between the parties, in one of which the young Nawáb was defeated. These deplorable events might, in the outset, have been summarily checked by the governor-general; but he declined to interfere, and the local anarchy had afterwards to be suppressed by Sir Charles Metcalfe. In 1833 a similar struggle for power occurred in Sindia's dominions, between Junkojee, the youth who had been adopted by Báiza Bye, the widow of Dowlut Ráo, and herself. In this quarrel, which threatened to affect the peace of all Central India, Lord William Bentinck absolutely refused to interfere; and though he visited Gwalior,

Bhopál.

Effects of non-interference.

Sindia's affairs.

left it without attempting any settlement. On July 10, the several brigades of disciplined troops, which had taken different sides, would have come into collision but for the personal efforts of the Resident, Colonel Stewart, whose representation of the serious danger which would ensue from any actual outbreak of hostilities, induced the governor-general to recognise the rajah, and Báiza Bye was obliged to retire from Gwalior. In the State of Jeypoor, another instance of mischief from the non-exercise of timely intervention resulted in the murder of Mr. Blake, the assistant to the Resident, in the streets of Jeypoor, in 1835. As at Bhopál and Gwalior, there was a minor prince at Jeypoor; and the regency was conducted by his mother, assisted by a banker, named Jóta Rám, believed to be her paramour. A rivalry ensued between the chiefs of the State and this person, which proceeded from bad to worse; and though it might have been prevented, had timely measures been taken, the non-interferent policy prevailed. A chief named Byree Sál was eventually elected to the office of minister by the nobles of the State; but the struggle between him and Jóta Rám continued; and the latter, believing the Resident, Major Alves, to have been the author of his loss of power, determined to destroy him and his cortége on the occasion of an official visit to the minister. The plan was prematurely carried out, and the Resident escaped with a slight wound, though Mr. Blake perished.

Settlement of the quarrel.

Jeypoor.

Murder of Mr. Blake.

Non-interference.

Its consequences.

It is needless to multiply examples. One decisive act of interference would have been sufficient to prove, throughout all native States, that disorder would not be permitted; instead of which, it was allowed to proceed without check, until the parties were compromised by their acts, and had incurred the penalty of absolute punishment. It was advanced in Lord William Bentinck's justification, that his policy proceeded out of a desire to make the rulers of native States responsible to their subjects; but though such a motive was most laudable and desirable, it was never declared as a basis of non-interference; and the instances in which intervention was necessary to suppress public disorder, arose out of struggles for power between the highest authorities in the several States, whose conduct and proceedings could not possibly have been affected by their people at large, and in regard to which the British Government was the only real arbiter.

Lord William Bentinck's motives for non-interference.

Among the political events of Lord William Bentinck's incumbency, his famous interview with Runjeet Singh at Roopur, on the banks of the Sutlej, in 1831, must not be passed over.

It was the most magnificent spectacle of the period; and while the Sikh ruler was accompanied by 16,000 of the flower of his army and of his chivalry, the governor-general contented himself with a comparatively small escort. The intercourse of the two potentates was most harmonious, and they separated with assurances of mutual good-will. The only political event of importance was the embassy to Sinde, conducted by Major Pottinger, which forestalled the intentions of Runjeet Singh in that quarter, and will be more prominently noticed hereafter. The last act of the governor-general's administration, was the creation of a medical college in Calcutta, in 1835. Except the ancient Hindoo, Grecian, and Arabian systems, no means of medical instruction existed in India. Of surgery, as based on anatomy, there was profound ignorance, and the village barber was the usual operator as surgeon, in cases of wounds, or hurts; while those who had traditional knowledge of simples were the physicians. Now, however, the whole range of European medical science, surgery, and anatomy, was opened to the pupils, who became at once very numerous; and the blessings of true medical instruction have since been widely extended.

Interview with Runjeet Singh.

Medical college.

Lord William Bentinck had already sent home his resignation, and having reached Calcutta from the Neilgherry hills, where he had proceeded on account of his health, sailed for England on March 20, 1835. Sir Charles Metcalfe held a commission as provisional governor-general, and succeeded him. It will have been estimated by the narrative, that in respect to administrative reform and moral progress, Lord William's incumbency had been unequalled in India; but two other efforts in the cause of civilisation and humanity, which were spread over the whole period of his tenure of office, deserve brief record. By the treaty of 1818, the district of Mairwarra, as part of Ajmere, fell into the possession of the British Government. The people, Mairs, were found to be unredeemed savages, like the Bheels, who lived by rapine, and were the dread of the surrounding country. For fourteen years Captain Hall laboured among this rude people, with singular perseverance, in their reclamation from many criminal practices, and his successor, Captain Dixon, completed what had been so ably begun. He constructed many great reservoirs for water, built a city, and converted an almost savage wilderness into the seat of vast agricultural improvements. The results of these local administrations will be found detailed in Dixon's 'Mairwarra,' a work full of interest to all students of Indian subjects.

Lord William Bentinck leaves India.

Sir Charles Metcalfe succeeds.

Mairwarra.

Captain Hall's and Captain Dixon's reforms.

Infanticide was one of those social crimes by which the higher castes of Indian society were, and may still to some extent be, infected. At the close of the eighteenth century, when Benares became a British province, it was found to exist among the Rajpoots, by Mr. Jonathan Duncan, the local commissioner, who, in some degree, interposed checks upon it. He followed up his good work when, as governor of Bombay, he discovered that in Kutch, Guzerat, Malwah, and Rajpootana, the practice of destroying female children was even more prevalent than in Bengal. But though some effect was produced, and some children had undoubtedly been preserved, the cruel rite was by no means eradicated. In 1833–4 the question was taken up again with great ardour by the late Sir John P. Willoughby, Mr. Wilkinson, Sir P. Melvil, and others; and though it is impossible, within the scope of this work, to follow the various preventive measures that were resorted to, it is due to the officers to record the humanity of their motives, and their earnest and persevering endeavours to suppress a practice repugnant to every good feeling of human nature. Whether the restrictive measures imposed upon the Rajpoots by registration of female births, and other means, have been entirely successful, may still unhappily be doubted; but there is at least no question, that the crime has greatly diminished, even in the strongest holds of its former unchecked prevalence.

Infanticide.

Its prevalence.

Measures for its suppression.

Another intervention in the cause of humanity belongs more especially to the Madras Presidency; but was encouraged and assisted by Lord William Bentinck to the utmost of his power. The Khónds, an aboriginal people, inhabiting the hills and forests west of the Northern Circars, were discovered in 1829 to be in the habit of sacrificing annually, to the 'Earth' goddess, numbers of children and adults, kidnapped or bought from the population of the low countries: and the suppression of the practice became imperative. But it was no easy task to prevent a rite which had been indulged from a period of great antiquity, and on which the Khónds believed their crops and their material prosperity depended. Captain Campbell was the first officer deputed to the Khónd districts for the purpose of preventing the rite; and he laboured for four years unremittingly for its suppression, rescuing from a horrible death many hundreds of prepared victims; but ill-health drove him from the province, and the relapse into the original practices became painfully apparent. His successor Major Macpherson's endeavours were equally well directed; but an insurrection broke out against him, which, owing to the nature of the country, was suppressed with much difficulty; and his proceed-

The Khónds of Goomsoor.

Human sacrifices.

Captain Campbell's efforts.

Insurrection of the people.

ings became the subject of acrimonious discussion, which was not closed till a much later period. He was replaced by Captain, now Colonel, Campbell, with greater success than before; and it may be hoped that the authority established over this wild race has led to an entire abandonment of the cruel rite; for it is many years since any detection of its commission has been reported, and the Khónds, by means of education, and nearer contact with a civilised power, have lost many distinctive features of their original savagery.

CHAPTER XII.

THE ADMINISTRATION OF SIR CHARLES METCALFE AND LORD AUCKLAND, 1835 TO 1837.

It was reserved for Sir Charles Metcalfe to withdraw the last restrictions under which the press of India had laboured for so many years. During the incumbency of Lord William Bentinck, it had been virtually, if not actually, free from interference; but the old law was still in existence, and might at any time be resorted to by any ruler of its originator Mr. Adams's tone of mind. The public of Calcutta had submitted a memorial for the abolition of this law before the departure of the governor-general; but he had declined to interfere, and the solution of the question remained to his successor. Nor was it long held in abeyance. Supported cordially by Mr. Macaulay, the Act was passed in the month of September, 1835, and Sir Charles Metcalfe had the satisfaction to receive the grateful acknowledgements of all classes, European and native, upon the freedom he had now practically established. But the measure raised a storm against him in the Court of Directors, for which he was not prepared. Of all the traditional prejudices which had been longest in existence, the restriction upon the press was perhaps the most dearly cherished there. With all his liberal opinions, held by many to be extreme, Lord William Bentinck had declined to pass an Act which, without consultation or warning, had now become law, and was irrevocable; and the man whose policy at Hyderabad had been supported faithfully, even to a memorable and extreme collision with the Board of Control, was the author of the so-esteemed deliberate indignity. The offence was unpardoned and unpardonable; and from thenceforth the long and eminent services of Sir Charles Metcalfe were virtually cancelled. The government of Madras, which he had been

Freedom of the press.

The Act passed.

The measure disapproved by the Court of Directors.

Consequences to Sir Charles Metcalfe.

led to expect, was curtly denied him: and as the presidency of Agra had been reduced, by an arrangement made in England, to a lieutenant-governorship, Sir Charles Metcalfe retired from India in 1836, after an unbroken residence there of thirty-six years. 'No man,' writes Mr. Kaye, his biographer, 'ever left India carrying with him so many lively regrets, and so many cordial good wishes from all classes of the community.' The remainder of his official life was passed in the employment of the Crown, and in the administration, successively, of Jamaica and Canada; and he eventually received the highest distinction that could be conferred upon him, in being raised to the peerage; but his connection with the company was never renewed, nor was any recognition made by the court of the faithful services of one of their most useful and most distinguished servants.

He retires from India, and enters the service of the Crown.

He is raised to the peerage.

In succession to Lord William Bentinck, the Hon. Mountstuart Elphinstone was offered the post of governor-general; but he declined the honour, in consideration of the state of his health, and Lord Heytesbury was appointed. In consequence of a change of ministry, however, this nomination was cancelled, and Lord Auckland dispatched to India, who reached Calcutta on March 3, 1836. One of the first Acts passed by him, on May 9, provided that no person was to be considered exempt in civil suits from the jurisdiction of the native judges who had been established. This regulation, which affected Europeans, who had hitherto held the privilege of appeal to the supreme court, was vehemently opposed in India, and became the subject of much acrimonious discussion, under the appellation of the 'Black Act.' The question was transferred to England, and debated in Parliament, on a motion by Mr. Ward; but it was defeated, and the Act confirmed.

Lord Auckland becomes governor-general.

The 'Black Act.'

The first political question which Lord Auckland had to decide, was the succession to the throne of Oudh. The king, Nasir-ood-deen Hyder, died on July 7, 1837: he left no issue, and having been an only son, the right of succession was not a little involved. Saadut Ally, the grandfather of the late king, had had ten sons; and the two elder being dead, the third, Nasir-ood-Dowlah, became heir according to Mahomedan law. It was asserted, however, by the chief Bégum, widow of the deceased, that her husband had adopted two boys during his life, one of whom had now become heir; and the queen-mother, as she may be styled, took measures to procure his succession by force of arms. Her retainers suddenly took posses-

Succession to the throne of Oudh.

Variety of claims.

sion of the palace by forcible entry, and were followed by the Bégum, with her protégé, Moona Ján, and she immediately proclaimed the boy king and installed him. Colonel Low, who had reached the palace, protested against the act, and escaped with some difficulty; but the king to be, Nasir-ood-Dowlah, remained her prisoner. Colonel Low gave no time for the insurrection to gain head. Having summoned the queen-mother, he allowed her a quarter of an hour for a reply, at the end of which, as she was still defiant, the palace-gate was blown open by a gun, and the courtyard cleared of her adherents, with some loss to them, while the Bégum and Moona Ján were taken prisoners. Nasir-ood-Dowlah was then brought out of his apartments, and enthroned by Colonel Low, who placed the crown on the king's head with his own hands.

Colonel Low's decided conduct.

Nasir-ood-Dowlah enthroned and crowned.

On the announcement that the right of succession had fallen on him, Nasir-ood-Dowlah had been required by Colonel Low to execute a paper, by which he agreed to sign 'any new treaty that the governor-general may dictate.' Colonel Low's spirited conduct throughout the disturbance received the governor-general's 'high approbation,' but of the agreement he was not so certain. He 'would have been better pleased,' he wrote, 'if Colonel Low had not accepted the unconditional engagement of submissiveness which the new king has signed. . . . the expediency of obtaining from His Majesty the signature of a previous agreement is the only point on which he feels that difference of opinion may be entertained.' And in reference to the Oudh question at large, the whole of Lord Auckland's minute deserves perusal. Two other claimants to the throne subsequently appeared, and petitioned the Indian Government and the Court of Directors on the subject of succession; but the original decision was maintained.

Lord Auckland's minute on Oudh.

It will be remembered that, in the year 1819, the descendant of Sivajee, rescued from the imprisonment in which he and his family had been kept by the Péshwah, had been presented with the territory of his ancestor, and with Sattara as its capital. Here he had continued to reign, at first in an unobtrusive manner; but latterly, many acts of intrigue were brought home to him: attempts to tamper with the fidelity of native soldiers of the Bombay army were detected: and it was evident that the naturally weak mind of the rajah was being inflated by adventurers of all descriptions. He was warned on several occasions, in a kindly and friendly spirit, but in vain; and on September 5, 1839, he was finally deposed, under a proclamation by the governor-general, and his brother received

Case of the Rajah of Sattara.

He is deposed.

investiture as rajah in his room—but with no modification of the original treaty—and the ex-rajah was sent to reside at Benares. The folly and presumption of his conduct, the schemes by which he proposed to re-establish the Mahratta power, are unparalleled in the histories of such efforts in India, and are only accountable by the weakness of his own intellect and the unceasing intrigues of the unscrupulous Brahmins and women by whom he was surrounded and influenced.

Sterner and more extensive subjects than the insurrection at Lukhnow or the affairs of Sattara were now to occupy Lord Auckland's attention. Runjeet Singh had become involved in a war with Dost Mahomed, ruler of Afghanistan. While Shah Soojah was occupied in an attempt to regain his dominions, Runjeet Singh had crossed the Indus, in 1835, and occupied the province of Peshâwur, up to the mouth of the Khyber pass; and about the same time he had assembled an army on the northern frontier of Sinde, with the view of attacking the Ameers, who, in nowise dismayed, prepared to meet the Sikhs. This quarrel was arranged by Colonel Pottinger, the political agent in Sinde; but that with the Afghans proceeded. Dost Mahomed, hoping to recover Peshâwur, caused a holy war to be preached against the Sikhs, and a large force descending the passes, appeared before Peshâwur. The agents of Runjeet Singh had, however, been at work, and on the desertion of Sooltan Mahomed from his brother, the whole Afghan army broke up and dispersed.

War between the Sikhs and Afghans.

Dost Mahomed now addressed himself to the governor-general, who replied that he would send an officer 'to discuss questions of commerce,' but he declined any interference with the affairs of the Punjâb. Left to his own resources, Dost Mahomed assembled another army, and sent it against Peshâwur, under his son, Akbur Khan, by whom, on April 30, 1837, the Sikh forces were completely defeated near Jumrood, at the entrance to the Khyber. The victory, however, was of little use, for Runjeet Singh sent heavy reinforcements to his army, and the Afghans were again driven into the passes. At that time, Lord Auckland's envoy, Lieutenant Burnes, had reached Kabool, and his proceedings there must be briefly reviewed, as they formed the basis of the Afghan war.

Dost Mahomed applies to the governor general.

Burnes at Kabool.

CHAPTER XIII.

THE ADMINISTRATION OF LORD AUCKLAND—THE AFGHAN WAR, 1837 TO 1839.

Burnes's mission to Dost Mahomed.

In September 1837, Lieutenant Alexander Burnes reached Kabool as envoy from Lord Auckland to Dost Mahomed. The governor-general had not delayed the fulfilment of his promise to send an officer to discuss questions of commerce. After his mission to Runjeet Singh, in 1831, Lieutenant Burnes had proceeded to Kabool, where he was hospitably entertained by Dost Mahomed, and thence travelled into Central Asia, as far as Bokhára, returning to Bombay by way of Persia; and his book of travels, soon afterwards published, is full of information in regard to countries then imperfectly known in England. No one better fitted for the deputation to Dost Mahomed could, therefore, have been found; for Lieutenant Burnes's acquaintance with the languages and the people of Central Asia and Persia was then unrivalled. He was received hospitably by the Ameer, with every demonstration of welcome, and a commercial treaty was duly discussed; but it was evident from the first that this was a very secondary object in the Ameer's mind. He was chafing under the loss of Peshâwur; and his whole endeavours were applied to regain it. The governor-general had certainly given him no room to hope for assistance; but, as communications among Eastern potentates usually represent one thing, and mean quite another, the Ameer perhaps concluded that Burnes's mission, openly in regard to trade, meant, in reality, the discussion of the politics of Afghanistan and the Punjâb. He had also discovered that a morbid dread of Russian influence existed in India; and he knew that the people, credulous and ignorant, had already become impressed with the possibility of Russian interference. Dost Mahomed, therefore, contrived to fill Burnes's mind with apprehension of Russian intrigue, which was confirmed by news from Persia; and on December 19, 1837, Captain Vicovich, an aide-de-camp of the Russian consul-general at Orenburgh, arrived at Kabool, with a letter from Count Simonich, the Russian ambassador at Tehran.

Dost Mahomed's opinions.

Arrival of Captain Vicovich.

Burnes's opinion of the mission.

There was nothing definite in the letter; but the expressions, 'trust him with your secrets,' and 'I beg you will look upon him as myself, and take his words as if from me,' might mean a great deal. If Burnes had considered for a moment the impossibility of any sudden advance by Russia, or the equal impossibility of any real impression by Persia on the Afghans, in furtherance of Russian designs, he would not have written as he did to Lord Auckland, that 'much more rigorous proceedings than Government might wish or contemplate are necessary to counteract Russian or Persian intrigue in this quarter than have yet been exhibited.' When an explanation was sought by the British Government, Captain Vicovich's proceedings were entirely disowned by Count Nesselrode; but meanwhile, Vicovich had been the means of bringing the affairs of Burnes's mission to a crisis. Dost Mahomed would have infinitely preferred an alliance with the English; but the envoy's instructions left no loophole for a political treaty, and in proportion as the truth became more and more evident, the encouragement of Vicovich became the more impressive. Lord Auckland's letters to Dost Mahomed were also, unhappily, of a curt and dictatorial nature; for they not only held out no hope of friendly intervention between him and Runjeet Singh, but bade him dismiss Vicovich and the Russians, and allow matters with the Sikhs to remain as they were. At this crisis, too, Dost Mahomed was labouring under the pressure of other perplexities. The chiefs of Kandahar, his brothers, had, under Russian influence, thrown themselves into alliance with Persia; and the King of Persia, assisted by Russian money, Russian officers, and the presence of Count Simonich himself, had laid siege to Herát. By what means that important place was defended by a young English artillery officer, Edward Pottinger, who was travelling in Central Asia, and was at Herát when it was invested, forms one of the most interesting episodes of the period. The Persians were ultimately obliged to raise the siege, in 1838, and retire; but the complicity of the Russians was too public to escape animadversion, and, added to the apprehension which Burnes's dispatches had produced, no doubt excited much uneasiness in India, as well to the Government as among the people.

Lord Auckland's letters.

Persian intrigues.

Defence of Herát.

Lord Auckland considered one of three courses must be followed. First, strict adherence to the line of the Indus; to assist Dost Mahomed; or to re-establish Shah Soojah, the ex-king, in Kabool, assisted by men and money. He unhappily decided on the latter course. To assist Dost Mahomed and his brothers at Kandahar would at once provoke the enmity of Runjeet Singh, and the only safe and consistent course—to guard the Indus, and abandon Central Asian politics and intrigues—was thrown aside. Accordingly, Mr. Macnaghten, then secretary to Government, was dispatched to Runjeet Singh; and after detailing the views of the governor-

Lord Auckland's opinion.

Mr. Macnaghten's negotiations.

general, succeeded in negotiating a tripartite treaty between the British, the Sikhs, and Shah Soojah, the ex-king of Afghanistan, who, for many years a fugitive from his country, had resided at Loodhiana on a pension granted him by the Government of India.

Execution of the tripartite treaty.

In Kabool, Dost Mahomed had continued to hope to the last. On April 23, 1838, he frankly informed Burnes that, as he had now no expectation from the British Government, the necessities of the country required that he should seek for assistance elsewhere—a conclusion not surprising, when the Persians, assisted by the Russians, were, it was considered, on the point of taking Herát—when his brothers of Kandahar had already joined the Persians—and when the needlessly supercilious letter of Lord Auckland contained expressions which not only forbade hope, but were offensive enough to provoke retaliation. His last letter to Burnes, however, is calm, truthful, and friendly in spirit, and its conclusion runs as follows:—'I expected very much from your Government, and hoped for the protection and enlargement of Afghanistan. Now I am disappointed, which I attribute, not to the ill-favour of the English, but to my own bad fortune.' Lieutenant Burnes left Kabool on April 26, on his return to India, and for the present, his diplomatic opponent, Vicovich, remained there, triumphant.

Its effect upon Dost Mahomed.

To strengthen Mr. McNeill's position with the Persian Court, Lord Auckland directed the Bombay Government to dispatch a small expedition to Karrack, an island in the Persian Gulf: which, consisting of 400 men, arrived there on June 19, 1838; but as no war had been declared against Persia, no notice beyond a complimentary offer of the place was taken of the movement by the Persian court. It was, nevertheless, the means of procuring the execution of a paper of several important clauses by the king; one of which guaranteed Herát from any future molestation by Persia. The whole of these entangled affairs might very well have rested here. Herát was saved and made safe for the future; the Russian instigations of Persia had failed of effect. Dost Mahomed could not but see that, apart from Persia, the Russian promises meant nothing, and the interposition of good offices between him and Runjeet Singh would, there is little doubt, have been accepted by both. The governor-general, and his secretaries—for there is no question now, that they had far more to do with the succeeding measures than he had—were, however, determined to carry out their original plan: to displace Dost Mahomed, and to replace him by Shah Soojah; and on October 1, 1838, the celebrated manifesto was issued at Simlah, which explained the grounds of

Expedition from Bombay to Karrack.

Its effect in Persia.

The Simlah manifesto.

procedure on the part of the Government of India in a distinct and authoritative manner.

It is a recapitulation of all the previous events; but it is as weak in argument as untrue in the assumptions it indulged in; unfair to Dost Mahomed, unjust to the people of Afghanistan, in forcing upon them an unpopular monarch already expelled from his throne, and whose repeated attempts to regain it had been resented and defeated; and in respect to the object of the expedition, altogether as delusive as it was dangerous and inexpedient. It is unfair, however, to throw the whole obloquy of the measure on Lord Auckland. Sir John Hobhouse, the President of the Board of Control, openly declared in the House of Commons, that he had authorised, perhaps directed, the interference; but as his dispatch has never become public, it is impossible to state how far its provisions agreed with the manifesto drawn up by the Indian secretaries. With the exception of Sir John Hobhouse, however, every Indian statesman of consideration disapproved of the war in the strongest terms, and between Lord William Bentinck, the Duke of Wellington, Lord Wellesley, and the Hon. Mr. Elphinstone, there was no difference of opinion—which, indeed, was shared by all reflective men in England and in India. But the die was cast: and towards the close of November 1838, one of the best equipped armies that India had ever furnished assembled at Ferozepoor, and on December 10 commenced its march, under the command of Sir Willoughby Cotton—Sir Henry Fane the commander-in-chief, remaining in India. Lord Auckland and Runjeet Singh met at Ferozepoor, where the army was inspected, and an interchange of magnificent hospitalities took place; but the ceremonies did not pass over without an occurrence which was accepted by the Sikhs as a disastrous omen. In proceeding to inspect two highly-finished guns, which were part of the presents to be made to him, Runjeet Singh stumbled, and fell flat on his face before them. He was not injured, but the omen was not the less considered evil.

Its character.

Sir John Hobhouse's policy.

Opinions of Indian statesmen.

An Indian army marches for Afghanistan.

Before the final departure of the troops, news of the abandonment of the siege of Herát, and the collapse of the Russo-Persian intrigue, had been received. It afforded an opportunity for the reversement of the whole policy of the movement, which ought not to have been neglected; but the actors in the great drama were too far compromised by the manifesto to recede, and after retaining a portion of the army, the rest proceeded to Dádur, on the northern frontier of Sinde, to form a

The Bengal force waits in Sinde.

junction with the Bombay force of 5,000 men advancing from Bombay by way of Sinde, under Sir John Keane.

When the Bombay army landed at Vikhur, on the south coast of Sinde, there seemed every probability of its having to fight its way through the country. As long as the fate of Herát was doubtful, the Ameers, it was alleged, had intrigued deeply with Persia. Persian envoys had been received at their capital, and the British agent, Captain Eastwick, had been insulted, and even threatened with assassination. The Ameers had most reluctantly submitted to the treaty of 1832, which precluded that military stores or troops should pass along the line of the Indus, by land or by water; but they were now informed by the governor-general, that in the present emergency, the provisions of this article must be suspended. Before two British armies, one on the north and one on the south, the Ameers were, however, perfectly helpless. They were obliged to pay a proportion of arrears of tribute, which had not been demanded for thirty years, and for which they held Shah Soojah's solemn acquittance, in consideration of a sum of three lacs of rupees, paid to him in 1833; and on the arrival of Sir John Keane's force at Hyderabad, they executed a subsidiary treaty, on February 5, 1839, which had already been prepared, binding them to pay three lacs a year for the support of troops to be stationed in Sinde. It was their only alternative, as Colonel Pottinger informed them, against complete subjection, if not annihilation; and the important fort of Bukkur was obtained from the Ameers of Northern Sinde by Sir Alexander Burnes under similar intimidation. There was no doubt, as Lord Auckland wrote to the Secret Committee, that 'our political and military ascendency in that country (Sinde) is now finally declared and confirmed;' but the means employed, and in particular the exaction of the obsolete tribute from the Ameers, and the imposition of a subsidiary treaty, have left these transactions under a stigma which they will never recover.

Movements of the Bombay force.

Conduct of the Ameers.

Subsidiary treaty executed.

Intimidation.

The Bengal and Bombay armies, now united under the command of Sir John Keane, advanced from Sinde into Afghanistan, by the Bolán and Khójuk passes—tremendous narrow defiles between precipices several thousands of feet high. At Quettah, between the Bolán and Khojuk passes, the army halted for a few days, already much straitened for want of provisions; and on the 25th of the same month, Shah Soojah, at the head of his own troops, entered Kandahar without opposition, where, on the arrival of the rest of the army, he was formally enthroned on May 8, 1839.

Advance by the Bolán pass.

Shah Soojah enthroned at Kandahar.

CHAPTER XIV.

LORD AUCKLAND'S ADMINISTRATION (*continued*)—THE AFGHAN WAR, 1839 TO 1841.

MR. KAYE'S 'Afghan War,' Havelock's narrative, Eyre's narrative of military operations, and other publications, independently of the official documents, give so complete and vivid an account of the progress of events, that varied and interesting as those in Afghanistan were, it is only possible here to give a brief detail of the most important. On June 27, the British army was in a condition to recommence its march from Kandahar upon Kabool; and proceeded by way of Ghuzny, the ancient capital of Mahmood, the conqueror of India, where it arrived on July 20. This fortress was found to be much stronger than had been anticipated. The battering guns had been left at Kandahar, and to call them up would have delayed the army for an indefinite period. Ghuzny was strongly garrisoned and well provisioned, and the only hope of reducing it was by a *coup de main*, directed against one of the gates; the wet ditch, the high escarpment of the eminence on which the walls were built, and the lofty rampart, rendering escalade impossible. On the 21st a reconnaissance was made, and information received from a nephew of Dost Mahomed, of the interior defences. The northern or Kabool gate was selected as the point of attack, and during the darkness and stormy condition of the night, 300 pounds of gunpowder, sewed into bags, was placed against the gates without being perceived by the enemy, by Captain Peat of the Bombay Engineers, assisted by Lieutenants Durand and Macleod of the Bengal Engineers, who fixed and lighted the fuse and retired The effect of the explosion was tremendous; the gate was blown in, and Colonel Dennie, at the head of H.M.'s 13th Light Infantry, rushed in. It was still dark, and though the Afghans rallied, and opposed the stormers with much resolution, they were driven back with heavy loss, and at daylight the British flag was hoisted on the citadel. Colonel Sale, who had followed with the main body of attack, was informed by a wounded officer that the advance party had failed, and a retreat was even sounded; but the error was retrieved as soon as made, and all opposition was quickly overcome. Brigadier Sale was, however, severely wounded, and his combat, hand to hand, with a brave adversary, whom he slew, is spiritedly described by Havelock. More than 500 of the

The British army advances on Ghuzny.

The storm of Ghuzny.

enemy had fallen, and 1,600 were taken prisoners, with the governor, Hyder Khan, the brother of Dost Mahomed. The loss of the British army was 180 in killed and wounded, of whom eighteen were officers; and the renown of the victory was enhanced by the moderation and good conduct of the soldiers by whom it was won.

Colonel Wade's advance by the Khyber.

After a halt for a week, the army resumed its progress without opposition; and at the same time Colonel Wade was advancing with the king's forces and the Sikh contingent through the Khyber pass, which was ill defended. These combined operations induced Dost Mahomed to send his brother, Jubbur Khan, to the envoy, Mr. Macnaghten, to negotiate terms of peace. The Ameer proposed to acknowledge Shah Soojah as king, and required that he should be nominated prime minister. These terms were rejected; but the Ameer was promised an honourable residence in India, an alternative which he refused, and unable to rally any force for the defence of Kabool, he left the city on August 2, on his way towards the mountains of Bámian. He was pursued, though in vain, by Captain Outram. On August 7, the army reached Kabool, and Shah Soojah made a triumphal entry into his capital, after an absence of thirty years in exile.

Dost Mahomed treats for peace.

The army enters Kabool.

Honours conferred by Parliament.

Profuse honours were showered upon many concerned in the expedition. The thanks of the Houses of Parliament and the Court of Directors were accompanied by the presentation of an earldom to Lord Auckland. Sir John Keane was raised to the peerage; Mr. Macnaghten and Colonel Pottinger were made baronets, and some of the superior officers received the order of the Bath in different degrees. Shah Soojah also established the Dooránee order, in three classes, which was conferred on officers named by him, and struck a medal to be given to all officers and soldiers present at the capture of Ghuzny.

Khelát captured.

Other achievements.

The main object of the expedition having been accomplished, the Bombay column was directed to return to India; but the greater part of the Bengal troops remained at Kabool. Tranquillity was not yet assured. Kamrán of Herát was busy with intrigues with Persia and Russia, and the Ghilzyes of the mountains were turbulent and disaffected. On its way back, a force from the Bombay column, under General Willshire, was dispatched against Khelát, which was captured by him, in a spirited assault, on November 13. Mehráb Khan, its chief, was killed in its defence, with 400 of his adherents, and 2,000 were taken prisoners. Other operations against rebellious chiefs followed, in all of which the British forces were triumphant. Many of these affairs were attacks upon strongholds bravely defended, which gave occasion for the display of great gallantry by the men and officers who assailed them. It was impossible, indeed, for organised rebellion to gain head, and the petty insurrections were the normal condition of a people and country always lawless and distracted, and resenting the imposition of a settled and apparently powerful government.

Meanwhile, the evil omen to Runjeet Singh, which has been incidentally mentioned, was literally fulfilled. On June 27, 1839, he died at Lahore, aged fifty-seven. In the course of the forty years of his career, he had not only consolidated the heretofore distracted Sikh chieftains and interests, but he had created an army of 80,000 men of all arms, with 300 admirable guns, disciplined by two French officers, Monsieurs Ventura and Allard, who, in 1822, had joined him as military adventurers. They were good soldiers, and by their skill, temper, and personal bravery, had not only won their positions, but had formed a better army than Sindia's under De Boigne, the Nizam's under Raymond, or Holkar's under Dudrenec. They had better material in men, and had India been free for their operations, would have overrun Hindostan. But Runjeet Singh was too conscious of the power of the English to provoke collision with them. From the day on which he had signed the treaty negotiated by Metcalfe, up to the day of his death, he never swerved from his good faith, and it was not till he was no more, that it was discovered that he alone perhaps, of all the Sikh authorities, had been truly honest in his professions and in his acts.

Death of Runjeet Singh.

Runjeet Singh was succeeded by his son, Kurruk Singh, who was totally unfitted to reign; and Náo Nihál Singh, with Dhyán Singh of Jummoo, became possessed of the real executive power. A change in the attitude of the Lahore court was speedily, and very inconveniently, manifest; remonstrances were made against the transmission of British troops and stores through the Punjâb, and communications with disaffected Afghan chiefs by the Sikh authorities on the frontier were detected. Sir William Macnaghten's remonstrances were loud and constant: and he even advised Lord Auckland to break with the Sikhs altogether. Such a course was, however, manifestly impossible; but the anxiety imposed by their attitude was not the less constant. Fresh apprehensions, too, were excited by the Russian expedition to Khiva, in November 1839, which was fatal to most of the troops employed; and proved, if more proof were necessary, that any advance by Russia,

Kurruk Singh succeeds.

Anxiety in regard to the Sikhs.

if made at all, must be the work of years, while the melancholy fate of Stoddart and Conolly at Bokhára, and the impossibility of interference to rescue or protect them, threw a gloom over the Central Asian question, which time has not removed.

The Bala Hissar given up to the king.

The winter of 1839 was passed by Shah Soojah and Sir William Macnaghten at Jellalabad; and on the king's return to the capital, he required that the Bala Hissar, a fort and palace situated on an eminence overlooking the city, should be made over to him. It was in vain that the most experienced military officers protested against its evacuation, and showed the danger which would attend the location of the British forces in any other position; the Bala Hissar was given up, and to this suicidal act, the disastrous termination of the occupation of Kabool may, in a great measure, be attributed. During the whole of the spring and summer of 1840, Afghanistan was unusually excited and turbulent; and in Beloochistan, the chief who had been elected to rule over Khelát was driven out by the adherents of Mehráb Khan, who had been killed in the first assault of the fort, and his son occupied the place. General Nott had, therefore, to march from Kandahar and retake Khelát. Meanwhile, Dost Mahomed was a perpetual source of apprehension. He had first proceeded to Bokhára, but was ill received there, and obtained protection from the Wullee of Khooloom; where, having raised some rude Oozbek levies, he attempted to invade Afghanistan, but was met and defeated by Colonel Dennie, on September 18. The Ameer was now obliged to fly from place to place, and on November 2, he was attacked at Purwándurrah, by a force under Sir Robert Sale. On this occasion, the 2nd Bengal Native Cavalry disgraced themselves by flight before not more than 200 Afghan horse, who accompanied the Ameer, and the number of the regiment was subsequently erased from the record of the army. On that occasion, Dost Mahomed escaped; but finding resistance hopeless, he next day rode to Kabool, and meeting Sir W. Macnaghten in his evening ride, surrendered himself to him, and claimed his protection. His brother, Jubbur Khan, had previously surrendered, and with all the ladies of the family had been sent honourably to India. On November 12, Dost Mahomed followed them, and Sir W. Macnaghten having written warmly in his behalf, an allowance of two lacs—20,000*l.*—per year, was settled on him by the governor-general, whose honoured guest he remained.

Local disturbances.

Proceedings of Dost Mahomed.

Misbehaviour of 2nd Bengal Cavalry.

Dost Mahomed surrenders,

and is pensioned in India.

Insurrections.

The insurrections in various parts of the country, partially suppressed in 1840, recommenced in the spring of 1841; and it is impossible, within the limits of this manual, to follow them and their various causes and results. The absence of Dost Mahomed, so far from contributing to the peace and security of Afghanistan, seemed only to increase disorder; and in proportion as partial insurrections were quelled, a desire seems to have sprung up among the principal Afghan chiefs to rid themselves, by one combined effort, of English domination. There is no doubt that the English, at this time, were more unpopular than the Shah: and Sir Alexander Burnes, who was in charge of the city of Kabool, probably the most unpopular among them; but neither he nor the envoy saw any cause for alarm. Unhappily, Sir Willoughby Cotton, who had hitherto commanded the forces in Afghanistan, resigned his post, and was succeeded by General Elphinstone, an aged and infirm person, entirely unfitted for a duty which, at any time, might require constant and severe exertion in the field. After the evacuation of the Bala Hissar, the troops had been cantoned in the plain without the city of Kabool, but they were not massed together, and they were separated from their stores and provisions. Warnings of the plot which was now in progress were not wanting either to the envoy or to Sir Alexander Burnes, but they were treated with disdain, if not with incredulity, and orders for the return of considerable portions of the Kabool and Kandahar forces to India were not suspended.

Unpopularity of the English.

The new cantonment.

In England, the enormous expense of the expedition and its political charges had alarmed the Court of Directors; and they advised a general retirement from Afghanistan at the very earliest period. It would have been well if this judicious order or direction had been literally carried out; but it was very evident that Shah Soojah's authority had not been firmly established: it was considered inexpedient, if not dishonourable, to abandon him, and Lord Auckland, by a majority in Council, determined that the forces should remain. The utmost economy and retrenchment of actual expenditure was urged upon the envoy, and the pecuniary measures adopted in regard to the Eastern Ghilzye chiefs, and other influential persons, only hastened the catastrophe. On November 1, at a secret meeting of the chiefs in the city of Kabool, Abdoolla Khan, one of those who, it is admitted, had been grossly insulted by Sir Alexander Burnes, proposed that his house should be attacked next day. Burnes was warned of this conspiracy by several native friends; but he was incredulous, though he applied for a reinforcement of his escort, and even after a visit from the Shah's prime minister, Oosman Khan, who implored him to proceed to a place of safety, he remained. The

The Court of Directors advise retirement.

but the forces remain.

Plot of the chiefs.

particulars of the closing scene need not be related: his house was forced, and in a vain attempt to escape in disguise, he and his brother Charles were literally cut to pieces by the mob, and his escort perished to a man. No attempt was made by the envoy or General Elphinstone, though they knew of the gathering tumult, to suppress it, or to rescue the officers in the city; and it is impossible to read the accounts of their irresolution without indignation. The only effort was made by the king himself, who dispatched a regiment of his own troops to the assistance of Sir Alexander Burnes; but the mob held possession of the streets and houses of the city—he was already dead—and it was beaten back with a loss of 200 men, and only saved by a reinforcement sent by Brigadier Shelton from the Bala Hissar.

Sir A. Burnes murdered.

Irresolution.

CHAPTER XV.

ADMINISTRATION OF LORD AUCKLAND (*concluded*)—THE RETREAT FROM KABOOL, 1841 TO 1842.

Besides the force actually at Kabool, there were Bombay troops at Kandahar, under the command of General Nott, which were under orders to return to India. Only a portion of them, under Colonel Maclaren, had commenced their march, when General Nott, on November 14, received a despatch from Kabool, dated the 3rd, requiring him to march thither with all his forces. This, however, was impossible, on account of deep snow, which had rendered Colonel Maclaren's progress impossible, and he was recalled. Sir Robert Sale was also ordered back from the eastern passes; but the enemy had occupied the defiles in force, and he was obliged to throw himself into Jellalabad for winter quarters. The only reinforcement which arrived at Kabool was the 37th Bengal Native Infantry, which had been stationed at the head of the Khoord Kabool pass, and which arrived in perfect order in the course of a few hours. No steps were taken either to reinforce Brigadier Shelton, who was in the Bala Hissar, or to organise any attack upon the insurgents, now hourly increasing in numbers. In Afghanistan, every man is armed and a soldier, and thousands speedily flocked into the city from the country around. On the afternoon of November 3, a weak detachment, under Major Swayne, was sent to open a communication with the city, but it was forced to return. Ensign Warren with 100 men of the 5th Native Infantry held the commissariat fort for the whole of the 4th, but was obliged

General Nott is unable to advance on Kabool.

Events at Kabool.

to evacuate it during the night. Another fort which commanded the British position, was indeed stormed and taken; but the commissariat fort remained in the hands of the enemy, and was plundered of all it contained. Other affairs followed, with varied results, and some provisions were obtained; but no impression worth recording was made on the rebels. On November 9, Brigadier Shelton was ordered into cantonment from the Bala Hissar, and on his arrival he opposed the occupation of that strong position, which was alike urged by the Shah, the envoy, and General Elphinstone: and under an incredible infatuation, his perversity was allowed to prevail.

Matters continued in the same state till the 23rd, when the enemy, who had posted two guns on the Beymároo hills, were attacked by Brigadier Shelton, who, after maintaining a desultory fight all day, was at last driven back into the cantonment in confusion. The Shah then renewed his solicitations for the whole of the force to take possession of the Bala Hissar; but though Sir W. Macnaghten pressed the measure, the military authorities refused to move. An interview between the envoy and the insurgent chiefs on November 25, ended without result; the chiefs demanded the unconditional surrender of the British troops, which was indignantly refused, and there remained only the issue of war. But day by day the provisions grew less, no other supplies were obtainable, and the troops, European and native alike, were demoralised by hunger, cold, and weakness.

General Shelton defeated at Beymároo.

Scarcity of provisions.

Akbur Khan, the son of Dost Mahomed, was now the avowed head of the insurgent chiefs. Since his arrival, the energy displayed by the enemy had been greater; all the roads were watched, and the supplies obtained from the villages around completely cut off. On December 11, the envoy proposed a meeting with him, which took place near the river. Sir W. Macnaghten had prepared a treaty which he took with him to discuss with the chiefs, and which related to the evacuation of Afghanistan by the English forces, the return of Dost Mahomed with his family, and the safe departure of Shah Soojah, should he determine to accompany the English. No objections were made, and Akbur Khan himself agreed to escort the forces through the passes. Meantime, however, the envoy was conducting a miserable set of intrigues with the Ghilzye and Kuzzilburh chiefs, lavishing upon them both money and promises for their support; and he was artfully drawn into another with the principal Barukzyes, by which—for the articles were drawn up—Akbur Khan was to become the Shah's minister, the British troops were to remain, and thirty

Akbur Khan becomes leader of the insurgents.

Sir W. Macnaghten's treaty.

His intrigues with the Ghilzyes

and Barukzyes.

lacs, with an annual stipend of four lacs, were to be paid to him, It had evidently been the purpose of Akbur Khan to exhibit to his confederates the small reliance they could have upon the envoy's faith, in the conclusion of a treaty with him, of an entirely opposite and contradictory character to what had already been settled; and in this, which involved the envoy's fate, he perfectly succeeded. Sir William Macnaghten's own defence forms his best and only apology for these miserable transactions. 'The lives of 15,000 human beings,' he said, 'were at stake, and he did the best he could to secure them,' and he confirmed the false treaty with Akbur Khan, by a writing in his own hand. On the 23rd he went again to meet Akbur Khan. One of his staff declared this 'to be a trap;' and General Elphinstone, to whom he confided his plan before he set out, warned him and remonstrated against the whole proceeding; but in vain. It is probable that Akbur Khan only intended to carry off the whole party, as the envoy's three companions, Trevor, Mackenzie, and Lawrence, were seized, and placed behind horsemen; but Sir William Macnaghten struggled with Akbur Khan, who drew a pistol and shot him. Trevor fell from horseback and was killed by the Ghilzyes, but the others were protected, though confined.

His defence.

Murder of Sir W. Macnaghten.

The troops would, there is little doubt, have now attacked the city, or made an effort to avenge the envoy's murder: but they were restrained, and the chiefs renewed their negotiations; but their demands were raised: the treasure must be surrendered, and all the guns but six; while the married men, with their wives and children, should remain as hostages and guests, until the arrival of Dost Mahomed. The two first articles were agreed to, and on January 6, 1842, the troops began their march. There were about 4,500 soldiers with 12,000 followers. Snow was lying heavily on the ground, and the cold was intense: and the first night, instead of clearing the Khoord Kabool pass, they bivouacked near the river. On the 7th they marched to Bootkhák, only four miles; and again halted at the request of Akbur Khan, who demanded fresh hostages—Pottinger, Lawrence, and Mackenzie—who went to him. On the 8th the force again moved on into the Khoord Kabool pass. It was lined by Ghilzyes, who poured a deadly fire upon the struggling mass, of which, about 3,000 fell; but the ladies and children reached Khoord Kabool, where Akbur Khan besought Captain Skinner to induce them to place themselves under his protection: he succeeded in his mission, and their lives were thus saved.

Terms proposed by the chiefs.

The march to India begins.

The army is attacked.

The ladies saved.

On the 10th, there only remained of the whole army, fifty artillerymen, 250 of the 44th, and 150 cavalry, with about 4,000 camp-followers. The rest had perished in the Tunghee Tareekee, a defile not more than ten feet wide, through which the troops had struggled, while volleys of musketry and stones were poured upon them by the Ghilzyes from the rocks above. Akbur Khan now promised to save the fighting men if they would lay down their arms; but the offer was indignantly rejected by the General and Brigadier Shelton, and forming an advance and rear guard, with the followers between, the remains of the force pushed on to Jugdulluk. Here ensued another conference: and the general, Brigadier Shelton, and Captain Johnstone, having attended Akbur Khan, were detained as hostages for the evacuation of Jellalabad. After this the wreck of men and officers passed on to Gundamuk, which was reached on the morning of the 13th, when, of all the army, twenty officers and forty-five men only remained; and while Major Griffith, their leader, was endeavouring to obtain terms, the little party was overwhelmed by a rush of the furious and bloodthirsty Ghilzyes. Captain Souter of the 44th, who had wrapped the colours of the regiment round his waist, and a few privates were taken prisoners, and six officers escaped, of whom, only one, Dr. Brydon, wounded, and mounted on a sorry pony, reached Jellalabad. With the exception of those who had been detained as hostages, and a few prisoners, the whole of the army and its followers had perished in the snow, and by massacre which not even money could restrain. Akbur Khan had followed the troops to the last, and declared that he had lost all control over the infuriated mountaineers, which in some respects perhaps was the truth. It is impossible to conceive a more total destruction of an army, with all its matériel of war; and yet it is little to say, that though some privations might have been endured in the Bala Hissar at Kabool, the greater part of the troops might, under ordinary capacity by its superior officers, not only have defied all local efforts, but have remained absolutely triumphant.

Remains of the army.

Fresh hostages.

Final attack at Gundamuk.

The surviving officer, Dr. Brydon, reaches Jellalabad.

Fate of the army.

General Sale was not intimidated: and his memorable defence of Jellalabad was a brilliant and triumphant episode of the war. A brigade was dispatched under Colonel Wylde to succour him, but it failed to force the defile; the Sikh troops mutinied at Peshâwur and refused to march. General Sale persisted in his resolution not to give up the place, and its defence continued. At Kandahar, General Nott defeated the insurgents and was left in comparative peace; but at Ghuzny, Colonel Palmer, who commanded the fort, after

General Sale defends Jellalabad.

General Nott defeats the insurgents at Kandahar.

a long resistance in the citadel, capitulated on March 6, an act for which he was severely blamed, and the garrison, which was composed of Sepoys, was attacked on the following day by the Afghans, in the quarters which had been assigned to them. Shumsh-ood-deen, the Afghan commander, offered to secure the lives of the officers if they would leave their men; but this they honourably refused to do, and on the 10th, the men, unable to endure their condition longer, and praying their officers to accompany them, made an attempt to escape. It was, however, fruitless; they were followed, and massacred to a man; but the officers, though often ill-treated, were in the sequel given up.

Capitulation of Ghuzny.

By this time, a new and more vigorous man had arrived in India as governor-general. Lord Ellenborough, who had been dispatched to relieve Lord Auckland, reached Calcutta on February 28, and found his predecessor prostrated in mind and body by the events which had occurred. The only effort which had been made to redeem the national honour, was the dispatch of Colonel Wylde's brigade, and that, owing to ill-equipment, and absence of military skill, had failed. Another force under General Pollock was in preparation, but had made no attempt as yet to advance.

Lord Ellenborough reaches India.

Except the Afghan war there is only one other incident of Lord Auckland's administration which deserves notice. All connection between the English Government of India and Hindoo temples and their idolatrous ceremonies was abolished under imperative orders from the Court of Directors and the Board of Control. All revenues derivable from these sources were abandoned, and the temples and their endowments placed under the management of their own priests. It will hardly now be credited, how much honour had used to be accorded to idols and their worship before this most necessary exactment of April 20, 1840. Up to this time troops had been paraded at festivals, salutes fired, and offerings by the company presented to idol deities; and the European functionary of the district was obliged, often most unwillingly, to take a part in heathen ceremonies, originally conceded to conciliate the people, but which had grown by usage into a portion of the ceremonies themselves. It is still stranger to record, that it was not till the lapse of years, that a final disseverance from and abandonment of Pilgrim Taxes was effected.

Acts of Lord Auckland's government. Connection with Hindoo temples ceases.

BOOK VIII.

CHAPTER I.

THE ADMINISTRATION OF LORD ELLENBOROUGH—THE EVACUATION OF AFGHANISTAN, 1842.

Causes of tranquillity in India.

IT was fortunate that no excitement among native States existed to increase the anxiety attendant on the disasters in Afghanistan; but the reason for this is very evident. The Sikhs, now the only real military power in India, were in alliance with the English; and except the disciplined troops of Sindia, with their splendid park of artillery, there was no other military force extant which could excite apprehension, or which could not, by a few simple movements, have been immediately overthrown. The Mahrattas, content under a liberal and protective government, had literally turned their swords into ploughshares. The Rajpoots were unmoved by the current events; and though there might be still thousands of unquiet spirits in India, there was no leader round whom they could rally, or any one bold enough to attempt the temerity of once more trying conclusions in the field. Lord Ellenborough, therefore, a man of much brilliant talent, and apparent determination, possessing ample theoretical experience in Indian affairs, and filled with ambition to distinguish himself in the actual government of India, with the details of which he was familiar—undertook the office of governor-general at a period of profound local tranquillity, which enabled him to apply all his energy to the retrieval of the Afghan disasters of his predecessor; and the advance of General Pollock's forces upon Jellalabad was the first step to be accomplished.

Difficulties at the Khyber pass.

This, however, was not so easy a task as was assumed. Four native regiments, lying at the foot of the Khyber pass, were in a dangerously mutinous condition, not only refusing to enter the defile, but by their emissaries endeavouring to excite other troops at a distance to uphold them in their determination. They were also very much weakened by a prevailing fever, and were, in a great degree, supported by the example of the Sikhs, who from an early period in the war had successfully resisted the efforts of their government to employ them under the terms of the treaty. But all these discouraging symptoms were gradually overcome by the tact and resolution of General Pollock; and on April 5, 1842, he advanced to the attack of one of the most formidable defiles in the world. Crowning the heights on both sides of the pass, the British troops gallantly drove the Afghans from the summits of their mountains, while the main body of the force advanced securely through the pass, and the fort of Ally Musjid, the key to the position, was occupied with comparatively little resistance. Pursuing his march, General Pollock arrived at Jellalabad, on April 15, and found the long-beleaguered garrison unmolested; the enemy had retired, and though unable to move, the brave defenders of the place were triumphant.

The Khyber pass forced.

Jellalabad relieved.

It is impossible to follow in detail the previous occurrences at Jellalabad, the narratives of which possess intense and singular interest. When Sir Robert Sale took possession of the town on November 13, he had only two days' provisions left, the country was in arms to a man, and the townspeople attempted to resist the occupation of the place. The latter were routed on the 14th by Colonel Dennie, and so sharp had been the lesson, that no further instance of revolt occurred. With indomitable energy and perseverance, and under the skilful direction of Captain Broadfoot, the defences were repaired, and the front cleared of all obstructions or cover. As yet the defenders were not molested from without; but demands came, first from Akbur Khan, and afterwards from Shah Soojah, to evacuate the town, and return to India. How these were refused, and how Broadfoot's energy in opposition to any attempt at movement, prevailed over more timid counsels, can only be understood by perusal of the narrative of the siege, and the opinions of the principal officers. It was clear to Captain Broadfoot and some others from the first, that after Brigadier Wylde's defeat, any present hope of obtaining relief was impossible: and that any attempt to move would be attended with the same results as had befallen the Kabool force. The new ramparts were thrown down and broken by an earthquake on February 18; but the damage was quickly repaired, and soon afterwards, by a skilful movement, large herds of cattle and sheep were captured, and driven into the town.

Events at Jellalabad; the gallant defence.

Early in March, Akbur Khan, finding that he could not obtain Jellalabad by negotiation, or by order of General Elphinstone, his hostage, arrived from Kabool at the

Arrival of Akbur Khan.

head of a considerable force; but he was unable to make any impression on the town, though his troops prevented the usual foraging parties from bringing in fodder and provisions. On April 7, the garrison sallied in three columns, attacked Akbur Khan's camp, and totally routed the whole of his force, capturing their guns, baggage, and ammunition, and burning their tents; but the gallant Colonel Dennie was unhappily killed in an assault on one of the little forts in the plain, which need not have been noticed. No more was seen of Akbur Khan or his army; the country around Jellalabad submitted, and supplies of provisions of all kinds became almost superabundant. Such was the condition of the 'illustrious garrison' on the arrival of General Pollock, after a trying but gallant defence of five months.

The garrison attacks and routs Akbur Khan.

At Kandahar, General Nott had received a summons like that to Jellalabad, to evacuate the place; but he never entertained a doubt as to his true course of action. He called in his detachments, concentrated his forces, and bid defiance to the enemy. On March 10, when he had sallied out against a body of insurgents, a treacherous attempt was made at night by a body of fanatics, incited by a chief believed to be in the English interest, to carry the town; but it was happily defeated with a loss of 600 men to the assailants. As had been done for the relief of Jellalabad, a force under General England had been sent up the Bolán pass, from Sinde, to reinforce Kandahar; but on March 28, the general was slightly checked at a village named Hykulzye, and though no more than ninety-eight men had been killed and wounded, retreated, in face of the indignant protestation of the officers of his force, to Quettah, whence he wrote to General Nott, that whenever he retired from Kandahar, 'assistance would be rendered to him.' General England was, however, peremptorily ordered to advance, and did so; when the defences at Hykulzye were found to be as contemptible as they had previously been supposed by every officer, except the general.

General Nott at Kandahar.

General England at Hykulzye.

There were now two opposing forces lying between the boundaries of Afghanistan; but a strange indecision as to further operations possessed Lord Ellenborough. He had left Calcutta after issuing a notification in regard to the abandonment of the policy of the tripartite treaty, and evacuation of Afghanistan; but, as he wrote, not before 'the establishment of our military reputation, by the infliction of some signal and decisive blows upon the Afghans, which may make it appear to them, to our own subjects, and to our allies, that we have the power of inflicting punishment upon those who commit atrocities

Indecision of the governor-general.

and violate their faith,' &c. Nevertheless, on April 19, he announced to the commander-in-chief, Sir Jasper Nicolls, his determination that the forces of Generals Pollock and Nott should evacuate Afghanistan, and return to India direct. No mention was made of the rescue of the captive officers, ladies, and children, and they were apparently to be left to their fate.

Public feeling in India.

This change of sentiment produced a very strong manifestation of indignant feeling throughout India. So cowardly and dishonourable a proceeding, after the previous official declaration, would have been witnessed with contempt by every native court in India, and happily it was averted. General Pollock opposed it in a dispatch of May 13, to the commander-in-chief, and he was directed to remain, until October, at Jellalabad. General Nott and Major Rawlinson at Kandahar, feeling their recovered strength, had become confident in their position; and the garrison of Khelát-i-Ghilzye had repulsed a desperate attack on the fort with heavy loss to the assailants, There was no possibility of refusing to obey the order of the governor-general; but the time of withdrawal had been left to the general and Major Rawlinson, and allowed a wide margin for contingencies. Yet the uncertainty prevailed till July, when Lord Ellenborough wrote to General Nott, suggesting the possibility of his return by way of Ghuzny and Kabool, but he at the same time

Dispatches to Pollock and Nott.

pointed out the great risk which would attend this course, and left the decision to the general himself, who was thus obliged to incur the responsibility of failure should it occur. At the same time, and under similar terms, General Pollock was left at liberty to advance on Kabool to meet General Nott. On the part of neither of these brave men—brave

Their determination.

morally as well as physically—was there the least hesitation. General Nott, after once more defeating the insurgents, left Kandahar on August 7, and General Pollock marched on the 20th of the same month, with a noble force of 8,000 men, both armies directing their course upon Kabool.

Murder of Shah Soojah.

The unhappy object of all the waste of blood and treasure, Shah Soojah, existed no longer. From the departure of the British forces, he had remained in the Bala Hissar, nominally acknowledged as king, though the real power of the State remained with Akbur Khan and his confederates. On April 5, the king was induced to leave the citadel to receive the homage of the army to be employed against Jellalabad, and was shot by the way. His son, Futteh Jung, recovered his body, and was himself proclaimed king: but parties ran high in the city,

Akbur Khan becomes supreme.

there was perpetual fighting in the streets, and on Akbur Khan's arrival from Jellalabad, an action was fought in the field, which resulted in his victory over the factious chiefs, and the restoration of nominal tranquillity.

Throughout India and Europe, the movements of the English forces upon Kabool were watched with intense interest. Kabool might indeed be reached, but would the captives be rescued? Akbur Khan had already threatened to remove them to Khooloom, and distribute them among the Oozbeks if Jellalabad were not evacuated, and Pollock's force did not return to India. On an advance on Kabool, therefore, it was apprehended that this threat would be put into execution; but no consideration of private interest delayed the march. The captives had, on the whole, been well treated; and Lady Sale's journal describes the life they led, at Tézeen, at Buddeabád, again at Tézeen, and a fort near Kabool. General Elphinstone indeed died in April, but his remains were sent to Jellalabad, by order of Akbur Khan, and interred with military honours.

Difficulty of recovering the captives.

Death of General Elphinstone.

General Pollock's operations were skilfully directed, and eminently successful. After destroying all the small forts around Jellalabad, he reached Gundamuk on August 23, where he halted for several days; but on September 7 Jugdulluk was gained, and on the 13th he met Akbur Khan at Tézeen at the head of an army of 16,000 men, which had taken up a formidable position commanding the before fatal Huft Kotul pass. Here the skeletons of the victims of the retreat strewed the ground; and the British troops, native as well as European, were excited to the last degree. The splendid Afghan horsemen fled before the charges of dragoons and native cavalry; the British infantry, European and native, crowned the heights with ringing cheers, and the enemy, hardly awaiting their approach, fled in the utmost disorder. The British loss was only 32 killed and 130 wounded. On the 14th the army was at Khoord Kabool, and on the 15th it encamped at Kabool itself, where the flag of England was hoisted on the Bala Hissar on the 16th, and saluted by salvos of artillery and the cheers of the army.

General Pollock's advance.

Victory of Tézeen.

Kabool re-occupied.

On the side of Kandahar, General Nott had been equally fortunate. He had marched, after being joined by the garrison of Khelát-i-Ghilzye: and such had been the discipline he had preserved, that the people of Kandahar lamented the departure of the English troops with tears, embracing them as friends, and bidding them God speed. General England had been dispatched by way of Quettah to Sinde with the heavy stores. General Nott's picked force, lightly though perfectly equipped, was capable of any fatigue or exertion, and all were in

Proceedings of General Nott.

the highest health and spirits. No resistance was encountered till the force reached Ghuzny: where, on August 30, the governor, Shumsh-ood-deen, attempted to dispute the advance, but was easily defeated. The fortifications of Ghuzny were blown up, and the so-called gates of Somnáth, in regard to the possession of which Lord Ellenborough had written special instructions, were brought away. Up to within twenty miles of Kabool, General Nott experienced no further opposition. On September 14, he found about 12,000 Afghans drawn up to dispute the road; but they were forthwith attacked, and, as he simply wrote, 'our troops beat them and dislodged them in gallant style.' On the 17th, two days after General Pollock's arrival, the Kandahar brigade marched into Kabool.

The fortifications of Ghuzny blown up.

The gates of Somnáth.

General Nott's force reaches Kabool.

To effect the release of the captives was now almost the only remaining object. On August 25, they had been sent off to Bamián, and would have been removed beyond the Hindoo Koosh mountains; but the commander of their escort, Saleh Mahomed, had been offered, through Mohun Lall, 20,000 rupees, and a pension of 12,000 rupees a year, which, under General Pollock's success, was irresistible; and, confiding the offer to Major Pottinger, and Captains Lawrence and Johnstone, they confirmed it. Pottinger, however, found that the people of the country were friendly: and nominating one of the local chiefs to the office of governor, he was soon at the head of a considerable number of partisans. Before, however, any trial of their fidelity occurred, 600 Persian horsemen, led by Sir Richmond Shakespeare, had followed up the captives, and marching ninety miles in two days, arrived on September 17, and they were safe. Two days afterwards they joined the column which had been dispatched under Sir Robert Sale, and finally thirteen ladies and nineteen children arrived at Kabool, to receive the welcome of the whole army, after a captivity of eight months.

The captives.

Sir Richmond Shakespeare rescues the captives.

The successful operations against Istaliff on September 28 and 29, and against Charikar, conducted by General McCaskill, were the last military operations in Afghanistan; and after destroying the noble bazaar at Kabool, on the ground that Sir William Macnaghten's mangled remains had been exposed in it (a needless act of comparative barbarism), the whole British army left Kabool on October 12, on its return to India, traversing the once fatal passes, and the Punjáb, without incident. It was accompanied by the family of Shah Soojah, who, having now no hope in their own country, returned to the protection of the British Government.

The last military operations.

The British army leaves Kabool.

CHAPTER II.

THE ADMINISTRATION OF LORD ELLENBOROUGH (*continued*)— THE CONQUEST OF SINDE, 1843.

LORD ELLENBOROUGH had prepared a noble welcome for the armies of Afghanistan. He formed a camp at Ferozepoor, as well for the pomp of reception, as to be ready to check the Sikhs should any hostile demonstrations occur in regard to the movements of Pollock and Nott. So far the arrangement at Ferozepoor was entitled to credit; but those who were received in theatrical pomp were ashamed of it, and the terms of the notification of October 1, 1842, if substantially true, need not have recapitulated errors which were admitted on all hands. More wilful, and more curiously absurd, was the proclamation in regard to the gates of the temple of Somnáth, or what were at first supposed to be them. 'My brethren and friends,' wrote the governor-general to the native rulers and people of India, 'our victorious army bears the gates of Somnáth in triumph from Afghanistan, and the despoiled tomb of Mahmood looks on the ruins of Ghuzny. The insult of 800 years is avenged.' The remainder of the bombast need not be repeated. A translation had to be read at every native court in India, and Residents and political agents blushed while they read it; and while, to every Mahomedan, many descendants of the old Afghan warriors who had conquered India, it was a direct insult, by the Hindoos it was received with incredulity and scorn. For, after all, were the gates those of Somnáth? As the governor-general proceeded to Agra, the gates received worship by some of the Brahmins of Muttra; but on their arrival at Agra, they were wisely deposited in the magazine, whence they have never since emerged. Happily, the indignity of causing Dost Mahomed to be present at the Ferozepoor pageant was not inflicted; he was dismissed kindly by the governor-general, and to his death declared that the honour and consideration with which he had been treated in India could not have been exceeded; yet 15,000,000*l*. and 20,000 lives had been sacrificed in removing him from a power to which he was now free to return.

The welcome at Ferozepoor.

The gates of Somnáth.

Dost Mahomed returns to his position.

During the operations in Afghanistan, the Ameers of Sinde had continued to observe, submissively and faithfully, the treaties which had been imposed on them. Troops and military stores passed up and down the Indus without molestation,

The Ameers of Sinde.

and from Upper Sinde the army at Kandahar derived much of the supplies without which it could not have remained there. It can hardly be supposed that, after the loss of their independence, the Ameers could have been very cordial friends; but at least they were passive, and no instance of bad faith occurred. On the contrary, and to the last, the assistance from Sinde to General Nott, and the columns ascending and descending the Bolán pass, never wavered. It might have been supposed that such signal and practically useful services would have been recognised by some public reward or acknowledgment, or by a relaxation of the provisions of the subsidiary treaty; but it was not so to be. The Ameers were not a united body; they had separate dominions with separate interests; and the chiefs of Hyderabad, of Meerpoor, and Upper Sinde were each in possession of hereditary territories.

Major Outram (Sir James) was then British Resident in Sinde, and found it necessary to report unfavourably of some of the chiefs; but his report was received with some misgiving by Lord Ellenborough, and the utmost caution in inquiry enjoined. Had the direction of political affairs remained with the Resident, it is probable they might have been concluded without war; but Sir Charles Napier was appointed to the supreme charge of the civil and military affairs of the province. It is impossible to deny high military skill, ability, and bravery to Sir Charles; but in regard to knowledge of the country and its people, temper, or ordinary courtesy to native princes, a worse selection could not have been made; while the provisions of the new treaty now to be submitted to the Ameers were so harsh and unexpected, that it was only by tact and good management that a collision with them was to be averted. In place of a payment of three lacs a year for the subsidiary force, territory of a like value was demanded; English steamers were to be supplied with wood from the Ameers' plantations; the Ameers were to be deprived of the right of coining money, and there were other clauses, alike humiliating and objectionable. Major Outram's charges, which after all were of a very trifling character, and referred to letters which were strongly suspected (and afterwards admitted) to be forgeries, were disposed of by Sir Charles Napier against the Ameers, and a draft of the new treaty was transmitted to him, in which, by an inadvertence, a greater portion of territory was named than the three lacs of the subsidiary treaty warranted. Of this, nevertheless, Sir Charles at once took possession, and after much misgiving and hesitation, and only in dread of further consequences, the Ameers submitted.

Outram's report. — *Appointment of Sir Charles Napier.* — *His ignorance of the people.* — *Provisions of a new treaty.* — *The new treaty.*

Among them was a traitor—Ally Morád—who saw that he could serve his own ambition at the expense of his kinsmen. One of the Ameers had the dignity of the 'Turban,' and was acknowledged chief; and the office was held by Meer Roostum, Ally Morád's eldest brother, a man of eighty-five years of age, universally beloved and respected; but Ally Morád had succeeded in obtaining the ear of Sir Charles Napier, and filled his mind with tales of treachery to be apprehended, and the ill-faith of his kinsmen; and having succeeded in inducing Meer Roostum to repair to his fort of Deejee, extorted from him a resignation of the 'Turban,' with lands of the value of six lacs a year. By this nefarious proceeding, and the previous confiscations of Sir Charles Napier, only six lacs remained to the Ameers, out of twenty, the revenue of the whole province; but their remonstrances were utterly disregarded.

Base conduct of Ally Morád.

The first act of hostility, without any declaration of war, was the capture of Emámgurh, on January 9, 1843. This was a fort in the desert, unapproachable by ordinary measures. In four days, Sir Charles reached it with 350 Europeans, mounted on camels; but he found it abandoned, and destroyed it. In order to discuss the treaty with Major Outram, the Ameers assembled at Hyderabad. They denied the treasonable letters, and demanded they should be produced. Meer Roostum protested against the treachery of Ally Morád; and while the negotiation with Major Outram was proceeding, Sir Charles Napier was advancing rapidly on Hyderabad. On February 12, the Ameers executed the treaty, affixing their seals; but the effect of the proceedings upon the Belóchee chiefs was not to be controlled. It was evident to them that their rulers had been disgraced, dishonoured, and deprived of two-thirds of their territory, and they became uncontrollable. On the 15th the Residency at Hyderabad was attacked by a mob, and Major Outram obliged to take refuge in a steamer. For two days previously the Ameers had importuned him to go away, but that was manifestly impossible.

Sir Charles Napier takes Emámgurh.

Execution of the treaty.

Its effects.

Sir Charles Napier now advanced, and on February 17, he met the Belóch army, 20,000 strong, with fifteen guns, at Meeanee; and though his own force was under 3,000, he attacked them at once, and after a bloody fight, in which the enemy lost, it is said, 5,000 men—for they would neither retire nor take quarter—they were totally defeated: the loss of the English force was 250 in killed and wounded. On the 20th Sir Charles took possession of Hyderabad, and of the valuables and treasures of the Ameers, which became prize-money, and yielded him 70,000*l.*; but Major Outram

Advance of Sir Charles Napier.

Victory of Meeanee.

Hyderabad captured.

nobly refused his share of 3,000*l.*, protesting against the whole of the transaction as unjustifiable, and the amount was distributed to charitable institutions in India. On March 22, the Belóchees again assembled at Dubba, not far from Hyderabad, under the Ameer Shére Mahomed, and were again defeated with terrible loss.

Belóchees defeated at Dubba.

The conquest of Sinde was indeed achieved; but it had been based upon violence, injustice, and deliberate perfidy, which, questionable as many transactions in the English conquest of India may be, has happily no parallel. No one ventured to vindicate it, and the acquisition proved so worthless in point of revenue, that its surrender to the Ameers would have been a policy as just as economical. Lord Ellenborough, though he confirmed the conquest, cannot be considered wholly responsible for it. The student has only to read how much was withheld from him—how much, in Sir Charles Napier's own words, 'rascality' was committed, to absolve him from all, except the grand error of committing the fate of the country and its rulers to a man who went upon his mission under a foregone conclusion from which he never swerved. The mischief did not end here. When ordered to take their turn of duty in Sinde, as in an ordinary province of India, the 14th Bengal Native Infantry, the 34th and the 69th, the 7th Cavalry, and some artillery mutinied: and thus was laid the foundation of that insubordination which culminated in 1857. With the Madras Sepoys the duty in Sinde was equally unpopular; and indeed, under the dread of being sent into Afghanistan, a feeling nigh akin to mutiny had been manifested at Secunderabad, Nagpoor, and other stations of the Madras army, and caused great uneasiness. The new province was, therefore, occupied by troops from the Bombay army, which have since remained. There is no doubt of its value in a strategical point of view; but the mode of its acquisition forms one of the darkest records of British Indian history.

Character of the conquest.

Disaffection of Bengal troops.

CHAPTER III.

THE ADMINISTRATION OF LORD ELLENBOROUGH (*concluded*)—AFFAIRS OF GWALIOR, 1843 TO 1844.

On February 7, 1843, Junkoojee Ráo Sindia died childless. His widow, Tára Bye, was a girl of barely thirteen years old, and the Resident, Colonel Speirs, recommended that she should be allowed to adopt a relative who should be

Death of Junkoojee Sindia.

recognised by the British Government, and this was accordingly done; but it by no means brought affairs at Gwalior to an amicable settlement. Two persons were in rival opposition for the regency: the Máma Sahib, or maternal uncle of the late rajah, and Dáda Khásjee Walla, the chief chamberlain and treasurer. Of the two, the governor-general's choice, for many valid reasons, fell upon the former; but the Ranee and her partisans would have preferred the latter, and as usual in Mahratta courts, a serious rivalry sprang up, which gave rise to unceasing intrigues against the regent, who had obtained a guarantee of support from the British Government. Nothing could have been more unpalatable to the large army of the Gwalior State. It consisted of 30,000 disciplined infantry, 10,000 Mahratta horse, and the famous park of artillery, which had remained since the days of De Boigne. Every attempt to reduce this force had been opposed by a threatening attitude, if not actual mutiny, with such success that the troops had become confident in their own strength; and the contingency of British interference which might be brought by the regent to bear upon them, was to be opposed at all hazards. Intrigues between the Ranee and the troops against the regent were carried on by a clever slave girl, who acquired great influence, and the Resident obliged her to withdraw on a pension. The Dáda refused the office of carrying the ashes of the deceased rajah to Benares, and shortly afterwards the Ranee wrote to the governor-general that, for many reasons of complaint against him, she had dismissed the regent. Lord Ellenborough did not support him, for he had perceived that he was weak and incompetent; but the mode of his dismissal was a deliberate insult to British authority, which could not remain unnoticed, and the Resident left the court.

Máma Sahib becomes regent.

The army of Gwalior.

The regent is dismissed by the Ranee.

The Dáda Khásjee had assumed the charge of affairs, and rallied round him all who were disaffected to the English; but the army had become uncontrollable even by him, and mutinous, and the local affairs fell into the last degree of confusion. In her extremity the Ranee turned to the governor-general, praying him to allow the Resident to return; but this was refused, unless the Dáda was given into his custody. This was rejected in turn: but the Dáda was attacked by a party who were adverse to him, and confined. He escaped, however, and became stronger than ever, advancing large sums for the payment of the arrears of the troops, and otherwise strengthening his position. It became impossible for the governor-general to allow this defiance of the paramount authority to continue; and his minute of November 1, 1843, is a very masterly and dignified ex-

The Ranee applies to the governor-general.

position of the affairs of Gwalior, and as an exposition of the political affairs of India in general at this juncture should be read by every student of Indian history. A bloody revolution had occurred in the Punjâb, when the British forces were clear of it, and the violence and uneasiness well known to prevail in Lahore, might be augmented by the spectacle of a successful resistance of British authority at Gwalior. It was therefore necessary—indeed unavoidable—to establish a friendly government there. Between the Sikhs and Gwalior, whose united forces amounted to 120,000 men, with 500 excellent guns, intercourse was more than suspected; and in any case, their relative position was one of extreme peril to the peace of Northern India. The Resident, who still remained absent from his post, urged the Ranee at least to send the Dáda to Agra to meet the governor-general; but Lord Ellenborough reached Agra on December 11, and there were no signs of his coming. He now addressed another definitive letter to the Ranee, and ordered the forces which had been assembled under Sir Hugh Gough, the commander-in-chief, to advance. 'The British Government could not,' his lordship wrote, 'permit the friendly intercourse which had existed for forty years with the house of Sindia to be interrupted,' and that the march of the British forces would not be stayed, until the establishment of complete order within the Gwalior territories was effected.

The governor-general's minute.

Position of the Sikhs and Gwalior.

The British forces advance on Gwalior.

The letter and the movement excited the utmost alarm at Gwalior; the Dáda was at once forwarded as a prisoner to the British camp, and the Ranee trusted that she had escaped further animadversion. The hollowness of the whole was, however, perfectly apparent to the governor-general, and he wrote to Colonel Sleeman, now Resident in room of Colonel Speirs, that without guarantee of tranquillity, and the establishment of a strong and friendly government, the British armies must advance. A proposal was then made for the Ranee and the young Máhárajah to meet the governor-general at Dhólpoor, whence they could return to Gwalior together; but it seemed by no means probable that this arrangement could be effected, and the governor-general proposed that the interview should take place wherever the respective camps should meet; and a village named Hingona, between Dhólpoor and Gwalior, was decided upon. An advanced British brigade crossed the Chumbul, the boundary of the Gwalior State, on December 21; the governor-general's camp followed on the 22nd, and by the 26th the whole of the right wing of the army was in position at Hingona. The governor-general awaited the arrival

Measures of the governor-general.

He proposes to meet the Ranee.

of the Ranee and the young Máhárajah for two days; but there was no appearance of their coming, and the superior officers of the Gwalior State, who had been placed in attendance on the governor-general, left suddenly and privately, and returned to the capital.

The governor-general was, however, not without hope of bringing matters to a peaceful conclusion, and the army marched on the 28th, when a small advanced guard was cannonaded from a position at Máhárájpoor, which had been intermediately taken up by the Mahratta forces. It was impossible to refuse so deliberate a challenge; but Sir Hugh Gough made no reconnaisance, and the next morning the army advanced as usual in ordinary order of route, accompanied by the ladies in camp and the governor-general. On reaching the vicinity of Máhárájpoor, the Mahratta guns, which had been masked and were of powerful calibre, opened on the leading troops. Dispositions for attack were hastily made, and as the light artillery of the British force was too feeble to silence that of the Mahrattas, there only remained the alternative of storming their position. This was gallantly done with repeated charges of infantry, and the result of a complete victory, though the old Mahratta infantry made a desperate resistance. The enemy's loss was computed at 3,000, with fifty-six guns, most of which were superb pieces cast in bronze. The number of killed and wounded on the side of the British was 797. Lord Ellenborough continued on the field, and showed much humane attention to the wounded. On the same day, and about the same time, the division of General Grey, which had advanced through Bundelkhund, defeated another portion of the Mahratta army, at Punniár, within twelve miles of Gwalior, which consisted of 12,000 men with forty guns, most of which were captured. A decoration of a bronze cross cast from the metal of the captured guns was conferred on all ranks, in commemoration of these victories. It transpired afterwards, that the troops had prevented the Ranee and their prince from going to meet the governor-general at Hingona, and that they had left Gwalior in the highest spirits at the prospect, of what they considered would be certain victory.

Battle of Máhárájpoor.

The Mahrattas defeated.

Victory of Punniár.

On December 30, the Ranee and the Máhárajah visited the governor-general in camp, and were informed of his decision. The State was to remain in its integrity; but the treaty of 1804, which had been concluded with Dowlut Ráo, the provisions of which in regard to a subsidiary or contingent force had never been executed, was now brought forward as the basis of a new settlement. The Ranee was deprived of the authority of regent, and pensioned on an allowance of three lacs a

Revisal of the treaty of 1804.

year—30,000*l*. The affairs of the regency were to be conducted, till the rajah's majority, at eighteen years of age, by a council of six principal chiefs and officers, and the Resident's advice was to be given when needed. The army was to be reduced to 9,000 men, with thirty-two guns, and a contingent force was formed of 10,000 men, under officers selected from the British army, on the same principle as that of his Highness the Nizam, and a portion of territory was assigned for its maintenance. It was to be regretted that so many men were re-enlisted from the late mutinous army which had just been defeated; but they were chiefly from Oudh—the brethren, so to speak, of the British Sepoys—and it was thought better to retain them, than to throw so many unemployed soldiers on their own resources.

Council of regency.

Reduction of the army.

The proceedings at Gwalior were the last of Lord Ellenborough's eventful government. He had come out to India, he declared, to ensure peace, and had entered upon a career of war with an ill-disguised fascination. Relations with the Sikhs were extremely uncertain, and were the example of Sinde to be followed, it was impossible to say what native powers might not be next coerced or annihilated. The terms of his proclamations, especially that of the gates of Somnáth, excited wonder and apprehension among the decorous and sober-minded directors; and it appeared to them that he held the civil service in contempt, and had sympathy only with the military. All these were assumed to be elements of danger. To the Vice-President in Council, Mr. Wilberforce Bird, may be attributed the abolition of slavery throughout India—Act V. of 1843: the reform of the police—Act IV. of 1844; and the suppression of lotteries—Act V. of 1844, were the only measures of importance which were passed during Lord Ellenborough's incumbency. On April 21, 1844, the recall of Lord Ellenborough was announced in the House of Commons by Sir Robert Peel, and on July 14 he left Calcutta: his brother-in-law, Sir Henry Hardinge, an officer of large military experience, being appointed to succeed him, who reached the presidency on the 23rd of the same month. Among the last political questions which came under Lord Ellenborough's notice were the affairs of Shórapoor. The regent had died, and the officer in political charge, Captain Meadows Taylor, was directed to assume the entire conduct of the administration until the rajah should attain his majority. On his arrival in England, Lord Ellenborough was created an earl for his services; but the precise grounds of his recall have never transpired. Although objections may be taken to his proceedings in many cases, yet it must not be forgotten that his prompt action

Recall of Lord Ellenborough.

Sir Henry Hardinge succeeds him.

in regard to the mutinous army of Gwalior, not only saved that State, but prevented its coalition with the Sikhs, whose attitude was hardly now to be mistaken, and whose ultimate hostility with the English he distinctly predicted.

CHAPTER IV.

THE ADMINISTRATION OF SIR HENRY HARDINGE—THE FIRST SIKH WAR, 1845.

No political events of importance occurred for the first few months after the governor-general's arrival. He addressed himself with great ability and assiduity to master the details of civil government, and especially to the extension of education. The discipline of the Bengal native army, there was little doubt, had become lax; its tone had deteriorated; and after mature deliberation, the measure of corporal punishment for serious offences, which had been abolished by Lord William Bentinck, was re-established. The effect produced by the act was beneficial, and the necessity for the punishment was of very rare occurrence.

Re-establishment of corporal punishment in the army.

The Punjâb, however, required the utmost vigilance; and those who had censured Lord Ellenborough's haughty treatment of Gwalior, soon acknowledged its essential wisdom and foresight, in the suppression of a lawless and uncontrollable force, which was ready to cast in its lot with any disturbers of the public peace. Lord Ellenborough had foreseen also the probabilities of a revolution at Lahore, and its consequence in disturbances on the frontier; and in some measure had made provision against such a contingency. Without any display, he had gradually augmented the frontier forces to 18,000 men, with seventy guns; but the stations were divided by considerable intervals; and yet to increase the troops on the frontier, without any apparent urgent necessity, would, the governor-general considered, excite alarm among the Sikhs, and hasten a conclusion which, indeed, sooner or later appeared inevitable. Troops were, therefore, massed in reserve at Umballa and other stations, till the frontier army amounted to 40,000 men with 100 guns, and the progress of events at Lahore was looked to with almost unparalleled anxiety throughout India.

State of the Punjâb.

Lord Ellenborough's foresight.

Precautionary measures.

Khurruk Singh, the son of Runjeet Singh, died on November 5, 1840, and was succeeded by his son Náo Nihál Singh, who had already displayed much vigour and

Events at Lahore.

capacity. On returning from the performance of his father's funeral ceremonies, a gateway, whether from design or accident, fell upon him, and he died the same day of the injury. The widow of Khurruk Singh now became regent: and the widow of Náo Nihál Singh being pregnant, it was hoped she might bear a son who would be the legitimate heir to the State. Shére Singh, who was a reputed son of Runjeet Singh, was friendly to the English, and having, by a successful revolution, obliged Ranee Chánd Koowur to retire to an estate which was provided for her, he thereupon became supreme; but he was under the control of the Dogra family of Jummoo. The soldiers of the army, who dictated their own terms, had already rid themselves of the French generals who had commanded them, and had become so uncontrollable, that Shére Singh actually applied to Lord Auckland, in 1841, for a force to overawe them. Happily this proposition was not acceded to, as a rupture with the Sikh army would, at that period, have been attended with disastrous consequences. On September 15, 1843, Shére Singh was shot on the public parade by Ajeet Singh, a chief who had been in exile, but who was restored to favour at the instance of Dhyán Singh of Jummoo, the executive minister; and on the same day, Pertáb Singh, the son of Shére Singh, and the minister Dhyán Singh, were also murdered. These acts were avenged by the troops, who, led by Heera Singh, the son of Dhyán Singh, stormed the citadel of Lahore next day, and Ajeet Singh was seized and put to death. After these atrocities, the troops placed on the throne Dhuleep Singh, the reputed son of Runjeet Singh: and Heera Singh remained in possession of the executive power as regent. He felt keenly the subordinate position to which he was reduced by the army, who, by means of delegates from the various regiments, had established Puncháyets, or councils, and had thereby become supreme. In this mood they were addressed by the Ranee and her brother Jowáhir Singh, and gained over to their cause; perceiving which, Heera Singh fled with the Pundit Julla, a celebrated Brahmin astrologer who had been his adviser; but they were pursued and put to death.

Shére Singh shot. *Pertáb Singh murdered.* *Ajeet Singh murdered.* *Dhuleep Singh succeeds.* *Heera Singh murdered.*

Jowáhir Singh, who now assumed the direction of affairs, had for his colleague, Lall Singh, the paramour of his sister, a woman of most licentious habits. The army was conciliated by fresh advances of pay: but it was in the last degree exactive and turbulent, and to find them occupation, they were directed to march against Gooláb Singh of Jummoo, from whom they extorted thirty-five

Jowáhir Singh regent. *Turbulence of the army.*

lacs of rupees—350,000*l.* Moolráj, the governor of Mooltan, another wealthy individual, had become semi-independent: and besides large arrears of revenue, had refused to pay a fine of 1,000,000*l.* sterling, which had been imposed on him. He was, however, reduced in time, and paid eighteen lacs—180,000*l.*—to the army. Early in 1845, Peshóra Singh, an adopted son of Runjeet Singh, rose in rebellion, but was taken prisoner in the month of August, and put to death by order of Jowáhir Singh—an act which so incensed the army, that the death of Jowáhir Singh was determined on in a full meeting of the Puncháyets, and he was taken to the parade-ground by the troops, and executed, in the middle of September.

Position of Moolráj.

Jowáhir Singh executed.

The Ranee assumed the charge of affairs, but the troops actually offered the office of regent to the highest bidder. Gooláb Singh, who was temporarily the most popular, and Téj Singh, the governor of Peshâwur, both declined the perilous honour; and the Ranee continued the regency, aided by her paramour Lall Singh as executive minister, and by Téj Singh as commander-in-chief. But the condition of the army was rapidly approaching a crisis, and the existing government had no means left of satisfying the troops, or of paying their arrears and extra gratuities. On November 17, after several previous consultations with the delegates of the army, the invasion of the British territories was determined upon, and the order issued to advance. It was the last desperate act of two desperate men, and a violent and utterly unprincipled woman, to rid themselves of troops by whom they might at any time be murdered, and the treasury of the State with all the private property in Lahore and Umritsir plundered. If the army conquered the British, as it was in the highest degree hopeful of doing, it would advance upon Dehly and Benares, and the subjection of all India would follow; if it were defeated, it would be eventually destroyed, and would trouble them no more. Such were the grounds of their proceedings. The troops themselves became suspicious of the Ranee's intentions and of her urgency, and for three weeks refused to move; and it was only on the receipt of a letter of remonstrance from the governor-general by the Ranee, that, urged by her bitter taunts as well as commands, the army, 60,000 strong, with 200 guns and 40,000 armed followers, themselves equal, or superior to, ordinary Indian levies, marched for the Sutlej.

Ranee Chánd Koowur's regency.

Invasion of the British territories decided on.

Major Broadfoot was the British agent on the frontier, and before the Sikhs moved from Lahore, wrote urgently to the governor-general to hasten on troops. Sir Henry Hardinge was then in camp, intending to visit the frontier in the course of a tour of inspection: but he was by no means prepared for an immediate attack by the Sikhs; and the small distance—only fifty miles—which intervened between Lahore and the Sutlej, gave him little time for ordering up the reserves, from a distance of 150 miles. On December 13, the first division of the Sikh army crossed the Sutlej, and on the 16th, the whole of it was encamped near Ferozepoor, then held by Sir John Littler with 10,000 men and thirty-one guns. He was a brave and skilful officer, and why he had not disputed the passage of the Sutlej by the Sikhs has never been publicly explained.

The British frontier unprepared for the invasion.

The Sikhs cross the Sutlej.

Like the news of Napoleon's movement received at Brussels, the intelligence of the passage of the Sutlej by the Sikhs arrived at Umballa on the day (December 11) on which a great ball was to be given by the commander-in-chief, and he moved next day at the head of all the available troops. In six days the force marched 150 miles, getting little food and less rest; and on December 18, after a long march of twenty-one miles, at four o'clock in the afternoon, the cavalry of Lall Singh's division of the Sikh army attacked the leading divisions of the British forces at Moodkee. On the confirmation of Major Broadfoot's news the governor-general had published a manifesto, by which, in consideration of an unprovoked attack on a friendly power, all the Sikh possessions east of the Sutlej were declared forfeit. He then threw 5,000 men from Loodhiana into Busseán, where Major Broadfoot had collected provisions and stores. Meanwhile, Lall Singh, passing Sir John Littler, had pushed on to Feroze Shéher, where he formed a vast intrenched camp: and hearing that the British force advancing was a slight one, had moved on the 18th with 20,000 men and twenty-two guns to oppose it.

British troops advance.

Manifesto issued by the governor-general.

While it lasted, the battle of Moodkee was sharp and bloody: and at first, Sepoys, and even English soldiers, exhausted as they were, reeled under the excellent fire and energetic attack of the Sikh infantry; but before night finally closed, seventeen guns had been taken, and the Sikh army retreated with heavy loss: that on the side of the British—872 (215 killed and 657 wounded)—included Sir Robert Sale and General McCaskill, both deeply regretted. On the 19th and 20th, the army halted, and two European and two native regiments joined the commander-in-chief.

Battle of Moodkee.

It was now determined to assault the great Sikh entrenchments at Feroze Shéher on the 21st, and Sir John Littler was directed to join on that day, with

Battle of Feroze Shéher.

as many troops as he could spare from Ferozepoor. He therefore marched with 5,000 infantry, two regiments of cavalry, and twenty-one guns, and took up his place in the general disposition of the troops about noon. Had the army—17,000 strong, with sixty-nine guns—advanced at once, much precious time would have been saved, the action would have been more decisive, and the loss and confusion of the night averted; but the commander-in-chief had formed no definite plan, beyond, as were his only tactics, storming batteries and carrying them by the bayonet; and in moving troops from place to place, and making such hasty and imperfect arrangements as ensued, four precious hours were wasted. At about four in the afternoon of the shortest day in the year, when but little daylight remained, the British forces were led, in three divisions—the right by Sir Hugh Gough, the left by Sir John Littler, and the centre by the governor-general—to the attack of a strong intrenchment, a mile and a half long by half a mile wide, defended by 35,000 of the flower of the Sikh army, with 100 guns. There were weak points in the Sikh works which might have been discovered by previous reconnaissance; but they were overlooked or neglected, and the very strongest portions were assaulted. H. M.'s 50th regiment, directed by Captain Pringle O'Hanlon of the staff, was the first to gain a footing in the Sikh camp, and the combat everywhere became general; but the enemy were as resolute in defence as the British troops were persevering in assault. Regiment after regiment of Sir John Littler's division staggered under the tremendous fire of grape and musketry by which they were met. H. M.'s 62nd regiment was much shattered; and at nightfall this division was obliged to retire. Sir Harry Smith, whose brigade had carried and occupied the village of Feroze Shéher, was unable to hold it during the night, and also drew off; but General Gilbert's division held what it had won. During the hottest part of this furious combat the 3rd Dragoons rode through the Sikh camp, from end to end, with a desperate valour only equalled by the charge of the Light Brigade at Inkermann.

Attack on the entrenched position.

Severe fighting.

Before the camp was carried, darkness fell upon the scene, and the night that ensued was truly designated as the 'night of horrors.' Portions of the camp were held by the English troops, others by the still unconquered Sikhs. A hard frost set in; the English forces had had neither food nor water for many hours, and the intense cold aggravated their sufferings. Men of different regiments, European and native, separated in the darkness and confusion, huddled together; and the noble 'Husseinee Pultun,' the 16th Bengal Native Infantry, under Colonel Hall, victorious and unbroken, was a rallying point for many a weary soldier dur-

The 'night of horrors.'

ing the night. By the bright starlight, the Sikh artillery from time to time fired upon the exhausted troops, and one large gun in particular did so much execution, that about two in the morning, Sir Henry Hardinge, calling upon H.M.'s 80th and the 1st European regiment, among whom he was lying, led them to attack and spike it, driving away the Sikh infantry by whom it was guarded. When daylight broke, order was restored; the various regiments on the field took up their positions in line with alacrity, and leading their respective divisions, Sir Hugh Gough and the governor-general advanced steadily, swept through the camp with cheers, and changing front on the centre, completed the victory.

Final advance and victory.

But, at this juncture Téj Singh brought up from the Sutlej a fresh force of 20,000 regular and irregular infantry, 5,000 superb cavalry, and 70 guns, and the action was partially renewed. It was at this crisis that the greatest peril existed; for the ammunition of all arms was nearly expended; the formation of regiments was by no means complete; and the troops were thoroughly exhausted alike by fatigue, thirst, and want of food. The advance of the Sikh cavalry, accompanied by horse-artillery, is described as the most splendid sight of the campaign. Their horses caracolling and bounding, and the bright sunlight flashing from steel armour, sabres, and spears, they came on at a rapid pace to within 400 yards of the British line, which, availing itself of such cover as could be found, awaited the charge with little hope of repelling it. Suddenly, however, after firing a few shots from their guns, the whole, as if stricken by a sudden panic upon a movement of English cavalry on their flank, wheeled about and retired as they had come. It was rumoured that Téj Singh had been bribed by English gold: but this has never been substantiated, and his retreat is accounted for by the fact that what he had come to save was already lost, and subordinate as he was to Lall Singh, who had fled to the Sutlej, he was bound to follow his commander. What he did, 'was,' as he said, 'to save his honour as a soldier.'

Téj Singh's movements.

Téj Singh suddenly retires.

The British loss had been very severe in 694 killed and 1,721 wounded, with a large proportion—103—of officers, among whom were many very distinguished men: Broadfoot, who had won a high reputation in Afghanistan, and who had proved invaluable as a political officer, Somerset, D'Arcy Todd of Herát fame, and many others. On the part of the Sikhs, the loss was estimated at 8,000 men; and 73 noble guns and many standards remained in the hands of the victors.

Severe losses.

In the Sikh camp, during the night, dissensions had run high, and the military chest of Lall Singh, who had fled at an early period, was plundered by the exasperated soldiery. Under a better and braver leader the result might indeed have been very different; for never before had so hardly-contested a battle been fought in India, nor, with eventual victory, had ever such great peril of defeat been encountered.

Conduct of Sikh soldiery.

CHAPTER V.

THE FIRST SIKH WAR, AND ADMINISTRATION OF LORD HARDINGE (*continued*), 1845 TO 1848.

THE British forces could not immediately follow up the success they had achieved; heavy guns, stores, and ammunition were all wanting, and till their arrival from Dehly, no forward movement could be made. The Sikhs, attributing this delay to fear, took heart, and towards the middle of January, Sirdar Runjoor Singh recrossed the Sutlej and threatened the station of Loodhiana, then weakly garrisoned. Sir Harry Smith was therefore detached with four regiments of infantry, three of cavalry, and eighteen guns to relieve it. He had been cautioned against approaching the fort of Buddewál, which lay on his route; but, nevertheless, moving under its walls, suffered sharply from its fire and from the splendid artillery of Runjoor Singh, lost some of his baggage, and was only saved from further disaster by the dashing charges of the cavalry under Colonel Cureton. Being reinforced, however, by his junction with the Loodhiana troops and Brigadier Wheeler's brigade, Sir Harry Smith now advanced in turn to attack the enemy, who had taken up an entrenched position at Aliwál, and had been reinforced by 4,000 men of the best disciplined Sikh infantry. Their army amounted by estimate to 15,000 men, with 56 guns; that of the British was about 10,000 men, with 32 guns. On January 28 the Sikhs had advanced from their entrenched camp to meet Sir Harry Smith, and a brilliant action ensued. The Sikh squares were penetrated and overthrown by charges of cavalry, in which H. M.'s 16th Lancers, under Colonel Cureton, in particular, were nobly distinguished. Position after position, battery after battery, were stormed; 67 guns were taken; and the enemy, driven to the bridge of boats they had constructed, fled precipitately across the Sutlej, many of them perishing in the stream, and under the fire of the artillery, which played with great effect upon the boats.

New advance of the Sikhs.

Combat of Buddewál.

Battle of Aliwál.

Defeat of the Sikhs.

Although the Sikh army had suffered three notable defeats, they still continued to retain their mischievous and turbulent predominance in the State. Gólab Singh, who had undertaken the office of minister from which Lall Singh had been deposed, although he entered into negotiations with the governor-general, who demanded the dismissal of the Sikh army, declared that he was helpless to effect it. No act of submission or peaceful overtures from the army having been offered, hostilities were resumed on the arrival of the siege-train from Dehly, which reached camp on February 8. For some weeks, the Sikhs, under the direction of a Spanish officer named Huerba, had been employed in constructing a remarkably powerful *tête de pont*, at the village of Soobráon, to cover a bridge of boats which they had thrown across the river Sutlej, below the ford of Hurreekee, and it was now completed in a series of half-moon bastions, connected by curtains, and covered by a ditch in front, both flanks resting on the river. This great work, two-and-a-half miles in length, was protected by batteries on the right bank of the river, so as to command the passage, and manned by 35,000 of the best of the Sikh troops, with sixty-seven heavy guns. It had been difficult to restrain the British army during its inaction in the presence of the daily progress of this entrenchment; but one day only intervened between the arrival of the heavy guns, stores, and ammunition, and the assault. The British army consisted of 15,000 men, of whom 5,000 were Europeans; and under cover of a fog, on the morning of February 10, all the dispositions for attack were made without being noticed by the enemy.

Negotiations.

Hostilities resumed.

Position of Soobráon.

When they were complete, about seven in the morning, the fog suddenly rolled away, displaying the British forces in order of battle; and the heavy guns opened on the Sikhs; but they made no impression on the earthworks; the enemy's fire was not checked, and the only resource that remained was a general assault, which was forthwith carried out, amidst the thunder of 120 pieces of artillery on both sides. About nine o'clock, the whole of the infantry divisions advanced. Of Sir Robert Dick's division on the left, the horse-artillery, under Colonel Lane, gallopped up to within 300 yards of the Sikh batteries, and delivered their fire, while the brigade under Colonel Storey, H.M.'s 10th and 53rd regiments, with the 43rd and 59th Native Infantry, advancing in line with the regularity of a parade movement, were the first to reach the entrenchment; and the Sikhs gathered to defend it, which they did by a withering fire that checked the leading troops, but did not repulse them. The divisions of Sir Harry Smith on the right,

Battle of Soobráon.

Storm of the Sikh position.

and General Gilbert in the centre, were led on in turn, and after a severe carnage, the entrenchment was won. The Sikh troops, fighting desperately to the last, retired to the bridge, where their retreat became a flight: and the British horse-artillery coming up at a gallop, poured grape and shrapnel on the flying masses, till the stream, now barely fordable, was choked with corpses, and the water dyed with blood. Nearly 10,000 Sikhs perished in two hours, and the whole of their guns, sixty-seven in number, with standards and immense military stores, remained as trophies to the victors. The battle had begun in earnest at nine o'clock, and by eleven there was not a single Sikh soldier, except the dead and wounded, on the left bank of the river. The British loss was also severe, amounting to 2,383 in killed and wounded, and General Sir Robert Dick, who fell in the assault.

Decisive victory.

No time was lost in throwing the British army across the Sutlej by a bridge of boats, which was constructed by Major Abbott with the boats which Lord Ellenborough had procured from Sinde; they crossed on the night of the action, and on the 11th envoys arrived from Lahore, followed by Rajah Goláb Singh on the 15th, and the boy, Máhárajah Dhuleep Singh, on the 17th. On the 20th, having advanced by easy marches, the army encamped on the plain of Meean Meer, without Lahore, and the citadel was partly occupied by British troops. Sir Henry Hardinge, on February 22, issued a public notification reviewing the events that had occurred, and dwelling with a proud satisfaction on the fact that in sixty days he had defeated the flower of the Khulsa army in four general actions, and taken from them 220 pieces of artillery; that only 14,000 of their great army remained, and that he was 'now dictating a treaty, the conditions of which will tend to secure the British provinces from the repetition of a similar outrage.' On the 23rd, at a public durbar, the treaty itself was executed. All the Sikh territories on the left bank of the Sutlej, with the Jullunder Dooáb, a fertile tract lying between the Sutlej and the Beyas, were to become British; 1,500,000*l.* to be provided, partly by cash, and partly by the sale of the mountain territory, which includes Kashmere; all the mutinous troops to be disbanded, and the army for the future to consist of twenty-five battalions of 800 each, or 20,000 men with 12,000 cavalry. Goláb Singh became the purchaser of Kashmere for a million sterling, and a separate treaty was made with him on March 16, at Umritsir, which secured to him and his heirs the sovereignty of the districts he had purchased. The sale of Kashmere was sharply criticised at the time; but its inaccessible

Advance of the British army.

Lahore reached and occupied.

Notification.

Treaty with the Sikh government.

Purchase of Kashmere by Goláb Singh.

character, and the still uncertain relations with the Punjâb, are conclusive reasons as to the necessity of then abandoning it.

Subsidiary treaty.

On March 6, a subsidiary treaty was made with the Lahore State in regard to the retention of a body of British troops during the reconstruction of the government and the army, and was to be in force till the end of the year only. Major, afterwards Sir Henry, Lawrence was left in charge of affairs. The army brought away all the captured ordnance; and 250 superb guns, with their equipments, were marched through the British territories, and, halting at every station, were saluted by the troops, until they reached Calcutta, where they were publicly received with all honours. Without this demonstration it seemed probable that the British victories would have been considered as fictions by most of the native courts, so impossible did the occurrences of this short but decisive war appear. In England the accounts of it were received with enthusiasm. The thanks of both Houses of Parliament were voted to the army, and the governor-general and Sir Hugh Gough were raised to the peerage; Sir Harry Smith was created a baronet, and honours of the Bath were freely distributed. Upon the army the governor-general conferred a donation of twelve months' batta, or extra allowance. Thus the first Sikh war ended, and with it the policy and foresight of Lord Ellenborough, in regard to Gwalior, were amply confirmed. If the Mahratta army had continued to exist in its lawless and disaffected condition, the counterpart of that of the Sikhs, it could not have been restrained, and under the fierce attack of the Sikhs in front, and that of Gwalior in the rear, the peril would have been extreme.

Procession of the Sikh guns to Calcutta.

Proceedings in Sinde and Belóchistan.

Although Sir Charles Napier had conquered Sinde proper by his defeat of the Ameers, there remained many unsubdued Belóche tribes to the north-west, inhabiting the strong country of Cutch Gundáva, Murrees, Boogtees and others, which had, for an unknown period, defied alike Sinde and Persia, and, as habitual marauders, preyed upon Sinde with impunity. It was impossible to bring their chiefs to terms, and the perpetual menace of their forces, which were computed at 18,000 men, rendered a campaign against them unavoidable. This, with all his accustomed energy and skill, Sir Charles conducted in person, and moved into the enemy's territories on January 13, 1845. In spite of a more rugged country than had even been anticipated, bristling with strongholds, and after considerable resistance, the chief rebel, Beejá Khan, was defeated and eventually captured; and by March 9, this local war was at end. Nothing could have been more complete or meritorious than the

Successful campaign.

whole of Sir Charles Napier's military operations; they were those of a brave soldier and an eminent tactician; but his civil administration, upon which he most prided himself, and which is detailed in 'The Administration of Sinde,' though it effected many reforms of the preceding vicious native government, could not make a poor country rich, nor, although Sir Charles issued a memorable proclamation in Lord Ellenborough's style 'to his soldiers,' announcing and asserting the financial success of his measures, were either the Government or the public satisfied that it was true. The student of Indian affairs should not, however, neglect to read the works extant upon the bitterly-disputed question of Sinde, from Sir James Outram's commentary on 'The Conquest of Sinde,' to other works of Sir Charles Napier and his brother William in reply. The whole of the Sinde question, its conquest and its administration, are discussed in these volumes.

Civil government.

The weakest part of the new arrangements at Lahore was the confirmation of Lall Singh as executive minister: a man of low origin, and the notorious paramour of the Ranee, faithless alike to the Sikhs and to the English. The Ranee herself was recognised as nominal regent, and the advice and direction of Major Lawrence were to be available on all occasions. Lall Singh's perfidy was soon manifest. He had incited a rebellion in Kashmere against Goláb Singh, which was only suppressed by Major Lawrence himself, at the head of troops which had lately been fighting against English armies; his own orders in writing to the insurgent Imám-ood-deen were produced by that person, and Lall Singh was tried by an assembly of Sikh chiefs, found guilty, and banished from Lahore to Benares on a pension.

Administration of Lahore.

Trial of Lall Singh.

Before the time arrived for the withdrawal of the British troops according to the terms of the treaty, the leading Sikh chiefs, convinced of the entire impossibility of forming or continuing a united or harmonious administration, viewed the approaching departure of the English with dismay, and besought a continuance of assistance and direction until the rajah should attain his majority. Lord Hardinge, after every consideration of their request, gave a very reluctant assent: for he saw clearly that there was in reality no alternative between new disturbances in the Lahore State and their probable prevention by local British authority; and he chose the latter. On December 16, 1846, a new treaty was executed by all the principal chiefs of the Punjâb, fifty-two in number, which provided that a council of regency of eight of them should be directed by the British Resi-

Continuance of British control requested.

Lord Hardinge consents.

Execution of a new treaty.

dent; and that twenty-two lacs of rupees should be allotted for the support of British troops to be stationed in the Punjáb. There seemed indeed to be every probability that this measure, arising from the spontaneous request of the chiefs, would last its time; but the sequel proved the contrary, as will be shown hereafter.

It was not only for the vigorous prosecution and successful termination of the Sikh war that Lord Hardinge's administration of three years remains a memorable record in the history of India. The army, which had been very largely increased since 1838, was reduced by 50,000 infantry, without any curtailment of officers, and augmented in irregular cavalry. The frontier was protected by 54,000 men, distributed in stations between Umballa, Meerut, and the Sutlej. Moveable brigades were established in the Punjáb; and, as far as was possible, every future contingency was provided for. In his financial arrangements, the governor-general was equally successful, and the public expenditure was reduced within the ordinary income. The great Ganges canal, which had been begun during Lord Auckland's incumbency, and suspended in that of Lord Ellenborough, was recommenced in March 1847. The question of railways, then in its infancy, was materially furthered; and in a true spirit of humanity, Lord William Bentinck's edict against Suttee was extended to the territories of native princes and chiefs, accompanied by earnest requests that the suppression of female infanticide and slavery should follow. A strange portion of old customs had remained in Sunday labour in all departments of the State, which was finally abolished. Amidst so benevolent and so wise a career, the unexpected return of Lord Hardinge to England was a subject of universal regret; and he finally sailed on March 15, 1848, having won the reputation of a great soldier and statesman, which the lapse of time has materially enhanced.

Review of Lord Hardinge's government.

He leaves India.

CHAPTER VI.

THE ADMINISTRATION OF LORD DALHOUSIE—THE SECOND SIKH WAR, 1848 TO 1849.

THE successor to Lord Hardinge was Lord Dalhousie, who had been President of the Board of Trade under the administration of Sir Robert Peel, and had displayed much ability in the arduous duties of his office; but he had no knowledge of the affairs of India, and its details had

Lord Dalhousie appointed governor-general.

to be acquired by local experience. He landed at Calcutta on January 19, 1848, and had the benefit of receiving from Lord Hardinge full information in regard to the general policy of the State. Lord Dalhousie was only thirty-six years old, and in the full vigour of his extraordinary talents; and, so far as could be foreseen, his administration promised to be one of peace and progress only. This hope was, however, soon roughly dissipated. Moolráj, the Sikh governor of Mooltan, broke into rebellion in four months after Lord Dalhousie's arrival, and the second Sikh war began.

Events at Mooltan.

It will be remembered that before the invasion of British territory by the Sikhs, Moolráj, the Dewán of Mooltan, who had succeeded his father, Sáwun Mull, in 1844, had been required to pay a million sterling as a fine on succession, which he had compromised with the army for eighteen lacs of rupees; but he had not yet paid this sum, and his position being in the last degree equivocal, a force was sent against him after the re-establishment of the government, with no result. Major Lawrence had been obliged to return to England for his health, and his place was occupied for a time by his brother, Mr. John, afterwards Lord, Lawrence, and ultimately conferred upon Sir Frederick Currie, formerly political secretary to Government, who was practically acquainted with Sikh affairs, and assumed charge on April 6, 1848. Finding entire evasion of the payment he had agreed to make impossible, Moolráj, under the guarantee of Mr. Lawrence, had previously visited Lahore, and made arrangements for the fulfilment of his engagements; but he then tendered his resignation of office, which was accepted, and Khan Singh, accompanied by Mr. Vans Agnew, a young civilian, and Lieutenant Anderson, Moolráj having preceded them, were dispatched from Lahore to take charge of the provinces, and they reached Mooltan on April 18. A small force, consisting of a Goorkha regiment 600 strong, 500 cavalry, and a troop of horse-artillery, was also dispatched to occupy Mooltan, and arrived there on the same day as Mr. Agnew. On this day, Moolráj, with apparent good faith, had paid two visits to the Eedgah, a fortified enclosure which had been assigned to Mr. Agnew, and arranged that the fort was to be given up on the following day. Nothing doubting, Mr. Agnew repaired to the fort, of which two companies of the Goorkhas had been placed in charge; but as he was returning in company with Moolráj, who rode by his side, he was speared by a man in the gateway, wounded with sword-cuts, and, rescued with difficulty, was carried back to the Eedgah by Khan Singh and Rung Rám, the brother of Moolráj; at the same time, Lieutenant Anderson was attacked

Mr. Vans Agnew wounded.

and desperately wounded, but was also brought in by the Goorkhas. Mr. Agnew was able to write a report of the occurrence, and to summon Moolráj, who had ridden off to his country-house, to account for the treachery; but Moolráj was then engaged in strengthening his position by appeals to his soldiery, declared they would not let him move, and the Goorkha escort and Sikh cavalry, seeing the turn affairs had taken, left the unfortunate officers to their fate. Khan Singh alone remained with them to the last: and in the afternoon a mob rushed into the Eedgah with frantic yells, and brutally murdered the wounded and helpless men, hacking off their heads, which were taken to Moolráj and afterwards blown to pieces. It was evident that two great and deplorable errors had been committed. The forces of Moolráj, and the probabilities of their resistance to a new governor, had not been ascertained at all. The sincerity of Moolráj's resignation was not in any way tested, and the force sent with the political agents and the new governor was altogether too slight, even had it been faithful, to have opposed Moolráj, or obliged him to evacuate a place, to defend which was a point of family honour, and upon the maintenance of which the support of all the retainers of his house depended. But the evil had been done, and it remained to apply the remedy.

Mr. Vans Agnew and Lieutenant Anderson murdered.

It is little to say that had prompt measures been adopted, had one or two of the moveable brigades, specially organised for such emergencies by Lord Hardinge, been set in motion, supported by a movement from Upper Sinde, the insurrection might have been nipped in the bud; but this was not done. Sir Frederick Currie, though he put troops under orders to march, waited the final orders of the commander-in-chief. Lord Gough hesitated because it was the hottest season of the year, and Lord Dalhousie confiding in the views of persons of local experience, he himself having none, acquiesced in the measure of delay. It was clear that Moolráj could not escape, and his punishment could be safely deferred to a more convenient season.

Inconsequent proceedings.

Meanwhile, a young officer, Lieutenant, afterwards Sir Herbert, Edwardes, who was employed in settling the province of Bunnoo, had received a letter from Mr. Agnew, informing him of his peril, which was followed by news of his murder. He immediately crossed the river Indus, but, finding his troops unfaithful, returned. Colonel Cortlandt, an officer in the Sikh service, had, however, a faithful regiment, which became the nucleus of other levies; the Nawáb of Báháwulpoor forwarded a contingent of indifferent retainers, and after assisting Cortlandt to defeat an attack upon him of 6,000 men sent by Moolráj,

Spirited conduct of Lieutenant Edwardes.

He is joined by Colonel Cortlandt.

Moolráj defeated.

the young commander, with a spirit worthy of Clive, again defeated Moolráj in person at Kineyree on June 18. Edwardes could only implore the Resident to reinforce him with regular troops: but the commander-in-chief was still impracticable, and Sir Frederick Currie would not assume any military responsibility. Edwardes was, however, on the 28th, reinforced by 4,000 men under Imám-ood-deen, the former rebel of Cashmere, but now a loyal subject, and had now no less than 18,000 men, with twenty-two guns, under his command; and, advancing on Mooltan, was met at Suddoosain by Moolráj, with an army of 10,000 men with eleven guns, whom he defeated with heavy loss, and Moolráj was driven into the fort of Mooltan, whence he was unable to emerge. The whole of these proceedings and collateral events, now briefly sketched, are vividly described at length in Sir Herbert Edwardes's work, 'A Year in the Punjâb,' which will well repay perusal, and proves how little able Moolráj would have been to withstand a combined advance of British troops, had it been early and promptly made.

Moolráj again defeated by Edwardes.

Perhaps Edwardes had become over-confident from success: for he held the capture of Mooltan to be a comparatively light affair; and on July 10, Sir Frederick Currie took upon himself to order General Whish to proceed to Mooltan with a battering-train, thus anticipating Lord Gough's decision, supported by that of the governor-general, dated July 11, that an immediate advance would be expedient. It only therefore remained to carry out the operation with vigour; the force was doubled by Lord Gough's orders, and on July 24, the general marched for Mooltan, at the head of 8,000 men of all arms, in two columns, one on the right and one on the left bank of the river Sutlej.

General Whish advances on Mooltan.

Mooltan was reached on September 4, and General Whish found it invested by Lieutenant Edwardes, with 7,700 infantry and 4,000 cavalry, the Báháwulpoor contingent, under Lieutenant Lake, of 5,700 infantry and 1,900 cavalry, and a Sikh force, under Sirdar Shére Singh, of 900 infantry and 3,800 cavalry; thus forming a total of 32,000 men, with forty-five guns, and four mortars. To oppose these united forces, Moolráj had but 12,000, with fifty-four heavy guns, and four mortars; but he had made Mooltan, by earthen defences outside the ditch, one of the strongest forts in India, and it was not inappropriately termed a second Bhurtpoor. After a formal summons of the garrison on the 4th, strange to say, in the name of the Queen of England, as the ally of the Máharajah Dhuleep Singh, which served to confirm a fast-spreading opinion that the Punjâb was about to be formally annexed —the siege began in earnest on the 7th: and after a spirited

Mooltan invested.

Its great strength.

Siege of Mooltan.

action, the enemy, who resisted stoutly, were driven within the defences. At this juncture, Shére Singh, whose conduct had been long suspicious, openly joined the enemy, and, to prove his devotion to the Sikh cause, marched to join his father Chutter Singh, already in open rebellion; when, under the determination of a council of war, the siege of Mooltan was for the present suspended.

Shére Singh joins the enemy.

The siege is suspended.

Meanwhile, under the active intrigues of the Máháranee, the whole of the Punjáb had become a scene of covert disaffection—almost every chief who had united in imploring the British to remain had signed a covenant to drive them from the Punjáb. The Ranee's intrigues spread rapidly to native courts in India, urging an effort to drive the British into the sea: and at length they became too notorious to be neglected or overlooked, and she was removed to Benares. But the mischief had been done: and the seeds of revolt, so deeply sown, were already springing up vigorously in various directions.

Intrigues of the Máháranee.

She is removed to Benares.

Reinforcements from Bombay only reached Mooltan late in December, and on their arrival the siege was recommenced, on the 27th of that month. General Whish had meanwhile taken up a position near the city, and had not been seriously molested; but in the interim the defences of the fort had been much improved and strengthened. The siege was now pressed with science and vigour, and a spirited sally was beaten back by Edwardes's force, against which it was directed. On the 30th, the great magazine in the city, which had contained 400,000 pounds of powder, was exploded by a shell, causing vast destruction. On January 2, two breaches in the city wall were reported practicable, and by one the place was carried; but in the other the real city wall was found entire, beyond a deep ditch, on the counterscarp of which a new and huge rampart of earth had been constructed. On the capture of the city, Moolráj retreated to the citadel with the remnant of his force, about 3,000 men; but on January 29 two breaches were effected, and Moolráj, with the survivors of his brave garrison, surrendered themselves at discretion. He was afterwards tried at Lahore, and sentenced to death; but he was spared, and imprisoned for life, and not long afterwards died.

The siege of Mooltan renewed.

Storm of the fort.

Moolráj surrenders the citadel.

His death.

CHAPTER VII.

THE SECOND SIKH WAR (*concluded*), AND ANNEXATION OF THE PUNJÂB, 1848 TO 1849.

'Unwarned by precedent, uninfluenced by example, the Sikh nation has called for war; and, on my word, Sir, they shall have it with a vengeance.' Such was Lord Dalhousie's memorable expression at a farewell banquet before he left Calcutta, on October 10, 1848, on his way to the upper provinces. Although the whole of the Punjâb was seething with disaffection, Chutter Singh was the only chieftain to begin the war openly in the field. He applied for aid to Dost Mahomed, agreed to deliver Pesháwur to him if he would join the Sikhs against the English; and this strange compact between people who hated each other mortally was actually made. Major, afterwards Sir George, Lawrence, was then in charge of Pesháwur, with 8,000 Sikh troops, whose fidelity was in the last degree questionable; but he contrived to keep them to their duty, until Sooltan Mahomed, the brother of Dost Mahomed, a person to whom he had shown the utmost kindness, treacherously seduced them, and, on October 24, led them to attack him in the Residency. Major Lawrence and his companions were conducted to Kohát, but afterwards delivered or sold to Chutter Singh, who confined them at Pesháwur. Meanwhile, Shére Singh, who had marched from Mooltan, had joined his father, and round their standards collected most of the old soldiers of the Sikh army.

The second Sikh war opens.

Afghan and Sikh alliance.

Major Lawrence confined.

The forces assembled at Ferozepoor for operations in the Punjâb were completed in equipment during October 1848, and under the personal command of Lord Gough, crossed the Rávee (Beyas) on November 16. They consisted of fifteen regiments of infantry—four European and eleven native—three regiments of English and ten of native regular and irregular cavalry, with sixty field guns and eighteen heavy guns, the latter now, for the first time, drawn by elephants instead of bullocks. On November 22, Lord Gough found Shére Singh encamped at Ramnugger, on the right bank of the Chenáb, with 15,000 men and a powerful artillery, with an advanced force on the left bank covered by his batteries. It was too strong a position to assail in front; but the advanced Sikh force was attacked and driven back without material result, and in a charge of the British cavalry to clear the left bank of the river, it was

The British forces advance into the Punjâb.

Indecisive action of Ramnugger.

rendered helpless in the sands, and suffered heavily from the Sikh guns on the right bank. In this desultory and ineffective skirmish Colonel Cureton, of the Lancers, who commanded the cavalry division, and Colonel William Havelock, the 'el chico blanco' of many a Peninsular fight, lost their lives, to the universal regret of the army. A flank movement, which might have been made at first, was now arranged: and on December 2, Sir Joseph Thackwell, with 8,000 men, crossed the river at Wuzeerabad, twenty-four miles above Ramnugger. It was proposed that he should advance upon Shére Singh's camp from the right flank, while the main army crossed the river in front. Shére Singh, however, did not await this issue. Abandoning his entrenchments, he marched to attack General Thackwell, whom, with a diminished force, he met at Sadoollapoor; but did not close with him, and after sustaining a heavy but ill-directed cannonade, which lasted till evening, General Thackwell discovered during the night that the Sikhs, now 30,000 strong, with forty guns, had retired towards the Jhelum. Lord Gough, in his dispatch, claimed the movement as a victory over the Sikh army, and even asserted its dispersion; but the fact was soon evident that Shére Singh had only retired to a better position, and had carried with him all his guns and equipment unmolested.

Colonels Cureton and Havelock killed.

The position chosen by Shére Singh was one of singular strength, and its selection displayed his skill as a general in no mean degree. To have followed him up, and forced him to fight at disadvantage, would probably have been effected by Lord Gough after the affair at Ramnugger; but he was restrained by the governor-general for upwards of three weeks, and unable to interfere with Shére Singh, who was thus able to carry out his plans leisurely and without interruption. On January 11, however, Lord Gough reviewed his forces, and on the 12th they advanced twelve miles to Dinjee, and on the 13th were near the Sikh entrenchments at Chillianwallah, which were held by them with 30,000 men and sixty guns. Of this place no reconnaissance had been made, nor were the enemy's dispositions understood, as they were covered by the thick jungle; and Lord Gough was about to encamp for the night, when the Sikhs fired upon him from some advanced guns, and he rashly gave orders for an immediate attack. The whole of the Sikh guns now opened fire; after enduring which for upwards of an hour, the British troops advanced on the position. The first regiment which reached the Sikh batteries was H.M.'s 24th, which was overwhelmed by a fearful fire of grape and musketry; 459 men, with twenty-three officers, were at once killed

Shére Singh retires to a new position.

Sikh entrenchment at Chillianwallah

Is attacked by Lord Gough.

Desperate combat.

and wounded. General Colin Campbell, afterwards Lord Clyde, had carried the position before him, spiking the guns; and other divisions under Sir Walter Gilbert, with brigades under Penny, Mountain, and others, though suffering heavily, finally conquered, and the Sikhs retired into the forest behind them. The cavalry had been less successful. Charged by a comparatively small body of Sikh horse, the 14th Dragoons, under a false order, uttered, it was supposed, by some coward in its ranks, went about, and galloped to the rear, pursued by the Sikhs; and the misadventure was only redeemed by a desperate charge made by Captain Unett. It was found impossible to hold the field during the night, now closing in, and Lord Gough unwillingly withdrew the army to Chillianwallah for water and rest. During the night the Sikh troops returned, carried off all the captured guns except twelve, and barbarously murdered all the wounded who could not be recovered before the close of the action. The loss in this inconsequent battle, which had nearly been a disastrous defeat, was 2,357 men, and 89 officers in killed and wounded; three regiments had lost their colours, and four horse-artillery guns had been taken.

The British forces retire for the night.

Heavy losses.

After the conclusion of the siege of Mooltan, General Whish moved up to reinforce the commander-in-chief. Shére Singh perceiving this movement, and probably desiring to destroy General Whish's force before it could cover Lahore or form a junction with the main army, left his entrenched camp at Russool on February 6, and marched in the direction of Lahore; but if the conception had been that of a clever tactician, its execution was extremely indifferent. He allowed British detachments to occupy the fords of the Chenáb, and, thus foiled, took up a position at Goojerát. He had been joined by his father, Chutter Singh, and a considerable force, and by Akrám Khan, a son of Dost Mahomed, with a division of Afghans; and the whole Sikh army, now collected in one place, amounted to upwards of 50,000 men, with sixty guns. On the other hand, Lord Gough, reinforced by General Whish on February 20, had under him 20,000 men and 100 guns. It will have been remarked in all Lord Gough's battles that artillery had been an arm of only very secondary consideration; and its disuse was even freely commented upon by the Sikh generals to Major George Lawrence, and so became the subject of open conversation. Lord Gough was urged by all the best officers of the army, and even by the governor-general, to employ it in the next engagement, and he happily consented to do so, though, it was said, against conviction.

Movement of General Whish.

Ineffective manœuvre by Shére Singh.

Position of Goojerát.

Relative forces.

On February 27, 1849, the British army advanced in line in

parade order upon the Sikh position at Goojerát. The centre was composed of eighty-four guns, many of heavy calibre, drawn by elephants, and when within easy range of the Sikh batteries, the whole opened fire, forming a magnificent spectacle. The effect was just what had been anticipated. The Sikh fire, in two hours and a half, was nearly silenced, and the British infantry, advancing from both flanks, carried the entrenched villages one by one, and drove out the Sikh infantry without a check. One brilliant charge was made by the Sikh and Afghan horse, but it was gallantly met and defeated by the 9th Lancers and the famous Sinde Horse, under Captain Malcolm, and hurled back. Finally, the British cavalry charged the now broken Sikh infantry, and pursued it for fifteen miles beyond the field of battle, doing immense execution. The whole of the British loss in this brilliant and scientifically fought battle was only 92 killed and 682 wounded, and 53 guns were taken, with many standards. It was impossible to estimate fully the loss of the Sikhs, but it amounted to several thousands, and the whole army had become totally broken and disorganised.

Battle of Goojerát.

Lord Gough's victory.

Rout of the Sikhs.

The pursuit of Shére Singh was taken up by General Gilbert, with 12,000 men and 40 guns; but the Sikh general was in no condition to renew the struggle. Having been joined by Major George Lawrence, who had been allowed absence to Lahore on parole, and whose good faith in returning was welcomed with enthusiastic shouts by the Sikh soldiers, negotiations were entered into with General Gilbert, who consented to receive the submission of the Sikhs if they laid down their arms unconditionally. On March 12, at the great Booddhist monument of Manikyalah, Shére Singh and the wreck of his army, about 8,000 men, met General Gilbert, and Shére Singh set the example by delivering up his sword. Then followed an astonishing and affecting spectacle. Chief after chief laid his sword at the general's feet, and after them the brave Sikh soldiers, one by one, passed by, casting their arms, sometimes in silent grief and tears, sometimes with passionate exclamations, upon the heaps which received them. Forty-one more guns were surrendered, the last of the parks of the old army, which had been buried 'till they should be needed.' This finished, General Gilbert with the cavalry hunted the Afghans back to the passes, into which they fled ignominiously, and, as the Sikhs said, 'like dogs.' The Sikhs had submitted honestly and without shame to a power which they now respected, and to which, since then, they have been admirably faithful in many trying scenes.

General Gilbert's pursuit.

Shere Singh negotiates.

The Sikh army lays down its arms.

Submission of the Sikhs.

During the progress of the war the British civil officers, with a wonderful skill and perseverance, held their posts; and many brilliant affairs, into which it is impossible to enter, occurred in different localities. Of these the most remarkable was the retention of the Jullunder Dooáb, the province lately ceded by Mr., the present Lord, Lawrence, who, without regular troops, and with a few hastily-collected levies of Sikhs and hill-men, routed the rebels, and overawed all attempts of local disaffection. Major Herbert, too, had defended the fort of Attock against many attacks, and received the emphatic thanks of the governor-general.

Minor combats.

The fate of the Punjâb was not long in suspense: and by a proclamation of March 29, 1849, the governor-general, reviewing past events, and the fact of the Lahore territories having been already once spared after a treacherous attack upon its allies, coupled with the uncertainty which would remain in future, boldly annexed the whole territory—a measure which no one then ventured to impugn, or which has since been questioned. On the young Máhárajah Dhuleep Singh a pension of five lacs of rupees (50,000*l.*) a year was conferred. He is now a Christian, and an English country gentleman, owning large estates in Suffolk; one of the best shots in England, and respected by all who know him. The chiefs were settled in their hereditary villages on pensions according to their rank, and the whole of the population submitted with extraordinary unanimity to the new rulers. Lord Dalhousie was created a marquis, Lord Gough an earl, and the honours of the Bath were conferred upon several of the most distinguished officers; but there were some, nevertheless, who, deserving as much or more than others, were unaccountably passed over. Thus ended the second and final Sikh war. With it the conquest of India, within its natural boundaries, the Indus, the Himalayas, and the ocean—more universal and more complete than any by which it had been preceded—had, after many vicissitudes, been effected in less than a hundred years by the English nation.

Annexation of the Punjâb.

Máhárajah Dhuleep Singh pensioned.

Honours conferred.

Conquest of India completed.

CHAPTER VIII.

THE ADMINISTRATION OF LORD DALHOUSIE (*continued*), 1849 TO 1853—NATIVE STATES—AND THE SECOND BURMESE WAR.

ON January 24, 1849, the Court of Directors, with whom the Board of Control agreed, wrote as follows to the governor-general, in regard to the State of Sattara, the rajah of which had died on April 5, 1848, without issue:—'By the general law and custom of India, a dependent principality like that of Sattara cannot pass to an adopted heir without the consent of the paramount power. We are under no pledge, direct or constructive, to give such a consent; and the general interests confided to our charge are best consulted by withholding it.' This declaration of a fixed principle in regard to adoption of heirs by native princes, formed the ground of subsequent proceedings; but in the case of Sattara it was the first in which Lord Dalhousie was called upon to give a final decision. As the rajah lay on his death-bed, he had adopted a boy, who, though distantly related, had no direct claim to succession by family descent; but who, according to Hindoo law and custom, could become heir to his personal property, and perform the necessary ceremonies at his decease. The question therefore arose, whether he should succeed to the State by the right of adoption, or whether that should be considered applicable only to the personal property; and it was argued with great ability by Sir George Clerk, the Governor of Bombay, a man of large Indian experience, in favour of the adoption; and by his predecessor, Lord Falkland, as also by Members of Council—in particular by Mr., afterwards Sir John P., Willoughby, whose exhaustive minute on the subject comprised every point under discussion. The State had been created, as will be remembered, at the close of the Mahratta war in 1819: and it was under the treaty by which it had been established, that the right to succession existed, so far as heirs of the body were concerned; but it did not include the right, or recognise the principle, of adoption, which Mr. Willoughby considered could not be recognised in this instance, and which had been resorted to without the concurrence, or even the previous knowledge, of the paramount authority.

Case of Sattara.

Question of the right of adoption.

Sir John Willoughby's minute.

Lord Dalhousie reviewed all the minutes and other documents submitted to him with great patience and ability; and on many grounds, which will be found by the student

Lord Dalhousie's minute.

in detail in the 'blue-book' on the case of Sattara, coincided with Mr. Willoughby's opinion. 'The Government,' he remarked, 'on such occasions, is bound to act with the purest integrity and the most scrupulous good faith. Wherever a shadow of doubt can be shown, the claim should be at once abandoned; but when the right to territory by lapse is clear, the Government is bound to take that which is legally and justly its due, and to extend to that territory the benefit of our sovereignty, present and prospective.' Thus illustrated by argument, and by all the investigation that could be made, the question of Sattara was referred to the court, and the reply given which has been already quoted. Upon the receipt of this opinion the final annexation of Sattara was confirmed.

Final annexation of Sattara.

As the question of permitting adoption in general has been set at rest for ever by Her Majesty's gracious proclamation, and every prince in India, without natural heirs, has now the full power to adopt a successor, the question of the expediency or non-expediency of the Sattara measure need not be discussed. The abstract right of the Government to do as it did, cannot be questioned. Beyond the immediate retainers of the little State, few had any interest in its maintenance. The perpetuation of the line of Sivajee in a direct manner would perhaps have been acceptable to the Mahratta people, as a tribute to former national greatness; but this sympathy was not extended to a boy who had no pretensions to royal descent: the annexation was looked upon as a consequence that could not have been averted: and when a period of excitement subsequently arrived, the people at large remained indifferent to any attempts that were made to arouse their sympathies. The court's opinion in the case of Sattara was not, however, extended to Kerowly, a small Rajpoot State. In this instance the court opposed annexation on the ground that the State had not been of British creation, and therefore that adoption, as a Hindoo custom, should be sanctioned; and thus rested the question between two separate illustrations and decisions.

Merits of the question.

Difference between Kerowly and Sattara.

The affairs of the royal family of Dehly had for some time been subjects of consideration: and the position of the king was warmly debated in England and in India during 1849-50. The questions were, whether the nominal sovereignty should be continued to the successors of Bahadur Shah, the present king: and whether the family should be allowed to continue to reside in the palace at Dehly—which, as a strategical position, was of immense value, and which was notoriously the focus of perpetual intrigues. The king, Bahadur Shah, was old and infirm; the successor to the throne, according to Mahomedan

The royal family of Dehly.

law, was now Prince Fukhr-ood-deen, the son of Prince Dára Bukht, the heir-apparent, who died in 1849; and an agreement was made with him, that on the death of the king he was to surrender the palace and remove to the Kootub, a royal residence a few miles from the city, on condition of being secured the existing pension attached to the family, with some personal addition. The succession of Prince Fukhr-ood-deen was, however, opposed by the king, in favour of his own son, Prince Jowán Bukht, by the Queen Zeenut Mahál; and another claimant subsequently appeared in Prince Mirza Korash, the eldest son of the king, who, finding the queen all powerful with his father, referred his claims to the consideration of the British Government. Although the question was referred to England, and opposed there, no action could be taken upon it during the king's life, and eventually a sterner and more tragic settlement awaited the whole affair than was ever contemplated by those concerned in its discussion.

After the Sikh war, there was a peace in India for three years, which afforded the governor-general ample leisure to consolidate the new government of the Punjâb, and to mould it after his own plans. Some of his most prominent measures will be mentioned hereafter. The results of Lord Gough's management of the army in the field, and particularly the battle of Chillianwalla, had excited alarm in England, and Sir Charles Napier, who had returned from Sinde, was at once selected for the office; with his usual energy he left England at once, believing that he should find the army in the last degree of disorganisation, and the losses in the field irretrievable. On the voyage out, he heard of the splendid victory of Goojerat, gained with a nominal loss, and that there was, in fact, nothing left for him to do in the Punjâb, which had been annexed; but he landed in India with two foregone conclusions: first, that the native army of the Bengal Presidency was in a state of covert mutiny and treachery, which he alone could drag to light, and punish; and secondly, that his position was almost, if not entirely, independent of the governor-general. As may be supposed, both these opinions led to collisions of a serious nature.

Condition of the native army of Bengal.

Sir Charles Napier's opinion.

There was no doubt then, nor has there been any since, that the disaffection which broke into open mutiny in 1857, had existed in many forms since the Afghan war. The Sepoys brooded over the sacrifice of their comrades, and considered that Government had taken an undue advantage of their services. This spirit was manifested on several occasions: but as yet only turned upon differences in the rates of pay, the Sepoys claiming the full extra allowances for foreign service, in

Long existence of disaffection.

the Punjâb and Sinde, and refusing to consider that annexation had reduced those provinces to the condition of ordinary British possessions. Sir Charles Napier's experience had been confined to the Bombay army, which had a more exact internal discipline than the Bengal. On these points, the contrast between the men of the two armies at the siege of Mooltan was very evident; the Bombay Sepoys were taunted with performing ordinary duties which had never been imposed upon the high-caste Brahmins of the Bengal army, and opinions and discussions had run high in camp and throughout India on the subject. These matters, and the conduct of Bengal regiments at Bukkur and Sikarpoor, in the Afghan war, subsequently formed the grounds for the foregone conclusions held by Sir Charles, which were soon visible in severe general orders, and sharp stinging remarks to officers on discipline, in his own peculiar trenchant style. Instances of refusing to receive pay on the reduced scale occurred in the 13th, 22nd, 32nd, and 41st Bengal Native Infantry, and many persons were tried and punished. The 66th Bengal Native Infantry, which partially mutinied at the fort of Góvindgurh, was summarily disbanded, and a Goorkha regiment put in its place. The pay of the army in the Punjâb was also remodelled in a slight degree; and all these acts were done by Sir Charles on his own responsibility, without any reference to the governor-general or the Council of India. A correspondence ensued, in which Sir Charles lost, while Lord Dalhousie preserved, his temper; but he told the commander-in-chief expressly, that while his proceedings were confirmed, the power under which such orders could be issued belonged to the governor-general in Council alone, and that Sir Charles's assumption of it would not for the future be permitted. Upon this, Sir Charles resigned office, and returned to England in March 1851.

Misconduct of Bengal regiments.

Sir Charles Napier's acts.

Sir Charles resigns office.

On a review of the whole circumstances by the Duke of Wellington, the decision of Lord Dalhousie was confirmed; but although Sir Charles Napier's opinion had taken the form of exaggerated expression and undue action, there was no doubt that the covert disaffection of the Bengal army after the second Punjâb war had increased, and was a notorious fact. The fire which blazed forth in 1857 was then smouldering: and it would have been wise, during a time of profound peace, to have gone to the root of the evil, and applied a remedy. Unfortunately, the violence of Sir Charles Napier to expose, and on the other hand, the apparent determination of the governor-general to ignore, the existing evil, resulted in complete inaction; and the lax discipline, against which very many European officers were ready

Disaffection continues.

to protest, had they dared to do so, not only continued to exist, but increased.

Burmese affairs.

Nothing of a satisfactory character had followed the peace of 1826 with the kingdom of Burmah. The treaty of February 24, 1826, had included commercial subjects, and protection of merchants and their transactions, as well as the residence of an envoy at the court: but the latter was found impracticable, without insult, by two successive envoys, and the former had been almost a dead letter from the first. In 1851, the complaints of merchants at Rangoon had increased to such an extent, that in the absence of any representative at the court of Ava, Lord Dalhousie sent Commodore Lambert, in H. M.'s s. 'Fox,' to demand satisfaction and explanation. This had some apparent effect, in the removal of the governor of Rangoon, and the appointment of another officer; but it is questionable whether it was not, in reality, a further proof and exhibition of arrogance, as the new governor was found to be more insulting and impracticable than his predecessor, and the officers deputed with official communication were denied access to him, and insulted.

Commodore Lambert's mission.

Blockade of Rangoon.

Commodore Lambert, therefore, in pursuance of the spirit of his instructions, placed the port of Rangoon under blockade, and took possession of one of the Burmese king's ships as security for the indemnity required. He offered, if the governor of Rangoon would visit the 'Fox,' and apologise for the insult that had been given, to salute the Burmese flag and receive him with due honours; but this was declined, and on moving from his anchorage, with the ship in tow, the Burmese batteries opened on the frigate, but were soon silenced. A haughty remonstrance was addressed by the governor of Rangoon to the governor-general, which was answered by the President in Council—Lord Dalhousie being then absent in the upper provinces—repeating the previous demands. The Americans had as much at stake in Burmah as the English—perhaps more; and the American frigate 'Susquehanna,' then at Calcutta, was prepared to assert the national rights; but Lord Dalhousie, who returned rapidly to Calcutta, took the quarrel on himself, and after repeated denials of justice or apology, resolved, with the unanimous consent of his Council, upon punishing an arrogance which could no longer be endured.

The English frigate fired upon.

War ensues.

First employment of the Sikhs.

Preparations for war were now commenced in earnest. 5,800 men, chiefly at Madras, were equipped for the service, including a regiment of Sikhs, the first whom Government had employed in war, and who, on the refusal of the 38th Bengal Native Infantry to embark from Calcutta, took their places with a high and cheerful spirit. In the former war, only one small steamer had been available. Now times were changed; and nineteen steamers, mounting 159 guns, and carrying 2,270 seamen and marines, were employed. The fleet arrived off Rangoon on April 2, 1852. The 'Proserpine,' carrying the governor-general's letter to the King of Burmah, was fired upon as she ascended the river, and the military and naval operations begun. Martaban was taken by assault, and while a detachment of the flotilla proceeded up the river to Kemmendine, the fortifications of Rangoon, which were found to have been greatly strengthened since the former war, were attacked on the 12th, and finally stormed, and the city captured by assault, by General Godwin, on the 14th, in spite of a gallant and persevering resistance by the enemy, who numbered 10,000 men, with 100 pieces of cannon. Bassein, garrisoned by 5,000 Burmese, was taken on May 17; the capture of Prome followed on July 9; and General Godwin declining to advance on Prome, Lord Dalhousie arrived on July 27, in order to satisfy himself of the situation of affairs. He saw that extensive reinforcements were needed, and proposed to increase the invading army to 20,000 men; and on October 9, General Godwin had advanced to Prome, which he found undefended and comparatively deserted.

Naval armaments.

Rangoon captured.

Lord Dalhousie arrives in Burmah.

Meanwhile, Major Hill, who had been left in charge of Pegu with 400 men of the 5th Madras Native Infantry, when it was taken in June, was besieged by 6,000 Burmese; and his memorable and arduous defence of the place forms the most notable incident of the war. In reply to his urgent application for reinforcements, General Godwin proceeded with 1,600 troops to his relief, and to his great joy found him still in possession of what he had so gallantly maintained. The Burmese at once evacuated the province, and the inhabitants with one accord prayed to be delivered from their long-endured tyranny, and taken under English protection: indeed, they had manifested a friendly spirit so constantly in the present, as well as in the former war, that it would have been an act of barbarity to abandon them a second time. Military operations were now suspended, for it seemed useless to prosecute war upon an enemy that could not fight, or a court prepared to abscond from Ava at any further approach of the English. The use of steam-vessels had completely paralysed all Burmese spirit, and the temporary defence of Rangoon was the only real action of the war. The question that remained was, what to do with the Burmese, and how to obtain satisfaction for injury and the cost of the war: for either, any application to the distracted Burmese court was useless. After mature deliberation, Lord Dalhousie determined to annex the

Major Hill's gallant defence of Pegu.

province of Pegu, for which a precedent had been established in the first war with Burmah, when the Arracan, Assam, and Tenasserim provinces had been annexed to British India. Yet this annexation, though confirmed by the Court of Directors and the Board of Control, was at first looked upon with no favourable eye by many parties in England and in India. It extended, it was urged, the British possessions too far; it was indefensible and unproductive, and would be a permanent expense, instead of profit, to the Government of India. These gloomy anticipations have however proved, as Lord Dalhousie asserted they would prove, entirely unfounded. The prosperity of the country has increased beyond precedent, and the value of exports and imports are now reckoned by millions sterling. The population is easy to manage, thoroughly content, and increasing both in numbers and material wealth; and it is little to say that, to the admirable success of Colonel Sir Arthur Phayre's management, these brilliant and almost unlooked-for results are attributable.

Annexation of Pegu.

Results of the measure.

While arrangements were being made for the occupation of the province, a revolution occurred at Ava, and the king was dethroned by his brother. In consequence of the British occupation of the river Irrawaddy, the utmost scarcity had prevailed at Ava, the prosecution of the war became unpopular, and so long as the power and counsels of the old king prevailed, peace was impossible. The Burmese estimated truly the impossibility of continuing the war, and on April 4, 1853, commissioners arrived at Prome to discuss a new treaty. They agreed to the annexation of Pegu, if the frontier were not extended to Meeaday, where it had been fixed, and this point was acceded to; but on May 9 they returned from Ava, and having found the king impracticable, no real treaty was prepared by them. Subsequently, however, the king, in a letter to the governor-general, virtually conceded all the British demands, and on June 30, 1853, a proclamation of peace was issued by Lord Dalhousie, which hitherto has suffered no interruption.

The King of Burmah dethroned.

Proclamation of peace.

CHAPTER IX.

LORD DALHOUSIE'S ADMINISTRATION (*continued*)—HYDERABAD AND OTHER NATIVE STATES, 1853 TO 1854.

IN 1853 the affairs of Hyderabad came to a crisis, which had long been impending. In the year 1843, finding that it was impossible to carry on the government, his official credit being thoroughly exhausted, Rajah Chundoo Lall resigned office. Since the transaction, mentioned in Chap. V., Book VII., he had continued to borrow on very usurious terms and interest, to which the rates of Messrs. Palmer & Co. were trifling in comparison; to mortgage the State districts; to encourage and maintain costly levies of foreign mercenaries, from whom he could obtain advances; and by his revenue collectors to rack-rent the country to such a degree, that the revenue had become very seriously impaired. It was a common saying at Hyderabad, that those who accepted new district offices in payment of advances, rode out of the city with their faces to their horses' tails to see who followed them. In the districts, rival Talookdars went to war with each other; the people were ground by exactions; and crops of villages might be seen standing under attachment, eaten by the birds and destroyed by the rains, long after the season of harvest was past. Of administration in the departments of public justice and police, and of the regulation of the irregular army, which amounted to 50,000 men, of whom 16,000 were Arabs and half-caste Arabs—there was not even a pretence; and local disorders, robberies of mail-posts, and the oppression of foreign mercenaries—Arabs, Rohillas, Sikhs, and Patáns—was grievous and notorious. Remonstrance had had no effect, and any remedy short of assuming the administration appeared impossible. The State was also drifting into serious debt to the British Government, which, animadverted upon severely and justly by the Court of Directors, became the foundation of subsequent proceedings. The contingent force, normally four months, but frequently more deeply in arrear, required to be paid, and there were other dues from the Nizam for stipends and pensions, settled by treaty after the last Mahratta war, which were never regularly settled, and had fallen into arrear.

Affairs of Hyderabad.

Bad effects of Rajah Chundoo Lall's administration.

Debt to the British Government.

After Rajah Chundoo Lall's resignation, the Nizam professed his intention to appoint a minister, but did not. He then carried on public affairs himself in a desultory

Conduct of the Nizam.

manner for some time, through an agent, or vakeel, Suráj-ool-Moolk, the grandson of the great Meer Allum, who, in 1846, was finally appointed Dewán, or prime minister. Suráj-ool-Moolk's intentions were excellent, and his ability considerable; but his power of executing reform was very limited, and his best attempts to restore good government, and check the corruption which had heretofore flourished, were defeated by intrigues, which the Nizam too frequently countenanced. In 1848, Suráj-ool-Moolk was removed from office, and another nobleman, Amjud-ool-Moolk, appointed, a man without the slightest pretensions either to influence or ability. He also was removed, and Shumsh-ool-Oomra, a nobleman of high rank and great experience, took his place; but he shortly after resigned. Meanwhile, the debt to the British Government had continued to increase, and Lord Dalhousie had no resource, under the stringent orders of the court, but to declare it must be put in course of liquidation by the end of 1850. After trials of two other persons as financial ministers, all hope of arrangements by the Nizam had broken down by April 1851, and he was called upon by the governor-general to make arrangements for the transfer of territory in satisfaction for the amount owed, and for the future payment of the contingent. Certain districts were also proposed for cession, including Berar; but the Nizam still hoped to evade the necessity, and again appointed Suráj-ool-Moolk as minister, who proposed to set apart several districts for the provision of the necessary funds. The resources of these districts were ample for the purpose; and if the arrangement had been maintained inviolate, any necessity for further proceedings would have been averted. The debt to the company now amounted to about eighty lacs of rupees—800,000*l.*—of which forty lacs—400,000*l.*—was paid in August 1851.

Ministry of Suráj-ool-Moolk,

who is removed from office.

Others in succession.

Demands of the governor-general.

Suráj-ool-Moolk resumes office.

General Fraser retired from the service in November 1852, and was succeeded as Resident at Hyderabad by Colonel (now General Sir John) Low. Public affairs were by no means improved; the debt to the English Government had again risen to nearly half a million sterling, and any hope of obtaining payments, even for current demands, was completely at an end. The necessity of ceding territory was again laid before the Nizam; several somewhat stormy interviews took place between him and Colonel Low, which are graphically described in the 'blue-book,' and in the end, the Nizam yielded, though reluctantly. He had, indeed, displayed more ability in the discussion than he had been thought capable of; reviewing past

The Nizam's debt increases.

The Nizam yields a reluctant consent.

treaties and transactions, and in particular exposing the discreditable resumption of the péshcush of the Northern Circars on account of 'Palmer's claim.' He was, however, on the horns of a dilemma. On the one hand, he could not bring himself to part with the contingent force, which the governor-general offered to disband; on the other, he had no means of paying the debt, or the charges of the contingent. The new treaty provided thirty-six lacs as the new cost of the contingent, the previous amount being reduced by six lacs—and all the Nizam's or local officers were pensioned. Three districts—Berar, Nuldroog, and the Ráichore Dooáb—were finally assigned to English management, the Nizam retaining his sovereign rights, and the British Government covenanting to render just accounts of the receipts and disbursements.

Lord Dalhousie has been severely censured for these transactions by many writers; but if some over-strong expressions in correspondence, the result of irritation, be excepted, there is nothing objectionable or overbearing in the result. It is impossible to pity, or sympathise with, the wilful extravagance and mismanagement of the Nizam's government, during a period of twenty-five years, and under repeated warnings of their consequences, or to allow that plea for the non-fulfilment of obligations. It is equally impossible to overlook the fact, that under General Fraser's arrangements of 1851, the settlement remained in the hands of the Nizam's government alone. As to the contingent force, it had continuously repressed disorder throughout the country, it was the only check the Nizam possessed against his lawless mercenaries, and it had rendered many special services. Its cost was well known to, and admitted by, the Nizam. It might have been discharged in 1829; but was deliberately retained, while its cost was materially reduced. It is, therefore, unjust to Lord Dalhousie to attribute to him motives which did not exist; and he had the satisfaction of delivering the Nizam, and his own Government, from very painful relative positions. The treaty of 1853 was subsequently modified in 1860, and, as will be noted in its proper place, all causes of discontent were then removed. Suráj-ool-Moolk, after a long illness, died very shortly after the treaty had been executed, and his nephew, Salar Jung, young in years but of great ability and promise, was appointed minister, and whose admirable administration still continues. At the period of the assignment of territory by the Nizam, the Rajah of Shórapoor attained his majority, and his country was made over to him. The revenues had been doubled during nearly twelve years of careful management, and every inducement existed to hope that he might continue

Review of the transactions.

Shórapoor.

what had been established. His fate was, however, a miserable end, as will be hereafter stated.

Ally Morád of Sinde.

In 1852–3, Ally Morád, one of the Ameers of Sinde, whose traitorous conduct to his eldest brother will be remembered, was found guilty, after his trial by a commission, of forgery, and the lands he had obtained were resumed.

Death of the Nawáb of the Carnatic.

Pension of his family.

The Nawáb of the Carnatic died childless in 1853, and his uncle, Azim Jáh, claimed the throne as the nearest collateral heir. Lord Harris, then governor of Madras, opposed any succession not recognisable by treaty, and was supported by his Council. They recommended that the family should be liberally provided for, and their debts paid; but that its recognition as local royalty should cease. With these views Lord Dalhousie concurred, and the decision was confirmed by the Court of Directors. By another death in the same year a considerable annual pension of eight lacs—80,000*l.*—lapsed to Government.

Death of Bajee Ráo, ex-Péshwah.

His adopted son, Dhundoo Punt,

applies for continuance of the pension.

Its refusal.

Bajee Ráo, the ex-Péshwah, died at Bithoor, in the month of January, having adopted an heir—Dhóndoo Punt, the Nána Sahib of subsequent infamous memory—who inherited the personal property of the Péshwah, which was acknowledged to be twenty-eight lacs of rupees—280,000*l.*—though believed to be much more. Nána Sahib's application for the continuance of the Péshwah's pension was refused, for it had been a grant for Bajee Ráo's life only; but the town and territory of Bithoor were conferred upon him for life. Not content with this decision, the Nána sent an agent to London, who made even more preposterous demands, which were in turn rejected. Bajee Ráo had received two and a half millions sterling during the period of his deposal, and was of notoriously penurious habits; and while his savings were not interfered with, the recognition of any hereditary right to the pension in an adopted heir was manifestly impossible.

Railways.

If the nature and variety of all these political questions of 1853, apart from the current business of the State, be considered, it will be evident how severely the governor-general's powers, great as they were, had been taxed; but in addition there were other subjects under review and settlement, the most important of which was that of the projected railways.

Lord Dalhousie's minute.

On April 20, 1853, Lord Dalhousie submitted a minute to the Court of Directors, which, thoroughly and practically acquainted with the subject as he had become while President of the Board of Trade in England, formed the basis of all those great works since completed, or now under construction, which will be detailed hereafter. The minute embraced every subject, political, military, and commercial; and as one of Lord Dalhousie's most comprehensive State papers, amply repays perusal: and the result of experience and time has amply proved the value of the counsel then given. The electric telegraph communication was spread over India in an almost incredibly short space of time, by the exertions of Dr., now Sir William, O'Shaughnessy. He had been sent to England expressly, in 1852, to assist in passing the question, to which no opposition was made in the Court of Directors, and to form an establishment. Before the end of 1853, the work was in rapid progress, and has continued to be extended wherever necessary; and Lord Dalhousie's hope, that the Indian might ultimately be united with the European systems, has been accomplished, and is being gradually perfected—it need hardly be said with what advantage to the Government or to the community.

Electric telegraph established.

Finally, in 1853, the East India Company's charter—which had been extended, in 1833, for twenty years, came to an end. It was not abolished, neither was any further term specifically assigned to it; but the constitution of the Court of Directors was considerably modified. The number of directors was reduced from twenty-four to eighteen —twelve to be elected as before, and six nominated by the crown—and their subordination to the Indian minister of the crown was thus rendered more complete, though the independence of the body was not yet extinguished. Their patronage was, however, curtailed, by throwing open the civil service to competition; and, reviewing the past, it will be more than ever apparent to the student, as the effects of the administration of the Court of Directors are traced to their sources, that the collision of the court with the minister of the crown in the famous 'mandamus' case, in regard to the affairs of William Palmer & Co., formed the foundation of their subsequent comparative weakness and eventual dissolution.

Charter of the East India Company ends.

Modification of the Court of Directors.

Under the new arrangements also, Bengal was created a separate government, with a lieutenant-governor; thus liberating the governor-general from a large portion of local detail, and providing a responsible authority for that of the senior member of Council whenever the governor-general was absent, which had been usually ineffective.

Bengal created a separate government.

CHAPTER X.

LORD DALHOUSIE'S ADMINISTRATION (*continued*)—NAGPOOR AND JHANSY, 1853 TO 1854.

Of all the period of Lord Dalhousie's administration, the year 1853–1854 most abounds with remarkable occurrences. The Burmese war had closed; but the diversity of the subjects which successively occupied the attention of the governor-general, show forth his versatility of talent and capacity of judgment more strongly, if possible, than the direction of war, or the ordinary course of civil administration. It is necessary to place them in order, if not of date of importance, for that reference to details which, impossible to be given here, should not be omitted by the student.

Affairs of Jhansy.

Death of the Rajah of Berar.

In this year (1853), the Rajah of Jhansy died, on November 11, without heirs, and on the 27th of the same month, Rughoojee Bhóslay, rajah of Berar, also died, under similar circumstances. The former State was comparatively insignificant; but the latter was of considerable importance, having an area of 76,500 square miles, with a population of 4,650,000; and it remained to be concluded whether both should be annexed to the British dominions, or whether the adoption of successors should be permitted. The case of Nagpoor was first decided; and, under a proclamation by the Government of India, it was annexed in the month of December, 1853. The deceased rajah, though during the last two years of his life he had been repeatedly urged to do so by the Resident, Mr. Mansel, had declared no heir, and expressed aversion to the discussion of adoption. There was no one on the male side recognisable by Hindoo law who could claim a right to the succession, and the rajah's widows, though, under Mahratta usage, they might have made an adoption, and subsequently offered to do so, could only instance persons of descent in the female line, and their request was rejected. The question, therefore, remained to be decided on grounds of expediency, not of right. In favour of continuing the State by adoption, or recognition of some claimant to the succession, Mr. Mansel, the Resident, pleaded strongly, and was supported in the Supreme Council by Sir John Low, in an able minute, which set forth the alarm already existent

Case of Nagpoor.

The State annexed.

The rajah declines to adopt an heir.

Mr. Mansel's minute supported by Sir John Low.

among native States, consequent upon the annexations of Sinde and the Punjâb, the necessity of maintaining public faith inviolate, and the advisability of allowing the widows of the rajah and the chief men of Nagpoor to make their own arrangements in regard to a successor.

Opinion of the governor-general.

These views were, however, diametrically opposed to that of the governor-general. 'The State of Nagpoor,' he wrote, 'conferred on the rajah and his heirs in 1818 by the British Government, has reverted to it on the death of the rajah without any heir.' But this assumption, which formed the basis of his lordship's decision, was that the State, like Sattara and Mysore, had been the free and new gift of the British Government, after conquest of the territory, and when no valid claim on the part of the original possessors existed. In this case, however, it was not so. After the treachery of Appa Sahib, in 1818, the State of Nagpoor, though it lay at the mercy of the British Government, was not annexed; but, on the contrary, continued without interruption to the heir adopted by the Ranee (Chap. V., Book VII.). Consequently, on the terms of the court's decision in the cases of Sattara and Kerowly, previously mentioned, Nagpoor appears clearly to lie in the category of the latter, and of Sindia and Holkar, &c., not of the former. The question of expediency, and whether or not the people, as indeed has been triumphantly proved, would be more content and prosperous under the British than under a native government, is beside the subject, and should not have entered into its discussion. The annexation was, nevertheless, decided upon, and undoubtedly caused much alarm and discussion in native society throughout India. The new policy could not be understood, when, in the instances of Holkar, Sindia, Oorcha, Duttea, Oodypoor, Kerowly, and others, native independent States originally created, and held in descent from their founders by adoption, were recognised without demur, and without challenge as to the person adopted being of either near or distant relationship. Nagpoor had been founded as an independent State before the British had exercised any political power whatever, and its existence had been continued without interruption. If natives admitted the abstract right of the British Government to do as it pleased with what had become its own by conquest, or to revoke any gifts previously made, they considered, and it must be admitted with justice, that States recognised by treaty as independent should be exempt from interference in cases of succession, and left to their own arrangements Such rights have in fact been since recognised and established by law; but the then unsettled state of these questions produced what was termed the annexation policy of Lord Dalhousie, which

Difference between Nagpoor and Mysore, &c.

Native discussion on the subject.

he maintained to the last, under the support of the Court of Directors and the Board of Control.

Objectionable means used to carry out the measure.

If the annexation of Nagpoor was an unpopular and alarming measure, the mode in which it was carried out increased the dissatisfaction of the native public of India, and in a great measure the European also, in no small degree. The governor-general, though he might confiscate the State, had surely nothing to do with the private property of the deceased rajah; and the rough manner in which it was seized, and, to all outward appearances, confiscated, and sold by auction—jewels, horses and the like—savoured, to the native mind, more of the confiscations of old Mahomedan tyrants than of the benignity of British rule. It would be little to say that few, even now, understand that the proceeds—200,000*l.*—were invested in a fund for the benefit of the Ranees and family of Nagpoor; but the property did not realise half its estimated value, and it was a great, but irredeemable error, to have interfered with it in any way. Independent of the fund, the Ranees and family receive liberal pensions from the revenues of Nagpoor.

The private property is seized,

and sold by auction.

The proceeds invested on account of the Ranees.

Case of Jhansy.

Jhansy was the next case. This small territory had been one of the Péshwah's first acquisitions from the Moghuls, and a Mahratta Brahmin family had been appointed to its management, under the title of Soobahdar. It was not an independent State, though the office was hereditary according to Mahratta usage, and part of the revenue was doubtless remitted to the State treasury. The Soobahdar was faithful to the British cause in the war of 1804, and a treaty was made with him by Lord Lake, which was confirmed by another in 1817, on the cession, under the treaty of Bassein, by the Péshwah, of all his rights in Hindostan, by which the Jhansy territory was continued to the ruler and his 'heirs and successors.' In 1832, Lord William Bentinck, in recognition of his loyalty and his well-ordered government, conferred the title of 'Máhárajah' on Rám Chunder Ráo, who adopted the English flag as his own, hoisted it on his citadel, and saluted it with a hundred guns. Rám Chunder died in 1835, and having no male heir, the succession devolved on the male representative of his grandfather's line, which was confirmed; and Gunga Dhur Ráo, continuing all the good faith of his predecessors, died on November 11, 1853. Before his death, having no heir, he adopted Anund Ráo, a boy of five years old—'My grandson, through my grandfather,' as he wrote: but which in reality, meant the adoption of the nearest male in descent from his great-grandfather, Sheo Ráo.

Adoption of an heir by the rajah.

On his death-bed, as it proved, the Máhárajah wrote to the governor-general that he had taken this step in case he should not survive: and that his wife, Gunga Bye, was to be considered regent during the boy's minority. This letter was read in the presence of the political agent for Bundelkhund, the day before the Máhárajah's death, and duly forwarded. The adoption was not, however, allowed, and the State was confiscated; and the grounds adduced for the proceeding were, that Jhansy was not originally an independent native State, but a dependency of the Péshwah's, to which the British Government succeeded under the treaty of Bassein, but which it had continued to the person found in possession; and that Sir Charles Metcalfe had on a former occasion decided against the principle of adoption in this State. On that occasion, however, there was a real heir living, and Sir Charles would not allow him to be set aside: it was not the principle of adoption that was then objected to, but adoption to the prejudice of a real heir. Sir John Low on this occasion agreed with the governor-general; but while he and Mr. Halliday could not controvert the arguments his lordship had adduced, they trusted the example of Kerowly might be followed. The annexation was not carried out with a show of force, and it was evident that the popular sympathy of the whole of Bundelkhund and the north-west provinces was in favour of the dispossessed Ranee and her family.

His letter to the governor-general.

Discussion in Council.

Native sympathy with the family.

Looking back on the past, this annexation, though based upon an exercise of abstract right, on the basis of the treaty of Bassein, appears to have been inexpedient, and not a little forced and ungenerous, considering the previous uniform good faith displayed and material assistance rendered by the Jhansy family on many occasions, and their recognition, by regular treaties, as independent princes. If necessary, which the small value of the principality put out of consideration, reduction might have been made in the amount of territory, to the original limits of the State; but entire confiscation, following immediately upon that of Nagpoor, increased the prevalent apprehensions to a painful extent. The measure was, however, confirmed by the Court of Directors, and for a time no more was heard of Jhansy.

Considerations of the policy.

CHAPTER XI.

THE ADMINISTRATION OF LORD DALHOUSIE (*concluded*)—THE ANNEXATION OF OUDH, 1854 TO 1856.

The Santál insurrection.

On June 30, 1855, a vast body of Santáls, an aboriginal tribe occupying the hills and forests on the north-west frontier of Bengal, assembled in rebellion, or, as they alleged, with the purpose of proceeding to Calcutta to lay their grievances before the head of the Government, and set out on their march. Their advanced guard, with their leaders, amounted to 30,000 men. They soon ate up the cakes they had brought with them, and beginning to plunder villages, put to death a native officer of police. This was their first overt act of rebellion, and it occurred on July 7. The Santál war, as it was called, ended with the year; and, as in relation to the great famine of 1770, reference was given to Mr. W. W. Hunter's admirable 'Annals of Rural Bengal,' so in the case of the Santáls, the student is referred to the same interesting work, not only for an account of this petty war, but for its causes and effects, as well as for a description, ethnological and otherwise, of the Santáls, which is unequalled in Indian literature. When the causes of the outbreak, which resembled those of the Kole war (Chapter X., Book VII.), were understood, the most efficient remedy was provided against a recurrence of discontent, in the separation of the Santál from the ordinary regulation districts, and the nomination of a special commissioner—an arrangement which has fulfilled all the intentions of its establishment.

The annexation of Oudh.

No subject in relation to the policy of Lord Dalhousie has received more searching commentary than the annexation of Oudh. It has been reviewed again and again in contemporary histories, in Parliamentary returns, in the publication of every document connected with it, and by the public press both of England and India, and will continue to be discussed in every succeeding history as long as India remains under the government of Great Britain. Any review of the whole of the transactions would be manifestly impossible in a work like the present, which only professes to point out facts for the guidance of the student, leaving him, as has been repeatedly stated, to refer to the details, and form his own judgment. There is no question that the misgovernment of Oudh had approached a crisis, at which interference was not only justifiable, but necessary and unavoidable. The successive reports of Colonel Sleeman and General Outram, both avowedly the staunch friends of native dynasties, teem with details of the sufferings of the people, the lawlessness of the population, and the brutal tyranny and exactions of the local aristocracy. There is equally no doubt of the profligate character of the king; of his inability and unfitness to govern; his frivolity, his sensuality, his attachment to miserable favourites and parasites, singers, dancers, buffoons, and even menial servants; his disregard of, and indifference to, warnings repeated again and again with the utmost earnestness and good faith, by Lord William Bentinck, Lord Auckland, and Lord Hardinge, in, it cannot be questioned, the sincere hope that he would make an attempt to overcome the local disorders, and to regain the confidence he had all but forfeited.

Condition of Oudh.

Character of the king.

But these hopes were vain. There was not only no improvement, but the local administration, practically effete, made no effort to redeem its position, and sunk lower and lower, even in the eyes of its own subjects. All these are patent facts, which no one, even among the most bitter censurers of the annexation, has ever disproved, or sought to disprove; and yet the question remains open as to whether the course pursued was justified by the emergency, and whether the abrogation of treaties, and cancelling of all claims by a dynasty on which, in its sorest times of need, the British Government of India had relied without ever experiencing disappointment, and to which its obligations had been placed on record for nearly a hundred years, was not a breach of national faith.

The question of interference in Oudh was one of those which, from its magnitude, and perpetually recurring causes of complaint in one form or other, had rested constantly under consideration of the executive government of India; but it had never been grappled with and decided. No temporary remedial measures could be applied, warnings had become useless, and were most likely considered as mere threats, which had been uttered again and again, and were of no real significance. They did not drive the king from his low indulgences, nor did they affect the aristocracy, who, confident in their own local power, scorned them. Of all warnings, that of Lord William Bentinck, in 1837, was perhaps the most emphatic and most solemn. It was submitted to the king in writing, so that it could not be ignored in the future; and Lord Hardinge's subsequent limit of two years only, before any final step was taken, pledged the British Government to action if it were necessary. That was in 1847, and instead of two years, seven had elapsed without change,

Repeated warnings to the Oudh government.

or without execution of the orders of 1834, issued by the Court of Directors, which formed the basis of the remonstrance of Lord William Bentinck in 1837. For upwards of fifty years, the kingdom of Oudh had enjoyed perfect immunity from war, and from outward danger of every kind; and had it possessed an ordinarily capable administration, it might have become the richest and most prosperous native State in India; but for these fifty years, neglect and indifference had uniformly prevailed, and were now irremediable.

That the assumption of the administration was a public necessity there can be little doubt. No one denied it then, or denies it now. The question rather is, whether the dynasty should have been extinguished or allowed to remain as it was, on the footing of the Nawábs of Moorshidabad or of the Carnatic. On this point the student has the benefit of the minutes of Lord Dalhousie, of the members of his Council, including Sir John Low and Mr., now Sir, Charles Halliday, Sir J. P. Grant, Mr. Dorin, and Sir Barnes Peacock; and in England of the Court of Directors, the President of the Board of Control, and the Cabinet. Of the Indian minutes, Lord Dalhousie's advised complete assumption of the administration, but not the extinction of the dynasty; on the contrary, that the king should retain the sovereignty, receiving a share of the general revenues, with provisions for all the members of the royal family. That the measure, moreover, could only be adopted with the king's consent, which, his lordship wrote, 'is indispensable to the transfer of the whole or any part of his sovereign power to the government of the East India Company: it would not be expedient or right to extract this consent by means of menace or compulsion.' Sir John Low, who had opposed the governor-general in the case of Nagpoor, advised the 'assumption of the government exclusively and permanently;' and that the king should retain his title for life, but not the sovereignty. But these documents need not be further reviewed, since they are open to those who may desire to read them. All are conclusive as to the 'assumption of the administration;' but they vary in respect to the continuance of the sovereignty, and the disposal of the surplus revenues. It is necessary, however, to quote a paragraph of Colonel Sleeman's report, to show how nearly the opinion of Lord Dalhousie coincided with his. 'If therefore,' writes Colonel Sleeman, 'our Government does interfere, it must be in the exercise of a right arising out of the existing relations between the two States, or out of our position as the paramount power in India. These relations, under the treaty of 1837, give our Government the right to take upon itself the

Official minutes on the question.

Lord Dalhousie's opinion.

Sir John Low's.

Colonel Sleeman's report.

administration under present circumstances; and indeed imposes on our Government the duty of taking it; but, as I have already stated, neither these relations, nor our position as the paramount power, give us any right to annex or confiscate the territory of Oudh. . . . We have only the right to secure for the suffering people that better government which their sovereign pledged himself to secure for them, but has failed to secure.'

Nothing can be clearer or juster than this: and it would have been well had these views, which were confirmed by those of the governor-general, been adopted in England, in lieu of the extreme measure of final annexation, and the extinction of the dynasty; but the authorities in England were unanimous in deciding upon entire confiscation, and the opinions of Lord Dalhousie were overruled. It is therefore manifestly unjust to lay upon him the sole burden of the responsibility of the ultimate measure, to which, in one of his most remarkable and exhaustive minutes, he had recorded a deliberate objection and dissent.

Agreement between Lord Dalhousie and Colonel Sleeman.

Opinion in England.

But, unfortunately, Lord Dalhousie had pledged himself to carry out the decision of the home authorities, and he remained, though sorely broken in health, for this especial purpose. By this course he did not do himself justice: and when the decision arrived, he might well have declined to execute what his mature judgment had not confirmed. Had he done so, time would have been given for consideration, and the final decree might have been modified. But, throughout his administration, Lord Dalhousie had been careful to obey orders from home when they were issued, and in this case he did not act upon impulse.

On February 7, 1856, the territory of Oudh ceased to exist as an independent sovereignty, and was annexed by proclamation to the British dominions. The most painful duty ever performed by Sir James Outram, the Resident, was the communication of the final decision to the king, who submitted, with tears, to an inevitable result, though to the last he refused to sign the deed of resignation; but the mandate had gone forth, and must be obeyed. One of the king's last acts—perhaps his very last—was to issue a proclamation to his subjects enjoining on them peaceful submission to the British Government. With the territory, the private property of the king was also confiscated and sold, which was the more to be regretted as it reawakened and augmented the odium already incurred in the case of Nagpoor. As he was to reside in Calcutta, the king might easily have removed his property, or, if he had pleased, sold it; but to consider it under the circumstances as belonging to the

The annexation of Oudh is proclaimed.

Conduct of the king.

The king's property sold.

State, and therefore to the British Government, was a deplorable and ungracious mistake, and awakened a degree of sympathy which would not perhaps have been otherwise displayed. An allowance of twelve lacs of rupees—120,000*l.*—a year was settled upon the king during his life.

Odium of the sale.

The annexation of Oudh may be considered the closing act of Lord Dalhousie's administration, for he sailed from India a month afterwards, on March 6, 1856, leaving a celebrated minute as the record of the events and measures of his incumbency. He believed India to be perfectly secure and peaceful, and he left it with a sincere and honest conviction that it would so remain.

Lord Dalhousie leaves India.

Mr. Marshman, in the third volume of his 'History,' has specially devoted the closing portion to a review of all the acts of Lord Dalhousie's administration, with much skill and eloquence, which will be read with interest; but while it is impossible to detail and illustrate them, as Mr. Marshman has done, the satisfaction of quoting a passage from a celebrated article in the London 'Times' of that period may not be denied. Nothing more just or true could be written.

'He, Lord Dalhousie, could point to railways planned on an enormous scale, and partly constructed; to 4,000 miles of electric telegraph spread over India, at an expense of little more than 50*l.* a mile; to 2,000 miles of road, bridged and metalled, nearly the whole distance from Calcutta to Peshâwur; to the opening of the Ganges Canal, the longest of its kind in the world; to the progress of the Punjâb canals, and of many other important works of irrigation all over India, as well as to the reorganisation of an official department of public works. Keeping equal pace with these public works, he could refer to the postal system which he introduced in imitation of that of Rowland Hill, whereby a letter from Peshâwur to Cape Comorin, or from Assam to Kurrâchee, is conveyed for three-farthings, or one-sixteenth of the old charge; to the improved training for the civil service, covenanted and uncovenanted; to the improvement of education and prison discipline; to the organisation of the Legislative Council, to the reforms which it had decreed—such as permitting Hindoo widows to marry again, and relieving all persons from the risk of forfeiting property by a change of religion. Many more items might be added to this list, were it necessary to prove the largeness and benevolence of the views and measures of this great statesman; and there is no doubt, from his recorded opinions, that the annexation measures so bitterly urged against him, were founded on the conviction that, in effecting them, he had delivered millions from the irregularities and oppression of native govern-

Article from the 'Times.'

ments, and secured for them the prospective advantages of protection and peace. No one can record, for few knew, of his daily toil, or how, with a delicate frame, he overcame it; toil which overworked and destroyed his physical powers, and in 1860 sent him to his grave. "I have played out my part," he said sadly, in reply to an address from the people of Calcutta, "and while I feel that in my case the principal act in the drama of my life is ended, I shall be content if the curtain should now drop on my public career."'

BOOK IX.

CHAPTER I.

THE ADMINISTRATION OF LORD CANNING, 1856 TO 1857.

THE successor to Lord Dalhousie, chosen in England, was Lord Canning, who, after several years' service in the Cabinet of Sir Robert Peel, had become postmaster-general in 1853. His moderate views and great powers of application to business, probably induced his selection. Lord Dalhousie had, it was considered, done enough for the present; and his measures might be worked out and perfected by one who perhaps would introduce few of his own or interfere with those of his great predecessor. Lord Canning assumed the office of governor-general on February 29, 1856, a few days before Lord Dalhousie's final departure; and it is probable, received from him a general explanation of the policy which had been pursued. India itself seemed to be in a state of profound tranquillity and content; receiving the vast impetus which had been given to her material progress in education—male and female—railways, telegraphs, canals, roads, &c., during Lord Dalhousie's tenure of office, with outward equanimity, if not with demonstrative appreciation. There was no political danger or apprehension looming on the horizon; and the native States that existed retained no elements of present or prospective danger. At its outset, therefore, the administration of Lord Canning seemed likely to be employed in the regulation of details only; and yet it proved one of the most terrible and momentous that had ever been witnessed in the history of the world.

Lord Canning appointed governor-general.

State of India.

Looking deeper, however, than the surface, there were latent causes of uneasiness which largely pervaded the minds of the native classes of all ranks and creeds. The system of education, now so much enlarged and progressing, was entirely opposed to Hindoo faith and doctrine, and in an equal

Influence of education.

degree to Mahomedan. Schools, English and vernacular, were crowded with Hindoo scholars, who, in everything they learned, could not fail to be imbued with convictions essentially antagonistic to their hereditary faith. By Mahomedans, indeed, they were comparatively little resorted to; but by Hindoos with eager thirst for knowledge, and active competition in its acquirement. In schools presided over by missionaries of all denominations, Christianity was professedly part of the course of instruction, and these were attended as numerously as those of Government, in which Christian teaching was necessarily forbidden. The subjects taught in all schools were discussed in the homes of the scholars, under all the bigotry of their old faith, by the parents and relatives of the scholars: and the deductions made were, as may be imagined, the causes of apprehension of the effects of the system in progress, impotent to check advance, but nevertheless existent, and prevalent to a very large extent, in all quarters of India.

Effects of material progress.

There was no question either that the material progress of India was unintelligible to the natives in general. A few intelligent and educated persons might understand the use and scope of railways, telegraphs, steam-vessels, and recognise in them the direction of a great government for the benefit of the people; but the ancient listless conservatism of the population at large was disturbed by them. 'The English,' it was said, 'never did such things before; why do they do so now? These are but new devices for the domination of their rule, and are aimed at the destruction of our national faith, caste, and customs! What was it all to come to? Was India to become like England? The earlier company's servants were simple, but wise men, and we respected them; we understood them, and they us; but the present men are not like them; we do not know them, nor they us.' No one cared perhaps very much for such sentiments, and few, very few, English heard them; but they will not have been forgotten by those who did.

Effects of sudden progress.

For nearly a century, the English in India, supported by the Court of Directors in England, had preserved neutrality in regard to, if not a direct conservatism of, the hitherto existent social and religious systems and prejudices of India; any change was deprecated, and as long as possible withstood. The demands of the younger English school of progressionists were coldly received and jealously restrained; but in the end they could not be resisted, and the immense efforts of Lord Dalhousie, suddenly, as it were, brought to bear on the previous restrictive policy, were too marked in their character and effects to be viewed with indifference by the people.

Few measures of importance passed through the Council of India in 1856. A bill for prohibiting or restraining the polygamy of the Kooleen Brahmins of Bengal, which was supported by many very influential natives, was discussed, but set aside for the present. On the other hand, the native army was affected by the promulgation of an order to enlist no Sepoys who would not take an oath to serve wherever they might be ordered to go, either in India or beyond sea. By many officers of the old school, who had taken a curious but absurd pride in the 'high caste' of their men, the order was contemplated with apprehension; but it had become unavoidably necessary in Bengal, and in Madras and Bombay, where 'high caste' Sepoys were mingled with others, it had been found productive of no inconvenience. It was judicious, moreover, to check the high caste domination which had led to mutinies, and affected the morale of the whole Bengal army. The penal code, commenced by Lord Macaulay, and discussed in England by the most eminent of English jurists, was brought forward by Mr., now Sir, Barnes Peacock; and though not finally passed, was sent for trial to the Punjâb, to the Hyderabad commission for the districts assigned by the Nizam, and other localities where the 'regulations' were not in use.

Legislative enactments. *General service oath.* *The penal code.*

Royal family of Dehly.

The question of the future location as well as the privileges of the royal family at Dehly, in regard to which so much discussion had taken place under Lord Dalhousie's administration, was resumed in 1856. The previous condition in which it was left by Lord Dalhousie will be found detailed in Chap. VII., Book VIII., and the final decision by the governor-general was now communicated to those concerned. The circumstances of the family had become altered in a material degree. The Prince Fukhr-ood-deen, who had been recognised as heir-apparent, and with whom the agreement in regard to the evacuation of the palace had been made, died on July 10, 1856, not without strong suspicions of having been poisoned; and an intrigue began, directed by the Queen Zeenut Mahál, to secure the heirship for her son. The king, indeed, made an official request that this might be done; but the course would have involved a breach of Mahomedan law, and Mirza Koraish, the next in legal succession to Fukhr-ood-deen, was recognised by the governor-general in Council, on the terms of the agreement made with the deceased prince, with this essential difference, that the conditions were not of agreement or bargain, as before, but as an independent decree on the part of Government.

Final settlement in Council.

It cannot be doubted that this final award, however just in regard to the succession, or necessary in a military point of view as regarded possession of the palace, was bitterly resented, as indeed was only natural, by the royal family: that, remembering the old relations between the company and the empire, the immense benefits originally conferred on them, and the admitted position of the company as servants of the State, it was only natural they should now be accused of perfidy. The efforts and intrigues of the spirited queen and several of the princes were now redoubled, locally as well as in foreign quarters; and India, especially the north-west provinces, became filled with the most alarming rumours, which, as the peculiar superstitious crisis advanced, agitated the minds of Hindoos and Mahomedans alike. The questions alike of the succession, the title of king, and possession of the palace, were to be decided by sterner measures than orders in Council; and the narrative of events will supply the particulars in their proper order.

Towards the close of 1855, a series of studied insults to the British envoy in Persia, Mr. Murray, obliged him to leave Teheran, and retire to Bagdad; and a Persian army again attacked, and on this occasion captured, Herât, in defiance of the former treaty, which engaged that it should not be molested. Under orders from England, war was proclaimed against Persia on November 1, 1856, and an army of about 6,000 men was dispatched from Bombay to the Persian Gulf, to be under the command and direction of Sir James Outram, when he should join it. Before his arrival, however, hostilities had commenced by an attack upon Rushair, a fort near the city of Bushire, on December 7, which, though the place was carried with trifling loss, proved that the Persian and Arab defenders were no mean antagonists. The day following, Bushire was attacked, and after a spirited defence, the garrison surrendered, and to the number of 2,000—many having escaped—laid down their arms; their guns, sixty-five in number, being taken possession of.

The Persian war.

On January 27 Sir James Outram reached Bushire, and assumed the command; and having been joined by one of the brigades of Havelock's division, marched, on January 3, 1857, upon Burrasjoon, where the Persian army had assembled with the intention of recapturing Bushire. After a fatiguing march of forty-one miles, he reached the position on the 5th, but found it deserted; and destroying the military stores found there, he commenced his return on the 7th by a night march. In his progress, being annoyed by attacks on the baggage made by the Persian cavalry, he halted and waited for daylight. When day dawned, after a night of miserable cold and rain, the Persian army was seen drawn up in battle array at a comparatively short distance on the left flank, and was immediately attacked; the cavalry, consisting of the Poona Horse and 3rd Bombay regi-

Night attack on Sir James Outram's force.

ment, making brilliant charges, one of which became memorable from the breaking of a square of disciplined Persian infantry by the 3rd Cavalry, and its almost entire destruction. The enemy did not wait the approach of the British infantry, but fled, leaving 700 dead on the field and many wounded. The force then returned to Bushire, having had only ten killed and sixty-two wounded in this spirited combat.

Attack on Mohamrah.

No further actions took place till March 26, when the strong fort and position of Mohamrah, situated on the Karoon river, a branch of the Euphrates, were attacked by the fleet and army in combination. Here the Prince Khan Mirza, with a powerful force, had established his headquarters, and considerable resistance was anticipated. Beyond, however, sustaining a cannonade from the fort and batteries, which was quickly silenced by the ships, none was experienced; for the prince and his army were found to have abandoned the camp, and to be in full retreat. The final movement of the war was a small expedition sent up the Karoon on the 29th, under Commodore Rennie, who on April 1 found the Persians, about 7,000 strong, posted at Ahwáz. The latter again fled without attempting to dispute the advance, leaving their camp to be taken possession of, with all the stores it contained.

Peace ensues.

Meanwhile, the preliminaries of a peace had been adjusted at Paris. The Shah again renounced all pretensions to Herát, and agreed to withdraw his troops from Afghanistan; and protection to British trade, and the continuance of the measures for the suppression of the slave trade, were also guaranteed. It is probable, however, that the attitude of Dost Mahomed, the ruler of Afghanistan, and his renewed connection with the Government of India, had contributed as much to the termination of the war as the actual attack upon the southern dominions of Persia. Early in January 1857, Sir John Lawrence, governor of the Punjâb, had met Dost Mahomed by appointment near Peshâwur. Old animosities were put aside by the Dost, who in the frankest good faith declared they were forgiven and forgotten, and that henceforth till his death he would be true to a nation who, in his exile, had treated him with respect and honour. But substantial advantages were guaranteed to him, in a subsidy of twelve lacs—120,000*l.*—a year so long as the war with Persia should last; 4,000 stand of arms were presented to him, and on his own part he engaged to maintain an army of 18,000 men. The speedy termination of the war afforded him no opportunity of meeting the Persians in the field; but there can be no doubt that a renewal of friendship with Dost Mahomed served the purposes of peace most materially. He

Friendly negotiations with Dost Mahomed.

was as good as his word, and to the day of his death his faith remained unquestioned and unbroken.

The war with China, which began in the latter end of 1856, had little connection with India beyond the employment there of troops of the Indian army, and it does not, therefore, belong to Indian history. It may be mentioned, however, that before the month of November, 1856, the forts at the entrance of the Canton river had been stormed and taken by the English fleet, Canton had been twice bombarded, and all the British factories had been burned in retaliation. Reinforcements were urgently applied for, and Lord Elgin was dispatched by the Ministry as special commissioner to the Chinese Government, to be followed by troops from England and from India. Those from India were in course of preparation, to be placed under the command of General Ashburnham; but they had happily not been dispatched when the occurrence of momentous events rendered the employment of eve E uropean who could bear arms an imperative necessity which had not been foreseen, and against which there was but scanty provision.

War with China.

CHAPTER II.

THE ADMINISTRATION OF LORD CANNING (*continued*)—THE SEPOY MUTINY, 1857.

AT last had arrived the Hindoo 'Sumbut' 1914 (1857-58), the hundredth year after the battle of Plassy, when, on a certain conjunction of the planets, it had been declared by astrologers, that the ráj, or reign, of the company, was to continue for a hundred years, but no more. It is impossible to overrate the effect of this strange prediction among a people who, ever credulous and superstitious in the last degree, look to astrological combinations for their guidance in every circumstance and action of life, and who will neither marry, make a bargain, set out on a journey, nor even have their nails pared or put on new clothes, without a favourable conjunction of the planets. Sumbut 1914, therefore, with its accompanying prognostications of dire events, of tumults, of wars, of pestilence and death—and above all, the cessation of the dominant power, agitated India in a most profound degree in all quarters. In every Hindoo almanac, the public recital of which, to every village community in every part of India, forms part of the ceremony of the first day of the new year, the predictions of the year,

The prediction of Plassy.

Hindoo almanacs.

made upon the aspects of the planets, are invariably declared. On this occasion, for the mysterious Sumbut 1914, along with the prophecies of good or bad fortune in crops and harvests or in trade, were mingled fatal auguries to ruling powers, which were believed as the infallible deductions of a hundred years before. The company's power had indeed as yet triumphed over all opposition, because it had kept faith with the people of India: and Mahratta, Mahomedan, and Sikh had alike succumbed to what it was hopeless to resist; but it was to cease. During the period preceding this Sumbut (1856–57), there had been a frightful visitation of cholera, which in strict accordance with prediction had swept away thousands and thousands of the people, and tremendous floods in Bengal had destroyed the industry of years. These were only indices of what was to come, and were recognised as earnests of the reality. Comparatively few Englishmen, perhaps, removed as most were, by their official or social position, from any but the most superficial acquaintance with native society, knew of these feelings, or if they did know, thought little of them. An astrological prediction, in their estimation, was but one of a series of idle superstitions prevalent among the natives, which had, and could have, no foundation in reality.

Warnings.

Early in the year 1857, many Englishmen were warned to be on their guard by native friends, sometimes anonymously, sometimes personally, and even adjured to retire from India, while they could do so in safety, or at least to send home their wives and children. Nothing decided could be elicited; and those who perhaps believed that all might not be so serene as the surface appeared to be, were scouted as alarmists, and becoming silent, patiently awaited the issue. Whether any such warnings reached the head of the Government at this early stage has never transpired; if they did, they were naturally treated with scorn, and thrown aside. At the latter end of February, however, or early in March, a very remarkable Mahratta letter or petition was received by Lord Elphinstone, the governor of Bombay, which contained a solemn announcement of treason, accompanied by the enumeration of causes of general discontent, one of which was the proceedings of the Inam commission, or investigation into tenures of rent-free lands, and urging effectual and speedy reform. The paper was anonymous, and its author could not be discovered; but its style and purport could not be mistaken as a well-meant, and to all appearances well-founded, admonition and warning of evil to come.

Mischievous reports.

Letter to Lord Elphinstone.

It is impossible to attempt to describe the various rumours with which, as the people expressed themselves, the very air was filled.

Nothing was too absurd to be believed, and there is not a work belonging to the period, and they have been published almost by scores, which does not teem with the details in every conceivable variety of form and matter. Those given in the first volume of Mr. Kaye's great and most interesting work on the 'Sepoy War,' and other histories of the time, so far from being exaggerated, do not adduce a tenth of the foul and mischievous calumnies that were disseminated broadcast through all quarters of India, and believed by the ignorant and credulous of all classes. From their tenor and sudden promulgation, it may be inferred that special agency was employed for the purpose. The princes of Dehly, from time to time, in the years immediately preceding the outbreak, had asked for leave to travel in India, and were allowed to do so freely and without suspicion of motive. One of them, afterwards active in the rebellion, visited Hyderabad, in the Deccan, where he was coldly received; but he journeyed leisurely through the provinces, obtaining hospitable reception from native princes and nobles, Hindoo and Mahomedan, wherever he went. Nor is there much doubt that these preparatory missions were intended to re-awaken loyalty to the throne of Dehly, and to secure adherents. In addition to these, though it is impossible to review the voluminous details, may be mentioned intrigues between the King of Dehly and the King of Persia, and the proclamations of the latter to the Mahomedans in India, which no doubt were widely disseminated, and of which a specimen was discovered during the Persian war. In all these, the queen, Zeenut Mahál, took an active part: and for some time before any mutiny or outbreak took place, the question of a revival of the Mahomedan empire had not only been actively and almost openly discussed in the palace of Dehly, but had caused very considerable excitement and uneasiness among the turbulent population of the city and of the districts around it. A great movement was expected; and it is more than probable that the revolt of the Sepoy army was, even then, the means looked to by the king and his partisans.

Dissemination of calumnies.

Previous plots.

The princes of Dehly.

Intrigues at Dehly.

The Nána Sahib of Bithoor, little suspected indeed, had been busy with plots, perhaps for years. In every province where latent disaffection existed, in the newly annexed States, and in the Deccan, where the Brahmin progenitors of his family had held regal sway, his emissaries were actively employed, while his correspondence with foreign rulers was kept up without intermission. His agent to England, Azim Oolla Khan, a clever and utterly unscrupulous plotter, had returned to India after visiting the Crimea, and told to his master, and to the willing ears of

The Nána Sahib.

his accomplices, exaggerated tales of England's weakness and humiliation, which were greedily believed and widely disseminated. England, it was declared, had exhausted all her resources; it was to India alone that she could look for assistance in the Russian war; and the country, already denuded of English troops, would be soon called upon to send more.

Advantage taken of the mutiny.

It may be doubtful whether any direct attempt had then been made, or was even in progress, to corrupt the Sepoys of the Bengal army. That perhaps, the general disaffection of the Sepoys being known, was left to the progress of events; for it must have been evident how small the chances of success would have been, had either the King of Dehly or the Nána, or both combined, attempted to rouse the people at large into rebellion by their own means, or their treasonable intrigues. Yet when the mutiny of the Sepoys broke out, the first rebel forces from Meerut marched directly upon Dehly, and joined the king, in the interval of a night only—a circumstance which could not have been fortuitous; and being joined by most of the subsequent mutineers, leads irresistibly to the conclusion that it was a preconceived and pre-arranged plan, to be carried out when matters were ripe. Instances of discontent and mutual combination against authority and discipline have already been mentioned in regard to the native troops of Bengal, which not only showed a latent feeling of strong disaffection to have been existent, but which only required the stimulus of some event to change into open rebellion. Nor was this long wanting.

The governor-general's position.

Of this condition of the people and of the native army the governor-general was necessarily ignorant. If he heard rumours, how was he, fresh from the peace and security of England, and from the quiet routine of a purely administrative office, to comprehend them? The Dalhousie and Napier controversy about the condition of the native army had passed away; and belief in the doubtful allegiance of the Sepoys did not extend to his councillors and his staff. Later, indeed, when Henry Lawrence told him what he knew, he might have wished he had understood it earlier; but in January 1857, even Lawrence himself would have denied any imminent danger. Lord Canning was a cold, impassive man, to whom few would have ventured to make known the public agitation at the close of 1856, and opening of 1857: and he may be entirely acquitted of the charge of not having made himself acquainted with, or not following up, if he did hear them, what were as yet mere intangible and confused rumours. Who could have ventured to tell him that it was believed the very land itself was to be put in chains by the railway and the electric telegraph;

What was believed by the people.

that as soon as these were accomplished, every native, of every caste and creed, would be required to receive baptism; and that *he* had been specially selected by the queen to abolish all distinctions of caste and proclaim Christianity! Yet these absurdities, following up the rapid material progress of Lord Dalhousie's administration, were, in that mad period of delusion, credited by millions, and it only remained to be seen in what form the horrible and tyrannical measure would be carried out.

In 1856, Enfield rifles were sent from England, and schools of musketry instruction were established at many, if not all, stations of the army. By the end of January 1857, the Sepoys at Barrackpoor, near Calcutta, had taken up a rumour which was believed to have originated from among the Brahmins of Calcutta itself: that the cartridges of these rifles were greased with cows' and pigs' fat, and were thereby rendered impure, to the end of first depriving the Sepoys of caste, when the conversion of the people would easily follow. The Sepoys held nightly meetings to discuss the subject, set fire to officers' houses and other buildings, and taking advantage of a detachment proceeding to Berhampoor, opened communication with the 19th, stationed there. In the course of a month the mutinous feeling not only included Berhampoor, but Ráneegunje; and on February 19, the men of the 19th regiment refused to receive the cartridges served out on parade, and broke into open mutiny. They were restrained from violence by Colonel Mitchell, who commanded them; but they remained sullen, and as soon as H.M.'s 84th arrived from Burmah, they were marched down to Barrackpoor, and disbanded on the 31st. They professed penitence, and declared themselves ready to serve anywhere; but their sentence 'for open and defiant mutiny' had been inexorably determined, and with a cheer to the noble veteran General Hearsey, who had performed the disagreeable duty, and execrations on the 34th, who had seduced them, they were marched out of the station and forwarded to their homes.

Arrival of the Enfield rifles.

The greased cartridges.

Mutiny of the 19th Native Infantry.

On March 29, two days before the 19th were disbanded, Mungul Pándy, a private Sepoy of the 34th, broke into open mutiny on the parade-ground at Barrackpoor, and called upon his comrades to join him. He wounded two officers in a hand-to-hand combat, in presence of the quarter guard, which did not interfere; and ultimately, when escape was impossible, shot himself, but not fatally, and was tried, and hanged acknowledging the justice of his sentence, on April 22. Meanwhile news of these occurrences, with infinite exaggerations, passed on to station after station in Upper India, and were thoroughly

Mungul Pándy.

Spread of the disaffection.

credited. As the discharged men of the 19th made their way to their homes in Oudh and Bundelkhund, they disseminated reports which aggravated the existent rumours, and it came to be actually believed by the Sepoys, as well as by the people, that not only were the cartridges greased, but that the public wells, and the flour, and ghee or clarified butter, sold in the bazaars, had been defiled by ground bone-dust and the fat of cows and pigs, while the salt had been sprinkled with cows' and hogs' blood. Lord Canning and the commander-in-chief issued order after order to satisfy the Sepoys; and in a proclamation dated May 16, the governor-general addressed the people at large, warning them of false reports, and disclaiming any attempt at deprivation of caste.

Exaggerated rumours.

Orders and proclamations.

For all the use they were, these documents need not have been issued. They were looked upon as traps to the unwary, and they were utterly discredited, and so failed of effect. It was even said that Government must have had sinister designs, or it would not have been at the pains to deny them. The fever of excitement was at its height, and the disease—for such it was—must run its course. If, instead of orders and proclamations, some bold member (had there existed one) in the Chief Council had at once admitted the danger, and advised the governor-general in March, or even April, to issue orders for strong positions to be taken up in every cantonment by the European troops, and a constant watchfulness to be maintained, much of the subsequent misery might have been prevented; but it is doubtful whether, even by these means, the actual outbreak of rebellion could have been restrained.

What might have been done.

At Umballa, at Meerut, and at other stations, the same constant occurrence of fires defied detection, as had been the case at Barrackpoor and Ráneegunje. From the commencement of 1857 the rural districts along the course of the Ganges and Jumna, and all over Central India, as far south as the frontiers of Berar, had been strongly agitated by the passing of baked flour-cakes (chupátees) from village to village. Whence they originated was never discovered, nor was the token professedly understood; but it spread through the country with marvellous rapidity, and was evidently a signal of warning or of preparation.

Fires in the large stations.

On May 10 the native troops at Meerut, the 3rd Cavalry, eighty-five men of which had been tried and convicted on a charge of refusing to use ordinary cartridges, with the 11th and 20th regiments of Native Infantry, rose in open mutiny and rebellion, shot down Colonel Finnis and other officers and ladies, set fire to their lines and to private houses, and, unchecked and unpursued, went off in a body to Dehly. At that time there were in the station not only European horse-artillery, but the 6th Dragoons (Carbineers) —only partially mounted, it is true, but still available on foot—and H.M.'s 60th Rifles. They were not much inferior to the natives in actual numbers, and if properly led, would have utterly routed and destroyed the mutineers; but, after melancholy inaction and confusion, the rebels eluded General Hewitt, who commanded the force, and having released all the prisoners in the gaol, together with their comrades, marched on to Dehly in the night, and left the general to defend the ruined cantonment.

The men of the 3rd Cavalry, dreading pursuit by the Carbineers, rode hard to Dehly—a distance of forty miles—and an advanced party of them entering the city soon after daybreak, proclaimed the success of the night before; and as the Meerut troops straggled in, they all, as if by previous concert, proceeded to the king. The people of the city—notoriously turbulent and lawless—rose at once; and the butchery of Europeans, men, women and children, commenced. It is not needful to repeat the details of these horrible atrocities, which have been so often and so vividly described,[1] nor of the subsequent butchery in the royal palace. One by one the three native regiments at Dehly, the 38th, 54th and 74th, caught the infection, shot many of their officers, and marching into the city, saluted the king. One point alone held out for a while, which was the famous arsenal, containing military stores for the whole of the north-west provinces. It was maintained with desperate courage by Lieutenant Willoughby, with Lieutenants Raynor and Forrest, and six other Englishmen, and when no longer tenable was blown up. Willoughby, with some companions, escaped to Meerut, but arrived only to die from the injuries he had received.

The surviving Europeans, men, women and children, with some still faithful remains of the native regiments, held the 'flagstaff tower' for a while; but they had no provisions or means of defence, and in despair set out for Meerut and Kurnál, enduring in their wanderings fatigues and privations which are hardly conceivable. Thus the first great step in the mutiny was accomplished.

[1] Vibart's 'Narrative,' &c.

CHAPTER III.

THE MUTINY (*continued*), 1857.

About this time, Nána Sahib of Bithoor, and his agent, Azim Oolla Khan, were proceeding from station to station in the north-west provinces and Oudh, fanning the flame of mutiny and rebellion. Such an opportunity as had been afforded by the conduct of the Sepoys, and the panic among the people, was too entirely consonant with their own plans to be neglected, and they were successful perhaps beyond their hopes. In Oudh, the new administration, which had promised fairly at first, became in the last degree unpopular, from the mistaken and over-zealous proceedings of the commissioner, Mr. Coverley Jackson, and his subordinates; and though Mr. Jackson was removed and Sir Henry Lawrence appointed in his room, the evil already done could not be remedied. As early as April, the 48th Native Infantry, stationed at Lukhnow, had shown symptoms of disaffection. On May 2, the 7th local Native Infantry mutinied at their station, some miles from the city; and as the troops advanced on them, broke and fled. Much as he strove to gain a clue to the real causes of the disaffection, even Henry Lawrence was baffled. On May 4, it was determined by the governor-general in Council to disband the 34th Native Infantry, still at Barrackpoor; on the 6th, the measure was carried out, and 500 men, disgraced and stripped of their uniforms, were banished from the station, and returned, vowing revenge, to their native province Oudh, to swell the discontent already existing there.

The Nána's progress.

Mistakes in Oudh.

Mutiny of native regiments in Oudh.

The 34th Native Infantry disbanded.

Before the rebels could cut the telegraph wires, the news of events at Meerut and Dehly had been widely disseminated. It was received at Ferozepoor (commanded by Brigadier Innes) on the 12th, where the presence of H.M.'s 61st Foot and 300 European artillery alone prevented an outbreak, and the loss of the immense magazine of military stores. An attempt to take this depot was made on the 13th by the 45th Native Infantry, but defeated; and while the greater portion of the 54th laid down their arms, and were allowed to remain, the 45th were disbanded and turned out of the cantonment; not, however, before they had succeeded in doing considerable damage by setting fire, during the night, to public and private buildings. They were pursued by the 10th Cavalry, and some of them were

Events at Ferozepoor.

killed or taken prisoners; but the greater number escaped, and joined the rebels at Dehly. The brigadier's proceedings, in not having at once disarmed both the native regiments, were severely censured, and he was deprived of his command. By timely succour, sent from the station of Jullunder, to Phillour, where another great magazine existed, any chance of rising there was prevented; and the same prompt action saved Umritsir.

And at Phillour.

At Lahore, the native troops, the 8th Bengal Cavalry, the 16th, 26th and 49th Native Infantry, paraded on the morning of May 13, by Brigadier Corbett, with H.M.'s 81st Foot and the artillery, were ordered to lay down their arms, and in terror of the Europeans obeyed; and at the same time the citadel was occupied, the wing of the 26th Native Infantry being disarmed by three companies of the 81st Foot. Thus Lahore was saved; but Pesháwur was still in danger, and the result of the telegraphic message was looked to with intense anxiety. There was, however, no hesitation at Pesháwur, where Brigadier Cotton commanded; and on the morning of the 15th, the 5th Native Cavalry, the 24th, 27th and 51st Native Infantry, were disarmed; but the 21st, to whom no suspicion was attached, remained for duty. At Murdán, a small station in the Punjâb, the 55th Native Infantry followed the example of Meerut, and went off in the direction of Swát; but it was followed, and so fearfully punished by Colonel Nicholson, that but few escaped, and those to suffer even a worse fate among the mountain tribes of the frontier. With the exception of the 21st at Pesháwur, not a single regiment of the old Bengal Sepoys in the Punjâb had proved untainted, and the decided measures adopted, here but very briefly sketched, had alone prevented the fulfilment of their designs. There had never been good feeling between the Sikhs and the Bengal Sepoys; and the readiness with which armed levies of Sikhs and Mahomedans, to check them, were made by the English authorities, and many of the Sikh chiefs, was a cheering proof that the latest enemies of the English had been converted into their staunchest friends. This, however, might not have followed, if the Sepoy rising had been simultaneous in all quarters, when the danger would have been immensely increased. There is little doubt, from the result of subsequent investigations, that a general outbreak had been fixed for May 31, by which time the rebel arrangements would have been complete; but the hurried action at Meerut precipitated the rising, and horrible as it was, became a main element of comparative general safety.

The native troops at Lahore disarmed.

Events at Pesháwur.

The native troops disarmed.

The 55th Native Infantry.

Simultaneous rising prevented.

The commander-in-chief, General Anson, had hurried down

from Simlah on receiving the news from Meerut, followed by three English regiments, to Umballah; where, on May 10, two native corps—the 5th and 60th—evidently by concert, had assembled in arms on their parades and threatened their officers; but had resumed their duties: and on the 17th the strong English brigade arrived. General Anson, urged thereto by Lord Canning on the one hand, and Sir John Lawrence on the other, at once prepared to advance on Dehly; but there were unforeseen delays in every material point—supplies, carriage, ammunition—and some very valuable days were lost. As yet the magnitude of the combination to be overcome, and the strength of the rebel position at Dehly, was underrated both by Lord Canning and Lawrence, whose opinions, though widely separated, were in unison—that the European force then at their disposal was sufficient for the destruction of the rebels; and the being apparently expected to do more than he had the means of doing, evidently added to General Anson's anxiety. On the 27th, the general had reached Kurnál, where he died of cholera, to the great regret of the army; and the command devolved upon Sir Henry Barnard, who, by June 4, had advanced to within twenty miles of Dehly. Here he was joined by Brigadier Wilson from Meerut, who, on May 30, at Ghazee-ood-deen Nugger, and again on the day following, had encountered strong forces of Sepoys, sent from Dehly to intercept his troops, and completely defeated them. With Brigadier Wilson's reinforcements, Sir H. Barnard's army now amounted to about 4,000 men, chiefly English soldiers.

The commander-in-chief takes the field.

His death.

Sir Henry Barnard succeeds.

But other localities of mutiny need mention, though it is impossible to follow the details of the several episodes in the great drama, which have but one character: mutiny of the native troops; murder of some, and escape from fearful death and privation of other, English men and women, and plunder of the stations. On May 20, at Aligurh, four companies of the 9th Native Infantry broke away and went off to Dehly, leaving the station at the mercy of the populace, by whom it was plundered; and on the 23rd three other companies of the same regiment, at Mynpoorie, followed their example. On the 29th, the 15th and 30th Bengal Native Infantry, with a company of native artillery, stationed at Nusseerabad, in Rajpootana, beat off the 1st Bombay Lancers, and marched for Dehly. On the 31st, at Bareilly, the 8th Irregular Cavalry, and the 18th and 68th Native Infantry, did the same; and on June 2, their example was followed by the 72nd and other troops at Neemuch. Between May 21 and June 3, the troops and detachments of all

Mutiny of the 9th Native Infantry at Aligurh.

Mutiny of the forces at Nusseerabad

and at Bareilly;

at Neemuch;

the stations in Rohilkhund, including Bareilly, Morádabad, Saharunpoor, Shahjehánpoor, Badaon, and Almórah, had mutinied; and at Bareilly the Mahomedans had risen, under Khan Baháidoor Khan, the descendant of Hafiz Rehmut Khan, of the time of Warren Hastings. Most of these risings were accompanied by the murder of such English officers as could be found, and the country was in possession of the rebels. The lieutenant-governor of the north-west provinces, Mr. John Colvin, resided at Agra, where the 44th and 67th Native Infantry formed part of the garrison, with H.M.'s 3rd Foot and a company of European artillery. The native troops seemed faithful, but were necessarily suspected. On May 20, Mr. Colvin issued a weak and ill-timed proclamation to 'soldiers engaged in the late disturbances,' which was at once repudiated by Lord Canning, and another more suited to the emergency substituted. Sindia sent his own bodyguard to Agra for Mr. Colvin's defence; but in the sequel it proved as deeply tainted as the British Sepoys. At the end of May a detachment from Gwalior at Muttra shot the English officers, plundered the treasury, and went off to Dehly; and on June 1, the 44th and 67th were disarmed, and the men, for the most part, escaped to Dehly.

In Rohilkhund.

Rise of Mahomedans at Bareilly.

Events at Agra.

While these events were in progress, the mutiny was fast extending to the stations in Bundelkhund, Nowgong, Banda, Chutterpoor, Futtehpoor, Humeerpoor, Jalown (a recently annexed principality), and several others, and hardly differs in detail from those already enumerated. The history of the annexation of Jhansy has already been given, and the widowed Ranee, Lukshmee Bye, was not slow to strike a blow for the recovery of lost power. The story of Jhansy is one of the most fearful of the sad records of massacre, for not one of the English there survived. The outbreak occurred on June 4, and until the 8th the English survivors defended themselves in the palace fort, and surrendered on the oaths and assurances of the mutineers that their lives should be spared; but, immediately afterwards, they were all, men, women and children (seventy-five persons), ruthlessly butchered, by, it was said, and there is little reason to doubt it, the orders of the Ranee Lukshmee Bye. She now proclaimed the independence of her State, and soon gathered round her an army of 14,000 men.

Mutinies in Bundelkhund.

The Ranee of Jhansy.

Massacre of Europeans.

On May 16, the Meerut news reached Futtehgurh, where the 10th Native Infantry was stationed; but the regiment, though agitated, was for a time very faithful. Here there was a larger proportion of Europeans than at other

Events at Futtehgurh.

stations: and the greater number of them—merchants, traders and some civilians—embarked on June 4, to the number of 166, in boats, making for Cawnpoor. Of these, 126 reached that station on the 12th, and about forty were protected by Hurdeo Buksh, a loyal Zemindar, in his fort of Dhurrumpoor. The 10th, with its officers and some other Englishmen, remained at Futtehgurh, and took possession of the fort. On June 18, the 41st Native Infantry, which had mutinied in Oudh, succeeded in crossing the river, and joined by some of the 10th, proclaimed the Nawáb of Futtehgurh as their sovereign, but met with little encouragement. These regiments then seized the treasure, and broke up; many proceeding to their homes, others joining the 41st in a siege of the fort. How this place was resolutely defended from that time till July 4, must be read in detail to be appreciated and understood. On that day, the fort being no longer tenable, the survivors quitted it in boats, and of them, only forty-seven reached Cawnpoor, ignorant, as they were enticed on shore, of the fate of that unhappy garrison.

Conduct of the 10th and 41st Native Infantry.

Gallant defence the fort.

At Cawnpoor were stationed the 1st, 53rd and 56th regiments of Native Infantry, with the 2nd Light Cavalry. There was no English regiment, and only sixty artillerymen. Of European succour there was no hope; but Sir Henry Lawrence sent eighty men of the 32nd Foot, and subsequently fifty-one of the 84th, and fifteen of the Madras Fusileers arrived, making 200 English soldiers in all. The general provided, as well as he could, against an outbreak, and intrenched the large European hospitals, laying up a store of provisions; but all through May the Sepoy regiments were at least quiet, and the Nána Sahib of Bithoor, close by, was profuse in his assurances of sympathy and assistance. The mutiny began on the morning of June 5. The native regiments used no violence to their English officers, but could not be restrained, and after plundering the treasury, and opening the doors of the gaol, set off towards Dehly. They were followed by the Nána, and brought back; and on the 6th, his hostile intentions were clearly manifested.

Cawnpoor.

Arrival of English soldiers.

Mutiny of native troops.

Oudh had not stirred since the disbandment of the 7th Native Infantry, but every day made its situation more perilous. Sir Henry Lawrence early provided against surprise and against future contingency. A massive castellated building, the Mutchie Bhówan, was provisioned, and with the residency formed a strong post. On May 30, the whole of the native troops, the 13th, 48th and 71st Native Infantry, and the 7th Cavalry, broke into mutiny, set fire to their lines and

Events in Oudh.

Mutiny of the native troops at all the stations.

the private houses. The 41st Native Infantry, at Seetápoor, murdered most of their officers, and went off to join the 10th at Futtehgurh; and at Sooltanpoor, Fyzabad, and Azimgurh, the same terrible scenes were enacted. At Allahabad, on June 5, the 6th regiment, just publicly complimented by Lord Canning for their loyal offer to serve against Dehly, suddenly shot down most of their officers; and it was only by the presence of mind and gallantry of Captain Brasyer, who commanded a corps of Sikhs in charge of the great fortress, that it was saved. Thus the progress of the mutiny has been sketched from Meerut to Peshâwur westward, to Allahabad and Oudh eastward, and into Rajpootana, as far as Neemuch. All details are necessarily wanting, as they would swell this work to volumes, and will be found in the histories of the war by Mr. Kaye, and other writers.[1] It only remains to sketch the progress of its extinction in this vast tract of country. From May 10 to June 5, the whole of the events detailed, and many other minor outbreaks, had occurred. The catastrophe was sudden, and for the time overwhelming; but the Meerut action had been twenty days too soon, and instead of a simultaneous rising from Peshâwur to Benares, as had been planned, the various occurrences were broken in character, and some of the most serious had been anticipated and prevented.

and of the 6th Native Infantry at Allahabad.

CHAPTER IV.

THE MUTINY (*continued*), 1857.

THIS is not the place for telling the story of Cawnpoor. In all its mournful and ghastly intensity, it may be read in Mowbray Thompson's narrative, in Mr. Trevelyan's pages, in the history of Mr. Kaye and other writers, and in many other authentic documents. More deliberately treacherous than the catastrophe of the 'Black Hole,' a hundred years before—more intensified and prolonged—the fate of those who perished there forms a tragedy, so full of terrible misery, of heroic endurance, and the deepest pathos, that it will be read with a shuddering tribute of tears, to the latest generation of Englishmen. On June 6, as mentioned in the last chapter, the native troops set out from Cawnpoor towards Dehly, with intent to join the king; but it was no part of the purpose of Nána Sahib that they should do

The story of Cawnpoor.

[1] Kaye's 'Sepoy War;' Trotter's 'History of British Empire;' 'History of India,' by Montgomery Martin; 'History of India,' by Beveridge, &c., &c.

so. The purpose of the Nána—one of the many delusions which appeared at this period—was to establish a Hindoo empire in his own person; and his first step was to induce the Cawnpoor mutineers to join him. There was much division among them; but he succeeded in turning them back, and before noon the frail buildings of refuge were invested. Including officers, soldiers, merchants, planters, clerks, and their families, there were not many less than a thousand Christian souls who had taken refuge in the miserable place of refuge and intrenchment prepared.

Defence.

Into the details of the defence from June 6 to 24, it is impossible in this limited manual to enter; but it was prolonged, under a blazing, scorching sun, until all the medicines for the sick, and well nigh all the ammunition and food, were consumed; after one building was burned, and the rest, riddled with shot, might at any time fall on those within; after the loss of many of the best officers and men, and the increasing debility of the remainder—without any hope of succour or rescue. In this condition of affairs, an emissary arrived from the Nána—an old lady named Greenway who had been taken prisoner, and brought an offer of a safe transmission to Allahabad, on condition that whatever the intrenchment contained should be given up.

Terms offered.

Had the defenders not been encumbered with helpless women and children, they would have preferred to cut their way through the Sepoys; but, under existing circumstances, that was impossible, and fearing no treachery, the Nána's offer was accepted.

and accepted.

On the 27th, the survivors, men, women and children, were marched down to the boats which had been prepared for them, in number about 450, and were no sooner embarked, than a murderous fire was opened upon them with grape from guns on the bank, and musketry.

Treacherous massacre.

Many perished, others got off in their boats; but their crews had deserted them, and one by one they were again captured. A considerable number of the Christians were at once shot, and otherwise put to death; but 122 were reserved for a while, to be in the end, as Havelock advanced, butchered, along with the survivors of the fugitives from Futtehgurh. Of the whole party who left the intrenchment on June 27, only four escaped and survived: Lieutenants Delafosse and Thompson, and privates Murphy and Sullivan, who, after many hairbreadth escapes, were protected by a friendly Oudh chief, Rajah Deeg Beeja Singh, and were able to join Havelock's force as it advanced.

The four survivors.

Like the defence of the intrenchment at Cawnpoor, the history of the siege of the position taken up at Lukhnow by Sir Henry Lawrence cannot be told here. It is an episode in itself, as interesting, as full of devoted heroism, in

Siege of the residency at Lukhnow.

this case, of Sepoys as well as English soldiers, as Cawnpoor; but attendant with no tragedy except the casualties of war, among which, the death of the noble and chivalrous Henry Lawrence, on July 4, is the most prominent incident. Up to June 30, he was comparatively unmolested; but on that day he sallied out at the head of all the men he could spare, for the purpose of reconnoitring the rebel forces at Chinhut, near Lukhnow, and himself badly wounded, was driven back with considerable loss to the residency; and on the same afternoon, the investment of the English position commenced. On July 1 the Mutchie Bhówan was given up, and the troops concentrated in the residency. How it was defended, without hope of succour, for three months; how gallant men fought, and brave enduring women helped; how mines were sprung by the enemy, and their breaches defended; how countermines were made, and sickness from wasting fever endured; and yet how the persevering enemy was again and again beaten back on every point, is modestly yet graphically told in Sir John Inglis's admirable report, and in the governor-general's public notification. There was hope, at the end of July, that they would be speedily relieved by Havelock; but this proved false: nor was it till September 22 that they were finally delivered, and that, too, under the most imminent peril they had as yet endured.

Final deliverance.

But more upon Dehly than upon Oudh and Lukhnow was the anxiety of all the British in India centred. There was apparently no means of increasing the English forces there. Reinforcement of them from the south was as impossible as from the east, and Sir Henry Barnard had already with him, it was believed, every man available from the stations of the north-west provinces. Against him had collected all the mutinied Sepoy regiments above Cawnpoor, and crowds of lawless undisciplined soldiery of the country, who had thronged together for plunder, and a final effort to re-establish the ancient dynasty of the Moghuls. In this crisis, Sir John (now Lord) Lawrence, trusted the Sikhs, and was trusted in turn; and yet, for some time, the condition of the Punjâb was as desperate as any other portion of Upper India, and it was only the cool, determined will of its chief ruler that saved it, and made it the turning point of eventual triumph.

Anxiety in regard to Dehly.

Sir John Lawrence and the Sikhs.

Mutiny had not been extinguished by disarmament of the native regiments in the Punjâb. On July 7, at Jullunder, the 6th Cavalry, and the 36th and 61st Native Infantry, who had been previously disarmed, rose at night by concert, and after much confusion and plunder, which was only checked by a troop of native horse-artillery, still faithful, and the levies of the Sikh Rajah of Kupoorthala, they left

Events in the Punjâb. Mutiny at Jullunder.

the station, and marched towards Dehly. As they passed the station of Phillour, they were joined by the 3rd Native Infantry, and though checked for a while by a small body of men under Lieutenant Williams, and Mr. Ricketts of the civil service, succeeded in crossing the Sutlej to Loodhiana, which they left wrecked, and eventually reaching Dehly. The attempt at pursuit from Jullunder had been abortive.

Other Punjab mutinies.

On July 8, the 14th Native Infantry at Jhelum, on being disarmed by three companies of the 24th Foot, resisted, and were not defeated without the loss of seventy-six Europeans in killed and wounded. Nearly 100 of the regiment were subsequently caught and executed, but a large proportion escaped to Dehly. Brigadier Nicholson, at the head of a moveable column, now disarmed the 59th at Umritsir; but on the 9th, the 9th Cavalry and 46th Native Infantry mutinied at Sealkote, and marched for Dehly. They were, however, pursued by Nicholson on the 10th, who, making a forced march of upwards of fifty miles, came up with them on the 12th at Trimmoo, on the Ravee, and after a sharp fight, drove them across the river, to an island which they defended till the 15th, when the position was stormed, and the whole bayonetted or drowned in the attempt to escape.

Native regiments at Lahore.

It has been already related that the three native regiments at Lahore had been disarmed, and were closely watched; but they were excited and uneasy, and on July 30, the 26th Native Infantry murdered their commander, Major Spencer, and took to flight in a furious dust-storm, which concealed their movements. Next day they were trying to cross the Ravee, opposed by a local native officer at the head of some Sikh police levies, when they were pursued by Mr. Cooper, of the civil service, at the head of ninety Sikh horsemen, and the remainder of the survivors, who had taken refuge on an island in the river, 282 in all, surrendered. Of these, 237 were forthwith hanged or shot; and the remainder, who had been confined in a small bastion, were found dead or dying from suffocation. This action was, and still is, heavily blamed by many; but it was recognised as a necessity, stern and terrible indeed, but justified under the murder of Major Spencer, and the general exigency, by Sir John Lawrence and Mr. Montgomery; there was no doubt that its effect restrained others from outbreak, or attempt to join the rebel forces, and in the end saved many lives. A similar fate attended the 51st Native Infantry at Peshâwur, who, upon a search for concealed arms in their lines, in which many were found, broke into mutiny on August 20, but were at once overpowered, and fled towards the Jumrood pass. They

Mr. Cooper's pursuit.

Its result.

The 51st Native Infantry at Peshâwur.

were pursued by the newly-raised levies, by police, and the people of the country, and not a man escaped: 700 perished; and on the 29th, 'lay dead in three deep trenches.' After these terrible examples, there was no further attempt to escape, and the Sepoy regiments in the Punjâb remained tranquil.

On June 8, Sir Henry Barnard advanced from Allypoor towards Dehly, and attacked the advanced division of the enemy at Budlee Serâi, where it was strongly posted. *Combat of Budlee Serâi.* The combat was short and decisive, and the Sepoys fled to Dehly, leaving six heavy guns to the victors. The army then pursued its march to the heights on the north-west of Dehly, from which the enemy was soon dislodged; and the weary troops, under cover of the ridge, had a little time for rest. Towards evening, the rebels advanced heavy masses of men, with an apparent intention of attacking the ridge; but their courage failed them, and they returned into the city. *The investment of Dehly.* The first step to the investment of Dehly had thus been gained, with the comparatively small loss of fifty-one killed and 132 wounded. The loss of the Sepoys was about 400, with thirteen guns. So far all had been well, and it was clear that in the field the Sepoys would have no chance of success, had they even dared to attempt to gain it; but they held a position strong by nature and art, well protected by massive fortifications; *Position of the mutineers.* they were at least 30,000 strong, and the roads to the south and east were open to their constantly arriving reinforcements of revolted stations and garrisons. There was abundance of provision, a very powerful artillery in heavy and light guns, with ample supplies of shot, shell, and powder. It is not therefore surprising, that they were confident, or that the siege, when it began, was prolonged. On June 13, *The siege commences.* an enterprise to capture the city by blowing open two gates was planned, which was called 'the gamester's throw;' but day broke before the preparations were completed, and it was judiciously abandoned. It is certain that failure then, which might have ensued, would have been most dangerous.

It is impossible to follow in detail the results of daily combats maintained in almost all parts of the British position. After the arrival of two newly-mutinied regiments from Nusseerabad, a sharp attack was made on the right rear of the English lines on June 19, which was defeated, and was repeated on the 20th with the same result. Joined by the regiments from Jullunder and Phillour, another attack was made on the British lines *Attacks on the British position.* on June 23, the anniversary of the battle of Plassy; and the rebel Sepoys, it was acknowledged, fought better than on any previous occasion, while their movements, particularly in the employment of clouds of skirmishers, proved them to be directed with much military skill; nor did they flinch from the bayonet. But they were forced back on every point with heavy loss, and in one place, 150 lying dead from bayonet wounds were counted. Their loss was estimated at 800 men, and that of the English was 160 in killed and wounded.

Meanwhile, and till the first week in July, the new levies from the Punjâb had been steadily arriving, bringing in supplies, stores and money, with every other necessary that the thoughtful and indefatigable Sir John Lawrence could supply; and it was felt throughout the army, now 7,000 strong, that Dehly might be taken. On the other hand, the mutineers were reinforced by the arrival of four new regiments of infantry, one of cavalry, and a battery of artillery from Rohilkhund, and others were on their way. At Agra, the Kotah contingent, with mutineers from Neemuch and Mehidpoor, sought to besiege the fort; but were attacked on July 4 by Brigadier Polwhele, at the head of a small force, and compelled to retire. But the rebels nevertheless claimed a victory, for the English were too weak to pursue them; and the Agra news was received with great rejoicing when it reached Dehly.

Progress of the siege.

Reinforcements to the enemy.

Action at Agra.

On the same day Sir Henry Barnard, already much exhausted by exposure and incessant anxiety, was attacked by cholera, and died. Brigadier Reed, the next senior officer, took up the command, but he resigned on the 17th, and was succeeded by Brigadier Archdale Wilson. Passing by, though with regret, the brilliant combats of the 9th, 14th, 18th, 23rd of July, and 2nd of August, and Lieutenant Hodson's able march to clear the country as far as Rhotuck up to the 22nd, it is cheering to record the account of a new reinforcement sent by Sir John Lawrence, as fully equipped as the preceding, which reached Dehly on August 14. It consisted of H.M.'s 52nd and a wing of the 61st Foot, Green's Punjâb Rifles, Bourchier's field-battery, and 200 Mooltan Horse, under the command of Brigadier John Nicholson, whose dealings with the mutineers of Sealkote, on July 12, have already been mentioned in this chapter. With this efficient reinforcement the British army, deducting the sick absent, exceeded 8,000 men, and a heavy siege-train was in progress from Ferozepoor. An attempt to intercept it was made by a rebel force of 7,000 men, but they were followed and attacked by Nicholson at Nujufgurh on August 25; and with a comparatively small loss of twenty-five killed and seventy wounded—though the brave Lumsden

Death of Sir Henry Barnard.

Brigadier Wilson succeeds.

Reinforcements from the Punjâb.

Siege-train from Ferozepoor.

Action at Nujufgurh.

was slain in the action—the enemy's strong position was carried, and thirteen guns with all their stores taken. Thus matters continued, sometimes with days of comparative inaction, and again recurrence of attacks and skirmishes, until September 6, when the long looked-for siege-train arrived, and on the 7th the siege operations were commenced in reality. Hitherto maintenance of position was the only object attainable, for the artillery was too weak to attempt the breach of the city walls; but the position on the ridge had proved a rock, against which every effort of the mutineers had been broken.

Danger of the crisis.

It is almost needless to explain the danger which existed everywhere at this crisis. The long inaction, as it had appeared, before Dehly, had given rise almost universally among natives, to the opinion that the English could not take it, and that the Sepoys and the king would in the end be masters. Even the Punjâb was seething, and while insurrection was repressed, there was many a wild chieftain who only waited to strike in when a general *mêlée* should ensue.

CHAPTER V.

THE MUTINY (*continued*), 1857.

State of feeling in Calcutta.

It is now necessary to follow the progress of events in Calcutta and Bengal generally, to the period at which the last chapter terminates. Until the receipt of the news from Meerut, no steps had been taken to provide for any emergency. Lord Canning, necessarily ignorant of the Sepoys, of the existing alarms, and the state of native feeling, may well be excused for not perceiving intuitively, what he might have learned from others, had there been any—except perhaps one, the veteran Hearsey—who dared to tell him; and it is little to say that through April, and till the final outbreak took place in May, the apathy, indifference, or real want of perception in the highest and most experienced officials of Calcutta, appears now unaccountable. When the mystery was solved, however, by the electric telegraph on May 12, its agency alone, for which the Government was indebted to the foresight of Lord Dalhousie, enabled the governor-general not only to comprehend the extent of the calamity, but to make provision against it. He is blamed for having been slow at first; but the reasons are so evident as to preclude blame. The attribute of prescience, indeed, was not possessed by him; but when the trouble came upon him,

The governor-general unjustly blamed.

his clear calm mind, and true, if slow, judgment, caused him to rise immeasurably above all by whom he was surrounded. Henry Lawrence's telegram from Lukhnow on May 16 was not neglected; and while on the 14th the 35th Foot had been summoned from Burmah, on the 16th Lord Harris at Madras, and Lord Elphinstone at Bombay, were requested to send all the European troops at their disposal to Calcutta. The P. and O. mail-steamer took a message from the governor-general to Ceylon for reinforcements, and Lord Elgin and General Ashburnham were called upon to spare every available soldier from the Chinese war. In addition to this, the hands of every commander and head civil officer in India were strengthened by powers to act on emergent occasions. The commander-in-chief, Sir John Lawrence, Mr. Colvin, and every other high official holding responsible posts, and frequently men of lower degree, who had done, or were doing, good work, were cheered and encouraged by autograph letters, as men like to be cheered in times of great danger; and considering all these acts, and many more, it is impossible to deny to Lord Canning the possession and exercise of great determination and foresight.

Measures.

The execution of his measures were, however, not commensurate with his will; and the miserably slow progress of driblets of men up the country was most disheartening. Twenty European soldiers a day, sent off in carts from the end of the railway at Ráneegunje, was not the way in which Cawnpoor and Lukhnow could be succoured. The 10th Foot at Dinapoor could not be spared, as they were watching three native regiments not yet disarmed. The 84th was detained at Calcutta for the same reason, as regarded the native troops at Barrackpoor; but Bengal was tranquil: and as all March and April had passed without an attempt to reinforce the upper provinces, so also May; when, on the 20th, Lord Canning publicly thanked the 70th Native Infantry for volunteering for service at Dehly, but declined the offer of the Europeans of all nations in Calcutta to form a volunteer corps.

Delay in transmission of troops.

On May 23, Colonel James Neill, with the 1st Madras Fusileers, arrived, and at once proceeded *en route* to Benares; and in the first few days of June, the 64th Foot and 78th Highlanders were soon followed by the 35th Foot from Burmah. These regiments, as fast as they arrived, were sent on by the now better organised system of transit, which sometimes took 100 men a day, but was still too inefficient for the emergency; and till the river should fill, the steamers were next to useless. On June 12, the governor-general invited the Europeans of Calcutta to form a volunteer corps, as they had pre-

Arrival of the Madras Fusileers and other English regiments.

viously offered to do—a request which was responded to cheerfully, and promoted a sense of security which had long been wanting. On the 14th, Brigadier Hearsey disarmed the native regiments at Barrackpoor, which had shown decided symptoms of mutiny; whereupon, notwithstanding the cool, staunch bearing of the governor-general, a panic, disgraceful in many respects, pervaded Calcutta, which it is almost shameful to record. Next day, however, under the pressure of his Council, Lord Canning passed an act of severe restriction upon the press, which no doubt aggravated the alarm which the measure was intended to suppress, and for which the imprisonment of the ex-King of Oudh in Fort William was a poor equivalent. On the 17th, Sir Patrick Grant and Brigadier-General Henry Havelock reached Calcutta, and on the 23rd the latter proceeded to join Colonel Neill at Allahabad.

Panic at Calcutta.

Restrictions on the press.

At the station of Secrole, near Benares, were the 13th Irregular Cavalry, a regiment of Sikhs, and the 37th Native Infantry; and to check them were three guns manned by Europeans and 150 of the 10th Foot. On June 3, Colonel Neill arrived, with sixty of his men, and the disarming of the 37th was determined upon. As the combined force of Europeans and Sikhs were moving down upon them, the 37th flew to arms, and fired irregularly; but the Sikhs, hitherto unsuspected, now fired upon the Europeans, and then with the Irregular Cavalry broke and fled. The mutiny was, however, quelled; and the Rajah of Benares, Ráo Narráin Singh, and Soorut Singh, a Sikh chieftain, who was a state prisoner, proved by their fidelity and assistance to Mr. Carre Tucker, the commissioner, and Mr. Gubbins, the magistrate, that order could be maintained even among the excitable and fanatical population of the city. The exertions and bearing of the civil officers of Benares, at this juncture one of the most dangerous spots in India, were beyond all praise.

Mutiny at Benares.

On June 5, the Sikh detachment at Jounpoor rose, shot down their officers, and plundering the treasury they were guarding, made off into the country. At Azimgurh, which the civilians had deserted, Mr. Venables, an indigo planter of much local influence, maintained order in a manner most creditable to himself and beneficial to Government; and on the 9th, Benares and its neighbourhood being tranquil, Neill set out for Allahabad, with forty men of his corps, and reached the great fortress on the 11th. He found the place invested on the land side by swarms of the rebels, and its only defenders some European invalids from Chunar, and Brasyer's Sikhs; but Sikhs in Neill's eyes found no favour after the Benares affair, and he quietly put them out of the fort. Subsequently these

Mutiny at Jounpoor.

Neill reaches Allahabad.

Sikhs earned his confidence by their good behaviour in clearing the villages around of rebels, and were of material use in the advance to Cawnpoor; and had it not been for a severe visitation of cholera, the admirably effected occupation of Allahabad would have been attended with no material loss. Every endeavour was now made to march upon Cawnpoor, but the tardy arrival of the men prevented this until June 30, when 400 of the Fusileers and 300 Sikhs, with two guns, marched under Major Renaud.

Advance on Cawnpoor by General Havelock.

On the same day General Havelock arrived, and on July 7, a column set out under his own command, to avenge the butchery at Cawnpoor, which it had been too late to prevent. To the last, Neill and Havelock had clung to the hope that the garrison of the intrenchment would be able to hold out; but the news which had arrived before the column could march, had extinguished hope.

Havelock's column, including Renaud's force, consisted of about 2,000 men, European and Sikhs, a company of Royal Artillery, and fifty horse, of whom twenty were English officers and gentleman under Captain Barrow. On the 10th he received news that the Sepoy regiments from Bithoor were advancing; and making two forced marches, he joined Renaud near Futtehpoor on the 12th. Without having time to rest the men, he found himself obliged to attack the enemy, about 4,000 strong, with twelve guns. The Sepoys did not await his advance, but scared by the execution of the Enfield rifles, fled, abandoning their guns; and want of cavalry alone prevented the action from being more decisive; but not one English soldier had been lost. On the 15th, crossing the bridge at Pandoo Nuddee, after a sharp combat, in which he lost Major Renaud and twenty-five men, but took four guns from the enemy, Havelock found himself on the 16th opposed by 5,000 Sepoys, under, it was said, the command of the Nána himself, strongly posted in a succession of villages. The odds were very heavy against the English force; but village after village was carried by the men of each regiment in turn, without a check, and the whole of the rebel army were driven from their position, fleeing into Cawnpoor, and leaving seven guns and 250 dead behind them. The English force had lost eight killed and eighty-eight wounded, or disabled by sunstroke.

Incidents of the march.

It was impossible to do more, for the evening was closing in: and the men, weary and hungry, lay down to rest near the great parade-ground of the station. They had heard again, as they marched up, of the destruction of Wheeler's garrison; but also that more than a hundred English people were still in confinement. Would they have the glory and the happiness of rescuing them?

Havelock reaches Cawnpoor.

Alas no! After the defeat on the Pandoo Nuddee on the 15th, it was debated by the Nána and Azim Oolla whether the remainder of the prisoners should not be put to death; and on its being decided that this course alone, as at Jhansy, would prevent further advance, they were all brutally destroyed on the 16th, some by shot, some by sword-cuts; while there is no doubt that many who survived wounds for a while, and little children, were thrown alive into the well which received, by most accounts, 210 bodies. Early on the 17th, Havelock's brigade marched into the station, and soon reached the scene of massacre. What was seen there, in all its sickening horror, need not be described again; but was it marvellous that the mournful blood-stained relics, the little shoes and scraps of clothing, the deep well filled with fresh dead—caused every British soldier to make an inward vow of revenge, which to the last was sternly fulfilled? Over that well, now enclosed by a rich Gothic screen, stands an angel in marble, with folded wings and crossed arms, an emblem of the rest of the dead beneath, who await the Lord's coming.

Massacre of the English prisoners.

Havelock did not delay at Cawnpoor. Reinforced by Neill with 200 men, and the party which had come up in the steamer, he marched to Bithoor on the 19th, blew up the magazine, and burned the palace, but found no enemy; and, returning to Cawnpoor, left Neill, now brigadier-general, in command of the station, and crossed over into Oudh. How Neill did his work there, restoring confidence, re-establishing the administration, and punishing rebels—making the worst of them clean up the blood of the murdered prisoners, and while he protected the well disposed, became a terror to evil-doers—how piles of plundered effects were, as it were, laid at his feet, does not require repetition; but Havelock's progress needs to be followed. On the 29th, he advanced from Mungulwar towards Lukhnow, and beat the enemy at Oonáo; but from disease, sunstroke, and casualties in action, he had lost 150 men in one march, and he returned to his camp and awaited reinforcements from Neill. Again, on August 4, with 1,300 men and thirteen guns, he advanced, and met the enemy, 20,000 strong, at Busherat Gunj, and, nothing daunted by numbers, attacked and defeated him; but advance was impossible, for cholera and dysentery were fast striking down his men. He therefore again retired to Mungulwar, and on the 13th, finding it impracticable to force the thirty-six miles of road to Lukhnow with the troops at his disposal, he recrossed the Ganges, in time to save Neill from some inconvenience: for, encouraged by the weakness of his force, the rebel troops had gathered round him in considerable

Havelock's operations.

Neill at Cawnpoor.

Havelock's advance towards Lukhnow.

He returns to Cawnpoor.

numbers. On the 15th, they had advanced close to the cantonment, where they were attacked by Neill and driven off, and the day after, a heavy body of them, drawn up near Bithoor, was engaged by Havelock, and routed; but there was no cavalry to pursue. Henceforth the brigade at Cawnpoor was not molested; but by sickness and casualties it had been reduced to little more than 700 able men, and it was evident that considerable reinforcements must arrive ere Lukhnow could be relieved.

Combat at Bithoor.

The progress of the relieving detachments was, however, delayed by events at and near Dinapoor, where, on July 25, three native regiments—the 7th, 8th, and 40th—mutinied, and succeeded in leaving the station unopposed. To the last General Lloyd, who commanded them, had believed in the good faith of these men, and refused to disarm them. The mutineers crossed the Soane, plundered Arrah, and, joined by Köer Singh, a Zemindar who had rebelled, attacked a house in which sixteen Englishmen with fifty Sikh police had taken refuge and fortified. The defence of this position forms a most interesting episode of the war: and it is satisfactory to record that the services of Mr. Boyle, an engineer, who had fortified the house, and conducted the defence, have been recognised by his admission to the Order of the Star of India. An attempt to relieve the besieged party, made from Dinapoor by a detachment of the 10th and 37th Foot, was attended with serious loss, owing to incautious proceedings, and forced to retire; and the fate of the Englishmen appeared inevitable, when, collecting such men as were available, Major Vincent Eyre, of the Artillery, formed a small field force, with which he defeated the rebels, with severe loss, on August 2, and on the 3rd had the satisfaction of releasing the gallant men who had so bravely defended themselves.

Mutiny at Dinapoor.

Gallant defence at Arrah.

Meanwhile extensive reinforcements of English soldiers had reached Calcutta: Sir Colin Campbell had arrived as commander-in-chief, Sir James Outram had come up as far as Allahabad, and, on September 16, he had joined Havelock and Neill with 1,400 men. Outram was the senior officer and might have assumed the command; but he generously waived his rank, and acted only as civil commissioner. On the 19th and 20th, 2,500 English soldiers crossed the Ganges, and on the 21st encountered the rebel army, which was sharply put to flight, losing four guns, taken by Outram at the head of the volunteer cavalry; and on the 23rd, a much superior force was attacked at the Alumbágh, near Lukhnow, routed, and pursued almost to the city. On the 24th, General Havelock gave his men rest before the final struggle,

Arrival of Sir Colin Campbell.

Second advance on Lukhnow.

which he saw would be severe, and on September 25, Neill leading, the defences of Lukhnow were attacked. These consisted of at least two miles of narrow lanes, streets, and massive buildings, defended with skill and desperation, and the fire poured upon the assailants was tremendous; but they were never checked, and as the evening closed, the victors, and those they rescued, had clasped hands, thanking God that deliverance had been effected. Such a combat had necessarily caused heavy loss, and the killed, wounded, and missing were 464 men; among them, to the grief of the whole army, and of the English nation, the gallant James Neill met his death from a chance shot almost at the entrance of the British position, and in the moment of victory. There had been few men more popular in the army, and few, if any, whose real military skill and dashing bravery inspired more confidence, or were more deeply respected.

Rescue of the garrison.

Death of Colonel Neill.

CHAPTER VI.

OPERATIONS AT DEHLY AND CURRENT EVENTS, SEPTEMBER TO NOVEMBER, 1857.

BEFORE Havelock was able to make his final endeavour to reach Lukhnow, the siege of Dehly was in active progress. As had been previously stated, it was opened in reality on September 7; for what preceded it was simply retention of position. The ground between the British position on the ridge and the city was first cleared as much as possible of walls and buildings during several days of constant skirmishing. Between the 7th and 11th, three batteries of heavy and one of light guns had been constructed and armed, in spite of the furious musketry fire from the walls of Dehly; and fifty guns poured shot and shell against the curtains between the water and the Kashmere bastions, without cessation, day or night. It was acknowledged by all that the rebel defenders did their utmost in never flinching from the fire, even after all their guns were disabled and dismounted; maintaining an unceasing discharge of musketry, making sallies on the works, and endeavouring with their cavalry to force the rear of the position. By the 13th, the massive walls were reduced to ruin, and at night, Greathed, Home, Lang, and Medley, officers of the Engineers, crept to the foot of the breaches, and returned safely, reporting them practicable. There was no time for delay, which was desired by none; for every

The siege of Dehly.

Batteries.

Conduct of the rebels.

Breaches are practicable.

day's skirmishing and protection of the batteries only decreased the number of effective soldiers and swelled the list of non-effectives, now over 3,000 men. At three in the morning of September 14, three assaulting columns had formed in the trenches. One, under Brigadier Nicholson, 1,000 strong, was to storm the breach of the Kashmere bastion; the second, under Brigadier Jones, 850 strong, that of the water bastion; and the third, 950 strong, under Colonel Campbell, to attack the Kashmere gate, when it should be blown down—in all, 2,800 men. Other columns were formed for reserve and for attack upon the suburb of Kissengunj, and, with the exception of a trifling force left to protect the camp, the whole of the British troops were employed. At the main breach, as the counterscarp had not been blown in, the dry ditch, eighteen feet deep, was a formidable obstacle under the furious fire opened upon the stormers; but it was crossed, the wall beyond climbed, and in a few minutes the breach was won.

Storm of Dehly.

At the Kashmere gate the powder-bags were laid by Lieutenants Home and Salkeld of the Engineers, with a party of volunteers for this desperate service, of whom the two foremost were shot dead as they laid the bags. Salkeld was wounded in two places as he tried to fire the train, and Sergeant Burgess, who took the match from him, was also shot dead as he applied it: but the explosion followed, and the bugler of the 52nd, attached to the party, sounding the advance, the stormers rushed in over the ruins of the just fallen gate, and carried all before them. But Dehly was not yet won. As the various columns advanced into the city, they were met by an unceasing and deadly fire from terraced houses, from massive buildings and mosques, and in an attempt to storm a narrow street which led to the Burn bastion, the gallant John Nicholson was struck down by what proved to be a mortal wound. After a vain attempt to carry the great Jumma mosque, the wearied troops rested on the ground they had won.

The Kashmere gate.

Death of Brigadier Nicholson.

Outside the walls, the right attack, under Major Reid, had failed: and the Kashmere contingent lost their guns, Major Reid being badly wounded. The columns retired to the ridge, but their retreat had been bravely covered by the cavalry under Hope Grant, and three of the rebels' guns in Kissengunj, which had done much execution, were spiked. All the northern ramparts, from the church to the Kabool gate, had been cleared of the enemy, and thirty-seven guns had been taken; but the loss had been very severe, in 280 killed and 1,170 wounded, and many of the enemy's strongest positions remained intact. Early next day these were shelled by the

Failure of right attack.

Operations in the city.

mortars which had been brought up, and the magazine having been breached, was stormed and taken. It contained 170 guns, many of the largest calibre, which might now be employed against the enemy; but the mortars were doing their work effectively upon the palace and other positions, the rebel fire manifestly slackened, and the English line of attack, carefully maintained and supported during the 17th and 18th, advanced steadily through the city.

On the 19th, the Burn bastion, the strongest point of the rebel defences, was surprised and carried, and on the morning of the 20th, the Lahore gate and Garstin bastions followed. Hodson, with his horse, finding the Dehly gate open, made his way to the Jumma Musjid unopposed, and shortly afterwards the gates of the palace were forced open, and the last stronghold captured; but it was unoccupied, except by some wounded Sepoys, and a few fanatics who had retreated into it and there met their doom. General Wilson had ordered no quarter to be given to men with arms in their hands; but beyond rebels, it was a joyful consideration of the victors, that amidst all the plunder, devastation, and, at one time, drunkenness, of the troops, who had fallen upon stores of liquors purposely placed in their way, no women or children, and few, if any, of the peaceable inhabitants and traders of the populous and wealthy city had suffered. The capture of Dehly had occupied six days of hard fighting in narrow streets and at every disadvantage; but the triumph had been complete, and not a rebel soldier remained alive in it. Alone, and as Lord Canning happily expressed it in his proclamation, 'before a single soldier of the many thousands who are hastening from England to uphold the supremacy of the British power has set foot on these shores,' Wilson's army had achieved a success which, from the character and obstinacy of the resistance, was unparalleled in the history of India, and by few, if any, in that of war.

The palace occupied.

Possession of Dehly.

Proclamation.

Contrasting the utterly inadequate force with which Sir Henry Barnard invested Dehly with that which took it, the undying glory of assistance rests upon Lord Lawrence. Under the domination of his powerful will, Sikh levies, Goorkhas, the troops of Sikh rajahs and feudatories, the powerful siege-train, supplies, money, and English soldiers had successively reached the camp on the ridge, and one and all contributed to the result, while the dauntless bravery of English and native soldiers crowned all. But the cost in dead and disabled men had been heavy. From the beginning of the investment to the close of the siege and storm of the city, 3,837 were killed, wounded, or disabled, in the following proportions:—Europeans killed, 572; wounded,

Assistance by Lawrence.

English losses.

1,566; missing, 13—total, 2,151. Natives killed, 440; wounded, 1,229; missing, 17—total, 1,686. The rebels' loss could never be estimated; but their dead lay literally in heaps in some places, and the whole was necessarily very great. Those that escaped broke into two bodies, one proceeding into the Dooáb, another along the line of the river Jumna. It was at first supposed that they had taken the king with them: but on the 21st it was ascertained that he was at the tomb of the Emperor Hoomáyoon, his ancestor, at a short distance from the city, and he was brought in with his family by Captain Hodson, and lodged in his own palace. Next day Hodson, taking a hundred of his own men, went again to the tomb, and seized two of the king's sons, and his grandson, in the midst of a crowd of armed retainers, who, overawed by his bearing, laid down their weapons; but as the princes proceeded in a native carriage to the city, it was surrounded near the gates by a threatening crowd, and anticipating an attempt at rescue, Hodson shot both of them, and taking their bodies to the most public place in the city, they were exposed, as men who had caused the helpless English women and children to be murdered on May 11 and 12. Thus closed the terrible tragedy of Dehly, blood-stained from the earliest period of its foundation to the close of its greatness.

The rebels.

The king brought from Hoomáyoon's tomb.

Hodson shoots two of the princes.

With what eagerness the news of the final result was looked for throughout India can hardly be expressed: and while the six days of fighting in the city, and the apparently slow progress made in its capture, could only be understood by those who estimated the nature of the warfare and were assured of final success, there were many who yet feared there might be failure, and dreaded the result. To all well-affected natives the news was as joyful as to the English; to others it was a deathblow of hope. By it many a wavering chieftain was restrained from outbreak, for no prominent head to the rebellion now existed: and those who might have rejoiced in the chance of a new sovereignty of Dehly refused the domination of mutinous Sepoys, without leaders, without any common bond of union, and without resources. Day by day the mighty power of England was becoming manifest in the arrival of fresh soldiers, and was aided not a little by the loyal demonstrations of native princes and people in every part of India.

Anxiety in India regarding Dehly.

Effects of the victory.

Two flying columns were at once dispatched from Dehly to pursue the mutineers and prevent them from making head in the country. That under Brigadier Greathed, sweeping down upon Allygurh, and dispersing and shattering every rebel band, was pursuing its way to

Pursuit of rebels from Dehly;

Greathed's column.

Cawnpoor, when an urgent message from Mr. Reade at Agra met him at Hattras. Mr. Colvin, the lieutenant-governor of the north-western provinces, had died on September 9, and for his successor, Colonel Fraser, Mr. Reade was officiating. While the English forces were occupied with Dehly, a considerable army of mutineers from Indoor, Gwalior, and other southern stations had assembled at Dhólpoor, on the Chumbul, hoping to be joined by the Gwalior contingent; but as yet it had not moved, for Sindia had been able to restrain it: the others could not remain inactive, and Agra, weakly defended, seemed an easy prey, and, could it be gained, would be a rallying point for all other bodies of mutineers now in the field. It was indeed fortunate the Dhólpoor rebels had not moved sooner; but Greathed, making a forced march, reached Agra on the morning of September 10, and as the men were resting, unaccoutred, a sharp fire was opened upon them from masked rebel guns. During the previous night, the rebel force, 7,000 strong, had marched from Dhólpoor with the intention of surprising the fort, but were happily forestalled. The action was short but decisive; and with the loss of their twelve guns, their camp, and 500 dead, the rebels were pursued by the cavalry and horse-artillery for five miles, when the weary troops could do no more, and the rebels, scattering themselves among the fields of tall maize, escaped. This essential service performed, the column marched on to Cawnpoor, which it reached on October 10.

Events at Agra.

Defeat of the rebels at Agra.

With a like success, another column from Dehly, under Brigadier Showers, took the forts of Kanoud and Jhájur, and cleared the country of all rebel bands and plunderers that infested it, restoring order, and re-establishing the executive government. To the south, many spirited affairs had taken place, into the details of which it is needless to enter; but success had attended all, and the loyal Bombay troops had at last struck in, beating a large body of rebels at Mundissoor in good style; and Brigadier Stuart, at Dhár, was doing good service with the Malwah field force, part of which was composed of the cavalry and infantry of the Hyderabad contingent. During July and August, Colonel Davidson, the Resident at Hyderabad, had, with excellent judgment, assembled a strong brigade of the contingent at Mulkapoor in Berar; and throughout the subsequent campaigns no force rendered more able or gallant service than the Nizam's contingent, which, composed as it was of the same elements in men as the Bengal army, and excited by the prevalent rumours and events, might, under inaction, have proved mutinous.

Showers's column.

Stuart's Bombay column.

Hyderabad contingent.

The country now became, as it were, dotted with smaller

events and actions, as everywhere that they could be discovered bands of rebels and mutineers were successively attacked. Near Azimgurh the Goorkhas of Jung Bahádoor of Nipál, led by Captain Boileaux and Mr. Venables, defeated a large body of the enemy on September 20. On October 2, Major English, with a wing of the 53rd and a few Sikhs, attacked a large rebel force at Chuttra and routed them, taking four English six-pounder guns, ten elephants, and all their camp-equipage, with 50,000 rupees in cash. On November 1, with part of the Naval Brigade and some detachments of English regiments, Colonel Powell attacked the Dinapoor regiments at Kájwah, and though he lost his life, the victory was won by Captain Peel, whose seamen here had their first brush with the enemy. All these movements and actions were, however, of secondary importance before the great combinations of Sir Colin Campbell, which were now in progress.

Varied minor events and combats.

CHAPTER VII.

THE SECOND RELIEF OF LUKHNOW, AND FIELD OPERATIONS, NOVEMBER AND DECEMBER, 1857.

Outram's defence of Lukhnow.

AFTER the first relief of the garrison of Lukhnow on September 25, Sir James Outram assumed the command. The rebel forces, so far from retiring from the city, now pressed the siege more closely, with augmented numbers, and for the succeeding two months the defence rivalled that of the preceding. The details form an instructive lesson in the art of war, from the manner in which advantage was taken of every building and cover, however slight, and the incessant mining and countermining against the native attack, which in this respect was peculiarly ingenious and persevering. At the crisis at which the former relief took place, two mines had been carried under the very centre of the English position, which were fortunately discovered; and during the second defence General Outram records that shafts aggregating 200 feet in depth and 3,291 feet of 'gallery,' were executed by his troops. It had been impossible either to send away the sick and wounded of the previous siege, or to retire from Lukhnow; and though in some peril from the duration of the attack and shortness of provision, it was a happy circumstance that the position was maintained without the necessity of attempting to retire.

Native mines and countermines.

Meanwhile, reinforcements from England were arriving daily in Calcutta, and were forwarded consecutively to Cawnpoor, which was the point of rendezvous for all detachments and flying columns; and on November 9, Sir Colin Campbell advanced for the relief of General Outram to Buntara, on the Lukhnow road, where, on the 12th, and afterwards on the 14th, he was joined by other troops and detachments, which brought up his force to about 5,000 men of all arms, with thirty guns. The daring feat of Mr. Kavanagh in carrying news from General Outram to Sir Colin through the rebel forces, is a well-known incident of the war, and met with a merited reward in the Victoria Cross and a handsome donation of 2,000*l.*

Reinforcements.

Sir John Campbell's advance.

On the 14th, the advance against the rebel positions began: and one after another they were carried at the point of the bayonet, the Sikhs and Punjâbees vying with the English soldiers for pre-eminence in the varied combats. The Sikunder Bágh, a large enclosure, strongly garrisoned by the enemy, was breached and stormed by the Highlanders, the 53rd Foot, and 4th Punjâbees, when every soul found within it perished, and more than 2,000 of the enemy's dead were afterwards taken out and buried. The day's proceedings were wound up by the capture of the Shah Nujuf, a mosque, surrounded by a loopholed wall, where the Naval Brigade greatly distinguished themselves, bringing up their heavy guns, in the thick of the fire, close to the building. The capture of this position brought the assailants into communication with the garrison. The Mess-house, another fortified rebel post, was not carried till the afternoon of the 17th; but the women, sick, and wounded, could not be removed till the 19th, when they all happily reached the Sikunder Bágh in safety.

Operations against Lukhnow.

Next day the position, defended so nobly for six weary months, was evacuated under such admirable precautions that the enemy, ignorant of the movement, continued firing on it long after no one remained there. Sir Colin Campbell's dispatch forms an eloquent record of the services performed by all, which were liberally rewarded by Government, by honours, distinctions, and extra allowances. Considering the severity of the fighting, the loss of the British force in the last movement was not heavy, in 122 killed and 414 wounded. That of the rebels could never be ascertained, but was believed to have been about 6,000: and it was mainly owing to Sir Colin's care in not employing his men in assaults till the powerful artillery had done its work, that the comparatively small loss may be attributed. It was no part of Sir Colin's Campbell's plan to attack the city

Evacuation of the British position.

Sir Colin Campbell's dispatch.

itself on this occasion. With the small force at his disposal, it would have been impossible to have done so with effect, and any partial operation was out of the question. On the 23rd, the whole of the troops were safe at Dilkoosha, near the city, where, on the 24th, the noble Sir Henry Havelock died from dysentery, and was buried at the Alumbágh. Here General Outram was left with 4,000 men, and on the 27th Sir Colin commenced his return to Cawnpoor with a large convoy. He had only reached Bunnee, when sounds of a heavy cannonade in the direction of Cawnpoor induced him to push on, the more especially as he had not heard from General Windham, whom he had left with 2,000 men in charge of the entrenchment, for several days.

Death of Havelock.

The Gwalior contingent, heretofore neutral, and restrained by Sindia, though they had mutinied in June when several of their officers were shot by them, had at last marched to join the rebel forces under the Nána and his brother, Bala Sahib; and their united troops amounted to 20,000 men, with forty guns. The Gwalior contingent was one of the finest and most perfectly disciplined native levies in India, and among the rebel leaders, Tantia Tópee, a Mahratta Brahmin, but a soldier of singular ability, now appeared for the first time as a general. As the rebel forces advanced on Cawnpoor, General Windham went forth to meet them on the 26th, with about 1,200 men and twelve guns, and routed the first body he came up with, near the Pandoo river; but he had evidently no conception of their entire numbers, and next day, finding himself outflanked, retired on his entrenchment in some confusion, losing the camp-equipage, which had been collected for the army, and much stores. The enemy now closed upon the entrenchment, gaining possession of the city of Cawnpoor, and it was only by severe fighting on the 28th that the entrenchment itself was preserved from bombardment, while there was the utmost danger that the bridge of boats across the Ganges, by which alone Sir Colin Campbell's force could gain Cawnpoor, would be destroyed. His hurried march forward, therefore, was an able stroke of generalship; and on the 29th and 30th the whole of the convoy and troops had safely reached their destination.

The Gwalior contingent.

Action at Cawnpoor.

There was no doubt that the English force at Cawnpoor had been handled unskilfully, while that of the rebels had been cleverly directed, and it was evident they must be driven from their position, which was every day becoming stronger; but till Sir Colin Campbell was free of all impediments and anxieties in regard to sick and wounded, he made no step in advance. All these were dispatched to Calcutta, with the garrison of Lukhnow, by December 5, and on the 6th the enemy was attacked with infinite spirit and resolution, the Naval Brigade winning fresh renown by the manner in which they moved and handled, as it was described, 'like playthings,' their heavy 24-pounder guns. All the troops, combined and admirably led, routed the right wing of the enemy, taking seventeen guns, twenty-five waggons, and all their stores; and the pursuit, taken up by General Little, was continued for fourteen miles. Meanwhile their left wing was attacked by General Mansfield in the rear, and totally routed; and on the 7th not a man of the great rebel army could be seen for miles around Cawnpoor. The British loss had been singularly small, in thirteen killed and eighty-six wounded.

The enemy defeated at Cawnpoor.

Mansfield's success.

Making sure of overtaking at least a portion of the rebels, who had made off to the ferry called Serái Ghát, twenty-five miles above Cawnpoor, Brigadier Hope Grant, after discovering a large amount of treasure at Bithoor, pursued them with a brigade of 2,000 infantry and 500 cavalry. He found them on the 9th where he had expected, and won a complete victory, taking fifteen guns, and their waggons, much ammunition, and some standards; while it is more surprising to relate that not one man of his force was even hurt: the rebels, on the contrary, sustaining heavy loss from a noble charge by the cavalry, the 9th Lancers and 5th Punjâbees. In two actions the Gwalior contingent had lost thirty-two guns, the arm in which they had most prided themselves.

Brigadier Hope Grant's skirmish.

Combat of Serái Ghát.

The commander-in-chief was now free to undertake a general campaign against the rebels in Oudh and Rohilkhund. It was ably planned and as ably executed. Separate columns under himself, Hope Grant, Seaton from Dehly, and Walpole, cleared the country as far as Furrukabad, in the course of the month of December; and at Futtehgurh a brilliant victory over the rebel Nawáb of that place was won by Colonel Kinleside, who took twelve guns and their waggons and stores from the enemy, who left 700 dead on the field and in their pursuit for seven miles. On the 27th, Colonel Seaton routed the enemy at Mynpooree, taking six guns: and in both these affairs the British loss was strangely small.

The campaign opens.

Various combats.

At Lukhnow, Outram had not been idle. On December 22, he sallied out with two regiments at night, and routed a body of rebels who had taken up a position on the Cawnpoor road; and on the 26th, Mahomed Hussein, a rebel leader, with 5,000 men, posted at Majowlee, was also defeated by Colonel Rowcroft. Jung Bahádoor of Nipál was advancing to co-operate with the British forces, with 10,000 Goorkhas from

Other operations.

his frontier; and at Furrukabad were now collected 10,000 troops under the commander-in-chief. Elsewhere, before the close of the year, many districts had been cleared of rebels. The mutineers of Dacca were perishing in the jungles of Bhootán, to which they had retreated. In Sylhet, the last remnant of the 34th Native Infantry had been destroyed by Captain Byng; and thus, eastward from Dinapoor, all was already safe and tranquil. In Central India, Saugor was held by the 31st Native Infantry and 3rd Cavalry, both faithful to the last. Brigadier Stuart had routed, near Mundissoor, the rebel force, which was attacking Neemuch. Rewah, the spirited rajah of which was throughout faithful, had been purged of rebels by the gallant young political agent, Lieutenant Osborne. At Mhow, and Holkar's Indoor, order had been completely restored: for on December 15, the three mutinous regiments there were disarmed. Thus, the future war was restricted to Oudh, Rohilkhund, and part of Bundelkhund; and for operations to the southward two columns under Sir Hugh Rose (now Lord Strathnairn) and Brigadier Whitlock, of the Madras army, were already in motion.

Much retributive justice had been dealt out to prominent rebels. The Nawáb of Jhájur, the Meer Nawáb, and other men of rank, taken in arms, were tried by commission, and hanged at Dehly. No mercy was shown in any case, either to great men or subordinates: and all who were connected with murders or massacres, as at Dehly, were for the most part hunted down and executed. Yet, though the people of disaffected districts had already perished by thousands, the cry for more revenge, more blood—raised furiously in Calcutta, and repeated by the press of India almost without intermission for many months—still continued, and Lord Canning was assailed in India and in England by a hurricane of abuse, which was indeed hard to endure, but which passed over him unheeded. Time, and subsequent events, have done ample justice both to his motives and to his much-abused 'clemency.' While, at the outset, he endowed every person in authority with extra powers, he found, as the circle of rebellion and resistance narrowed, and as almost indiscriminate slaughter was carried on, that restraint was needed, and he resolutely imposed it by his order on July 31. Real criminals were not the less brought to condign punishment; but the burning of suspected villages and indiscriminate slaughter of the people, were checked in time, and the pacification of disturbed districts and the establishment of order were rapidly effected. Even at Dehly, before the end of 1857, most of the inhabitants had returned to their houses; trade and usual occupations had been resumed; the fortifications had been saved from a wild cry that had gone out for their destruction; and little but the ruins of the bastions and breaches remained to tell of the fierce contest that had raged there. Lastly, the north-western provinces were separated from the regulation districts, and for the present placed under the able administration of Sir John Lawrence.

CHAPTER VIII.

MILITARY OPERATIONS, JANUARY TO JUNE, 1858.

ON January 27, a military commission, of which Colonel Dawes of the Bengal Artillery was president, assembled in the palace at Dehly, the scene of the glories and vicissitudes of the great imperial family for 330 years, for the trial of Mahomed Bahádoor Shah, the last king. After twenty days' proceedings, the king was found guilty of having ordered the murder of forty-nine Christians at Dehly; of waging war upon the British Government; and of exciting the people of India, by proclamations, to destroy the English. Sentence of death was recorded against him, but commuted into one of transportation. His favourite wife, Zeenut Mahál, and his son Jumma Bukht, decided to accompany him, and they were eventually forwarded to Tounghoo in Burmah. In the state of existing feeling against the royal family, it might have gone hard with the queen if she had been put on her trial; but no prosecution was entered against her or her son. The commutation of sentence raised afresh the clamour against Lord Canning's clemency, and in self-defence he reviewed, in a minute for the Court of Directors, all his own acts, in so admirable a spirit of fairness and justice to the people of India at large, that his worst enemies were silenced by his calm magnanimity.

Trial of the king of Dehly.

Lord Canning's minute.

On January 2, the commander-in-chief, driving the rebels from its vicinity, became master of Furrukabad, and lay there while Hope Grant routed them in Rohilkhund on the 27th, with his usual success. On the 12th, at Lukhnow, Sir James Outram defeated a very imposing attack upon his position at the Alumbágh, by an army of the rebels estimated at 30,000 men, after a combat which lasted from sunrise till late in the afternoon; and on the 16th, a second, and even more desperate assault from the same army met with a like result. The month of January passed away without any move on the part of the commander-in-chief, for he had received orders from the governor-general, which directed an entire change in the plan of

Events of the campaign.

his campaign; and it is to be regretted he was ever interfered with. In admirable good temper, however, Sir Colin made new arrangements and preparations for attacking Oudh, instead, as he had before determined, of first clearing Rohilkhund, and reserving Oudh for his final effort. Meanwhile, Brigadier Franks, driving the enemy before him, had advanced to the south-east frontier of Oudh, and joined Jung Bahádoor's Goorkhas, thus completing the cordon in that direction.

The campaign.

The Bombay column under Sir Hugh Rose, which had steadily advanced into Central India, took possession of the strong fort of Rátgurh, and the road was thus opened for the relief of Saugor. Some alarm was caused by a partial mutiny of Madras troops at Nagpoor on January 18, which was, however, instantly suppressed by the remainder, and Sir Hugh Rose's force was enabled to continue its march. Again, on February 21, General Outram was attacked by 20,000 men, the Bégum of Oudh being herself in the field: and repulsed them with a fearful carnage, losing, on his part, only nine men wounded. On the 23rd, Sir Hope Grant captured the town of Meeán Gunj, in the direction of Lukhnow, taking six guns, and destroying 1,000 of the rebels, his own loss being only two killed and nineteen wounded;

Brigadier Franks' victory.

and on the 19th, Brigadier Franks, with his force of 6,000, attacked the army of Mahomed Hussein Nazim, estimated at 20,000 strong, near Chunda, and took six guns, and again at Waree, the same evening, putting him to flight. On the 23rd, out-manœuvring the enemy's general, Franks again attacked his army, now 25,000 strong, with twenty-five guns, very strongly posted between Badshah Gunj and Sooltanpoor; and, turning his right flank by an admirable movement, routed the whole, want of cavalry alone preventing him from following up his victory. As it was, twenty-one guns were captured, and nearly 2,000 of the enemy lay dead or wounded on the field. Again it is surprising to record that in the two days' fighting General Franks had only lost two men killed and sixteen wounded. On March 1, General Franks brought his brilliant independent operations to a close by joining the general camp before Lukhnow.

The campaign in Oudh continued.

On February 20, the seamen of the 'Pearl' frigate, under Captain Sotheby, joined by Colonel Rowcroft, with some Nipálese levies, captured two forts near Fyzabad, taking all the guns. On the 26th, after a sharp fight, Jung Bahádoor's Goorkhas stormed the curiously strong fort of Berozepoor, slaying all the defenders. On March 5, his troops, under General Khurruk Bahádoor, defeated and utterly routed the remains of Mahomed Hussein Nazim's army at the Kandoo river, taking their only remaining gun, and slaying and wounding 600 of them.

These operations complete the affairs in Oudh during February, and considerably aided the plans of the commander-in-chief.

To the south and west, Sir Hugh Rose, on February 10, drove the mutineers and rebels from the almost impregnable fort and position of Gurra Kóta, and soon afterwards defeated them at the pass of Muddunpoor, which they had disputed. General Roberts, now at the head of a column of 6,000 men, was sweeping through Malwah in the direction of Kóta. General Whitlock's column from Nagpoor, long delayed there by want of draught cattle for his siege guns, was entering Bundelkhund; and in Rewah, Colonel Hinde and Captain Osborne, the political agent, had, unaided by regular troops, taken six forts, sixty-two guns, and completely established order in that principality.

Campaign in Central India.

The events of March were more important. Sir Colin Campbell's arrangements were complete; he had conferred with the governor-general, who was now at Allahabad, and on the 2nd, with a noble army of 25,000 men, of which hardly less than 16,000 were English troops, the largest number ever brought together in India, the second attack on Lukhnow commenced. It is impossible either to enumerate the various troops employed in the field, all now veterans, or to follow the operations in detail so admirably described in the official dispatches, and in Mr. Russell's 'Diary' and letters to the 'Times.' There was no doubt, from the strength of the defences, the number of the mutineers and rebels, and the obstinate character of the contest, that the vast preparations of Sir Colin Campbell had been unavoidable to ensure success; and that it would have been bad policy in a political point of view to have run any risk of check or failure. The last of the siege-trains reached Lukhnow on the 4th, and the operations commenced in earnest. It was impossible to invest a city the circumference of which was twenty miles; but as the commander-in-chief states in his dispatch, 'some avenues of supply or relief might be closed.' On the 6th, therefore, a pontoon-bridge of casks and rafts was thrown across the river Goomtee, and Sir James Outram, at the head of the 1st Brigade, crossed, with instructions to clear the defences north of the city, and obtain the command of the two great bridges. By this operation, which involved some severe fighting in the capture of several important positions, the enemy's first line was turned by the 9th, when the Martinière was stormed by the 42nd, 53rd, and 90th Foot, under Lugard and Hope; and the 42nd Highlanders and 4th Punjâb Rifles following, cleared the line of outward defences, by which time Sir James Outram had established himself to the north of the Iron Bridge.

The second attack on Lukhnow.

Attack of March 6.

Continued attacks on positions.

Early on the 11th, a great block of buildings in the second line of the defence, called the Bégum Kóthee, was stormed and taken by the 93rd Highlanders, the 4th Punjâbees, and 1,000 Goorkhas, led by Brigadier Adrian Hope, and upwards of 500 of the enemy's dead were afterwards buried. It was, in fact, the key of the enemy's position, and was gallantly but fruitlessly defended. On this day, also, Jung Baháдoor arrived, with 9,000 Goorkhas and twenty-four guns, and was allotted a post on the canal covering the left attack. On the 14th, the Imámbára position was carried by assault, and Brasyer's Sikhs, pressing on, gained the Kaiser Bágh, and thus the third line of defence was penetrated. Next day, crossing the river by a pontoon-bridge, Outram took the Iron Bridge in reverse, and captured it; and pursuing his course through the Muchee Bhowán and the Imámbára, reached the residency. So far the city was captured; but most of the rebels had been able to escape by the various outlets. The Queen of Oudh, Huzrut Mahál, still, however, held the Moosee Bágh, a large palace with enclosed gardens about it, with 7,000 men; and the fanatic Moulvee of Fyzabad remained in the heart of the city with his adherents. These bodies were successively attacked, the Moosee Bágh on the 19th by Sir James Outram, who drove out the enemy with heavy loss, but did not succeed in capturing the queen; the Moulvee's position by Sir Edward Lugard on the 21st, with a similar result.

Arrival of Goorkhas under Jung Bahádoor.

Concluding operations.

Trifling British loss.

As on other occasions, Sir Colin Campbell had carefully protected his troops by artillery, of which he had a great preponderance; and the loss during the whole of the operations amounted to only 127 killed and 505 wounded—a marvellous contrast indeed with the results of battles under Lord Gough. Among the officers killed was the brave Captain Hodson, the hero of a hundred combats; and Captain Sir William Peel, of the 'Shannon,' the dashing leader of the Naval Brigade, having been severely wounded, was recovering when he was attacked by small-pox, and died on April 27. Of the enemy, upwards of 3,000 were buried, but of their loss in wounded no account could ever be gained. When victory had attended the British arms in November, Lukhnow was the scene of a fresh tragedy in the murder, under the orders of the fanatic Moulvee, of nineteen persons, some of them English ladies. They were taken out of their prison and shot by a party of the 71st Native Infantry. The only survivors, the widow of Captain Orr, and the sister of Sir Mountstuart Jackson, were rescued on the 16th by Captains McNeil and Boyle, with a party of Goorkhas, who had been guided to

Death of Sir William Peel.

Loss of the enemy.

Murder of English prisoners in Lukhnow.

Rescue of two ladies.

them by a friendly native, a feat which formed one of the many romantic episodes of the capture of the great city. On the 23rd, General Grant overtook a large body of fugitives on the road to Seetápoor, captured their guns, and routed them with heavy loss; and this affair brought the present military operations to a close. The rebels had indeed been driven out of Lukhnow, but they were to be the occasion of many a spirited combat before peace was restored to Northern India.

Lukhnow cleared of rebels.

The change in the plan of the commander-in-chief directed by the governor-general has been previously noticed, and as had been expected, the rebels had now united for the most part at Bareilly, where Khan Bahádoor Khan held sway, and as yet had not been molested. He was supported by the fanatical Mahomedans; but, from his oppressive conduct, the Hindoos of the province were already sighing for the return of their old masters, the English. With Khan Bahádoor Khan were now Prince Feróze of Dehly, the Bégum of Oudh, the fanatic Moulvee, and the Nána of Bithoor.

Operations against Bareilly.

Leaders of the rebellion.

For operations in Rohilkhund, three columns were employed under Generals Seaton, Walpole, and Jones. At a place called Rodamow, on April 14, during a rash assault upon a petty fort, which occasioned a greater loss of men than many a general action, the gallant young Brigadier-General Adrian Hope was killed, amidst the regret of the whole army. On the 23rd, Walpole beat the rebels handsomely at Sirsa, taking ten guns—a victory which left their bridge and the road to Bareilly open. Sir Colin Campbell was now advancing from Cawnpoor; and having joined Walpole, marched on Bareilly by way of Shahjehánpoor; while Jones's column, driving in the rebels' posts, approached the city from the opposite direction, on May 5, as Sir Colin's army was coming up. The object of the combined movement was to allow no one to escape. As it neared the city, the head of Sir Colin's advanced column was furiously attacked by a band of fanatics, sword in hand: but they were all bayonetted on the spot, to the number of 133. On the 6th, the heavy guns opened on the city, which was speedily taken, with all its magazines and stores; but the rebel leaders had effected their escape. The Moulvee now turned back upon Shahjehánpoor, where a weak force had been left; and a reinforcement under Brigadier Jones, which followed the enemy, had much ado to hold its own, obliging Sir Colin himself to hasten to its assistance on the 18th, when the rebels made off beyond the frontier of Oudh.

Campaign in Rohilkhund.

Death of Brigadier-General Adrian Hope.

Bareilly taken; the rebel leaders escape.

Sir E. Lugard's column from Lukhnow was directed against the rebel Köer Singh, who was still active in Báhar and the districts about Oudh. He was pursued from place to place by Brigadier Douglas, suffering much loss, and being himself wounded; but, on April 23, he turned upon a small force under Captain Le Grand from Arrah, and defeated it in a manner which caused much animadversion on its commander; when Douglas taking up the pursuit, chased the rebels into the jungles beyond, where, throughout June, a most harassing warfare was carried on; nor was it till the lapse of several months that the district was left in peace.

Sir E. Lugard's operations.

The manner in which the rebels contrived to re-unite in large bodies during May and June surprised the British commanders. On June 12, General Hope Grant was obliged to march from Lukhnow to Nawábgunj for the attack of 16,000 men, who had collected there; and after a sharp combat, the enemy was routed, with the loss of six guns and some 600 men left dead on the field. Shortly afterwards, however, their leader, the Moulvee, was killed in an attack upon a fort belonging to the Rajah of Powain, which proved to be a severe loss to the rebel cause. Mahomed Hassan tried to supply his place, and scattered bodies of rebels collected round him in the Górukpoor district; but on June 9 and 18 they were beaten and dispersed by Colonel Rowcroft's small force of soldiers, sailors, and Goorkhas, and were not allowed to re-unite.

Events of May and June.

Many attempts were made by bands of rebels, driven out of the upper provinces and now become banditti, to penetrate into the Eastern Gangetic districts; but they found themselves everywhere opposed and routed by the moveable columns watching these provinces; not, however, without several desperate combats—that with a small body of sailors encamped near the town of Cháibassa, in which for the first time the Koles of Singhbhoom took part with the rebels, and fought with much resolution, being the most remarkable.

CHAPTER IX.

MILITARY OPERATIONS AND EVENTS IN CENTRAL INDIA AND THE DECCAN, 1858.

No portion of the war against the mutineers and rebels was carried on with more brilliant spirit and success than the operations of Sir Hugh Rose, with his army of Bombay troops and the Hyderabad contingent. The military operations in Oudh and Rohilkhund had been conducted in an open and well-peopled country; those of Sir Hugh Rose, on

Sir Hugh Rose's campaign.

the contrary, were for the most part in one of the most rugged portions of India, the jungles, ravines, and broken ground of the Vindhya range, and Bundelkhund, the population of which had defied, for several hundred years, the continued efforts of the Mahomedan emperors. Having relieved Saugor on February 3, Sir Hugh marched towards Jhansy, which had not as yet been molested, and in which city the Ranee had fully established her authority. His success at the pass of Muddunpoor has been previously noticed. On March 17, Chandéree was captured by the First Brigade; and on the 23rd, Sir Hugh invested Jhansy, one of the strongest fortresses in Upper India. The siege operations had hardly commenced, when Tantia Tópee and the Rajah of Bánpoor, with an army of 20,000 men, advanced to the Ranee's assistance; and on March 31, their signal—an immense bonfire—that they had crossed the Betwah, was saluted by the fort batteries. Without slackening the siege attack, Sir Hugh took possession, during the night, of the road leading from the Betwah river towards Jhansy, with about 1,200 men of all arms, of whom nearly 700 were English soldiers. The numerical odds against him were immense, but the issue was a magnificent success. As the rebels advanced, before daylight, on April 1, they were met by Sir Hugh, totally defeated, and pursued for nine miles across the Betwah, losing 1,500 men with eighteen guns and all their military stores.

Jhansy invested.

Battle of the Betwah.

Defeat of the rebels.

This defeat cut off all hope of succour to the Ranee. Most of the guns of the fort had been silenced, and by April 2 a practicable breach had been effected. She had made negotiations for surrender, but the terms she offered were inadmissible with reference to the murders she had caused to be perpetrated in June; and on the 3rd, the breach was stormed with perfect success, and a lodgment made in the city. During the night, the Ranee contrived to evade the outposts, and fled on horseback, with a small escort of her cavalry. She was pursued for twenty miles, but finally escaped into the jungles. Next morning, the final attack on the citadel and town was made. So complete was the cordon about the walls, that none of the rebels escaped, and 5,000 of them perished; for in memory of the past events, no quarter was given or asked for. The whole British loss amounted to thirty-eight killed and 215 wounded. It is satisfactory to record, that the famishing women and children were fed by the English soldiers from their own rations, and afterwards supported by Sir Hugh Rose with the grain found in the fort.

Storm of Jhansy.

Escape of the Ranee.

The citadel taken.

Great loss of the rebels.

Some days elapsed in resting the men of the force, who, under constant hard work and the fierce heat which prevailed, had become thoroughly exhausted: but fresh laurels were in store for them. The Ranee of Jhansy had joined Tantia Tópee at Kalpy, where the rebel army had again concentrated, to the number of 20,000 men, and had thrown up entrenchments about the town of Koonch. Here, on May 7, they were attacked by Sir Hugh; who, piercing their strong line of defence in the centre, forced them to retire, which they did in good order, until pursued by the cavalry and horse-artillery their ranks were shattered, and the 52nd Bengal Native Infantry, which had mutinied at Jubbulpoor in September, killed almost to a man. Nine guns were taken, with all their stores and ammunition, and 600 Sepoys were slain on the field; the number of wounded being, as usual, impossible to ascertain. It was hopeless to do more on account of the heat, which affected alike victors and vanquished. The men had marched and fought for sixteen hours with the thermometer at 115° in the shade, but the rebels were nevertheless pursued for eight miles. Sir Hugh Rose, on this day, had four successive attacks of sunstroke, and was recovered with difficulty, and forty-six men were stricken down; but only five were killed, and twenty-six wounded, in the action.

Battle of Koonch.

Rout of the rebels.

Trifling English loss.

The rebel forces rallied again at Kalpy, a strong fort on the Jumna, and now amounted to 15,000 men; and on May 19, supported by a column from Cawnpoor under Colonel Maxwell, and another from the northward under Colonel Riddell, the place was attacked. On the 20th, the rebel army made a spirited sally upon Sir Hugh's force, but were beaten back. On the 22nd, being between a double fire, they again attacked Sir Hugh's troops, and were only driven into the town after an obstinate combat, suffering very heavily under the charges of cavalry and the guns of the horse-artillery. All that night, Kalpy was cannonaded by Maxwell, and early on the morning of the 23rd, Sir Hugh Rose's troops advanced to assault the town in two columns; but they encountered no resistance, for the enemy had fled, and the whole of the great rebel arsenal was taken possession of. Here were found fifty guns, with an immense quantity of stores, powder and ammunition. Nor did the rebels escape free: followed by the cavalry under Gall, and guns under Lightfoot, the pursuit was maintained, the Sepoys were cut down by hundreds, and every gun they possessed brought into camp.

Attack on Kalpy.

Assault of Kalpy.

Capture of the rebel arsenal.

Supposing that the labours of the Central India field force had come to an end, Sir Hugh Rose issued an order which is too remarkable to be omitted. 'Soldiers!' wrote Sir Hugh, 'you have marched more than a thousand

Sir Hugh Rose's general order.

miles, and taken more than a hundred guns. You have forced your way through mountain passes and intricate jungles, and over rivers; you have captured the strongest forts and beat the enemy, no matter what the odds, wherever you met him; you have restored extensive districts to the Government, and peace and order now reign where before, for twelve months, were tyranny and rebellion; you have done all this, and you have never had a check. I thank you with all my sincerity for your bravery, your devotion and your discipline. When you first marched, I told you, that you, as British soldiers, had more than enough of courage for the work which was before you, but that courage without discipline was of no avail; and I exhorted you to let discipline be your watchword. You have attended to my orders. In hardships, in temptations and in dangers you have obeyed your general, and you have never left your ranks. You have fought against the strong, and you have protected the rights of the weak and defenceless, of foes as well as friends. I have seen you, in the ardour of combat, preserve and place children out of harm's way. This is the discipline of Christian soldiers, and it is this which has brought you triumphant from the shores of Western India to the waters of the Jumna, and establishes without doubt that you will find no place to equal the glory of your arms.' The whole campaign, indeed, formed an exploit never surpassed in Indian warfare, and by few in the history of war.

But the labours of the force were not yet over. After his defeat at Koonch, Tantia Tópee had proceeded secretly to Gwalior, which was fixed as the next rallying point of the rebel army, and organised a conspiracy against Sindia, to be supported by the rebel troops as they should arrive. It was discovered by the Máhárajah and his minister, Dinkur Ráo, who advised a defensive policy till the arrival of British troops from Agra; but Sindia, eager to strike a blow at his faithless contingent and their comrades, and considering them to have lost organisation and spirit by the defeats they had endured—relying also on his household troops, whom he believed faithful—attacked the enemy at Barragaom on June 1, with 8,000 men and twenty-four guns. The result was unfortunate; Sindia's troops either joined the rebel forces, or returned to camp, and his army melted away, leaving him with a comparatively small escort. His special bodyguard, indeed, fought with their old Mahratta spirit, and suffered heavily; but it was impossible to rally the rest, and equally so to return to Gwalior. Sindia therefore rode off in the direction of Dhólpoor, on the Agra road, where, after providing for the safety of the Báiza Bye and the Ranees, Dinkur Ráo joined

Tantia Tópee at Gwalior.

Sindia attacks the rebels,

and is deserted by his troops.

Gwalior occupied by the rebels.

him in the evening. Gwalior, with all its guns, stores, and treasure, was now lost. Means of re-equipment of the rebel forces were ample, and speedily used; and the Nána Sahib of Bithoor was proclaimed Péshwah. Six months' pay was issued to the troops, and thus, as it were, a new army of 18,000 men, with all the famous Gwalior artillery, rose out of the ruins of the old, more powerful in resources that its predecessors.

Nána Sahib proclaimed Peshwah.

When this astounding news reached Sir Hugh Rose, he reassumed the command he had laid down, and leaving General Whitlock in charge of Kalpy, marched with two brigades under Stuart and Napier for Gwalior, on June 7; and being joined by a brigade from Agra under Colonel Riddell, the enemy was attacked in their post of the Morar cantonments on the 16th, and driven from it with heavy loss. It was a surprise; for the rebel Sepoys could not believe that troops which had already made a long night march, would assault them without rest; but the English brigades were led into the action without halting. Sir Hugh now waited the junction of Brigadier Smith's column from the westward, which came up in the course of the 17th, driving the enemy before him, from all the heights south of the city; and in the last charge by a squadron of the 8th Hussars attached to the force, the fierce Ranee of Jhansy, Lukshmee Bye, was killed by a trooper, without her sex being discovered. Dressed in male attire, she had been present in every action since her escape from Jhansy. With her, was killed another lady, supposed to be her sister, but who proved to have been a concubine of the late rajah. It was said that the Ranee had courted death on the field, to save herself from the ignominious fate she dreaded; nor is this at all improbable.

Sir Hugh Rose marches on Gwalior.

Surprise of the rebels at Morar.

The Ranee of Jhansy killed.

On the 18th, the whole of the rebel entrenchments and positions were stormed and captured, with all their guns, and their forces again obliged to take to flight; but their retreat was more compact and orderly than on former occasions, and they took with them no less than thirty field-pieces. Of this day's fighting Sindia was witness, having ridden in from Agra the day before; and on the 20th, under the salutes of the troops, and rejoicings of all his loyal subjects, he again took possession of his palace and capital. The mutineers had sacked both as far as possible, and in treasure, jewels, and property, Sindia's loss was estimated at fifty lacs of rupees—500,000*l*. On the same day Brigadier Robert Napier, with 600 cavalry and six field-guns, followed the enemy, and came up with them next day at Jourah Alipoor, where, dashing into their midst with-

Storm of the rebel position.

The rebels retreat.

Sindia restored.

Napier's victory closes the campaign.

out a check, he put them to utter flight, taking twenty-five guns; a feat which, considering the number—6,000—and as yet complete organisation of the rebels, and their numerous field-artillery, was, as the last, unsurpassed among the many brilliant feats of the campaign. Operations were now closed for the season, and Sir Hugh Rose finally resigned his command on June 20.

Meanwhile the column of General Roberts, on March 30, had attacked the mutineers of the Kóta contingent, who held possession of that city. About 400 of them were slain in the storm of the place; for, in consequence of their murder of Major Burton, the political agent, and his two sons, in the month of October, no quarter was given; but the greater number of them, with a considerable amount of treasure, succeeded in retiring to Jhansy, and were not pursued. General Whitlock, whose advance from Nagpoor has been already noticed, marched in the direction of Banda, by way of Chirkáree and Punnah; and on April 19, defeated the rebel troops of the Nawáb before the town of Banda, taking four guns, and leaving 500 of the enemy dead on the field. Thence General Whitlock pursued his way to Kalpy, of which place he was left in charge by Sir Hugh Rose.

General Roberts in Rajpootana.

Although the narration of the mutiny and its consequences has been confined to the transactions in Northern India, there were occurrences in other localities to the south, which need a brief notice. They were, in truth, escapes from great perils; for had the mutinous and rebellious proceedings been allowed to gain head in any case, they might have infected the Sepoys of the Bombay and Madras armies, neither of which were wanting in elements of danger. Poona and Bombay were by no means free from seditious intrigues in the early period of the mutiny; but they were chiefly on the part of Mahomedan fanatics, and were suppressed. Among the purely Mahratta portion of the Bombay army, no instance of disaffection occurred; but there were several regiments in which men from Oudh and Bundelkhund had been numerously enlisted; and in one of these, the 27th Native Infantry, 140 of all ranks mutinied at Kolapoor on July 31, and contrived, in the darkness and heavy rain of the night, to make off, having plundered the camp treasury of 50,000 rupees, and murdered three officers. By what means these men hoped to gain Hindostan, it is fruitless to imagine. Seventy-four were captured next day, and in the course of a few days most of the rest perished; for Captain Kerr, commanding the Mahratta Horse, with fifty troopers, marched from Sattara to Kolapoor—seventy-six miles—in twenty-

Mutinies in the Deccan.

Disaffection at Bombay and Poona.

Mutiny of 27th Native Infantry at Kolapoor.

Pursuit by Captain Kerr.

four hours, and pursuing the mutineers, came up with them in a temple where they were resting, and slew most of them. Of the whole regiment, sixty-three were executed, and sixty-six transported for life. The 21st Native Infantry, and three Oudh recruited regiments, showed a mutinous spirit as late as September 1857, being then at Kurrachee in Sinde, and were disarmed; but beyond these regiments, no symptoms of disaffection appeared in the native army of Bombay; and the conduct of the native troops of that presidency employed in Central India, which has been detailed, is entitled to the highest praise.

The 21st Native Infantry at Kurrachee.

The same eulogium attends the Hyderabad contingent, composed for the most part of men from Oudh and Northern India. They were sorely tempted to strike in with the rebels; but to none of the native troops with him did Sir Hugh Rose record a higher tribute of praise. Yet the 1st Nizam's Cavalry, stationed at Aurungabad, were in a state of mutiny early in June; and on the arrival of a column of Bombay troops under General Woodburn, a part of the regiment broke into open revolt, when they were fired on by the artillery, and pursued by the dragoons, many of them being captured and brought to trial; while those who escaped, proceeding to the station of Mominabad and to Hyderabad, excited much alarm throughout the country. Fortunately the infantry and artillery of the contingent remained loyal; for, if possible, better organised than the Gwalior force, the mutiny of the whole would have been extremely difficult to overcome, and would have extended rebellion to the Madras presidency.

The Nizam's contingent.

Partial mutiny of the 1st Nizam's Cavalry.

During the early part of the mutiny, and indeed until the capture of Dehly, the city of Hyderabad, with its immense population, was in a most critical condition; and the arrival of some of the mutineers from Aurungabad excited the fanatic Mahomedans to the utmost. Seditious sermons were preached in many of the mosques, and the 'faithful' urged to rise against the 'infidel' English. But the Nizam took no part in the movement, the minister, Salar Jung, though young in years, was firm and faithful, and made over to the Resident, Colonel Davidson, twelve of the Aurungabad men who had been apprehended in the city. This produced a slight outbreak, when some Rohillas and local fanatics attacked the residency on July 17, but were easily repulsed, and no further attempts at insurrection followed. The Arabs in the city, from whom violence had been apprehended, were under the control of the minister, and their chiefs and men were not to be seduced into rebellion.

City of Hyderabad.

Loyal conduct of the Nizam and his minister.

Attack on the residency.

A very widespread conspiracy was attempted in the Southern Mahratta districts of the Bombay presidency, towards the close of 1857, which, however, only produced two outbreaks—one of the Rajah of Nurgoond, who treacherously murdered Mr. Manson, the political agent, who had gone to remonstrate with him. The fort of Nurgoond, which resisted, was afterwards captured and dismantled. The second, by a Brahmin named Bheem Ráo, who gained temporary possession of the strong fortress of Kópul Droog, in the Ráichore Dooáb, and tried to raise the country, but failed. He was soon afterwards attacked by a Madras force from Bellary under Colonel Hughes, when he was killed in an attempt to retire to the upper works. There was no doubt, from intelligence received by the Resident at Hyderabad at this period, that the young Rajah of Shórapoor was deeply implicated in this treason; and having been a ward of the British Government during a long minority, Colonel Davidson sent his assistant, Captain Rose Campbell, to remonstrate with him, and if possible to save him. But no impression could be made upon the rebellious spirit that prevailed, and Captain Campbell's life being threatened, a portion of the contingent force stationed at Lingsoogoor, under Captain Wyndham, went to his assistance. This was treacherously attacked on February 7, 1858, by the rajah's tribe of Beydurs, with some Arabs and Rohillas; but after fighting all night they were repulsed, and early in the morning the moveable column under Colonel Hughes, which had been watching the Beydur districts, came up by a forced march, and uniting with Captain Wyndham, drove the Beydurs back into the town of Shórapoor, a position of immense natural strength. The day after, a Bombay column under Colonel Malcolm also arrived, and preparations were being made to assault the place, when it was discovered to be entirely deserted. The rajah had fled, and his Beydur militia and Rohilla and other levies had dispersed. The town was taken possession of, and the rajah, a few days afterwards, apprehended at Hyderabad. He was tried by a Commission, and sentenced to death; but his life was spared, and his sentence, in consideration of his youth, and the evil influences by which he had been surrounded, commuted to an imprisonment in the fort of Vellore for five years. On his way thither, however, the unfortunate young man shot himself—as was believed, by accident—with a revolver which he was examining. The transactions at Shórapoor were the last attempts at rebellion or mutiny in the Deccan. The principality of Shórapoor was attached, and with the Ráichore Dooáb, placed under the authority of Captain Meadows Taylor.

Rebellion in the Southern Mahratta country.

Bheem Ráo killed.

The Rajah of Shórapoor attacks a British force, but is defeated.

The rajah flies to Hyderabad.

CHAPTER X.

CURRENT EVENTS, INDIA AND ENGLAND, 1858 TO 1859

WHILE military operations were suspended during the rainy season, Lord Canning was occupied with considerations in regard to Oudh which need to be briefly reviewed. On March 31, 1858, he had sent Sir James Outram the draft of a proclamation to be issued in Oudh, which, with the exception of six landholders who had been loyal, confiscated the possessions of all others remaining, and declared the whole proprietary right in the soil of Oudh to belong to the British Government. If the abstract right of the question be considered, there can be no doubt that the principle upon which Lord Canning acted, apart from any consideration of rebellion, was correct. The Talookdars, as they were termed, were not landholders in freehold, but farmers or middlemen, between the government and the people; holding by authority from the government the office of arranging and collecting the revenues derived from the land, on an aggregate of villages or counties, or as it might be. No doubt these offices had, in many instances, become hereditary; and in most cases the Talookdars were locally too powerful to be displaced by an effete government like that of Oudh under the king; but Lord Canning considered it most expedient to assert the full right of Government to the land, leaving the cases of individual proprietorship or hereditary occupation to be settled hereafter. He could not recognise any real title of proprietary possession in what had never been admitted to be such by the former government; and the records of the country showed that much of the assumed right had been consequent on fraud and violence.

Proclamation for Oudh.

The Talookdars.

The measure was, however, a blow against the proudest and most powerful local aristocracy in India; the speedy pacification of the province was an event of all others to be desired, and admitting the proprietary right of Government in the land as a position not to be disputed, there might be, on the part of the Talookdars, many claims of ancient hereditary occupancy, of feudal tenure, and recognition of that tenure by preceding governments, extending to periods even antecedent to the Mahomedan conquest. Oudh had, for ages, been one of the strongholds of the Aryan people; and the claims of the descendants of their chieftains could not be ignored by a

Considerations against confiscation.

sweeping confiscation of all, without distinction or investigation. So thought Sir James Outram, who made a spirited and earnest remonstrance against the proclamation. He protested against confiscation at large, not only as unjust in principle, but as calculated to perpetuate disaffection; and asserted that before the conquest many of the Talookdars had been unjustly dealt with by the English settlement officers, whose injudicious proceedings had mainly incited them to rebellion. While Lord Canning was obliged to admit that such had been the case, he allowed Outram to soften the terms of the proclamation in some degree; but its main purport was not altered, and the speedy submission of the landholders was more consequent perhaps upon Sir James Outram's personal character, and the judicious proceedings of his successor, Mr. Robert Montgomery, than on any actual trust in the subsequent mercy of Government. Sir James was soon afterwards promoted to the Supreme Council.

Outram's remonstrance.

The terms of Lord Canning's proclamation were repudiated in England by means of a harsh and sarcastic dispatch from Lord Ellenborough, the President of the Board of Control; but the work of settlement had already gone on well under the effect of the measures taken by Mr. Montgomery. New titles were granted to Talookdars, and they were constituted magistrates; new settlements of revenue were made with them, and, as a local aristocracy, they became not only more secure than they had been before, as well in their possessions as against arbitrary exaction and demands, but every incentive to exertion in the improvement of their dependents was held out to them. Had the annexation of Oudh been followed by a similarly just and conciliatory policy, there can be little doubt that all or most of the great Talookdars would not only have abstained from rebellion, but assisted Government to subdue the mutiny. Their action was in fact produced by the dread of abolition of their hereditary rights and privileges, which, under the attempt to introduce the land settlement measures of the north-west provinces, were being ignored and swept away. As had been the case in Sinde and the Punjâb, Oudh was disarmed, and the number of arms collected was very large. Six hundred and eighty four cannon, 186,177 fire-arms, 565,321 swords, 50,311 spears, and 636,683 weapons of other descriptions were destroyed, while 1,569 forts, great and small, were demolished or dismantled.

Repudiation of Lord Canning's proclamation in England.

The new settlement.

On July 8, 1859, peace was proclaimed by Lord Canning; and July 28 was fixed as a day of general thanksgiving, 'a humble offering of gratitude to Almighty God for the many mercies vouchsafed.'

Proclamation of peace.

The events of 1857 had aroused in the people of England a degree of interest in Indian affairs which had never before existed. Under a national struggle, impending between England and a cruel enemy, under widespread affliction, and the terror of losing what it had taken a century to gain, the feelings of all classes were excited beyond any former precedent, and it was soon manifest in what form their demonstration would have practical effect. There could at least be no further double government; responsibility could no longer be bandied about between the company and the crown; and in regard to responsibility for the outbreak—whether it resulted from the greased cartridges alone, or whether it was the effect of previous disaffection and combination in the native army; of long existing and rapidly gathering mistrust and misapprehension among the people—suspicion of proselytism, of material improvements, of confiscations, of Mahomedan and Hindoo fanaticism and intrigue, or that general antagonism to progress and change, in which history only repeats itself—it was bootless to inquire. Henceforward, one government only could be permitted; and that of the crown must succeed that of the company, which long since virtually, was now actually dead.

Feeling aroused in England.

In the eyes of the people of India, the rule of the company, in accordance with the popular superstition, had ceased with the mutiny. Whose were the thousands of English soldiers? whose the generals that commanded them? whose the ships that brought them? None but the Queen's. The company was dead. The Queen had taken up her sceptre to rule India, and would do it, as many hoped, graciously, with honour to herself and respect to her people. At best, as the people said, the company was now known to have been a mere farmer (Ijáradar) of the land; and it was not honourable or endurable that princes and nobles should be farmed out in common, with the contingency of unchecked absorption of their territories whenever the company pleased. All the former prestige of the 'Koompany Bahádoor' had departed with the unequivocal display of its weakness; but the government of the Queen could not, indeed, be disputed; and all India was witness to the spirit and energy of the mighty nation which had put forth its resources in a manner not to be mistaken. If there were many who feared the principles of the new power more than those of the old; who had believed in the conservatism of the company, and its unwillingness either for absorption of territory or proselytism of the people; whose worst fears during the religious panic seemed about to be confirmed—the time was past when such opinions could have weight with the people at large, who, wit-

Confirmation of the prophecy of Plassy.

Native opinion.

nessing the result of local combination for resistance, passively submitted to whatever might befal; nor were others wanting, who dreaded that the old 'farm' might be renewed, who considered that the company would spend millions to secure it, and that once secured, with extended power, the last term of charter would be worse than the preceding, and was in proportion to be dreaded.

Among all these, and innumerable phases of popular feeling in India, some indescribably childish and absurd, others grave and thoughtful; and after a prolonged consideration by the Parliament of England, the Act that provided for the sole dominion of the crown in India passed into law on August 2, 1858. On November 1, a year after the rule of the company had fallen into abeyance, the gracious proclamation of Queen Victoria was issued by the governor-general at Allahabad, translated into all the vernacular languages of India, read at every native court, and freely circulated to all classes of the people. It was admirably worded, and fell like oil upon troubled waters. By it, all existing dignities, rights, usages, and treaties were confirmed: all grounds of suspicion of tampering with caste or religious faith removed: and from the highest to the lowest ranks of society, a reliant spirit of calm assurance and acquiescence in its simple provisions was at once effected. Lying at the feet of the conqueror, it was felt that much that was new might have been imposed on the people of India; but the gracious words established no new principles, and the security established by the Queen's edict communicated a like feeling throughout the country, which was too genuine to be mistrusted. From henceforth, a new era had dawned upon India.

Dominion of the queen.

Proclamation.

Its beneficial effects.

Before the close of the year, the commander-in-chief, now Lord Clyde, was again in the field, and the last efforts of mutineers in Oudh were gradually crushed. The Queen's proclamation had promulgated amnesty to all, except those directly concerned in the murders of the mutiny, and many availed themselves of it, and surrendered; but there were others still defiant and desperate, and against these Lord Clyde and forces under several commanders, proceeded to act without delay. On November 9, the Rajah of Améthie submitted; but the Sepoys who had gathered round him, supposed to be 20,000 strong, got away with their guns. Rajah Bénee Mádhoo, after offering terms of submission, which could not be accepted, escaped from Lord Clyde and Sir Hope Grant's forces, and took the field with his army, his guns, and his treasure. He was pursued from place to place; other bodies of rebels being routed as they were encountered, and finally, the

The last campaign against mutineers.

Rajah Bénee Mádhoo.

whole, with their leaders, among whom were the Nána and his brother, Bála Ráo, were driven by the close of the year across the Raptee river into the Terái jungles of Nipál, having lost all their guns, stores, and well nigh means of subsistence. Here, with the way of escape back into Oudh carefully closed, and access to Nipál proper denied, the rebel Sepoys suffered fearfully from the pestilential climate. Many perished by the forces of Rowcroft, Kelly, and the Nipálese; and by hundreds, those that survived came to the British posts, and surrendered themselves. Bénee Mádhoo was killed by the Nipálese, and the Nána, his brother, and Azim Oolla, died in the jungles, with many other men of note who had been actively engaged in the rebellion, in which, as Lord Clyde recorded, 150,000 native troops had been subdued.

The rebels are driven into the Terái.

Fate of the principal leaders.

Lord Canning's progress through the country was a succession of brilliant assemblies, at which the loyal princes and people were received with all the magnificence which the occasion demanded. Many were decorated by him, many rewarded, and it was evident that the effects of the tumult were fast passing away. In England the new constitution of the Council, consisting of the Secretary of State for India, with twelve members, chosen from the late Court of Directors and the Indian services, worked surely and harmoniously under Lord Stanley; and in India, while no new administrative measures were brought forward, the old were strengthened and improved.

Lord Canning's progress.

Constitution of the new Council.

The war was dying out everywhere. The last effort was made by Prince Feróze, in concert with Tantia Tópee. The former foreseeing destruction in Nipál, dashed through Oudh, and joined Tantia, who, with what remained of his army, was still eluding the various columns which strove to hem him in. From Rajpootana to Berar, the pursuit never slackened, and his attempts to break into the Deccan were skilfully frustrated; but this could not long endure. His last hiding-place was betrayed, and, on April 7, 1859, he was seized while asleep in the Parone jungle, two miles from Seepree, in Malwah, and there he was tried and executed. Mán Singh, his fellow-rebel and leader, had surrendered on the 2nd, and directed Major Meade to Tantia's last camp. The fate of the other rebel chiefs need not be followed in detail.

The last effort of the war.

Tantia Tópee executed.

The rest of Lord Canning's incumbency might have passed away without any material event; but discontent in the European portion of the company's army at one time threatened very serious consequences. On the amalgamation of the company's with the Queen's troops, it would have

Discontent of European troops.

been wise to have allowed a small bounty on re-enlistment. The men protested against being transferred from one service to another without special provision or agreement; and, under Lord Canning's order, demanded their discharge, which, with a free passage to England, could not be denied them. They were accordingly sent home, and thus the Government, by an unwise economy or obstinacy, lost the services of nearly 10,000 seasoned veterans, whose passages to England cost far more than the small bounty which would have satisfied them. One regiment only, the 5th Bengal Fusileers, broke into mutiny at Berhampoor, and threatened violence; but their discontent was happily brought to a conclusion without a resort to force; and after the measure of amalgamation was passed, the establishment of nine regiments of royal infantry, three of cavalry, and additions to the Engineers and Artillery corps, absorbed the remainder, both officers and men, of the old local European troops of the company.

European troops

CHAPTER XI.

LORD CANNING'S ADMINISTRATION (*concluded*), 1859 TO 1862.

Lord Lawrence's opinion of the mutiny.

THE opinion of Lord Lawrence in regard to the mutiny was, 'that it had its origin in the army itself; it is not attributable to any external or antecedent conspiracy whatever, although it was afterwards taken advantage of by disaffected persons, to compass their own ends; the approximate cause was the cartridge affair, and nothing else.' There was, no doubt, much foundation for this opinion; but it may hardly be considered to reach the depth of the occurrence, and the general feeling of uneasiness, which prevailed at the end of 1856, and beginning of 1857, though it might not have caused mutiny of the native soldiery, or rebellion of the people, nevertheless helped to encourage their progress. The conduct of the people, even in the most disturbed districts, was, for the most part, singularly neutral. The agricultural, mercantile, and manufacturing population took no part in the rebellion, or in demonstrations in its favour. The only Zemindar, among the hundreds of Bahár, who rebelled, was Köer Singh, a man whose embarrassments had rendered him notoriously desperate. All Bengal was perfectly tranquil. The noble aid given by the Sikhs, at the call of Sir John Lawrence, proves that they had no desire to re-establish a national independence, and were content with the local government. When Khan Bahádoor Khan, the chief of Rohilkhund,

Conduct of the people.

imposed his authority upon the province, the Hindoos submitted because they had no power to resist, and soon found by his exactions and oppressions, as well as by interference with their religious observances, that a fanatical Mahomedan rule would be unendurable, and they hailed the re-establishment of the English Government with unfeigned rejoicings. All Rajpootana was tranquil and well affected; and the substantial aid rendered by the Sikh chiefs west of the Sutlej, formed a memorable and gratifying proof of their entire loyalty. Counting the number of actual rebels in Central India, the Ranee of Jhansy, the Nawábs of Banda and Futtehgurh, the Rajah of Bánpoor, and a few other minor chiefs and persons; and comparing them with the loyal princes, Sindia, Holkar, the Máhárajahs of Jeypoor, Joudhpoor, Alwur, and Oodypoor, the Rajahs of Rewah, Bhurtpoor, and Kóta, the Bégum of Bhopál, the Nawáb of Rampoora, and others whose independent territories almost cover Central India, the preponderance on the side of attachment to the British Government was enormous.

Condition of Western and Southern India.

As will have been seen by the narrative of events, neither the rulers nor the people south of the Nerbudda took any part in the disaffection. The Gáikwar of Baroda; the people of the lately annexed provinces of Sattara and Berar; the Nizam, and the whole of his populous dominions; the great Mahratta families who possess independent territories; the Mahratta people at large, who might have been stirred to action by a new Péshwah and the memories of their plunder of India; with those of Mysore, and the whole of the south—were loyal and tranquil during the excitement of the period, and never seem to have entertained a doubt of the ultimate triumph of the English, over an outbreak as sudden as it was fearful. The only element of apprehension was the Mahomedans, who were most affected by fanaticism; and without doubt there were many of the southern Mahomedans of Arcot and Vellore, the descendants of the old Moghul and Patán soldiers and colonists, who, never perfectly reconciled to Christian domination, looked eagerly and anxiously to news of success at Dehly, and were ready to make a diversion in the king's favour, should there be opportunity. As for the Hindoos, as soon as the first excitement had passed away, they relapsed into their usual condition of passive obedience. The weird prophecy in regard to Sumbut 1914 had indeed been fulfilled: but war and tumult had passed away without affecting them.

Position of the English.

Triumphantly, then, had England come out of the ordeal; and with renewed confidence. The test which many had dreaded, had been suddenly and fiercely applied; and never was disaffection in possession of such powerful auxiliaries as a disciplined army of 150,000 men, with ample material of war, and a general excitement of the people from other causes; yet no one rose except a few disaffected nobles and State officials, who, without territory or subjects, were supported only by the lawless scum of the districts in which they lived—hereditary robbers and marauders, whom a powerful government had been able to restrain, but who returned at once to ancient evil ways directly its authority ceased, temporarily, to exist. If the loyal classes of the convulsed districts needed any confirmation of motives of attachment to the British Government, it was furnished to them in the insecurity which prevailed as long as its functions were suspended, and the security which accompanied their re-establishment.

It has not been possible to follow the course of events in the minor presidencies; and indeed there is little to record, after the first shock of the mutiny had been endured. Lord Harris at Madras, and Lord Elphinstone at Bombay, proved invaluable coadjutors to the governor-general; and the manner in which troops were forwarded to Calcutta, and the Madras and Bombay columns despatched for service in Central India, is entitled to the highest praise. Bombay had indeed the largest share in those operations, and endured the most keen alarm; but Lord Elphinstone's prompt and decisive action against the first demonstration of the Nána's intrigues, and Mahomedan fanaticism, prevented any chance of their further development. Exhausted, however, by the climate, and by anxiety, he went to England in 1860, only to die. So also the chivalrous James Outram, who, with his constitution thoroughly impaired, was unable to retain his seat in Council, and retired, also only to die. Sir John Lawrence, too, equally suffering, was saved by a speedy retirement to England, where he was appointed to the Council of India, and was succeeded in the Punjâb by Mr., now Sir Robert, Montgomery, from Oudh.

Minor presidencies.

Deaths of Lord Elphinstone and of Sir James Outram.

In 1860 and 1861, reforms of the administration of justice were carried out in the amalgamation of the Supreme or Queen's and the Sudder or Company Courts, under one chief justice, with assistant judges, some practising barristers, some civilians of not less than ten years' standing. Natives were also eligible for appointment to the latter offices. The courts of the assistant judges formed courts of appeal from others beneath them, and their jurisdiction extended to criminal as well as civil cases and suits. The penal code, now improved by trial and extension, also became law, and was made applicable to all localities in India. In this year also, the first Indian minister of finance, Mr. Wilson, took his place in the General

Judicial reforms.

Mr. Wilson's income-tax.

Council of India, and the most material of his proposed measures was an income-tax, applicable at large to natives as well as Europeans. Against so fair an impost, and against the taxation at all of sections of the community on which, under native administrations, heavy burthens had been laid, Sir Charles Trevelyan, then governor of Madras, protested vehemently, and to an extent for which, as it amounted to positive insubordination, he was superseded in his government.

Sir Charles Trevelyan's protest.

Unfortunately Mr. Wilson died before his financial measures could be matured, and was succeeded by Mr. Laing, whose principal reform was the establishment to some extent of a paper currency. The redemption of the land revenue for money payments was also determined by the governor-general in council, as well as the sale of waste lands; but it does not appear that in either case any material progress has been experienced.

Death of Mr. Wilson.

No sooner had war ceased, than the great public works of India, which had been suspended during its existence, were resumed with spirit. The North-Western Railway progressed rapidly towards Dehly; the Great Indian Peninsular Railway had advanced to Sholapoor, in the Deccan, and very materially towards Jubbulpoor. The Sinde Railway from Kurrachee, along the line of the Indus, the Madras Railway to connect the eastern with the western coasts, were also in course of completion. Along with railways, canals were making great progress: the great Ganges Canal was extended in several branches; the Bárce Dooáb Canal in the Punjâb was under completion. The noble works on the Krishna and Godavery rivers were in active operation in the Madras Presidency, and a canal for irrigation and traffic from the Toombuddra river to Madras had been projected, and has since been partially executed. The metalled trunk road which reaches from Calcutta to Peshâwur, a distance of 1,500 miles, was finished; and it is impossible to detail the many other works, in metalled roads, which were under execution in all the presidencies. It had been recognised, at last, as a public duty, that a portion of the revenue of India should be applied to guarantees of interest upon railways, and to an enlarged system of public works, and the impetus given by this measure to the railways was only what had been expected.

Resumption of public works; details.

The only check to the universal and fast extending prosperity of India was caused by the famine in the north-western provinces of 1860—1861. No rain fell, and between the Jumna and the Sutlej the sufferings of the people were frightful. No less than 500,000 human beings are believed to have perished, and the whole of the population, notwithstanding the benevolent exertions of Government, of individuals, and

Famine in the north-western provinces.

the receipt of large subscriptions from England, endured misery which it was hopeless to alleviate in proportion to the existing necessity. During its continuance, the exertions of Sir Robert Montgomery in the Punjâb, of Mr. Edmonstone in the north-western provinces, and of Colonel Baird Smith, the engineer-in-chief, can never be overrated; and to the regret of all India, the latter, prostrated by his exertions, died soon after he had left Calcutta, on his voyage to England.

Death of Colonel Baird Smith.

In November 1861, the governor-general suffered a severe affliction in the loss of Lady Canning, and prepared to return to England. His last splendid court was assembled at Allahabad, where, on November 1, he conferred the order of the Star of India, newly established, upon those of the native princes of the north-west who had afforded the most material aid during the mutiny. These were Sindia, the Sikh chief of Puttiala, the Bégum of Bhopál, and the Nawáb of Rampoora. To His Highness the Nizam the same decoration was forwarded, and on November 25, he was invested with the insignia by Colonel Davidson, the Resident. His Highness had already received some very substantial acknowledgments of obligations. In 1860 a new treaty was made in regard to the assigned territory, by which Berar alone, the revenues of which had materially increased under British management, was retained, and the other large provinces, Daraseo and Nuldroog on the west, and the Ráichore Dooáb on the south-west, were restored to him. The province of Shórapoor, which had been confiscated after the rajah's treason, was also conferred upon him, and yielded an annual net revenue of three and a half lacs of rupees—35,000*l.*—and the balance of his debt, the principal of which amounted to fifty lacs of rupees—500,000*l.*—was altogether cancelled. In addition, a princely gift of various choice articles of English manufacture, valued at 10,000*l.*, or a lac of rupees, a magnificent diamond ring, and a jewelled sword, were sent as a khillut or present of honour, accompanied by gifts of the value of 3,000*l.* each, to Salar Jung the prime minister, who was afterwards created a knight of the Star of India, and to the Nawáb Shumsh-ool-Oomra, chief of the Hyderabad nobles. It is possible that the Nizam may have been disappointed by the measures of Lord Dalhousie being still retained; but any reversal of the final settlement in regard to the pay of the contingent, and other obligations of His Highness's government, was considered inadmissible. There was, however, a claim for surplus upon the management of the assigned districts from the commencement, and this was under consideration for final adjustment.

Lord Canning's farewell Durbar.

The Star of India.

His Highness the Nizam.

It is hardly necessary to follow the details of honours and rewards, which were conferred upon individuals who had proved faithful or done good service during the mutiny; but before his final departure from India, in March 1862, Lord Canning had the satisfaction of bringing them to a close. As he was leaving India, addresses from all sections of the community, both English and native, bade him an affectionate farewell; and it was evident that the first fierce clamour against his clemency had been softened by a late, but full, recognition of its justice and necessity. But India and his anxieties had proved too much for his constitution, and he died shortly after his arrival in England, on June 17. The last governor-general of the company had become the viceroy of the Queen, and during his term of office had had to encounter and overcome the fiercest storm that had ever broke over the English power. Future historians, while they may notice his natural slowness of conception and of action, will not fail to recognise the inherent firmness and unostentatious greatness of his character, which, through the double storm of English animadversion and the fierce contest of the mutiny, enabled him to surmount both in an honest, unswerving, practical endeavour to do his duty to his country, and to the people committed to his charge. At the worst period, and when surrounded by panic-stricken men, he never lost confidence in himself or his means, and his calm courage and perseverance, while they cheered and encouraged every subordinate authority, gained him an eventual success, the value of which will be enhanced by time.

Honours and rewards.

Lord Canning leaves India.

His death

and character.

CHAPTER XII.

VICEROYALTIES OF LORD ELGIN AND SIR JOHN LAWRENCE, 1862 TO 1865.

Lord Elgin, who had been employed as H.M.'s plenipotentiary in China, and had brought the transactions there to a conclusion, was appointed Lord Canning's successor, and assumed the office of Viceroy of India on March 12, 1862. Sir Charles Trevelyan was appointed finance minister, in succession to Mr. Laing, who had retired; and the Legislative Council of India, extended under the term of the new Act of 1861, now contained three native members, all men of note and mark: the Sikh Rajah of Puttiala, Rajah Déo Narráin Singh of Benares, and

Lord Elgin succeeds as viceroy.

Sir Charles Trevelyan as minister of finance.

Appointment of native councillors.

Rajah Dinkur Rao, the minister of Sindia. Three gentlemen not belonging to the service, Messrs Cowie, Fitzwilliam and Forbes, gave an appearance of freedom and representative constitution to an assembly which, for latter times, had been too restricted. On February 5, 1863, Lord Elgin left Calcutta for the upper provinces, holding public receptions or durbars, which were attended by the chiefs and nobles of the various districts through which he passed. That at Agra was a most magnificent spectacle, and again collected the princes of Rajpootana and Central India, as had been the case under Lord Canning. The viceroy proceeded to Simlah; but he was already suffering under a chronic disorder, and on his return he died at Dhurmsalla, in the Himalayas, on November 20, 1863. His brief tenure of office allowed of no opportunity or proof of his capacity, and was simply one of routine. During its continuance, a conspiracy among the Wáhábee fanatics of Patna was found to have extended to Sittána, on the Afghan frontier, and to have had for its design a rising of Mahomedans in the east, as well as in the west, with considerable sympathy, if not assistance in money, from the south. Had not the conspiracy at Patna been discovered and checked by the local magistrate, Mr. Tayler, early in 1857, it might have assisted the rebellion in some degree; but though the bitter spirit and malignant intention of the latter attempt were clearly manifest, its impotence was patent to all but its originators.

Durbar at Agra.

Death of Lord Elgin.

Wáhábee conspiracy.

The idea of a new Mahomedan conspiracy in India, however, excited apprehension in England: and the locality in which armed demonstration had occurred, Sittána, on the north-west frontier of the Punjâb, demanded the presence of one who should be able to apply personal acquaintance with the people to the suppression or prevention of war. Sir John Lawrence, therefore, was chosen to succeed Lord Elgin. Though not desiring office, he at once responded to the call, and proceeded to Calcutta without delay. Meanwhile the campaign against the Sittána fanatics had assumed somewhat formidable dimensions. Other Afghan hill-tribes were taking part with the Sittána rebels; and, as it was termed, the 'Umbeyla campaign,' threatened to bring about a coalition of all the Afghans of the mountains against the British power, and an invasion of the Punjâb. General Neville Chamberlain, who had conducted the first operations, was severely wounded, and a retirement of the forces from what appeared to be a fruitless mountain warfare—a warfare which in the time of the Emperor Akbur had caused the destruction of a fine army—was almost determined upon by the Council of Calcutta, in spite of the remons-

Sir John Lawrence appointed viceroy.

Campaign against Sittána fanatics.

Proposed retirement.

trances of Sir Hugh Rose, who had succeeded Lord Clyde as commander-in-chief. At this crisis, Sir William Denison, the governor of Madras, reached Calcutta, to act as viceroy till the arrival of Lord Elgin's successor. He saw at once the inadvisability of retirement, and directed Sir Hugh Rose to press the operations against the fanatics. This was done with spirit and judgment, and during the ensuing month the primary object of the campaign was attained, and submission made by the chiefs of the frontier tribes.

Sir William Denison takes charge of the viceroyalty.

The Umbeyla campaign renewed.

In many respects, both operations were remarkable. The Sittána fanatics resided chiefly in the town and district of Mulka, on the north side of a mountain which separated the Indus from the Kabool river, just above their junction; and Mulka could only be approached through the territories of other mountain-tribes, the Eusofzyes and Bonáirs, with whom there was no intention of interfering. On October 20, 1863, the British force, which consisted of two English and six native regiments, advanced to the Umbeyla pass, a proclamation having been issued to explain the motive of the campaign. As it progressed, the people were found civil and obliging; but near Umbeyla, shots were fired, a skirmish ensued, and for several days in succession the fighting was almost continuous, the object of the enemy being to close the pass behind the British force. On the 26th, the position which had been taken up was attacked with much resolution by a large body composed of men from Swát and from Mulka, who had joined the Bonáirs of Umbeyla. The enemy was repulsed in every attack; but it was impossible not to see that progress onwards, into even wilder defiles, and without supplies, was impossible, and that were any advance made, the pass behind must inevitably be closed. From the time the army took up its position and began to clear a road, until November 20, there were daily combats, attended with much actual hand-to-hand fighting. The 'Eaglecrag' picket was twice taken by the enemy and retaken, and in his last and third assault for its recovery, General Chamberlain was badly wounded. Reinforcements were, however, coming up, and the force held its ground, now less molested than before; but the enemy were known to be collecting men in large numbers. This was the period at which retirement was contemplated by the Council of Calcutta, but opposed by Sir William Denison: and when Sir Hugh Rose was at liberty to give the necessary order for advance, it was made effectively.

Details of operations.

For some days negotiations with the Akhoond of Swát, and other heads of tribes, had been in progress; but they came to nothing, and on December 15, General Garnock, now in command, moved to attack the enemy's position at Laloo, about two miles distant, with his whole force. It was very strong, and held by some thousands of the enemy; but it was stormed with a rush, and the Afghans fled. Umbeyla was assaulted next morning, the enemy retiring into the fastnesses of the mountains above, with the exception of one party, which attacked the 23rd Native Infantry and Pioneers, sword in hand, and did considerable mischief, but were in turn put to flight. The Bonáirs now submitted, and a party of them volunteered to accompany a detachment of English troops to Mulka and destroy the place. The village was found deserted, but the powder-factory was blown up, the houses burned, and the object of the campaign—the lesson sought to be impressed on these rude tribes, that no resistance or difficulty of access could prevent the attainment of a desired object—seemed to be duly appreciated. On Christmas-day, 1863, the force left the Chumla valley, and regained the plains; but the road which had been made by the troops was immediately destroyed.

Successful attack on the enemy's position.

Mulka captured.

In 1862–1863, the cessation of supplies of cotton from America, owing to the civil war, produced a corresponding demand for Indian produce, and the prices rose an enormous extent. Surat cotton, of which the former value in England was from threepence to fourpence a pound, had risen, in cases of good quality, to nearly two shillings, while all others had increased in proportion. The value of exports rose in Bombay from 43,000,000*l.* to 63,000,000*l.* sterling in a single year; and the importation of the precious metals, silver and gold, was of immense amount. Nor was there any sudden cessation either of demand or extra value; both were steadily maintained. This influx of wealth changed the condition of the people of Western India very materially, and combined with the large expenditure on public works, had the effect of increasing the values of food, of labour, and of manufactures in an extraordinary manner throughout India. Much apprehension was felt in Europe at the immense absorption of gold and silver by India; but it was unavoidable, as it would have been impossible to pay in manufactures only, for what was exported under the exceptional demand.

Rise in value of cotton.

Its effect in Western India.

Sir John Lawrence arrived in Calcutta on January 12, 1864. It is little to say he was enthusiastically received by all ranks and all classes, European as well as native. He had many personal friends among both; and one who had so nobly done his part in the period of alarm and disaster, whose influence and exertions had so materially checked

Arrival of Sir John Lawrence.

the tide of rebellion, was evidently the most fitted to follow up what Lord Canning had begun, and in which he himself had borne so large a part. As from his seat in the Indian Council of England he had been able to follow the course of events without check, so he took up his office at the interval of a month, without any break in his knowledge of what was passing. He found India at peace; the Umbeyla campaign was at an end, and provincial exhibitions of local produce and manufactures were begun by that in the Punjâb, which was eminently successful, and rightly directed by Sir Robert Montgomery.

The viceroy at Lahore.

Sir John Lawrence did not remain long in Calcutta; he proceeded to Simlah for the hot season, and at the close of the monsoon went direct to Lahore. Here, after six years, he had the gratification of meeting his old Sikh friends and addressing them in their own language, in an eloquent but simple speech. He told them of the interest which the Queen of England felt in them all, how she had charged him to be careful of them, and how deeply she and Prince Albert desired their prosperity. He reviewed the measures of his own, his brother's, and successive administrations; how taxation had been lightened, how canals and roads had been constructed, and how means of education had been provided; and concluded by a prayer, which must have moved all hearts present, that God would guard and protect them, and give them all needful for their benefit. Few great assemblies in India have resembled this, at once solemn and joyful, with thankful remembrances of the past, and bright anticipations for the future.

Measures for the improvement of English soldiers.

During 1864, Sir John Lawrence's exertions to improve the condition of English soldiers in India were begun earnestly, and to the last period of his tenure of office never ceased. For their occupation and amusement he sanctioned reading-rooms, gardens, workshops, means of athletic exercise and games—in short, everything calculated to improve their moral and physical condition. Nor were means of religious study and improvement omitted, but, on the contrary, facilitated by provision of religious works, and apartments for their private study. Their barracks also were surveyed and improved, and in many places altogether reconstructed: the old sanatarium in the hill-stations enlarged, and other localities in India which enjoyed a cool climate, with fresh mountain air, sought out. Nor was sanitary reform confined to the location of European troops. Outbreaks of cholera, of fever, of small-pox, fall so heavily and so unexpectedly upon India, that investigation of the causes by a sanitary commission, opened in 1861, and continued throughout the country, not only brought to light many unknown causes of malaric influence, but suggested remedial measures.

A quarrel with the State of Bhótan was in progress on the viceroy's arrival in India, which had arisen out of claims by the Bhótanese Láma upon portions of cultivated territory, called Dooars, lying at the foot of the mountains in Assam. These had been annexed after the province came into possession, and a sum of money, to be paid annually, was agreed to in compensation. The same arrangement was made with the Bengal Dooars, but it did not restrain the Bhótanese from making inroads into them, kidnapping British subjects, and committing other excesses. The money payment was therefore refused, until security should be obtained; a measure which led to reprisals on the part of the Bhótanese. In November 1863, the Hon. Ashley Eden was sent as ambassador to the capital of Bhótan, with a view to arrange a definite treaty, accompanied by a small escort. His mission was an unwise one, in every respect. It was impossible to protect him; from first to last he was ill-treated and insulted by every means of indignity, and finally a release of the Dooars was extorted from him, when he was suffered to retire.

Bhótan war.

Causes of the war.

The Hon. Ashley Eden's mission.

His conduct, and the treatment he had met with, alike produced an outburst of indignation; and in November 1864, war was declared against Bhótan. It was badly conducted, and the country proved very unhealthy, nevertheless, some positions were occupied, and maintained; but one, Dewángiry, was retaken by the enemy, with some spirit, and so far from the Bhótanese showing any disposition to submit, they appeared more reliant in their resources. A new campaign was therefore necessary, and a heavy force was assembled. Dewángiry was retaken, Dalimkote captured and held; but it was not till 1865, by which time the troops in occupation had suffered frightfully from the climate, that it was determined to conquer and annex the whole territory. This produced a disposition to treat on the part of Bhótan, and peace ensued; but it may be said it was purchased, by an agreement to pay 25,000 rupees per annum for the Bengal Dooars. The whole proceeding, from first to last, was unfortunate and ill-managed. Had sufficient forces been thrown into the Dooars in the first instance, and the passes watched, the Bhótanese might have been defied till they were obliged to become suppliants for restoration of their assumed rights.

War declared.

Second campaign.

Unsatisfactory conclusion of the war.

CHAPTER XIII.

THE ADMINISTRATION OF SIR JOHN LAWRENCE (*continued*), 1865 TO 1867.

Temple's administration of the central provinces.

In the year 1862, Mr., now Sir Richard, Temple had been nominated chief commissioner of the 'central provinces,' an aggregate of previous smaller and separate jurisdictions, including Nagpoor, the Saugor and Nerbudda territory, and part of Bundelkhund. It comprised an immense area of about 250,000 square miles, with a very varied population, in some localities sparse, in others populous, and included some of the most rugged country, as well as the wildest aboriginal tribes of India. To mould this into shape as it were, to connect previous local systems of administration into one harmonious whole, required more than ordinary ability and power of application; and it was a fitting and welcome task to a man who, with great physical energy, possessed a mind capacious and ingenious, which had already found congenial occupation in the affairs of the Punjâb, where, as well in the revenue as the judicial departments, Sir Richard Temple had gained considerable experience. In the central provinces, Sir Richard's measures were eminently successful; and his administrative reports show wonderful powers of endurance, in long and rapid journeys, in the constant overlooking of every detail of administration, to which alone the result is attributable, and in his friendly intercourse with every native chief or landholder of the various districts. Larger in extent than the Punjâb, infinitely more diversified in natural features, in language, population, and in products, he had mastered all details, harmonised all working measures, and laid the foundation of future progress. Too little is known by the people of England of such undertakings and their results, or of the means by which they have been achieved; of the management by one individual and a few subordinates, of the affairs of provinces as large as France or Spain, uniting many different races and languages, and requiring daily toil of which there is little conception. Among such administrative exploits, Sir Richard Temple's tenure of the central provinces claims prominent notice; and at the close of the year 1865, he

Industrial exhibition at Nagpoor.

was able to apply a gratifying test of the success of his harmonising measures in an industrial exhibition held at Nagpoor, to which every district made contributions in produce and manufactures, and at which all classes of the people, from the semi-savage aborigines, Góndṡ, Bheels, and Kookoos, to the civilised Hindoos and Mahomedans, for the first time in their history mingled together in common. After the preceding war, devastation, and bloodshed, the effects of Sir Richard Temple's labours are more than ordinarily gratifying to contemplate; and few of the provincial administrative reports possess so high and so varied an interest as his.

Results of over speculation in Bombay.

The great influx of money into Bombay, and the enormous fortunes suddenly realised by adroit speculators, produced a mania of local joint stock companies, which exceeded in its results anything that had ever before appeared in India. Old means of investment trebled and quadrupled, for the time, in actual value. The shares in a company formed for the reclamation of land from the sea rose to twelve times their value—1000*l.* to 12,000*l.* and upwards—and others in proportion. With a plethora of wealth, the wildest schemes were entertained and put into execution; but after the custom of such events, the collapse was as sudden as the rise, and many were ruined. Nor was it till the end of the year, that commercial confidence was in some degree restored. Similar in some respects to the Bombay, Colaba and Backbay reclamation schemes and companies of Bombay, was the Port Canning Company of Calcutta. As year after year the navigation of the Hooghly became more difficult, the Mutlah, another branch of the Ganges, east of Calcutta, was fixed upon as the site of a new commercial capital; a railway was constructed from Calcutta, and warehouses were built; but although the navigation was much easier from the sea, no large ships ascended to the new Port Canning, and the scheme, if not entirely abandoned, became abortive. The only chance of the new port being frequented appears to lie in the stream of the Hooghly becoming too shallow for large vessels.

Projected port on the Mutlah.

In the course of the year under review, the college of civil engineers for the north-western provinces was founded at Roorkhee; an establishment which, whether in regard to Europeans or natives, has already sent forth many able men, and is in active operation. The institution owes its origin to the suggestions of Sir Hugh Rose, who, as a means of employment for many unemployed officers, considered that a public college course would be the best method of fitting many for the department of public works—a hope which has been fully justified.

College for civil engineers founded at Roorkhee.

The year 1866 is memorable from the great famine of Orissa. There had been a failure of rain in the season of 1865, and scarcity began to prevail, which passed into abso-

Famine in Orissa.

lute famine almost without notice, and certainly without precaution. Till it had reached an alarming height, the government of Bengal were inactive; and the time passed by in which supplies of grain could have been sent by sea. When the people were perishing in thousands, no vessel could approach the coast, and the supplies forwarded by land were utterly insufficient to meet the general wants. The lieutenant-governor of Bengal, Sir Cecil Beadon, and his Council, defended themselves to the best of their power; but they could not, and did not, escape the severe animadversions of the viceroy and of the press of England. Lord Napier, governor of Madras, took active measures for the relief of the people under his jurisdiction; and at a later period, Orissa was relieved; but the intermediate destruction of life was estimated at 2,000,000, and the amount of human suffering had been incalculably great. A plan had been formed, before the famine, of turning the waters of the Máhánuddy river to use in the irrigation of the Delta of Orissa, and the works were under execution by a private company. After a long discussion, which much retarded their progress, the company, for want of means, was obliged to make over its works to Government.

Orissa irrigation scheme.

The Currency Commission, which was instituted in this year, applied itself laboriously to the questions of silver, gold, and paper circulation; but it may be said to have been premature, as beyond a recommendation for the continued trial of the paper currency, and some suggestions as to detail of working measures, it gave no opinion upon the question of a general gold medium, which had many supporters, though it recommended that gold should continue to be a legal tender in payment of revenue. In the face of the constantly fluctuating market value of gold, it was indeed impossible to come to any other conclusion.

Currency question.

In 1866, Sir Richard Temple was promoted from the office of commissioner of the central provinces to the political department, as Resident at Hyderabad. He was succeeded by Mr. Strachey, who did ample justice to his predecessor's immense exertions, which may be briefly summarised. New and uniform land settlements had been completed all over the various provinces, and the demand fixed for from twenty to thirty years. Every class, every individual, general proprietors as well as occupants of fields, knew what their rights and obligations were, and all questions as to proprietary rights over waste lands were settled. The police department was reformed, and many native gentlemen were created honorary magistrates, and performed 'one-fifth' of the whole

Land settlements and other measures of the central provinces.

business satisfactorily. The civil courts of the provinces were enlarged, and the proceedings simplified; and improvement was manifest in the number of suits instituted, which rose from 19,000 to 45,000. 1,570 public vernacular schools were established, and fifty-six public dispensaries had afforded relief to 150,000 patients. Vaccination was extended to thousands, and sanitary regulations enforced in towns and villages. Four hundred miles of road had been bridged and metalled, and other branch lines in connection with the railway to Jubbulpoor were under construction. In addition to these, court-houses, police-stations, barracks, rest-houses for travellers, churches and wells, might be named; but the detail, after all, would hardly convey an idea of the impetus given to this long-neglected territory by Sir Richard Temple, or of his practically benevolent exertions in securing it. 'Whatever of progress,' writes his successor, Mr. Strachey, 'has been noted, was secured during Mr. Temple's rule. No such progress had ever been seen in this part of India before. Much of it may—must be, due to the action of natural, commercial, and social forces; but something, at any rate, may have been the result of good government, and must have been due to the personal exertions of Mr. Temple—to the system he introduced, and the officers he trained.' Sir Richard could not indeed be resisted; and while he achieved more in practical results, unaided, except by the subordinates, into whom he had to infuse his own energy, during his incumbency of little more than four years, these results rival, if they do not exceed, any in the history of the British administration of India.

Death of Bishop Cotton.

On October 6, as Dr. Cotton, the Bishop of Calcutta, was on a tour of visitation in Assam, he was accidentally drowned, to the great grief of the Christian community. During his incumbency, he had laboured very zealously and effectually in the cause of the Church, had visited every station in his vast diocese, and had stimulated the ministers of religion by his example and discipline; and a very sincere tribute to his memory and admirable labours was recorded by the viceroy in council.

The high courts established.

In conformity with the Act of Parliament for the government of India, two provincial high courts were established in 1866, one for the Punjâb at Lahore, one for the north-western provinces at Agra. These were presided over by chief justices appointed by the crown, and serve as the local courts of appeal, from all lower courts, as well as courts of first instance.

Irrigation.

The question of irrigation in India had been warmly taken up by Lord Cranborne during his tenure of office as Secretary of State for India, and the deplorable famine of Orissa had opened the way to a clearer perception of the necessity and practical value of these useful works. The scarcity of rain in that province had been followed by floods almost as destructive; but the advantage of regular and controllable supplies of water was not the less evident. Colonel Strachey was therefore sent from England as commissioner for works of irrigation, and arrived early in 1867, for the purpose of furthering these great undertakings; but some time necessarily elapsed before details could be decided upon. Even in this year the continuance of distress was severely felt in Orissa: and the viceroy stated at a public meeting convened in Calcutta, that 27,000 tons of rice would still be required, and 1,500 orphan children already, with 2,000 more in prospect, would have to be maintained.

The census of the central provinces, taken on November 5, 1866, with much care, was promulgated early in 1867. The result was perfectly unexpected in the great majority of Hindoos over Mahomedans, and was as follows:—

Census of central provinces.

Hindoos	6,864,770
Mahomedans	237,922
	7,102,692

Of those classed under Hindoo, were the aboriginal tribes, numbering about two millions. The result gave only seventy-nine souls to the square mile, which is attributable to the immense preponderance of forest, jungle, and uncleared, and for the most part unculturable, land.

Little more of general or historical interest marks the year 1867, but as it was closed with a discussion in regard to extension of railways, those under completion up to this period may be briefly noted:—

1. Lord Dalhousie's projected line from Calcutta to Dehly, called the East Indian, to be prolonged to Attock, in the Punjâb, with an extension south to Jubbulpoor.

2. The Great Peninsular Railway from Bombay to Jubbulpoor, to meet the East Indian, as well as a line *viâ* Sholapoor to meet the Madras line, near the Toombuddra river, with an extension from Sholapoor to Hyderabad.

3. The Bombay, Baroda, and Ahmedabad line.

4. The Sinde line, connecting Sinde *viâ* Mooltan with the East Indian line, in the Punjâb.

5. The Oudh and Rohilkhund line.

6. The Great Southern of India.

7. Eastern Bengal.

8. Calcutta and South-Eastern.

9. Madras and Western Coast.

By the report up to the year under notice, it appeared that, out of 5,599½ miles of projected railways, 3,934½ miles had been completed, and 1,665 miles remained to be finished.

The whole of the questions noted in this chapter are of a purely administrative character; but as they serve to illustrate the progression of events in India, are not without historical importance.

CHAPTER XIV.

THE ADMINISTRATION OF SIR JOHN LAWRENCE (*concluded*), 1868.

THE details of works of irrigation, in operation, in their construction, or projected, were reviewed by Sir John Lawrence in Council on March 31, 1868, with the following results:—

Review of great irrigation works.

I. In the Punjâb:—1. A new canal from the Sutlej was roughly estimated at 2,000,000*l.* sterling; the work, it was hoped, would be begun next season. 2. The remodelling of the Báree Dooáb canal and that of the Western Jumna. 3. Surveys for canals from the Sutlej to Feróżepoor and Mooltan, and for the extension of the canal system on the right bank of the Indus.

II. In the North-west Provinces:—1. A new canal projected from below Dehly to irrigate the Agra and Muttra districts, at the cost of 500,000*l.* 2. The improvement of the Ganges canal for navigation, in order to complete a water communication from Lahore to Dehly, Agra, the Dooáb and Oudh. 3. Works in Rohilkhund for irrigation and drainage, as also in Bundelkhund in respect to utilising the waters of the three largest rivers. 4. In Oudh, a canal from the Sarda; would be not inferior to the Ganges canal, at a cost of 2,000,000*l.*

III. In Bengal several projects:—1. To utilise the waters of the Gunduk. 2. A canal from the Ganges, near Ráj Mahál, perhaps as far as Calcutta. 3. A canal from the Damoodra, for navigation and irrigation, through the coal district of Raneegunje, to the Hooghly. 4. A canal from the Soane; the project, originally, of the East India Irrigation Company. 5. The works of the same company in Orissa, already in progress.

IV. In the Central Provinces, two promising projects were in course of survey.

V. In the Madras Presidency:—1. The completion by extension of branches of the great works on the Krishna and Godavery rivers. 2. Two very large tanks near Madras itself. 3. The extension of irrigation from the Pennaar river into the Vellore district. 4. A project for the utilisation of the waters of a river in

Travancore, to be applied to the province of Madura. 5. Extension and improvement of the works of the Cavery river.

VI. In the Presidency of Bombay:—1. A project for a large canal from the Indus at Róree, to irrigate the Hyderabad collectorate in Sinde, with improvements of other existing works. 2. In Guzerat a project, already sanctioned, of a canal from the Tapty river. 3. In Khandésh, a work of irrigation of considerable importance, already in progress. 4. In the Deccan, several undertakings in various stages of progress, and several new projects which would be submitted to Government.

VII. In Mysore, a large sum would be applied from the surplus revenues in furtherance of irrigation works.

The Secretary of State had already sent out thirty civil engineers of experience, who would be distributed to various localities, and others would follow in the coming year; and 'generally,' his Excellency states, 'it might be affirmed that the Government of India had taken all necessary steps to inaugurate the policy of extending irrigation to the utmost. It had already established in every province a separate head to the irrigation branch of the public works department, and would be ready to consider favourably every proposal having in view the improved administration of this class of works.'

Measures for extending irrigation.

From the foregoing detail, which necessarily excludes all former works executed and in actual working operation, it will be seen that new irrigation projects extended to all the three presidencies of India; that the importance of such projects had been fully recognised; and that no doubt existed, not only of those detailed being executed as rapidly as funds could be provided, but that they would be succeeded by others in every province where the means of obtaining water supplies, and of disposing of them to advantage in the irrigation of the soil, appear to be practicable and profitable. To all such undertakings, it is evident that the viceroy had given his best consideration and encouragement.

Importance of the question.

Small wars are seldom absent from India, and early in 1868, an insurrection of the Wághurs—an aboriginal tribe in the province of Kattiawar, in the Bombay presidency—arose, which required force for its suppression. The Wághurs had originally possessed the district of Okamundel, in which they resided, which was sold to the Gáikwar in 1815. In 1857, the district was re-transferred to the British Government, and it was found that the Wághurs had never abandoned their hereditary occupations of plunder and lawless conduct. Collision with the new administration was inevitable; but a small force under Colonel Anderson encountered and routed a body of them—not, however,

Waghur insurrection.

without losing two valuable officers, Captains La Touche and Hibbert. A partial insurrection of Bheels followed in another part of Guzerat, but was promptly suppressed.

Black Mountain campaign.

The military operations of the year closed with a campaign against the Afghans of the Black Mountain, on the north-west of the Punjâb—near the locality of the Umbeyla campaign—who, like the Sittána fanatics, had been excited by the Wáhábees of Patna and Southern India; a strange circumstance, when it is considered that those who sought to excite rebellion, and those who entered into it, were separated by 1,500 miles. But the conspirators were not without system; they had forwarded supplies and money, by agents, through the railways to their destination, and, no doubt, succeeded in making considerable preparations. The tribe now seduced was the Hussunzye, inhabiting the Agrór valley, in the Black Mountain range. They attacked a police station as a commencement of hostilities, and showing no disposition to submit, a campaign against them became inevitable. Troops were therefore massed upon the frontier under the command of General Wylde; and marching on September 26, two brigades advanced to Oghee on October 3, whence the operations continued till the 7th, when a village belonging to the Paráree Syeds, having been destroyed, the chiefs of several of the clans, finding further resistance impossible, came into camp for terms, which were accelerated by the results of other attacks upon their positions and villages, in which the enemy were uniformly routed. By the 10th, however, all had submitted, and the force was withdrawn. It was considered by many that enough punishment had not been inflicted to have a permanent effect in the prevention of outrage; but Government was satisfied that ill-will would only be perpetuated by the continued destruction of villages, and that the present submission of the clans might be received in earnest of future good behaviour. Enough had been done on the Black Mountain, as well as at Umbeyla, to prove that no natural obstruction and no armed opposition could prevent progress, when it was needful, into the wildest and most inaccessible regions of the mountains.

General Wylde's operations.

The question of the western frontier, which had occupied all successive Governments of India, from the Mahomedan period up to the present time, is still an open one; but much progress has been made in it, and there are good grounds for believing that the tribes, though not under our own Government, nor, indeed, many of them under that of Afghanistan, but wholly independent, are becoming more amenable to civilised influences than before, while the sharp lessons that have been occasionally read to them have not been entirely without effect.

The Ameer Dost Mahomed of Afghanistan died in 1863. Up to the period of his death he had not only preserved perfect good faith with the Government of India, but had maintained tranquillity in his dominions. After his death, though he had appointed his son, Shére Ally Khan, to succeed him, the nomination was opposed by his brothers Afzool Khan and Azim Khan; and a series of struggles took place, in one of which Shére Ally was dethroned, and Afzool Khan became ruler. He did not live long afterwards, and his son, Abdool Rahmán, waived his claim in favour of his uncle, Azim Khan, who had been for some time a fugitive in British territory. Ultimately, however, Shére Ally regained his throne, and the opposing faction was gradually overcome.

Affairs of Afghanistan: death of Dost Mahomed.

Disputed succession.

During the whole of this prolonged contest the policy of the viceroy was much criticised both in England and in India. By many, especially in India where a powerful army was burning for a further field of action, he was blamed for not interfering in force for the support of Shére Ally, or in any case for the pacification of Afghanistan. While in a disturbed condition, it was assumed to be at the mercy of Persian, or worse, Russian intrigue: and nothing but a decided interference in arms could, it was alleged, prevent the Russians from crossing the Oxus to the assistance of Shére Ally, Azim Khan, Abdool Rahmán, or whichever party should bid highest for their support. The assemblage of General Wylde's magnificent force against the Black Mountain tribes gave colour to the supposition that a movement into Afghanistan was projected: but the policy of the viceroy was a perfect neutrality, and was supported by remarkable reasoning which is well explained in the 'Edinburgh Review' of April, 1870 (No. 268). It is not necessary to enter into the details of the subject, further than to state that the designs of Russia, should she have any, would only be furthered by a fresh British advance into Afghanistan, and that the best policy would be to support the *de facto* ruler of the country, without entering into the intricate mazes of its domestic politics; or that intrigue on the part of Persia was an idle bugbear, the weakness of which had been already sufficiently demonstrated to need any fresh illustration. It is very possible that the army was disappointed by Sir John Lawrence's pacific policy; but there can be no question of its expediency.

Policy of the viceroy.

In this year a precautionary measure was sanctioned for the construction of fortified posts in many of the large stations, as well to protect the arsenals, as to afford refuge in case of need. That such works would have proved invaluable during the mutiny will have been manifest from the narrative of events. In the Punjâb, at Jullunder and Sealkote; in

Fortified posts.

India, at Nowgong in the central provinces, at Umballa, and at Hyderabad in the Deccan, these fortified arsenals were to be constructed, while at Mooltan, at Peshâwur, and Rawul Pindee more extensive forts were to be executed. It is perhaps a strange fact, that, with the exception of the presidencies, the English have erected no fortifications in India. In a few localities, as at Dehly, Allahabad, and Agra: Ahmednugger in the Deccan, Bellary, Vellore, &c., native fortifications have been improved, and used as magazines; but in no other part of the country do they exist, and the siege of Dehly formed an impressive lesson against trusting them, in case they were constructed, to any but English soldiers. In barracks, indeed, the expenditure, under Sir John Lawrence's administration, had been munificent, nearly seven millions sterling having been applied to this purpose alone.

Legislative enactments.

The details of purely administrative measures are subjects hardly fitted, by their local and often intricate character, for discussion in a manual of history: but a few belonging to Sir John Lawrence's incumbency may be briefly enumerated. The Municipal Improvement Act of 1868 was applied to the formation and guidance of municipalities in the north-west provinces. The local municipal committees consist of a proportion of official and non-official members, and their duties are the conservancy of towns and villages, and their improvements; the expenses being defrayed from taxes levied on houses and the octroi duties which have been imposed. Under the operation of this Act much has already been effected, especially in the conservancy of towns, a subject much neglected before; and as an incitement to efforts in local management of details, which were almost beyond the province of the collector or magistrate, they are practically useful and encouraging.

Tenancy questions.

Two Acts—XIX. and XXVIII.—of 1865 are, however, of more important character. The former relates to the rights of cultivators in Oudh, the latter a similar measure in regard to the Punjâb. By these Acts, the definitions of the rights of tenants, whether hereditary or at will, and so-called tenant-right upon improvements, are expressed and confirmed; but neither measures have passed without strong opposition and lengthened discussions, into which it is impossible to enter. In taking up the subject, it was evidently the intention of Sir John Lawrence to secure the rights of hereditary occupancy of land to those who have possessed them for generations. Such tenancies are well known and well defined in Madras and Bombay, where, so long as the stipulated rent or land-tax was paid, the occupant had a proprietary right in the land he cultivated. Other tenants, being tenants at will without hereditary right, had occupancy from year to year, or by lease as might be agreed. In the case of Oudh, hereditary right was defined by a thirty years' occupancy, dating back from February 1856; but it is advanced, and perhaps admitted, by the cultivators, that there are no classes in Oudh to which the designation of hereditary occupant, or, as he would be termed in Bombay or Madras, 'Merasdar,' can be applied; and the Talookdars of Oudh have protested against the interference which a recognition of such rights would involve. Equally in the Punjâb, rights which in other parts of India have been guarded with the most jealous care by the people, and respected by all preceding native governments, as before explained, are apparently unknown or unclaimed, and are thus accounted for by Sir John Lawrence:—'Under the Sikh rule, the position of the hereditary cultivators was practically very much on a par with that of proprietors in the same village. And although the Sikhs, in their social relations to each other, set a high value on proprietary rights in land, more particularly when these were ancestral, their rulers acted very differently, and cared little who held, or who cultivated, these lands, provided that the revenue was punctually paid.'

This exemplifies the present condition of the Punjâb hereditary tenures, and shows the results of disturbed and oppressive administrations, which not only did not protect existing rights in land, but overthrew them in mere consideration of revenue. The condition of Oudh exhibits exactly the same result, from the same causes. The hereditary landholders had been unable to retain their rights in opposition to a grasping administration in the Punjâb, and to the unlimited and unquestioned power of the Talookdars in Oudh.

Sir John Lawrence's motive in these Bills was the protection, by legal recognition, of the hereditary occupant, and the security of his tenure: and considering the additional value which land in India is acquiring under a settled government and moderate assessment, there is no question that Sir John's large experience led him directly to the root of the question, in the establishment of definite rights, and, therefore, titles to the land, wherever they could be proved. The working of these two Acts is, therefore, a subject of much interest, but certainly, as yet, undefinable; and in the case of hereditary occupants, cannot fail to ensure the gratitude of those concerned on a point which, in former settlements in the Bengal presidency, had been much or entirely overlooked, and which in the Punjâb and in Oudh might have shared the same fate in being irredeemably swept away, but for his wise and timely interposition.

At the close of 1868, Sir John Lawrence's term of office having nearly expired, Earl Mayo, Chief Secretary for Ireland under Mr. Disraeli's administration, was appointed viceroy, and arrived in Bombay before the end of the year. If Sir John Lawrence's policy as viceroy be reviewed, it will not be found barren of fruit. The long list of administrative acts, his adjustment of progressive measures, his extension, as far as practicable, of education, his liberality in public works, his Bills for the protection of tenants in Oudh and in the Punjâb, are peculiarly his own, and may be separated from the heterogeneous Acts passed by the Legislative Council. All evince a benevolence of purpose, a deep desire to further and secure the interests of the people whom he had known so long, and over whom he became in turn chief ruler. His foreign policy was peculiarly his own, and has not been impugned. With all these great points in his favour, and with the certainty of having by his mere presence and authority repressed latent disaffection, it must be admitted that his rule was not popular as viceroy, though it was great and powerful. His own service was doubtless jealous of a member who had belonged to their ranks and had overstepped all; yet there was no one who watched more vigilantly over its rights, or whose patronage was more pure. Popularity in India, however, unless accompanied by corresponding vigour, is the lowest meed of praise that can be accorded to a viceroy, and was a distinction never sought by Lord Lawrence, or attempted to be sought, either from Europeans or from natives. Enough for him that he did his duty, strictly, sternly perhaps, without bending; and in this respect, the character and administration of Lord Lawrence, apart from his Punjâb acts, will rise in proportion with the lapse of time. On his retirement from the office of viceroy, his long and great services were recognised and rewarded by his elevation to the peerage.

Earl Mayo appointed viceroy.

Review of Sir John Lawrence's policy.

CHAPTER XV.

THE ADMINISTRATION OF EARL MAYO, AND CONCLUSION: 1869 TO 1870.

THE appointment of Earl Mayo to the office of viceroy was severely criticised and opposed both in England and in India; and indeed to succeed one so perfectly conversant with the affairs of India as his predecessor, was to induce a comparison which might prove disadvantageous. Earl Mayo belonged to the Conservative party of England; but his appointment was nevertheless ratified by Mr. Gladstone's Whig Cabinet—a wise measure in relation to the people of India, as proving to them that the man considered most capable would be selected for their governor, without reference to home politics. But the progress of Earl Mayo, while it has surprised those to whom he was unknown, has fully justified the selection originally made. His great capacity has been developed, and the experience he is gaining bids fair to place him in the rank of the most illustrious men who have preceded him. Among all classes, European and native, he has established a widespread popularity and respect, as much due to his public measures as to his magnificent hospitality. So far, indeed, he appears to be one of those characters which can only be estimated by having been placed in a position in which his natural powers are increased by exercise of great responsibilities. Unfettered and unprejudiced by any former association with, or opinion upon, Indian questions, and without any former local ties, he is able to apply a fresh, clear, and powerful judgment to the consideration of all local affairs, and to the general well-being of the empire. The results of a year's incumbency leave little room for comment, though events have already occurred, not only to develop great and independent decision of character, but to afford a key, as it were, to future results.

Earl Mayo's qualifications.

The foreign policy of Lord Lawrence has been briefly noticed in the last chapter. It was strictly non-interferent as regards Afghanistan, but reticent—perhaps overmuch. While it professed to encourage Shére Ally, the ruler of Afghanistan, it was cold in demeanour and in practical effect; and Lord Mayo, while he strictly retained the principles of non-interference, went a step further, in giving to the Ameer Shére Ally hearty and generous recognition, assistance, and hospitality. There may have been obstacles to such a course during Lord Lawrence's viceroyalty which have not transpired. If this were the case, Lord Mayo availed himself of the first moment at which they were withdrawn to redeem his predecessor's views from a coldness which might grow into positive marks of mistrust, if not aversion, on the part of the Ameer. A cordial invitation to Ameer Shére Ally to visit India, and confer upon matters relating to Afghanistan and the security of the frontier, was therefore forwarded to Kabool, and was responded to in the same spirit in which it was given. On March 27, 1869, the Ameer met the viceroy at Umballa, and was sumptuously *fêted* and entertained: receiving not only presents of great intrinsic value, but, what was of more consequence to him, entire recognition of his rights and position, with means of

Foreign policy.

The Ameer Shére Ally visits the viceroy.

defending them in a supply of arms, and a money subsidy of twelve lacs of rupees, or 120,000*l.* per year. By this generous proceeding, Earl Mayo has not only secured the personal attachment of the Ameer, but enabled him to judge of the magnitude of the British resources in India, of the progress of the country, and condition of its people in comparison with his own, which can hardly fail of having future good effect. The results of the Ameer's visit, the honour which was accorded to him, together with the good feeling which existed on both sides, have ere now become known to all the nations and tribes of Central Asia. They have already effected much that was needful to the consolidation of the Ameer's power; and the knowledge that it is not only recognised, but supported by the authority of the viceroy, backed by all the resources at his disposal, cannot fail to repress intrigue and disaffection. Under such circumstances, the peace and gradual improvement of Afghanistan can hardly be doubtful; and it is impossible for its people not to perceive that all bitter memories of the past have given place to more generous and hopeful feelings on the part of the British Government.

Apprehended deficit in the budget of 1868–69.

Following the brilliant reception of Ameer Shére Ally, the discovery of a considerable estimated deficit in the budget of the year 1868–69 was an unlooked for and unpleasant contingency which had not been anticipated, and the financial report of Sir Richard Temple was met with sharp criticism in India and England. In this question the viceroy is now engaged. Retrenchments and an enhanced income-tax are not less unpopular measures now than they have ever been found to be; but the necessity for real economy cannot be relaxed, and while the actual condition of the revenue cannot be exactly ascertained until the close of the session of Parliament, there is every reason to believe that by a vigorous effort this temporary check may be overcome, and by the period of the budget of 1869–70 that the proper equilibrium of revenue and expenditure may be attained and confirmed.

Visit of Prince Alfred to India.

While these pages were being written, Prince Alfred, Duke of Edinburgh, the second son of Queen Victoria, had completed a tour of India. He arrived in Calcutta on December 22, 1869, in his noble frigate the 'Galatea,' and was received with every demonstration of loyal welcome and rejoicing. He was entertained with truly regal pomp and splendour by Earl Mayo, and invested with the Grand Cross of the Star of India by him as its Grand Master, amidst a gathering of native princes and nobles, Hindoo and Mahomedan, such as Calcutta never witnessed before, nor may, perhaps, witness again. The events are too recent to need any description in these pages; and while the progress of the prince was marked by eager welcome and profuse hospitality, English and native, throughout the country, its moral effect in familiarising the people of India with the royal family which now rules them, in uniting the bond between the native and alien races, and in securing the grateful acknowledgment of the Queen for her son's reception, can hardly be overrated. With this event, the year 1869 closed in India, amidst profound peace and general rejoicing, and the year 1870 opened with their continuance. The cloud of suffering with which 1869 was overcast in the north-west provinces and Rajpootána, by the famine which prevailed, has also cleared away, and there is every hope that abundance may ensue in the coming harvest. At this happy juncture, therefore, this history of India closes.

Prospects of 1870.

As a student's manual only, necessarily restricted in size, it has been impossible to review events as they have occurred with the fulness which can only be attained in an elaborate history. Yet it may be hoped that sufficient detail has been given to induce the student to follow up the works of the various historians of India, which will not fail both to instruct, and, by their wonderful and varied interest, to gratify him. From the dim early ages of Aryan invasion to the establishment of Hindoo power; from the decadence of that power under Mahomedan invasion and dominion, to the establishment of the sway of the Christian nation of England over both, the long record of more than 3,000 years has been completed through the varied stages of progress—from aboriginal savagery and barbarism, to the civilising influences of the nineteenth century. Of the Hindoo period, the records are indeed scanty; but from the literature and science which have survived, there is evidence that during its existence the Aryan people were as far in advance of their Western brethren in intellectual culture as they are now below them, and that what they were then in religion, in capacity, in ingenuity, and in social habits, so, for the most part, they are now. Three thousand years—a period of time hardly realisable by mere numbers—has seen change certainly among them; but comparatively it has been very slight, and the institution of caste, and the religion of Brahma, still resist the influences of Mahomedanism and Christianity. If other impressions are gaining strength in the land under the influence of Christian teaching and secular education, they are necessarily slow of development; and it must be remembered that the recently-declared Brahmóism, from which much appears to be expected, is not Christianity, but the resuscitation of that simple Theism which was the religion of the Védás 4,000 years ago, and as yet has made a very limited progress.

Concluding remarks.

Hindoo period.

What the future of the great Hindoo race, for the most part Aryan, may be, is at present dark; but may become, under Divine guidance, both bright and glorious.

Through all the Mahomedan period and its variations, the student has been conducted with more ample definition of events than the Hindoo; for the Mahomedans, wherever they settled or conquered, have furnished excellent historians, and India, in this respect, has proved no exception. Their magnificent conquests, their splendour, their cruelty, their often savage fanaticism, their massacres of 'infidel' Hindoos, and their occasional benevolence and statesmanlike greatness, in laws, in revenue settlements, and in political measures, have been followed as nearly and fully as was practicable. That they had deteriorated in all great qualities long before the virtual destruction of their power by the Mahrattas, will be evident from the events which followed the reign of Aurungzebe, their only monarch who can be said with truth to have been Emperor of India. What remains of their period of sway are magnificent mosques, mausoleums, palaces, and fortresses, unequalled in the world: memorials of individual and dynastic wealth, and greatness only. There was no science and no literature to survive. It has been a favourite subject with popular writers to contrast the comparatively niggardly spirit and feeble execution of English works with those of the Mahomedans, and to depreciate what has been effected by India's last conquerors; but the accusation was unjust and unmerited. Englishmen, though they might govern large provinces, were yet poorly paid in proportion to Mahomedans in the same positions; and where the one might spend enormous sums upon his mausoleum, might found mosques and colleges, or build a palace from the revenues at his disposal, the corresponding English officer lived in a humble bungalow, accounted to his government for every penny he collected, and when he died rested under a simple stone or monument. Mahomedan emperors made no roads, no harbours, and but few bridges or canals—these, too, defective in scientific construction. Yet they ruled for more than 700 years with, for the greater part of the time, the resources of the whole of India at their disposal.

Mahomedan period.

The English, who have struggled into local power during the last hundred years, were, for the first half of it, little more than commercial adventurers, who, when the opportunity occurred, and they were insensibly drawn into the existing local struggles, struck in boldly for supremacy, and won it; and in the record of the last half of the century must the effects of their progress be looked for. Gradual, very gradual, and perhaps timorous at first, it received its final impetus from the Marquis of Dalhousie, and since then has never stopped. The early

The English.

rigid conservative policy is regretted by many; but it must be borne in mind that English civilisation is not Indian, and that to have urged on what existed in England before a way had been provided for it in India, would have been to incur a risk which might have lost all that has been gained.

Mutual progress under English rule.

So, now at last the field is open, and the progress swift and sure, England can look with pride upon many thousands of miles of metalled and bridged roads constructed—over mountain-passes, and through forests, where before there were barely foot-tracks; over rivers at their highest floods, morasses, and plains, impassable in the monsoons, now traversable with safety in all seasons; to 15,000 miles of railways which will be eventually constructed—of which, as stated by Lord Mayo at Jubbulpoor in April—4,000 miles are already opened, 1,000 are in progress, and 9,000 are about to be immediately commenced, carrying with them greater civilising influences than it is possible yet to imagine, while they enlarge the commerce and develop the resources of the country; to several thousands of miles of navigable and irrigating canals, the only rivals to which are the ancient Hindoo irrigation works of the Madras presidency; to at least 15,000 miles of electric telegraph; to a uniform and certain postal system at a very low rate; to a progressive system of public education; and, above all, to the maintenance of peace throughout India, in contrast with the never-ending strife, rapine, and butchery of the Mahomedan and Mahratta periods. Of the early Hindoo ages the records are indeed dimmer; and yet, from what has been ascertained, there is every reason to conclude that the condition of the country was not materially different. For more than a thousand years, at least, there are unvarying records of war and desolation, till they culminated in the acts of the Mahrattas and Pindhárees; and from these, as from all other public scourges, the power of England has delivered the long-suffering people of India. Greater than these are the moral effects of universal security of property, the rapid progression of national wealth, industry, and intelligence, and the conversion of purely military and predatory classes into productive members of the community. It is no little triumph to have been able to turn swords into ploughshares among alien races; and yet the examples of the Mahrattas, the Sikhs, and many other classes, are examples which admit of no denial. Let the student review in his mind the results of native rule which this history has furnished, and he will, I think, be unable to resist the conviction that the intervention of England at the crisis of confusion, and striving for mastery at which it occurred, was providentially directed and sustained.

It is at once admitted that the condition of some parts of the

Mahomedan period have had their parallel in European history: that its fierce contests, its fanatical massacres, may find equivalents in Christian nations, and that the murders and assassinations of its kings and princes, and tortures, have had, too, their Western representatives. But while the West emerged out of comparative barbarism into a brilliant civilisation, the Indian Mahomedan had not altered; nor has he shown as yet, for the most part, any symptom of regeneration; on the contrary, all change is hated and avoided, except by those upon whom orthodox Mahomedanism hangs more loosely than upon their forefathers.

Mahomedans.

Enough, however, of comparison of the past and the present. English rule may not be loved, may not be everywhere popular; but, tested by the fierce convulsion of the Mutiny, and compared with the condition of the Mahomedan rule at its hundredth year of existence, it is more popular, and better loved. It has in it no element of pomp or display, by which the imaginations of an excitable people can be enthralled; but, on the contrary, in a hard, perhaps mechanical, adherence to routine, just to the people, painstaking and hardworking—it is sincerely respected. It prevents and suppresses crime, and it dispenses justice to all: it is honest, because its servants are incorruptible either by money or influence, and the test of rebellion only served the more firmly to establish its power and its preference over that of the native. It is rapidly creating wealth by development of natural resources and their employment, by extension of production, and by internal and external commerce; while it may be questioned whether any State in the civilised world shows more practical benevolence in the desire for, or utilisation of, improvement, than the widespread British provinces of India.

Character of English rule.

Urged as they are by example, by encouragement to exertion, and by surrounding progress, it is painfully evident how backward and defective most independent native States still remain in ordinary means of protection, justice, or public convenience to their people, and how slow they are to adopt more enlightened measures of reform. Wherever elements of improvement exist in them, they will continue to develop progress, and to maintain their positions: wherever they fail, they must inevitably, in process of time, drop into the great and irresistible tide of advancement which is fast spreading over the land. Meanwhile England does not wait. The history of the first ten years of the administration of the Crown shows not only no halting or faltering in purpose, but the reverse. The desire of England is India's greatness, prosperity, and happiness, as an essential part of

Independent native States.

her own; and the simple but affecting prayer of Queen Victoria, which closes her proclamation to the people of her dominions, is this:—

'May the God of all power grant unto us, and to those in authority under us, strength to carry out these our wishes for the good of our people.'

APPENDIX

To Page 120, *Book II.*

NIZAM-OOD-DEEN AHMED BUKSHY observes in his History that Feróze introduced many excellent laws, which were current in his time. Among others were the following regulations:—The first was the abolition of the practice of mutilating criminals—a mode of punishment which he would not allow to be inflicted on any of his subjects, Mahomedan or Hindoo; the second regulation limited very much the demand on cultivators, by which he increased not only the population but the revenue. . . . . He caused his regulations to be carved on the Musjid of Ferózabad, of which the following may be taken as a sample.

'It has been usual in former times to spill Mahomedan blood on trivial occasions, and for small crimes to mutilate and torture them by cutting off the hands and feet and noses and ears, by putting out eyes, by pulverising the bones of the living criminal with mallets, by burning the body with fire, by crucifixion and by nailing the hands and feet, by flaying alive, by the operation of ham-stringing, and by cutting human beings to pieces. God, in His infinite goodness, having been pleased to confer on me the power, has also inspired me with the disposition, to put an end to these practices. It is my resolution, moreover, to restore, in the daily prayers offered up for the royal family, the names of all those princes, my predecessors, who have reigned over the empire of Dehly, in hopes that these prayers, being acceptable to God, may in some measure appease His wrath and ensure His mercy towards them. It is also hereby proclaimed that the small and vexatious taxes under the denomination of Cotwally, &c., payable to the public servants of Government, as perquisites of officers, by small traders; that licences for the right of pasturage from shepherds on waste lands belonging to the Crown; fees from flowersellers, fishsellers, cottoncleaners, silksellers, and cooks; and the precarious and fluctuating taxes on shopkeepers and vintners, shall henceforward cease throughout the realm; for it is better to relinquish this portion of the revenue than realise it at the expense of so much distress occasioned by the discretionary power necessarily invested in tax-gatherers and officers of authority; nor will any tax hereafter be levied contrary to the written law of "the book."

'It has been customary to set aside one-fifth of all property taken in war for the troops, and to reserve four-fifths for the Government. It is hereby ordered that in future four-fifths shall be distributed to the troops, and one-fifth only reserved for the Crown. I will on all occasions cause to be banished from the realm persons convicted of the following crimes:—Those who profess Atheism or who maintain schools of vice; all public servants convicted of corruption, as well as persons paying bribes. I have myself abstained from wearing gaudy silk apparel and jewels, as an example to my subjects. I have considered it my duty to repair every public edifice of utility constructed by my predecessors—such as caravanserais, musjids, wells, reservoirs of water, aqueducts, canals, hospitals, almshouses, and schools—and have alienated considerable portions of the revenue for their support. I have also taken pains to discover the surviving relatives of all persons who suffered from the wrath of my late lord and master, Mahomed Toghluk, and having pensioned and provided for them, have caused them to grant their full pardon and forgiveness to that prince, in the presence of the holy and learned men of their age, whose signatures and seals as witnesses are affixed to the documents, the whole of which, as far as lay in my power, have been procured and put into a box, and deposited in the vault in which Mahomed Toghluk is entombed. I have gone and sought consolation from all the most learned and holy men within my realm, and have taken care of them. Whenever my soldiers have been rendered inefficient for service by wounds or by age, I have caused them to be pensioned on full pay for life. Two attempts have been made to poison me, but without effect.'—Extract from 'History of the Rise of the Mahomedan Power in India,' Briggs's 'Trans. of Ferishtta,' vol. i. pp. 162–164.

II.

INDIAN STATISTICS.

The annual 'Statistical Abstract relating to British India' has been issued by the India Office:—

It states that there are 910,853 square miles of territory under British administration, containing a population of 155,348,090 souls; the native States under the Government of India comprise (as far as can be ascertained) 646,147 square miles, with a population of 46,245,888; and the foreign States comprise 188 square miles under the French Government, with a population of 203,887, and 1,066 square miles under the Portuguese Government, with a population of 313,262. The total presents an area of 1,558,254 square miles, and a population of 202,111,127 souls. In those portions of British India for which the occupations of the people are stated, not including Bengal (Lower Provinces) or Bombay, 60,000,000 among 102,000,000 are described as engaged in agriculture; 53,000,000 are males, 48,000,000 females; 78,000,000 are Hindoos, 17,000,000 Mahomedans, 1,700,000 are Parsees, Jains, and Buddhists; 1,000,000 are Sikhs, and 523,875 Christians, 57,421 of these being Europeans. The gross revenue of British India for the year ending March 31, 1869, was 49,262,691*l.*, and the gross expenditure in India and England, 53,407,334*l.*, leaving a deficiency of 4,144,643*l.*; the public debt amounted to 102,866,189*l.*, and the interest upon it to 5,025,014*l.* Revenue, expenditure, debt, and interest are all higher than in any other of the ten years, 1860–69, included in this little volume of statistics. The imports into British India by sea in the financial year 1868–69, including treasure, amounted in value to 50,943,191*l.*, and the exports to 53,706,830*l.* The imports of merchandise amounted to 35,793,767*l.*; among them were cotton goods, 15,483,476*l.*; cotton twist and yarn, 2,531,656*l.*; metals, manufactured and unmanufactured, 3,211,408*l.*; metal manufactures, 451,379*l.*; railway materials, 1,526,780*l.*; machinery, 730,295*l.*; raw silk, 703,840*l.*; silk goods, 381,836*l.*; woollen goods, 722,262*l.*; apparel, 483,551*l.*; jewellery and precious stones, 370,637*l.*; salt, 683,455*l.* The exports included raw cotton of the value of 19,707,877*l.*; cotton goods, twist and yarns, 1,329,944*l.*; opium, 10,695,654*l.*; dyes, 3,023,146*l.*; grain and pulse, 2,650,898*l.*; jute, and jute manufactures, 2,070,242*l.*; raw silk, 1,269,468*l.*; seeds, 1,927,989*l.*; coffee, 1,111,027*l.*; hides and skins, 1,230,932*l.*; tea, 974,519*l.*; ivory and ivory ware, 224,802*l.*; saltpetre, 310,757*l.* The moneys coined at the mints of the several presidencies in the year amounted to 5,457,083*l.*, almost all silver. The Government currency notes in circulation averaged 10,145,533*l.*; the reserve in coin, 6,618,191*l.* The expenditure on public works sanctioned by the Government in the year 1868–69 was 7,040,000*l.*—viz., 2,400,000*l.* on military works, 829,321*l.* on civil buildings, 2,561,505*l.* on public improvements, and 1,249,174*l.* on establishments, tools, plant, &c. The expenditure by the Government on schools and colleges in the year was 590,452*l.*; the average attendance of pupils reached 757,767, in schools and colleges belonging to or aided by the Government. The number of letters and newspapers transmitted through the post-office of British India in the year reached 74,664,817—a great advance on previous years. The troops employed in British India in the year were 184,858—64,858 being Europeans and 120,000 natives. The number of emigrants embarked from British India is stated at 13,358—6,377 proceeding to the West Indies, 5,014 to British Guiana, and 1,967 to Mauritius. Railway progress has already been reported by Mr. Juland Danvers.—*Homeward Mail, August* 19, 1870.

INDEX.